27th Pacific Asia Conference on Language, Information and Computation 2013

(PACLIC 27)

Taipei, Taiwan
21 - 24 November 2013

ISBN: 978-1-63266-288-0

Printed from e-media with permission by:

Curran Associates, Inc.
57 Morehouse Lane
Red Hook, NY 12571

Some format issues inherent in the e-media version may also appear in this print version.

Printed by Curran Associates, Inc. (2014)

Association for Computational Linguistics
209 N. Eighth Street
Stroudsburg, Pennsylvania 18360

Phone: 1-570-476-8006
Fax: 1-570-476-0860

acl@aclweb.org

Additional copies of this publication are available from:

Curran Associates, Inc.
57 Morehouse Lane
Red Hook, NY 12571 USA
Phone: 845-758-0400
Fax: 845-758-2634
Email: curran@proceedings.com
Web: www.proceedings.com

Conference Dates: November 21-24, 2013
Conference Venue: Administration Building, National Chengchi University
Organizer: Department of English, National Chengchi University
Co-organizers: Institute of Linguistics, Academia Sinica
Graduate Institute of Linguistics, National Chengchi University
Department of Computer Science, National Chengchi University
Supporting Organizations: Linguistic Society of Taiwan (LST)
Association for Computational Linguistics and Chinese Language Processing (ACLCLP)

Sponsors:
National Science Council, Executive Yuan, R.O.C.
Institute of Linguistics, Academia Sinica
NCCU Office of Research and Development

Welcome Message from Conference Honorary Chair

On behalf of ILAS, a co-host of this conference with National Chengchi University, I would like to welcome you all to the 27th Pacific Asia Conference on Language, Information and Computation (PACLIC27).

The PACLIC conference has a long history,dating back to 1982 where the first conference of this series was organized with the original name "Korea-Japan Joint Conference on Formal Linguistics". It was the consensus of the organizer of the 1994 Joint Conference of the Asian Conference on Language, Information and Computation (ACLIC) and the Pacific Asia Conference on Formal and Computational Linguistics (PACFoCoL) that the two conferences would continue to be held jointly in the future as the Pacific Asia Conference on Language, Information and Computation, with the 1995 conference being numbered the 10th. Over the years the conference series has developed into one of the leading conferences in the Pacific-Asia region. Like the previous PACLIC conferences, PACLIC27 has received 123 submissions (workshop and main conference included) in the fields of theoretical and computational linguistics, and participants coming from 27 countries.

The long tradition of the conference has been the keynote and invited speakers, and this year is no exception. The 5 eminent scholars who kindly agreed to deliver keynote speeches for this year are Professor Alec Marantz (New York University, USA), Professor Junichi Tsujii (Microsoft Research Asia, Beijing), Professor Wen-Lian Hsu (Academia Sinica, Taiwan), Professor Yukio Tono (Tokyo University of Foreign Studies, Japan),and Professor Stefan Th. Gries (University of California, Santa Barbara, USA). Furthermore the 3 distinguished scholars for the invited talks are Professor Chengqing Zong (Chinese Academy of Sciences, China), Professor KingkarnThepkanjana (Chulalongkorn University, Thailand) and Professor Aesun Yoon (Pusan National University, Korea). I have no doubt that in the three days there will be many opportunities for you to explore the intellectual fascination of theoretical and computational linguistics with these internationally renowned scholars and the other participants as well. It is my sincere hope that some of these interactions will lead to possible collaborations in the future or ring a bell in your memory in the years to come.

Thank you!

Chiu-yu Tseng (Conference Honorary Chair)
Director, Institute of Linguistics, Academia Sinica

Welcome Message

The 27th Pacific Asia Conference on Language, Information, and Computation (PACLIC 27) is being held at National Chengchi University in Taipei, Taiwan from 21-24 November 2013. PACLIC is hosted annually by different academic institutions in the Asia-Pacific region. It has been nine years since the conference was first held in Taiwan, when PACLIC 19 was hosted by the Academia Sinica in 2005, and we are truly honored that National Chengchi University has the opportunity to take up the task this time.

For the past years, PACLIC has provided platforms for scholars to share new ideas about language, information, and computation, and, as such, has developed into one of leading conferences on the synergy of language studies and computational analysis. PACLIC 27 in Taiwan aims to carry on the mission of providing a great opportunity for linguists and computer scientists to gain stimulation from the exchange of the most up-to-date knowledge. A pre-conference workshop on Computer-Assisted Language Learning that represents an exemplary synergy of language, information, and computation is organized to address the study of computers and information technology in language teaching and learning. The theme is 'Corpora and Language Learning'. Together with the main conference, PACLIC 27 provides the best access to the current trends in both linguistics and computational linguistics among the international research community, and most importantly, allows for the generation of synergies among research approaches and findings.

We received paper submissions representing enormous diversity, with authors from 27 countries or regions, namely, Canada, China, the Czech Republic, Denmark, France, Germany, Hong Kong, India, Iran, Ireland, Japan, Korea, Libya, Macao, Malaysia, Morocco, the Netherlands, the Philippines, Portugal, Singapore, Switzerland, Taiwan, Thailand, Turkey, the United Kingdom, the United States, and Vietnam. All submissions were rigorously reviewed by three reviewers to ensure the quality of all of the accepted papers. Of the 114 submissions, 39 papers (34%) were accepted for oral presentations, and another 17 papers (15%) for poster presentations. The research topics this year include grammar and syntax, language generation, discourse and pragmatics, lexical knowledge learning, speech perception, language learning, language acquisition, corpus compilation and analysis, machine translation, phonetics, lexical semantics, morphology and syntax, and sentiment analysis. The turnout reflects a diverse, inspiring and high-quality collection of research.

The key to the guarantee of high-quality results lies in the tremendous efforts and professional contributions of the program committee members from 18 countries, to whom we must extend our greatest gratitude, and the conference is enriched by the resulting combination of keynote speeches, invited talks and oral and poster presentations. The five keynote speeches for the main conference are given by internationally well-known scholars—Professor Alec Marantz from New York University, Professor Wen-Lian Hsu from Academia Sinica, Professor Yukio Tono from the Tokyo University of Foreign Studies, Professor Stefan Th. Gries from the University of California, Santa Barbara, and Professor Junichi Tsujii from Microsoft Research Asia in Beijing. The three invited talks are given by Professor Chengqing Zong from the Chinese Academy of Sciences, Professor Aesun Yoon from Pusan National University, and Professor Kingkarn Thepkanjana from Chulalongkorn University. Professor Yukio Tono and Professor Jason S. Chang from National Tsing Hua Univeristy present their keynote speeches in the workshop. The chance to hear first hand of their respective expertise definitely provides us with inspiring insights for research. On behalf of the organizing committee, we express our wholehearted appreciation to them. We would also like to thank the steering committee for their supervision, to Professor Zhao-Ming Gao from National Taiwan University and Professor Jyi-Shane Liu from National Chengchi University for organizing the workshop, to Professor Siaw-Fong Chung from National Chengchi University, Professor Jing-Shin Chang from National Chi Nan University and Liang-Chih Yu from Yuan Ze University for their efforts of compiling the proceedings, and to the local staff members at National Chengchi University for their exceptional dedication and coordination in their work.

Finally, we hope that you will enjoy the conference, and take advantage of this special occasion to renew contacts, and exchange ideas and the results of the latest developments. More importantly, you cannot miss the chance to explore and discover the beauty of Formosa, and to experience the great hospitality of this island.

Conference Chair and Co-Chair:
Huei-ling Lai and Kawai Chui (National Chengchi University)

Program Committee Chairs:
Chao-Lin Liu (National Chengchi University)
Shu-Chuan Tseng (Academia Sinica)

Steering Committee:

Standing Members:

Chae, Hee-Rahk, Hankuk University of Foreign Studies, Seoul
Huang, Chu-Ren, The Hong Kong Polytechnic University, Hong Kong
Roxas, Rachel, De La Salle University-Manila, Manila
Sun, Maosong, Tsinghua University, Beijing
Tsou, Benjamin, City University of Hong Kong, Hong Kong
Yoshimoto, Kei, Tohoku University, Sendai
Zhang, Min, Institute for Inforcomm Research, A-STAR, Singapore

Ex Officio Members:

Harada, Yasunari, Waseda University, Tokyo (Digital Archivist)
Lai, Huei-ling, National Chengchi University, Taipei (PACLIC 27 Local Organizer)
Manurung, Ruli, University of Indonesia, Depok (PACLIC 26 Local Organizer)
Otoguro, Ryo, Waseda University, Tokyo (Associate Digital Archivist)

Honorary Chair:

Tseng, Chiu-yu (Academic Sinica)

Conference Chair:

Lai, Huei-ling (National Chengchi University)

Conference Co-Chair:

Chui, Kawai (National Chengchi University)

Program Committee:

Chairs:

Liu, Chao-Lin (National Chengchi University)
Tseng, Shu-Chuan (Academic Sinica)

Co-Chairs:

Bond, Francis (Nanyang Technology University)
Ji, Donghong (Wuhan University)
Kwong, Olivia (City University of Hong Kong)
Manurung, Ruli (University of Indonesia)
Otoguro, Ryo (Waseda University)
Roxas, Rachel (De La Salle University-Manila)

Yeom, Jae-Il (Hongik University)

PC Members:

Aroonmanakun, Wirote (Chulalongkorn University)
Baldwin, Tim (University of Melbourne)
Bressan, Stephane (National University of Singapore)
Chae, Hee-Rahk (Hankuk University of Foreign Studies)
Chang, Chia-Hui (National Central University)
Chang, Claire H.H. (National Chengchi University)
Chang, Jung-Hsing (National Chung Cheng University)
Chang, Tao-Hsing (National Kaohsiung University of Applied Sciences)
Chang, Yungli (Institute of Linguistics, Academia Sinica)
Chen, Chun-Yin Doris (National Taiwan Normal University)
Chen, Hsin-Hsi (National Taiwan University)
Chen, Kuang-Hua (National Taiwan University)
Cheng, Pu-Jen (National Taiwan University)
Chng, Eng-Siong (Nanyang Technological University)
Daille, Beatrice (University of Nantes)
Dalrymple, Mary (Oxford University)
De Busser, Rik (National Chengchi University)
Dong, Minghui (Institute for Infocomm Research)
Fu, Guohong (Heilongjiang University)
Harada, Yasunari (Waseda University)
Her, One-Soon (National Chengchi University)
Hong, Munpyo (Sungkyunkwan University)
Hsiao, Yu-Chau E. (National Chengchi University)
Hsieh, Shelley Ching-Yu (National Cheng Kung University)
Hsieh, Shu-Kai (National Taiwan University)
Hsu, Dong-Bo (National Taiwan Normal University)
Huang, Chiung-Chih (National Chengchi University)
Huang, Meei-Jin (Shih Chien University)
Huang, Xuanjing (Fudan University)
Inui, Kentaro (Tohoku University)
Ji, Donghong (Wuhan University)
Kim, Jong-Bok (Kyung Hee University)
Kordoni, Valia (Saarland University and DFKI GmbH)
Kwong, Oliver (City University of Hong Kong)
Lai, Bong Yeung Tom (City University of Hong Kong)
Law, Paul (City University of Hong Kong)

Lee, Yae-Sheik (Kyungpook National University)
Lenci, Alessandro (University of Pisa)
Levow, Gina-Anne (University of Washington)
Li, Haizhou (Institute for Infocomm Research)
Lin, Chuan-Jie (National Taiwan Ocean University)
Lin, Jo-Wang (National Chiao Tung University)
Lin, Shou-De (National Taiwan University)
Liu, Qun (Dublin City University & ICT Chinese Academy of Sciences)
Lu, Wen-Hsiang (National Cheng Kung University)
Ma, Qing (Ryukoku University)
Ma, Yanjun (Baidu)
Maekawa, Takafumi (Hokusei Gakuen University Junior College)
Matsumoto, Yuji (Nara Institute of Science and Technology)
Matsushita, Mitsunori (Kansai University)
Morey, Mathieu (Nanyang Technological University)
Ng, Vincent (University of Texas at Dallas)
Nie, Jian-Yun (Universit de Montral)
Ogihara, Toshiyuki (University of Washington)
Otoguro, Ryo (Waseda University)
Paris, Cecile (CSIRO - ICT Centre)
Park, Jong C. (KAIST)
Prévot, Laurent (Aix-Marseille Université)
Qi, Haoliang (Heilongjiang Institute of Technology)
Qiu, Long (Institute for Infocomm Research)
Ranaivo-Malançon, Bali (Universiti Malaysia Sarawak)
Roxas, Rachel (De La Salle University-Manila)
Sah, Wen-Hui (National Chengchi University)
Shaikh, Samira (State University of New York - University at Albany)
Shyu, Shu-Ing (National Sun Yat-sen University)
Siegel, Melanie (Hochschule Darmstadt)
Singhapreecha, Pornsiri (Thammasat University)
Smith, Simon (Coventry University)
Sornlertlamvanich, Virach (National Electronics and Computer Technology Center)
Su, Keh-Yih (Behavior Design Corporation)
Su, Lily I-Wen (National Taiwan University)
Su, Yi-Ching (National Tsing Hua University)
Sung, Li-May (National Taiwan University)

Tabata, Tomoji (The University of Osaka)
Thompson, Henry S. (University of Edinburgh)
Tsai, Ming-Feng (National Chengchi University)
Tsai, Richard Tzong-Han (Yuan Ze University)
Tseng, Yuen-Hsien (National Taiwan Normal University)
Van Genabith, Josef (Dublin City University)
Villavicencio, Aline (Federal University of Rio Grande do Sul, University of Bath)
Wan, I-Ping (National Chengchi University)
Wang, Haifeng (Baidu)
Wang, Houfeng (Peking University)
Wang, Hsu (Yuan Ze University)
Wang, Hui (National University of Singapore)
Wang, Yu-Fang (National Kaohsiung Normal University)
Wu, Jing-Lan Joy (National Taiwan Normal University)
Wu, Jiun-Shiung (National Chung Cheng University)
Yang, Cheng-Zen (Yuan Ze University)
Yeh, Jui-Feng (National Chia-Yi Universty)
Yeom, Jae-Il (Hongik University)
Yokoyama, Satoru (Tohoku University)
Zhang, Jiajun (Chinese Academy of Sciences)
Zhang, Min (I2R)
Zhao, Hai (Shanghai Jiao Tong University)
Zock, Michael (CNRS-LIF)
Zong, Chengqing (Chinese Academy of Sciences)

Workshop Chairs:

Liu, Jyi-Shane (National Chengchi University)
Gao, Zhao-Ming (National Taiwan University)

Publication Chairs:

Chung, Siaw-Fong (National Chengchi University)
Chang, Jing-Shin (National Chi Nan University)
Yu, Liang-Chih (Yuan Ze University)

Table of Contents

Main Conference Keynote Speeches

Workshop Keynote Speeches

Main Conference Invited Talks

PACLIC 27 Papers

Oral Presentation Session 1A: Grammar and Syntax

Oral Presentation Session 1B: Language Generation

Oral Presentation Session 2A: Discourse and Pragmatics

Oral Presentation Session 2B: Lexical Knowledge Learning

Oral Presentation Session 3A: Speech Perception

Oral Presentation Session 3B: Language Learning

Oral Presentation Session 4A: Language Acquisition

Oral Presentation Session 4B: Corpus Compilation and Analysis

Oral Presentation Session 5A: Grammar and Syntax

Oral Presentation Session 5B: Machine Translation

Oral Presentation Session 6A: Morphology and Syntax

Oral Presentation Session 6B: Phonetics

Oral Presentation Session 7A: Semantics

Oral Presentation Session 7B: Sentiment Analysis

Poster Session 1

Poster Session 2

Workshop Session 1

Workshop Session 2

Workshop Session 3

Words and Rules Revisited: Reassessing the Role of Construction and Memory in Language

Alec Marantz
New York University, USA
marantz@nyu.edu

Abstract

Pinker's influential presentation of the distinction between the combinatoric units of language (the "words") and the mechanisms that organize the units into linguistic constituents (the "rules") rested on a strong, but ultimately incorrect, theory about the connection between a speaker's internalized grammar and his/her use of language: that what is linguistically complex, and thus constructed by the grammar, is not memorized; thus experience with complex constituents (as measured in corpus frequency, for example) would have no effect on processing such complex constituents. I argue that recent results within linguistics and within psycho- and neuro-linguistics show instead that memory and frequency effects are irrelevant to the linguistic analysis of language but always influence processing, across simple and complex constituents. Phrases and words can be shown always to decompose down to the level of morphemes both in representations and in processing, and, contrary to Pinker's claim, the "memorized" status of a complex structure holds no import for its linguistic analysis. On the other hand, speakers' experience with language is always reflected in their use of language, so frequency effects are always relevant to processing, even for completely regular combinations of words and morphemes. I will present neurolinguistic evidence for full decomposition of irregular forms (such as English irregular verbs), as well as evidence for frequency effects for regular combinations of morphemes and words.

A Principle-Based Approach for Natural Language Processing: Eliminating the Shortcomings of Rule-Based Systems with Statistics

Wen-Lian Hsu
Institute of Information Science, Academia Sinica
hsu@iis.sinica.edu.tw

Abstract

In natural language processing, an important task is to recognize various linguistic expressions. Many such expressions can be represented as rules or templates. These templates are matched by computer to identify those linguistic objects in text. However, in real world, there always seem to be many exceptions or variations not covered by rules or templates. A typical approach to cope with this situation is either to produce more templates or to relax the constraints of the templates (e.g., by inserting options or wild cards). But the former could create many similar case-by-case templates with no end in sight; and the latter could lead to lots of false positives, namely, matched but undesired linguistic expressions. Thus, the flexibility of rule matching has troubled the natural language processing (NLP) as well as the artificial intelligence (AI) community for years so as to make people believe that rule-based approach is not suitable for NLP or AI in general. On the other hand, fine-grained linguistic knowledge cannot be easily captured by current machine learning models, which resulted in mediocre recognition accuracy. Therefore, how to make the best out of rule-based and statistical approaches has been a very challenging task in natural language processing.

This paper describes a partial matching scheme that enables a single template to match a lot of semantically similar expressions with high accuracy, which we refer to as the Principle-Based Approach (PBA).

In PBA, we use a collection of frames to represent linguistic concepts or rules. Each frame is a collection of slots (also called components) with relations specified among them. A slot can be a word, phrase, semantic category, or another frame concept. One can specify position relations, collocation relations, and agreement relations and others among its slots. Unlike normal templates that involve mostly left-right relations among its components in a sentence, relations within frames can be multi-dimensional. For example, one slot could be a variable indicating the topic which other slots belong to.

To illustrate our partial matching scheme, consider a simple frame concept involving 5 components such that their relations in a sentence are arranged as 1, 2, 3, 4, 5 from left to right. Suppose in a sentence we can identify components 2, 3, and 5 in that order. So 1 and 4 are missing (deletion), and there maybe words inserting between 2 and 3 (insertion), and also between 3 and 5. Furthermore, a match for slot 5 could be on word-sense rather than on the word themselves (substitution). Our partial matching scheme allows for insertion, deletion and substitution. An insertion is given a positive score if it tends to collocate with its left or right matched components in general (otherwise, negative). A deletion can be harmless if slots 2, 3, and 5 contain a key combination for the frame. Note that many such key combinations can be pre-specified as indices of the frame. Collocation and bigram statistics can be incorporated in such score estimation. A substitution is given a lower score depending on their closeness in a semantic tree. After all these scores are determined, we can use an alignment algorithm to measure the fitness score and to decide how well the frame matches with the sentence.

PBA is inspired by the fact that when one studies a foreign language, he or she is usually presented with a collection of rules. These rules and their possible extensions and variations are practiced over and over again in real life to be mastered by the learner. PBA is flexible in that, it tends to relieve the burden of having to match with something "exactly" as specified and fine-grained linguistic knowledge can be more easily adopted to help estimate the scores of insertion, deletion and substitution in a PBA frame match.

We believe PBA can model more linguistic phenomena than current machine learning models, and is more suitable for NLP and AI in general. More details and examples of PBA will be covered in the talk.

Extracting "Criterial Features" for the CEFR Levels Using Corpora of EFL Learners' Written Essays

Yukio Tono
Tokyo University of Foreign Studies
y.tono@tufs.ac.jp

Abstract

In this talk, I will report on the on-going project on systematic extraction of criterial features from multiple source corpora based on the Common European Framework of Reference for Languages (CEFR). First, a brief description of the CEFR itself, the project and the design of several different corpora newly compiled for the project will be given, followed by methodological issues regarding how to extract criterial features from CEFR-based corpora using machine learning techniques.

The CEFR-J and Reference Level Descriptions

The project aims to support the implementation of the CEFR-J, an adaptation of the CEFR into English language teaching in Japan (Tono & Negishi 2012). After the release of Version 1 of the CEFR-J in March, 2012, we launched a new government-funded project called the "CEFR-J Reference Level Description (CEFR-J RLD)" Project. RLD is a term used for the CEFR to prepare an inventory of language (lexis and grammar) for each individual language for the purpose of level specification.

Table 1 shows the list of corpora to be used for the project:

Type of Corpora	Name	Features
Input corpus	ELT materials corpus (to be completed)	ELT course books Major textbooks that claim to be CEFR-based
Interaction corpus	Classroom observation data	30 hours secondary school ELT classes
Output corpus	JEFLL Corpus (0.7 million)	Written, secondary school, CEFR level
	NICT JLE Corpus (2 million)	Spoken, interview test scripts, 1,280 participants, CEFR level
	ICCI (0.6 million)	Written, primary & secondary school, 9000 samples, CEFR level
	GTECfS Corpus (to be comleted)	Written, exam scripts, 30,000 samples, CEFR level
	MEXT Corpus	S/W 2000 students randomly

	MEXT Corpus (S: 8,000 words) (W:3,0000 words)	S/W 2000 students randomly selected from all over Japan

Table1: Corpora used for the project

Three types of corpora have been either newly compiled or re-organised: input, interaction, and output corpora. For input corpora, major ELT publishers' CEFR-based course materials have been scanned and processed by OCR. For output corpora, major learner corpora for Japanese EFL learners, the JEFLL Corpus and the NICT JLE Corpus, have been selected, but for our project, the essays originally classified according to the school grades or oral proficiency test
scores, have been re-classified according to the estimated CEFR levels assigned by trained raters based on their holistic scorings. Two additional corpora have been made available. One is an exam-based corpus called the GTEC for STUDENTS Writing Corpus, provided by the Benesse Corporation. It consists of more than 30,000 students essay data with approximately 5,000 samples aligned with correction data. The other is the data collected by Ministry of Education (MEXT), in which more than 2,000 students were randomly selected from all over Japan. They were given written and oral proficiency exams in English. This data shows the average performance of EFL learners in Japan, after the three year instructions in secondary school.

Finally, a corpus of classroom interaction between teachers and students has been added to the resource. This is an on-going project and the size is relatively small, but I hope that it will shed light on the understanding of what is happening in the classroom.

Our aim is to identify criterial features by looking at input and output corpora across CEFR levels. The language presented in the input corpora may not be produced in the output corpora. By examining both input and output, descriptions of criterial features will become more systematic. The interaction corpus also helps better understand the learning/acquisition process in the classroom. Input from textbooks as well as input and interactions in the actual classroom will play an important role in learning a target language. The major goal is to find out criterial features for the levels specified in the CEFR-J and complete the inventory of grammar and vocabulary for teaching and assessment, with a special reference to teaching and learning contexts in Japan.

In the past few years, various linguistic criteria have been proposed as "criterial", but they need to be validated against a particular learner group like Japanese EFL learners because the data used in Europe are very different from our learner group. Also each proposed criterial feature should be evaluated and weighed in terms of usefulness as CEFR-level "classifiers". Then a bundle of criterial features have to be tested and validated to find out which combinations of criterial features work best to predict the CEFR-levels. In a way, for assessment purposes, it is sufficient to identify the most salient criterial feature that can distinguish all the levels clearly. For teaching purposes, however, all the learning items need to be somehow evaluated against their 'criteriality.'

There are various ways of extracting criterial features from the data. Machine learning techniques such as random forest seem to be very promising for this purpose. For instance, random forest is very useful in that it gives estimates of what variables are important in the classification. Table 2 shows the results of variable importance measure by Gini impurity criterion. Basically, the higher the score is, the more important the variable is. By using this kind of information, one can profile which linguistic feature will be most effective in classifying texts into CEFR levels. The major aim of the project is to decide on which machine learning algorithms to take, and evaluate a range of criterial features for its effectiveness as assessment and teaching points.

Linguistic features	MeanDecreaseGini
Total n. of words	440.3
Total n. of sentences	134.8
N. of VPs	277.2
N. of clauses	182.4
N. of T-units	121.3
N. of dependent clauses	102.6
N. of complex T-units	114.6
N. of complex nominals	210.2

Table2: Variable importance measured by Mean Decrease of Gini

In this paper, I will report on the performance of different machine learning techniques, including random forest, support vector machine, decision tree (C4.5), and naïve Bayes over CEFR-level classified texts and compare which programs produce the best result and useful additional information to evaluate the importance of criterial features.

References

Hawkins, J.A. & Filipović, L. (2012). Criterial Features in L2 English. Cambridge: Cambridge University Press.

Tono, Y. 2012a. Developing corpus-based word lists for English language learning and teaching: A critical appraisal of the English Vocabulary Profile. In J. Thomas & A. Boulton (eds). Input, Process and Product: Developments in Teaching and Language Corpora (pp.314-328). Brno: Masaryk University Press.

Tono, Y. 2012b. International Corpus of Crosslinguistic Interlanguage: Project overview and a case study on the acquisition of new verb co-occurrence patterns. In Y. Tono, Y. Kawaguchi & M. Minegishi (eds.) Developmental and Crosslinguistic Perspectives in Learner Corpus Research (pp.27-46). Amsterdam: John Benjamins.

Tono, Y. & Negishi, M. 2012. The CEFR-J: Adapting the CEFR for English language teaching in Japan. JALT Framework & Language Portfolio SIG Newsletter No.8 (September, 2012), pp. 5-12.

It's about Time: More and More Sophisticated Statistical Methods in Corpus Linguistics

Stefan Th. Gries
University of California, Santa Barbara
stgries@linguistics.ucsb.edu

Abstract

By its very nature, corpus linguistics is a discipline not just concerned with, but ultimately based on, the distributions and frequencies of linguistic forms in and across corpora. This undisputed fact notwithstanding, for many years, corpus linguistics has been dominated by work that was limited in both computational and statistical ways. As for the former, a lot of work is based on a small number of ready-made proprietary software packages that provide some major functions but can of course not provide the functionality that, for instance, programming languages provide. As for the latter, a lot of work is very unstatistical in nature by relying on little more than observed frequencies or percentages/conditional probabilities of linguistic elements.

However, over the last 10 years or so, this picture has changed and corpus linguistics has evolved considerably to a state where more diverse descriptive statistics and association measures as well as multifactorial regression modeling, other statistical classification techniques, and multivariate exploratory statistics have become quite common. In this talk, I will survey a variety of recent studies that showcase this new-developed methodological variety in both synchronic and diachronic corpus linguistics; examples will include applications of generalized linear (mixed-effects) models, different types of cluster-analytic algorithms, principal components analysis and other dimension-reduction tools, and others.

Linking Text with Data and Knowledge Bases

Junichi Tsujii
Microsoft Research Asia
Beijing, China
jtsujii@microsoft.com

Abstract

In the last two decades, we have witnessed the rapid development of techniques in statistical modeling of language, which exploit large collections of text to reveal statistical regularities in language uses. However, the statistics-based approach to language,which tends to ignore or deemphasize structural issues of language, has shown its own limitations. The approach in its strictest form, for example, fails to treat the systematic mapping between syntax and semantics of language (i.e. the compositional aspect of meaning).An increasing number of researchers have become interested in combining linguistic theories, which treat the compositional aspect of meaning, with statistical modeling of language.

On the other hand, the community of knowledge-mining and semantic search has constructed large knowledge bases such as Freebase, Yago and Wikipedia. Although these knowledge-bases have been constructed independently of the interests in the NLP research community, they provide essential resources for research on Natural Language Understanding, which aims to develop a system which understands language as human being does. The first step of such an understanding system is to relate surface forms of language with corresponding units in knowledge-bases. Once text is mapped to representation in the knowledge domain, one can perform inferences of various sorts by combining it with knowledge in the knowledge base. Inferences, which combine information embedded within text with human knowledge which is external to text, are deemed essential in text understanding.

The two streams of research in the above seem to be tackling the same problem of how surface expressions in text can be linked with extra-linguistic representation in the knowledge domain, and what roles the structure of language plays in such a linking process.

With this broad perspective in mind, I will address the following research topics which I have been involved in:

(1) Parsing and Semantics: While the performance of a syntactic parser has been improved substantially of late, it still fails to treat semantically crucial constructions. In order to resolve the difficulties which remain in parsing, we have to treat semantics of language more systematically than the current state of the arts parsers do. I would argue that we cannot resolve the difficulties without referring

to proper theories of syntax.

(2) Entity linking: Disambiguation in entity-linking has been carried out by using characteristics specific to individual entities. However, in order to treat long-tail problems in entity-linking, not only properties of individual entities but also classes of entities and their properties in knowledge bases have to be exploited. The results of our recent experiments will be presented, in order to illustrate how structures in knowledge bases can be used for interpretation of expressions in language.

(3) Relation linking: The same relation in the knowledge domain can be expressed by diverse surface expressions in language. To gather surface relation expressions for a given set of relations in the knowledge domain is a crucial step of linking text with knowledge. Some of our recent studies in relation extraction will be presented as the next step of linking text with knowledge bases.

(4) Paraphrasing and structures of sentences: While semantics of words have been studied extensively both in distributional semantics and traditional linguistics (e.g. synonyms, antonyms, etc.), semantics of larger units such as phrases and clauses have not been studied with similar degrees of details. Paraphrase recognition by structure alignment will provide a framework to capture semantics of larger units in language than words. We discuss how structures of sentences together with inferences based on meaning can give fine grained explanation of paraphrases, and how such research will contribute to the task of linking text with knowledge.

Mining Language Learners' Production Data for Understanding of L2 Learning Systems

Yukio Tono
Tokyo University of Foreign Studies
`y.tono@tufs.ac.jp`

Abstract

In this workshop, I will share my experience in the field of learner corpus research (LCR). First I will define learner corpora in terms of its design criteria. Second, I will show how L2 learners' production data as corpora can be exploited to find linguistic features that characterize the progress in L2 learning systems. Third, such transitional competence should be explained by various internal and external factors such as cognitive, affective, and instructional effects. I would like to discuss with the participants how to model L2 learning systems by showing various examples of features marking different stages of learning in English as a foreign language.

Introducing Linggle: From Concordance to Linguistic Search Engine

Jason S. Chang
Department of Computer Science
National Tsing Hua University
son.jschang@gmail.com

Abstract

We introduce a Web-scale linguistics search engine, *in e*, that retrieves lexical bundles in response to a given query. Unlike a typical concordance, *in e* accepts queries with keywords, wildcard, wild part of speech (PoS), synonymous words, and additional regular expression (RE) operators, and returns bundles with frequency counts. In our approach, we argument Google Web 1T corpus with inverted file indexing, PoS information from BNC, and semantic indexing based on Latent Dirichlet Allocation. The method involves parsing the query to transforming the query to several keyword retrieval commands, retrieving word chunks with counts, filtering the chunks again the query as a RE, and finally displaying the results according the count, similarity, and topic. Clusters of synonymous or conceptually related words are also provided. In addition, *in e* provide example sentences from *e e or i es* on demand. The current implementation of *in e* is the most comprehensive functionally, and is in principle language and dataset independent. We plan to extend *in e* to provide a fast and convenient access to a wealth of linguistic information embodied in Web scale datasets including *oo e We* and *oo e oo s ra* for many major languages in the World.

For non-native speakers, doubts concerning the usage of a preposition, the mandatory presence of a determiner, the correctness of the association of a verb with an object or the need for synonyms of a term in a given context are problems that arise frequently when writing in English. Printed collocation dictionaries and reference tools based on compiled corpora offer limited coverage of word usage while knowledge of collocations is vital for the competent use of a language. We propose to address these limitations with a comprehensive system that truly aims at letting learners "know a word by the company it keeps". *in e* (**linggle.com**) is a broad coverage language reference tool for English as Second Language learners (ESL). The system is designed to access words in context under various forms.

First, we build inverted file index for the *oo e We ra* to support queries with RE-like patterns including PoS and synonym matches. For example, for the query "$V $D +important role", *in e* retrieve 4-gram chunks that start with a verb and a determiner followed by a *i portant* synonym and the keyword *ro e* (e. g., *p a a e part* 15,900). A natural language interface is also available for users that would be less familiar to pattern based search. For example the question " *o an es ri e a ea* would retrieve two word chunks with count such as "*san ea* 413,300" and "*ro ea* 16,800". The n-gram search implementation is achieved through filtering, re-indexing, and populating Web 1T ngram in a HBase database and augmenting them with the most frequent PoS for words (without disambiguation) derived from the British National Corpus.

The n-grams resulting from the queries can then be linked to examples extracted from the New York Times Corpus in order to provide full sentential context for more effective learning. In some situations, users might need to search for words in a specific syntactic relation (i. e., *o o ates*). Let's consider the example "absorb $N" that queries all the objects of the verb *a sor* . In this case, grouping the words that belong to similar domains together offers a better overview of the usage of the verb than a list of objects ordered by frequency. For example the verb *a sor* takes clusters of objects related to the topic *i i ener* , but also to the topics *one no e e* or *pop ation.*

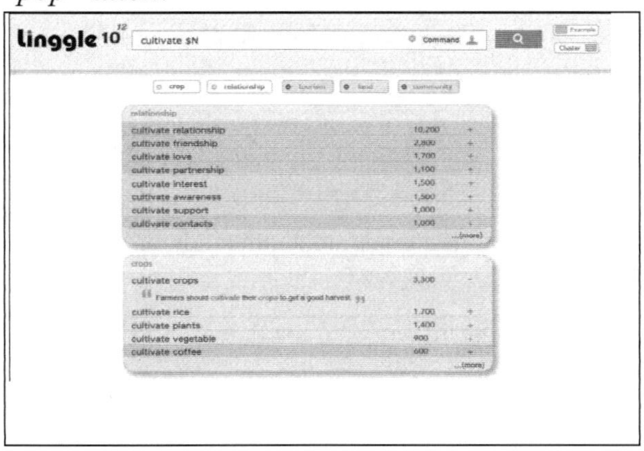

This tendency of predicates to prefer certain classes is defined by Wilks (1978) as selectional preference and widely reported in the literature. *in e* proposes *pre erre* clusters of synonymous query arguments of adjectives, nouns and verbs. The clustering is achieved by building on Lin and Pantel (2002)'s large-scale repository of dependencies and word similarity scores and on an existing method for selectional preference induction with a Latent Dirichlet Allocation (LDA) model.

*** Formatting Issue - Best Available Paper/Graphic ***

References

Chang, Jason. S. 2008. Linggle: a web-scale language reference search engine. Unpublished manuscript.

Fletcher, William H. 2012. Corpus analysis of the world wide web." In *e n ope ia o pp ie in isti s.*

Kilgarriff, Adam, and David Tugwell. 2001. Word sketch: Extraction and display of significant collocations for lexicography. In *ro ee in s o o p tationa tra tion na sis an p oitation or s op*, pp. 32-38.

Kilgarriff, Adam. 2007. Googleology is bad science." *o p tationa in isti s* 33(1), pp. 147-151.

Lin, Dekang, and Patrick Pantel. 2002. Concept discovery from text. In *ro ee in s o* .

Lin, Dekang, Kenneth Church, Heng Ji, Satoshi Sekine, David Yarowsky, Shane Bergsma, Kailash Patil et al. 2010. "New tools for web-scale n-grams." *ro ee in s o* .

Potthast, Martin, Martin Trenkmann, and Benno Stein. Using Web N-Grams to Help Second-Language Speakers. 2010. In *ro ee in s o We ra Wor s op*, pages 49-49.

Wu, Shaoqun, Ian H. Witten, and Margaret Franken. 2010. Utilizing lexical data from a Web-derived corpus to expand productive collocation knowledge." *e* 22(1), pp. 83-102.

Wilks, Yorick. 1978. Making preferences more active. *rti i ia nte i en e* 11(3), pp. 197-223.

Statistical Machine Translation Based on Predicate-Argument Structure

Chengqing Zong
Institute of Automantion, Chinese Academy of Sciences
No. 95, Zhong Guan Cun East Road, Beijjing 100190, China
cqzong@lpr.ia.ac.cn

Abstract

As we have well known that it is always a basic requirement for statistical machine translation (SMT) to maintain semantic equivalence between a source sentence and its translation. However, nearly all of the existing translation models do not deal with the semantic structure between two languages at all. In this talk, I will present a novel translation method based on semantically-motivated framework, using predicate-argument structure (PAS). Generally, PAS depicts the semantic relation between a predicate and its associated arguments, and it always indicates the semantic frame and skeleton structure of a sentence. Thus, we believe the PAS would be much beneficial for machine translation in grasping the semantics of sentences. Furthermore, after analysis of the weakness of PAS representation during translation, I will propose a concept of syntax-complemented PAS (SC-PAS). It effectively overcomes the drawback of the prevalent gaps in PAS and provides more useful knowledge for SMT.

We also call the semantically-motivated framework as Analysis-Transformation-Translation (ATT) framework, which is just based on the PAS and SC-PAS. As the following figure shows, this framework divides the whole translation process into three steps: (1) Analysis: to analyze the source sentences and obtain their PASs (or SC-PASs) automatically; (2) Transformation: to convert the source-side PASs (or SC-PASs) to target side by predicate-aware transformation rules; (3) Translation: this step is further divided into two parts: (a)element translation is to translate each element of PAS (or SC-PAS); (b)translation by global reordering is to combine the resulting translation candidates to translate the entire structure. By taking advantage of PAS (or SC-PAS), the ATT framework can well keep the semantic structure consistency of the source language and the target language and consequently show the great potential to improve translation quality.

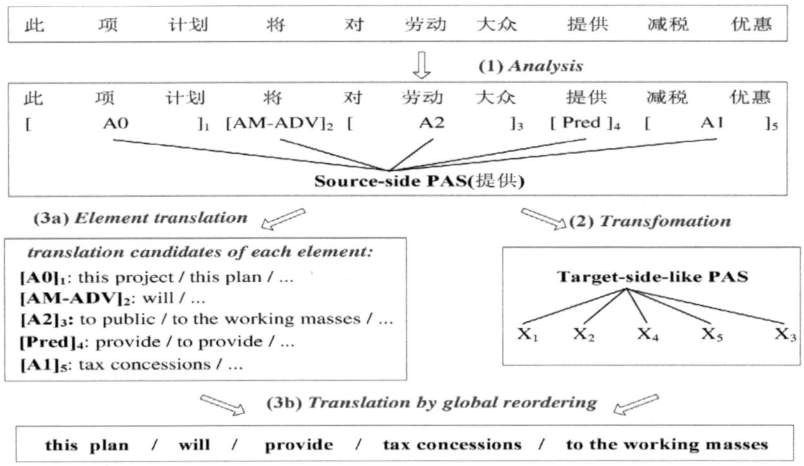
此 项 计划 将 对 劳动 大众 提供 减税 优惠
(1) Analysis
此 项 计划 将 对 劳动 大众 提供 减税 优惠
[A0]1 [AM-ADV]2 [A2]3 [Pred]4 [A1]5
Source-side PAS(提供)
(3a) Element translation
(2) Transfomation
translation candidates of each element:
[A0]1: this project / this plan / ...
[AM-ADV]2: will / ...
[A2]3: to public / to the working masses / ...
[Pred]4: provide / to provide / ...
[A1]5: tax concessions / ...
Target-side-like PAS
X1 X2 X4 X5 X3
(3b) Translation by global reordering
this plan / will / provide / tax concessions / to the working masses

Using Hierarchically Structured Lexicon as Key Clues Solving Data Sparseness Problems in Word Sense Disambiguation: a Case for Korean and Its Applications to English and Chinese

Aesun Yoon
Korean Language Processing Laboratory
Dept. of French
Pusan National University
Busan, 609-735, Rep of Korean
asyoon@pusan.ac.kr

Minho Kim, Hyuk-Chul Kwon
Korean Language Processing Laboratory
Dept. of French
Pusan National University
Busan, 609-735, Rep of Korean
{karma, hckwon}pusan.ac.kr

Abstract

Word sense disambiguation (WSD) determines the accuracy of almost all tasks in natural language processing. Korean Processing Laboratory of Pusan National University has been working on efficient automatic WSD methods, especially for Korean language. This paper presents our unsupervised model using hierarchically-structured lexicon, i.e. Korean WordNet (KorLex). KorLex can provide us with key clues for solving data sparseness problems, which are inherent in the unsupervised WSD. The proposed model shows 91.14% average accuracy, which is 26.95% higher than the best performance obtained by a supervised method (Lesk's dictionary-based WSD). Our model obtains also a higher accuracy for English and Chinese, using Princeton WordNet and HowNet.

Effects of Constituent Orders on Grammaticalization Patterns of the Serial Verbs for 'Give' in Thai and Mandarin Chinese

Kingkarn Thepkanjana
Chulalongkorn University
Phayathai Road, Bangkok 10330
THAILAND
Kingkarn.T@chula.ac.th

Satoshi Uehara
Tohoku University
41 Kawauchi, Aoba-ku, Sendai
980-8576 JAPAN
uehara@intcul.tohoku.ac.jp

Abstract

The verbs meaning 'give' across languages are known to be among the most highly grammaticalized verbs, which exhibit a high degree of polyfunctionality. This paper aims to (i) present commonalities and differences in the grammaticalization of the verbs for 'give' in Thai and Mandarin Chinese, namely, hây in Thai and gěi in Mandarin Chinese, and (ii) investigate how different constituent orders of the head vis-à-vis the modifier and complement in Thai and Mandarin Chinese bear on patterns of grammaticalization of the two verbs. It is found that the functions that hây in Thai and gěi in Mandarin Chinese share in common are (1) the ditransitive verb use, (2) the dative-marking use, (3) the benefactive-marking use, and (4) the causative-marking use. As for different functions of hây and gěi, hây exhibits the clause connective use, which is lacking in gěi, whereas gěi exhibit the passive-marking use, which is lacking in hây. It is argued that the head-modifier order in Thai seems to be compatible with postverbal grammaticalized morphemes whereas the modifier-head order in Mandarin Chinese seems to be compatible with preverbal grammaticalized ones.

1 Introduction

It is generally known that Thai and Mandarin Chinese are typologically similar in many respects. They are isolating, topic-prominent, serializing, have the SVO basic word order and rich with grammaticalized morphemes. However, there is one important difference between them, i.e. difference in constituent order. Mandarin Chinese has the modifier-head order whereas Thai has the head-modifier one. This paper investigates how the difference in constituent order in Thai and Mandarin Chinese bears on patterns of grammaticalization of serial verbs in the two languages. The serial verbs for 'give' in Thai and Mandarin Chinese, i.e. hây and gěi, are used as a case study. The verbs meaning 'give' across languages are known to be among the most highly grammaticalized verbs, which exhibit a high degree of polyfunctionality. The analysis in this paper is based on the findings of a synchronic contrastive study of hây and gěi presented in Thepkanjana and Uehara (2008).

2 Commonalities and differences

Thepkanjana and Uehara (2008) make a synchronic contrastive study of the polysemous morphemes hây and gěi in Thai and Mandarin Chinese. It is found in Thepkanjana and Uehara (2008) that hây and gěi share four main uses, namely, the ditransitive (main) verb use, the dative-marking use, the benefactive-marking use and the causative-marking use. As for differences between hây and gěi, one important use that is missing in hây is the passive-marking use whereas one that is missing in gěi is the clause connective function. The commonalities between the two verbs are discussed in section 2.1 and the differences in section 2.2. The examples provided are drawn from Thepkanjana and Uehara (2008).

2.1 Commonalities between hây and gěi

The first common function between hây and gěi is the ditransitive main verb use. Hây and gěi in this use co-occur with two NPs following each other in a row. The structural schemas of the ditransitive verbs hây and gěi and some examples of this use are given below. Notice that the semantic roles of NP1 and NP2 in Thai and Mandarin Chinese are different.

Ditransitive verb use

Thai: [hây + NP1 + NP2]
(thing) (recipient)

(1) sǒmsàk hây ŋən sǒmchay
Somsak give money Somchay
'Somsak gave Somchay some money.'

Mandarin Chinese: [gěi + NP1 + NP2]
(recipient) (thing)

(2) Zhāngsān gěi Lǐsì qián
Zhangsan give Lisi money
'Zhangsan gave Lisi some money.'

Dative-marking use

Thai: [V + NP1 +hây+ NP2]
(thing) (recipient)

(3) sǒmsàk sòŋ ŋən hây sǒmchay
Somsak send money give Somchay
'Somsak sent some money to Somchay.'

Mandarin Chinese: 2 schemas

Schema 1: postverbal *gěi*
[V + NP1 + gěi + NP2]
(thing) (recipient)

(4) Zhāngsān jì-le yì fēng
Zhangsan send-ASP one CLS
xìn gěi Lǐsì
letter give Lisi
'Zhangsan mailed a letter to Lisi.'

Schema 2: preverbal gěi
[gěi + NP1 + V + NP2]
(recipient) (thing)

(5) Zhāngsān gěi Lǐsì mǎi
Zhangsan give Lisi buy
yì běn shū
one CLS book
'Zhangsan bought a book for (and gave it to) Lisi'

Notice that the dative hây in Thai occurs postverbally whereas the dative gěi occurs both preverbally and postverbally.

Newman (1993b) argues that an act of giving naturally results in some kind of benefit to the recipient. Even a non-giving action, such as driving, speaking and cleaning can also be done for the benefit of someone. The person who benefits from the agent's action is usually called a beneficiary. Therefore, it is natural that hây and gěi can also function as benefactive markers. The notion of benefactive is more complicated than generally assumed. Three types of benefactive are postulated in this paper as below.

(a) Recipient benefactive: The beneficiary gains a benefit by virtue of being a recipient of a concrete entity, for example, John bought a sweater for Mary.
(b) Benefit benefactive: The beneficiary gains a more or less abstract benefit from somebody's action, for example, John sang a song for Mary.
(c) Behalf benefactive: The beneficiary gains a benefit from somebody who performs an action on his/her behalf, for example, John drove a car for Mary because she was drunk.

It is found that the Thai hây can be used to mark the three types of benefactive as shown below.

Recipient benefactive

(6) sǒmsàk súuu sɯ̂anǎaw hây
Somsak buy sweater give
sǒmchay
Somchay
'Somsak bought a sweater for Somchay.'

Benefit benefactive

(7) sǒmsàk tàt phǒm hây sǒmchay
Somsak cut hair give Somchay
'Somsak cut hair for Somchay.' Or
'Somsak cut Somchay's hair.'

Behalf benefactive

(8) sǒmsàk khàprót hây sǒmchay
Somsak drive a car give Somchay
'Somsak drove a car for Somchay.'

It is noted that the benefactive hây is ambiguous between the recipient benefactive and behalf benefactive readings if the main verb incorporates the sense of giving or involves the the manipulation of an entity as shown in (9) and (10).

(9) sǒmsàk sòŋ còtmǎay hây sǒmchay
Somsak send letter give Somchay
'Somsak sent a letter to Somchay.' Or
'Somsak sent a letter on Somchay's behalf.'

(10) sǒmsàk suɯ́ɯ nǎŋsuɯ̌ɯ hây
Somsak buy book give
*s*ǒmchay
Somchay
'Somsak bought a book and gave it to Somchay.' Or
'Somchay bought a book on Somchay's behalf.'

It is found that the Mandarin Chinese gěi can be used to mark the recipient benefactive and the benefit benefactive in some cases as shown below.

(11) Zhāngsān gěi Lǐsì mǎi
Zhangsan give Lisi buy
yì běn shū
one CLS book
'Zhangsan bought a book for (and gave it to) Lisi'

(12) Zhāngsān gěi wǒme*n* chàng
Zhangsan give us sing
yì shǒu gē
one CLS song
'Zhangsan sang a song for us.'

The structural schemas of the benefactive hây and gěi are given below.

Benefactive-marking use
Thai: [V + (NP1) + hây + NP2]
(beneficiary)

Mandarin Chinese: [gěi + NP1 + V+ (NP2)]
(beneficiary)

Notice that the benefactive hây and gěi occur in different positions. The former occurs postverbally, i.e. after the main verb, whereas the latter occurs preverbally, i.e. before the main verb.

The third common use of hây and gěi is the causative use. The causative constructions with the causative-marking hây and gěi in Thai and Mandarin Chinese have the same syntactic schema as below.

Causative-marking use
Thai and Mandarin Chinese:
[NP1 + hây/gěi + NP2 + VP]
(causer) (causee)

(13) sǒmsàk hây sǒmchay ʔɔ̀ɔk pay
Somsak give Somchay exit go
'Somsak had Somchay go out.'

(14) Zhāngsān gěi Lǐsì kàn
Zhangsan give Lisi look
'Zhangsan let Lisi look.'

The NP1 in the schema above is the causer whereas the NP2 is the causee. The causer is typically human whereas the causee is typically animate. The causative verbs hây and gěi express an indirect causation in which the causer intentionally causes an event to take place by doing something to prompt the causer to act or by not doing something which prevents that event to take place. The causee is the person who directly causes the event to take place. Notice that the causative gěi occurs in the same position as the benefactive gěi in Mandarin Chinese, which results in ambiguity between the causative and benefactive readings in some cases as shown in (15), which is taken from Newman (1996:20).

(15) wǒ gěi nǐ kàn
I give you look
'I let you look.' (causative) Or
'I look on your behalf.' (benefactive)

According to Yap and Iwasaki (1998), native speakers of Mandarin Chinese tend to interpret gěi in (15) as the benefactive marker rather than the causative one as in (16).

(16) tā gěi *wǒ* *zào*-le
s/he give me build-ASP
yì dòng fángzi
one CLS house
'S/he built a house for me.' (preferred)
'S/he had me build a house.' (awkward)

Yap and Iwasaki (1998) note that Mandarin Chinese prefers the causative verbs ràng and jiào to the verb gěi in expressing indirect causation as in (17).

(17) tā *gěi/ràng/jiào háizi shuì-jiào
s/he CAUSE child sleep
'She let the child sleep.

The use of ràng and jiào rather than gěi to express causation helps prevent the ambiguity between the causative and benefactive readings that can arise if gěi is used as the causative verb, which occurs in the same position as the benefactive gěi. It is therefore not surprising that the use of the causative gěi in Mandarin Chinese is much more restricted than the use of the causative hây in Thai because the latter does not create ambiguity as the former.

2.2 Differences between hây and gĕi

Hây and gĕi are different in two ways. There is one important use of hây which is missing in gĕi, namely, clause connective use, and one important use of gĕi which is missing in hây, namely passive-marking function. The clause connective use, which is missing in gĕi is discussed first.

The connective hây in Thai takes place in complex constructions in which hây functions as a subordinator which links two predicates or two clauses. The first clause in the complex construction is the matrix clause and the other is the subordinate one. The complex constructions in which *hâ*y functions as the subordinator can be classified into three types, namely, a purposive construction, a jussive construction and a complementation construction. The purposive construction is a complex construction in which the subordinate clause functions as a purpose of the performance of an action denoted by the matrix clause. The jussive construction expresses a command, request or demand made by one participant towards another in order for the latter to perform an action (Van Valin and LaPolla, 1997). The complementation construction is a complex construction in which the subordinate clause functions as a complement of the desiderative predicate of the matrix clause. The structural schema of the connective hây and some examples of the three types of complex constructions containing hây are given below.

Clause connective use
Thai: $_{S1}$[NP1 + VP1] + hây+ $_{S2}$[NP2 + VP2]

From Rangkuphan (1997:36)
Purposive construction
(18) nuan phlàk kæ̂æw hây
Nuan push Kaew give

*k*lîŋ pay rɯ̂ayrɯ̂ay
roll go continually
'Nuan pushed the glass in order for it to keep rolling.'

(19) nuan khon námtaan hây lalaay
Nuan stir sugar give melt
'Nuan stirred the sugar in order for it to melt.'

Jussive construction
(20) sŏmsàk bɔ̀ɔk hây sŏmchay maa
Somsak tell give Somchay come
'Somsak told Somchay to come.'

(21) sŏmsàk sàŋ hây sŏmchay
Somsak order give Somchay
klàp bâan
return home
'Somsak ordered that Somchay go home.'

Complementation
(22) sŏmsàk yàak hây sŏmchay
Somsak want give Somchay
m*aa* *hăa*
come see
'Somsak wanted Somchay to come to see him.'

(23) sŏmsàk tɔ̂ŋk*aan* hây lûuk
Somsak want give child
rian phæ̂æt
study medicine
'Somsak wanted his child to study medicine.'

Thepkanjana and Uehara (2008) argue that each type of complex construction results from a reanalysis of hây from the causative verb to the subordinator. In the reanalysis process, the causative hây is semantically bleached out and loses its verbal properties to varying degrees in the three types of complex construction. In other words, hây in the three types of complex construction has different degrees of function word properties. It is argued in Thepkanjana and Uehara (2008) that the connective hây in the complex constructions is derived, extended or grammaticalized from the causative hây. The hây's in all of these cases are followed by a clause or a predicate. The causative hây functions as the main verb in the causative construction whereas the connective hây is preceded by a main verb and followed by a clause or a predicate. It is found that there is an intention that an event take place in the subject of the matrix clause in all of the three types of complex construction and in the subject of the causative hây. It is argued in Thepkanjana and Uehara (2008) that the notion of indirect causation has the highest degree of saliency in the causative hây but has decreasing degrees of saliency in the purposive, jussive and complementation constructions.

On the other hand, one important use of gěi which is missing in hây is the passive-marking function. The passive-marking function is alternatively called the agentive-marking function. The structural schema of the passive-marking gěi and some examples are given below.

Passive-marking use
Mandarin Chinese: [NP1 + gěi+ NP2 + VP]
From Haspelmath (1990:48)
(24) Lǐsi gěi Zhāngsān kànji*àn*-le
Lisi give Zhangsan see-ASP
'Lisi was seen by Zhangsan.'

From Newman (1993b:471)
(25) jīnyú gěi m*āo* chī-le
goldfish give cat eat-ASP
'The goldfish was eaten by the cat.'

According to Xu (1994), the passive gěi is used in colloquial speech whereas the other passive marker, bèi, is used in formal speech. In addition, a verb which co-occurs with the passive gěi must be marked by the aspect marker le, otherwise the sentence with gěi will not be interpreted as a passive sentence. Many works, such as Newman 1993a, b), Xu (1994), Yap and Iwasaki (1998, 2003) argue correspondingly that the passive gěi is directly derived from the causative gěi via the reflexive context. An important question is why the development from a causative use into a passive one does not take place in Thai. Yap and Iwasaki (1998) found out that hây in Thai takes only a volitional causer. Yap and Iwasaki (2003) argue that only nonvolitionality on the part of the causer can allow a passive interpretation to emerge. Therefore, the high degree of volitionality of the causer prevents hây from developing into a passive marker in Thai.

2.3 Summary

In summary, hây in Thai occurs in four constructions, namely, the ditransitive construction, the prepositional phrase, the causative construction and the complex construction. Hây functions as the ditransitive main verb, dative and benefactive markers, causative verb and clause connector or subordinator, respectively. Each of the four constructions has its own structural schema as below. The syntactic category of hây in each construction and function is specified under each structural schema in the rightmost column.

No.	Construction type Containing hây	Function of hây	Structural Schema
1	ditransitive construction	ditransitive (main) verb	hây+ NP1 + NP2 main verb
2	prepositional phrase	dative marker; benefactive marker	VP+$_{PP}$[hây +NP] preposition
3	causative construction	causative verb	NP1+hây+NP2+ VP causative verb
4.	complex sentence	clause connector	$_{S1}$[NP1+VP2] + hây + $_{S2}$[NP2+VP2] subordinator

Table 1. Functions and Structural Schemas of Hây

On the other hand, gěi in Mandarin Chinese appears in four constructions, namely, the ditransitive construction, the prepositional phrase, the causative construction and the passive construction. Gěi functions as the ditransitive main verb, dative and benefactive markers, causative verb and passive marker, respectively. The constructions in which gěi appears, the functions and the structural schemas of all constructions containing gěi appear in Table 2.

No.	Construction type Containing gěi	Function of gěi	Structural Schema
1	ditransitive construction	ditransitive (main) verb	gěi+ NP1 + NP2 main verb
2	prepositional phrase	dative marker	VP + $_{PP}$[gěi + NP] preposition
			$_{PP}$[gěi + NP] + VP preposition
		benefactive marker	$_{PP}$[gěi + NP] + VP preposition
3	causative construction	causative verb	NP1+gěi+NP2+ VP causative verb and passive marker
4	passive construction	passive marker	

Table 2. Functions and Structural Schemas of Gěi

Some observations can be made regarding the functions, the structural schemas and the productivity of hây and gěi in the functions specified in the tables above as follows.

(a) The clause connector use is possible for hây in Thai but is lacking for gěi in Mandarin Chinese.
(b) The passive-marking use in possible for gěi in Mandarin Chinese but is lacking for hây in Thai.
(c) The gěi-marked dative PP in Mandarin Chinese can occur both before and after the main VP whereas the hây-marked dative PP can occur only after the main VP. That means there are two structural schemas of the dative gěi whereas there is only one of the dative hây.
(d) Even though the gěi-marked dative PP in Mandarin Chinese is claimed by many researchers to occur both before and after the main VP, only the preverbal gěi-marked dative PPs, not the postverbal ones, are attested in a Beijing Mandarin speech corpus (Sanders and Uehara, 2012).
(e) The gěi-marked benefactive PP in Mandarin Chinese can occur only before the main verb phrase.
(f) The postverbal [hây+NP] in Thai and the preverbal [gěi+NP] in Mandarin Chinese can be ambiguous between the dative and benefactive interpretations if the main VP incorporates the sense of giving.

(g) The structural schemas of the causative and the passive gěi are identical.
(h) The causative use of hây in Thai is productive but that of gěi in Mandarin Chinese is not.

In section 3, we will argue for the relationship between constituent orders in Thai and Mandarin Chinese on the one hand and patterns of grammaticalization of hây and gěi on the other.

3. Effects of constituent orders on patterns of grammaticalizationof hây and gěi

In this section, we will point out how constituent orders in Thai and Chinese bear on patterns of grammaticalization of hây and gěi in both languages. The constituent orders to be discussed in this section are those of a head vis-à-vis a modifier and those of a head vis-à-vis a complement. A complement is a syntactic category that is selected or subcategorized for by the head of a phrase. A complement is therefore semantically necessary for the head to become semantically complete. Some examples of complements are below.

(26) I cut <u>a tree</u>.
(27) She put <u>a book</u> <u>on the table</u>.

In (26) and (27), the direct object nominals *a* tree and *a* book function as complements of the verbs cut and put respectively. In addition, the prepositional phrase *on* the table also functions as another complement of the verb put in (27) because the verb put is semantically incomplete without it. On the other hand, a modifier is an expression which limits or qualifies the meaning of a word, a phrase or a sentence. It is less semantically crucial to the meaning of a head than a complement. In other words, a modifier is more semantically peripheral than a complement. The underlined parts in (28) and (30) illustrate the modifiers in the sentences.

(28) The tree is <u>very</u> tall.
(29) She *read* the newspaper <u>in the living room</u>.
(30) She went to see *a* movie <u>after dinner</u>.

In (28), very modifies tall. In (29) and (30), the phrases i*n* the living room and after dinner modify the predicates in the clauses. The three sentences above are semantically complete without the modifiers. However, Langacker (1987) acknowledges that the demarcation between modification and complementation is sometimes hard to draw because the difference between them is a matter of degree.

It is generally known that the constituent orders in Thai and Mandarin Chinese are different in that Thai has the head-modifier constituent order whereas Mandarin Chinese has the modifier-head one. The difference in constituent order in the two languages is illustrated below. The adverbial modifiers in the examples are underlined.

Thai

(31) khun	pay	<u>kɔ̀ɔn</u>
you	go	first

'You go first.'

Mandarin Chinese

(32) nǐ	<u>xiān</u>	zǒu
you	first	go

'You go first.'

However, in case of the head and complement, the constituent orders in Thai and Mandarin Chinese are identical, that is, head-complement order. Therefore, in Mandarin Chinese, the modifier appears before the head whereas the complement appears after the head. On the other hand, in Thai, both the modifier and the complement appear after the head. In this section, we will point out that the constituent orders of the head and modifier and of the head and complement in Thai and Mandarin Chinese have some effects on patterns of grammaticalization of hây in Thai and gěi in Mandarin Chinese. To be specific, we will provide answers to the following questions in terms of different constituent orders in Thai and Mandarin Chinese.

1. Why does the benefactive [gěi+NP] occur only in the preverbal position, not the postverbal position, in Mandarin Chinese?
2. Unlike the benefactive [gěi+NP], the dative [gěi+NP] occurs both preverbally and postverbally in Mandarin Chinese. Why does the dative [gěi+NP] behave differently from the benefactive [gěi+NP]?
3. Why do the dative [hây+NP] and the benefactive [hây+NP] not occur in the preverbal position in Thai?
4. Why is the causative gěi not productive in Mandarin Chinese?
5. Why is gěi not used as a clause subordinator in Mandarin Chinese? In contrast, why is hây used as a clause subordinator in Thai? Moreover, why is the clause subordinator hây used highly productively in Thai?

The first question is why the benefactive [gěi+NP] occurs only in the preverbal position, not the postverbal position, in Mandarin Chinese. In order to answer this question, we have to understand the role of the benefactive PP in a sentence. The benefactive PP in a sentence serves as a modifier, rather than a complement, of the main VP because it is peripheral and can be omitted. It functions like an adverbial phrase modifying the main VP. It merely adds an extra piece of information regarding who benefits from the agent's action. Therefore, the preverbal benefactive [gěi+NP] matches the modifier-head constituent order in Mandarin Chinese. The postverbal benefactive [gěi+NP] would violate this constituent order in the language.

The second question is why the dative [gěi+NP] behaves differently from the benefactive [gěi+NP] in Mandarin Chinese. That is, the dative [gěi+NP] occurs both preverbally and postverbally whereas the benefactive [gěi+NP] occurs only preverbally. We argue that a dative constituent, which expresses a participant receiving a thing in a transfer event, is located somewhere on a continuum between a complement and a modifier. A recipient is sometimes analyzed as a semantically crucial participant for a transfer event to be semantically complete. This is because the transfer event is usually analyzed as consisting of three crucial participants, namely, a giver, a thing given and a recipient. However, the recipient is in some contexts perceived as not as semantically crucial as the other two participants as in J*ohn* donates bl*ood* every month. On the other hand, the recipient in Jo*hn* gave a*n* expensive birthday present t*o* his mother, can be perceived to be a semantically crucial participant. That means the recipient can be perceived as a complement in some contexts and as a modifier in some others. Since the dative PP denoting a recipient fluctuates on the complement-modifier continuum, it is not surprising that the dative PP in Mandarin Chinese can occur both preverbally and postverbally according to the head-complement and modifier-head constituent orders in Mandarin Chinese. However, Sanders and Uehara (2012) found that the dative [gěi+NP] occur only preverbally in a speech corpus of Beijing Mandarin Chinese. This fact may suggest that the dative [gěi+NP] in spoken Beijing Mandarin Chinese is perceived to be modifier-like rather than complement-like. The examples below illustrate the preverbal dative [gěi+NP] in spoken Beijing Mandarin Chinese.

Data from Sanders' and Uehara's personal communication

(33) méi gěi nǐ xiě
not give you write
'I haven't written to you.'

(34) wǒ gěi nǐmen shuō ya
I give you (pl.) say PART.
'Let me tell you.'

The third question is why the dative and benefactive [hây+NP] do not occur preverbally in Thai. In the grammaticalization process, a string of [V1+NP1] + [V2+NP2] is reanalyzed into [V+NP1] + [P+NP2]. That is, the second verb is grammaticalized into a preposition marking a dative and benefactive NP. The PP functioning as a complement and a modifier occurs after the main VP. Therefore, the fact that the dative and benefactive [hây+NP] constituents do not occur preverbally matches the predominant head-complement/modifier constituent order in Thai.

The fourth question is why the causative gěi is not productive in Mandarin Chinese. Unlike the benefactive gěi and the dative gěi, which are grammaticalized into prepositions, the causative gěi is more verb-like in that it can be negated. Notice that the causative gěi appears in the same position as the benefactive gěi, i.e. the preverbal position, which bears two consequences. The first consequence is that the preverbal gěi tends to be analyzed as the benefactive marker functioning as a modifier of the main VP, which corresponds to the predominant modifier-head constituent order in Mandarin Chinese, rather than as the causative verb. The second consequence is that the preverbal gěi in some cases can give rise to ambiguity between the causative and the benefactive readings. It is found that the other causative verbs ràng and jiào are used more frequently than gěi in order to avoid ambiguity as stated earlier in the paper.

The last question is why gěi is not used as a clause subordinator in Mandarin Chinese but hây is in Thai? Moreover, why is the clause subordinator hây used highly productively in Thai? A complex construction consists of a matrix clause and a subordinating clause. Most subordinating clauses function as modifiers of the matrix VPs. In Mandarin Chinese, modifiers precede heads. Therefore, the postverbal position is not a perfect site for a verb to be grammaticalized into a subordinator in Mandarin Chinese. This is the reason why we do not find the postverbal subordinator gěi in Mandarin Chinese. In contrast, the postverbal position is a perfect site for a verb to be grammaticalized into a subordinator introducing a subordinating clause in Thai because it matches the head-modifier constituent order in the language. That is why hây is used as subordinator with a high degree of productivity in Thai.

However, it is noted in some previous works that gěi is used as a subordinator to introduce an adverbial clause occurring after a matrix clause in the head-adverbial clause order. This use of gěi is exemplified by (35).

(35) Zhāngsān chàng gē gěi
Zhangsan sing song give
tā tīng
he/she hear
'Zhangsan sang a song for him/her to hear.'

However, this construction is not attested in a Beijing Mandarin speech corpus according to Sanders and Uehara (2012). To express this meaning, the benefactive gěi is used instead as in (36).

(36) Zhāngsān gěi tā chàng
Zhangsan give he/she sing
gē
song
'Zhangsan sang a song for him/her.'

The fact that the subordinator gěi is not found in spoken Beijing Mandarin Chinese confirms our hypothesis that the postverbal position is not a perfect site for gěi to be grammaticalized into a subordinator.

Another observation can be made regarding the grammaticalized passive marker gěi in Mandarin Chinese. It is noted in Thepkanjana and Uehara (2008) that the passive gěi in the structural schema [gěi + NP + VP] has been developed into what Newman (1993b: 477) calls "the prefixal gěi in passive constructions" as in (35).

From Newman (1993b: 477)
(37) tā gěi-mà-le
he PASSIVE-scold-ASP
'He/She was scolded.'

This phenomenon, which indicates that the second verb becomes the head which the prefix gěi is attached to, corresponds with the modifier-head pattern constituent order in Mandarin Chinese.

4 Conclusion

This paper presents commonalities and differences in the grammaticalization of hây in Thai and gěi in Mandarin Chinese and argues how different constituent orders in Thai and Mandarin Chinese bear on patterns of

Grammaticalization of the two verbs in the two languages. It is found that the common functions shared by hây and gěi are (1) the ditransitive main use, (2) the dative-marking use, (3) the benefactive-marking use and (4) the causative-marking use. As for differences, hây, not gěi, is used as a subordinator connecting two clauses in a complex construction whereas gěi, not hây, is used as a passive marker. Five questions are posed regarding different patterns of grammaticalization of hây and gěi in Thai and Mandarin Chinese. Facts about different patterns of grammaticalization of the two morphemes under discussion are accounted for in terms of different constituent orders in Thai and Mandarin Chinese, i.e. head-modifier/complement in Thai, modifier-head and head-complement in Mandarin Chinese. It is argued that the head-modifier constituent order in Thai seems to be compatible with postverbal grammaticalized morphemes whereas the modifier-head order in Mandarin Chinese seems to be compatible with preverbal grammaticalized ones.

Acknowledgments

This research work is partially supported by the Ratchadaphiseksomphot Endowment Fund of Chulalongkorn University (RES560530179-HS) awarded to the first author and a Grant-in-Aid for Scientific Research from the Japan Society for the Promotion of Science (No. 24520416) awarded to the second author.

References

Dan Xu. 1994. The Status of Marker Gei in Mandarin Chinese. Journal of Chinese Linguistics, 22(2): 363-394.

Foong Ha Yap and Shoichi Iwasaki. 1998. 'Give' Constructions in Malay, Thai and Mandarin Chinese: A Polygrammaticization Perspective. Proceedings of the 34th Annual Meeting of the Chicago Linguistic Society, 421-438.

Foong Ha Yap and Shoichi Iwasaki. 2003. From Causative to Passive: A Passage in Some East and Southeast Asian Languages. In Eugene H. Casad and Gary B. Palmer (eds.) Cognitive Linguistics and Non-Indo-European Languages. Mouton de Gruyter, Berlin & New York, 419-445.

John Newman. 1993a. A Cognitive Grammar Approach to Mandarin Gei. Journal of Chinese Linguistics, 21(2): 313-336.

John Newman. 1993b. The Semantics of Giving in Mandarin. In Richard A. Geiger and Brygida Rudzka-Ostyn (eds.) Conceptualizations and Mental Processing in Language. Mouton de Gruyter, Berlin & New York. 433-485.

John Newman. 1996. Give: A Cognitive Linguistic Study. Mouton de Gruyter, Berlin & New York.

Kingkarn Thepkanjana and Satoshi Uehara. 2008. The Verb of Giving in Thai and Mandarin Chinese as a Case Study of Polysemy: A Comparative Study. Language Sciences, 30(6): 621-651.

Martin Haspelmath. 1990. The Grammaticalization of Passive Morphology. Studies in Language, 14(1): 25-72.

Robert D. van Valin, Jr. and Randy J. LaPolla. 1997. Syntax: Structure, Meaning and Function. Cambridge University Press, Cambridge.

Robert M. Sanders and Satoshi Uehara. 2012. A Syntactic Classification of the Synchronic Use of Gěi in Beijing Mandarin: A Spoken Corpus-based Case Study of its Polyfunctionality. Chinese Language and Discourse, 3(2): 167-199.

Ronald W. Langacker. 1987. Foundations of Cognitive Grammar, volume I. Theoretical Prerequisites. Stanford University Press, Stanford, California.

Suda Rangkupan. 1997. An investigation of haŷ complex constructions in Thai. Available from: <http://www.buffalo.edu/soc-sci/linguistics/people/students/ma_theses/rangkupan/RANGKMA.PDF>

Global Approach to Scalar Implicatures in Dynamic Semantics

Jae-Il Yeom
Hongik University
English Language and Literature
94 Wausan-ro, Sangsu-dong, Mapo-gu
Seoul 121-791
KOREA
jiyeom@hongik.ac.kr

Abstract

It has been disputed whether scalar implicatures (= SIs) arise globally or locally. Basically SIs should be global because they arise by comparing strengths of whole alternative statements. On the other hand, there are a lot of examples in which local SIs are preferable. Linguists like Chierchia (2002) and Fox (2006) even claim that SIs arise by applying an operator to syntactic constituents to get their stronger meanings. In this paper, I claim that SIs are global and seemingly local implicatures are effects of contexts on global implicatures. Moreover, I will show that no syntactic analyses work.

1 Introduction

Scalar implicatures (SIs) arise on the basis of the maxim of quantity by Grice (1975):

(1) The maxim of quantity:

a. Make your contribution as informative as is required (for the current purposes of the exchange).

b. Do not make your contribution more informative than is required.

It is the first maxim of quantity that is relevant to SIs. When a stronger statement is relevant to the context and a speaker utters a weaker statement, it is implicated that the stronger statement is not true in the speaker's information state. Assuming that the speaker is well-informed and that he knows the stronger alternative is false, the hearer accepts the implicature as true.

Grice did not explicate the precise procedure of getting a SI. Horn (1972, 1989) suggested that a SI arises by comparing a set of alternative statements that arises by replacing a scalar term in the original statement with a stronger scalar alternative expression in the language system. Behind this idea lies the assumption that a set of scalar terms, which is called a **scalar set**, is given in the language system. Sauerland (2004) gives a more precise procedure, within the Neo-Gricean tradition that a SI arises based on a set of scalar alternatives. He assumes that SIs have an epistemic status, following Gazdar (1979), but deviates from his idea by assuming that the maxim of quantity gives rise to only uncertainty inferences, which he calls primary implicatures. Primary implicatures have the form of 'K', in which K means 'know' and is a stronger alternative sentence of the original utterance. The hearer tentatively strengthens each of the primary implicature of the form 'K'. If the stronger implicature is compatible with the meaning of the statement and all the primary implicatures, it gets the status of a SI, which he calls a secondary implicature.

His idea is illustrated in the following:

(2) John broke some glasses.

(3) a. ScalAlt(some) = {all, many, some}

b. ScalAlt(John broke some glasses) = {John broke all glasses, John broke many glasses, John broke some glasses}

c. (2) primarily implicates the following: ¬K(John broke all glasses) ¬K(John broke many glasses)

d. secondary implicatures: K¬(John broke {all, many} glasses)

The use of *some* yields a stronger statement ϕ (= 'John broke {all, many} glasses') and the primary implicature is $\neg K\phi$, which can be strengthened into $\neg K\phi$ since it is compatible with the statement itself plus all the primary implicatures.

Neo-Griceans naturally accepted that SIs are calculated from a whole statement. In this respect, they can be called globalists. SIs are inferences based on the maxim of quantity by Grice (1975). Implicatures are supposed to be calculated from utterances, which are always dealt with as a whole. This implies that SIs only arise from stronger statements than the original statement.

However, linguists like Chierchia (2002) claim that implicatures are included in the meaning of a statement, as part of the strengthened meaning (= the literal meaning plus its implicatures) of a CHUNK of a statement as a scope-site of a scalar expression, in the process of compositional semantic interpretation, following Krifka (1995), and the strengthened meaning of the sentence chunk is combined with the meaning of the rest of the sentence. The plain meaning of an expression α is represented as $[\![\alpha]\!]$ and the implicature is $\neg$S(α^{ALT}), where S(α^{ALT}) is the weakest alternative of α that entails α. Thus the strengthened meaning of α is the conjunction of the two meanings: $[\![\alpha]\!] \wedge \neg$S($\alpha^{ALT}$), which entails other strengthened meanings from the stronger alternatives of α. Chierchia introduces the negation operator to get a stronger meaning. For the same purpose, Fox (2006) instead introduces the exhaustivity (exh, hereafter) operator. They can be called localists.

Their analysis is illustrated in the following:

(4) Mary believes that John broke some glasses.

(5) a. LF: Mary believes that [[some glasses]$_i$ [John broke t$_i$]]

b. $[\![$[[some glasses]$_i$ [John broke t$_i$]]$]\!]$ = some'(student')(λx.broke'(j,x))

c. $[\![$[[some glasses]$_i$ [John broke t$_i$]]$]\!]^S$ = some'(student')(λx.broke'(j,x)) $\wedge$ $\neg$S([[some glasses]$_i$ [John broke t$_i$]]^{ALT}) = some'(student')(λx.broke'(j,x)) $\wedge$ $\neg$many'(student')(λx.broke'(j,x))

d. $[\![$(4)$]\!]^S$ = believes'(m, ˆ(some'(student')(λx.broke'(j,x)) $\wedge$ $\neg$many'(student')(x.broke'(j,x))))

It is assumed that the quantifier *some glasses* is Quantifier-raised witin the complement clause of the propositional attitude verb *believes*. And a SI from the use of *some* is calculated when the strengthened meaning of the complement clause is obtained in (5c). The strengthened meaning of the complement clause is the conjunction of the plain meaning and a SI of the clause, the latter of which is expressed as $\neg$S(ϕ^{ALT}), where ϕ is the complement clause *[some glasses [John broke t$_i$]]*. We are assuming that the weakest stronger alternative of *some* is *many*. The alternative meanings are derived in a similar way to the alternative semantics by Rooth (1985) for focus. The strengthened meaning of the complement clause is combined with the meaning of the rest of the sentence, as in (5d).

Localists' approaches may look more systematic, manageable and more constrained than globalists', because they are based on syntactic structures and calculation of SIs is precisely defined. However, one theoretically serious problem with localists is that, as Horn (1989) pointed out, SIs do not arise within downward entailing contexts and that SIs are based on strengths of statements as a whole. Even if they calculate SIs locally, they have to check whether an alternative involved in the calculation makes the whole sentence a stronger statement to see if it really leads to a valid SI. In this respect, SIs are inherently global.

Empirically, actual data do not take part with either of the two positions. Consider the following examples:

(6) Some students who drank beer or wine were allowed to drive.

a. Some students who drank beer or wine, but NOT both, were allowed to drive.

b. NOT[some students who drank both were allowed to drive]
(= No students who drank both were allowed to drive.)

(7) Every linguistics student at MIT has read LGB or Syntactic Structures. (Modified from Sauerland 2004, (58))

a. NOT[Every linguistics student at MIT has read LGB and Syntactic Structures]

b. Every linguistics student at MIT NOT[has read LGB and Syntactic Structures]
(= No linguistics students at MIT have read LGB and Syntactic Structures.)

In (6), it is plausible that no students who drank both beer and wine were allowed to drive, which is calculated by negating the whole stronger alternative. In (7), a linguist at MIT is likely to have read one of the two books, and the global SI is more likely. On the other hand, the following two examples show the opposite:

(8) Some students who watched TV or played games failed math.
   a. Some students who watched TV or played games, but not did both, failed maths. (conveyed)
   b. NOT[Some students who watched TV and played games failed maths] (global SI)

(9) Every student wrote a paper or made a classroom presentation.
   a. Every student wrote a paper or made a classroom presentation but did not do both.
   b. NOT(every student wrote a paper and made a classroom presentation)

In (8), it is more likely that a student who watched TV and played games failed math. For this reason the global SI that no students who watched TV and played games failed math is not acceptable. Similarly, in (9), if either of the two requirements is sufficient to get a grade, it is more plausible to assume that no students satisfied both requirements. This corresponds to the local SI. Thus we do not get the global SI that not every student did both.

Then we could take a position in which we exploit both ways of calculation of SIs. But if we cannot provide clear criteria for when we get global SIs and when we get local ones, it is not an explanation at all. Moreover, if syntactic structures are not what we directly deal with in calculating SIs, we cannot choose a localistic approach anyway. In this paper I will show that calculation of SIs needs more fine-grained structures than syntactic structures. And I will also show that local SIs are contextual effects on global SIs.

2 SIs corresponding to no syntactic constituents

2.1 SIs embedded in syntatic structures

In a syntactic analysis the operator that applies to a constituent which yields a SI is of semantic type of a proposition. In Chierchia (2002), the negation operator applies to a scope site of a scalar expression. A scope site has a semantic type of a proposition, or a clause, in more common terms. In Fox (2006), *exh* applies to a constituent that has the semantic type of a proposition and takes both the meaning of the constituent as a proposition and a set of alternative propositions to that, as its arguments. However, there are cases where we can get a SI from a NP:

(10) Some boys who read some of the books passed the test.

From the use of *some of the books* a global approach predicts the SI that no boys who read all of the books passed the test, which is implausible. A local approach predicts that the sentence conveys the meaning that some boys who read some, but not all, of the books passed the test. This does not exclude the possibility that some other boys who read all of the books passed the test. The original statement conveys the meaing that reading some of the books was sufficient to pass the test. This indicates that the local SI is not plausible, either. A more plausible SI can be one of the following:

(11) a. No boys read all of the books.
   b. The boys who passed the test did not read all of the books.

The two possible SIs correspond to the following structures:

(12) a. some boys who read some of the books
   b. Some boys who passed the test read some of the books.

The first SI corresponds to the NP *some boys who read some of the books*, and the second corresponds to a quite different sentence than the original. Moreover, the second SI anaphorically refers to the boys who passed the test, which does not have a corresponding constituent in the original sentence.

The two implicatures in (11) do not come from any syntactic constituent of semantic type of a proposition. This shows that SIs depend on contents, not on structures. To deal with contents of statements, we need to deal with semantic representations, instead of syntactic structures. Since SIs do not depend on syntactic structures, they are not calculated compositionally. They should be calculated after the statement is interpreted into a semantic representation.

Since we do not depend on syntactic structures, we will have to resort to a global approach. On the other hand, we have seen some SIs that could be calculated by a localistic approach. In order for a SI to be like a local SI, a SI has to have the effect of being embedded even if we calculate it after we finish interpreting the statement. One way to make such an effect is to deal with semantic representations in dynamic semantics:

(13) Mary met a doctor. He lived near Brooklyn.
$\simeq$ Mary met a doctor who lived near Brooklyn.

Even though the pronoun *he* is used in a new sentence, the whole text seems to have the meaning of a sentence in which the second sentence is embedded in a relative clause in the first sentence. A similar effect can be expected when a SI of a statement is calculated after the statement is interpreted:

(14) Some boys who read some of the books passed the test. They did not read all of the books.
$\simeq$ Some boys who read some of the books, but did not read all of them, passed the test.

In this example, the pronoun *they* refers to the boys who read some of the books and passed the test. The second sentence is added after the first statement is finished and it is taken to be a SI of the first sentence. The effect is the same as the sentence in which the SI is embedded in the relative clause of the statement.[1] This is one way of getting the effect of a local SI from a global SI. Note that this effect comes from anaphora across sentences in dynamic semantics.

2.2 SIs not based on scalar terms

Horn (1972, 1989) proposed a set of scalar terms to capture SIs. However, there are scales that are not based on scalar terms or any explicit expressions. This can be observed in examples like (6–9). Consider the pair of (6) and (8). When a student who drank beer or wine was allowed to drive, a student who drank both beer and wine is not likely to have been allowed to drive. Drinking either beer or wine is the **upper limit** for being allowed to drive. A SI that is compatible with this background knowledge survives, and a SI that is not dies. In (8), on the other hand, when a student who watched TV or played games failed math, a student who did both is more likely to fail math. Watching TV or playing games is understood as the **lower limit** for failing math. The difference between (6) and (8) lies in the opposite directionality of the scalar likelihood, independently of the semantic strengths of alternatives.

The scalarity of likelihood cannot be captured by any syntactic constituent and it is not a matter of semantics either. This can be captured by ordering possible worlds according to some knowledge about likelihood of states of affairs. SIs generally have the effect of strengthening the original statement. If the strengthening goes in the opposite direction to the scalar likelihood, the SI is rejected. In (8) the global SI is that no students who watched TV and played games failed math, which is less likely than the original sentence. Therefore it is rejected. We can get a weaker SI than this. At the moment I will call it a local SI, but I will show below that it is also a global SI. In (6), the global SI that no students who drank both beer and wine were allowed to drive is more likely than the original statement. And it is accepted. Note that this is a case where a semantic scalarity is in opposite direction to a pragmatic likelihood.

3 Global SIs with the effect of local SIs

As we have seen, sometimes we get global SIs and other times we get local SIs. It is not just that whether a global or local SI is plausible is determined by a context, but that a global SI has the effect of a local SI in a certain context. This is what I am going to show in this section.

3.1 Disjunction structures and SIs

As I said in the introduction, Saulerland (2004) assumes that the scalar alternatives of *or* is {and, L, R, or}. When a disjunct includes a scalar expression and the latter is replaced with a stronger alternative, the disjunct itself becomes a stronger

[1] It is sometimes pointed out that there is a subtle difference between the two sentences, but the effect is clearly what we need. And even if we admit the difference, a more intuitively correct meaning is obtained by the first one rather than the one in which the SI is embedded. When the SI is embedded in the relative clause, there is a possibility that some other boys who read all of the books passed the test. This possibility is not necessarily legitimate.

alternative and its stronger alternative is also an alternative of the whole statement, as follows:

(15) John spilt wine or broke some glasses. (= p)

(16) a. ScalAlt(p) = {John spilt wine and broke all glasses, John spilt wine and broke some glasses, John spilt wine, John broke all glasses, John broke some glasses, p}

The assumption of the operators L and R has the effect of projecting a local implicature from each disjunct into the main context. Thus the statement implicates the following:

(17) ¬(John spilt wine and broke all glasses)
¬(John spilt wine and broke some glasses)
¬(John broke all glasses)

Here the SI that John did not break all glasses arises from a stronger alternative of the second disjunct. This is a case where the disjunction structure is transparent for the projection of a SI.

However, it does not have to be the case. There are cases where a stronger alternative of a disjunct yields only a local SI:

(18) a. John broke all or some glasses.
b. John wanted hot or at least warm water.
c. John won the lottery or made some easy money.

In these examples, the use of the second disjuncts implicates that the first disjuncts do not hold. Take the first example. If the second disjunct is understood as meaning John broke some (or all) glasses, the use of the disjunction operator is infelicitous. For this reason, the second disjunct has to mean that John broke some but not all glasses, and this has to be a local implicature. Otherwise it would contradict the first disjunct:

(19) #John broke all or some glasses. He did not break all glasses.

The discourse is not inconsistent because we could conclude that John broke only some of the glasses. However, the discourse is incoherent. A speaker who can truly assert the second sentence would not utter the first sentence.[2] We can say the same thing about the other two examples.

One thing in common among the three examples is that the two disjuncts are not independent of each other. This contextual information makes the implicatures from the second disjuncts stay in the second disjuncts, making them local implicatures. However, contextual information should be put aside when we discuss the way that SIs are calculated. As I said, we can always assume global SIs and the meanings of local SIs are derived by the help of contextual information.

I propose that the meaning of a statement and its implicatures are captured by their informational effects on the current information state. Suppose that ϕ is uttered in the current information state and changes it into s′. Then a (global) SI $\neg\psi$ (, where ψ asymmetrically entails ϕ,) is added to s′ and changes it into s″. Then the net effect of ψ on s′ is the set of possible worlds eliminated by $\neg\psi$, i.e., $(s'\backslash(s' + \psi)$, where "\" is a set minus). This is the actual effect of the SI on the current information state.

(20) $s + \phi = s'$
$s' + \neg\psi = s''$

(21) net effect of $\neg\psi = s'\backslash(s'+\neg\psi)$
$= s'\backslash(s'\backslash(s'+\psi)) = s'+\psi$

The composition of the set of the possible worlds determines the actual SI. Consider (15) first. With the information state s, since the two disjuncts are independent of each other, we can assume that s+(15) includes the following three sets of possible worlds:

(22) a. a set of possible worlds in which John only spilt wine
b. a set of possible worlds in which John only broke some glasses
c. a set of possible worlds in which John did both

In this context, the SI from *some* has the following effect on the information state, following (21):

(23) $(s+(15))\backslash(s+(15)+SI_{some})$
$= s+(15)\cap\{w|$ John spilt wine or broke many/all glasses$\}$

[2]A simple way of distinguishing coherence and consistency is that a discourse is coherent if it is asserted by the same speaker, but a discourse is consistent if it does not lead to the absurd information state if uttered by different speakers. In the example at hand, if the two sentences are uttered by two different speakers, it does not lead to the absurt information state. But they cannot be uttered by the same speaeker felicitously.

= s+(15)∩{w| John broke many/all glasses}

The net effect of the use of *some* is what we get by updating s+(15) with a stronger alternative. But (15) and the stronger alternative share the possible worlds in which the first disjunct holds. Therefore the net effect of the stronger alternative is the same as the effect of the second disjunct. Since the two disjuncts are independent of each other, the set of possible worlds eliminated by the global SI consists of those in which John only broke many/all glasses and those in which John both spilt wine and broke many/all glasses. They are possible worlds in which the second disjunct of the stronger alternative holds, regardless of whether the first disjunct holds. That is, the SI has the overall effect on the information state, regardless of whether the first disjunct holds or not. Thus the SI has the effect of a global SI, even though the net effect only comes from the second disjunct of the stronger alternative.

Next, consider (18.a), where a SI from one disjunct does not project. In a given context, the two disjuncts are not independent of each other, but there is a subset relation:

(24) a. a set of possible worlds in which John broke all glasses
b. a set of possible worlds in which John broke some glasses (and possibly all)
c. (a) $\subseteq$ (b)

In this situation, the net effect of the SI from the use of *some* is the following:

(25) s′ = s + "John broke all or some glasses"

(26) the net effect of "¬(John broke all or many/all glasses)"
= s′+John broke all or many/all glasses
= s′∩{w| John broke all or many (but not some) glasses in w}

Since the first disjunct is shared by the two alternatives, the net effect is determined by the second disjunct. Therefore the SI has the effect that John broke many (but not some) glasses. However, this does not have the overall effect on the current information state, because the two disjuncts are not independent of each other. If it did, the speaker would simply say that John broke some glasses. Then there would be no possible worlds in which John broke all glasses. There should be some possible worlds in s′ that John broke all glasses.[3] Then the net effect of the SI only applies to the possible worlds in which John did not break all glasses. That is, it eliminates possible worlds in which John broke not all but more than just some glasses. This is the way the global SI has the effect of a local implicature.

3.2 Other cases of local SIs

In a conditional, the antecedent clause and the consequent clause are not independent of each other. In normal cases, a SI from the consequent clause is not supposed to have the effect of a local SI. This can be explained easily:

(27) s + "if ϕ, then ψ" = s+[$\neg\phi \vee \psi$][4]

(28) For a stronger alternative ψ' of ψ, the net effect of the global SI
= s′+[if ϕ, then ψ']
= s+[$\neg\phi \vee \psi$] + [$\neg\phi \vee \psi'$]
= s+[[$\neg\phi \vee \psi$] $\wedge$ [$\neg\phi \vee \psi'$]]
= s+[$\neg\phi \vee [\psi \wedge \psi']$]
= s+[$\neg\phi \vee \psi'$]
= s+ [if ϕ, then ψ']

The net effect of the global SI ¬(if ϕ, then ψ') is limited to the possible worlds in which ϕ hold. This is the effect of restricting the SI to the consequent clause. Thus the global SI has the effect of a local SI.

On the other hand, when the antecedent clause is trivially satisfied in the current information state, a global SI has a overall effect.

(29) If you want to, you may have some apples.

In the given context, it is likely that the hearer wants to have some apples. In this context, the an-

[3]This is the effect of the felicity condition that each disjunct should make a non-trivial meaning contribution to the meaning of a whole sentence. This is beyond the scope of this paper.

[4]The way a sentence is interpreted has to be defined so that anaphoric dependency relations can be captured. For this purpose, a conditional sentence has to be interpreted as follows:

i. s + "if ϕ, then ψ" = s\((s+ϕ)\(s+ϕ+ψ)) = s′

That is, a pronoun in the antecedent clause can refer to something in the main context, and a pronoun in the consequent clause can refer to something in the main context or the antecedent clause. We can assume this rule, but it would lead to a more complex calculation. For convenience's sake, I assume a propositional logic in which a conditional is equivalent to the disjunction of the negation of the antecedent clause and the consequent clause.

tecedent clause is trivially satisfied in the current information state and thus the antecedent clause does not change the current information state. The conditional does not have the effect of a conditional but the consequent clause. Therefore the (global) SI from the use of *some* in the consequent clause affects the current information state directly and has the effect of a global SI:

(30) s + "you want to have some apples" = s
s + "If you want to, you may have some apples"
= s\((s+"you want to have some apples")\(s+ "you want to have some apples"+"you may have some apples"))
= s\(s\(s+"you may have some apples"))
= s+"you may have some apples"

As shown above, the conditional has the same meaning as the consequent clause, which makes a SI from the consequent clause a global effect on the current information state.

In Chierchia (2002), it is claimed that a scalar expression in a propositional attitude context yields a local SI. This is not explained by the mechanism I have used so far.

(31) Mary believes that John broke some glasses.
+> Mary believes that John did not broke all glasses.

(32) s + Mary believes that John broke some glasses
= {w∈s| for every w′ in Dox(m,w), John broke some glasses in w′} = s′

(33) net effect of "¬(Mary believes that John broke many/all glasses)" =
s′\(s′+"Mary believes that John broke many/all glasses")
= {w∈s| for every w′ in Dox(m,w), John broke some glasses in w′, there are some possible worlds w″ in Dox(m,w) such that John did not broke many/all glasses in w″}
= It is not the case that Mary believes John broke many/all glasses.
≠ Mary believes John did not break many/all glasses.

The SI that it is not the case that Mary believes John broke many/all glasses does not mean that Mary believes John did not break many/all glasses. But intuitively we seem to get the latter inference. However, it is not reliable to discuss belief contexts and draw a conclusion. When we talk about Mary's belief, we can think of Mary's statements the speaker heard, and they are likely to yield SIs, which are also taken to be part of Mary's belief even in the speaker's report. Another reason for not relying on discussions of belief contexts is that a belief operator is not generally accepted as a universal quantifier over doxastic alternatives. It seems to be due to the lack of an existential counterpart.

Consider an epistemic unviersal quantifier *must* and a obligation operator:

(34) John must have broken some glasses.
+> John may not have broken all glasses.
+/> John cannot have broken all glasses.

(35) John must read some of the books.
+> John does not have to read all of the book.
+/> John must not read all of the books.

Considering the fact that the deontic operator behaves just the way we expected it to, we cannot claim that SIs should be local. On the other hand, epistemic operators tend to allow stronger SIs than what is predicted by the theory. For some reason, an epistemic operator tends to have wide scope, even over the operator introduced to calculate a SI.

In this section, I have shown that the actual effect of a SI on the current information state can be captured by dealing with possible worlds, rather than expressions. It allows us to accout for how global SIs get the effects of local GIs. This allows us to dispense with local SIs. In the previous section, I also showed that SIs from syntactically embedded can have global effects and that they can be dealt with in dynamic semantics. Dynamic seantics assumes that the meaning of a sentence is a context change potential which takes an information state as an input and yields an updated information state by adding the information conveyed by the sentence to the input information state. In the next section, I will propose a new analysis reflecting the two necessary components to account for SIs and their observations.

4 SIs in dynamic semantics

4.1 Basics of dynamic semantics

In this paper, I will use a (slightly modified) DRT (discourse representation theory) in representing the meaning of a sentence for various reasons. First, it allows us to be able to manage meanings as representations. Second, it provides more fine-grained chunks of meanings than the classical predicate logic or syntactic structures, which allows us to account for some SIs which do not correspond to a syntactic constituent. Third, anaphoric relationships are easily captured, which is necessary to account for the effect of being embedded of a SI even when it is added to the DRS (discourse representation structure) after the sentence is interpreted. A variable in a SI can be free or bound by a variable in the previous DRS, and the mechanism allows us to get various SIs, depending on whether variables in a stronger alternative statement are free or bound by the variables in the original statement. Let's see how it works.

Anaphoric relations are restricted by accessibility paths given by the DRT. The accessibility paths can be restricted as follows:

(36) a. A DRS is a pair of a set of variables and a set of conditions on the variables, <var, con>.

b. A variable in (i) is accessible for a variable in (ii), but a variable in (ii) is not accessible for a variable in (iii), and not vice versa, in one of the following configurations:
<var(i), ...<var(ii),... >...>
<var(i),<var(ii),...>∨<var(iii),...>>
<var(i),...>⇒/∀<var(ii),...>

A variable newly introduced in a DRS is accessible for any variable in the conditions in it. In a disjunction structure, a variable in one disjunct is not accessible to a variable in another disjunct. In a conditional, a variable introduced in the antecedent clause is accessible for a variable in the consequent clause, but not vice versa.

On the other hand, we will assume an information state with respect to which a DRS is interpreted. This is necessary to account for cases where a global SI has the effect of a local SI.

(37) An information state is a set of pairs of a possible world w and an assignment g.

(38) A set of variables var includes a variable v for possible worlds.

(39) A DRS is interpreted with respect to a model <W, D, F, G>, where W is a set of possible worlds, D a set of individuals, F an interpretation function of constants, and G a set of assignment functions.

(40) A DRS <var, con> is supported in an information state s iff for every member <w,g> in s, {<w, g∪var>} supports every condition in con.

(41) {<w,g>} supports P_v(x) iff g(v)=w and g(x) ∈ F(P)(w)

(42) {<w,g>} supports < var(i), con(i)> ∨ <var(ii), con(ii)> iff <w, g∪var(i)> supports every condition in con(i) or <w, g∪var(ii)> supports every condition in con(ii).

(43) {<w,g>} supports < var(i), con(i)> ⇒ <var(ii), con(ii)> iff <w, g∪var(i)> does not support every condition in con(i) or <w, g∪var(i)∪var(ii)> supports every condition in con(ii).

An information state is a set of pairs of a possible world and an assignment. To interpret a DRS with respect to possible worlds, I introduce a variable for possible worlds in DRSs. This is a deviation from the standard DRS, in which each DRS is interpreted with respect to a model. In this paper, possible worlds are included in a model. This makes a DRS more like a semantic representation. This would yield no problems. After a DRS is interpreted, we get an information state which supports the DRS. We only deal with information states we get after a statement is interpreted, so we do not need dynamic interpretation rules. Instead, we need support conditions. A DRS is supported by an information state iff each pair of a possible world and an assignment supports each condition in the DRS. A disjunction structure is supported by a pair of a world and an assignment iff one of the disjuncts is supported by the pair. A conditional is dealt with like a disjunction of the negation of the antecedent clause and the consequent clause.

I do not have to follow the Neo-Gricean tradition, because it is assumed that a SI arises by comparing the meanings of alternative statements. However, scalar alternatives make themselves more salient than others. In this respect it does not do any harm to assume a set of scalar alternatives. But it is not necessary to assume them.

4.2 SIs from non-clauses

Now we can deal with cases where SIs arise from some non-clause constituents. Such cases are problematic with localistic approaches. One example is given in (10), which is given here again. It is interpreted into a DRS as follows:

(10) Some boys who read some of the books passed the test.

(44)
$$\begin{array}{|l|}\hline v\ \mathrm{X\ Y\ Z\ k} \\ \hline \mathrm{boys}_v(\mathrm{X}) \\ \mathrm{books}_v(\mathrm{Z}) \\ \mathrm{Y}\subseteq\mathrm{Z} \\ \mathrm{read}_v(\mathrm{X,Y}) \\ \mathrm{test}_v(\mathrm{k}) \\ \mathrm{passed}_v(\mathrm{X,k}) \\ \hline \end{array}$$

This is just the interpretation of (10), but I will assume that it is the first sentence and constitutes the main DRS. Suppose that this is supported in an information state s. In the result information state, we calculate a SI from the use of *some of the books*. We get a global SI by negating a stronger alternative of the whole statement:

(45)
$$\neg\begin{array}{|l|}\hline v\ \mathrm{X'\ Y'\ Z'\ k'} \\ \hline \mathrm{boys}_v(\mathrm{X'}) \\ \mathrm{books}_v(\mathrm{Z'}) \\ \begin{array}{|l|}\hline \mathrm{l} \\ \hline \mathrm{l}\in\mathrm{Z'} \\ \hline\end{array} \Rightarrow \begin{array}{|l|}\hline \\ \hline \mathrm{read}_v(\mathrm{X',l}) \\ \hline\end{array} \\ \mathrm{test}_v(\mathrm{k'}) \\ \mathrm{passed}_v(\mathrm{X',k'}) \\ \hline \end{array}$$

This is embedded in the main DRS and we have to see if some variables in it can be bound in the main DRS:

(46)
$$\begin{array}{|l|}\hline v\ \mathrm{X\ Y\ Z\ k} \\ \hline \mathrm{boys}_v(\mathrm{X}) \\ \mathrm{books}_v(\mathrm{Z}) \\ \mathrm{Y}\subseteq\mathrm{Z} \\ \mathrm{read}_v(\mathrm{X,Y}) \\ \mathrm{test}_v(\mathrm{k}) \\ \mathrm{passed}_v(\mathrm{X,k}) \\ \neg\begin{array}{|l|}\hline \mathrm{X'\ Y'\ Z'\ k'} \\ \hline \mathrm{boys}_v(\mathrm{X'}) \\ \mathrm{books}_v(\mathrm{Z'}) \\ \begin{array}{|l|}\hline \mathrm{l} \\ \hline \mathrm{l}\in\mathrm{Z'} \\ \hline\end{array} \Rightarrow \begin{array}{|l|}\hline \\ \hline \mathrm{read}_v(\mathrm{X',l}) \\ \hline\end{array} \\ \mathrm{test}_v(\mathrm{k'}) \\ \mathrm{passed}_v(\mathrm{X',k'}) \\ \hline \end{array} \\ \\ \hline \end{array}$$

The process is quite similar to the presupposition projection in van der Sandt (1992). Since we are talking about the same possible world, v is bound by the same variable in the matrix DRS. Variables like Z′ and k′ are introduced by presuppositions and are supposed to be bound by Z and k respectively. Therefore conditions on them are not negated:[5]

(45′)
$$\begin{array}{|l|}\hline v\ \mathrm{X\ Y\ Z\ k} \\ \hline \mathrm{boys}_v(\mathrm{X}) \\ \mathrm{books}_v(\mathrm{Z}) \\ \mathrm{Y}\subseteq\mathrm{Z} \\ \mathrm{read}_v(\mathrm{X,Y}) \\ \mathrm{test}_v(\mathrm{k}) \\ \mathrm{passed}_v(\mathrm{X,k}) \\ \neg\begin{array}{|l|}\hline \mathrm{X'} \\ \hline \mathrm{boys}_v(\mathrm{X'}) \\ \begin{array}{|l|}\hline \mathrm{l} \\ \hline \mathrm{l}\in\mathrm{Z} \\ \hline\end{array} \Rightarrow \begin{array}{|l|}\hline \\ \hline \mathrm{read}_v(\mathrm{X',l}) \\ \hline\end{array} \\ \mathrm{passed}_v(\mathrm{X',k}) \\ \hline \end{array} \\ \\ \hline \end{array}$$

This leads to the following SIs:

(47) a. No boys read all of them(= the books) and passed it(= the test).

b. No boys read all of them(= the books).

All conditions considered, we get (47a) as a SI, but intuitively it is not plausible. When some boys who read only some of the books passed the test, a boy who read all of the books is more likely to pass the test. And we already know some boys passed the test. Thus we can ignore the last condition in the DRS:

(45″)
$$\begin{array}{|l|}\hline v\ \mathrm{X\ Y\ Z\ k} \\ \hline \mathrm{boys}_v(\mathrm{X}) \\ \mathrm{books}_v(\mathrm{Z}) \\ \mathrm{Y}\subseteq\mathrm{Z} \\ \mathrm{read}_v(\mathrm{X,Y}) \\ \mathrm{test}_v(\mathrm{k}) \\ \mathrm{passed}_v(\mathrm{X,k}) \\ \neg\begin{array}{|l|}\hline \mathrm{X'} \\ \hline \mathrm{boys}_v(\mathrm{X'}) \\ \begin{array}{|l|}\hline \mathrm{l} \\ \hline \mathrm{l}\in\mathrm{Z} \\ \hline\end{array} \Rightarrow \begin{array}{|l|}\hline \\ \hline \mathrm{read}_v(\mathrm{X',l}) \\ \hline\end{array} \\ \\ \hline \end{array} \\ \\ \hline \end{array}$$

Here comes in the more fine-grainedness of a DRS. Notice that what was in the relative clause in the sentence is not embedded in the DRS but put in the main DRS. Moreover, each condition can be

[5] We are talking about the actual world, and we do not assume a new variable for possible worlds.

freely considered or ignored in calculating SIs to get a contextually relevant SI.

In my analysis, since a SI is calculated after the sentence is interpreted, all infomation in the sentence can be considered to be presuppositions, following Stalnaker (1978, 2006). Thus even X' can be bound by X in the main DRS.

(45‴)

v X Y Z k
$\text{boys}_v(X)$ $\text{books}_v(Z)$ $Y \subseteq Z$ $\text{read}_v(X,Y)$ $\text{test}_v(k)$ $\text{passed}_v(X,k)$ $\neg$ [[l | $l \in Z$] $\Rightarrow$ [| $\text{read}_v(X,l)$]]

(They (= some boys who read some of the books) did not read all of them (= the books))

Even though the SI is calculated separately from the original sentence, it gives rise to the effect of embedding the SI in the relative clause of the original sentence as in the following:

(48) Some boys who read some of the books, but not all of them, passed the test.

It is just a coincidence that the SI goes into the relative clause. A SI can go anywhere in the main DRS, but syntactically it can be realized in a relative clause or in the restrictor or the nuclear scope of a quantifier, depending on where a relevant scalar expression occurs in the sentence.

5 Conclusion

In this paper, I claim that SIs are always global and that SIs are calculated in the framework of dynamic semantics. I used the DRT as a semantic tool, but my analyses does not rely on a particular framework. Any dynamic semantics will do. I have shown that global SIs can have the effect of local SIs in some contexts. This effect is obtained in various ways. First, a global SI can get the effect of being embedded in a purely syntactic island, and this is possible due to the dynamic binding. Another way in which a global SI can get the effect of a local is the role that a context plays. This is not a matter of structure but a matter of information contained in an information state. A third factor is background knowledge. Background knowledge determines the scalarity of likelihood of states of affairs. This is a pragmatic matter. Hence it is not captured by the semantic ordering of scalar terms.

References

Chierchia, G. 2002. Scalar Implicatures, Polarity Phenomena, and the Syntax/Pragmatics Interface. In A. Belletti (ed.), *Structures and Beyond*, Oxford University Press, Oxford. pp. 39–103.

Gazdar, G. 1979. *Pragmatics: Implicature, Presupposition, and Logical Form*. Academic Press, New York.

Grice, P. 1975. Logic and Conversation. In P. Cole and J. L. Morgan (eds.), *Speech Acts*. Academic Press, NY, pp. 4158.

Horn, L. R. 1972. *On the Semantic Properties of Logical Operators in English*. PhD thesis, University of California, LA.

Horn, L. 1989. *A Natural History of Negation*. University of Chicago Press, Chicago.

Kamp, Hans. 1981. A Theory of Truth and Semantic Representation. In J. Groenendijk and others (eds.). *Formal Methods in the Study of Language*. Amsterdam: Mathematics Center.

Krifka, M. 1995. The Semantics and Pragmatics of Polarity Items. *Linguistic Analysis* 25: 209-257.

Rooth, M. 1985. *Association with Focus*. Ph. D. Diss., University of Massachusetts, Amherst.

van der Sandt, R. A. 1992. Presupposition Projection as Anaphora Resolution. *Journal of Semantics* 9:333-377.

Sauerland, U. 2004. Scalar implicatures in complex sentences. *Linguistics and Philosophy* 27, 367391.

Stalnaker, R. 1978. Assertion. In P. Cole (ed) *Syntax and Semantics 9: Pragmatics*. Academic Press, New York.

Stalnaker, R. 2006. Assertion revisited: on the interpretation of two-dimensional modal semantics. In Garcia-Caripintero, M. and Macia, J. (eds.), *Two Dimensional Semantics*. Oxford University Press.

Unification of Numeral Classifiers and Plural Markers: Empirical Facts and Implications

One-Soon Her
Graduate Institute of Linguistics & Research Center for Mind, Brain, and Learning
National Chengchi University
Taipei, Taiwan
hero@nccu.edu.tw

Yun-Ru Chen
Graduate Institute of Linguistics
National Chengchi University
Taipei, Taiwan
99555015@nccu.edu.tw

Abstract

The use of an obligatory numeral classifier (C) on N in general does not co-occur with mandatory plural marking (PM) (Greenberg 1990[1972], Sanches and Slobin 1973). Borer (2005) and Her (2012a) take this generalization further and see Cs and PMs as the same category. This unification implies that C/PM are mutually exclusive on N. In this paper, we first provide a mathematical foundation for this unification, i.e., C/PM both function as a multiplicand with the precise value of *1* (Her 2012a), and then explore empirically to what extent C/PM's complimentary distribution is borne out. We obtain from the WALS database a total of 22 languages with both Cs and PMs, including Mandarin, Japanese, and Vietnamese. Our survey finds C/PM co-occurring on N in 11 languages. We then set out to formally account for the unification of C/PM and explain its exceptions, taking Mandarin as an example, with a double-headed classifier construction. This study thus adds merit to the unification of C/PM and concludes with its implication on a universal lexical count/mass distinction.

1 Introduction

Greenberg (1972) and Sanches and Slobin (1973) made the initial observation that languages with obligatory numeral classifiers (Cs) on nouns do not have compulsory morphological marking of nominal plurality, and vice versa. This generalization has been supported by a number of researchers, e.g., Tsuo (1976), Borer (2005), Her (2012a), Doetjies (2012), among others. To explain this generalization, Greenberg (1972) links the emergence of Cs in a language to its loss of plural markers (PMs), and as Peyraube (1998) observes, this is true for the rise of Cs in Chinese.

However, this generalization is noncommittal on the complimentary distribution of Cs and PMs, as it says nothing about the cases where either C or PM is optional. Borer (2005:94) and Her (2012a:1682) take this generalization further and claim that Cs and PMs are the same category. The *–s* suffix in English, for example, applicable to all count nouns, is seen as a general classifier, similar to the Chinese *ge* in (1a) (Her 2012a:1682); the two thus share the same constituent structure, as in (2).

(1) a. 三 個 杯子
san ge beizi
3 C cup
b. three cups

(2)

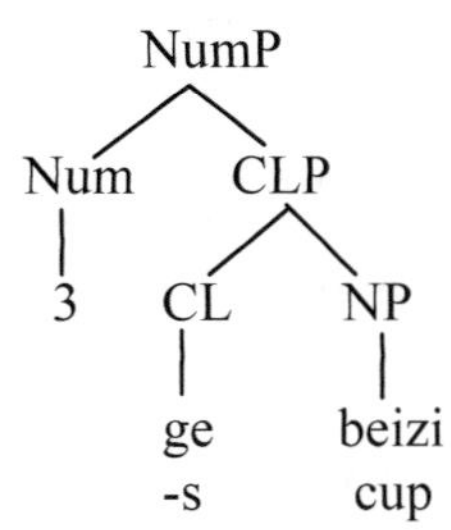

The C/PM unification predicts the two to be in complimentary distribution on N. Yet, it does not preclude the scenario where the two coexist in a language but do not co-occur on N. The first objective of this paper is purely empirical: to identify to what extent these two predictions are borne out. We then set out to account for the general pattern of distribution between Cs and PMs across languages as well as the exceptional cases where C/PM do co-occur on N. The paper is organized as follows. Section 2 offers a mathematical interpretation of Cs and PMs as the functional basis for their unification. Section 3 then obtains from the WALS database 22 languages that employ Cs and PMs and examines the distribution of the two on N in each language. Section 4 consists of discussions of the empirical facts obtained in the previous section and offers a formal syntactic account of Mandarin C/PM co-occurrence. Section 5 examines the implication that C/PM unification has on the controversy of count/mass distinction in languages. Section 6 concludes the paper.

2 Unification of Cs and PMs

In classifier languages, the C position in relation to a numeral (Num) and N can also be occupied by a measure word (M). Her and Hsieh (2010) and Her (2012b) demonstrate that, while C/M belong to the same category, they differ semantically. Specifically, while M is semantically substantive, C is semantically null, in the sense that it does not contribute any additional semantic information to N that N does not already have. Thus, if the grammatically required C is omitted for stylistic considerations, the meaning is not affected, as in (3), taken from Her (2102b:1219 (16)).

(3) 五 (張) 餅 二 (條) 魚
wu zhang bing er tiao yu
5 C loaf 2 C fish
'5 loaves and 2 fish.'

Based on the insight from Greenberg (1990[1972]:172), Au Yeung (2005), and Yi (2011), Her (2012a) proposes to account for C's semantic redundancy mathematically in seeing [Num C] as [$n \times 1$]. In a multiplicative operation, for a multiplicand to be null, its value can only be *1*. This view unifies all Cs under the concept of a multiplicand with the precise value of *1*.[1] To illustrate, (3) can be seen mathematically as (4).

(4) [[5 ($\times 1$)] loaf] (+) [[2 ($\times 1$)] fish]

[1] The only mathematical difference between Cs and Ms is that the value of an M is anything but *1*, e.g., 2 in the case of 雙 *shuang* 'pair', 12 in the case of 打 *da* 'dozen', and kilo in the case of 公斤 *gongjin* 'kilo' (Her 2012a).

Having established Cs as the multiplicand *1* entering a multiplicative relation with Num as the multiplier in [Num C N], we now compare the Chinese example in (1a), repeated in (5), with its English counterpart in (6): the only difference is that Chinese employs a C and English uses a PM *–s*, which can also be seen as the multiplicand *1*.

(5) Chinese: [[3×1] cup] = [3 *ge* beizi]
(6) English: [[3×1] cup] = [3 *–s* cup]

Surface word orders set aside, the two languages are identical in their nominal expressions with numerals, if C *ge* and PM *–s* are taken to be the two sides of the same coin. Indeed, like Chinese C, which is generally required, the generally required *–s* can be omitted without affecting the meaning. Thus, though (7a) is ill-formed in an argument position, its meaning is unmistakable. Also, in some languages, e.g., Hungarian, Tibetan, Archaic Chinese, among others, the counterpart of (7a) is well-formed in argument positions. Likewise in (7b), *three-cup*, well-formed as a modifier, still has the plural reading. And then, there are cases like those in (7c), where the omission of *–s* is obligatory, but a plural reading still must obtain.

(7) a.*three cup
b. a three-cup bra
c. three fish/deer/sheep

Note also that PM *–s* is still required when Num's value is smaller than *1*, and thus not *1*, e.g., *0.5 apples* and *0 apples* and not **0.5 apple* and **0 apple*, indicating that *–s* here has little to do with plurality. The PM *–s* thus serves the same function as a general C in highlighting the discreteness or countability of N. However, there is a caveat: PM *–s* is not allowed when Num has the value of *1*, as in (8), and yet, the counterpart C *ge* in Chinese is well-formed.

(8) He bought one cup(*s).
(9) *Ta mai-le (yi) ge beizi.*
he bought 1 C cup
'He bought a cup.'

Her (2012a:1682) offers an explanation likewise based on mathematics. In [1×1], either the multiplier (Num) or the multiplicand (C/PM) can be omitted without changing the result. Both options are found in languages. As seen in (10a), in Chinese Num is *optionally* omitted, but only when its value is *1*; in contrast, in Persian, when Num is *1*, it is *obligatorily* omitted, as in (10b) (Gebhardt 2009:212). In Khasi, an Austro-Asiatic language in India, when Num is *1*, it is C that is obligatorily omitted, as in (10c) (Temsen 2007: 6); the same is true in Tat (Greenberg, 1990[1972]:168), Amis, a Formosan language (Tang 2004:389), and Tetun, an Austronesian language (van Klinken, 1999). English, shown in (10d), is thus rather like Khasi; the only difference is that the multiplicand *1* is expressed as PM in English, C in Khasi. Incidentally, Indonesian is interesting in that the generally optional C is obligatory with the numeral *1* (Sneddon 1996).

(10) Options of Num, Num=*1*
 a. Chinese [[*1* × *1*] cup] = [(1) C cup]
 b. Persian [[*1* × *1*] cup] = [*1 C cup]
 c. Khasi [[*1* × *1*] cup] = [1 *C cup]
 d. English [[*1* × *1*] cup] = [1 *–s cup]

To summarize, Cs and PMs can be unified under the view that they both enter into a multiplicative relation with Num and function as a multiplicand with the precise value of *1*, which explains why both are semantically superfluous.

3 Potential Exceptions in 22 Languages

The unification of Cs and PMs as the same category means that they occupy the same syntactic position and share the same constituency structure. Consequently, Cs and PMs must be mutually exclusive on N. Yet, there has not been any serious attempt in finding out to what extent this prediction is borne out empirically. In the *World Atlas of Language Structures* (WALS) database, there are two studies that may shed light on this very issue, though indirectly: Gil (2008) looks at 400 languages and found Cs in 140, and Haspelmath (2008) examines 291 languages and 163 have PMs. What interests us is that 114 languages are covered in both studies, as shown in Table 1.

Table 1. C/PM Distribution in 114 languages

	PM×	**PM√**
C×	8	80
C√	4	**22**

Out of the 114, only 8 are without Cs and PMs, which will be examined in Section 5. The majority employs PMs only, while 4 employ Cs only. Cs and PMs thus do seem to be largely complimentarily distributed in languages. However, 22 languages have both, as seen in Table 2.

Table 2. Cs and PMs in 22 languages

	Optional C	Obligatory C
Human Ns, optional	Hatam	Mandarin Japanese
All Ns, optional	Ainu Indonesian Khmer Tetun Chantyal	Garo Jacaltec Nivkh Teribe Ulithian Vietnamese
All Ns, optional in inanimates	None	Belhare
Human Ns, obligatory	None	Taba Kathmandu-Newar
All Ns obligatory	Hungarian Turkish Tuvaluan	Kham Mokilese

The 4 languages with obligatory Cs and PMs, if confirmed, are certain challenges, as C/PM co-occurring on N is certain. Yet, in fact all 22 languages may present problems for C/PM unification, if C and PM co-occur on N, whether optionally or obligatorily. In 3.1 are listed the 11 languages where Cs and PMs are found to be in complimentary distribution, and 3.2 presents the 11 languages that do allow Cs and PMs to co-occur on N.

3.1 C/PM mutually exclusive

Garo (Tibeto-Burman): optional Cs and PMs, PMs not used where numerals denote plurality (Burling 1961, *p.c.*).

Indonesian: optional Cs and optional PM by way of reduplication (Sneddon 1996), does not allow C/PM co-occurrence (Johnny Lee, *p.c.*).

Kham (Tibetan): obligatory PM on all Ns, but the putative Cs are in fact 'not true classifiers in the classical sense defined by Greenberg (1972) and others..' (Watters, 2002:180).

Jacaltec (a Mayan language of Guatemala): obligatory Cs and an optional PM on all Ns. However, we suspect that the putative PM *heb'* is an adjective or quantifier (see the discussions of Mokilese and Vietnamese below), not a morphological PM. See (11).

(11) *ca-wan heb' naj winnaj*
 2-NumCL PL C man
 'the 2 men' (Craig, 1986:246)

Mokilese (Micronesian): plurality marked on the determiner, not N (Harrison, 1976), no C/PM co-occurrence on N (Doetjes 2012).

Teribe (a Chibchan language of Panama): obligatory Cs, optional PMs, do not co-occur (Quesada, 2000).

Tetun (an Austronesian language of Timor): optional Cs and an optional PM on all Ns (van Klinken *et al*, 2002), no examples of the two co-occurring (John Hajek, *p.c.*).

Tuvaluan (an Austronesian language of Tuvalu): some classifier-like elements, which led to its inclusion by Gil (2005). Yet, Besnier (2000:367) is emphatic that 'Polynesian languages do not have classifier systems, and Tuvaluan is no exception.'

Turkish: optional Cs and PMs (Kornfilt, 1997; Göksel and Kerslake, 2011), no C/PM co-occurrence on N (Jaklin Kornfilt, *p.c.*).

Ulithian (Austronesian): obligatory Cs, but plurality is marked on demonstratives, not on Ns (Lynch *et al*, 2002).

Vietnamese: obligatory Cs, optional PMs on all Ns. Note, however, that the so-called 'pluralizers' or 'plural markers' are in fact quantifiers, not morphological PMs on N, and carry various explicit quantifier meanings and (in)definiteness (Thompson, 1965:180; Schachter, 1985:38). See (12).

(12) *các con ngựa đen*
PL-def C horse black
'the black horses' (Nguyen 2004:18)

3.2 C/PM *not* mutually exclusive

For each the 11 languages where Cs and PMs co-occur on N, a reference and an example are given.

Ainu (an indigenous language of Hokkaido): optional Cs and an optional PM for all Ns (Bugaeva, 2012)

(13) *okkaypo utar tu-n*
young.man PL 2-C
'these 2 young men' (Anna Bugaeva, *p.c.*)

Belhare (a Kiranti language of Nepal): obligatory Cs and optional PM on inanimate Ns.

(14) *sip-paŋ maʔi-chi*
2-C person-PL
'2 people' (Bickel 2003:563)

Chantyal (an endangered language of Nepal): optional Cs and an optional PM for all Ns.

(15) *tin-ta jəmməy naku-ma*
3-C all dog-PL
'all 3 dogs' (Noonan 2003:318)

Hatam (West Papuan): optional Cs and PMs.

(16) *di-kindig-bat-nya i-bou can*
1sg-brother-COLL-PL 3PL-C 2
'my 2 brothers' (Reesink 1999:83)

Hungarian: optional Cs, PMs obligatory on all Ns but do not co-occur with numerals.

(17) *ex-ek a szem-ek rohadt-ak*
this-PL the C-PL rotten-PL
'These rotten ones.'

(18) *három takaró-(*k)*
3 blanket-PL
'3 blankets' (Csirmaz and Dékány, 2010:13)

However, Csirmaz and Dékány (to appear) suggests that [Plural demonstrative + def. article + CL + N-PL] is not well-formed.

(19) *??az-ok a fej salátá-k*
that-PL the C lettuce-PL
'those heads of lettuce

Japanese: obligatory Cs and an optional PM on human Ns.

(20) *Sono-gakusei-tati san-nin kita.*
that-student-PL 3-C came
'The 3 students came' (Amazaki, 2005:224)

Kathmandu Newar (Tibeto-Burman): obligatory Cs and PMs on animate Ns.

(21) *nya-mhə pasa-pĩ:*
5-C friend-PL
'5 friends.' (Hale and Shrestha 2006:93)

Khmer (Austroasiatic and official language of Cambodia): optional Cs and an optional PM on all Ns (Gilbert, 2008; Gorgoniyev, 1966).

(22) *proas (proas) bei nak*
man-man 3 C
'3 men' (Soksan Ngoun, *p.c.*)

Mandarin: obligatory Cs and an optional PM for human Ns.

(23) *san wei laoshi-men*
3 C teacher-PL
'3 teachers' (Her 2012a)

Nivk (language isolate of Siberia): obligatory Cs and optional PMs on all Ns.

(24) *ku-umguo ʁla-gu men*
that-girl-PL 2 C
'those 2 girls' (Panfilov 1962:158)

Taba (Austronesian): obligatory Cs and an optional PM on human Ns.

(25) *mapin-ci mat-tol*
woman-PL C-3
'3 women' (Bowden 2001:256)

4 A Formal Account for Mandarin

These 11 languages present a significant challenge to the unification of C/PM; however, a thorough and comprehensive examination of all 11 cases is clearly too wide in scope for the present paper. We thus focus on Mandarin, a quintessential classifier language believed to have the largest inventory of Cs (T'sou, 1976). Traditionally it has been claimed that C/PM do not co-occur on N in Mandarin. However, recent data from corpus and the Internet indicate that C and *–men*, a PM for human nouns, do co-occur, indicating variation in grammaticality judgment among Mandarin speakers (e.g., Her 2012a). To explain this C/PM co-occurrence, we propose a formal account with the following grammatical characterizations.

(26) a. The category CL consists of the two subcategories: Cs and PMs.
b. The morpheme *–men* is a suffix that carries the feature [pl] and [def].
c. Cs are clitics and require a proper host (Yang 2002, Chen 2012).
d. Numerals project NumP and carry [pl], except *1*, which has [sg].
e. There are two null numerals, Ø[sg] and Ø[pl].
f. Ø[pl] subcategorizes for PM, all other numerals, C.

With that, we account for (27) with the structure and derivation in (28). The suffix *-men* attracts N to raise to CL. Given that *–men* carries a definite reading (e.g., Huang *et al*, 2009:8.4.1), the N-*men* phrase thus raises to Num and then to D to fill the empty heads.

(27) *laoshi-men*
teacher-PL

(28) a.
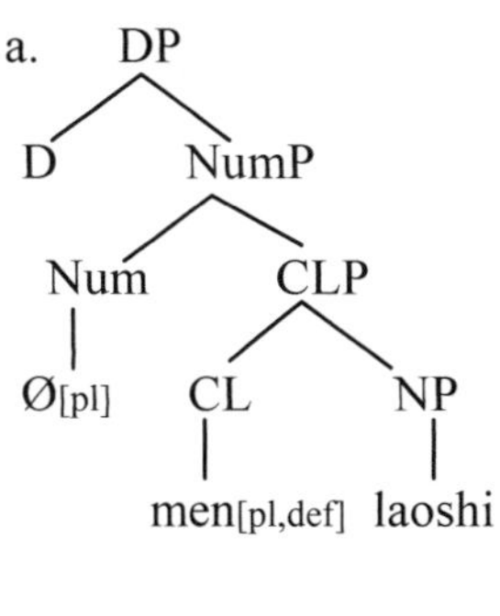

b.
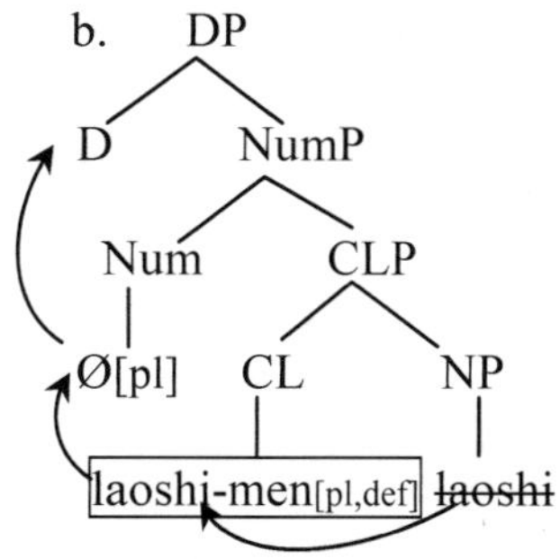

In contrast, numeral *san* '3' in (29) is ill-formed, becuase overt numerals subcategorize for Cs, not *–men* (see (26f)). The example in (30) is thus well-formed; the clitic *wei* raises to an Num, as in (31). Following Huang *et al* (2009, chp.8), we assume (30) is ambiguous between a quantity reading with NumP, and an individual reading, thus with a null D projecting a DP and taking NumP as complement.

(29) **san laoshi-men*
3 teacher-PL

(30) *san wei laoshi*
3 C teacher
'3 teachers'

(31)
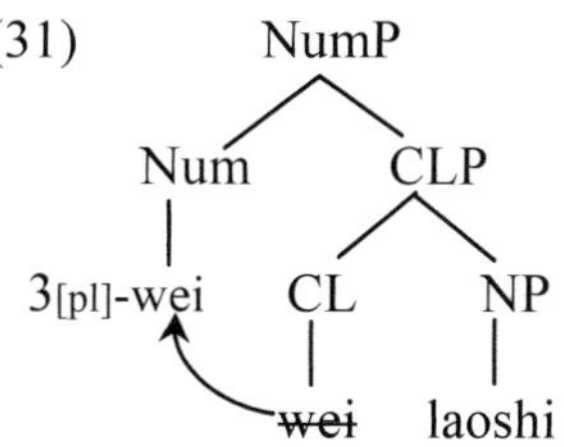

The bare classifier phrase in (32) is ill-formed, for Cs, as clitics in Mandarin, require a proper host. The example in (33), where an overt numeral serves as the host for C, is thus well-formed with or without the overt D.

(32) **wei laoshi*
C teacher

(33) (*zhe*) *yi wei laoshi*
the 1 C teacher
'(the) one teacher'

(34)
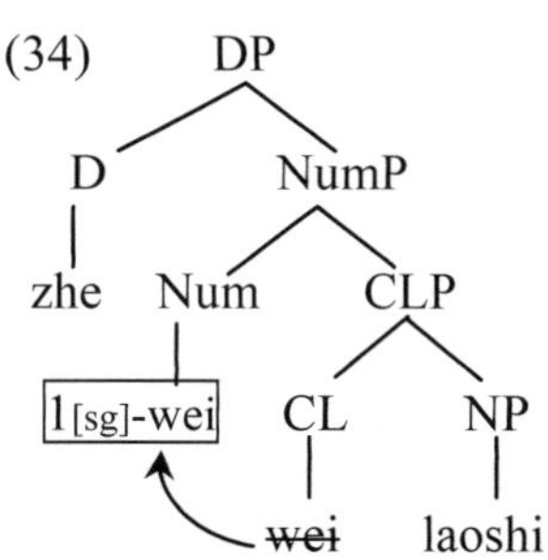

As mentioned earlier, the numeral *1* can be omitted. The example in (35) is thus well-formed with or without the numeral *1*, as long as there is an overt D serving as host for C.

(35) *zhe wei laoshi*
the C teacher
'this teacher'

(36) a.

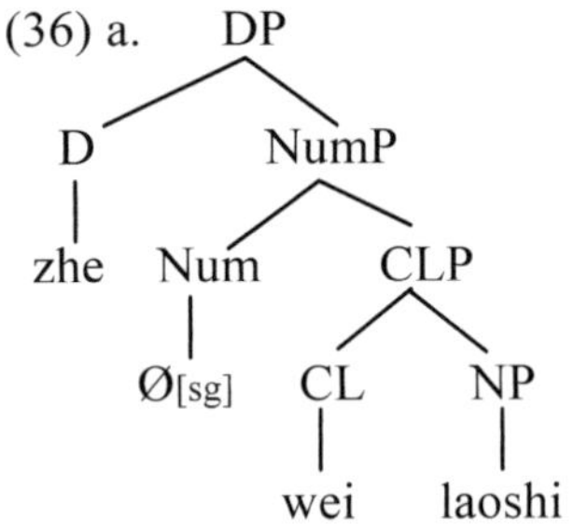

b.

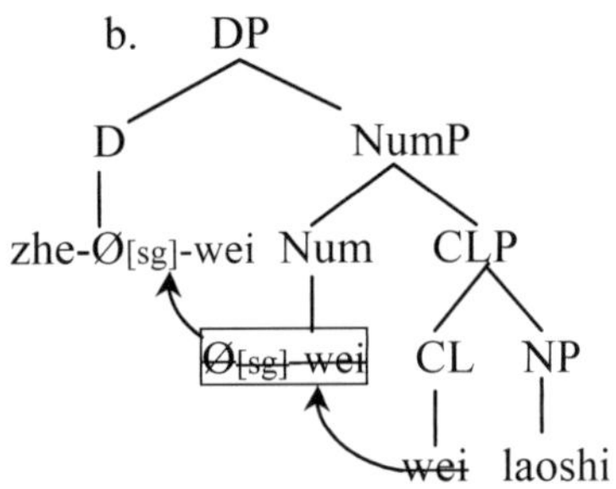

Finally, for the co-occurrence of C and–*men*, it should be noted that any analysis proposed should ideally reflect its marked nature, as C/PM co-occurring on N is clearly the exception, not the norm. An example is given in (37), the derivation of which is illustrated in (38a-c). Note the difference between (38) and (31); the latter is without –*men* and thus without DP.

(37) *san wei laoshi*(-*men*)
3 C teacher-PL
'(the) 3 teachers'

(38) a.

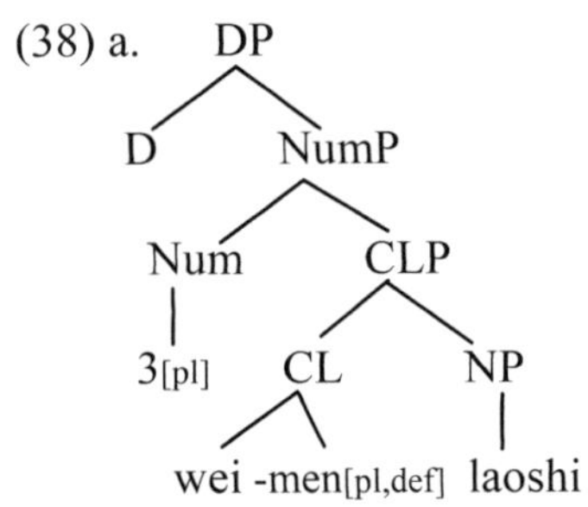

b.

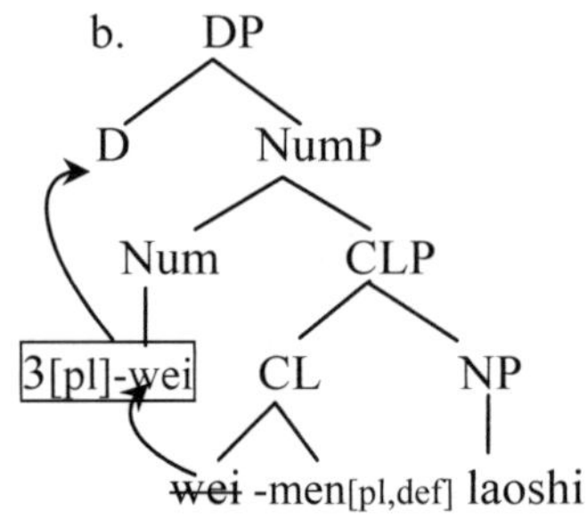

c.

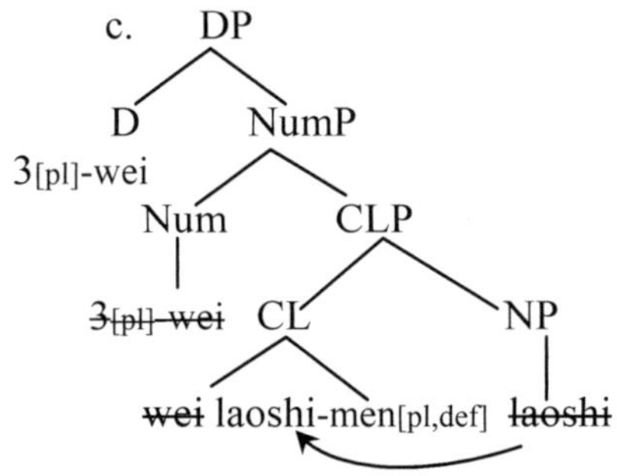

What's marked about the structure is that CL is double-headed, with a C and a PM, each undergoing its normal derivation. In (38c), the Num-C phrase thus raises to D to fill its empty head for definiteness, the only compatible reading with the CLP due to *-men*. Thus, the DP structure of (38) remains the same with an overt D, e.g., *zhe* 'the'. The double-headed CL is independently motivated by the so-called 'CL copying construction', coined by Zhang (2013:169). Two examples are given in (39), and the proposed derivation of (39a) in (40), which, like (30) and unlike (37) with –*men*, is a NumP.

(39) a. *san duo hua*(-*duo*)
3 C flower-C
'3 flowers'

b. *san pi ma*(-*pi*)
3 C horse-C
'3 horses'

(40) a.

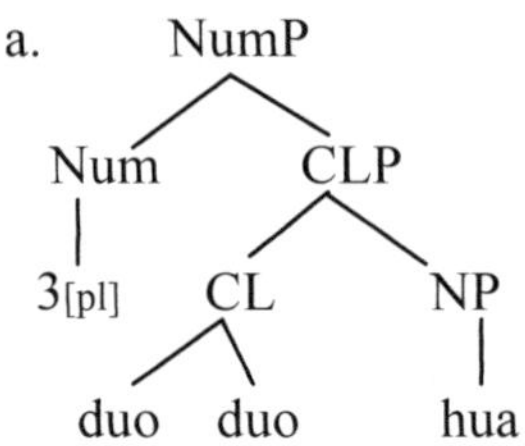

b.

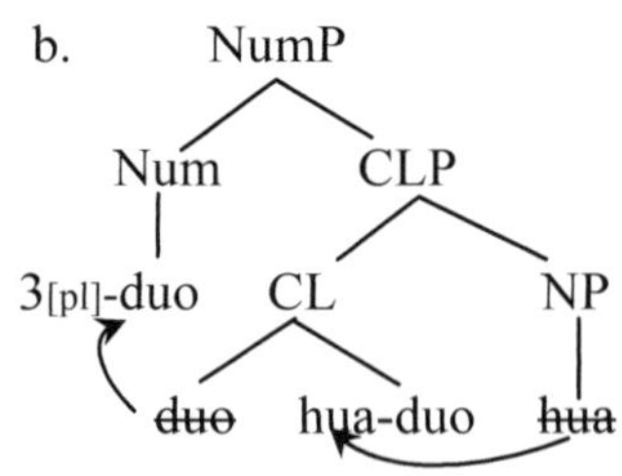

There is also cross-linguistic evidence of double-headedness, e.g., appositional compounds (*woman doctors*, *women doctor*) (Bresnan, 2001), the double-headed VV structures in Classical Chinese (Feng 2002), and a double-headed verbal phrase structure for serial verb constructions in some African languages (e.g., Baker, 1989; Hiraiwa and Bodomo, 2008; Aboh, 2009).

5 Implication on the Count/Mass Issue

The discussions thus far indicate that Cs and PMs are two typological choices serving the same cognitive function of highlighting the discrete or count nature of a noun. In other words, the existence of C/PM in a language entails a count/mass distinction in that language. Thus, to the extent that C/PM is universal, so is the count/mass distinction. The C/PM unification thus supports Yi's (2009, 2011) and Her's (2012a) rejection of the thesis that classifier languages, unlike PM languages, have no count nouns, a thesis held prominently by Quine (1969b:35ff), Allan (1977), Krifka (1995), and Chierchia (1998), among others. This leaves us with two issues to explore further. First, is the count/mass distinction made universally at the lexical or syntactic level? Second, is there any evidence for the count/mass distinction in languages without C/PM?

5.1 Syntactic or lexical distinction

Borer (2005) contends that all nouns in all languages are mass at the lexical level and a count/mass distinction only exists at the syntactic level, i.e., a noun is count only when it appears as the complement in the syntactic configuration projected by C/PM. Her view is based primarily on data showing fairly robust convertibility between putative count nouns and mass nouns in English, as in (41) and (42).

(41) A wine/wines, a love/loves, a salt/salts (on count reading)
(42) There is dog/stone/chicken on the floor (on mass reading)

Borer's view thus predicts that all putative mass nouns can be marked with a PM and be coerced into count, as in (41), and in the case of classifier languages, all putative mass nouns can appear with a C and thus turn into count. But this prediction is too strong to be true. Many putative mass nouns in English cannot be quantified by numerals, unlike putative count nouns.

(43) a.*one conspicuousness
b.*one beautifulness
c.*one precariousness
(44) a.*three conspicuousnesses
b.*three beautifulnesses
c.*three precariousnesses

Likewise, many putative mass nouns in Mandarin cannot appear in the [Num C N] configuration either, again unlike putative count nouns in the language.

(45) a.*三 個 空氣
san ge qi
3 C air
b.*三 個 酒精
san ge jiujing
3 C alcohol
c.*三 個 不銹鋼
san ge buxiugang
3 C stainless-steel

The problem is easily solved, however, if the traditional view is adopted, where a count/mass distinction is made at the lexical level.

5.2 Languages without C/PM

Given the lexical count/mass distinction in languages with C/PM and the fact that the majority of the world's languages have either Cs or PMs or both (again, see Table 1, repeated below), the implication is that the count/mass distinction is universal.

Table 1. C/PM Distribution of in 114 languages

	PM×	PM√
C×	**8**	80
C√	4	22

Out of the 114 languages covered by both Gil (2008) and Haspelmath (2008), only 8 are without C/PM. Early Archaic Chinese is another example. Since grammatically, count nouns, by definition, can be counted without the help a measure word, a language must logically have numerals, count quantifiers, e.g., *several* and *many*, or count determiners, e.g., *these* and *those*, for it to have count nouns. So, we shall have a closer look at the numeral systems in these 8 languages and Early Archaic Chinese. The nine languages are divided into two groups, those with restricted numerals only and those with a (semi-)productive system.

Group 1: restricted numerals

Imonda, a Papuan language, has numerals 1 to 5 only: 1, 2, 1+2, 2+2, and 2+2+1 (Chan, 2013).

Pirahã, an Amazonian language isolate, has no numerals (Frank *et al*, 2008).

Yidiny, a nearly extinct Australian language, has only numerals 1–5 (1991:224).

Yingkarta, an Australian language *a.k.a.* Yinggarda and Inggarda, has numerals 1-4 only: 1, 2, 3, and 2+2 (Chan, 2013).

Group 2: (semi-)productive systems

Early Archaic Chinese already has a very mature decimal system.

Chimariko, a Hokan language of California, now extinct, has quinary and decimal system (Jany 2007:110).

Kombai, a Papuan language, has a semi-productive body tally system (Chan, 2013).

Mapudungun, an Araucanian language of Chile, has a decimal system (Chan, 2013).

Salt-Yui, a Papuan language, has a finger-and-toe tally system with a 2, 5, and 20-based cyclic pattern (Chan, 2013).

We will take Early Archaic Chinese as an example for Group 2, and Pirahã, for Group 1. Early Archaic Chinese in the Shang oracle-bone inscriptions, or Oracular Chinese, from 18th-12th centuries BC, is known to have neither Cs nor PMs (Xu, 2006). It does, however, have a well-developed decimal numeral system and also a number of plural quantifiers. Evidence of count/mass distinction comes from the fact that numerals can quantify an N directly, as in (46). Without exception, such Ns are all putative count nouns, indicating a lexical count/mass distinction.

(46) a.五 人 一 牛 (Hu 1983 (01060)
wu ren yi niu
5 person 1 ox
'5 persons and 1 ox'

b.鳥 二百十二， 兔 一 (Hu 1983 (41802))
niao er-ba-shi-er tu yi
bird 2-hundred-ten-2 hare 1
'212 birds and 1 hare'

Pirahã, on the other hand, is anumeric and also makes no distinction between singular and plural (Everett, 2005). More significantly, experiments conducted by Gordan (2005) and Everett and Madora (2012) show that monolingual Pirahã speakers are only able to conceptualize an exact numerical quantity equal to or smaller than three. However, the notion of 'count' only requires the concept of *individual* via the notion of *one* (Yi, 2009:219). In other words, the notion of exact quantity above three is not a necessary condition for either the conceptual or the linguistic distinction between count and mass. Clear evidence for a count/mass distinction in Pirahã comes from the two different quantifiers in (47), both indicating a large quantity in approximation (Nevins *et al* 2009).

(47) a. xaíbái 'many' (count nouns only)
b. xapagí 'much' (non-count nouns only)

The fact that a language without numerals is still able to make a lexical distinction of count/mass, coupled with the fact that pre-linguistic infants are capable of representing precise numbers (1-3) as well as approximating numerical magnitudes (see Feigenson *et al*, 2004, for an excellent summary and review), suggests that the count/mass distinction is universal.

6 Conclusion

This study confirms the generalization that numeral classifiers (Cs) and plural markers (PMs) are largely complimentarily distributed in languages. We concur with Her (2012a) that this generalization exists because it reflects C/PM's identical mathematical function as a multiplicand with the value of *1* and the cognitive function of highlighting the discreteness, or the count nature, of the noun. However, genuine exceptions, where C/PM co-occur on N in 11 languages out of 114 examined, do pose a challenge to the unification of Cs and PMs. These 11 languages are Ainu, Belhare, Chantyal, Hatam, Hungarian, Japanese, Kathmandu Newar, Khmer, Mandarin, Nivk, and Taba. We take Mandarin as an example and account for its [D Num CL N] construction, where the C/PM co-occurrence involves a marked structure with a double-headed CL.

Furthermore, the unification of Cs and PMs also has significant implications on the debate over the count/mass distinction in languages. Our preliminary survey of 9 languages without C/PM, with special attention on Pirahã, indicates that the existence of a numeral system in a language is in fact not a prerequisite for the count/mass distinction. Thus, to the extent that the unification of Cs and PMs is on the right track, the implication is that the count/mass distinction is made on the lexical level and it is universal.

References

Aboh, Enoch. 2009. Clause structure and verb series. *Linguistic Inquiry* 40(1):1-33.

Allan, K. 1977. Classifier. *Language* 53: 285-311.

Amazaki, Osamu. 2005. *A Functional Analysis of Numeral Quantifier Constructions in Japanese*. PhD dissertation, State University of New York at Buffalo.

Au Yeung, W.-H. Ben, 2005. *An interface program for parameterization of classifiers in Chinese*. PhD Dissertation, Hong Kong University of Science and Technology.

Baker, Mark. 1989. Object sharing and projection in serial verb constructions. *Linguistic Inquiry* 20(4):513-553.

Besnier, Niko. 2000. *Tuvaluan: A Polynesian Languages of the Central Pacific*. Routledge, London and New York.

Bickel, Balthasar. 2003. Belhare. In *The Sino-Tibetan languages*, eds., Graham Thurgood and Randy LaPolla, 546-569. Routledge, London.

Bowden, John. 2001. *Taba: Description of a South Halmahera Language*. Pacific Linguistics, Canberra.

Bresnan, Joan. 2001. *Lexical-Functional Syntax*. Blackwell, Oxford.

Bugaeva, Anna. 2012. Southern Hokkaido Ainu. In *The Languages of Japan and Korea*, ed., Nicolas Tranter. Routledge.

Burling, Robbins. 1961. *A Garo Grammar*. Deccan College Postgraduate and Research Institute Poona.

Chan, Eugene. 2013. *Numeral systems of the world's languages*. Available online at http://lingweb.eva.mpg.de/numeral/. Accessed on 2012/03/01.

Chen, Ching Perng. 2012. *On the Bare Classifier Phrase in Mandarin Chinese*. MA thesis, Graduate Institute of Linguistics, National Chengchi University

Chierchia, Gennaro. 1998. Reference to kinds across languages. *Natural Language Semantics* 6:339-405.

Craig, Colette. 1986. Jacaltec noun classifiers: A study in grammaticalization. *Lingua* 70:241-284.

Csirmaz, Aniko and Éva Dékány. To appear. Hungarian is a classifier language. In *Word Classes*, eds., Simone Raffaele and Francesca Masini. John Benjamins, Amsterdam.

Dan Gusfield. 1997. *Algorithms on Strings, Trees and Sequences*. Cambridge University Press.

Doetjes, Jenny. 2012. Count/mass distinction across languages. In *Semantics: An International Handbook of Natural Language Meaning*, Part III, eds., Claudia Maienborn, Klaus von Heusinger and Paul Portner, 2559-2581. De Gruyter, Berlin.

Dixon, Robert. 1991. *Words of Our Country*. University of Queensland Press.

Everett, Caleb and Keren Madora. 2012. Quantity recognition among speakers of an anumeric language. *Cognitive Science* 36(1):130-141.

Everett, Daniel 2005. Cultural constraints on grammar and cognition in Pirahã: Another look at the design features of human language. *Current Anthropology* 46:621-646.

Feigenson, Lisa, Stanislas Dehaene, and Elizabeth Spelke. 2004. Core systems of number. *Trends in Cognitive Science* 8(7):307-314.

Feng, Shengli. 2002. A formal analysis of the origin of VR-constructions in Chinese. *Yuyanxue Luncong* 26:178-208. Commercial Press, Beijing.

Frank, Michael C., Daniel L. Everett, Evelina Fedorenko, and Edward Gibson. 2008. Number as a cognitive technology: Evidence from Pirahã language and cognition. *Cognition*, Volume 108(3):819-824.

Gebhardt, Lewis. 2009. *Numeral Classifiers and the Structure of DP*. PhD Dissertation, Northwestern University.

Gil, David. 2008. Numeral classifiers. In *The World Atlas of Language Structures Online*, eds., Martin Haspelmath, Mathew Dryer, David Gil, and Bernard Comrie, chapter 55. Max Planck Digital Library. Available online at http://wals.info/feature/55.Accessed on 2012/5/21.

Göksel, Asli and Celia Kerslake. 2005. *Turkish: A Comprehensive Grammar*. Routledge, London and New York.

Gordon, Peter. 2004. Numerical cognition without words: Evidence from Amazonia. *Science* 306:496-499.

Greenberg, Joseph. 1990[1972]. Numerical classifiers and substantival number: problems in the genesis of a linguistic type. In *On Language: Selected Writings of Joseph H. Greenberg*, eds., Keith Denning and Suzanne Kemmer, 166-193. Stanford University Press. [First published 1972 in *Working Papers on Language Universals* 9:1-39.]

Hale, Austin and lswaranand Shresthachrya. 1973. Is Newari a Classifier Language? *Nepalese studies* 1(1):1-21.

Harrison, Shelly. 1976. *Mokilese Reference Grammar*. University Press of Hawaii.

Haspelmath, Martin. 2008. Occurrence of nominal plurality. In *The World Atlas of Language Structures Online*, eds., Martin Haspelmath, Mathew Dryer, David Gil, and Bernard Comrie, chapter 34. Max Planck Digital Library. Available online at http://wals.info/feature/55. Accessed on 2012/5/21.

Her, One-Soon. 2012a. Distinguishing classifiers and measure words: A mathematical perspective and implications. *Lingua* 122(14): 1668-1691.

Her, One-Soon. 2012b. Structure of classifiers and measure words: A lexical functional Account. *Language and Linguistics* 13(6):1211-1251.

Her, One-Soon and Chen-Tian Hsieh. 2010. On the semantic distinction between classifiers and measure words in Chinese. *Language and linguistics* 11(3):527-551.

Hiraiwa, Ken and Adams Bodomo. 2008. Object-sharing as symmetric sharing. In *Proceedings of the 26th West Coast Conference on Formal Linguistics*, eds. Charles B. Chang and Hannah J. Haynie, 243-251. Cascadilla Proceedings Project, Somerville, MA.

Hu, Houxuan (ed.). 1983. *Jiaguwen heji* 'The great collection of the oracle inscriptions'. China Social Sciences Publishing House, Beijing.

Huang, C.-T. James, Audrey Y.-H. Li, and Yafei Li. 2009. *The Syntax of Chinese*. Cambridge University Press.

Jany, Carmen. 2007. *Chimariko in Areal and Typological Perspective.* PhD Dissertation, University of California, Santa Barbara.

Krifka, Manfred. 1995. Common nouns: a contrastive analysis of Chinese and English. In *The Generic Book*, eds., Gregory N. Carlson and Francis Jeffry Pelletier, 398-411. University of Chicago Press.

Nevins, Andrew, David Pesetsky, and Cilene Rodrigues. 2009. Piraha Exceptionality: a Reassessment. *Language* 85(2):355-404.

Nguyen, Tuong-Hung. 2004. *The Structure of the Vietnamese Noun Phrase*. PhD dissertation, Boston University.

Noonan, Michael. 2003. Recent Language Contact in the Nepal Himalaya. In *Language Variation: Papers on Variation and Change in the Sinosphere and in the Indosphere in Honour of James A. Matisoff*, eds., David Bradley, Randy LaPolla, Boyd Michailovsky, and Graham Thurgood, 35-51. Pacific Linguistics, Canberra.

Panfilov, Vladimir. 1962. *Grammatika nivkhskogo iazyka* [Grammar of Nivkh] 1. Leningrad: Izdatel'stvo akademii nauk.

Peyraube, Alain. 1998. On the history of classifiers in Archaic and Medieval Chinese. In *Studia Linguistica Serica*, ed. Benjamin K. T'sou, 131-145. Language Information Sciences Research Centre, City University of Hong Kong.

Reesink, Ger P. 1999. *A grammar of Hatam: Bird's Head Peninsula, Irian Jaya*. Pacific linguistics, Canberra.

Quine, Willard van Orman. 1969. *Ontological Relativity & Other Essays*. Columbia University Press, New York.

Sanches, Mary and Linda Slobin. 1973. Numeral classifiers and plural marking: An implicational universal. *Working Papers in Language Universals* 11:1-22.

Schachter, Paul. 1985. Parts-of-speech. In *Language Typology and Syntactic Description: Clause Structure Vol. 1,* ed., Timothy Shopen, 3-62. Cambridge University Press.

Sneddon, James N. 1996. *Indonesian: A Comprehensive Grammar*. Routledge, New York.

Tang, Chi-Chen J. 2004. Two types of classifier languages: A typological study of classification markers in Paiwan noun phrases. *Language and Linguistics* 5(2): 377-407

Thompson, Laurence. 1965. *A Vietnamese Grammar*. University of Washington Press, Seattle, WA.

T'sou, Benjamin K. 1976. The structure of nominal classifier systems. In *Austoasiastic Studies,* eds., Phillip N. Jenner, Stanley Starosta, and Laurence C. Thompson, 1215-1247. University of Hawaii Press.

van Klinken, Catharina L. 1999. *A grammar of the Feban dialect of Tetun: An Austronesian language of West Timor*. Pacific Linguistics, Canberra.

Watters, David E. 2002. *A Grammar of Kham*. Cambridge University Press

Xu, Dan. 2006. *Typological Change in Chinese Syntax*. Oxford University Press.

Yang, Rong. 2002. *Common nouns, Classifiers, and Quantification in Chinese*. PhD Dissertation, State University of New Jersey.

Yi, Byeong Uk. 2009. Chinese classifiers and count nouns. *Journal of Cognitive Science* 10:209-225.

Yi, Byeong Uk. 2011. What is a numeral classifier? Philosophical Analysis 23:195-258.

Zhang, Niina Ning. 2013. *Classifier Structures in Mandarin Chinese*. Mouton de Gruyter, Berlin & New York.

Head-internal Relatives in Japanese as Rich Context-Setters

Tohru Seraku
St. Catherine's College
Manor Road, Oxford, UK
OX1 3UJ
tohru.seraku@scatz.ox.ac.uk

Abstract

Head-Internal Relatives (HIRs) in Japanese are regarded as rich context-setters within Dynamic Syntax (DS): the propositional tree of the HIR clause is mapped onto a 'partial' tree, which establishes a rich context for the embedding clause to be parsed. This partial tree contains a situation node decorated with the Relevancy restriction and a node for an internal head. This account handles some new data and makes a novel prediction. Further, it is shown that the past DS analysis of HIRs in fact models change relatives (but not HIRs).

1 Introduction

Japanese displays so-called HIRs (Head-Internal Relatives), where the relative clause lacks a gap, the head is found inside the relative clause, and the relative clause ends with the particle *no*.

(1) [*Ringo-ga* *tsukue-no-ue-ni*
[apple-NOM table-GEN-top-at
oite-atta *no*]-*o* *Kiki-ga* *tabeta.*
place-existed NO]-ACC K-NOM ate
'An apple was on a table and Kiki ate it.'

This paper addresses Japanese HIRs in Dynamic Syntax (DS; Cann et al., 2005; Kempson et al., 2001). Sect. 2 surveys previous studies. Sect. 3 introduces DS. Sect. 4 argues that the past DS account of *no* (Cann et al., 2005) fails to capture the non-nominality of HIRs. Sect. 5 presents an alternative DS account. Sect. 6 argues that the past DS account of *no* models change relatives (but not HIRs). Sect. 7 concludes the paper.

2 Previous Studies

Several papers collected in Kuroda (1992) as a point of departure, the Japanese HIR has been extensively explored (Kitagawa, 2005; Kuroda, 2005; see references therein). Two approaches stand out. First, some scholars note parallelisms between HIRs and E-type anaphora and make use of the E-type mechanism for HIRs (Hoshi, 1995; Kim, 2007, 2008a/b, 2009; Matsuda, 2002; Shimoyama, 1999, 2001). The most advanced work in this camp is Kim's analysis. Second, others postulate the null functional head ChR (Choose Role) as a sister to VP, and assume that ChR picks out the internal head by choosing a salient thematic role in the eventuality denoted by VP (Grosu, 2010; Grosu & Landman, 2012).

Kim's E-type analysis and the ChR analysis are the two most influential accounts of HIRs in the literature, but they seem need revisions. First, it is widely held that the head in the HIR denotes a maximal set of individuals that satisfy the HIR clause description (Hoshi, 1995). For instance, for (1) to be felicitous, the situation must be the one where Kiki ate **all** of the apples on the table. But maximality effects are shown to be derived **pragmatically**. Thus, for (2) to be felicitous, a situation must be the one where each passenger puts no more than one ticket in the checker, even though he has multiple tickets, provided our world knowledge that the insertion of multiple tickles may cause malfunction of the checker (Kubota & Smith, 2007: 154).

(2) *Dono-zyookyaku*$_i$*-mo* [e$_i$ *saifu-ni*
every-passenger-too [wallet-in
kaisuuken-ga *haitteita* *no*]-*o*
coupon.ticket-NOM was.present NO]-ACC
toridashite *kaisatsu-ni* *ireta.*
pick.up ticket.checker-to put
'Every passenger picked up a coupon ticket that she/he had in (her/his) wallet and put it in the ticket checker.'

In Kim's account, maximality effects obtain due to the feature [+*definite*] of the head D, and in the ChR account, they emerge due to the feature

[MAX] of the head C. Thus, both accounts do not predict the context-dependency of maximality.

Second, HIRs are not sensitive to islands. For instance, Mihara (1994: 239) shows that the HIR (3) is not sensitive to the complex NP island.[1]

(3) [*Taro-ga* [*Hanako-ga subarashii ronbun-o*
[T-NOM [H-NOM excellent paper-ACC
kaita toiu uwasa]-*o kiiteita*
wrote TOIU rumour]-ACC has.heard
no]-*ga tsuini syuppansareta.*
NO]-NOM finally was.published
'Taro has heard a rumour that Hanako wrote an excellent paper, and the paper was finally published.'

Kim's account cannot model island-insensitivity of HIRs because it concerns only the eventuality denoted by the **highest** clause in the HIR clause (cf., Grosu (2010: 250)). In the ChR account, a null operator at Spec, ChRP undergoes cyclic A'-movement and this predicts island-sensitivity of HIRs. This prediction is said to be borne-out by considering data in Watanabe (2003), but without taking into account the examples such as (3).

Finally, it has been widely believed that the HIR clause cannot license negation (Hoshi, 1995; Grosu & Landman, 2012). The present paper, however, observes that negation is licensed if the existence of the individual denoted by the head is inferable. For instance, negation is licensed in the HIR (4) because it is inferable that there was a wallet somewhere other than a safe.

(4) *Dorobo-wa* [*saifu-ga kinko-ni*
thief-TOP [wallet-NOM safe-at
haittei-naka-tta no]-*o*
put.inside-NEG-PAST NO]-ACC
manmato nusumi-dashita.
successfully steal-took.away
'A wallet was not inside a safe (but outside the safe), and a thief successfully stole it.'

In the ChR account, they might argue that *saifu* moves over NegP at LF so that it out-scopes the negator. But this remedy is untenable since ChR cannot select NegP, anyway. This is because it is assumed that (i) VP denotes an open proposition with an event slot; (ii) ChR selects such an open proposition; but (iii) NegP closes the proposition over the event slot before it is selected by ChR (Grosu & Landman, 2012: 176). Kim's account, on the other hand, seems to correctly treat (4). In her analysis, the head denotes the maximal set of individuals that satisfy a salient property and a salient thematic role in the state denoted by the HIR clause. In (4), the property is identified with *saifu*' and the role is identified with Theme. So, the head *saifu* is correctly detected. As illustrated in (5), however, the negation data display long-distance dependency. Given that Kim's account concerns only the state denoted by the highest clause in the HIR (cf., discussion around (3)), it cannot detect the head *hoseki* in (5).

(5) *Dorobo-wa* [*aru-yumeijin-ga*
thief-TOP [certain-celebrity-NOM
[*ie-de-wa hoseki-o kinko-ni*
[house-at-TOP jewellery-ACC safe-at
irete-nai to] *TV-de itteita*
put.inside-NEG COMP] TV-at said
no]-*o manmato nusumi-dashita.*
NO]-ACC successfully steal-took.away
'A celebrity said in a TV programme that she did not put her jewellery in a safe, and the thief successfully stole it.'

These data undermine the recent works on the HIR. In this paper, I shall propose an alternative account within Dynamic Syntax.

3 Dynamic Syntax (DS)

Dynamic Syntax (DS) is a formalism that models 'knowledge of language,' construed as a set of procedures to build up an interpretation on the basis of word-by-word parsing in real time (Cann et al., 2005; Kempson et al., 2001). DS assumes semantic representation **without** a separate level of syntactic representation. So, a string is directly mapped onto a semantic structure as it is parsed left-to-right online.

3.1 A Sketch of the Formalism

DS models gradual updates of an interpretation as progressive growth of a semantic tree. The initial state is specified by the Axiom:

(6) Axiom
?t, ◊

The Axiom sets out a node decorated with ?t, a requirement that this node will be of type-t. A pointer ◊ indicates a node under development. A parser updates this initial tree state by executing general, lexical, and pragmatic actions. Every

[1] Kuroda (2005) suggests that the Complex NP Constraint may be at work. At the same time, however, he notes that the HIR involving the complex NP is not totally degraded.

time a node is created, it comes with a set of requirements, and every tree update is driven by some form of requirements. A DS tree is said to be well-formed iff no outstanding requirements remain. A string is said to be grammatical iff there is a tree update that leads to a well-formed tree. For instance, if a parser processes (7), it gradually updates the initial state (6) by running general, lexical, or pragmatic actions until the well-formed tree (8) emerges, where there are no outstanding requirements. (Throughout this paper, tense is set aside; see Cann (2011).)

(7) *Kiki-ga hashi-tta.*
K-NOM run-PST
'Kiki ran.'

(8) *hashi'*(*Kiki'*)(*SIT*) : t, ◇
SIT : e_S *hashi'*(*Kiki'*) : $e_S \to t$
Kiki' : e   *hashi'* : $e \to (e_S \to t)$

DS trees are binary-branching, an argument being on the left and a functor on the right. Each node is decorated with a pair α : β, where α is a semantic content and β is a set of labels that show various properties of the content such as logical type. In (8), *hashi* (= 'run') takes not only the subject term *Kiki'* but also the situation term *SIT*. DS assumes that all verbs select a situation term of type-e (cf., Davidson (1967)). The type of situation term is notated as e_S.

The backbone of DS trees is LOFT (Logic Of Finite Trees; Blackburn & Meyer-Viol (1994)). LOFT is a language to talk about node relations. Two operators are of particular relevance to this paper. $<\downarrow_0>$ refers to an argument daughter and $<\downarrow_1>$ refers to a functor daughter, together with their inverses: $<\uparrow_0>$ and $<\uparrow_1>$. These operators may be used in conjunction with labels. Thus, $<\downarrow_0>(e_S)$ states that the argument daughter is of type-e_S. This holds at the top node in the tree (8).

As stated above, a set of requirements drives the application of general, lexical, or pragmatic actions to update a tree state. An action package is in the following conditional format:

(9) IF (input condition)
THEN (action; if the condition is met)
ELSE (action; if it is not met)

The IF-block is a condition on the node marked by the pointer ◇. The THEN-block specifies an action to be run if the condition is met whereas the ELSE-block specifies an action to be run if the condition is not met. Let us consider an action package that is encoded in a verb. Since Japanese is pro-drop, it is assumed that all verbs project a propositional template. For instance, the verb *hashi* (= 'run') generates the tree (10).

(10) Parsing *hashi* (= 'run')
?t
U : e_S ?($e_S \to t$)
V : e   *hashi'* : $e \to (e_S \to t)$, ◇

Each argument node is annotated with a meta-variable, a place-holding device to be saturated with a term such as *Kiki'*. The action package to generate the tree (10) is formulated as follows:

(11) Entry of *hashi* (= 'run')
IF ?t
THEN make/go($<\downarrow_0>$); put(U : e_S); go($<\uparrow_0>$)
make/go($<\downarrow_1>$); put(?($e_S \to t$));
make/go($<\downarrow_0>$); put(V : e); go($<\uparrow_0>$)
make/go($<\downarrow_1>$); put(*hashi'* : $e_S \to (e \to t)$)
ELSE ABORT

The IF-block declares that a parser performs the actions in the THEN-block iff a current node is a type-t-requiring node. (If this is not met, ABORT applies; the tree update is quitted.) The THEN-block consists of primitive actions. make/go(α) is an action to create a node α and move a pointer ◇ to the node. Since $<\downarrow_0>$ refers to an argument daughter, make/go($<\downarrow_0>$) is an action to create an argument daughter and moves a pointer ◇ to the node. put(α) is an action to decorate a current node with α. So, put(?($e_S \to t$)) decorates a current node with ?($e_S \to t$). These atomic actions build the tree (10).

DS adopts the epsilon calculus for modelling quantification. The epsilon calculus, proposed by David Hilbert, is the logic of arbitrary names in natural deduction in Predicate Logic (Kempson et al., 2001). All quantified NPs are mapped onto an epsilon term, a type-e term defined as a triple: a binder, a variable, and a restrictor. For instance, *neko* (= 'a cat')[2] is mapped onto (ε, x, *neko'*(x)), where ε is an epsilon binder (analogous to ∃), x a variable, and *neko'*(x) a restrictor. A situation term is notated as *SIT* in (8) but it is precisely

[2] Japanese lacks determiners. Thus, the quantificational force of bare NPs is contextually determined.

expressed as an epsilon term such as (ε, s, *S*(s)). (For the situation predicate *S*, see Cann (2011).)

Once a proposition emerges, each epsilon term is evaluated for scope. This process, Quantifier-Evaluation (Q-Evaluation), explicates the scope dependencies; the restrictor of a term is enriched with the other predicates in the proposition. For instance, the proposition (12) contains two terms. Suppose that the situation term (ε, s, *S*(s)) outscopes the subject term (ε, x, *neko*'(x)).

(12) *hashi*'(ε, x, *neko*'(x))(ε, s, *S*(s))

A term having a narrow scope is Q-Evaluated first. So, (ε, x, *neko*'(x)) is evaluated first, to the effect that (12) is updated to (13). The evaluated epsilon term, abbreviated as a, reflects not only the original predicate *neko*' but also the predicate *hashi*' into the restrictor, with the connective & for existential quantification.

(13) *neko*'(a)&*hashi*'(a)(ε, s, *S*(s))
where a = (ε, x, *neko*'(x)&*hashi*'(x)(ε, s, *S*(s)))

The same procedure then applies to the situation term, and (13) is updated into (14).

(14) *S*(b)&[*neko*'(a_b)&*hashi*'(a_b)(b)]
where b = (ε, s, *S*(s)&[*neko*'(a_s)&*hashi*'(a_s)(s)])
a_b = (ε, x, *neko*'(x)&*hashi*'(x)(b))
a_s = (ε, x, *neko*'(x)&*hashi*'(x)(s))

The technical detail here is unimportant. What is essential is that (i) Q-Evaluation algorithmically applies to a term in the reverse-order of the scope relation, (ii) each evaluated term reflects the full content of the proposition into the restrictor, and (iii) the output such as (14) explicates the full scope dependency.

In closing this DS exegesis, the LINK device needs to be mentioned. So far, only individual trees have been considered, but two discrete trees may be built up in tandem and paired in virtue of a shared term. This formal tree pairing is called 'LINK.' The LOFT operator <L> refers to the LINKed node from the perspective of a current node. The inverse is defined as $\langle L^{-1}\rangle$. For details, see Sect. 4 and, especially, Sect. 5.1.

3.2 A Sample Tree Update

Progressive growth of a DS tree vis-à-vis left-to-right parsing is illustrated with the string (15). The initial state is the Axiom (16), and a parser incrementally updates this initial tree by running general, lexical, or pragmatic actions.

(15) *Neko-ga hashi-tta.*
cat-NOM run-PST
'A cat ran.'

(16) Axiom
?t, ◇

First, the actions encoded in *neko* and *ga* induce a subject node decorated with the content of *neko* and the logical type e.[3]

(17) Parsing *Neko-ga*

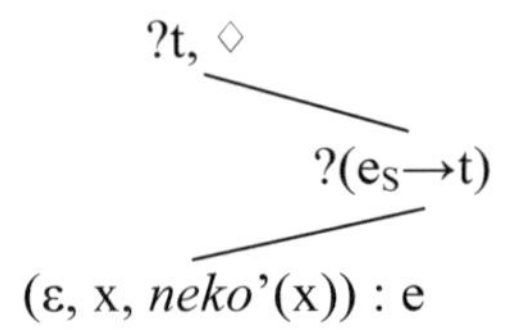

Next, *hashi* (= 'run') projects a propositional schema, where a situation and a subject node is decorated with a meta-variable (cf., (10)). Note that a subject node is already present in (17). This pre-existing node harmlessly collapses with the subject node created by *hashi*.

(18) Parsing *Neko-ga hashi-tta* (ignoring tense)

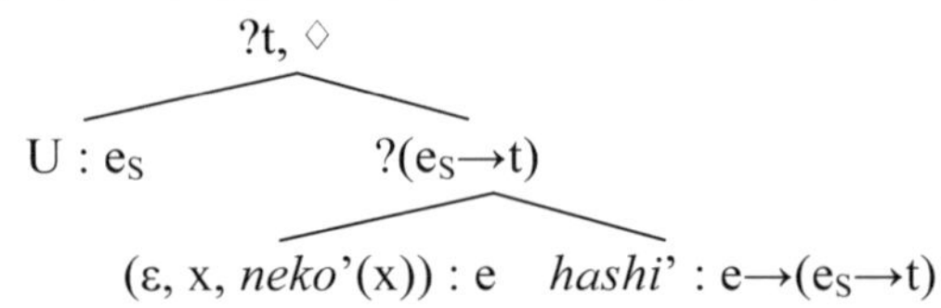

Two daughter nodes at the bottom are specified for content and type. Thus, functional application and type deduction compute the content and type of the mother node. This process, formulated as the general action Elimination, also applies to the intermediate argument-functor pair, yielding the decoration at the top node.

(19) Elimination (twice)

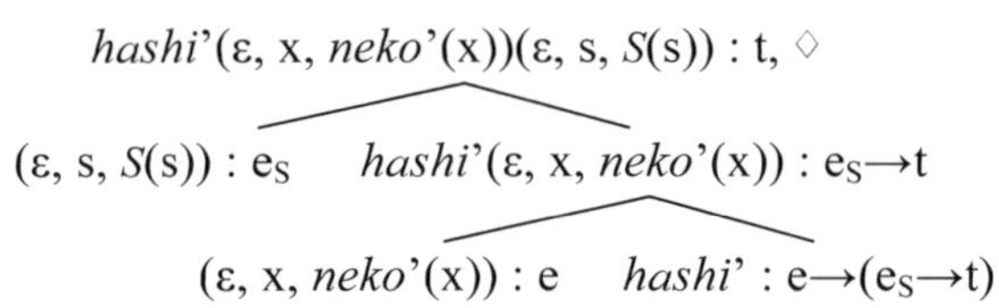

[3] Formally, the general action Local *Adjunction induces an unfixed node, to be decorated by *neko* and to be fixed as a subject node by the nominative case particle *ga*.

This is a well-formed final state in that it has no outstanding requirements. The proposition at the top node is Q-Evaluated; see (14) for the output.

4 A Previous DS Account

Building on Kurosawa (2003), Cann et al. (2005) and Kempson & Kurosawa (2009) propose that *no* in HIRs is a LINK-inducing nominaliser. For instance, consider (20). The parse of (20) up to *oite-atta* yields the tree (21). The proposition at the top node in (21) is Q-evaluated as in (22):

(20) [*Ringo-ga* *oite-atta* *no*]-*o*
[apple-NOM place-existed NO]-ACC
Kiki-ga *tabe-ta.*
K-NOM eat-PST
'There was an apple and Kiki ate it.'

(21) Parsing the string (20) up to *oite-atta*

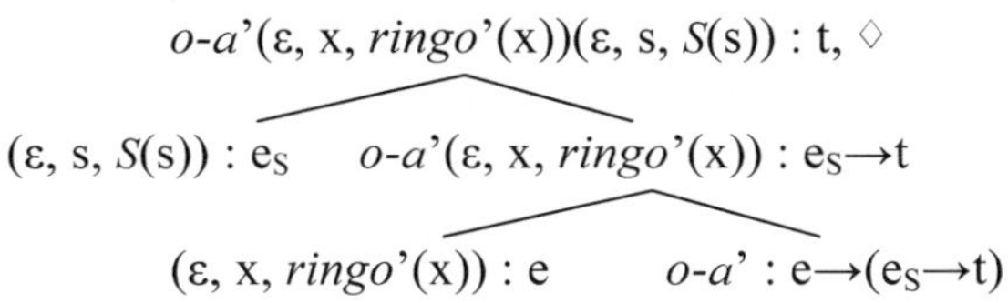

(22) Evaluating the proposition in (21)
$S(b)\&[ringo'(a_b)\&o\text{-}a'(a_b)(b)]$
where $b = (\varepsilon, s, S(s)\&[ringo'(a_s)\&o\text{-}a'(a_s)(s)])$
$a_b = (\varepsilon, x, ringo'(x)\&o\text{-}a'(x)(b))$
$a_s = (\varepsilon, x, ringo'(x)\&o\text{-}a'(x)(s))$

Now, *no* (i) initiates a LINK relation to a type-e-requiring node and (ii) decorates the node with a term in the evaluated proposition (in this case, a_b in (22)). In the tree display (23), a LINK relation is expressed by a curved arrow:

(23) Parsing the string (20) up to *no*

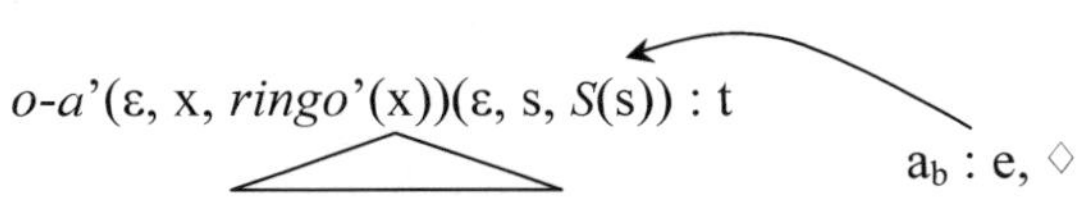

where a_b is as defined in (22).

The rest of the process is as usual. Especially, the node decorated with a_b is identified as an object node by the accusative case particle *o*, and *tabe-* projects a propositional schema, where the object node collapses with the pre-existing object node.

The heart of this analysis is that *no* is regarded as a **nominaliser**: it maps a proposition onto a term denoting an entity reflecting the proposition. Seraku (in prep.) demonstrates that this entry of *no* models FRs (Free Relatives), where *no* is seen to have the nominal status (Tonosaki, 1998).

Unlike FRs, however, HIRs possess a number of **non-nominal** characteristics. First, when the nominaliser *no* denotes a human, it has a (mostly, derogatory) connotation (cf., Kuroda (1992)). So, *no* in the FR (24) may have such connotation but *no* in the HIR (25) does not. This suggests that individuals are not denoted in HIRs.

(24) [*Naita no*]-*o* *Kiki-ga* *nagusameta.*
[cried NO]-ACC K-NOM consoled
'Kiki consoled a person who cried.'

(25) [*Tomodachi-ga naita no*]-*o*
[friend-NOM cried NO]-ACC
Kiki-ga nagusameta.
K-NOM consoled
'A friend cried and Kiki consoled him.'

Second, the relative clause is modifiable by demonstratives in FRs but not in HIRs (Tonosaki, 1998). Given that only individual-denoting items may be modified, it seems that an individual is denoted in the FR (26) but not in the HIR (27).

(26) *Sono* [*Kiki-ga* *katta* *no*]-*o*
that [K-NOM bought NO]-ACC
Jiji-ga *tabeta.*
J-NOM ate
'Jiji ate that thing which Kiki bought.'

(27) **Sono* [*Kiki-ga* *ringo-o* *katta*
that [K-NOM apple-ACC bought
no]-*o* *Jiji-ga* *tabeta.*
NO]-ACC J-NOM ate
'Kiki ate that apple and Jiji ate it.'

Third, FRs but not HIRs may offer an answer to *wh*-questions asking about an individual (cf., Matsuda (2002)). For instance, the *wh*-question *Who did Kiki console?* may be answered by the FR (28) but not by the HIR (29).

(28) [*Naita no*]-*o* *nagusameta.*
[cried NO]-ACC consoled
'Kiki consoled a person who cried.'

(29) #[*Tombo-ga* *naita no*]-*o* *nagusameta.*
[T-NOM cried NO]-ACC consoled
Int. 'Kiki consoled Tombo, who cried.'

Finally, a focus position in clefts is occupied by FRs, but not HIRs. Given that only a nominal item is focussed in Japanese clefts (Seraku, in prep.), it follows that FRs, but not HIRs, denote a nominal entity.

(30) [*Kiki-ga* *tabeta* *no*]-*wa* [*Osono-ga*
[K-NOM ate NO]-TOP [O-NOM
yaita *no*] *da.*
baked NO] COP
'It is [the thing that Osono baked] that Kiki ate.'

(31) *[*Kiki-ga* *tabeta* *no*]-*wa* [*Osono-ga*
[K-NOM ate NO]-TOP [O-NOM
pan-o *yaita* *no*] *da.*
bread-ACC baked NO] COP
'It is Osono's baked bread that Kiki ate.'

To sum up, it seems reasonable to assume that HIRs do not denote individuals; see also Seraku (in prep.) for further sets of data that point to the same conclusion. Thus, while the entry of *no* in Cann et al. (2005) deal with nominalisation data appropriately (Seraku, in prep.), it cannot predict the **non-nominal** status of HIRs.

Further, the entry of *no* in Cann et al. (2005) fails to account for why **only** HIRs (but not other types of relatives) are subject to the Relevancy Condition (Kuroda, 1992). The detail is still a controversy (Kim, 2007) but it requires that the event described by the HIR clause should be a relevant sub-event of the event described by the embedding clause. One construal of relevancy is 'temporal contiguity'; for instance, the HIR (25) cannot be interpreted as: 'A friend cried 1 year ago and Kiki consoled him today.' By contrast, this reading is possible in the FR (24). So, if *no* in Cann et al. (2005) applies to both HIRs and FRs, the Relevancy Condition asymmetry is left as a mystery.

5 A New DS Account

5.1 Proposal

I now propose an alternative DS account of HIRs. The last section has argued for the non-nominal status of HIRs. What remains unclear is why the HIR clause is case-marked, though case particles are usually attached to nominal items.

This apparent conflict is solved if HIRs are regarded as **rich context-setters**: the proposition of the HIR clause is mapped onto a propositional structure that is **partially articulated** when it is introduced. The embedding clause will be parsed with this partial tree as **context**. The partial tree contains two nodes. First, a situation node comes with the requirement that the situation term in this main tree will be in a 'Relevancy' relation to the situation node of the HIR clause. Second, a node for an individual term is present and it is decorated with the content of a head. This makes sure that the head, though internal to the relative clause, is selected by the embedding verb. The position of the node is guided by the case particle. For instance, in the sequence *no-ga*, where *ga* is a nominative-case particle, the node of the head is identified as a subject node. I shall propose that this tree update is lexically triggered by the sequence '*no* + case particle.'[4]

(32) Proposal (see (40) below for formal details)
The unit '*no* + case particle' maps the tree of the HIR clause onto a **partial** tree which involves (i) a situation node decorated with the 'Relevancy' requirement and (ii) a node for an internal head. The node position of the head is signalled by the case particle.

To illustrate (32), consider the HIR (33). The parse of (33) up to *oite-atta* yields the tree (34) (cf., (21)). The proposition at the top node is then Q-Evaluated as in (35) (cf., (22)).

(33) [*Ringo-ga* *oite-atta* *no*]-*o*
[apple-NOM place-existed NO]-ACC
Kiki-ga *tabe-ta.*
K-NOM eat-PST
'There was an apple and Kiki ate it.'

(34) Parsing the string (33) up to *oite-atta*

o-a'(ε, x, *ringo*'(x))(ε, s, *S*(s)) : t, ◇

(ε, s, *S*(s)) : e_S *o-a*'(ε, x, *ringo*'(x)) : $e_S \rightarrow t$

(ε, x, *ringo*'(x)) : e   *o-a*' : $e \rightarrow (e_S \rightarrow t)$

(35) Evaluating the proposition in (34)

S(b)&[*ringo*'(a_b)&*o-a*'(a_b)(b)]

where b = (ε, s, *S*(s)&[*ringo*'(a_s)&*o-a*'(a_s)(s)])
a_b = (ε, x, *ringo*'(x)&*o-a*'(x)(b))
a_s = (ε, x, *ringo*'(x)&*o-a*'(x)(s))

Now, *no-o* drives lexical actions. First, it LINKs the type-t node onto the type-t-requiring node.

---

[4] Seraku (in prep.) argues that the sequence '*no* + the topic particle *wa*' models clefts. Like HIRs, a propositional tree is mapped onto another propositional tree. In this view, clefts are regarded as **context-setters**: the pre-*no-wa* part sets a context for the focus item to be parsed. But unlike HIRs, the mapped tree in clefts **lacks** internal structure (i.e., it is not partially articulated when it is induced.) Hence, clefts as context-setters, and HIRs as rich context-setters.

(36) Parsing (33) up to *no-o*: the part (i)

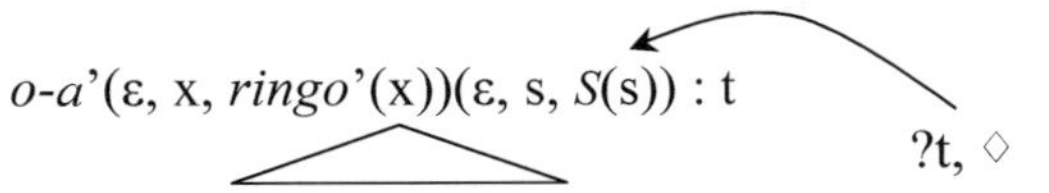

Second, a parser creates a situation node with the requirement that the term will contain as a sub-term a situation term in the previous proposition, in the present case, the situation term b in (35). This is expressed as $?\exists x.Fo(x)\&[b☆x]$. *Fo* is a formula predicate (Kempson et al., 2001) and ☆ stands for whatever relation holds between the events denoted by the HIR and the matrix clauses, as governed by the Relevancy Condition.

(37) Parsing (33) up to *no-o*: the part (ii)

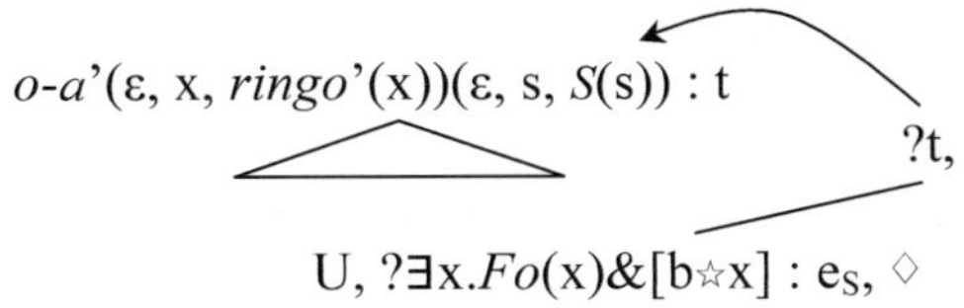

where b is as defined in (35)

Finally, a parser creates a node for a head. In the present case, this is decorated with a_b in (35).[5] The node position is guided by the case particle; in (33), the accusative case particle signals that the term a_b is at an **object** node.

(38) Parsing (33) up to *no-o*: the part (iii)

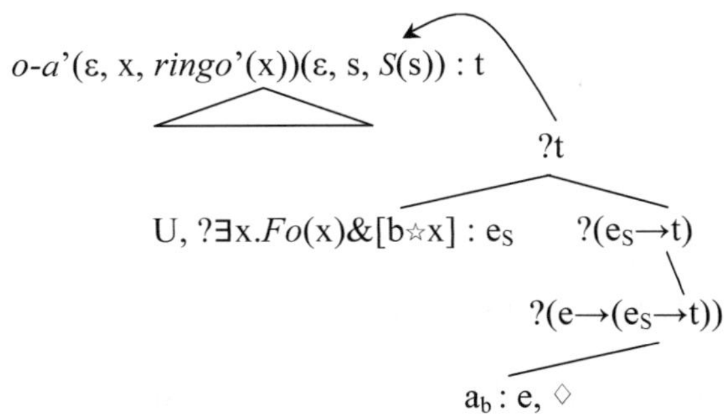

where a_b and b are as defined in (35)

This partial tree is a rich context against which the matrix clause is subsequently parsed. Within this partial tree, (i) *Kiki-ga* introduces a subject node; (ii) the matrix verb *tabe* (= 'eat') projects a propositional schema; (iii) each argument node collapses with the pre-existing nodes. The final tree state is given in (39).

(39) Parsing the whole string (33): final state

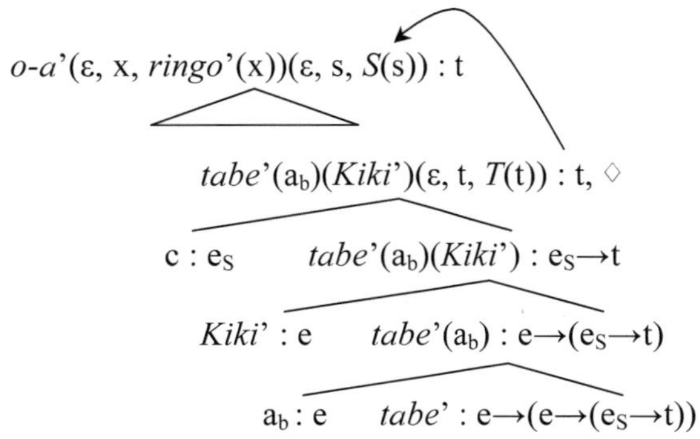

where $c = Fo(\varepsilon, t, T(t))\&[b☆(\varepsilon, t, T(t))]$
a_b and b are as defined in (35)

The entry of '*no* + case particle' is formally presented as follows:

(40) Entry of the unit '*no* + case particle'

```
IF      t
THEN IF       φ[(α : e_S), (β : e)]
     THEN  make/go(<L^-1>); put(?t);
           make/go(<↓0>);
           put(U, ?∃x.Fo(x)&[α☆x] : e_S);
           go(<↑0>); make/go(<μ>);
           put(β : e)
     ELSE  ABORT
ELSE ABORT
```

where $\mu \in \{\downarrow_1\downarrow_0, \downarrow_1\downarrow_1\downarrow_0, \downarrow_1\downarrow_1\downarrow_1\downarrow_0, \ldots\}$

φ stands for an evaluated proposition of the HIR clause. α is a situation term occurring in φ and β a non-situation term occurring in φ. μ stands for some LOFT-relation and its value is fixed by a case particle: the nominative case particle selects $\downarrow_1\downarrow_0$ (i.e., subject), the accusative case particle $\downarrow_1\downarrow_1\downarrow_0$ (i.e., object), and the dative case particle $\downarrow_1\downarrow_1\downarrow_1\downarrow_0$ (i.e., indirect object). I shall assume only these three case specifications here, but the set could be enriched (Seraku, in prep.).

One may object that (40) is a stipulation, but Seraku (in prep.) shows that (40) is defined based on the entries of the nominaliser *no* and the cleft marker *no-wa*; see Seraku (in prep.) Further, the fusion of *no* and a case particle is diachronically plausible; these fusions yielded many sentential connectives such as *no-ni* (= 'though'). Kuroda (2005: 230, fn 37) suggests that such connectives may have developed from the sequence '*no* + case particle' through the use of HIRs.

5.2 Non-nominal Nature of HIRs

The entry (40) models the non-nominal features of HIRs in Sect. 4. First, *no* in HIRs is no longer

[5] The selection of a term is pragmatically determined. This models the indeterminacy of HIR heads (Kuroda, 1992).

regarded as a nominaliser as conceived in FRs. Thus, the lack of connotation in the HIR (25), repeated here as (41), is anticipated.

(41) [*Tomodachi-ga naita no*]-*o*
[friend-NOM cried NO]-ACC
Kiki-ga nagusameta.
K-NOM consoled
'A friend cried and Kiki consoled him.'

Second, in our analysis, the tree of the HIR clause is mapped onto a **type-t**-requiring node. This is contrasted with FRs, where *no* maps the tree of the relative clause onto a **type-e**-requiring node. Provided that demonstratives only modify a type-e item, it is thus expected that they cannot modify HIRs. Consider (27), re-cited here as (42).

(42) **Sono* [*Kiki-ga ringo-o katta*
that [K-NOM apple-ACC bought
no]-*o Jiji-ga tabeta.*
NO]-ACC J-NOM ate
'Kiki ate that apple and Jiji ate it.'

Third, since the mapped tree is of **type-t**, it is also expected that HIRs cannot offer an answer to *wh*-questions asking about individuals. This is why the HIR (29), repeated here as (43), cannot answer to the question *Who did Kiki console?*

(43) ♯[*Tombo-ga naita no*]-*o nagusameta.*
[T-NOM cried NO]-ACC consoled
Int. 'Kiki consoled Tombo, who cried.'

For the same reason, the HIR (31), reproduced here as (44), cannot be at a type-e focus position.

(44) *[*Kiki-ga tabeta no*]-*wa* [*Osono-ga*
[K-NOM ate NO]-TOP [O-NOM
pan-o yaita no] *da.*
bread-ACC baked NO] COP
'It is Osono's baked bread that Kiki ate.'

In the literature, there is some indication that HIRs exhibit a nominal property (Hoshi, 1995; Kuroda, 2005). In the HIR (45), the *no*-part looks as though it stands as a nominal that licenses the numeral quantifier *san-mai.*[6]

(45) *Kiki-wa* [*pan-ga teiburu-ni*
K-TOP [bread-NOM table-on
oiteatta no]-*o san-mai tabeta.*
place.existed NO]-ACC 3-CL ate
'Kiki ate 3 slices of bread on a table.'

But (45) does not show the nominality of HIRs. In our analysis, the unit *no-o* introduces an object node and decorates it with the evaluated content of the head *pan.* It is this **content** that licenses the numeral quantifier *san-mai.* In fact, as shown in (46), *san-mai* may be licensed even if there is no overt host NP as long as there is a proper content that denotes a salient object, say, bread. (In DS terms, the object meta-variable posited by *tabe* (= 'eat') is pragmatically substituted with a content denoting a salient object such as bread.)

(46) *Kiki-wa san-mai tabeta.*
K-TOP 3-CL ate
'Kiki ate 3 slices of something (e.g., bread).'

5.3 Maximality, Islands, and Negation

Another benefit of the entry (40) is that the data in Sect. 2 also follow. First, (40) says nothing about maximality effects. For instance, the term of the internal head in (35), namely a_b, as re-cited here as (47), only involves the epsilon binder ε, which is analogous to the existential operator ∃.

(47) $a_b = (\varepsilon, x, ringo'(x) \& o\text{-}a'(x)(b))$
$b = (\varepsilon, s, S(s) \& [ringo'(a_s) \& o\text{-}a'(a_s)(s)])$
$a_s = (\varepsilon, x, ringo'(x) \& o\text{-}a'(x)(s))$

So, the term a_b itself does not encode maximality. This models the context-dependent nature of the maximality effect as illustrated in (2).

Second, in the entry (40), β is a term of the internal head. Importantly, (40) does not impose any structural restriction on where β is detected within the evaluated proposition. This captures island-insensitivity of HIRs (3).

Third, negation data are also handled. DS has not explored negation but it is reasonable to hold that the negator interacts with quantifiers to fix the scope. In (4), Q-Evaluation may give rise to a proposition where the term of *saifu* (= 'a wallet') out-scopes the negator. A parser makes a copy of this term and puts it at an object node built by the sequence *no-o*.

5.4 The Relevancy Condition

The Relevancy predicate ☆, though it does not spell out the Relevancy Condition, offers a basis for modelling that only HIRs are subject to the condition. A research avenue is to substantiate ☆

[6] One may claim that *san-mai* is licensed by the internal head *pan* (= 'bread') and it is then floated out of the HIR clause. But this analysis is not plausible because quantifier float is clause-bounded; see Hoshi (1995: 36-50).

by representing aspects and tense within situation terms (cf., (Cann, 2011)).

Still, the entry (40) at its present form makes a novel prediction: the condition holds between the HIR clause and its **immediate** embedding clause. Consider (48). The HIR clause has to be relevant to the intermediate clause *Kiki-ga tabeta* but not to the matrix clause *Jiji-ga itta*. Thus, (48) may have the reading: 'There was an apple and Kiki ate it. Then, 3 years later, Jiji said about it.' This restriction is predicted by the entry (40) since ☆ is put at a situation node in the structure of the **immediately** embedding clause.

(48) [[*Ringo-ga oite-atta no*]-*o*
[[apple-NOM place-existed NO]-ACC
Kiki-ga tabeta to] *Jiji-ga itta.*
T-NOM ate COMP] J-NOM said
'Jiji said that [there was an apple and Kiki ate it].'

Is this generalisation expressible in previous works? In Kim's E-type analysis, the HIR clause moves and adjoins to a higher AspP. So, it must be assumed that it does not move over the AspP for *Kiki-ga tabeta*. In the ChR account, the null OP at Spec of ChRP may undergo successive cyclic A'-movement. Thus, it must be assumed that the null OP does not move up to Spec of CP within the matrix clause. These assumptions may be justified in terms of computational economy, but no such justification is as yet provided.

6 Change Relatives (CRs)

It is argued that Cann et al.'s (2005) entry of *no* is not applicable to HIRs. Then, is this entry to be eliminated? The answer is negative. First, it treats *no*-nominalisation data (Seraku, in prep.). Second, as will be argued below, it also accounts for CRs (Change Relatives), a much less studied type of Japanese relatives.

CRs denote the 'state of change,' as illustrated in (49) (Tonosaki, 1998: 144).

(49) [*Otamajyakushi-ga kaeru-ni natta*
[tadpole-NOM frog-COP became
no]-*ga niwa-o haneteiru.*
NO]-NOM garden-in is.hopping
'A frog which is the result of changing from a tadpole is hopping in the garden.'

CRs are quite similar to HIRs at a surface level: the head is inside the relative clause without a gap and the relative clause ends with *no*. Yet, Tonosaki (1998) claims that CRs behave more like FRs than HIRs.[7] A convincing set of data concerns modifiability: like FRs and unlike HIRs, *sono* may be put in CRs as exemplified in (50).

(50) *Sono* [*otamajyakushi-ga kaeru-ni*
that [tadpole-NOM frog-COP
natta no]-*ga niwa-o haneteiru.*
became NO]-NOM garden-in is.hopping
'That frog which is the result of changing from a tadpole is hopping in the garden.'

I shall provide additional pieces of data. First, like FRs and unlike HIRs, CRs may be used to answer *wh*-questions asking about individuals. For instance, the *wh*-question *What is hopping in the garden?* may be properly answered by (51).

(51) [*Otamajyakushi-ga kaeru-ni natta*
[tadpole-NOM frog-COP became
no]-*ga haneteiru.*
NO]-NOM is.hopping
'A frog which is the result of changing from a tadpole is hopping in the garden.'

Second, like FRs but unlike HIRs, CRs may be at a focus position in clefts.

(52) [*Haneteiru no*]-*wa* [*otamajyakushi-ga*
[is.hopping NO]-TOP [tadpole-NOM
kaeru-ni natta no] *da.*
frog-COP became NO] COP
'It is [a frog which is the result of changing from a tadpole] that is hopping.'

Finally, like FRs but unlike HIRs, the Relevancy Condition is inert in CRs. For instance, (49) may be interpreted as: 'A tadpole became a frog 2 years ago and it is now hopping in the garden.'

These additional data corroborate Tonosaki's claim that CRs are more like FRs than HIRs. Given that the entry of *no* in Cann et al. (2005) models FRs (Seraku, in prep.), it is reasonable to assume that this entry of *no* applies to CRs (but not HIRs). More specifically, the parse of (49) up to *natta* yields a propositional content and the nominaliser *no* then picks out a term within the evaluated proposition and annotates a new type-e node with the term. This node is reflected into the propositional tree constructed by the matrix verb *haneteiru*. For details, see Seraku (in prep.).

[7] Contrary to our expectation, CRs do not have connotation when they denote humans (Tonosaki, 1998). In this respect, CRs behave more like HIRs. This is a residual problem.

7 Conclusion

This paper views Japanese HIRs as rich context-setters: the unit '*no* + case particle' encodes the procedures to map the tree of the HIR clause onto a partially-articulated tree. This partial tree is a 'rich' context against which the immediately embedding clause is processed. The partial tree contains two nodes:

- First, there is a situation node annotated with the relational predicate ☆. This provides a basis for modelling that only HIRs are subject to the Relevancy Condition.
- Second, there is an individual term decorated with the content of a head. This ensures that the head, though internal to the HIR clause, is licensed by the embedding verb.

This account predicts a range of HIR properties, including the data that would pose a problem for recent analyses of HIRs (e.g., maximality, island-insensitivity, negation, the locality restriction on the Relevancy Condition). It has also been shown that the nominaliser *no* (Cann et al., 2005) does not model HIRs but CRs. For additional sets of predictions, see Seraku (in prep.).

Acknowledgements

I am grateful to anonymous PACLIC reviewers for their helpful comments on the earlier version of the present paper. I would also like to thank Ruth Kempson and Jieun Kiaer for constructive exchange. All inadequacies are solely due to the author. This work is supported by the Sasakawa Fund Scholarship.

References

Blackburn, P. & Meyer-Viol, W. 1994. Linguistics, logic and finite trees. Bulletin of the IGPL 2: 3-31.

Cann, R. 2011. Towards an Account of the English Auxiliary System, In Kempson, R. et al. (Eds.) The Dynamics of Lexical Interfaces. CSLI, Stanford.

Cann, R., Kempson, R., and Marten, L. 2005. The Dynamics of Language. Elsevier, Oxford.

Davidson, D. 1967. The logical form of action sentences. In Rescher, N. (Ed.) The Logic of Decision and Actions. UPS, Pittsburgh.

Grosu, A. 2010. The status of the internally-headed relatives of Japanese/Korean within the typology of *definite* relatives. JEAL, 19: 231-274.

Grosu, A. & Landman, F. 2012. A quantificational disclosure approach to Japanese and Korean internally headed relatives. JEAL, 21: 159-196.

Hoshi, K. 1995. Structural and Interpretive Aspects of Head-Internal and Head-External Relative Clauses. Ph.D. dissertation, University of Rochester.

Kempson, R. & Kurosawa, A. 2009. At the syntax-pragmatics interface. In Hoshi, H. (Ed.) The Dynamics and Mechanism of Language. Kuroshio, Tokyo.

Kempson, R., Meyer-Viol, W., and Gabbay, D. 2001. Dynamic Syntax. Blackwell, Oxford.

Kim, M. J. 2007. Formal linking in internally headed relatives. NALS, 15: 279-315.

Kim, M. J. 2008a. Relevance of grammar and pragmatics to the Relevancy Condition. Language Research, 44: 95-120.

Kim, M. J. 2008b. Event Structure and Internally-headed Relative Clauses. VDN Verlag Dr. Mueller, Saarbrucken.

Kim, M. J. 2009. E-type anaphora and three types of *kes*-construction in Korean. NLLT, 27: 345-77.

Kitagawa, C. 2005. Typological variations of head-internal relatives in Japanese. Lingua, 115: 1243-76.

Kubota, Y. & Smith, E. A. 2007. The Japanese internally headed relative clause is not an E-type pronoun. In Miyamoto, Y. & Ochi, M. (Eds.) MITWPL 55. MIT Press, MA, Cambridge.

Kuroda, S.-Y. 1992. Japanese Syntax and Semantics. Kluwer, Dordrecht.

Kuroda, S.-Y. 2005. Nihongo-kara Mita Seisei Bunpo. (Generative Grammar from the Perspective of Japanese) Iwanami, Tokyo.

Kurosawa, A. 2003. On the Interaction of Syntax and Pragmatics. Ph.D. thesis, King's College London.

Matsuda, Y. 2002. Event sensitivity of head-internal relatives in Japanese. In Akatsuka, N. et al. (Eds.) Japanese/Korean Linguistics 10. CSLI, Stanford.

Mihara, K. 1994. Nihongo-no Togo Kozo. (Syntactic Structure of Japanese) Syohakusya, Tokyo.

Seraku, T. in prep. Clefts, Relatives, and Language Dynamics. D.Phil. thesis, University of Oxford.

Shimoyama, J. 1999. Internally headed relative clauses in Japanese and E-type anaphora. JEAL, 8: 147-82.

Shimoyama, J. 2001. *Wh*-Constructions in Japanese. Ph.D. dissertation, University of Massachusetts, Amherst.

Tonosaki, S. 1998. Change-relatives in Japanese. Journal of Japanese Linguistics, 16: 143-60.

Watanabe, A. 2003. *Wh* and operator constructions in Japanese. Lingua, 113: 519-58.

An Abstract Generation System for Social Scientific Papers

Michio Kaneko
Graduate School of Integrated Basic Sciences
Nihon University, Tokyo, JAPAN
m-kaneko@chs.nihon-u.ac.jp

Dongli Han
Department of Information Science,
College of Humanities and Sciences
Nihon University, Tokyo, JAPAN
han@chs.nihon-u.ac.jp

Abstract

Abstracts are quite useful when one is trying to understand the content of a paper, or conducting a survey with a large number of scientific documents. The situation is even clearer for the domain of social science, as most papers are very long and some of them don't even have any abstracts at all. In this work, we narrow our attention down to the social scientific papers and try to generate their abstracts automatically. Specifically, we put weight on three points: important keywords, readability as an abstract, and features of social scientific papers. Experimental results show the effectiveness of our method, whereas some problems remain and will need to be solved in the future.

1 Introduction

Abstracts are expected to help readers who are trying to understand the outline of a paper, or conducting a survey with a large number of scientific documents. The situation is even clearer for the domain of social science, as most papers in this area tend to be very long and some of them don't even have any abstracts at all.

There have been many methods proposed for Japanese summarization (e.g., Ochitani et al. 1997; Hatakeyama et al., 2002; Mikami et al., 1999; Ohtake et al., 1999; Hatayama et al., 2002; Tomita et al., 2009; Fukushima et al. 2011). However, most existing proposals are made towards general text summarization instead of abstract generation for scientific papers. Here, it is important to distinguish between a summary and an abstract. According to a Japanese dictionary, an abstract contains the most important stuffs or the important matter that has been stated in a document, and a summary is a short text transformed from a long text containing all the important points in the original text (Umesao et al., 1995).

With the difference between summaries and abstracts in mind, we attempt to propose a new method to generate abstracts for social scientific papers in this paper. Specifically, we put weight on three points: important keywords, readability as an abstract, and features of social scientific papers.

In this paper, we first describe our proposal in Section 2, 3, 4 and 5. Specifically, Section 2 gives a brief introduction on the necessary language resources for the development of the subsequent modules. Section 3, 4 and 5 describe the sentence processing, importance degree estimation, and abstract generation respectively. Finally, we discuss some experiments conducted to evaluate the effectiveness of our approach in Section 6.

2 Necessary Language Resources

In this work, in order to perform textual analysis and importance degree estimation for words or phrases, we create the following five lexicon-files beforehand.

<Adverb Lexicon>:
created from (Nitta, 2002) containing adverbs describing degrees (like *e p asis*).
<Sentence-End Expression Lexicon>:
extracted from (Morita and Matuki, 1989) containing all expressions functioning similarly to auxiliary verbs in Japanese.
<Conjunction Transformation Lexicon>:

containing the corresponding relations between conjunctive particles and conjunctions.

<Indispensable-case Lexicon>:
generated from EDR [1] containing all the necessary cases of predicates.

<Conjunction Lexicon>:
containing the conjunctions used to expand one affair to multiple affairs, and the copulative conjunctions used to connect two affairs in Japanese as shown in Figure 1 (Ichikawa, 1978).

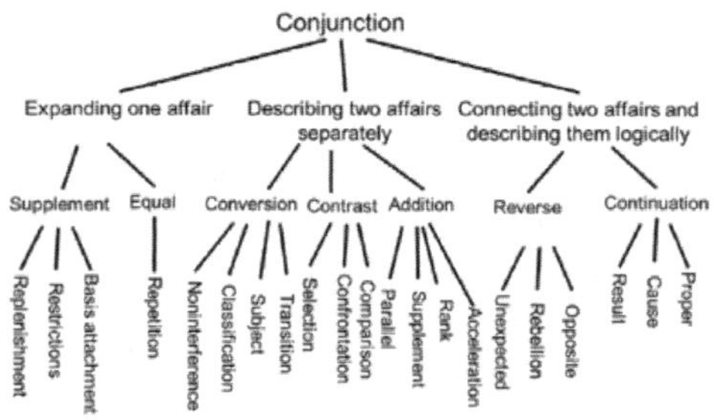

Figure 1. Conjunction classification

Moreover, we have created three lexicons specialized in social science. The first one is a called Keyword Dictionary containing the words extracted from two sociological dictionaries (Uchida et al., 2001; Imamura, 1988).

The second lexicon is the Noun-phrase Dictionary. Based on the idea that noun phrases play important roles in sentences (Minami, 1974), we extract five kinds of noun phrases from a social scientific literature database according to the following definitions

- Expressions ending with the continuous form of a nominalized verb
- Nominalized verb + "カタ", "ブリ" ("ップリ"), "ヨウ", "バ", "バショ", "トコロ" ("ドコロ"), "トキ" ("ドキ"), etc.
- Adjective + "サ"
- Noun + Noun.
- Adnominal form of an inflectable word + noun

The social scientific literature database we have created in advance is composed of 221 social scientific papers obtained from the Web containing 63,056 sentences.

The third lexicon, Mutual-information Table, is also generated from the scientific literature database. It contains mutual information between nouns appearing in each literature. Mutual information between nouns is calculated with Formula 1 (Church , 1990).

$$(\ , \ ) = \log \frac{(\ , \ )}{(\ ) (\ )} \qquad (1)$$

and in Formula 1 indicate the occurrence probability of noun A and noun B respectively, and indicates the co-occurrence probability of noun A and noun B in the same sentence of the database.

3 Sentence Processing

After conducting a morphological analysis on the input social scientific paper, we execute a series of processing on each sentence of the paper: keyword extraction, parenthesis processing, third-person sentence removing, sentence segmentation, and sentence-information assignment. Here, we describe them in each sub-section respectively.

3.1 Keyword Extraction

Keywords are extracted for subsequent importance degree estimation. Here, words and phrases are extracted from the paper as *e or s* if they also appear in the Keyword Dictionary. Similarly, the noun-phrases matching the Noun-phrase Dictionary are extracted as *e or s*. Another sort of keyword is called *e or s*, which stands for common noun or compound noun, and has been extracted during the morphological analysis using Mecab [2], a free Japanese morphological analyzer. Meanwhile, the occurrence frequency of each extracted keyword and the place it appears (i.e., the number of paragraph it appears in) are also recorded.

3.2 Parenthesis Processing

Generally, texts enclosed in round parentheses tend to act as supplement or modification to the texts prior to it. Therefore, round parentheses could be simply removed without influencing the basic meaning of the original texts in most cases. However, there is one exception. When the texts contained in the round parentheses are less than 15 characters, they will be extracted as another sort of keyword, *e or s*. Here, the number 15 indicates the maximum keyword-length in the Keyword Dictionary.

[1] http://www2.nict.go.jp/out-promotion/techtransfer/EDR/J_index.html

[2] http://mecab.sourceforge.net/

3.3 Third-person Sentence Removing

One of our goals in this work is to extract the text that expresses the author's opinions most directly and correctly. For this reason, we consider that sentences holding third-person subjects are inappropriate to appear in the final abstract. Sentences fulfilling the following conditions are recognized automatically as third-person subject sentences, and excluded from final sentence candidates for abstract generation.

- sentences containing either "は" or "が", and the previous morpheme being a proper personal name.
- sentences containing either "は" or "が", the previous morpheme being a suffix, and the morpheme prior to the suffix being a personal name.
- sentences containing either "は" or "が", and the previous morpheme being a third-person pronoun such as "彼" (he) or "彼女" (her).

3.4 Sentence Segmentation

Social scientific papers in Japanese often contain long sentences. In most cases, only one part of the sentence is important and expected to be included into the final abstract, whereas the rest part might be unnecessary and redundant. Along this idea, we segment long sentences in accordance with the rules in Table 1.

Original	After Segmentaiton
Verb(+Suffix) +"、"	verbal +"。"+ "そして" +"、"
Conjunctive particle + "、"	verbal +"。"+ Conjunction +"、"

Table 1. Rules for sentence segmentation

Here in Table 1, "、" and "。" indicate comma and period in Japanese, and "そして" means "then" in English.

Moreover, in the lower case of Table 1, i.e., when the original sentence is in a form of "conjunctive particle + comma", a transformation will be executed using the Conjunction Transformation Lexicon described in Section 2. Table 2 shows some examples in the Conjunction Transformation Lexicon.

Conjunctive particle	Conjunction
が	だが
て	そして
で	そして
ので	なので
ば	ならば
や	それに

Table 2. Example rules of the conjunction transformation lexicon

3.5 Sentence-information Assignment

The last process in this module is to assign some required information to sentences: cohesive relation and position information.

A cohesive relation indicates a strong relation lying between two sentences. Specifically, we use the following four patterns to match two sentences where cohesive relations exist in between.

- The sentence containing an interrogative and the subsequent sentence.
- The sentence containing a demonstrative and the preceding sentence.
- Two sentences connected by conjunctions that are used for connecting two affairs logically.
- Two sentences connected by conjunctions that are used to expand and describe the previous affair.

In the first pattern, if the sentence containing an interrogative appears at the end of the paper, no cohesive relation will be assigned. Similarly, in the second pattern, if the sentence containing a demonstrative is the first sentence, or the demonstrative is pointing to something within the current sentence, no cohesive relation will be assigned either. The third and the forth pattern are defined based on the conjunction classification tree in Figure 1.

Position information is associated with the position of the sentence. We have carried out an investigation on 40 social scientific papers with regard to the position where important sentences tend to appear. It turns out that the first paragraph and the last paragraph of each chapter, and the whole last chapter have an inclination to contain important sentences. The system records the number of chapter and paragraph as the position information of the current sentence which will be used for importance degree estimation afterward.

4 Importance degree Estimation

An abstract is expected to contain the most important part of the original paper. In this section, we describe our proposal to estimate the importance degree of each keyword in the first step and that of each sentence in the second step for a particular social scientific literature.

4.1 Importance degree Estimation for Keywords

Four kinds of keywords (i.e., *e or s*, *e or s*, *e or s*, and *e or s*) are considered as the candidates to be included in the final abstracts. We calculate the importance degree of each keyword (denoted as *s ore* hereafter) using its occurrence frequency and distribution as shown in Formula 2.

$$\_s\ ore = \quad \times (\frac{p}{p} + 1) + e\ n \qquad (2)$$

Here, indicates the occurrence frequency of the keyword under calculation, *p* and *p* indicate the number of the paragraph the keyword appears in and the total number of paragraphs contained in the whole paper. Meanwhile, *e n*, abbreviated from "extra information" acts to make difference between each kind of keywords.

We have defined two kinds of *e n* for different keywords. First, for *e or s*, *e or s*, and N *e or s*, the *e n* amounts to the occurrence frequency of the keyword within important positions, i.e., the first paragraph and the last paragraph of each chapter, and the whole last chapter. Then, for *e or s*, we consider the total number of characters is more informative than the position information, and therefore plug it into *e n* .

Obtained importance degrees of keywords are recorded and will be used for sentence-importance estimation in Section 4.2.

4.2 Importance degree Estimation for Sentences

This sub-section describes the method for calculating the importance degree of each sentence in a paper. This information will become the basis of abstract generation in Section 5.

The importance degree of a sentence (denoted as *s ore* hereafter) is computed following Formula 3.

$$\_s\ ore = \sum_{i=1}^{n} \{\ \_\ \ ore(\ e\ \ or\ _i)\} \times \alpha \qquad (3)$$

Basically, *s ore* can be acquired as the total value of all *s ores* otained in Section 4.1. Here we denote the total number of keywords in the sentence as *n*. In case shorter keywords are contained in longer keywords, we employ the *on est at prin ip e* and put a high priority on longer keywords.

α in formula 3 is a weighted value for the following four kinds of special expressions.

- emphasis expressions
  existing in the Adverb Lexicon
- sentence-end expressions
  existing in the Sentence-End Expression Lexicon
- theme expressions
  nouns prior to "は"
- cohesive relations

If any of the above expressions is found within the sentence under calculation, the total value of all *s ores* will be multiplied by α (> 1.0) for times. is the total count of the above expressions contained in the sentence.

5 Abstract Generation

We have obtained the importance degrees for all the sentences in Section 4. However, we still need to cut the unnecessary part in each sentence to keep each sentence in the final abstract appear plain and sophisticated. This function is called sentence simplification in this paper. Then we are going to conduct constituent-sentence acquisition, cohesive sentence insertion, and abstract assembling eventually to generate the final abstract. In this section, we describe each function in detail.

5.1 Sentence Simplification

We attempt to cut the unnecessary part and simplify a sentence using three kinds of information: indispensable cases, dependency relations between segments, and mutual information.

An indispensable case is a necessary case of a predicate, such as "ガ" or "ヲ" expressing *a ent* case and *o e t* case respectively. A sentence tends to appear unnatural if its main predicate lacks one or more indispensable cases. We use the Indispensable-case Lexicon described in Section 2 to put a mark on each segment containing an indispensable case.

Dependency relations are usually obtained with the help of a Japanese dependency analyzer. Here, we use Cabocha [3] to analyze the dependency relations between segments in a Japanese sentence. Figure 2 is the analyzing result of an example sentence, "政治階級という言葉は階級という言葉とともに死語と化したのである" (The word *estate o ern ent* turned into the dead language along with the word *estate*).

In Figure 2, there are six segments in the input sentence, and the main segment is "化したのである" (turned). We can also see that three segments are modifying directly, or depending on in other words, the main segment, while the rest two are not.

Our idea is to employ this difference to cut the unnecessary part, i.e., the segments which are not depending on the main segment. However, if an indispensable-case exists in a segment, even the segment is not depending on the main segment directly, it is still left in the sentence otherwise the sentence will appear odd.

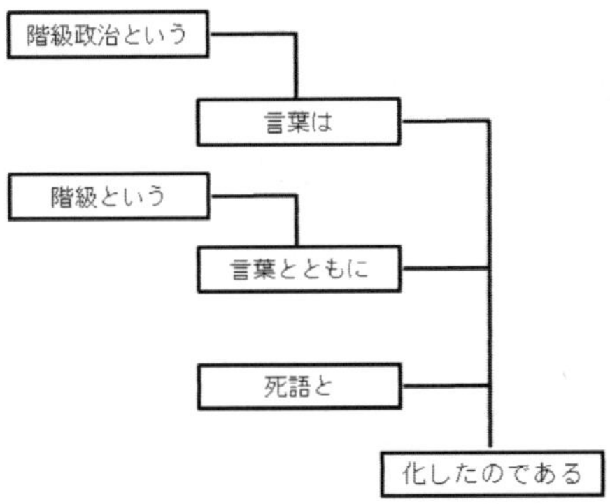

Figure 2. The analyzing result of an example sentence

Meanwhile, if we can find a sufficiently-high mutual information in the Mutual-information Table for a noun (denoted as $noun_a$) in any of the remaining segments, and another noun (denoted as $noun_b$) in the deleted segments, the segment containing $noun_b$ will be left undeleted in the sentence. Table 3 shows some examples from the Mutual-information Table.

All the simplified sentences inherit the importance degrees of the original sentences.

Noun	Noun	Mutual Information
サミット	ミーイズム	1.588042
サミット	世界	0.458759
サミット	論説	2.043721
サミット	各国	1.628684
サミット	自国	2.365649
サミット	利益	0.780687
サミット	形骸	3.365649
サミット	経済	1.687578

Table 3. Some examples from mutual information table

5.2 Constituent-sentence Acquisition

Constituent sentences are the sentences extracted from the original paper to compose the final abstract. Basically, the system just picks out the topmost *n%* simplified sentences based on their importance degrees. Here, *n* stands for the target compression rate which is set by the user before generating the abstract. Three ways have been proposed to determine the total number of constituent sentences or characters. We denote them as , , and as shown below.

- = *n%* × total number of sentences in the original paper
- = *n%* × total number of characters in the original paper
- = + cohesive sentences

is the simplest way for determining necessary number of constituent sentences. Unlike with , uses the number of characters to calculate necessary constituent number. For example, if the original paper contains 1000 characters, and *n* has been set to 20, the system will extract simplified sentences in order of their importance degrees until the total number of extracted characters is equal to or larger than 200. The difference between and lies in the consideration of cohesive sentences. At the time the total number of extracted characters becomes larger than the calculated constituent number (200 in the above example), if the last-extracted sentence is the first sentence of a cohesive sentence pair, the system will extract the second sentence of the pair as well. Otherwise, the last-extracted sentence is removed from the constituent-

[3] http://code.google.com/p/cabocha/

sentence set. We attempt to make the final abstract appear as natural as possible in this way.

We will give a further discussion on the difference among , , and in Section 6.1.

5.3 Cohesive Sentence Insertion

As stated in Section 5.2, a cohesive sentence pair is composed of two sentences holding strong association in between.

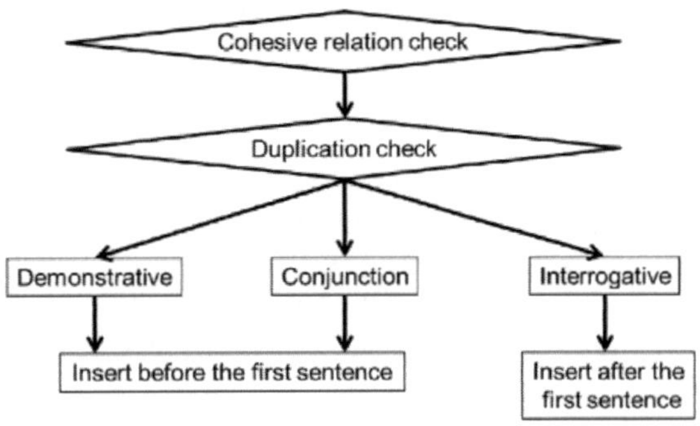

Figure 3. The flow of cohesive sentence insertion

If one and only one sentence has been selected as an abstract constituent, another sentence in the pair should also be extracted and attached to the first sentence in order to keep the final abstract coherent and natural. The appending position is determined according to the type of cohesive relation as shown in Figure 3.

5.4 Abstract Assembling

We have described the procedure to extract constituent sentences so far. The next step is to assemble all the constituent sentences in the order they have appeared in the original paper to compose the abstract. Finally, we conduct the following adjustment to format the abstract.

- connect two sentences coming from the same sentence in the original paper using the rules in Table 2 in the opposite direction.
- replace the theme in the subsequent sentence with a demonstrative if the preceding sentence has the same theme.
- start a new paragraph whenever the chapter changes according to the position information of each sentence.

6 Experiments and Evaluations

We have conducted several experiments to examine the effectiveness of our approach. Here in this section, we first introduce a set of experiments on different manners to determine the number of constituent sentences, then describe a subjective assessment on the system-generated abstract in comparison with another two abstracts. Finally, some discussions are made about the problems and their potential solutions.

6.1 Experiments on the Difference between NC_1, NC_2, and NC_3

In order to figure out the difference between three constituent-extraction manners, we calculate the standard deviations of the total character-number in the generated abstracts with , , and respectively.

We select six social scientific papers as the experimental objects. Each paper has been input into three prototypes following the definitions of , , and respectively. The average value of the ratios of the number of characters contained in each generated abstract divided by that of each original paper has been shown in Figure 4, 5 and 6.

A comparison with the target ratio from 5% through 30% has been made to figure out how close the actual number of characters is to the calculated target number.

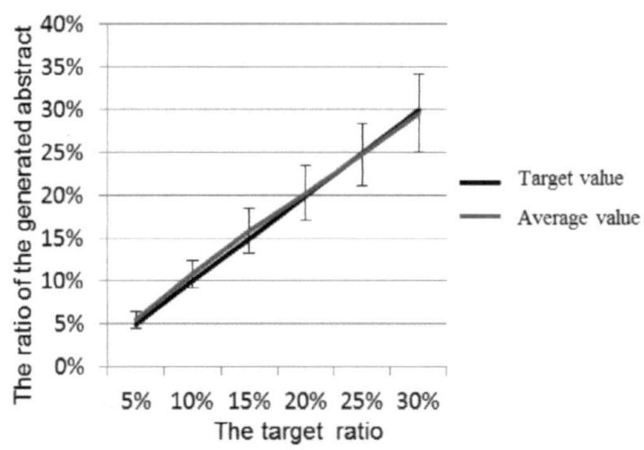

Figure 4. Experimenal results with

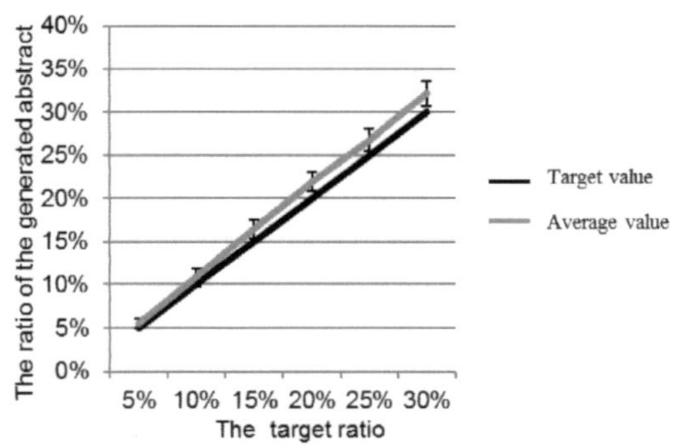

Figure 5. Experimenal results with

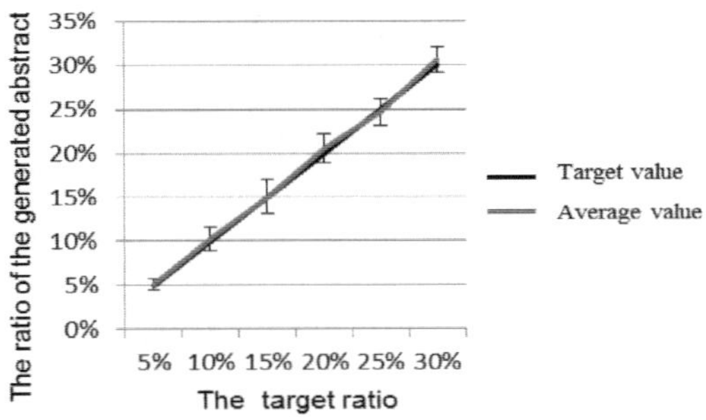

Figure 6. Experimenal results with

From the above figures, we can see that the average-value curve for is the most accurate one. The standard deviation for each constituent-extraction manner has also been calculated. They are 0.92%~4.60% for , 0.56%~1.40% for , and 0.66%~1.95% for . There is little difference between the deviations of and , both of which use a character-based calculation to extract constituent sentences. On the other hand, has exhibited relatively more volatility, which shows the instability nature of sentence-based calculation

As a result, we decide to use character-based calculation to estimate the necessary number of constituents for abstract generation in subsequent processing.

6.2 A Subjective Assessment

We conduct a subjective assessment using three kinds of abstracts.

- The abstract written by the authors (called as *a stra t* hereafter).
- The abstract created by the system. (called as *a stra t* hereafter)
- The abstract created by Microsoft Word 2003 (called as *W a stra t* hereafter)

In this experiment, the papers as specified in Table 4 were used.

	Number of paragraphs	*Number of sentences*	*Number of words*	*Publication type*
Paper1	51	448	12138	bulletin
Paper2	38	175	5461	journal article
Paper3	23	155	5514	bulletin

Table 4 . Paper information

Four graduate students and fourteen undergraduate students all majoring in natural language processing have supported us with the subjective assessment. They are divided into five groups each with three or four students. All the three kinds of abstracts are provided to each group without explicit information on which is , or *W a stra t*. After 30 minutes' personal reading and 20 minutes' group discussion, each group is asked to rank the three abstract on the following four questions

- Q. 1: Is the abstract grammatically natural?
- Q. 2: Is the Japanese easy to understand?
- Q. 3: Are sentences naturally connected with each other?
- Q. 4: Do you think the text is appropriate as an abstract?

The reason we adopt groups' opinions instead of individuals' ones lies in the awareness that examinees tend to be more responsible for the group they belong to, rather than the case when they behave as individuals. Table 5 shows the results of the assessment. Each figure in Table 5 indicates an average evaluation-value of the five groups for Q.1, Q.2, Q3 or Q4 towards one of the three abstracts.

$$ae = \frac{(\ \times 3 + \ \times 2 + z \times 1)}{5} \qquad (4)$$

An average evaluation value (*ae*) is calculated following Formula 4. Here, , , *z* indicates the number of groups that have assessed the abstract as the first place, second place, or third place respectively in regard to the corresponding question. A larger figure implies a better evaluation.

	A-abstract	*S-abstract*	*W-abstract*
Q. 1	2.8	1.2	1.4
Q. 2	2.6	1.4	1.6
Q. 3	2.6	1.8	1.6
Q. 4	2.4	2.2	1.2

Table 5. Results of the subjective assessment

As we have expected, the abstract written by the authors is the best for all the evaluation items. Also, our system seems to have shown the same or better performance than the summarization function of Microsoft Word 2003. Especially, our system achieves 2.2 for the question *o o t in t e te t is appropriate as an a stra t*, which is almost the same with that from *a stra t.*

However, there are still some problems remaining. In an interview with the examinees after the assessment, we have got some valuable comments such as "Pronouns are met too frequently" or "Too many long sentences exist in the abstract". In the following sub-section, we are going to make some discussions about these problems and try to conduct a validation.

6.3 Discussions

In regard to the issues observed by the examinees in the subjective assessment, we might have ways to adjust our approach. For example, we can skip the theme replacement function in abstract assembling described in Section 5.4, so that the total number of pronouns will decrease. On the other hand, to get a clearer look at the adequate length of a sentence in the abstract, we have conducted an investigation.

We have randomly selected 20 social scientific papers each with an abstract written by its original authors. Another abstract is produced by the system for each paper with the same number of sentences in the original abstract. The investigation is carried out by measuring the length (i.e., the total number of characters) of sentences in the original abstract, and that of the abstract generated by the system. Figure 7 and Figure 8 show their distributions.

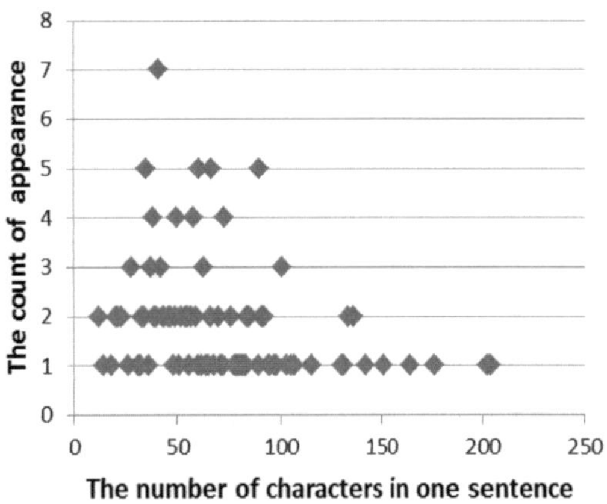

Figure 7. Distribution of the number of characters in original abstracts

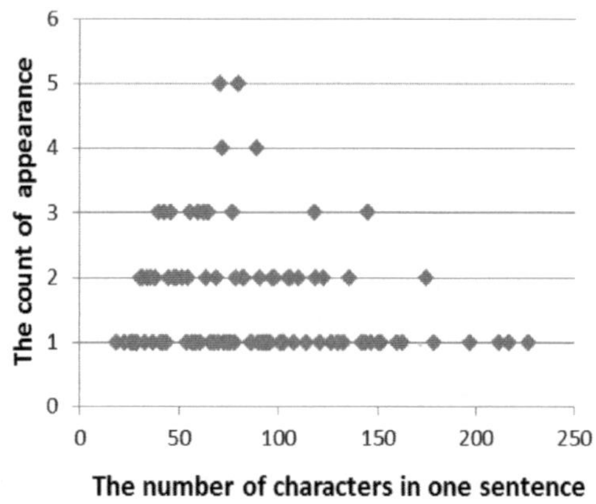

Figure 8. Distribution of the number of characters in abstracts generated by the system

The average numbers of characters in the original abstracts and the system-generated abstracts are 38.5 and 53.3 respctively. Moreover, The median value for the original abstracts is 64.5, whereas the median value for the abstracts generated by the system is 79.0. This might have been the reason of the unsatisfied results in Section 6.2 for Q.1 and Q.2. We could figure out some strategies to cope with this issue. For example, we can leave the cohesive relation out of our consideration when extracting constituent sentences, or just impose a restriction on the number of characters or segments when simplifying a sentence for the abstract.

7 Conclusion

In this paper, we propose a method to generate abstracts for social scientific papers. We put weight on three points: important keywords, readability as an abstract, and features of social scientific papers. Three main modules have been developed in our system to generate the abstract: sentence processing, importance degree estimation, and abstract generation.

Experimental results have shown the effectiveness of our proposal in comparison with another existing summarization tool, especially when we use character-based calculation to estimate the necessary number of constituents for abstract generation.

However, there is still room to improve. Results of an investigation on sentence length exhibit the future possibility to enhance our method and improve the quality of the abstract.

References

Church K. Ward and Hanks Patrick. 1990. Word Association Norms, Mutual Information, And Lexicography. Computational Linguistics, 16(1):22-29.

Fukushima Takahiro, Ehara Terumasa, and Shirai Katsuhiko. 2011. Partitioning long sentences for text summarization. Journal of Natural Language Processing, 6(6):131-147. (in Japaense).

Hatayama Mamiko, Matsuo Yoshihiro, and Shirai Satoshi. 2002. Summarizing Newspaper Articles Using Extracted Informative and Functional Words.Journal of Natural Language Processing, 9(4):55-73. (in Japaense).

Ichikawa Takasi. 1978. Kokugo Kyouiku No Tame No Bunsyouron Gaisetu. Kyouiku-shuppan. (in Japaense).

Imamura Hitoshi. 1988. Gendai Sisou Wo Yomu Ziten. Kodansha Ltd.(in Japaense).

Mikami Makoto, Masuyama Shigeru, and Nakagawa Seiichi. 1999. A Summarization Method by Reducing Redundancy of Each Sentence for Making Captions of Newscasting. Journal of Natural Language Processing, 6(6):65-81. (in Japaense).

Minami Hujio. 1974. Gendai Nihongo No Kouzou. Taishukan Publishing Co., Ltd.(in Japaense).

Morita Yosiyuki and Matsuki Masae. 1989. Nihongo Hyougen Bunkei Yourei Tyuusin Hukugouzi No Imi To Youhou. ALC.(in Japaense).

Nitta Yosio. 2002. Fukushiteki Hyowugen No Shosou. Kurosio Syuppan. (in Japaense).

Ochitani Ryo, Nakao Yoshio, and Nishino Fumihito. 1997. Goal-Directed Approach for Text Summarization. In Proc. of the ACL Workshop on Intelligent Scalable Text Summarization, 47-50.

Ohtake Kiyonori, Funasaka Takahiro, Masuyama Shigeru, and Yamamoto Kazuhide. 1999. Multiple Articles Summarization by Deleting Overlapped and Verbose Parts.Journal of Natural Language Processing, 6(6):45-64. (in Japaense).

Tomita Kohei, Takamura Hiroya, and Okumura Manabu. 2009. A New Approach of Extractive Summarization Combining Sentence Selection and Compression. IPSJ SIG Notes(NL).2009(2):13-20. (in Japaense).

Uchida Mituru, Imamura Hiroshi, Tanaka Aiji, Tanifuji Etsushi, and Yoshino Takashi. 2001. Dictionary of Contemporay Japanese Government and Politics. Brensyuppan(in Japaense).

Umesao Tadao, Kindaichi Haruhiko, Sakakura Atuyosi, and Hinohara Sigeaki. 1995. Nihongo Daiziten Kodansha kara ban dai2han. Kodansha Ltd. (in Japaense).

*** Formatting Issue - Best Available Paper/Graphic ***

Automatic Utterance Generation in Consideration of Nominatives and Emoticon Annotation

Yusuke Nishio
Graduate School of Integrated Basic Sciences
Nihon University, Tokyo, JAPAN

Mirai Miura
Graduate School of Information Science
Nara Institute of Science and Technology
Nara, JAPAN

Dongli Han
Department of Information Science
College of Humanities and Sciences
Nihon University, Tokyo, JAPAN
han@chs.nihon-u.ac.jp

Abstract

The demand is increasing recently for non-task-oriented conversation system in various scenes. Previous studies provide various strategies to enrich the methods for generating utterances, thus making the conversation systems or agents appear more interesting. However, most previous works tend to rely on templates and therefore are not able to perform flexible conversation-utterance generation. We propose here in this paper a thorough modification to a previous work to address this problem. Specifically, we introduce an automatic utterance generation in consideration of the embedded structure of sentences based on the principle of nominative maintenance. Moreover, emotion presumption has been implemented to add entertaining elements into the conversation with a user. The experimental results show that our approach proposed in this study has helped improve the performance of a conversation system.

1 Introduction

Non-task-oriented conversation systems have been developed during the past decade. They pay more attention to continuing the conversation by any means rather than the rigorousness of the utterance's content in comparison with task-oriented ones. However, the insufficiency in methods for generating utterances still remains as a critical issue unsolved.

For example, Higuchi et al. concentrate on modalities appearing in human's utterances, and try to incorporate them into the process of utterance generation (Higuchi et al., 2008). Song et al. (Song et al., 2009) and Han et al. (Han et al., 2010) present a strategy to provide new topics for users in a free conversation system at the point the system "considers" that the user has lost interest in the current topic. As just described, most previous studies provide various strategies to enrich the methods for generating utterances, so that the user might feel interested in the system and intend to continue the conversation. However, none of them could escape from the fact that they all generate utterances depending mainly on some particular kinds of templates or augmented templates.

As a case study to cope with this problem, Han et al. develop a free conversation system employing Markov sequences as shown in Figure 1 (Han et al., 2011; Nishio and Han, 2012). They use the topic-word pair extracted beforehand to search the Twitter for snippets that contain a noun in the beginning and a verb or adjective in the end, and then generate an utterance employing a Two-starting-word style Markov connection.

Although this approach has been proven quite effective in promoting the human-like qualities of utterances, a significant problem has been observed simultaneously: Utterance Focus usually spreads around too widely. This seems to come from the nature of the two-starting-word method which tends to generate comparatively long computer-utterances.

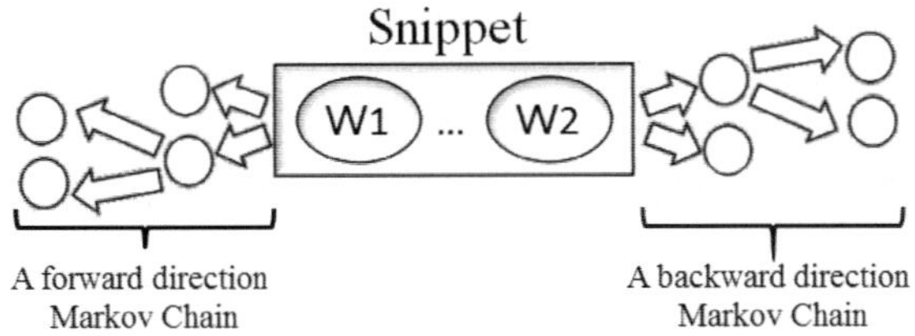

Figure 1: Processing schema of multiple-word Markov connection

Here we propose a strategy to cope with this issue. Specifically, we incorporate some restrictive rules to improve this situation by limiting the total number of words or characters contained in the generated utterance. Moreover, to add more entertaining elements into the system, we implement an Emoticon Annotating function to assign an emoticon to the utterances.

In this paper, we first describe the theoretical basis and specific steps of the utterance generation process in Section 2 and 3. Then we propose a method to presume possible emotions for an input text in Section 4. Section 5 elaborates the function we have implemented to annotate an emoticon to a computer-generated utterance based on the results of emotion presumption. Finally, we give some experimental results for verifying the effectiveness of our approach in Section 6.

2 Theoretical Basis

As we have mentioned in Section 1, utterance generation in the previous work is conducted based on Markov chains. The snippet is extracted randomly instead of using any restriction rule. As a result, long utterances are easily generated whose focuses tend to spread around too widely. To address this issue, we have to figure out some strategies to limit the total number of words or characters contained in the generated utterance. In this section, we introduce two concepts: Embedded Structure and the principle of nominative maintenance.

2.1 Embedded Structure

Various reasons are conceivable to cause long utterances. One of them is the situation that two or more subordinate clauses or sentences are embedded into one snippet. Such Grammatical structure is called *e e e str t re* (Shibatani, 1978). In an *e e e str t re*, there usually exists a special sign. It is called *o p e ent senten e in i ator* and includes four kinds of linguistic expressions: "～こと[~koto]", "～の[~no]", "～と[~to]", and "～ように[~youni]". A *o p e ent senten e in i ator* indicates the end of an independent purport, which will not exert influence on the whole sentence.

A snippet which contains a *o p e ent senten e in i ator* is considered unsuitable for generating brief utterances. In other words, when we try to put a restriction on the length of a snippet, we can remove the part containing a *o p e ent senten e in i ator* from the snippet.

2.2 Nominative Maintenance

It is said that a nominative noun, or a nominative noun clause is indispensable for generating a logically and grammatically correct Japanese sentence (Shibatani, 1978). Here are two examples.

赤ちゃんはもう歩けるよ。
(The baby can already walk.)

赤ちゃんにもう歩けるよ。
(can already walk to a baby.)

The first example contains a nominative noun clause, while the second example doesn't contain a nominative noun clause, and hence is not grammatically correct.

To put it another way, if a snippet contains two or more nominative noun clauses, we will have reason to believe that the snippet might have multiple subordinate sentences. In order to obtain a shorter utterance, it is desirable to select the snippet which consists of a single sentence, or possesses a simple structure. In this way, nominative noun clause can be used as another indicator for avoiding the extraction of long snippets.

3 Utterance Generation

With the concepts stated in Section 2 in mind, we propose a method to generate utterance based on the two-starting-word Markov-chain model devised in the previous work (Nishio and Han, 2012). Section 3.1 describes the rough flow and Section 3.2 presents the specific formula to estimate the priority of each snippet candidate.

3.1 Flow of the Utterance Generation

As described in Section 2.1, one of the reasons for the emergence of long utterances is the situation that two or more subordinate clauses or sentences are embedded into one snippet. Here arises the necessity to select a snippet fragment from the snippet-candidate set extracted from Twitter.

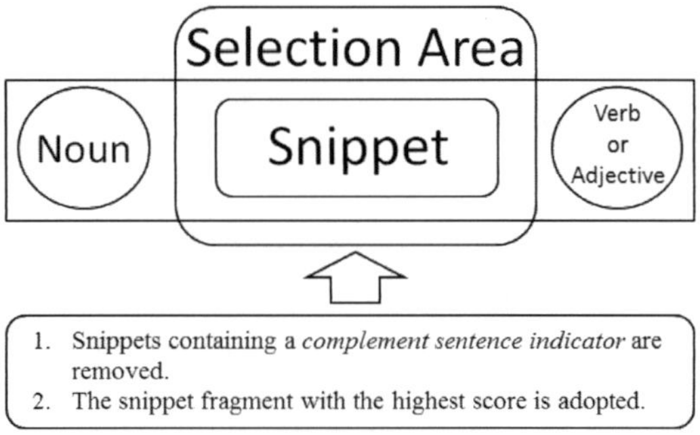

Figure 2: Processing schema of snippet selection

Figure 2 shows the overall view. Snippets containing a *o p e ent senten e in i ator* are removed from the snippet-candidate set first, then the snippet fragment with the highest priority is selected. The method to estimate the priority score for each snippet fragment will be explained in Section 3.2.

Another reason for the emergence of long utterances might have existed in the backward- or forward-direction Markov processing.

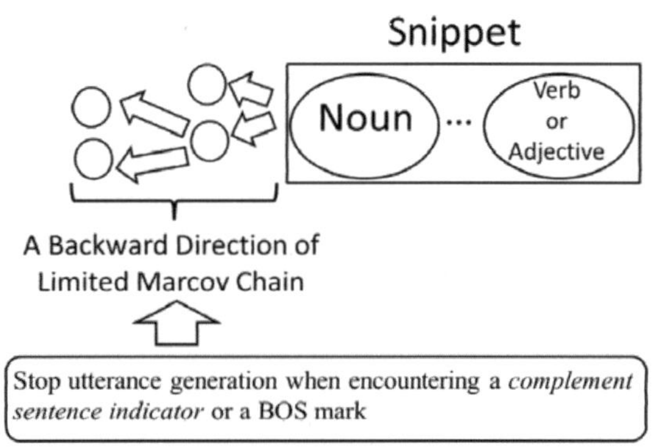

Figure 3: Processing schema of backward utterance generation

Backward-direction Markov processing starts with a noun, and extends to the left direction based on a bi-directional Markov dictionary as shown in Figure 3. The process will stop when encountering a *o p e ent senten e in i ator* or a BOS (Beginning of Sentence) mark.

Similarly, the forward-direction Markov processing starts with a verb or adjective, and extends to the right direction (as shown in Figure 4). The process will continue only when morphemes other than an independent word serve as a chain candidate. An independent word tends to take a pivotal role in a sentence, and is therefore likely to start a completely new statement which might lead to a long sentence finally. Moreover, if a punctuation or a EOS mark is encountered, the process will terminate at that time.

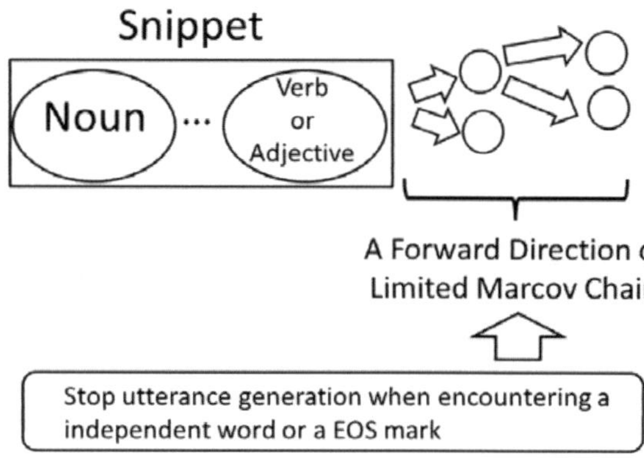

Figure 4: Processing schema of forward utterance generation

3.2 Priority Estimation of Snippet Fragment

With the above concepts in mind, we define a measure below to calculate the priority score for each snippet-fragment candidate.

$$Score_i = \begin{cases} 0 & if\ (FL_i = Subst_i + Decl_i) \\ \frac{1}{M_i} & if\ ((FL_i > Subst_i + Decl_i) \& (N_i \leqq 1)) \\ \frac{1}{N_i \cdot M_i} & if\ ((FL_i > Subst_i + Decl_i) \& (N_i > 1)) \end{cases}$$

Here, $Score_i$ stands for the score assigned to each snippet fragment. $_i$ indicates the total number of characters contained in the snippet fragment, and $_i$ indicates the number of case particles that are possible to appear with nominatives in the snippet fragment. $_i$ is the number of morphemes in the snippet fragment. st_i indicates the length of the noun at the beginning of the snippet fragment, and e_i indicates the length of the verb or adjective at the end of the snippet fragment.

$_i$ is compared with the sum of st_i and e_i to determine whether the snippet fragment is composed only of the noun and the declinable word. Only when additional characters exist, a score other than 0 is assigned to the snippet fragment. The score varies inversely with the number of morphemes in the snippet fragment, and even gets $_i$ times lower when more than 2 potential nominatives might exist.

4 Emotion Presumption

In order to add more entertaining elements into the system, we implement an Emoticon Annotating function to assign an emoticon to the computer-generated utterances. Our Function consists of two steps: emotion determination and emoticon annotation. In this section, we elaborate the process to determine an emotion for a generated sentence based on machine learning techniques.

4.1 Extraction of Emotion Trigger

Our basic idea is to infer the corresponding emotion according to a particular textual clue. For example, in a sentence "突然雨が降ってきたので、残念だ" (It was regrettable that it suddenly started to rain), "突然雨が降ってきた" acts as an emotion trigger, together with the conjunction "ので" implying a causal relationship between "突然雨が降ってきたので" and "残念だ" (regrettable).

If we can find some disciplinary rules or patterns from the usage of emotion triggers, we might be able to infer the emotion even for an incomplete sentence (i.e., a sentence that doesn't contain any explicit emotion expression such as *re retta e* or *app* .

Tokuhisa et al. have employed the combination of a conjunction and an emotion as the keyword to search the Web for emotion triggers, and performed a kNN-based similarity calculation between an input sentence and the emotion-trigger corpus to infer the emotion for the input sentence (Tokuhisa et al., 2008). In another study, Matsumoto et al. have created some sentence patterns from a small Japanese lexicon manually each with a pre-assigned emotion (Matsumoto et al., 2006). When the input sentence matches a sentence pattern, the emotion of the corresponding sentence pattern will be assigned to the input sentence.

Both works attempt to find patterns to infer emotions from input sentences. However, Tokuhisa et al. have used a very simple algorithm considering the method for pattern matching, whereas Matsumoto et al. have a major issue in the scale of data source (i.e., the small lexicon).

In this study, we combine the advantages of the above two works, and propose a new method to infer emotions based on Predicate-Argument Structure. Specifically, we collect an emotion trigger corpus from the Web in a similar way Tokuhisa et al. have done, while conduct the pattern matching using each predicate and its arguments contained in the emotion trigger corpus.

Given this perspective, the first task in our study is to extract the emotion triggers from the Web for a particular type of emotion. Here, we use Twitter as the Web data source, and search it taking the conjunction combined with the emotion expression as the clue word for emotion triggers as shown in Figure 5.

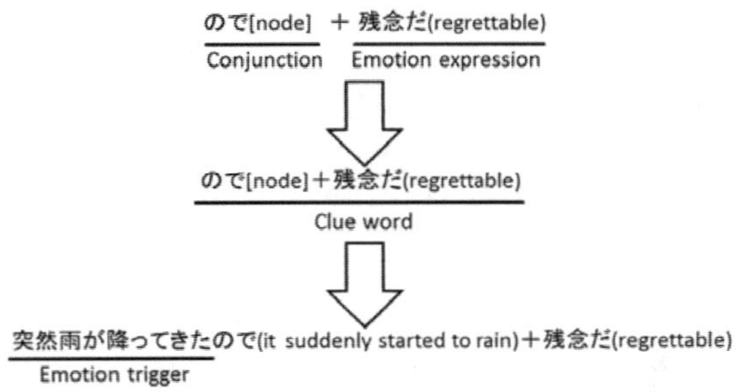

Figure 5: Flow of emotion trigger extraction

Based on the experience of Tokuhisa et al., we have used nine kinds of conjunctions including "ので" [node], "から" [kara], "ため" [tame], "のは" [nowa], "のが" [noga], "ことは" [kotowa], "ことが" [kotoga], "て" [te], and "で" [de]. Similarly, nine types of emotions and their concrete expressions are extracted from (Nakamura, 2003) and used here as emotion expressions. They include: "哀" (sorrow), "安" (ease), "厭" (hate), "喜" (hope), "驚" (surprise), "好" (like), "恥" (shame), "怒" (angry), and "怖" (fear) .

4.2 Extraction of Predicate Arguments

The emotion triggers obtained in Section 4.1 are then analyzed to extract predicate arguments using KNP [1], a free Japanese dependency analyzer. A predicate argument is the argument appearing together with a predicate.

For example, the analytical result from KNP for the sentence "私は食堂でカレーを食べた" (I ate curry at the dining hall) includes three arguments for the predicate "食べた" (ate): "私は" (I), "食堂で" (dining hall), and "カレーを" (curry). "〜は" (I), "〜で", and "〜を" are called Ga-case, De-case, and Wo-case respectively in Japanese. Our idea is to collect the pair of a

[1] http://nlp.ist.i.kyoto-u.ac.jp/index.php?KNP

predicate and one of its arguments, and find the relation between a predicate argument structure and an emotion statistically. Here, we take the three-element combination (predicate, case, noun) as the basic feature in our machine learning process. For example, for the above sentence, we are able to obtain three instances for the basic feature.

(eat, Ga-case, I)
(eat, De-case, dining hall)
(eat, Wo-case, curry)

However, since the combination of declinable words, cases, and nouns could be infinite, we might need a way to abstract the basic features to avoid the data-sparseness problem. Here we use a thesaurus called Nihongo Goi Taikei (NTT Communication Science Laboratories, 1997) to accomplish this task. This thesaurus classifies all the concepts in Japanese into superordinate ones and subordinate ones in different hierarchies. For example, "flower" and "tree" are abstracted into "plant", and "pace" and "footwork" are abstracted into "operation of hand and foot". We generate abstracted features from the set of basic features in this way, and create a training data set containing 779,638 instances. Later in Section 6, we will talk about the different effects in using these two sorts of features.

4.3 Polarity Annotation

Abstraction is considered as a means to address the sparseness problem when generating predicate arguments. However, in case two nouns with opposite polarities have the same superordinate concept, abstraction might become kind of side effect. For example, both "矜持" (pride) and "おごり" (arrogance) are abstracted into the same superordinate concept "自信・誇り・恥・反省" (faith・glory・shame・serious), which is not desirable for subsequent machine learning. To solve this issue and make the abstraction more accurate, we annotate a polarity property to the abstracted element as shown in Figure 6. Here, we have three kinds of polarities: P, N and E, indicating Positive, Negative, and Even respectively.

It is not only during the process of abstraction that polarity is important. Suppose we have two noun phrases: "きれいな人" (a pretty person) and "失礼な人" (a rude person). The head is common to both, while the meanings are completely different because of the modifiers with opposite polarity. In most cases, we consider that the polarity of the modifier is more important than the head noun itself. In this situation, we also need to assign a polarity to the head noun, otherwise we will obtain a lot of self-contradictory feature instances, and finally impair the performance of the machine-learning based classifier.

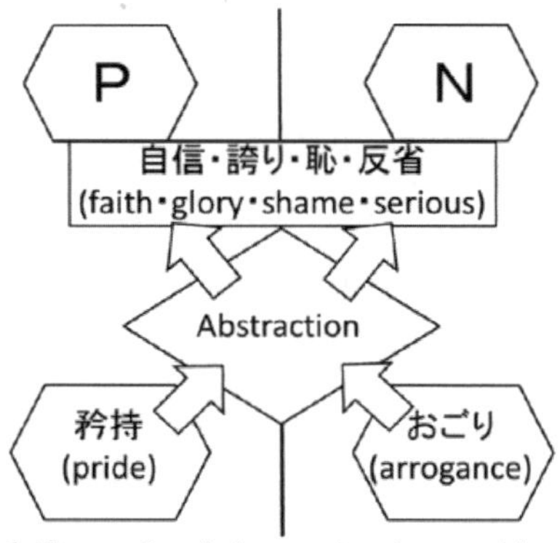

Figure 6: Example of abstraction in consideration of PN value

We annotate a polarity to the head noun according to the polarity of the modifier as shown in Table 1. Polarity information used in this study comes from two dictionaries (Kobayashi et al., 2004; Higashiyama et al., 2008; Takamura et al., 2005).

Modifier	Head noun
P	P
N	N
E	Polarity of the head noun itself

Table 1: Polarity annotation rules for modificands

4.4 Emotion Classification

Using the training data set we have created in Section 4.2 and 4.3, we employ the Naive Bayes algorithm as the basic machine learning method to generate an emotion classifier. Formula 1 shows the basic idea of Naive Bayes classifier, where e ,   , e , and e indicate the probability of a emotion, the probability of a emotion trigger, the probability of an emotion provided with a particular emotion trigger, and the probability of an emotion trigger provided with a particular emotion.

$$(e|\ ) = \frac{(\ |e) \times (e)}{(\ )} \quad (1)$$

e is calculated as the ratio of the total number of the instances holding a particular emotion divided by the total number of the whole corpus. e could be estimated by Formula 2.

$$
\begin{aligned}
&(\ | e) \\
&= ({}_1 \wedge \cdots \wedge \ \ | e) \qquad (2) \\
&\approx \prod_{i=1} ({}_i | e)
\end{aligned}
$$

${}_i e$ represents the probability of the ith feature provided with a particular emotion. We calculate e for each emotion classification and identify the classification with the largest probability as the emotion for the provided emotion trigger.

5 Emoticon Annotation

In this section, we describe the procedure to annotate an emoticon to a computer-generated utterance based on the result of emotion presumption.

An emoticon could be one or more characters or symbols, or a combination of both sometimes. Generally users want to express some sort of facial expression through emoticons. Here are some examples: "＼（ˆ ˆ）／", " <(` ^´)> ", "o(^◇^)o".

Some previous studies have been carried out for emoticon analysis. Urabe et al. quantify the emotions expressed by emoticons through a questionnaire (Urabe, 2013). Similarly, Emura et al. create an emoticon collection and classify the emoticons according to a questionnaire (Emura, 2012).

Both works aim at providing emoticon candidates for a text input by the user. Different from the previous works, our purpose is to annotate the emoticon to a computer-generated utterance based on the emotion presumption. We adopt an emoticon database built by Kawakami in our study (Kawakami, 2008). This database contains 31 kinds of basic emoticons belonging to five emotion categories each with its own relative strength.

However, as described in Section 4, our schema has nine kinds of emotion-classification, which is different from that of Kawakami. For this reason, we have adjusted our classification to conform with the previous work as shown in Figure 7.

Figure 7: Emotion-classification consolidation

6 Experiments and Evaluations

We have built two kinds of prototypes based on the algorithm devised in the previous work (Han et al., 2011 & Nishio et al., 2012) and our approach respectively. Then by running each prototype constantly, we have collected a lot of execution results and conversation log data. Several evaluations are conducted to examine the effectiveness of our methods based on these results and data.

6.1 Evaluation on Utterance Generation

A subjective assessment on utterance generation is carried out with 14 college students who haven't involved in this work so far. Three conversation fragments for both prototypes are randomly extracted from the conversation log data and given to all the examinees together with some simple instructions. Then the examinees are told to compare each pair of conversation log data without being informed which log data is coming from our system in two points: Association between Utterances, and Utterance Focus. The former evaluation item indicates the association between continuous utterances, i.e., how good has the conversation topic transited? The latter item, Utterance Focus, evaluates the quality of a generated utterance sentence.

For both evaluation items, 12 students have given their votes to our system indicating that most examinees consider our system as a better solution compared with the previous work. This reveals the effectiveness of our approach to cope with the issue of long utterances occurred in the previous work, while maintaining the Two-starting-word style Markov connection and the natural transition between utterances simultaneously.

6.2 Evaluation on Emotion Presumption

Following the steps described in Section 4.1, we have extracted 779,638 emotion triggers from Twitter. The whole dataset is divided into two parts, 90% as the training data and the remaining 10% as the test data. Then we conduct a series of experiments to examine the performance of the machine-learning based emotion classifier.

According to the description in Section 4.2 and 4.3, we have employed four kinds of feature in different experiments. Table 2 shows the name of each experiment and a brief explanation on its feature. The baseline indicates the method where 2-gram model are used instead of predicate-argument structure.

Experiment	Feature
baseline	2-gram model
no_abs	not abstracted feature
abs	abstracted feature
abs_pn	abstracted feature with PN value
abs_pn'	abstracted feature with PN value from modifier

Table 2: Differences among experiments

Figure 8 shows the emotion classifying accuracies of each method varying with the volume of training data. When we use only 2,000 emotion triggers as the training data, all the methods show the poorest performance. As we increase the volume of the training data, the accuracy of each method begins to increase except the 2-gram model. Before the data volume reaches 200,000, methods using abstracted features have kept outperforming those not abstracted. This is what we have expected. When we don't have enough training data to conduct machine learning, we will encounter the data-sparseness problem. Abstraction is expected to be an effective solution to this issue. What have been observed in Figure 8 proves the effectiveness of feature abstraction. Among the three methods involved feature abstraction, abs_pn and abs_pn' performs better than abs, proving the usefulness of Polarity. However, there is no obvious difference between abs_pn and abs_pn during the whole process. This is what we haven't expected and should be exhaustively investigated until the reason is clear.

On the other hand, little difference is observed when the data volume is more than 400,000, no matter the features are abstracted or not. This might indicate the turning point of data sparseness. In other words, 400,000 or more emotion triggers are likely to be sufficient for machine-learning based emotion classification.

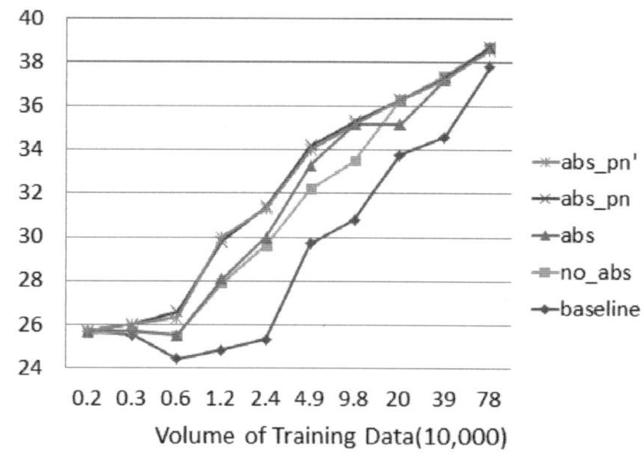

Figure 8: Change of accuracies with the volume of training data

Generally, although the classification performance is not as good as we have expected, our approach has got a better performance than the baseline method.

6.3 Evaluation on Emoticon Annotation

We randomly select five conversation fragments as the evaluation data. With the support of the examinees described in Section 6.1, we conduct another subjective assessment. The emoticon annotation function has been applied to the utterances in each fragment. Then two kinds of fragments are shown to the examinees: the original fragments and their emoticon-versions. Here are the questions in the questionnaire.

- Q.1
  Do you think conversation fragments annotated with emoticons are more interesting than those containing plain text only?
- Q.2
  For the utterances annotated with emoticons, do you think the atmosphere the emoticons are conveying conforms with the text? (1-yes, 2-intermediate, 3-no)

The questions inquire about the overall significance and the specific precision. Table 3 shows the average evaluation results calculated from all the examinees based on the five fragments.

Question	Average Result
Q.1	66%
Q.2	1.9

Table 3: Evaluation results on emoticon annotation

According to the evaluation results, 66% of the examinees agree that the emoticon annotation will enhance the entertaining aspect of conversation systems, and our approach seems effective to accomplish this task.

7 Conclusion

In this paper, we propose some significant improvement-strategy to a previously developed non-task-oriented conversation system.

Specifically, we introduce an automatic utterance generation in consideration of the *e e e str t re* of sentences and the principle of nominative maintenance. Meanwhile, emoticon annotation based on emotion presumption has been implemented to add entertaining elements into the conversation interface with a user. The experimental results show that our approach proposed in this study has helped improve the performance of a conversation system.

However, the result is not as good as we have expected. For example, We have focused on the snippets containing nominatives while neglected the grammatically incorrect sentences during the process of sentence generation. There might exist a need to utilize the incomplete sentences too in order to increase the diversity and number of candidate snippets. Another problem lies in the emoticon annotation function. It is impossible to determine the emotion for a generated sentence if it lacks case particles according to the current method. We are going to incorporate some new strategies into the system to address these issues.

References

Emura Yuka and Seki Youhei. 2012. Facemark Recommendation based on Emotion, Communication, and Motion Type Estimation in Text. Journal of Natural Language Processing Volume 19, Number 5, 401-418. (in Japanese)

Han Dongli, Kinoshita Yasuhiro, Fukuchi Ryu, and Tsurugi Kousaki. 2011. Utterance Generation Using Twitter Replying Sentences and Character Assignment. International Journal of Digital Content Technology and its Applications, Vol. 5, No. 10, 119-126.

Han Dongli, Song Xin, and Maeda Kazuki. 2010. Topic Presentation for a Free Conversation System Based on the Web Texts. International Journal of Digital Content Technology and its Applications, vol.4, no.3, 7-14.

Higashiyama Masahiko, Inui Kentaro, and Matsumoto Yuji. 2008. Jyutugo No Sentakushikousei Ni Chakumoku Shita Meishi Hyouka Kyokusei No Kakutoku. Proceedings of the 14th Annual Conference of the Natural language Processing, 2G3-01. (in Japanese)

Higuchi Shinsuke, Rzepka Rafal, and Araki Kenji. 2008. A Casual Conversation System Using Modality and Word Associations Retrieved from the Web. Proceedings of the 2008 Conference on Empirical Methods in Natural Language Processing, 382-390.

Kawakami Masahiro. 2008. The Database of 31 Japanese Emoticon with their Emotions and Emphases. Osaka Shoin Women's College human science research bulletin, 7, 767-782. (in Japanese)

Kobayashi Nozomi, Inui Kentaro, Matsumoto Yuji, Tateishi Kenji, and Fukushima Toshikazu. 2004. Collecting Evaluative Expressions for Opinion Extraction. The 1st International Joint Conference on Natural Language Processing, 584-589.

Matsumoto Kazuyuki, Ren Fuji, and Kuroiwa Shingo. 2006. Emotion Estimation System Based on Emotion Occurrence Sentence Pattern. Lecture Notes in Artificial Intelligence 7114 (Computational Intelligence), Springer, 902-911.

Nakamura Akira. 2003. Kanjyo Hyougen Jiten. Toukyoudou Shuppan, Japan. (in Japanese)

Nishio Yusuke and Han Dongli. 2012. Automatic Utterance Generation by Keeping Track of the Conversation's Focus within the Utterance Window. Lecture Notes in Artificial Intelligence 7614 (Advances in Natural Language Processing), Springer, 322-332.

NTT Communication Science Laboratories. 1997. Nihongo Goi Taikei. Iwanami Shoten, Japan. (in Japanese)

Shibatani Masayoshi. 1978. Nihongo No Bunseki Seisei Bunpou No Houhou. Taishukan Shoten, japan. (in Japanese)

Song Xin, Maeda Kazuki, Kunimasa Hiroyuki, Toyota Hiroyuki, and Han Dongli. 2009. Topic Control in A Free Conver-sation System. Proceedings of the 2009 IEEE International Conference on Natural Language Processing and Knowledge Engineering, 529-534.

Takamura Hiroya, Inui Takashi, and Okumura Manabu. 2005. Extracting Semantic Orientations of Words using Spin Model. Proceedings of the 43rd Annual Meeting of the ACL. 133–140.

Tokuhisa Ryoko, Inui Kentaro, and Matsumoto Yuji. 2008. Emotion Classification Using Massive Examples Extracted from the Web. Proceedings of the 22nd International Conference on Computational Linguistics (COLING-2008), 881-888.

***** Formatting Issue - Best Available Paper/Graphic *****

Urabe Yuki, Rzepka Rafal, and Araki Kenji. 2013. Kaomoji No Arawasu Kanjyou Wo Motiita Kaomoji Suisen Syetem No Koutiku. Proceedings of the 19th Annual Conference of the Natural 1language Processing. P3-20, 648-651. (in Japanese)

Gap in pagination due to unavailable paper.

Pages 75-84

Prosodic Convergence, Divergence, and Feedback: Coherence and Meaning In Conversation

Li-chiung Yang
Faculty of Humanities
Tunghai University, Taichung, Taiwan
yang_lc@thu.edu.tw,
lichiung.yang@gmail.com

Abstract

A key goal for participants in language communication is to bring about a mutually shared experience of ideas, event narratives, and emotional responses. This goal is achieved not only through the exchange of lexical meaning, but also through interactive signaling to coordinate information status. Our results show that prosodic synchrony (convergence) and dissynchrony (divergence) both occur in conversation, and that synchrony is achieved gradually as participants cooperate to build up a shared information and involvement state. Our analysis further indicates that feedback is a critical component of cooperative adaptation to new information, bringing about convergent speaker states.

1 Introduction

Human language provides an especially cogent platform for studying the phenomenon of imitative and convergent behaviors in human communication, as speech communication integrates a complex mix of cognitive, emotional, and interactive social processes that are expressed in a number of different forms: the language specific choice of lexical items to communicate meaning, visually-based information exchange of gestures and facial expressions, and the shaping of the oral and aural environment through variations in prosodic flow. Scientific studies have shown convergent behavior in body movements and gesturing in conversation (Condon and Sander, 1974; Nagaoka, et al., 2007, Campbell and Stefan, 2010), and in speech (Gratch, et al., 2007; Jonsdottir, et al., 2007, Buschmeier, et al. 2011, Lelong and Bailly, 2011; Heylen, et al., 2011; Ward, 2006), and focused on their role in creating harmony and rapport between conversational participants through the use of feedback markers, and through timing and frequency of non-verbal facial and movement gesturing (Lelong and Bailly, 2011; Heylen, et al., 2011).

Spontaneous conversation is multi-functional in both its goals and processes: the most evident goal of transmitting information simultaneously carries a social goal of building rapport and the sharing of attitudes and emotions towards the information transmitted. In the conversational process, speakers provide propositional and emotional and information through prosody, gesturing, and feedback, and engage in interactional probing to build a shared knowledge state and guide topic in a mutually desired direction. Prosody plays a key role in this process, as it provides a powerful and informative resource to communicate multiple levels of coherence and meaning by providing a direct and immediate link to fundamental expressive states.

2 Goal and perspective

The current study presents our results on prosodic convergence and divergence in spoken dialogues, drawing from extended conversational data in Mandarin Chinese. Because of the multi-dimensional goals at work in language, synchrony is approached as both building social interactional harmony, and also reflecting informational, organizational and expressive processes in conversations. The coherence achieved in a successful dialog is a shared coherence, one that is constructed through interactions of participants to discover and overcome respective inadequacies of information state. Thus, in addition to imitative speech patterns, prosodic convergence and divergence are considered as information-rich

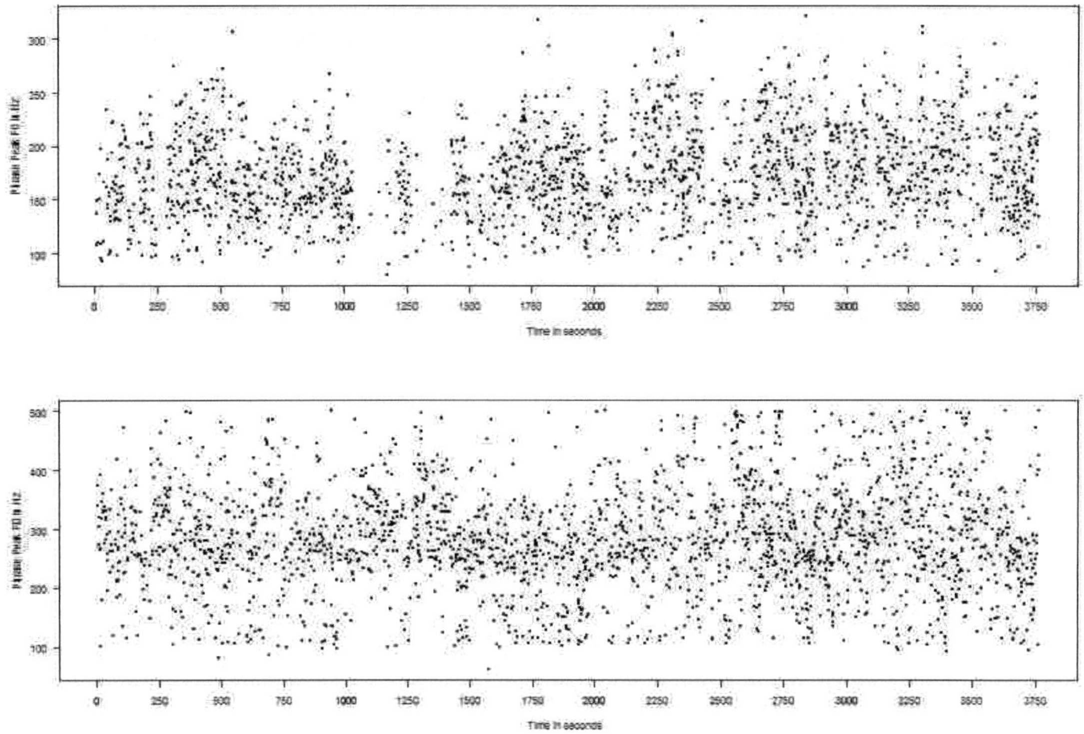

Figure 1: Times series of phrase peak f_0 in Hz for the male speaker (top), and female speaker (bottom) in a 62-minute long conversation. The x-axis is time in seconds and the y-axis is pitch in Hz.

patterns that speakers use to monitor comprehension, communicate disinterest or encouragement, and signal different levels of agreement and judgment on topic.

3 Data and methodology

For this study, our data corpora consist of two extended spontaneous conversations in Mandarin Chinese, each approximately one hour in length. The Mandarin data are a subset of Academia Sinica's Mandarin Conversational Dialogue Corpus (MCDC)[1] of natural conversations between newly-met participants (Tseng, 2004). The conversations were recorded in stereo in a quiet room and both conversations selected were mixed-gender pairs, with 1 male and 1 female participant. For these conversations, there were no preset topics and the speakers were free to talk about anything that arises naturally from the communication process (see Tseng, 2004 for a detailed account of the recording and processing procedures). For ease of processing, each conversation was subdivided into 20 subsections, with approximately 3 minutes per episode. For the current study, the conversational data were further segmented to the phrase level, i.e. phrase-size chunkets, based on a combination of lexical, syntactical, semantic as well as acoustical criteria, and target tokens of interest were annotated and extracted. Measurements of fundamental frequency (f_0) and amplitude were automatically computed, and normalized to each speaker's pitch mean and range. For each speaker and each phrase, low, average, and high values for both f_0 and amplitude were extracted as a means to show global pitch and amplitude movement variation. The acoustic measurements were then examined and correlated with incidence of feedback response and speaker interactions. Altogether there were 1,246 phrases for the female speaker and 2,273 phrases for the male speaker in mcdc01, and 2,256 for the female speaker and 2,014 for the male speaker in mcdc05, resulting in 3,519 phrases for mcdc01 and 4,280 for mcdc05 with a total of 7,799 phrases. Figure 1 shows the Times series of phrase peak f_0 in Hz for the both speakers.

[1] For detailed information about the Mandarin Conversational Dialogue Corpus (MCDC), please see http://mmc.sinica.edu.tw/mcdc_e.htm

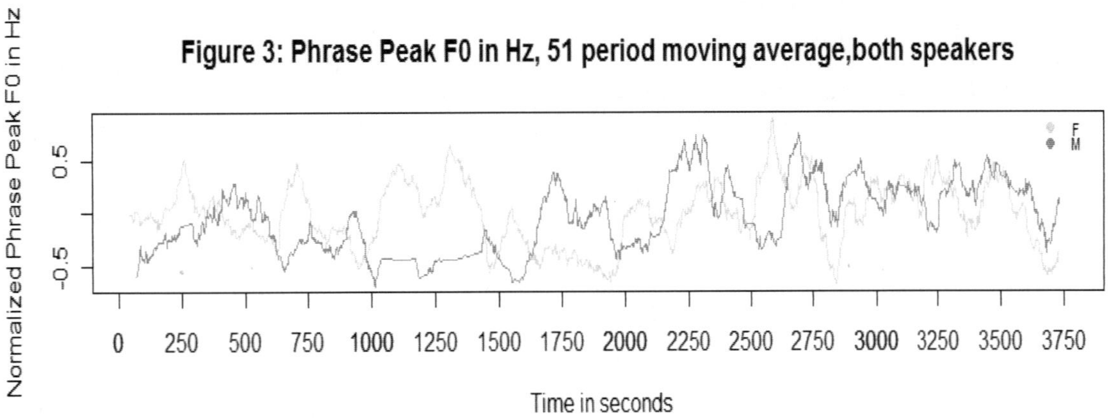

Figure 2: Normalized phrase peak with 51 period moving average for both speakers in MCDC conversation

4 Analysis and results

4.1 Conversational structure and prosodic convergence

By prosodic convergence (synchrony), we mean that speakers often use corresponding or matching movements in phrase pitch level to signal agreement on the current topic hierarchy. Our results show that both convergence and divergence in prosody occur at both local inter-phrase level pitch level changes, as well as over dialogue sections extending globally across topics and subtopics. Figure 2 compares the normalized global phrase movement for the two speakers in the Mandarin dialogue depicted above, and the moving correlation at lag 0.

The main pattern for the Mandarin conversational corpora is that prosodic synchrony is arrived at gradually, with an initial probing stage where topic is negotiated, followed by mixed convergence and divergence as options are explored or overturned from a one-sided viewpoint, until speakers arrive at a mutually fulfilling topic theme, where convergence is frequent. Near conversation end, participants converge in a descending pitch pattern in a shared recognition of the coming conclusion.

By comparison to talks between friends, conversations between newly-met participants may be more susceptible to lags in convergence, as speakers work to construct a common conversational outlook. The current results indicate that prosodic lags go in both directions, as speaker roles change and new topics are brought up during the course of the conversation. At the local level, prosodic synchrony at phrase-to-phrase pitch movement is common: convergence is associated with agreement or encouragement of topic, whereas divergence is associated with disagreement, doubt, or non-interest.

4.2 Feedback and prosodic convergence

Speaker role was found to be important in the incidence and location of feedback tokens with respect to the prosodic patterns. Feedback markers of high interest or surprise such as '*oh*', and encouraging markers such as '*um*' or '*umhum*' occur more frequently in areas of high pitch and convergence, and less frequently in divergent prosodic sections. The marker '*dui*' *right* occurs more frequently in areas of convergence and stretches of extended rise as the hearer provides added encouragement or confirmation respectively. Thus, feedback markers often provide explicit marking of the same underlying relational states that are provided by synchrony phenomena.

Our data indicate that speakers differ greatly in their use of feedback in different conversations, in both frequency and distribution, as depicted in Figures 2-3, which show the incidence of feedback for *oh* and *dui* across 20 continuous 3-minute episodes of conversations mcdc05 (due to space limitation, the 01 figures are not shown in this paper). As seen in Tables 1-2, the frequency of feedback for conversation mcdc01 is less than half of that for conversation mcdc05: for mcdc05, the male and female *oh* and *dui* feedback over all episodes totals 305, or 43.1% of mcdc05's total feedback frequency of 707. The use of feedback by the female speaker in mcdc01 is especially low for both *oh* and *dui,* with only 111 instances total.

Comparing the speaker usage of feedback markers *dui* and *oh*, we can see that in these two conversations, both female speakers' use of *oh* is relatively greater than *dui*: there are 82 *oh's* vs. 29 *dui's* in mcdc01, and 207 *oh's* vs. 169 *dui's* in mcdc05. Conversely, the male speakers' use of *dui* in both conversations is *much* greater than their use of *oh*: 171 *dui's* vs. 23 *oh's* in mcdc01 and 322 *dui's* vs. 9 *oh's* in mcdc05. The males have a striking near exclusion of the use of *oh* in both conversations.

MCDC01	Female		Male	
Token	oh	dui	oh	dui
Counts	82	29	23	171
Subtotal	111		194	
MCDC05	Female		Male	
Token	oh	dui	oh	dui
Counts	207	169	9	322
Subtotal	376		331	

Table 1: Counts of feedback markers *oh* and *dui* by speaker for 2 conversations, mcdc01 and mcdc05

MCDC01	Female		Male	
Token	oh	dui	oh	dui
Mean	4.05	1.45	1.15	8.55
Stdev	3.99	1.86	1.31	3.67
MCDC05	Female		Male	
Token	oh	dui	oh	dui
Mean	10.35	8.45	0.45	16.1
Stdev	7.84	3.32	0.80	11.11

Table 2: Mean counts of feedback markers *oh* and *dui* by speaker for 2 conversations, mcdc01 and mcdc05

The temporal distribution of feedback within conversations also varies greatly by speaker and conversation. In mcdc01, the female speaker has a higher concentration of feedback responses in the first 7 episodes of the conversation, and gradually reduces her feedback in the latter half of the conversation, while the male's feedback distribution is more uniform across the conversation. By contrast, the feedback for both speakers in mcdc05 occurs with higher frequency across the conversation, and also exhibits cyclical behavior.

4.3 Patterns of feedback distribution in conversation

Feedback markers are key interactive signals that communicate the adequacy of information exchange, and the distribution of specific markers is closely linked to their specific functions and to the emotional and involvement states of speakers and interactivity level of the conversation. Imbalances in participant state commonly give rise to different degrees of cognitive certainty or uncertainty, and feedback provides immediate signals to speakers that adjustment or restatement of information may be necessary.

For example, *oh, dui,* and *umhum* are three of the most frequent feedback markers in Mandarin (Tseng, 2004; Yang, 2006), and each signals different degrees of cognitive uncertainty and receptivity towards communicated information. While *oh* functions as a response to information, marking surprise, unexpectedness or newness, and necessitating a cognitive adjustment (reorientation), *dui* acts as confirmation and agreement to information received, and implied as already known or accepted. The predominant function of *umhum (uhhuh),* on the other hand, is expression of acknowledgment or encouragement. Thus, o*h, dui,* and *umhum* each has its unique different functions and occurs under different informational environments. The specific functions of these markers have great significance for their frequency and distribution in any given conversation.

If we take a closer look at the following figures and tables where we tabulated and plotted the occurrences of these three feedback markers through time in mcdc05 by speaker, we can see a clearer pattern: there is a clear gender difference and preference for the use of these markers. In this conversation, the male speaker has a mean of 7.6 instances of *umhum* per episode, just 26% of the female's mean frequency of 29.1 for the same marker. A similar large gap exists for *oh,* with the female speaker having about *20 times* as many *oh's* as the male speaker. Conversely, the male speaker used *dui* about twice as often as the female speaker, with mean episode counts of 16.1 for the male speaker vs. 8.45 for the female.

The relationships for *oh* and *dui* in mcdc05 are consistent with the results for mcdc01, with female *oh* and male *dui* having the higher relative frequencies, as presented earlier. The much greater use of *oh* and *umhum* by the female and greater use of *dui* by the male speaker presented here suggest that there exists some social-cultural expectations of greater male control and greater female supportiveness in male-female social interactions, and this feature might be especially marked in conversations where politeness and role-conformity could be expected to exert greater force.

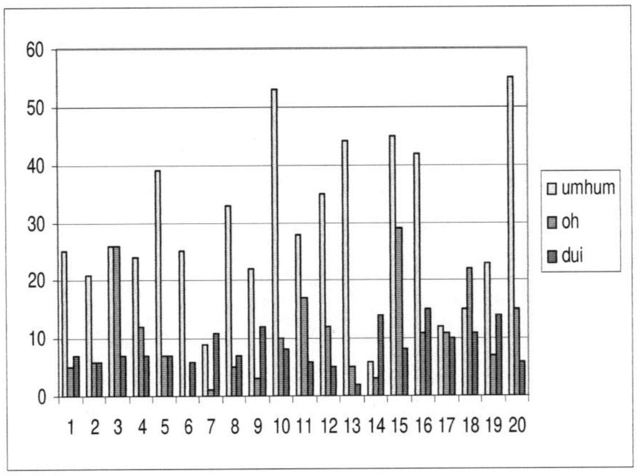

Figure 3: Frequency counts of feedback markers *umhum*, *oh*, and *dui* of the female speaker in mcdc05 by episode

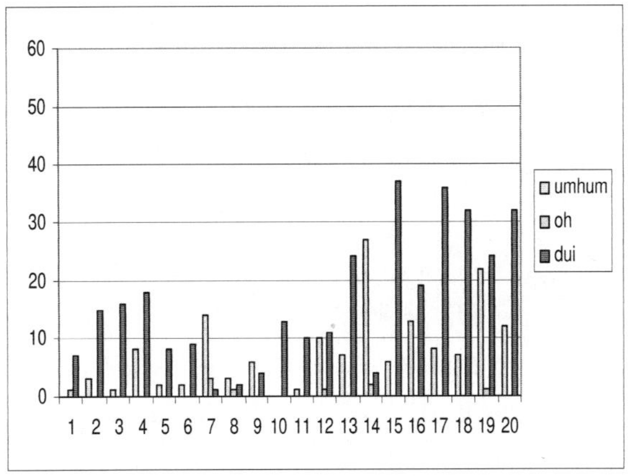

Figure 4: Frequency counts of feedback markers *umhum*, *oh*, and *dui* of the male speaker in mcdc05 by episode

	Male			Female		
Feedback	umhum	oh	dui	umhum	oh	dui
Mean	7.6	0.45	16.1	29.1	10.35	8.45
Stdev	7.05	0.80	11.11	13.57	7.84	3.32
Counts	152	9	322	582	207	169

Table 3: Mean counts of feedback markers *umhum*, *oh* and *dui* by speaker for mcdc05

	mcdc01				mcdc05			
Gender	Female		Male		Female		Male	
Token	oh	dui	oh	dui	oh	dui	oh	dui
Counts	82	29	23	171	207	169	9	322
Subtotal	111		194		376		331	
Total	305				707			

Table 4: Counts of feedback markers *umhum*, *oh* and *dui* by speaker for mcdc01 and mcdc05

4.4 Feedback and changing speaker state

The progression of feedback use in this conversation follows the activities of each speaker as they interact to bring about a successful conversation. At the start of this conversation, both participants explore several topics in sequence, with the female speaker more open in sharing information and responsive to the male speaker in the first half of the conversation. The initial topics serve as self-introductions and as search activity to arrive at a mutually satisfying topic.

As shown in Figures 3-4 and Table 5, the relatively low feedback activity of the male speaker in the initial episodes is matched by a high frequency of encouraging *umhum* feedback by the female speaker, to provide support for the male speaker. In episodes 7-9, the female speaker started an extended narration to tie her own experience and viewpoint to the male speaker's account, which is an essential cohesion-building strategy. The male speaker stays relatively silent during this period, and this results in very low use of both *oh* and *dui* for both speakers in those episodes. After the repeated rapport-building activities by the female speaker, the male speaker gradually becomes more open and emotionally expressive, and this transformation is reflected in his increased use of feedback from that point on.

In discourse, participants may unintentionally hit an area of high interest, and participants may become very involved. In this conversation the topic hits a major turning point in episode 14. At that point, both participants suddenly discover something unexpected but highly relevant and meaningful to both of them, and this transforms the nature of the conversation, with a high intensity of involvement by both participants, as evidenced by the greatly increased use of feedback markers from that episode on. This effect is especially dramatic for the male speaker.

As can be seen in Table 6, the male speaker's use of feedback increases greatly after the turning point, with *umhum* increasing to over 3 times its pre-turning point average, and *dui* about 2.5 times, while his use of *oh* decreased slightly, indicating his increased confidence and certainty associated with this newfound identity. By comparison, the female speaker's use of feedback is also increasing, and consistent over the conversation, with *umhum* occurring at the same frequency, and *oh* and *dui* increasing by about 2/3.

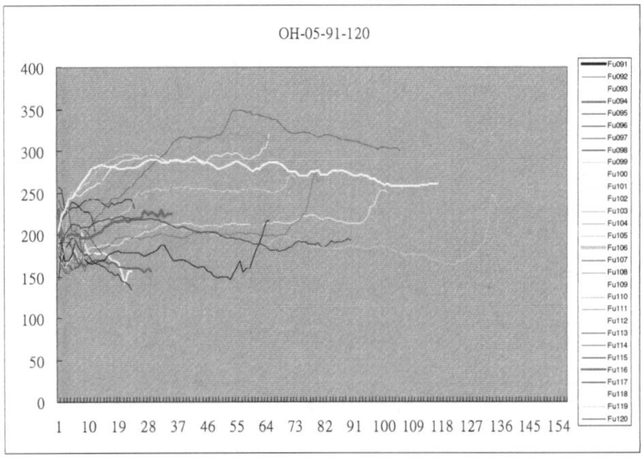

Figure 5: A selection of 30 instances of the female speaker's *oh*s in mcdc05, approximately occurring from episode 11 to the beginning of episode 14, showing different forms relating to different states and functions in spontaneous conversation

The result of our finding suggests that the use of feedback to encourage rapport can consist of a feedback loop that increases rapport between participants and leads to more synchronous feedback patterns over time. Our finding further provides evidence that convergent patterns occur as speakers cooperatively achieve a shared common ground, and that feedback is a key element of how speakers reach this goal in communication (Yang, 2006).

Our findings show that speaker role plays a significant role in the incidence and location of feedback markers with respect to the prosodic patterns. Feedback markers of high interest or surprise such as *oh*, and encouraging markers such as *um* or *umhum* occur more frequently in areas of high pitch and convergence, and less frequently in divergent prosodic sections. The marker *dui 'right'* occurs more frequently in areas of convergence and stretches of extended rise as the hearer provides added encouragement or confirmation respectively. Thus, feedback markers often provide explicit marking of the same underlying relational states that are provided by synchrony phenomena. Figure 5 provides an illustration of how meaning is effectively encoded in such short feedback utterances for spoken communication.

	Male			**Female**		
Ep.	uhm	oh	dui	uhm	oh	dui
1	0	1	7	25	5	7
2	3	0	15	21	6	6
3	1	0	16	26	26	7
4	8	0	18	24	12	7
5	2	0	8	39	7	7
6	2	0	9	25	0	6
7	14	3	1	9	1	11
8	3	1	2	33	5	7
9	6	0	4	22	3	12
10	0	0	13	53	10	8
11	1	0	10	28	17	6
12	10	1	11	35	12	5
13	7	0	24	44	5	2
14	27	2	4	6	3	14
15	6	0	37	45	29	8
16	13	0	19	42	11	15
17	8	0	36	12	11	10
18	7	0	32	15	22	11
19	22	1	24	23	7	14
20	12	0	32	55	15	6
T			483			958

Table 5: Counts of feedback markers *umhum*, *oh* and *dui* by speaker and episode: mcdc05

	Male			**Female**		
	umhum	oh	dui	umhum	oh	dui
Pre TP	57.0	6.0	138.0	384.0	109.0	91.0
Post TP	95.0	3.0	184.0	198.0	98.0	78.0
Pre mean	4.4	0.5	10.6	29.5	8.4	7.0
Post mean	13.6	0.4	26.3	28.3	14.0	11.1

Table 6: Mean counts of feedback markers *umhum*, *oh* and *dui* by speaker, before and after the turning point for mcdc05

5 Conclusions

Our analysis suggests that prosodic synchrony phenomena occur as a mirror of topically and emotionally synchronized or dis-synchronized participant states and that convergence and divergence phenomena are not only strategies to encourage rapport, but also act as organizational indicators providing key information on the degree of understanding, on emotional synchrony, and on the perceived status of a mutually fulfilling topic flow. This universal feature is essential to communication and interaction, and should be utilized greatly in current multimodal communication environment research.

Acknowledgment

The research is supported by National Science Council of Taiwan under grant no. NSC97-2410-H-029-026. The funding support is gratefully acknowledged by the author.

References

Amélie Lelong & Bailly, Gérard. 2011. Study of the phenomenon of phonetic convergence thanks to speech dominoes. In A. Vinciarelli, K. Vicsi, C. Pelachaud and A. Nijholt (eds.) *Analysis of verbal and nonverbal communication and enactment: the processing issue*, 280–293.

Buschmeier, H., Z. Malisz, M. Włodarczak, S. Kopp, and P. Wagner. 2011. 'Are you sure you're paying attention?'–'Uh-huh'. Communicating understanding as a marker of attentiveness. *Proceedings of INTERSPEECH 2011*, Florence, Italy, 2057–2060.

Campbell, Nick, and Scherer, Stefan. 2010. Comparing measures of synchrony and alignment in dialogue speech timing with respect to turn-taking activity. *Proceedings of Interspeech 2010,* 2546–2549.

Chika Nagaoka, Masashi Komori, & Sakiko Yoshikawa. 2007. Embodied synchrony in conversation. In Toyoaki Nishida (ed.) *Conversational informatics: an engineering approach*, Wiley Series in Agent Technology. John Wiley & Sons. 331–352.

Condon, W. S., Sander, L. W. 1974. Neonate movement is synchronized with adult speech, interactional participation and language acquisition. *Science*, Vol.183, 99–101.

D. Heylen, Bevacqua, E., Pelachaud, C., Isabella Poggi, Gratch, J., and Schröder, M. 2011. Generating listening behaviour. In P. Petta et al. (eds.), *Emotion-Oriented Systems*, Cognitive Technologies, Springer-Verlag Berlin Heidelberg. 321–347

Emanuel Schegloff. 1982. Discourse as an interactional achievement: some uses of *uh huh* and other things that come between sentences. *GURT 1981 Analyzing Discourse: Text and Talk*, ed. by D. Tannen. Georgetown University Press, 71–93.

G. Jonsdottir, Gratch, J., Fast, E., and Thórisson, K. 2007. Fluid semantic back-channel feedback in dialogue: challenges and progress. In C. Pelachaud et al. (Eds.): *IVA 2007*, LNAI 4722, Springer-Verlag Berlin, Heidelberg, 154–160

Herbert Clark. 1996. *Using language*. Cambridge: Cambridge University Press.

Howard Giles and P. Smith. 1979. Accommodation theory: Optimal levels of convergence. In H.Giles & R. St. Clair (Eds.), *Language and social psychology,* 45-65. Oxford: Blackwell.

Jennifer Pardo. 2006. On phonetic convergence during conversational interaction. *Journal of the Acoustic Society of America* 119(4): 2382–93.

Jennifer Pardo. 2010. Expressing oneself in conversational interaction. In *Expressing oneself/Expressing one's self: communication, cognition, and identity*, ed. E. Morsella (Taylor & Francis London), 183–196.

Kawai Chui. 1994. *Information Flow in Mandarin Chinese Discourse*. PhD dissertation. National Taiwan Normal University.

Li-chiung Yang. 1995. Intonational Structures of Mandarin Discourse, PhD dissertation, Georgetown University.

Li-chiung Yang. 2006. Integrating prosodic and contextual cues in the interpretation of discourse markers. In *Approaches to Discourse Particles*, ed. By Fischer, Kerstin, Elsevier, 265–297.

Lixing Huang, Morency, L., and Gratch, J. 2010. Learning backchannel prediction model from parasocial consensus sampling: A Subjective Evaluation. *The 10th International Conference on Intelligent Virtual Agents (IVA 2010),* Philadelphia, PA, USA, 159–172.

Lixing Huang and Gratch, J. 2012. Crowdsourcing backchannel feedback: understanding the Individual Variability from the Crowds. *The Interdisciplinary Workshop on Feedback Behaviors in Dialog,* Portland, Oregon.

Nigel Ward. and Tsukahara, W. 2000. Prosodic Features which cue back-channel responses in English and Japanese. *Journal of Pragmatics*, 23, 1177–1207.

P. Sadler, Ethier, N., Gunn, G.R, Duong, D, and Woody, E. 2009. Are we on the same wavelength? Interpersonal complementarity as shared cyclical patterns during interactions. *Journal of Personality & Social Psychology*, 97(6):1005–20.

Jens Allwood, Nivre, J. and Ahlsén, E. 1992. On the semantics and pragmatics of linguistic feedback. *Journal of Semantics,* 9:1–26.

Jonathan Gratch, Wang, N., Gerten , J., Fast, E., & Duffy, R. 2007. Creating rapport with virtual agents. *The 7th International Conference on Intelligent Virtual Agents*. Paris, France, 125–138.

S. P. Gill. 2012. Rhythmic synchrony and mediated interaction: towards a framework of rhythm in embodied interaction. *AI & Society,* 27, 111–127.

Shu-Chuan Tseng. 2003. Taxonomy of spontaneous speech phenomena in Mandarin conversation. In *SSPR-2003*, ISCA & IEEE Workshop on Spontaneous Speech Processing and Recognition, Tokyo Institute of Technology, Tokyo, Japan.

Shu-Chuan Tseng. 2004. Processing spoken Mandarin corpora. *Traitement automatique des langues. Special Issue: Spoken Corpus Processing,* 45(2): 89–108.

Shu-Chuan Tseng. 2008. Spoken corpora and analysis of natural speech. *Taiwan Journal of Linguistics,* vol. 6.2, 1–26.

Susan Brennan, & Herbert Clark. 1996. Conceptual pacts and lexical choice in conversation. *Journal of Experimental Psychology: Learning, Memory, and Cognition*, 22(6), 1482–1493.

Wallace Chafe. 1994. *Discourse, consciousness and time*. Chicago: University of Chicago Press.

Wallace Chafe. 2008. The analysis of discourse flow. In *The Handbook of Discourse Analysis*. Oxford: Blackwell, 673-687.

A Quantitative Comparative Study of Prosodic and Discourse Units, the Case of French and Taiwan Mandarin

Laurent Prévot
Aix Marseille Université
CNRS, LPL
Aix-En-Provence, France
laurent.prevot@lpl-aix.fr

Shu-Chuan Tseng
Academia Sinica
Institute of Linguistics
Taipei, Taiwan
tsengsc@gate.sinica.edu.tw

Alvin Cheng-Hsien Chen
National Changhua
University of Education
English Department
Changhua City, Taiwan
alvinworks@gmail.com

Klim Peshkov
Aix Marseille Université
CNRS, LPL
Aix-En-Provence, France
klim.peshkov@lpl-aix.fr

Abstract

Studies of spontaneous conversational speech grounded on large and richly annotated corpora are still rare due to the scarcity of such resources. Comparative studies based on such resources are even more rarely found because of the extra-need of comparability in terms of content, genre and speaking style. The present paper presents our efforts for establishing such a dataset for two typologically diverse languages: French and Taiwan Mandarin. To the primary data, we added morpho-syntactic, chunking, prosodic and discourse annotation in order to be able to carry out quantitative comparative studies of the syntax-discourse-prosody interfaces. We introduced our work on the data creation itself as well as some preliminary results of the boundary alignment between prosodic and discourse units and how POS and chunks are distributed on these boundaries.

1 Introduction

Interest for the studies of discourse prosody interface has arisen in the last decade as illustrated by the vitality of the events and projects in this domain. However, while theoretical proposals and descriptive works are numerous, quantitative systematic studies are less widespread due to the cost of creating resources usable for such studies. Indeed, prosodic and discourse analysis are delicate matters requiring lower-level processing such as the alignment with speech signal at syllable level (for prosody) or at least basic syntactic annotation (for discourse). Moreover, many of these studies are dealing with read or monologue speech. The extremely spontaneous nature of conversational speech renders the first levels of processing complicated. Previous works (Liu and Tseng, 2009; Chen, 2011; Bertrand et al., 2008; Blache et al., 2009; Afantenos et al., 2012) give us the opportunity to produce conversational resources of this kind. We then took advantage of a bilateral project for working on conversational speech in a quantitative fashion, and this for two typologically diverse languages: French and Taiwan Mandarin. We believe this combination of linguistic resources and skills for these two languages is a rather unique situation and allows for comparative quantitative experiments on high-level linguistic analysis such as discourse and prosody.

Our objective is to understand the commonalities and the differences between discourse prosody interface in these two languages. More precisely, we look at how prosodic units and discourse units are distributed onto each other.

In spirit, our work is closely related to the one of (Simon and Degand, 2009; Lacheret et al., 2010; Gerdes et al., 2012), however our focus here are the insights we can get from a comparative study. Moreover our dataset has a more conversational nature than the datasets studied in their work. About the data, (Gerdes et al., 2012) wanted to have an interesting spectrum of discourse genres and speaking styles while we focused on conversations both for making possible the comparative studies and to make sure to have enough coherent instances in the perspective of statistical studies. Also, while (Lacheret et al., 2010) requires a purely intuitive approach, we used a more balanced approach combining explicit criteria from different language domains. Finally, our annotation experiments are largely produced either by automatic tools (trained on experts data) or by naive coders. This is a major difference with the studies listed above that are based on experts annotations since it allows us scale up in data size more easily.

The paper is structured as follows. We will start in section 2 by presenting how we built a comparable dataset from existing corpora. Then we will address in section 3 and 4 respectively the creation of prosodic and discourse units. Based on these new datasets, we will investigate the discourse prosody interface in a comparative and quantitative way (Section 5). Finally, in section 6 we will pay some attention at what is happening syntactically at various types of boundaries as defined in the preceding section.

2 Building comparable corpora

lge	dur(m)	syll	tokens	PU	DU
fr	89	23631	20233	6057	2130
tw	205	54615	37637	8563	5673

Table 1: Size of the data set

First of all, corpora from both languages were recorded in very similar conditions. There are both face-to-face interaction in an anechoic room and speech was recorded via headsets on separate channels. The original recordings are also very comparable in size. The raw figures of both datasets are presented in Table 1.[1] We had to decide which linguistic information and which part from the full corpora to include in our joint dataset. About the later point, we extracted narrative sequences from the French data that included also more interactive topic negotiation sequences. About the linguistic levels, our study concerned prosodic and discourse levels but we wanted to be able to perform fine-grained study involving syntactic and phonetic aspects. We therefore agreed to include syllables, tokens and part-of-speech information in our data as can be seen in Table 2. As the POS tagsets are different in both languages, we established a matching table to make the POS information mutually understandable (Table 3).

Description	**Tier Name**	Tier Content
Syllable	Syllable	STRING-UTF8
Token	Word	STRING-UTF8
Part-Of-Speech	POS	STRING-UTF8
Prosodic Units	PU	PU
Discourse Units	DU	{ DU, ADU}

Table 2: Contents of the joint dataset

tw	fr	Category
N	N	Nouns *(N)*
Nh	P	Pronouns *(Pro)*
Ne	D	Determiners *(Det)*
V	V	Verbs *(V)*
T,I,FW	I	Particles, DM[2]... *(Part)*
D	R	Adverbs *(Adv)*
A	A	Adjectives *(Adj)*
P	S	Prepositions *(Prep)*

Table 3: Correspondence of the most frequent POS tags

2.1 Creation of the French dataset

The ORCHID.fr Dataset is a subset of the Corpus for Interactional Data (CID) (Bertrand et al., 2008) consisting of 1.5 hour of conversational speech produced by 3 female and 3 male speakers. The CID corpus is a collection of 8 hours of free conversation in French. All the speaker turn boundaries are time-aligned with the speech signal at phone level by using forced alignment techniques (Illina et al., 2004). Moreover, the corpus had been entirely POS-tagged (See (Blache et al., 2008) for a presentation of the probabilistic technique used). Finally, in the framework of the OTIM and ORCHID projects an annotation campaign for annotating prosodic phrasing and segmenting the corpus into discourse units had been ran. In the present project, we modified the

[1] See sections 3 and 4 for Prosodic Units, Discourse Units and Abandoned DU definitions.

criteria for labeling discourse units according to the commonly defined operational guidelines for French and Taiwan Mandarin data processing.

2.2 Creation of the Taiwan Mandarin dataset

The ORCHID.tw Dataset is a subset of the Taiwan Mandarin Conversational Corpus (the TMC Corpus), consisting of 3.5 hours of conversational speech produced by 7 male and 9 female speakers (Tseng, 2013). The TMC Corpus is a collection of 42 hours of free, task-oriented and topic-specific conversations in Taiwan Mandarin. All the speaker turn boundaries as well as syllable boundaries were human-labeled in the ORCHID.tw Dataset. Boundaries of words and POS tags were automatically generated based on the syllable boundary information and the output of the automatic word segmentation and POS tagging system developed by the CKIP at Academia Sinica (Chen et al., 1996). Previously, the ORCHID.tw dataset has been annotated with boundaries of prosodic units as defined in (Liu and Tseng, 2009) and with boundaries of discourse units in (Chen, 2011). In the present ORCHID project, we modified the criteria for labeling discourse units according to the commonly defined operational guidelines for French and Taiwan Mandarin data processing. The definition for prosodic units remains unchanged.

3 Producing prosodic units

3.1 French data

The definition of prosodic units is adopted mainly from prosodic phonology (Selkirk, 1986; Nespor and Vogel, 1986) that proposed a universal hierarchy of prosodic constituents. At least two levels of phrasing above the word have been admitted in French: the lowest level of phonological phrases (Post, 2000) or accentual phrases (AP) (Jun and Fougeron, 2000) and the highest level of Intonational phrases (IPs). The accentual phrase is the domain of primary stress. This latter is realized on the final full syllable of a word with longer duration and higher intensity than non-final syllables, and associated with a melodic movement. The secondary stress, more variable and optional, is generally realized on the initial stressed syllable of the first lexical word. It is associated with a rise movement. The Intonational Phrase contains one or more accentual phrases. It is marked by a major final rise or fall (intonation contour), a stronger final lengthening and can be followed by a pause (Hirst and Di Cristo, 1984; Jun and Fougeron, 2000). More recently, a few studies attempted to show the existence of an intermediate level of phrasing (intermediate phrase, ip) that would be realized with stronger prosodic cues than the ones associated with AP and weaker than those associated with IP (Michelas and D'Imperio, 2010).

For the French dataset, both phonetic and phonological criteria have been used to annotate the boundaries of prosodic units. Once primary and secondary stresses are identified, the main acoustic cues are: (1) specific melodic contour, (2) final lengthening, (3) pitch reset. Moreover, disfluencies were annotated separately and silent pauses have not been systematically associated with a boundary (Portes et al., 2011). In a previous study involving two experts, we have shown the reliability of annotation criteria for the higher level of constituency (IP) (see (Nesterenko et al., 2010)). In a second stage, we elaborated a guideline for transcribing prosodic units in French by naive annotators. They have to annotate 4 levels of prosodic break defined in terms of a ToBI-style annotation (ref) (0 = no break; 1 = AP break; 2 = ip break; 3 = IP break) in Praat (Boersma, 2002).

Based on this break annotation we created *Prosodic Units (PU)* that are basically resulting from considering any break of level 2 or 3 as boundaries for our PUs. The merging of breaks of level 2 and 3 has been made to match the annotation style of the Taiwan Mandarin data but also to improve the reliability of the data produced. Indeed, the inter-annotator agreement was overall higher when levels 2 and 3 are collapsed. Finally, we added breaks on pauses over 400ms. We computed a κ-score for our data set by taking each token as a decision point and counting the number of matching and non-matching boundaries across annotators. This method of calculation yielded a κ-score of 0.71 for our dataset which is a nice score for naive coders on prosodic phrasing task.

Cohen's kappa (Cohen and others, 1960) (and see (Carletta, 1996; Artstein and Poesio, 2008) for further discussion) is a measure designed to measure inter-coder agreement. It corrects the raw agreement by an estimation of the agreement by chance. The issue here is that it is a segmentation task, therefore we have to decide on what are the decision points. We are using the tokens as decision points rather than a fixed sample (as it is done in some annotation tools) because the French guidelines are using words as the base units for instructing where to put the boundaries. Agreement on no-boudary (0-0) is therefore an agreement for this decision task and there is no satisfying way to evaluate a kappa score if these agreements are left out. Other measures need to be introduced (Pevzner and Hearst, 2002; Fournier and Inkpen, 2012) if one wants to measure a different aspect of the segmentation agreement. However to be perfectly transparent with the annotation results, Figure 1 presents the contingency table for the Orchid's style prosodic units (See also (Peshkov et al., 2012) for deeper evaluation of the annotation of the whole CID corpus).

A/B	(0-1)	(2-3)
(0-1)	12242	1987
(2-3)	581	5272

Figure 1: Contingency table for the French prosodic units

3.2 Taiwan Mandarin data

The definition of prosodic units is adopted mainly from that of *Intonation Unit* in the field of discourse analysis (Chafe, 1994; Tao, 1996), but emphasizing on the concept of prosodic phrasing, instead of a coherent intonation pattern. We are in the opinion that prosodic phrasing is definitely not purely linear and sequential, as language planning should work with a certain kind of structure and hierarchy, which expectedly result in different types of prosodic phrasing. Nevertheless, the design of a single layer of prosodic phrasing will provide segmentation boundaries for further distinguishing the types of prosodic units and it is easier to achieve a reasonable inter-labelers agreement. Boundaries of prosodic units were annotated based on four main cues perceived by the labelers: (1) pitch reset (a shift upward in overall pitch level), (2) lengthening (changes in duration), (3) alternation of speech rate (changes in rhythm), and (4) occurrences of paralinguistic sounds (disjunction or disruption of utterances such as pauses, inhalation, and laughter). The annotation of prosodic units of the ORCHID.tw Dataset has been accomplished in an earlier project (Liu and Tseng, 2009). Three labelers were trained to annotate prosodic units on a subset of 150 speaker turns until a satisfactory consistency rate was achieved. The rest of the dataset was completed by the three labelers independently.

Although the French and Taiwan Mandarin datasets were annotated based on different theories, but the annotation criteria were comparable. To ensure the comparability of the criteria, a cross-language segmentation experiment was conducted on a small subset of our data by the authors of this paper. Each tried to annotate prosodic units in the other language. The annotation results conducted by the non-native labelers confirmed that the main cues used for segmenting the prosodic unit boundaries were in principle uniform, except for those caused by repairs and restarts.

4 Producing discourse units

Concerning discourse units, the annotation campaign also involved naive annotators that have segmented the whole corpus (half of it being cross annotated). This annotation was performed without listening to the signal but with timing information. It was performed with Praat (Boersma, 2002) but without including the signal window, only the time-aligned token tiers. The segmentation was performed by adopting a set of discourse segmentation guidelines, inspired from (Muller et al., 2012) and (Chen, 2011). We combined semantic criterion *(Vendler's (Vendler, 1957) style eventualities identification and Xue's proposition identification (Xue, 2008))*, discourse criterion *(presence of discourse markers)* and pragmatic criterion *(recognition of specific speech acts)* to perform the segmentation.

More practically the task consisted in first identifying a main predicate, and then all its complements and adjuncts as illustrated in (1) and (2). Mandarin spontaneous speech presents an additional challenge in the task of DU annotation for its lack of tense-marking verbal system. Our segmentation proceeds on the basis of the semantic bonding between predicates identified (Givón, 1993). Additional cues such as discourse connectives articulating discourse units were also used. Finally, mainly because of the interactive dialogic phenomena (e.g question-anwser pairs) we added a few pragmatic criterion for allowing short utterances *(e.g yeah)* or fragments *(e.g where?)* (Ginzburg et al., 2007) to be acceptable discourse units.

(1) French Discourse Units
[on y va avec des copains]$_{du}$ [on avait pris le ferry en Normandie]$_{du}$ [puisque j'avais un frère qui était en Normandie]$_{du}$ [on traverse]$_{du}$ [on avait passé une nuit épouvantable sur le ferry]$_{du}$
[we going there with friends]$_{du}$ [we took the ferry in Normandy]$_{du}$ [since I had a brother that was in Normandy]$_{du}$ [we cross]$_{du}$ [we spent a terrible night on the ferry]$_{du}$

(2) Taiwan Mandarin discourse units
[qishi ta jiang de na ge ren yinwei ta you qu kai guo hui]$_{du}$ [ta hai you jiang]$_{du}$ [keneng shi ye bu zhidao wei she me]$_{du}$
[in fact the one he mentioned had the meeting]$_{du}$ [he said in addition]$_{du}$ [probably (he) did not know why, either]$_{du}$

Manual discourse segmentation with our guidelines has proven to be reliable with κ-scores ranging between 0.74 and 0.85 for the French data and reaching 0.86 for the Taiwan Mandarin data.

Moreover we distinguished between several units in discourse: *discourse units* and *abandoned discourse units*.[3] The later are units that are so incomplete that it is impossible to attribute them a discourse contribution. They are distinguished from *false starts* (that are included in the DU they contributed) by the fact that the material they introduced cannot be said to be taken up in the following discourse unit.

(3) French abandoned discourse units
[et euh mh donc t(u) avais si tu veux le sam- + le]$_{adu}$ [pour savoir qui jouait tu (v)ois]$_{du}$
[and err mm so tu had if you want the sat- + the]$_{adu}$ [in order to know who play you see]$_{du}$

(4) Taiwan Mandarin abandoned discourse units
[danshi muqian]$_{adu}$ [yinwei shezhiyu]$_{adu}$ [wo you ting renjia jiang]$_{du}$ [man kuazhang]$_{du}$
[but for the moment]$_{adu}$ [because even though]$_{adu}$ [I heard some people say]$_{du}$ [it is incredible]$_{du}$

[3]We actually had also a *parenthetical* category but it was not consistently annotated at the current stage and therefore this distinction was not included in this paper.

5 Discourse Prosody Interface

5.1 Size of units

From Table 1, we can deduce the size of our units presented in Table 4. The significantly smaller French PUs (up to 40% depending to the units taken to compare) might partially be attributed to the difference in the segmentation style and the extraction of the subsets. The Taiwan Mandarin dataset contains only very long speaker turns, thus reducing the number of shorter prosodic units which are more often produced in interactive conversational speech. For DUs in which guidelines are basically identical we get very similar DU size in terms of duration and number of syllables (roughly 15% difference), French units host more tokens (43%) and therefore included shorter words.

	dur (s)	# syll	#tokens	# PU
PU-fr	0.88	3.9	3.3	-
PU-tw	1.44	6.4	4.4	-
DU-fr	2.51	11.1	9.5	2.8
DU-tw	2.17	9.6	6.6	1.5

Table 4: Comparative size of the units produced

Moreover from Table 1 we can see, that the French dataset included a larger part of abandoned discourse units (11% for 6,5% in the Taiwan Mandarin dataset). This is in line with the more spontaneous style conversations already mentioned in the French dataset.

5.2 Association of prosodic and discourse units

We examined the different types of association between prosodic and discourse units by means of boundary alignment. We follow (Chen, 2011) classification that starts from discourse units and that distinguishes 8 situations resulting from combining two parameters: (i) the presence of a prosodic boundary within the discourse unit (inner boundary vs. no-inner-boundary) ; (ii) the match of discourse and prosodic unit at either left, right, both or none boundaries. Such a classification resulted in the distribution illustrated in Fig 2.

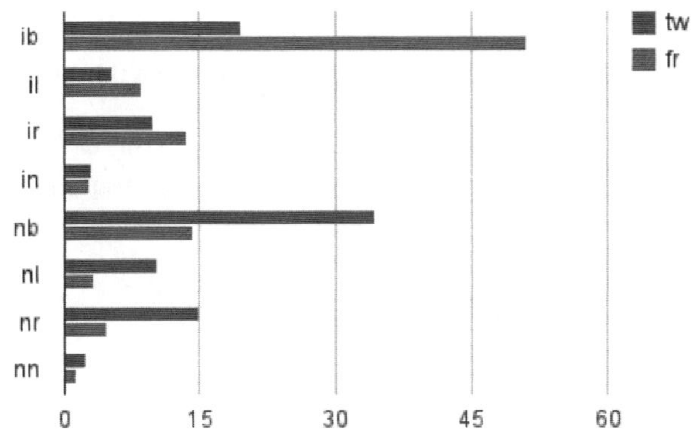

Figure 2: Distribution of PU/DU association types

In French data, perhaps because of the comparatively smaller prosodic units in the French data, discourse units host much more systematically several prosodic units. It is striking to see in figure 3 that more than half of the time and for both language discourse units are providing the starting and ending boundaries for the prosodic units. Overall, we see in figure 3 that once atomic and composite (in terms of PUs) DUs are collapsed their split in the alignment types are quite similar.

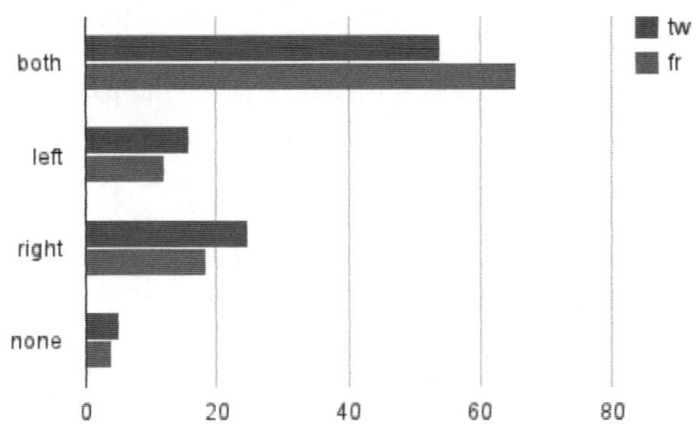

Figure 3: Distribution of PU/DU simplified association types

6 Syntactic categories at boundaries

Making use of the mapping table of POS information (Table 3) we established we are able to compare the distribution of POS at the boundaries. More precisely we looked at places where there was a match between PU-DU initial boundaries (Fig. 4) and PU-DU final boundaries (Fig. 5).

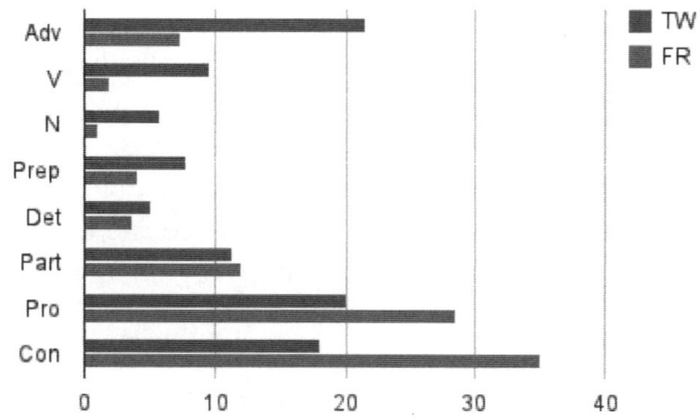

Figure 4: POS distribution at Initial matching boundaries

Interestingly, French units tend to begin more often with connectives and pronouns. In Taiwan Mandarin, the percentage of pronouns is lower and that of adverbs is higher. This may be due to fact that in conversation, sentences are often zero-subject or with the focus moved to sentence-initial positions.

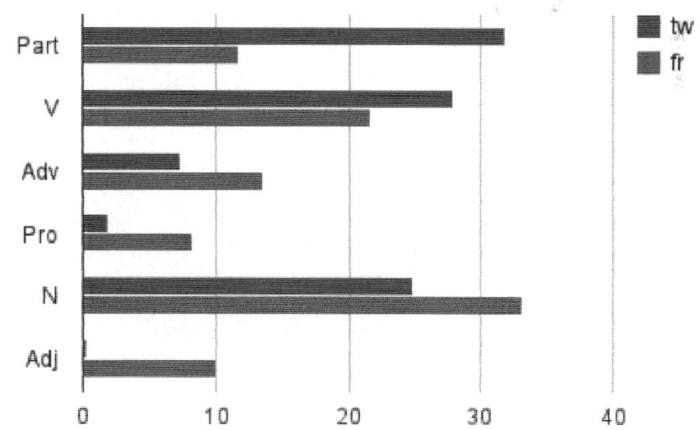

Figure 5: POS distribution at Final matching boundaries

For final matching boundaries, Taiwan Mandarin ends often with sentence-final particles, which is expected in conversation. Moreover, French ends more often at nouns than verbs, Taiwan Mandarin more verbs than nouns. Our preliminary studies on the word categories only provide information for the boundary. More work on the sentence structure is required to conduct in-depth studies on language production.

7 Chunks as processing units

Chunks (Abney, 1991) can be seen as an intermediate level of syntactic processing. They are the basic structures built from the tags but do not deal with long dependencies or rich constituence. They are basically units centered on a syntactic head, a content word. As reminded by Abney, chunks can be related to ϕ-sentences (Gee and Grosjean, 1983) which have a more intonational nature. An idea defended in these early works is that chunks are indeed language processing units from a cognitive viewpoint. The break-up of experimental linguistics as renewed the interest for this hypothesis and is attempting to make it more precise (Blache, 2013) and relate to other empirical evidences such as eye-tracking (Blache and Rauzy, 2012).

With this idea in mind, we will investigate our prosodic and discourse units in terms of chunk size and constituency. The first basic hypothesis we are testing is if tokens are syntactic units and chunks more processing units, the structure of PUs and DUs in terms of tokens does not have to match across languages while it should in terms of chunks. More precisely, we expect a significant variation of PU/DU size across languages in terms number of tokens but not in terms of chunk size.

7.1 Creating chunks

VC	Verbal Chunk
NC	Nominal Chunk
AdvC	Adverbial Chunk
PC	Prepositional Chunk
IC	Intractional Chunk
DisfError	Disfluencies or tagging errors
AdjC	Adjectival Chunk

Table 5: Chunks category created

From the chunking definition, we retain the importance of the head. We therefore designed simple rules using POS-tag patterns for creating the chunks listed in Table 5. This was done by looking at most frequent patterns first. We processed in three different steps involving three different type of rules:

1. Propose for most frequent POS pattern a chunking rule *(e.g Pro Pro V $\rightsquigarrow$ VC ; Det N N $\rightsquigarrow$ NC)*
2. Propose a set of rules aggregating tags and chunks into coherent chunks *(e.g Prep NC $\rightsquigarrow$ PC ; VC Part $\rightsquigarrow$ VC)*. This is done iteratively until stabilization of the number of sequences.
3. Simplification of the sequences by merging certain categories *(Det, Pro)* (or sequences of them) into some existing chunks *(e.g [Det|Pro]+ VC $\rightsquigarrow$VC)* and simplifying some chunks sequences *(IC IC $\rightsquigarrow$ IC)*

The two first types of rule are strongly language dependent while the third type is common to both languages.

Using pre-trained existing chunker was problematic. The rules used were defined to handle spontaneous spoken constructions. To our knowledge, existing chunkers are trained on written data which makes them impractical for our purposes. Moreover, in the rule-based design the rules are accessible to the linguists and this allow to compare them directly across languages rather than comparing chunking quality. Indeed, we are not interested in the chunks from an applicative perspective (such as named entity recognition) but as good approximation of semantic processing units. On the longer term, it could be however interesting to improve and evaluate and improve pre-trained chunking steps but this will require a large amount of manual work which we cannot afford for the time being.

7.2 Size in chunks

We then try to validate our hypothesis based on the chunks created and computed the size of PUs and DUs in terms of chunks (Table 6) and more precisely in terms of their length (in chunks) distribution (Figures 6 and 7).

Taiwan Mandarin and French size and size distribution exhibit however very different figures. About French PUs, it could be due to the sampling of the data (shorter PUs compared with the sampling of

lge	Size-PU	Size-DU
fr	1,48	3,69
tw	2,05	2,27

Table 6: Average size of units (in chunks)

long speaker turns data of Taiwan Mandarin) and the annotation criteria of PU. About the DUs, the distribution is also different but for this category we are more thinking at an issue with the tagging and chunking process. While we tried to keep the rules for producing the chunks coherent across the language, we might need either a more careful joint rules crafting or, perhaps a completely systematic chunking rules system. However, we do not have annotated chunks on this kind of data for training a supervised machine learning approach. Moreover, the dataset is significant but most likely not sufficient for unsupervised methods. In this context, crafting a simple rule-based system was appealing.

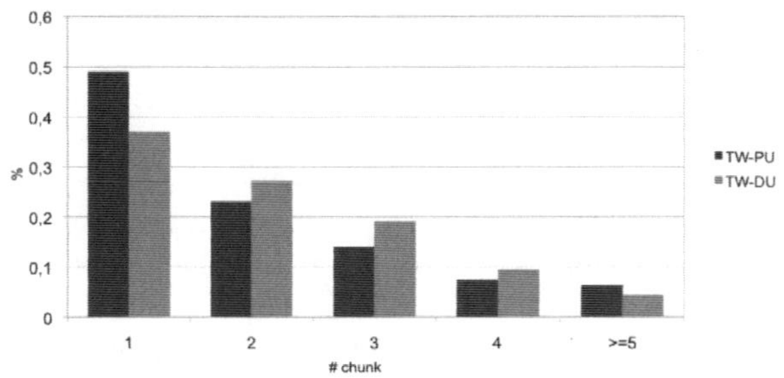

Figure 6: Comparison of Units size of the TW dataset

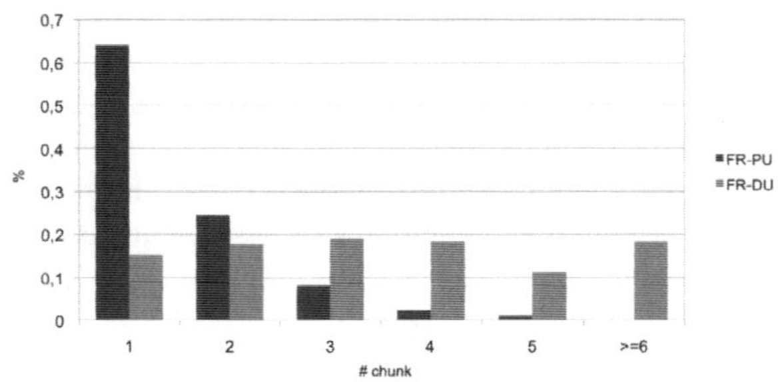

Figure 7: Comparison of Units size of the FR dataset

8 Conclusion and Future work

This work has shown that to create perfectly comparable corpora, one needs to start from joint design. However, this is a rare scenario and most of comparative datasets of richly annotated corpora will try to re-use at least part of their previous monolingual studies. Here we tried to make use of extremely similar resources for producing comparable corpora. We believe that although this data set could still be improved and benefited from an even more similar starting point, we have a unique resource for performing quantitative comparative studies of the kind initiated here. Equipped with this dataset, we are in position to conduct a series of deeper comparative studies. The chunking systems used in this paper are just a first attempt in this direction. Although the results for the chunk size are not conclusive for our hypothesis, we did get to know better the structures present in the units we are investigating and we would like to push further our exploration in this direction. We are currently looking at the distribution of the mono-,bi- and tri-chunks PUS and DUs sequences in order to get finer in the language comparison without going into a full syntactic analysis which is out of reach for this kind of data. In parallel, we will also attempt a shallower but more robust approach consisting in counting simply the number of content words in the units. This is even more basic than chunking but we would like to see whether it could be an interesting shortcut to the basic semantic structure of these units.

Acknowledgements

This work has been realized thanks to the support of the France-Taiwan ORCHID Program, under grant 100-2911-I-001-504 and the NSC project 100-2410-H-001-093 granted to the second author, as well as ANR *OTIM* BLAN08-2-349062 for initial work on the French data. We would like also to thank our colleagues for the help at various stage of the Data preparation, in particular Roxane Bertrand, Yi-Fen Liu, Robert Espesser, Stéphane Rauzy, Brigitte Bigi, and Philippe Blache.

References

Steven Abney. 1991. Parsing by chunks. In Robert Berwick, Steven Abney, and Carol Tenny, editors, *Principle-Based Parsing*. Kluwer Academic Publishers, Dordrecht.

Stergos Afantenos, Nicholas Asher, Farah Benamara, Myriam Bras, Cécile Fabre, Mai Ho-dac, Anne Le Draoulec, Philippe Muller, Marie-Paule Péry-Woodley, Laurent Prévot, et al. 2012. An empirical resource for discovering cognitive principles of discourse organisation: the annodis corpus. In *Proceedings of LREC*.

Ron Artstein and Massimo Poesio. 2008. Inter-coder agreement for computational linguistics. *Computational Linguistics*, 34(4):555–596.

R. Bertrand, P. Blache, R. Espesser, G. Ferré, C. Meunier, B. Priego-Valverde, S. Rauzy, et al. 2008. Le cid-corpus of interactional data-annotation et exploitation multimodale de parole conversationnelle. *Traitement Automatique des Langues*, 49(3):1–30.

Philippe Blache and Stéphane Rauzy. 2012. Robustness and processing difficulty models. a pilot study for eye-tracking data on the french treebank. In *24th International Conference on Computational Linguistics*.

Philippe Blache, Stéphane Rauzy, et al. 2008. Influence de la qualité de l'étiquetage sur le chunking: une corrélation dépendant de la taille des chunks. *Actes, Traitement Automatique des Langues Naturelles*, pages 1–10.

Philippe Blache, Roxane Bertrand, and Gaëlle Ferré. 2009. Creating and exploiting multimodal annotated corpora: the toma project. *Multimodal corpora*, pages 38–53.

Philippe Blache. 2013. Chunks et activation: un modèle de facilitation du traitement linguistique. In *Proceedings of Traitement Automatique des Langues Naturelles*.

P. Boersma. 2002. Praat, a system for doing phonetics by computer. *Glot international*, 5(9/10):341–345.

Jean Carletta. 1996. Assessing agreement on classification tasks: The kappa statistic. *Computational linguistics*, 22(2):249–254.

Wallace Chafe. 1994. *Discourse, consciousness, and time: The flow and displacement of conscious experience in speaking and writing*. University of Chicago Press.

Keh-Jiann Chen, Chu-Ren Huang, Li-Ping Chang, and Hui-Li Hsu. 1996. Sinica corpus: Design methodology for balanced corpora. In *Proceedings of the Eleventh Pacific Asia Conference on Language, Information and Computation*, pages 167–176.

A. C. Chen. 2011. *Prosodic phrasing in Mandarin conversational discourse: A computational-acoustic perspective*. Ph.D. thesis, Graduate Institute of Linguistics, National Taiwan University.

Jacob Cohen et al. 1960. A coefficient of agreement for nominal scales. *Educational and psychological measurement*, 20(1):37–46.

Chris Fournier and Diana Inkpen. 2012. Segmentation similarity and agreement. In *Proceedings of the Conference of the North American Chapter of the Association for Computational Linguistics: Human Language Technologies*, pages 152–161, Montréal, Canada.

James Paul Gee and François Grosjean. 1983. Performance structures: A psycholinguistic and linguistic appraisal. *Cognitive psychology*, 15(4):411–458.

Kim Gerdes, Sylvain Kahane, Anne Lacheret, Arthur Truong, and Paola Pietrandrea. 2012. Intonosyntactic data structures: The rhapsodie treebank of spoken french. In *Proceedings of the Linguistic Annotation Workshop @ COLING*.

Jonathan Ginzburg, Raquel Fernandez, Howard Gregory, and Shalom Lappin. 2007. Shards: Fragment resolution in dialogue.

Talmy Givón. 1993. *English grammar: A function-based introduction*, volume 2. John Benjamins, Amsterdam.

Daniel Hirst and Albert Di Cristo. 1984. French intonation: a parametric approach. *Die Neueren Sprachen*, 83(5):554–569.

Irina Illina, Dominique Fohr, Odile Mella, Christophe Cerisara, et al. 2004. The automatic news transcription system: Ants some real time experiments. In *8th International Conference on Spoken Language Processing-ICSLP*, page 4.

S.A. Jun and C. Fougeron. 2000. A phonological model of French intonation. *Intonation: Analysis, modelling and technology*, pages 209–242.

Anne Lacheret, Nicolas Obin, and Mathieu Avanzi. 2010. Design and evaluation of shared prosodic annotation for spontaneous french speech: from expert knowledge to non-expert annotation. In *Proceedings of the Fourth Linguistic Annotation Workshop*, pages 265–273. Association for Computational Linguistics.

Y.-F. Liu and S.-C. Tseng. 2009. Linguistic patterns detected through a prosodic segmentation in spontaneous Taiwan Mandarin speech. In S.-C. Tseng, editor, *Linguistic Patterns in Spontaneous Speech*, number A25 in Monograph Series, pages 147–166. Institute of Linguistics, Academia Sinica.

Amandine Michelas and Mariapaola D'Imperio. 2010. Accentual phrase boundaries and lexical access in french. In *Proceedings of Speech Prosody*.

Philippe Muller, Marianne Vergez-Couret, Laurent Prévot, Nicholas Asher, Benamara Farah, Myriam

Bras, Anne Le Draoulec, and Laure Vieu. 2012. Manuel d'annotation en relations de discours du projet annodis. Technical Report 21, CLLE-ERS, Toulouse University.

Marina Nespor and Irene Vogel. 1986. *Prosodic phonology*. Dordrecht.

Irina Nesterenko, Stephane Rauzy, and Roxane Bertrand. 2010. Prosody in a corpus of french spontaneous speech: perception, annotation and prosody˜ syntax interaction. In *Speech Prosody 2010-Fifth International Conference*.

Klim Peshkov, Laurent Prévot, Roxane Bertrand, Stéphane Rauzy, and Philippe Blache. 2012. Quantitative experiments on prosodic and discourse units in the corpus of interactional data. In *Proceedings of SemDial 2012: The 16th Workshop on the Semantics and Pragmatics of Dialogue*.

L. Pevzner and M. A. Hearst. 2002. A critique and improvement of an evaluation metric for text segmentation. *Computational Linguistics*, 28(1):19–36.

Cristel Portes, Roxane Bertrand, et al. 2011. Permanence et variation des unités prosodiques dans le discours et l'interaction. *Journal of French Language Studies*, 21(1).

Brechtje Post. 2000. *Tonal and phrasal structures in French intonation*, volume 34. Thesus.

Elisabeth Selkirk. 1986. *Phonology and syntax: The relation between sound and structure*. The MIT Press.

Anne Catherine Simon and Liesbeth Degand. 2009. On identifying basic discourse units in speech: theoretical and empirical issues. *Discours. Revue de linguistique, psycholinguistique et informatique*, (4).

Hongyin Tao. 1996. *Units in Mandarin conversation: Prosody, discourse, and grammar*, volume 5. John Benjamins Publishing Company.

S.-C. Tseng. 2013. Lexical coverage in taiwan mandarin conversation. *International Journal of Computational Linguistics and Chinese Language Processing*, 1(18):1–18.

Zeno Vendler. 1957. Verbs and times. *The philosophical review*, pages 143–160.

Nianwen Xue. 2008. Labeling chinese predicates with semantic roles. *Computational Linguistics*, 34(2):225–255.

*** Formatting Issue - Best Available Paper/Graphic ***

Corpus-based Research on Tense Analysis and Rhetorical Structure in Journal Article Abstracts

Pin-ning Tu
National Taiwan University of Science and Technology, Taiwan/ #43, Sec. 4, Keelung Rd. Da'an Dist., Taipei 106, Taiwan (R.O.C.)
promise523@hotmail.com

Shih-Ping Wang
National Taiwan University of Science and Technology, Taiwan/ #43, Sec. 4, Keelung Rd., Da'an Dist., Taipei 106, Taiwan (R.O.C.)
spwang2005@yahoo.com.tw

Abstract

There has long been a growing interest in journal articles (JA) abstract writing, and this pervading interest has boosted the exigency for further instructive research. This current study aims to investigate both the variant application of the verb tense as well as the rhetorical structure within JA abstracts. A 9.9 million word corpus of 1000 JAs was collected based on four prestigious journals, i.e., *o rna o ra ati s o rna o esear in ea in o rna o e on an a e Writin* and *ea in an Writin* , respectively. The quantitative analysis indicates the tendency of tense shown in the commonly applied reporting verbs. On the other hand, the qualitative analysis shows the prevailing adoption of three-, four-, and five-move theories in terms of the CARS model, the IMRD structure, and the IPMPrC structure. The results not only reveal the explicit tendency of the variance within reporting verbs but also suggest a distinct pervasiveness of the IMRD structure over the other models. These findings not only present a more systematic pattern within JA abstracts, but also show potentials for enlightening further pedagogy-oriented composition instruction for JA abstract.

1. Introduction

Previous studies have highlighted the indispensable importance of JA abstract in the contemporary flow. The pivotal role of JA abstract has received considerable attention in academic written genre among the international community. Swales (1990) appeals to the academia, claiming that the research in JA abstracts ought not to be ignored inasmuch of its influential significance upon the genre investigation and disciplinary discourse communities.

As the knowledge of proficient preferences for language choice as well as rhetorical structure has a great influence on academic written genre, many investigators have recently turned to the relevant research in relation to genre analysis, thematic organization, formulaic language, rhetorical structure, etc. (Cortes, 2004; Hyland, 2008a; Lorés, 2004; Martín, 2002; Swales, 1990; Wang & Chan, 2011; Wang & Kao, 2012). Furthermore, research in terms of corpora decoding for rhetorical structures such as moves and steps is also regarded as one of the recommendations for further research expansion by Flowerdew (2010).

Taking the contribution of the previous studies, this current reserach sets out to explore the variation of tense within the reporting verbs among the transitions of moves via the structural analysis in JA abstracts.

2. Literature review

In the respect of genre analysis, move analysis has been always considered to be one of the most influential elements. A move is a rhetorical element which serves the function of correlating and cohering within the written or spoken context (Lorés , 2004; Swales, 2004). However, it is not a definite unit which is constraint to perform in a fixed pattern because it is able to vary along with the context. In other words, move functions as a communicative role between each transition of the rhetorical structure.

A brief elaboration of the most pervasive move theory in terms of three-, four-, and five-moves is described in sequence.

2.1. Three-move theory

Create a Research Space (CARS) model, proposed by Swales (1990), has been widely used by scholars to outshine their publication in this competitive academia (Cheng, 2006). CARS model is divided into three moves, including establishing a territory, establishing a niche, and occupying the niche (Swales, 1990).

In other words, Move 1: establishing a territory can be commensurate with "goal" and "current capacity," synthesizing the research aim with the previous research (Swales, 1990, p. 142). As a consequence, Move 2: establishing a niche functions as offering a space for research gap and possible research questions (Swales, 1990). Under this circumstance, Move 3: occupying the niche will provide a "solution of criteria of evaluation" that taps into the intricacies which came up with in Move 2 section (Swales, 1990, p. 142).

2.2. Four-move theory

The most well-known and considerably applied structure in academic writing is the IMRD structure (i.e., Introduction, Methods, Results, and Discussion) (Golebiowski, 2009). It was first proposed by Ventola (1994).

To illustrate the content in depth, the introduction segment would cover the further elaborations of the purpose and objective of the current research. Lorés (2004) additionally comments that any other questions that could possibly bring out further open discussion might also be included in this Introduction segment. When it comes to the second stage – Method, a clarification of the scheme adopted in the research will be described (Lorés, 2004). As the lines progress, the Result segment is expected to offer critical information in relation to the findings from the implement of the research (Lorés, 2004). The final Discussion section is required to contain a further discussion of the findings, an exploration of possible research space and practical application (Lorés, 2004).

2.3. Five-move theory

Differing from the above discussed structures, the five-move theory – IPMPrC structure, proposed by Hyland (2004), is especially designed to access the RA abstracts. Nevertheless, it is clarified in the first place that the aim of setting this five move structure lies in providing an assertion in relation to JA abstract conducting as well as an inter-textual projection in terms of the significance of each research instead of addressing definite move steps (Hyland, 2004).

In an attempt to provide a clearer framework of the main characteristics of the IPMPrC structure, Table 1 elaborates the primary functions of each move in the five-move theory (Hyland, 2004, p. 67).

Move	Function
Introduction	Establishes context of the paper and motivates the study or discussion.
Purpose	Indicates purpose, thesis or hypothesis, outlines the intention behind the paper.
Method	Provides information on design, procedures, assumptions, approach, data, etc.
Product	States main findings or results, the argument, or what was accomplished.
Conclusion	Interprets or extends results beyond scope of paper, draws inferences, points to applications or wider implications.

Table 1: IPMPrC structure

3. Methodology

In an attempt to shed lights on the various dimensions that are possibly exposed from the academic written genre, a total of 1000 journal articles, which comprises 9,983,482 tokens out of 117,855 types of distinct words, were extracted evenly from four prestigious academic journals: *o rna o ra ati s* (JOP), *o rna o esear in ea in* (JRR), *o rna o e on an a e Writin* (JSLW), and *ea in an Writin* (R&W).

In accordance with the principle aim of this current research, that is, to specify the variation of verb tense and rhetorical structure in JA abstracts, 1000 abstracts were additionally extracted from the retrieved research materials, and constructed as the primary research corpora. Table 2 compares the tokens and types of the five primary corpora.

Type of Corpora	No.	Tokens	Types
JOP abstracts corpus	250	47,074	6,068
JRR abstracts corpus	250	39,699	4,001
JSWL abstracts corpus	250	45,520	4,265
R&W abstracts corpus	250	45,700	3,679
1,000 abstracts corpus	1,000	177,945	9,711

Table 2: Comparison among research corpora

The data analysis is twofold. On the one hand, the quantitative analysis focuses on the investigation of verb tense, especially set out for reporting verbs, by manipulating the analytical instruments such as *ono on ro* and *Wor it ersion* .

On the other hand, the qualitative analysis of consists in the assessment of the rhetorical structure in accordance with CARS model, the

IMRD structure, and the IPMPrC structure. Table 3 below illustrates the comparison of different transitions among the applied theories from three to five moves.

Three moves CARS model	**Four moves** IMRD structure	**Five moves** IPMPrC structure
Context	Introduction	Introduction
Gap	Methods	Purpose
Present study	Results	Methods
	Discussion	Product
		Conclusion

Table 3: Comparison of move theories

4. Results

The current study reports on two dimensions in JA abstracts: verb tense and rhetorical structure. Firstly, the analysis of verb has uncovered a prevailing application of be-verbs, such as *is*, *are*, *as*, *ere*, as well as reporting verbs such as *s o , e a ine*, *s est*, *in esti ate*, and *in* , in applied frequency sequence. It is reasonably assumed that the different application pattern of be-verb contains two possibilities: plain statement as well as passive voice.

Prior to tackling the various findings on the different tense of verbs, a clearer comparison of how be-verb is applied in each of the research corpora is shown in Table 4.

Form	JOP	JRR	JSLW	R&W	ALL
is	**526**	200	275	173	1204
are	**329**	206	213	153	901
was	75	**300**	134	**355**	864
were	83	**374**	243	**442**	1142
be	192	110	140	94	536
total	1,205	1,190	1,005	1,217	4,647

Table 4: Frequency of be-verbs

As can be seen from Table 4, it is apparent that JOP has its tendency to use present tense whereas JRR and R&W has similar tendency to apply past tense. This finding also reflects on the results obtained from the reporting verbs, as shown in Table 5.

Form	JOP	JRR	JSLW	R&W	ALL
show	**63**	21	32	19	135
-s	22	8	11	2	43
-ing	3	6	1	4	14
-ed	13	**77**	26	**88**	204
examine	**19**	16	21	40	96
-s	**32**	16	25	5	78
-ing	7	3	12	7	29
-ed	14	**53**	24	**81**	172
suggest	26	31	39	46	**142**
-s	15	23	23	7	**68**
-ing	2	8	9	9	28
-ed	9	9	20	12	50
investigate	**19**	19	18	25	81
-s	**20**	5	16	5	46
-ing	5	4	6	5	20
-ed	13	**32**	28	**46**	119
find	5	15	14	5	39
-s	2	1	----	----	3
-ing	----	----	2	----	2
-ed	**38**	**54**	**51**	**60**	**203**

Table 5: Frequency of reporting verbs

It can be seen from the data shown in Table 5 that the each research corpus has its tendency towards the application of tense as stated in the analysis of be-verbs, except for the single peculiar example "find." When it comes to the reporting verb "find," it was found that this particular word possesses its consistent tendency of past tense or passive voice in all reserach corpora. The practical examples of past tense and passive voice extracted from each research corpus are demonstrated below.

- *ina t e st* ***found*** *t at i e t e a orit o t e o p aints on rip isor an e onsi ere in ire t or t ir part o p aints t ere ere ne ert e ess so e e a p es t at r t e ire t in ire t i oto* (JOP – past tense)
- *t* ***was found that*** *a t o t e sa e is o rse o e iti ation t e i e is se in so e o t e ar ents a ressers app t eir o n e perien e to t eir ie s o t is is o rse an t s reate opposin ar ents* (JOP – passive voice)
- *We* ***found*** *an asso iation et een t e an et ni it in i atin t at t a orit i ren an i ren ro i a i ies a in enera t e ost sti atin s* (JRR – past tense)
- *t* ***was found that*** *etter no e e as spe i i a re ate to t e e e op ent o p one e se entation in pre iterate i ren* (JRR – passive voice)

***** Formatting Issue - Best Available Paper/Graphic *****

- *W i e so e **found that** peer o ents ere ie e it s epti is an in e itt e re ision ot ers **found that** t e i e p earners to i enti an raise a areness o t eir stren t s an ea nesses in ritin* (JSLW – past tense)
- *e est eas re **was found** to e tota or s in error ree a ses* (JSLW – passive voice)
- *prin ipa o ponents ana sis **found** partia isso ia i it et een i er e e s i s in in rea in o pre ension o a ar an print e pos re an o er e e s i s in in e o in an spe in in a t rea ers* (R&W – past tense)
- *ot or rea in an o pre ension **were found to be** i sta e an eneti in en es ere pri ari responsi e or t at sta i it* (R&W – passive voice)

Turning to the exploration of the move analysis has revealed a wide application of three-, four-, and five-move theory in JA abstracts. The distribution of the applied rhetorical structure is shown in Table 6.

JA Abstract Corpora	CARS model		IMRD structure		IPMPrC structure	
	N	%	N	%	N	%
JOP	48	19.2	119	47.6	83	33.2
JRR	32	12.8	166	66.4	52	20.8
JSLW	71	**28.4**	95	**38**	84	**33.6**
R&W	22	8.8	159	63.6	69	27.6
ALL	173	17.3	539	**53.9**	288	28.8

Table 6: Application of move theories

As can be seen in Table 6, IMRD structure is the most commonly applied rhetorical structure. There are 53.9% over half of the JA abstracts which were found out to be written in accordance with the IMRD structure. Table 7 illustrates the transitions of the moves in IMRD structure, which was randomly selected from the JRR abstract corpus.

Move	JA abstract from JRR corpus
I	This semi-longitudinal study **examined** the development of narrative writing quality of young Turkish second language learners in mainstream Dutch-only education, and the impact of student-level and classroom-level predictors of narrative writing quality, using hierarchical linear modelling.
M	Writing samples of 106 third graders and 111 fourth graders of seven Flemish primary schools **were** collected at the beginning and at the end of the school year. Measures included one holistic primary trait judgement, and six objective indices of text quality. Student-level predictors included age, SES and home language, while the classroom-level predictor focused on the home language pattern of the classroom.
R	There **was** a significant mean growth for each index in each grade, but effect sizes differed from quite large for content and word level indices over moderate for sentence level indices to small for the text level index. Home language (Turkish) had a significant negative effect on all but one variables, particularly in Grade 4, while the negative effect of low SES was much more limited. A supplementary negative effect was found for homogeneity of classroom population.
D	**Implications** of the study highlight the importance of student and classroom characteristics in writing achievement as well as the need to consider the poor performance of Turkish children.

Table 7: Example of IMRD structure

Table 7 shows that the JA abstract was constructed with (I) the specific research focus, (M) the sampling and participants, (R) main findings, and (D) the derived implications. It can be especially observed from the highlighted boldfaced words in Table 7 that the tendency of verb tense and the reprting verb choice were found out to be reflecting the findings, which indicated the tendency of past tense as well as passive voice applied in JRR corpus, stated in the former sections.

The second example, randomly selected from JSLW corpus (see Table 8), is the IPMPrC structure, which was found out to contain 28.8% of the JA abstracts written in this structural pattern.

Move	JA abstract from JOP corpus
I	Hedges and boosters **are** important metadiscursive resources for writers to mark their epistemic stance and position writer–reader relations.
P	Building on previous research that suggests notable cross-cultural and cross-linguistic differences in the use of hedges and boosters in academic discourse, this comparative study **investigates** the use of such discourse markers in academic article abstracts.
M	Based on a **corpus** of 649 abstracts collected from 8 journals of applied linguistics, this study **examines** if hedging and boosting strategies differ (a) between applied linguists publishing in Chinese- and English-medium

	journals and (b) between authors of empirical and non-empirical academic articles.
Pr	Quantitative analyses indicated that abstracts published in English-medium journals featured markedly more hedges than those published in Chinese-medium journals and that abstracts of empirical research articles used significantly more boosters than those of non-empirical academic articles. Textual analyses further revealed that the distinct patterning of hedges and boosters in Chinese and English abstracts had a joint, interactive effect on the authorial certainty and confidence conveyed therein.
C	These results **are discussed** in terms of culturally preferred rhetorical strategies, epistemological beliefs, lack of facility in English as a second/foreign language, and the nature of supporting evidence drawn on for knowledge claims in different types of academic writing.

Table 8: Example of IPMPrC structure

Table 8 presents the trasitions of the five-move theory from (I) establishing the context, (P) staing the main purpose, (M) methodology, (Pr) emerged observations, and (C) discussions. Interestingly, the contrary tendency of present tense is also reflected in the randonly selected example, as shown in Table 8.

Turning now to the findings of the three-move structure. It was revealed that only 17.3% of the JA abstracts were written in accordace with the CARS model; however, the minority does not shatter the irreplacable importance that each move theory possesses. The example randomly selected from the JSLW abstract corpus is demonstrated in Table 9.

Move	JA abstract from JSLW corpus
1	English as an Additional Language (EAL) students' textual borrowing in disciplinary writing **has attracted** wide research interest in recent years.
2	**However**, much of the research was conducted in the regular curriculum setting while the relevance of the issue in a writing-for-publication context has largely been overlooked. In particular, disciplinary experts' perspectives concerning textual borrowing **have not been explored in-depth**.
3	The present study **fills** such a gap in the literature by looking into how an expert writer, a professor of biochemistry in a Chinese university, perceived novices' textual borrowing in their initial drafts and eliminated such borrowing as he redrafted novice texts for publication. The study **revealed** that the expert had complete tolerance for his students' copying and that his elimination of it during redrafting was guided by his genre expertise and rhetorical skills for publishing. The paper also **pointed out** that the shortage of explicit teaching from the supervisor to his students as well as the lack of active participation of his students in the writing process was bound to the publication pressure in the local institutional context.

Table 9: Example of CARS model

It is clear that the transition of the three-move theory set out from (1) appealing to readers' attention, (2) indicating the gap, and (3) presenting the current findings. The highlighted boldfaced words imply the impartial selection of tense shown in the JSLW abstract corpus.

5. Concluding remarks

This current research aimed to investigate tense analysis as well as rhetorical structure in JA abstracts. The implemented data analysis has indicated the variant but consistent tendency of verb tense in each discipline. The findings of the verb tense are reflected in the assessment as shown in the transitions of rhetorical structure. It is believed that the variations of verb tense as well as the rhetorical structure are strongly connected and interrelated. Despite the lack of pedagogical experiment design that has led this study to the limitation of not knowing the actual benefit of the research findings for language learners, it is determined that the acquired language use and the structural pattern suggest authentic disciplinary conventions on linguistic productions.

References

Cheng, A. (2006). Analyzing and enacting academic criticism: The case of an L2 graduate learner of academic writing. *o rna o e on an a e Writin* (4), 279-306.

Cortes, V. (2004). Lexical bundles in published and student disciplinary writing: Examples from history and biology. *n is or pe i i rposes* (4), 397-423.

Flowerdew, L. (2010). Using corpora for writing instruction. In A. O'keeffe & M. McCathy (Eds.), *e ro t e e an oo o orp s in isti s* (pp. 444-457). London: Routledge.

*** Formatting Issue - Best Available Paper/Graphic ***

Golebiowski, Z. (2009). Prominent messages in Education and Applied Linguistics abstracts: How do authors appeal to their prospective readers? *o rna o ra ati s* (4), 753-769.

Hyland, K. (2004). *is ip inar is o rses o ia intera tions in a a e i ritin* . Ann Arbor: The University of Michigan Press.

Lorés, R. (2004). On RA abstracts: from rhetorical structure to thematic organisation. *n is or pe i i rposes* (3), 280-302.

Martín, P. M. (2002). A genre analysis of English and Spanish research paper abstracts in experimental social sciences. *n is or pe i i rposes* (1), 25–43.

Swales, J. M. (1990). *enre ana sis n is in a a e i an resear settin s*. Cambridge, UK: Cambridge University Press.

Swales, J. M. (2004). *esear enres p oration an app i ations*. Cambridge, UK: Cambridge University Press.

Ventola, E. (1994). Abstracts as an object of linguistic study. In S. Cmejrkova, F. Danes & E. Havlova (Eds.) *Writin s pea in an a e e t is o rse o ni ation.*(pp. 333–52). Tubingen: G. Narr.

Wang, S.P., & Chan, C.W. (2011). Research on wordlists, lexical bundles and text structures of journal article abstracts. In R.F. Chung, et al. (Eds.), *i ersit o an a es apers in onor o ro essor en sao on t e asion o is etire ent* (pp. 369-381). Taipei: Crane Publisher Co.

Wang, S.P., & Kao, C.L. (2012). Wordlists, clusters and structure in research article introductions. *t ies in n is an a e an iterat re,* , 27-43.

A Novel Schema-Oriented Approach for Chinese New Word Identification

Zhao Lu
Dept. of Computer Science and Technology, East China Normal University
zlu@cs.ecnu.edu.cn

Zhixian Yan
Samsung Research America, Silicon Valley, USA
zhixian.yan@samsung.com

Junzhong Gu
Dept. of Computer Science and Technology, East China Normal University
jzgu@cs.ecnu.edu.cn

Abstract

With the popularity of network applications, new words become more common and bring the poor performance of natural language processing related applications including web search. Identifying new words automatically from texts is still a very challenging problem, especially for Chinese. In this paper, we propose a novel schema-oriented approach for Chinese new word identification (named "ChNWI"). This approach has three main steps: (1) we suggest three composition schemas that cover nearly all two-character up to four-character Chinese word surfaces; (2) we employ support vector machine (SVM) to classify Chinese new words of three schemas using their unique linguistic characteristics; and (3) we design various rules to filter identified Chinese new words of three schemas. Our extensive evaluations with two corpora (Chinese news titles and CIPS-SIGHAN 2012 CSMB) show ChNWI's efficiency on Chinese new word identification.

1 Introduction

With the rapid development of information technology, as well as the growth of social networks (e.g., Chinese Microblog, WeChat), Chinese new words are constantly being created and their usages have become an inevitable phenomenon. Automatic identification of new words plays an important role in a number of areas in Chinese language processing, such as automatic segmentation, information retrieval and machine translation (Zhang et al., 2010; Duan et al., 2012). In the Chinese new word identification (NWI) task, new words refer to new composition words that are not registered in the dictionary of a Chinese segmenter.

Statistical approaches are the most widely used methods in NWI. The previous methods extract some linguistic features of new word compositions, i.e., *word composition probability*, *cooccurrence probability*, *mutual information*, and *word frequency*, while they assume above linguistic features playing the same impact on various word surfaces (Chang and Lee, 2003; Li et al., 2008; Zhang et al., 2010). Some methods also have binary decision, either "new words" or "not new words". A SVM-based method (Li et al., 2008) aims at two word surfaces, NW11 and NW21, and the method uses same linguistic features for the two surfaces. Other statistical models, for instance, a latent discriminative model (Pang et al., 2009), a linear-time incremental model (Zhang et al., 2012) and conditional random fields (CRFs) model (Wang et al., 2012), are designed for NWI.

Recently, some hybrid methods have been suggested. These hybrid methods employ more or fewer rules for statistical methods to obtain an optimal efficiency of identification. However, the rules these methods used are created by the people, which cause these methods are not suitable for other new word composition schemas (Zhang et al., 2006; Jiang et al., 2011; Xi et al., 2012).

Despite the wide studies of new word identifications, accurately identifying Chinese new words from texts automatically is still a very challenging task because of the following reasons:

- Most existing studies focus on English and these methods are not suitable for Chinese. Chinese new words have less morphology variations than many other languages, and there is a lack of capital clues as in English. In Chinese, there are not special symbols implying boundaries between two words and any adjacent characters can form a word. This is one main reason of the difficulty to recognize new words from texts.

- A survey of the literature indicates that there are eleven surfaces of four-tuple Chinese words, while those methods focus on two surfaces (i.e., NW11 and NW21). They use same linguistic characteristics and same filtering rules for the two surfaces. The two aspects cause the lower accurate rate and the problem of data sparseness.

To address these challenges, in this paper, we propose a schema-oriented Chinese new word identification approach which combining SVM and rules, it is called "ChNWI". The ChNWI approach has two main parts, i.e., (1) ChNWI training process, in which we first define three word composition schemas, their particular linguistic characteristics, and one basic feature model with other three feature models for three schemas; (2) ChNWI testing process, in which we identifying new words of three schemas from segmented fragments using various filtering rules of three schemas. Concluded, this paper has the following three main contributions:

- We classify eight of eleven surfaces of four-tuple Chinese words into three composition schemas, i.e., single-character schema, affix schema and NW22 schema. We study their special linguistic characteristics of the three schemas.

- We design a rich set of features models for the three schemas by analyzing their linguistic characterises. We hereinafter apply SVM as our basic classifier due to its robustness, efficiency and higher performance than other classifiers, for instance, Perceptron, Naive Bayes and kNN (Li et al., 2008). Furthermore, we design filter rules for the three schemas to refine the NWI decision.

- We evaluate ChNWI on two corpora, *i.e.*, a collected Chinese news title dataset and a popular MicroBlog dataset. The experimental results show the efficiency of ChNWI on Chinese new word identification.

The remaining sections of this paper are organized as follows. Section 2 presents the main framework of our ChNWI approach. Section 3 introduces three new word composition schemas, their linguistic characteristics and their feature models. Section 4 discusses the training process and the test process of ChNWI. We conduct several experiments and analyze experimental evaluations in section 5. Finally, we conclude this paper and discuss future work.

2 Our ChNWI appraoch

In this section, we first formulate the task in this paper, then we present our approach in general.

The task of identifying Chinese new words in this paper is concluded as: after extracting strings of three kinds of schemas from segmented fragments, we compute the confidence degree of these strings using both their special linguistic characteristics, together with SVM; we select these strings with their confidence degree larger than a certain threshold as new word candidates.

The confidence degree of a Chinese new word with the feature set x belongs to the category y is defined as the co-occurrence probability $p(x, y)$ of the category y and the feature set x. The category y refers to "Chinese new words" or "not Chinese new words", and x is the feature vectors of a new word. Formally, given a training sample set, $T = \{(x_1, y_1), (x_2, y_2), ..., (x_n, y_n)\}$, where $x_i \in R^n, y_i \in \{-1, 1\}$. x_i refers to the feature vectors of new words, y_i is the category of a new word.

The framework of ChNWI is shown in Figure 1. Two main parts of the suggested ChNWI approach are the training process and the testing process.

The training process includes: (1) we first segment and POS tagging the training corpus using a Chinese word segmenter; (2) After extracting linguistic characteristics of three schemas, we generate three feature vectors for three schemas using their positive samples and negative samples; (3) Three feature models for the three schemas are generated using the SVM classifier.

The steps of the ChNWI testing process are: (1) we segment and POS tagging the test corpus and extract potential strings of three schemas using two suggested algorithms; (2) we extract three feature vectors for three schemas using the extracted linguistics characteristics during the ChNWI training process; (3) we identify new word candidates of three schemas using the three generated SVM models. Finally, we suggest various rules to filter all candidates.

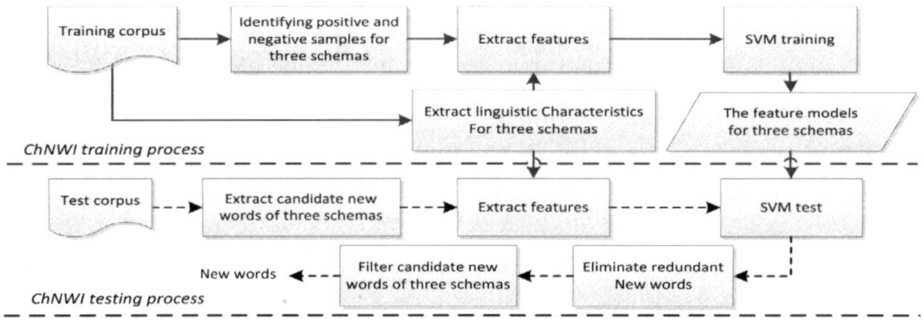

Figure 1: The ChNWI Framework

3 Three schemas of Chinese new words and their feature models

In this section, we present three schemas of Chinese new words and define their feature models.

3.1 Various surfaces of Chinese new words

Literature (Jiang et al., 2011) shows that, all four-tuple Chinese new words can be classified into 11 compositions, i.e., 53 % new words of NW11, 31% new words of NW21, 5% new words of NW12 and NW31, and 11% other schemas. Here, NW is the abbreviation of New Word, 1 refers to a single character, 2 refers to a binary word, 3 refers to a ternary word. After investigating the features of these compositions, we classify four-tuple Chinese new words into three schemas, i.e., *single-character schema*, *affix schema* and *NW22 schema*. The three schemas cover nearly above 11 compositions.

3.1.1 Single-character schema

The new words of *single-character schema* are composed of up to four consecutive single characters. The single-character schema includes, NW11, NW111 and NW1111. Some examples of single-character schema are:

(1) NW11, 蚁/ng 族/n (yi/ng zu/n)

(2) NW111, 经/n 适/n 房/n (jing/n shi/n fang/n)

(3) NW1111, 反/n 独/d 促/v 统/vi (fan/n du/d cuc/v tong/vi).

There are less linguistic characteristics for new words of single-character schema mainly because of most of all single characters have no combined features with their neighboring ones, thus up to four adjacent characters can be viewed as a new word.

3.1.2 Affix schema

The second surface type is "affix schema". A new word of affix schema is composed by a single character and an existing word. Affix schema can be further classified as *prefix schema* and *suffix schema*. Prefix schema includes NW12 (a single character with an existing binary word) and NW13 (a single character with an existing ternary word), e.g., 反通胀(Anti inflation). Suffix schema includes NW21 (an existing binary word with a single character) and NW31 (an existing ternary word with a single character), for example, 国土部(Ministry of Land and Resources).

Both prefix schema and suffix schema have strong linguistic characteristics. The first character is easy to combine with a binary word to compose a ternary new word, or with a ternary word to constitute a four tuple new word. These kinds of first characters are viewed as *prefix letters*, such as, 零(zero), 软(soft) and 反(anti).

The last character (or the tail character) of suffix schema is easy to combine a binary word to form a ternary new word, or with a ternary word to form a four tuple new word. We view the kinds of tail characters as *suffix letters*, for instance, 部(department), 率(rate) and 式(style).

3.1.3 NW22 schema

New words of NW22 schema are mainly composed by two binary words. Some examples are 人口普查(Census) and 热带风暴(Tropical storm). Unlike single-character schema and affix schema, this kind of new words have less special linguistic characteristics for the reason of two adjacent binary words can compose a new word of NW22. Since there are not significant characteristics of NW22, it is difficult to identify these new words.

3.2 Feature models for three schemas

We first suggest a base feature model for three schemas, then we propose a special feature model for each schema.

3.2.1 Basic feature model

For new words of three schemas, some linguist characteristics are important, i.e., co-occurrence, mutual information, word frequency and adjunct categories. The base feature model (Base_F) for three schemas is defined as follows,

$$Base_F\{F_F, F_{COP}, F_{MI}, F_{AV}\} \quad (1)$$

here, F_F refers to word frequency, F_{COP} is co-occurrence probability or average co-occurrence probability, F_{MI} is mutual information or average mutual information, F_{AV} is adjacent categories.

Word frequency is a basic characteristic of new words, especially for NW22 schema. This characteristic is an important aspect of determining whether a string is a new word or not. We view a string S in a corpus is a new word candidate if its frequency is larger than a pre-defined threshold. In this paper, we set the threshold to 2 for the aim of covering mostly new word candidates.

Co-occurrence probability show the tightness degree of two Chinese characters or two words A and B. The higher their co-occurrence probability, the higher the tightness degree of A and B is. The greater the tightness degree is, the more easier A with B to compose a new word.

Mutual information indicates the relevant degree of two continuous strings A and B. Mutual information not only reflects the possibility of the combination of two continuous strings to be a word, but also measures the internal relevant degree of a word. We use *average mutual information* to indicate the coupling degree of continuous characters or words in a string S (Luo and Sun, 2003). The higher the average mutual information of S is, the higher its coupling degree is. Which means the higher possibility of S is to be a new word (Zhou, 2005).

Adjacent category represents the relevant degree among a word (or a string) with its context. Adjacent category $AV(S)$ can be further divided into *left adjacent category* (L_{AV}) and *right adjacent category* (R_{AV}). Given a Chinese string S, its adjacent category is defined as follows,

$$AV(S) = min\{L_{AV}(S), R_{AV}(S)\} \quad (2)$$

here, $L_{AV}(S)$ and $R_{AV}(S)$ refer to the numbers of the words in which the string S appearing in the left or in the right of the words respectively.

In a sentence, a string is viewed as a word if it satisfies that, its cohesive degree is higher and its coupling degree with its context is lower. For a term, its various contexts cause its left adjacent category and its right adjacent category are large numbers. From this consideration, for a Chinese string S, if its left adjacent category value or its right adjacent categories are larger than a predetermined threshold, which means that the string S is loose with its context and it is higher possibility of being a Chinese new word. That is the reason we view the two adjacent categories with lower values to be the adjacent category of the string S in Equation (2).

3.2.2 Feature model for single-character schema

As a new word of single-character schema is a string of continuous characters in a segmented fragment, for single-character schema, we add *independent word probability* (IWP) into the base feature model to get a new feature model, which is called as the feature model of single-character schema (F_{single}) as follows,

$$F_{single}\{F_{IWP}, F_F, F_{COP}, F_{MI}, F_{AV}\} \quad (3)$$

Independent word probability of a string S ($S = c_1, c_2, ..., c_n$) is defined as the joint probability of all characters in the string. We assume that, the higher the independent word probability of a string S is, the higher the probability of S being a new word is. Based on the assumption, we take a string as a new word candidate if its $IWP(S)$ is larger than a pre-defined threshold.

3.2.3 Feature models for affix schema

New words of affix schema have relatively significant linguistic features. That is the probability of the affix characters appearing in the head or the tail of a word is very high. That is to say, the affix characters are easy to compose new words together with existing words or other characters. From this observation, we can compute the head-character word probability $IWP(C, f)$ and the tail-character word probability $IWP(C, l)$ for a word of affix schema. We further classify the feature model of affix schema into two categories, the prefix feature model (F_{prefix}) and the suffix feature model (F_{suffix}), as follows,

$$F_{prefix}\{F_{IWP}(f), F_F, F_{COP}, F_{MI}, F_{AV}\} \quad (4)$$

$$F_{suffix}\{F_{IWP}(l), F_F, F_{COP}, F_{MI}, F_{AV}\} \quad (5)$$

here, $F_{IWP}(f)$ and $F_{IWP}(l)$ refer to the head-character word probability and the tail-character word probability respectively.

3.2.4 Feature model for NW22 schema

The third schema type is NW22 schema. The new word of NW22 schema is a combination of two existing words. It is obvious that, word probability, head-character word probability or tail-character word probability do not reflect the unique characteristics of NW22 schema. To NW22 schema, both the degree of combination between two existing words and the context of two words are important features. Therefore, we use the base feature model for NW22 schema only.

4 ChNWI training and testing process

4.1 The training process of ChNWI

We first determine positive samples and negative samples for three schemas respectively.

For single-character schema, positive samples mainly refer to words up to four characters in the dictionary of a segmenter, i.e., ICTCLAS, and any substrings of these words are not words. For example, 逃逸(escape), 麦当劳(McDonald's) and 说三道四(make irresponsible remarks) are words in the dictionary, while any sub-strings of the three words are not registered in the dictionary. Negative samples are the extracted continuous strings of NW11, NW111 and NW1111 in segmented fragments, while these strings are not registered as words in the segmenter.

The positive samples of affix schema are ternary words or quaternary words in the dictionary of a segmenter, and parts of these words are words also. For example, the first two characters of the word 户口本(hukou ben) is a word, and the last three characters of the word 喝西北风(he xibeifeng) is a word also. The negative samples of affix schema are these strings combined with a character and a word of NW12, NW13, NW21 and NW31, while they are not words in the dictionary.

For NW22 schema, positive samples are quaternary words in the dictionary, and half of these words are words also. Such as 历史纪录(historical record) and 汉语拼音(Chinese pinyin), parts of the two words are binary words. Negative samples are these strings combined by two binary words while they are not words in the dictionary.

Then we use LibSVM (Chang and Lin, 2011) to gain three SVM models for three schemas using positive samples and negative samples. In order to improve the accuracy of the SVM training model, we manually choose some negative samples as positive sample for three schemas respectively.

4.2 ChNWI testing process

4.2.1 Extracting new word candidates of three schemas

We suggest three methods to extract new word candidates of three schemas respectively.

(1) Extract new word candidates of single-character schema

As we discussed above, a new word of single-character schema is made up of two or more continuous characters in segmented fragments. That is, given a segment fragment $T = \{X_1X_2...X_i...X_n\}(1 \leq i \leq n)$, here, X_i is a word or a character. If there is a string $NW(i, j) = \{X_iX_{i+1}...X_j\}$ in T and each X_i in NW is a character, then we view the string NW as a new word candidate of single-character schema. If the length of NW is larger than 2, then its all sub-strings with lengths larger than or equal to 2 are new word candidates also. If $i = 0$ or X_{i-1} is not a character, and if $j = n$ or X_{j+1} is not a character, then $NW(i, j)$ is viewed as the *longest new word candidate*. For example, both 经适(jing shi) and 适房(shi fang) in 经适房(jing shi fang) are all viewed as new word candidates of single-character schema, 经适房(jing shi fang) is a longest new word candidate.

Given three strings of single-character schema, A, B and C, if there is $A = B + C$, and the lengths of B and C are smaller than or equal to 2, A is viewed as the *parent string* of B and C and both B and C are viewed as two *sub-strings* of A.

We present the process of extracting new word candidates of single-character schema as follows: firstly, we extract the longest new word candidates from the segmented test corpus, and count their frequencies using Algorithm 1; then, for each longest new word candidates, it's all substrings are extracted and their frequencies are counted using Algorithm 2.

Algorithm 1: The Candidate New Word Detection Algorithm(CND)

```
Input: SSTC
Output: slpuw, spuw
begin
    for each a_i in SSTC do
        get a_i = w[0]w[1]...w[k];
        for each w[j]w[j+1] in a_i do
            if the length of w[j] == 1 then
                if the length of w[j+1] == 1 then
                    add to spuw;
                else
                    N(w[j]w[j+1]) ++;
    set temp to null;
    for each w[j] in a_i do
        if length(w[j]) == 1 then
            w[j] appended to temp;
        else
            If length(temp) > 1 if temp not in slpuw then
                add temp to slpuw;
                set temp to null;
            else
                N(temp) ++;
                set temp to null
```

We use Algorithm 1 to extract all longest new word candidates of single-character schema in a segmented text $SSTC$. Here, $a = \{w[0]w[1]...w[k]\}$ is a segmented fragment in n $SSTC$. w is a part of a, it is maybe a word, a Chinese character, a number or an English character. $N(w)$ is the frequencies of w in the segmented fragments, $length(w)$ is the length of w, $slpuw$ is the longest new word candidate set of single-character schema, $spuw$ is the new word candidate set of affix schema.

Algorithm 2 is a sliding window algorithm which is used to extract all sub-strings of each longest new word candidate and their frequencies. The input and output of Algorithm 2are $spluw$ (the longest new word candidate set) and the new word candidate set. The main idea of Algorithm 2 is to traverse each longest new word candidate using a sliding window algorithm to extract all substrings with their lengths are larger than or equal to 2, and to count their frequencies.

(2) Extract new word candidates of affix schema

Algorithm 2: The Candidate New word Detection Algorithm(CND)

```
Input: slpuw
Output: A set subset of substring
begin
    for each c_k in slpuw do
        let s = c_k, j = 2, substring is null;
        for (; j < length(s); j++) do
            for (i = 0; i+j-1 < length(s); i++) do
                substring = s.sub(i, i+j);
                if substring not in subset then
                    added to subset;
                    N(substring) = N(s);
                else
                    N(substring) ++;
```

All new word candidates of two kinds of affix schema are collected using Algorithm 1 also. The main steps of extracting new word candidates of affix schema are: firstly, we traverse each segmented fragment, collect all strings of NW21 or NW31 as new word candidates and add them into the new word candidate set of suffix schema; then we collect all strings of NW12 or NW13 as new word candidates, and add them into the new word candidate set of prefix schema.

(3) Extract new word candidates of NW22

For new words of NW22 schema, the extraction process is: collect all strings of NW22 schema as new word candidates, and add them into the new word candidate set of NW22 schema also.

4.2.2 Eliminating redundant new word candidates

After extracting all new word candidates of three schemas, we will further eliminate all new word candidates with their frequencies less than 2, and eliminate all redundant new word candidates. For all new word candidates of single-character schema, since we collect all longest new word candidates and their sub-strings as new word candidates, there are redundant candidates in the collection.

The main steps of eliminating these redundant strings are as follows: given a parent string $C_iC_{i+1}...C_{i+j+1}$, its two substrings $C_{i+1}C_{i+2}...C_{i+j+1}$ and $C_iC_{i+1}...C_{i+j}$, the differences between the frequency of $N(C_iC_{i+1}...C_{i+j+1})$ and the frequencies of its substrings, $N(C_{i+1}C_{i+2}...C_{i+j+1})$ and

$N(C_iC_{i+1}...C_{i+j})$, is marked as a. If a is smaller than a predefined threshold b, then we view the two sub-strings are redundant. We remove the two strings and only keep the parent string. On the contrary, if the frequency $N(C_iC_{i+1}...C_{i+j})$ is larger than the frequency $N(C_iC_{i+1}...C_{i+j+1})$, or the frequency $N(C_{i+1}C_{i+2}...C_{i+j+1})$ is larger than the frequency $N(C_iC_{i+1}...C_{i+j+1})$, and the difference between them is larger than b, then we remove the parent string, and keep two sub-strings. In this paper, we set $b = 2$ for the minimum length of Chinese word is 2.

4.2.3 Filtering new word candidates

We design various filtering rules for the single-character schema and the affix schema.

For single-character schema, we use stop words to filter new word candidates. For example, 在(zai), 将(jiang), 称(chen) are often used in texts, while they with other characters or words cannot compose new words. So, for all candidates of single-character schema, if a word starts or ends with these characters, we will eliminate these candidates.

For affix schema, we use a head-character list and a tail-character list for the aim of filtering new word candidates. Some prefix characters, examples including "副, 近, 新" (fu, jin, xin) are often used in prefix schema. During the training process, we have added the top N of characters with their $IWP(f)$ values are bigger into the head-character list. For suffix schema, some suffix characters, for example, " 门, 热, 控" (men, re, kong) are used often. During the training process, we also add the top N characters with their $IWP(l)$ values are bigger into the tail-character list. We design the filtering rules of affix schema as: if the first character in a new word candidate of prefix schema is found in the tail-character list, then we ignore the new word candidate. For example, the first character 案(an) of a new word candidate 案抓获(an zhua huo) is in the tail-character list, so we remove the candidates. Similarly, if the tail character in a new word candidate of suffix schema is found in the head-character list, then we ignore the candidates.

For NW22 schema, there are not special rules to filter new word candidates of NW22 schema.

5 Experimental results and analysis

As we discussed above, new words studied in this paper related to the dictionary of the ICTCLAS segmenter [1], a popular segmenter developed by the Chinese Academy of Sciences. To test the efficiency of our approach, we design three experiments on three corpora. The first corpus is set of the domestic news titles on Sina.com.cn from June 2010 to July 2012, which contains 0.12 Million news titles. We divide the corpus into two parts, one is the testing corpus and the other is the training corpus. The second one is the MicroBlog corpora of CIPS-SIGHAN CLP 2012 Chinese Segmentation on MicroBlog Bakeoff (CSMB) (Duan et al., 2012), which contains 5,000 sentences.

In each ChNWI training process, we use cross-validation method to obtain the optimal training parameters. We divide the training corpus averagely into 10 parts, one is used to verify, the others are used for training. The numbers of features are: four features for single-character schema, six features for affix schema and four features for NW22 schema. The training time of every experiment for ChNWI models is not more than 4 minutes and the testing time is not more than 5 second using a laptop with an Intel(R) Core(TM) i3 CPU and 2.92G RAM.

For evaluation, we adopt the same evaluation method defined in the CSMB bake-off task, precision (P), recall(R) and F-measure.

$$P = \frac{\text{Number of new words correctely identified}}{\text{Number of new words are identified}} \quad (6)$$

$$R = \frac{\text{Number of new words correctely identified}}{\text{Number of new words in the corpus}} \quad (7)$$

$$F = \frac{2 * P * R}{P + R} \quad (8)$$

5.1 Experiments on the first corpus

In the first experiment, we investigate the related contributions of each feature model of each schema of ChNWI. The experimental results are shown in Figure 2. In Figure 2, #1 and #2 refer to $Base_F$ and F_{single}+Filtering rules of Single-character schema, #3 and #4 are $Base_F$ and F_{prefix}+Filtering rules of Prefix schema, #5 and #6 refer to $Base_F$ and F_{suffix}+Filtering rules of Suffix schema, and #7 refers to $Base_F$ of NW22 schema respectively.

[1]ICTCLAS, http://www.ictclas.org/

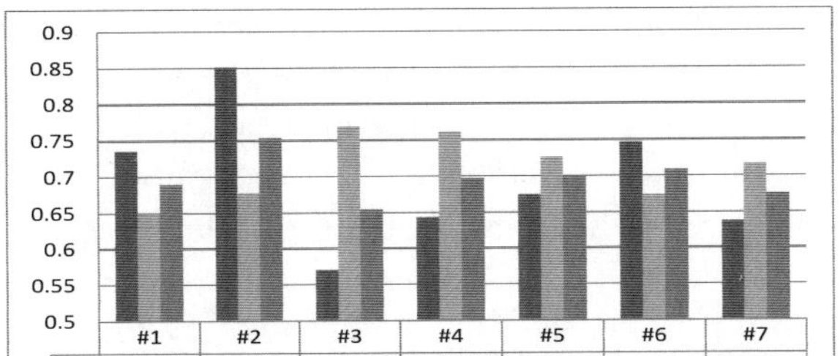

	#1	#2	#3	#4	#5	#6	#7
P	0.7356	0.8511	0.5706	0.6433	0.6742	0.746	0.6376
R	0.6492	0.6767	0.769	0.7603	0.7268	0.6731	0.7164
F	0.69	0.7539	0.6549	0.697	0.6995	0.7077	0.6747

Figure 2: Experiments on contributions of various feature models

Test on single-character schema

In the feature model F_{single}, independent word probability is a special linguistic characteristic. To show the effectiveness of independent word probability, we first use the base model, $Base_F$, then we use the feature model F_{single} of single-character schema, together with the corresponding filtering rules.

In Figure 2, #1 and #2 are the experimental results of single-character schema. To some extent, our approach can identify new words of single-character schema effectively. Especially we add the feature F_{IWP} and the relevant filtering rules to the base model, the precision rates improves 11.6% and F-value also increase 6.39%.

Test on Affix schema

Affix schema can be divided into prefix schema and suffix schema.

The feature model for prefix schema is F_{prefix}. In which, the first word probability is an important linguistic characteristics. To show the contribution of first word probability, we first use the base model, $Base_F$, then, we use F_{prefix} with the corresponding filtering rules. The experimental results of prefix schema are shown as #3 and #4 of Figure 2. Our approach has good effectiveness of identifying new words of prefix schema also. Using F_{IWP} and filtering rules, the correct rate improves 7.27%, while F value improves 4.21%.

In the feature model F_{suffix} of suffix schema, the tail word probability is also an important feature. We first use the base model $Base_F$, then we employ F_{suffix} and the relevant filtering rule. The experimental results of suffix schema are #5 and %6 of Figure 2. Similar to prefix schema, our method has better efficiency on identifying new words of suffix schema. After using $F_{IWP(l)}$ and filtering rules, the correct rate improves 7.18% and F-value improves 0.8%.

Test on NW22 schema

As we discussed above, there are less linguistic characteristics of NW22 schema, so we use the base model $Base_F$ as the feature model of NW22 schema. The experimental result of NW22 schema is #7 of Figure 2. #7 shows that our method has better effectiveness on identifying new words of NW22 schema. The F-score of NW22 schema is more than 67%.

5.2 Experiment on MicroBlog Corpora

We perform the second experiment to find how ChNWI improves the performance of a Chinese segmenter. We test ChNWI on the MicroBlog Corpora suggested by CIPS-SIGHAN-2012 CSMB. The corpora includes 294 new words (14%) and 252 rule-based combination of words (12%). Both the two words are unregistered words to a segmenter. The performance of the two test points is, the max correct numbers of the two test points are 65 (22.1%) of new words and near 70 (27.8%) of rule-based combination of words (Duan et al., 2012). Which shows that the systems submitted may not deal with unregistered words well.

The CIPS-SIGHAN-2012 CSMB provides no training set, we train ChNWI on the training corpus used in the first experiment. In the second experiment, we select the ICTCLAS segmenter and the suggested ChNWI is used as post processing. The experimental results are shown in Figure 3 and Figure 4. All data of the maximal (Max) and the average (Avg) performance of Figure 3 and Figure 4 are from the report (Duan et al., 2012).

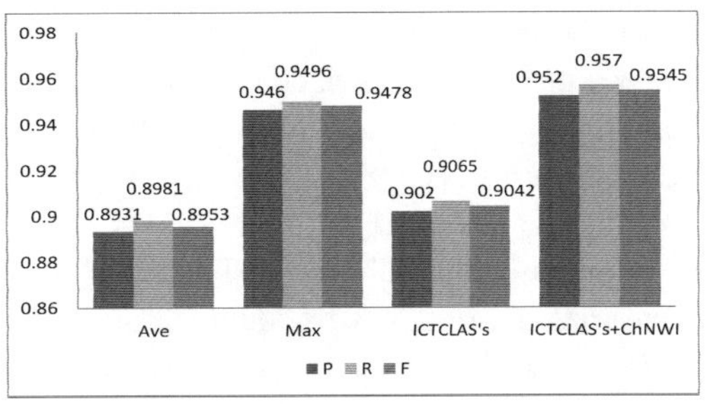

Figure 3: Experimental results of ICTCLAS's with ChNWI on MicroBlog corpus

Figure 3 shows that, compared with ICTCLAS's, F-score of ICTCLAS's + ChNWI is improved near 5%. Compared with Avg and Max,

F-scores of ICTCLAS's + ChNWI are improved 0.6% and near 6 % respectively.

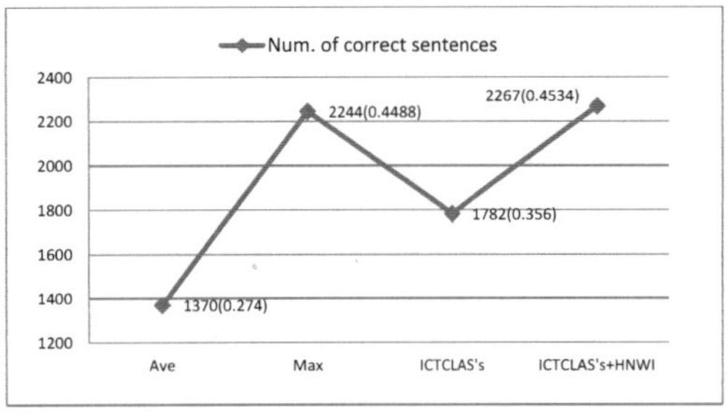

Figure 4: Numbers (and percentages) of correct sentences segmented by ICTCLAS's with ChNWI in MicroBlog corpus

Figure 4 shows the numbers (and percentages) of correct sentences segmented by ICTCLAS's and ICTCLAS's+ChNWI. The number and percentage of correct sentences are improved 485 and 9.7% respectively.

6 Conclusion and future work

In this paper, we propose the ChNWI approach to identify Chinese new words of three schemas. We first summarize three schemas based on eight surfaces, they are single-character schema (covers NW11, NW111 and NW1111), affix schema (spans NW21, NW31, NW12 and NW13) and NW22 schema. Next, we represent that four linguistics features, i.e., *word frequency*, *co-occurrence probability*, *mutual information* and *adjacent category*, play same impacts on the three schemas, while *independent word probability* is important to single-character schema, *head-character word probability* and *tail-character word probability* are key facts to prefix schema and suffix schema respectively. Our experimental results on two corpora show that, new words are categorized into three schemas and employing their unique features not only improve the accuracy score but also improve the recall rate of identification.

We also test the ChNWI approach on the domain-related (Mobile Communication) corpus with 80 thousand sentences. All these sentences are collected from Baidubaike and Wikipedia. With the development of new business in the Mobile Communication domain, there are a considerable amount of new words which are not registered in the dictionary of a segmenter. We test our approach in identifying new words of the three schemas contained in the domain-related corpus. The ChNWI approach gets three accuracy rates, 80%, 68% and 71%, for single-character schema, affix schema and NW22 schema respectively.

In future, we further improve the ChNWI approach from the following three aspects: (1) apply automatic feature selection and check the performance; (2) consider the combination of different schemas for other surfaces (i.e., NW211 and NW112). (3) study additional schemas rather than the three suggested schemas.

Acknowledgement

This work is sponsored by the grant from the Shanghai Science and Technology Foundation (No. 11511504002).

References

Chih-Chung Chang, and Chih-Jen Lin. 2011. Libsvm: A library for support vector machines. *ACM Transactions on Intelligent Systems and Technology.*

Guodong Zhou. 2005. A chunking strategy towards unknown word detection in Chinese word segmentation. *Lecture Notes in Computer Science*, 3651:530–541.

Haijun Zhang, Shumin Shi, Chaoyong Zhu, and Heyan Huang. 2010. Survey of Chinese New Words Identification. *Computer Science*, 37(3):6–11.

Hongqiao Li, Chang-Ning Huang, Jianfeng Gao, and Xiaozhou Fan. 2005. The use of SVM for Chinese new word identification. *First international joint conference on Natural Language Processing*, 723–732.

Huiming Duan, Zhifang Sui, Ye Tian, and Wenjie Li. 2012. The CIPS-SIGHAN CLP 2012 ChineseWord Segmentation onMicroBlog Corpora Bakeoff. *Second CIPS-SIGHAN Joint Conference on Chinese Language Processing*, 35–40.

Jiahen Zheng, and Wenhua Li. 2002. A Study on Automatic Identification for Internet New Words According to word-building Rule. *Journal of Shanxi University (Natural Science Edition)*, 25(2):115–119.

Kaixu Zhang, Maosong Sun, and Changle Zhou. 2012. Word Segmentation on Chinese Mirco-Blog Data with a Linear-Time Incremental Model. *Second CIPS-SIGHAN Joint Conference on Chinese Language Processing*, 41–46.

Longye Wang, Derek F. Wong, Lidia S. Chao, and Junwen Xing. 2012. CRFs-Based Chinese Word Segmentation for Micro-Blog with Small-Scale Data. *Second CIPS-SIGHAN Joint Conference on Chinese Language Processing*, 51–57.

Ning Xi, Bin Li, Guangchao Tang, Shujian Huang, Yinggong Zhao, Hao Zhou, Xinyu Dai, and Jiajun

Chen. 2012. Adapting Conventional ChineseWord Segmenter for Segmenting Micro-blog Text. *Second CIPS-SIGHAN Joint Conference on Chinese Language Processing*, 63–68.

Shengfen Luo, and Maosong Sun. 2003. Two character Chinese word extraction based on hybrid of internal and contextual measure. *Second SIGHAN Workshop on Chinese Language Processing*, 24–30.

Tao-Hsing Chang, and Chia-Hoang Lee. 2003. Automatic Chinese unknown word extraction using small-corpus-based methodmeasure. *1st IEEE International Conference on Natural Language Processing and Knowledge Engineering*, 459-464.

Wenbo Pang, Xiaozhong Fan, Yijun Gu, and Jiangde Yu. 2009. Chinese Unknown Words Extraction Based on Word Level Characteristics. *9th International Conference on Hybrid Intelligent System*, 361–366.

Xiao Sun, Degen Huang, Haiyu Song, and Fuji Ren. 2011. Chinese new word identification: a latent discriminative model with global features. *Journal of Computer Science and Technology*, 26(1):14–24.

Xin Jiang, Yanjiao Cao, and Zhao Lu. 2011. Automatic Recognition of Chinese Unknown Word for Single-Character and Affix Models. *Sixth International Conference on Intelligent Systems and Knowledge Engineering*, 435–444.

Yisu Xu, Xuan Wang, Buzhou Tang, and Xiaolong Wang. 2008. Chinese Unknown Word Recognition using improved Conditional Random Fields. *8th International Conference on Intelligent Systems Design and Applications*, 363–367.

Ziru Zhang, Qiangjun Wang, and Xuedong Tian. 2006. Chinese New Words Extraction Based on Machine Learning Approach. *2006 International Conference on Machine Learning and Cybernetics*, 3380–3384.

A Study of the Effectiveness of Suffixes for Chinese Word Segmentation

Xiaoqing Li [†] **Chengqing Zong** [†] **Keh-Yih Su** [‡]
[†]National Laboratory of Pattern Recognition, Institute of Automation, Chinese Academy of Sciences, Beijing, China
[‡]Behavior Design Corporation, Taiwan
{xqli, cqzong}@nlpr.ia.ac.cn, kysu@bdc.com.tw

Abstract

We investigate whether suffix related features can significantly improve the performance of character-based approaches for Chinese word segmentation (CWS). Since suffixes are quite productive in forming new words, and OOV is the main error source for CWS, many researchers expect that suffix information can further improve the performance. With this belief, we tried several suffix related features in both generative and discriminative approaches. However, our experiment results have shown that significant improvement can hardly be achieved by incorporating suffix related features into those widely adopted surface features, which is against the commonly believed supposition. Error analysis reveals that the main problem behind this surprising finding is the conflict between the degree of reliability and the coverage rate of suffix related features.

1 Introduction

As words are the basic units for text analysis, Chinese word segmentation (CWS) is critical for many Chinese NLP tasks such as parsing and machine translation. Although steady improvements have been observed in previous CWS researches (Xue, 2003; Zhang and Clark, 2007; Wang et al., 2012; Sun et al., 2012), their performances are only acceptable for in-vocabulary (IV) words and are still far from satisfactory for those out-of-vocabulary (OOV) words. According to the Zipf's law (Zipf, 1949), which states that the frequency of a word is inversely proportional to its rank in the frequency table for a given corpus, it is unlikely to cover all the words of a language in the training corpus. OOV words are thus inevitable in real applications.

To further improve the performance for OOV words, various approaches have been proposed. Most of them aim to add additional resources, such as external dictionaries (Low et al., 2005; Zhao et al., 2010; Li et al., 2012) or unlabeled data (Zhao and Kit, 2008; Sun and Xu, 2011). However, additional resources are not always available and their coverage for OOV words is still limited. Researchers, especially linguists (Dong et al., 2010), thus seek to further improve the performance of OOV words by characterizing the word formation process (Li, 2011).

According to the internal structures of OOV words, they can be divided into three categories: (1) character-type related OOV, which consists of Arabic digits and foreign characters, and usually denotes time, date, number, English word, URL, etc. This kind of OOV can be well handled by rules or character-type features if the character-type information can be utilized (Low et al., 2005; Wang et al., 2012); (2) morpheme related OOV, which mainly refers to a compound word with prefix/suffix or reduplication (e.g. "高高兴兴" (happily)). According to (Wang et al., 2012), the errors related with suffix are the major type (more than 80%) within this category; (3) others (such as named entities, idioms, terminology, abbreviations, new words, etc.), which are usually irregular in structure and are difficult to handle without additional resources. Since extra knowledge about character-type and additional resources are forbidden in the

SIGHAN closed test (Emerson, 2005), which is widely adopted for performance comparison, we will focus on the second category to investigate how to use suffix related features in this paper.

Generally speaking, Chinese suffixes are very productive and many words can be formed in this way. For example, the word "旅行者" (traveler) is composed of a stem ("旅行", travel) and a suffix ("者", -er). Although the character and character co-occurrence features (adopted in most current approaches) are able to partially characterize the internal structure of words (Sun, 2010), and some OOV words are indeed correctly handled when compared to pure word-based approaches (Zhang et al., 2003; Gao et al., 2005), suffix related errors still remain as an important type of errors. Therefore, it is natural to expect that suffixes can be explicitly utilized to provide further help.

Furthermore, prefix/suffix related features were claimed to be useful for CWS in some previous works (Tseng et al., 2005; Zhang et al., 2006). However, in their works, the prefix/suffix features are just a part of adopted features. The performances before and after adopting prefix/suffix features are never directly compared. So we could not know how much improvement actually results from those prefix/suffix related features. Besides, those features have only been adopted under discriminative approaches (Xue, 2003; Peng, 2004). We would also like to know whether the suffix related features would be effective for the generative approach (Wang et al., 2009; Wang et al., 2010).

In comparison with the discriminative model, the generative model has the drawback that it cannot utilize trailing context in selecting the position tag (i.e. **B**eginning, **M**iddle, **E**nd and **S**ingle) (Xue, 2003) of the current character. Therefore, incorporating suffix information of the next character is supposed to be a promising supplement for the generative approach. So the real benefit of using suffixes is checked for the generative model first.

To make use of the suffix information more completely, a novel quantitative tagging bias feature is first proposed to replace the context-independent suffix list feature adopted in the literature. Compared with the original suffix-list feature, the proposed tagging bias feature takes the context into consideration and results less modeling error. A new generative model is then derived to incorporate the suffix related feature.

However, experimental results have shown that the performance cannot be considerably improved by adding suffix information, as what we expected. Furthermore, no improvement can be achieved with the suffix list when we re-implemented the discriminative approach of (Tseng et al., 2005; Zhang et al., 2006). This negative conclusion casts significant doubt on the above commonly believed supposition that suffix information can further improve the performance of CWS via incorporating it into surface features. The reasons for this surprising finding are thus studied and presented in this paper.

2 Extracting suffix information

In linguistic definition[1], a suffix is a morpheme that can be placed after a stem to form a new word. Also, a suffix cannot stand alone as a word. According to this definition, only a few characters can be regarded as suffixes, such as '者' (-er), '化' (-ize), '率' (rate), etc. However, the character '湖' (lake) in the words "昆明湖" (Kunming Lake) and "未名湖" (Weiming Lake) can help recognize those OOV words, although it can also appear as an independent word in the phrase "在/湖/中间" (in the middle of the lake). We thus loosen the constraint that a suffix cannot stand alone as a word in this paper to cover more such characters. That is, if a character tends to locate at the end of various words, it is regarded as if it plays the role of a suffix in those words. In this way, many named entities (such as the two location names mentioned above) will be also classified as suffix related words.

2.1 Difficulties in recognizing suffixes

Nonetheless, we cannot distinguish suffixes from those non-suffixes by just checking each character because whether a character is a suffix highly depends on the context. For example, the character '化' is a suffix in the word "初始化" (initial-ize). However, it becomes a prefix when it comes to the word "化纤" (chemical-fibre). Also, whether a character is a suffix varies with different annotation standards adopted by various corpora. For example, the character '厂' (factory) is a suffix in words such as "服装厂" (clothing-factory) in the PKU corpus provided by the SIGHAN 2005 Bakeoff (Emerson, 2005). Nevertheless, it is regarded as a single-character

[1] http://zh.wikipedia.org/wiki/%E8%A9%9E%E7%B6%B4

word in similar occasions in the MSR corpus. For these two reasons, suffixes cannot be directly recognized by simply locating some pre-specified characters prepared by the linguist.

2.2 Extracting a suffix-like list

Due to the difficulty in recognizing real suffixes, previous works (Tseng et al., 2005; Zhang et al., 2006) extract a suffix-like list beforehand from each corpus in context-free manner. Specifically, Tseng et al. (2005) considers characters that frequently appear at the end of those rare words as potential suffixes. In their approach, words that the numbers of occurrences in the training set are less than a given threshold are selected first, and then their ending characters are sorted according to their occurrences in those rare words. Afterwards, the suffix-like list is formed with those high-frequency characters. Zhang et al. (2006) constructs the list in a similar way, but without pre-extracting rare words.

In order to reduce the number of suffix errors resulted from the above primitive extraction procedure, we propose to obtain and use the suffix-list in a more prudent manner as follows:

- Having considered that suffix is supposed to be combined with different stems to form new words, we propose to use the *suffix productivity* as the criteria for extracting suffix list, which is defined as the size of the set $\{w \mid w \in IV, [w+sc] \in IV\}$, where w is a word in the training set, sc is a specific character to be decided if it should be extracted as a *suffix character*, and IV denotes in-vocabulary words. The cardinality of this set counts how many different IV words can be formed by concatenating the given suffix character to an IV word. Therefore, larger suffix productivity means that the given suffix character can be combined with more different stems to form new words, and is thus more likely to be a suffix.
- According to our investigation, most OOV with suffix are composed of a multi-character IV and a suffix, such as "旅行者" (i.e., "旅行" + "者"). So we set the suffix status for a given character to be true only when that character is in the suffix list and its previous character is the end of a multi-character IV word. In this way we can avoid many over-generalized errors (thus improve the precision for OOV with suffixes) and it only has little harm for the recall.

2.3 Adopting tagging bias information

There are two drawbacks to adopt the above suffix-like list: (1) The associated context that is required to decide whether a character should be regarded as a suffix is either completely not taken into account (in previous approaches) or treated too coarsely (in the above proposed approach). (2) The probability value (a finer information) that a given character acts as a suffix is not utilized; only a hard-decision flag (in or outside the list) is assigned to each character.

To overcome these two drawbacks, we introduce the *context-dependent tagging bias level*, which reflects the likelihood that the next character tends to be the beginning of a new word (or be a single-character word) based on the local context. This is motivated by the following observation: if the trailing character is biased towards 'S' or 'B', then the current character will prefer to be tagged as 'S' or 'E'; on the contrary, if the trailing character is biased towards 'M' or 'E', then the current character will prefer to be tagged as 'B' or 'M'.

Having considered that the surrounding context might be unseen for the testing instances, we introduce four different kinds of tagging bias probabilities as follows (and they will be trained in parallel for each character in the training-set):

- *Context-free tagging bias level* (qf_i): which is the quantized value of $P(t_{i+1} \in \{E,M\} \mid c_{i+1})$ that is estimated from the training corpus. In our experiments, we quantize $P(t_{i+1} \in \{E,M\} \mid c_{i+1})$ into five different intervals: [0.0-0.2], [0.2-0.4], [0.4-0.6], [0.6-0.8] and [0.8-1.0]; therefore, qf_i is a corresponding member of {-2, -1, 0, 1, 2}.
- *Left-context-dependent tagging bias level* (ql_i): Compared with qf_i, $P(t_{i+1} \in \{E,M\} \mid c_i^{i+1})$ is used instead of $P(t_{i+1} \in \{E,M\} \mid c_{i+1})$. The quantization procedure is the same.
- *Right-context-dependent tagging bias level* (qr_i): Compared with qf_i, $P(t_{i+1} \in \{E,M\} \mid c_{i+1}^{i+2})$ is used instead of $P(t_{i+1} \in \{E,M\} \mid c_{i+1})$. The quantization procedure is the same.
- *Surrounding-context-dependent tagging bias level* (qs_i): Compared with qf_i, $P(t_{i+1} \in \{E,M\} \mid c_i^{i+2})$ is used instead of $P(t_{i+1} \in \{E,M\} \mid c_{i+1})$. Quantization is the same.

3 Incorporating Suffix Information

3.1 For the generative model

Wang et al. (2009) proposed a character-based generative model for CWS as follows:

$$\bar{t}_1^n \equiv \arg\max_{t_1^n} \prod_{i=1}^{n} P([c,t]_i \mid [c,t]_{i-2}^{i-1}) \quad (1)$$

where $[c,t]_1^n$ is the associated character-tag-pair sequence for the given character sequence c_1^n.

To overcome the drawback that it cannot utilize trailing context, we propose to incorporate the suffix information of the *next* character (denoted by q_i), which can be either the suffix-list binary indicator or the above tagging bias level, into the model and reformulate it as follows:

$$\hat{t}_1^n = \arg\max_{t_1^n} P(t_1^n \mid c_1^n, q_1^n) = \arg\max_{t_1^n} P(t_1^n, c_1^n, q_1^n)$$

$P(t_1^n, c_1^n, q_1^n)$ is then approximated by $\prod_{i=1}^{n} P([t,c,q]_i \mid [t,c,q]_{i-2}^{i-1})$, and its associated factor is further derived as below:

$$\begin{aligned} & P([t,c,q]_i \mid [t,c,q]_{i-2}^{i-1}) \\ & = P(q_i \mid [t,c]_i, [t,c,q]_{i-2}^{i-1}) \times P([t,c]_i \mid [t,c,q]_{i-2}^{i-1}) \\ & \approx P(q_i \mid t_{i-1}^{i}, c_{i-2}^{i}) \times P([t,c]_i \mid [t,c]_{i-2}^{i-1}) \\ & \approx P_{tq[i]}(m_i \mid t_{i-1}, c_{i-2}^{i}) \times P([t,c]_i \mid [t,c]_{i-2}^{i-1}) \end{aligned} \quad (2)$$

where m_i indicates whether t_i matches the suffix information of c_{i+1} or not, and $tq[i]$ specifies the corresponding type of probability factor to be adopted (i.e., qf_i, ql_i, qr_i, qs_i). For those three different suffix features (previous suffix-list, proposed suffix-list, and proposed tagging bias), m_i will be decided as follows:

- For the previous suffix-list feature, m_i will be a member of {Match, Violate, Neutral}. If c_{i+1} is in the suffix-list, when t_i is assigned with the position tag 'B' or 'M', m_i will be 'Match'; otherwise m_i will be 'Violate'. If c_{i+1} is not in the suffix-list, m_i will always be 'Neutral', no matter what position tag is assigned to t_i.
- For the proposed suffix-list feature, m_i will also be a member of {Match, Violate, Neutral}. If c_{i+1} is in the suffix list and c_i is the end of a multi-character IV word, when t_i is assigned position tag 'M', m_i will be 'Match'; otherwise m_i will be 'Violate'. If c_{i+1} is not in the suffix list or c_i is not the end of a multi-character IV word, m_i will always be 'Neutral'.
- For the proposed tagging bias feature, m_i will be a member of {Match[q_i], Violate[q_i], Neutral}, where q_i is a member of { qs_i, ql_i, qr_i, qf_i } and is selected according to whether the context c_i^{i+2} in the testing sentence is seen in the training corpus or not. Specifically, if c_i^{i+2} is seen in the training corpus, then q_i will be qs_i; else if c_i^{i+1} is seen, then q_i will be ql_i; else if c_{i+1}^{i+2} is seen, then q_i will be qr_i; otherwise, q_i will be qf_i. When $q_i > 0$ (i.e., c_{i+1} tends to be the beginning of a new word), if t_i is assigned 'S' or 'E', then m_i will be $\text{Match}[q_i]$; otherwise, m_i will be $\text{Violate}[q_i]$. On the contrary, when $q_i < 0$ (i.e., c_{i+1} tends not to be the beginning of a new word), if t_i is 'B' or 'M', then m_i will be $\text{Match}[q_i]$, otherwise, m_i will be $\text{Violate}[q_i]$. For example, if $q_i = 2$ and $t_i = E$, then m_i will be 'Match[2]'. On the contrary, if $q_i = -2$ and $t_i = E$, then m_i will be 'Violate[-2]'. Also, we will have four different $P_{tq[i]}(m_i \mid t_{i-1}, c_{i-2}^{i})$ (associated with {*qs*, *ql*, *qr*, *qf*}, respectively), and *tq*[*i*] indicates which one of them should be adopted at c_i. Afterwards, according to the context of each testing instance, a specific $P_{tq[i]}(m_i \mid t_{i-1}, c_{i-2}^{i})$ will be adopted.

It is reasonable to expect that the two factors in Equation 2 should be weighted differently in different cases. Besides, the second character-tag trigram factor is expected to be more reliable when c_{i-1}^{i} is seen in the training corpus. Therefore, these two factors are combined via log-linear interpolation. For the suffix-list feature, the scoring function will be:

$$\begin{aligned} Score(t_i) = & \ \alpha_k \times \log P([c,t]_i \mid [c,t]_{i-2}^{i-1}) \\ & + (1-\alpha_k) \log P(m_i \mid t_{i-1}, c_{i-2}^{i}); \quad 1 \le k \le 2 \end{aligned} \quad (3)$$

where α_k is selected according to whether c_{i-1}^{i} is seen. The values of α_k will be automatically decided in the development set via MERT (Och, 2003) procedure.

For the tagging bias feature, the scoring function will be:

$$Score(t_i) = \alpha_{tq,k} \times \log P([c,t]_i \mid [c,t]_{i-2}^{i-1}) + (1-\alpha_{tq,k}) \log P(m_i \mid t_{i-1}, c_{i-2}^{i}); 1 \le tq \le 4, 1 \le k \le 2 \quad (4)$$

where $\alpha_{tq,k}$ is selected according to which tagging bias probability factor is used and whether c_{i-1}^{i} is seen. Therefore, we will have eight different $\alpha_{tq,k}$ in this case.

3.2 For the discriminative model

We adopt the following feature templates under the maximum entropy approach that are widely adopted in previous works (Xue, 2003; Low et al., 2005):

$(a)\ C_n (n = -2, -1, 0, 1, 2);$

$(b)\ C_n C_{n+1} (n = -2, -1, 0, 1);$

$(c)\ C_{-1} C_1$

where C represents a character, and n denotes the relative position to the current character of concern.

To further utilize the suffix information, (Tseng et al., 2005) proposed a suffix-like list based feature as below.

$(d)\ s_0$, which is a binary feature indicating whether the current character of concern is in the list. In our modified approach, the suffix status will be true when the character c_0 is in the suffix-list and also c_{-1} is the end of a multi-character IV word.

Besides the above feature, (Zhang, 2006) also utilized some combinational features as follows:

$(e)\ c_0 s_{-1}, c_0 s_1, c_{-1} s_0, c_{-2} s_0$, where c denotes a character, s denotes the above suffix-like list feature.

In addition, we also tested the case of context-free tagging bias (proposed in Section 2.3), under this discriminative framework, by adding the following template.

$(f)\ qf$, which is the context-free tagging bias level. Please note that qs (also ql and qr) is not adopted because it will always be qs in the training-set (and thus will be over-fitted). Therefore, only qf is adopted to make the training and testing conditions consistent.

4 Experiments and Discussions

4.1 Setting

All the experiments are conducted on the corpora provided by SIGHAN Bakeoff 2005 (Emerson, 2005), which include Academia Sinica (AS), City University of Hong Kong (CITYU), Peking University (PKU) and Microsoft Research (MSR). For tuning the weights in Equation 3 and Equation 4, we randomly select 1% of the sentences from the training corpus as the development set.

For the generative approaches, the SRI Language Model Toolkit (Stolcke, 2002) is used to train $P([c,t]_i \mid [c,t]_{i-2}^{i-1})$ with the modified Kneser-Ney smoothing method (Chen and Goodman, 1996). The Factored Language Model in SRILM is adopted to train $P(m_i \mid t_{i-1}, c_{i-2}^{i})$, and it will sequentially back-off to $P(m_i \mid t_{i-1})$. For the discriminative approach, the ME Package provided by Zhang Le[2] is adopted to train the model. And trainings are conducted with Gaussian prior 1.0 and 300 iterations. In addition, the size of the suffix-like list in all approaches is set to 100[3], and the occurrences threshold for rare words in (Tseng et al., 2005) is set to 7. Typical F-score is adopted as the metric to evaluate the results.

4.2 Results of generative approaches

The segmentation results of using different generative models proposed in Section 3.1 are shown in Table 1. "Baseline" in the table denotes the basic generative model corresponding to Equation 1; "With Suffix-Like List" denotes the model that adopts the suffix-like list related features, corresponding to Equation 3; each sub-row right to it indicates the method used to extract the list. "With Tagging Bias" denotes the model that adopts tagging bias related features, corresponding to Equation 4. Bold entries indicate that they are statistically significantly different from their corresponding entries of the baseline model.

Table 1 shows that the improvement brought by the tagging bias approach is statistically significant[4] from the original model for three out of four corpora; however, the difference is not much. Also, for the suffix-like list approaches, the performance can only be slightly improved when the suffix-list is extracted and used in our

[2] http://homepages.inf.ed.ac.uk/lzhang10/maxent_toolkit.html

[3] This size is not explicitly given in their papers; so we tried several different values and find that it only makes little difference on the results. So is the threshold for rare words.

[4] The statistical significance test is done by the bootstrapping technique (Zhang et al., 2004), with sampling size of 2000 and confidence interval of 95%.

		PKU	AS	CITYU	MSR
Baseline		0.951	0.948	0.945	0.970
With Suffix-Like List	Tseng	0.951	0.948	0.946	0.970
	Zhang	0.951	0.948	0.946	0.970
	Proposed	0.952	0.949	**0.947**	0.970
With Tagging Bias		**0.953**	**0.950**	**0.947**	0.970

Table 1: Segmentation results for generative approaches in F-score

	PKU	AS	CITYU	MSR
Baseline	0.946	0.951	0.943	0.960
Tseng	0.946	0.949	0.942	0.961
Tseng+	0.946	0.949	0.942	0.960
Zhang	0.946	0.949	0.941	0.959
Zhang+	0.945	0.949	0.941	0.960
With qf	0.946	0.950	0.941	0.960

Table 2: Segmentation results for discriminative approaches in F-score

proposed way. To inspect if the quality of the suffix-list will affect the performance, we manually remove those characters which should not be regarded as suffixes in each list (such as Arabic numbers, and characters like "斯", "尔", which always appear at the end of transliteration). However, the performances are almost the same even with those cleaned lists (thus not shown in the table). The reasons will be found out and explained in Section 5.

4.3 Results of discriminative approaches

Table 2 shows the segmentation results for various discriminative approaches. 'Baseline' in the table denotes the discriminative model that adopts features (a)-(c) described in Section 3.2; 'Tseng' denotes the model with additional feature (d); and 'Tseng+' adopts the same feature set as 'Tseng', but the suffix-like list is obtained and used in our proposed way; similarly, the same interpretation goes for 'Zhang' and 'Zhang+'. Last, 'with qf' denotes the model with additional feature (f), instead of features (d) and (e). Please note that qs (also ql and qr) is not adopted (explained above in Section 3.2).

The results in Table 2 show that neither the suffix-like list related feature nor the context-free tagging bias feature can provide any help for the discriminative approach. Similar to the generative approach, no significant benefit can be brought in even if the list is further cleaned by the human. This seems contradictory to the claims given at (Tseng et al., 2005; Zhang et al., 2006) and will be studied in the next section.

5 Problems Investigation

5.1 Suffix information is unreliable when associated context is not seen

Whether a character can act as a suffix is highly context dependent. Although context has been taken into consideration in our proposed suffix-list approach and tagging bias approach, the preference implied by the suffix list or tagging bias level becomes unreliable when the context is unfamiliar. Table 3 shows the percentage that the preference of different tagging bias factors matches the real tag in the training set. It can be seen that the matching rate (or the influence power) is higher with broader seen context. When no context is available (the last column; the suffix-list approach), it drops dramatically. As a result, many over-generalized words are produced when qf must be adopted. For example, two single-character words "该/局" (this bureau) are wrongly merged into a pseudo OOV "该局". As another example, the first three characters in the sequence "冠军/奖碟" (championship award-tray) are wrongly merged into a pseudo OOV "冠军奖" (championship-award). Because the related context "奖碟" is never seen for the character '奖', it is thus regarded as a suffix in this case (as it is indeed a suffix in many other cases such as "医学奖" (medicine-prize) and "一等奖" (first-prize)).

Corpus	qs	ql	qr	qf
PKU	0.996	0.977	0.923	0.686
AS	0.993	0.970	0.899	0.662
CITYU	0.997	0.976	0.919	0.653
MSR	0.992	0.970	0.898	0.662

Table 3: The matching rates of various tagging bias factors in the training set

Corpus	qs	ql	qr	qf
PKU	0.457	0.135	0.135	0.002
AS	0.374	0.083	0.082	0.004
CITYU	0.515	0.148	0.149	0.008
MSR	0.299	0.060	0.060	0.0003

Table 4: Unseen ratios for qs, ql, qr and qf in the testing set

5.2 Required context is frequently unobserved for testing instances

However, according to the empirical study of Zhao et al., (2010), the OOV rate can be linearly reduced only with an exponential increasing of corpus size, roughly due to Zipf's law; and n-gram is expected to also follow this pattern (Marco, 2009). Therefore, the sparseness problem gets more serious for the n-gram with a larger "n" (i.e., with wider context) because its number of possible distinct types would become much greater. As a consequence, there will be much more unseen bigrams than unseen unigrams in the testing set (Of course, unseen trigrams will be even more). Table 4 shows the unseen ratios for *qs*, *ql*, *qr* and *qf* in the testing set. It is observed that the unseen ratio for *qs* is much larger than that for *qf*. However, according to the discussion in the previous subsection, the preference of tagging bias level is not reliable for *qf*. Therefore, more reliable a suffix-feature is, less likely it can be utilized in the testing-set. As the result, no significant improvement can be brought in by using suffix related features.

6 Conclusion

Since suffixes are quite productive in forming new words, and OOV is the main error source for all state-of-the-art CWS approaches, it is intuitive to expect that utilizing suffix information will further improve the performance. Some papers even claim that suffix-like list is useful in their discriminative models, though without presenting direct evidence. Against the above intuition, the empirical study of this paper reveals that when suffix related features are incorporated into those widely adopted surface features, they cannot considerably improve the performance of character-based generative and discriminative models, even if the context is taken into consideration. Error analysis reveals that the main problem behind this surprising finding is the conflict between the reliability and the coverage of those suffix related features. This conclusion is valuable for those relevant researchers in preventing them from wasting time on similar attempts.

Last, the reason that humans can distinguish suffixes correctly is largely due to their ability in utilizing associated syntactic and semantic knowledge of the plain text. We still believe suffix information can help for CWS if such knowledge can be effectively incorporated into the model. And this will be our future work.

Acknowledgments

The research work has been partially funded by the Natural Science Foundation of China under Grant No. 61003160 and Hi-Tech Research and Development Program ("863" Program) of China under Grant No. 2012AA011101 and 2012AA011102.

References

Andreas Stolcke. 2002. SRILM - an extensible language modeling toolkit. In *Proceedings of the International Conference on Spoken Language Processing*, pages 311-318.

Baroni Marco. 2009. Distributions in text. In A. Lüdeling and M. Kytö (eds.), *Corpus linguistics: An international handbook*. Mouton de Gruyter, Berlin, Germany.

Franze Josef Och. 2003. Minimum error rate training in statistical machine translation. In *Proceedings of the 41st Annual Meeting on Association for Computational Linguistics*, pages 160-167, Sapporo, Japan.

Fuchun Peng, Fangfang Feng and Andrew McCallum. 2004. Chinese segmentation and new word detection using conditional random fields. In *Proceedings of COLING*, pages 562–568.

George Kingsley Zipf. 1949. Human Behavior and the Principle of Least Effort: An Introduction to Human Ecology. Addison-Wisley. Oxford, UK.

Hai Zhao, Chang-Ning Huang, Mu Li and Bao-Liang Lu. 2010. A Unified Character-Based Tagging Framework for Chinese Word Segmentation. *ACM Transactions on Asian Language Information Processing (TALIP)*, 9 (2). pages 1-32.

Hai Zhao and Chunyu Kit. 2008. Unsupervised Segmentation Helps Supervised Learning of Character Tagging for Word Segmentation and Named Entity Recognition. In *Sixth SIGHAN Workshop on Chinese Language Processing*.

Hai Zhao, Yan Song and Chunyu Kit. 2010. How Large a Corpus do We Need : Statistical Method vs. Rulebased Method. In *Proceedings of LREC-2010*. Malta.

Huaping Zhang, Hongkui Yu, Deyi Xiong and Qun Liu. 2003. HMM-based Chinese lexical analyzer ICTCLAS. In *Proceedings of the Second SIGHAN Workshop on Chinese Language Processing*, pages 184-187.

Huihsin Tseng, Pichuan Chang, Galen Andrew, Daniel Jurafsky and Christopher Manning. 2005. A Conditional Random Field Word Segmenter for Sighan Bakeoff 2005. In *Proceedings of the Fourth SIGHAN Workshop on Chinese Language Processing*, pages 168-171.

Jianfeng Gao, Mu Li, Andi Wu and Chang-Ning Huang. 2005. Chinese word segmentation and named entity recogni-tion: a pragmatic approach. *Computational Linguistics*, 31(4), pages 531-574.

Jin Kiat Low, Hwee Tou Ng and Wenyuan Guo. 2005. A Maximum Entropy Approach to Chinese Word Segmentation. In *Proceedings of the Fourth SIGHAN Workshop on Chinese Language Processing*, pages. 161-164, Jeju Island, Korea.

Kun Wang, Chengqing Zong and Keh-Yih Su. 2009. Which is more suitable for Chinese word segmentation, the generative model or the discriminative one? In *Proceedings of PACLIC*, pages 827-834, Hong Kong, China.

Kun Wang, Chengqing Zong and Keh-Yih Su. 2010. A Character-Based Joint Model for Chinese Word Segmentation. In *Proceedings of the 23rd International Conference on Computational Linguistics*, pages 1173-1181, Beijing, China.

Kun Wang, Chengqing Zong and Keh-Yih Su. 2012. Integrating Generative and Discriminative Character-Based Models for Chinese Word Segmentation. *ACM Transactions on Asian Language Information Processing*, Vol.11, No.2, June 2012, pages 7:1-7:41.

Nianwen Xue. 2003. Chinese Word Segmentation as Character Tagging. *Computational Linguistics and Chinese Language Processing*, 8 (1). pages 29-48.

Ruiqiang Zhang, Genichiro Kikui and Eiichiro Sumita. 2006. Subword-based Tagging for Confidence-dependent Chinese Word Segmentation. In *Proceedings of the COLING/ACL*, pages 961-968, Sydney, Australia.

Stanley F. Chen and Joshua Goodman. 1998. An empirical study of smoothing techniques for language modeling. *Technical Report TR-10-98, Harvard University Center for Research in Computing Technology*.

Thomas Emerson. 2005. The second international Chinese word segmentation bakeoff. In *Proceedings of the Fourth SIGHAN Workshop on Chinese Language Processing*, pages 123-133.

Weiwei Sun. 2010. Word-based and character-based word segmentation models: Comparison and combination. In *Proceedings of the 23rd International Conference on Computational Linguistics (Coling 2010)*, pages 1211-1219, Beijing, China.

Weiwei Sun and Jia Xu. 2011. Enhancing Chinese Word Segmentation Using Unlabeled Data. In *Proceedings of the 2011 Conference on Empirical Methods in Natural Language Processing*, pages 970-979, Edinburgh, Scotland, UK.

Xiaoqing Li, Kun Wang, Chengqing Zong and Keh-Yih Su. 2012. Integrating Surface and Abstract Features for Robust Cross-Domain Chinese Word Segmentation. In *Proceedings of the 24th International Conference on Computational Linguistics (COLING)*. Pages 1653-1669, Mumbai, India.

Xu Sun, Houfeng Wang and Wenjie Li. 2012. Fast Online Training with Frequency-Adaptive Learning Rates for Chinese Word Segmentation and New Word Detection. In *Proceedings of the 50th Annual Meeting of the Association for Computational Linguistics*, pages 253-262, Jeju Island, Korea.

Ying Zhang, Stephan Vogel and Alex Waibel, 2004. Interpreting BLEU/NIST scores: How much improvement do we need to have a better system. In *Proceedings of LREC*, pages 2051–2054.

Yue Zhang and Stephen Clark, 2007. Chinese Segmentation with a Word-Based Perceptron Algorithm. In *Proceedings of ACL*, pages 840-847, Prague, Czech Republic.

Zhengdong Dong, Qiang Dong and Changling Hao. 2010. Word segmentation needs change - from a linguist's view. In *Proceedings of CIPS-SIGHAN Joint Conference on Chinese Language Processing*. Beijing, China.

Zhongguo Li. 2011. Parsing the Internal Structure of Words: A New Paradigm for Chinese Word Segmentation. In *Proceedings of the 49th Annual Meeting of the Association for Computational Linguistics: Human Language Technologies*, pages 1405--1414, Portland, Oregon, USA.

Gap in pagination due to unavailable paper.

Pages 126-135

Towards a Revised Motor Theory of L2 Speech Perception

Yizhou Lan
Department of Chinese, Translation and Linguistics
City University of Hong Kong
Tat Chee Avenue, Kowloon, Hong Kong
ylylan2-c@my.cityu.edu.hk

Abstract

This study aims to review, through experiment proof of a salient effect of articulatory gestures on L2 perception, the time-honored but still put-to-sideways motor theory of speech perception. On one hand, previous studies in support to motor theory were largely done by tests of mismatch in duplex perception of acoustic/speech data; or by L1 development observations. On the other hand, L2 learning studies had seldom followed the motor theory framework. The current study employed two experiments on experienced L2 English speakers from a Cantonese L1 background to finish discrimination tasks on both 1) same allophone [tr] and [tʃ] but with different gestural overlapping in real words 2) the crucial acoustic cue of distinguishing the gestural differences of the same contrast by native speakers in isolation -- namely, the CV transitions. Results showed that non-native speakers could perform native-like in experiment 2 but not in experiment 1. Though both experiments contain the same acoustic information, only experiment 1 contains the entire gestural information. It is concluded that, at least, errors in second language acquisition has a gestural basis, which might partly support the motor theory from a new perspective.

1 Introducing the theoretic dispute

Acoustic-based perception mechanisms claim that human speech is perceived by a psycho-acoustic device which is capable of normalizing incoming sound tokens and extracting acoustic cues from acoustic sounds to form phonological categories (Pisoni, 1985; Kuhl, 2000). But the myth these theories failed to give explicit clarification to lies in the multiplicity and high variability of acoustic signal in one same percept of speech sound. Upon this possible discrepancy, it is suggested by motor theorists that the human percept for speech sounds lies in the articulatory gestures and production is based on that accordingly (Liberman and Mattingly, 1985).

Inconsistencies between the two theories of speech perception lie in what the primitive percept of speech is and the nature of processes of perception are. Acoustic perception theorists insist that human beings actively detect the acoustic information in the flow of speech, which is recognized as speech sounds. In motor theory, however, sound waves are but the product of intended articulatory gestures, which constitute an independent "language module". In terms of process, the acoustic perception of speech inevitably introduces two systems consisting of phones, the physical property of acoustic signals; and phonemes, the mental representation or classification of meaningful sound units (Ladefoged, 1993). However, the motor theory believes that we only perceive speech sounds (not other acoustic signal) through gestures because only linguistic sounds own gestural properties.

Despite the difference, an important common ground shared by both models is that both models separate phonetics (physical stimuli) and phonology (mental representation) with different instruments. For acoustic models, the two systems are separated by two levels of processing; for motor theory, a completely torn-apart module was introduced by claiming that the ability to detect gestures is "purely linguistic" and differs from acoustic perception fundamentally (ibid.).

Previous studies supporting the motor theory of speech perception had largely adopted the methodology of duplex perception (Rand, 1974; Whalen & Liberman, 1987) to show that segmentation of speech sounds by using acoustic detail is not plausible for human language perception because experiments has shown that humans perceive CV transitions (primarily stops and fricatives) in speech sounds (part of a word) more accurately and context-dependent than non-speech acoustic sounds, like bird chirps.

More recent studies on animal perception of language (Kuhl, 2000) provided arguments against the motor theory because the ability to perceive gestures, as it was put, can also be captured by other mammals. On its basis, Best (1995) brought forward another gesture-based theory of speech perception entitled the direct-realist view. Its basic viewpoint, different from the motor theory, is that language perception is not innate, because although without intended gestures, other animals can still distinguish human vowels. Rather, human beings perceive speech by generalizing others' gestures, no matter he or she have such knowledge of gesture.

Even so, the direct realist theory faces two challenges. Firstly, it did not specify what are the gestures being utilized as categories, not like motor theory's predecessors' work with articulatory gestures (Browman and Goldstein, 1987, 1992), and is inherently phonemic. The other limitation is that it did not fully explain how sounds are learned, although there are hints that it was through frequency-based statistical learning. Maybe the cause was the fear to be labeled another auditory-based theory, because statistical learning of speech sounds is inherently normalization of psycho-acoustic data. Both challenges cannot be resolved by only using L1 data. The reason is shown in the section below.

2 Employing L2 as a condition to unveil the motoric nature of speech perception

Second language acquisition of speech is believed to be influenced by the native language of the learners. Especially, experienced learners who are considered near-native in proficiency will often establish stable intermediate categories in an audio-based learning model, the most widely renowned being the Speech Learning Model (SLM, Flege, 1987; Flege et al., 2003). In essence, L2 provides another dimension to testify language perception models by providing an intermediate, if not impoverished, level between L1 and L2 in the speaker's ontogeny (Major, 2002), and thus may depict different perceptual accuracy in acoustical or phonological tasks.

The motor theory is not exactly what others (Massaro and Chen, 2008) has criticized that perception comes through multiple sources. According to Liberman and Mattingly (1985) "...the string of phonetic segments is overlapped in the sound ... [with] no acoustic boundaries. Until and unless the child (tacitly) appreciates the gestural source of the sounds, he can hardly be expected to perceive, or ever learn to perceive, a phonetic structure." Under an experiment design of L2 perception, it will be even more demanding for L2 speakers to tactically retrieve intended gestures which are different from that in L1.

The basic rationale of motor theory is that gestures are invariant (and that acoustics are too variable), and thus more prone to be regarded as the percept under the ecological mechanism of human perception (Galantucci et al., 2006). This claim has been more amplifiably proven by this experiment because variations in gestures have caused serious perceptual problems, but not the 'crucial' acoustic cue of formant transition in L2 perceivers.

However, empirical studies seldom provided counter-evidence to the claims it has made. Nor did the auditory-motor debate ever been explicitly carried on in the scope of L2 acquisition. Actually, using L2 as an examining condition for the speech perception theories has its own inherent merits. Investigating this question through L2 has a very profound implication towards which of the two theories are more explanatory. In results in L1 that distinguishes accuracy in acoustic/speech sound perception, we can either say the salient different result of perceiving full CV words and CV transitions is because of the normalization of acoustic sound into speech sound category through extensive statistical learning; or, alternatively, we can also say that gestures are the distal objects that humans perceive directly as categories. However, in L2, it is easier to see whether pure acoustic sounds are perceived as linguistic sound, or if gestures play a part too. If the latter is true, the learnability of L2 speakers in one sound may be discovered to be different in different gestural environments. This is something L1 data cannot provide since L1 perceptions are almost always accurate in linguistic settings; even native listeners hear purely acoustic sounds. The current study examines the tongue tip and tongue body gestures of /r/ in CrV, which may vary in degrees of overlapped gestural constellations introduced by vowel contexts (/i/, where gestures are not heavily loaded and /u/, where gestures are more in conflict).

3 Gestural difference in Cantonese L2 speech of English *tr-* cluster

Cantonese speakers were reported by previous literature to have an inclination to mispronounce English C-r clusters. They either deleted the [r] or substituted it to [w] (Hung, 2002; Chan, 2006). However, for alveolar clusters (tr- and dr-), previous studies showed that considerable affrication was a feature of their production (Lan and Oh, 2012). According to SLM, Cantonese speakers should be able to perceive them in a *tr-/ch-* contrast in the initial position, given that they had ample experience in using English.

Even for native speakers, the acoustic signals of [r] in C-r production with the two vowel contexts are very similar. However, the *tr-* clusters in two vowel conditions, /i/ and /u/, were observed to have different gestures. The gestural difference can be shown in the following four schematic scores (following Browman and Goldstein, 1987) of gestures of CV syllables in *true*, *chew*, *tree* and *Chee*, respectively (See Figure 1). TT stands for Tongue Tip constriction degree. If the tongue tip moves forward or frontward, the magnitude would be high; TB stands for Tongue Body constriction degree. If the tongue body moves backward, the magnitude would be high.

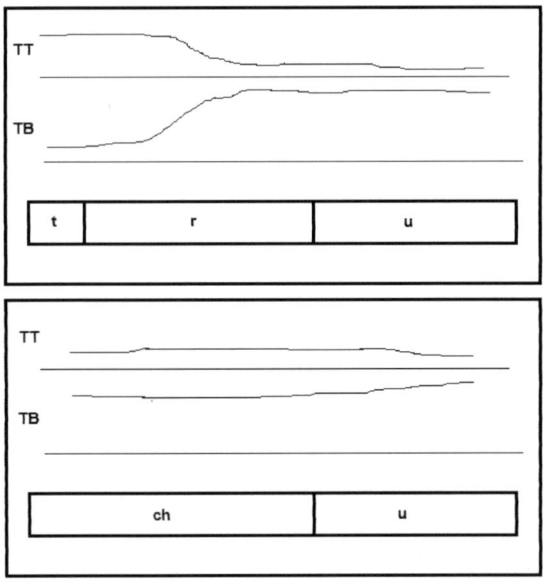

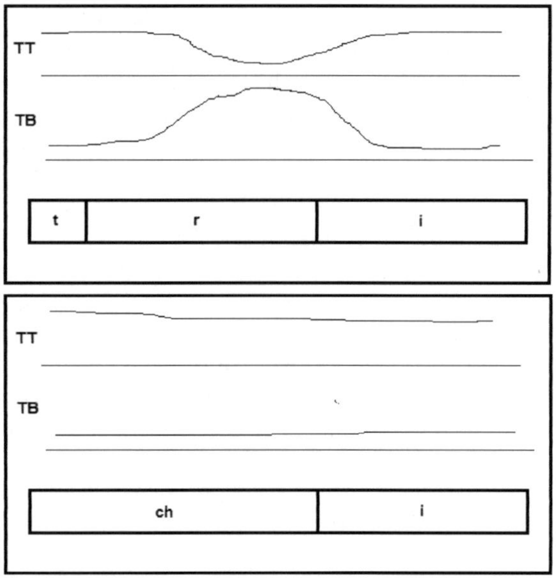

Figure 1: Schematic gestural scores for *true*, *chew*, *tree* and *Chee*, from top to bottom.

Note that the contrast of gestural scores for the [r] part in *tr-i* and *ch-i* is clear, because the [r] in /i/ environment shows both TT backward and TB retraction; whereas in *ch-i*, TT was always in forward position and TB always in rest position. However, the contrast of in *tr-u* and *ch-u* is more opaque because the TT and TB for both *tr-* and *ch-* words are eventually attaining the same position. Temporal overlap has made the sound contrast even more indiscernible to L2 learners.

One possible concern is, as has been pointed out earlier in this section, that although gesturally the [r] productions varied considerably for TT and TB constellations in /i/ and /u/ contexts, the acoustic properties of these two environments, nevertheless, were invariant in both conditions. Thus phonetically, the two conditions cannot constitute an allophonic variation. The two spectrograms in Figure 2 show that both sounds had considerable F3 rise, which is a signature characteristics for the presence of /r/.

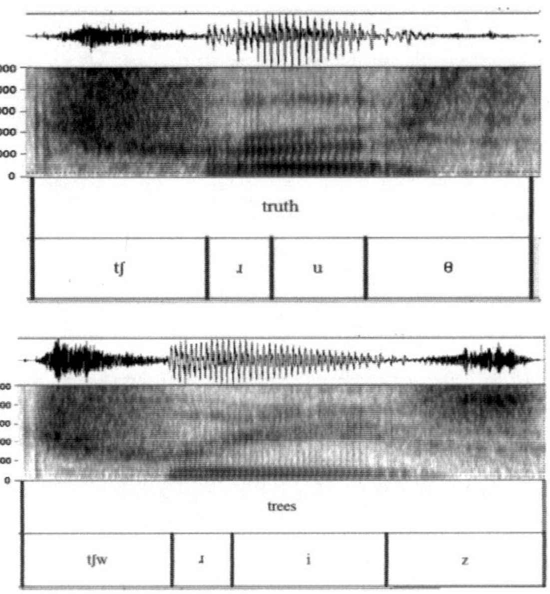

Figure 2: Spectrograms of truth and trees by native English speakers.

Apart from the impressionistic data, 92 of these tokens (46 *trees* and 46 *truth* productions) by native English speakers were analyzed for F3 in the [r] part and the results were sent to an independent variable t-test. Result showed that the difference of F3 in two vowel context was insignificant [t=-2.09, df=90, p=.305].

4 Experiment protocols for current study

The two experiments employed a contrast of word perception and non-speech acoustic detection respectively. In experiment 1, speakers were presented *tr-i* and *tr-u* sounds with *ch-i* and *ch-u* sounds as contrasts for discrimination perception. And in experiment 2, the CV formant transition parts are elicited from the speech and participants were asked to distinguish the acoustic segments from *tr-i* and *ch-i*, as well as *tr-u* and *ch-u*.

If the results are in support to auditory perception, as suggested by SLM, then the perceptual accuracy, no matter high or low, should be the same for L2 speakers because in both vowel contests, [r] sounds fully represents the acoustic data which is needed for L2 speakers to successfully/unable to distinguish the target sound contrast. The accuracy rate depends on the degree to which Cantonese speakers categorize the /r/ sound into phonemes correctly.

If the results support the classic motor theory, provided the difficulty in gestural contrast of *tr-* in the /u/ context by the learners, then the perceptual accuracy for full words should be better than the acoustic differences because of prior duplex experiments on native speakers has shown that acoustic perception of elicited "perceptual cues" should be poorer if not supported by the information of intended gestures by complete words. Also, the higher predicted accuracy may be attributed to the motor theorists' belief that human perception of speech sounds is modular and universal, which enables the universal grammar to help L2 learners perceive the intended gestures. A further prediction is that the accuracy for vowel contrasts of /i/ and /u/ should be different because of the different gestural difficulty demonstrated by the previous section.

4.1 Participants

Participants were three adults (2 females and 1 male, mean age=27.5) working as administrative staff at City University of Hong Kong. They all spoke English fluently as their working language. None of them had exposure to other foreign languages except English. All participants were right-handed with no reported hearing or motor-control defects. They did not have prior exposure to musical training. For controlling, three native monolingual English speakers (2 females and 1 male, mean age=26.5) from California, U.S. also participated in the study and went through the same procedure.

4.2 Stimuli

The perception tests were carried out in the Phonetics Lab, City University of Hong Kong. The listening perception materials used in two experiments are elicited from the same set of language productions by a native speaker. Stimuli words were produced by another Native American English speaker in a carrier sentence of "Now I say_____".

Words for both experiments were designed as minimal pairs of trVC and chVC (e.g. *trep-twep*). Stimuli differ in five vowel contexts, /i/, /ɛ,æ/, /u/, /ʌ/, and /ɔ/. Each word was repeated for three times by the native English speaker and then the most clearly pronounced utterance was selected as an experiment word. Stimuli for experiment 1 were the words themselves. However, in experiment 2, only the CV transition, or /r/ part, which was defined strictly as the start of voicing to the steady state of vowel, was used. In both experiments, test tokens were added with the equal numbers of fillers. In each experiment, stimuli were repeated for 10 times and randomized. In total, 600 tokens were tested (6 participants × 2 experiments × 5 vowels × 10 repetitions).

4.3 Procedure

Both experiments utilize the discrimination paradigm of the sounds in the minimal pairs. In this paradigm, three consecutive words (e.g., *treek/tweek/tweek*) were played, where the third word was identical to either the first or the second one. The participants were asked to circle the correct word on the answer sheet. The inter-stimulus intervals (ISI) were set at 250 milliseconds for both tasks.

To resolve a possible problem that might hinder reliability of stimuli induced by acoustic differences other than from the critical consonant part, the original vowel parts of the stimuli were replaced with the identical vowel which was sectioned from one token so that vowel quality remained consistent for the tasks. For instance, the [i] in one clear production of "treek" was used for all tokens with /i/ vowels in both experiments.

5 Results

5.1 Results by participant groups

For the sake of contrasting the two experime and highlighting the difference, the results w first presented with Cantonese and native Engl contrast and then by experiments.

Native English speakers showed an aver accuracy rate of 98.8% in discerning the *tr-/* contrast in words (N=300, std=.111). T difference between experiment 1 and 2 was 10 and 97.5%, which was statistically significant [2.259, df=298, p<.05]. The difference betw subjects was not significant [F(2, 297)=.3 p=.740]. The effect of vowel was not signific in experiment 2 [F(4, 145)=1.021, p=.398]. It v not significant in experiment 1 either.

For native Cantonese speakers, the overall accuracy rate was 81% (N=300, std=.397). The difference between experiment 1 and 2 was 66% and 95% [t=5.534, df=298, p<.0001]. The difference between subjects was insignificant [F(2, 297)=1.557, p=.214]. The effect of vowel was not significant in experiment 2 [F(4, 145)=.511, p=.728]. However, it was significant in experiment 1. [F(4, 145)=3.031, p<.05]. Among the vowel members, Tukey's post-hoc tests showed that the difference of vowel /i/ and /u/ were significant [/i/: md=.45, std.E=.145, p=.02; /u/: md=.45, std.E=.145, p=.02] (See Figure 3).

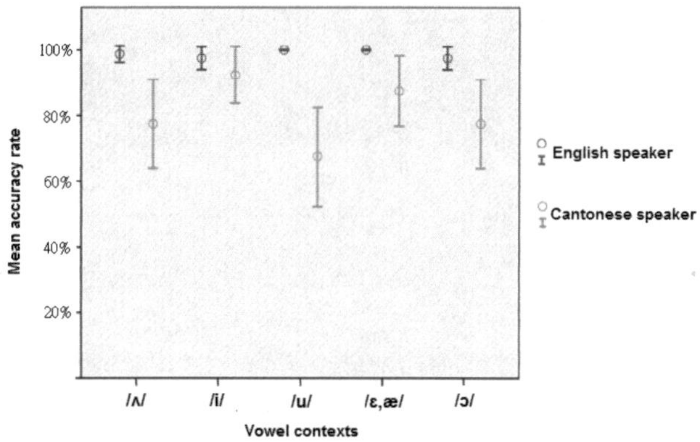

Figure 3: Accuracy rates of English and Cantonese speakers plotted by vowel types.

5.2 Results by experiments

The comparison of Cantonese and native English speakers' accuracy rate in each experiment was done, too. For experiment 1, the difference was significant [t=10.116, df=298, p<.0001]. However, for experiment 2, the difference was insignificant [t=1.136, df=258, p=.257] (See Figure 4).

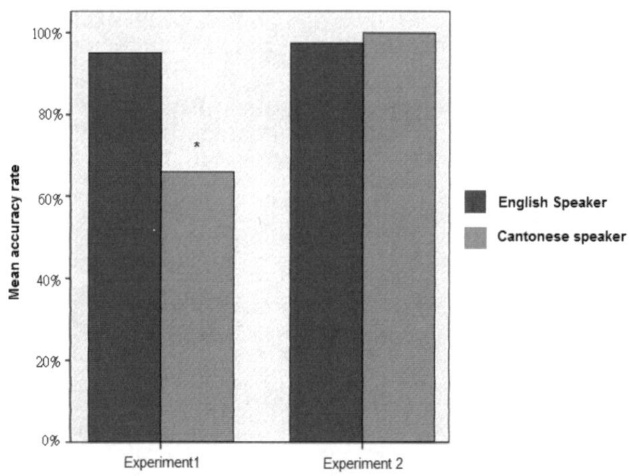

Figure 4: Accuracy rate of two experiments plotted by English/Cantonese speakers.

6 Discussions

The results of the two experiments may help giving some evidence to, if not settle, some of the theoretical disputes. For both experiments, native English speakers performed almost perfectly. The uniform high perception rate is not fruitful to support either of the competing theories. The analyze-worthy result lies in the comparison of English and Cantonese speakers as well as the comparison between two experiments for Cantonese speakers, together with the effect of vowel contexts. It was shown that the first experiment witnessed a significantly different perceptual accuracy in two vowel contexts, with Cantonese speakers having a lower accuracy rate and a bigger discrepancy between vowel contexts; whereas the accuracy in second experiment was equally high in two groups and the high accuracy rates were not affected by vowel contexts. This showed that articulatory gestures in context might help establish categories and influence the acquisition of speech sounds, rather than acoustic information only. Therefore, the acoustic model cannot explain all of the L2 phonological acquisition patterns.

However, the results were also not in line with a purely motor theory either, because the traditional motor theory will predict that word perception should be better than acoustic perception because linguistic aids are provided. Instead, the results showed that word perception rate is poor for experienced Cantonese speakers.

A new "gestural-learning model" for L2 perception, based on Best's direct-realist theory, is hereby brought about. It has three major hypotheses. 1) perception of speech sounds is neither purely acoustical nor linguistically innate; 2) the process of learning of speech sounds is in fact the learning gestures through a distributive manner, which is influenced by the sensitiveness to gestural categories, and specifically, number and density of the categories being intervened with each other; 3) The learning process of an L2 ontogeny is gradual and gradient.

The model offers a way to explain for the results of this study. It may explain (1) why the accuracy rate in experiment 2 is better than experiment 1. In experiment 2, no gestural information is used so it's natural to perceive acoustic, non-linguistic sounds correctly because the focus is on acoustic detail; (2) why /i/ showed a higher accuracy rate than /u/. Since L2 learners are hard or insensitive to internalize much tokens of the gestural information in /u/ because of the complexity of the gesture. /i/ tokens are more salient to be perceived and are thus more prone to have gone through distributive learning. However, /u/ tokens are often neglected by its gestural complexity and thus be equivalently categorized with the *ch-* category, resulting in less distributive learning.

The major difference between the two classic theories and the current model is that language is neither purely linguistic nor acoustic. It involves a gradual learning process of intended gestures and gesture constellations. The direct- realist theory (Best 1995, Best et al, 2001) has already mentioned that the gestures in speech perception could also be learned through experience and not inherently acquired by the linguistic module. More than that, the current model combines the distributive learning model with the scope of second language speech learning, and adopts a gradual perspective into the learning process.

The possible drawback for the motor theory to reconcile to a distributive acquisition model is because of the idea that linguistic perception is modular and different from acoustic perception. This is partly real as confirmed by the results of this study. However, in this way, phones and phonemes are so apart that L2 speakers cannot learn phonemes through phones because they lack the certain intended gestures in development. Nevertheless, the results, as has discussed earlier, suggest that L2 speakers can still perceive more than 80% of the tokens correctly in some vowel contexts. This proves the ability for L2 learners to extract gestural information from L2 linguistic experience, hence the new model of speech perception. The table below is a sketch of the three models being compared (SFee Table 1).

Acoustic-based	Motor theory	Gestural learning
Frequency-based statistical learning	Purely innate as a single modular/device	Frequency-based statistical learning
Normalized prototype-another type of invariant	Direct perception of distal gestures	Direct perception of distal gestures

Table1: Comparison of three theoretic models.

One limitation of the study is that it failed to provide longitudinal data as direct evidence to support the third hypothesis of the model. However, from the experiment we see that for different vowel contexts, the accuracy rate was different, and the overall accuracy rate for the *tr-* category is 66%, which is in between perfect (100%) and chance (50%), representing an intermediate and gradual level of learning. Limitation also lies in the small number of participants and languages.

7 Conclusions

The study summarizes the different predictions the traditional acoustic approach and motor theory would give to Cantonese L2 speakers' perception of *tr-* cluster in two vowel contexts. The result shows that Cantonese speakers perform poorly in real-word perception tests but near-ceiling in acoustic sound perception. This shows that acoustic sound is not a basis for L2 speech perception and the results supports the motor theory that speech is not perceived through sounds exclusively. However, the result that L2 speakers having an intermediate rate of successfully perceiving the L2 sounds raises questions towards motor theory's claim that the language modular is innate and cannot be shaped by experience.

Through these results, a new model of gestural learning was proposed through the discussions above. This model would bring fine-grained gestural percepts and frequency-based normalizing process of category formation together. Further investigations, such as more sound contrasts from more L1 and L2 linguistic backgrounds, as well as real-time EMA or fMRI imaging of L2 speakers' articulations may be done to testify it in detail.

Acknowledgments

The author is grateful to Dr. Dong Yanping for her advice, which gave birth to an initial idea of this study.

References

A. M. Liberman and I. G. Mattingly. 1985. The motor theory of speech perception revised. Cognition 21 (1), 1–36.

B. Galantucci, C. A. Fowler, and M. T. Turvey. 2006. The motor theory of speech perception reviewed. Psychonomic bulletin & review, 13(3), 361-377.

C. P. Browman and L. Goldstein. 1987. Tiers in articulatory phonology, with some implications for casual speech. Haskins Laboratories Status report on speech research, 1-30.

C. P. Browman and L. Goldstein. 1992. Articulatory phonology: an overview. Phonetica, 49, 155-180.

C. T. Best. 1995. A Direct Realist View of Cross-Language Speech Perception. In Strange, W. (ed.). Speech perception and linguistic experience: Issues in cross-language research, 171-204.

C. T. Best, G. W. McRoberts, and E. Goodall. 2001. Discrimination of non-native consonant contrasts varying in perceptual assimilation to the listener's native phonological system. Journal of Acoustics Society of America, 109(2), 775–94.

D. B. Pisoni. 1985. Speech perception: Some new directions in research and theory. Journal of the Acoustical Society of America, 78, 381-388.

D. H. Whalen. 1981. Effects of vocalic formant transition and vowel quality on the English [s]-[S] boundary. Journal of the Acoustical Society of America, 69, 275-282.

D. W. Massaro and T. H. Chen. 2008. The motor theory of speech perception revisited. Psychonomic bulletin & review, 15 (2), 453-457.

J. E. Flege. 1987. The production of "new" and "similar" phones in a foreign language: evidence for the effect of equivalence classification, Journal of Phonetics, 15, 47-65.

J. E. Flege, C., Schirru., and I. R. A. MacKay. 2003. Interaction between the native and second language phonetic subsystems, Speech Communication, 40, 467-491.

P. K. Kuhl. 2000. A new view of language acquisition. Proceedings of the National Academy of Sciences, 97(22), 11850-11857.

P. Ladefoged. 1993. A course in Phonetics. Harcourt Brace Jovanovich College Publishers.

R. C. Major. 2001. Foreign Accent: The Ontogeny and Phylogeny of Second Language Phonology. Mahwah, NJ: Lawrence Erlbaum Associates.

T. C. Rand. 1974. "Letter: Dichotic release from masking for speech". The Journal of the Acoustical Society of America, 55 (3), 678–680.

T. N. Hung. 2002. Language in contact: Hong Kong English phonology and the influence of Cantonese. In Kirkpatrick, A. (ed.). Englishes in Asia: Communication, Identity, Power and Education. Melbourne: Language Australia,191-200.

V. A. Mann and A. M. Liberman. 1983. Some differences between phonetic and auditory modes of perception. Cognition, 14, 211-235.

Y. Chan. 2006. Strategies used by Cantonese speakers in pronouncing English initial consonant clusters: Insights into the interlanguage phonology of Cantonese ESL learners in Hong Kong, IRAL proceedings, 44, 331-355.

Difficulties in Perception and Pronunciation of Mandarin Chinese Disyllabic Word Tone Acquisition: A Study of Some Japanese University Students

Yuting Dong
Japan Society for the Promotion of Science
Graduate School of Human and Environment Studies,
Kyoto University
amydyt@gmail.com

Yasushi Tsubota
Academic Center for Computing and Media Studies,
Kyoto University
tsubota@media.kyoto-u.ac.jp

Masatake Dantsuji
Academic Center for Computing and Media Studies,
Kyoto University
mdantsuji@mediakyoto-u.ac.jp

Abstract

Tonal errors pose a serious problem to Mandarin Chinese learners, making them stumble in their communication. The purpose of this paper is to investigate beginner level Japanese students' difficulties in the perception and pronunciation of disyllabic words, particularly to find out which combinations of tones these errors mostly occur in. As a result, the errors made by the 10 subjects were mostly found in tonal patterns 1-3, 2-1, 2-3, 3-2 and 4-3 in both perception and pronunciation. Furthermore, by comparing the ratio of tonal errors of initial to final syllables, we can tell that the initial syllables appear more difficult than the final syllables in perception, but in pronunciation this tendency is not found. Moreover, there seems to be some connection between learners' perception and pronunciation in their acquisition process.

1 Introduction

Many Southeast Asian languages are tonal languages including Mandarin Chinese. Mandarin Chinese is a well-known example of a tonal language, in which each syllable has its own fixed tone, including both high-low distinctions and rising-falling variations. The acoustic characteristics of tones are mainly determined by pitch value. Tones are relatively defined. This so-called "relativity" is the stability of pitch within the pitch range of an individual speaker.

In general, learners start learning the Mandarin Chinese pronunciation by practicing monosyllabic words. From educators' experiences, it seems that learners tend to make fewer errors when they pronounce monosyllabic words. However, one of the most important characteristics of Mandarin Chinese is the collaborative pattern of tones in spontaneous speech, such as the rules of tone sandhi and the patterns of tone combinations. This factor influences learners much more when they pronounce disyllabic words in longer sentences. To improve learners' tonal pronunciation, Zhu (1997) argues that the teaching of tone combinations ought to focus on disyllabic words. Firstly, almost all combination patterns of monosyllabic words in spontaneous speech are included in disyllabic words. Therefore, disyllabic words could be regarded as the foundation. Secondly, modern Chinese contains a large number of disyllabic words. According to Xian Dai Han Yu Pin Lv Ci Dian, there are only 3751 monosyllabic words, but 22941 disyllabic words that make up 73.63% of the total word number. Practicing disyllabic words could solve most problems with tone combinations. The changes of Chinese tones in connected speech pose a serious problem to learners of Mandarin Chinese. It is also found in classroom settings that Japanese students often stumble in their communication because of their tonal errors. The purpose of this paper is to investigate beginner level Japanese students' difficulties in the perception and pronunciation of disyllabic words, particularly to find out which tones these errors mostly occur in. The paper also compares the tonal error patterns between the pseudo-disyllabic word /mama/ and real disyllabic words. Furthermore, comparisons will also be made between perception and pronunciation experiment results because the relationship between these two factors in the acquisition process is another interest of the paper. This study will hopefully play an important role in teaching the 4 Chinese tones to Japanese students.

2 Literature Review

2.1 The Phonetic Features of Chinese and Japanese

In Chinese each syllable has its fixed tone. The high and low, falling and rising pitches depend on the vibration rate of the vocal cords. The constitution of Chinese tones is not determined only by pitch level, but also by transition patterns. There are level, rising, falling, and falling-rising tones, which are caused by changes in pitch. In addition to pitch, the intensity and duration of the sound are also relevant to the make-up of the tone. Intensity indicates the weight or strength of a sound. For instance, the neutral tone in Chinese is related to sound intensity. The easiest and the most effective way to transcribe and record tones is the system of tone-letter proposed by Chao (1968). It classifies tone pitch into five degrees, and divides a perpendicular line into four parts to signify the particular location of the tone pitch on the scale. The low, mid-low, middle, mid-high, and high pitches are indicated by the numbers 1

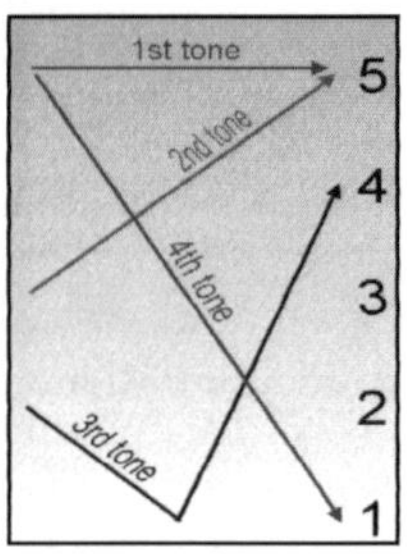

Figure 1. The location of Mandarin Chinese tone

to 5 respectively (Figure 1). The accurate tone-letter of each tone is represented by the high and low pitch, the rising and falling pitch, or the fluctuation of pitch. In a Chinese disyllabic phrase, the tones of the first and the second word are compromised for the sake of being euphonious (Wu, 1992). It is natural to make the pitch in the second syllable lower than that in the first. Take a disyllabic word with two rising pitches for example, the second rising pitch turns into low-rising (Figure 2).

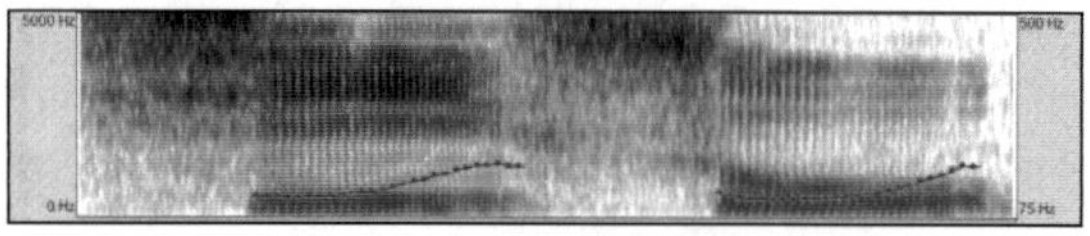

Figure 2. Word of tone 2-2 (xísú, custom) pronounced by a Chinese native speaker. (The underline signifies tone.)

In a disyllabic word with two falling pitches, both syllables are lower due to the mutual influence of these two falling pitches (Figure 3).

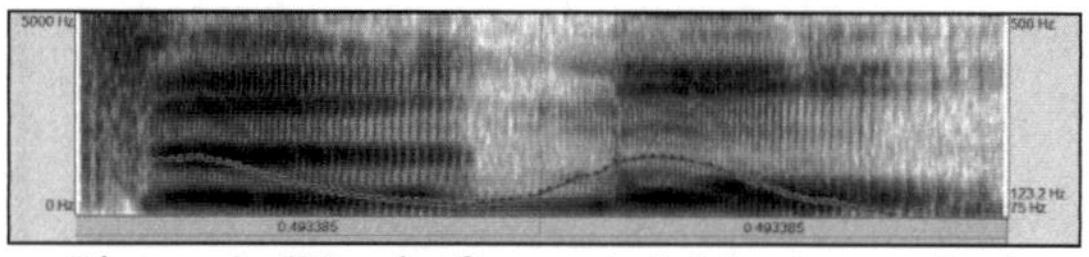

Figure 3. Word of tone 4-4 (zìmù, caption) pronounced by a Chinese native speaker.

Among Japanese phonetic features, accent bears the closest relationship to Chinese tone. There are two types of accents in the languages of the world (Hiroshi, 2003). One is "stress accent", which uses the intensity of sounds to differentiate various lexical items. The other is "pitch accent", which uses the pitch of sounds to distinguish one word from another. Japanese is classified as a pitch accent language. According to several researchers (Vance, 1986; Wang, 1997; Jun, 2001; Kubozono, 2006), the Japanese accent can be classified into two types—flat and non-flat. "Mora" in Japanese means the duration of a sound. The accent in Japanese displays in the mora instead of in the syllable. For example, the word [shimbun] (newspaper) has two syllables but four moras.

The difference between flat and non-flat type lies in the existence of the accent. The accent means there is a transition from high to low pitch in a word. The flat type does not have the accent, whereas the non-flat type does. The transition of the non-flat type can also be classified into three patterns—H-L, L-H-L, and L-H.

In general, a noun of n short syllables can have any of n+1 possible pitch patterns (Vance, 1986). When an isolated word is followed by other enclitic particles, the accent will also follow the pitch of the last mora, because in standard Japanese (Tokyo dialect), if the pitch in a word falls once, it will not rise up again (Kubozono, 2006).

According to the patterns stated above, the accent in standard Japanese (Tokyo dialect) has the following characteristics. First, there can only be one part with high pitch in a word (with one mora or several consecutive moras). Second, the pitches of the first and the second moras must differ. If the first mora is pronounced with high pitch, the second one must be with low pitch. In the same way, if the first is with low pitch, the second must be with high pitch. Third, the pitch in plural morals in Japanese undergoes less change than those in Chinese. Then, within one syllable, the change of pitches causes a change of meaning in Chinese but not in Japanese. All these factors are assumed to affect Japanese students when they are speaking Chinese.

The Japanese accent and Chinese tone seem to be represented by pitch change. In Japanese, the accent is represented in the pitch change of each mora within a word. The basic component is a mora. However, in Chinese, tone is displayed in the pitch change within each syllable. The basic tone-bearing unit is a morpheme.

2.2 The Tonal Errors of Japanese Students Learning Chinese

When Japanese students listen to Chinese disyllabic words, they often fail to judge which tone is the one they have heard. According to previous studies (Yang, 1999; Nishi, 2004; Liu, 2008; Dong, 2011), Japanese students showed a common error tendency: ① the final syllables and initial syllables received quite different percentage from the right answer, ② tone 2 and tone 3 were more difficult for students to master, ③ the pseudo-word /mama/ received more right answers than the real words. However, they did not point out whether students had the same problems when they pronounced the disyllabic words.

On the other hand, there are three common errors made by Japanese students in pronouncing Chinese (Zhu 1994)—flat tone, mispronunciation of multi-syllabic words, and stress of the neutral tone. Many Japanese students of Chinese pronounce disyllabic words in Chinese with rising-falling tones, regardless of their original tones, such as in the example of [chūnfēng] (spring breeze) changing to [chúnfēng] (pure breeze), and also in [fāngbiàn] (convenient) changing to [fángbiàn] (room convenient). The cause of this mispronunciation is related to the "euphonic change" in Japanese. Whatever the original pitch pattern is, when two words are combined into one lexical item, only the L-H-L pattern is allowed. For example, the original pitch of [waseda] belongs to the H-L pattern while that of [daigaku] (university) the L-H pattern. When these two words are combined, the pitch of [wasedadaigaku] (Waseda University) turns into the L-H-L pattern. This is because in Japanese, there cannot be two pitch changes in one word, which means that only one pitch peak is allowed in Japanese compounds. It is very difficult for Japanese students to pronounce distinguishably tone 3 from tone 4, tone 2 from tone 3, and tone 2 from tone 4 in Chinese (He, 1997). They easily mistake tone 3 for tone 2.

So far, even though the previous studies have identified some tendencies in the perceptional test of disyllabic words, it is still not clear whether the results can be accepted in pronunciation. Also, the "euphonic change" which does not appear in monosyllabic words, has not been discussed yet from both perception and pronunciation fields. This study is aimed at the two points mentioned above.

3 Methodology

3.1 Subjects

10 Japanese students of Kyoto University participated in the experiment of this study. They had Chinese classes for 3 hours per week, continuing for 1 year. They come from different regions of Japan and their native language is Japanese. All subjects were required to read out the disyllabic words shown to them on the slides. Then, they had to mark down the tones they heard from an audio file on an answer sheet.

3.2 Design of Word Chart

This study is going to deal with two kinds of disyllabic words. One is real words, which appear in the subjects' textbook. These words are supposed to be familiar to the subjects and practiced in the classes. The other is the pseudo-word /mama/ which is very easy to pronounce so that the subjects are able to concentrate more on four tones. In some cases, /mama/ can be interpreted into the meaning of "mother". However, it must be read as /māma/, in which case the second syllable is neutral tone, and not the research target in this study. Moreover, /màmǎ/ is another pattern, which may have the meaning of "scolding the horse" but it is not a typical disyllabic word. Therefore, in this study all tonal patterns of /mama/ will be treated as pseudo-words ignoring any possible meaning transfer.

There are four tones in Chinese. If all four tones are arranged into disyllabic words, sixteen combination pairs are retrieved. However, when 3-3 is pronounced, it changes into 2-3 so it is omitted. In this study, the neutral tone is not included in the word chart. The numbers 1, 2, 3, 4 represent the high pitch, rising pitch, falling-rising pitch, and falling pitch, respectively, as illustrated below.

1-1, 1-2, 1-3, 1-4
2-1, 2-2, 2-3, 2-4
3-1, 3-2, , 3-4
4-1, 4-2, 4-3, 4-4

Moreover, for each pattern, five real disyllabic words with different phonetic syllables were chosen for the speaking part. Ideally, every tone pair should be selected from the same set of syllables to control the segmental structure, considering the potential effects of syllabic structure on tone. However, since the words had to be known by all subjects, the range of the word list was limited. Finally, there were altogether 75 words selected.

To avoid the expectation of a pattern from the subjects, the order of the words were rearranged. Every word was supplemented with Chinese phonetic symbols (Pinyin) and all the disyllabic words listed came from the basic vocabulary contained in the subjects' textbook. Before the recording, the subjects were familiarized with the demo word slides with no time limit, and were not informed of the correct pronunciation. During the formal recording, if the subjects made any mistakes, they were not allowed to make self-corrections until the same word appeared again. Each word was read four times in order to reduce mispronunciations, such as inserting fillers, repetition, and so on. In the analysis, unless a word was pronounced correctly four times, it was judged as failing to pronounce. Then, the mispronounced words became the target for analysis by software.

In the listening part, besides fifteen pseudo-word /mama/ with different tone patterns, six words were selected for each tone pattern making a total of ninety real words. Half of the words contained in the material were chosen from the textbook and the other half were from outside the textbook, because if the subjects listened to a word they knew, they might get the right answer without any effort. In order to reduce this risk, unfamiliar words were also chosen. The material used in this experiment was pronounced by two native Mandarin Chinese speakers; one male and one female. Each word was read out four times, twice by the male and twice by the female speaker in random order. The material was played by a digital speaker and we made sure the subjects could hear the voice very clearly.

3.3 Procedure

This study was divided into three parts. The first part was to let subjects read the pseudo-disyllabic word /mama/ so as to collect the data with little phonetic influence. The second part was to ask the subjects to read out the disyllabic words on the slides. To prevent the subjects from predicting the answers without hearing the sounds, the words appeared in random order. The third part was to ask the subjects to listen to the pseudo-words and the real disyllabic words with four tones and write down the right answer on the answer sheet.

3.4 Methods of Analysis

On one hand, the results of the perceptual test were collected by counting the answers on the answer sheets, not only marking the right or wrong answers, but also listing what kinds of mistakes the subjects made. On the other hand, the pronunciation test results were analyzed in two ways. First, a perceptual analysis was performed by 4 Mandarin Chinese native speakers to identify the tonal errors made by the 10 subjects in pronouncing those disyllabic words, and to take a record of how subjects mispronounced the tones. Although the neutral tone was not included in the test word chart, the subjects actually pronounced some tones, similar to the neutral tone so it was added into the native speakers' judgment. Then, the data was analyzed with the phonetic analysis software Praat, too. Finally, we investigated the pseudo-words to real words tonal error ratio in perception and pronunciation.

4 Results and Discussion

4.1 Ratio of Tonal Errors in Perception

It is quite obvious that the 3-1 pattern of pseudo-words and the 1-3 pattern of common words were the most difficult ones for the subjects in the listening test. Both of them contained tone 1 and tone 3 but in a different order. Besides the 1-3, 2-1, 2-3, 3-2, 3-4, 4-2 and 4-3 patterns of pseudo-words, 1-2, 2-1, 2-3, 3-2, 3-4, 4-2 and 4-3 patterns of real words also received higher mistake rates than average. Particularly, 7 kinds of patterns were included in both the pseudo-words and the real words. If the subjects make the same mistakes in their pronunciation, we can suppose that there is some connection between their perception and pronunciation.

4.2 Ratio of Tonal Errors in Pronunciation

From Table 2 we can see that the tonal errors of the 10 subjects are mostly concentrated in tonal patterns 1-3, 1-4, 2-1, 2-3, 2-4, 3-2 and 4-3. Although the highest mistake rates in the pseudo-words and the real words are different from the results of the listening test, the 1-3, 2-1, 2-3, 3-2 and 4-3 patterns seem to be difficult for subjects in both perception and pronunciation (Table 3).

By comparing the ratio of tonal errors of initial to final syllables, we can tell that the initial syllables seem more difficult than the final syllables in perception, but in pronunciation we received the opposite results. It means that the tone of the final syllable is influenced by the initial syllable so that the subjects mispronounced the tone heavily. At the same time, in the pseudo-word /mama/, listening to a word and choosing the right tone seemed to be harder than pronouncing the same word. The same tendency also can be found in the real words.

Table 1. Ratio of perceptual tonal errors of two types of disyllabic words (%)

	/mama/ (n=150)		Real words (n=900)	
	Number of mistakes	Ratio (%)	Number of mistakes	Ratio (%)
1-1	1	0.67	6	0.66
1-2	3	2.00	29	3.22
1-3	5	3.33	32	3.56
1-4	1	0.67	4	0.44
2-1	7	4.67	22	2.44
2-2	3	2.00	12	1.34
2-3	5	3.33	29	3.22
2-4	0	0	13	1.44
3-1	7	4.67	18	2.00
3-2	4	2.67	28	3.11
3-4	5	3.33	21	2.33
4-1	2	1.34	11	1.22
4-2	5	3.33	26	2.89
4-3	5	3.33	23	2.56
4-4	0	0	13	1.44
Average	3.53	2.36	19.13	2.13

Table 2. Ratio of pronouncing tonal errors of two types of disyllabic words (%)

	/mama/ (n=150)		Real words (n=900)	
	Number of mistakes	Ratio (%)	Number of mistakes	Ratio (%)
1-1	0	0	3	0.40
1-2	1	0.67	6	0.80
1-3	4	2.67	18	2.40
1-4	2	1.33	13	1.74
2-1	2	1.33	14	1.87
2-2	0	0	11	1.47
2-3	5	3.33	15	2.00
2-4	3	2.00	20	2.67
3-1	1	0.67	3	0.40
3-2	2	1.33	15	2.00
3-4	1	0.67	7	0.94
4-1	2	1.34	3	0.40
4-2	0	0	1	0.13
4-3	5	3.33	14	1.87
4-4	0	0	8	1.07
Average	1.87	1.25	10.07	1.34

Table 3. The sum of perception and pronunciation test results (%)

		1-1	1-2	1-3	1-4	2-1	2-2	2-3	2-4	3-1	3-2	3-4	4-1	4-2	4-3	4-4
Percep-tion	/mama/	0.67	2.00	3.33	0.67	4.67	2.00	3.33	0	4.67	2.67	3.33	1.34	3.33	3.33	0
	Real words	0.66	3.22	3.56	0.44	2.44	1.34	3.22	1.44	2.00	3.11	2.33	1.22	2.89	2.56	1.44
Pronunci-ation	/mama/	0	0.67	2.67	1.33	1.33	0	3.33	2.00	0.67	1.33	0.67	1.34	0	3.33	0
	Real words	0.40	0.80	2.40	1.74	1.87	1.47	2.00	2.67	0.40	2.00	0.94	0.40	0.13	1.87	1.07

Table 4. Ratio of tonal errors of initial and final syllables (%)

Type / Tonal Pattern	Perception				Pronunciation			
	/mama/		Real words		/mama/		Real words	
	initial	final	initial	final	initial	final	initial	final
1-1	0.67	0	0.44	0.22	0	0	0.13	0.27
1-2	0.67	1.33	1.33	1.89	0.67	0	0.67	0.13
1-3	1.33	2.00	1.78	1.78	0	2.67	0.67	1.73
1-4	0.67	0	0.33	0.11	0.67	0.67	0.67	1.07
2-1	3.33	1.33	2.00	0.44	1.33	0	1.47	0.40
2-2	1.33	0.67	0.67	0.67	0	0	1.20	0.27
2-3	2.00	1.33	1.11	2.11	0.67	2.67	0.67	1.33
2-4	0	0	1.22	0.22	1.33	0.67	1.60	1.07
3-3	2.67	2.00	1.67	0.33	0.67	0	0.13	0.27
3-2	2.00	0.67	1.89	1.22	1.33	0	1.60	0.40
3-4	2.67	0.67	2.11	0.22	0	0.67	0.67	0.27
4-1	0.67	0.67	0.78	0.44	0.67	0.67	0.27	0.13
4-2	1.33	2.00	1.33	1.56	0	0	0.13	0
4-3	1.33	2.00	0.56	2.00	0	3.33	0.40	1.47
4-4	0	0	1.00	0.44	0	0	0.40	0.67
Total	20.67	14.67	18.22	13.56	7.33	11.33	10.67	9.47

4.3 Some Typical Tonal Errors in Each Group

Table 5. Typical tonal error patterns of perception

	/mama/		Real words	
	initial	final	initial	final
1-3	1→4	3→2	1→4/2/3	3→2/4
2-1	2→3	1→2	2→3/1/4	1→2
2-3	2→3	3→2	2→4/1/3	3→2
3-2	3→2/4	2→3/4	3→2/4	2→3/4/1
4-3	4→3	3→2	4→2/3	3→2/4

From Table 3 we can see that tonal patterns 1-3, 2-1, 2-3, 3-2 and 4-3 are typical tonal errors in both perception and pronunciation. In this section, we will present how the subjects mistook the tones in the listening test. In addition, we will show the pitch contour of tonal patterns mentioned above to clarify some error tendencies.

Table 5 indicates two important things: firstly, the answers to the pseudo-words and the real words share similar error patterns; secondly, the subjects made various types of errors when they listened to real words. More specifically, tone 1 of the initial syllable was mostly mistaken for tone 4, sometimes for tone 2 or 3 in the real words. Tone 2 of the initial syllable was often mistaken for tone 3, which also has a rising tendency. When tone 3 is in the initial position, it is likely to be heard as tone 2 or tone 4. On the other hand, initial tone 4 was heard as tone 2 or tone 3. For the final syllable, except for the 3-2 pattern, the other tones were mostly mistaken for tone 2. This is a very interesting phenomenon of Japanese students.

Table 6. Typical tonal error patterns of pronunciation

	/mama/		Real words	
	initial	final	initial	final
1-3		3→0/2	1→4	3→0/2/4
2-1	2→3/4		2→3/1/4	1→2/4
2-3	2→4	3→0/4	2→4/1	3→0/4/1
3-2	3→1/2		3→1/2/4	2→1
4-3		3→0/2	4→1/3	3→0/4/1/2

From Table 6 we can see that no subject made mistakes in some of the syllables of the pseudo-words. This is different from the perceptional test results. Moreover, when the subjects pronounced the real words, they made more mistakes than in the pseudo-words. This is the same tendency as in perception.

If we compare Table 5 and Table 6, we can see that the subjects share the same tonal pattern errors in some aspects of their perception and pronunciation. For instance, they heard the pseudo-word of tonal pattern 1-3 as 1-2, and also pronounced them in the same way. We may see more details in Table 7.

Table 7. Common tonal error patterns shared by perception and pronunciation

	/mama/		Real words	
	initial	final	initial	final
1-3		3→2	1→4	3→2/4
2-1	2→3		2→3/1/4	1→2
2-3			2→4/1	
3-2	3→2		3→2/4	2→1
4-3		3→2	4→3	3→2/4

We also found several differences between perception and pronunciation. For example, as mentioned before, there were fewer mistakes in pronunciation than in perception. No one mispronounced the first syllable of the 1-3/4-3 patterns, or the second syllable of the 2-1/3-2 patterns. In addition, when subjects pronounced disyllabic words, they made different mistakes from listening to those words. For example, the most obvious difference was in the final syllable of tone 3. In the listening test, it was mostly mistaken for tone 2, but in the pronunciation test, it was always pronounced as neutral tone (tone 0).

In the following paragraphs, we are going to select some typical words and make comparisons of pitch contour between subjects and native speakers.

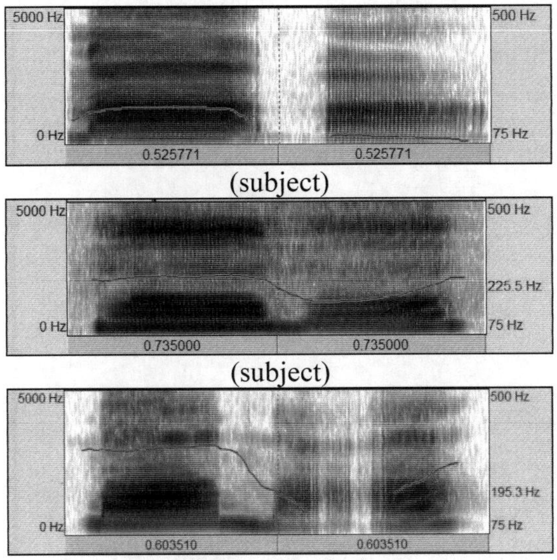

Figure 4. Pitch contour of /māmǎ/

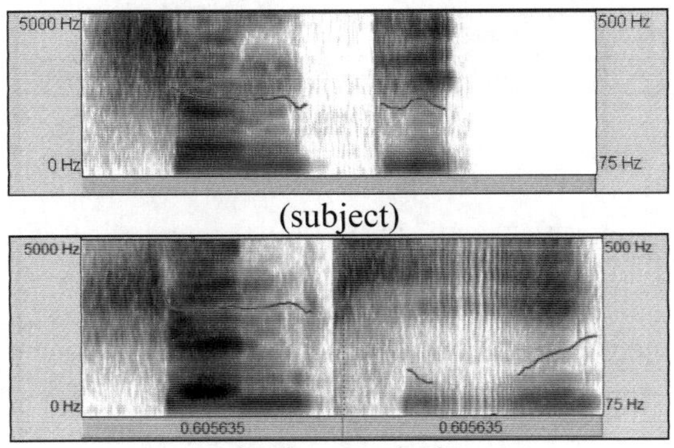

Figure 5. Pitch contour of /shēn tǐ/

First of all, let us start with the pseudo-disyllabic word /mama/, which is pronounced with typical tonal errors. Figure 4 shows that some subjects have problems pronouncing the final rising-falling tone (tone 3). We can hardly see the falling-rising procedure in the upper pictures in Figure 4, but the native speaker's pitch contour shows the process very clearly. Most subjects mispronounced it as a neutral tone or even a rising tone. The same tendency can also be found in real words (Figure 5).

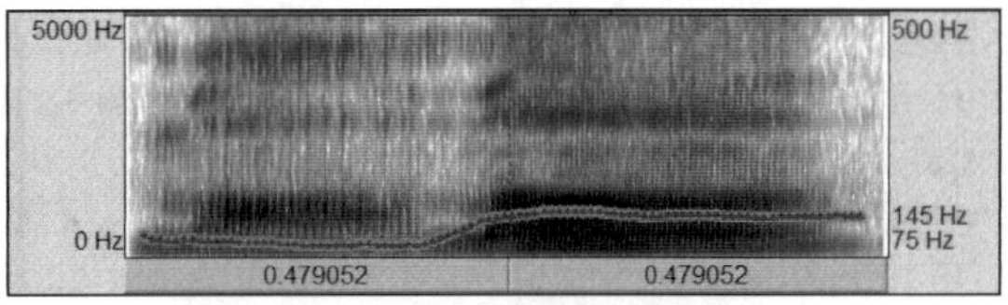

(subject)

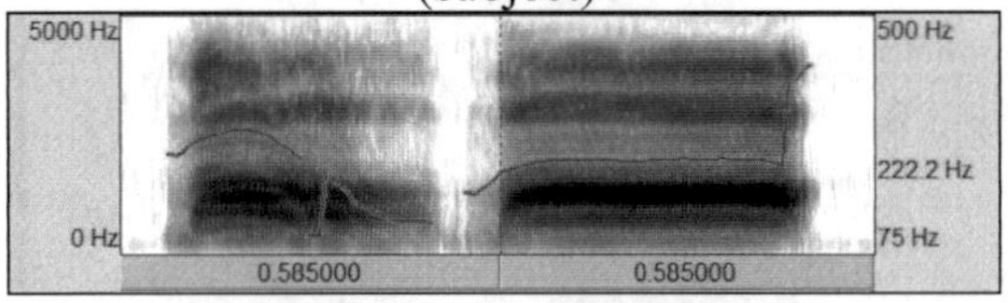

(subject)

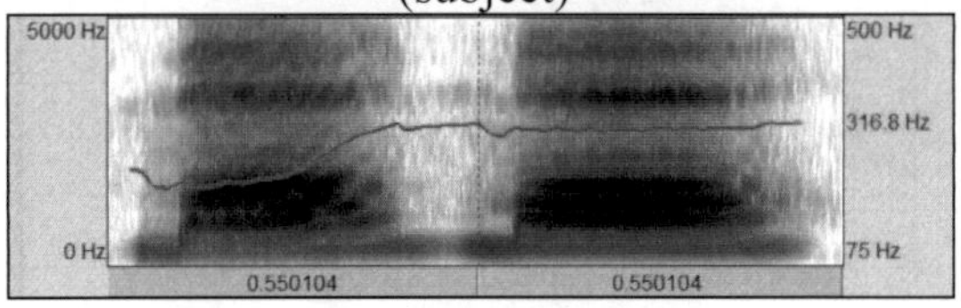

(native speaker)

Figure 6. Pitch contour of /mámā/ (subject)

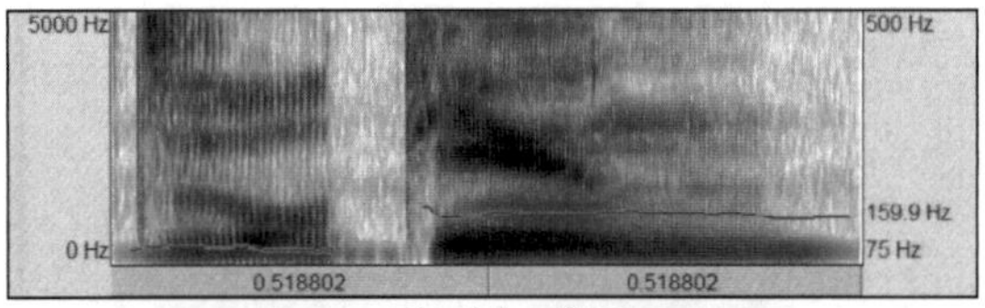

(subject)

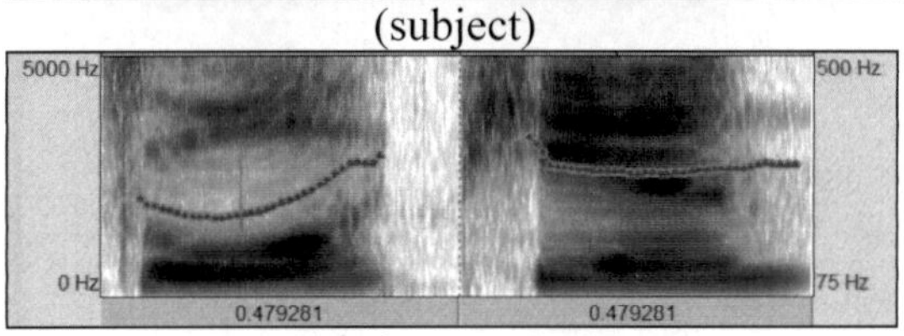

(native speaker)

Figure 7. Pitch contour of /zuó tiān/

The initial tone 2 (rising tone) requires a swift rising of the voice. However, we can hardly see this tendency from the subject's pitch contour in Figure 6 and 7, in which tone 2 is even lower than the level of tone 1. As a result, it sounds like tone 3 of the first syllable in the native evaluation.

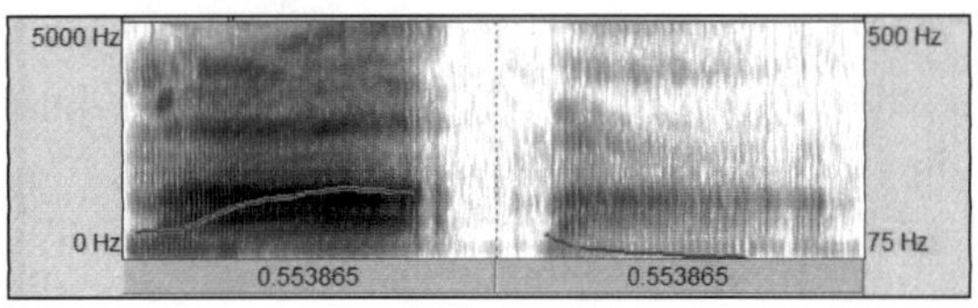

(subject)

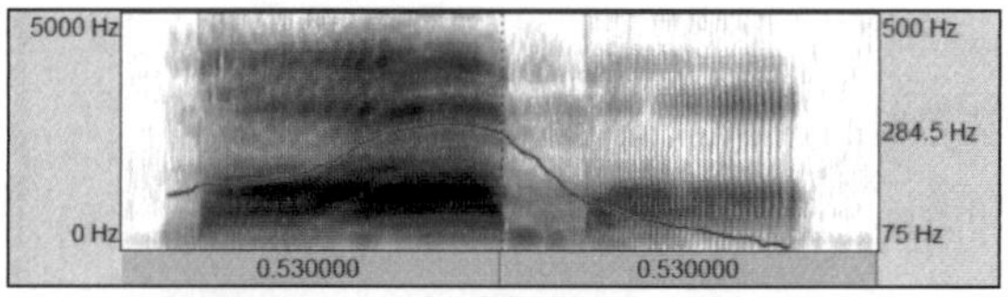

(subject)

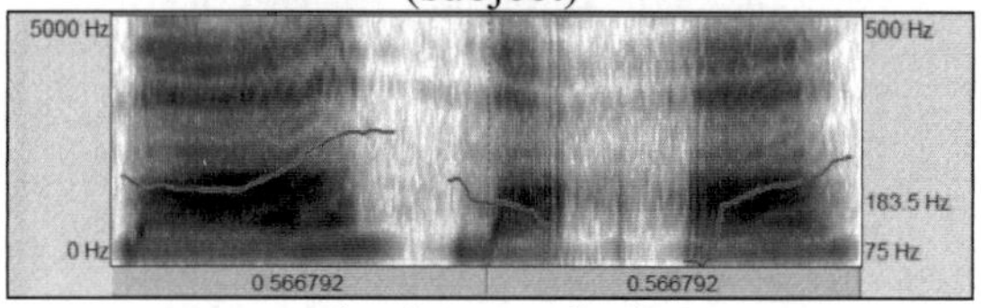

(native speaker)

Figure 8. Pitch contour of /mámǎ/

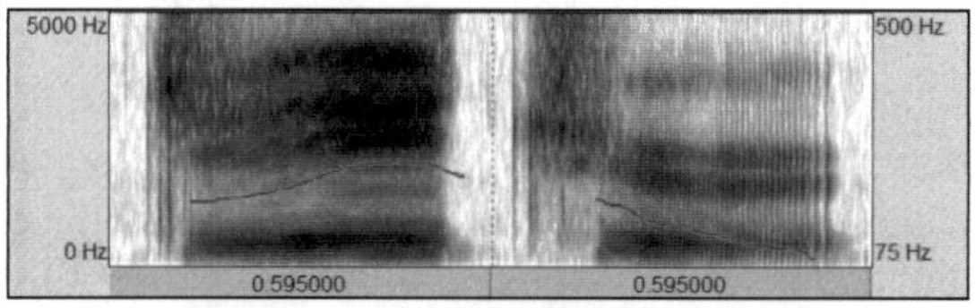

(subject)

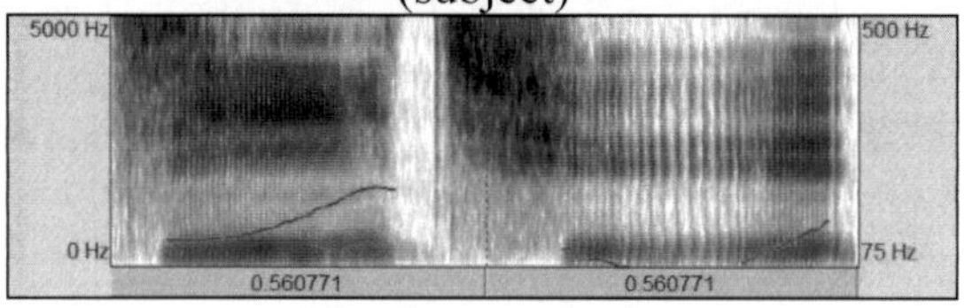

(native speaker)

Figure 9. Pitch contour of /jí qǔ/

Also with an initial tone 2, when the final tone is tone 3, the rising trend is much clearer than in the 2-1 pattern. On the other hand, almost all subjects failed to pronounce tone 3 in the correct falling-rising process (Figure 8, Figure 9). Their pitch contour fell down without rising.

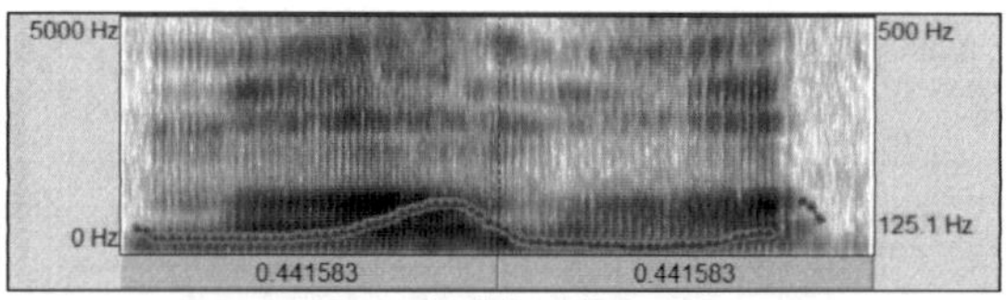

(subject)

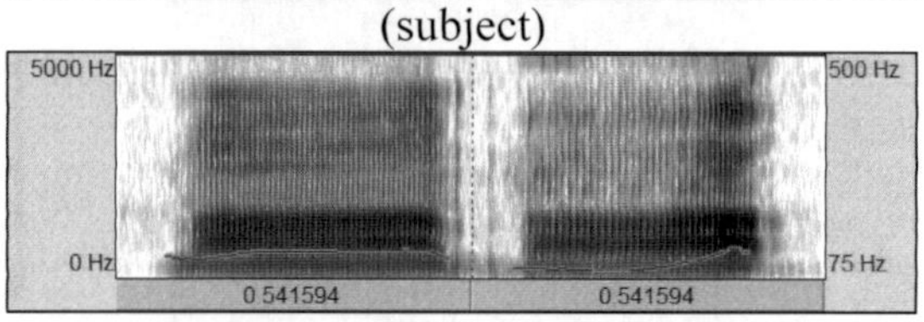

(subject)

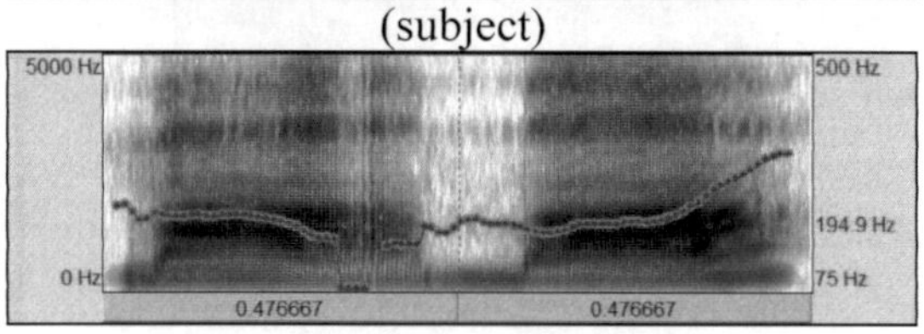

(native speaker)

Figure 10. Pitch contour of /mǎmá/

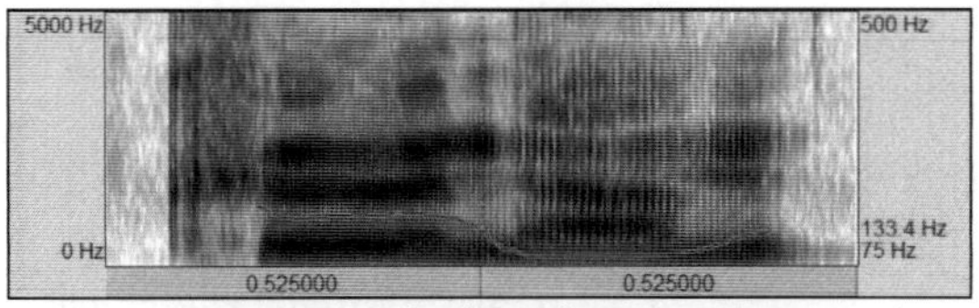

(subject)

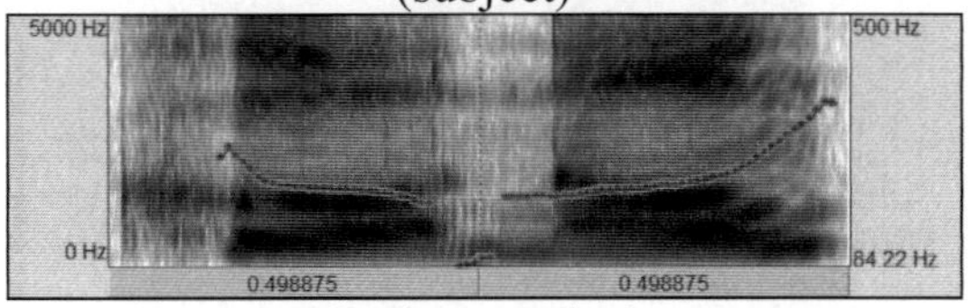

(native speaker)

Figure 11. Pitch contour of /kě néng/

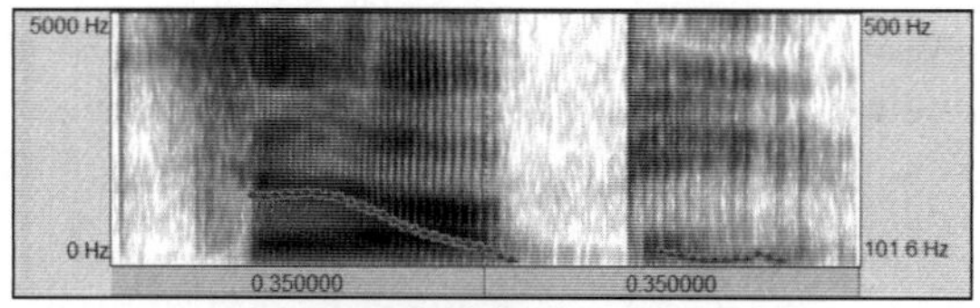

(subject)

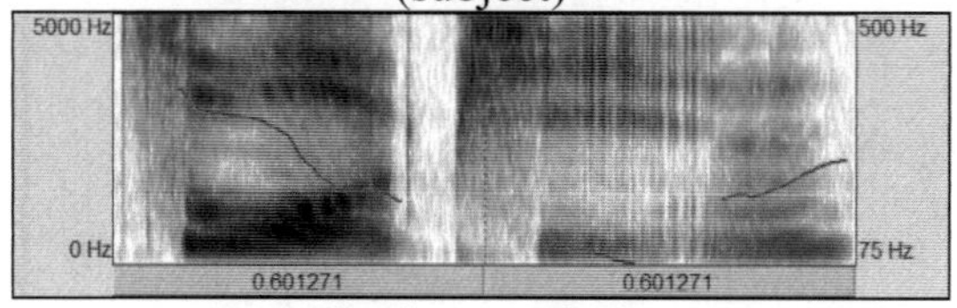

(native speaker)

Figure 13. Pitch contour of /zuò pǐn/

In Mandarin Chinese, the 3-2 pattern is a difficult tonal combination for learners. The voice must be suppressed into a low level first and then raised immediately (Figure 10, Figure 11, native speaker). In this study, some subjects were successful, while others failed. In the failed cases, we can hardly see any difference between initial and final tones (Figure 10, Figure 11, subject).

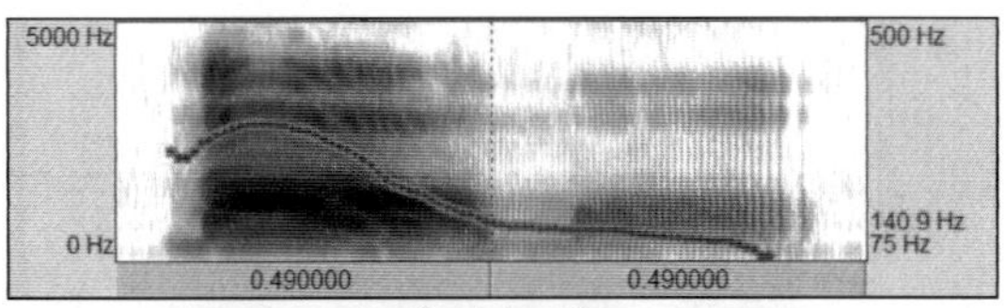

(subject)

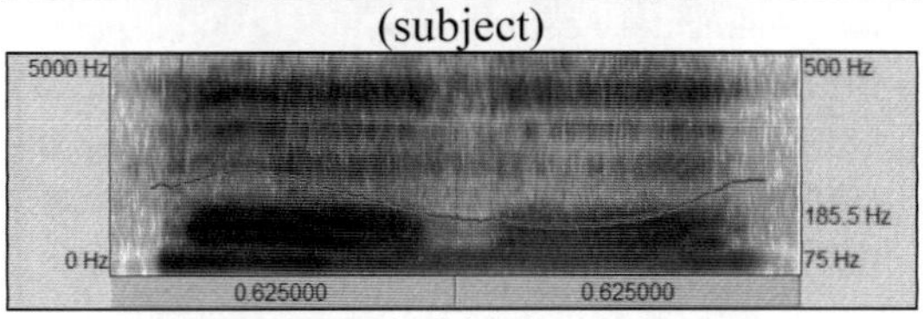

(subject)

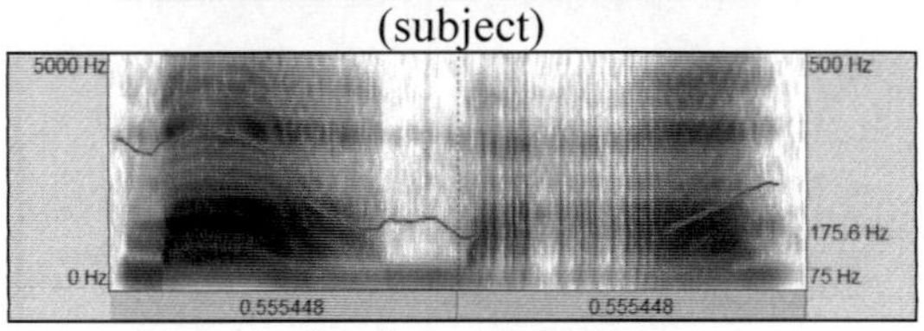

(native speaker)

Figure 12. Pitch contour of /màmǎ/

By comparing the pitch contour of the subject's and the native speaker's, it becomes obvious that the subjects pronounced tone 4 with little difficulty but still failed to pronounce tone 3 correctly. They made mistakes in one of two ways: the voice was either suppressed without rising or not suppressed enough. In the first case, it sounded like neutral tone and in the second case, it sounded like tone 2.

From the tonal pitch contour analysis we can see why tonal patterns 1-3, 2-1, 2-3, 3-2 and 4-3 are most easily mispronounced by all subjects. When they pronounce initial tone 1 (flat tone), the start is not high enough to distinguish from the following tone. Then, the pronunciation of initial tone 2 (rising tone) is too moderate so the listener cannot identify it very clearly. Also, the subjects failed to pronounce tone 3 in the correct falling-rising process no matter whether it was the initial or the final tone. Finally, if subjects pronounced tone 4 win short or moderate falling trend, the voice would sound like the neutral tone.

5 Conclusion

This study focused only on disyllabic words. In Japanese, the pitches of the first and the second moras must differ. If the first mora is pronounced with high pitch, the second one must be with low pitch. In the same way, if the first is with low pitch, the second must be with high pitch (Kubozono, 2006). A rising-falling pattern was proposed (Zhu, 1994) based on the pitch changes of Japanese students and it was argued that regardless of the original pitch in Japanese, new compounds are always of Low-High-Low tones. The tonal errors of the ten Japanese students in this current study are also similar to this pattern because of the negative transfer from the students' mother tongue.

In this study, the errors made by the 10 subjects were mostly found in tonal patterns 1-3, 2-1, 2-3, 3-2 and 4-3. They mistook these five patterns the most in both perception and pronunciation. Particularly, the 3-1 pattern of the pseudo-words and 1-3 pattern of the real words were the most difficult for the subjects in the listening test. About pronunciation, they pronounced initial tone 1 (flat tone) not high enough and initial tone 2 (rising tone) too moderately to distinguish from the following tone. Also, the subjects had problems mostly with tone 3 no matter whether it was initial or final.

Furthermore, by comparing the ratio of tonal errors of initial to final syllables we can tell that the initial syllable seems to be more difficult than the final syllable in perception, but in pronunciation this tendency was not found.

Moreover, the subjects quite often mispronounced the words the same way as they misheard them. We also found several differences between perception and pronunciation. As mentioned before, there were fewer mistakes in pronunciation than in perception. In addition, there were more variations of pronunciation mistakes than perceptional ones.

This study discussed the tonal errors by only 10 subjects. It is recommended that in a future study of related issues more subjects should be included to make the experimental results more representative. Also, words with a carrying phrase should be added in further studies to obtain a more complete picture of the acquisition of Chinese tones.

Since the functions of Chinese tones and Japanese pitch accent differ, by means of contrastive analysis one can help teachers pay special attention to those tones learners frequently confuse, so as to make them fully acquainted with the correct tone production in various tone combinations.

References

Chao L.- J. 2003. Special Phonetic Instruction in Chinese to Japanese Students. *Journal of Yunnan Normal University*, 1(3): 66-67.

Chao Y. R. 1968. *A Grammar of Spoken Chinese*. Berkeley: University of California Press.

Dong Y. T, Tsubota Y and Dantsuji M. 2011. The Perceptional Error Patterns of Japanese Mandarin Chinese Learners in the Disyllabic Words, *Proceedings of the 9th National Congress of Japan Association of Chinese Language Education*, 15-19.

He P. 1997. Studies in Basic Phonetic Instruction in Chinese to Japanese Students. *Language Teaching and Linguistic Studies* 3, 49-50.

Hiroshi W. 2003. The Theory of Japanese Stress and Phonetic Categorization. *Journal of Wu Feng Institute of Technology* 11, 283-286.

Jun S. 2001. Problems and Solutions of Japanese Learning Chinese Tones. *Proceedings of the International Symposium in Teaching Chinese to Japanese Students* 172. Peking: Chinese Social Science.

Kubozono H. 2006. *Akusento no Hosoku*. Tokyo: Iwanami Shoten.

Liu J. P. 2008. RiBen LiuXueSheng HanYu ShuangYinJi Ci ShengDiao PianWu DiaoCha BaoGao, *ShangYe WenHua*, Vol. 3, 33-34.

Nishi T. 2004. Nihongo Bogowasha no Chugokugo Seicho Kikitori ni Kansuru Ichi Kousatsu – Dainisei to Daisansei no Kondou, *Tagen Bunka*, Vol. 4, 15-27.

Vance T. J. 1986. *An Introduction to Japanese Phonology*. Albany: State University of New York Press.

Wu Z.- J.& Lin M-Z. 1989. *An Outline of Experimental Phonetics*. Peking: High Education Press.

Wu Z.- J. 1992. *Introduction to the Phonetics of Modern Chinese*. Peking: Chinese Language Teaching.

Wang S.- Y. 1992. Japanese Tone and Pronunciation. *Foreign Languages in Fujian* 2, 24-26.

Yang L. M. 1999. Chugokugo no Seicho Chikaku ni Kansuru Jikkenteki Kenkyu – Seicho Kyoiku no Tame no Kisoteki Kenkyu, *Meiji Daigaku Jinbun Kagaku Kenkyusho Kiyo*, Vol. 45, 294-307.

Zhu C. 1994. Contrastive Experiments on the Suprasegmental Features of Chinese and Japanese. *Journal of East China University* 1, 85-86.

Zhu C. 1997. *The Strategies of Foreign Students for the Phonetic Learning in Chinese.* Peking: Beijing Language and Culture University Press.

Exploring the Chinese Mental Lexicon with Word Association Norms

Oi Yee Kwong
Department of Chinese, Translation and Linguistics
City University of Hong Kong
Tat Chee Avenue, Kowloon, Hong Kong
Olivia.Kwong@cityu.edu.hk

Abstract

Our internal repository of words, often known as the mental lexicon, has primarily been modelled by psychologists as some kind of network. One way to probe its organisation and access mechanisms is by means of word association techniques, which have rarely been applied on Chinese. This paper reports on the design and implementation of a pilot word association test on native Hong Kong Cantonese speakers. The test contains 500 stimulus words, carefully selected and controlled on important factors including word frequency, part-of-speech, syllabicity, concreteness and vocabulary type. The resulting association norms based on 58 participants reveal interesting properties of the Chinese mental lexicon, such as the dominance of disyllabic and nominal concepts, and collocational associations. Despite its current small scale, the word association norms obtained from this study do not only offer first-hand psycholinguistic evidence for investigating the Chinese mental lexicon but also provide a useful resource to inform future studies in Chinese lexical access, lexical semantics and lexicography.

1 Introduction

Humans know tens of thousands of words, and their language behaviour suggests that the words are systematically organised and efficiently accessed in their internal word repository, often known as the mental lexicon. For a long time, psychologists have hypothesised the mental lexicon as a massive network of inter-connected nodes. The organisation and access mechanisms of the mental lexicon have primarily been studied with experimental approaches, using a variety of tasks like lexical decision, semantic verification, word association, etc. Despite some intrinsic weaknesses, word association techniques offer first-hand psycholinguistic evidence of our mental lexicon especially for revealing the extensiveness of the network and the different kinds of semantic associations among concepts in it. However, large-scale association norms obtained from native Chinese speakers comparable to those in English and other languages are lacking. This study, as a pilot attempt, intends to produce a set of word association norms from native Hong Kong Cantonese speakers, to complement other experimental methods and offer more insight for further studies on the Chinese mental lexicon.

Hong Kong Chinese is our focus in this study. Written vocabularies from Modern Standard Chinese and spoken vocabularies from the Cantonese dialect are supposed to co-exist in the mental lexicon of its speakers. It is therefore theoretically and practically interesting to explore how such mixed forms, together with other Chinese-specific factors like logographic meanings, syllabicity and the fuzziness of the word notion, as well as other general factors like word frequency, part-of-speech, concreteness and polysemy, shape the organisation of the Chinese mental lexicon.

Stimulus words were thus chosen carefully and systematically, with due consideration for the various important factors. The resulting word association norms are expected to shed light on a wide range of research questions on the Chinese mental lexicon, some of which are particularly addressed in the current study:

- What is the basic unit in the semantic memory of Chinese speakers?
- What kinds of semantic associations are found, and which kind (taxonomic, thematic, or otherwise) dominates?

- How do the associations differ for words of different frequency, part-of-speech, and concreteness?
- Are written and spoken vocabulary items stored together or separately?

In Section 2, we briefly review related work. In Section 3, the design and implementation of our word association test, and the compilation of word association norms, will be described. Preliminary analysis of the data will be discussed in Section 4, followed by a conclusion with further research agenda in Section 5.

2 Studies on the Mental Lexicon

As Aitchison (2003) pointed out, the general picture of the mental lexicon so far is one in which there are a variety of links between words, some strong, some weak. Strictly speaking, our knowledge of words includes phonological, morphological, syntactic, and even other lower level features like radicals, shapes and strokes. Hence network models in different forms and complexity have been proposed under the connectionist roof. For example, McClelland and Rumelhart's (1981) interactive activation model assumes three levels of processing (feature, letter, and word) which occur simultaneously with excitatory or inhibitory interactions. Others (e.g. Bock and Levelt, 1994; Caramazza, 1997) suggested that a lexical network should also connect a lemma level and a lexeme level for syntactic and phonological properties respectively, in addition to the conceptual level for semantic relations. Models for Chinese need to account for the role of radicals and their positions in a character, as well as the combination of characters to form words (e.g. Taft, 2006). The focus of this study is primarily on the semantic connections among words, or semantic memory.

The psychological reality of the network models receives support from experimental psychology, which often employs methods like lexical decision, semantic verification, etc. The spreading activation model of lexical access suggested in Collins and Loftus' (1975) classic study has been most influential especially with its account for the associative priming effects. Frequency effect and concreteness effect have been observed regarding lexical organisation (e.g. Kroll and Merves, 1986; Bleasdale, 1987). The role of polysemy with respect to lexical representation and word recognition, in isolation or in context, has also been widely studied (e.g. Rayner and Frazier, 1989; Klein and Murphy, 2002; Rodd et al., 2002). Similar studies on Chinese, though not as many, have identified some Chinese-specific properties of the mental lexicon, including the fuzziness of the word notion (e.g. Hoosain, 1992), word frequency (but not character frequency) effects and the competition between homophonic morphemes (e.g. Zhou and Marslen-Wilson, 1994), relations between morphemes and words (e.g. Myers, 2006), polysemy and meaning representation in the mental lexicon (e.g. Lin and Ahrens, 2010). Most of these studies on Chinese, however, were based on Mandarin Chinese, and the effect of concreteness has not been widely studied.

Word association techniques have also been a traditional approach to probe the mental lexicon. They can be used within experimental approaches, but more often, the resulting word association norms offer another useful resource for us to explore the mental lexicon from a broader perspective, which may in turn inform and complement experimental studies. Word association tests ask human subjects for the first word they can think of upon seeing or hearing a stimulus word and the percentage of subjects producing each response is computed from a large group of subjects to give the word association norms, which are useful in many respects (e.g. de Groot, 1989; Hirsh and Tree, 2001; Guida and Lenci, 2007). Examples of famous English word association norms include the 1952 Minnesota word association norms (Jenkins, 1970) and the Birkbeck word association norms (Moss and Older, 1996). Large-scale word association data are also available for other languages like Japanese (Joyce, 2005) and German (Schulte im Walde et al., 2008). However, comparable large-scale association norms obtained from native Chinese speakers are lacking. The pilot study reported in this paper thus intends to fill this gap with a focus on the mental lexicon of native Hong Kong Chinese, and to capitalise on the range of association data thus produced for qualitative and quantitative analyses with respect to various important factors.

3 Word Association Test

In this study, human subjects were asked to give the first word which occurs to them upon seeing a certain stimulus word, and thus it is a *discrete* word association test. The responses need not be in any particular part-of-speech, and thus they lead to a set of *free* association norms. In the following, we describe the design and implementation of the test. Chinese examples are listed with Cantonese transcription in Jyutping (in italics) and an English gloss (in quotes) alongside.

3.1 Test Platform

Online version of the association test was developed. Registered participants were given instructions in English and Chinese (Figure 1), and asked to input their response on the web interface (Figure 2). The English and Chinese instructions are more or less equivalent. It was additionally specified in the Chinese instructions that there was no restriction on the part-of-speech and syllabicity for the responses. There is also slight difference in the example given in the instructions. In English, possible responses to "butter" are exemplified with "bread", "milk", "fat" and "spread"; while in Chinese, for the equivalent stimulus word 牛油 *ngau4-jau4* 'butter', the example responses given are 麵包 *min6-baau1* 'bread', 牛油果 *ngau4-jau4-gwo2* 'avocado', 牛奶 *ngau4-naai5* 'milk', 肥膩 *fei4-nei6* 'fatty', 黃色 *wong4-sik1* 'yellow', and 搽 *caa4* '(to) spread'. The inclusion of "avocado" and "milk" for the Chinese examples was to demonstrate the Chinese-specific cases as they share morphemes with the stimulus word.

3.2 Participants

All 58 participants (20 males and 38 females) were undergraduate students of the City University of Hong Kong. They were recruited from the Department of Chinese, Translation and Linguistics, and the Department of Computer Science. All of them are native Hong Kong Cantonese speakers. Each participant was rewarded with a shopping voucher upon completion of all test sessions.

3.3 Selection of Stimulus

To maximise the usefulness of the pilot collection of data and the resulting association norms, a balanced and representative sample of stimulus words was selected. The selection was done with systematic control on various factors deemed important in human lexical processing, which include word frequency (High, Mid, Low)[1], part-of-speech (Noun, Verb, Adjective, Fluid), syllabicity (Monosyllabic, Disyllabic, Trisyllabic), concreteness (Concrete, Abstract), and vocabulary type (Written, Spoken)[2]. As far as polysemy is concerned, most of the disyllabic and trisyllabic words are unambiguous. The categorially fluid ones are by default ambiguous, and the monosyllabic words are mostly ambiguous in Chinese. They were not particularly controlled for the number of meanings they possess. Altogether 500 stimulus words were selected. Their distribution with respect to the various factors and some examples for each category are shown in Table 1. All stimulus words were randomly divided into five test sessions with 100 words each.

3.4 Association Norm Preparation

The initially collected responses were checked for obvious typos (e.g. changing 普通詰 *pou2-tung1-kit3* to 普通話 *pou2-tung1-waa2* for 'Putonghua') and correcting homophones (e.g. changing 快子 *faai3-zi2* to 筷子 *faai3-zi2* for 'chopsticks'). For specific responses, we had to double check with participants and asked them to clarify, to help our subsequent classification of the responses. Similar responses (e.g. 蛋 *daan2* 'egg' and 雞蛋 *gai1-daan2* 'egg') were marked. In a word association test, the general patterns of responses from large groups of subjects are compiled into a set of word association norms. The percentage occupied by a certain response is assumed to indicate the associative strength between the stimulus and that response. The percentage of individual response types for each stimulus word was thus computed and the association norms were listed accordingly. Two examples are shown in Figure 3.

---

[1] The frequency distinction for the current study was based on a 2.6-million-character Chinese corpus collected over the web, which is composed of texts from three newspapers and five magazines covering a variety of topics. The corpus was word segmented. Two word lists were compiled from the news subcorpus and the magazine subcorpus respectively. The word-frequency list from the news subcorpus was divided into three frequency bands according to the cumulative percentage: Hi (below 80%), Mid (80-90%) and Low (above 90%). Only words appearing in both subcorpora were included as candidates.

[2] By written vocabularies, we mean those lexical items which can be acceptably used in standard written Chinese texts. In fact most of these items are also used in Cantonese speech. The spoken vocabularies, on the other hand, are often considered inappropriate to be used in formal written contexts.

Please read each word displayed on screen and then input the first word it brings to mind. Type your response in the textbox provided. For example, if the given word is "butter", the first word you think of might be "bread" or "milk" or "fat" or "spread" or something else. Please note that we are interested in the word that comes to mind immediately, and there is no right or wrong "answer", so you only need to give your immediate response, not after thinking about it for a while. Do not go back and change your mind after you have given your first response. Your responses should primarily be in the same language as the given words, but if it really happens that you immediately think of a word in another language, you may just input that word. Each test session contains 100 words. Try to finish one whole session without interruption at a time. Now please click "Start" to begin.

請觀看螢光幕顯示的詞語，然後盡快在空格內輸入第一個您即時聯想到的詞語，音節及詞性不限。 例如：當螢光幕顯示「牛油」一詞，大家可能會聯想到「麵包」、「牛油果」、「牛奶」、「肥膩」 、「黃色」、「搽」等等，您可以使用任何一種自己慣用的輸入法，盡快輸入您想到的第一個詞語。 我們旨在觀察一般人聯想的特點和規律，沒有對錯之分，所以您只需靠即時反應，不用特別思考，也不要更改已輸入的詞語。您應盡量以測試詞語的語言回應，但若您確實只能聯想到另一語言的詞語，也可輸入該詞。每一節測試包含 100 個詞語。每次請一氣呵成完成整節測試。現在請點擊 Start 開始測試。

Figure 1. Instructions Given to Participants

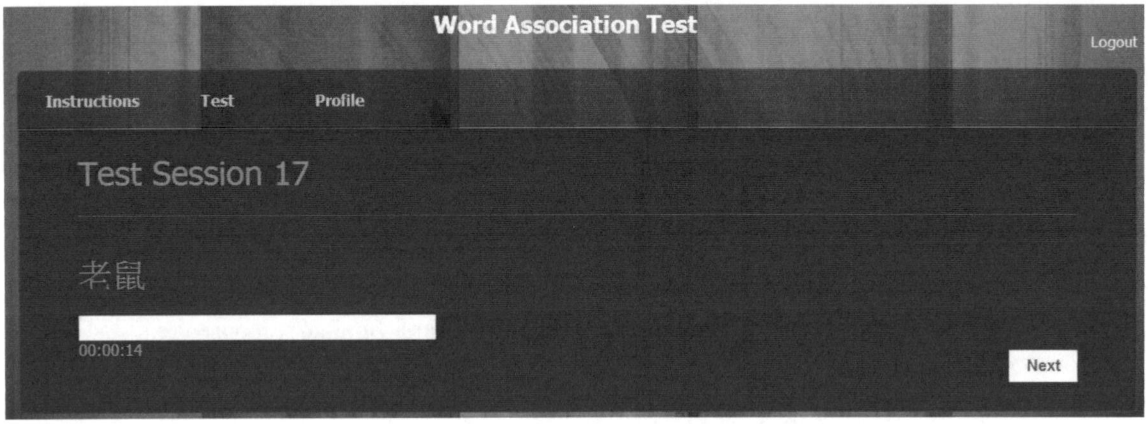

Figure 2. Online Platform for Submitting Association Responses

戒指 'ring'			**閱讀 '(to) read'**		
結婚	'marriage'	41.4%	書本	'book'	29.3%
承諾	'promise'	8.6%	書	'book'	20.7%
訂婚	'engagement'	8.6%	書籍	'book'	8.6%
鑽石	'diamond'	8.6%	小說	'fiction'	5.2%
求婚	'propose'	6.9%	理解	'comprehension'	5.2%
婚姻	'marriage'	5.2%	圖書	'(picture) book'	5.2%
無名指	'ring finger'	3.4%	計劃	'plan'	3.4%
戴	'wear'	3.4%	習慣	'habit'	3.4%
決定	'decision'	1.7%	文章	'article'	1.7%
所羅門	'Solomon'	1.7%	全文	'full article'	1.7%
金色	'gold (colour)'	1.7%	有益	'beneficial'	1.7%
很貴	'very expensive'	1.7%	困難	'difficult'	1.7%
閃	'shiny'	1.7%	知識	'knowledge'	1.7%
情人	'lover'	1.7%	眼鏡	'spectacles'	1.7%
責任	'responsibility'	1.7%	喜好	'preference'	1.7%
電影	'movie'	1.7%	報告	'report'	1.7%
			報章	'newspaper'	1.7%
			廣泛	'widely'	1.7%
			課外書	'leisure book'	1.7%

Figure 3. Examples of Association Norms

VOC	SYL	POS	CON	FRQ	Examples	
Wrt	Di	Noun	Abs	Hi	文化 *man4-faa3* 'culture'	事業 *si6-jip6* 'career'
				Mid	性格 *sing3-gaak3* 'personality'	治安 *zi6-ngon1* 'public order'
				Lo	良知 *loeng4-zi1* 'conscience'	潛質 *cim4-zat1* 'potential'
			Con	Hi	電腦 *din6-nou5* 'computer'	手袋 *sau2-doi2* 'handbag'
				Mid	畫家 *waa2-gaa1* 'painter'	菜刀 *coi3-dou1* 'chopper'
				Lo	花生 *faa1-sang1* 'peanut'	藥膏 *joek6-gou1* 'ointment'
		Verb	Abs	Hi	明白 *ming4-baak6* 'understand'	應付 *jing3-fu6* 'handle'
				Mid	珍惜 *zan1-sik1* 'cherish'	抗拒 *kong3-kui5* 'resist'
				Lo	猶豫 *jau4-ji4* 'hesitate'	承繼 *sing4-gai3* 'inherit'
			Con	Hi	畢業 *bat1-jip6* 'graduate'	參考 *caam1-haau2* 'refer'
				Mid	散步 *saan3-bou6* 'stroll'	挑選 *tiu1-syun2* 'select'
				Lo	徘徊 *pui4-wui4* 'linger'	溜冰 *lau4-bing1* 'ice-skate'
		Adj	--	Hi	明顯 *ming4-hin2* 'obvious'	重要 *zung6-jiu3* 'important'
				Mid	低調 *dai1-diu6* 'low-key'	慷慨 *hong2-koi3* 'generous'
				Lo	幼稚 *jau3-zi6* 'naive'	脆弱 *ceoi3-joek6* 'fragile'
		Fluid	--	Hi	服務 *fuk6-mou6* 'serve/service'	計劃 *gai3-waak6* 'plan'
				Mid	指揮 *zi2-fai1* 'conduct(or)'	練習 *lin6-zaap6* 'exercise'
				Lo	推斷 *teoi1-dyun3* 'infer(ence)'	青春 *cing1-ceon1* 'young/youth'
	Mono	Noun	Con	Hi	手 *sau2* 'hand'	海 *hoi2* 'sea'
				Mid	菜 *coi3* 'vegetable'	碳 *taan3* 'carbon'
				Lo	氧 *joeng5* 'oxygen'	虎 *fu2* 'tiger'
	Tri	Noun	Con	Hi	身分證 *san1-fan2-zing3* 'ID card'	辦公室 *baan6-gung1-sat1* 'office'
				Mid	小朋友 *siu2-pang4-jau5* 'child'	牛仔褲 *ngau4-zai2-fu3* 'jeans'
				Lo	天花板 *tin1-faa1-baan2* 'ceiling'	伺服器 *si6-fuk6-hei3* 'server'
Spk	--	--	--	--	回水 *wui4-seoi2* '(to) refund'	屋企 *uk1-kei2* 'home'

Table 1. Distribution and Examples of Stimulus Words by Various Factors
(Each group contains 20 stimulus words, amounting to 500 words altogether.)

3.5 Classification of Responses

All responses were then classified according to their syntactic and semantic nature. The syntactic classification, as shown in Table 2, categorises each response with respect to its constituent unit (WRD for words, PHR for phrases, SEN for sentences and INC for incomplete), vocabulary type (WRT for written words, SPK for spoken words, ENG for English or foreign words, and MIX for code-mixed items), and part-of-speech (NN for common nouns, VB for verbs, AJ for adjectives, PN for proper nouns, and OT for all other categories). For example, one of the responses to 三文治 *saam1-man4-zi6* 'sandwich' is 好食 *hou2-sik6* 'delicious', and this response is classified as WRD (word), SPK (spoken), and AJ (adjective). The semantic classification, on the other hand, had to consider the relation between individual stimulus words and responses. The granularity of classification may vary according to different purposes of analysis (e.g. Guida and Lenci, 2007; McRae et al., 2012). In this study, four main types of relations, from narrow to broad, are considered, namely taxonomic, collocational, thematic, and other relations. As exemplified in Table 3, taxonomic relations[3] comprises ANT for antonymy, HYP for hypernymy/hyponymy, MER for meronymy/holonymy, PRP for properties/attributes, SBL for siblings or coordinate terms, and SYN for (near-)synonymy. Collocations (COL) cover strongly collocated stimulus-response pairs or common syntagmatic patterns. Thematic relations (THM) include all broad and contextual relations between the stimulus and response, which can usually be connected within a given theme or context. Situational and personal associations, and those

[3] For simplicity, properties/attributes and part-of relations are grouped with other conventional taxonomic relations in this study.

involving subjective perception and value judgement, are grouped into the last category (OTH), which accommodates all other cases that cannot fit into any of the above types.

Category	Examples
Constituent Unit	
WRD	互聯網 *wu6-lyun4-mong5* ‘Internet’
PHR	賣豬肉 *maai6-zyu1-juk6* ‘sell pork’
SEN	知識就是力量 *zi1-sik1-zau6-si6-lik6-loeng6* ‘Knowledge is power’
INC	其實我 *kei4-sat6-ngo5* ‘actually I’
Vocabulary Type	
WRT	乞丐 *hat1-koi3* ‘beggar’
SPK	老豆 *lou5-dau6* ‘dad (colloquial)’
ENG	iPhone
MIX	做 GYM *zou6-zim1* ‘work out in gym’
Part-of-Speech	
NN	大提琴 *daai6-tai4-kam4* ‘cello’
VB	打架 *daa2-gaa3* ‘(to) fight’
AJ	宏偉 *wang4-wai5* ‘grand’
PN	陳奕迅 *can4-jik6-seon3* ‘Eason Chan’
OT	若然 *joek6-jin4* ‘if’

Table 2. Syntactic Classification of Responses

Type		Examples	
		Stimulus	Response
TAXONOMIC	ANT	樂觀 *lok6-gun1* ‘optimistic’	悲觀 *bei1-gun1* ‘pessimistic’
	HYP	老鼠 *lou5-syu2* ‘mouse’	動物 *dung6-mat6* ‘animal’
	MER	引擎 *jan5-king4* ‘engine’	飛機 *fei1-gei1* ‘airplane’
	PRP	石頭 *sek6-tau4* ‘stone’	堅硬 *gin1-ngaang6* ‘hard’
	SBL	長褲 *coeng4-fu3* ‘trousers’	短褲 *dyun2-fu3* ‘shorts’
	SYN	開心 *hoi1-sam1* ‘happy’	快樂 *faai3-lok6* ‘happy’
COL		解決 *gaai2-kyut3* ‘solve’	問題 *man6-tai4* ‘problem’
THM		機場 *gei1-coeng4* ‘airport’	旅遊 *leoi5-jau4* ‘travel’
OTH		頸鏈 *geng2-lin2* ‘necklace’	討厭 *tou2-jim3* ‘detest’

Table 3. Semantic Classification of Responses

4 Preliminary Analysis and Discussion

4.1 Basic Profile of Data

Among the 29,000 responses to 500 stimulus words from 58 participants, there are about 16,000 distinct stimulus-response pairs. The response types elicited by individual stimuli range from 7 to 49, averaging at 32.

Among all response tokens, the majority falls under written vocabularies. Less than 1% of the responses are non-Chinese (English or numeric) or code-mixed items. Spoken vocabularies occupy about 4% of all responses. Nevertheless, for the 20 spoken stimulus words, slightly more than 13% of the responses are spoken items. This suggests that while spoken and written items co-exist in the mental lexicon of Hong Kong Chinese, spoken items remain the minority but they are more closely linked together and more readily activate one another.

Excluding non-Chinese and code-mixed responses, the majority of the response tokens (about 74%) are disyllabic, followed by about 14% of monosyllabic responses, 8% of trisyllabic ones, and the remaining (less than 4%) are quadrisyllabic or longer. For monosyllabic stimuli alone, 40% of the responses are also monosyllabic, and disyllabic responses occupy only 50%. On the other hand, for trisyllabic stimuli alone, monosyllabic responses fall back to a general 13% whereas trisyllabic responses occupy about 11%. In general, about 5% of the responses are obviously non-words. Most of these are phrases, and there are some sentences, and only a few incomplete constituents.

For the part-of-speech (POS) and semantic nature of the responses, we consider only those which appeared twice or more. Among them, nominal responses occupy about 59%, verbal responses 19%, and adjectival responses 17%. Proper nouns account for less than 4% of the responses. It is interesting to note that the proportion of nominal responses stays the largest regardless of the POS of the stimulus words (54% for nominal stimuli, 70% for verbal stimuli, and 61% for adjectival stimuli). Nevertheless, associations between verbs and adjectives are apparently weaker as compared to verb-verb and adjective-adjective associations respectively. For instance, for verbal stimuli, there are 20% verbal responses but only 7% adjectival responses. For adjectival stimuli, there are 23% adjectival responses but only 15% verbal responses. This suggests the central role of nominal nodes in the mental lexicon. Verbs and adjectives have their own mass of associations, but most of the time they are more strongly associated to nominal concepts. In other words, paradigmatic relations may be more salient for nominal concepts, whereas syntagmatic relations, especially noun-verb and noun-adjective associations, are more significant for the learning and memory of verbs and adjectives.

Regarding the semantic associations between the stimuli and responses, taxonomic relations account for about 20%, collocational relations 42%, thematic relations 21%, and the remaining 17% (others) are mostly non-linguistic associations which often involve personal experience and judgement. Previous analysis of word association norms reveals that there are several common relations found between the responses and the stimuli, including coordination (e.g. salt to pepper), superordination (e.g. colour to red), synonymy (e.g. hungry to starved), collocation (e.g. net to butterfly), attributes (e.g. comfortable to sofa) and functions (e.g. rest to chair) (e.g. Aitchison, 2003), though their distribution is not clear. It appears that for Chinese, at least from the pilot data in this study, narrow taxonomic relations (including attributive and part-of relations) are relatively minor, whereas collocational and thematic associations have the largest share.

4.2 Frequency, POS and Concreteness

Figure 4 shows the distribution of the various kinds of semantic associations for concrete stimuli, including nouns and verbs of high and low frequency. Figure 5 shows similar results for abstract stimuli.

Some interesting facts are observed on the semantic associations with respect to the frequency, POS and concreteness of the stimulus words. First, collocational associations are particularly prominent for abstract stimuli. For nouns and verbs alike, abstract words were mostly responded with collocational items. Second, while collocational responses still occupy a large share for concrete verb stimuli, their importance for concrete noun stimuli is taken over by thematic associations. In other words, concrete words tend to elicit more thematic responses, and this is particularly true for nouns. Third, in general nouns tend to elicit more taxonomic relations than verbs, except for high frequency abstract nouns and verbs. Fourth, the role of the rather constant proportion of other non-linguistic associations in the semantic memory should by no means be ignored.

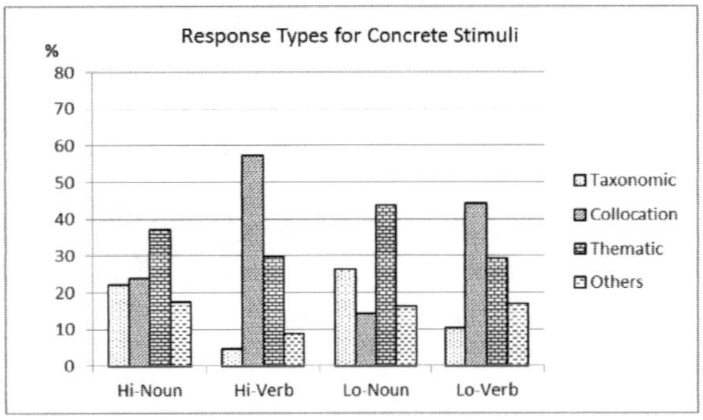

Figure 4. Response Types for Concrete Words

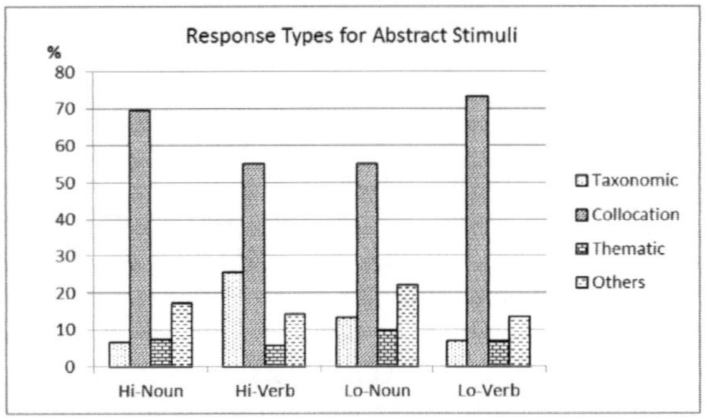

Figure 5. Response Types for Abstract Words

4.3 Some Implications

Referring to the questions raised in Section 1, the preliminary observations and analysis of the pilot association norms above thus suggest certain possibilities for the Chinese mental lexicon for further investigation.

Regarding the basic units, disyllabic words apparently dominate the Chinese mental lexicon. This is not only evident from the overall 74% disyllabic responses. In fact, the large number of monosyllabic items especially in response to monosyllabic stimulus words also points to the significance of disyllabic concepts. Many of the monosyllabic responses are not really elicited because of their morphemic meaning, but are intended to be combined with the stimulus to form a disyllabic word. For example, the stimulus 字 *zi6* 'character' elicited responses like 打 *daa2* '(to) hit' and 體 *tai2* 'body', probably because they form common words 打字 *daa2-zi6* '(to) type' and 字體 *zi6-tai2* 'font' respectively, and these disyllabic words are also among the responses for the same stimulus. There also remains the philosophical distinction between concepts and lexical items in the mental lexicon. To a certain extent, the mental lexicon is not like a dictionary of words, but rather a repository of words superimposed with a semantic network of concepts. Hence different responses may simultaneously point to the same concept. For instance, among the responses for 閱讀 *jyut6-duk6* '(to) read' in Figure 3, the top three responses (書本 *syu1-bun2* 'book', 書 *syu1* 'book', and 書籍 *syu1-zik6* 'book') all refer to the same concept "book" except that they might be more conventionally used in different contexts or registers. This is quite specific to Chinese given its word formation mechanisms and may suggest a slightly different organisation of the mental lexicon for Chinese from that for English which is worth further investigation.

Regarding the semantic associations, although previous studies have identified several prominent kinds of responses particularly under narrow taxonomic relations, in this study we nevertheless found that the broader but less mentioned collocational relations and thematic relations made up the majority of the responses. This is in fact quite an unexpected finding, especially for nouns, though less so for verbs and adjectives. While taxonomic relations are by definition confined to stimulus and response under the same part-of-speech, collocational and thematic relations may apply to intra- or inter-POS pairs. Past studies on the semantic memory tend to focus on the connection of nominal concepts, and semantic lexicons often emphasise their taxonomic connections. When it comes to free association, however, it happens that even for nominal stimuli, taxonomic associations are not always more readily activated than collocational and thematic associations. This suggests that the associative strengths for pure ontological relations may not be as strong as others which are probably continuously reinforced through personal and media contact. The diversity of relations exhibited in word association norms should not be under-estimated, especially in view of the "Others" category which covers situational associations and personal judgement. For instance, one response for 漢堡包 *hon3-bou2-baau1* 'hamburger' was 好吃 *hou2-hek3* 'delicious' which appears to be a property of hamburgers, but it is nevertheless too subjective to be taken as a genuine semantic association as being delicious is hardly an intrinsic attribute for any food. This suggests that while the organisation of the mental lexicon as a network may be something universal, the semantic associations and associative strengths in individuals' semantic memory may be a personal copy containing the universal structure and ontological connections, but to a large extent augmented and shaped by one's experience, perception, and exposure to interpersonal as well as cultural and media influence. We must therefore be cautious in interpreting the association norms. The top responses for individual stimulus words may be considered more universal and they are expected to inform and correspond to what one designs for semantic lexicons. The infrequent responses, which make up the majority, constitute only personal mental pictures, and may not even be properly considered very weak associations in general.

Regarding the role of frequency, POS and concreteness, taxonomic relations as well as thematic relations are apparently more accessible for nouns than verbs, especially concrete nouns. The concreteness effect is also exhibited in the dominance of collocational responses among abstract stimuli. The frequency effect does not seem to be significant, except that high frequency abstract verbs were found to elicit unexpectedly many taxonomic associations. The dominance of nominal concepts in the mental lexicon is nevertheless obvious as nominal responses made up the majority regardless of the POS of the stimuli.

Regarding the organisation of written and spoken vocabulary items, the above preliminary analysis reveals that they co-exist in the mental lexicon of Hong Kong Chinese. While most lexical items can be used both in written and spoken form (and hence all considered written items), spoken items are more or less confined to specific contexts and registers, and are more readily activated when the stimulus word is also a spoken item. It seems that when prompted with a spoken item, participants tend to feel greater acceptability of colloquial spoken items to be given as responses.

4.4 Potential Applications

Results from word association norms have a direct role for advancing our understanding of the mental lexicon and the development of psycholinguistic models for human lexical processing. Upon quantitative and qualitative analyses of the norms, we can draw up hypotheses on the nature and strengths of semantic associations, the degree of isolation or distinctiveness for particular concepts, the dispersion or diversity of the network, etc. for further investigation. One possible direction of study concerns the asymmetry of associative strength and thus readiness of activation between concepts. The traditional spreading activation model suggests that activation strengths depend, to a certain extent, on the number of connections (or density of nodes) from a concept and the distance in the activation path. With real data from the association norms (for example, the top response for the stimulus 衣櫃 *ji1-gwai6* 'wardrobe' is 衣服 *ji1-fuk6* 'clothing' (39.7%), but conversely, when 衣服 *ji1-fuk6* 'clothing' is the stimulus, 衣櫃 *ji1-gwai6* 'wardrobe' only accounts for 5.2% of the responses), this notion can be subject to more systematic investigation.

The association norms can also provide support for other areas including natural language processing, computational lexicography, and language pedagogy.

For natural language processing, the analysis of word association norms may reveal various kinds of semantic associations in relation to different salient factors including frequency, polysemy and concreteness, to inform the design of word sense disambiguation systems to better address the issue of lexical sensitivity, allowing a better exploitation of various knowledge sources with respect to different kinds of target words. For instance, Kwong (2012) suggested that concrete and abstract senses may be best distinguished and thus disambiguated by different knowledge sources.

For computational lexicography, the very notion of association plays an important role, and has thus significantly influenced the design of many lexical resources. WordNet (Miller et al., 1990) is perhaps the most typical example in this regard, as it started out as a psycholinguistic project on network models for the mental lexicon, but turned out to be one of the most popular semantic lexicons in computational linguistics. With the availability of large corpora, many studies have subsequently tried to simulate the observations from word association norms statistically from large corpora, and such statistical simulation provides concrete and scalable data to enhance lexicography (e.g. Church and Hanks, 1990; Wettler and Rapp, 1993; Ferret and Zock, 2006). Having a set of Chinese word association norms available will certainly enhance work in this regard.

Despite that participants were clearly asked to give the first "word" which the stimulus word brings to mind, responses other than words are still seen. This echoes that the concept of "word" is not really a clear and unambiguous one even for native speakers of Chinese. Monosyllabic responses comprise morphemes and words, and multi-syllabic responses contain phrases, sentences, and even non-constituent in addition to words. The many responses in the "Others" category involving extra-linguistic associations and personal mental pictures do not only reveal the organisation of the mental lexicon (especially of the younger generation) but also the influence of media and culture, which should be informative to educators to reflect on language pedagogy, even for L1 teaching.

5 Future Work and Conclusion

In this paper, we have reported on the design and implementation of a pilot word association test for Hong Kong Chinese. Preliminary analysis of the resulting association norms has revealed the dominance of disyllabic and nominal concepts, and collocational associations in the Hong Kong Chinese mental lexicon. The concreteness effect was also observed. In addition to traditional linguistic relations, semantic associations based on subjective experience and value judgement were also constantly found. More detailed quantitative and qualitative analysis of the responses is underway, and a larger-scale data collection will be planned. Notwithstanding the limitation of discrete word association, a benchmarking set of word association norms, which is currently lacking for Hong Kong Chinese, can offer a snapshot of the mental lexicon to inform and complement experimental studies. Further investigation on how the conventional spreading activation model may account for the asymmetry of associations will be done. The association norms will also be useful to other related areas like natural language processing, computational lexicography, and language pedagogy.

Acknowledgements

The work described in this paper was supported by grants from the City University of Hong Kong (Project No. 7002798 and funding from the Department of Chinese, Translation and Linguistics).

References

Aitchison, J. (2003) *Words in the Mind: An Introduction to the Mental Lexicon*. Blackwell Publishers.

Bleasdale, F.A. (1987) Concreteness dependent associative priming: Separate lexical organization for concrete and abstract words. *Journal of Experimental Psychology: Learning, Memory, and Cognition, 13*, 582-594.

Bock, K. and Levelt, W. (1994) Language production: Grammatical encoding. In M.A. Gernsbacher (Ed.), *Handbook of Psycholinguistics*. San Diego: Academic Press.

Caramazza, A. (1997) How many levels of processing are there in lexical access? *Cognitive Neuropsychology, 14*: 177-208.

Church, K.W. and Hanks, P. (1990) Word Association Norms, Mutual Information, and Lexicography. *Computational Linguistics, 16(1)*:22-29.

Collins, A.M. and Loftus, E.F. (1975) A spreading-activation theory of semantic processing. *Psychological Review, 82(6)*:407-428.

Ferret, O. and Zock, M. (2006) Enhancing electronic dictionaries with an index based on associations. In *Proceedings of COLING-ACL 2006*, Sydney, Australia, pp.281-288.

Groot, A.M.B. de (1989) Representational Aspects of Word Imageability and Word Frequency as Assessed Through Word Association. *Journal of Experimental Psychology: Learning, Memory, and Cognition, 15(5)*:824-845.

Guida, A. and Lenci, A. (2009) Semantic Properties of Word Associations to Italian Verbs. *Italian Journal of Linguistics, 19(2)*: 293-326.

Hirsh, K.W. and Tree, J.J. (2001) Word association norms for two cohorts of British adults. *Journal of Neurolinguistics, 14*:1-44.

Hoosain, R. (1992) Psychological reality of the word in Chinese. In H-C. Chen and O.J.L. Tzeng (Eds.), *Language Processing in Chinese*. Amsterdam: Elsevier Science Publishers, pp.111-130.

Jenkins, J.J. (1970) The 1952 Minnesota word association norms. In L. Postman and G. Keppel (Eds.), *Norms of Word Association*. New York: Academic Press, pp.1-38.

Joyce, T. (2005) Constructing a Large-Scale Database of Japanese Word Associations. (Special issue: Kanji corpus research, edited by Katsuo Tamaoka), *Glottometrics, 10*.

Klein, D.E. and Murphy, G.L. (2002) Paper has been my ruin: conceptual relations of polysemous senses. *Journal of Memory and Language, 47*: 548-570.

Kroll, J.F. and Merves, J.S. (1986) Lexical access for concrete and abstract words. *Journal of Experimental Psychology: Learning, Memory, and Cognition, 12*:92-107.

Kwong, O.Y. (2012) Psycholinguistics, Lexicography, and Word Sense Disambiguation. In *Proceedings of the 26th Pacific Asia Conference on Language, Information and Computation (PACLIC 26)*, Bali, Indonesia, pp.408-417.

Lin, C-J. C. and Ahrens, K. (2010) Ambiguity Advantage Revisited: Two Meanings are Better than One When Accessing Chinese Nouns. *Journal of Psycholinguistic Research, 39*:1-19.

McClelland, J.L. and Rumelhart, D.E. (1981) An interactive activation model of context effects in letter perception: Part 1. An account of basic findings. *Psychological Review, 88*: 375-407.

McRae, K., Khalkhali, S. and Hare, M. (2012) Semantic and Associative Relations in Adolescents and Young Adults: Examining a Tenuous Dichotomy. In V.F. Reyna, S.B. Chapman, M.R. Dougherty and J. Confrey (Eds.), *The Adolescent Brain: Learning, Reasoning, and Decision Making*. American Psychological Association.

Miller, G.A., Beckwith, R., Fellbaum, C., Gross, D. and Miller, K.J. (1990) Introduction to WordNet: An On-line Lexical Database. *International Journal of Lexicography, 3(4)*:235-244.

Moss, H. and Older, L. (1996) *Birkbeck Word Association Norms*. Hove, U.K.: Psychology Press.

Myers, J. (2006) Processing Chinese compounds: A survey of the literature. In G. Libben and G. Jarema (Eds.), *The Representation and Processing of Compound Words*. Oxford: Oxford University Press, pp.169-196.

Rayner, K. and Frazier, L. (1989) Selection mechanisms in reading lexically ambiguous words. *Journal of Experimental Psychology: Learning, Memory, and Cognition, 15(5)*, 779-790.

Rodd, J., Gaskell, G. and Marslen-Wilson, W. (2002) Making Sense of Semantic Ambiguity: Semantic Competition in Lexical Access. *Journal of Memory and Language, 46*:245-266.

Schulte im Walde, S., Melinger, A., Roth, M. and Weber, A. (2008) An Empirical Characterisation of Response Types in German Association Norms. *Research on Language and Computation, 6(2)*: 205-238.

Taft, M. (2006) Processing of characters by native Chinese speakers. In P. Li, L.H. Tan, E. Bates and O.J.L. Tzeng (Eds.), *The Handbook of East Asian Psycholinguistics, Volume 1: Chinese*. New York: Cambridge University Press.

Wettler, M. and Rapp, R. (1993) Computation of word associations based on the co-occurrences of words in large corpora. In *Proceedings of the 1st Workshop on Very Large Corpora: Academic and Industrial Perspectives*, Columbus, Ohio, pp.84-93.

Zhou, X. and Marslen-Wilson, W. (1994) Words, morphemes and syllables in the Chinese mental lexicon. *Language and Cognitive Processes, 9(3)*:393-422.

Towards Automatic Error Type Classification of Japanese Language Learners' Writing

Hiromi Oyama
Graduate School of Information Science
Nara Institute of Science and Technology
8916-5 Takayama, Ikoma, Nara, Japan
hiromi-o@is.naist.jp

Mamoru Komachi
Graduate School of System Design
Tokyo Metropolitan University
6-6 Asahigaoka, Hino, Tokyo, Japan
komachi@tmu.ac.jp

Yuji Matsumoto
Graduate School of Information Science
Nara Institute of Science and Technology
8916-5 Takayama, Ikoma, Nara, Japan
matsu@is.naist.jp

Abstract

Learner corpora are receiving special attention as an invaluable source of educational feedback and are expected to improve teaching materials and methodology. However, they include various types of incorrect sentences. Error type classification is an important task in learner corpora which enables clarifying for learners why a certain sentence is classified as incorrect in order to help learners not to repeat errors. To address this issue, we defined a set of error type criteria and conducted automatic classification of errors into error types in the sentences from the **NAIST Goyo Corpus** and achieved an accuracy of 77.6%. We also tried inter-corpus evaluation of our system on the **Lang-8** corpus of learner Japanese and achieved an accuracy of 42.3%. To know the accuracy, we also investigated the classification method by human judgement and compared the difference in classification between the machine and the human.

1 Introduction

Automatic error detection is one area that has been widely studied. One of the challenges in this work is generalizing the great number of error patterns. Given that the different types of learners' errors are too numerous to detect, some researchers have broken down the error detection task according to the types of errors, such as spelling errors, mass count noun errors and preposition errors. If the error type classification is made in advance, it will help the automatic error detection system more accurate.

Classifying error types has other advantages. First, it will help resulting learner corpora useful in linguistic research. It can offer teachers with effective feedback on patterns of errors repeatedly made by students. Secondly, through classification of errors, learners are able to correct their own errors by comparing acceptable and unacceptable sentences.

Learner corpora are useful for statistical analysis of learner output and provide positive and negative examples that contribute to improving writing skills. According to Ellis's input theory (Ellis, 2003), both positive and negative input are required in learning a second language. Positive input provides grammatically correct and acceptable models of the language. Negative input is comprised of incorrect sentences that are made by non-native speakers. It teaches learners the sentences they should not produce. Learners' writing skills are improved by exposure to both. A system to organize both correct sentences (for positive evidence) and incorrect sentences that language learners are likely to produce (for negative evidence) would benefit language learners considerably. To master a foreign language, it is very effective to see where a problem lies and what caused it, rather than merely learning the correct expression.

We propose a machine learning-based approach on automatic error type classification in Japanese learners' writing by looking at the local contextual cues around a target error.

In Section 2, we give a brief overview of previous related work. Section 3 then outlines our annotation schema for the Japanese learners' errors. Then, we propose a machine learning-based approach to automatic error type classification in the writing of learners of Japanese learners by looking at the local contextual cues around a target error in Section 4. We discuss the experimental results with both in-domain and out-of-domain settings and also compare the characteristics of the classification between the machine and the human in Section 5.

2 Previous Work

Automatic Error Detection Systems: In the writing of learners of English, automatic grammatical error detection is used for spelling error (Mays et al., 1991), countable or uncountable noun errors (Brockett et al., 2006; Nagata et al., 2006), prepositional errors (De Felice and Pulman, 2008; Tetreault and Chodorow, 2008; Gamon et al., 2008) and article errors (Han et al., 2006; De Felice and Pulman, 2008; Gamon et al., 2008). Sun et al. (2007) focus on discriminating between erroneous and correct sentences without considering error types.

As for texts by Japanese learners, most of the research focuses on correcting errors with particles (postpositions) (Imaeda et al., 2003; Suzuki and Toutanova, 2006; Nampo et al., 2007; Oyama and Matsumoto, 2010; Ohki et al., 2011; Imamura et al., 2012). Besides, Mizumoto et al. (2011) consider error correction in the language learners' writing handling any error types.

As for automatic error type classification, Swanson and Yamangil (2012) deal with 15 error type classification in English learners' essays in the Cambridge Learner Corpus(CLC [1]). However, they did not report an inter-corpus evaluation.

Japanese Language Learners' Corpora: Japanese language learner corpora include Taiyaku DB, which is a multilingual database of Japanese learners' essays compiled by the National Institute of Japanese Language [2] consisting of 1,565 essays written by learners from 15 different countries. The KY corpus (Kamata and Yamauchi, 1999) has spoken data of Japanese language learners at different proficiency levels. There are several Japanese language learners' corpora with error annotation, such as the Teramura corpus at the Osaka University (Teramura, 1990) (3,131 sentences with error tag annotations among the 4,601 sentences), the learner corpus at Nagoya University (Oso et al., 1998) (756 files), the "Online Japanese Error corpus dictionary[3]" (40 files are error tagged) and the Japanese language learners' corpus at Tsukuba University (Li et al., 2012)[4] (540 files).

Our work aims to add error type annotation on learner corpora. Unlike previous research which depend on entirely manual annotation, we focus on semi-automatic annotation method to reduce human cost and to improve consistency in annotation.

3 Error Tag Annotation on the NAIST Goyo Corpus

We needed an error annotated corpus for our experiment, but some of the corpora we mentioned have different error annotation schema from each other and from ours, as well. We also needed essays from a variety of the nationalities so as to take in a wider range of errors; therefore, we used the Taiyaku DB for annotating errors with our error schema.

The 313 essays in the Taiyaku DB are already corrected by professional Japanese teachers. We annotated those essays manually with error tags.

To simplify this experiment, we utilized a compressed set of 17 essential error tags out of 76 in total. "Verb" takes in "verb conjugation" and the "Spelling" category includes "hiragana" or "katakana", and so forth. We briefly introduce here the 17 essential error tags as we use for our experiment in Section 4. The sets of error types and examples are shown in Table 1.

Postposition (P) includes omission, addition or choice of a wrong postposition or compound particles.

Word Choice (SEM) includes inappropriate word selection due to not considering context.
Spelling (NOT) includes wrong use of the three types of Japanese characters: Hiragana, Katakana and Kanji.

Missing (OM) indicates that the sentence has a missing element.

Verb (V) covers a wide range of types, such as verb conjugation, transitive or intransitive verb form choice, passive voice, tense/aspect and so forth.

Unnecessary (AD) indicates that unnecessary words or expressions are written in a sentence, making it ungrammatical or unnatural.

Inappropriate register (STL) covers the wrong choice of a sentence ending. A Japanese essay text must be consistent, using ei-

[1] `http://www.cambridge.org/elt/corpus/clc.htm`

[2] `http://jpforlife.jp/contents_db`

[3] `http://cblle.tufs.ac.jp/llc/ja,wrong/index.php?m=default`

[4] `http://www34.atwiki.jp/jccorpus/`

ther "da/dearu" or "desu/masu" throughout (the "da/dearu" ending preferable in formal writing).

Nominalization (NOM) in Japanese (as in "to watch/watching" in English) requires choosing "no" or "koto," depending on the context, which confuses learners. "*Shumi wa eiga wo miru **no** desu" is an error; "Shumi wa eiga wo miru **koto** desu (I enjoy **watching** a movie)" is correct. On the other hand, "Tori ga toby **no** wo mimashita (I saw a bird **flying** in the sky)" is used, but not "*Tori ga toby **koto** wo mimashita".

Connecting (CONJ) is an error in conjunction use (corresponding to the English "and","then", "because" and etc).

Adjective (ADJ) is usually a conjugational error. A Japanese adjective conjugates in its combinations with a verb, an adverb or a noun that follows it. The adjective suffix "-i" is used before nouns.

Demonstrative (DEM) includes the use of "ko", "so" or "a" which are divided into three categories according to the distance from the participants in a dialogue. These distinctions are not found in the native languages of many learners of Japanese language who often err here.

Word order (ORD) is also important; with the case particles in Japanese, word order is more flexible than in English.

The **Collocation (COL)** category consists of a wrong set of noun-particle-verb.

Use of "da" (AUX) follows grammatical rules unique to Japanese. Japanese complex sentences require that the subordinate clause should end in the copula "da," as in "Anohito wa kirei**da** to omoimasu (I think **that** that girl is pretty)". The copula "da" becomes "desu" at the end of a polite sentence. The difficulty of this distinction leads to errors like "*Anohito wa kirei**desu** to omoimasu", where "da" is replaced by "desu".

Negation (NEG) includes the use of "nakute " and "naide", which means "because not" and "without". "Ie ni irate**nakute** soto e ikimashita (I went out **because I just could not** stay in the house.)"; "*Ie ni irate**naide** soto e ikimashita" is not used. "naide" is more used as in "Kasa wo mota**naide** i.e. wo demashita. (I left home **without** bringing an umblera.)".

Some **adverb (ADV)** are used with either "ni" or "to" particles in Japanese, differentiated by the preceding word, while being completely interchangeable in some contexts.

For the **Pronoun (PRON)** category, both "*Kare**tachi**" and "Kare**ra**" have a meaning of "they" or "them" but should be differentiated according to their context.

Table 2 presents the proportion of error types according to the learners' national origin[5]. The most frequent error type is Word choice, followed by Postposition, Verb, Spelling, Phrase and Adjective. Phrase error includes the incorrect use of phrase patterns such as "...tari ...tari" in a sentence like "Kinou wa ne**tari** terebi wo mi**tari** shimashita. (I took a nap and watched TV yesterday.)". Whole alternation indicates errors that cannot be corrected word by word and the entire sentence needs rewriting. Whole alternation type errors do not enter into this experiment because our classifier handles only local information features. We also omit Phrase type errors, which consist of discontinuous multiple word expressions and which is therefore an extremely difficult task with a window size of only one to three words.

4 Learning-Based Error Type Classifier

We propose an approach for automatic error type classification which uses a machine learning method. We performed two experiments; one is a 10-fold cross-validation (in-domain) in the NAIST Goyo Corpus and the other is to apply our method to an out-of-domain test data from the Lang-8 corpus to see whether the method is applicable to any type of learner corpora.

4.1 Problem Setting

Figure 1 shows the work flow of automatic error type classification.

From an annotated sentence, the error part *(x)*, the correct part *(y)* and their error type *(t)* are extracted as *(x, y, t)*. The following sentence meaning *Everyone has a right to smoke* provides as examples:

- *Dare **ni**mo tabako wo suu kenri ga aru
- Dare **de**mo tabako wo suu kenri ga aru
- Use of Postposition (P)

The particle "ni[6]" *(x)* is taken as an error; "de[7] "

[5]The number is a proportion to the number of learners' essays.

[6]When "ni" is used with "mo", it should be used with a negative ending.

[7]When "de" is used with "mo", it means "Any", which "Dare demo" mean "Anybody".

Table 1: Error types in the collapsed 17 class set
*φ in this table indicates missing of an element.
* # indicates the number of instances.

Description	Sample and Correction	English Translation	#
Postposition (P)	*Eigo **wo** wakaru Eigo **ga** wakaru	I can understand English	3,351
Word choice (SEM)	***bubun jin** **ichibu no hito**	**some people**	2,546
Spelling (NOT)	*nenp**a** no hito nenp**ai** no hito	the **elderly** people	1,838
Missing (OM)	*Nobu φ resutoran ni ikimashita Nobu **to iu** resutoran ni ikimashita	I went to a restaurant **whose name is** Nobu	1,441
Verb (V)	*Tegami wo ka**ki**nai Tegami wo ka**ka**nai	I **do not write** a letter	1,348
Unnecessary (AD)	***Tenki** ga samukute... φ samukute...	**The weather** is cold...	1,177
Inappropriate register (STL)	*Totemo taihen**ne** Totemo taihen**desu**	It is very hard	328
Nominalization (NOM)	*Shumi wa eiga wo miru **no**desu Shumi wa eiga wo miru **koto**desu	I enjoy **watching** a movie	300
Connecting (CONJ)	***Soshitemo** Pet to asobimasu **Soshite** Pet to asobimasu	**And then,** I played with my pet	196
Adjective (ADJ)	*Boku wa futo-**kute** hito desukara Boku wa futo-**i** hito desukara	I am a **fat** person	149
Demonstrative (DEM)	***Asoko** de tomodati ni aimashita **soko** de tomodati ni aimashita	I met a friend **there**	137
Word order (ORD)	***yori** shichigatsu shichigatsu **yori**	**From** July	121
Collocation (COL)	*Shiken **ni sankashimashita** Shiken **wo ukemashita**	I **took a test**	113
Use of "da" (AUX)	*Anohito wa kirei**desu** to omoimasu Anohito wa kirei**da** to omoimasu	I think **that** the girl is pretty	49
Negation (NEG)	*Ie ni irare**naide** soto e ikimashita Ie ni irare**nakute** soto e ikimashita	I went out **because I did not** want to stay at home	26
Adverb (ADV)	*Nonbiri **ni** sugoshita Nonbiri **to** sugoshita	I spend a day They **at leisure**	24
Pronouns (PRON)	*kare**tachi** kare**ra**	**they /them**	16

Table 2: The proportion of error types on the NAIST Goyo Corpus (top 10)
VN indicates learners from Vietnam, TH Thai, CN Chinese, ML Malaysia, MN Mongolia, KH Cambodia, KR Korea and SG Singapore

	VN	TH	CN	ML	MN	KH	KR	SG
Word choice (SEM)	35.0	27.0	17.2	22.8	29.2	12.8	25.2	23.8
Postposition (P)	21.8	23.1	20.6	24.2	22.1	17.4	17.3	30.6
Verb (V)	13.8	15.3	16.8	12.1	14.2	15.9	14.6	10.2
Spelling (NOT)	9.8	10.1	19.8	16.9	12.7	33.6	15.5	6.8
Phrase	6.2	7.0	2.6	7.3	5.2	1.7	3.4	4.9
Nominalization (NOUN)	2.5	2.6	3.5	1.4	3.4	2.0	4.4	2.9
Adjective (ADJ)	2.0	0.9	2.6	1.5	1.9	1.7	1.5	1.5
Whole alternation	2.0	2.6	1.2	3.4	0.7	1.4	2.4	2.4
Inappropriate register (STL)	1.7	1.2	2.3	6.0	4.1	6.1	3.1	6.3
Word order (ORD)	1.0	1.3	1.2	0.3	0.4	1.2	0.6	0.0

Table 3: Features

Features	Error / Corrected samples
Error part	ni
Correct part	de
Error type	Postposition
POS and root form of Error part	Postposition, ni
POS and root form of Corrected words	Postposition, de
Word, POS at the window size of W±1	dare (who), Noun, mo (also), Postposition
Word, POS at the window size of W±2	BOS, tabako (tobacco), Noun
Word, POS at the window size of W±3	BOS, wo (object-particle), Postposition

(y) as a correction and "particle (or postposition) error" *(t)* as its error type.

Then, we extracted the contextual information as features to train the Maximum Entropy classifier. We created multiple instances out of sentence pairs that contain multiple errors and corrections.

Table 3 shows that features and samples from "Dare demo tabako wo suu kenri ga aru (Everyone has right to smoke.)" as an example.

For the test data, after aligning the learners' sentences and corrected sentences, we extracted an error part, a correct part and also the contextual information with error type unknown. Finally, the test instance is judged by the classifier.

4.2 Data

We used the error-annotated corpus, which we call the NAIST Goyo Corpus. For the first experiment, we performed a 10-fold cross-validation with 13,152 instances from the NAIST Goyo Corpus (in-domain) .

For the second experiment, we used as test data 1,090 erroneous sentences from the Lang-8 corpus for an out-of-domain text. The Lang-8[8] offers a social network service (SNS) of multi language essay-correction for foreign language learners. The service has over 400,000 registered members at present and supports 98 languages, facilitating multilingual communication. When learners write a passage in their target language, native speakers of the language on the web correct the errors for them. This service can provide a huge corpus of language learners' essays, a useful resource for language teachers and learners (Mizumoto et al., 2011).

4.3 Features

Features include the error and the correct words, the part of speech (POS) and the contextual information with their surface forms. The context window ranges from 1 to 3 before and after the target error and correct part.

[8] `http://www.lang-8.com`

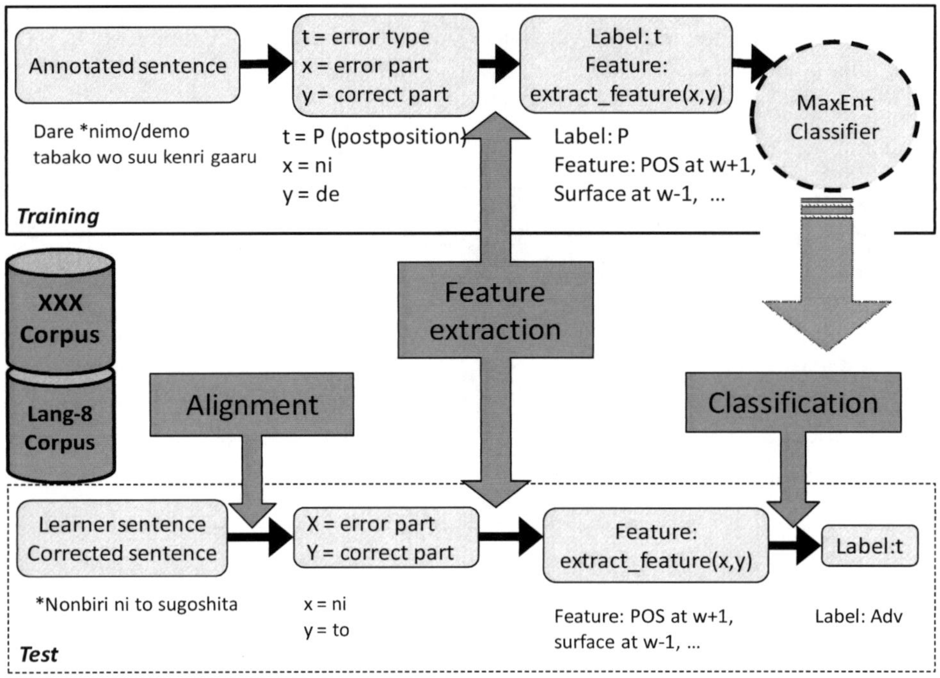

Figure 1: Work flow

We used the Maximum entropy method for the classification[9]. We aligned the erroneous and correct sentences by the dynamic programming method (Fujino et al., 2012)[10]. We assign POS from UniDic-2.1.1 dictionary using the MeCab-0.994[11].

To see how much this approach has contributed to the accuracy, we set a baseline where features are bags of words of both correct and error instances in place of the contextual information.

5 Result

5.1 Assessment measure

Recall (R) indicates the proportion of correctly classified sentences to the sentences belonging to each error type. Precision (P) indicates the correctly classified sentences in proportion to the sentences classified by the system. F-measure (F) shows the harmonic mean of precision and recall. Accuracy (A) shows the proportion of correctly classified sentences to all sentences, which is the proportion of true positives to true negatives over all sentences.

5.2 Experiment in the NAIST Goyo Corpus

The accuracy of the 10-fold cross validation in the NAIST Goyo Corpus is 77.6% with a window size of 1 on both sides, 77.1% with a window size of 2 on both sides, and 76.6% with the window size of 3 on both sides. Table 4 shows the recall, precision and F-measure. The baseline is 76.9%. Classification performance of "Postposition (P)", "Spelling (NOT)", "Missing (OM)" and "Unnecessary (AD)" show a high accuracy score, and lower accuracy with "Word order (ORD)", "Collocation (COL)", "Negation (NEG)" and "Pronoun (PRON)".

The error types with high accuracy are mostly with the window size of 1, which indicates the very local information would suffice to some error types such as "Word choice (SEM)", "Spelling (NOT)", "Missing (OM)", "Inappropriate register (STL)","Nominalization (NOM)", "Adjective (ADJ)", "Word order (ORD)", "Negation (NEG)" and "Pronoun (PRON)".

In this setting, we see from the results above that in general the larger number of instances, the more accurate the error type classification. However "Collocation (COL)" or "Word order (ORD)"

[9] http://homepages.inf.ed.ac.uk/lzhang10/maxent_toolkit.html

[10] https://github.com/tkyf/jpair

[11] http://mecab.googlecode.com/svn/trunk/mecab/doc/index.html

Table 4: Results of 10-fold cross validation in the NAIST Goyo Corpus (F-measure)
*# indicates the number of instances.

	F(%)	Precision (%)			Recall (%)			F-measure (%)			
Type	Baseline	W±1	W±2	W±3	W±1	W±2	W±3	W±1	W±2	W±3	#
P	94.82	95.18	95.38	95.17	96.27	96.42	96.18	95.71	**95.89**	95.67	3,351
SEM	65.88	62.73	62.28	61.42	69.52	69.84	67.40	**65.92**	65.73	64.22	2,546
NOT	72.58	76.83	77.84	75.26	71.03	69.40	67.77	**73.70**	73.22	71.22	1,838
OM	87.84	93.96	93.85	93.76	95.49	95.35	95.28	**94.68**	94.57	94.49	1,441
V	**66.30**	64.49	61.87	61.18	66.83	64.75	67.27	65.60	63.10	64.01	1,348
AD	86.42	83.02	84.05	83.71	88.61	89.38	88.02	85.66	**86.58**	85.76	1,177
STL	54.75	56.45	55.69	52.83	54.36	54.95	48.80	**55.17**	54.92	50.60	328
NOM	57.92	67.26	65.16	65.77	53.17	51.84	51.17	**59.13**	57.35	57.12	300
CONJ	**42.14**	43.74	40.25	43.32	33.74	30.68	35.39	37.48	34.36	38.29	196
ADJ	33.21	42.94	44.15	39.36	38.38	31.67	33.00	**40.05**	36.41	35.57	149
DEM	**65.06**	65.40	66.68	64.20	54.84	62.86	62.86	59.32	64.27	63.19	137
ORD	7.38	32.50	30.00	18.89	9.94	5.77	5.00	**14.89**	9.37	8.45	121
COL	7.75	12.00	19.17	11.43	4.55	8.94	6.29	6.32	**11.70**	7.73	113
AUX	22.46	27.50	27.50	36.50	18.50	21.00	19.00	21.94	23.17	**23.21**	49
NEG	14.28	45.00	13.89	21.88	11.67	6.67	13.33	**18.53**	12.22	17.50	26
ADV	10.85	20.83	23.23	23.61	15.00	23.33	28.33	17.71	20.97	**23.15**	24
PRON	0.00	6.67	7.14	0.00	10.00	5.00	0.00	**8.00**	7.14	0.00	16
ALL	46.82	52.74	51.07	49.90	46.58	46.34	46.18	48.84	47.70	47.07	13,152

types show a very low accuracy against their total number. The reason being that they require more contextual information, which needs to be extracted from widely separated sentence constituents.

5.3 Experiment in the Lang-8 corpus

We performed classification on the Lang-8 data. Accuracy in the Lang-8 was 42.3% with a window size of 1 on both sides, 40.0% with a window size of 2 on both sides, and 41.6% with a window size of 3 on both sides. The baseline is 41.5%. Although we mentioned the error types with high accuracy are mostly with the window size of 1 in the NAIST Goyo Corpus, "Word choice (SEM)" in the Lang-8 performs the best score with a window size of 3. We can assume that window size of 3 gives enough information to the classifier if we use out-of-domain data, like the Lang-8.

Table 6 presents the confusion matrix of error types in the Lang-8. The table indicates that many sentences in the Lang-8 are likely to be classified into the "Word choice (SEM)" category. "Word choice (SEM)" achieves a rather high rate in the NAIST Goyo Corpus but it results in 34.5% with the Lang-8 corpus. The reason may come from that the domain of vocabulary plays an important role and that the domain-sensitive feature is required to improve the classification performance over those categories.

5.4 How do humans judge the error type?

We also conducted an additional classification over error types by human judgement. We asked 11 Japanese teachers to judge 20 instances randomly taken from the Lang-8, especially the ones the machine misclassified. Similar to the machine learning method, the most confusing type was "Word choice (SEM)" followed by "Verb (V)" as in Table 7.

We also investigated what the teachers take into consideration in classifying those instances. We found that they judged mainly by the very local cues, such as, the error and correct part and one word previous or following only, even though whole sentences are presented to them. In addition, in case of "Postposition (P)" error type, they tried to focus on the verb which is in a relationship of the dependency. Similar to this, in case of "Adverb (ADV)", they tried to focus also on the verb which the adverb depends on.

Table 5: Results in the Lang-8 (F-measure)

	F(%)	Precision (%)			Recall (%)			F-measure (%)			
Type	Baseline	W±1	W±2	W±3	W±1	W±2	W±3	W±1	W±2	W±3	#
P	**75.79**	69.23	68.22	68.93	83.72	84.88	82.56	**75.79**	75.65	75.13	86
SEM	24.44	20.92	20.88	23.37	74.76	78.64	66.02	32.70	32.99	**34.52**	103
NOT	**42.65**	40.30	37.04	32.76	38.03	28.17	53.52	39.13	32.00	40.64	71
OM	**71.79**	53.40	54.90	54.37	98.21	100.00	100.00	69.18	70.89	70.44	56
V	**46.41**	36.31	35.16	35.68	53.98	56.14	57.89	43.42	43.24	44.15	113
AD	**63.95**	57.53	55.71	51.95	67.74	63.93	65.57	62.22	59.54	57.97	62
STL	34.48	44.44	39.66	35.71	35.71	41.07	35.71	39.60	**40.35**	35.71	56
NOM	**20.20**	53.33	46.15	50.00	9.76	7.32	10.98	16.49	12.63	18.00	82
CONJ	45.22	65.00	66.67	57.58	35.62	16.44	26.03	**46.02**	26.37	35.85	73
ADJ	32.76	60.47	51.28	61.54	33.77	25.97	20.78	**43.33**	34.48	31.07	77
DEM	**75.00**	89.74	93.75	87.18	59.32	50.85	57.63	71.43	65.93	69.39	59
ORD	0.00	50.00	33.33	100.00	3.03	3.03	6.06	5.71	5.56	**11.43**	33
COL	5.56	16.67	66.67	22.22	3.45	6.90	6.90	5.71	**12.50**	10.53	29
AUX	7.55	50.00	33.33	37.50	6.00	2.00	6.00	**10.71**	3.77	10.34	50
NEG	**15.09**	100.00	75.00	75.00	4.17	6.25	6.25	8.00	11.54	11.54	53
ADV	**12.82**	75.00	33.33	26.67	4.69	4.69	6.25	8.82	8.22	10.13	64
PRON	0.00	0.00	0.00	0.00	0.00	0.00	0.00	0.00	0.00	0.00	23
ALL	33.75	51.90	47.71	48.26	36.00	33.90	35.77	34.01	31.51	33.34	1,090

Table 6: Confusion matrix over error type in Lang-8
*Row represents the actual classes and column represents the system predicted classes.

	P	S	N	O	V	A	St	No	C	Aj	D	Or	Co	Au	Ne	Av	Pr
P	0	1	0	3	1	3	3	1	0	0	0	0	0	0	0	0	0
SEM	0	0	10	0	11	0	1	0	0	2	0	0	2	0	0	0	0
NOT	2	24	0	0	12	0	0	0	0	1	0	0	0	0	0	0	0
OM	0	0	0	0	1	0	0	0	0	0	0	0	0	0	0	0	0
V	1	37	4	2	0	0	4	1	1	0	0	0	2	0	0	0	0
AD	14	1	0	0	0	0	3	0	0	0	0	1	0	1	0	0	0
STL	0	6	1	7	15	3	0	1	0	0	0	0	1	2	0	0	0
NOM	3	24	3	21	10	9	0	0	0	2	1	0	0	0	0	1	0
CONJ	10	9	1	3	16	2	0	1	0	5	0	0	0	0	0	0	0
ADJ	0	35	7	0	5	1	1	0	2	0	0	0	0	0	0	0	0
DEM	0	17	2	1	0	1	1	1	1	0	0	0	0	0	0	0	0
ORD	0	26	2	1	0	1	0	0	1	1	0	0	0	0	0	0	0
COL	0	18	0	0	8	0	0	0	0	1	0	0	0	0	0	0	0
AUX	2	10	1	9	9	7	5	0	3	1	0	0	0	0	0	0	0
NEG	0	14	3	0	18	0	7	1	2	1	0	0	0	0	0	0	0
ADV	0	50	3	1	0	2	0	0	2	3	0	0	0	0	0	0	0
PRON	0	13	0	0	0	0	0	0	0	0	0	0	0	0	0	0	0

Table 7: Confusion matrix of the human judge over error type in Lang-8
*Row represents the actual classes and column represents the system predicted classes.

	P	S	N	O	V	A	St	No	C	Aj	D	Or	Co	Au	Ne	Av	Pr
P	1	1	0	0	0	1	2	0	0	0	0	0	0	0	0	0	0
SEM	0	5	0	0	1	0	0	0	0	0	0	0	0	0	0	0	0
NOT	0	0	6	2	0	0	0	0	0	0	0	0	0	0	0	0	0
OM	0	0	0	0	1	0	0	0	0	0	0	0	0	0	0	0	0
V	1	3	0	0	7	0	0	0	0	0	0	0	0	0	0	0	0
AD	0	0	0	1	0	2	0	0	0	0	0	0	0	0	0	0	0
STL	0	1	1	0	0	2	5	0	1	0	0	0	1	0	0	0	0
NOM	0	0	0	0	0	0	0	0	0	0	0	0	0	0	0	0	0
CONJ	0	4	0	1	5	1	0	0	5	1	0	0	0	0	0	0	0
ADJ	0	0	0	0	0	0	0	0	0	0	0	0	0	0	0	0	0
DEM	1	1	0	0	0	1	0	0	0	0	3	0	0	0	0	0	0
ORD	0	0	0	0	0	0	1	1	0	0	0	4	0	0	0	0	0
COL	0	4	1	0	1	0	0	0	0	0	0	0	0	0	0	0	0
AUX	0	2	0	3	4	0	0	0	3	2	0	0	0	1	0	0	0
NEG	0	3	0	0	4	1	0	0	1	1	0	0	0	0	0	0	0
ADV	2	9	0	0	0	1	0	0	1	0	0	0	0	0	0	2	0
PRON	0	3	0	0	0	0	0	0	0	0	0	0	0	0	0	0	0

6 Conclusion

This paper presented an approach to classifying error types in the writing of learners of Japanese language in an error annotated corpus. We performed classification experiment with the NAIST Goyo Corpus and the Lang-8 corpus. Although context features, such as what words precede or follow and error and correction, play in an important role in determining the error types, features considering a long distance dependency will be required for the categories with the low accuracy such as the "Collocation (COL)" , "Pronoun (PRON)" or "Word order (ORD)" categories.

For the inter-corpus experiment, the result was lower than the ones of in-domain corpus. We assume that the difference of domain has affected the performance. We consider how to compromise the difference of the domain since there are a variety of text data in a real setting.

For the experiment by the human judgement, we concluded that the types of "Word choice (SEM)", "Missing (OM)" and "Unnecessary (AD)" can be included in any other error types, which causes the confusion regardless of the machine or the human classification. Thus, in the error type classification, it is beneficial to keep two stages separate; to classify those three types of 'Word choice (SEM)", "Missing (OM)" or "Unnecessary (AD)" in the first place and then to classify the other error types. We also found that many teachers consider the dependency of the error part. We will take those aspects into the future trial.

Currently, a huge body of web-based corpora of language learners' writing have being constructed. They are difficult to use directly for the linguistic or educational research because they have both correct and incorrect sentences altogether. Classifying those miscellaneous texts into meaningful groups according to their errors will benefit language researchers by shedding light on the linguistic findings on how people learn the second language. It also provides learners feedback to inform the reasons why the errors are made.

Acknowledgments

We are deeply grateful for the Lang-8 web organizer to offer the text data for our classification experiment.

References

C. Brockett, W.B. Dolan, and M. Gamon. 2006. Correting ESL errors using phrasal SMT techniques. In *Proceedings of the 21st International Conference on*

Computational Linguistics and 44th Annual Meeting of the Association for Computational Linguistics (ACL), pages 249–256, Sydney, Australia.

R. De Felice and S.G. Pulman. 2008. A classifier-based approach to preposition and determiner error correction in L2. In *Proceedings of the 22nd International Conference on Computational Linguistics (COLING 2008)*, pages 169–176, Manchester, U.K.

N.C. Ellis. 2003. Constructions, chunking, and connectionism:the emergence of second language structure. In C. Doughty and M. Long, editors, *The handbook of second language acquisition*. Blackwell.

T. Fujino, T. Mizumoto, M. Komachi, M. Nagata, and Y. Matsumoto. 2012. Word segmentation for automatic error correction in the Japanese language learners' essays. In *Proceedings of The Eighteenth Annual Meeting of The Association for Natural Language Processing*, pages 26–29.

M. Gamon, J. Gao, C. Brockett, A. Klementiev, W.B. Dolan, D. Belenko, and L. Vanderwende. 2008. Using contextual speller techniques and language modelling for ESL error correction. In *Proceedings of the 3rd International Joint Conference on Computational Linguistics (IJCNLP 2008)*, pages 449–456, Hyderabad, India.

N. R. Han, M. Chodorow, and C. Leacock. 2006. Detecting errors in English article usage by non-native speakers. *Natural Language Engineering*, 12(2):115–129.

K. Imaeda, A. Kawai, Y. Ishikawa, R. Nagata, and F. Masui. 2003. Error detection and correction of case particles in Japanese learner's composition. In *Proceedings of the Information Processing Society of Japan SIG*, pages 39–46.

K. Imamura, K. Saito, K. Sadamitsu, and H. Nishikawa. 2012. Grammar error correction using pseudo-error sentences and domain adaptation. In *Proceedings of the 50th Annual Meeting of the Association for Computational Linguistics (ACL)*, pages 388–392.

O. Kamata and H. Yamauchi. 1999. KY corpus version 1.1. Report, Vocaburary Acquisition Study Group.

J. Li, G. Lin, Y. Miyaoka, and H. Shibasaki. 2012. Creation of Japanese language learners' corpus with application of the natural language precessing. In *Proceedings of the Spring Meeting of the Society of Japanese Language and Linguistics in 2012*.

E. Mays, F.J. Damerau, and R.L. Mercer. 1991. Context based spelling correction. *Information Processing and Management*, 23(5):517–522.

T. Mizumoto, M. Komachi, M. Nagata, and Y. Matsumoto. 2011. Mining revision log of language learning SNS for automated Japanese error correction of second language learners. In *Proceedings of the 5th International Joint Conference on Natural Language Processing (IJCNLP)*, pages 147–155.

R. Nagata, T. Wakana, A. Kawai, K. Morihiro, F. Masui, and N. Isu. 2006. Recognizing errors in English writing based on the mass count distinction. *The Institute of Electronics, Information and Communication Engineers (IEICE), Transactions on Information and Systems*, J89-D(8):1777–1790.

R. Nampo, H. Ototake, and K. Araki. 2007. Automatic error detection and correction of Japanese particles using features within bunsetsu. In *Proceedings of the Information Processing Society of Japan SIG*, pages 107–112.

M. Ohki, H. Oyama, S. Kitauchi, T. Suenaga, and Y. Matsumoto. 2011. Error detection in the system mannual texts by non-Japanese native speakers. In *Proceedings of The 17th Annual Meeting of The Association for Natural Language Processing*, pages 1047–1050.

M. Oso, M. Sugiura, Y. Ichikawa, M. Okumura, S. Komori, H. Shirai, N. Takizawa, and T. Sotoike. 1998. A learners' corpus of Japanese compositions: Digitalizing and sharing the data. Report, University of Nagoya.

H. Oyama and Y. Matsumoto. 2010. Automatic error detection method for Japanese particles. *Polyglossia Vol.18*, pages 55–63.

G. Sun, X. Liu, G. Cong, M. Zhou, Z. Xiong, J. Lee, and C.Y. Lin. 2007. Detecting erroneous sentences using automatically mined sequential patterns. In *Proceedings of the 45th Annual Meeting of the Association for Computational Linguistics (ACL)*, pages 81–88, Prague, Czech Public.

H. Suzuki and K. Toutanova. 2006. Learning to predict case makers in Japanese. In *Proceedings of the 21st International Conference on Computational Linguistics and 44th Annual Meeting of the Association for Computational Linguistics (ACL)*, pages 1049–1056.

B. Swanson and E. Yamangil. 2012. Correction detection and error type selection as an ESL educational aid. In *Proceedings of the Conference of the North American Chapter of the Association for Computational Linguistics (NAACL)*, pages 357–361.

H. Teramura. 1990. Examples of error sentences for the Japanese language learners–conjunctions and adverbs–. Technical report, Osaka University and The Natonal Iinstitute of Japanese Language.

J. Tetreault and M. Chodorow. 2008. The ups and downs of preposition error detection in ESL writing. In *Proceedings of the 22nd International Conference on Computational Linguistics (COLING 2008)*, pages 865–872, Manchester, U.K.

The Development of Coherence in Narratives: Causal Relations

Wen-hui Sah
Department of English, National Chengchi University
whsah@nccu.edu.tw

Abstract

This study explored Mandarin-speaking children's ability in maintaining narrative coherence. Thirty Mandarin-speaking five-year-olds, 30 nine-year-olds and 30 adults participated. The narrative data were elicited using *Frog, where are you?* Narrative coherence was assessed in terms of causal networks. The results displayed children's development in achieving narrative coherence by establishing causal relations between narrative events. Results were considered in relation to capacities for working memory and theory of mind. Narrators' differences in communicative competence and cognitive preferences were also discussed.

1 Introduction

Previous research relied on a variety of schemes to explore how narrators relate categories of information in a narrative (e.g., Berman and Slobin, 1994; Trabasso et al., 1992). Some researchers examine narrative structure (Peterson and McCabe, 1983); some concern more about the conceptual basis for relating narrative information (Trabasso and Nickels, 1992; Trabasso et al. 1992). Regarding cognitive processing, capacities for working memory and theory of mind were considered relevant to a narrator's ability to organize and integrate narrative information (Trabasso et al., 1992). Given the significant role of narratives in children's development (Chang, 2004), the present work aimed to explore Mandarin-speaking children's progress in relating events and hence in maintaining coherence in narratives.

One intriguing assumption of the research by Trabasso et al. (1992) is that narrators tend to encode a protagonist's actions as relevant to a goal plan. They suggested that knowledge of goal/plans serves as the conceptual basis under-pinning narrative representations. Children, with increasing age, were found to be more advanced in applying knowledge of goal/plans to integrate narrative events coherently.

Acknowledging the significance of goal/ plan knowledge aside, Trabasso et al. (Trabasso and Sperry, 1985; Trabasso and van den Broek, 1985) indicated that it is causal inferences that unite elements (such as goals, actions, and outcomes) in a goal-plan. Similarly, Stein and Albro (1997) suggested that causal reasoning is required to organize content and structure coherently. In other words, causal relation is regarded as a basic mechanism for integrating episodic and thematic information. As Karmiloff-Smith (1985) indicated, coherence refers to global representation of story meaning and connectedness, which is embodied in the temporal and causal structure of a story.

Given the significance of causal relations for narrative construction, Trabasso and Sperry (1985) outlined procedure to identify causal networks so as to assess causal connectivity between linguistic units in a narrative. Research has shown that causal networks provide explanations for variance in story recall (Trabasso et al., 1984). In particular, compared with measures of story grammar, causal networks were found to be a more reliable predictor of story recall (Trabasso and van den Broek, 1985). Research has also shown that the derived causal connections correlated with the importance ratings for narrative events (Trabasso and Sperry, 1985). Additional credence of the predictive power of causal networks is given by Diehl et al.'s (2006) research, which revealed that the system of causal networks is a potential tool to assess narrative coherence.

In recent decades, most developmental research of Mandarin-speaking children's narrative ability has focused on typically-developing preschool children (e.g., Chang, 2004; Chen et al., 2011; Li, 2012). Many of these studies used high-point analysis or story grammar to analyze preschoolers' narrative structure. However, very little is known about older Mandarin children's ability to relate narrative events. Even less is known about Mandarin children's progress in maintaining narrative coherence. Much prominent research on other languages adopted a cross-sectional research paradigm to investigate narrative development by examining data based on the frog story (e.g., Bamberg and Marchman, 1990; Berman and Slobin, 1994); nevertheless, only a few studies (Chang, 1995; Li, 2012; Sah, 2013) on Mandarin-speaking children followed this paradigm. Among them, Chang's (1995) and Sah's (2013) research included both preschool and school-age children, while the other studies focused on only preschoolers (Li, 2012). Nevertheless, we still lack of knowledge about Mandarin children's development in maintaining narrative coherence. It is, however, important for us to understand more about this, for such ability is integral to narrative construction. To extend the line of frog-story-based research and to replicate previous findings based on causal networks, the present study explored how Mandarin-speaking children maintain narrative coherence by posing the following research questions.

(1) Is there any difference in Mandarin-speaking five- and nine-year-olds' ability to encode events in the causal chain?
(2) Is there any difference in five- and nine-year-olds' ability to establish causal connections between narrative events?
(3) Is there any difference between the two groups of children in encoding events with different levels of causal connectedness?

2 Method

2.1 Participants

Participants included 60 children and 30 adults. The children were divided into two age groups: 30 five-year-olds (M_{age}= 5;8) and 30 nine-year-olds (M_{age}= 9;6). They were all typically developing children, with no learning disabilities, or speech or hearing problems. Additionally, 30 college students (M_{age}= 19;5) participated in this study. There were an equal number of participants of each gender in each group. All the participants were from similar middle-class socio-economic backgrounds.

2.2 Material

Much research of narrative development has focused on data based on the picture book *Frog, where are you?* (Mayer 1969), considered a reliable tool to tap children's narrative abilities (Bamberg and Marchman, 1990; Berman and Slobin, 1994). To control the content of the narrative data, we also used the frog story to elicit narratives. This book depicts an elaborate series of events which allow narrators to provide various links among events, so it is suitable to our research goal.

2.3 Procedure

The interviews were carried out individually, and consisted of an initial warm-up conversation followed by a narrative task based on *Frog, Where are You*. Participants were first asked to look through the entire book and then asked to tell a story while looking at the pictures. The interviews were audio-taped and transcribed.

2.4 Data Analyses

Clauses were used to quantify story length. A clause consists of a verb and its arguments, and corresponds roughly to a single event. Children's ability to maintain narrative coherence was examined in terms of events in the causal chain and causal connections (Diehl et al., 2006; Trabasso and Sperry, 1985).

A causal connection was established between a pair of events when the criterion of necessity was satisfied.[1] The necessity was tested by using counterfactual argument of the form: If not A then not B. In other words, if event A had not happened in the story, then event B would not have happened. Accordingly, the two events are considered causally connected. For instance, in the story, event A is "the dog smashed the jar"; the ensuing event B is "the boy was angry with the dog". If the dog had not smashed the jar, the boy would not be angry with it. As such, these two events are judged as causally connected. Based on this criterion, we identified inter-connections between events, which not only signal causal dependency between events but quantify relative importance of story events.

Apart from causal connections between events, we examined the causal chained events encoded by narrators. Causal chained events form the gist of a story (Trabasso and Sperry, 1985). To determine these, we first identified

[1] The criterion of necessity was originally proposed by lawyers (Hart and Honoré , 1959) and reviewed by Mackie (1980). It provides reliable identification of causal relations in stories and has been used extensively (Diehl et al., 2006; Trabasso and Sperry, 1985).

opening and closing events. The opening events include setting information, which introduces the protagonist, time and place, and the initiation part, which triggers the ensuing episodes. The closing events refer to protagonists' goal attainment/failure. The events with causes and consequences which can be traced from the opening through closing of the narratives belong to the causal chain (Appendix).

The pattern of causal connectedness within each narrative was also examined. To this end, four types of causal connectedness were differentiated, namely, C_0, C_1, C_2, and C_{3+}. C_0 type refers to the discrete event which has no connection with other events in the story; the C_1-event has connection with only one other event; the C_2-event has connections with two other events. And events with three or more connections were collapsed into the category C_{3+} because they were used infrequently.

3 Results

Since analyses regarding causal chains and causal connections were considered in relation to story length, the overall story length for three groups of participants was first established. To this end, the number of clauses was used as an indication of story length. The mean numbers of clauses were, respectively, from the youngest to oldest group, 35.93, 41.23 and 72.03. Kruskal-Wallis test indicated a significant age main effect, χ^2=43.46, $p < .001$. Post-hoc Mann-Whitney tests revealed significant pair-wise differences: adults produced significantly more clauses than both nine-year-olds (U = 81.50, $p < .001$) and five-year-olds (U = 62.50, $p < .001$). The mean numbers of different words were, from the youngest to oldest group, 113.80, 139.87 and 228.63. A significant age main effect was also obtained here, χ^2 =45.71, $p < .001$. Post-hoc Mann-Whitney tests revealed significant pair-wise differences between adults and nine-year-olds (U = 106.00, $p < .001$) and between adults and five-year-olds (U = 34.00, $p < .001$). For both story length and variety of words, the differences between the two groups of children, however, were non-significant.

Causal chained events and causal connections were relied on to infer children's development of narrative coherence. In the analysis based on 'plot' components, researchers found developmental increases in children's ability to establish global plotline (Aksu-Koç and Tekdemir, 2004; Berman and Slobin, 1994). In light of this, we predicted that, compared with nine-year-olds, five-year-olds would be less sensitive to the global plotline so they might encode less causal chained events. In addition, previous research also found age-related increases in applying knowledge of goal/plans to relate narrative information (Sah, 2013; Trabasso et al., 1992). Given this, we presumed that, along with advancement in knowledge of goal/plans, children would be more likely to encode causal relations between narrative events. Thus narratives produced by nine-year-olds would be more causally connected, and more coherent than those by five-year-olds.

Regarding the first research question, our data revealed age-related increases in mean number of causal-chained events. One-way ANOVA (analyses of variance) yielded a significant age main effect for it. Post-hoc analyses further displayed significant pair-wise differences: adults encoded significantly more chained events than nine-year-olds; nine-year-olds, more than five-year-olds. The reverse pattern, however, is shown for the density of causal-chained events.[2] Regarding this, one-way ANOVA yielded a significant age main effect. The post-hoc analysis revealed significant differences: children outperformed adults. The difference between two groups of children did not reach significant level (Table 1).

With respect to the mean number of causal connections, as predicted, one-way ANOVA yielded a significant main effect of age. Post-hoc analyses confirmed the developmental trend: adults encoded significantly more causal connections than did children; nine-year-olds outperformed five-year-olds. For the density of causal connections, a significant age main effect was again obtained from ANOVA. Subsequent analyses revealed that densities of causal connections for both adults and nine-year-olds were significantly larger than that for five-year-olds. Measures of causal connections suggested that, with increasing age, children were more likely to establish causal relations between narrative events, hence, more skillful in enhancing narrative coherence (Table 1).

[2] To control overall story length, we also measured story connectedness in terms of the density for causal chained events and that for causal connections (Diehl et al., 2006). The densities were obtained through dividing the total number of causal chained events and that of causal connections in each story, respectively, by the total number of clauses in that story.

	5-year-old (N=30) M (SD)	9-year-old (N=30) M (SD)	Adult (N=30) M (SD)	F
Number of chained events	14.27 (4.96)	18.4 (3.86)	23.13 (3.56)	33.97*
Density of chained events	.41 (.09)	.46 (.09)	.34 (.09)	11.64*
Number of causal connections	25.86 (12.93)	41.73 (13.04)	65.93 (17.67)	55.47*
Density of causal connections	.65 (.28)	1.00 (.12)	.93 (.12)	29.82*

* p< .001

Table 1: Number and density of causal chained events and causal connections

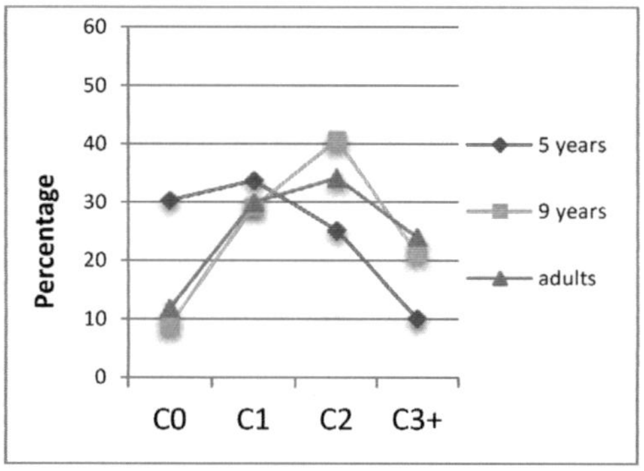

Fig.1 Distribution of events for each type of causal connectedness

Next, four types of causal connectedness were differentiated: C_0, C_1, C_2, and C_{3+}. We calculated proportions of events for each type within each story. Arc sine transformations were applied to the percentage data to normalize the distribution; two-way ANOVA were performed.

The statistical analyses yielded significant Age x Type interaction, $F(6, 261) = 14.65$, $p<.001$, $\eta^2_{partial} = .25$. Further examination shows age-related preferences for encoding events with different types of causal connectedness. Figure 1 reveals that five-year-olds were far more likely to encode discrete events (C_0 events) than did nine-year-olds and adults. Reverse patterns were shown for the use of C_2 and C_{3+} types of events; namely, nine-year-olds and adults tended to encode events with more causal connections than did five-year-olds. ANOVA yielded significant age main effects for all types (Table 2). Post-hoc analyses displayed age-related differences for each type. For C_0 events, five-year-olds were significantly more likely to employ them than did nine-year-olds and adults. A reverse pattern, however, is shown for C_{3+} events. While C_1 event is the dominant type for five-year-olds, C_2 event was preferred by nine-year-olds. C_{3+} events were encoded more by both adults and nine-year-olds.

4 Discussion

Most cross-sectional narrative studies on

	5-year-old	9-year-old	Adult	F
C_0	30.32	8.92	11.82	15.34*
C_1	33.73	29.20	29.99	3.94*
C_2	25.15	40.61	34.18	13.75*
C_{3+}	10.8	21.26	24.01	20.56*

* p < .001

Table 2. Proportions of events for each type of causal connectedness (%)

Mandarin-speaking children focused on preschoolers' narrative performance (e.g., Chang, 2004; Chen et al., 2011; Li, 2012). Scarcity is the research included both preschool and school-age children (Chang, 1995; Chang, 2001; Sah, 2013). Given so, we know little about Mandarin children's progress in establishing narrative coherence from preschool to school years. Another limitation of previous studies is that only a few of them based on the frog story to tap Mandarin children's narrative ability (Chang, 1995; Chen et al., 2011; Li, 2012; Sah, 2013). The present work thus aimed to fill the gap by examining development of coherence in narratives by including both preschool and school-age children and by eliciting narratives based on the frog story, which combined makes it possible to compare findings of other cross-sectional research out of similar research paradigms (e.g., Trabasso et al., 1992).

Though developmental differences in basic narrative measures were not significant, age-related increases manifested in number of causal chained events, which suggest that, with increasing age, children were more sensitive to the relative causal importance of narrative events. On the other hand, the density of chained events reversed the above pattern in which children outperformed adults. Given the fact that adults produced far more clauses than did children, the seemingly contradictory pattern of density is explicable since adults' markedly larger amount of clauses might lead to their lower density.

Consistent with our prediction, the results revealed children's developmental progress in inferring and establishing causal relations, which is largely compatible with findings in previous studies on English-speaking children (Trabasso and Nickels, 1992; Trabasso et al., 1984). The increasing ability in establishing causal relations gains additional support from the preferred types of events used by participants of different age groups. While the youngest group preferred C_0 and C_1 events, nine-year-olds and adults were more likely to encode events with more causal connections. To sum up, with increasing age, children appear to be more capable of encoding essential narrative elements and of integrating them into a coherent whole via causal relations.

Among earlier endeavors, only Chang's (1995) research examined Mandarin children's narrative development by means of causal networks. The researcher relied on causal connections to assess narrative coherence, but did not detect significant age effect for it. Unlike Chang's work, we included a larger sample with wider age span, and confirmed the age-related progress in enhancing narrative coherence found in English-speaking children (Trabasso and Nickels, 1992; Trabasso et al., 1992).

The developmental progress detected here might be explicated from an information processing standpoint. Working memory is an integral part of the information-processing system (Baddeley and Hitch, 1974). Its storage and processing components are presumably relevant to constructing narratives based on a picture book, since narrators need not only to understand individual events portrayed in pictures but also to integrate and store the information as a memory representation. Better performance in narrating a picture-book story, therefore, would require larger working-memory capacity. In the narrative study by Trabasso et al. (1992), one finding is suggestive: younger children's insufficiency in encoding planning components was partly attributed to their limited working-memory capacity. As Gathercole et al. (2004) noted, age-related increases in working-memory capacity manifested for participants from age four through fifteen. In view of this, adults would be expected to have larger working-memory capacity than do children, and nine-year-olds would have an advantage over five-year-olds. As such, the developmental difference in working-memory capacity is likely to contribute to the age-related differences found in the present study. This interpretation is, however, open to further empirical inquiry.

Other than storing and organizing information, a successful narrator needs to possess communicative competence, which ensures the narrator to construct a narrative that is understandable to listeners by selecting what is relevant based on the listener's needs. The knowledge about listeners' needs may embody in the extent to which a narrator conforms to the Gricean maxims (Grice, 1989). Children of different ages may have different assumptions about communicative necessity. Trabasso et al. (1992), for instance, reported that older children showed a better understanding of Grice's maxim of quantity than did younger children. They presumed that younger children's limited communicative competence related to the absence of certain essential information in narratives. Likely, in this study, five-year-olds' less causally-connected narratives may be relevant to their difficulty in adhering to the maxims, for they may have insufficient knowledge about what their listeners need. Further research is needed to test such speculation.

Apart from working-memory capacity, children's ability in theory of mind (ToM) is also relevant to how well they relate narrative information (Colle et al., 2008). As indicated by Tager-Flusberg and Sullivan (1995), ToM is essential to narrative construction, for a successful narrator relies on ToM not only to elaborate the internal states of story characters to account for their actions, but also to take account of listeners' needs. The intertwined relationship between ToM ability and narrative representation is also noted in Sah's (2013) research, in which the absence of emotion attribution by five-year-olds was considered reflecting their limited ToM ability. In view of this, we speculate that five-year-olds' limited ability in ToM might relate to their insufficient communicative competence, which presumably led to less causal connections encoded by them, and, hence, contributed to the developmental differences exhibited in this study.

Children's progress in enhancing narrative coherence implies their increasing ability to integrate essential narrative information. It is a cognitive tendency to integrate elements into a higher level of organization (Frith and Happé, 1994). The gradual unfolding of the ability to integrate relevant information is evident in research of narrative development (e.g., Bamberg and Marchman, 1990; Trabasso et al., 1992). For instance, it is noted that, initially, preschoolers are likely to encode narratives in terms of discrete events; gradually, they evolve to infer and establish proper interrelationships between events (Berman and Slobin, 1994). The progress from differentiation to integration may relate to cognitive preferences of children in different ages. According to Piaget (1969), children between ages four and seven belong to the intuitive period of cognitive development. During this period, their understanding of objects or events mainly relies on the most salient perceptual features of the target items, rather than on logical or rational thinking processes. This cognitive preference is also evident in Perner's (1991) research of distinction between appearance and reality, in which preschoolers' responses were mostly based on apparent perceptual features. Nine-year-olds, however, belong to a different developmental stage, the concrete operational stage, and they perform better in providing logical links between things. Such difference in cognitive preferences helps to explain why children of different ages performed differently in the present study: five-year-olds mostly valued salient details so they preferred to encode C_0 and C_1 events; comparatively, nine-year-olds focused more on relations between events, so they constructed narratives with more causal connections, hence their narrations more coherent. Put another way, the tendency to value piecemeal details at the expense of the whole picture of things may presumably render five-year-olds' narrative less coherent.

To sum up, the present study advanced our knowledge about Mandarin-speaking children's development of maintaining coherence in narratives. It also demonstrated that the system of causal network provides an alternative to quantitatively assess narrative coherence.

References

Aksu-Koç, Ayhan, & Tekdemir, Göklem. (2004). Interplay between narrativity and mindreading: A comparison between Turkish and English. In S. Strömqvist & L. Verhoeven (Eds.), *Relating events in narrative: Typological and contextual perspectives* (pp. 307-327). Mahwah, NJ: Lawrence Erlbaum.

Baddeley, Alan., & Hitch, Graham. (1974). Working memory. In G. H. Bower (Ed.), *The Psychology of Learning and Motivation* (pp. 47-89). New York: Academic Press.

Bamberg, Michael, & Marchman, Virginia. (1990). What holds a narrative together? The linguistic encoding of episode boundaries. *Papers in Pragmatics, 4*, 58-121.

Berman, Ruth A., & Slobin, Dan I. (1994). *Relating events in narrative: A crosslinguistic developmental study*. Hillsdale, NJ: Lawrence Erlbaum.

Chang, Chien-Ju. (2004). Telling stories of experiences: Narrative development of young Chinese children. *Applied Psycholinguistics, 25*, 83-104.

Chang, Pao-Yueh. (1995). The development of child's story schema: A causal network discourse analysis (Unpublished master's thesis). National Taiwan Normal University.

Chen, Hsin-Hsi., Chang, Chien-Ju., & Chen, Hsiu-Fen. (2011). Developing narrative structure in preschoolers' retelling of a story book: Episodic analysis. *Bulletin of Educational Psychology, 42*(3), 359-378.

Colle, Livia., Baron-Cohen, Simon., Wheelwright, Sally., & van der Lely, Heather. (2008). Narrative discourse in adults with high-functioning autism or Asperger syndrome. *Journal of Autism and Developmental Disorders, 38*(1), 28-40.

Diehl, Joshua, Bennetto, Loisa, & Young, Edna. (2006). Story recall and narrative coherence of high-functioning children with autism spectrum disorders. *Journal of Abnormal Child Psychology, 34*(1), 87-102.

Frith, Uta, & Happé, Francesca. (1994). Autism: Beyond 'theory of mind'. *Cognition, 50*, 115-132.

Gathercole, S., Pickering, S., Ambridge, B., & Wearing, H. (2004). The structure of working memory from 4 to 15 years of age. *Developmental Psychology, 40*, 177-190.

Grice, Paul. (1989). *Studies in the way of words*. Cambridge, MA: Harvard University Press.

Hart, Herbert, & Honoré, Antony. (1959). *Causation in the law* (pp. xxxii, 454). Oxford: Clarendon Press.

Karmiloff-Smith, Annette. (1985). Language and cognitive processes from a developmental perspective. *Language and Cognitive Processes, 1*(1), 61-85.

Li, Yun-Chen. (2012). Analysis of picture-elicited narrative in three- and five-year-old preschoolers (Unpublished master's thesis). National Kaohsiung Normal University.

Mackie, J. (1980). *The cement of the universe: A study of causation*. Oxford: Clarendon Press.

Mayer, Mercer. (1969). *Frog, where are you?* New York: Dial Press.

Perner, J. (1991). *Understanding the representational mind*. Harvard, MA: MIT.

Peterson, Carole, & McCabe, Allyssa. (1983). *Developmental psycholinguistics: Three ways of looking at a child's narrative*. New York: Plenum.

Sah, Wen-Hui. (2013). Global and local connections in Mandarin-speaking children's narratives: A developmental study based on the frog story. In A. McCabe & C. J. Chang (Eds.), *Chinese Language Narration: Culture, cognition, and emotion*. John Benjamins (in press).

Stein, Nancy, & Albro, Elizabeth. (1997). Building complexity and coherence: Children's use of goal-structured knowledge in telling stories. In. M. Bamberg (Ed.), *Narrative development: Six approaches* (pp. 5-44). Mahwah, NJ: Lawrence Erlbaum.

Tager-Flusberg, Helen, & Sullivan, Kate. (1995). Attributing mental states to story characters: A comparison of narratives produced by autistic and mentally retarded individuals. *Applied Psycholinguistics, 16*, 241-256.

Trabasso, Tom, & Nickels, Margret. (1992). The development of goal plans of action in the narration of a picture story. *Discourse Processes, 15*, 249-275.

Trabasso, Tom, Secco, Tom, & van den Broek, Paul. (1984). Causal cohesion and story coherence. In H. Mandl, N. L. Stein, & T. Trabasso (Eds.), *Learning and comprehension of text* (pp. 83-111). Hillside, NJ: Lawrence Erlbaum.

Trabasso, Tom, & Sperry, Linda L. (1985). Causal relatedness and importance of story events. *Journal of Memory and Language, 24*, 595-611.

Trabasso, Tom, Stein, Nancy, Rodkin, Philip, Munger, Margaret, & Baughn, Camille. (1992). Knowledge of goals and plans in the on-line narration of events. *Cognitive Development, 7*, 133-170.

Trabasso, Tom, & van den Broek, Paul. (1985). Causal thinking and the representation of narrative events. *Journal of Memory and Language, 24*, 612-630.

Appendix. Causal Chain and Causal Connections by One Child

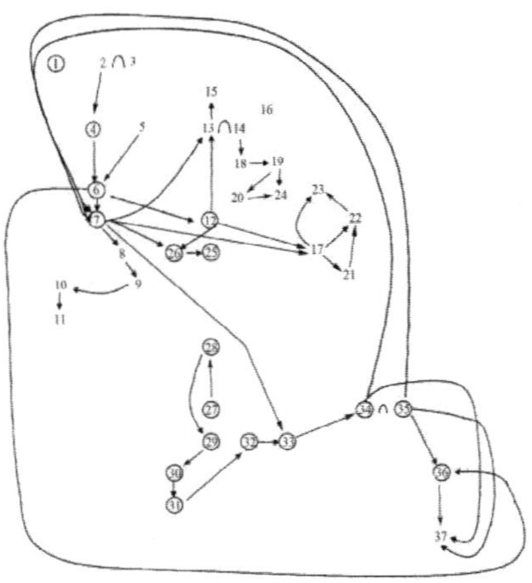

Note: Each number in the map stands for one story event. Circled numbers are the events on the causal chain; causal connections between events are represented by arrows. And arches connect co-occurring events. The story events corresponding to the numbers in the map are given below.

1. xiao nanhai you liang ge chongwu
'(One) little boy has two pets.'
2. you yi tian xiao nanhai zai shuijiao
'One day when the little boy is sleeping,'
3. han xiaogou zai shuijiao
'and his dog is sleeping,'
4. qingwa jiu cong guanzi li pao chulai le
'the frog runs out of the jar.'
5. ranhou tian liang le
'Then the sky gets brighter,'
6. tanmen jiu faxian qingwa bujian le
'they realize the frog has gone.'
7. tamen jiu daochu zhaozhaokan
'They look everywhere.'
8. tamen dakai chuanghu
'They open the window'
9. zhao qingwa
'to look for the frog.'
10. ranhou xiaogou buxiaoxin diao xiaqu le
'Then, the dog falls down out of its carelessness.'
11. ba qingwa de quzi shuaihuai le
'(It) breaks the frog's house.'
12. ranhou tamen dao senlin fujin zhao
'Then they search nearby the forest.'
13. xiao nanhai zai dongkou li zhao
'The little boy searches inside the hole.'
14. nage xiaogou kan shu shang de fengwo
'That dog looks at the beehive in the tree.'
15. di limian pao chu yi zhi yanshu
'A gopher runs out of the hole on the ground.'
16. fengwo li you mifeng
'There are bees inside the beehive.'
17. xiao nanhai pa shang shu
'The little boy climbs up to a tree.'
18. xiaogou buxiaoxin yao shu
'The dog carelessly shakes the tree.'
19. ba fengwo neng diao le
'(It) knocks down the beehive.'
20. mifeng dou pao chulai le
'All the bees run out.'
21. xiao nanhai dao shu shang de dong li zhao
'The little boy searches (the frog) in the tree-hole.'
22. yi zhi maotouying jiu fei chulai
'One owl flies out.'
23. xiao nanhai jiu die xiaqu le
'The little boy then falls down.'
24. mifeng jiu zhui zhe xiaogou pao
'The bees then chase the dog.'
25. xiao nanhai pa shang shitou
'The little boy climbs up a rock'
26. zhaozhaokan qingwa
'to look for the frog.'
27. ranhou yi zhi lu pao chulai
'Then a deer runs out.'
28. xiao nanhai jiu die dao ta shen shang
'The little boy then falls onto the deer.'
29. lu jiu dai zhe xiao nanhai pao
'The deer then carries the little boy around.'
30. ranhou tanen diao jin shanggu li le
'Then they fall into the valley.'
31. zuihao tamen die jin chitang li
'Finally they fall into the pond.'
32. tamen qilai dao an shang
'They get up onto the bank.'
33. ranhou dao mudui qianmian zhao
'Then (they) look for (it) in front of a pile of woods.'
34. zhaodao le liang zhi qingwa

'(They) find two frogs'

35. haiyou zhaoao shengxia de xiao qingwa
'and find the rest of the little frogs.'

36. xiao nanhai jueding ba qingwa dai huijia
'The little boy decides to take the frog home'

37. jiu gen naxie qingwa shuo zaijian
'Then (he) says good-bye to those frogs.

Clausal-Packaging of Path of Motion in the Second Language Acquisition of Russian and Spanish

Kawai Chui **Hsiang-lin Yeh** **Wen-Chun Lan** **Yu-Han Cheng**
National Chengchi University,
NO.64, Sec.2, ZhiNan Rd.,Wenshan District,Taipei City 11605 Taiwan (R.O.C.)
kawai@nccu.edu.tw verayeh@nccu.edu.tw wenchun@nccu.edu.tw 101555001@ nccu.edu.tw

Abstract

Given that Mandarin is a verb-serializing language, Russian a satellite-framed language, and Spanish a verb-framed language, the current study examines Mandarin college students' acquisition of Russian and Spanish as L2, to understand the strength of L1 preferences for expression of PATH on Russian and Spanish majors' second language acquisition in Taiwan. Based on oral narrative data, the study focuses on lexicalization and concatenation preferences in L1 and L2 languages. First, Russian majors' morphosyntactic preferences show that L1 Mandarin affects students' acquisition of Russian at the elementary level. However, in the acquisition of Spanish, learners' native language does not hold strength; Spanish majors' morphosyntactic patterning conforms more to that in L2 Spanish for both elementary and intermediate levels. Moreover, the Spanish majors appear to be developing their L2 concatenation patterning in a way that is divergent from the target L2 Spanish. The findings provide a deeper understanding of the different degrees of L1 influence on learners' acquisition of L2 Russian and of L2 Spanish at various levels of proficiency.

1 Introduction

The packaging of PATH and MANNER of motion at the level of the clause has been discussed since the typological distinction between 'satellite-framed' languages and 'verb-framed' languages was proposed (Talmy, 1985, 1991), in that the former incorporate motion with MANNER in the main verb and express PATH with a verb particle or a satellite, whereas the latter incorporate motion with PATH in the main verb and express MANNER in the subordinated verb. Later, Slobin (2004: 249) added a group of 'equipollently-framed' languages to the typology, where "[p]ath and manner are expressed by equivalent grammatical forms" and the typical construction type for verb-serializing languages is MANNER VERB + PATH VERB. Mandarin Chinese, as a verb-serializing language in both spoken and written discourse (Slobin, 2000, 2004; Huang and Tanangkingsing, 2005; Chen, 2007; Chen and Guo, 2009; Chui, 2009), belongs to the equipollently-framed group. The use of manner-path verbs such as *fēi-chū* 'fly-exit' or manner-path-deictic verbs such as *fēi-chū-qù* 'fly-exit-out' are common in Mandarin oral narratives and daily conversations (Chui, 2009, 2012).

Russian is a satellite-framed language and Spanish is a verb-framed language (Talmy, 1985, 1991; Slobin 2004). Together with Mandarin, the three languages have their own language-specific lexicalization patterns for the expression of motion events, as illustrated by the following examples from Slobin (2004: 224). The appearance of the movement of an owl is encoded by the manner-path serial verb *fēi-chū* in Mandarin, by *vy-skočila* 'jump' – a manner verb with the path prefix *vy-* in Russian, and by the path verb *sale* 'exit' in Spanish.

Mandarin: Fei1-chu1 yi1 zhi1 mao1 tou2 ying1. (=Fly out one owl.)
Russian: Tam vy-skočila sova. (=There out-jumped owl.)
Spanish: Sale un buho. (=Exits an owl.)

"Cross-linguistic differences in surface forms and accompanying linguistic conceptualizations raise potential problems for L2 learners" (Brown and Gullberg, 2011: 81). Then, in Mandarin speakers' second language acquisition of Russian and Spanish in Taiwan, does the typical patterning of motion in L1 Mandarin transfer to students' L2, be it Russian or Spanish, during their learning in Taiwan? If such is the case, does the effect of such transfer differ in the case of the learning of Russian and in that of Spanish? Does the transfer continue throughout the four years of study in college?

None of these questions have as yet been well investigated, and they will be addressed in the current study.

Brown and Gullberg (2010, 2011, 2012, 2013) have done a series of research on L1-L2 influence in second language acquisition, based on the expression of PATH and/or MANNER in Japanese and English at the clause level. In Brown and Gullberg (2010, 2011), they focused on different PATH components and examined the performance of the same speakers in the L1 and L2. With regard to the lexicalization and concatenation patterns, the studies demonstrated "a strong influence of the L1 on the L2 and a more subtle influence of the L2 on the L1" (2011: 90). Considering both PATH and MANNER, Brown and Gullberg (2012) found that not only learners' first language (L1) affected the acquisition of an L2, but also L2 had influence on L1, owing to learners' multicompetence. Finally, learners' established and emerging linguistic systems could become similar as a result of L1-L2 convergence (Brown and Gullberg, 2013). Following this line of research, the present study looks at the clausal packaging of PATH of motion in typologically different L1 and L2 languages, to understand learners' emerging grammar of motion and whether L1 Mandarin strongly affects the acquisition of L2 Russian and that of Spanish.

Specifically, the present study investigates the morphosyntactic patterning of PATH and the concatenation of the lexical and adverbial expressions of PATH in L1 and L2 languages. The research questions include: What are the typical morphosyntactic devices used in the L1 and L2 expression of PATH during speaking? How many path elements tend to be concatenated within a clause in L1 and L2? Do the typical usages in the L1 and the target L2 languages transfer to students' L2, be it Russian or Spanish? If such is the case, to what extent and in what way do learners' L2 Russian and their L2 Spanish follow the preferred patterns in L1? Does the effect of such transfer differ at various levels of proficiency during acquisition? Is there any cross-linguistic difference between the acquisition of Russian and that of Spanish?

The study contributes to understanding the nature of the relationship between established L1 and emerging L2 within the multilingual mind. It also has implications for language pedagogy and assessment.

2 Data and methodologies

Participants

In this study, there were five groups of participants. Three of the groups were comprised of native speakers, the other two of learners. All of the participants were students at National Chengchi University (NCCU). Group 1 was comprised of five native speakers of Mandarin producing L1 Mandarin; they were freshmen aged 18 or 19 in 2002. They were neither majors in Russian or Spanish nor did they study foreign languages as L2 at the university. Group 2 was comprised of five native speakers of Russian producing L2 Russian, aged from 19 to 27, studying in a Chinese or an academic program at NCCU. Group 3 was comprised of five native Spanish speakers producing L2 Spanish; they aged from 21 to 29, also studying in a Chinese or an academic program.

The other two groups were comprised of learners. They were Russian or Spanish majors at some point in time (Years 1, 2, 3 or 4) in the four years of college at NCCU in the 2012/13 academic year. They produced learners' L2 Russian and learners' L2 Spanish, respectively. The number of Russian participants and Spanish participants totaled twenty for each language, with five students from each grade. They were all native Mandarin speakers aged from eighteen to twenty-two. They were studying Russian or Spanish as a foreign language in a non-immersion context, and had little or no knowledge of these two languages prior to entering college.

Stimulus for L1 and L2 production

To compare the data from the various language groups on a common basis, we elicited all of the spoken data from the same stimulus - a seven-minute-long cartoon episode of the 'Mickey Mouse and Friends' series. The soundtrack of the cartoon includes music and only a very small amount of dialogue. The episode contains numerous motion events: Mickey, Minnie, Pluto and a bull are holding a party at the beach, and eating and playing around, and then they have a fight with an octopus. Finally, Mickey and his friends win.

Procedure

The participants across the five groups were not informed about our particular research interests. They were told that they were taking part in a study of storytelling. They were paid for their participation.

All of the participants were tested individually. First, each of them viewed the cartoon episode two times on TV or a laptop computer in a quiet classroom. Immediately afterwards the participant was led to another classroom and requested to retell the story to an adult listener, knowing that the listener had not viewed the episode. The participant sat on a classroom chair with no armrests, facing the listener who was about 90cm away. The recounting in Mandarin, Russian, or Spanish as L1 or L2 was filmed by a visible video camera. Details about the duration of narrations can be found in Table 1.

The spoken data were documented in the NCCU Spoken Corpus of Mandarin, the NCCU Learner Corpus of Russian, and the NCCU Learner Corpus of Spanish.

L1 Mandarin	7 min. 17 sec.
L2 Russian	7 min.
L2 Spanish	3 min. 50 sec.
Learners' L2 Russian	6 min. 8 sec.
Learners' L2 Spanish	3 min. 6 sec.

Table 1. Average duration of narration in the five language groups

Transcription, segmentation, and coding of data

The L1 Mandarin narratives were transcribed by graduate students with Mandarin as their L1. The storytellings in L2 Russian (produced by native speakers), L2 Spanish (produced by native speakers), learners' L2 Russian, and learners' L2 Spanish were transcribed by students majoring in either Russian or Spanish and then checked by a professor of Russian or a professor of Spanish, respectively. All of the data were first segmented into clauses, i.e., ''any unit that contains a unified predicate... (expressing) a single situation (activity, event, state)'' (Berman and Slobin, 1994: 660). Complements were not separated.

Next, motion-event clauses containing path information were identified and coded. The occurrences across the five datasets are: 128 instances in L1 Mandarin; 45 instances in L2 Russian; 44 instances in L2 Spanish; 51 instances in learners' L2 Russian; and 46 instances in learners' L2 Spanish. As to learners' L2 production, the Russian and Spanish majors in the first two years of college were considered as elementary learners; those in the third and fourth years as intermediate learners. Whether the acquisition of an L2 differs with respect to the two levels of proficiency will be investigated in Section 4. Finally, the clauses were coded for (1) the lexical form of a motion verb, and (2) the adverbial elements encoding path information about the same motion event, including particles, adverbs, and adpositional phrases expressing location, source, goal, direction, etc.

3 Clausal packaging of PATH in L1 and L2 production: Mandarin, Russian, and Spanish

In every language, lexical verbs and adverbials can be used to express PATH in a single clause. That multiple adverbials can be stacked to provide more PATH descriptions is language-specific. Some languages allow several path components outside the verb, while others require a separate verb for each component (Slobin, 2004). This section investigates the morphosyntactic preferences for the expression of PATH and the stacking of PATH components in the three languages spoken by native speakers.

3.1 L1 Mandarin production

The lexicalization and concatenation of PATH elements in L1 Mandarin can be illustrated by two examples. The clause in Example 1 is about Pluto hiding under a picnic table and the octopus pouncing up on top of it. The pouncing event is represented by the serial manner-path-deictic verb *pū-shàng-qù* 'pounce-go up-go', encoding the manner *pū* 'pounce', the upward direction *shàng* and the deictic movement *qù* 'go'. In Example 2, the clause is about a sausage being dropped into the sea. The dropping event is expressed lexically by the manner verb *diào* 'drop' and adverbially by the prepositional phrase of GOAL *dào* 'to' *hǎi* 'sea' *lǐmiàn* 'in'.

(1) ..rānghòu nà zhī... zhāngyú jiù
then that CL octopus then
pū- le **shàng-qù**
pounce PRF go up-go
'Then, the octopus pounces onto (Pluto).'

(2) ..nàge.. nàcháng.. **diào dào hǎi lǐmiàn**
that sausage drop to sea inside
'That..sausage..was dropped into the sea.'

There are 128 motion clauses conveying path information in the Mandarin dataset. As shown in Table 2, Mandarin speakers have two lexical preferences: (1) use of serial verbs (47.7%), among which manner-path-deictic verbs like *pǎo-chū-lái* 'run-exit-come' are the majority; and (2) use of single manner verbs accompanied by path adverbials (43%). Second, it is also common to convey path information outside the verb: 53.9% (69 clauses) of all of the motion clauses realize different components of a path, including location, source, goal, and direction. Among all the 77 occurrences of PATH components in the data, the expression of GOAL constitutes the majority (66.2%).

Verb types		PATH adverbials	
manner verb (with path adverbial)	43.0%	location	11.7%
path verb	6.3%	source	9.1%
deictic verb	3.1%	goal	66.2%
path-deictic verb	7.8%	direction	13.0%
manner-path verb	0.8%	Total	100.0%
manner-deictic verb	2.3%		
manner-path-deictic verb	36.7%		
Total	100.0%		

Table 2. Morphosyntactic expression of PATH in L1 Mandarin

The concatenation of PATH elements lies in the number of path elements in the verbal or adverbial form per clause. Mandarin allows stacking path components outside the verb within a clause, yet the spoken data shows a strong preference by the speakers (82.8%) to mention a single path element. See Table 3.

1 path element	2 path elements	3 path elements
82.8%	16.4%	0.8%

Table 3. Number of path elements in L1 Mandarin

3.2 L2 Russian production

Lexical verbs in Russian can take a path prefix, such as 'за-' 'into' in Example 3. The Russian native speaker in the example talks about a motion event involving Mickey Mouse going into the sea. It is encoded lexically by the deictic verb ходить 'go' accompanied by the path prefix 'за-', and adverbially by the prepositional phrase of GOAL в воду 'into water'.

(3) ... Микки Маус преспокойно
Mickey Mouse extremely.calmly
за-ходит в воду
into-go into water
'Mickey Mouse goes into the water extremely calmly.'

There are in total 45 motion clauses encoding PATH in the L2 Russian dataset. 37.8% of all of the motion clauses are of the PATH PREFIX + MOTION VERB type; manner verbs taking path adverbials are also common (33.3%), and path/deictic verbs also constitute a substantial portion (28.9%). Moreover, the occurrence of path adverbials is 73.3% (33 clauses) of all of the motion clauses speakers. Among all the 35 occurrences of PATH components, GOAL (62.9%) was mostly brought up. See Table 4.

Verb types		PATH adverbials	
manner verb (with path adverbial)	33.3%	location	11.4%
path verb	20.0%	source	17.1%
deictic verb	8.9%	goal	62.9%
path prefix-deictic verb	17.8%	direction	8.6%
path prefix-manner verb	20.0%	Total:	100.0%
Total:	100.0%		

Table 4. Morphosyntactic expression of PATH in L2 Russian

Slobin (2004) noted that Russian, a satellite-framed language, expresses PATH primarily in a wide range of adverbials; thus, more PATH segments per clause would be brought up for the discussion of a motion event. In our data, the occurrence of path adverbials in Russian is higher than that in Mandarin (73.3% vs. 53.9%). Moreover, Table 5 shows that as many as 44.4% of all clauses encode two path elements in Russian (cf. 16.4% in Mandarin).

1 path element	2 path elements
55.6%	44.4%

Table 5. Number of path elements per clause in L2 Russian

3.3 L2 Spanish production

The use of path verbs is regarded as the typical pattern for the expression of PATH in verb-framed languages like Spanish (Talmy,

1985, 1991; Slobin, 2004). As shown in Example 4, the Spanish native speaker tells that the cow goes into the water. The motion event is expressed lexically by the path verb *entra* and adverbially by the prepositional phrase of GOAL *al agua* 'to the water'.

(4) ..la vaca **entra al agua**
the cow enter to.the water
'The cow goes into the water.'

Besides path verbs, manner verbs could also be used to characterize certain types of motion events (Aske, 1989; Slobin and Hoiting, 1994; Slobin 1996; Naigles et al., 1998). Aske (1989) found that resultative events with a source or a definite endpoint, such as *to the house*, were described by path verbs, whereas events taking place at or in a single location, such as *in the house*, could be characterized by manner verbs. Slobin and Hoiting (1994) distinguished between boundary-crossing events and non-boundary-crossing events; the former would be described by path verbs and the latter by manner verbs. Similar results were also found in Naigles et al. (1998), with ten black-and-white line drawings of ordinary intransitive motion events and twelve colored dynamic videos of common intransitive motion events as stimuli. These findings suggest that the use of manner verbs is not a rarity. This is borne out by our narrative data: While the use of path verbs and deictic verbs constitutes the majority (54.5%) of all the 44 motion events in the L2 Spanish dataset, a substantial portion of the clauses comprise manner verbs and adverbial expression of PATH (45.5%). See Table 6. Finally, just as in the case of the other two languages, the rate of the occurrence of path adverbials is high (72.7%, 32 out of all the 44 clauses). GOAL, again, is the most frequently brought up component in Spanish narration.

Verb types		PATH adverbials	
manner verb (with path adverbial)	45.5%	location	6.3%
path verb	38.6%	source	3.1%
deictic verb	15.9%	goal	84.4%
Total:	100.0%	direction	6.2%
		Total:	100.0%

Table 6. Morphosyntactic expression of PATH in L2 Spanish

Regarding the concatenation of PATH elements, Slobin (2004: 244) found that the description of PATH components in Spanish typically requires separate verb clauses, so that "V-language writers in the sample almost never used a motion verb with more than one ground.... V-language writers and frog story narrators prefer to provide ground information in scene-setting descriptions rather than in clauses with motion verbs." The statistics in Table 7 support the occurrence of less path information within a clause, as most of the clauses include merely one path element (72.7%).

1 path element	2 path elements
72.7%	27.3%

Table 7. Number of path elements per clause in L2 Spanish

In summary, the three languages spoken by native speakers have their own language-specific lexicalization and concatenation patterns in narrative discourse. L1 Mandarin speakers encode PATH primarily in a range of serial verbs comprising at least one path component and also utilize single manner verbs with path adverbials. Such typical patterns of usage are different from the common use of motion verbs with a path prefix, manner verbs, and path/deictic verbs in Russian, and also from the use of path/deictic verbs and manner verbs in Spanish.

The expression of PATH both lexically and adverbially is predominant and most of the speakers mention the GOAL component across the three languages. As to the number of path elements per clause, both Mandarin and Spanish prefer one element. In Russian, however, a significantly higher number of clauses convey two path elements – one in the verb and the other in a prepositional phrase. The next section examines the acquisition of Russian and that of Spanish by elementary and intermediate learners to understand the strength of preferences for expression of PATH in L1 on learners' second language acquisition with respect to two levels of proficiency, and whether the acquisition of Russian and that of Spanish differ.

4 Clausal packaging of PATH in learners' L2 production: Spanish and Russian

Given that Mandarin is a verb-serializing language, Russian a satellite-framed language, and Spanish a verb-framed language, how do learners of Russian and of Spanish each develop their L2 in the presence of knowledge from two typologically different languages? Is there any difference in the L1 transfer, if there any, between these two groups of learners, and between the elementary and the intermediate learners in each language group?

4.1 Learner's L2 Russian production

The Russian majors produced 51 PATH clauses; 40 of them consisting of path adverbials (80.4%). The learners did not use the PATH PREFIX+MOTION VERB pattern frequently, probably because of its language-specificity and grammatical optionality. See Table 8. For differences in the use of manner verbs and the use of path/deictic verbs, the chi-square value shows significant difference between L2 production at elementary level and that at intermediate level (X^2=4.21, d.f.=1, p<.05). In other words, elementary learners prefer manner verbs (60%) and intermediate learners prefer path/deictic verbs (58.0%). Nonetheless, the use of path adverbials is prevalent in L2 production, regardless of proficiency levels: 85% for elementary learners; 77.4% for intermediate learners.

Verb types	Years 1 & 2	Years 3 & 4
manner verb	60.0%	32.3%
path verb	5.0%	19.4%
deictic verb	25.0%	38.6%
path-deictic verb	10.0%	6.5%
path-path verb	0.0%	3.2%
Total:	100.0%	100.0%
PATH adverbials	Years 1 & 2	Years 3 & 4
location	0.0%	0.0%
source	5.9%	12.5%
goal	88.2%	62.5%
direction	5.9%	25.0%
Total:	100.0%	100.0%

Table 8. Morphosyntactic expression of PATH in L2 Russian

The concatenation patterns do not differ between the two groups of Russian learners, as evidenced by the statistically insignificant chi-square value with regard to the distribution of one-path-element, two-path-element, and three-path-element clauses (X^2=2.64, d.f.=2, p<.05). See Table 9.

	1 path element	2 path elements	3 path elements
Years 1 & 2	70.0%	30.0%	0.0%
Years 2 & 3	48.4%	48.4%	3.2%

Table 9. Number of path elements per clause in L2 Russian

4.2 Learner's L2 Spanish production

There are in total 46 PATH clauses in the L2 Spanish production, among which adverbials encoding PATH constitute 38 clauses (82.6%). The use of path/deictic verbs is predominant with no statistically significant difference between the elementary and the intermediate learners (X^2=2.88, d.f.=1, p<.05). The occurrence of path adverbials is higher in the narratives of intermediate learners (89.3%) than in those of elementary learners (72.7%). Nonetheless, the GOAL component, again, is most frequently brought up in the storytellings, regardless of level of proficiency. See Table 10.

Verb types	Years 1 & 2	Years 3 & 4
manner verb	5.6%	25.0%
path verb	50.0%	32.1%
deictic verb	44.4%	42.9%
Total:	100.0%	100.0%
PATH adverbials	Years 1 & 2	Years 3 & 4
location	7.7%	4.0%
source	0.0%	0.0%
goal	92.3%	96.0%
direction	0.0%	0.0%
Total:	100.0%	100.0%

Table 10. Morphosyntactic expression of PATH in L2 Spanish

	1 path element	2 path elements
Years 1 & 2	33.3%	66.7%
Years 2 & 3	35.7%	64.3%

Table 11. Number of path elements per clause in L2 Spanish

The concatenation patterns are also consistent between the two groups of Spanish learners (X^2=0.274, d.f.=1, p<.05). They manifest a preference to express two path elements in a clause, 66.7% in elementary students' production and 64.3% in intermediate students' production. See Table 11.

When comparing the production of Russian learners and Spanish learners, we found that the two groups of students acquire the two L2 languages in different ways. Learners of Russian at elementary level mainly use manner verbs while those at intermediate level prefer the path/deictic verbs. Levels of proficiency, however, do not affect the preference of learners of Spanish to use path/deictic verbs. Another difference lies in the quantity of path information: While learners of Russian mostly produce a single path element in each clause, learners of Spanish frequently produce two elements. Finally, the similarities between the learners of Russian and those of Spanish are found in the high occurrence of path adverbials and of the GOAL component.

5 Strength of L1 on second language acquisition

Section 3 has shown that native speakers of L1 Mandarin, L2 Russian, and L2 Spanish utilize their own typical language-specific morpho-syntactic patterns in the expression of PATH of motion. In Section 4 it was demonstrated that the second language acquisition of Spanish is not in complete alignment with that of Russian. Based on the findings, this section will compare the patterning of L1 Mandarin, L2 Russian, and L2 Spanish to understand how Mandarin learners acquire the knowledge of a different linguistic system, and the strength of L1 preferences on Russian and Spanish majors' second language acquisition.

<u>Does learners' L2 Russian pattern like L1 Mandarin or L2 Russian?</u>

A lexicalization pattern commonly used in Russian is the co-occurrence of a path prefix and a motion verb, yet learners rarely use this optional language-specific pattern to express PATH. See Table 12. Regarding the choice between manner verbs and path/deictic verbs, native Mandarin speakers prefer to use manner verbs but native Russian speakers use more path/deictic verbs. These two languages influence learners in different ways: The preference for manner verbs along with PATH adverbials in elementary L2 production resembles L1, without a significant difference between Mandarin and elementary L2 Russian (X^2=2.02, d.f.=1, p<.05). A significant difference was found between Mandarin and intermediate L2 Russian (X^2=19.7, d.f.=1, p<.05). The usage rate of path/deictic verbs is significantly higher on the part of intermediate learners.

Groups of speakers	Manner verb	Path/deictic verb	Path prefix+ motion verb
L1 Mandarin	82.1%	17.9%	--
L2 Russian	33.3%	28.9%	37.8%
Learners' L2 Russian (Years 1 & 2)	60.0%	30.0%	10.0%
Learners' L2 Russian (Years 3 & 4)	32.3%	58.1%	9.6%

Table 12. Lexicalization of PATH in Mandarin and Russian

L1 transfer is also found in the patterning of the concatenation of the path elements. Just like native Mandarin speakers, elementary learners typically encode one path element per clause, with no significant difference between the L1 and the L2 production (X^2=2.26, d.f.=2, p<.05). On the contrary, intermediate learners significantly mention two path elements in their narration (X^2=16.3, d.f.=2, p<.05). See Table 13.

Groups of speakers	1 path element	2 path elements	3 path elements
L1 Mandarin	82.8%	16.4%	0.8%
L2 Russian	55.6%	44.4%	0.0%
Learners' L2 Russian (Years 1 & 2)	70.0%	30.0%	0.0%
Learners' L2 Russian (Years 3 & 4)	48.4%	48.4%	3.2%

Table 13. Concatenation of PATH in Mandarin and Russian

In brief, the L1 effect is not consistent with respect to the two levels of proficiency: Elementary learners are more affected by their native language; the language produced by intermediate learners resembles the target language more.

<u>Does learners' L2 Spanish pattern like L1 Mandarin or L2 Spanish?</u>

According to the narrative data produced by native Spanish speakers in Table 6, the use of manner verbs with a path adverbial is nearly as frequent as that of path verbs and deictic verbs. Nevertheless, learners prefer to use path/deictic verbs. See Table 14. In other words, given the distribution of the frequency of manner verbs and path/deictic verbs, the significant differences between L1 Mandarin and the two groups of L2 Spanish (X^2=37.0, d.f.=1, p < .05 for elementary learners; X^2=28.4, d.f.=1, p < .05 for intermediate learners) provide evidence that L1 Mandarin with its prevalent use of manner verbs does not affect learners' acquisition of Spanish.

Groups of speakers	Manner verb	Path/deictic verb
L1 Mandarin	82.1%	17.9%
L2 Spanish	45.5%	54.5%
Learners' L2 Spanish (Years 1 & 2)	5.6%	94.4%
Learners' L2 Spanish (Years 3 & 4)	25.0%	75.0%

Table 14. Lexicalization of PATH in Mandarin and Spanish

Groups of speakers	1 path element	2 path elements	3 path elements
L1 Mandarin	82.8%	16.4%	0.8%
L2 Spanish	72.7%	27.3%	0.0%
Learners' L2 Spanish (Years 1 & 2)	33.3%	66.7%	0.0%
Learners' L2 Spanish (Years 3 & 4)	35.7%	64.3%	0.0%

Table 15. Concatenation of PATH in Mandarin and Spanish

With regard to the concatenation patterns, the production of the Spanish learners, different from that of the Russian learners, reveals an idiosyncrasy in the development of learners' L2 language. As shown in Table 15, both Mandarin and Spanish native speakers tend to encode one path element per clause, either lexically or adverbially. L2 Spanish learners, on the other hand, mostly express two elements, one lexical and one adverbial. This preference for quantity is found to be the same for both elementary and intermediate learners. The significant chi-square values are: X^2=22.8, d.f.=2, p<.05 for L1 Mandarin and elementary learners' L2 Spanish; X^2=28.1, d.f.=2, p<.05 for L1 Mandarin and intermediate learners' L2 Spanish; X^2=8.36, d.f.=1, p<.05 for L2 Spanish and elementary learners' L2 Spanish; X^2=9.64, d.f.=1, p<.05 for L2 Spanish and intermediate learners' L2 Spanish.

In brief, the L1 effect was not found in the acquisition of Spanish. Spanish majors' morphosyntactic patterning conforms more to that in L2 Spanish, regardless of proficiency levels. Finally, the Spanish majors appear to be developing their L2 concatenation patterning in a way that is divergent from the target L2 Spanish. More data are needed to testify as to the nature of this apparently idiosyncratic development.

By examining the morphosyntactic and concatenation preferences in the L1 and L2 languages, the current study found that the distinct preferences in Mandarin, Russian, and Spanish affect learners' second language acquisition of Russian and of Spanish in various ways. More importantly, the findings as a whole provide understanding of the different degrees of L1 influence on learners' acquisition of L2 Russian and of L2 Spanish at two levels of proficiency. The question as to why Mandarin influences the acquisition of Russian rather than that of Spanish awaits future research.

6 Conclusion

Three typologically different languages were investigated in the present study: Mandarin, a verb-serializing language; Russian, a satellite-framed language; and Spanish, a verb-framed language. The acquisition of Russian and of Spanish as L2s was examined across the four years of study in college in Taiwan to understand the ways in which learners develop their L2 with knowledge from two typologically different languages, and the strength of L1 preferences for the expression of PATH within the clause on learners' development of each of the L2s.

The findings of this study contribute to the understanding of the nature of the relationship between established L1 and L2 languages and learners' emerging L2 languages, and to the linguistic conceptualization of PATH of motion in the bilingual mind. The findings may also provide a base for language pedagogy and assessment.

In the future, learners' written production in class should also be examined to obtain a more complete picture of learners' L2 production and of L1 effect on second language acquisition. Moreover, the ways in which learners' knowledge of a second language may affect performance in their first language can be studied to understand more about learners' multi-competence (Cook 1991; Brown and Gullberg 2013).

Acknowledgments

This research was funded by grants from The Aim for the Top University and Elite Research Center Development Plan, National Chengchi University. We would like to thank the reviewers for their insightful comments and helpful suggestions. All errors of interpretation are our own responsibility.

References

Aske, J. (1989). Path predicates in English and Spanish: A closer look. In K. Hall, M. Meacham, & R. Shapiro (Eds.), *Proceedings of the Fifteenth Annual Meeting of the Berkeley Linguistics Society* (pp. 1-14). Berkeley: Berkeley Linguistics Society.

Berman, R. A., & Slobin, D. I. (1994). *Relating events in narrative: A crosslinguistic developmental study.* Hillsdale, N.J.: Lawrence Erlbaum Associates.

Brown, A., & Gullberg, M. (2010). Changes in encoding of path of motion after acquisition of a second language. *Cognitive Linguistics*, *21*, 263-286.

Brown, A., & Gullberg, M. (2011). Bidirectional cross-linguistic influence in event conceptualization? Expressions of Path among Japanese learners of English. *Bilingualism: Language and Cognition*, *14*, 79-94.

Brown, A., & Gullberg, M. (2012). Multicompetence and native speaker variation in clausal packaging in Japanese. *Second Language Research*, *28*, 415-442.

Brown, A., & Gullberg, M. (2013). L1-L2 convergence in clausal packaging in Japanese and English. *Bilingualism: Language & Cognition*, *16*, 477-494.

Chen, L. (2007). *The Acquisition and Use of Motion Event Expressions in Chinese*. München: LINCOM Europa.

Chen, L., & Guo, J. (2009). Motion events in Chinese novels: Evidence for an equipollently-framed language. *Journal of Pragmatics*, *41*(9), 1749-1766.

Cook, V. (1991). The poverty of the stimulus argument and multicompetence. *Second Language Research*, *7*, 103-17.

Huang, S., & Tanangkingsing, M. (2005). Reference to motion events in six western Austronesian languages: Toward a semantic typology. *Oceanic Linguistics*, *44*, 307-340.

Slobin, D. I. (1996). Two ways to travel: Verbs of motion in English and Spanish. In M. Shibatani, & S. Thompson (Eds.), *Grammatical constructions: Their form and meaning* (pp. 70–96). Oxford: Oxford University Press.

Slobin, D. I. (2000). Verbalized events: a dynamic approach to linguistic relativity and determinism. In S. Niemeier, & R. Driven (Eds.), *Evidence for linguistic relativity* (pp. 107-138). Amsterdam: John Benjamins Publishing.

Slobin, D. I. (2004). The many ways to search for a frog: linguistic typology and the expression of motion events. In S. Strömqvist, & L. Verhoeven (Eds.), *Relating events in narrative: Typological and contextual perspectives* (pp. 219-257). Hillsdale, N.J.: Lawrence Erlbaum Associates.

Slobin, D. I., & Hoiting, N. (1994). Reference to movement in spoken and signed languages: Typological considerations. In S. Gahl, A. Dolbey, & C. Johnson (Eds.), *Proceedings of the twentieth annual meeting of the Berkeley Linguistics Society* (pp. 487-505). Berkeley: Berkeley Linguistics Society.

Talmy, L. (1985). Lexicalization patterns: semantic structure in lexical forms. In T. Shopen (Ed.), *Language typology and syntactic description* (Vol. 3, pp. 57-149). Cambridge: Cambridge University Press.

Talmy, L. (1991). Path to realization: a typology of event conflation. In L. A. Sutton, C. Johnson, & R. Shields (Eds.), *Proceedings of the Seventeenth Annual Meeting of the Berkeley Linguistics Society* (pp. 480-519). Berkeley: Berkeley Linguistics Society.

*** Formatting Issue - Best Available Paper/Graphic ***

Age Related Differences in Language Usage and Reading between English Monolinguals andBilinguals

Dylan Marshall
De La Salle University
Manila, Philippines
marshalld@ismanila.org

Hamid Gomari
De La Salle University
Manila, Philippines
h.gomari@yahoo.com

Abstract

This study investigates age related differences in standardized tests scores of *an a e sa e* and *rea in* from elementary to high school for students who are either monolinguals whose L1 is English or bilinguals whose L1 is not English. An interactioneffect between *ra e e e* and*rea in* and *an a e sa e* standardized test scores was hypothesized because as bilinguals become proficient in *o niti e a e i an a e ro i ien* in English,they are able tonarrow the 'achievement gap'in comparison to their monolingual classmates and even experience cognitive advantages (Cummins, 1999).Participants were 1081 students from an international school. *an a e sa e* and *rea in* were measured using MAP standardized achievement tests.The2x2 ANOVA showed an interaction between *ra e e e* and *an a es spo en* on *an a e sa e* ($p<0.05$).There was a main effect for *an a es spo en* and *ra e e e* on *an a e sa e* ($p<0.05$). No interaction was found for *ra e e e* and *an a es spo en* on *rea in* ($p>0.05$). A main effect was found for *an a es spo en* and *ra e e e* on *rea in* ($p<0.05$).Significant differences exist between bilingual and monolingualsand these differences *an e* over time. As bilingual students are immersed in English education, their performance on standardized tests catches up with their monolingual counterparts by grade 5 for *an a e sa e* but not for *rea in* , but no cognitive advantages are shown.

1Introduction

We live in an increasingly globalized world where bilingualism is very common as global societies become more interconnected. In this context, it is of vital importance to understand how bilingualism relatesstudents' language abilities, cognitive abilities and academic performance.Understanding differences between monolinguals and bilinguals is particularly relevant in the context of reading and language usage in international schools where the medium of instruction is English. These schools are often extremely diverse linguistic communities and many students are known as Third-Culture Kids (TCKs) who have grown up in a different culture to their passport country. Many students come from family backgrounds where there is no spoken English, and their main English input comes from their school life. It is important to find out whether being monolingual or bilingual can account for differences in performance in standardized test scores to understand how the monolingual and bilingual experience in international schools impacts students' performance in reading and language usage.

Early research on bilingualism proposed that bilinguals were at a disadvantage linguistically compared to monolinguals. Peal and Lambert (1962) studied the effect of bilingualism on cognitive functioning which led to a shift in our understanding of the effects of bilingualism. Their study found that the bilinguals outperformed monolinguals on almost all the tests, particularly on the tests involving mental organization; therefore, they concluded that bilinguals profited from *enta e i i it* and being bilingual was an asset. Since then, a considerable number of studies have been conducted on this topic and they havefound enhanced meta-linguistic awareness in bilingual children (Bialystok, 2009).

When considering language development in the school environment, it is important to consider the different levels and types of language proficiency.Cummins (1976) proposed that there are two *t res o* levels of linguistic proficiency: first, it is necessary for bilingual children to reach the lower threshold to avoid cognitive disadvantages and the second, higher threshold is necessary to make it possible for beneficial aspects of bilingualism to influence cognitive growth.

Cummins (1976)also proposed a distinction between *asi nterpersona o ni ation i s* (BICS)which account for children's ability to deal with the use of language in "peer-appropriate ways in everyday face-to-face situations" (Cummins, 1984, p.4) and *o niti e a e i an a e ro i ien* (CALP) which are the academically-related aspects of language proficiency. Bilingual children need to develop their proficiency in CALP for academic success in school, and this takes time. Indeed, Cummins (1999) states that "in second language acquisition contexts, immigrant children often acquire peer-appropriate conversational fluency in English within about 2 years but it requires considerably longer (5-10) years to catch up academically in English" (Cummins, 1999,p.2).

Another factor proposed by Cummins (2001) that relates to second language acquisition is Common Underlying Proficiency (CUP). Cummins believes when a child learns one language he/she acquires a set of skills and implicit meta-linguistic knowledge that he/she can draw upon when learning another language. The CUP provides the base for the development of students' native language (L1) and the second language (L2). This suggests that it is very important for students to maintain their L1. In most international schools students learn all their lessons through the medium of English,but there are additional programs in place to encourage students to maintain their non-English L1 languages, so it may be that bilinguals whose L2 is not English may experience some *o niti e a anta es* of being bilingual by the time they have spent 5-7 years immersed in English education.

There are differences between monolinguals and bilinguals in terms of how they process information when reading. Jimenez, Garcia and Pearson (1996) studied the strategic reading processes of 8 bilingual Latina/o children who were identified as successful English readers, in order to explore how bilingualism affectsmeta-cognition. They found Latina/o readers were able to actively transfer information across languages, translate from one language to another and openly access cognate vocabulary while reading.Furthermore, while encountering unknown vocabulary items whether reading an English or Spanish text, such readers utilized a *ran e o strate i pro esses* to determine the meanings of the unknown words. Less successful Latina/o readers employed *e er strate ies* and were found to be less effective in resolving comprehension problems in either language so that they could identify the unknown words, but were not able to come up with appropriate interpretations of text.The successful Anglo readers, due to their access to the well-developed prior knowledge, rarely encountered unknown vocabulary and were able to use considerable cognitive resources to the act of comprehension.

Martinez and Lesaux (2010) conducted a longitudinal study to examine the process of English reading comprehension for low achieving English Spanish bilingual childrenat the age of 11. The researchers evaluated the influence of growth rates, from early childhood (age 4.5) to pre-adolescence (age 11), in vocabulary and word reading skills on English reading comprehension. They used structural equation modeling (SEM) and annually administered standardized tests of word reading accuracy and productive vocabulary in English and Spanish, and they administered an English reading comprehension test at age 11. They found that English skills accounted for *a* unique variance in English reading comprehension outcomes.This shows that the level of L1 proficiency amongst bilinguals is not necessarily related their L2 proficiency.

The Age-of-Acquisition (AoA) of L2 language for bilinguals is also important in determining later proficiency. Bialystok and Miller (1999) conducted a research study on three groups of participants. They were given a grammaticality judgment test based on five structures of English grammar in both oral and written form. The first group consisted of native speakers of Chinese, the second, native speakers of Spanish, and the third, native English speakers. The two learner groups were divided into those who had begun learning English at a younger (less than 15 years) or older (more than 15 years) age. Performance was measured for both accuracy of judgment and time taken to respond. The results of their study showed that those who had started learning English *ear ier* performed *etter* than those who had learnt English later on the English grammar tests.

Furthermore, Kaushanskaya and Marian (2007) studied AoA effects in the development of *i in a a anta e* for word-learning among 30 monolingual speakers of English and 30 high-proficient English Spanish bilinguals. They further divided the bilingual participants into two groups of *ear* (15) and *ate* (15) bilinguals. The results of their study revealed that the AoA affected word-learning performance, and early bilinguals performed *etter* than monolinguals on the word-learning task. Based on the examination of AoA effects in the development of the bilingual cognitive advantage for foreign word learning, they suggested that earlier acquisition age amplifies bilingual *o niti e a anta e*. This clearly shows that those who acquire their second language earlier have a distinct advantage over those who acquire it later on.

Indeed, Bialystok (2009) proposes that the longer bilingual students have been immersed in their L2 language education the better their performance is on executive control tasks. They identified executive control as the mechanism that explains how bilingualism connects to bilingual *o niti e a anta e* Luc, deSa and Bialystok (2011) examined young adult bilinguals and found that *ear i in a s* (who were activity bilingual before the age of 10) had higher level of English proficiency than *ate i in a s*.

However, Bialystok et al. (2010) studiedvocabulary differences in the language of schooling (i.e., English) between monolingual and bilingual children using the Peabody Picture Vocabulary Test (PPVT) standard scores of a total of 1,738 children. The overall PPTV score was found to be *i er* for monolinguals than for bilinguals.

Further evidence for this phenomenon comes from Han (2011) who carried out a longitudinal study with a very large sample of 16,380 students on bilingualism and academic performance and found that bilingual children whose L1 was not English performed worse in tests of *rea in* and *ra ar* in third grade but they were able to *ose t e ap* on their monolingual counterparts as they progressed through school by the time they reachedfifth grade.This means that by the time they were in middle and high school, the bilingual students' performance was similar to that of monolinguals.

Taken together, the findings of the aforementioned research studies suggest that significant differences exist at a *o n a e* between bilingual and monolingual students, but these differences *an e* over time. As the bilingual students whose L1 is not English are immersed in English education, their performance catches up with their monolingual counterparts and they may experience cognitive advantages.

The current study seeks to investigate whether there are changes between the grades 3 to 10 (7 to 16 years of age) in the standardized test scores of *an a e sa e*and *rea in* for bilingual students with an L1 that is not English and monolinguals whose L1 is English.

This study is significant because it examines differences in performance between monolingual and bilinguals across grade levels in a K-12 international school. There seems to be a gap in the research on this area as no previous studies have examined this topic in this particular context. It is important to know the relationship between languages spoken and students' academic performance, because this knowledge can help schools to provide optimum support for students as they progress from elementary school to middle school and then high school. Once the relationships between these variables are understood, administrators and teachers can identify the key grade levels where extra support should be given to students. In particular, the main focus of this study is to answer the following questions:

- Are there any significant differences in *an a e sa e* and *rea in* standardized test scores between monolingual and bilingual students across grades 3 to 10?
- Do bilingual students *ose t e ap* on their monolingual counterparts on *an a e sa e* and *rea in* standardized test scores after being immersed for 4-10 years in English education?

*** Formatting Issue - Best Available Paper/Graphic ***

2Methodology

2.1 Participants

The participants were 1081 students from a K-12 international school.The school has students from varied ethnic andcultural backgrounds. There are 65 nationalities represented in the school. The medium of instruction is English throughout the school. The sample consisted ofelementary (*n*), middle (*n*) and high school (*n*) students of mixed gender. All participants had high socio-economic status. Students were L1 English monolinguals *n* and bilinguals whose L1 is not English *n* The languages represented in the sample of bilinguals wereKorean, *n* , Japanese *n* , Chinese *n* , Filipino, *n* , Hindi, *n* , Spanish, *n* , Dutch, *n* , Indonesian, *n* , French, *n* , Norwegian, *n* , Urdu, *n* , Swedish, *n* , Malay, *n* , Bengali *n* , German, *n* , Vietnamese *n* , Portuguese, *n* , Arabic, *n* , and others not specified *n* . Due to confidentiality reasons and an agreement with the school, no further details with regards to the participants could be provided.

2.2 Instruments

The Northwest Evaluation Association (NWEA) (2012) Measures of Academic Progress (MAP) standardized achievement test was used to measure *an a e sa e* and *rea in* . This is a widely used and reliable measure of academic performance in international schools and North America. The theoretical framework used for the scale construction was the Rasch Model (Rasch, 1961). MAP is a computerized adaptive assessment, this means that as a student responds to questions, the test responds to him/her, and the next question is either more or less difficult than the previous one. MAP produces an RIT Score (Rasch Unit) for the student in *an a e sa e*and *rea in* . The RIT Scale is an equal interval scale from high to low, and average scores all have the same meaning regardless of grade level (Northwest Evaluation Association, 2012).

For the *an a e sa e* test, students are required to do tasks demanding them to use correctpunctuation, grammar, sentence structures, capitalization and spelling. For the *rea in* test, students' ability to analyze and understand text is measured. Students are given a number of reading comprehension tasks on several texts. High reliability was established for students MAP RIT Scores in *an a e sa e*(α. =.78) and *rea in* (α. =.74) through analyzing the Chronbach's Alpha (α) of the test scores.

2.3 Procedure

Data was gathered in the fall MAP testing sessions in 2012. Letters were sent to parents to inform them that their child would be completing the MAP tests. The test was administered on computers from 7.30 to 9.30 am in the morning. On arrival in school, students went to the computer room and the computers were already logged on to the MAP test software. The test was supervised by MAP proctors who have attended specialized training in the administration of MAP tests.

Students were instructed to follow the information given on the screen to complete the questions given. Upon completion of the tests, the resultswere submitted electronically to the Northwest Evaluation Association (NWEA) central office in Portland, Oregon, USA. The results were analyzed and shared with the school through the NWEA MAP school portal two months after testing.

The MAP RIT scores were downloaded from the NWEA MAP school portal by the elementary school Assistant Principal and collated in a Microsoft Excel document. Students MAP RIT scores for *an a e sa e* and *rea in* were matched with their demographic information from the schools registrar's office online PowerTeacher database on the *an a es spo en*for each student. All personal details of participants were kept entirely confidential in accordance with the APA (2002) ethical guidelines. Raw data was analyzed using SPSS statistical software.

3 Results

The aim of the study is to examine whether there are age related differences between monolingual and bilingual students (*an a es spo en*) on standardized achievement tests scores of *rea in* and *an a e sa e* RIT scores. Two-way between subjects 2x2 ANOVAwere used to analyze differences between grade levels for monolinguals and bilinguals on *an a e sa e* and *rea in* standardized test scores.Descriptive statistics for the measures of students' *rea in* and *an a e sa e* scores from grades 3 to 10 are presented in Table 1 in Appendix A.

The two-way ANOVA that was conducted examined the effect of *an a es spo en* and *ra e e e* on *an a e sa e*RIT scores. There was a significant interaction between the effects of *ra e e e* and *an a es spo en* on *an a e sa e*RIT scores, (6, 1067) = 2.126, *p* = .048 ($p<0.05$). This interaction effect can be seen in Figure 1. Simple main effects analysis showed a main effect for *an a es spo en* monolingualsscored significantly higher thanbilinguals on *an a e sa e* RIT scores. (1, 1067)= 27.4237, p=.000 ($p<0.05$). A main effect was also found for *ra e e e* on *an a e sa e*RIT scores (6, 1067)= 217.234, p=.000 ($p<0.05$).

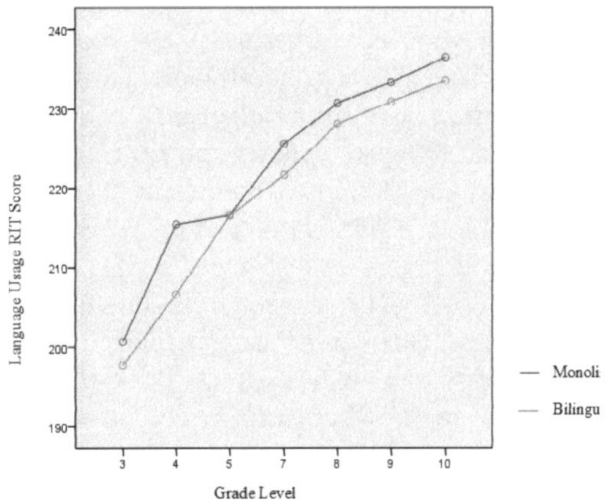

Figure 1.Language Usage RIT scores by grade level for monolinguals and bilinguals.

The two-way ANOVA that was conducted examined the effect of *an a es spo en* and *ra e e e* on *rea in* RIT scores. There was no significant interaction between the effects of *ra e e e* and *an a es spo en* on *rea in* RIT scores, (6, 1066) = 1.372, *p* = .223 ($p>0.05$).Simple main effects analysis showed a main effect for *an a es spo en* monolinguals scored significantly higher than bilinguals on *rea in* RIT scores. (1, 1066)= 47.372, p=.000 ($p<0.05$). A main effect was also found for *ra e e e* on *rea in* RIT scores (6, 1067) = 221.062, p=.000 ($p<0.05$), these main effects can be seen in Figure 2.

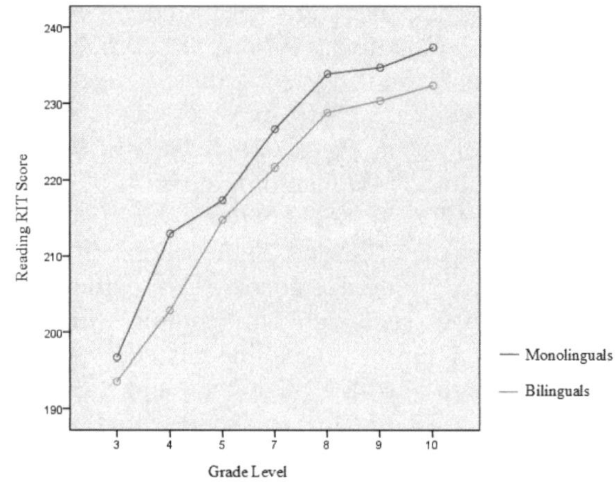

Figure 2.Reading RIT scores by grade level for monolinguals and bilinguals.

4 Discussion

In relation to the first research question, the result shows that there are significant differences in *an a e sa e* and *rea in* standardized test scores between monolinguals and bilinguals for students across grades 3 to 10. For *an a e sa e*, the main effect for *an a es spo en* shows that scores for monolinguals and bilinguals are significantly different across the grade levels. The general trend is that the performance of both monolinguals and bilinguals increases as the students' progress through the grade levels. This may be due to both groups of students developing their skills in language as they progress through schooling and deal with increasingly complex linguistic input. Furthermore, in all grades apart from grade 5, the monolinguals outperform the bilinguals. This shows that for *an a e sa e*, the bilingual students do *ose t e ap* on their monolingual counterparts by grade 5, but the gap then widens again after that.

The hypothesis of the study is supported by the significant interaction between *ra e e e* and *an a es spo en*for *an a e sa e* scores. This is interesting because it provides empirical support for Cummins (1999) proposition that it takes 5 to 10 years for bilinguals to gain *o niti e a e i an a e ro i ien* (CALP).This also supports Han's (2009) finding that bilinguals reach the same level as monolinguals on tests of grammar by grade 5. By the time the students finish elementary school and enter middle school in grade 5, the monolingual and bilingual's performance is the same. The immersionof bilinguals in the English language in elementary school education has enabled them to perform just as well as their monolingual counterparts by grade 5. However, contrary to the hypothesis, the result showed that from grade 7 through to grade 10 the gap then widens between the monolinguals and bilinguals. The monolinguals outperform the bilinguals, so the *o niti e a anta es* of bilingualism do not demonstrate themselves in the students' performance in *an a e sa e* in their second language.

For *rea in* the monolinguals outperform the bilinguals across all grade levels, and performance of both groups also increases with age. There is a narrowing of the gap in performance at grade 5 between the monolinguals and bilinguals, but the interaction effect is not significant, not supporting the hypothesis. The gap in performance between monolinguals and bilinguals narrows more for *an a e sa e* than for *rea in*

This connects to the findings of Bialystok et al. (2010) who found that monolinguals had higher scores on vocabulary tests than bilinguals. Because vocabulary and reading are closely related and this may help explainthe difference in *rea in* performance between the monolinguals and bilinguals found in the current study,as this may be connected to the vocabulary differences between the two groups.

The findings connect to Jimenez et al.'s (1996) study because they found that those who were successful in reading comprehension tasksemployed several meta-cognitive strategies, but those who were less successful did not. This suggests that specific techniques should be taught to bilinguals to help improve their reading comprehension skills, because the current study shows their performance to be consistently lower than monolinguals in *rea in*

As discussed by Martinez and Lesaux (2010), English native speakers bring much to the process of learning to read; by about age 6, they have acquired approximately 90% of adult language structures. What such English monolinguals needto do is just learn to recognize printed words which are more likely to be part of their oral vocabulary. On the other hand, forbilingual learners (like Spanish English bilinguals in Martinez and Lesaux's study) school can be considered as the first formal encounter with the English language; therefore, such learners need to learn vocabulary and linguistic structures at the same time,so as to make the meaning of the printed words. Accordingly, it can be said that the difference in the vocabulary size of English monolinguals and bilinguals might affect their performance in *rea in* comprehension tests leading to better performance of English monolinguals.

In relation to Peal and Lambert's (1962) and Bialystok's (2009) assertions that bilinguals profit from *enta e i i it* the result of this study suggests that this mental flexibility does not show itself though increased performance in *an a e sa e* and *rea in* , because the monolinguals continue to outperform the bilinguals through until grade 10. Cummins' (1976) threshold hypothesis proposes that students need to reach a lower threshold to avoid cognitive disadvantages and a higher threshold to gain the beneficial effects of bilingualism. In the context of thefast paced educational environment of international middle and high school, it appears that the bilingual students struggle to meet the higher threshold that allowsthem to experience the *o niti e a anta es* of bilingualism (Bialystok, 2009).In the school in which this study was carried out, the majority of teachers and students are native speakers of English and this makes it a challenging linguistic environment for the bilingual students. The bilingual students are continually being challenged by more complex linguistic input as they progress through school and they find it difficult to catch up with the monolinguals.

The results show that bilinguals do notexperience a great disadvantage, but apart from *an a e sa e*scores in grade 5, their performance is consistently lower than their monolingual counterparts. This suggests that it may take even longer than from grades 3 to 10 for the bilinguals to develop *o niti e* *a e i an a e ro i ien* (CALP).Perhaps it is not until after even more years of immersion in English, such as university studies in an English speaking country the bilinguals develop CALP on par with native speakers, and then start to experience the *o niti e a anta es* of bilingualism.

However, in relation to the differences between *ear* and *ate* bilinguals the findings of previous research are supported by this study.Bialystok and Miller (1999) and Luc, deSa and Bialystok (2011) also found that early bilinguals outperformed late bilinguals on grammaticality judgment tests and tests of English proficiency. These findings relate to the current study because bilinguals *ose t e ap* on the monolinguals by grade 5 for *an a e sa e* This is because that grade contains a cohort of *ear i in a s* who have developed their English skills in their elementary schooling, which supports Bialystok (1999) proposition that it takes 5-10 years to achieve proficiency in CALP.

However, this finding does not support those of Kaushanskaya and Marian (2007) who found that early bilinguals experience bilingual *o niti e a anta es* over monolinguals in word learning tasks, because in the current study no *o niti e a anta es* for bilingualism were shown in terms of performance in *an a e sa e*and *rea in* Perhaps this is because *an a e sa e* and *rea in* unlike word learning are not the domains in which *o niti e a anta es* related to *e e ti e ontro* are present.

A limitation of this study is that it did not include a non-linguistic measure in order to examine whether bilingualism leads to *o niti e a anta e* in other domains. More research is needed into difference in performance between monolinguals and bilinguals on non-linguistic tests such as performance in mathematics, to see whether the *o niti e a anta es* of bilingualism transfer themselves to that domain.

A factor to consider in this particular context is that many of the students are Third-Culture Kids (TCKs) who have grown up in a different culture to their passport country and they may have lived in several countries as their families move from one country to another. This means that the quality of the English education they would have received may have varied between the different schools they have attended andthis is not controlled for in the current study. To address this issue, research using a longitudinal rather than a cross-sectional design could be used.

Another factor is that students come from different family background where there is variation in the level of English input and students AoA. A limitation of the study and this is not controlled for in this study, so future research could examine the role of English input and AoA in the home on the development of a student's acquisition of English CALP.

The findings of this study suggest that more support is needed for bilinguals in their schooling. They need to be supported at the transition to middle school, because at grade 5, when middle school starts, they have closed the gap on their monolingual counterparts, but the gap widens out as they progress through middle school to high school. In middle school additional support in English should be targeted at bilinguals to make sure they do not fall behind the monolinguals. This support would allow them to perform at the same level as monolinguals or even outperform them.

Further research is needed to address the influence on English input outside of the school setting on CALP development in bilinguals, and also to see whether cognitive advantages are transferred to domains other than *an a e sa e* and *rea in* More research is also needed into the gap in performance between monolinguals and bilinguals widens after grade 5.

In conclusion, the findings of the current study show that significant differences exist between bilingual and monolingual students in *an a e sa e* and *rea in* standardized test scores but these differences *an e* over time. As the bilingual students whose L1 is not English are immersed in English education, their performance catches up with their monolingual counterparts by grade 5 for *an a e sa e* but not for *rea in* . For *an a e sa e* monolinguals outperform bilinguals from grades 3 to 4 and grades 6 to 10, but not for grade 5. For *rea in* monolinguals outperform bilinguals from grades 3 to 10 and no *o niti e a anta es* to bilingualism were shown in this context.

References

American Psychological Association.(2002). *t i a rin ip es o s o o ists an o e o on t* Retrieved from http://www.apa.org/ethics/code/index.aspx

Bialystok, E., & Miller, B. (1999). The problem of age in second-language acquisition: Influences from language, structure, and task. *i in a is an a e an o nition*, 2, 127-145.

Bialystok, E. (2009). Bilingualism: The good, the bad, and the indifferent. *i in a is an a e an o nition* , 3–11.

Bialystok, E., Luk, G., Peets, F. K., & Yang S. (2010).Receptive vocabulary differences in monolingual and bilingual children. *i in a is an a e an o nition* (4) 225-231.

Cummins, J. (1976). The influence of bilingualism on cognitive growth: A synthesis of research findings and explanatory hypotheses. *Wor in apers on i in a is* 1-43.

Cummins, J. (1979). Cognitive/academic language proficiency, linguistic interdependence, the optimum age question and some other matters.*Wor in apers on i in a is* 121-129.

Cummins, J. (1981). *e ro e o pri ar an a e e e op ent in pro otin e ationa s ess or an a e inorit st ents* In California State Department of Education (Ed.), Schooling and language minority students: A theoretical framework. Los Angeles: Evaluation, Dissemination and Assessment Center, California State University.

Cummins, J. (1984) *i in a ation an pe ia ation ss es in ssess ent an e a o* San Diego: College Hill.

Cummins, J. (1999). Biliteracy, empowerment, and transformative pedagogy. In J. V. Tinajero & R. A. DeVillar (Eds.), *e po er o t o an a es* (pp. 9-19). New York: McGraw-Hill.

Cummins, J. (2001). *e otiatin i entities ation or e po er ent in a i erse so iet* Ontario, CA: California Association of Bilingual Education.

Han, W. (2011).Bilingualism and Academic Achievement. *i e e op ent* 300–321.

Jimenez, T. R., Garcia, E. G., and Pearson, D. P. (1996).The reading strategies of bilingual Latina/o students who are successful English readers: Opportunities and obstacles. *ea in esear arter* (1) 90–112.

Kaushanskaya, M., & Marian, V. (2007). Age-of-acquisition effects in the development of a bilingual advantage for word learning. *ro ee in s o t e n nn a oston ni ersit on eren e on an a e e e op ent.*Cascadilla Press; Somerville, MA.

Luk, G., DeSa, E., & Bialystok E. (2011). Is there a relation between onset age of bilingualism and enhancement of cognitive control?. *i in a is an a e an o nition* , 488-495.

Martinez, M. J., & Lesaux, N. (2010).Predictors of reading comprehension for struggling readers: The case of Spanish-speaking language minority learners. *ationa s o o* (3), 701–711.

Northwest Evaluation Association, (2012). *eas res o a e i ro ress* Retrieved 2nd April 2012 fromhttp://www.nwea.org/products-services/computer-based-adaptive-assessments

Peal, E., & Lambert, W. (1962). The Relation of Bilingualism to Intelligence, *s o o i a ono rap s*, 76, 1–23.

Rasch, G. (1961). On general laws and the meaning of measurement in psychology, pp. 321–334 in *ro ee in s o t e o rt er e e posi on at e ati a tatisti s an ro a i it* , IV. Berkeley, California: University of California Press.

Appendix A

Table 1.

Descriptive Statistics for Reading and Language Usage Scores.

Variable	Group	Grade	N	Mean	SD
Reading	Monolingual	3	196.66	79	12.836
	Bilingual	3	193.58	48	12.123
Language Usage	Monolingual	3	200.67	79	12.444
	Bilingual	3	197.67	48	13.145
Reading	Monolingual	4	212.94	77	10.612
	Bilingual	4	202.86	50	11.992
Language Usage	Monolingual	4	215.42	77	9.190
	Bilingual	4	206.62	50	12.734
Reading	Monolingual	5	217.33	88	9.450
	Bilingual	5	214.76	51	10.869
Language Usage	Monolingual	5	216.58	88	8.963
	Bilingual	5	216.53	51	9.995
Reading	Monolingual	7	226.62	89	9.174
	Bilingual	7	221.65	63	14.937
Language Usage	Monolingual	7	225.60	89	8.415
	Bilingual	7	221.67	63	12.654
Reading	Monolingual	8	233.87	116	9.954
	Bilingual	8	228.77	62	12.661
Language Usage	Monolingual	8	230.69	116	8.434
	Bilingual	8	228.11	62	10.331
Reading	Monolingual	9	234.70	103	11.761
	Bilingual	9	230.33	82	13.232
Language Usage	Monolingual	9	233.31	103	9.178
	Bilingual	9	230.89	83	10.700
Reading	Monolingual	10	237.35	100	10.171
	Bilingual	10	232.33	72	13.343
Language Usage	Monolingual	10	236.47	100	8.807
	Bilingual	10	233.57	72	11.115

Compiling a Corpus of Taiwanese Students' Spoken English

Lan-fen Huang
Language Centre, Shih Chien University
200 University Road
Nei-men, Kaohsiung 845 Taiwan
Lanfen.huang@gmail.com

Abstract

This paper reports the compilation of a corpus of Taiwanese students' spoken English, which is one of the twenty sub-corpora of the *Louvain International Database of Spoken English Interlanguage* (*LINDSEI*) (Gilquin et al., 2010). *LINDSEI* is one of the largest corpora of learner speech. The compilation process follows the design criteria of *LINDSEI* so as to ensure comparability across sub-corpora. The participants, procedures for data collection and process of transcription are all recorded. Sixty third- or fourth-year English majors in Taiwan are interviewed and recorded in English. Each interview is accompanied by a profile which contains information about such learner variables as age, gender, mother tongue, country, English learning context, knowledge of other foreign languages, amount of time spent in English-speaking countries and such interviewer variables as gender, mother tongue, knowledge of foreign languages and degree of familiarity with the interviewees. Another variable, the learners' English proficiency level based on the results of international standardised tests is collected; this is not available in other sub-corpora of *LINDSEI*. The participants' proficiency is similarly distributed across B1 to C1 levels in the Common European Framework of Reference. This paper concludes with a discussion of the contributions and research potential of the corpus.

1 Introduction

Corpus compilation, as it has developed, can be traced back to the 1960s (Sinclair, 1991). Research on corpora has mostly focused on written English and contributed a great deal of corpus-based grammatical description and explanation. In contrast, relatively few studies have emerged of corpora of spoken languages, which call for a time-consuming and laborious transcribing process. Yet it is widely acknowledged that this is an area which needs to be further explored (Carter and McCarthy, 1995). A similar trend is found in the field of learner corpora. Learner corpora have been used to study the written language of learners from different backgrounds, in terms of mother tongue. However, little research has been done on the spoken language produced by learners. One of the few major accomplishments in the corpus studies of learners' spoken English is the compilation of *the Louvain International Database of Spoken English Interlanguage* (*LINDSEI*) version 1 (Gilquin et al., 2010), which includes spoken English produced by learners from eleven different first languages (L1s). The present paper first introduces *LINDSEI* and then reports the compilation process of the Taiwanese sub-corpus, before discussing its contributions and potential for future research.

2 Overview of *LINDSEI*

The *LINDSEI* project began in 1995 and in 2010 published its first version, which includes sub-corpora of eleven L1s: Bulgarian, Chinese, Dutch, French, German, Greek, Italian, Japanese, Polish, Spanish and Swedish[1]. It involved 544 informal interviews and roughly one million tokens in total, with an average of 1,949 tokens in each one. About one third of the spoken data comes from the interviewers and two thirds from the learners.

In order to have comparable data across sub-corpora and to avoid the heterogeneity of interlanguage, the sub-corpora of *LINDSEI* must

[1] Another nine are in progress, including this Taiwanese sub-corpus. Please see *LINDSEI Partners* (Gilquin, 2012a) at http://www.uclouvain.be/en-307845.html (assessed on 22 August 2013).

meet an established set of criteria. Each corpus consists of 50 to 53 informal interviews between a learner and an interviewer. All learners are third- or fourth-year English-major students in countries where English is used as a foreign language and more than half the interviewers (64%) are native speakers (NSs) of English (Gilquin et al., 2010).

Each interview takes about 15 minutes to cover three tasks: set topics[2], free discussion and picture description. The first task serves as a warm-up activity. One of three topics is chosen by the interviewee. This lasts five to six minutes, including some follow-up questions put by the interviewer. The second task, taking seven to eight minutes, consists of free discussion of general topics, such as life at university, hobbies, travel experience, what the student hopes to do after university, family, etc. The object is not to stress and embarrass the interviewees with difficult questions but to get them to talk spontaneously. In the last few minutes, the interviewer asks the interviewee to look at a sequence of four pictures and tell the story that they illustrate. The student should not be given either the time or opportunity to make notes before describing the picture. It should be an improvised description.

All the interviews are orthographically transcribed and marked up according to the transcription guidelines (Gilquin, 2012b). Each transcription is accompanied by a profile which contains information about such learner variables as age, gender, mother tongue, country, English learning context, knowledge of other foreign languages, amount of time spent in English-speaking countries and such interviewer variables as gender, mother tongue, knowledge of foreign languages and degree of familiarity with the interviewees.

The eleven sub-corpora of *LINDSEI* offer a wide range of possibilities of research into Contrastive Interlanguage Analysis (CIA)[3]. The comparison can be done between different interlanguages as well as between any interlanguage and the native speech in the *Louvain Corpus of Native English Conversation* (*LOCNEC*), which is compiled by De Cock (2004), using the same structure as *LINDSEI*.

In addition, the written counterpart of *LINDSEI*, the *International Corpus of Learner English* (*ICLE*) (Granger et al., 2009) is a corpus of argumentative essays written by learners from sixteen L1 backgrounds. *LINDSEI* and *ICLE* share ten mother tongue backgrounds, which makes it possible to compare spoken and written interlanguages.

3 Taiwanese Sub-corpus of Spoken English

The compilation of the Taiwanese sub-corpus of *LINDSEI* began in October 2012 and went on for one year, sponsored by the National Science Council, Taiwan, under grant number NSC101-2410-H-158-012.

3.1 Recruitment of Participants

The participants were 60[4] third- or fourth-year undergraduate students majoring in English in the six universities in Taiwan, listed in Table 1 below.

	University	Number of participants
1	Shih Chien University	7
2	Wenzao Ursuline College of Languages	10
3	National Cheng Kung University	16
4	National Pingtung University of Education	12
5	National Taiwan University of Science and Technology	9
6	National Kaohsiung University of Applied Sciences	6
	Total	60

Table 1. Universities participating in the Taiwanese sub-corpus of *LINDSEI*

[2] The three set topics are: 1) *An experience you have had which has taught you an important lesson. You should describe the experience and say what you have learnt from it.* 2) *A country you have visited which has impressed you. Describe your visit and say why you found the country particularly impressive.* 3) *A film/play you've seen which you thought was particularly good/bad. Describe the film/play and say why you thought it was good/bad* (Gilquin et al., 2010, p. 8).

[3] The term, Contrastive Interlanguage Analysis (CIA) was coined by Granger (1996; 1998).

[4] The *LINDSEI* team requires all contributors to a sub-corpus to submit 50 recordings and their accompanying profiles. In case of problems such as unintelligible sound quality or an incomplete learner profile for any of the contributors, 60 recordings were made. 50 out of the 60 learners will be sent to the *LINDSEI* team, who will further process them. Therefore, the data in the Taiwanese sub-corpus of *LINDSEI* reported in this paper will differ slightly from the final version included in the second version of *LINDSEI*.

The participants were recruited through an advertisement on campus or at the invitation of their instructors. They were informed that the collected spoken data would be used for research purposes and had to give their permission by signing a learner profile questionnaire (see Appendix A) on the day of the interview. The questionnaire used for the Taiwanese corpus was slightly adapted from that in *LINDSEI* by adding one question: *Have you ever taken an English proficiency test? If yes, please give the name of the test, your result and date of the test.* Most of the learners gave their TOEIC scores, but some had IELTS, TOEFL, BULATS, GEPT and CSEPT grades [5]. Table 2 below lists the distribution of the 60 learners' English proficiency in the four levels of the Common European Framework of Reference (CEFR). The learners' proficiency is similarly distributed across the B1 to C1 levels; therefore, it is best described as ranging from intermediate to advanced. The Taiwanese sub-corpus is similar to other sub-corpora in *LINDSEI*. Although information about the learners' proficiency in *LINDSEI* was not available, a tentative study, based on a random sample of five learners from each sub-corpus, indicates that 64% were rated as high-intermediate (and lower) and 36% advanced (Gilquin et al., 2010, pp. 10-11).

Level	Number	Percentage
B1	14	23.3%
B2	18	30.0%
C1	19	31.7%
C2	1	1.7%
n/a	8	13.3%
Total	60	100%

Table 2. The distribution of the 60 learners' English proficiency in the four levels of CEFR

Four interviewers, one American, one British and two Taiwanese teachers of English, were involved in the data collection (see Table 3). Ideally, the interviewers should have been NSs of English, since it may be easier to develop natural communication when the learners talk with someone who does not share the same L1. However, to fit in with the availability of the interviewers who were NSs, the learners and the researcher, 70% of interviews were done by NSs and the remainder by Taiwanese teachers of English. They were briefed beforehand on how to conduct the interview and fully aware of the use of the transcripts and audio files for research purposes.

Inter-viewer	Gender	Mother tongue	Number of interviews (Percentage)	Transcript Number
1	Male	British English	22 (36.7%)	TW011-032
2	Male	American English	20 (33.3%)	TW001-010 TW033-042
3	Male	Chinese	9 (15.0%)	TW043-051
4	Female	Chinese	9 (15.0%)	TW052-060
			60 (100%)	

Table 3. The interviewers' gender and mother tongue

3.2 Procedures for Informal Interviews

On the day of the interview, the learners of English were asked to fill in a profile questionnaire (Appendix A), with the assistance of the researcher. This form included information about learner variables and was signed and dated to signify written consent to use the recorded interviews for research purposes. In order to make the best use of time without keeping the interviewers waiting, this task of filling the questionnaire was done by some learners after the interviews. Either way, the learners were well aware of being recorded.

After filling in the questionnaires, the learners were given at least five minutes to prepare to talk on one of the three set topics. Then, the learners were invited to enter a classroom or meeting room where two electronic recorders had been set up. The researcher left the room as soon as she had made sure that the recorders were working, because the students might have felt under pressure if two people had been listening to them.

As reported in the previous section, the whole informal interview took about 15 minutes. During this period, the interviewer tried his/her best to be friendly and to help students talk more by giving quick responses and specific questions, and the learners were given neither the time nor

[5] The Test of English for International Communication (TOEIC), International English Language Testing System (IELTS), Test of English as a Foreign Language (TOEFL), and Business Language Testing Service (BULATS) are internationally recognised certificates. The General English Proficiency Test (GEPT) and College Student English Proficiency Test (CSEPT) are locally developed tests in Taiwan.

the opportunity to write notes. This interview aimed to collect spontaneous speech from the learners.

After the interviews, the learners were given a voucher for NT$200 (US$1 equals NT$30) to spend. The recordings and learner profiles were coded for the transcribing process.

3.3 Process of Transcription

The 60 interviews were orthographically transcribed and marked up by two research assistants following the guidelines provided by the *LINDSEI* project (Gilquin, 2012b). The transcription work for a 15-minute interview might take five to ten hours, depending on the transcribers' experience of transcribing. The two transcribers spent more time to begin with, when they were not yet very familiar with the transcription guidelines. All the transcripts were double-checked by the researcher. Each of them took about 30 to 60 minutes to finish.

In the process of transcription, two pieces of computer software were used, *Audacity* (2013) and *Windows Media Player*. *Audacity* was used to edit the sound recordings, in particular for deleting redundant time at the beginning and end of the interviews. It also made it possible to manipulate the sound file, e.g. by reducing its speed, playing it back several times, etc.

The task of orthographic transcribing needed less skill. The mark-up process required more training. Of the twenty aspects of transcription in the guidelines, the marking-up of overlapping speech was most difficult and time-consuming.

4 Contributions of the Taiwanese sub-corpus of *LINDSEI*

The establishment of the Taiwanese learner corpus of spoken English will make contributions in three ways: 1) by increasing the visibility of Taiwanese learners in the international academia; 2) by informing the teaching of spoken English to Taiwanese students; and 3) by serving as a model for the compilation of corpora of spoken English in Taiwan.

First, Taiwanese learners represent one group of Chinese speakers, as well as the Chinese sub-corpus compiled in mainland China, in the fields of corpus studies and interlanguage research. *LINDSEI* is currently the most comprehensive learner corpus project and includes international collaboration from twenty groups. Being one of the sub-corpora of *LINDSEI*, without doubt, increases the visibility of Taiwan in international academia and contributes to the research on spoken English. The spoken data collected in Taiwan will be shared with other groups of L1s. This, compared with a self-designed learner corpus, enables researchers worldwide to conduct a wider range of investigations. Furthermore, the learner speech collected in Taiwan in 2012 and 2013 offers the most recent data of this kind, while those in the Chinese sub-corpus were compiled in 2001 (Gilquin et al., 2010). The information in the learner profiles of the Chinese sub-corpus shows that 48 out of 53 learners (90.6%) had received six years of English education at school before they began their first degree and none of the learners had ever stayed in an English-speaking country. By contrast, the learners in the Taiwanese sub-corpus had much greater exposure to English. They had on average nearly ten years of English learning before entering university and 21 out of 60 (35%) learners had stayed in countries where English is spoken for an average of 6.8 months.

Second, the usage patterns of Taiwanese learners can be identified to facilitate and improve the teaching of spoken English. The importance of corpus studies and applications has been stated in recent international conferences on Applied Linguistics held in Taiwan (e.g. the 18th International Symposium on English Teaching: Internet- and Corpus-based English Instruction (13-15 November 2009), the 2012 International Conference on Applied Linguistics and Language Teaching: Technological and Traditional Teaching and Learning (19-21 April 2012), and the 2012 LTTC International Conference: The Making of a Translator (28-29 April 2012)). However, there has hitherto been no learner corpus of spoken English available for research purposes. It is worth noting that the Language Training and Testing Centre in Taiwan has undertaken to transcribe the speaking tests of GEPT, which was developed in Taiwan, but it might take some time for the learner corpus to be published. In mainland China, some learner corpora have been made available, for example, the *Spoken and Written English Corpus of Chinese Learners*, version 1.0 (Wen et al., 2005) and version 2.0 (Wen et al., 2008); and the *Chinese Learner Spoken English Corpus* (Yang and Wei, 2005). The data in these corpora were collected from speaking tests which involve retelling a story, describing a picture and discussing a topic. In the test-taking context, learners' speech was restricted and unnatural. In contrast, the spoken English produced in the informal interviews for *LINDSEI* was relatively authentic. The learners were voluntary and the setting was outside the classroom and not exam-oriented.

Third, this corpus will be the first publicly available learner corpus in Taiwan. It will serve as a model for the compilation of corpora. In Taiwan, the development of corpus studies is still in its infancy. This project, in collaboration with the *LINDSEI* team in Belgium, provides research training for the researcher as well as the team members. The researcher benefits from interacting with international researchers in the field of Corpus Linguistics and from being involved in the process of transcribing, which is seen as an analytical tool (Swann, 2010). Both these advantages will help the researcher to exploit the potential of the collected data. The team members gain research experience and broaden their scope in the expectation that more corpus studies will be done in future.

5 Research Possibilities

The corpus of Taiwanese students' spoken English provides a range of possibilities for research. As mentioned in Section Two, the sub-corpora in *LINDSEI* have been employed in CIA, in which two types of comparison can be made: 1) between NS and learner languages (in this case, *LOCNEC* (De Cock, 2004) and the Taiwanese sub-corpus) and 2) between speakers of different mother tongues (the Taiwanese sub-corpus and any other sub-corpora of *LINDSEI*). There is a growing interest in quasi-longitudinal studies, i.e. comparing learners of the same L1 at different proficiency levels. Information about learners' English proficiency levels is available (see Table 2) and reliable, because it based on the results of international standardised tests of English proficiency. In both CIA and quasi-longitudinal studies, a number of investigations can be pursued, such as lexis, phraseology, organization of spoken discourse, and features of spoken English.

Among the five features of spoken English 1) deictic expressions, 2) situational ellipsis, 3) headers, tails and tags, 4) discourse markers and 5) polite and indirect language, vague language and approximations (Carter and McCarthy, 2006), discourse markers have attracted much research attention (e.g. on Chinese learners: He and Xu, 2003; Fung and Carter, 2007; Liu, 2010; Huang, 2011). The quantitative corpus studies have revealed the usage of discourse markers by learners. Such research has been conducted across the eleven sub-corpora by Gilquin and Granger (2011; forthcoming). These researchers point out that using *LINDSEI* as an aggregate may conceal variations between learners of different L1s as well as between learners in one specific corpus. It seems that the L1 plays an important role for ESL learners.

In terms of practical applications, the learner corpus research has certainly helped us to improve our understanding of learner language and to inform English Language Teaching. However, there is always more work to do. As De Cock (2010) notes in her call for more studies using spoken learner corpora in the classroom, the compilation of the Taiwanese sub-corpus of *LINDSEI* will certainly facilitate research on Chinese-speaking learners, which is one of the biggest groups to use English as a foreign language.

Acknowledgments

This work was supported by the National Science Council, Taiwan, under grant number NSC101-2410-H-158-012. Without this funding, the Taiwanese sub-corpus of *LINDSEI* would not have been possible. My gratitude goes to the *LINDSEI* team at the Centre for English Corpus Linguistics of the Université Catholique de Louvain, Belgium, in particular, the project leader, Prof Sylviane Granger and the coordinator, Dr Gaëtanelle Gilquin. The efforts of my project team members, Ms Hsiao-hui Lin, Ms Miranda Yu-ting Huang, Dr Jon Nichols, Mr Simon Kubelec, Mr Alex Jou and Mr Chih-hao Hsueh are most appreciated. Special thanks are due to my contacts in the six universities participating in this corpus and the Taiwanese learners who agreed to be interviewed and recorded.

References

2013 members of the Audacity development team 2013. Audacity (Version 2.0.3). Available at http://audacity.sourceforge.net/.

Anping He and Manfei Xu. 2003. Small words in Chinese EFL learners' spoken English. Foreign Language Teaching and Research, 35(6), 446-453.

Binmei Liu. 2010. Discourse Marker Use by L1 Chinese EFL Speakers. (PhD thesis), University of Florida.

Gaëtanelle Gilquin and Sylviane Granger. 2011. The use of discourse markers in corpora of native and learner speech: From aggregate to individual data. Paper presented at the Corpus Linguistics Conference 2011, Birmingham.

Gaëtanelle Gilquin, Sylvie De Cook, and Sylviane Granger (Eds.). 2010. LINDSEI Louvain International Database of Spoken English Interchange. Handbook and CD-ROM. Louvain-la-Neuve: Presses universitaires de Louvain.

Gaëtanelle Gilquin. 2012a. LINDSEI Partners. Retrieved 26 August, 2013, from http://www.uclouvain.be/en-307845.html

Gaëtanelle Gilquin. 2012b. Transcription guidelines. Retrieved 26 August, 2013, from http://www.uclouvain.be/en-307849.html

Gaëtanelle Gilquin, and Sylviane Granger. forthcoming. Learner language. In D. Biber and R. Reppen (Eds.), *Cambridge Handbook of Corpus Linguistics*. Cambridge: Cambridge University Press.

Joan Swann. 2010. Transcribing spoken interaction. In S. Hunston and D. Oakey (Eds.), Introducing applied linguistics: Concepts and skills (pp. 163-176). Abingdon: Routledge.

John Sinclair. 1991. Corpus, Concordance, Collocation. Oxford: Oxford University Press.

Lan-fen Huang. 2011. Discourse markers in spoken English: A corpus study of native speakers and Chinese non-native speakers. (PhD thesis), University of Birmingham, UK. Retrieved from http://etheses.bham.ac.uk/2969/

Loretta Fung and Ronald Carter. 2007. Discourse markers and spoken English: Native and learner use in pedagogic settings. Applied Linguistics, 28(3), 410-439.

Ronald Carter and Michael McCarthy. 1995. Grammar and the spoken language. Applied Linguistics, 16(2):141-158.

Ronald Carter and Michael McCarthy. 2006. Cambridge Grammar of English. Cambridge: Cambridge University Press.

Sylviane Granger, Estelle Dagneaux, Fanny Meunier, and Magali Paquot (Eds.). 2009. International Corpus of Learner English (2nd ed.). Louvain-la-Neuve: Presses universitaires de Louvain.

Sylviane Granger. 1996. From CA to CIA and back: An integrated approach to computerized bilingual and learner corpora. In K. Aijmer, B. Altenberg and M. Johansson (Eds.), Languages in Contrast. Text-based cross-linguistic studies. Lund Studies in English 88 (pp. 37-51). Lund: Lund University Press.

Sylviane Granger. 1998. The computer learner corpus: A versatile new source of data for SLA research. In S. Granger (Ed.), Learner English on Computer (pp. 3-18). Harlow: Longman.

Sylvie De Cock. 2004. Preferred sequences of words in NS and NNS speech. Belgian Journal of English Language and Literatures, New Series 2:225-246.

Sylvie De Cock. 2010. Spoken learner corpora and EFL teaching. In M. C. Campoy, B. Bellés-Fortuño and M. L. Gea-Valor (Eds.), Corpus-based Approaches to English Language Teaching (pp. 123-137). London: Continuum.

Appendix A. Learner Profile (adapted from Gilquin et al., 2010, pp. 110-111)

LEARNER PROFILE

==

Text code: (to be filled in by the researcher)

==

Surname: **First name(s)**:

Age:

Male ☐ Female ☐

Nationality:

Country:

Native language:

Father's mother tongue:

Mother's mother tongue:

Language(s) spoken at home: (if more than one, please give the average % use of each)

Education:

Primary school - medium of instruction:

Secondary school - medium of instruction:

Current studies:

Current year of study:

Institution:

Medium of instruction:

English only ☐

Other language(s) (specify) ______________ ☐

Both ☐

==

Years of English at school:

Years of English at university:

Stay in an English-speaking country:

Where?

When?

How long?

Have you ever taken an English proficiency test? If yes:

Name of the test:

Result: Date:

==

Other foreign languages in decreasing order of proficiency:

==

I hereby give permission for my interview to be used for research purposes.

Date: .... Signature: ....

****

Section to be filled in by the interviewer

Interviewer: Male ☐ Female ☐

Native language:

Foreign languages (in decreasing order of proficiency):

Relation with learner: Familiar ☐ Vaguely familiar ☐ Unfamiliar ☐

(If possible, please be more specific, e.g. learner's professor, TA, etc: ……...……………………...)

BCCWJ-TimeBank: Temporal and Event Information Annotation on Japanese Text

Masayuki Asahara **Sachi Yasuda** **Hikari Konishi**
Mizuho Imada **Kikuo Maekawa**
Center for Corpus Development, National Institute for Japanese Language and Linguistics
10-2, Midori-cho, Tachikawa, Tokyo, Japan, 190-8561
masayu-a@ninjal.ac.jp

Abstract

Temporal information extraction can be split into the following three tasks: temporal expression extraction, time normalisation, and temporal ordering relation resolution. This paper describes a time expression and temporal ordering annotation schema for Japanese, employing the *Balanced Corpus of Contemporary Written Japanese*, or BCCWJ. The annotation is aimed at allowing the development of better Japanese temporal ordering relation resolution tools. The annotation schema is based on an ISO annotation standard – *TimeML*. We extract verbal and adjective event expressions as ⟨EVENT⟩ in a subset of BCCWJ. Then, we annotate temporal ordering relation ⟨TLINK⟩ on the above pairs of event and time expressions by previous work. We identify several issues in the annotation.

1 Introduction

Temporal information processing in natural language texts has received increasing scholarly attention in recent years. Since temporal order of events often has implications for causal relations (*cause and effect*), identifying them is an essential task for deep understanding of language. Several types of resource for English temporal information processing have been developed, such as an annotation specification *TimeML* (Pustejovsky et al., 2003) and annotated corpora *TimeBank* (Pustejovsky et al., 2010) and *Aquaint TimeML Corpus*. The English annotation specification has been extended as an ISO standard of a temporal information mark-up language – ISO TimeML (ISO, 2008), which covers Italian, Spanish, Chinese and other languages. Temporal information-annotated corpora in various languages have been developed and shared by natural language processing researchers. TempEval-2 (Verhagen et al., 2010), a task for the SemEval-2010, and TempEval-3 (UzZaman et al., 2013), a task for the SemEval-2013, have been proposed as shared temporal-relation reasoning tasks. In these shared tasks, datasets for English, Italian, Spanish, Chinese, and Korean are provided.

However, there is no such resource for the Japanese language. In this paper, we present a means of porting ISO-TimeML into the Japanese language and also describe the basic specifications of '*BCCWJ-TimeBank*' which is a realisation of the temporal information annotation of the *Balanced Corpus of Contemporary Written Japanese*, or BCCWJ (Maekawa, 2008).

2 Related Research

This section explains two related research areas. One is ISO-TimeML, which is an ISO standard for temporal information mark-up languages. The other is BCCWJ, on which we annotate temporal information tags.

2.1 ISO-TimeML

The ISO Technical Committee (TC 37) proposes several standards for language resources, under the collective category 'Terminology and other language and content resources'. Four structures of the committee (SC) are established: TC 37/SC 4 [1] is charged with looking at annotation standards for all areas of natural language resources. TC 37/SC 4 includes six working groups (WG) to design language annotation specification mark-up languages such as stand-off mark-up and XML. TC 37/SC 4/WG 2, the semantic annotation WG, discusses semantic annotation standards. The original TimeML developers and TC 37/SC

[1] http://www.tc37sc4.org/

4/WG 2 defined ISO-TimeML as Semantic Annotation Framework(SemAF)-Time (ISO-24617-1:2012) within the context of TC 37/SC 4.

TimeML and ISO-TimeML define four types of entities — ⟨TIMEX3⟩, ⟨EVENT⟩, ⟨MAKEINSTANCE⟩, and ⟨SIGNAL⟩. The ⟨TIMEX3⟩ tag specifies various attributes of time expressions, such as tid, type, quant, freq, mod, and value. The time expressions are categorised into four types: DATE, TIME, DURATION, and SET. The attribute @value includes the normalised values of the time expressions in a machine-readable format. The ⟨EVENT⟩ tag specifies various attributes of event expressions, including the class of the event, tense, grammatical aspect, polarity, and modal information. The ⟨MAKEINSTANCE⟩ tag presents the event instances expressed by ⟨EVENT⟩-tagged expressions. Finally, the ⟨SIGNAL⟩ tag annotates elements to indicate how temporal objects are related amongst themselves.

TimeML and ISO-TimeML also define several types of links. Among these, ⟨TLINK⟩ expresses temporal order among instances of time expressions and/or event expressions.

2.2 BCCWJ

BCCWJ was publicly released in 2011 by NINJAL , Japan. It consists of three sub-corpora: 'Publication', 'Library', and 'Special purpose'. 'Publication' consists of samples extracted randomly from the whole body of books, magazines, and newspapers published during 2001-2005. 'Library' consists of randomly extracted samples in circulation in libraries in the period 1986-2005. Finally, the 'Special purpose' sub-corpus consists of several mini-corpora without any statistical sampling method being used. It includes text from Yahoo! Answers, Yahoo! Blogs, white papers, and school textbooks. The total size of BCCWJ is about 100 million words.

The part of BCCWJ called 'CORE' , manually annotates word boundaries, base phrase boundaries, and morphological information. CORE consists of six registers in 'Publication' and 'Special purpose': books (PB), magazines (PM), and newspapers (PN) from 'Publication', and Yahoo! Answers (OC), Yahoo! Blogs (OY), and white papers (OW) from 'Special purpose'. The size of CORE is about 1.3 million words.

CORE has received linguistic annotations from several research institutes (e.g. for syntactic dependency structures, by NAIST and NINJAL; predicate-argument relations, by NAIST, named entities by TITECH , modality, by Tohoku and Yamanashi Universities; Japanese framenet , by Keio University, and so on). The CORE samples are split into annotation priority sets from A to E to allow the annotations to overlie as much as possible. Table 1 shows the basic statistics and priority sets of BCCWJ CORE. The word unit is based on the 'Short Unit Word', UniDic standard (Den et al., 2008); UniDic is a lexicon for Japanese morphological analysis.

3 Specification for Japanese Temporal Information Annotation

This section presents a specification for Japanese temporal information annotation. The annotation is realised as BCCWJ-TimeBank. The specification is based on TimeML (Pustejovsky et al., 2003) and adapted to the Japanese language. Figure 1 shows an example of the annotation. Below, we overview the specification of TimeML tags: ⟨TIMEX3⟩ for temporal expressions, ⟨EVENT⟩ and ⟨MAKEINSTANCE⟩ for event expressions, and ⟨TLINK⟩ for temporal ordering. We also mention other tags which we exclude from Japanese temporal information annotation.

3.1 ⟨TIMEX3⟩

The target temporal expressions of ⟨TIMEX3⟩ are DATE, TIME, DURATION, and SET by @type. We do not permit any nests of ⟨TIMEX3⟩ . We clip the expressions by character-based since Japanese does not have word delimitation spaces.

The attributes of @tid, @type, @value, @freq, @quant, and @mod have been inherited from the original TimeML.

There is an issue regarding which calendar to use in porting TimeML to Japanese. In Japan, we use not only the Western calendar but also a native Japanese calendar based on the year of the Emperor's reign. We introduce a new attribute @valueFromSurface to address this issue. @valueFromSurface includes a @value-like like string to indicate a machine-readable datetime value, whereas @value includes the normalised version of value, @valueFromSurface includes the non-normalised version of the value, which can be generated on rewrite rules. @valueFromSurface

PN23_00001 Sample in BCCWJ CORE

```
<TIMEX3 @value="2002-04-11" @definite="true" @tid="t0"
functionInDocument="CREATION_TIME" type="DATE"/>

<sentence>  地方自治体が<EVENT @class="NULL" @eid="e25">運営する</EVENT>公営地下鉄二十六路線のうち
<TIMEX3 @value="FY2000" @definite="FALSE" @valueFromSurface="FY2000" @tid="t4" @type="DATE">
二〇〇〇年度</TIMEX3>決算で経常損益が黒字なのは、
札幌市南北線など四路線に<EVENT @class="I_ACTION" @eid="e26">とどまった</EVENT>ことが、公営交通事業協会
が
<TIMEX3 @value="2002-04-10" @definite="true" @valueFromSurface="XXXX-XX-10" @tid="t5"
type="DATE">十日</TIMEX3><EVENT @class="I_ACTION" @eid="e27">まとめた</EVENT>報告書で
<EVENT @class="I_STATE" @eid="e28">分かった</EVENT>。</sentence>

<MAKEINSTANCE @eventID="e26" @eiid="ei26"/>
<MAKEINSTANCE @eventID="e27" @eiid="ei27"/>
<MAKEINSTANCE @eventID="e28" @eiid="ei28"/>

<TLINK @relTypeA="after" @relTypeB="after" @relTypeC="during" @task="DCT"
@timeID="t0" relatedToEventInstance="ei26"/>
<TLINK @relTypeA="after" @relTypeB="after" @relTypeC="after" @task="DCT"
@timeID="t0" @relatedToEventInstance="ei27"/>
<TLINK @relTypeA="after" @relTypeB="after" @relTypeC="after" @task="DCT"
@timeID="t0" @relatedToEventInstance="ei28"/>

<TLINK @relTypeA="vague" @relTypeB="equal" @relTypeC="during" @task="T2E"
@timeID="t4" @relatedToEventInstance="ei26"/>
<TLINK @relTypeA="vague" @relTypeB="before" @relTypeC="before" @task="T2E"
@timeID="t4" @relatedToEventInstance="ei27"/>
<TLINK @relTypeA="vague" @relTypeB="before" @relTypeC="before" @task="T2E"
@timeID="t4" @relatedToEventInstance="ei28"/>
<TLINK @relTypeA="after" @relTypeB="before" @relTypeC="during" @task="T2E"
@timeID="t5" @relatedToEventInstance="ei26"/>
<TLINK @relTypeA="contains" @relTypeB="after" @relTypeC="finishes" @task="T2E"
@timeID="t5" @relatedToEventInstance="ei27"/>
<TLINK @relTypeA="contains" @relTypeB="equal" @relTypeC="before" @task="T2E"
@timeID="t5" @relatedToEventInstance="ei28"/>

<TLINK @relTypeA="vague" @relTypeB="before" @relTypeC="contains" @task="E2E"
eventInstanceID="ei26" @relatedToEventInstance="ei27"/>
<TLINK @relTypeA="before" @relTypeB="before" @relTypeC="before" @task="E2E"
eventInstanceID="ei27" @relatedToEventInstance="ei28"/>
```

English Translation:
Municipal Transportation Works Association published a report on April 10th. The report shows that only 4 public tube railways (e.g. Sapporo City Nanboku line) from 26 have a surplus.

Figure 1: An Example of Japanese BCCWJ TimeBank annotation

can encode Japanese calendars. For example, '平成 25 年' (*the 25th year of the Heisei era*) is encoded in the `@valueFromSurface` of `'H25'` and normalised as the `@value` of `'2013'` in the ISO-8601-like format.

The difference between `@value` and `@valueFromSurface` shows the use of the normalisation procedure. However, we cannot judge whether the ⟨`TIMEX3`⟩ is fully normalised (fully specified) or under-specified. We introduce another new attribute `@definite` to indicate whether the ⟨`TIMEX3`⟩ is fully-specified `'true'` or under-specified `'false'`.

3.2 ⟨EVENT⟩ and ⟨MAKEINSTANCE⟩

Next, we need to annotate the event expressions and instances to link the temporal ordering to ⟨`TIMEX3`⟩.

The event expression candidates are automatically extracted from the BCCWJ of morphological information. We define long word units with verbs and adjectives — 4,953 expressions — as the event expression candidates. First, the candidates are judged by two annotators as to whether the target expression is an event expression or not. If the expression boundaries are not valid, a longer expression covering the candidate is redefined by the annotators. Second, the annotators judge whether the target expres-

Table 1: BCCWJ CORE: Registers and its priority set

Register	(Abbr.)	Priority Set	# of Samples	# of Words
White Paper	OW	A to D	62	197,011
Books	PB	A to D	83	204,050
Newspapers	PN	A to E	340	308,504
Yahoo! Answers	OC	A to B	938	93,932
Magazines	PM	A to D	86	202,268
Yahoo! Blog	OY	A to B	471	92,746

sion has any instances on the timeline or not. If an instance is recognised, the annotators define a ⟨MAKEINSTANCE⟩ in the corpus. The ⟨MAKEINSTANCE⟩ is a stand-off from the event expression, but is linked on the ⟨EVENT⟩ tag by the @eid attribute. Third, the annotators annotate the @class attribute on the ⟨EVENT⟩. @class attributes are nine: seven for event instances (OCCURRENCE, REPORTING, PERCEPTION, ASPECTUAL, I_ACTION, I_STATE, STATE) and two for non-instances (NULL and NONE). The difference between NULL and NONE is that the former is applied by ⟨EVENT⟩ annotators and the latter by ⟨TLINK⟩ annotators below. The instances are doubly checked by both ⟨EVENT⟩ and ⟨TLINK⟩ annotators. [2]

- OCCURRENCE: Event expressions without event arguments describing something that happens or occurs in the world (the argument event). Most event expressions belong to this class.
- REPORTING: Event expressions with an event argument describing the action of an animate actor declaring, narrating, or informing about the argument event.
- PERCEPTION: Event expressions with an event argument describing the physical perception of the argument event.
- ASPECTUAL: Event expressions with an event argument describing some aspectuality of the argument event.
- I_ACTION: Intensional action expressions with an event argument describing an action or situation to introduce the argument event, from which we can infer something given its relation with the I_ACTION.
- I_STATE: Intensional state expressions with an event argument referring to an alternative or possible world.
- STATE: State expressions in the timeline. We only annotate when an instance is introduced and becomes an argument of the other event expressions.
- NULL, NONE: Non-instance expressions.

The annotator discriminates whether the target is an event or a state (STATE). Then, he or she judges whether the target has any event argument or not (OCCURRENCE). Finally, he or she categorises any target with an event argument into one of the five categories of REPORTING, PERCEPTION, ASPECTUAL, I_ACTION, and I_STATE.

The two annotators and two supervisors defined a detailed linguistic annotation specification employing some Japanese language tests based on linguistic research (Kudo, 1995; Kudo, 2004; Nakamura, 2001). The two annotators are trained by the specification until the agreement rate reaches 75%.

3.3 ⟨TLINK⟩

⟨TLINK⟩ defines the temporal ordering of temporal information expressions and event expressions. We use a variant of Allen's interval algebra as ⟨TLINK⟩ labels; there are 13 labels for temporal ordering and three for event-subevent relations. We also have one label 'vague' for underspecified relations. Figure 2 shows the 13 + 3 labels. The three underlined labels — 'is_included', 'identity', and 'include' — are event-subevent versions of 'during', 'equal' and 'contains', respectively. Strictly, we can also define event-subevent

[2] Though the original TimeML defines 7 @class attributes on non instance event expressions, we do not define it. This is because our main research objective is annotating temporal ordering on the event instances.

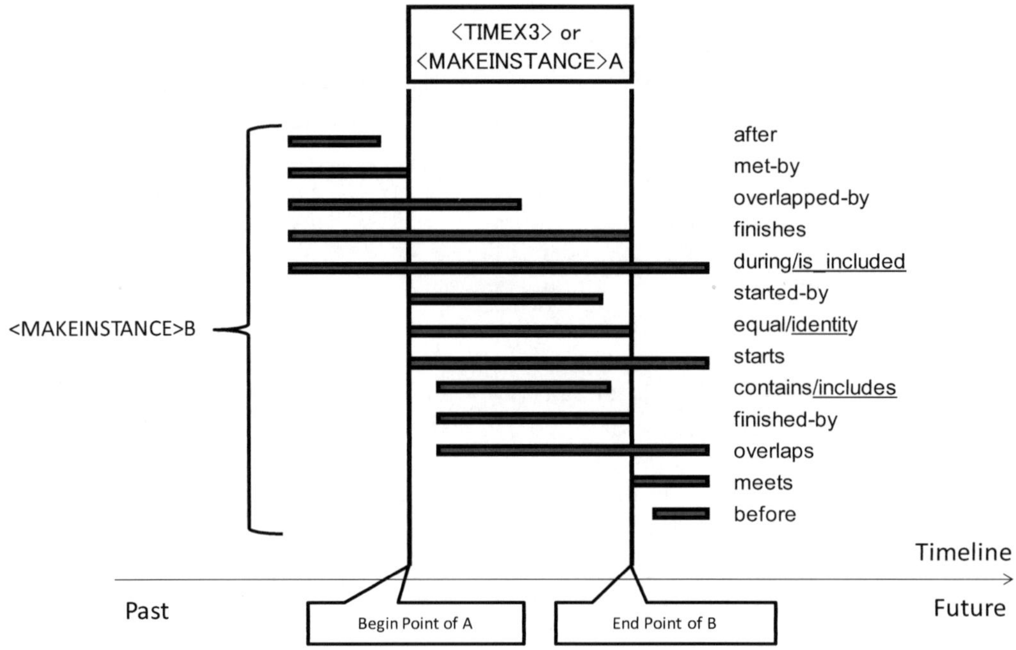

Figure 2: ⟨TLINK⟩ : Labels

versions of 'finishes', 'started-by', 'starts', and 'finished-by'. However, we did not define these, because they are rare and because TimeML did not define them.

⟨TLINK⟩ annotators are different from ⟨EVENT⟩ and ⟨MAKEINSTANCE⟩ annotators. Three annotators annotate the ⟨TLINK⟩ labels on part of pairs among ⟨TIMEX3⟩ and ⟨MAKEINSTANCE⟩. The number of ⟨TLINK⟩ candidates are square of the number of ⟨TIMEX3⟩ and ⟨MAKEINSTANCE⟩. It is hard to check all possible pairs in the documents; therefore, we limit the target pairs to the following four types of relations:

- 'DCT': relations between a ⟨TIMEX3⟩ of document creation time (DCT) and an event instance;
- 'T2E': relations between a ⟨TIMEX3⟩ (non DCT) and an event instance within one sentence;
- 'E2E': relations between two consecutive event instances; and
- 'MAT': relations between two consecutive matrix verbs of event instances.

If the relation is between two different possible worlds, we use the label 'vague'. When we regard the 'vague' relations as disjoint links , the connected subgraph indicates the different possible worlds.

The value of ⟨TIMEX3⟩ is regarded not as a time point but as a time interval. The event instance of a punctual verb is regarded as a time point occurrence, whereas the other event instances are regarded as time interval occurrences.

3.4 Other Tags in the original ISO-TimeML

In the original TimeML, ⟨SIGNAL⟩, ⟨SLINK⟩ , and ⟨ALINK⟩ are defined. ⟨SIGNAL⟩ is used with some temporal prepositions and conjunctions in English, ⟨SLINK⟩ is used for subordination relations, and ⟨ALINK⟩ is used for non-constituent aspectual relations. Currently, we are not using these with the BCCWJ-TimeBank.

4 BCCWJ-TimeBank

This section presents basic statistics on BCCWJ-TimeBank, the Japanese corpus annotated for temporal information. We also consider the annotation environment of BCCWJ-TimeBank.

4.1 ⟨TIMEX3⟩

We use XML Editor oXygen [3] for ⟨TIMEX3⟩ annotation. We define DTD for BCCWJ-TimeBank.

[3] http://www.oxygenxml.com/

The DTD enables us to use the machine-aided (in terms of, XML validation, a completion mechanism, and so on) environment of oXygen. An annotator performs inline annotation on the original text corpus. We introduce a pair-programming-like method in which a display is shared by an annotator and supervisor. Though the method is stressful for both annotator and supervisor, the data becomes more consistent and annotation errors are reduced.

Table 2 shows annotation target samples for ⟨`TIMEX3`⟩. The column 'W/TIMEX' shows the number of samples or sentences which include at least one temporal information expression. Some samples in the registers OW (white paper), OC (Yahoo! Answers), and OY (Yahoo! Blogs) do not include any temporal information expressions.

Table 3 shows the basic statistics of ⟨`TIMEX3`⟩ annotations. The table shows the number of ⟨`TIMEX3`⟩ by `@type` and `@definite` and the relation of {`@value` and `@valueFromSurface`}. `@type` has four labels: `DATE`, `TIME`, `DURATION`, and `SET`. We exclude document creation time (DCT), which is given in corpus metadata, from the statistics. Then, we analyse the statistics on the basis of two perspectives. The first is whether `@definite` is '`true`' or '`false`', in other words, whether the temporal information expression is fully specified or under-specified. The former can be mapped on the timeline, while the latter cannot. The other perspective is whether `@value` and `@valueFromSurface` are identical ('=') or not ('≠'). The former have undergone some normalisation procedure from the annotators, while the latter have not.

A total of 5,297 temporal information expressions are annotated in the corpus. Of those, 1,639 (30%) are fully specified expressions without any normalisation procedures applied. 2,023 (37%) of that can be normalised by contextual information, and 1,875 (34%) cannot. The third group need more external information to be normalised.

In the 'DATE' expressions, most of the fully-specified expressions(`@definite` '`true`'; 61%) have had manual normalisation performed (`@value` ≠ `@valueFromSurface`;50%). This fact shows that the normalisation procedure is important for temporal information processing. The normalisation includes conversion from Japanese to western calendar, conversion from 2-digit to 4-digit western calendar, and completion year (taken from document creation time).

Table 4: ⟨`TIMEX3`⟩ : Statistics in PN (A)

⟨`TIMEX3`⟩ `@type`	
DCT (DATE)	54
DATE	727
TIME	107
DURATION	291
SET	19
ALL	1,198

Table 5: ⟨`EVENT`⟩ : Statistics in PN(A)

⟨`EVENT`⟩`@class`	Count
non-instance	(1,129)
`NULL`	1,114
`NONE`	15
event instance w/o event arg	(2,352)
`OCCURRENCE`	2,352
event instance w/ event arg	(1,291)
`REPORTING`	126
`PERCEPTION`	27
`ASPECTUAL`	63
`I_ACTION`	880
`I_STATE`	195
state instance	(181)
`STATE`	181

In the 'TIME' expressions, most fully specified expressions have had manual normalisation performed. The normalisation includes completion date (from document creation time) and resolution of a.m./p.m. ambiguity.

In the 'DURATION' and 'SET' expressions, `@definite` 'true' means that the length of the temporal region on the timeline can be uniquely determined. When we map on the timeline, we need ⟨`TLINK`⟩ information with 'DATE' or 'TIME' expressions or event expressions.

Note that we reduce the annotation target samples of ⟨`EVENT`⟩ , ⟨`MAKEINSTANCE`⟩ , and ⟨`TLINK`⟩ PN register (A) — 54 samples. The reason is that only the PN (newspaper) sample has date-level document creation time information as metadata. Table 4 shows the statistics of ⟨`TIMEX3`⟩ in PN (A) samples.

Table 2: ⟨TIMEX3⟩ : Annotation target samples

Register		# of Samples ALL	W/ TIMEX		# of Sentences ALL	W/ TIMEX		# of Words ALL
OW	(A)	17	16	(94%)	1,439	405	(28%)	58,336
PB	(A)	25	25	(100%)	2,568	289	(11%)	57,929
PN	(A,B)	110	110	(100%)	5,582	1,562	(28%)	116,834
OC	(A)	518	250	(48%)	3,479	488	(14%)	60,086
PM	(A)	23	23	(100%)	3,066	413	(13%)	59,372
OY	(A)	257	198	(77%)	3,986	765	(19%)	63,459

Table 3: ⟨TIMEX3⟩ : @type × @definite × {@value , @valueFromSurface}

@definite	true (fully-specified)						false (under-specified)					
@value and @valueFromSurface	all		=		≠		all		=		≠	
DATE	2,214	(61%)	381	(10%)	1,833	(50%)	1,438	(39%)	1,275	(35%)	163	(4%)
TIME	188	(37%)	1	(0%)	187	(37%)	315	(63%)	239	(48%)	76	(15%)
DURATION	1,129	(92%)	1,128	(92%)	1	(0%)	99	(8%)	99	(8%)	0	
SET	131	(85%)	129	(84%)	2	(1%)	23	(15%)	22	(14%)	1	(1%)
ALL	3,662	(66%)	1,639	(30%)	2,023	(37%)	1,875	(34%)	1,635	(30%)	240	(4%)

4.2 ⟨EVENT⟩ and ⟨MAKEINSTANCE⟩

We annotate ⟨EVENT⟩ and ⟨MAKEINSTANCE⟩ tags only on PN register (A). Table 5 shows the statistics of ⟨EVENT⟩ tags by @class. Event instances by ⟨MAKEINSTANCE⟩ are defined on the last seven @class in the tables. The number of ⟨MAKEINSTANCE⟩ is 3,839.

4.3 ⟨TLINK⟩

The three annotators are independently trained for ⟨TLINK⟩ annotation. The annotation is performed on four types of relations: 'DCT', 'T2E', 'E2E', and 'MATRIX'.

Table 6 shows annotation agreement among the 13+3+1 labels by three annotations and relation types. The three ∩-connected numbers are the label counts by each of the three annotators. The right number after '=' is the agreed count.

The agreed counts for 'after', 'during', 'contains', and 'before' are higher than the others. These relations do not exhibit boundary matching between the two time intervals. The relation 'equal' is the most frequent of those that do include interval boundary matching. Other relations are infrequent and show low agreement count among the three annotators. These findings show that a judgment of interval boundary matching is rare among and difficult for human annotators.

The relation 'vague' was agreed on 314 times by the three annotators. This fact shows that the discrimination of possible worlds might be doable by annotation.

Table 7 shows agreement rates by relation type across the three evaluation schemata. We define the schemata as follows: 'Label 13+3+1' is the most fine-grained evaluation schema; in it, all 13+3+1 relations are discriminated. 'Label 13+1' is a schema without event-subevent discrimination, in which 'is_included', 'identity', and 'includes' are regarded in the same light as 'during', 'equals', and 'contains', respectively. 'Label 5+1' is a TempEval-like schema in which 13+3+1 relations are generalised into 5+1 relations: 'BEFORE', 'BEFORE-OR-OVERLAP', 'OVERLAP', 'OVERLAP-OR-AFTER', 'AFTER', and 'VAGUE'.

The agreement rate across all relations is 65.3% (Cohen's kappa 0.733) using the most fine-grained evaluation schema (Label 13+3+1). We perform ⟨TLINK⟩ annotations on fixed relation pairs of four types. TimeBank 1.2 jointly performs ⟨TLINK⟩ annotations without fixing relation pairs. In this method, the ⟨TLINK⟩ relation agreement rate is 77% and the relation pairs agreement 55%. We believe that the BCCWJ-TimeBank ⟨TLINK⟩ relation agreement rate is in no way inferior to that of TimeBank 1.2. Among the four relation types, the agreement rate of 'DCT' is the highest and that of 'T2E' second-highest. The relation between a temporal information expression and an event instance is easier than the relation between two event instances. This is because the interval of

Table 6: ⟨TLINK⟩ : Annotation agreement by Annotator × Label × Relation type

Relation types	DCT	T2E	E2E	MATRIX	All
Count	3,839	2,188	2,972	1,245	10,244
after	2,352∩2,326∩2,133=1,961	396∩441∩432=315	627∩631∩639=432	292∩284∩277=198	3,667∩3,682∩3,481=2,906
met-by	0∩0∩0=0	5∩10∩2=2	18∩12∩3=2	7∩3∩2=1	30∩25∩7=5
overlapped-by	11∩5∩4=2	59∩52∩42=20	3∩3∩2=0	0∩0∩1=0	73∩60∩49=22
finishes	2∩8∩1=0	10∩1∩11=0	5∩8∩5=1	1∩0∩0=0	18∩17∩17=1
during	449∩424∩650=217	105∩100∩113=62	206∩139∩225=67	112∩86∩134=43	872∩749∩1,122=389
started-by	1∩0∩0=0	9∩2∩8=0	3∩14∩6=2	0∩3∩0=0	13∩19∩14=2
equal	1∩17∩0=0	37∩70∩51=19	263∩412∩307=154	62∩140∩90=29	363∩639∩448=202
starts	2∩0∩0=0	30∩9∩14=2	6∩16∩2=0	0∩1∩1=0	38∩26∩17=2
contains	164∩85∩144=63	830∩853∩868=671	299∩292∩344=117	148∩152∩188=64	1,441∩1,382∩1,544=915
finished-by	0∩0∩0=0	3∩3∩0=0	6∩7∩6=0	1∩3∩0=0	10∩13∩6=0
overlaps	2∩2∩4=1	75∩84∩70=32	6∩27∩5=0	1∩4∩3=0	84∩117∩82=33
meets	1∩13∩0=0	25∩26∩2=2	88∩88∩32=22	9∩15∩0=0	123∩142∩34=24
before	739∩767∩746=572	389∩360∩383=288	1,058∩994∩1,098=713	418∩436∩422=294	2,604∩2,557∩2,649=1,867
is_included	0∩0∩0=0	0∩0∩0=0	19∩2∩6=1	6∩0∩1=0	25∩2∩7=1
identity	0∩0∩0=0	0∩0∩1=0	11∩7∩24=2	16∩5∩15=2	27∩12∩40=4
includes	0∩0∩0=0	0∩0∩0=0	27∩10∩2=1	18∩2∩0=0	45∩12∩2=1
vague	115∩191∩157=38	212∩177∩191=100	327∩309∩265=128	154∩111∩111=48	808∩788∩724=314

Annotator A ∩ Annotator B ∩ Annotator C = Agreed count

Table 7: ⟨TLINK⟩ : Annotation agreement by Relation type across three evaluation schemata

Relation types	DCT	T2E	E2E	MATRIX	ALL
Count	3,839	2,188	2,972	1,245	10,244
Label 13+3+1	0.743(2854)	0.691(1513)	0.552(1642)	0.545(679)	0.653(6688)
Label 13+1	0.743(2854)	0.691(1513)	0.561(1667)	0.560(697)	0.657(6731)
Label 5+1	0.748(2873)	0.734(1605)	0.627(1862)	0.623(776)	0.695(7116)

Agreement rate(Agreed count)

the temporal information expression is more easily defined on the timeline than the interval of the event instance is. Under the relaxed relation evaluation schema, the agreement rates of 'E2E' and 'MATRIX' increase. This means that while interval boundary matching in these event instances is hard for the annotators to agree upon, interval anteroposterior relations can be agreed on.

Finally, table 8 shows agreement by two entity types: DCT and TIMEX of ⟨EVENT⟩@class. Relations with STATE tend to show low agreement rates, and relations between DCT/TIMEX and STATE are lower than relations between DCT/TIMEX and other event instances. This is because recognition of the time interval boundaries of state expressions is difficult for the annotators. In event instances with event arguments, relations with REPORTING, I_ACTION tend to show high agreement rates than averages.

5 Conclusions

This paper presents a temporal information-annotated Japanese specification and corpus. We adapt the temporal information annotation specification of the original TimeML and ISO-TimeML to the Japanese languages in several layers: ⟨TIMEX3⟩, ⟨EVENT⟩, ⟨MAKEINSTANCE⟩, and ⟨TLINK⟩. We construct BCCWJ-TimeBank as the realisation of the specification. Achieved temporal ordering agreement rates are 65.3%.

As ongoing research, we will continue to look into machine-learning-based temporal ordering estimation. In English temporal ordering, the tense and aspect information in ⟨MAKEINSTANCE⟩ are important features. However, in Japanese temporal ordering, the morphologically overt information is ' る (-ru)' vs ' た (-ta)' for non-past and past tense and ' る (-ru)' vs ' ている (-teiru)' for limited aspect. We will report the results of this temporal ordering estimation.

Further, as future research, we intend to take advantage of BCCWJ's status as the first balanced large-scale shared corpus of Japanese and analyse our annotation as compared to the syntactic and semantic annotations conducted on BCCWJ by several Japanese research institutes, as mentioned in section 2.2. Since Japanese is a modality-rich language, the modality annotations by these other institutes will be important for temporal ordering.

Acknowledgements

References

Y. Den, J. Nakamura, T. Ogiso, and H. Ogura. 2008. A proper approach to Japanese morphological analysis: Dictionary, model, and evalua-

Table 8: ⟨TLINK⟩ : Annotation agreement by {DCT, ⟨TIMEX3⟩ , ⟨EVENT⟩@class} × ⟨EVENT⟩@class

	DCT	TIMEX	OCC	REP	PER	ASP	I_A	I_S	STA	ALL
OCCURRENCE	0.739	0.702	0.551	0.625	0.286	0.718	0.559	0.592	0.422	0.656
Abbr. OCC	(2,352)	(1,320)	(1,602)	(104)	(7)	(39)	(494)	(130)	(102)	(6,159)
REPORTING	0.881	0.697	0.663	0.222	1.000	0.667	0.519	0.368	0.500	0.694
Abbr. REP	(126)	(66)	(95)	(9)	(2)	(3)	(52)	(19)	(12)	(385)
PERCEPTION	0.815	0.700	0.444	NaN	0.000	NaN	0.500	1.000	0.000	0.646
Abbr. PER	(27)	(10)	(18)	(0)	(1)	(0)	(6)	(1)	(1)	(65)
ASPECTUAL	0.714	0.615	0.545	1.000	0.000	0.000	0.643	0.000	0.000	0.627
Abbr. ASP	(63)	(52)	(44)	(6)	(2)	(2)	(14)	(1)	(1)	(185)
I_ACTION	0.808	0.720	0.576	0.690	0.667	0.765	0.631	0.527	0.333	0.698
Abbr. I_A	(880)	(567)	(491)	(29)	(6)	(17)	(309)	(55)	(51)	(2407)
I_STATE	0.651	0.686	0.490	0.250	0.750	0.429	0.545	0.875	0.333	0.594
Abbr. I_S	(195)	(86)	(145)	(4)	(4)	(7)	(55)	(16)	(15)	(527)
STATE	0.492	0.398	0.356	0.600	1.000	0.444	0.431	0.333	0.238	0.424
Abbr. STA	(181)	(83)	(118)	(5)	(3)	(9)	(51)	(9)	(21)	(481)
ALL	0.743	0.691	0.548	0.618	0.560	0.649	0.573	0.562	0.374	0.653
	(3,839)	(2,188)	(2,524)	(157)	(25)	(77)	(984)	(233)	(203)	(10,244)

Agreement rate (Agreed count)

tion. In *the 6th Language Resources and Evaluation Conference(LREC-2008)*, pages 1019–1024.

ISO. 2008. Iso dis 24617-1: 2008 language resource management – semantic annotation framework - part 1: Time and events. International Organization for Standardization.

M. Kudo. 1995. *Asupekuto, Tensu-Taikei to Tekusuto — Gendai Nihongo-no Jikan-no Hyougen.* Hituzi Syobo.

M. Kudo. 2004. *Nihongo-no Asupekuto, Tensu, Muudo-Taikei Hyoujun-go Kenkyu-wo Koete (in Japanese).* Hituzi Syobo.

K. Maekawa. 2008. Balanced Corpus of Contemporary Written Japanese. In *Proc. of the 6th Workshop on Asian Language Resources (ALR-8)*, pages 101–102.

C. Nakamura. 2001. *Nihongo-no Jikan Hyougen.* Kuroshio Shuppan.

J. Pustejovsky, J. Casta no, R. Ingria, R. Saurí, R. Gaizauskas, A. Setzer, and G. Katz. 2003. TimeML: Robust Specification of Event and Temporal Expressions in Text. In *Proceedings of the 5th International Workshop on Computational Semantics (IWCS-5)*, pages 337–353.

J. Pustejovsky, K. Lee, H. Bunt, and L. Romary. 2010. ISO-TimeML: an International Standard for Semantic Annotation. In *Proceedings of LREC-2010*, pages 394–397.

N. UzZaman, H. Llorens, L. Derczynski, J. Allen, M. Verhagen, and J. Pustejovsky. 2013. Semeval-2013 task 1: Tempeval-3: Evaluating time expressions, events, and temporal relations. In *Second Joint Conference on Lexical and Computational Semantics (*SEM), Volume 2: Proceedings of the Seventh International Workshop on Semantic Evaluation (SemEval 2013)*, pages 1–9, Atlanta, Georgia, USA, June. Association for Computational Linguistics.

M. Verhagen, R. Saurí, T. Caselli, and J. Pustejovsky. 2010. SemEval-2010 Task 13: TempEval-2. In *Proceedings of the 5th International Workshop on Semantic Evaluations (SemEval-2010)*, pages 57–62.

A Corpus-Based Approach to Linguistic Function

Hengbin Yan and Jonathan Webster
The Halliday Centre for Intelligent Applications of Language Studies
Department of Chinese, Translation and Linguistics
City University of Hong Kong
{hbyan2, ctjjw}@cityu.edu.hk

Abstract

In this paper, we present our recent experience in constructing a first-of-its-kind functional corpus based on the theoretical framework of Systemic Functional Linguistics. Annotated on selected texts from the Penn Treebank, the corpus was built by a collaborative team on web-based annotation platform with several advanced features. After a discussion on the background and motivation of the project, we present our solutions to some of the challenges encountered in the collaborative annotation process. With fine-grained annotations of an initial corpus now available, the corpus can serve as a valuable linguistic resource that complements existing semantically annotated corpora and aid in the development of a larger-scale resource crucial for automated systems for analysis of linguistic function.

1 Introduction

Recent years have seen data-driven approaches to natural language processing successfully applied to a wide range of problems including syntactic (Collins, 2003; Klein and Manning, 2003) semantic (Gildea and Jurafsky, 2002; Pradhan et al., 2004) and discourse (Hernault et al., 2010) analysis. Computational processing of functional aspects of linguistic data, on the other hand, is a relatively underexplored research area. In linguistics, functional analysis refers to the study of language use in context. Among the theories for analyzing the functions of language, Systemic Functional Linguistics (SFL, Halliday and Matthiessen, 2004) is a linguistic framework that is becoming increasing influential in recent years. SFL provides an ideal handle to exploring language as intentional acts of meaning, complementing more syntactically oriented approaches to linguistic study. Despite its power, traditional analysis with SFL is done manually, a time- and effort- consuming process.

We are motivated in our study to extend the power of the framework to computational analysis. The difficulty in automating analysis of linguistic functions lies in both the fuzziness in the functional domain and a lack of relevant computational resources. The most significant lack of resource is a high-quality reference corpus crucial to statistical analysis and modeling. In the following sections, we discuss our initial efforts in constructing such a resource on a collaborative annotation platform and present the initial results from the corpus. The corpus is our first step in bridging the gap between the linguistic theory and application of such theory including automated analysis of language functions.

2 Related Works

Over the past decades, the construction of prominent linguistic corpora to account for the syntactic (Marcus, 1993), semantic (Kingsbury et al., 2002) and discourse (Carlson and Okurowski, 2002; Prasad et al., 2008) structures of linguistic information has deepened our understanding in each layer and made possible automated data-driven analysis based on them. Although the advantages of a functional-semantic orientation are apparent to text analysis, the complexity arising from annotation of multi-level functional-semantic information, such as that found in SFL, has led to a scarcity in large-scale, high-quality corpora annotated with such information (Honnibal and Curran, 2007). While the possibility and suitability of SFL in its application to computational analysis have been duly discussed (Halliday and Webster, 2006) and successfully applied in a number of NLP applications, particularly in Natural Language Generation (Teich, 1999) a lack of high-quality SFL-based computational resources, especially a large-scale reference corpus, has impeded its applications in wider range of problems.

A number of tools have been developed for annotating multi-layered functional structures, such as Gensys (Kumano et al., 1994), PALinkA (Orasan, 2003) and UAM CorpusTool (O'Donnell, 2008). Despite addressing some of the difficulties in functional annotation, these tools still exhibit certain significant drawbacks such as: (1) inability to represent discontinuous and embedded units; (2) incompatibility with other annotation structures and formats; (3) lack of visualization of annotated structures; (4) overcomplicated interface; (5) nil collaboration among annotators; and (6) poor support for multi-language tagging.

Efforts have been made to circumvent the difficulties in manual annotation by attempting to convert the Penn Treebank to an SFL corpus (Honnibal and Curran, 2007). The project has been partially successful in aligning basic functional components with syntactic structures in the Penn Treebank. It is argued that the partial success in converting the basic functional categories is due to the consistent annotation schemes of the Penn Treebank, and the SFL's remarkable agreement with other linguistic theories on the distinction of syntactic components, despite its emphasis on feature structures rather than syntactic representation. However, the work has been mostly concerned with the surface features of the SFL that are more or less syntactically oriented, while being unable to produce fine-grained functional-semantic categories that are crucial for any in-depth analysis of texts based on SFL. A high-quality functional corpus is still needed to fill this gap.

A number of linguistic resources annotated with shallow semantic roles have been produced over the years. Notable among them are the following three: FrameNet, VerbNet and Propbank.

The FrameNet database (Baker et al., 1998) is a semantic corpus annotated on the British National Corpus. The corpus annotates the frames of sentences using three components: lexicons, frames, and example sentences. Frames, or the context-sensitive conceptual structure, organized hierarchically, are composed of frame elements specific to a particular frame. Such annotations provide valuable context-specific knowledge and are useful for capturing certain semantic or syntactic patterns.

VerbNet (Schuler, 2005) is a domain-independent verb lexicon with linkage to other lexical resources such as FrameNet and WordNet. It provides complete descriptions of verbs based on Levin's original classification (Levin, 1993), with substantial refinement. Each verb class in VerbNet is annotated with syntactic descriptions called syntactic frames, which define the surface realization of the predicate-argument structure for transitive, intransitive, prepositional phrases etc, and thematic roles (e.g. Agent, Location, Theme) of its arguments. Semantic selectional restrictions (human, animate, organization etc.) specify what thematic roles are allowed in the classes.

Propbank (Kingsbury and Palmer, 2002) is another semantically-labeled resource. Annotated on one million words of the Wall Street Journal section of the Penn Treebank, it provides detailed description of the predicate-argument structure of the annotated texts. The theoretical assumption underlying the annotations are fundamentally the same as that of the VerbNet: the semantics of sentences are reflected in the syntactic frames associated with a verb of a particular verb class according to Levin's classification. The argument structure are labelled arg0, arg1, arg2, etc., based on the semantic role they play in a sentence and regardless of their syntactic positions. Thus in the sentences: *John broke the window*, and *The window broke*, although the window is the syntactic object in the first and subject in the second, it is given the same argument label. This allows us to capture the similarities in transitivity alternations in sentences that are syntactically different.

The annotation of such semantically-oriented resources is important contributions to the study of the complex phenomenon of language meanings. Each of them is grounded on a particular framework with certain assumptions, one more suited for certain applications than the others. However, to account for a fuller spectrum of the multifaceted nature of language meanings, multiple complementary resources are often linked and combined. With a focus on language functions (language use in context), the work on the proposed functional corpus provides an alternative view to the semantic and functional aspect of language that can be useful in problems and applications not directly targeted by those pre-existing resources, such as Critical Discourse Analysis and Automatic Text Generation.

3 Corpus Construction

3.1 Corpus Texts

To leverage existing resources, the new corpus is annotated on the Penn Treebank (Marcus, 1993) with texts taken from the Wall Street Journal section. The same raw texts form a common basis of three well established corpora: the Penn Treebank, the RST Discourse Treebank (Carlson and Okurowski, 2002), and the Penn Discourse Treebank (Prasad et al., 2008), making it possible for easy automatic alignment (establishing word-to-word correspondence) among the corpora. We align our functional-semantic features with each of these corpora to create a multilayered interlinked information structure that can be used to explore the interactions and correlations of syntactic, discourse and functional information.

3.2 Annotation Infrastructure

The corpus is annotated using a web-based collaborative Tagger that we recently developed (see Figure. 2). The Tagger aims at providing a theory-neutral annotation framework for annotating heterogeneous (syntactic, semantic, functional, discourse) layers of linguistic information, multimodal data (e.g. images, sounds, videos) and metadata (e.g. user management, access control, time and geographical information).

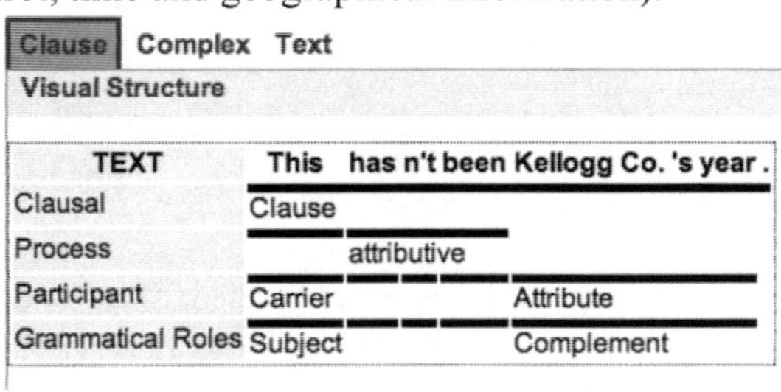

Figure 1: A structured view of a clause in the annotated corpus, taken from the web-based interface.

The Tagger is built on a generic, multifunctional database framework compatible with the Annotation Graph (Bird and Liberman, 1999), an abstract annotation framework capable of representing a wide range of common linguistic signals (text, speech, image, video, multimodal interactions etc.), with properties particularly suited for collaborative annotation. This generic layered framework lends flexibility to alignment of noncontiguous words and other linguistic resource, useful for the nonconventional segmentation of functional components (such as the common anticipatory '*it*' as in "*It is a good thing that he stepped down as President.*") in SFL.

The Tagger features immediate annotation feedback through visualization, a process known to improve the quality and efficiency of annotation. For instance, when tagging at a particular layer (e.g. syntactic structure), information of the other layers (e.g. semantic properties) is immediately visible in a hierarchical structured format. This visualized information serves as additional references to the current layer being annotated, especially when they are closely related in terms of function or meaning. When annotation errors (e.g. misalignment, mismatched labeling) are made they are immediately visible from the annotation interface for appropriate actions such as deletion or modification to be taken.

3.3 Quality assurance

Annotation quality and consistency are maintained by standard measures such as online documenting guidelines, trainings and tutorials, and multiple passes. In annotating functional-semantic features, we seek a balance by preserving reasonable alternative interpretations, while striving to reduce annotation errors. A logging and tracking mechanism is introduced that tracks all online activities in real time, for supervisors to review annotation and provide real-time feedback to annotators for correction and improvement.

The tool uses a Wiki-like message board for discussions between annotators and public users, a process known to improve quality of collaborative knowledge construction (Kittur and Kraut, 2010). Questions and feedback, along with a set of constantly updated guidelines, are recorded in a version-controlled database to be retrieved whenever needed and to guide new annotators and future annotations where similar scenarios arise. Each change made on the annotation tool is traceable, allowing for rollback at a later time (e.g. in case of a critical error).

One major difficulty in ensuring the annotation quality of the proposed functional corpus lies in the inherent ambiguity in language functions. Even in a restricted context, there can be multiple interpretations of the same text. Unlike transformational grammars which study syntactic properties independent of context, functional theories such as SFL is grounded on the belief that language functions that a particular text serves can only be seen by taking into account all the related contextual factors, which are often culturally and socially dependent and subject to subjective interpretation. This leads to difficulties in disambiguating language meanings and functions. In annotating the functional corpus, the boundaries of some of the functional concepts are not always clear-cut. For example, apart from the three major functional types of process, material, mental and relational, there are three other types of processes that lie between the boundaries of any two of them: verbal, behavioral and existential. With such indeterminate boundaries, classification of the process types can often be difficult (see Section 4 for some examples). For the purpose of preserving alternative interpretations that also reflect the functional diversity of the structure, we choose to preserve multiple annotations of the same components. The annotations are ordered in terms of the perceived plausibility, resulting in primary annotations and secondary annotations that coexist.

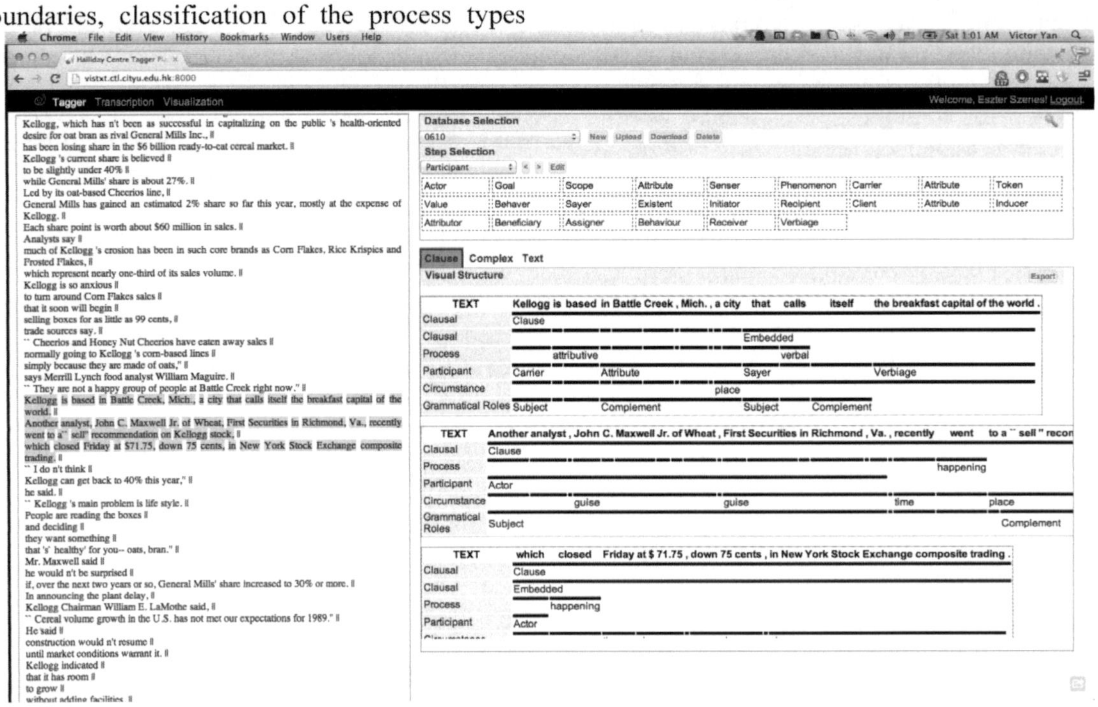

Figure 2: A view of the web-based collaborative tagger for annotating the functional and discourse structures of multilingual texts. The web-based interface is divided into three operation panels, namely, the text panel (left), annotation panel (top right) and visual structure panel (bottom right).

3.4 Corpus Details

We adopt Halliday's seminal works (Halliday, 1994) on the theory to provide standard reference due to the maturity and wide adoption of the works. Specific guidelines on the annotation task are designed in accordance with these reference materials.

In SFL-based analysis, three strata of meaning (called metafunctions) operate in parallel: the ideational, interpersonal, and textual metafunctions. As the other two layers are more syntactically oriented and convertible from syntactically parsed trees, we focus our annotation on the ideational metafunction, and more specifically a major subcategory, the experiential metafunction, whose categorization is largely functionally oriented and less lexically/syntactically dependent.

The experiential metafunction, as its name suggests, has to do with functions relating to world experience. Linguistically, it involves a configuration of processes and participants involved (such as Actor, Goal), and the accompanying circumstances (such as time, place, manner). Such configuration allows one to look beyond the sentence surface to probe into the semantic aspect of the text.

The annotation was done in three successive layers, in which each of the following constituents is annotated:

Clausal: clausal boundaries, including boundaries of embedded clauses. The clause boundaries are aligned with the RST Treebank where clausal boundaries are also annotated, with fine-grained changes made to make it more suited for SFL's definitions of clauses.

Process: processes are the center of a clause, typically realized by a verbal group headed by the root verb of the clause. As described in (Halliday, 1994), there are six common types of processes (material, behavioral, mental, verbal, relational, existential), subdivided into ten more refined types. Each of the process types is associated with a set of nuclear and non-nuclear participants. A summary of the process with its related participants is given in Table 1.

Participant: participants are the central nominal groups of the clause typically realized by subject or objects of the clause.

Circumstance: more-peripheral units related to time, place, manner etc., typically realized by adverbial groups. There are in total nine broad types of circumstances: *Extent, Location, Manner, Cause, Contingency, Accompaniment, Role, Matter,* and *Angle,* each with its own subtypes. The *Extent* circumstance, for example, is subdivided into three subtypes: *duration, frequency,* and *distance.*

Process type	Nuclear participants	Non-nuclear participants
material: action event	Actor, Goal	Initiator, Recipient, Client, Scope
mental: perception affection cognition	Senser, Phenomenon	Inducer
Relational: attributive	Carrier, Attribute	Attributor, Beneficiary
identifying	Token, Value	Assigner
behavioural	Behaver, Target	Behaviour, Scope
verbal	Sayer, Target	Receiver, Verbiage
existential	Existent	

Table 1: A summary of the process types and participants in the corpus

4 Annotation Statistics

The construction of the functional corpus is an on-going project. The current corpus is constructed by a small team of annotators, all linguistic majors at graduate or undergraduate levels with formal training in the theoretical framework. After an initial three months of annotation we have constructed a small-scale corpus. In total we have annotated 81 documents from the Penn Treebank, with a total number of 43351 words, divided into 1621 sentences and 4620 clauses. The statistics of the top five types of annotated processes, participants, and circumstances are shown in Table 2.

Process Type	Number	Percentage
doing	1871	44.63%
happening	673	16.05%
verbal	585	13.96%
attributive	464	11.07%
identifying	216	5.15%
Participant Type	**Number**	**Percentage**
Goal	1608	23.85%
Actor	1300	19.28%
Verbiage	1153	17.10%
Sayer	517	7.67%
Attribute	469	6.96%
Circumstance Type	**Number**	**Percentage**
place	841	33.71%
quality	288	11.54%
degree	265	10.62%
guise	260	10.42%
comparison	125	5.01%

Table 2: Number of occurrences and percentage of each of the functional types

In total, we have identified 912 verb types. The verb types are identified by extracting the core verb from each verbal group and then lemmatized using WordNet's lemmatizer (Bird et al., 2009). For example, in the clause *The movement is called a vibration*, the process, as realized by a verbal group is *is called*, while the core verb in the verbal group is *called*, which is lemmatized to its base form *call.* In total, 218 word types have more than one process type (details of the number of each process type as represented by verb types are shown in Table 4).

Process Type	Lexical Meaning	Example (processes are underlined)
material: action	phoning somebody	The president called him earlier tonight.
relational: identification	identify; describe	This movement is called a vibration.
verbal	say loudly	The butcher's son called out a greeting.
mental: cognition	consider; regard	This act can hardly be called generous.

Table 3: Examples of the process *call* with four different process types

# of Process Types	1	2	3	4	5	6
# of Verb Types	714	168	37	7	4	2

Table 4: Number of verb types and the number of process types that a verb type has.

We calculate the inter-annotator agreement statistics on the three functional components: Process types, Participants and Circumstances. We consider agreement to be cases where both the boundaries and types of functional labels are the same. The agreement ratio is 93.78% for Process types, 87.47% for Participants, and 86.13% for Circumstances. The lower agreement in Participants and Circumstances is due to the fact that sometimes the boundaries of the structure that represent these functional components are not universally agreed upon. Although there is definitely still room for improvement, the agreement is already high considering the fact that functional labels are often inherently more subjective than their lexical/syntactic counterparts.

5 Conclusion & Future work

In this paper, we discuss our work on constructing a functional corpus based on an influential theoretical framework. We present our initial attempts at building the corpus on a collaborative annotation platform. Although the scale of the functional corpus is still relatively small, its construction has made it possible to study basic functional properties computationally.

As an experiment, a prototypical classification system is built based on the annotated results for automatically classifying the functional processes of clauses using machine-learning algorithms such as Support Vector Machine (Tong and Koller, 2002), results from which are to be presented in another paper. The potential use of the functional corpus is promising, with prospects of further developing into an important resource for carrying out fully automated functional analysis. The corpus and the experimental classifier will be further employed to build a large-scale functional corpus with substantially less effort. We plan to continue to expand the current corpus before releasing it to the community for researchers to further explore its potential application in a wide range of areas.

References

Baker, C. F., Fillmore, C. J., & Lowe, J. B. (1998). The berkeley framenet project. In *Proceedings of the 17th international conference on Computational linguistics-Volume 1* (pp. 86–90).

Bird, S., Klein, E., & Loper, E. (2009). *Natural language processing with Python*. O'reilly.

Bird, S., & Liberman, M. (1999). Annotation graphs as a framework for multidimensional linguistic data analysis. In *Towards Standards and Tools for Discourse Tagging–Proceedings of the Workshop*.

Carlson, L., & Okurowski, M. (2002). RST discourse treebank.

Collins, M. (2003). Head-driven statistical models for natural language parsing. *Computational linguistics*.

Gildea, D., & Jurafsky, D. (2002). Automatic Labeling of Semantic Roles. *Computational Linguistics*, 28(3), 245–288.

Halliday, M., & Webster, J. (2006). *Computational and quantitative studies*.

Halliday, Michael A., & Matthiessen, C. M. (2004). An introduction to functional grammar.

Halliday, Michael AK. (1994). An Introduction to Functional Grammar. London: Edward Arnold.

Hernault, H., Prendinger, H., DuVerle, D. A., & Ishizuka, M. (2010). HILDA: A Discourse Parser Using Support Vector Machine Classification. *Dialogue & Discourse*, 1(3), 1–33.

Honnibal, M., & Curran, J. J. R. (2007). Creating a systemic functional grammar corpus from the Penn treebank. *Proceedings of the Workshop on Deep Linguistic Processing - DeepLP '07*, (June 2005), 89.

Kingsbury, P, Palmer, M., & Marcus, M. (2002). Adding semantic annotation to the penn treebank. *Proceedings of the Human Language Technology Conference*.

Kingsbury, Paul, & Palmer, M. (2002). From TreeBank to PropBank. In *LREC*.

Kittur, A., & Kraut, R. E. (2010). Beyond Wikipedia: coordination and conflict in online production groups. In *Proceedings of the 2010 ACM conference on Computer supported cooperative work* (pp. 215–224).

Klein, D., & Manning, C. D. C. (2003). Accurate unlexicalized parsing. *Proceedings of the 41st Annual Meeting on Association for Computational Linguistics ACL 03*, 1(July), 423–430.

Kumano, T., Tokunga, T., Inui, K., & Tanaka, H. (1994). GENESYS: An integrated environment for developing systemic functional grammars. In *Proceedings of the International Workshop on Sharable Natural Language Resources* (pp. 78–85).

Levin, B. (1993). English verb classes and alternations: A preliminary investigation (Vol. 348). University of Chicago press Chicago.

Marcus, M. (1993). Building a large annotated corpus of English: The Penn Treebank. *Computational linguistics*.

O'Donnell, M. (2008). Demonstration of the UAM CorpusTool for text and image annotation. *Proceedings of the 46th Annual Meeting of the Association for Computational Linguistics on Human Language Technologies Demo Session - HLT '08*, (June), 13–16.

Orasan, C. (2003). PALinkA: A highly customisable tool for discourse annotation. In *Proceedings of the 4th SIGdial Workshop on Discourse and Dialog* (pp. 39–43).

Pradhan, S., Ward, W., & Hacioglu, K. (2004). Shallow semantic parsing using support vector machines. *Proceedings of HLT/NAACL*, 233.

Prasad, R., Dinesh, N., & Lee, A. (2008). The penn discourse treebank 2.0. *Proceedings of the 6th International Conference on Language Resources and Evaluation (LREC 2008)*, 2961–2968.

Schuler, K. K. (2005). VerbNet: A broad-coverage, comprehensive verb lexicon.

Teich, E. (1999). Systemic functional grammar in natural language generation: Linguistic description and computational representation.

Tong, S., & Koller, D. (2002). Support vector machine active learning with applications to text classification. *The Journal of Machine Learning Research*, 2, 45–66.

A Case Study of a Free Word Order

Vladislav Kuboň and **Markéta Lopatková** and **Jiří Mírovský**
Charles University in Prague
Faculty of Mathematics and Physics
Czech Republic
{vk,lopatkova,mirovsky}@ufal.mff.cuni.cz

Abstract

The paper aims at the investigation of free word order. It concentrates on the relationship between (formal) dependencies and word order. The investigation is performed by means of a semi-automatic application of a method of analysis by reduction to Czech syntactically annotated data.

The paper also presents the analysis of introspectively created Czech sentences demonstrating complex phenomena which are not sufficiently represented in the corpus. The focus is on non-projective structures, esp. those connected with the position of clitics in Czech. The freedom of word order is expressed by means of a number of necessary shifts in the process of analysis by reduction.

The paper shows that this measure provides a new view of the problem, it is orthogonal to measures reflecting the word order freedom based on a number of non-projective constructions or clitics in a sentence. It also helps to identify language phenomena that generally pose a problem for dependency-based formalisms.

1 Introduction

The phenomenon of word order freedom plays an important role in natural language processing. The less rigid the word order, the bigger challenge for all kinds of parsing algorithms it constitutes.

In this paper we are going to study the relationship between *(formal) dependencies* – defined through analysis by reduction, a stepwise simplification of a sentence preserving its correctness (Lopatková et al., 2005)– and *word order*. We want to gain better insight into the problem by means of the application of a semi-automatic procedure to syntactically annotated data. This method can verify the concept of the analysis by reduction (introduced in Section 2) against real data and, at the same time, it can shed more light on the relationships between these two syntactic phenomena, dependency and word order.

Our goal is twofold:

First, we focus on typical, 'core' (projective) word order. We are going to quantify how many sentences can be completely processed by a simple analysis by reduction (i.e., sentences are (correctly) reduced until only the predicate is left in the sentence). In order to be able to perform this task for a large volume of data, namely syntactically annotated data from the Prague Dependency Treebank (PDT) (Hajič et al., 2006)), we have developed an automatic procedure (requiring, of course, a subsequent manual checking) on a relatively large subset of the PDT data. The results are presented in Section 3.

Second, we present an analysis of more 'peripheral' word order. When it is impossible to perform simple reduction (without violating the correctness constraint), we strengthen the analysis by reduction by the concept of 'shifts' – word order modifications which help to preserve the correctness constraint. Such data provide a very interesting material for the analysis of individual linguistic phenomena involved in complicated sentences (Section 4). We are primarily concentrating on the analysis of sentences which have been discovered as problematic in previous research, see esp. (Holan et al., 2000).

1.1 The Background

In the world of dependency representation, there are three essential (and substantially different) syntactic relationships, namely 1. *dependencies* (the relationship between a governing and a modifying sentence member, as e.g. a verb and its object, or a noun and its attribute), 2. *'multiplication'* of two or more sentence members or clauses (esp. coordination), and 3. *word order* (i.e., the linear sequence of words in a sentence).[1]

In this paper we are concentrating on the phenomena 1 and 3, i.e., on the relationships of dependency and word order. The interplay between these two basic syntactic relationships is relatively complex especially in languages with a higher degree of word order freedom. The reason is simple – while the dependency relations are indicated primarily by morphological means (as morphological cases and agreement (Daneš et al., 1987)), the word order expresses primarily phenomena like communicative dynamism and topic-focus articulation (Hajičová and Sgall, 2004).

Within dependency linguistics, these relationships have been previously studied especially within the Meaning-Text Theory: the approach aiming at the determination of dependency relations and their formal description is summed up esp. in (Mel'čuk, 2011). An alternative formal description of dependency syntax can be found in (Gerdes and Kahane, 2011). Our approach is based on the Czech linguistic tradition represented mainly in (Sgall et al., 1986).

Let us now formulate the basic principle underlying the *analysis by reduction*: roughly speaking, if one of the words creating a possible governor-modifier pair can be deleted without changing the distribution properties of the pair (i.e., the ability to appear in the same syntactic context) then it is considered as a modifying one (dependent on the latter one). This is applicable on so called endocentric constructions (as, e.g. *small table, Go home!*); for exocentric constructions (as *Peter met Mary*), the principle of analogy on the part-of-speech level is applied, see (Sgall et al., 1986; Lopatková et al., 2005).

The reason for exploiting the analysis by reduction is obvious: it allows for examining dependencies and word order independently. The method has been described in detail in (Lopatková et al., 2005),its formal modeling by means of restarting automata can be found in (Jančar et al., 1999; Otto, 2006; Plátek et al., 2010). A brief description of its basic principles follows in Section 2.

There is a number of approaches aiming at formalization of word order complexity – let us mention especially the notions of non-projectivity (Marcus, 1965; Holan et al., 2000), (multi-)planarity, gap-degree and well-nestedness – a thorough overview is provided in (Kuhlmann and Nivre, 2006). All these approaches are based on the interplay between the ordering introduced by edges in a tree and the linear ordering of tree nodes. All these approaches look at the problem from the point of view of *complexity of word order*.

An alternative approach to the problem of measuring the word-order freedom has been introduced in (Kuboň et al., 2012). This approach is based on a number of word order shifts[2] necessary for correct analysis by reduction. Contrary to tree-based measures, the number of shifts can somehow express the degree of word order freedom (or the number of *strict word-order constraints* applied). It was shown that number of shifts is 'orthogonal' to the non-projectivity, see (Kuboň et al., 2012).

The experiments in (Kuboň et al., 2012) showed that – with only basic constraints on the analysis by reduction carried out on the limited set of sentences from the PDT – the minimal number of shifts enforced did not exceed one. Here we present a special construction in Czech requiring at least two shifts (Section 4.1), which disproves the hypothesis.

2 Methodology – Analysis by Reduction

Let us first describe the main ideas behind the method used for sentence analysis. *Analysis by reduction (AR)* is based on a stepwise simplification of an analyzed sentence. It defines possible sequences of reductions (deletions) in the sentence – each step of AR is represented by *deleting* at least one word of the input sentence; in specific cases, deleting is accompanied by a *shift* of a word form to another word order position.

Let us stress the basic constraints imposed on the analysis by reduction, namely:
(i) the obvious constraint on preserving individual word forms, their morphological characteristics and/or their surface dependency relations, and
(ii) the constraint on preserving the correctness (a

[1](Tesnière, 1959) considers linear order vs. structural order and also divides the structural relationships between connexion (now dependency) and junction (coordination).

[2]The shift operation should not be confused with (syntactic) movement in transformational or derivational theories as it is not limited to discontinuous constituents or displacement.

grammatically correct sentence must remain correct after its simplification).

Note that the possible order(s) of reductions reflect dependency relations between individual sentence members, as it is described in (Plátek et al., 2010). The basic principles of AR can be illustrated on the following Czech sentence (1).

Example 1.
Petr se bojí o otce.
'Peter - *refl* - fears - for - father'
'Peter fears for his father.'

The analysis by reduction can be summarized in the following scheme:

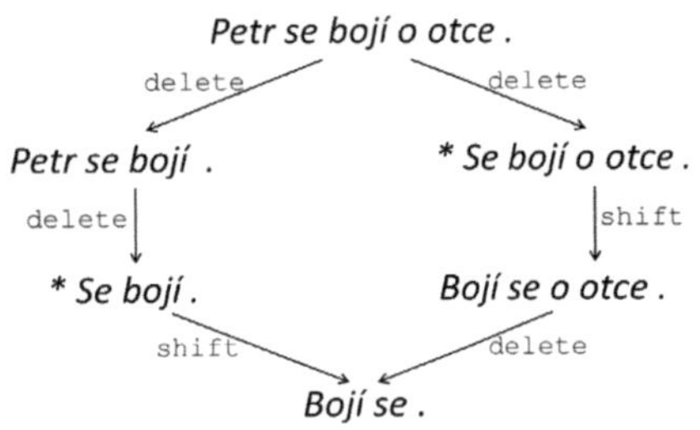

Sentence (1) can be simplified in two ways:
(i) Either by simple deletion of the prepositional group *o otce* 'for father' (following the constraint on correctness of the simplified sentence, the pair of word forms must be deleted in a single step; see the left branch of the scheme).
(ii) Or by deleting the subject *Petr* (the right part of the scheme).[3] However, this simplification results in an incorrect word order variant starting with a clitic[4] **Se bojí o otce*; thus the change of word order (the shift operation) is enforced $\rightarrow_{shift}$ *Bojí se o otce*.

Now, we can proceed in a similar way until we get the minimal correct simplified sentence *Bojí se*.

We can notice that the order of reductions reflects the dependency relations in the corresponding dependency tree. Informally, the words are 'cut from the bottom of the tree'; i.e., a governing node must be preserved in a simplified sentence until all its dependent words are deleted, see (Lopatková et al., 2005).[5] In other words, AR corresponds to the dependency tree for sentence (1):

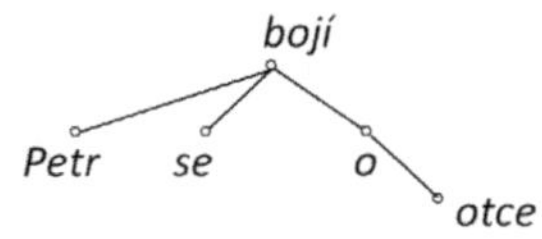

2.1 Exploiting AR in Experiments

Let us now briefly list the conditions which we have applied in our experiments with AR:

1. *Data selection.*
As we have already mentioned, we focus on the interplay between dependency relations in a sentence (i.e., binary relations between modified and modifying sentence members) and its (linear) word order. Thus, in the initial phase of our investigations, we concentrate on sentences which do not contain phenomena of obviously non-dependent character (esp. coordination, apposition, and parentheses). We also focus only on sentences with a single finite verb (and thus typically consisting of a single clause only).

2. *Shift limitations – the application of the shift operation is limited to cases where it is enforced by the correctness preserving principle of AR.*
In other words, shift operation can be applied only in those cases where a simple deletion would result in a sentence with erroneous word order and a shift (word order modification) can correct it, as in sentence (1).

3. *Optimality – we presuppose a choice of an 'optimal' shift.*
Although we are working with a single syntactic structure for a sentence, there are typically several possibilities how to perform AR (as in sentence (1) with two possible branches of AR). We focus on those branches of AR that show a minimal number of shifts. However, the condition of optimality may sometimes be difficult to achieve, the optimal shifts are not obvious in complicated sentences combining more linguistic phenomena, as it is discussed in Section 4.2.2.

4. *Projectivity – we allow only for projective reductions.*
Reduction of non-projective dependencies is not

[3]Note that Czech is a pro-drop (null-subject) language. Thus it is possible to reduce a sentence subject (if present at all) at any moment – provided that all words depending on the subject have already been reduced; the sentence remains syntactically correct.

[4]Czech has strict grammatical rules for clitics – roughly speaking, they are usually located on the sentence second (Wackernagel's) position, see esp. (Avgustinova and Oliva, 1997; Hana, 2007).

[5]As described in the cited article, the relations between the preposition and its 'head' noun as well as between the verb and his clitic is rather technical as both words involved in the relation must be reduced within a single step. Here we adhere to the practice used for the PDT annotation.

allowed.[6] In other words, a dependent word in a distant position cannot be deleted (with the only exception of limited technical non-projectivities caused, e.g., by prepositions).

The constraint allowing only projective reductions makes it possible to describe a core projective word order. It shows that – even within projective constructions – certain constraints on word order exist, esp. in connection with the position of clitics. Thus a measure based on the number of necessary shifts does not correlate with non-projectivity, see also (Kuboň et al., 2012).

Let us demonstrate the processing of non-projective reductions on the following example (2) (based on (Holan et al., 2000), modified).

Example 2.
Petr se Marii rozhodl tu knihu nekoupit.
'Peter - *refl* - Mary - decided - the book - not-to-buy'
'Peter decided not to buy the book to Mary.'

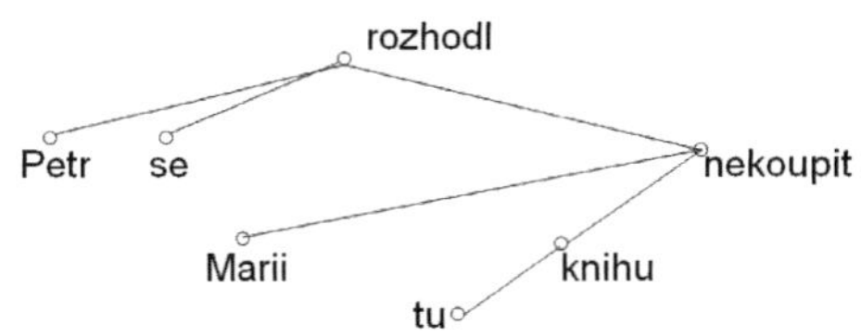

The word *Marii* (indirect object of the verb *nekoupit* 'not-to-buy') cannot be reduced as it is 'separated' from its governing verb by the main predicate *rozhodl* 'decided' (i.e., by the root of the dependency tree) and thus the relation *Marii – nekoupit* 'to-Mary – not-to buy' is represented by the non-projective edge in the dependency tree. Thus within projective AR, the shift must be performed to make the reduction possible: $\rightarrow_{shift}$ *Petr se rozhodl Marii tu knihu nekoupit.* $\rightarrow_{delete}$ *Petr se rozhodl tu knihu nekoupit.*

3 A Semi-Automatic Application of AR on the PDT Data

3.1 The Data

For humans, especially for native speakers of a particular natural language, it is easy to apply the analysis by reduction, at least when simple sentences are concerned. However, this application exploits the fact that the human understands the sentence and that (s)he is naturally able to reduce it step by step. When we are aiming at applying AR automatically, we have to 'substitute' (at least to some extent) the understanding using the syntactically annotated data (with subsequent manual correctness checking).

For our experiments, we make use of the data from the Prague Dependency Treebank 2.0 (PDT, see (Hajič et al., 2006)).[7] The syntactic structure – a single dependency tree for a single sentence – actually guided the process of AR.

The PDT contains very detailed annotation of almost 49,500 Czech sentences. The annotation is performed at multiple layers, out of which the analytical (surface syntactic) layer is the most relevant for our experiments; we are taking into account only training data (38,727 sentences).

3.2 Searching the Data

For obtaining a suitable set of test sentences for AR as well as for searching the data, we exploit a PML-TQ search tool. PML-TQ is a query language and search engine designed for querying annotated linguistic data (Pajas and Štěpánek, 2009), based on the TrEd toolkit (Pajas and Štěpánek, 2008). TrEd with the PML-TQ extension (primarily designed for processing the PDT data) allows users to formulate complex queries on richly annotated linguistic data. Let us exemplify some types of queries used for obtaining the subset of the PDT data for automatic analysis by reduction.

The output of the first (simplified) example query provides a set of test sentences with the required properties (line 3 - sentence length is limited to 10-25 tokens; 4,5 - no coordination and apposition nodes; 6,7 - no parentheses; 8,9 - just one finite verb; 10,11 - no numerals in test sentences):

```
1 t-root
2 [atree.rf a-root $r :=
3   [descendants()≥ 10, descendants()≤ 25,
4     0x descendant a-node
5     [afun in {"Coord", "Apos"}],
6     0x descendant a-node
7     [is_parenthesis_root="1"],
8     1x descendant a-node
9     [m/tag ~ "^V[Bipqt]"],
10    0x descendant a-node
11    [m/tag ~ "^C" ] ] ] ;
```

Out of the 38,727 sentences of the training data of PDT, only 2,453 sentences remained after the application of this preprocessing filter. Although this number constitutes only 6.33% of the training set, it is still too big for manual testing. This fact

[6] Informally, projective constructions meet the following constraint: having two words n_{gov} and n_{dep}, the second one being dependent on the first one – then all words between these two words must also (transitively) depend on n_{gov}.

[7] http://ufal.mff.cuni.cz/pdt2.0/

clearly shows the necessity of a semi-automatic method of applying AR to the data.

The second query gives a set of non-projective sentences from PDT where the non-projectivity is not caused by a preposition (AuxP) or by emphasizing words (AuxZ) or by some particles (AuzY) (line 5). Note that the output must be filtered in order to merge possible multiple results (line 9).

```
1 t-root
2 [atree.rf a-root $r :=
3   [descendant a-node $p :=
4    [1+x same-tree-as a-node
5     [ afun !~ "Aux[PYZ]$", !ancestor $p,
6     ((ord < $c.ord & ord > $p.ord)
7     V (ord > $c.ord & ord < $p.ord)) ],
8     a-node $c := [ ] ] ] ] ;
9 >> for file() & "#" & $r.id
     give $1 sort by $1
```

The second query gives 6,357 non-projective sentences (out of 38,727 sentences in the training data, i.e. 16.41%), in which non-projectivity is not caused by the 'technical' decisions how to annotate prepositions, particles and emphasizing words.

3.3 The Automatic AR Procedure

The automatization of the AR requires a very careful approach. It is necessary to guarantee the correctness of the analyzed sentences in each step of the AR. Let us briefly sketch individual rules guiding the automatized AR:

1. *Reduction rules.* The process is oriented bottom-up, it starts with the leaves of the dependency tree and it removes all nodes marked by analytical functions for attributes, adverbials, objects and subjects, whenever possible. One very important word-order condition is preserved, namely the one guaranteeing that the neighboring nodes are removed first, followed by those which are connected by projective edges.

2. *Preserving non-projectivity.* A node cannot be reduced if this reduction would result in some non-projective edge becoming projective.

3. *Prepositions.* If a node is governed by a preposition, it is necessary to reduce both nodes at once, in a single step. This also has a consequence for the relationship of immediate neighbourhood – prepositions are ignored in this relationship. Prepositions are also ignored when projectivity is tested – i.e., if the only source of a non-projective edge is a preposition, the sentence is treated as projective (this is justified by rather technical annotation of prepositions in PDT).

4. *Clitics.* Clitics may be reduced only together with their governing word. There is also one very important constraint preventing ungrammatical constructions – no reduction may be performed which would leave a clitic on the first sentence position.

5. *Comparison.* Pairwise constructions *čím – tím* 'the – the' cannot be reduced. Other types of comparisons *jako, než* 'as, than' are being reduced together with their last children.

6. *Particles.* Particles are in principle being reduced with regard to the word order constraint, unless they belong to a set of special cases – *coby, jako, jakoby, jakožto* 'as, like' are being reduced together with their parent, similarly as in the case of comparison.

7. *Emphasizing expressions.* If the word order permits it, they can be reduced in the same way as, e.g., adverbials. If a prepositional group is involved, it is reduced as a single unit.

8. *Punctuation and graphical symbols.* Reduction can be applied when the governing word is being reduced.

9. *Full stop.* Sentence ending punctuation is reduced as a final step of AR.

Note that in some cases, we do not insist on a complete reduction (with only the predicate left at the end). Even with the set of test sentences mentioned above and the incomplete reductions, the automatic AR gives us interesting results – see the resulting tables in the following section. Apart from the numerical results, this approach also helped to identify other minor phenomena which do not have a dependency nature.

3.4 Analysis of the Results of the Automatic Procedure

Here we quantify and analyse the results of the automatic AR applied on the test sentences from the PDT. First of all, the following table provides numbers of sentences where specific problematic phenomena appear (from the complete set of the training data from PDT, i.e., from 38,727 sentences).

	phenomenon
12,345	sentences containing clitic(s)
	out of which 3,244 non-projective (26.3%)
850	with the comparison or complement introduced by *coby, jako, jakoby, jakožto*
	out of which 451 non-projective (53.1%)
895	with the comparison expressed by *než*
	out of which 323 non-projective (36.1%)
844	with the comparison with ellipsis
	out of which 302 non-projective (35.8%)
32	with the comparison expressed by *čím-tím*
	out of which 17 non-projective (53.1%)

Let us mention the reasons why we consider these phenomena problematic from the point of view of AR. First, clitics have a strictly specified position in a Czech sentence; thus they may cause a complex word order (including number of non-projective edges, see Section 4). Second, a comparison (frequently accompanied by ellipses) has also complex and non-dependency character.

Let us now look at the results of simple (projective) reductions as described in the previous subsection. The first column describes the number of nodes (= word forms) to which the processed sentences were reduced; the second column gives the number of corresponding sentences and the third column gives their proportion with respect to the whole test set of 2,453 sentences:

nodes	sentences	%	cumulative coverage
1	1,640	66.86	
2	29	1.18	68.04
3	354	14.43	82.47
4	235	9.58	92.05
5	113	4.61	96.66
6	44	1.79	98.45
7	21	0.86	99.31
8	10	0.41	99.72
9	5	0.20	99.92
10	2	0.08	100.00

We can see that our 'careful' automatic model of simple AR (projective AR without shifts) can process almost 67% of the test set (plus 15.6% sentences are reduced into simple structures with 2 or 3 nodes). Note that 282 (out of 2,453 test sentences) 308 sentences were non-projective (i.e., 11.50% sentences cannot be fully reduced in the course of projective AR).

After a manual analysis of the sentences that were reduced automatically to two nodes (29 in total), we can see that 23 sentences contain a clitic (dependent on the predicate) that prevents the full reduction, or an auxiliary verb (6 cases) or punctuation (1 case) (both auxiliary verbs and punctuation are represented as separate nodes in PDT). Further, 5 sentences which start with subordinating conjunction complete the list (as, e.g., → *Že rozeznáte* 'That (you) recognize').

resulting in 2 nodes	phenomenon	resulting in 3 nodes
29	total sentences	354
23	clitic(s)	310
6/1	aux. verb / punctuation	74
n/a	non-projectivity	37
5	others	0

In order to illustrate the most complicated cases, let us look at one sentence from the 'bottom' part of the table. → *Složení by se nemělo měnit v takové míře jako dosud.* 'The composition should not keep changing in such a degree as so far.' (10 nodes remain as a result of the simple AR).

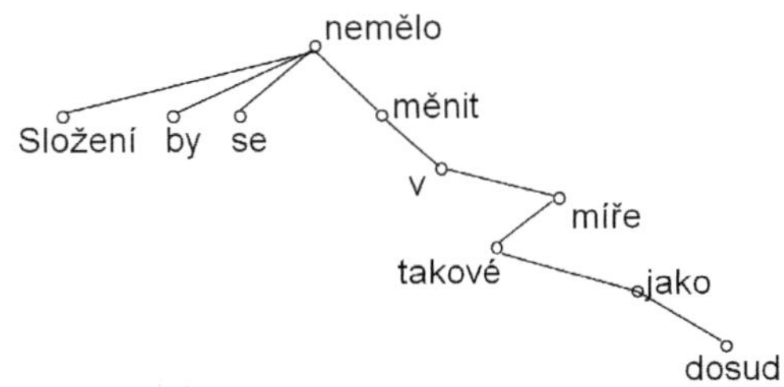

The first word *Složení* must be preserved in order to preserve correct position of the clitics *by* and *se* (an auxiliary verb and a reflexive particle); further, the non-projective edge *takové – jako dosud* 'such – as so far' in the comparison ('separated' by the governing node *míře* 'degree') stops the process of AR.

The results presented in the previous tables actually support the claim that the automatic procedure works surprisingly well given the complexity of the task. It is able to reduce more than 92% of input sentences to trees with 4 or less nodes. On top of that, it fails to reduce the tree (by a failure we understand the reduction to 7 or more nodes) in 1.55% of cases only.

4 Manual Analysis of Sentences Requiring a Shift within AR

Let us focus on sentences that cannot be reduced (in the course of AR) by simple step-by-step deletion: such attempt would result in a sentence with incorrect word order, see sentence (1). In order to deepen our understanding of the phenomena under investigation, we decided to analyze selected sentences manually. A further automatization might be attempted in the subsequent phases of our investigation.

As it was shown in the previous sections, the role of shifts during the analysis by reduction is twofold:
1. *To keep the correctness preserving constraint*, which concerns primarily the cases when an input sentence contains a clitic (as in sentence (1)); this issue is addressed in Section 4.1.
2. *To enable projective AR of non-projective sentences*, as it was exemplified on sentences (2); this issue is addressed in Section 4.2.

We will present the analysis of these interesting cases step by step, by looking at typical examples. For the sake of simplicity, we will present only 'optimal' branches of AR, i.e., those branches that require a minimal number of shifts (see principle 3 in Section 2.1). This is a purely technical simplification, we are looking for *minimal* necessary number, therefore investigating all possible branches does not make sense, it would give identical results as our 'optimal' approach.

4.1 Number of Necessary Shifts within AR

The crucial question is how many shifts are necessary. The first attempt to get some estimation of the maximal number of necessary shifts in Czech sentences described in (Kuboň et al., 2012) suggested that this number might equal one. This observation had been performed on a small sample of PDT. However, our further research, which included some additional interesting examples created introspectively, indicated that this number might be higher even if the principle of projectivity is not applied, i.e., if we allow for non-projective reductions.

First of all, let us present a counter example to the claim published in (Kuboň et al., 2012) concerning the number of necessary shifts (≤ 1) in Czech sentences. The following sentence requires at least two shifts in the course of the AR (note that the sentence is non-projective):

Example 3.
S těžkým se bála pomoci úkolem.
'with - difficult - *refl* - (she) was afraid - to help - task'
'With a *difficult* task, she wanted to help.'

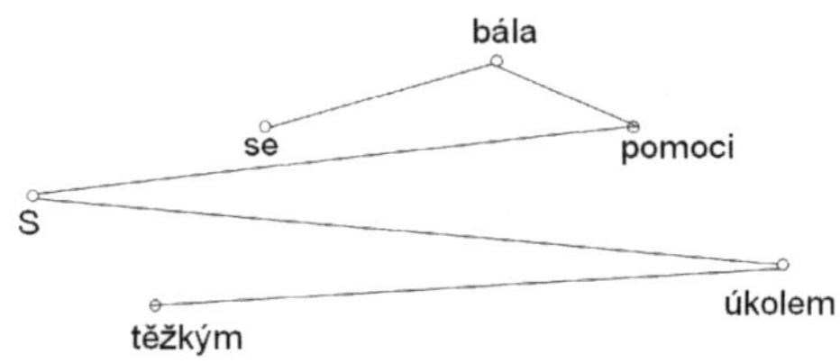

Due to the dependency relations present in the sentence there is only one possibility how to reduce it, the reduction of the adjective *těžkým* 'difficult'. Unfortunately, it results in syntactically incorrect word order: $\rightarrow_{delete}$ **S se bála pomoci úkolem.*
This situation can be corrected in two possible ways, we will sketch only one of them:
$\rightarrow_{shift}$ *S úkolem se bála pomoci* . (A shift of the noun *úkolem* 'task' next to the preposition.)
$\rightarrow_{delete}$ **Se bála pomoci* . (Unfortunately, the next reduction must remove the prepositional group *s úkolem* 'with task' making the sentence again ungrammatical.)
$\rightarrow_{shift}$ *Bála se pomoci.* (Now we can repair the sentence by shifting the verb *bála* to the left.)
The same result will be gained in other branches of AR.

Regardless of the possible reduction sequences, it is necessary to apply at least two shifts. However, although the sample sentence is rather strange, the splitting of the prepositional group is a grammatical construction in Czech. It allows to put a strong stress on an adjective modifying the noun and not on the whole prepositional group, see (Hajičová and Sgall, 2004).

4.2 Projectivization within AR

The principle of projectivity (Section 2.1) constitutes a relatively strong constraint on AR. Its role may be illustrated by the following example of a (simplified) sentence from PDT.

Example 4.
Pomocí může být systém ECM.
'help - can - to be - system - ECM'
'The ECM system may be a help.'

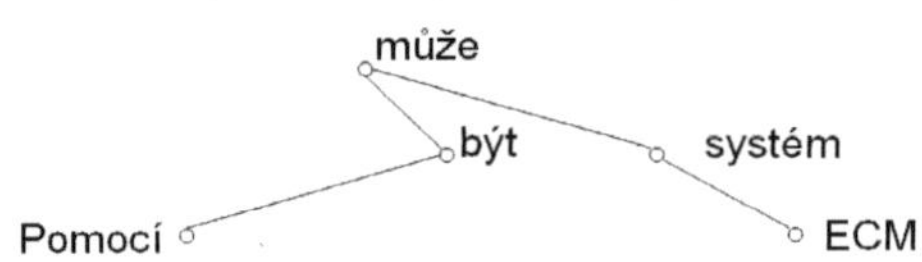

The first two steps are easy, we will get rid of the subject *systém ECM* 'the ECM system' by a stepwise deletion: $\rightarrow$ *Pomocí může být.*
The remaining three words constitute a non-projective 'core' of the original sentence with the non-projective edge *být – pomocí* 'to be – help'.

The AR with non-projective reductions (without the principle of projectivity applied) would not require any shift operation, the word *pomocí* 'help' would be reduce first, followed by the verb *být* 'to be'; these steps would result in the correct simplified sentence *Může.* '(It) can'. However, with the principle of projectivity we have to make the sentence projective first, otherwise no reductions would be possible. For this, we have the following options:
(a) We can make the sentence projective by shifting the *dependent* word pomocí 'help': $\rightarrow$ *Může pomocí být.* (or $\rightarrow$ *Může být pomocí.*)
(b) We can also make it projective by shifting the *governing* word *být*: $\rightarrow$ *Pomocí být může.* (or $\rightarrow$ *Být pomocí může.*).
The application of both options (a) and (b) in example (4) requires one shift, so the score with the principle of projectivity applied (i.e., only projective reductions are allowed) increases.

In general, it is also possible to use (c) a shift of the *main verb* of the sentence. If a non-projective core of the sentence has a simple structure with only a single non-projective edge involved, the shift of the main verb has the same results as either (a) or (b). However, in general (with more non-projective edges present in the core of the sentence), the shift of the main verb may result in a word order different from those achieved by the options (a) and (b), see esp. example (6) below.

4.2.1 Clitics and Non-Projectivity in Projective AR

The results on the test sample without the principle of projectivity applied showed that the number of non-projective constructions in a sentence and the number of clitics are not directly reflected in the necessary number of shifts (presented in (Kuboň et al., 2012)).

With the principle of projectivity (i.e., only projective reductions are allowed), the sentences requiring more than one shift not necessarily contain any special constructions, just the combination of clitics and non-projectivities is enough to raise the number of shifts over one:

Example 5.
Tu knihu se rozhodl věnovat nadaci.
'this - book - *refl* - decided - donate - to a foundation'
'He decided to donate this book to a foundation.'

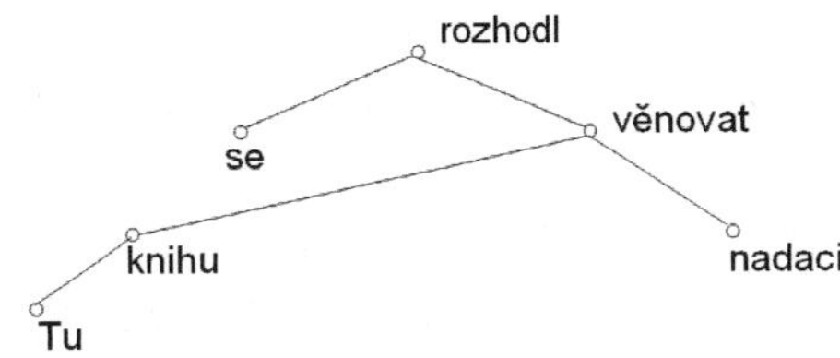

The first two deletions are obvious, the words *tu* 'this' and *nadaci* 'foundation' can be reduced in an arbitrary order: $\rightarrow$ *Knihu se rozhodl věnovat.*
There are two possibilities how to projectivize the sentence, (a) shifting the dependent word, or (b) shifting the governing word, as mentioned in example (4). Let us sketch here only the former variant (the latter results in the same number of shifts):
$\rightarrow_{shift}$ **Se rozhodl knihu věnovat.* (Reduction of the dependent word *knihu* 'book'.)
This shift results in the ungrammatical sentence, therefore it is necessary to perform a shift operation again, this time by shifting the predicate of the sentence to the sentence first position (thus eliminating the ungrammaticality caused by the clitic in the first position).
$\rightarrow_{shift}$ *Rozhodl se knihu věnovat.*
The remaining reductions are then obvious:
$\rightarrow_{delete}$ *Rozhodl se věnovat.* $\rightarrow_{delete}$ *Rozhodl se.*
Regardless of the variant used, we arrive at a score of 2 shifts. This actually indicates that the constraints applied to the AR help to capture the interplay of clitics and non-projectivities in a more subtle way than the original measure presented in (Kuboň et al., 2012).

4.2.2 Number of Shifts in Projective AR

Let us now show that the resulting number of shifts cannot be simply calculated as a sum of the number of non-projective constructions and the number of clitics in a sentence. The following sentence contains two instances of each phenomenon – the clitics *se* and *mu* and the non-projective dependency edges *knihu – věnovat* 'book – to donate', and *mu – věnovat* 'him – to donate', respectively:

Example 6.
Tu knihu se mu rozhodl věnovat.
'this - book - *refl* - him - (he) decided - donate'
'(He) decided to donate this book to him.'

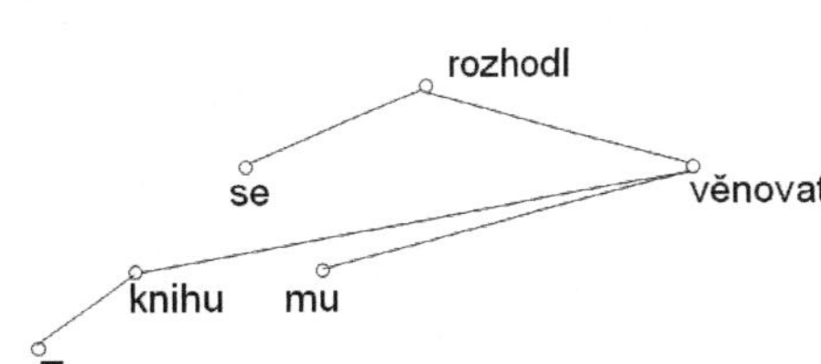

Let us now quickly sketch the AR.
$\rightarrow_{delete}$ *Knihu se mu rozhodl věnovat.* (Reduction of the pronoun *tu* 'this'.)
If we now apply the shift operation on the pronoun *mu* 'him' with the aim at reducing the number of non-projectivities, we will get $\rightarrow_{shift}$ *Knihu se rozhodl mu věnovat.*[8] After the reduction of the dependent pronoun *mu* 'him' we will get one of the intermediate results from the previous example (5), $\rightarrow_{delete}$ *Knihu se rozhodl věnovat.* We already know that in order to reduce this sentence completely we need two more shift operations, therefore the total number of shifts reaches 3.
However, in this case the application of the option (c) mentioned in example (4), shifting the main verb, Section 4.2, brings a better result. If (after the first projective reduction of *tu* 'this') we now shift the word *knihu* 'book' to a projective position $\rightarrow_{shift}$ **Se mu rozhodl knihu věnovat.*, a complementary second shift of the main verb *rozhodl* 'decided' will make the sentence projective (and grammatically correct) $\rightarrow_{shift}$ *Rozhodl se mu knihu věnovat.* and by subsequent application of the reduction of dependent words *mu* 'him' and *knihu* 'book' in an arbitrary order we will get $\rightarrow$ *Rozhodl se věnovat.* This sentence can be further reduced $\rightarrow$ *Rozhodl se.* Overall, only 2 shift operations are necessary in this case (regardless of the number of the studied phenomena involved).

Searching for the minimal necessary number of shifts may be relatively complicated even for sentences whose complexity is lower than in the previous examples. The naive estimation of a number of necessary shift operations for projective reduction in the course of AR can rely on a number of clitics and a number of non-projective edges. However, the next example shows that a single shift operation may 'fix' several non-projectivities. It also shows an example of a sentence where the complex word order is not caused by a clitic.

Example 7.
Prostředí zde máme za úkol vytvořit dobré.
'environment - here - (we) have - as a task - to create - good'
'We have a task to create a good environment here.'

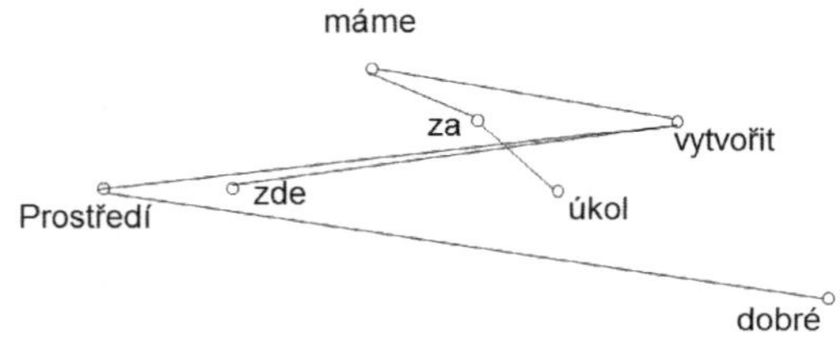

This sentence contains a topicalized noun *prostředí* 'environment'. The dependency tree includes three non-projective edges which are caused by the topicalization. Again, the first reduction is simple and straightforward, the prepositional group *za úkol* can be reduced immediately: $\rightarrow$ *Prostředí zde máme vytvořit dobré.* Then we have several possibilities in which order and by what type of shift to proceed. Again, we will focus on (one of) the 'optimal' sequences of reductions:
$\rightarrow_{shift}$ *Prostředí máme zde vytvořit dobré.* (The reduction of *zde* 'here' is possible only after a shift moves it next to the governing infinite verb *vytvořit* 'create'.)
$\rightarrow_{delete}$ *Prostředí máme vytvořit dobré.*
$\rightarrow_{shift}$ *Máme vytvořit dobré prostředí.* (Here we are shifting the governing noun *prostředí*.)
$\rightarrow_{delete}$ *Máme vytvořit prostředí.* (The reduction of the dependent adjective *dobré* 'good'.)
$\rightarrow_{delete}$ *Máme vytvořit.* (Reduction of the dependent noun *prostředí* 'environment'.)
$\rightarrow_{delete}$ *Máme.* (Final reduction.)
In this 'optimal' branch we have achieved all reductions with the help of only 2 shifts.

This example shows that even without clitics we need at least 2 shifts in the process of projective AR.

Conclusion and Perspectives

In this paper we have tried to achieve a deeper insight into the phenomenon of word order freedom. We have concentrated upon the relationship between (formal) dependencies and word order in Czech. The investigation of this relationship has been performed by means of a semi-automatic analysis of a subset of a large corpus. This analysis proved the applicability of AR on a vast majority of sentences and, at the same time, it helped us to identify problematic phenomena.

Further, manual analysis of complicated sentences proved that the relationship between the number of necessary shifts in the process of AR is orthogonal to the number of clitics or non-projective constructions in a sentence.

[8] The group *Knihu se rozhodl* may be understood as a single unit, see (Hana, 2007), and thus the clitic *mu* 'him' still occupies the correct 'sentence second' position.

Our research helped to analyze concrete phenomena in Czech which influence the word order, namely strict position of clitic(s) and non-projective constructions, and their mutual interplay. The number of necessary shifts with a constraint on projectivity of reductions allows for a more subtle expression of differences between certain configurations of a word order than the measures introduced in previous papers. The range of values of the original measure of word order freedom has been increased.

In the future we would like to continue the research by examining more linguistic phenomena, by testing the measure on other languages with various degrees of word order freedom and by experimenting with a different or modified set of constraints applied on the shift operation. We would also like to expand the research scope to other important phenomena, especially coordination. It would also be interesting to develop a (semi-)automatic method for an optimal application of the shift operation.

Acknowledgments

The research reported in this paper has been supported by the Czech Science Foundation GA ČR, grant No. GA P202/10/1333. This work has been using language resources developed and/or stored and/or distributed by the LINDAT-Clarin project of MŠMT (project LM2010013).

References

Tania Avgustinova and Karel Oliva. 1997. On the Nature of the Wackernagel Position in Czech. In *Formale Slavistik*, pages 25–47. Vervuert Verlag, Frankfurt am Main.

František Daneš, Miroslav Grepl, and Zdeněk Hlavsa, editors. 1987. *Mluvnice češtiny 3*. Academia, Praha.

Kim Gerdes and Sylvain Kahane. 2011. Defining dependencies (and constituents). In *Proceedings of DepLing 2011*, pages 17–27, Barcelona.

Jan Hajič, Jarmila Panevová, Eva Hajičová, Petr Sgall, Petr Pajas, Jan Štěpánek, Jiří Havelka, M. Mikulová, Z. Žabokrtský, and M. Ševčíková. 2006. *Prague Dependency Treebank 2.0*. LDC, Philadelphia.

Eva Hajičová and Petr Sgall. 2004. Degrees of Contrast and the Topic-Focus Articulation. In *Information Structure – Theoretical and Empirical Aspects*, volume 1, pages 1–13. Walter de Gruyter, Berlin; New York.

Eva Hajičová, Jiří Havelka, Petr Sgall, Kateřina Veselá, and Daniel Zeman. 2004. Issues of Projectivity in the Prague Dependency Treebank. *The Prague Bulletin of Mathematical Linguistics*, 81:5–22.

Jiri Hana. 2007. *Czech Clitics in Higher Order Grammar*. Ph.D. thesis, The Ohio State University.

Tomáš Holan, Vladislav Kuboň, Karel Oliva, and Martin Plátek. 2000. On Complexity of Word Order. *Les grammaires de dépendance – Traitement automatique des langues (TAL)*, 41(1):273–300.

Petr Jančar, František Mráz, Martin Plátek, and Jörg Vogel. 1999. On monotonic automata with a restart operation. *Journal of Automata, Languages and Combinatorics*, 4(4):287–311.

Vladislav Kuboň, Markéta Lopatková, and Martin Plátek. 2012. Studying formal properties of a free word order language. In G. Youngblood and Philip McCarthy, editors, *Proceedings of FLAIRS 25*, pages 300–3005, Palo Alto. AAAI Press.

Marco Kuhlmann and Joakim Nivre. 2006. Mildly non-projective dependency structures. In *Proceedings of the COLING 2006 and ACL 2006 (Poster Sessions)*, pages 507–514, Sydney.

Markéta Lopatková, Martin Plátek, and V. Kuboň. 2005. Modeling Syntax of Free Word-Order Languages: Dependency Analysis by Reduction. In *Proceedings of TSD 2005*, volume 3658 of *LNAI*, pages 140–147, Berlin Heidelberg. Springer-Verlag.

Solomon Marcus. 1965. Sur la notion de projectivité. *Zeitschrift fur Mathematische Logik und Grundlagen der Mathematik*, 11(1):181–192.

Igor A. Mel'čuk. 2011. Dependency in language. In *Proceedings of DepLing 2011*, pages 1–16, Barcelona.

Friedrich Otto. 2006. Restarting Automata. In *Recent Advances in Formal Languages and Applications, Studies in Computational Intelligence*, volume 25, pages 269–303, Berlin. Springer-Verlag.

Petr Pajas and Jan Štěpánek. 2008. Recent Advances in a Feature-Rich Framework for Treebank Annotation. In *Proceedings of CoLING 2008*, volume 2, pages 673–680, Manchester, UK. The Coling 2008 Organizing Committee.

Petr Pajas and Jan Štěpánek. 2009. System for Querying Syntactically Annotated Corpora. In *Proceedings of the ACL-IJCNLP 2009 Software Demonstrations*, pages 33–36, Singapore. ACL.

Martin Plátek, František Mráz, and Markéta Lopatková. 2010. (In)Dependencies in Functional Generative Description by Restarting Automata. In *Proceedings of NCMA 2010*, volume 263 of *books@ocg.at*, pages 155–170, Wien. Österreichische Computer Gesellschaft.

Petr Sgall, Eva Hajičová, and Jarmila Panevová. 1986. *The Meaning of the Sentence in Its Semantic and Pragmatic Aspects*. Reidel, Dordrecht.

Lucien Tesnière. 1959. *Eléments de syntaxe structurale*. Librairie C. Klincksieck, Paris.

Some Formal Properties of Higher Order Anaphors

R. Zuber
Laboratoire de Linguistique Formelle,
CNRS and University Paris-Diderot
Richard.Zuber@linguist.univ-paris-diderot.fr

Abstract

Formal properties of functions denoted by higher order anaphors like *each other* and syntactically complex expressions containing *each other* are studied. A partial comparison between these functions and functions denoted by (simple and complex) reflexives is draw. In particular it is shown that both types of function are predicate invariant (in a generalised sense). These results allows us to understand the anaphoric character of both reflexive and reciprocal expressions.

1 Introduction

By higher order anaphor, I mean expressions like *each other*, sometimes called basic higher order anaphors, and various complex expressions syntactically containing *each other*. These complex anaphors include Boolean compounds like *each other and most students, each other and themselves* and various modifications of *each other* like *only each other* or *at least each other*. Higher order anaphors are also expressions formed by the application of a *higher order anaphoric determiner* like *each other's* or *every ...except each other* to a common noun (CN). All such expressions will be called reciprocals and sentences containing them (in object position) will be called reciprocal sentences.

Higher order anaphors can be opposed to (logically) simple anaphors whose basic example is the reflexive pronoun *himself/herself/themselves*. This simple basic anaphora can also occur in Booleanly complex anaphors like *himself and most students* or in modified expressions like *only himself, even themselves*. So the distinction between simple and higher order anaphors is of logical nature: as we will see below functions denoted by higher order anaphors take binary relations (or binary relations and sets) as arguments and give sets of type $\langle 1 \rangle$ quantifiers as output whereas simple anaphors have arguments of the same type as higher order ones (that is their arguments are binary relations or sets and binary relations) but their output are sets (of individuals).

The semantics of reciprocal sentences is a complex matter (as shown for instance in Dalrymple *et al.*, 1998; Cable, forthcoming; Dotlačil, forthcoming; Mari, forthcoming). In fact there does not seem to be any general agreement concerning the data and the interpretation of reciprocal constructions (cf. Beck, 2000). In this paper I am not, strictly speaking, interested in the semantics of higher order anaphors but in the formal properties of functions denoted by higher order anaphors. Two types of such properties will be discussed: those which are similar to properties of functions denoted by simple anaphors and those which make them different from functions denoted by simple anaphors. Formal properties of functions denoted by simple anaphors have been studied in Keenan (2007), Zuber (2010b) and Zuber (2011) and some formal properties of higher order anaphors are given in Sabato and Winter (2012) and Peters and Westerståhl (2006). As far as I can tell, no comparison between the two types of function have been made. Moreover, only basic anaphors (that is syntactically simple anaphors) have been taken into consideration.

2 Formal preliminaries

We will consider binary relations and functions over universe E which is supposed to be finite. If a function takes only a binary relation as argument, its type is noted $\langle 2 : \tau \rangle$, where τ is the type of the output; if a function takes a set and a binary relation as arguments, its type is noted $\langle 1, 2 : \tau \rangle$. If $\tau = 1$ then the output of the function is a set of individuals and thus the type of the function is $\langle 2 : 1 \rangle$. For instance the function $SELF$, defined as $SELF(R) = \{x : \langle x, x \rangle \in R\}$, is of this type. The case we will basically consider here is when τ corresponds to a set of type $\langle 1 \rangle$ quantifiers and thus τ equals, in Montagovian notation, $\langle\langle\langle e, t \rangle t \rangle t \rangle$. In short, the type of such functions will be noted either $\langle 2 : \langle 1 \rangle \rangle$ (functions from binary relations to sets of type $\langle 1 \rangle$ quantifiers) or $\langle 1, 2 : \langle 1 \rangle \rangle$ (functions from sets and binary relations to sets of type $\langle 1 \rangle$ quantifiers).

Let R be a binary relation. Then : $dom(R) = \{x : \exists_y \langle x, y \rangle \in R\}$ and $rg(R) = \{x : \exists_y \langle y, x \rangle \in R\}$. Furthermore, for any $a \in E$, $aR = \{x : \langle a, x \rangle \in R\}$ and $Ra = \{x : \langle x, a \rangle \in R\}$. The relation R^{-1} is the converse of R (that is $R^{-1} = \{\langle x, y \rangle : \langle y, x \rangle \in R\}$) and the relation R^S is the maximal symmetric relation included in R, that is $R^S = R \cap R^{-1}$. A type $\langle 2 : 1 \rangle$ or type $\langle 2 : \langle 1 \rangle \rangle$ function F is convertible iff $F(R) = F(R^{-1})$. Relation I is defined as $I = \{\langle x, x \rangle : x \in E\}$. The relation R^t is the transitive closure of the relation R, that is the smallest transitive relation in which R is included.

Basic type $\langle 1 \rangle$ quantifiers are functions from sets (sub-sets of E) to truth-values. In this case they are denotations of subject NPs. However, NPs can also occur in oblique positions and in this case their denotations do not take sets (denotations of verb phrases) as arguments but rather denotations of intransitive verb phrases, that is relations, as arguments. To account for this eventuality it has been proposed to extend the domain of application of basic type $\langle 1 \rangle$ quantifiers so that they apply to n-ary relations and act as arity reducers, that is have as output an (n–1)-ary relation. Since we are basically interested in binary relations, the domain of application of basic type $\langle 1 \rangle$ quantifiers will be extended by adding to their domain the set of binary relations. In this case the quantifier Q can act as a"subject" quantifier or a "direct object" quantifier giving rise to the *nominative case extension* Q_{nom} and *accusative case extension* Q_{acc} respectively. They are defined as follows (Keenan, 1987; Keenan and Westerståhl, 1997):

D1: For each type $\langle 1 \rangle$ quantifier Q, $Q_{nom}(R) = \{a : Q(Ra) = 1\}$.

D2: For each type $\langle 1 \rangle$ quantifier Q, $Q_{acc}(R) = \{a : Q(aR) = 1\}$.

From now on $Q_{nom}(R)$ will be noted $Q(R)$. Nominative and accusative extensions can thus be considered as functions from binary relations to sets. By type $\langle 1 \rangle$ quantifiers I will mean basic type $\langle 1 \rangle$ quantifiers as well as their nominative and accusative extensions.

Given that type $\langle 1 \rangle$ quantifiers and their arguments form Boolean algebras, every quantifier Q has its Boolean complement, denoted by $\neg Q$, and its post-complement $Q\neg$, defined as follows: $Q\neg = \{P : P \subseteq E \wedge P' \in Q\}$ (where P' is the Boolean complement of P). The dual Q^d of the quantifier Q is, by definition, $Q^d = \neg(Q\neg) = (\neg Q)\neg$. A quantifier Q is self-dual iff $Q = Q^d$. These definitions work also for extended type $\langle 1 \rangle$ quantifiers. It easy to see for instance that $\neg(Q_{acc}) = (\neg Q)_{acc}$ and $(Q^d)_{acc} = (Q_{acc})^d$. A type $\langle 1 \rangle$ quantifier Q is *positive* iff $Q(\emptyset) = 0$.

A special class of type $\langle 1 \rangle$ quantifiers is formed by *individuals*, that is ultrafilters generated by an element of E. Thus I_a is an individual (generated by $a \in E$) iff $I_a = \{X : a \in X\}$. Ultrafilters are special (principal) filters. A (principal) filter generated by the set $A \subseteq E$ is the following quantifier: $Ft(A) = \{X : X \subseteq E \wedge A \subseteq X\}$. Thus ultrafilters are principal filters generated by singletons.

One property that we will use is the property of *living on*. The basic type $\langle 1 \rangle$ quantifier lives on the set A (where $A \subseteq E$) iff for all $X \subseteq E$, $Q(X) = Q(X \cap A)$. If E is finite then there is always the smallest set on which a quantifier Q lives: it is the meet of all sets on which Q lives. The fact that A is the smallest set on which the quantifier Q lives will be noted $Li(Q, A)$. If $A \in Q$ then A is called the witness set of Q: $A = wt(Q)$. The quantifier Q is called *plural*, noted $Q \in PL$, iff $\exists_{a,b \in E}$ such that $Q \subseteq I_a \cap I_b$.

Functions from pairs of sets to truth-values or binary relations between sets are type $\langle 1, 1 \rangle$ quantifiers. In NLs they are denoted by (unary) nominal determiners, that is expressions which take one CN as argument and give a NP as output. Denotations of nominal determiners obey various constraints. Recall first the constraint of conservativity for type $\langle 1, 1 \rangle$ quantifiers. A well-known definition of conservativity is given in D5:

D3: $F \in CONS$ iff for any property X, Y one has $F(X, Y) = F(X, X \cap Y)$

Definition D3 can be generalised so that it applies to type $\langle 1, 2 : \tau \rangle$ functions (cf. Zuber 2010a):

D4: A function F of type $\langle 1, 2 : \tau \rangle$ is conservative iff $F(X, R) = F(X, (E \times X) \cap R)$

Observe that the above definition does not depend on the type τ of the result of the application of the function. So obviously it can be used with higher order functions. Type $\langle 2 : 1 \rangle$ functions can also be (predicate or argument) invariant and invariance is a property depending on the type of the output of the function. Thus (see Keenan and Westerståhl, 1997):

D5: A type $\langle 2 : 1 \rangle$ function F is predicate invariant iff $a \in F(R) \equiv a \in F(S)$ whenever $aR = aS$.

For instance the function $SELF$ is predicate invariant. The following definitions are generalisations of predicate invariance applying to type $\langle 2 : \langle 1 \rangle \rangle$ and type $\langle 1, 2 : \langle 1 \rangle \rangle$ functions:

D6: A type $\langle 2 : \langle 1 \rangle \rangle$ function F satisfies **HPI** (higher order predicate invariance) iff for any positive type $\langle 1 \rangle$ quantifier Q, any $A \subseteq E$, any binary relations R, S, if $A = Wt(Q)$ and $Ft(A)R = Ft(A)S$ then $Q \in F(R)$ iff $Q \in F(S)$.
D7: A type $\langle 1, 2 : \langle 1 \rangle \rangle$ function F satisfies **D1HPI** (higher order predicate invariance for unary determiners) iff for any positive type $\langle 1 \rangle$ quantifier Q, any $A \subseteq E$, any binary relations R and S, if $A = Wt(Q_1)$ and $Ft(A)R \cap X = Ft(A)S \cap X$ then $Q \in F(X, R)$ iff $Q \in F(X, S)$.

3 Reciprocals and reflexives

In this section I briefly present simple syntactic, or categorial, similarities and, possibly, differences, between reflexives and reciprocals, both simple and syntactically complex.

We will consider sentences of the form given in (1):

(1) NP TVP GNP

In this schema, GNP is a generalised noun phrase. GNPs are linguistic objects that can play the role of syntactic arguments of transitive verb phrases (TVPs). So "ordinary" NPs or DPs (determiner phrases) are GNPs. However there are *genuine* GNPs which differ from "ordinary" NPs in that they cannot play the role of all verbal arguments; in particular they cannot occur in subject position. This is the case of anaphoric expressions.

The GNPs related to reflexives and reciprocals are *anaphoric noun phrases* (ANPs). Roughly, their ("referential") meaning depends on the meaning of another expression in the sentence, the so-called *antecedent of the anaphor*, by which it is bound. In the simplest case the antecedent is the subject NP. Thus a more specific form of sentences that we will consider of the form given in (2) instantiated in (3) and (4):

(2) NP TVP ANP.
(3) Most students washed themselves.
(4) Leo and Lea hate each other.

Thus the GNPs we consider are ANPs. In the above examples we have syntactically simple ANPs. Such ANPs can occur as syntactic parts of complex GNPs; in particular they can be parts of Boolean compounds and can be modified by categorially polyvalent modifiers such as *only, also, even, at least, let alone*, etc. :

(5a) Leo and Lea admire themselves and most teachers.
(5b) Leo and Lea admire each other, themselves and two teachers.
(6) Two monks hug each other only.

A special class of complex ANPs is formed by the application of *anaphoric determiners* (ADets), to CNs. Again, this can be done both with reflexive determiners and with reciprocal ones. Many languages have possessive anaphoric determiners. This is the case with Slavic languages which have the possessive "determiner-pronoun" $SVOJ$ (meaning, roughly 'ones own') which can be considered as ADet with reflexive meaning (cf. Zuber, 2011). Similarly, marking the simple reciprocal *each other* in English by the possessive marker results in a ADet with reciprocal meaning. This possibility is indicated in the following examples:

(7) Leo and Lea admire their own books.
(8) Leo and Lea admire each other's books.

Thus *their own* in (7) is a ADet with a reflexive meaning and *each other's* in (8) is an ADet with reciprocal meaning.

More interestingly it is possible to use an ordinary determiner (or its "part") and the simple ANPs *himself/herself/themselves* to form a ADet with reflexive meaning and to use an ordinary determiner and the simple ANPs *each other* to form an ADet with reciprocal meaning. Thus, roughly speaking (Zuber, 2010a), if *D* is an ordinary one place determiner, denoting monotone increasing function, then *D..., including himself* or *D...in addition to themselves* are ADets with the reflexive meaning. If *D* is a determiner denoting monotone decreasing functions then *D, not even himself* is an ADet as well. The following sentences contain various complex ADets with reflexive meaning:

(9) Two students admire most teachers in addition to themselves and Picasso
(10) Leo and Lea washed some vegetarians including at least themselves.
(11) Leo and Lea admires no philosophers, not even themselves or Socrates.

Quite similar procedure can be applied, though probably somewhat less productively, to (syntactically) simple and complex reciprocals in order to obtain ADets with reciprocal meaning. The following examples illustrate this possibility:

(12) Two students shaved most students including each other.
(13) Leo and Lea admire most logicians in addition to each other.
(14) Leo and Lea admire no philosopher, let alone each other.

As the following examples show simple and complex reflexives and reciprocals can occur also in other than direct object positions. The following example show that reflexives and reciprocals can be arguments of a verb taking three arguments:

(15) Leo protected himself/himself and Lea from Al.
(16) Leo and Lea protected every students from themselves.
(17) Most philosophers protect themselves from themselves.
(18) Most philosophers protect themselves and the president from themselves.
(19) Two monks protect themselves from the guru and themselves.
(20) Five philosophers protected each other from themselves.
(21) Leo and Lea/every student protected each other from Al.
(22) Leo and Lea protected every philosopher from each other.

This shows that reflexives can occur twice in a sentence in two different argumental positions of the verb. This is not the case with reciprocals:

?(23) Leo and Lea prevented each other from each other
?(24) Leo and Lea gave each other each other's book.

The above sentences are not acceptable, or at least not interpretable.

The difference pointed out by the above examples is related to the difference in the categorial status of reflexives on the one hand and reciprocals on the other. Thus it is usually assumed that ANPs with reflexive meaning are "argument" reducers: when applied to a di-transitive verb phrase they give a transitive verb phrase, and when applied to a transitive verb phrase they give just a VP.

The situation with reciprocals is different. Recall that ANPs are GNPs. GNPs apply to TVPs and give VPs as result. So what is the category of such VPs. Ignoring directionality, the subject NPs in the constructions we are interested in are of the category $S/(S/NP)$. This means that, in order to avoid type mismatch, verb phrases must be raised and have the category $S/(S/(S/NP))$. Then their denotational type is $\langle\langle\langle e,t\rangle t\rangle t\rangle$. Consequently, sentences of the form (1) are true iff the quantifier denoted by the NP is an element of the set denoted by $TVP\ GNP$. Thus ANPs with reciprocal meaning denote type $\langle 2 : \langle 1\rangle\rangle$ functions. This categorial difference is related to the following semantic difference. Consider the following examples:

(25a) Leo and Lea washed themselves
(25b) Bill and Sue washed themselves.

(26) Four persons, Leo, Lea, Bill and Sue washed themselves.
(27a) Leo and Lea hug each other.
(27b) Bill and Sue hug each other.
(28) Four persons, Leo, Lea, Bill and Sue hug each other.

Clearly (25a) in conjunction with (25b) entails (26) whereas (27a) in conjunction with (27b) does not entail (28). This means that the quantifiers denoted by the subject NPs in (27a) and (27b) do not apply to the predicate denoted by the complex VPs in these sentences and that the GNPs like *each other* denote type $\langle 2 : \langle 1 \rangle \rangle$ functions.

There are of course genuine type $\langle \langle \langle e, t \rangle t \rangle t \rangle$ (or type $\langle 2 : \langle 1 \rangle \rangle$ in our notation) functions, that is such that they are not lifts of simple type $\langle 2 : 1 \rangle$ functions.

4 Higher order anaphors

We have seen that higher order anaphors denote type $\langle 2 : \langle 1 \rangle \rangle$ functions. Any type $\langle 2 : 1 \rangle$ function whose output is denoted by a VP can be lifted to the type $\langle 2 : \langle 1 \rangle \rangle$ function. This is in particular the case with the acusative and nominative extensions of a type $\langle 1 \rangle$ quantifier. For instance the accusative extension of a type $\langle 1 \rangle$ quantifier can be lifted to type $\langle 2 : \langle 1 \rangle \rangle$ function in the way indicated in (29). Such functions will be called *accusative lifts*. More generally iff F is a type $\langle 2 : 1 \rangle$ function, its lift F^L, a type $\langle 2 : \langle 1 \rangle \rangle$ function, is defined in (30):

(29) $Q^L_{acc}(R) = \{Z : Z(Q_{acc}(R)) = 1\}$.
(30) $F^L(R) = \{Z : Z(F(R)) = 1\}$

The variable Z above runs over the set of type $\langle 1 \rangle$ quantifiers.

As we have seen, simple reflexives are interpreted by the function $SELF$. This function is of type $\langle 2 : 1 \rangle$, that is a function which takes binary relations as argument and gives a set as result. Complex reflexives are interpreted by corresponding Boolean combination of $SELF$ with (lifted) denotations of NPs being a part Boolean compounds or, in the case of modification by categorially polyvalent particles, by modifications of $SELF$. Obviously, they are also of type $\langle 2 : 1 \rangle$. These functions satisfy predicate invariance defined in D5. The function $SELF$, but not the functions denoted by complex reflexives, also satisfies the left predicate invariance:

D 8: A type $\langle 2 : 1 \rangle$ function F is left predicate invariant iff for any $a \in E$ and any binary relations R, S, if $Ra = Sa$ then $a \in F(R)$ iff $a \in F(S)$ where $Ra = \{x : \langle x, a \rangle \in R\}$.

Accusative extensions of type $\langle 1 \rangle$ quantifiers, which can also be considered as type $\langle 2 : 1 \rangle$ functions, satisfy a stronger condition than predicate invariance. They satisfy so-called *accusative extension* condition AE (Keenan and Westerståhl, 1997):

D 9: A type $\langle 2 : 1 \rangle$ function F satisfies AC iff for any $a, b \in E$ and any binary relations R, S, if $aR = bS$ then $a \in F(R)$ iff $b \in F(S)$.

It is important (Keenan, 2007) that functions denoted by reflexive expressions, simple and complex, do not satisfy AC and thus they are different from accusative extensions of type $\langle 1 \rangle$ quantifiers denoted by "ordinary" NPs in the object position. . In that sense, reflexive expressions are also genuine GNPs.

The corresponding higher order extension condition is defined in D10:

D10: A type $\langle 2 : \langle 1 \rangle \rangle$ function F satisfies **HEC** (higher order extension condition) iff for any positive type $\langle 1 \rangle$ quantifiers Q_1 and Q_2, any $A, B \subseteq E$, any binary relations R, S, if $A = Wt(Q_1)$ and $B = Wt(Q_2)$, and $Ft(A)R = Ft(B)S$ then $Q_1 \in F(R)$ iff $Q_2 \in F(S)$.

Functions which are accusative lifts satisfy **HEC**. We will see that functions denoted by higher order anaphors do not satisfy **HEC** because functions satisfying **HEC** have the following obvious property:

Proposition 1: Let F be a type $\langle 2 : \langle 1 \rangle \rangle$ function which satisfies **HEC** and let $R = E \times C$, for $C \subseteq E$ arbitrary. Then for any $X \subseteq E$ either $Ft(X) \in F(R)$ or for any X, $Ft(X) \notin F(R)$.

In order to present various properties of functions denoted by higher order anaphors I will discuss only some such functions and not define all functions which constructions discussed in the previous section denote. Some other functions are discussed in Zuber (2012).

Consider first the function given in (31):

(31) $RFL\text{-}RECIP(R) = \{Q : \exists_{A \subseteq E} A = Wt(Q) \wedge Q(Dom(A \times A) \cap (R \cap R^{-1})) = 1\}$

Informally, this function can be considered as the denotation of an anaphor like *each other or oneself or themselves*. In other words it does not make *a priori* a distinction between "purely" reflexive and "purely" reciprocal interpretation, as apparently it happens in many languages. Observe in particular that individuals can be in the output of this function. Furthermore, the meet of two individuals can be in the output of this function even if they are in the relation R with themselves only.

The following function excludes the "reflexive part" and interprets purely reciprocal anaphors (in their strong logical reading):

(32) $SEA(R) = \{Q : A = Wt(Q) \wedge |A| \geq 2 \wedge Q(Dom((A \times A) \cap (R \cap R^{-1}) \cap I')) = 1\}$, where I' is the complement of the identity relation I.

Consider now example (33), where, clearly, a Boolean composition of two higher order functions is involved, one of which is an accusative lift:

(33) Leo and Lea admire each other and most teachers.

We want to give a function interpreting the complex anaphor *each other and most teachers*. Obviously this function has to entail the function SEA above and be completed by the part corresponding to *most teachers*. It is given in (34):

(34) $SEA_Q(R) = \{Z : Z \in SEA \wedge Z \in Q^L_{acc}\}$

The above functions are based on the relation R^S. Sentences in (35) have somewhat illogical interpretation. Functions corresponding to these interpretations are given in (36):

(35a) Five students followed each other.
(35b) All pupils followed each other and two teachers.
(36a) $ILEA(R) = \{Z : \exists_{A \subseteq E}(Li(Z, A) \wedge A \times A \cap I' \subseteq R^t\}$

(36b) $ILEA_{Qconj}(R) = ILEA(R) \cap Q^L_{acc}(R)$

Let us see now some constraints on the above functions. First we have:

Proposition 2: Functions $RFL\text{-}RECIP$, SEA and SEA_Q satisfy **HPI**.

Proof We prove only that $RFL\text{-}RECIP$ satisfies **HPI**. Suppose that $A = Wt(Q)$ and that $Q \in REF\text{-}RECIP(R)$. We have to show that if for some binary relation S (i) holds (i): $\forall_{x \in A}(xR = xS)$ then $Q \in RFL\text{-}RECIP(S)$. Given the definition of $RFL\text{-}RECIP$ this happens when $Q(Dom((A \times A) \cap (S \cap S^{-1}) = 1$. But if (i) holds then $(A \times A) \cap (R \cap R^{-1}) = (A \times A) \cap (S \cap S^{-1})$. Hence $Q \in RFL\text{-}RECIP(S)$.

It is easy to prove, using proposition 1, that:

Proposition 3: Functions $RFL\text{-}RECIP$, SEA and SEA_Q do not satisfy **HAI**.

Proof: We prove only that the function $RFL\text{-}RECIP$ does not satisfy **HAI**. Given its definition in (31) we can see that for $C \subseteq E$ arbitrary , for any C_1 such that $C \subseteq C_1$ we have $Ft(C_1) \notin RFL\text{-}RECIP(E \times C)$ and for any $C_2 \subseteq C$ we have $Ft(C_2) \in RFL\text{-}RECIP(E \times C)$. Hence, given proposition 1, $RFL\text{-}RECIP$ does not satisfy **HPI**.

Here are some other properties:

Proposition 4: Let $F \in \{RFL\text{-}RECIP, SEA, ILEA\}$ and $R = S^{-1}$. Then $F(R) = F(S)$

Proposition 4 has an interesting consequence: since $R = (R^{-1})^{-1}$, it follows from Proposition 2 that functions $RFL\text{-}RECIP$, SEA and $ILEA$ are convertible.

The above properties do not hold for complex higher order functions that is functions denoted by syntactically complex reciprocals. For higher order functions based on the relation R^S the following proposition holds:

Proposition 5: Let $F \in \{RFL\text{-}RECIP, SEA, SEA_Q\}$, $R = S^{-1}$ and

$Dom(R) = Dom(S)$. Then $F(R) = F(S)$.

To illustrate Proposition 5 consider the following examples:

(37a) Five students followed each other.
(37b) Five students preceded each other.

If we consider that the relation expressed by *follow* is the converse of the relation expressed by *precede* that (37a) and (37b) are equivalent.

Observe that the property of functions expressed in Proposition 6 does not depend on the type of the output of the function. It is easy to see, for instance that many reflexives functions denoted by reflexives have a similar property. More precisely we have:

Proposition 6: Let $F \in \{SELF, SELF \otimes Q_{acc}\}$, where $\otimes$ is a Boolean connective, $R = S^{-1}$ and $Dom(R) = Dom(S)$. Then $F(R) = F(S)$.

Thus Propositions 5 and 6 express, informally, properties of functions sensitive to some aspects of their arguments only. Conservativity, as defined in D4 is such a property. Definition of conservativity given in D4 naturally applies to functions denoted by anaphoric determiners. The conservativity of anaphoric determiners giving rise to reflexives is discussed in Zuber (2010b). We are not directly interested here in the semantics of anaphoric determiners but it would be easy to show that the anaphoric determiner *Every...except each other* as it occurs in (38) denotes a conservative function:

(38) Two students washed every student except each other.

To conclude let us see some other properties of functions denoted by anaphors. These functions are "sensitive" to some aspects of their arguments, that is to some properties of the binary relations to which they apply. Consider the following definition:

D11: A type $\langle 2 : \tau \rangle$ function F is *symmetry sensitive*, $F \in SYMS$, iff $F(R) = F(S)$ whenever $R \cap R^{-1} = S \cap S^{-1}$.

Functions $SELF$, $RFL\text{-}RECIP$ and SEA are symmetry sensitive. Functions denoted by complex anaphors (reflexive or reciprocal) do not have this property. They have the following property:

D12: A type $\langle 2 : \tau \rangle$ function F is *symmetry and range sensitive*, $F \in SYMRS$ iff $F(R) = F(S)$ whenever $R \cap R^{-1} = S \cap S^{-1}$ and $Rg(R) = Rg(S)$.

Note that $SYMS \subseteq SYMRS$. Thus not only functions denoted by complex anaphors but also those denoted by simple anaphors are symmetry and range sensitive. This is what all anaphors have in common. In order to distinguish anaphors with purely reflexive meaning from those with purely reciprocal meaning the following definitions can be used:

D13: A type $\langle 2 : \tau \rangle$ function F is *symmetry only sensitive*, $F \in SYMOS$, iff $F(R) = F(S)$ whenever $R \cap R^{-1} \cap I' = S \cap S^{-1} \cap I'$ and $Rg(R) = Rg(S)$.
D14: A type $\langle 2 : \tau \rangle$ function F is *reflexivity and range sensitive*, $F \in REFLRS$, iff $F(R) = F(S)$ whenever $R \cap I = S \cap S \cap I$ and $Rg(R) = Rg(S)$.

For instance *only each other* denotes a symmetry only sensitive function and *himself* or *himself and most students* denote reflexivity and range sensitive functions.

Observe that $SYMOS \subseteq SYMRS$ and $REFLS \subseteq SYMRS$. Similarly $SYMS \subseteq SYNRS$. Thus purely reflexive anaphors denote functions which are not symmetry only sensitive and purely reciprocal anaphors denote functions which are not reflexivity sensitive but both classes are symmetry and range sensitive.

5 Conclusive remarks

It has been shown that it is preferable to treat simple and complex reciprocal expressions, belonging to the class of higher order anaphors, as denoting type $\langle 2 : \langle 1 \rangle \rangle$ functions (that is functions having relations as arguments and sets of type $\langle 1 \rangle$ quantifiers as result) and not as denoting type $\langle 1, 2 \rangle$ quantifiers, as usually proposed. The main reason for this treatment is the fact that the basic reciprocal expression *each other* can combine not only with NPs (which denote (extensions of) type $\langle 1 \rangle$

quantifiers) but also with expressions which denote functions which are not quantifiers (or their extensions). In that respect the reciprocals are similar to reflexives since functions interpreting reflexives (like function $SELF$, its modifications and its Boolean compounds) are neither quantifiers not extensions of a type $\langle 1 \rangle$ quantifier.

It is well-known (Keenan 2007; Zuber 2010b) that the existence of anaphors in NLs shows that the expressive power of natural languages would be less than it is if the only noun phrases we needed were those interpretable as subjects of main clause intransitive verbs. The reason is that anaphors like *himself, herself* must be interpreted by functions from relations to sets which lie outside the class of generalised quantifiers as classically defined. In this paper some preliminary results are presented to show that the existence of higher order anaphors even further extends the expressive power of NLs.

The move to consider that higher order anaphors denote genuine type $\langle 2 : \langle 1 \rangle \rangle$ functions allows us to understand the "non-Boolean" behaviour of the conjunction *and* in their context. Observe, for instance, that (39a) in conjunction with (39b) does not entail (40):

(39a) Leo and Lea hug each other.
(39b) Bill and Sue hug each other.
(40) Four people hug each other.

Functions denoted by higher order anaphors satisfy higher order invariance: they are predicate invariant in a generalised sense. They are different from quantifiers denoted by NPs on the direct object position because they do not satisfy the higher order accusative extension which accusative lifts satisfy. In that respect they similar to functions denoted by simple anaphors (reflexives) which are predicate invariant and do not satisfy the accusative extension condition.

Various conservativity-like properties of functions denoted by reciprocals have been also exhibited. Thus it has been indicated that both types of anaphoric determiners, those giving rise to reflexives and those giving rise to reciprocals, denote conservative functions. Moreover, it has been formally expressed how both types of functions are "sensitive'" only to some aspects of binary relations which are their arguments.

References

Sigrid Beck. 2000. Exceptions in Relational Plurals, *in* Brendan Jackson, and Tanya Matthews (eds), *SALT X*, Cornell University, 1-16

Seth Cable. forthcoming. Reflexives, Reciprocals and Contrast, forthcoming in *Journal of Semantics*

Mary Dalrymple, *et al.* 1998. Reciprocal expressions and the concept of reciprocity, *Linguistics and Philosophy* 21(2):159-210

Jakub Dotlačil. forthcoming. Reciprocals Distribute over Information States, forthcoming in *Journal of Semantics*

Edward L. Keenan. 1987. Semantic Case Theory, *in* Groenendijk, J. and Stokhof, M. (eds.) *Proc. of the Sixth Amsterdam Colloquium*

Edward L. Keenan. 2007. On the denotations of anaphors. *Research on Language and Computation* 5(1):5-17

Edward L. Keenan and Dag Westerståhl. 1997. Generalized Quantifiers in Linguistics and Logic, *in* Johan van Benthem and Alice ter Meulen (eds). *Handbook of logic and language*, Elsevier, Amsterdam, 837-893

Alda Mari. forthcoming. *Each other*, Asymmetry and Reasonable Futures, forthcoming in *Journal of Semantics*

Peters, S. and Dag Westerståhl. 2006. *Quantifiers in Language and Logic*, Oxford U.P.

Sivan Sabato, and Yoad Winter. 2012. Relational domains and the interpretation of reciprocals. *Linguistics and Philosophy* 35(3):191-241

Richard Zuber, 2010a. Generalising Conservativity, in Anuj Dawar, and Ruiz de Queiroz. (eds). *WoLLIC 2010*, LNAI 6188, Springer Verlag, 247-258

Richard Zuber. 2010b. Semantic Constraints on Anaphoric Determiners, *Research on Language and Computation* 8(4): 255-271

Richard Zuber. 2011. Semantics of Slavic anaphoric possessive determiners, *in* Ed Cormany, *et ali.* (eds). *Proceedings of SALT 19*, e-Language, 464-477

Richard Zuber. 2012. Reciprocals as higher order functions, in *Proceedings of the Ninth International Workshop of Logic and Engineering of Natural Language Semantics 9 (LENLS 9)*, 118-129

Richard Zuber. 2013. Some Higher Order Functions on Binary Relations, *in* Glyn Morrill, and Mark-Jan Nederhof (eds). *Formal Grammar 2012/2013*, LNCS 8036, Springer-Verlag, 277-291

ChinGram: A TRALE Implementation of an HPSG Fragment of Mandarin Chinese

Stefan Müller
Freie Universität Berlin
Stefan.Mueller@fu-berlin.de

Janna Lipenkova
Freie Universität Berlin
Janna.Lipenkova@fu-berlin.de

Abstract

In this paper, we present our effort in the development of a HPSG grammar for Chinese. We present the basic notions of the HPSG framework, review existing theoretical analyses and implementations of Chinese grammar fragments in HPSG and present a range of deep linguistic analyses that are part of our own implementation.

1 Introduction

This paper presents a grammar fragment of Chinese which is built in the framework of HPSG (Pollard and Sag 1994) and implemented in the grammar development system Trale (Meurers et al. 2002; Penn 2004). The grammar is one of the grammars that are developed in the CoreGram project (Müller 2013a). Apart from the Chinese grammar, which will be documented in Müller and Lipenkova (In Preparation), there are smaller fragments of several languages and larger fragments of German, Persian, Danish, and Maltese (see Müller (2013b) for details on size). These grammars share a common core und hence crosslinguistic generalizations are captured. We see the advantages of the HPSG framework for a formal analysis of Chinese as follows:

- HPSG provides a range of powerful formal tools for the description of linguistic expressions which are embedded into the logical framework of Typed Feature Structure Logic (Carpenter 1992) and allow a seamless implementation in logical programming paradigms.
- HPSG makes restricted use of *a-priori* theory-internal statements about the empiricial properties of linguistic signs. Since Chinese phenomena often cannot be explained using the terminology and assumptions of the Western linguistic tradition, HPSG provides us with a 'neutral' framework for the formalization of language-specific phenomena based on which more general principles can be derived.
- In contrast to most formal theories, HPSG is not a syntax-driven framework. That is, there is no central syntactic component from which a Phonological Form and a Logical Form is derived. Instead, the different levels of linguistic representation – phonology, syntax, semantics, pragmatics – have equal weight. This is especially beneficial for Chinese, which has a poor morphological system and exhibits a high degree of surface ambiguity. The use of a powerful semantic-pragmatic component with fine-grained definitions of semantic types and selectional restrictions and preferences thus helps disambiguation.

In the following, we first introduce the basic feature architecture and formal tools of the grammar formalism. Then, we review existing work in HPSG and grammar development for Chinese. Finally, we describe the theoretical and empirical basis of our research and provide a synopsis of the covered phenomena; the main analytical choices

* The work reported in this paper was supported by the grant ChinGram MU 2822/5-1 by the Deutsche Forschungsgemeinschaft.

** The following abbreviations are used:

- HPSG sign features: HD: head; SS: synsem; IND: index
- Tree arc symbols: Arg: argument daughter; Spr: specifier daughter; H: head daughter; NH: non-head daughter; Adj: adjunct daughter
- Glosses: CL: classifier; ATTR: attributive particle *de*; LOC: localizer particle

are illustrated using a subset of example phenomena.

2 Framework and implementation

This part provides a brief overview of the main principles and components of HPSG; for more detailed expositions, the reader is referred to the standard makeup described in Pollard and Sag (1994), Sag (1997), and Müller (2008b). The semantics follows Minimal Recursion Semantics as described in Copestake et al. (2005).

2.1 HPSG

The main characteristics of the HPSG framework are as follows:

- *Feature-based*: the universal format of representation are descriptions of typed feature structures (Carpenter 1992).
- *Model-theoretic*: generalizations on linguistic objects are formulated as declarative constraints; there are no transformations.
- *Lexicalist*: a great part of linguistic information, especially information about syntactic combination, is stored in the lexicon.
- *Monostratal*: multiple levels of linguistic representation (phonology, syntax and morphology, semantics, pragmatics and information structure) are modelled in parallel; no formal priority is given to the structural levels.

Formally, an HPSG grammar consists of two parts: a signature and a theory, the theory is subdevided into a lexicon and a grammar:

- *Signature*: ontology that contains types and their feature specifications; the signature is structured as an inheritance hierarchy allowing for multiple inheritance.
- *Lexicon* (constraints on linguistic signs of type *root*, *stem*, or *word*):
  - Lexical entries
  - Lexical rules, specifying systematic relationships holding between classes of lexical items (cf. Meurers 1999a and Meurers 2001, *i.a.*, for studies of the formal properties of lexical rules)
- *Grammar* (constraints on linguistic objects of type *phrase*):
  - Small set of broad-range principles holding of large subtypes of *phrase*, e. g. Head Feature Principle, Valence Principle, Semantics Principle for *headed-phrases*
  - Immediate dominance schemata, specifying the constituency of phrases
  - Linear precedence rules, ruling out impossible constituent orders

A linguistic sign is modelled with feature structures built according to a standardized architecture. The feature structures are sets of feature-value pairs; the value of a feature is either atomic or in itself a feature structure description. The types of values acceptable for a feature are specified in the *signature*, which is organized as a multiple inheritance hierarchy. The following figure shows the gist of the feature architecture of a linguistic sign:

(1)
$$\begin{bmatrix} \textit{sign} & \\ \text{PHON} & \textit{list(phon-symbol)} \\ \text{SYNSEM} & \begin{bmatrix} \text{LOC} & \begin{bmatrix} \text{CAT} & \begin{bmatrix} \text{HEAD} & \textit{head} \\ \text{SPR} & \textit{list(synsem)} \\ \text{COMPS} & \textit{list(arg)} \end{bmatrix} \\ \text{CONT} & \begin{bmatrix} \text{INDEX} & \textit{index} \end{bmatrix} \end{bmatrix} \\ \text{NONLOC} & \textit{nonloc} \end{bmatrix} \\ \text{RELATIONS} & \textit{list(rels)} \\ \text{C-CONT} & \textit{c-cont} \end{bmatrix}$$

At the highest level, features whose values can be constrained by selecting heads are collected under the SYNSEM attribute. SYNSEM is divided into local and nonlocal features, nonlocal features carrying information about items that participate in long-distance dependencies. The local feature bundle specifies a range of syntactic and semantic properties of the sign; CAT specifies the part-of-speech specific HEAD features which are propagated by a lexical head to the mother node. It also contains the valence features SPR and COMPS, which contain the specifier and the complements the sign must combine with in order to grow into a well-formed phrase. The value of SPR is a list of SYNSEM objects, whereas the value of COMPS is a list of objects of the type *argument*. This type specifies the SYNSEM value of the valent and tracks its realization with the boolean feature REALIZED:

(2) $\begin{bmatrix} \textit{argument} \\ \text{ARGUMENT } \textit{synsem} \\ \text{REALIZED } \textit{bool} \end{bmatrix}$

At the level of the lexical head, all valents start out with a negative REALIZED specification. Once the valent has been realized, its REALIZED feature switches to positive. The complex representation of valents is adopted for COMPS in place of the cancellation approach to valence as it is assumed in the traditional makeup of the framework: under the cancellation view, a valent are represented by a SYNSEM object which disappears from the valence list once the respective element has been realized. However, there are structures which require the SYNSEM value of realized dependents to be accessible at the mother node (Przepiórkowski 1999; Meurers 1999b; Müller 2008a; Bender 2008). In Chinese, we use this extended valence specification for specific types of serial verb constructions, as described in Section 6.4.[1]

The CONT(ENT) attribute specifies semantic features, the main information being an index variable which identifies a referential or situational argument.

Finally, besides SYNSEM, the three top-level features PHON, RELATIONS and C-CONT contain the phonological form, the semantic relations contributed by the elements composing the sign and the semantic contribution of the mother node. By placing these features outside of SYNSEM, we ensure that their values cannot be specified by selecting heads, which enhances a more constrained theory of selection.

Syntactic composition is mainly determined by the following two principles which are assumed to hold for most languages:

- Head Feature Principle (Pollard and Sag 1994, p. 34): the HEAD value of any headed phrase is structure-shared with the HEAD value of the head daughter.
- Valence Principle: in a headed phrase, for each valence feature F, the F value of the mother is determined as follows:
  - If the valence list of F consists of *synsem* objects, its value corresponds to the head daughter's F value minus the SYNSEM values of its sisters.
  - If the valence list of F consists of *argument* objects, its value corresponds to the head daughter's F value, whereby the valents that are realized as sisters get a positive REALIZED value.

Semantically, the relations list of the mother node is the concatenation of the relations of the daughters. Further, the index of the mother is identified with the index of the head daughter, adjunction structures being an exception because the index of the mother is projected from the adjunct daughter.

2.2 The implementation environment

There are two systems which are used for grammar engineering with HPSG: Trale (Meurers et al. 2002; Penn 2004; Müller 2007) and LKB (Copestake 2002). The implementation presented in this paper uses the Trale system. Trale is a Prolog-based grammar development environment that supports both parsing and generation. It comes with the user interface Grale which allows to display different kinds of linguistic descriptions (parse trees, lexical entries, lexical rules, types, macros etc.).

Additionally to the implementation of descriptions formulated using the tools provided by the framework, macros can be defined in order to make the grammar more readable. Just as the types in the signature, macros are generalizations over linguistic objects that can be organized in an inheritance hierarchy; additionally, macros allow for parametrization.

A Trale grammar can be distributed between an arbitrary number of files, different files containing sets or subsets of linguistic generalizations of a certain type. Thus, file sharing by multiple grammars is straightforward, which eases multilingual grammar development since constraints shared by multiple languages can be organized into separate files (Omitted 2013).

3 Previous work

On the one hand, since the 90's, several studies have provided theoretical HPSG analyses of specific phenomena of Chinese. Formal treatments have been proposed for the NP (Gao 1993; Xue and McFetridge 1995; Ng 1999), serial verb constructions (Lipenkova 2009; Müller and Lipenkova 2009) and the well-known *bǎ*-construction (?Lipenkova 2011). Besides, two

[1] For the sake of readability, we will use the cancellation notation for structures that do not require this additional information about the relization status of valents.

dissertations, namely Gang (1997) and Gao (2000), provide overall sketches of HPSG grammars for Chinese.

On the other hand, there are two ongoing efforts in grammar development for Chinese, presented in Wang et al. (2009), Yu et al. (2010), and Zhang et al. (2011, 2012).

Wang et al. (2009) and Yu et al. (2010) adopt a data-driven approach with the aim of developing a HPSG parser for Chinese. Starting out with a small set of assumptions about the grammar (sign structure, grammatical principles and schemata), they manually convert a Chinese treebank into an HPSG treebank; the resulting treebank is used for the extraction of a large-scale lexicon of Chinese.

Zhang et al. (2011) and Zhang et al. (2012) use the HPSG framework to combine grammar engineering and treebank compilation. Besides basic clause structures, the grammar covers the structure of NPs and locative phrases, topic constructions, coverbs, resultative verb compounds and simple *bǎ*- and *bèi*-constructions.

Both projects, though being oriented towards a large-scale data-driven grammar implementation, attempt to stay close to the original version of the framework and minimize the use of language-specific postulates. Our grammar aims to complement these efforts and refine some of the analyses by grounding them on findings from recent descriptive and theoretical research.

4 Theoretical and empirical grounding

Our implementation aims at a theoretically adequate analysis of Chinese which is based on research in theoretical linguistics, but can also be adapted for use in NLP applications.

In the last half-century, Chinese linguistics has been driven by three lines of research:

- The descriptive tradition (Chao 1968; Li and Thompson 1981; Zhū 1982, *i. a.*), mainly followed by native linguists, focusses on the description of semantics, pragmatics and discourse structure. Structural considerations often limit themselves to observations about surface order, whereas syntactic relations are treated in a rather permissive, loosely defined fashion.

- The cognitive line of research, starting with a series of papers by James H.-Y. Tai (Tai 1989, 1992, 1993, *i. a.*), seems to be a natural continuation of the descriptive tradition. Concepts of cognitive linguistics often do not impose strict structural constraints and provide a flexibility which allows for rather intuitive explanations of linguistic phenomena.

- The generative line of research, starting with Huang (1982) and continued in Li (1990), Huang (1992), Sybesma (1999) and Huang et al. (2009), *i. a.*, makes heavy use of theory-internal assumptions adopted from generative grammar. One of the drawbacks of this approach for Chinese is that it sometimes uses data for which empirical support is difficult to find.

In our work, we rely to a great part on descriptive research in order to improve the adequacy of the data and the compliance with intuitions of native linguists about aspects of meaning and usage of linguistic structures. Besides, two corpora, the *Lancaster Corpus of Mandarin Chinese* and the *Modern Chinese Corpus* hosted by Beijing University, are used to backup our empirical claims. Analyses in the generative and cognitive traditions are carefully considered against empirical evidence from these sources. In the following exposition, we often use simplified structures for purposes of illustration in order to ease understanding by non-Chinese speakers.

5 The coverage of the grammar

Our grammar contains a syntactic component which specifies linear order and constituency, a lexicon with about 900 lexical items and a number of lexical rules, as well as a set of macros which are used as 'abbreviations' for recurring descriptions of linguistic objects to ease the work of the grammar writer. The grammar is tested against a testsuite of sentences representing different constituent and clause structures of Chinese. Currently, we are testing the grammar against a larger corpus of real-usage examples of the covered phenomena and extending the lexicon and the grammar as new items and structures arise. The phenomena that can be analyzed at present are:

- NP structure:
  - Internal structure, combination with determiners, numerals and classifiers

- Prenominal modification: adjectival and possessive modifiers, relative clauses with subject, object and adjunct extraction

- Relative clauses
- Morphological variation: compounding, reduplication, affixation
- Basic clause structures and valence alternations: transitive, intransitive and ditransitive frames; *bǎ*- and *bèi*-construction; serial verb constructions; topic structures; unmarked passives; existential constructions
- Syntactic marking: nominal and verbal *de*-adjunction; verbal *de*-complementation
- Mood and aspect marking
- Modal verbs
- Locative and temporal adjuncts; linear orders of adjuncts
- Resultative and directional constructions

6 Example analyses

This section briefly describes some analyses adopted in the grammar. After describing the set of immediate schemata that we use for Chinese, we consider localizers and locative phrases, existential constructions with locative inversion, aspect marking and serial verb constructions. It should be kept in mind that HPSG works with recursive feature structures which can grow into very detailed and voluminous representations; in the following, we only provide partial descriptions, focussing mainly on the valence and category features as well as features that guide semantic composition. For the sake of readability, we often do not provide full feature path specifications; this has no impact on the theoretical analysis since the omitted feature paths can always be reconstructed using the feature specifications in the signature.

6.1 Set of immediate dominance schemata

We assume binary branching and use immediate dominance (ID) schemata for the combination of heads with complements, specifiers and adjuncts. Adjuncts and complements can combine with heads via two instances of the respective schemata which allow to differentiate between head-initial and non-head-initial phrases; two boolean head features responsible for word order – INITIAL for heads in head-argument structures and PREMODIFIER for modifiers in head-adjunct structures – determine which structure applies in a given phrase instance. Since specifiers always precede their head, only one schema is required for specifier-head combination. Complements and specifiers are selected by their heads, whereas adjuncts select their head. Additionally to these schemata which are common for analyses of different languages, we assume a language-specific ID schema for serial verb constructions. This additional assumption can be justified by the fact that serial verbs occur in languages of limited geographic areas which independently exhibit common structural characteristics (Seuren 1990).

6.2 Localizer phrases and locative PP adjuncts

'Localizers' are particles that specify the position of a figure relative to its ground. In most languages, this semantic relation is expressed by locative prepositions. Chinese has only one generic preposition for signaling the stative position of an entity relative to another entity, namely *zài*; this preposition basically indicates the proximity of two entities without providing more information about the nature of the locative relation. Further specification is required in most cases; in general, only proper names referring to geographic locations (names of cities, countries etc.) can combine with *zài* without additional lexical material that provides further information about the position:

(3) a. Tā zài Běijīng gōngzuò.
he in Beijing work
'He is working in Beijing.'

b. Tā zài wū-*(lǐ) gōngzuò.
he in room-inside.LOC work
'He is working in the room.'

Chinese thus has a small set of postnominal particles (*lǐ* ('inside'), *xià* ('under'), *pángbiān* ('at the side') etc.) which have to be used for further specification of the relative position of the figure.

We analyze localizers as heads selecting for NPs; their semantic index is of sort *locative-rel*. Figure 4 shows the combination of the localizer and the noun for the phrase *wū-lǐ* ('in the room') as used in (3b).

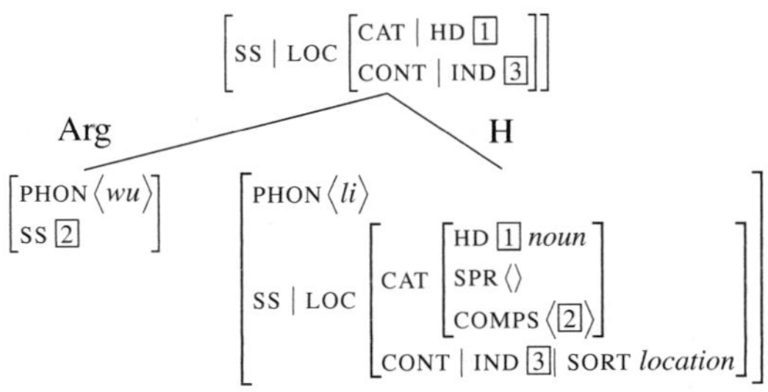

Figure 1: Structure of *wū-lǐ* ('in the room')

The resulting structure can be used in two contexts: on the one hand, they can be used as prepositional complements in locative adjuncts, as illustrated in (3b). On the other hand, they can act as subjects in presentational or existential constructions. Since these positions are prototypical NP positions, we refer to structures composed of an NP and a localizer particle as 'locative NPs'. In the following, we consider the latter usage; locative subjects will be analyzed in Section 6.5.

In locative adjuncts, locative NPs are selected by the generic locative preposition *zài* which signals the static proximity between figure and ground. The semantic combination is regulated by the following constraint in the lexical entry of *zài*:

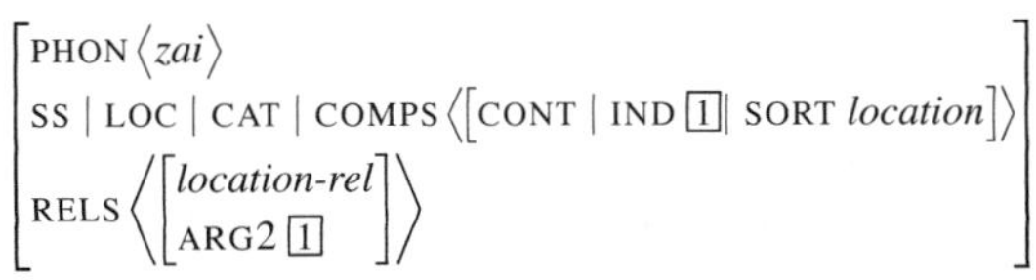

The direct combination of *zài* with names of geographical locations (3a) is ensured by specifying the indices of these names for the sort *location*.

The position of locative adjuncts is fixed to the position between subject and verb:

(4) a. Tā zài wū-lǐ kànjiàn le guǐ.
he in room-LOC see ASP ghost
'He saw a ghost in the room.'

b. * Zài wū-lǐ tā kànjiàn le guǐ.
in room-LOC he see ASP ghost
'He saw a ghost in the room.'

c. * Tā kànjiàn le guǐ zài wū-lǐ.
he see ASP ghost in room-LOC
'He saw a ghost in the room.'

In order to constrain the possible surface positions of adjunts, they are specified for the boolean head feature PRE-MODIFIER; if the value is positive, the adjunct has to precede the head. The locative preposition *zài*, along with other prepositions heading adjunct PPs, has a positive PRE-MODIFIER value and modifies a VP, that is a verbal projection with a single element in the SPR list and an empty COMPS list.

6.3 Locative inversion

Locative inversion is used to indicate the presence or existence of some entity at a location; the NP denoting the location appears in the specifier position, whereas the entity whose existence is asserted instantiates the complement slot of the existential verb:

(5) Běijīng yǒu hěn duō chē.
Beijing have very many car
'There are many cars in Beijing.'

The sentence-initial position can be occupied either by the name of a geographical location or by a locative NP; locative PPs are not possible in that position:

(6) (*Zài) Běijīng / jiē-shàng yǒu hěn duō chē.
in Beijing / street-on.LOC have very many car
'There are many cars in Beijing.'

Thus, the SPR slot of the verb in an existential construction is constrained to an NP that specifies a location (SORT *location*) by virtue of being the name of a geographical location or containing a localizer particle:

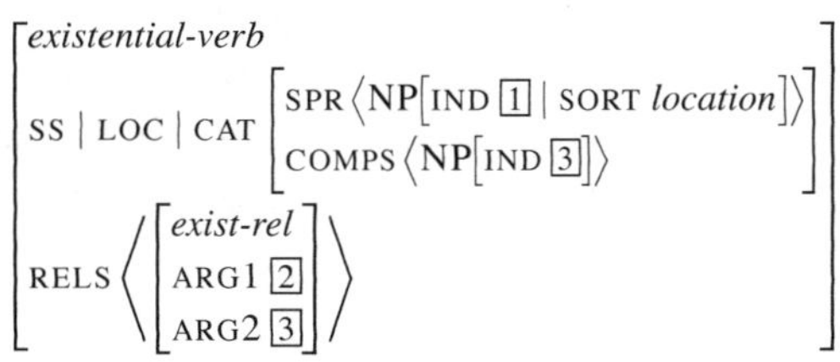

Whereas the verb *yǒu* does not additionally constrain the semantics of its complement, other existential verbs may allow only agentive or non-agentive complements (e. g. *zuò* ('to sit'), *táng* ('to lie') for agentive complements; *guā* ('to hang') for non-agentive complements). These verbs fall into different subclasses of *existential-verb*, the semantic constraints being formulated via selectional restrictions on the index of the complement NP.

6.4 Aspect marking

Chinese has three postverbal aspect markers, as illustrated in the following example:

(7) Tā kàn le / zhe / guo shū.
he read PFV / PROG / EXP book
'He read / is reading / once read the book.'

These markers mark the perfective, durative and experiential aspect, respectively. Naturally, they differ in the range of semantic classes of verbs with which they combine. Their syntactic distribution is identical: they immediately follow the verb. Additional surface material between verb and aspect marker is unacceptable.

In our grammar, aspect marking is analyzed by lexical rules. The rules take a verb as input and output a verb followed by an aspect marker. The relations list of the output verb is the result of appending the aspectual relation contributed by the aspect marker to the relations list of the input verb:

$$\begin{bmatrix} \text{PHON } \boxed{1} \\ \text{SS} \mid \text{LOC} \begin{bmatrix}\text{CAT} \mid \text{HEAD } \textit{verb} \\ \text{CONT} \mid \text{IND } \boxed{3}\end{bmatrix} \\ \text{RELS } \boxed{2}\end{bmatrix} \rightarrow \begin{bmatrix}\text{PHON } \boxed{1} \oplus \langle \textit{le} \rangle \\ \text{RELS } \left\langle \begin{bmatrix}\textit{perfective-rel} \\ \text{ARG } \boxed{3}\end{bmatrix}\right\rangle \oplus \boxed{2}\end{bmatrix}$$

Figure 2: Lexical rule for aspect marking

The lexical rule description specifies only output features which differ from the input. For instance, phonological material is added. The PHON value of the output lexical item is the concatenation of the PHON value of the input and the phonological material associated with the aspect marker. The RELS list starts with an additional *aspect-relation* which takes as argument the event index of the verb. In the example above, the aspectual relation is *perfective-rel*. Further lexical rules are posited for the durative and experiential aspect markers.

6.5 Serial verb constructions

In the basic form, the serial verb construction (SVC) resembles unmarked coordination: two VPs are juxtaposed without overt marking of the relation between them:

(8) Zhāngsān qù chéngshì zhōngxīn mǎi yīfu.
Zhangsan go city center buy clothes
'Zhangsan goes to the city center and buys clothes.'

Depending on the ways in which the two described events can be related by virtue of our world knowledge, different semantic relations can be established between the two VPs. Thus, in (8), the relation would most probably be interpreted as one of *purpose*: Zhangsan goes to the city *in order to* buy clothes. Other possible relations are *causative*, *manner-or-instrument* and *consecutive*. As can be seen in (8), the structure of the SVC may completely underspecify the relation between the two events.

SVCs occur in languages of delimited geographic areas which also share other important structural properties (Seuren 1990). The cross-linguistic occurrence of SVCs justifies the assumption of an additional ID schema, illustrated in Figure 3. The SVC is an instance of a non-headed structure which combines two non-head daughters. The first non-head daughter is a saturated VP; this can be followed from the specification of its COMPS list as a list of spirits.[2] The mother node has a non-empty C-CONT feature which specifies the semantic relation between the two events. Specifically, the RELS feature inside of C-CONT accommodates a relation of the type *svc-relation*, which has the subtypes *causative*, *purpose*, *manner-or-instrument* and *consecutive*.

As described in Gang (1997) and Müller and Lipenkova (2009), the semantic relation can be overtly indicated by perfective or durative aspect marking on one of the VPs. For example, marking of the first VP with the durative aspect marker *zhe* enforces a *manner-or-instrument* reading:

(9) Zhāngsān chàng zhe gē tiàowǔ.
Zhangsan sing DUR.ASP song dance
'Zhangsan sings a song while dancing.'

[2]A spirit is a valent that has already been realized, specified as follows:

(i) $\begin{bmatrix}\textit{argument} \\ \text{ARG } \textit{synsem} \\ \text{REALIZED } +\end{bmatrix}$

(cf. Section 2 on the treatment of valence).

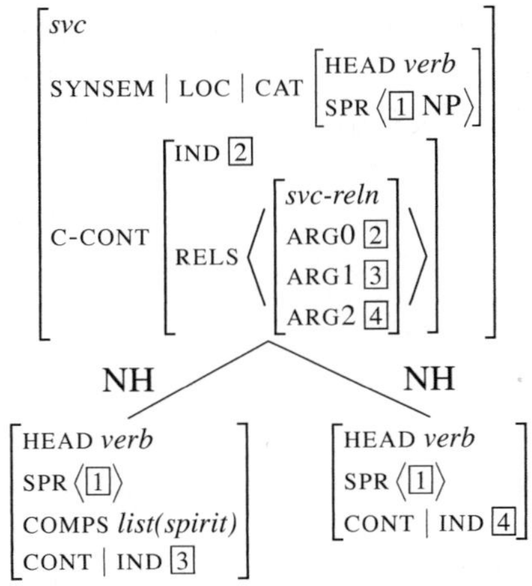

Figure 3: Immediate dominance schema for SVCs

$$\textit{shared-object-svc} \rightarrow \left[\text{NH-DTRS}\left\langle \left[\text{COMPS}\left\langle\begin{bmatrix}\text{ARGUMENT } \boxed{1}\\ \text{REALIZED } +\end{bmatrix}\right\rangle \oplus \textit{list}\right], \left[\text{COMPS}\left\langle\begin{bmatrix}\text{ARGUMENT } \boxed{1}\\ \text{REALIZED -}\end{bmatrix}\right\rangle \oplus \textit{list}\right]\right\rangle\right]$$

Figure 4: Valence specification in SVCs with shared objects

This is captured by complex antecedent constraints which relate aspectual relations of the daughters to the relation in the C-CONT feature of the mother. Thus, the following constraint applies for (9):

(10) $$\begin{bmatrix}\textit{svc}\\ \text{NH-DTRS}\left\langle\left[\text{RELS}\left\langle\textit{durative}\right\rangle\oplus\textit{list}\right]\right\rangle\end{bmatrix} \rightarrow \left[\text{C-CONT} \mid \text{RELS}\left\langle\textit{manner-or-instrument}\right\rangle\right]$$

A special structural subtype of the SVC is the SVC with a shared object (*shared-obj-svc*): if the objects of the first and the second verb refer to the same referent, the object in the second VP is left unrealized:

(11) Zhāngsān zhǒng cài mài.
Zhangsan plant vegetables sell
'Zhangsan plants vegetables and sells them.'

In this case, the reading is always a purpose reading:

(12) $$\textit{shared-object-svc} \rightarrow \left[\text{C-CONT} \mid \text{RELS}\left\langle\textit{purpose}\right\rangle\right]$$

In order to establish coreference between the objects in the two VPs and to prevent the realization of the object in the second VP, we make use of the REALIZED feature. Thus, the SYNSEM values of the object valent are identical for both VPs. The valent is realized in the first VP and left unrealized in the second VP (Fig. 4).

For a detailed analysis and formalization of SVCs, the reader is referred to Müller and Lipenkova (2009).

7 Conclusion

In this paper, we have presented our HPSG implementation of a Chinese grammar fragment; after laying out the basic assumptions and concepts of the framework, we have illustrated the use of the formal means provided by the framework for a range of phenomena of Chinese; specifically, we have considered localizers and locative phrases, locative inersion, aspect marking and serial verb constructions. The presented grammar is implemented in the Trale system and is tested against a testsuite which contains both positive and negative examples. Future work includes the extension of the theoretical coverage of the grammar and the systematic use of corpora for the construction of a broader empirical test environment.

References

Bender, Emily M. 2008. Radical Non-Configurationality without Shuffle Operators: An Analysis of Wambaya. In Stefan Müller (ed.), *Proceedings of the 15th International Conference on HPSG, NICT, Keihanna, Japan*, pages 6–24, Stanford, CA: CSLI Publications.

Carpenter, Bob. 1992. *The Logic of Typed Feature Structures*. Tracts in Theoretical Computer Science, Cambridge: Cambridge University Press.

Chao, Yuen Ren. 1968. *A Grammar of Spoken Chinese*. Berkeley: California University.

Copestake, Ann. 2002. *Implementing Typed Feature Structure Grammars*. Stanford: CSLI Publications.

Copestake, Ann, Flickinger, Daniel P., Pollard, Carl J. and Sag, Ivan A. 2005. Minimal Recursion Semantics: an Introduction. *Research on Language and Computation* 4(3), 281 – 332.

Ding, Picus Sizhi. 2000. A computational study of the *ba* resultative construction: parsing Mandarin *ba*-sentences in HPSG. In *Proceedings of PACLIC 14*, Tokyo, Japan.

Gang, Liu. 1997. *Eine unifikations-basierte Grammatik für das moderne Chinesisch – dargestellt in der HPSG*. Ph.D.thesis, University Constance, SFB 471, FG Sprachwissenschaft, Universität Konstanz, Germany.

Gao, Qian. 1993. Chinese NP Structure. In Andreas Kathol and Carl J. Pollard (eds.), *Papers in Syntax*, OSU Working Papers in Linguistics, No. 42, pages 88–116, Ohio State University: Department of Linguistics.

Gao, Qian. 2000. *Argument Structure, HPSG and Chinese Grammar*. Ph.D.thesis, Ohio State University.

Huang, C.-T. James. 1992. Complex predicates in control. In Richard K. Larson, Sabine Iatridou, Utpal Lahiri and James Higginbotham (eds.), *Control and Grammar*, Dordrecht: Kluwer.

Huang, C.-T. James, Li, Y.-H. Audrey and Li, Yafei. 2009. *The Syntax of Chinese*. Cambridge Syntax Guides, Cambridge, United Kingdom: Cambridge University Press.

Huang, James C.-T. 1982. *Logical relations in Chinese and the theory of grammar*. Ph.D.thesis, MIT, Massachusetts.

Li, Audrey Yen-Hui. 1990. *Order and Constituency in Mandarin Chinese*. Studies in Natural Language and Linguistic Theory, Dordrecht: Kluwer Academic Publishers.

Li, Charles N. and Thompson, Sandra A. 1981. *Mandarin Chinese: A Functional Reference Grammar*. Berkeley: University of California Press.

Lipenkova, Janna. 2009. *Serienverbkonstruktionen im Chinesischen und ihre Analyse im Rahmen von HPSG*. Masters Thesis, Freie Universitt Berlin.

Lipenkova, Janna. 2011. Reanalysis of obligatory modifiers as complements in the Chinese *bǎ*-construction. In Stefan Müller (ed.), *Proceedings of the 18th International HPSG Conference*, Stanford: CSLI Publications.

Meurers, Walt Detmar. 1999a. *Lexical Generalizations in the Syntax of German Non-Finite Constructions*. Ph.D.thesis, Eberhard-Karls-Universität, Tübingen.

Meurers, Walt Detmar. 1999b. Raising Spirits (and Assigning Them Case). *Groninger Arbeiten zur Germanistischen Linguistik (GAGL)* 43, 173 – 226.

Meurers, Walt Detmar. 2001. On Expressing Lexical Generalizations in HPSG. *Nordic Journal of Linguistics* 24(2), 161–217.

Meurers, Walt Detmar, Penn, Gerald and Richter, Frank. 2002. A Web-Based Instructional Platform for Constraint-Based Grammar Formalisms and Parsing. In Dragomir Radev and Chris Brew (eds.), *Effective Tools and Methodologies for Teaching NLP and CL*, pages 18 – 25.

Müller, Stefan. 2007. The Grammix CD Rom. A Software Collection for Developing Typed Feature Structure Grammars. In Tracy Holloway King and Emily M. Bender (eds.), *Grammar Engineering across Frameworks 2007*, Studies in Computational Linguistics ONLINE, Stanford: cslip.

Müller, Stefan. 2008a. Depictive Secondary Predicates in German and English. In Christoph Schroeder, Gerd Hentschel and Winfried Boeder (eds.), *Secondary Predicates in Eastern European Languages and Beyond*, Studia Slavica Oldenburgensia, No. 16, pages 255 – 273, Oldenburg: BIS-Verlag.

Müller, Stefan. 2008b. *Head-Driven Phrase Structure Grammar: Eine Einführung*. Stauffenburg Einführungen, No. 17, Tübingen: Stauffenburg Verlag, second edition.

Müller, Stefan. 2013a. The CoreGram Project: A Brief Overview and Motivation. In Denys Duchier and Yannick Parmentier (eds.), *Proceedings of HMGE 2013, Düsseldorf*.

Müller, Stefan. 2013b. The CoreGram Project: Theoretical Linguistics, Theory Development and Verification. Ms. Freie Universität Berlin.

Müller, Stefan and Lipenkova, Janna. 2009. Serial Verb Constructions in Mandarin Chinese. In Stefan Müller (ed.), *Proceedings of the 16th International Conference on HPSG, University of Göttingen, Germany*, Stanford: CSLI.

Müller, Stefan and Lipenkova, Janna. In Preparation. *Mandarin Chinese in Head-Driven Phrase Structure Grammar*. Empirically Oriented Theoretical Morphology and Syntax, Berlin: Language Science Press.

Ng, Say K. 1999. A Double-specifier Account of Chinese NPs Using Head-driven Phrase Structure Grammar. Master thesis, Department of Linguistics, University of Edinburgh.

Penn, Gerald. 2004. Balancing Clarity and Efficiency in Typed Feature Logic Through Delaying. In *Proceedings of the 42nd Meeting of the Association for Computational Linguistics (ACL'04), Main Volume*, pages 239–246, Barcelona, Spain.

Pollard, Carl J. and Sag, Ivan A. 1994. *Head-Driven Phrase Structure Grammar*. Studies in Contemporary Linguistics, Chicago, London: University of Chicago Press.

Przepiórkowski, Adam. 1999. On Case Assignment and "Adjuncts as Complements". In Gert Webelhuth, Jean-Pierre Koenig and Andreas Kathol (eds.), *Lexical and Constructional Aspects of Linguistic Explanation*, Studies in Constraint-Based Lexicalism, No. 1, pages 231–245, Stanford, CA: CSLI Publications.

Sag, Ivan A. 1997. English Relative Clause Constructions. *Journal of Linguistics* 33(2), 431–484.

Seuren, P. A. M. 1990. Serial Verb Constructions. In Z. A. M. Joseph Brian D. (ed.), *When Verbs Collide: Papers from the Ohio State Mini-Conference on Serial Verbs*, pages 14 – 32, Ohio: Ohio State University.

Sybesma, Rint. 1999. *The Mandarin VP*. Dordrecht: Kluwer.

Tai, James Y.-H. 1989. Towards a Cognition-based Functional Grammar of Chinese. In *Functionalism and Chinese Grammar*, pages 187 – 226, Chinese Language Teachers Association.

Tai, James Y.-H. 1992. Variation in Classifier Systems Across Chinese Dialects: Towards a Cognition-based Semantic Approach. In *Chinese Language and Linguistics 1: Chinese Dialects*, pages 187 – 226, Taiwan: Academia Sinica.

Tai, James Y.-H. 1993. Iconicity: Motivations in Chinese Grammar. In *Principles and Prediction: The Analysis of Natural Language*, pages 153 – 174, Amsterdam: John Benjamins.

Wang, Xiangli, Iwasawa, Shun'ya, Miyao, Yusuke, Matsuzaki, Takuya, Yu, Kun and ichi Tsujii, Jun. 2009. Design of Chinese HPSG Framework for Data-Driven Parsing. In Olivia Kwong (ed.), *Proceedings of PACLIC 2009*, pages 835 – 842, City University of Hong Kong Press.

Xue, Ping and McFetridge, Paul. 1995. DP structure, HPSG, and the Chinese NP. In *Proceedings of the 14th Annual Conference of Canadian Linguistics Association*, Montreal, Canada.

Yu, Kun, Miyao, Yusuke, Wang, Xiangli, Matsuzaki, Takuya and ichi Tsujii, Jun. 2010. Semi-automatically Developing Chinese HPSG Grammar from the Penn Chinese Treebank for Deep Parsing. In Chu-Ren Huang and Dan Jurafsky (eds.), *Proceedings of COLING 2010*, pages 1417 – 1425, Chinese Information Processing Society of China.

Zhang, Yi, Wang, Rui and Chen, Yu. 2011. Engineering a Deep HPSG for Mandarin Chinese. In *Proceedings of 9th WALR / IJCNLP*, ACL.

Zhang, Yi, Wang, Rui and Chen, Yu. 2012. Joint Grammar and Treebank Development for Mandarin Chinese with HPSG. In Nicoletta Calzolari et al. (ed.), *Proceedings of the LREC'12*, Istanbul, Turkey.

Zhū, Déxī. 1982. *Yǔfǎ jiǎngyì [A manual of grammar]*. Beijing: Shangwu yinshuguan.

Vietnamese to Chinese Machine Translation via Chinese Character as Pivot*

Hai Zhao[1,2†] **Tianjiao Yin**[3] **Jingyi Zhang**[1,2]
(1) MOE-Microsoft Key Laboratory of Intelligent Computing and Intelligent System
(2) Department of Computer Science and Engineering, Shanghai Jiao Tong University
#800 Dongchuan Road, Shanghai, China, 200240
(3) Facebook, Inc. 1601 Willow Rd. Menlo Park, CA 94025 USA
zhaohai@cs.sjtu.edu.cn, ytj000@gmail.com
zhangjingyizz@gmail.com

Abstract

Using Chinese characters as an intermediate equivalent unit, we decompose machine translation into two stages, semantic translation and grammar translation. This strategy is tentatively applied to machine translation between Vietnamese and Chinese. During the semantic translation, Vietnamese syllables are one-by-one converted into the corresponding Chinese characters. During the grammar translation, the sequences of Chinese characters in Vietnamese grammar order are modified and rearranged to form grammatical Chinese sentence. Compared to the existing single alignment model, the division of two-stage processing is more targeted for research and evaluation of machine translation. The proposed method is evaluated using the standard BLEU score and a new manual evaluation metric, understanding rate. Only based on a small number of dictionaries, the proposed method gives competitive and even better results compared to existing systems.

1 Introduction

The statistical machine translation (SMT) has been well developed from a basis of data-drive idea since the work of (Brown et al., 1993). However, a large amount of parallel corpora are always necessary to build a standard SMT system for a specific language pair, regardless of the possible useful linkages between these two languages. There is existing work that considered using helpful linguistic heuristics to enhance the current SMT (Chu et al., 2012), though their approaches still follow the standard processing pipeline of SMT. For those resource-poor languages, a pivot language will be used as an expedience (Utiyama and Isahara, 2007; Wu and Wang, 2009).

Figure 1: The phrase *Chinese character culture sphere* written in Chinese characters from different regions.

In this work, we focus on machine translation (MT) for language pairs with few parallel corpora but rich linguistic connections. A case study on Vietnamese and Chinese will be done. To exploit the shared linguistic characteristics between the language pair, the common written form, Chinese character, is adopted as a translation bridge. Being the oldest continuously used writing system in the world, Chinese characters are logograms that are still used to write Chinese (汉字/漢字 in Chinese, hànzì in Chinese pinyin) and Japanese (kanji). Such characters were used but are currently less frequently used in Korean (hanja), and were also used in Vietnamese (chữ Hán). All the countries that were historically under Chinese language and culture are unofficially referred to *Chinese character cultural sphere* or Sinosphere. These two terms are often used interchangeably but have different denotations (Matisoff, 1990). A Chinese character writing example of different regions is in Figure 1.

*This work was partially supported by the National Natural Science Foundation of China (Grant No.60903119, Grant No.61170114, and Grant No.61272248), and the National Basic Research Program of China (Grant No.2009CB320901 and Grant No.2013CB329401).

†corresponding author

Figure 2: Different scripts for Chinese characters.

There are tens of thousands of Chinese characters, though most of them are minor graphic variants only existing in historical texts as Figure 2. Mastering modern Chinese usually requires knowing 2,000-4,000 characters. Though most words in modern Chinese consist of two or more characters, each Chinese character may correspond to a spoken syllable with a distinct meaning. Being meaning-oriented representation units, Chinese characters are naturally suitable to act as a bridge of semantic representation for translation task. This process will be especially promising as we are working on a language like Vietnamese.

Vietnamese (tiếng Việt) is spoken by about eighty million people. Much of Vietnamese vocabulary has been borrowed from Chinese, and it formerly used a modified Chinese writing system, Chữ Nôm, and given vernacular pronunciation. The Vietnamese alphabet (Quốc Ngữ) in use today is a Latin alphabet with additional diacritics for tones, and certain letters.

In this paper, a novel two-stage approach is proposed for Vietnamese to Chinese MT by adopting Chinese characters as the pivot. Vietnamese syllables will first be converted into Chinese characters according to the meaning equivalence. Then Chinese character sequences in Vietnamese grammar order will be modified and reordered into grammatical Chinese. The proposed approach only requires a small number of linguistic resources, such as bilingual dictionaries and monolingual language model, to work effeciently.

2 Related Work

Only recently have researchers begun to be involved in the domain of Vietnamese language processing. Most work on Vietnamese language processing has to still focus on very basic issues such as corpus building, primary processing tasks, etc.

A few studies have been done on Vietnamese related MT, though nearly all MT studies on Vietnamese focus on English as source or target language. As Vietnamese is an under-resourced language, most Vietnamese MT systems adopted rule based methods (Le et al., 2006; Le and Phan, 2009; Le and Phan, 2010).

(Pham et al., 2009) used word-by-word translation incorporated with predefined templates to perform English-Vietnamese translation on weather bulletin texts. The similar strategy was also used in (Hoang et al., 2012) for Vietnamese to Katu language translation on the same domain.

Until very recently, the statistical approach was applied to Vietnamese related MT task. (Nguyen and Shimazu, 2006; Nguyen et al., 2008) used self-defined morphological transformation and syntactic transformation to beforehand solve reordering problem for Vietnamese-English translation. (Thi and Dinh, 2008) introduced a word re-ordering approach that makes use of the syntactic rules extracted from parse tree for English-Vietnamese MT. (Bui et al., 2010) proposed language dependent features to enhance Vietnamese-English SMT. (Nguyen et al., 2012) integrated more knowledge about the topic of the text, part-of-speech and morphology to resolve semantic ambiguity of words during translation. Based on empirical observation, (Nguyen and Dinh, 2012) proposed a group of heuristic patterns to discover the alignment errors. (Bui et al., 2012) proposed a group of rules to split long Vietnamese sentences based on linguistic information to enhance Vietnamese to English MT.

Few studies have been done for MT task between Vietnamese and Chinese as to our best knowledge. For such a low resource language pair, rule based MT systems are too hard to build, and statistical MT systems require too large parallel corpus that is also difficultly acquired. Though Chinese characters have been considered a useful intermediate form for MT, few studies made a full use of them. Instead, most existing approaches focus on the role of Chinese word during translation (Chang et al., 2008; Xu et al., 2008; Dyer et al., 2008; Ma and Way, 2009; Paul et al., 2010; Nguyen et al., 2010). (Chu et al., 2012) exploited shared Chinese characters between Chinese and Japanese to improve the concerned translation performance. The most recent work (Xi et al., 2012)

	Vietnamese	Chinese
Character script	Chữ Nôm	Chinese characters (official now)
Romanized script	Quốc Ngữ (official now)	pinyin

Table 1: Chinese vs. Vietnamese: writing systems

proposed using Chinese character as aligning unit. However, both of the above works are different from ours, in which Chinese characters are used as a pivot for translation task for the first time.

3 Chinese Elements inside Vietnamese

3.1 The Same and The Difference

Most linguists agree that Chinese and Vietnamese belong to two quite different language families. All varieties of modern Chinese are usually categorized as part of the Sino-Tibetan language family. However, opinions are divided on the language family that Vietnamese should belong to, though the most acceptable view is that it is part of the Mon - Khmer branch of the Austroasiatic language family according to the observation that Vietnamese and Khmer share a lot of cognates and basic grammar (Benedict, 1944; Nguyen, 2008).

A writing system comparison between Chinese and Vietnamese is shown in Table 1. An obvious distinction between Vietnamese and Chinese writing is on the role of the Romanized scripts. The Quốc Ngữ is official writing system of Vietnamese today, while pinyin is only an assistant language learning tool for Chinese today.

Both Chinese and Vietnamese, like many languages in East Asia, are analytic (isolating) languages[1]. Neither of them uses morphological marking of case, gender, number or tense. Both languages use word order and function words to convey grammar relationships. As word order or function words are changed, the meaning will be changed accordingly. Moreover, their syntax both conforms to subject-verb-object word order and possesses noun classifier systems.

As each Chinese character in Chinese represents a meaningful unit, a major feature of Vietnamese word-building is that each syllable may be separately used as a meaningful unit. Like Chinese, most Vietnamese words are bi-syllable. Chinese is written without blanks between words and Vietnamese is written with blanks between two syllables instead of words. Thus word segmentation becomes a primary processing for both languages.

Vietnamese is a prop-drop (pronoun-dropping) language, which means that certain classes of pronouns in Vietnamese may be omitted when they are in some sense pragmatically inferable. Chinese also exhibits frequent pro-drop features.

Both Chinese and Vietnamese allow verb serialization. Contrary to subordination in English where one clause is embedded into another, the serial verb construction is a syntactic phenomenon that two verbs are put together in a sequence in which no verb is subordinated to the other.

Different from Chinese on word order, Vietnamese is head-initial, i.e., displaying modified-modifier ordering, but number and noun classifier being before the modified noun. Thus, for example, the *Vietnamese language* in Vietnamese grammar order should not be *Vietnamese language* (Việt Nam tiếng) but *language Vietnamese* (tiếng Việt Nam).

3.2 Sino-Vietnamese

As a result of close ties with China for more than 2,000 years, quite a few of the Vietnamese lexical elements have Chinese roots. The elements in the Vietnamese derived from Chinese is called Sino-Vietnamese (Hán Việt; 漢越), which accounts for about 30-60% of the Vietnamese vocabulary (LUO, 2011). This vocabulary was originally written with Chinese characters, but like all written Vietnamese, is now written with the Quốc Ngữ, the Latin-based Vietnamese alphabet. Sino-Vietnamese words have a status similar to that of Latin-based words in English: they are used more in formal occasion than in everyday life. Most monosyllabic Sina-Vietnamese are used for word-building morphemes, though a few of them may be directly adopted as words as well.

A lot of Sino-Vietnamese words, such as those in Table 2, have the exactly same meaning as modern Chinese. Some Sino-Vietnamese words (Table 3) are written in the same Chinese characters but represent different meaning from their Chinese counterparts. Some Sino-Vietnamese words (Table 4)are entirely invented by the Vietnamese, which can be directly written in Chines characters

[1]A few linguists strictly define that an isolating language as a type of language with a low morpheme-per-word ratio is a closely related concept of the analytic language, but still different from the latter. In this paper, we do not strictly distinguish these two concepts.

Vietnamese words	Chinese characters	Chinese pinyin	meaning
lịch sử	歷史	lì shǐ	history
định nghĩa	定義	dìng yì	definition
phong phú	豐富	fēng fù	fruitful
thời sự	時事	shí shì	current events

Table 2: A list of Sina-Vietnamese words

Vietnamese in Latin	Vietnamese in chữ Hán	Chinese word	Chinese meaning
linh mục	靈牧	牧师	clergyman
lí thuyết	理說	理论	theory
bệnh cảm	病感	感冒	flu
khẩu trang	口裝	口罩	mask

Table 4: A list of Sina-Vietnamese words with similar writing and same meaning

but not used in Chinese or no longer used in modern Chinese. Interestingly, though not exactly the same in writing, there is always one character that is shared by both languages for words in Table 4.

Writing Sino-Vietnamese words with Quốc Ngữ may cause some confusions due to the large amount of homophones in Chinese and Sino-Vietnamese. For example, both '明'(*bright*) and '冥'(*dark*) are read or written as *minh* with Quốc Ngữ, thus only using Chinese character can one distinguish the two contradictory meanings of the word "*minh*".

4 Chinese Characters but not Chu Nom

4.1 Why it is Chinese Characters

A Chinese character is regarded as a unity of form (writing), sound (phonetics) and meaning (semantics). An illustrative example of Chinese character is given in Figure 3, which demonstrates a character with written form '福', sound 'fú'(pinyin) and meaning 'good luck'. However, it is not balanced for the three primary factors of Chinese character. The core functionality of Chinese character is being a meaning unit. In fact, Chinese character is neither a good carrier of pronunciation nor stable at written forms: different Chinese variants

Figure 3: Chinese character is a trinity.

and other languages such as Japanese and Korean usually borrow Chinese Characters semantically rather than phonetically, and the Chinese character scripts also continuously evolved in the past 3,000 years as shown in Figure 2.

Meanwhile, the meaning that Chinese character was initially invented to express seldom changes over time. Chinese characters used in the similar way for different languages also share the same or similar meaning, which is especially obvious for Chinese characters borrowed by Japanese (kanji). For example, although the character '山' in Figure 2, has more than 8 different writing scripts, and may be pronounced as *shan* in Mandarin Chinese, either *yama* or *san* in modern Japanese, it is always referred to the meaning 'mountain' in both languages.

In addition, Chinese character writing system is usually more accurate than alphabetic writing systems on expressive ability. In fact, Chinese, Vietnamese and Korean are the victims of a large amount of homophones in their vocabulary. However, modern Korean and Vietnamese that have adopted alphabetic writing systems are more easily plagued by this problem than Chinese as the latter may respite the difficulty by assigning different Chinese characters to respectively record different meanings of the same pronunciation.

4.2 Why it is not Chu Nom

Chữ Nôm is a system of modified and invented characters modeled loosely on Chinese characters, which, unlike the system of Chinese character (chữ Hán), allows for the expression of purely Vietnamese words to any extent.

The character set for Chữ Nôm is extensive, up to 20,000, arbitrary in composition and inconsistent in pronunciation [2]. The Chữ Nôm characters can be divided into two groups: those borrowed from Chinese and those invented especially for Vietnamese. The characters borrowed from Chinese are used to represent either Chinese loan words or native Vietnamese words. For the former case, the character may have more than one pronunciation. For the latter case, the character may be only used phonetically, regardless of the original standard meaning of it in Chinese. For example, the Chinese character '沒' (méi, means *none*

[2] Online resources on Chữ Nôm can be found at the following links, http://nomfoundation.org/ and http://www.chunom.org/.

Vietnamese Meaning	Vietnamese words	Chinese characters	Chinese pinyin	Chinese meaning
method	phương tiện	方便	fāng biàn	convenience
office building	văn phòng	文房	wén fáng	study room
rich	phong lưu	風流	fēng liú	romantic
full-grown	phương phi	芳菲	fāng fēi	flowers and plants

Table 3: A list of Sina-Vietnamese words with same writing but different meaning

Figure 4: The 20 most frequent Nom characters in which red bold ones are not used in Chinese.

in Chinese) is used to represent the Vietnamese word một (means *one* in Vietnamese).

Figure 4 shows top 20 most frequent Nom characters. As we are finding a pivot written form for Vietnamese to Chinese MT, Chữ Nôm looks like a good candidate. However, three reasons make Chữ Nôm unable to fulfill the task. First, too many characters in Chữ Nôm belong to the Vietnamese-only type, which can be neither recognized by modern Chinese nor naturally mapped to commonly used Chinese characters. Second, Chinese characters that are still popularly used in modern Chinese may be only phonetically borrowed by Chữ Nôm. Third, Chữ Nôm has never been standardized, which may lead to multiple writing choices for the same Vietnamese syllable.

5 The Proposed Approach

Chinese character is a powerful representation as an ideographic writing system, for text written with Chinese characters, even if grammatically incorrect, it is understandable and even readable for people who know Chinese characters but speak different languages of Sinosphere. Vietnamese as an analytical language, its individual syllable has similar ideographic property. Vietnamese is perhaps more suitable to adopt an ideographic writing system like Chinese characters. Therefore, we first attempt to find a proper Chinese character to record each syllable of Vietnamese text in accordance with its contextual meaning. In this way, we will have a Vietnamese text written with Chinese characters. Then, with additional processing, the Chinese character sequences in the Vietnamese grammar are converted into grammatical Chinese sentences. The proposed approach is divided into two stages as the following.

Stage 1: Syllable-to-Character Conversion

To find a matching Chinese character for a Vietnamese syllable, bilingual dictionaries are necessary to provide possible character candidates. However, we still need more heuristics to determine which character should be chosen according to the context in which the Vietnamese syllable is located. As multisyllable Vietnamese word usually has a unique Chinese equivalent, we propose to first perform word segmentation over the Vietnamese sentence and then convert the segmented words into Chinese. Relying on a pre-specified dictionary, the maximum matching algorithm as shown in Algorithm 1 that is traditionally used for Chinese word segmentation will be applied to Vietnamese word segmentation [3].

Two bilingual dictionaries are used for Vietnamese word segmentation and Chinese character conversion.

The first dictionary is a Sino-Vietnamese vocabulary. Sino-Vietnamese vocabulary will play a core role during the conversion. For all known Sino-Vietnamese words, we can simply determine their Chinese character equivalents without ambiguities. Vietnamese and Chinese actually share the same words on the Sino-Vietnamese vocabulary, and the only difference is behind the written forms, either Vietnamese Quốc Ngữ or Chinese characters. In this work, we use all bisyllable Sino-Vietnamese vocabulary from (LUO, 2011), which includes 10,900 Vietnamese-Chinese word pairs. This dictionary will be referred to D_s hereafter.

For the part beyond the Sino-Vietnamese words in Vietnamese text, there is no such a dictio-

[3]This algorithm is more precisely referred to as the forward maximal matching algorithm.

Algorithm 1 Maximal matching algorithm

INPUT1 Dictionary $D = \{w_i|\}$, and $maxlen$ is the maximal word length inside D.
INPUT2 Syllable sequence $c_0c_1..c_{n-1}$
Let i=0
while i<n **do**
  let m=$min(maxlen, n - i)$
  while m>1 **do**
    if $c_ic_{i+1}..c_{i+m-1}$ is a word in D **then**
      $i = i+m$, and set a segmentation mark before c_{i+m}.
      break
    else
      $m = m - 1$
    end if
  end while
  if m==1 **then**
    Set a segmentation mark before c_{i+1}
  end if
  $i = i + m$
end while

nary that meet our requirements, we have to seek help from online resources for a quick but inaccurate solution. We let a crawler collect Vietnamese texts[4] from the Internet and then feed the Google translator[5] with the text, so that we obtain a loose parallel corpus between Vietnamese and Chinese. After each Vietnamese monosyllable and each Chinese character segmented as a word, we may obtain an aligned phrase table by using bidirectional GIZA++ alignment (Och and Ney, 2003). We perform two steps of pruning on the phrase table. First, only those aligned phrases that have the same numbers for both Vietnamese syllables and Chinese characters will be kept. Second, If a Vietnamese phrase is mapped to multiple Chinese phrases, then only the one with the highest aligning probability will be conserved. Regarding both Vietnamese syllables and Chinese characters in the phrase table as words, we finally build the second bilingual dictionary D_g with 6.8 million word pairs.

Given a Vietnamese sentence, we apply the maximal matching algorithm twice to accomplish the word segmentation. When a word is segmented according to the Vietnamese part of bilingual dictionary, it will be automatically converted into Chinese characters according to the corresponding Chinese part of the dictionary. The Sino-Vietnamese dictionary D_s is first adopted. If there are still undetermined parts in the sentence after the first round of segmentation and conversion, then the dictionary D_g will be used.

Stage 2: Restating and Reordering

As Vietnamese uses a different modifier-modified order, which is the most difference from Chinese, its text, even though written in Chinese characters, cannot be fully understood by one who only knows Chinese. Therefore, we introduce this stage of processing to polish the Chinese character sequences in Vietnamese word order. Note that it is entirely a monolingual processing task.

The first difficulty that we should consider is that not all Vietnamese words are the exactly same as their Chinese counterparts. To alleviate this difficulty, we tentatively replace a Vietnamese word written in Chinese character by another related word. A Chinese synonym dictionary[6] with 77,000 items is therefore used to enumerate all these possible related words.

To determine each best related word and reorder the character sequence into Chinese word order, we use language model trained on Chinese text following equation (1).

$$\{w_0^*w_1^*..w_n^*\} = \operatorname*{argmax}_{\forall\omega(w_i)\text{and}\{w_0'w_1'..w_n'\}} \prod_{i=1}^{n}(P(\omega(w_i)'|\omega(w_{i-m+1})'\omega(w_{i-m})'..\omega(w_{i-1})')), \quad (1)$$

where $\omega(w_i)$ represent a related word of w_i and $\{w_0'w_1'..w_n'\}$ is a permutation of $\{w_0w_1..w_n\}$. To prevent from generating too many reordering possibilities, the distance between the original position of each word and its new location is limited to less than 4 words. The above output sequence can be decoded through a Viterbi style algorithm.

6 Experiments

We manually collect 2,046 sentence pairs as test set to evaluate the proposed approach. We report the MT performance using the original BLEU metric (Papineni et al., 2002). A trigram Chinese language model is trained on the text with segmentation that is extracted from the People' Daily[7]

[4]The Vietnamese corpus has 77 M bytes, 0.86 million Vietnamese sentences and 13 million Vietnamese monosyllables.

[5]http:// translate.google.com/?hl=en#vi/zh-CN/

[6]The Word Forest of Synonyms: http://www.ir-lab.org/

[7]It is the most popular newspaper in China.

Systems	Ours/Stage 1	Ours/Stage 1+2	Google
BLEU	14.5	18.6	20.3

Table 5: BLEU scores for the proposed system.

Systems	Ours/Stage 1	Ours/Stage 1+2	Google
/wo ref.	65.4	67.1	62.3
/w ref	62.3	63.6	60.7

Table 6: Understanding rates without any Vietnamese knowledge.

from 1993 to 1997. To segment the Chinese text, the maximal matching segmentation algorithm with Chinese side words of the above two bilingual dictionaries are used.

The results with Google translation comparison are given in Table 5. With limited support linguistic resources, the proposed approach gives a very competitive result as the Google translator does.

Although it goes without saying, actually all the state-of-the-art MT systems are far from the requirement of being serious publishing or any official usages. Most of the current MT outputs are used, tacitly in fact, for a rough understanding of texts written in other languages that readers do not know at all. We will evaluate the results of the proposed approach from this sense. A group of human evaluation experiments are done based on the following scoring rules. For each translated sentence, a human evaluator will determine if the rough meaning of the sentence is understandable, and the sentence will be given score (1) 1.0 if the sentence can be fully understood; (2) 0.5 if the sentence seems understandable but not so certain; (3) 0.0 if the meaning of sentence cannot be captured at all. We define understanding rate for the given test set, $U_r = \frac{\sum_{i=1}^{N} \alpha_i}{N}$, where N is number of sentences in the test set and α_i is the evaluation score given to the i-th sentence.

The first group of results with U_r are given in Table 6. There are two types of results in the table, the first human evaluator gives score without allowing to read the translation reference, while the second is allowed to read the reference to verify and modify his score after he already gives a score.

The second group of results are given on the condition that human evaluators are taught about grammar difference between Vietnamese and Chinese that Vietnamese is a head-initial language. The results are given in Table 7. The second group of human evaluation results are slightly better than the first group. With limited linguistic knowledge, human evaluator can finish the necessary grammar conversion by himself for better understanding on the translated text.

Systems	Ours/Stage 1	Ours/Stage 1+2	Google
/wo ref.	68.5	72.9	69.3
/w ref	66.1	71.6	67.7

Table 7: Understanding rates with limited Vietnamese knowledge.

Systems	Sentences
Source	Du khách Tây Ban Nha thưởng thứ trà tại Trâm Anh quán.
Target	西班牙游客在簪缨馆品茶。
Stage 1	游客 西班牙 赏识 茶 在 簪缨 店 .
Stage 2	西班牙 游客 赏识 茶 在 簪缨 店 .
Google	西班牙游客享受茶在英国的前哨基地。

Table 8: Vietnamese-to-Chinese translation.

Overall, the proposed approach gives satisfactory results on Vietnamese to Chinese translation with quite limited linguistic input. Our system gives competitive results as the existing system in terms of BLEU, and outperforms the latter according to the newly introduced evaluation metric. These comparisons show that though the translation output of our system is not up to its best on word transformation and ordering (that is mostly concerned by the BLEU score, and mostly determined by grammar translation stage.), but it possesses better understandability, which is mostly determined by semantic translation stage.

7 Error Analysis

Rough manual inspection shows that both work stages introduce factors that lead to poor translation. For Stage 1, most errors occur because the target Chinese characters are incorrectly given by the dictionary D_g at the very beginning. For those Vietnamese syllables that have multiple conversion options in writing as Chinese characters, it is surprising that we find few examples on such types of character selection errors. This observation suggests that a direct refine work on D_g may be hopeful to give significant performance improvement. Furthermore, it is also useful to enrich the current Sino-Vietnamese dictionary D_s as up to now it only includes bisyllable words.

For Stage 2, it looks like that word order adjusting does not work well, though one can see a BLEU score increasing after the processing of Stage 2. In fact, U_r scores in Table 6 and 7 demonstrate that word order only has a marginal effect over the understanding (or guessing) the translated sentence. Later, according to word order difference between Chinese and Vietnamese, we may especially adjust the order of Vietnamese words with specific part-of-speech so that the translation results can be further improved.

Table 8 shows an actual translation output by our system. For a detailed English explanation, please refer to the appendix.

8 Semantic Translation vs. Grammar Translation

Using Chinese character as an intermediate form, a two-stage MT approach has been proposed. We loosely refer the first stage as semantic translation, and the second as grammar translation. The semantic translation is called because syllable to character conversion is based on semantic equivalence rather than anything else, such as phonetics or written forms. The grammar translation includes two monolingual subtasks, word restating and reordering, to let the expression more fluent.

Standard SMT integrates semantic and grammar translation into one word/phrase alignment model, which partially make researchers working on MT lose focus. We say that the proposed two-stage MT processing strategy allows translation research more focused. For example, our experiments demonstrate a higher understanding rate but lower BLEU score for the same MT outputs. If we loosely regard that understanding rate measures the semantic aspect of MT performance and BLEU measures the grammar factor, then we now have a chance to see that a poor grammar translation is an obstacle on the way to let MT outputs become really useful on a formal occasion.

9 Other Language Pairs

Now we consider if the proposed approach can be extended to other language pairs. Though it is a two-stage translation, language specific properties are actually concerned only at Stage 1, and Stage 2 may work on any other target language in principle. Thus we may only focus on Stage 1.

A simple maximal matching algorithm with bilingual dictionaries can be adopted to perform semantic translation as Stage 1 because two essential language facts, (1) Vietnamese and Chinese share a very large vocabulary, and (2) They both belong to analytic (isolating) languages, which means that there is nearly a full correspondence between a single word/character/syllable and a single aspect of meaning. Motivated by this observation, it is possible to extend this work to other languages in Sinosphere, such as Korean and Japanese. The following gives reasons why both languages meet the above conditions.

Let us first consider the vocabulary. The exact proportion of Sino-Korean vocabulary is still a matter of debate. (Sohn, 2001) stated that it is between 50 - 60%. For Sino-Japanese, it usually has an estimation of 40-50%.

Both Korean and Japanese belong to agglutinative languages, which seems that the above second condition is not met. However, using Chinese character based writing traditionally or currently, a stable correspondence between meaning and writing for both languages can be generally found [8]. From the writing perspective, both Korean and Japanese are *quite isolating*.

10 Conclusions and Future Work

This paper presents a two-stage conversion method for the MT task between resource-scarce language pairs that both belong to the isolating language type, such as Vietnamese and Chinese, and other languages in Sinosphere that demonstrate observable isolating language characteristics.

Chinese character as the heart of the evolution of languages in Sinosphere is selected as an intermediate equivalent form during translation. In detail, Chinese character sequences subject to source language grammar play a pivot role. Compared to existing translation system, the proposed method, with a small number of linguistic resources, gives competitive or even better results in terms of standard BLEU score or a newly introduced human evaluation metric, understanding rate.

It is worth noting that we have only made a very preliminary attempt with respect to the proposed approach. For example, during semantic translation, in addition to bilingual dictionary, we do

[8]For example, though the meaning *moutain* is pronounced as *yama* or *san* in Japanese, it can be always written as the same Chinese character 山.

not use any other context information to effectively determine the target Chinese characters. During grammar translation, we do not use any language-specific features to improve the target language generation. Exploring all the potentials, it is expected to receive even better results.

References

Paul K. Benedict. 1944. Thai, Kadai and Indonesian: A new alignment in southeastern Asia. *American Anthropologist*, 44(2):576–601.

Peter F. Brown, Vincent J. Della Pietra, Stephen A. Della Pietra, and Robert. L. Mercer. 1993. The mathematics of statistical machine translation: parameter estimation. *Computational Linguistics*, 19(2):263–311.

Thanh Hung Bui, Le Minh Nguyen, and Akira Shimazu. 2010. Using rich linguistic and contextual information for tree-based statistical machine translation. In *2011 International Conference on Asian Language Processing*, pages 189–192, Harbin, China, December.

Thanh Hung Bui, Le Minh Nguyen, and Akira Shimazu. 2012. Sentence splitting for Vietnamese-English machine translation. In *2012 Fourth International Conference on Knowledge and Systems Engineering*, pages 156–160, Danang, Vietnam, August.

Pi-Chuan Chang, Michel Galley, and Christopher D. Manning. 2008. Optimizing Chinese word segmentation for machine translation performance. In *Proceedings of the Third Workshop on Statistical Machine Translation*, pages 224–232, Columbus, Ohio, USA, June.

Chenhui Chu, Toshiaki Nakazawa, Daisuke Kawahara, and Sadao Kurohashi. 2012. Exploiting shared Chinese characters in Chinese word segmentation optimization for Chinese-Japanese machine translation. In *Proceedings of the 16th EAMT Conference*, pages 35–42, Trento, Italy, May.

Christopher Dyer, Smaranda Muresan, and Philip Resnik. 2008. Generalizing word lattice translation. In *Proceedings of the 46th Annual Meeting of the Association for Computational Linguistics: Human Language Technologies*, pages 1012–1020, Columbus, OH, USA.

Thi My Le Hoang, Thi Bong Phan, and Huy Khanh Phan. 2012. Building a machine translation system in a restrict context from Ka-Tu Language into Vietnamese. In *2012 Fourth International Conference on Knowledge and Systems Engineering*, pages 167–172, Danang, Vietnam, August.

Manh Hai Le and Thi Tuoi Phan. 2009. Three algorithms for word-to-phrase machine translation. In *2009 International Conference on Asian Language Processing*, pages 328–331, Singapore, December.

Manh Hai Le and Thi Tuoi Phan. 2010. Lexical gap in English-Vietnamese machine translation: What to do? In *2010 International Conference on Asian Language Processing*, pages 265–269, Harbin, China, December.

Manh Hai Le, Chanh Thanh Nguyen, Chi Hieu Nguyen, and Thi Tuoi Phan. 2006. Dictionaries for English-Vietnamese machine translation. In *The 21st International Conference on the Computer Processing of Oriental Languages*, pages 363–369, Singapore, December.

Wenqing LUO. 2011. *A Study on Bi-syllable Sino-Vietnamese Words in Vietnamese: A Comparison with Chinese (in Vietnamese)*. World Publishing Corporation, Guangzhou, China.

Yanjun Ma and Andy Way. 2009. Bilingually motivated domain-adapted word segmentation for statistical machine translation. In *Proceedings of the 12th Conference of the European Chapter of the Association for Computational Linguistics*, pages 549–557, Athens, Greece, April. Association for Computational Linguistics.

James A. Matisoff. 1990. On megalocomparison. *Language*, 66(1):106–120.

Giang Thanh Nguyen and Dien Dinh. 2012. Improving English-Vietnamese word alignment using translation model. In *2012 IEEE International Conference on Computing and Communication Technologies, Research, Innovation, and Vision for the Future (RVIF)*, Ho Chi Minh City, Vietnam, February.

Thai Phuong Nguyen and Akira Shimazu. 2006. Improving phrase-based statistical machine translation with morphosyntactic transformation. *Machine Translation*, 20:147–166.

Vinh Van Nguyen, Thai Phuong Nguyen, Akira Shimazu, and Minh Le Nguyen. 2008. A reordering model for phrase-based machine translation. In *GoTAL - 6th International Conference on Natural Language Processing*, pages 476–487, Gothenburg, Sweden, August.

ThuyLinh Nguyen, Stephan Vogel, and Noah A. Smith. 2010. Nonparametric word segmentation for machine translation. In *Proceedings of COLING-2010*, pages 815–823, Beijing, China, August.

Quy Nguyen, An Nguyen, and Dien Dinh. 2012. An approach to word sense disambiguation in English-Vietnamese-English statistical machine translation. In *2012 IEEE International Conference on Computing and Communication Technologies, Research, Innovation, and Vision for the Future (RVIF)*, Ho Chi Minh City, Vietnam, February.

Thien Giap Nguyen. 2008. *A Brief History on Vietnamese Study (in Vietnamese)*. Vietnam Education Press, Hanoi, Vietnam.

Franz Josef Och and Hermann Ney. 2003. A systematic comparison of various statistical alignment models. *Computational Linguistics*, 29(1):19–51, March.

Kishore Papineni, Salim Roukos, Todd Ward, and Wei-Jing Zhu. 2002. BLEU: a method for automatic evaluation of machine translation. In *Proceedings of the 40th Annual Meeting on Association for Computational Linguistics*, ACL '02, pages 311–318, Stroudsburg, PA, USA. Association for Computational Linguistics.

Michael Paul, Andrew Finch, and Eiichiro Sumita. 2010. Integration of multiple bilingually-learned segmentation schemes into statistical machine translation. In *Proceedings of the Joint 5th Workshop on Statistical Machine Translation and MetricsMATR*, pages 400–408, Uppsala, Sweden, July. Association for Computational Linguistics.

Son Bao Pham, Giang Binh Tran, Dang Duc Pham, Kien Chi Phung, and Kien Trung Nguyen. 2009. An information extraction approach to English-Vietnamese weather bulletins machine translation. In *2009 First Asian Conference on Intelligent Information and Database Systems*, pages 161–166, Dong hoi, Quang binh, Vietnam, April.

Ho-Min Sohn. 2001. *The Korean Language*. Cambridge University Press, Cambridge, UK.

Hong-Nhung Nguyen Thi and Dien Dinh. 2008. A syntactic-based word re-ordering for English-Vietnamese statistical machine translation system. In *The Tenth Pacific Rim International Conference on Artificial Intelligence (PRICAI-08)*, pages 809–818, Hanoi, Vietnam, December.

Masao Utiyama and Hitoshi Isahara. 2007. A comparison of pivot methods for phrase-based statistical machine translation. In *Proceedings of NAACL HLT 2007*, pages 484–491, Rochester, NY, USA, April.

Hua Wu and Haifeng Wang. 2009. Revisiting pivot language approach for machine translation. In *Proceedings of the 47th Annual Meeting of the ACL and the 4th IJCNLP of the AFNLP*, pages 154–162, Singapore, August.

Ning Xi, Guangchao Tang, Xinyu Dai, Shujian Huang, and Jiajun Chen. 2012. Enhancing statistical machine translation with character alignment. In *Proceedings of the 50th Annual Meeting of the Association for Computational Linguistics*, pages 285–290, Jeju, Republic of Korea, July.

Jia Xu, Jianfeng Gao, Kristina Toutanova, and Hermann Ney. 2008. Bayesian semi-supervised chineseword segmentation for statistical machine translation. In *Proceedings of COLING-2008*, pages 1017–1024, Manchester, UK, August.

APPDENDIX

We now give a detailed English explanation to the translation example output by our system. A word-by-word translation is shown in Table 9. The meaning of source Vietnamese is that '*Spanish tourists enjoy tea at Tram Anh teahouse.*' We analyze two problematic words in our translation. The first word *thưởng thứ* is Sino-Vietnamese, its exact Chinese form is right '赏识'. Unfortunately, these two characters in Chinese as a word means '*appreciate*' instead of '*enjoy*' as its Vietnamese counterpart. Furthermore, Stage 2 also fails to rectify this meaning-drift word due to the limitation of our synonymous dictionary. However, if we only concern about the first character '赏' of the word '赏识', it will be acceptable for Chinese readers, as two basic senses of '赏' are '*enjoy*' and '*award*', though '赏茶' is not a usual expression in Chinese for saying '*enjoy tea*'. The second inexact conversion about '*quán*' comes from building the second bilingual dictionary D_g. As in the aligned phrase table, '*quán* is translated onto '店'(diàn in Chinese pinyin, means '*shop*' or '*building/facilities for business purpose*') with a higher probability than the expected exact one, ' 馆'(guǎn, means *building (group) for specific purpose*). Though the character '店' is not the expected translation, it is rough in line with the original meaning of source phrase and acceptable for most Chinese readers. Generally, most Vietnamese names are supposed to have standard forms written in Chinese characters. Using a pivot language, Vietnamese names are hard to exactly be translated into Chinese. For our example, in addition to the unique mismatched character, the named entity *Trâm Anh quán* has been exactly translated, which can be hardly done by Google translator, as we surmise, using English as a pivot language. In fact, the meaning of the Google translator output is '*Spanish tourists enjoy tea at the British outpost*'.

English	Vietnamese	Chinese	Stage 1
tourist	du khách	游客	√
Spain	Tây Ban Nha	西班牙	√
enjoy	thưởng thứ	赏识	?
tea	trà	茶	√
at	tại	在	√
Tram Anh	Trâm Anh	簪缨	√
house,inn,etc	quán	店	?

Table 9: Vietnamese-to-Chinese translation: word by word conversion.

Overall, by speculating that ' 赏识茶' is a typo of ' 赏茶', a Chinese reader can easily guess the true meaning of the source Vietnamese, '西班牙游客在簪缨馆赏茶(*Spanish tourists enjoy tea at Tram Anh shop*)' from the translation given by our system, '西班牙游客赏识茶在簪缨店(*Spanish tourists appreciate tea at Tram Anh shop*)'.

Transliteration Extraction from Classical Chinese Buddhist Literature Using Conditional Random Fields

Yu-Chun Wang
Department of Computer Science
and Information Engineering,
National Taiwan University, Taiwan
Telecommunication Laboratories,
Chunghwa Telecom, Taiwan
d97023@csie.ntu.edu.tw

Richard Tzong-Han Tsai*
Department of Computer Science
and Information Engineering,
National Central University,
Zhongli City, Taiwan
thtsai@csie.ncu.edu.tw

Abstract

Extracting plausible transliterations from historical literature is a key issues in historical linguistics and other resaech fields. In Chinese historical literature, the characters used to transliterate the same loanword may vary because of different translation eras or different Chinese language preferences among translators. To assist historical linguiatics and digial humanity researchers, this paper propose a transliteration extraction method based on the conditional random field method with the features based on the characteristics of the Chinese characters used in transliterations which are suitable to identify transliteration characters. To evaluate our method, we compiled an evaluation set from the two Buddhist texts, the Samyuktagama and the Lotus Sutra. We also construct a baseline approach with suffix array based extraction method and phonetic similarity measurement. Our method outperforms the baseline approach a lot and the recall of our method achieves 0.9561 and the precision is 0.9444. The results show our method is very effective to extract transliterations in classical Chinese texts.

1 Introduction

Cognates and loanwords play important roles in the research of language origins and cultural interchange. Therefore, extracting plausible cognates or loanwords from historical literature is a key issues in historical linguistics. The adoption of loanwords from other languages is usually through transliteration. In Chinese historical literature, the characters used to transliterate the same loanword may vary because of different translation eras or different Chinese language/dialect preferences among translators. For example, in classical Chinese Buddhist scriptures, the translation process of Buddhist scriptures from Sanskrit to classical Chinese occurred mainly from the 1st century to 10th century. In these works, the same Sanskrit words may transliterate into different Chinese loanword forms. For instance, the surname of the Buddha, Gautama, is transliterated into several different forms such as "瞿曇" (*qü-tan*) or "喬答摩" (*qiao-da-mo*), and the name "Culapanthaka" has several different Chinese transliterations such as "朱利槃特" (*zhu-li-pan-te*) and "周利槃陀伽" (*zhou-li-pan-tuo-qie*). In order to assist researchers in historical linguistics and other digital humanity research fields, an approach to extract transliterations in classical Chinese texts is necessary.

Many transliteration extraction methods require a bilingual parallel corpus or text documents containing two languages. For example, (Sherif and Kondrak, 2007) proposed a method for learning the string distance measurement function from a sentence-aligned English-Arabic parallel corpus to extract transliteration pairs. (Kuo et al., 2007) proposed a transliteration pair extraction method using a phonetic similarity model. Their approach is based on the general rule that when a new English term is transliterated into Chinese (in modern Chinese texts, e.g. newswire), the English source term usually appears alongside the transliteration. To exploit this pattern, they identify all the English terms in a Chinese text and measure the phonetic similarity between those English terms and their surrounding Chinese terms, treating the pairs with the highest similarity as the true transliteration pairs. Despite its high accuracy, this approach cannot be applied to transliteration extraction in classical Chinese literature since the prerequisite (of the source terms alongside the transliteration) does not apply.

Some researchers have tried to extract transliterations from a single language corpus. (Oh and Choi, 2003) proposed a Korean transliteration identification method using a Hidden Markov Model (HMM) (Rabiner, 1989). They transformed the transliteration identification problem into a sequential tagging problem in which each Korean syllable block in a Korean sentence is tagged as either belonging to a transliteration or not. They compiled a human-tagged Korean corpus to train a hidden Markov model with predefined phonetic features to extract transliteration terms from sentences by sequential tagging. (Goldberg and Elhadad, 2008) proposed an unsupervised Hebrew transliteration extraction method. They adopted an English-Hebrew phoneme mapping table to convert the English terms in a named entity lexicon into all the possible Hebrew transliteration forms. The Hebrew transliterations are then used to train a Hebrew transliteration identification model. However, Korean and Hebrew are alphabetical writing system, while Chinese is ideographic. These identification methods heavily depend on the phonetic characteristics of the writing system. Since Chinese characters do not necessarily reflect actual pronunciations, these methods are difficult to apply to the transliteration extraction problem in classical Chinese.

This paper proposes an approach to extract transliterations automatically in classical Chinese texts, especially Buddhist scriptures, with supervised learning models based on the probability of the characters used in transliterations and the anguage model features of Chinese characters.

2 Method

To extract the transliterations from the classical Chinese Buddhist scriptures, we adopt a supervised learning method, the conditional random fields (CRF) model. The features we use in the CRF model are described in the following subsections.

2.1 Probability of each Chinese character in transliterations

According to our observation, in the classical Chinese Buddhist texts, the Chinese characters chosen be used in transliteration show some characteristics. Translators tended to choose the characters that do not affect the comprehension of the sentences. The amount of the Chinese characters is huge, but the possible syllables are limited in Chinese. Therefore, one Chinese character may share the same pronunciation with several other characters. Hence, the translators may try to choose the rarely used characters for transliteration.

From our observation, the probability of each Chinese character used to be transliterated is an important feature to identify transliteration from the classical Buddhist texts. In order to measure the probability of every character used in transliterations, we collect the frequency of all the Chinese characters in the Chinese Buddhist Canon. Furthermore, we apply the suffix array method (Manzini and Ferragina, 2004) to extract the terms with their counts from all the texts of the Chinese Buddhist Canon. Next, the extracted terms are filtered out by the a list of selected transliteration terms from the Buddhist Translation Lexicon and Ding Fubao's Dictionary of Buddhist Studies. The extracted terms in the list are retained and the frequency of each Chinese character can be calculated. Thus, the probability of a given Chinese character c in transliteration can be defined as:

$$Prob(c) = \log \frac{freq_{trans}(c)}{freq_{all}(c)}$$

where $freq_{trans}(c)$ is c's frequency used in transliterations, and $freq_{all}(c)$ is c's frequency appearing in the whole Chinese Buddhist Canon. The logarithm in the formula is designed for CRF discrete feature values.

2.2 Language model of the transliteration

Transliterations may appear many times in one Buddhist sutra. The preceding character and the following character of the transliteration may be different. For example, for the phrase "於憍薩羅國" (*yu-jiao-sa-luo-guo*, in Kosala state), if we want to identify the actual transliteration, "憍薩羅" (*jiao-sa-luo*, Kosala), from the extra characters "於" (*yu*, in) and "國" (*guo*, state), we must first use an effective feature to identify the boundaries of the transliteration.

In order to identify the boundaries of transliterations, we propose a language-model-based feature. A language model assigns a probability to a sequence of m words $P(w_1, w_2, \ldots, w_m)$ by means of a probability distribution. The probability of a sequence of m words can be transformed into a conditional probability:

$$\begin{aligned} P(w_1, w_2, \cdots, w_m) &= P(w_1)P(w_2|w_1) \\ &\quad P(w_3|w_1, w_2) \cdots \\ &\quad P(w_m|w_1, w_2, \cdots, \\ &\quad w_{m-1}) \\ &= \prod_{i=1}^{m} P(w_i|w_1, w_2, \cdots, \\ &\quad w_{i-1}) \end{aligned}$$

In practice, we can assume the probability of a word only depends on its previous word (bi-gram assumption). Therefore, the probability of a sequence can be approximated as:

$$\begin{aligned} P(w_1, w_2, \cdots, w_m) &= \prod_{i=1}^{m} P(w_i|w_1, w_2, \\ &\quad \cdots, w_{i-1}) \\ &\approx \prod_{i=1}^{m} P(w_i|w_{i-1}) \end{aligned}$$

We collect person and location names from the Buddhist Authority Database[1] and the known Buddhist transliteration terms from The Buddhist Translation Lexicon (翻譯名義集)[2] to create a dataset with 4,301 transliterations for our bi-gram language model.

After building the bi-gram language model, we apply it as a feature for the supervised model. Following the previous example, "於憍薩羅國" (*yu-jiao-sa-luo-guo*, in Kosala state), for each character in the sentence, we first compute the probability of the current character and its previous character. For the first character "於" , since there is no previous word, the probability is $P(於)$. For the second character "憍", the probability of the two characters is $P(於憍) = P(於)P(憍|於)$. We then compute the probability of the second and third characters: $P(憍薩) = P(憍)P(薩|憍)$, and so on. If the probability changes sharply from that of the previous bi-gram, the previous bi-gram may be the boundary of the transliteration. Because the character "於" rarely appears in transliterations, $P(於憍)$ is much lower than $P(憍薩)$. We may conclude that the left boundary is between the first two characters "於憍".

2.3 Functional Words

We take the classical Chinese functional words into consideration. These characters have special grammatical functions in classical Chinese; thus, they are seldom used to transliterate foreign names. This is a binary feature which records the character is a functional word or not. The functional words are listed as follows: 之 (*zhi*), 乎 (*hu*), 且 (*qie*), 矣 (*yi*), 邪 (*ye*), 於 (*yu*), 哉 (*zai*), 相 (*xiang*), 遂 (*sui*), 嗟 (*jie*), 與 (*yu*), and 噫 (*yi*).

2.4 Appellation and Quantifier Words

After observing the transliterations appearing in classical Chinese literature, we note that there are some specific patterns of the characters follows the transliteration terms. Most of the characters following the transliteration are appellation or quantifier words, such as 山 (*san*, mountain), 海 (*hai*, sea), 國 (*guo*, state), 洲 (*zhou*, continent). For example, there are some cases like 耆闍崛山 (*qi-du-jui-san*, Vulture mountain), 拘薩羅國 (*jü-sa-luo-guo*, Kosala state), and 贍部洲 (*zhan-bu-zhou*, Jambu continent). Therefore, we collect the Chinese characters that are usually used as appellation or quantifiers following transliterations and then design this feature. This is also a binary feature that records the character is used as an appellation or quantifier word or not.

2.5 CRF Model Training

We adopt the supervised learning models, conditional random field (CRF) (Lafferty et al., 2011), to extract the transliterations in classical Buddhist texts. For CRF model, we formulate the transliteration extraction problem as a sequential tagging problem.

2.5.1 Conditional Random Fields

Conditional random fields (CRFs) are undirected graphical models trained to maximize a conditional probability (Lafferty et al., 2011). A linear-chain CRF with parameters $\Lambda = \lambda_1, \lambda_2, \ldots$ defines a conditional probability for a state sequence $\mathbf{y} = \mathbf{y}_1 \ldots \mathbf{y}_T$, given that an input sequence $\mathbf{x} = \mathbf{x}_1 \ldots \mathbf{x}_T$ is

$$P_\Lambda(\mathbf{y}|\mathbf{x}) = \frac{1}{Z_\mathbf{x}} \exp\left(\sum_{t=1}^{T} \sum_{k} \lambda_k f_k(\mathbf{y}_{t-1}, \mathbf{y}_t, \mathbf{x}, t)\right)$$

where $Z_\mathbf{x}$ is the normalization factor that makes the probability of all state sequences sum to one; $f_k(\mathbf{y}_{t-1}, \mathbf{y}_t, \mathbf{x}, t)$ is often a binary-valued feature function and λ_k is its weight. The feature functions can measure any aspect of a state transition, $\mathbf{y}_{t-1} \rightarrow \mathbf{y}_t$, and the entire observation sequence,

[1] `http://authority.ddbc.edu.tw/`

[2] `http://www.cbeta.org/result/T54/T54n2131.htm`

$\mathbf{x}$, centered at the current time step, t. For example, one feature function might have the value 1 when $\mathbf{y}_{t-1}$ is the state *B*, $\mathbf{y}_t$ is the state *I*, and $\mathbf{x}_t$ is the character "國" (*guo*). Large positive values for λ_k indicate a preference for such an event; large negative values make the event unlikely.

The most probable label sequence for $\mathbf{x}$,

$$\mathbf{y}^* = \arg\max_{y} P_\Lambda(\mathbf{y}|\mathbf{x})$$

can be efficiently determined using the Viterbi algorithm.

2.5.2 Sequential Tagging and Feature Template

The classical Buddhist texts are separated into sentences by the Chinese punctuation. Then, each character in the sentences is taken as a data row for CRF model. We adopt the tagging approach motivated by the Chinese segmentation (Tsai et al., 2006) which treat Chinese segmentation as a tagging problem. The characters in a sentence are tagged in **B** class if it is the first character of a transliteration word or in **I** class if it is in a transliteration word but not the first character. The characters that do not belong to a transliteration words are tagged in **O** class. We adopt the CRF++ open-source toolkit[3]. We train our CRF models with the unigram and bigram features over the input Chinese character sequences. The features are shown as follows.

- Unigram: s_{-2}, s_{-1}, s_0, s_1, s_2
- Bigram: $s_{-1}s_0$, s_0s_1

where current substring is s_0 and s_i is other characters relative to the position of the current character.

3 Evaluation

3.1 Data set

We choose one Buddhist scripture as our data set for evaluation from the Chinese Buddhist Canon maintained by Chinese Buddhist Electronic Text Association (CBETA). The scripture we choose to compile the training and test sets is the Samyuktagama (雜阿含經). The Samyuktagama is one of the most important scriptures in Early Buddhism and contains a lot of transliterations because it detailedly records the speech and the lives of the Buddha and many of his diciples.

[3] `http://crfpp.googlecode.com`

The Samyuktagama is an early Buddhist scripture collected shortly after the Buddha's death. The term agama in Buddhism refers to a collection of discourses, and the name Samyuktagama means "connected discourses." It is among the most important sutras in Early Buddhism. The authorship of the Samyuktagama is traditionally regarded as the most early sutra collected by the Mahakssyapa, the Buddha's disciple, and five hundred Arhats three months after the Buddha's death. An Indian monk, Gunabhadra, translated this sutra into classical Chinese in Liu Song dynasty around 443 C.E. The classical Chinese Samyuktagama has 50 volumes containing about 660,000 characters. Because the amount of Samyuktagama is too tremendous, we take the first 20 volumes as the training set, and the last 10 volumes as the test set.

In addition, we want to evaluate if the supervised learning model trained by one Buddhist scripture can be applied to another Buddhist scrupture translated in different era. Therefore, we choose another scripture, the Lotus Sutra (妙法蓮華經), to create another test set. The Lotus sutra is a famous Mahayana Buddhist scripture probably written down between 100 BC and 100 C.E. The earliest known Sanskrit title for the sutra is the Saddharma Pundarika Sutra, which translates to "the Good Dharma Lotus Flower Sutra." In English, the shortened form Lotus Sutra is common. The Lotus Sutra has also been highly regarded in a number of Asian countries where Mahayana Buddhism has been traditionally practiced, such as China, Japan, and Korea. The Lotus Sutra has several classical Chinese translation versions. The most widely used version is translated by Kumarajiva ("鳩摩羅什" in Chinese) in 406 C.E. It has eight volumes and 28 chapters containing more then 25,000 characters. We select the first 5 chapters as a different test set to evaluate our method.

3.2 Baseline Method

There are a few reseaches focusing on transliteration extraction from classical Chinese literature. However, in order to compare and show the benefits of our method, we construct a baseline system with widely used information extraction methods. Because many previous researches on transliteration extraction are based on phonetic similarity or phoneme mapping approaches, we also use these methods to construct the baseline system. First,

Table 1: Evaluation Results of Tranliteration Extraction

		Precision	Recall	F_1-score
Our Approach	The Samyuktagama test set	0.8810	0.9561	0.9170
	The Lotus Sutra test set	0.9444	0.9474	0.9459
Baseline	The Samyuktagama test set	0.0399	0.7771	0.0759
	The Lotus Sutra test set	0.0146	0.5789	0.2848

the baseline system use the suffix array method to extract all the possible terms for the classical Chinese Buddhsit scriptures. Then, the extracted terms are converted into Pinyin sequences by a modern Chinese pronunication dictionary. We also adopt the collected transliteation list used in section 2.1 and also convert the transliterations into Pyinyin sequences. Next, for each extracted terms, the baseline system measures the Levenshtein distance between the Pinyin sequences of the extracted terms and all the transliterations as the phonetic similairy. If the extracted term has a Levenshtein distance less than threshold (distance ≤ 3 in our baseline) from one of the transliterations we collect, the extracted term will be regarded as a transliteration; otherwise, the term will be dropped.

3.3 Evaluation Metrics

We use two evaluation metrics, recall and precision, to estimate the performance of our system. Recall and precision are widely used measurements in many research fields, sucn as information retrieval and information extraction. (Manning et al., 2008) In the digital humanities research field, a key issue is the coverage of the extraction method. To maximize usefulness to researchers, a method should be able to extract as many potential transliterations from literature as possible. Therefore, in our evaluation, we use recall, defined as follows:

$$Recall = \frac{|\text{Correctly extracted transliterations}|}{|\text{Transliterations in the data set}|}$$

In addition, the correctness of the extracted transliterations are also important. To avoid wasting time on the useless information, a method should be able to extract correct transliterations from literature as possible. Thus, we also use precision, defined as follows:

$$Precision = \frac{|\text{Correctly extracted transliterations}|}{|\text{All extracted transliterations}|}$$

With precision and recall, the F-score measurement is also adopted as a weighted average of the precision and recall. The F_1-score is defineds as follows:

$$F_1\text{-score} = \frac{2 \times recision \times recall}{precision + recall}$$

3.4 Evaluation Results

Table 1 shows the results of our method and the baseline system on different test sets. The gold standards of these two test sets are compiled by human experts who examine all the sentences in the test sets and regconize each transliterations for evaluation. The results show that our method can extract 95.61% transliterations on the Sumyuktagama and 94.74% on the Lotus Sutra. On the precision measurement, our method also achieves pretty good results, which show that most of the terms our method extract are actual transliterations. Our method outperforms the baseline system and the precision of the baseline system is very poor. The baseline system cannot extract most transliterations due to the limit of the suffix array method since the suffix array method only extracts the terms that appear twice or more in the context. Besides, the phonetic similarity is not effective to filter the transliteartions; the problem causes the low precision. These results demonstrate that our method can save a lot of labor-intensive work to examine the transliteration for the historical and humanity researchers.

4 Discussion

4.1 Effectiveness of transliteration extraction

Our method can extract many transliterations from the Samyuktagama such as "迦毘羅衛" (*jia-pi-luo-wei*, *Kapilavastu*, the name of an ancient kingdom where the Buddha was born and grew up), "尼拘律" (*ni-jü-lü*, *Nyagro*, the forest name in Kapilavastu kingdom), and "摩伽陀" (*muo-qie-tuo*, *Magadha*, the name of an ancient Indian kingdom). These transliteration do not appear in the training set, but our method can still identify them. In addition, our method also finds out many transliterations in the Lotus Sutra which are unseen in the Samyuktagama, such as "娑伽羅" (*suo-qie-luo*, *Sagara*, the name of the king of the sea world in ancient Indian mythology), "鳩槃茶/鳩槃荼" (*jiu-pan-cha/jiu-pan-tu*, *Kumbhanda*, one of a group of dwarfish, misshapen spirits among the lesser deities of Buddhist mythology), and "阿鞞跋致" (*a-pi-ba-zhi*, *Avaivart*, "not turn back" in Sanskrit). Since the characteristics of the Lotus Sutra are different from the Samyuktagama in many aspects, it shows that the supervised learning model trained by one Buddhist scripture may apply to other Buddhist scriptures translated in different eras and translators.

We also discovered that transliterations may vary even in the same scripture. In the Samyuktagama, the Sanskrit term "Chandala" (someone who deals with disposal of corpses, and is a Hindu lower caste, formerly considered untouchables) has two different transliterations: "旃陀羅" (*zhan-tuo-luo*) and "栴陀羅" (*zhan-tuo-luo*). The Sanskrit term "*Magadha*" (the name of an ancient Indian kingdom) has three different transliterations: "摩竭陀" (*muo-jie-tuo*), "摩竭提" (*muo-jie-ti*), and "摩伽陀" (*muo-qie-tuo*). The variations of the transliterations of the same word give the clues of translators and translation progress. These variations may help the study of historical Chinese phonology and philology.

4.2 Error cases

Although our method can extract and identify most transliteration pairs, some transliteration pairs cannot be identified. The error cases can be divided into several categories. The first one is that a few terms cannot be extracted, such as "闍維" (*she-wei*, *Jhapita*, cremation, a monk's funeral pyre). This transliteration is less used and only appears three times in the final part of the Samyuktagama. The widely used transliteration of the term "*Jhapita*" is "荼毘" (*tu-pi*). It may cause the difficulty for the supervised learning model to identify these terms.

The other case is incorrect boundary of the transliterations. Sometimes our method may extract shorter terms, such as "韋提" (*wei-ti*, correct transliteration is "韋提希", *wei-ti-xi*, *Vaidehi*, a female person name), "波羅" (*po-luo*, correct transliteration is "波羅柰", *po-luo-nai*, *Varanasi*, a location name in northen India), "瞿利摩羅" (*qü-li-muo-luo*, correct transliteration is "央瞿利摩羅", *yang-qü-li-muo-luo*, *Angulimala*, one of the Buddha's disciples). This problem is due to the probability generated by the language model. For example, the probability of the first two charactgers of the transliteration "央瞿利摩羅", P(央瞿), is very low. It causes the CRF model predicts the first character "央" (*yang*) does not belong to the transliteration. If more transliterations can be collected to build a better language model, this problem can be overcome.

In some cases, our method extracts much longer terms, like "阿那律陀夜" (*a-na-lü-tuo-ye*, correct transliteration is "阿那律陀", *a-na-lü-tuo*, *Aniruddha*, one of the Buddha's closest disciples), and "兒富那婆藪" (*er-fu-na-po-sou*, correct transliteration is "富那婆藪", *fu-na-po-sou*, *Punabbasu*, a kind of ghost in Buddhist mythology). In these cases, the previous or following characters are often used in transliterations. Therefore, it is very difficult to distinguish the boundary of the actual transliteration. In addition, there are some cases that a transliteration followed by another transliteration immediately. For example, our method extracts out the term "闡陀舍利" (*chan-tuo-she-li*), which comprises two transliteration terms such as "闡陀" (*chan-tuo*, *Chanda*, one of the Buddhist's disciples) and "舍利" (*she-li*, *Sarira*, Buddhist relics). It is also difficult to separate them without any additional semantic clues. Although our method sometimes might extract incomplete transliterations with incorrect boundary, checking the boundary of a transliteration is not difficult to a human expert. Therefore, the extracted incorrect transliteartions also have the benefits to help humanity researchers quickly find and check plausible transliterations.

5 Conclusion

The transliteration extrction of foreign loanwords is an important task in research fields such as historical linguistics and digital humanities. We propose an approach which can extract transliteration automatically from classical Chinese Buddhist scriptures. Our approach comprises the conditional random fields method with designed features which are suitable to identify transliteration characters. The first feature is the probability of each Chinese character used in transliterations. The second feature is probability of the sequential bigram characters measured by the language model method. In addiition, the functional words, appellation and quantifier words also be regarded as binary features. Next, the transliteration extration problem is formulated as a sequential tagging problem and the CRF method is used to train a model to extract the transliterations from the input classical Chinese sentences. To evaluate our method, we constructed an evaluation set from the two Buddhist texts, the Samyuktagama and the Lotus Sutra, which were translated into Chinese in different eras. We also construct a baseline system with proach with suffix array based extraction method and phonetic similarity measurementfor comparison. The recall of our method achieves 0.9561 and the precision is 0.9444. The results show our method outperforms the baseline system a lot and is effective to extract transliterations from classical Chinese texts. Our method can find the transliterations among the immense classical literatures to help many research fields such as historical linguistics and philology.

References

Y. Goldberg and M. Elhadad. 2008. Identification of transliterated foreign words in hebrew script. *Computational Linguistics and Intelligent Text Processing*.

J-S. Kuo, H. Li, and Y-K. Yang. 2007. A phonetic similarity model for automatic extraction of transliteration pairs. *ACM Trans. Asian Language Information Processing*, 6(2).

John Lafferty, Andrew McCallum, and Fernando CN Pereira. 2011. Conditional random fields: Probabilistic models for segmenting and labeling sequence data. *Proc. of ICML*, pages 282–289.

Christopher D Manning, Prabhakar Raghavan, and Hinrich Schütze. 2008. *Introduction to information retrieval*, volume 1. Cambridge University Press Cambridge.

G. Manzini and P. Ferragina. 2004. Engineering a lightweight suffix array construction algorithm. *Algorithmica*, 40(1):33–50.

J. Oh and K. Choi. 2003. A statistical model for automatic extraction of korean transliterated foreign words. *International Journal of Computer Processing of Oriental Languages*, 16(1):41–62.

L. Rabiner. 1989. tutorial on hidden markov models and selected applications in speech recognition. In *Proceedings of the IEEE*, volume 77.

T. Sherif and G. Kondrak. 2007. Bootstrapping a stochastic transducer for arabic-english transliteration extraction. *Proceedings of Annual Meeting- Association for Computational Linguistics*.

Richard Tzong-Han Tsai, Hsieh-Chuan Hung, Cheng-Lung Sung, Hong-Jie Dai, and Wen-Lian Hsu. 2006. On closed task of chinese word segmentation: An improved crf model coupled with character clustering and automatically generated template matching. *Proceedings of the Fifth SIGHAN Workshop on Chinese Language Processing*, pages 134–137.

Effects of Parsing Errors on Pre-reordering Performance for Chinese-to-Japanese SMT

Dan Han[1,2] **Pascual Martínez-Gómez**[2,3] **Yusuke Miyao**[1,2]
Katsuhito Sudoh[4] **Masaaki Nagata**[4]
[1]The Graduate University For Advanced Studies
[2]National Institute of Informatics, [3]The University of Tokyo
[4]NTT Communication Science Laboratories, NTT Corporation
{handan,pascual,yusuke}@nii.ac.jp
{sudoh.katsuhito,nagata.masaaki}@lab.ntt.co.jp

Abstract

Linguistically motivated reordering methods have been developed to improve word alignment especially for Statistical Machine Translation (SMT) on long distance language pairs. However, since they highly rely on the parsing accuracy, it is useful to explore the relationship between parsing and reordering. For Chinese-to-Japanese SMT, we carry out a three-stage incremental comparative analysis to observe the effects of different parsing errors on reordering performance by combining empirical and descriptive approaches. For the empirical approach, we quantify the distribution of general parsing errors along with reordering qualities whereas for the descriptive approach, we extract seven influential error patterns and examine their correlation with reordering errors.

1 Introduction

Statistical machine translation is a challenging and well established task in the community of computational linguistics. One of the key components of statistical machine translation systems are word alignment techniques, where the words from sentences in a source language are mapped to words from sentences in a target language. When estimating the most appropriate word alignments, it is unfeasible to explore every possible word correspondence due to the combinatorial complexity. Considering local permutations of words might be effective to translate languages with a similar sentence structure, but these methods have a limited performance when translating sentences from languages with different syntactical structures.

An effective technique to translate sentences between distant language pairs is pre-reordering, where words in sentences from the source language are re-arranged with the objective to resemble the word order of the target language. Rearranging rules are automatically extracted (Xia and McCord, 2004; Genzel, 2010), or linguistically motivated (Xu et al., 2009; Isozaki et al., 2010; Han et al., 2012; Han et al., 2013). We work following the latter strategy, where the source sentence is parsed to find its syntactical structure, and linguistically-motivated rules are used in combination with the structure of the sentence to guide the word reordering. The language pair under consideration is Chinese-to-Japanese, which despite their common roots, it is a well known language pair for their different sentence structure.

However, syntax-based pre-reordering techniques are sensitive to parsing errors, but insight into their relationship has been elusive. The contribution of this work is two fold. First, we provide an empirical analysis where we quantify the aggregated impact of parsing errors on pre-reordering performance. Second, we define seven patterns of the most common and influential parsing errors and we carry out a descriptive analysis to examine their relationship with reordering errors. We combine an empirical and descriptive approach to present a three-stage incremental comparative analysis to observe the effect of different parsing errors on reordering performance.

In Section 2, after a brief description on the pre-reordering method that we use for experiments, we will introduce some related works on parsing error analysis and analysis on the relation between parsing and machine translation. From a general perspective, we describe our analysis methods for this work in Section 3. Then, we carry out the analysis and exhibit the results in Section 4 and Section 5. The last two sections are dedicated to discussion, future directions and summarize our findings.

Vb-H	VV VE VC VA P
BEI	LB SB
RM-D	NN NR NT PN OD CD M FW CC ETC LC DEV DT JJ SP IJ ON

Table 1: Lists of POS tags for identifying words as Vb-H, RM-D, and BEI. (Han et al., 2013)

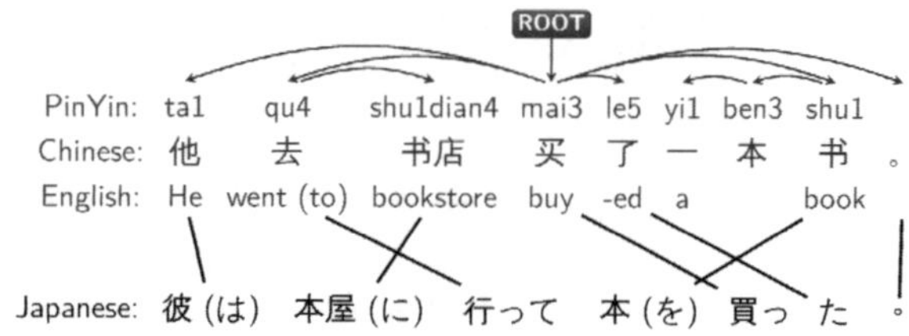

Figure 1: Example of unlabeled dependency parse tree of a Chinese sentence (SVO) with word aligned to its Japanese counterpart (SOV). Arrows are pointing from heads to dependents.

2 Background

2.1 Reordering Model

Since local reordering models which are integrated in phrase-based SMT systems do not perform well for distant language pairs due to their different syntactic structures, pre-reordering methods have been proposed to supply the need for improving the word alignment. Han et al. (2013) described one of the latest pre-reordering methods (DPC) which was based on dependency parsing. The authors were using an unlabeled dependency parser to extract the syntactic information of Chinese sentences, and then by combining with part-of-speech (POS) tags[1], they defined a set of heuristic reordering rules to guide the reordering. The essential idea of DPC is to move so-called verbal block (Vb)[2] to the right-hand side of its right-most dependent (RM-D) for a Subject-Verb-Object (SVO) language to resemble a Subject-Object-Verb (SOV) language's word order. Table 1 shows the POS tags that are used to identify words as Vb-H, RM-D, or BEI (a Vb-H involves in a bei-construction) in a sentence from Han et al. (2013).

Figure 1 shows an example of unlabeled dependency parse tree of a Chinese sentence aligned with its Japanese translation. According to the reordering method, "went" will be reordered behind of "bookstore" while "buy -ed" will be reordered to the right-hand side of "book", and thus the sentence will follow a SOV word order as Japanese. However, if "book" was wrongly recognized as the dependent of "went" in the dependency structure, "went" will be wrongly reordered to the right-hand side of "book". Therefore, syntactic structure based reordering methods highly rely on the parsing accuracy. In order to further improve word alignments or refine existing reordering models, it is important to observe the effects of parsing errors on reordering performance.

In this analysis, we borrow this state-of-the-art pre-reordering model for our experiments since it is a rule-based pre-reordering method for a distant language pair based on dependency parsing as well as its extensibility to other language pairs.

2.2 Related Work

Although there are studies on analyzing parsing errors and reordering errors, as far as we know, there is not any work on observing the relationship between these two types of errors.

One most relevant work to ours is observing the impact of parsing accuracy on a SMT system introduced in Quirk and Corston-Oliver (2006). They showed the general idea that syntax-based SMT models are sensitive to syntactic analysis. However, they did not further analyze concrete parsing error types that affect task accuracy.

Green (2011) explored the effects of noun phrase bracketing in dependency parsing in English, and further on English to Czech machine translation. But the work focused on using noun phrase structure to improve a machine translation framework. In the work of Katz-Brown et al. (2011), they proposed a training method to improve a parser's performance by using reordering quality to examine the parse quality. But they did not study the relationship between reordering quality and parse quality.

There are more works on parsing error analysis. For instance, Hara et al. (2009) defined several types of parsing error patterns on predicate argument relation and tested them with a Head-driven phrase structure grammar (HPSG) (Pollard and Sag, 1994) parser (Miyao and Tsujii, 2008). McDonald and Nivre (2007) explored parsing errors for data-driven dependency parsing by

[1] In this work, POS tag definitions follow the POS tag guidelines of the Penn Chinese Treebank v3.0.

[2] According to (Han et al., 2013), a Vb includes the head of the Vb (Vb-H) and an optional component (Vb-D).

comparing a graph-based parser with a transition-based parser, which are representing two dominant parsing models. At the same time, Dredze et al. (2007) provided a comparison analysis on differences in annotation guidelines among treebanks which were suspected to be responsible for dependency parsing errors in domain adaptation tasks. Unlike analyzing parsing errors, authors in Yu et al. (2011) focused on the difficulties in Chinese deep parsing by comparing the linguistic properties between Chinese and English.

There are also works on reordering error analysis like Han et al. (2012) which examined an existing reordering method and refined it after a detailed linguistic analysis on reordering issues. Although they discovered that parsing errors affect the reordering quality, they did not observe the concrete relationship. On the other hand, Giménez and Màrquez (2008) proposed an automatic error analysis method of machine translation output, by compiling a set of metric variants. However, they did not provide insight on what SMT component caused low translation performance.

3 Analysis Method

We combine an empirical approach with a descriptive approach to observe the effects of parsing errors on pre-reordering performance in three stages: preliminary experiment stage, POS tag level stage, and dependency type level stage. First, we provide a general idea of the sensitiveness of parsing errors on reordering method. Then, we use POS tags to identify parsing errors and quantify the aggregate impact on reordering performance. Finally, we define several concrete error patterns and examine their effects on reordering qualities.

In order to test for an upper bound of the reordering performance and examine the specific parsing errors that affect reordering, one way is to contrast the reordering based on error-free parse trees with the reordering based on auto-parse trees. Error-free parse trees are considered as gold trees.

In the preliminary experiment stage, we set up two benchmarks in two scenarios. For scenario 1, the benchmark is manually reordered Chinese sentence on the basis of Japanese reference. By measuring the word order similarities between the benchmark and the gold-tree based reordered sentence as well as between the benchmark and the auto-parse tree based reordered sentence separately, we quantify the extent of parsing errors that influence reordering. Meanwhile, the former measurement shows additionally the general figure of the upper bound of the reordering method. However, since it is not only time-consuming but also labor-intensive to set up the benchmark in scenario 1, we use the Japanese reference as the benchmark in scenario 2 and follow the same strategies as in scenario 1 to calculate the word order similarities. More detailed description on the preliminary experiment is given in Section 4.

In POS tag level stage, we compare the gold-tree with auto-parse tree along with reordering quality to explore the relationship between general parsing errors and reordering from two aspects: the percentages of top three most frequent dependent's POS tags that point to wrong heads and the percentages of top two most frequent head's POS tags that are recognized wrongly. The percentages of other POS tags are not provided because they are negligible. Our objective is to profile general parsing errors' distribution. However, this does not imply that those errors are the cause of the reordering errors. Section 5.1 includes more concrete analysis results.

In dependency type level stage, we classify the most influential parsing errors on reordering into three superclasses and seven subclasses according to the methodology of the reordering method. We then plot the distribution of these parsing errors for various reordering qualities. In Section 5.2, we illustrate these parsing errors with examples.

4 Preliminary Experiment

4.1 Gold Data

In order to build up gold parse tree sets for comparison, we used the annotated sentences from Chinese Penn Treebank ver. 7.0 (CTB-7) which is a well known corpus that consists of parsed text in five genres. They are Chinese newswire (NS), magazine news (NM), broadcast news (BN), broadcast conversation programs (BC), and web newsgroups, weblogs (NW).

We first randomly selected 517 unique sentences (hereinafter set-1) from all five genres in development set of CTB-7 which is split according to (Wang et al., 2011). However, we found that sentences in BC and NW are mainly from spoken language, which tend to have faults like repetitions, incomplete sentences, corrections, or incorrect sentence segmentation. Therefore, we randomly selected another 2, 126 unique sentences

	BN	BC	NM	NS	NW	Total
set-1	100	100	100	117	100	517
set-2	797	-	578	751	-	2,126
Total	897	100	678	868	100	2,643
AL	29.8	20.0	33.5	28.4	25.9	29.8
Voc.	$5.5K$	690	$5K$	$5.1K$	972	$9.5K$

Table 2: Statistics of selected sentences in five genres of CTB-7. AL stands for the average length of sentences, while Voc. for vocabulary.

	Baseline	Gold-DPC	Auto-DPC
M-reordered	0.82	0.90	0.88
Gold-DPC	-	-	0.95

Table 3: The average value of Kendall's tau (τ) of 517 Chinese sentences by comparing manually reordered sentences, unreordered sentences, and automatically reordered sentences. M-reordered is short for manually reordered.

(hereinafter set-2) within a limit to three genres: NS, NM, and BN. Table 2 shows the statistics of all selected sentences in five genres respectively.

For converting CTB-7 parsed text to dependency parse trees, we used an open utility Penn2Malt[3] which converts Penn Treebank into MaltTab format containing dependency information. Since the head rules that Penn2Malt recommended for converting on its website do not contain three new annotation types in CTB-7, we added three new ones for them as follows: FLR (Fillers) and DFL (Disfluency) head on right-hand branch; INC (Incomplete sentences) follows the same head rule as FRAG (Fragment).

Meanwhile, professional human translators translated all Chinese sentences in both set-1 and set-2 into Japanese. Thereafter, according to the Japanese references, Chinese sentences in set-1 have been manually reordered as the same word orders as their Japanese counterparts by a bilingual speaker of Chinese and Japanese for the experiments in scenario 1. For example, the Chinese sentence in Figure 1 is following the word order of "He bookstore went (to) a book buy (-ed) ." in the handcrafted reordered set since it resembles the Japanese word order.

4.2 Evaluation

We use Kendall's tau (τ) rank correlation coefficient (Isozaki et al., 2010) to measure word order similarities between sentences in two different scenarios. In the first scenario, we use the set of manually reordered Chinese sentences from set-1 as benchmark and compare it with the set of automatically reordered Chinese sentences. In the second scenario, we combine set-1 and set-2 to obtain a larger data set. The set of Japanese references plays the role of benchmark and is compared with the set of automatically reordered Chinese sentences. Word alignments are produced by MGIZA++ (Gao and Vogel, 2008).

In both scenarios, we carry out the reordering method DPC (See Section 2.1). Auto-parse trees are generated by an unlabeled Chinese dependency parser, Corbit[4] (Hatori et al., 2011). Gold trees[5] are converted from CTB-7 parsed text which are created by human annotators. More specifically, we refer to auto-parse tree based reordering system as Auto-DPC and to gold-tree based reordering system as Gold-DPC. Baseline system uses unreordered Chinese sentences.

Scenario 1 Preliminary observation about the effects of parsing errors on reordering performance is to compare word order similarities between manually reordered Chinese sentences and automatically reordered Chinese sentences from set-1. Table 3 shows the average τ value.

For baseline system, the average τ value shows how similar these 517 Chinese sentences between manually reordered ones and non-reordered ones are. Comparing with manually reordered Chinese, both Auto-DPC and Gold-DPC achieved higher average τ value than baseline, which imply that the reordering method DPC positively reordered the Chinese sentences and improved the word alignment. Nevertheless, a slightly lower average τ value of Auto-DPC shows that DPC is sensitive on parsing errors. This assumption is also confirmed by the average τ value between Auto-DPC and Gold-DPC. However, the difference of τ values are limited. We hence increase the test data by adding set-2 for further experiments in scenario 2.

Scenario 2 Since we do not have manually reordered Chinese sentences as benchmark for set-2, we calculate the Kendall's tau between Chinese sentences and their Japanese counterparts for both data sets by using the MGIZA++ alignment

[3]http://stp.lingfil.uu.se/ nivre/research/Penn2Malt.html

[4]http://triplet.cc/software/corbit

[5]Note that Corbit was tuned with the development set of CTB-7.

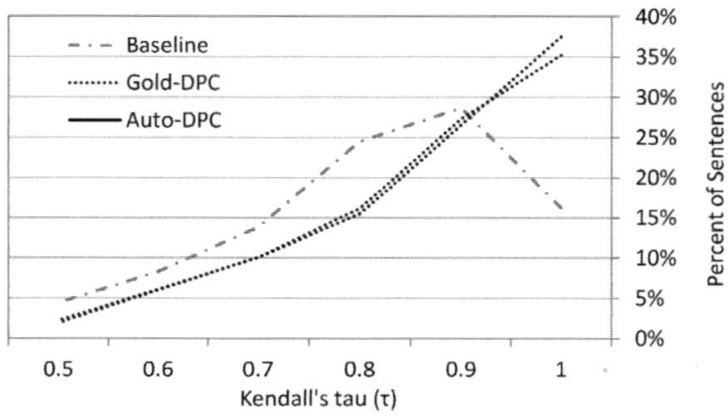

Figure 2: The distribution of Kendall's tau values for $2,236$ bilingual sentences (Chinese-Japanese) in which the Chinese is from three systems of baseline, Auto-DPC, and Gold-DPC.

file, `ch-ja.A3.final`. The comparison implies how monotonically the Chinese sentences have been reordered to align with Japanese. We use MeCab[6] (Kudo and Matsumoto, 2000) to segment Japanese sentences and also filter out sentences with more than 64 tokens. There are $2,236$ valid Chinese-Japanese bilingual sentences in total. Figure 2 shows the distribution of Kendall's tau from three systems in which the baseline is built up by using ordinary Chinese.

In Figure 2, baseline system contains a large numbers of non-monotonic aligned sentences, whereas both Auto-DPC and Gold-DPC increased the amount of sentences that achieved high τ values. Reordering based on gold-tree reduced more percentage of low τ sentences than reordering based on automatically parsed trees. Especially, the amount of sentence difference in $0.9 < \tau <= 1$ between Gold-DPC and Auto-DPC shows that reordering method DPC has a high sensitivity on parsing errors, which enhances the conclusions from the preliminary observation in scenario 1. Furthermore, the performance of reordering system Gold-DPC sketches the figure of upper bound of the reordering method.

5 Analysis on Causes of Reordering Errors

Preliminary experiments in Section 4 provide a general idea of the effects of parsing errors on reordering. In order to achieve more explicit relationship between specific parsing errors and reordering issues, we first identify concrete parsing errors by comparing gold-trees with auto-parse trees. Since the syntactic information that guides reordering in DPC is limited to dependency structure and POS tags, for analysis on the causes of reordering errors, we examine parsing errors from these two linguistic categories. In this section, the value of Kendall's tau measures the word order similarity between Gold-DPC and Auto-DPC.

[6]http://mecab.googlecode.com

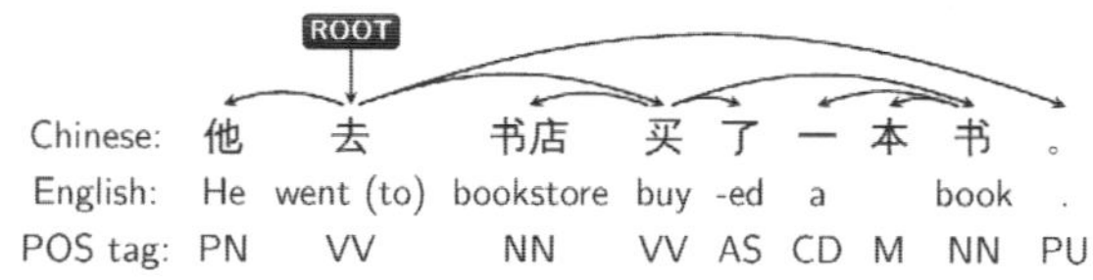

Figure 3: A possible wrong dependency parse tree of the example in Figure 1.

5.1 Part-of-Speech Tag Error

There are two types of parsing errors to a token in a dependency parse tree. One is that the token points to a wrong head, namely **dependent-error**, and another one is that the token is recognized wrongly as a head of other tokens, namely **head-error**. For example, Figure 3 presents a possible wrong parse tree of the example shown in Figure 1. By comparing with the gold-tree in Figure 1, tokens (POS tag) of "he (PN)", "went (VV)", "bookstore (NN)", "buy (VV)", "a (CD)", and ". (PU)" in the dependency tree in Figure 3 all point to different wrong heads, which are dependent-errors. Concurrently, tokens (POS tag) of "went (VV)", "buy (VV)", and "book (NN)" are wrongly recognized as heads of other tokens (e.g., "he", "bookstore", "a"), which are head-errors. According to the definition, every head-error has at least one corresponding dependent-error. However, in the case that a token is not the root in a gold-tree but is root in the wrong tree, this token is a dependent-error corresponding with no head-error. An example is the dependent-error "went (VV)" in Figure 3.

We count the number of POS tag mis-recognitions separately for dependent- and head-errors. In the example of Figure 3, dependent-error counts are for VV, 2 errors, and PN, NN, CD, PU each 1 error. The number of POS tag mis-recognitions for head-errors are VV with 2 errors, and NN with 1 error. In our analysis, we will compute these counts for all POS tags at every sentence in our data set. However, our reordering method performed differently at each sentence in our data set, and the reordering quality varied from

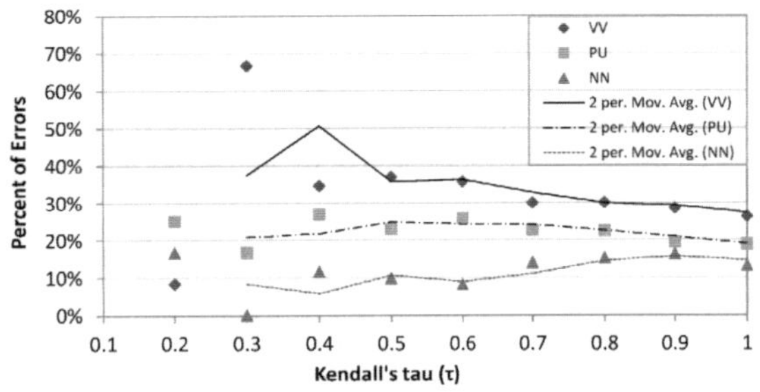

Figure 4: The distribution of top three dependent-error POS tags and their tendency lines.

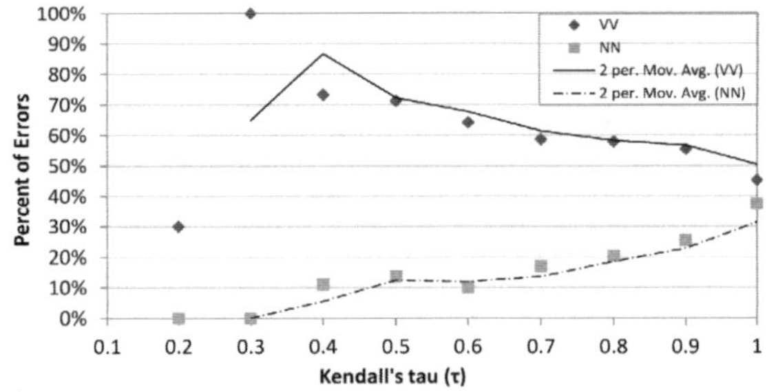

Figure 5: The distribution of top two head-error POS tags and their tendency lines.

sentence to sentence. With the objective of observing the correlation between reordering quality and each type of error, we will first group sentences according to their Kendall's τ values. Then, we will compute proportions of POS tag errors at each τ value, for every type of POS tag error.

Figure 4 shows the distribution of top three dependent-error POS tags, which means that they are the three most frequent POS tags that point to a wrong head in auto-parse trees. VV represents all verbs except predicative adjective (VA), copula (VC), and you3[7] as the main verb (VE). PU represents punctuation and NN represents all nouns except proper noun (NR), temporal noun (NT), and the ones for locations which cannot modify verb phrases with or without de0[8]. The dependent-error on VV accounts for a larger proportion in low reordering accuracy sentences whereas more NN dependent-error occurred in high reordering accuracy sentences. On the other hand, the proportion of PU dependent-error is more consistent.

Figure 5 shows the distribution of top two head-error POS tags, which means that they are the two most frequent POS tags that are recognized wrongly as heads in auto-parse trees. Comparing to Figure 4, the tendency of both VV and NN is the same but distincter.

The analysis results on the proportion distributions of dependent-error POS tags and head-error POS tags in different reordering quality sentence groups exhibit that there are more parsing errors on verbs than nouns in low reordering accuracy sentences and thus the parsing errors on verbs influence more on the reordering performance. However, it is still difficult to reveal the effects of more concrete parsing errors on reordering considering that not all verb parsing errors influence the reordering. As an illustration, in Figure 3, if the head of "bookstore" were "went", the VV head-error of "went" would not cause any reordering error since it would be reordered consistently to the right-hand side of its RM-D "bookstore". Consequently, we use a descriptive approach to analyze dependency types to explore the effects from more concrete parsing errors in the next section.

5.2 Dependency Type Error

As introduced in Section 2.1, DPC first identifies Vb, RM-D, and then reorders necessary words. Thus, DPC reorders not only Vb-H, but also Vb-D in a Vb, which means that the failure on identifying Vbs may also cause unexpected reordering on particles, such as aspect markers. However, in this work, we only focus on reordering issues of Vb-H candidates[9]. To discover the effects of more concrete parsing errors on reordering, we distinguish three categories of dependency types, i.e., **ROOT**, **RM-D**, and **BEI**. Among them, ROOT denotes whether the Vb-H candidate is the root of the sentence or not, RM-D is the right-most object dependent of the Vb-H candidate if it has one, and BEI denotes whether the Vb-H candidate is involved in a bei-construction.

According to the methodology of the reordering method DPC, we define seven patterns of parsing error phenomena and classify them into three types by comparing the gold-tree (GT) with auto-parse tree (Corbit-tree, CT). Table 4 lists all parsing error patterns in three error types, ROOT error, RM-D error and BEI error by considering three dependency types ROOT, RM-D and BEI. Symbols of "$\surd$", "$\times$", "?" represent the status of a cer-

[7]A Chinese character expresses possession and existence.

[8]A Chinese character is specially used to connect the verb phrase and its modifier.

[9]We use "Vb-H candidate" in this work for the reason that if the Vb-H is involved into a bei-construction, then it can not be Vb-H according to (Han et al., 2013).

	BEI		ROOT		RM-D	
	GT	CT	GT	CT	GT	CT
ROOT Error						
Root-C	×	×	×	√	×	×
Root-G	×	×	√	×	×	×
RM-D Error						
RM_D-C	×	×	×	×	×	√
	×	×	×	√	×	√
	×	×	√	×	×	√
	×	×	√	√	×	√
RM_D-G	×	×	×	×	√	×
	×	×	×	√	√	×
	×	×	√	×	√	×
	×	×	√	√	√	×
RM_D-D	×	×	×	×	√	diff.
	×	×	×	√	√	diff.
	×	×	√	×	√	diff.
	×	×	√	√	√	diff.
BEI Error						
BEI-C	×	√	√	?	×	?
	×	√	×	?	√	?
	×	√	√	?	√	?
BEI-G	√	×	?	√	?	×
	√	×	?	×	?	√
	√	×	?	√	?	√

Table 4: Seven error patterns (Root-C, Root-G, RM_D-C, RM_D-G, RM_D-D, BEI-C, BEI-G) that cause three types of reordering issues (ROOT error, RM-D error, and BEI error). GT stands for gold-tree, and CT stands for Corbit-tree. Symbols "√", "×", "?" represent the status of True, False, and Unknown, respectively. "diff." means that the RM-Ds exist in both GT and CT but are different.

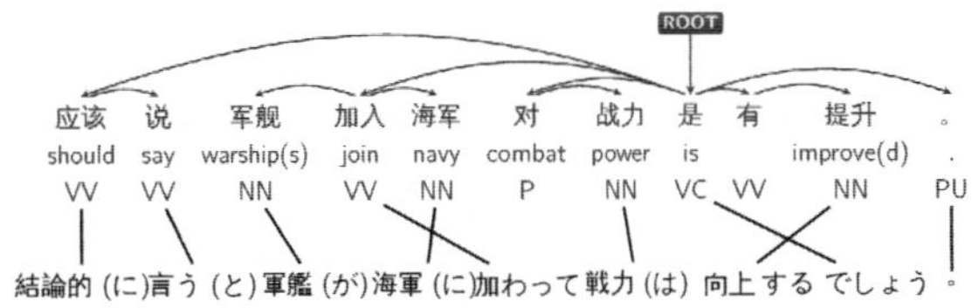

(a) Gold tree

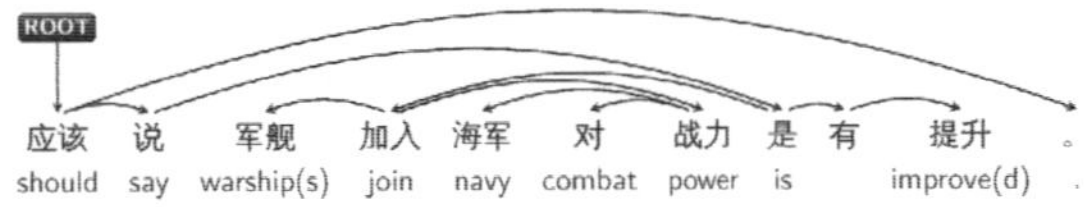

(b) A possible wrong parse tree.

Figure 6: An example for parsing error patterns of Root-C and RM_D-D. English translation: One should say that, the additions of warships will help to improve the navy's combat power.

tain dependency type in gold-tree or Corbit-tree. For every Vb-H candidate, the 6 status are conditions to match the error pattern. For example, to match a Root-C error pattern, the Vb-H candidate needs to satisfy the following conditions: in gold-tree, it is not the root, and does not have any RM-D or bei dependent; in Corbit tree, it does not have any RM-D or bei dependent, but it is the root.

Root-C is the case where a Vb-H candidate has been wrongly parsed as the root of the sentence. However, it only affects the reordering with two constrains, namely that RM-D of the Vb-H candidate does not exist and Vb-H is not involved in a bei-construction. For instance, the Vb-H "should" in the example of Figure 6 was recognized as root in auto-parse tree in Figure 6b. However, the actual root is the Vb-H "is" in gold tree of Figure 6a. Therefore, since "should" does not have any dependent as either BEI or RM-D in both GT and CT, it will be reordered incorrectly to the end of the sentence according to the CT whereas it will not be reordered according to GT, which is already in the same position as its Japanese counterpart.

Root-G is the opposite case of Root-C where a Vb-H candidate is the root of the sentence but was not parsed as the root in CT. This affects the reordering under the two same constraints as Root-C. Figure 7b shows an example of Root-G. In Figure 7a, the word alignment shows that the Vb-H "agree" should be reordered to the end of the sentence. However, it will not be reordered for the wrong parse tree shown in Figure 7b.

RM_D-C is the case where the RM-D of a Vb-H candidate exists in a CT but not in GT. In other words, a RM-D candidate was parsed wrongly on its head. There are four varieties of combination with the status of ROOT, BEI of the Vb-H candidate that lead to incorrect reorderings. The Vb-H "agree" in Figure 7c matches the last combination of RM_D-C, which will be reordered right after "journalist" instead of at the end of the sentence.

RM_D-G is the opposite case of RM_D-C where the RM-D of a Vb-H candidate was missed in a CT. There are also four cases of reordering errors according to the status of BEI, ROOT and RM-D. Vb-H "went" in Figure 3 matches the second combination of RM_D-G so that it will not be able to reorder after "bookstore".

RM_D-D is the case where a bei-construction-free Vb-H candidate obtains two different RM-D candidates in CT and GT, which causes the reordering issue. In Figure 6, Vb-H "join" received different RM-Ds in two trees. According to the

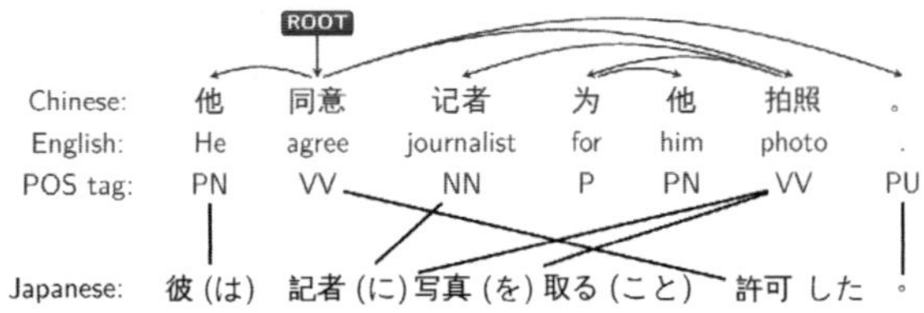

(a) Gold-tree.

(b) A possible erroneous parse tree.

(c) Another possible erroneous parse tree.

Figure 7: An example for parsing error patterns of Root-G and RM_D-C. English translation: He agreed to the journalist to take a picture of him.

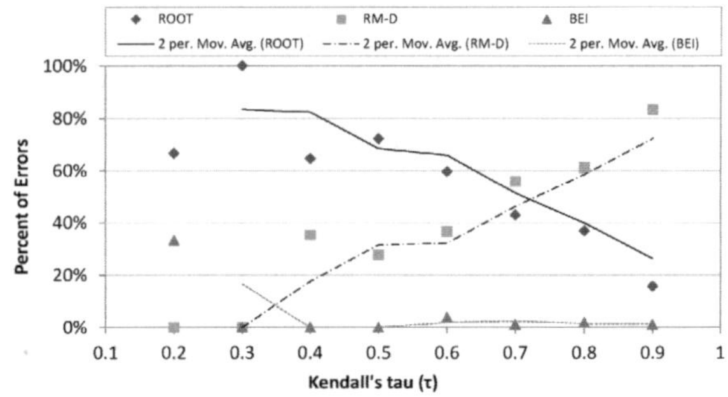

Figure 8: Distribution of three types of parsing errors in different τ groups and their trend curves.

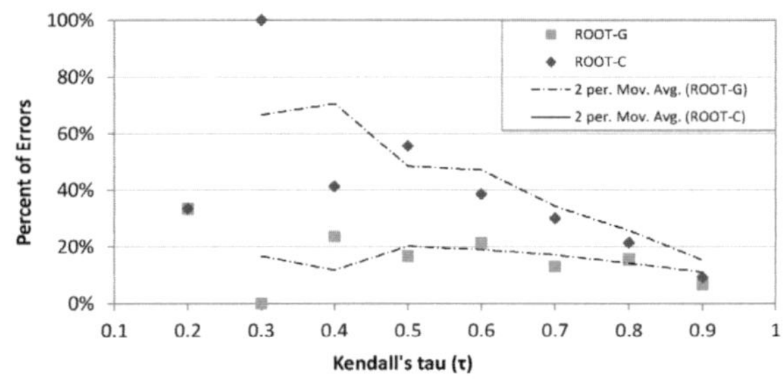

Figure 9: Distribution of patterns of ROOT error in different τ groups and their trend curves.

word alignment, it should be reordered next to "navy" instead of "combat power".

BEI-C is the case where a Vb-H candidate received a wrong BEI dependent in CT. This will prevent reordering independently on whether the Vb-H candidate has RM-D or is the root.

BEI-G is the opposite case of BEI-C, where Vb-H in GT will not be reordered but in CT it will.

After defining seven patterns of parsing errors and classifying them into three types, we calculate the average frequency proportions of each type in different τ value groups of sentences.

Figure 8 shows the distribution of the three types of parsing errors and their tendencies. In low τ value sentences, there are higher proportions of ROOT errors, and relatively lower proportions in high τ value sentences. RM-D errors follow the opposite tendency. This implies that the effects of ROOT errors on reordering are stronger than the effects from RM-D errors. The reason could be that ROOT errors cause long distance reordering failure while RM-D errors lead to more local reordering errors. Since there are very few BEI errors, it was difficult to capture their trends.

Figure 9 and Figure 10 provide the correlations between parsing error patterns and reordering accuracy. In ROOT errors types, Root-C had a larger percentage than Root-G in low reordering accuracy sentences which shows that the Vb-H candidate that does not have any object dependent tends to be recognized as root by parser. This is consistent with the distribution results that are shown in Figure 10. The error pattern of RM_D-G had larger percentage than the other two patterns, which also implies that a Vb-H candidate in a CT tends to have less or none object dependents.

5.3 Further Analysis Possibilities

Due to the time limitation, we only focused on analyzing parsing errors that cause reordering issues on Vb-H candidates while defining the error patterns. However, it is not only that Vb-H candidates are reordered in DPC, but also other words like Vb-D candidates and particles will be reordered. It is also meaningful to explore the parsing error patterns which cause unexpected reordering on these words and the correlation between them as well.

The current study on exploring influential parsing errors is not exhaustive, and another analysis possibility would be to explore what types of parsing errors do not affect reordering so that parsers can sacrifice their performance on those types of issues in order to improve on influential types.

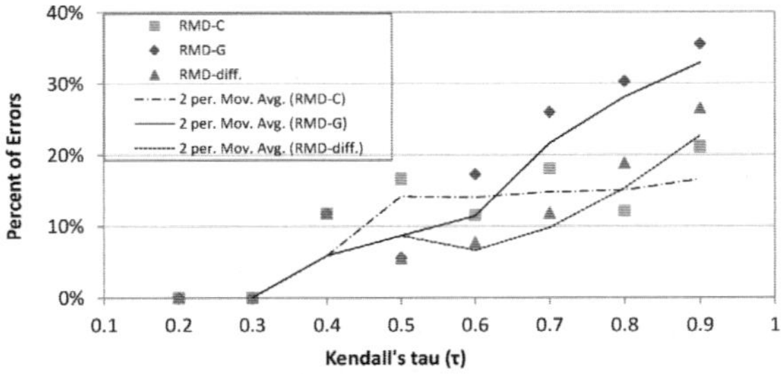

Figure 10: The distribution of different patterns of RM-D error in different τ groups.

6 Discussion and Future Work

Two important research directions concentrate on either improving parsers or developing linguistically motivated pre-reordering methods. We believe that analyzing the link between those directions can help us to refine future developments.

We observed relatively small effects on reordering quality in response of parsing errors. However, reordering quality affect word alignments, which in turn affect the quality of bilingual phrases that are extracted. It would be interesting to extend this work to quantify the propagation of parsing and reordering errors in SMT pipelines, to observe the factored effect on the overall MT quality.

We found that not all POS tagging and parsing errors correlate equally with reordering quality. In the case of DPC reordering method, mis-recognitions of VV words correlate with low reordering performance, whereas mis-recognitions of NN words had a smaller impact. Indeed, DPC heavily relies on detecting verbal blocks that are candidates for reordering, and systems that use the same strategy should choose POS taggers that display high accuracy of VV recognition.

One of the key characteristics of DPC is its ability to correctly reorder sentences with reported speech constructions. For that purpose, it is crucial for parsers to recognize the sentence root, and our analysis demonstrated that systems that follow similar strategy should rely on parsers that have a high accuracy to recognize the sentence root.

In general, we believe that future developments of syntax-based pre-reordering methods would benefit of preliminary analysis of POS tagging and parsing accuracies. In case of linguistically motivated pre-reordering methods, reordering rules could be designed to be more robust against unreliable POS tags or unreliable dependency relations. For automatically learned reordering rules, those systems could be designed to make use of N-best lists of certain POS tags or dependencies that are critical but that parsers cannot reliably provide.

There are other popular syntax-based pre-reordering methods that may use different types of parsing grammars (i.e. Head-driven phrase structure grammar), and similar analysis would also be interesting in those contexts, possibly with a larger set of gold parsed and reordered sentences. Additionally, researchers interested in developing POS taggers and parsers with the objective to aid pre-reordering could attempt to maximize the accuracy of POS tags or dependencies that are relevant to the reordering task, maybe at the expense of lower accuracies on other elements.

7 Conclusion

In this work, we carried out linguistically motivated analysis methods by combining empirical and descriptive approaches in three analysis stages to examine the effects of different parsing errors on pre-reordering performance. We achieved four objectives: (i) quantify effects of parsing errors on reordering, (ii) estimate upper bounds in performance of the reordering method, (iii) profile general parsing errors, and (iv) examine effects of specific parsing errors on reordering.

In the first stage, we set up benchmarks in two scenarios for reordered Chinese sentences. By calculating the word order similarity between the benchmarks and the dependency parse tree based auto-reordered Chinese sentences, we quantified the correlation between parsing errors and reordering accuracies as well as explored the upper bound in reordering quality of the reordering model.

In the second stage, we examined the effects of two types of parsing errors on reordering quality by using POS tag information. The distributions of parsing errors' POS tags provide a general view of the influential parsing error types and an approximation to the cause of the effects.

In the last stage, we defined several patterns of parsing errors that assuredly cause reordering errors by using the linguistic feature of dependency types based on a deep linguistic study of the syntactic structures and the reordering model. The analysis results assist us to achieve a better and more explicit understanding on the relationship between parsing errors and reordering performance. Furthermore, we captured the effects of more concrete parsing errors on reordering.

References

Mark Dredze, John Blitzer, Partha Pratim Talukdar, Kuzman Ganchev, Joao Graca, and Fernando Pereira. 2007. Frustratingly hard domain adaptation for dependency parsing. In *Proc. of the CoNLL Shared Task Session of EMNLP-CoNLL*, pages 1051–1055.

Qin Gao and Stephan Vogel. 2008. Parallel implementations of word alignment tool. In *Software Engineering, Testing, and Quality Assurance for Natural Language Processing*, pages 49–57.

Dmitriy Genzel. 2010. Automatically learning source-side reordering rules for large scale machine translation. In *Proc. of COLING*, pages 376–384.

Jesús Giménez and Lluis Màrquez. 2008. Towards heterogeneous automatic MT error analysis. In *Proc. of the 6th International Conference on Language Resources and Evaluation*, pages 1894–1901.

Nathan Green. 2011. Effects of noun phrase bracketing in dependency parsing and machine translation. In *Proc. of ACL-HLT, Student Session*, pages 69–74.

Dan Han, Katsuhito Sudoh, Xianchao Wu, Kevin Duh, Hajime Tsukada, and Masaaki Nagata. 2012. Head finalization reordering for Chinese-to-Japanese machine translation. In *Proc. of the ACL 6th Workshop on SSST*, pages 57–66.

Dan Han, Pascual Martínez-Gómez, Yusuke Miyao, Katsuhito Sudoh, and Masaaki Nagata. 2013. Using unlabeled dependency parsing for pre-reordering for Chinese-to-Japanese statistical machine translation. In *Proc. of the ACL Second Workshop on Hybrid Approaches to Translation*, pages 25–33.

Tadayoshi Hara, Yusuke Miyao, and Jun'ichi Tsujii. 2009. Descriptive and empirical approaches to capturing underlying dependencies among parsing errors. In *Proc. of EMNLP*, pages 1162–1171.

Jun Hatori, Takuya Matsuzaki, Yusuke Miyao, and Junichi Tsujii. 2011. Incremental joint POS tagging and dependency parsing in Chinese. In *Proc. of 5th IJCNLP*, pages 1216–1224.

Hideki Isozaki, Katsuhito Sudoh, Hajime Tsukada, and Kevin Duh. 2010. Head finalization: A simple reordering rule for SOV languages. In *Proc. of WMTMetricsMATR*, pages 244–251.

Jason Katz-Brown, Slav Petrov, Ryan McDonald, Franz Och, David Talbot, Hiroshi Ichikawa, and Masakazu Seno. 2011. Training a parser for machine translation reordering. In *Proc. of the 2011 Conference on EMNLP*, pages 183–192.

Taku Kudo and Yuji Matsumoto. 2000. Japanese dependency structure analysis based on support vector machines. In *Proc. of the EMNLP/VLC-2000*, pages 18–25.

Ryan McDonald and Joakim Nivre. 2007. Characterizing the errors of data-driven dependency parsing models. In *Proc. of the 2007 Joint Conference on EMNLP-CoNLL*, pages 122–131.

Yusuke Miyao and Jun'ichi Tsujii. 2008. Feature forest models for probabilistic HPSG parsing. *Computational Linguistics*, 34:35–80.

Carl Jesse Pollard and Ivan A. Sag. 1994. *Head-driven phrase structure grammar*. The University of Chicago Press and CSLI Publications.

Chris Quirk and Simon Corston-Oliver. 2006. The impact of parse quality on syntactically-informed statistical machine translation. In *Proc. of EMNLP*, pages 62–69.

Yiou Wang, Junichi Kazama, Yoshimasa Tsuruoka, Wenliang Chen, Yujie Zhang, and Kentaro Torisawa. 2011. Improving Chinese word segmentation and POS tagging with semi-supervised methods using large auto-analyzed data. In *Proc. of 5th IJCNLP*, pages 309–317.

Fei Xia and Michael McCord. 2004. Improving a statistical MT system with automatically learned rewrite patterns. In *Proc. of COLING*.

Peng Xu, Jaeho Kang, Michael Ringgaard, and Franz Och. 2009. Using a dependency parser to improve SMT for subject-object-verb languages. In *Proc. of NAACL*, pages 245–253.

Kun Yu, Yusuke Miyao, Takuya Matsuzaki, Xiangli Wang, and Junichi Tsujii. 2011. Analysis of the difficulties in Chinese deep parsing. In *Proc. of the 12th International Conference on Parsing Technologies*, pages 48–57.

Reduplication across Categories in Cantonese

Charles Lam
Linguistics Program, Purdue University
Beering Hall, Room 1289
West Lafayette, IN 47907
charleslam@purdue.edu

Abstract

This paper investigates the formal semantics of reduplication in Cantonese, i.e. how the meaning of reduplicated forms are encoded and computed with the given meaning from the base forms. In particular, this paper argues that reduplication denotes a summation function that adds up arguments (be they object-, event- or degree-arguments) and return a collection of the elements. The surface difference across categories is accounted for in terms of cumulativity and quantization (Krifka, 1998; Krifka, 2001; Rothstein, 2004). The present approach makes use of scalar structure and summation as formal tools to model the cross-categorial behaviour of reduplication. It provides the advantage of a unified theory for lexical composition across categories nouns, verbs and adjectives.

Keywords: *reduplication, formal semantics, cumulativity, cross-categorial behaviour*

1 Introduction

Reduplication is found across syntactic categories noun, verb and adjective in Cantonese. They all share a similar surface order, but the interpretation can be quite differently. Nominal reduplication denotes an exhaustive list such as 'everybody, every apple'. Verbal reduplication displays either durative or iterative reading, depending on the telicity of the verbal predicate. Adjectival reduplication shows a hedging and diminutive reading, as in 'a little fat' or 'reddish'

The goal of this paper is to establish a unified account for the cross-categorial reduplication that can interpret the various meanings. We argue that the common thread behind these interpretations is *summation*. Building on the notions of cumulativity and quantization, the interpretations of reduplication are predictable.

In what follows, section 2 lists out the distribution and characteristics of reduplication in Cantonese. Section 3 reviews previous studies and points out that they cannot account for the behaviour of reduplication across categories. Section 4 discusses the formal property of *cumulativity* (Krifka, 1998; Rothstein, 2004), which provides a basis to account for the surface differences across categories. To test the hypothesis, section 5 provides the details of the proposal and shows how various interpretations can be handled by the present cumulativity analysis. Section 6 discusses the advantage of this approach and also the theoretical implications.

2 Data

This section makes a few observations on reduplication in Cantonese. We will first focus on adjectives, then include nouns and verbs, which share a similar surface pattern. Consider the sentence (1), which provides a reduplicated adjectives denote a sense of hedging or diminution.

(1) *keoi5 gou1 gou1 dei2*
3sg tall tall Prt
'S/he is fairly tall.'

Uttering (1) means that the person is considered tall, but probably not the tallest person or not even 'very tall'. This can be seen in (2), which is infelicitous unless it is otherwise specified that all other members of the group are simply short.

(2) *keoi5 gou1 gou1 dei2, so2ji5 keoi5*
3sg tall tall Prt, therefore 3sg
zeoi3 gou1
SUPERLATIVE tall
'#S/he is fairly tall, so s/he is the tallest.'

The reduplicated adjective form with the particle *gou1 gou1 dei2* is in complementary distribution with (3), where an overt marker shows the magnitude of tallness. This requirement of degree marker in (3) is well-documented, see Grano (2011) for a recent discussion of its syntax and semantics.

(3) *keoi5 *(hou2 / gei2) gou1*
3sg very / fairly tall
'S/he is very / fairly tall.'

Third, adjective reduplication shows an interesting parallelism on the surface with nominal (4) and verbal (5) reduplication in Cantonese.

(4) *go2 go2 sai3lo6 *(dou1) hou2 lek1*
CL CL child DISTR very smart
'Every child is very smart.' [1]

(5) *ngo5 tai2 tai2 ha5 syu1 fan3 zo2*
1sg read read Dur book sleep Perf
'I fell asleep while reading.'

The data above show that reduplication can apply to lexical categories (i.e. nouns, verbs and adjectives). This parallelism is not unique to Cantonese: Chakraborty and Bandyopadhyay (2009) also report that reduplication in Bengali can denote repetition (e.g. 'every year'), plurality (e.g. 'the houses'), emphasis (e.g. 'deep red rose') and imperfective verbs (e.g. '*Talking about something*, suddenly he stopped.'), together with a few other meanings. It is therefore plausible that reduplication denotes some function that is more generic and applicable to different elements. This paper does not attempt to account for cross-linguistic data, but instead focuses on Cantonese. The working hypothesis is that reduplicated forms have a common semantic thread between them, and that that common thread is *summation*. What the summation function does is 'add up' atomic elements into a collection. Reduplicated nouns denote an exhaustive group. For example, (4) refers to a group of children, which is equivalent to 'every single child' in English. Reduplicated verbs denote a durative event, as in *tai2 tai2 ha5 syu1* 'reading (books)' in (5). An interesting feature is that the predicates denoted by reduplicated verbs must be an atelic event, which in turn suggests that reduplicated verbs denote a collection of homogeneous subevents, following the assumption that atelic events have 'subevental properties' (Bennett and Partee, 1972; Krifka, 2001). This paper applies the existing analysis of cumulativity to reduplication in the nominal and verbal domain and further extends the analysis to adjectival reduplication. We thus hypothesize the following:

(6) Reduplication in Cantonese denotes a summation function.

The hypothesis in (6) predicts that the result of the function is always a sum of the input. If the result of the reduplication does not denote a sum or total of the given input, one may claim that hypothesis (6) is falsified.

3 Previous studies

3.1 The complex nature of adjectives

In general, the denotation of adjectives or properties can be decomposed into semantic functions of dimension, scale and degree. A dimension is a choice of measurement, such as height or weight. Scale is an linear ordered set within the same dimension, such as *tall* or *short* for the same dimension of height and *heavy* or *light* for weight. A degree specifies a point along the scale. The degree can bear specific value, as in *full* or *empty* in English. For example, whenever a speaker perceives the water level in a cup to reach the maximum value (i.e. 100%), then it would be felicitous to say *The cup is full.* However, a degree can also bear a fuzzy value, which may vary depending on the context. For instance, one would have very different standard of 'being tall' for *John is tall* and *The Willis tower is tall.* This decomposed adjective phrase analysis is also known as the DegP-shell analysis. Based on this analysis (Xiang, 2005; Grano and Kennedy, 2012), this paper assumes that adjective phrases are internally complex. In terms of syntax, there are multiple heads within the traditional AdjP.

3.2 Cross-categorial reduplication in various languages

There is little discussion specifically on adjectival reduplication in the literature. Although adjectival reduplication is attested in many other languages, e.g. Basque (De Rijk and De Coene, 2008), Bengali (Chakraborty and Bandyopadhyay, 2009) and a handful of others (Rubino, 2011), little attention

[1] Abbreviations: CL- classifier, DISTR- distributive marker, Dur- durative aspect, Perf- perfect aspect, 3sg- third person singular pronoun, Prt- particle

is put on its formal semantic properties. Regier (1994) does provide a good summary of what reduplication can mean in various languages, but does not include Cantonese.

A recent study on adjective reduplication in Mandarin (Liu, 2012) provides an informal pragmatic account of some restrictions on adjectives that can undergo reduplication. Liu's account, like other works cited in this section, adopts an informal cognitive grammar approach to the issue. Also, Liu did not attempt to handle reduplication in nouns and verbs, thus the present analysis differs from Liu's analysis both in terms of the formal approach and scope of study.

Based on crosslinguistic data, Abraham (2005) suggests 'divisibility' as a criterion for base forms that undergo reduplication. He generalizes that reduplicated forms always denote predicates that are divisible, so these divisible predicates must always be a collection of some elements. Abraham (2005) also notes that this generalization would contradict the empirical data that some reduplication forms actually denote diminutive adjectives.

Kouwenberg and LaCharité (2005) address the apparent contradiction of diminutive or 'approximative' interpretation of reduplication and suggest that the diminutive reading is an extension from a dispersive interpretation. That means a diminutive reading of 'yellowish' would come from a dispersive 'yellow-spotted'. 'Dispersive' means that multiple instances of *yellow-ness*, such as spots or stains, are spread over or dispersed. This reading can therefore be construed as multiple instances of 'yellow'. For Kouwenberg and LaCharité (2005), this is a connecting context where reduplication first bears plurality. This reading can be extended to diminution, in the sense that yellowness is spread over the entity in a diluted way, instead of being individual spots or patches. However, such an account does not constrain when a language or an expression can perform semantic extension from dispersive to diminutive. It does work well for reduplication of colour adjectives in Cantonese, but not with adjectives of size and shape. For example, reduplication of predicates such as 'big' or 'tall' can never bear any dispersive reading, because the property of 'big' or 'tall' always predicates over the whole entity, not part of it. Kouwenberg and LaCharité (2005)'s theory of extension relies on the dispersive reading extending to diminution. Therefore, it cannot account for size and shape adjectives bearing diminutive reading, because the dispersive reading is impossible for size and shape adjectives. This paper takes the intuition that reduplication denotes a sense of multiplicity of elements, but does not assert that diminution comes from dispersion. Instead, this paper suggests that both diminutive and dispersive readings are the result of summation, as will be further discussed in section 5.3.

The theory in Abraham (2005) and Kouwenberg and LaCharité (2005) treats iconicity as a central property in reduplication. This paper takes the multiplication as an intuition that there is a summation process. In sections 4 and 5, we show that the formal properties of cumulativity and quantization can resolve the apparent contradiction that the same predicate can denote the sum of a collection and a subpart of the same collection.

4 Cumulativity and Quantization

The central claim of this paper is that summation is the underlying common thread in reduplication. Before we move on to the implementation, it is crucial to understand that cumulativity and quantization have a direct impact on the result of the elements undergoing summation. This section sets up the background of cumulativity in the literature on nouns and verbs.

Krifka (2001) defines cumulativity as the following:

(7) A predicate P is cumulative iff
(i) $\forall x, y[P(x) \wedge P(y) \rightarrow P(x \oplus y)]$
(ii) $\exists x, y[P(x) \wedge P(y) \wedge \neg x = y]]$

Condition (i) means when two entities x and y are added together, they can still be described with the same denotation. Condition (ii) ensures x and y are distinct elements. For example, in a situation when Mary said she saw that John left, and Jane also said she saw that John left, we cannot infer that John left twice or conclude that 'leaving' is cumulative. The reason is that 'John' in the two utterances is the same person.

Cumulative predicates include 'wine' or 'apples' [2]. If an object x called 'wine' is added to another object, which is distinct from x, let's call it y, which is also wine, we have a new object containing x and y. Since we can reasonably describe this

[2]Here the term predicate is used in a logical sense, not a linguistic sense. It bears no specification of category such as noun or verb, nor is it restricted to events or properties.

new object as 'wine' (as opposed to 'two wines', which is possible in a different context), we can conclude that 'wine' denotes a cumulative predicate. Typically, but not necessarily, cumulative predicates include mass nouns and count plural nouns. As noted in Rothstein (2004), there are several 'exceptions' like *line*, *sequence* or *fence* in English, which we will not discuss in detail here.

The same characteristic can be applied to verbal predicates. Atelic predicates are typically cumulative. Take *run* in English as an example. Two distinct instances of *run*, when put together, can also be described as 'run'. Likewise, putting *John built houses last year* and *John builds houses this year* together, one can still describe the whole event as 'building houses'.

In contrast, count nouns with number marking are characterized by the property of *quantization*. Krifka (2001) defines quantized predicates as:

(8) A predicate P is quantized iff
$\forall x, y[P(x) \wedge P(y) \rightarrow \neg y < x]]$

Using the example in Krifka (1998), if an element x can be called '3 apples', then it is impossible for any proper subset of x to be described as '3 apples'. This captures our intuition that part of '3 apples' can be an apple, or two apples, but not three apples. Similarly, a proper part of quantized events cannot be identical to its superset. If we say 'John made **four cakes**.', the part of the event, for example John making one cake, cannot be described as 'John made **four cakes**.' It shows that the verbal predicate 'make four cakes' is quantized.

The notions of cumulativity and quantization capture the human understanding of collective entities. There are two important messages. Firstly, summation of two elements (more precisely, two predicates) can often result in an element with same denotation, as seen in cumulative predicates 'apples' or 'run'. Note that the count-mass distinction is linguistic, which means that the encoding of whether a noun is count or mass is independent from ontology. For example, nouns like 'furniture' or 'footwear' are considered mass because they do not co-occur with numerals or the singular indefinite article, as in '*four furniture' or '*a footwear'. Second, the count-mass distinction is language-specific, meaning that an entity denoted by a mass noun in one language can be count in another language.

5 Summation as a common thread

The previous section shows that the behaviour or the interpretation of the sum (i.e. the returned value as a result of summation) can be used to indicate cumulativity and quantization. The denotation of 'SUM' in (9) is essentially 'every' in English (Heim and Kratzer, 1998).

(9) $[\![\text{SUM}]\!] = \lambda f \in D \,.\, \forall x \in D \rightarrow f(x) = 1$

This ensures all the individuals x are included in the sum D. From this formalization, we can see that whenever the sum shares the same denotation as its atomic elements, then we can see that the atomic elements must be cumulative. (e.g. 'some water' can be a collection of 'some water'). On the contrary, if a collection does not share the same denotation as its atoms (e.g. 'a chair' cannot have 'a chair' as its proper subset), the elements are quantized.

This section shows the implementation of summation in reduplication across the categories noun, verb and adjective in Cantonese.

5.1 Nouns

Cantonese nominals in general require classifiers on top of the noun. Nominal reduplication always applies to the classifier, as in (10). In (10) and (11), both the classifier and noun are present. The crucial difference between (10) and (11) is that the former reduplicates its classifier, which is acceptable, and the latter reduplicates its noun, which is unacceptable. Sentence (12) shows reduplication of the noun without a classifier, which is also unacceptable.

(10) *go2 go2 sai3lo6 dou1 hou2 lek1*
CL CL child DISTR very smart
'Every child is very smart.'

(11) **go2 sai3lo6 sai3lo6 dou1 hou2*
CL child child DISTR very
lek1
smart
Intended: 'Every child is very smart.'

(12) **sai3(lo6) sai3lo6 dou1 hou2 lek1*
child child DISTR very smart
Intended: 'Every child is very smart.'

The data show that Cantonese reduplication applies only to classifiers, but not nouns [3]. Both

[3]For detailed discussion syntax of classifier and noun in Cantonese, see Cheng, 2012), which points out two puzzles

the classifier and the noun must be present and whenever there is reduplication, it must apply to the classifier[4].

There are a few apparent exceptions to the generalization that reduplication always applies to the classifier, such as *jat6 jat6* 'day-day – every day', *jan4 jan4* 'person-person – everybody', *dou6 dou6* 'place-place – everywhere', where there is no classifier present. However, one can also observe that these nouns behave differently from other common nouns in other contexts. For example, these nouns can cooccur with numerals without any classifiers, as shown in (13). Also, exceptions like *jat6* 'day' or *nin4* 'year' are measurement units of time, which can never occur with classifiers (**saam1 go3 jat6* 'three-classifier-day' would be unacceptable for '3 days'). We can therefore treat these nouns as if they already carry the functional feature that classifiers add to common nouns. This observation conforms with (Zhang, 2013)'s view that individuation is not exclusively expressed by classifiers and bare nouns in classifier-languages can denote countable objects.

(13) *keoi5 heoi5 zo2 hon4gwok3 sap6*
3sg go Perf Korea ten
*(*go3) jat1*
CL day
'S/he went to Korea for ten days.'

Now with well-formed reduplication like (10), we can see that each single member 'child' in the group 'every child' is quantized, but not cumulative, because a proper subpart of a child would not qualify as a child, i.e. one cannot reasonably call a subpart, say the shoulder of a child, 'a child'. Formally:

(14) $[\![\text{SUM}]\!](\text{child}) = \lambda f \in D \, . \, \forall x \in D \rightarrow f(x)=1$
$= \forall x \in D \rightarrow \textbf{child}(x)=1$

The phrase 'every child' is true (truth value=1), iff each of the members in the domain D is a child. The Cantonese phrase *go3 sai6lo6* 'a child' (before reduplication) works the same way as its English counterpart. Since the phrase *go3 sai6lo6* 'a child' is quantized, we predict that a summation of such elements would result in a quantized entity. This prediction is borne out in the data. To see this, let us focus on the individual member first. Since the utterance (10) denotes an exhaustive group of 'every child', it means that the predicate 'very smart' would apply to each of the individual members. The interpretation is also supported by the self-contradiction in the utterance in (15). Since (15) is not acceptable, we can infer that the reduplicated noun must denote every single member of 'the children'.

(15) *#go2 go2 sai3lo6 dou1 hou2 lek1,*
CL CL child DISTR very smart
dan6hai6 jau1 jat1 go3 m4 lek1
but EXIST one CL Neg smart
'#Every child is very smart, but one of them is not.'

As predicted for the reduplicated form denoting 'every child', we can also observe the predicted result of a quantized entity. A proper subset of 'every child' cannot be also described as 'every child', for the reason that if a set y is the proper subset of a larger set x, y is necessarily smaller and thus does not include at least one of the members in x. Thus it is impossible to describe set y with the same denotation of x and we can conclude that the reduplicated noun phrase denotes a quantized predicate as well.

5.2 Verbs

Verbal reduplication in Cantonese shows a different pattern than nominals. Example (5) is repeated below as (16). The reading event must be interpreted as a prolonged, durative event, as its English translation suggests.

(16) *ngo5 tai2 tai2 ha5 syu1 fan3 zo2*
1sg read read Dur book sleep Perf
'I fell asleep while reading.'

As first suggested by Bennett and Partee (1972), all the subparts within an atelic event are homogeneous. It provides a basis to compare an atom of a durative event to a singular member in plural count nouns. That means, the durative reading event in (16) can be seen as a collection of atomic reading subevents. Since these subevents are homogeneous, the whole reading event is considered atelic.

about Cantonese classifier reduplication. While both Cantonese and Mandarin use classifiers in their nominals, only Cantonese allows classifier reduplication.

[4] For independent reason, presumably phonological, Cantonese reduplication often takes one syllable. The unacceptability of (12) shows that a partial reduplication (i.e. reduplicating only the first syllable) would not make the utterance acceptable.

Atelic events can be independently tested with duration modification, which is equivalent to the *for / in a period of time* test in English. If a predicate can be modified by 'for an hour' (or any other context-appropriate time interval), then the predicate is atelic. For example, *John read for an hour* is acceptable, whereas **John read in an hour* is not. It shows that 'read' is atelic. Cantonese does not use a prepositional phrase to show duration, but uses the verb copying construction like (17) instead[5]. Example (18) is equivalent to *in 3 minutes* in English. Since only (17) but not (18) is compatible with *tai2 syu1* 'read', we can conclude that *tai2 syu1* is atelic.

(17) *ngo5 tai2 syu1 tai2 zo2*
1sg read book read Perf
saam1-fen1-zong1
3-minute
'I read for 3 minutes.'

(18) **ngo5 hai2 saam1-fen1-zong1 zi1noi6*
1sg in 3-minute within
tai2 syu1
read book
'*I read (with)in 3 minutes.'

Because *tai2 syu1* 'read' is atelic, we can say that each instance of reading is identical to other instances within the same event.

What makes verbal reduplication such as (17) different from nominal reduplication is that the members of the reading events are non-quantized and cumulative. Conceptually, an instance of reading counts as reading, no matter how long it lasts. Also, adding up two instances of reading would also be interpreted reading. In other words, atelic predicates such as *tai2 syu1* 'read book' in Cantonese are cumulative. Let x and y be distinct atomic events, and *tai2 syu1* $[\![\text{read}]\!]$ be predicate over each of them. The interpretations above are formalized in (19) below:

(19) $[\![\text{read}]\!](x) \wedge [\![\text{read}]\!](y) = 1$
$[\![\text{read}]\!](x \oplus y) = 1$

What the durative interpretation of verbal reduplication tells us is that it must denote a sum of multiple subevents as members, otherwise one should be able to find verbal reduplication examples that are punctual (i.e. not durative). However, since the reduplicated verb still denotes one prolonged event, we must account for this difference from nominal reduplication (which denotes a collection of distinct, individuated members) in terms of cumulativity.

However, it is also possible for verb reduplication to contain non-cumulative and quantized subevents. Semelfactive verbs, such as *jump* and *knock* in English are always punctual, i.e. they cannot be durative. This is shown by the observation that *John jumps for an hour* would only give the iterative reading that there are more than one jumps in that hour, rather than the reading that one single jump lasts for an hour. The verb *tiu3* 'jump' in Cantonese works the same way as its English counterpart. Only (20), but not (21), is acceptable[6].

(20) *ngo5 tiu3 zo2 saam1-fen1-zong1*
1sg jump Perf 3-minute
'I jumped for 3 minutes.' (*iterative only*)

(21) **ngo5 hai2 saam1-fen1-zong1 zi1noi6*
1sg in 3-minute within
tiu3 (zo2)
jump Perf
'*I jumped (with)in 3 minutes.'

When the verb *tiu3* 'jump' is reduplicated, as in (22), the only reading allowed is that jumping is iterative, i.e. there must be more than one instance of repeated jumping.

(22) *ngo5 tiu3 tiu3 ha5 gok3dak1*
1sg jump jump Dur feel
tou5ngo6
hungry
'I (begin to) feel hungry while jumping.'
(*iterative reading only*)

The fact that (22) cannot be durative can naturally be explained by the cumulativity and quantization contrast.

(23) $[\![\text{jump}]\!](\text{x}) \wedge [\![\text{jump}]\!](\text{y}) = 1$

(24) $[\![\text{jump}]\!](\text{y}) \rightarrow \neg y < x = 1$

If (23) is true, then (24) is necessarily true, i.e. the atomic event y must not be a proper subpart of the atomic event x (cf. definition (8)). Since

[5] Note that the two occurrences in (17) are not contiguous, thus it is distinct from verb reduplication.

[6] Similar to English, one would judge (21) as acceptable if there was an implicit object that gives some other meaning. (21) intends only the literal meaning of 'jump'.

tiu3 'jump' is punctual and quantized, the sum of multiple instances of it must be a proper superset of each individual instance, therefore the reduplication is interpreted as an iterative event, but not a durative one.

This section has shown that the summation formulation naturally handles the two kinds of verb reduplication without stipulating summation itself. The choice between durative reading of one instance of the same event and the iterative reading that represents multiple instances can be predicted solely by the nature of the event denoted by the base verb. If the base form is cumulative, the summation function returns a durative event; if the base form is quantized, summation returns an iterative reading.

5.3 Adjectives

There are two independent issues in the interpretation of adjectives. The first one concerns the status of reduplication as a semantic function and a syntactic head in the domain of adjectives. The second issue is the apparent contradiction between summation and the hedging and diminutive reading. This section will show that reduplication is indeed one of the variants that denotes degree, alongside *hou2* 'very' and other degree markers, such as *gei2* 'fairly'. It will also be shown that the diminutive reading does not contradict summation or plurality in general, echoing previous studies on diminutive reduplication (Abraham, 2005; Kouwenberg and LaCharité, 2005).

Regarding the first issue, the distribution of reduplication shows that the reduplication morpheme should be a functional head asserting some sort of degree. By comparing (25) and (26) against the ungrammatical (27), we can see that adjectival predicates must either have *hou2* 'very' or reduplication to be acceptable.

(25) *go2 zek3 maau1 hou2 fei4*
that CL cat very fat
'That cat is very fat.'

(26) *go2 zek3 maau1 fei4 fei4 dei2*
that CL cat fat fat Prt
'That cat is fairly fat.'

(27) **go2 zek3 maau1 fei4*
that CL cat fat
'*Intended*: That cat is fat.'

Since reduplication and degree markers like *hou2* 'very' cannot cooccur and one of them must appear in the utterance, they are in complementary distribution and must denote similar function.

Section 3 showed that adjective predicates are internally complex, based on previous studies on scale and degrees. Following Grano (2011) and Grano and Kennedy (2012)'s analysis of Mandarin, elements like 'very' in Chinese denote a morpheme that turns a bare adjective into a degree-marked element[7]. More specifically, the assertion of the degree-marked adjective would involve a morpheme $[\![pos]\!]$, which provides the contextual standard to determine whether the object in question meets the standard for the given property. Since reduplication also denotes the assertion that an entity meets a certain standard, one can say that reduplication shares the same position as $[\![pos]\!]$, by the distribution shown above.

The second issue is the diminutive interpretation as a counterexample of to the present summation theory. Abraham (2005) investigates how reduplication can provide diminutive interpretation, assuming reduplication was a iconic manifestation of multiplicity. The data for diminitive reduplication cited in Abraham (2005) and Kouwenberg and LaCharité (2005) include verbs and adjectives, but the adjective examples are colour terms and other adjectives that can describe part of an entity, as in (28) and (29).

(28) a. Base form: *red* 'red'
b. *redi-redi* 'reddish, red-spotted'
Caribbean Creoles (Abraham, 2005, p.552)

(29) a. Base form: *brok* 'to break'
b. *brokii-brokii* 'as if broken all over'
Caribbean Creoles (Kouwenberg and LaCharité, 2005, p.538)

The explanation given in Kouwenberg and LaCharité (2005) is that there is an intermediate meaning of 'red-spotted' or 'as if broken all over' which denotes multiple instances of redness (or for (29), breaks). The dispersive reading ('red-spotted' or 'as if broken all over') is then extended to diminutive reading ('reddish' or 'fairly/

[7]Cantonese is similar to Mandarin in all the related aspects here. Grano (2011) also notes that (27) can provide implicit comparative reading in a contrastive context, but this is outside the focus of this paper.

slightly broken'). In such a theory, both Kouwenberg and LaCharité (2005) and Abraham (2005) claim that reduplication in form does denote a sense of multiplicity, only that the multiplicity is distributed to the same entity. (Kouwenberg and LaCharité, 2005) claim that '(t)he real-world effect of such scattered distribution of colour is to tone down rather than intensify the colour'. Therefore the multiple spots of the colour would result in a diminutive reading, through the dispersive reading.

However, the iconicity theory cannot explain the Cantonese examples like (26), where there cannot be a dispersive reading. Since the predicate *fei4* 'fat' applies to the whole entity 'cat', but not part of it, it is impossible to interpret *fei4 fei4 dei2* as 'being fat everywhere / all over' in (26). The cumulative analysis pursued in this paper avoids the problem with dispersive reading. Based on the discussion of distribution above, we can see that bare adjectives (27) are not allowed in the language. If we further assume that adjectival predicates should include the positive morpheme $[\![pos]\!]$ for any assertion, the Cantonese data would mean that bare adjectives do not denote the positive degree, since they cannot assert the positive degree.

The cumulativity analysis, on the other hand, explains the correct diminutive interpretation and why no intensification arises. Given the formulation of cumulativity in (7), a predicate is considered cumulative if the sum of the predicate has the same denotation of its atomic elements. Let x and y be two property-denoting variables, each predicated by $[\![\text{fat}]\!]$ as in (30a):

(30) a. $\textbf{fat}(x) \wedge \textbf{fat}(y) = 1$
b. $\forall x,y\ [\textbf{fat}(x \oplus y)] = 1$
c. $\forall x,y\ [\textbf{fat}(x) \wedge \textbf{fat}(y) \rightarrow \neg\, y < x] = 0$

(30b) is true because any two instances of being fat conjoined would denote $[\![\text{fat}]\!]$. For (30c) to be true, the property-denoting variable (i.e. bare adjectives *without* degree-marking) y must not be a proper subpart of x. However, this is not the case in the Cantonese data. For example, the belly of a fat cat can be described as fat. The proper subpart does share the same denotation of its whole. We thus conclude that adjectives in Cantonese must be cumulative. Section 5.2 has shown how cumulativity accounts for verb reduplication under durative interpretation. Adjectival reduplication shows a similar pattern. That is, the reduplicated form denotes a cumulative and non-quantized predicate. Cumulativity succeeds in preventing the wrong interpretation for reduplication to denote intensification in Cantonese. By extending the cumulativity analysis to adjectives, it can be seen that reduplication does not necessarily denote 'more' in the quantized sense, even though it denotes a summation function.

The apparent contradiction between summation and diminution comes from the wrong comparison. Since atomic bare adjectives do not denote any degree, it would be wrong to compare the degree denoted by reduplication and the non-existing degree denoted by the bare form. Instead, the reduplicated form should be compared to the default degree-marker *hou2* 'very', as in (25), when one is measuring the intensity or extent of the assertion. Recall that Cantonese requires overt degree-marking, as shown by the unacceptability of (27). Comparing the two options (25) and (26) to assert a positive degree, (25) with *hou2* would denote a neutral assertion of positive degree, but it can also be interpreted as emphasis or intensification, whereas (26) gives the diminutive, hedging reading ('slightly, fairly *Adj*'). Despite being a result of summation from the bare adjective, the degree denoted by reduplication should be compared to the canonical positive assertion, but not the atomic bare adjective. In other words, there is no contradiction between the summation formulation and the diminutive interpretation.

The present account is more powerful than the iconicity-based theory for two reasons. First, cumulativity is a property more widely observed across categories and languages, whereas iconicity is not as prominent in explaining behaviours of various constructions. The present account does not assume either iconicity or any form of symbolism and relies only on the notion of cumulativity, which is independently needed for count/mass distinction or durative events in the language. Second, the iconicity account does not explain the reduplication of adjectives that must describe the entity as a whole, but not a part, such as (26). On the contrary, cumulativity can handle such cases without relying on an intermediate dispersive reading, which is not always available.

The present cumulativity analysis makes the following two predictions: (i) in languages where reduplicated adjectives denote intensification, the adjectives are degree-marked and thus quantized;

(ii) in languages where reduplicated adjectives denote diminution, the adjectives are not marked with degree and thus cumulative. Cantonese adjectives would belong to type (ii). On the one hand, Cantonese adjective reduplication denotes diminution. On the other hand, Cantonese adjectives alone do not carry degree, as revealed by the observation that it requires degree marking.

This analysis does not exclude the possibility that the two options can co-exist in the same language, as we have already observed such cases in Cantonese verbs, where both cumulative and quantized predicates are possible within the same category. Our Cantonese adjectives are exclusively cumulative, but it does not mean that it is impossible for other languages to show category-internal variations in terms of cumulativity and quantization. What the present analysis predicts is that the two subtypes of adjectives would each display a different meaning in their respective reduplication forms, if they exist at all in such a language.

This section has explained that adjective reduplication in Cantonese should be treated as diminutive because the atomic bare adjective is cumulative. By showing that we should be comparing reduplication forms only to degree-marked adjectives, instead of the base form, we conclude that there is indeed no contradiction between the summation treatment to reduplication and its diminutive interpretation. By analogy, adjectives without degree-marking are similar to verbs without aspect-marking or nouns without classifiers or determiners, in the sense that bare verbs and bare nouns do not denote instantiated arguments, but only kinds of object or events in an abstract sense.

6 Implications

The present hypothesis that reduplication denotes summation is confirmed only with Cantonese data. However, it can also be tested by cross-linguistic data. Various pragmatic interpretation are discussed in the literature (Regier, 1994). Regier suggests notions like 'lack of specificity' and 'non-uniformity' as subtypes of meanings that can be denoted by reduplication. These can potentially be formalized as elements with fuzzy boundaries or multiple degrees along a scale. In languages where reduplication denotes intensification, the present analysis can also be extended to account for the increased degree through summation. This would then predict that the reduplicated elements are quantized, since the sum would have a distinct denotation.

The advantage of the present proposal is that the notions of cumulativity and quantization are independently testable without reduplication. For languages that show reduplication, knowing the cumulativity and quantization properties can predict the reading of reduplication. For unreduplicated base forms that are cumulative, such as *paau2 bou6* 'lit: run step, i.e. to jog' in (31), the present proposal predicts that its reduplicated form would denote the same predicate, i.e. a durative, atelic event. On the other hand, in a base form that is punctual, such as *tiu3 sing2* 'jump rope' in (32), each instance of jump must be quantized because the sum of two jumps cannot be described as a jump. In this case, it correctly predicts that the felicitous reading in sentence (32) must be iterative, but not a reading of a single prolonged jumping-action.

(31) *keoi5 paau2 paau2 ha5 bou6*
3sg run run Asp step
gok3dak3 tou5ngo6
feel hungry
'S/he feels hungry while jogging.'

(32) *keoi5 tiu3 tiu3 ha5 sing2 gok3dak3*
3sg jump jump Asp rope feel
tou5ngo6
hungry
'S/he feels hungry while jumping rope.'

The present analysis shows that reduplication can be formalized as a summation process[8], while the difference across categories in their respective interpretations can be resolved with the notions of cumulativity and quantization. This step allows us to apply semantic functions independently of syntactic categories. Since there can be variance of cumulativity and quantization within the same category, as observed in mass nouns and bare plural count nouns being cumulative and quantified count nouns being quantized, the cumulativity and quantization contrast in different cases of reduplication should not be solely attributed to a difference in category. This also raises the question

[8] A natural next step is to extend the current analysis to the bisyllabic full reduplications, commonly known as the AABB and ABAB patterns. This is, however, beyond the scope of this study.

of the traditional notion of 'category'. More precisely, if the semantic functions are shared across categories, then what is the role of categories in grammar? Independently, there are decompositional proposals in syntax that explicitly suggest parallel structure between the nominal and the verbal domains (Borer, 2005a; Borer, 2005b; Megerdoomian, 2008) and between the verbal and adjectival domains (Kennedy and McNally, 2005; Beavers, 2008; Ramchand, 2012). Wouldn't it be desirable to have a unified theory across lexical categories? Due to the limited scope of this study, we will leave the issue here for future research.

7 Conclusion

The main goal of this paper is to explain the cross-categorial behaviour of reduplication in Cantonese.

This paper has shown that it is possible to interpret reduplicated forms in lexical categories (i.e. nouns, verbs and adjectives) under the same function, *summation*. Whenever reduplication occurs, the atomic elements are added up and put into a collection. We argue that the difference in interpretations depends solely on the cumulativity and quantization of the element, but not its category. Nominal reduplication returns a superset of its elements, which conforms with the fact that classifier phrases in Cantonese denote individuated elements and is thus quantized. Verbal reduplication can be either cumulative or quantized, depending on the aktionsart of the individual verbal predicate. Adjectival reduplication is cumulative, due to its divisibility into subparts. The present analysis bears two implications. It captures the cross-categorial behaviour in semantic terms and provides a basis for future research on the formal semantic properties of reduplication across languages.

Acknowledgments

I thank Ronnie Wilbur and Chuck Bradley for sharing their insights and critical comments at earlier stages of this project. I am grateful to the three anonymous reviewers for constructive suggestions.

References

Abraham, W. (2005). *Intensity and diminution triggered by reduplicating morphology: Janus-faced iconicity*, pages 547–568.

Beavers, J. (2008). *Scalar complexity and the structure of events*, pages 245–265. Berlin: Mouton de Gruyter.

Bennett, M. and Partee, B. (1972). Towards the logic of tense and aspect in English. Report for the System Development Corporation. *Compositionality in Formal Semantics*, pages 59–109.

Borer, H. (2005a). *Structuring Sense: Volume 1: In Name Only*. Oxford University Press.

Borer, H. (2005b). *Structuring Sense: Volume II: The Normal Course of Events*, volume 2. Oxford University Press, USA.

Chakraborty, T. and Bandyopadhyay, S. (2009). Identification of reduplication in Bengali corpus and their semantic analysis: A rule-based approach. In *23rd International Conference on Computational Linguistics*, page 73.

Cheng, L. L. S. (2012). *Counting and classifiers*. Oxford University Press.

De Rijk, R. P. and De Coene, A. (2008). *Standard Basque: A progressive grammar*. MIT Press.

Grano, T. and Kennedy, C. (2012). Mandarin transitive comparatives and the grammar of measurement. *Journal of East Asian Linguistics*, 21:219–266.

Heim, I. and Kratzer, A. (1998). *Semantics in generative grammar*, volume 13. Wiley-Blackwell.

Kennedy, C. and McNally, L. (2005). Scale structure, degree modification, and the semantics of gradable predicates. *Language*, pages 345–381.

Kouwenberg, S. and LaCharité, D. (2005). Less is more: Evidence from diminutive reduplication in Carribbean Creole languages. pages 533–545.

Krifka, M. (1998). The origins of telicity. *Events and grammar*, 197:235.

Krifka, M. (2001). The mereological approach to aspectual composition. *Conference Perspectives on Aspect*. University of Utrecht, OTS.

Liu, C.-S. L. (2012). Reduplication of adjectives in Chinese: a default state. *Journal of East Asian Linguistics*.

Megerdoomian, K. (2008). Parallel nominal and verbal projections. *Current studies in linguistics series*, 45:73.

Ramchand, G. (2012). Scalar structure across categories: V, P vs. A*. CASTL, Univeristy of Tromsø.

Regier, T. (1994). A preliminary study of the semantics of reduplication.

Rothstein, S. (2004). *Structuring Events*. Blackwell.

Rubino, C. (2011). Reduplication. In Dryer, M. S. and Haspelmath, M., editors, *The World Atlas of Language Structures Online*. Max Planck Digital Library, Munich.

Xiang, M. (2005). *Some topics in comparative constructions*. PhD thesis, Michigan State University.

Zhang, N. N. (2013). *Classifier Structures in Mandarin Chinese*. Berlin: Mouton de Gruyter.

*** Formatting Issue - Best Available Paper/Graphic ***

Yet Another Piece of Evidence for the Common Base Approach to Japanese Causative/Inchoative Alternations

Tomokazu Takehisa
Niigata University of Pharmacy and Applied Life Sciences
265-1 Higashijima, Akiha-ku, Niigata 956-8603, Japan
takehisa@nupals.ac.jp

Abstract

This paper presents yet another argument for the view that both the causative and inchoative verbs in the Japanese causative alternation are syntactically equally complex, derived independently from common bases. While morphological considerations alone suggest that such an approach must be taken to account for cases involving equipollent alternations, which have overt morphemes for both the causative and inchoative affixes, the question remains unsettled as to whether there are cases where such processes as causativization of inchoative verbs or anticausativization of causative verbs are involved. In an attempt to answer this question, this paper examines the three approaches to the causative alternation by utilizing the possibility of having idiomatic interpretations as a probe into the syntactic structure. Evidence from idioms reveals that the common base approach still fares better. As a further consequence, postulation of a phonologically null morpheme is forced for some causative and inchoative affixes.

1 Introduction

It has been standard since the early days of generative grammar that causative verbs are assumed to be syntactically more complex than their inchoative counterparts, reflecting their semantic complexity. While specific analyses like Dowty (1979) are long gone, their spirit remains alive and well and has been instantiated in later theoretical constructs such as Lexical Conceptual Structure (e.g., Rappaport and Levin, 1988) and double VP structure (e.g., Hale and Keyser, 1993). Moreover, while structural complexity per se is independent of the issue of the derivational relationship between the causative and inchoative alternants, it has been also standard to assume that causatives are virtually derived from their inchoative counterparts via operations like Predicate Raising in Generative Semantics or Head Movement in the GB/MP framework. Thus, the causativization approach, which views causatives as based on inchoatives, has been influential across a variety of theoretical perspectives.

Two more approaches can be discerned as alternatives to handle the derivational relationship between the two alternants. One involves the process of anticausativization of causative verbs (e.g., Levin and Rappaport Hovav, 1995), and the other approach, proposed by researchers like Piñón (2001) and Alexiadou et al. (2006), is the common base approach, where both the causative and inchoative alternants are derived independently from an identical root. The three possible approaches to the causative/inchoative alternation are given in (1).[1]

(1) a. *e a sati ization pproa*
Causatives are derived from inchoatives.
b. *e nti a sati ization pproa*
Inchoatives are derived from causatives.
c. *e o on ase pproa*
Causatives and inchoatives are derived from their common bases.

Japanese sheds light on this issue of derivation from a different angle: the language is very well known for having rich derivational and in-

[1] See Haspelmath (1993) for a classification of the alternation in terms of markedness relations. In this paper, I focus on ways to relate the two alternants of a pair syntactically.

flectional systems of verbal morphology, and the morphosyntax of the causative/inchoative alternation is one of the well-studied domains of investigation. A list of the causative/inchoative affix pairs is given in (2), which is in large part based on Jacobsen (1992:258ff.).[2,3]

(2)	CAUS/INCH	e.g., √V-C-NPST/√V-I-NPST
a.	-e- /-ar-	ag-e-ru/ag-ar-u 'rise/raise'
b.	-s-/-r-	kae-s-u/kae-r-u 'return(C)/return(I)'
c.	-s-/-re-	kowa-s-u/kowa-re-ru 'break(C)/break(I)'
d.	-s-/-ri-	ta-s-u/ta-ri-ru 'add/suffice'
e.	-as-/-e-	korog-as-u/korog-e-ru 'roll(C)/roll(I)'
f.	-as-/-i-	nob-as-u/nob-i-ru 'extend/stretch'
g.	-os-/-i-	ot-os-u/ot-i-ru 'drop/fall'
h.	-akas-/-e-	obiy-akas-u/obi-e-ru 'threaten/fear'
i.	-e-/-or-	kom-e-ru/kom-or-u 'fill/become filled'
j.	-e-/-are-	wak-e-ru/wak-are-ru 'divide(C)/divide(I)'
k.	-as-/-Ø-	koor-as-u/koor-Ø-u 'freeze(C)/freeze(I)'
l.	-e-/-Ø-	ak-e-ru/ak-Ø-u 'open(C)/open(I)'
m.	-se-/-Ø-	ni-se-ru/ni-Ø-ru 'model after/resemble'
n.	-Ø-/-e-	mog-Ø-u/mog-e-ru 'pluck off/come off'
o.	-Ø-/-ar-	tog-Ø-u/tog-ar-u 'sharpen(C)/sharpen(I)'
p.	-Ø-/-Ø-	hirak-Ø-u/hirak-Ø-u 'open(C)/open(I)'

Unless powerful morphophonological rules manipulating the underlying phonological strings are assumed to apply,[4] morphological considerations alone suggest that the common base approach must be taken to account for equipollent alternations, as in (2)a–(2)j, which involve overt affixes for both the causative and the inchoative alternants. However, the same line of reasoning also suggests that causativization of inchoative verbs and anticausativization of causative verbs may be involved in (2)k–(2)m and (2)n–(2)o, respectively. Since there are no a priori reasons to reject the possibility that more than one system coexists in a language, the issue remains unsettled as to whether these two processes are called for to account for the above examples.

Thus, this paper takes up the issue by investigating data involving (2)k–(2)o in a different light, with the availability of idiomatic interpretations. Specifically, I will show that neither the causativization approach nor the anticausativization approach can be maintained even in cases where they initially appear to be plausible and thus that the common base approach should be taken all across the board, which in turn justifies postulating that some causative and inchoative morphemes are phonologically null.

The paper is organized as follows: in section 2, I will introduce the assumptions about idioms adopted in this paper. In section 3, I will examine the three approaches to the causative alternation in turn, in light of the availability of idiomatic interpretations, arguing for the common base approach. Section 4 briefly discusses ditransitive causatives and their related forms. Section 5 concludes the paper.

This paper is couched within the general framework of Distributed Morphology (Halle and Marantz, 1993), but, this work being of a descriptive nature, I believe the result can be imported into any other framework.

2 Idioms and Structures

Idioms have received much attention because they present the test case for the principle of compositionality (see the works in Everaert et al , 1995 and Nunberg et al., 1994). While they are not compositional, displaying varying degrees of semantic drift, phrasal idioms are structurally constrained as well as non-idiomatic phrases.

As proposed by O'Grady (1998), Everaert (2010) and Bruening (2010), the structural constraints can be reduced to the selectional properties of particular lexical items. Thus, for the

[2] The following abbreviations are used: ACC = accusative; CAUS, C = causative; COM = comitative; COMP = complementizer; DAT = dative; DIM = diminutive; DV = dummy verb; GEN = genitive; HON = honorific; INCH, I = inchoative; INST = instrumental; NPST = nonpast; PST = past; TRANS, T = transitive; √V = verbal root.

[3] In the following, the symbol Ø indicates either the presence of a phonologically null morpheme or the absence of a morpheme, depending on the approach one endorses.

[4] See Miyagawa (1998) for such an attempt (cf. Nishiyama, 1998). Under the causativization approach, he proposes a set of rules to the affix pairs in (2) within the framework of Distributed Morphology (Halle and Marantz, 1993).

present purposes, I assume, following O'Grady (1998), that idioms are subject to the Continuity Constraint: the component parts of an idiom must form a chain of selectional relations, expressed in terms of head-to-head relations.

According to the Continuity Constraint, an idiom like *i t e a it* has the following chain of relations, indicated by the arrows:

(3) [$_{VP}$ [$_{V}$ kick] [$_{NP}$ [$_{D}$ the] [$_{N}$ habit]]]

In (3), the chain is established via head-to-head relations: the verb selects the noun, which in turn selects the definite article.[5] This chain of relations serves as a unit for special meaning. In the following, I will call the smallest constituent containing such a chain a minimal idiomatic constituent (MIC for short) and indicate it with a circle, as illustrated in (4):[6]

(4)

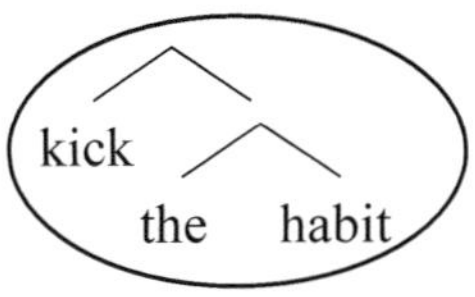

Moreover, if a structural relation involved in the chain is disrupted, then the related unit for special meaning is disrupted, making an idiomatic interpretation unavailable, as shown in (5):

(5)

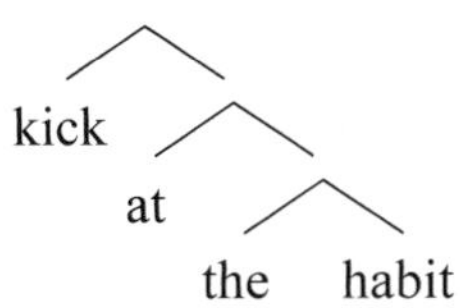

Furthermore, the Continuity Constraint also predicts that an idiom's component parts can be modified without losing its special meaning only if its chain of relations is not disrupted, as illustrated in (6):

(6) [$_{VP}$ [$_{V}$ kick] [$_{NP}$ [$_{D}$ the] [$_{AP}$ filthy] [$_{N}$ habit]]]

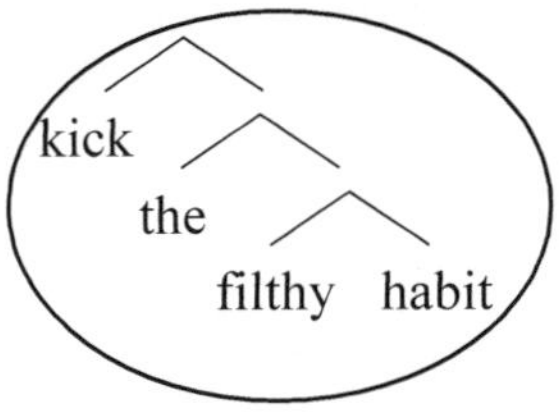

[5] It is crucial that D does not take NP as its complement, as Bruening (2010) also assumes.

[6] MIC is employed to indicate a unit for special meaning for the purpose of presentation.

Likewise, adding more structure does not affect an idiom if its chain is kept intact, as in (7).

(7)

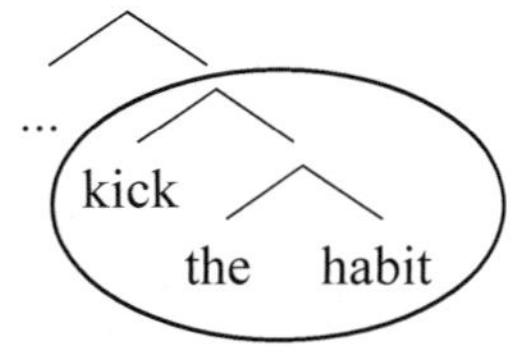

Given these assumptions, we will turn to the approaches to the causative alternation.

3 The Causative Alternation and Idioms

3.1 Causativization of Inchoative Verbs

The causativization approach takes it that causatives are derived from inchoatives by affixation of a causative morpheme. Consider the structures in (8), where B, I, and C represent a base (with extra materials such as NP), an inchoative morpheme, and a causative morpheme, respectively:

(8) Causativization

a. b. c.

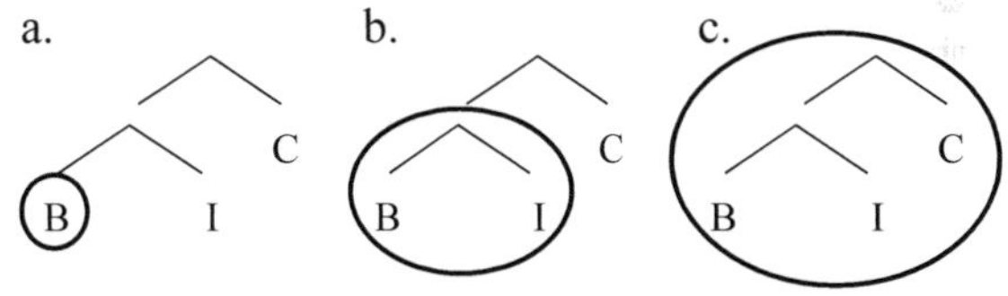

The possible combinations of MICs and idioms predicted in the causativization approach are shown in Table 1: for instance, if [B] is an MIC (i.e., (8)a), then it is expected that [B], [B I], and [[B I] C] can form idioms.

		Minimal Idiomatic Constituent		
		[B]	[B I]	[[B I] C]
Idiom	[B]	OK	*	*
	[B I]	OK	OK	*
	[[B I] C]	OK	OK	OK

Table 1: Predicted Combinations

The structural asymmetry encoded should be reflected in the realm of idiomatic interpretations. As McGinnis (2004) discusses, since the causative alternant contains its inchoative counterpart in the causativization approach, it is predicted that, if an idiomatic interpretation is possible with an inchoative, it should be possible with the causative counterpart as well. Moreover, not all causative idioms have the inchoative counterparts, another consequence of the assumption that the causative contains the inchoative.

Good candidates for this causativization treatment are the affix pairs in (2)k–(2)m, whose inchoative affixes are assumed to be phonologically null, or alternatively, it is also possible to assume that there is no inchoative affix involved and the base itself is an inchoative verb. If the latter assumption is adopted, the difference between (8)a and (8)b dissolves, but the aforementioned predictions made by the causativization approach are not affected at all.

This said, consider the causative/inchoative pairs in (9)–(11), where an inchoative verb can appear as part of an idiom, while its causative counterpart cannot. Since the pattern observed in these examples cannot be predicted, as shown in Table 1, it is clear that the causativization approach should be excluded even in cases where it might appear to be appropriate.

(9) a. * ude-o tat-e-ru
arm-ACC √stand-CAUS-NPST
b. ude-ga tat-Ø-u
arm-NOM √stand-INCH-NPST
'have good skills'

(10) a. * ki-o sum-as-u
mind-ACC √over-CAUS-NPST
b. ki-ga sum-Ø-u
mind-NOM √over-INCH-NPST
'console oneself, feel satisfied'

(11) a. * X-ni kyak.koo-o abi-se-ru
X-DAT foot.light-ACC √pour-CAUS-NPST
b. X-ga kyak.koo-o abi-Ø-ru
X-NOM foot.light-ACC √pour-INCH-NPST
'become the center of attention'

Let us see the other possible patterns displayed by the causative/inchoative pairs: in (12)–(14), both the alternants can form idioms, while only the causative alternant can in (15)–(17). These two patterns can be dealt with by (8)a and (8)c, respectively.

(12) a. X-to kata-o narab-e-ru
X-COM shoulder-ACC √line.up-C-NPST
'rival X'
b. X-to kata-ga narab-Ø-u
X-COM shoulder-NOM √line.up-I-NPST
'rival X'

(13) a. haba-o kik-as-u
width-ACC √take.effect-CAUS-NPST
'have great influence'
b. haba-ga kik-Ø-u
width-NOM √take.effect-INCH-NPST
'have great influence'

(14) a. on-ni ki-se-ru
gratitude-DAT √put.on-CAUS-NPST
'try to make someone feel indebted'
b. on-ni ki-Ø-ru
gratitude-DAT √put.on-INCH-NPST
'feel indebted'

(15) a. in'nen-o tuk-e-ru
fate-ACC √attach-CAUS-NPST
'make a false charge'
b. *in'nen-ga tuk-Ø-u
fate-NOM √attach-INCH-NPST

(16) a. kuti.ura-o aw-as-u
mouth.back-ACC √meet-CAUS-NPST
'rearrange a story so as not to contradict each other '
b. *kuti.ura-ga aw-Ø-u (>a-u)
mouth.back-NOM √meet-INCH-NPST

(17) a. X-ni hiya.mizu-o abi-se-ru
X-DAT cold.water-ACC √pour-C-NPST
'discourage X'
b. *X-ga hiya.mizu-o abi-Ø-ru
X-NOM cold.water-ACC √pour-I-NPST

In face of the counterexamples to the causativization approach in (9)–(11), one might wonder if their MICs are disrupted in the causative examples, where idiomatic interpretations are impossible. However, invoking structural disruption to account for the cases at hand would leave us with no account of the pairs in (12)–(14): it is quite unlikely that adding the same causative affix sometimes does and sometimes does not alter the structure of an MIC.

Therefore, we can conclude that the causativization approach makes too strong predictions about idiomatic interpretations. It is not always true that, if an idiom is possible with an inchoative, it is possible with its causative counterpart.

3.2 Anticausativization of Causative Verbs

The anticausativization approach predicts exactly the opposite to those made by the causativization approach. Specifically, it predicts that, if an idiomatic interpretation is possible with a causative, then it should be possible with its inchoative counterpart, as shown in Table 2 below. This is because the inchoative contains the causative in this approach, as represented in (18).

(18) Anticausativization

a. b. c.

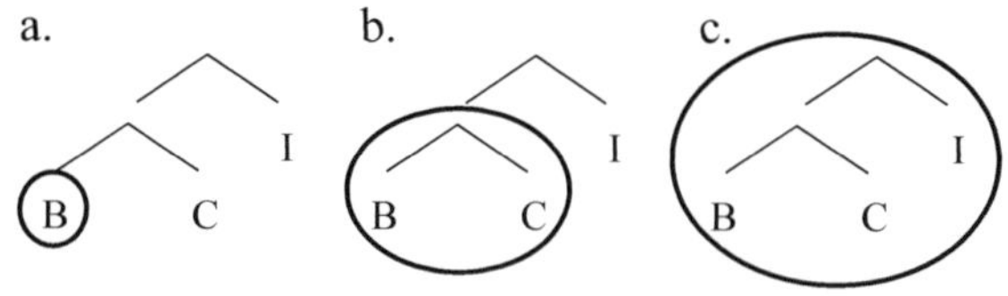

		Minimal Idiomatic Constituent		
		[B]	[B C]	[[B C] I]
Idiom	[B]	OK	*	*
	[B C]	OK	OK	*
	[[B C] I]	OK	OK	OK

Table 2: Predicted Combinations

Moreover, if an inchoative is part of an MIC, as in (18)c, then the idiomatic interpretation is not available with its causative counterpart.

The causative/inchoative affix pairs in (2)n and (2)o are considered, as an anticausativization analysis can be applied to them easily, with no need to assume powerful morphophonological processes. As is the case with the causativization approach, what is predicted not to exist can be detected: the pairs in (19) and (20) cannot be accounted for in this approach. The pairs in (21) and (22) and those in (23) and (24) can be accounted for by (18)a and (18)c, respectively.

(19) a. (ko-)mimi-ni hasam-Ø-u
DIM-ear-DAT √put.between-CAUS-NPST
'overhear, happen to hear'
b. * (ko-)mimi-ni hasam-ar-u
DIM-ear-DAT √put.between-INCH-NPST

(20) a. sira-o kir-Ø-u
white-ACC √detach-CAUS-NPST
'dissemble, pretend not to know'
b. * sira-ga kir-e-ru
white-NOM √detach-INCH-NPST

(21) a. hone-o or-Ø-u
bone-ACC √break-CAUS-NPST
'take the trouble'
b. hone-ga or-e-ru
bone-NOM √break-INCH-NPST
'be troublesome'

(22) a. te-o husag-Ø-u
hand-ACC √obstruct-CAUS-NPST
'have one's hands tied'
b. te-ga husag-ar-u
hand-NOM √obstruct-INCH-NPST
'one's hands are tied.'

(23) a. * kosi-o kudak-Ø-u
waist-ACC √crush-CAUS-NPST
b. kosi-ga kudak-e-ru
waist-NOM √crush-INCH-NPST
'chicken out'

(24) a. * oku.ba-ni mono-o hasam-Ø-u
molar-in stuff-ACC √put.btwn-C-NPST
b. oku.ba-ni mono-ga hasam-ar-u
molar-in stuff-NOM √put.btwn-I-NPST
'beat around the bush'

By the same token as in the last subsection, we cannot invoke structural disruption to handle the counterexamples without losing an account of the pairs such as in (21) and (22), where idioms are available with both the causative and the inchoative alternants.

However, up to this point, I have simplified the discussion somewhat, ignoring the possibility that there is a distinct syntactic head immediately above the constituent headed by a causative morpheme, i.e. Kratzer's (1996) VOICE or its equivalent, which introduces an agent argument. If this head is assumed to be present, we will need to consider the following structure as a possible MIC, in addition to those in (18) (and (8)).

(25)
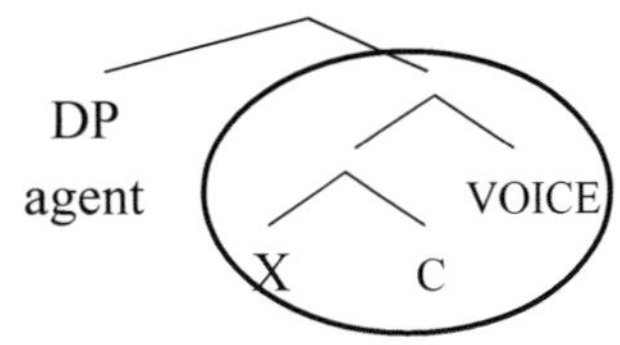

The MIC in (25) opens up the possibility of explaining examples like (19) and (20) (and also (15)–(17) in the last subsection) in terms of structural disruption. That is, the causative idioms have the MIC in (25), while their inchoative counterparts do not. As it appears, some causative idioms, such as (20)a, do indeed have the MIC in (25), instantiating the possibility just mentioned, while some like (19)a do not. As represented in the structure in (25), the divide is at the obligatory presence of an agent. Specifically, if a causative idiom has VOICE as part of its MIC, as in (25), then the presence of an agent is necessarily implied. On the other hand, if VOICE is not part of its MIC, then the presence of an agent is not required.

Evidence for the divide comes from data involving a classic constituency test known as *soo s r* replacement, the Japanese version of *o so* replacement. It is well known that this process has a constraint to the effect that a verb selecting a volitional agent must be replaced (Shibatani, 1978), as shown in (26).[7]

(26) a. *enti e er*
Taroo-ga hasir-ta(>hasit-ta), Ziroo-mo
T.-NOM run-PST Z.-also
{soo si-ta/ hasit-ta}
so do-PST/ run-PST
'Taroo ran. Ziroo did so, too.'

[7] I simply assume that "accidental" agents are not the same as (volitional) agents and should be treated differently. However, the question remains open on this point.

b. *on a enti e er*
Taroo-ga tentoo-si-ta, Ziroo-mo
T. -NOM fall-DV-PST Z.-also
{ *soo si-ta/ tentoo-si-ta}
so do-PST/ fall-DV-PST
'Taroo fell. Ziroo {did so, too/also fell}.'

Applied to (19)a and (20)a, this test yields the following results, suggesting that VOICE is part of the MIC in (20)a, but it is not in (19)a.

(27) a. Taroo-ga sira-o kir-Ø-ta (>kit-ta),
T.-NOM white-ACC √detach-CAUS-PST
Ziroo-mo {soo si-ta/ kit-ta}
Z.-also so do-PST/ (see above)
'Taroo dissembled. Ziroo did so, too.'

b. Taroo-ga uwasa-o ko-mimi-ni
T.-NOM rumor-ACC DIM-ear-DAT
hasam-Ø-ta (>hasan-da), Ziroo-mo
√put.between-CAUS-PST Z.-also
{*soo si-ta/ ko-mimi-ni hasan-da}
so do-PST/ (see above)
'T. overheard a rumor. Z. did so, too'

The upshot is that, even though some causative idioms involve an MIC like (25) and thus an analysis invoking structural disruption can account for the impossibility of idiomatic interpretations in, say, (20)b, causative idioms like (19)a cannot be analyzed as having the MIC in (25), and the contrast found in (19) remains a problem to the anticausativization approach.

Therefore, we can conclude that the anticausativization approach fails for the same reason as the causativization approach: it makes too strong predictions concerning idiomatic interpretations.

3.3 Causativization and Inchoativization of Common Bases

Unlike the approaches we saw above, the common base approach predicts no implicational relations between the causative and inchoative idioms, as neither alternant structurally contains the other, only sharing the common base, as depicted in (28). Note that an account invoking the MIC in (25) is available in this approach as well.

(28) The Common Base Approach

a. b. c.

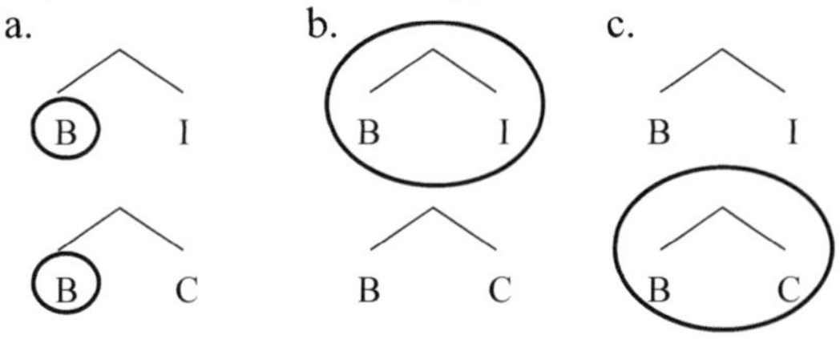

		Minimal Idiomatic Constituent		
		[B]	[B I]	[B C]
Idiom	[B]	OK	*	*
	[B I]	OK	OK	*
	[B C]	OK	*	OK

Table 3: Predicted Combinations

Importantly, as Table 3 shows, the common base approach can handle all the patterns properly: both the causative and inchoative alternants can form idioms, as in (29) and (30), only the inchoative alternant can form an idiom, as in (31) and (32), and only the causative alternant can form an idiom, as in (33) and (34).

(29) a. X-o haku.si-ni modo-s-u
X-ACC blank.paper-DAT √back-C-NPST
'bring X back to square one'

b. X-ga haku.si-ni modo-r-u
X-NOM blank.paper-DAT √back-I-NPST
'X goes back to square one'

(30) a. X-o ki-ni kak-e-ru
X-ACC mind-DAT √hook-CAUS-NPST
'have X in *one s* mind'

b. X-ga ki-ni kak-ar-u
X-NOM mind-DAT √hook-CAUS-NPST
'X is on *one s* mind'

(31) a. *X-ni o-hati-o mawa-s-u
X-DAT HON-bowl-ACC √roll-CAUS-NPST

b. X-ni o-hati-ga mawa-r-u
X-DAT HON-bowl-NOM √roll-INCH-NPST
'X's turn comes around'

(32) a. * X-to sooba-o kim-e-ru
X-COMP market-ACC √fix-CAUS-NPST

b. X-to sooba-ga kim-ar-u
X-COMP market-NOM √fix-INCH-NPST
'It is generally considered that X'

(33) a. (o-)tya-o nigo-s-u
HON-tea-ACC √muddy-CAUS-NPST
'varnish, patch up, cover up'

b. *(o-)tya-ga nigo-r-u
HON-tea-NOM √muddy-INCH-NPST

(34) a. ude-ni yori-o kak-e-ru
arm-DAT twist-ACC √hook-CAUS-NPST
'put all *one s* skills'

b. * ude-ni yori-ga kak-ar-u
arm-DAT twist-NOM √hook-INCH-NPST

Furthermore, the common base approach predicts that each of the alternants with an identical root can form a different idiom. This prediction is borne out, as shown in (35) and (36), though there are not so many examples of this kind.

(35) a. asi-o tuk-e-ru
foot-ACC √attach-CAUS-NPST
'establish a relation'
b. asi-ga tuk-Ø-u
foot-NOM √attach-INCH-NPST
'get traced, come to light'
(36) a. atama-o sag-e-ru
head-ACC √lower-CAUS-NPST
'apologize; thank'
b. atama-ga sag-ar-u
head-NOM √lower-INCH-NPST
'admire, respect; be impressed '

This also lends support to the common base approach to the causative alternation in Japanese.

4 Extension: Ditransitive Causatives

We have established that the causative alternation can be best analyzed in terms of the common base approach. We have also noted that an MIC like (25) is needed for idioms which require that the presence of an agent be implied.

The common base approach can account for further patterns displayed by verbal roots such as *i* '√see', which has three alternants, the ditransitive (causative), the transitive, and the intransitive (inchoative). As given in (37), each of the alternants can form a different idiom.

(37) a. me-ni mono-o mi-se-ru
eye-DAT thing-ACC √see-CAUS-NPST
'teach someone a lesson'
b. X-o oo.me-ni mi-Ø-ru
X-ACC large.quantity-DAT √see-T-NPST
'overlook X, pardon X'
c. X-ga me-ni mi-e-ru
X-NOM eye-DAT √see-INCH-NPST
'X is a foregone conclusion'

Even a cursory look at idioms based on the transitive alternant reveals that they display variability as to the interpretation of the nominative argument. First, we need to assume idioms like (38)b involve VOICE as part of their MICs, as in (39) (cf. (25)), and thus, no causative counterpart is available, as shown in (38)a.[8]

(38) a. * X-ni (Y-no) asimoto-o mi-se-ru
X-DAT Y-GEN foot-ACC √see-C-NPST
b. X-ga (Y-no) asimoto-o mi-Ø-ru
X-NOM Y-GEN foot-ACC √see-T-NPST
'X takes advantage of (Y's) weakness'

(39)

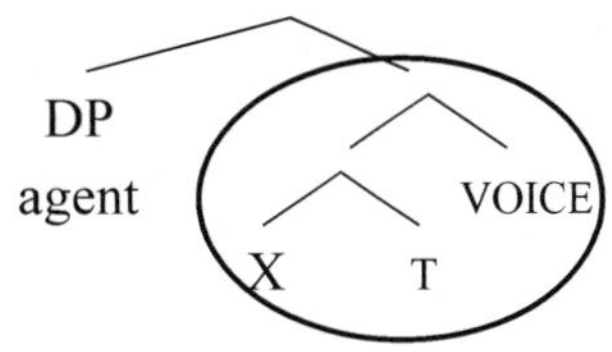

The following example corroborates that the nominative arguments in (38)b is associated with volition, the hallmark of agentivity.

(40) Taroo-ga kyaku-no asimoto-o mi-Ø-ta,
T.-NOM client-GEN foot-ACC √see-T-PST
Ziroo-mo soo si-ta
Z.-also so DV-PST
'Taroo took advantage of his client's weak point. Ziroo did so, too.'

Next, other transitive idioms have an MIC like (41), where APPL, a head comparable to VOICE, selects an affectee, a cover term for non-agentive arguments construed as perceiver, possessor, recipient and so on (cf. Pylkkänen, 2008).

(41)

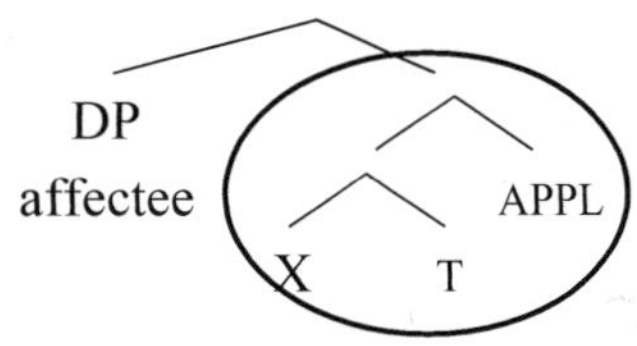

The relevant example is given in (42)b. Compare this to (42)a, which shows that the idiomatic interpretation is impossible with the ditransitive causative counterpart. Note that the nominative argument in (42)b cannot be construed as an agent, as shown in (43).

(42) a. * X-ni naki-o mi-se-ru
X-DAT cry-ACC √see-CAUS-NPST
b. X-ga naki-o mi-Ø-ru
X-NOM cry-ACC √see-TRANS-NPST
'X suffer for his/her own deed'
(43) Taroo-ga naki-o mi-Ø-ta, Ziroo-mo
T.-NOM cry-ACC √see-T-PST Z.-also
{*soo si-ta/ naki-o mi-Ø-ta}
so DV-PST/ cry-ACC √see-T-PST
'T. suffered for his deed. Z. did so, too'

The contrast in (42) shows again that the causativization approach is not viable even in the case of ditransitive causatives: it would be possi-

[8] The examples in (i) show the same contrast as in (38), but (i)a may receive a different treatment: *e* 'eye' can only be associated with the "subject" argument.
(i) a. *X-ni Y-o siroi me-de mi-se-ru
X-DAT Y-ACC white eye-INST √see-CAUS-NPST
b. X-ga Y-o siroi me-de mi-Ø-ru
X-NOM Y-ACC white eye-INST √see-INCH-NPST
'X looks coldly upon Y'

ble to form (42)a out of (42)b by having a causative morpheme and VOICE, an agent-introducing head, above the structure in (41). Given, moreover, that it is implausible to derive the transitive from the ditransitive causative considering the morphological makeup, the common base approach is the only approach that is left to account for the contrast in (42). Specifically, the MIC in (41) is not formed with the ditransitive causative, which does not involve a transitive morpheme. Although the details need to be more fully worked out, this line of thought can handle the puzzling pattern displayed by (42), and hopefully, provide a more coherent picture of the relationship between syntactic structure and idioms.

5 Concluding Remarks

This paper has presented an argument for the common base approach to the causative alternation in Japanese. The argument is of a simple, brute-force nature and takes into account various alternatives including even the ones which might be dismissed as implausible without a moment's thought. However, it clearly shows, by utilizing the locality requirements imposed on phrasal idioms, that the causative and inchoative verbs in the causative alternation are best analyzed in terms of the common base approach. Thus, it is not the case, at least morphosyntactically, that causatives are derived from their inchoative counterparts or the other way around. This conclusion, then, further justifies another conclusion: the symbol Ø in (2)k–(2)p must represent a phonologically null morpheme, not the absence of a causative or inchoative morpheme.

As a final note, the issue taken up in this paper is independent of other important ones concerning the morphology and semantics of the causative/inchoative alternation in Japanese. I hope that further research will clarify the conclusions reached here and their relations to other aspects of the alternation.

Acknowledgments

I am grateful to Sakumi Inokuma and three anonymous reviewers for PACLIC 27 for providing valuable comments on earlier versions of this paper. Needless to say, I am solely responsible for any misanalyses or shortcomings contained herein.

References

Alexiadou, Artemis, Elena Anagnostopoulou, and Florian Schäfer. 2006. The Properties of Anticausatives Crosslinguistically. In M. Frascarelli, ed., *ases o nterpretation*, pp.187-211. Mouton de Gruyter. Berlin.

Bruening, Benjamin. 2010. Ditransitive Asymmetries and a Theory of Idiom Formation. *in isti n ir* , 41(4):519-562.

Dowty, David. 1979. *Wor eanin an onta e ra ar er s an i es in enerati e e an ti s an onta e s* . D. Reidel, Dordrecht.

Everaert, Martin, Eric-Jan van der Linden, André Schenk, and Rob Schreuder, eds. 1995 *io s tr t ra an s o o i a erspe ti es*. Lawrence Erlbaum Associates, Hillsdale, NJ.

Everaert, Martin. 2010. The Lexical Encoding of Idioms. In M. Rapapport Hovav, E. Doron, and I. Sichel, eds., *e i a e anti s nta an ent tr t re*, pp.76-98. Oxford University Press, Oxford.

Hale, Kenneth and Samuel J. Keyser. 1993. On Argument Structure and the Lexical Expression of Syntactic Relations. In K. Hale and S.J. Keyser, eds., *e ie ro i in* , pp.53-109. MIT Press, Cambridge, MA.

Halle, Morris and Alec Marantz. 1993. Distributed Morphology and the Pieces of Inflection. In K. Hale and S.J. Keyser, eds., *e ie ro i in* , pp.111-176. MIT Press, Cambridge, MA.

Haspelmath, Martin. 1993. More on the Typology of Inchoative/Causative Verb Alternations. In B. Comrie and M. Polinsky, eds., *a sati es an ransiti it* , pp.87-120. John Benjamins, Amsterdam.

Jacobsen, Wesley M. 1992. *e ransiti e tr t re o ents in apanese*. Kurosio Publishers, Tokyo.

Kratzer, Angelika. 1996. Severing the External Argument from its Verb. In J. Orrick and L. Zaring, eds., *rase tr t re an t e e i on*, pp.109-137. Kluwer Academic Publishers, Dordrecht.

Levin, Beth and Malka Rappaport-Hovav. 1995. *n a sati it t t e nta e i a e anti s n ter a e*. MIT Press, Cambridge, MA.

McGinnis, Martha. 2004. Idiomatic Evidence for the Syntax of English 'Lexical' Causatives. Handout of the talk given at the University of Toronto on April 10, 2004.

Miyagawa, Shigeru. 1998. *ase* as an Elsewhere Causative and the Syntactic Nature of Words. *o rna o apanese in isti s*, 16:67-110.

Nishiyama, Kunio. 1998. The Morphosyntax and Morphophonology of Japanese Predicates. Ph.D. Thesis. Cornell University.

Nunberg, Geoffrey, Ivan A. Sag, and Thomas Wasow. 1994. Idioms. *an a e*, 70(3):491-538.

*** Formatting Issue - Best Available Paper/Graphic ***

O'Grady, William. 1998. The Syntax of Idioms. *at ra an a e an in isti eor* , 16(2):279-312.

Piñón, Christopher. 2001. A Finer Look at the Causative-Inchoative Alternation. *ro ee in s o e an ti s an in isti eor* , 11:273-293.

Pylkkänen, Liina. 2008. *ntro in r ents*. MIT Press, Cambridge, MA.

Rappaport, Malka and Beth Levin. 1988. What to Do with Theta-Roles. In W. Wilkins, ed., *nta an e anti s e ati e ations*, pp.7-36. Academic Press, New York.

Shibatani, Masayoshi. 1978. *i on o no nse i* [An Analysis of Japanese]. Taishukan, Tokyo.

Are Mandarin Sandhi Tone 3 and Tone 2 the Same or Different? The Results of Functional Data Analysis

Chierh Cheng[1] **Jenn-Yeu Chen**[1] **Michele Gubian**[2]
[1]Department of Chinese as a Second Language, National Taiwan Normal University, Taiwan
[2]Center for Language and Speech Technology, Radboud University Nijmegen, Netherlands
chierh.cheng@gmail.com, psyjyc@ntnu.edu.tw, M.Gubian@let.ru.nl

Abstract

Functional Data Analysis (FDA) is used to investigate Tone 3 sandhi in Taiwan Mandarin. Tone 3 sandhi is a tone change phenomenon that arises when two low tones occur in succession resulting in the first tone being realised as a rising tone. Tone dyads T2T3 and T3T3 were compared in terms of their F_0 contours and velocity profiles. No difference was found between the F_0 contours of the two tone dyads. In contrast, velocity profiles showed an increased difference in the later part of the seemingly similar rising movements of T2 and sandhi T3, with a steeper rising-falling movement in the former than the latter. This research demonstrates that FDA can elucidate more detail in the time dimension than that of conventional techniques commonly employed in the current phonetic literature.

1 Introduction

This paper aims to take a closer look at tone sandhi, and in particular Tone 3 sandhi, a traditional research question in Chinese linguistics. Tone sandhi occurs whenever a prosodic context is met for disyllabic units of certain tonal combinations; the tone of the first syllable is changed from its underlying tone in a systematic manner. Tone 3 sandhi and *yi* sandhi are the two major tone sandhi phenomena in Mandarin[1]. Tone 3 sandhi means that a low tone is realised as a rising one when followed by another low tone. For example, *zong3 tong3* ('總統', means 'president') is realised as *zong2 tong3*. Tone 3 sandhi is also seen to be cyclically applied according to a hierarchical prosodic structure (Shih, 1997). The scope of *yi* sandhi, on the other hand, is somewhat limited. *yi* here means the number 'one' in Mandarin and its underlying high-level tone (Tone 1) undergoes respective changes according to its following morpheme being a classifier of a specific tone.[2] That is to say, *yi* sandhi requires matching phonological and morphological contexts.

Myers and Tsay (2003) supplemented their study on tone sandhi in general with *yi* sandhi and concluded that more empirical data is needed to elucidate the most ubiquitous but still unclear nature of Tone 3 sandhi in Chinese phonology. Xu (2004, p. 796) similarly speculated the following on the mechanism of Tone 3 sandhi,

> "It is unclear whether the largely rising contour in the first L of L L is due to a complete change of the target to [rise] as in R or due to implementation of the same complex target as in isolated L with a time constraint. Further studies are needed to sort this out."

This paper follows their advice and experiments with a method called Functional Data Analysis (FDA) to see whether further details can be exposed via this advanced statistic method.

1.1 Previous findings and implications

It is important to note that the aspect which remains unclear in the majority of acoustic research on Tone 3 sandhi, and which also

[1] Tone 1 (high-level, H), Tone 2 (rising, R), Tone 3 (low, L) and Tone 4 (falling, F) are the four main tone categories in Mandarin. There is also a neutral tone, Tone 5, which is more frequently used in mainland China than in Taiwan.

[2] For example, *yi1* is realised as T2 when it is followed by a T4 classifier (e.g. *yi2 jian4* '一件', means 'one article') and is realised elsewhere as T4 when it is followed by T1, T2, or T3 (e.g. *yi4 zhang1* '一張, one piece of'; *yi4 zhi2* '一直, all along'; *yi4 zhong3* '一種, a kind of'). *yi* sandhi is sometimes mentioned together with *qi*(七)、*ba*(八)、*bu*(不), all of them go through similar variations.

influences psycholinguistic research, is whether (1) speakers replace the first low tone with a rising one by applying a phonological rule prior to articulation (i.e. a categorical change) or (2) no rule is specifically defined prior to articulation and a seemingly 'rising' pattern in the first syllable followed by a low tone is attributed to an online phonetic process (i.e. a gradient phonetic implementation). The gradient phonetic differences of sandhi T3 to that of underlying T2 could be due to speakers' inability to produce two low tones in quick succession, or the existence of an articulatory encoding stage to adjust the online articulatory operations prior actual articulation (Chen and Chen, in press).

Acoustic data supporting either the categorical or gradient view of Tone 3 sandhi is generally acquired by comparing 'underlying T2' (e.g. T2 in a **T2**T3 context) and 'sandhi T3' (e.g. T3T3→**T2**T3) in terms of several measurements as follows: F_0 values (maximum, minimum, mean, etc.), duration, and F_0 slope (for which the definition varies between studies). In general, if no statistically significant difference in the above measurements is found between underlying T2 and sandhi T3, then Tone 3 sandhi is suggested to be a 'categorical change'. On the other hand, if there is a statistically significant difference in either measurement, then Tone 3 sandhi is considered 'gradient'. If the results are of discernible differences, but these differences are not large enough to result in a statistical difference between the two rising F_0 contours, Tone 3 sandhi process is sometimes suggested to be in the process of 'merging' from underlying T3 to T2, i.e. the differences between underlying T2 and sandhi T3 are not fully neutralized phonetically (Peng, 2000).

1.2 Purpose of this study

The purpose of this study is to investigate T3 sandhi phenomenon in the time dimension. Like in traditional studies, we will compare F_0 contours extracted from 'underlying T2' (T2T3 dyads) and 'sandhi T3' (T3T3 dyads). Contrary to traditional studies, we will not rely on a few comprehensive measurements taken on F_0 contours such as duration, slope, etc. Rather, F_0 contours *as they are* will be input to statistical tools that perform a scan of the time axis and produce detailed results along the time dimension. This powerful extension of classic statistical analysis has two fundamental advantages. First, all the information carried by the shape of F_0 contours is preserved, since no selection of 'special points', such as peaks, is required. Second, results provide a detailed picture of the time dimension, rather than one comprehensive answer, e.g. in terms of overall significant difference. This approach is of particular interest for the investigation of T3 sandhi because, based on past studies, we expect that differences between tone dyad T2T3 and T3T3, if any at all, may be quantitatively small and localised in one or few specific phases of the whole articulatory gesture. The analysis will be carried out by applying Functional Data Analysis (FDA, Ramsay and Silverman, 2005; Gubian, 2013). In particular, a functional t-test will be employed, which extends the rationale of the well-known t-test to the time dimension in a principled way (Cheng et al., 2010).

To dig even deeper into the dynamics of the underlying articulatory gestures, our investigation will be carried out not only on F_0 contours, but also on their respective velocity contours, i.e. their first derivative with respect to time. These curves show the slope of their respective F_0 contours in time, i.e. take positive/negative values whenever the F_0 contour is rising/falling. This representation offers further insight in the underlying tonal targets, since the intention of the speaker to reach a certain target might not be evident by looking at the F_0 value at a certain time, but rather can only be revealed by looking at the rate with which this value is changing (Gauthier et al., 2007).

2 Methodology

2.1 Dataset

The data used is a subset from a systematically designed and collected corpus from the first author's previous research on bi-tonal variation and time pressure. Six male Taiwan Mandarin speakers recorded disyllabic /ma/+/ma/ sequences with a total of 16 (4x4) tonal combinations embedded in two carrier sentences. These two carrier sentences differ in the tone preceding the target sequence /ma/+/ma/, being H or L. The tone following the target sequence is always H. Various conditions were imposed to elicit different degrees of tonal reduction, including positions in a carrier sentence (initial, mediate and final), repetition time (1st, 2nd, and 3rd) and speech rate (slow, normal and fast). Three reduction types were labelled according to the integrity of the intervocalic /m/, *non-contracted* for a clear presence of an intervocalic nasal, *contracted* for a clear absence of nasal murmur and *semi-contracted* for intermediate cases. More details concerning the corpus can be found in Cheng et al. (2010).

In this study, we selected *non-contracted* T2T3 and T3T3 from a (T1#)/ma/+/ma/(#T1) context, where # delimits the target sequence and its surrounding tones. We chose non-contracted realizations in order to avoid the complex issues involved in tonal contractions, which are not relevant here, and we selected only one tonal context for consistency. In total 119 T2T3 dyads and 106 T3T3 dyads were selected.

2.2 F_0 extraction

Extraction of F_0 contours was first carried out with the vocal cycle marking of the Praat program (Boersma and Weenink, 2013) and then with manual repair of octave jumps and other distinct irregularities using a Praat script (Xu, 2013). For each target curve, 40 measurement points were generated, 20 equidistant points per syllable. This time sampling scheme implicitly produced an alignment of all contours on their syllabic boundary, because the 21st F_0 sample marks the beginning of the second syllable in all contours. This convenient fact will be used in the following steps. F_0 values are converted to semitones and the average of the 40 samples subtracted from all contours, which helps reduce variability owing to speaker identity.

2.3 From F_0 samples to functions of time

Functional Data Analysis (FDA) refers to a set of tools that extend ordinary multivariate statistics to the domain of functions. Any FDA session requires that the input curves are represented as functions, in our case functions of time *f(t)* (hence the term "functional" in FDA). Standard smooth interpolation techniques were customarily applied at this stage. In particular, we applied B-splines-based smoothing with roughness penalty (Ramsay and Silverman, 2005). B-splines are a family of polynomial functions that allow one to smoothly interpolate arbitrary contours defined by a finite number of samples (de Boor, 2001). Roughness penalty refers to a regularization procedure where fitting error, i.e. the difference between the exact sample values and the corresponding one read on the interpolating function *f(t)*, is traded for smoothness of *f(t)*. The latter is enforced in order to reduce unnecessary and rapidly varying shape detail, which in the case of F_0 contours is likely to be due to the limited precision of the F_0 tracker and to irrelevant microprosodic effects. An example of smoothing is shown in Figure 1.

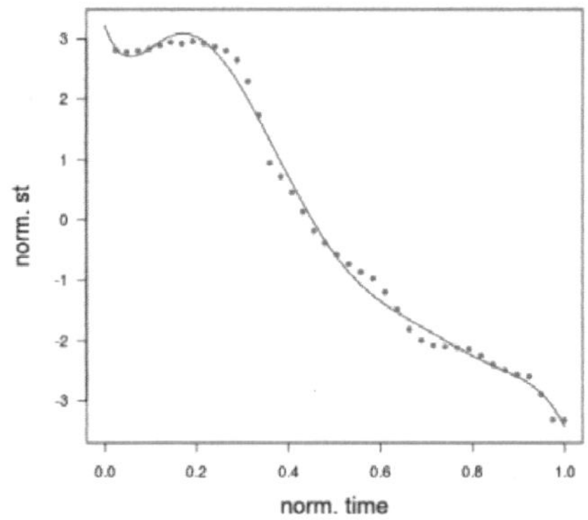

Figure 1: An example of smoothing applied to one of the F_0 contours in our data set. Red dots indicate original F_0 samples, the solid curve is the interpolating function *f(t)*.

A crucial aspect of the functional representation of data lies in the fact that the same time axis must be used in all curves. This means that all curves are normalised to have the same duration. Since the original tone dyads do not have the same duration, a proper normalization has to be carried out. In our case, we have divided the common time axis in two equal halves, the first half spans the first syllable, the second half the second syllable. This normalization was based on the sampling scheme described above. The total duration is conventionally indicated as 1 (i.e. *not* the average duration in seconds).

Velocity curves *v(t)*, i.e. first derivatives of the F_0 curves, were computed directly from the analytical form of *f(t)* before the application of time normalization. That is, the values of *v(t)* curves are from the original un-normalised F_0 contours (and are thus in units of semitones per second) before themselves being normalised in time.

2.4 Functional t-test

Functional t-test is a technique that extends the concept of t-test to continuous functions. Ordinary t-test compares the mean of two sets of numbers and determines whether those means are different, at a certain confidence level. Functional t-test compares the mean functions of two groups of functions sharing the same time axis and determines *where* those mean curves differ, at a certain confidence level. The mean curve is the curve obtained by averaging the values of all curves at each corresponding point in time. Operationally, a battery of ordinary t-tests is carried out in the time dimension. The confidence value for the test statistics are obtained by resampling techniques (see Ramsay and Silverman, 2005 for further details).

In this work, two separate functional t-tests have been conducted, one comparing the 119 T2T3 F_0 contours against the 106 T3T3 F_0 contours, and another comparing their respective velocity curves.

3 Results

The results of the two functional t-tests described above are shown in Figures 2 and 3 for F_0 contours and their velocity curves respectively. Figure 2a shows the mean F_0 contours for the T2T3 and T3T3 dyads. As mentioned earlier, the time axis is normalized to a common unitary duration, and the middle point t = 0.5 marks the boundary between the first and the second syllable for all contours, i.e. the onset of the second /m/ sound in all /mama/ sequence. Also the vertical axis is normalized, since the mean semitone value in time has been subtracted from each curve. Both curves appear very similar, the general trend is an initial fall, since the preceding tone is a high tone in all cases, followed by a rise, which realises the first target, and ending with a sharp fall, which realises the second target. The outcome of the functional t-test is shown in Figure 2b. The solid red line indicates the value of the test statistic along the time axis, which is the same axis as in Figure 2a. Blue curves in Figure 2b represent time dependent significant thresholds, the higher flat line representing a more conservative threshold. The test statistic locally reaches significance at 5% confidence whenever the red curve reaches above one of the blue ones. Figure 2b shows that there is no point in time where the small differences between the average T2T3 and T3T3 curves are significant, since the red curve always remains below both thresholds.

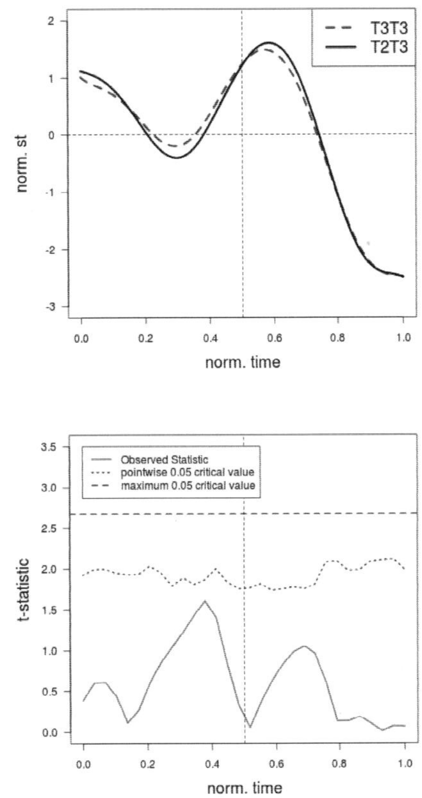

Figure 2: top (a) Normalised average F_0 contours of T3T3 (blue) and T2T3 (black); bottom (b) Functional t-test on the normalised averaged F_0 contours of T3T3 and T2T3.

Figures 3a and 3b show results for the velocity curves. Figure 3a shows that the velocity curves are qualitatively very similar on average. Crucially, their signs are almost always the same, meaning that at every instant in time, on average the F_0 contours are either both rising (positive velocity) or both falling (negative velocity). However, small quantitative differences are visible, especially around 0.5 normalised time units. Figure 3b shows that the mean velocity curves of Figure 3a differ significantly in an interval localized around 0.5 normalised time units, since the red curve surpasses one of the empirical confidence levels (i.e. pointwise 0.05 critical value). Returning to Figure 3a, this means that the difference in slope between T2T3 and T3T3 localized around the syllable boundary is systematic. T2T3 F_0 curves tend to increase more rapidly than sandhi T3T3 curves (i.e. T2T3 velocity curves reach a higher value) in the process of completing the realization of the first target and preparing for the second one.

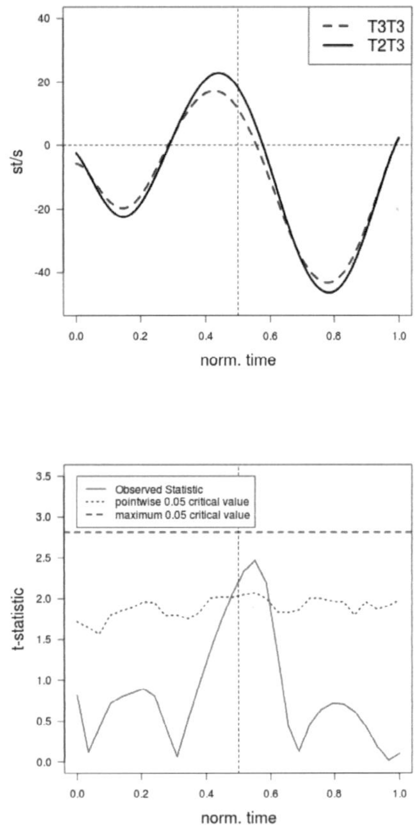

Figure 3: top (a) Normalised average F_0 velocity contours of T3T3 (blue) and T2T3 (black); bottom: (b) Functional t-test on the normalised averaged F_0 velocity contours of T3T3 and T2T3.

Finally, we check whether this result obtained using velocity contours could be the consequence of an overall difference in duration between the T2T3 and T3T3 syllable groups. The mean duration of the first syllable is 0.194 second for T2T3 and 0.181 second for T3T3, while the duration of the second syllable is almost identical for both dyads (0.175 second). The small duration difference in the first syllable is not significant (p-value > 0.05). That is, the higher velocity of the F_0 contour towards the end of the first syllable in the T2T3 group is unlikely to be attributed to a longer duration. From this, we conclude that the localised effect seen on velocity is real.

4 Discussion and Conclusion

Looking only at the statistical results obtained from performing a functional t-test on the F_0 contours, shown in Figure 2b, no significant difference is seen between underlying T2 and sandhi T3. However, applying a functional t-test to the first derivative of the F_0 contours (velocity) reveals interesting information in the time dimension—specifically, a significant difference is seen between tone dyads T3T3 and T2T3 velocity curves towards the end of the first syllable (Figure 3b). A significant difference in this region may suggest speakers' late modification of articulatory implementation. The increased difference in velocity also indicates a steeper rising-falling movement in T2T3 than that of T3T3. This may be an indication that the articulatory target for sandhi T3 is not as clearly defined as that of an underlying T2 followed by a low tone, thus resulting in a less 'prepared' rising-falling trajectory in the T3T3 context.

Responding to the question raised in the title of this paper, 'are Mandarin sandhi T3 and underlying T2 the same or different?', through analysing the velocity profiles along the time dimension, the current results demonstrate 'a difference' at a later part of the implementation of sandhi T3 to that of an underlying T2.

It is interesting to note that if the FDA comparison was made using only F_0 contours, sandhi T3 and underlying T2 could have been interpreted as 'the same'. It is worth mentioning that F_0 contours contain surface variations, for which articulatory movements are less exposed (compared to F_0 velocity) and should be taken with caution in pitch related research.

To conclude, in this paper, techniques from Functional Data Analysis have been applied to look at Tone 3 sandhi in Taiwan Mandarin. Applying a functional t-test to F_0 velocity contours demonstrated a difference between 'underlying T2' (T2T3) dyads from 'sandhi T3' (T3T3) dyads; the former F_0 contours exhibit a steeper rise than the latter near the end of the first syllable. This small yet systematic difference has not been previously reported in the literature. It is hoped that such quantitative findings on Mandarin Tone 3 sandhi can shed further light on the mechanism of tone sandhi in general.

Acknowledgements

Writing of this paper was supported by "Aim for the Top University Plan" of the National Taiwan Normal University and the Ministry of Education, Taiwan, R. O. C. The authors would like to thank Dr. Yi Xu and Dr. Rhodri Nelson for their valuable comments and suggestions to improve the quality of this paper.

References

Boersma, Paul and Weenink, David. 2013. Praat: doing phonetics by computer [Computer program]. Version 5.3.52, retrieved 12 June 2013 from http://www.praat.org/

Chen, Jenn-Yeu and Chen, Train-Min. In press. Mechanism and Locus of Tone 3 Sandhi during Mandarin Chinese Spoken Word Production. *Journal of Chinese Linguistics.*

Cheng, Chierh, Xu, Yi, and Gubian, Michele. 2010. Exploring the mechanism of tonal contraction in Taiwan Mandarin. *Proc. Interspeech, 2010*: 2010-2013.

de Boor, Carl. 2001. *A Practical Guide to Splines*, Revised Edition. Springer, New York.

Gauthier, Bruno, Shi, Rushen, and Xu, Yi. 2007. Learning phonetic categories by tracking movements, *Cognition*, 103: 80-106.

Gubian, Michele. 2013. Functional data analysis for speech research. [Online]. Available: http://lands.let.ru.nl/FDA

Myers, James and Tsay, Jane. 2003. Investigating the phonetics of Mandarin tone sandhi. *Taiwan Journal of Linguistics*, 1(1): 29-68.

Peng, Shu-Hui. 2000. Lexical versus 'phonological' representations of Mandarin Sandhi tones. *Papers in laboratory phonology V: Acquisition and the lexicon*: 152-167.

Ramsay, Jim and Silverman, Bernard. 2005. *Functional Data Analysis—2nd Ed.* Springer.

Shih, Chilin. 1997. Mandarin third tone sandhi and prosodic structure. *Linguistic Models*, 20: 81-124.

Xu, Yi. 2004. Understanding tone from the perspective of production and perception. *Language and Linguistics*, 5.4: 757-797.

Xu, Yi. 2013. ProsodyPro—A Tool for Large-scale Systematic Prosody Analysis. *Proc. Tools and Resources for the Analysis of Speech Prosody (TRASP 2013)*, Aix-en-Provence, France.

*** Formatting Issue - Best Available Paper/Graphic ***

An Application of Comparative Corpora of Interactional Data – toward the Sound Profiles of Sites of Initiation in French and Mandarin Recycling Repair

Helen Kai-yun Chen
Phonetics Lab, Institute of Linguistics, Academia Sinica
Taipei, Taiwan
helenkychen@gmail.com

Abstract

This study examines the sound profiles of sites of initiation in French and Mandarin recycling repair (also disfluent repetitions). 150 examples of disfluent repetitions were extracted from comparative speech corpora of naturally occurred, face-to-face Mandarin and French interaction. By the approach of *intera tiona proso* plus *i pressionisti ents*, each instance of recycling repair was annotated manually for its prosodic realization, including relative pitch height and duration between the R1/R2 of the repair, as well as silence and other sound cues for initiating the repair. Through comparing the results of acoustic measurements, it is suggested that interlocutors of the two languages may orient to different methods of initiating the repair in spontaneous interaction in that, French speakers tend to incorporate lengthening at the end of R1 plus optional filled pauses to initiate the repair, while Mandarin speakers employ quick cut-offs for repair initiation, followed by immediate repair.

1 Introduction

Repair is a commonly occurring phenomenon in face-to-face interaction. During the process of conversational exchanges, speakers often stop before the end of their turns to make adjustments, i.e. to correct, to elaborate, or to qualify what they have said (Jasperson, 1998). As have shown in previous studies by Schegloff (1979) and Schegloff et al. (1977) on repair in natural conversation by the approach of conversation analysis (CA), the type of *sa e t rn, se - initiate* repair occurs far more frequently than other-initiated repair. In terms of the sound environment for initiating the repair by CA approach, Schegloff (1979) suggested that the sites of initiation in English self repair may involve a limited number of forms that are sensitive to the most immediate sound environment during production, including *t o* , *pa se*, or *i er*. It should be noted that Schegloff further pointed out that the location of the site of initiation in English repair could be "after the first sound of a word or just before its last" (1979: 275). To extend Schegloff's observation on the site of initiation in self-repair further, Fox et al. (2009) reported a cross-linguistic investigation of sites of initiation in same-turn self-repair from seven languages (including Mandarin) with the goal to uncover the universal principles in shaping sites of initiation in recycling and replacement repairs across languages.

The current study provides detailed acoustic profiles for the sites of initiating self-repair, extracted from comparative speech corpora of naturally occurred, face-to-face Mandarin and French interaction. Specifically, this study examines the sound profiles of the particular example of *re in* repair (or disfluent repetitions, shortened as DR) which is defined as "a brief, sometimes a longer repeat or re-saying of part of the utterance occurring in a conversational turn", following Schegloff (1987: 71). Below are two examples of recycling repair in French and Mandarin respectively:

(1) **le [R1] le [R2]** terrain commençait à glisser beaucoup (Henry and Pallaud, 2003)
the the field begin to slip a lot
"**the the** field began to slip much"

(2) 他那時候**買- [R1] 買[R2]**這個送 ipod
tā nà shíhou **mǎi- mǎi** zhège sòng ipod
3sg DET time **buy buy** DET offer PN
"(At) that time, it was **buying- buying** this one and getting one IPod for free."

150 instances of recycling repair/DR in Mandarin and French were culled from comparative speech corpora of both languages (cf. Bertrand et al., 2008; Chen et al., 2012). By

the approach of *intera tiona proso* plus *i pressionisti* judgments (cf. Benkenstein and Simpson, 2003; Kelly and Local, 1989), each instance of recycling repair was annotated manually in terms of its prosodic realization for and around the site of initiation, including pitch, duration, silence around R1 and R2 while accomplishing the repair, as well as perceivable sound cues including cut-offs and/or sound stretch to initiate the DR. As an application to the previously established comparable corpora of Mandarin and French interactional data, the major goal of the current study is to provide detailed sound profiles for sites of initiation in recycling repair of both languages. Although Fox et al. (2009) has provided the cross-linguistic analysis on the sites of initiation in same-turn self-repair, their study wasn't able to cover much analysis on the sound realizations in repair initiations, due to some constraints on the data collected. As will be shown, the result of the present study suggests that speakers of the two languages seem to favor different methods of initiating recycling repairs in terms of the sound realization. Based on the comparative results of acoustic measurements, it will be demonstrated that Mandarin speakers tend to initiate the repair by cut-offs at the end of R1, followed immediately by the repair; while French speakers incorporate the sound cue of lengthening at the end of R1 with optional filled pauses to initiate the repair. With instances of DR annotated by their prosodic realizations in both languages, eventually the data from the current study may serve as yet another language resource for further exploration of cross-linguistic studies on how human interaction is reflected in sound and prosody, i.e. specifically how the initiation of repair in terms of prosodic realization could be associated with interlocutors' strategies for turn-taking and sequential organization of the interaction across languages.

The paper is organized as follows. Section 2 provides a brief review of related research on repair/disfluency. In section 3 it introduces the data incorporated in the current study and the methodology adopted for analyzing the sound production within and around the sites of initiation of recycling repair instances. Section 4 presents the results from acoustic measurements. Section 5 discusses the implications of the results based on the acoustic analysis. Finally, section 6 is the summary and future research.

2 Related Research

In the following 2.1, it introduces previous research that focused on repair and/or disfluency. Section 2.2 and 2.3 provide review of the studies discussing the phenomenon of disfluency in Mandarin interaction and French conversations respectively.

2.1 Research on Repair/Disfluency

The discussion of same-turn self-repair has been the centre of focus in studies of the relevant fields, including psycholinguistics (e.g. Levelt, 1983; Levelt and Cutler, 1983), computational linguistics (e.g. on disfluency in speech: Shriberg, 1994; 1995; Tseng, 2003), general linguistics (e.g. Fox et al., 1996; Fox et al., 2009), and also in conversation analysis (e.g. Jasperson, 1998; Schegloff, 1987; Schegloff et al., 1977).

Most of the earlier studies on repair/disfluency focused on the phenomenon mainly in English. It was not until Fox et al. (1996) that there had been discussion about repair in other languages such as Japanese. Some previous studies that focused on DR in other languages include: Benkenstein and Simpson's study on the phonetic correlates of self-repair involving word repetitions in German speech (2003); Henry and Pallaud discussed word segments and repeats in French speech (2003); and Tseng discussed repetitions in spontaneous Mandarin (2003; 2006).

2.2 Repetition Repair in Mandarin Conversation

As mentioned, the current study concentrates on the specific instances of *re in* repair as one of the method of repair in conversations. There are several reasons that this particular method of carrying out same-turn self-repair has been chosen as the main focus: first of all, as shown in some previous quantitative studies on Mandarin repair (cf. Tseng, 2003; 2006), this type of repetition repair is the most frequent type of repair in Mandarin conversation. Moreover, Fox et al. (2009) also suggested that Mandarin speakers consistently initiate repair after the word is recognizably completed, i.e. the initiation in or after the last sound of the word in repair while recycling. Most of all, with regard to research methodology; the preference of initiating Mandarin repair after recognizable completion provides a sound justification to compare the sound realization of repeated words or phrases while doing the repair: since the recycling would be a complete repetition of the same word or phrase, it actually allows for a straightforward comparison of the prosodic realizations between R1 and R2 of the DR.

Another study focusing on Mandarin recycling repairs was Chen (2011), which took the approaches of conversational phonetics and interactional prosody toward the analysis of sound patterns of Mandarin recycling repairs in natural conversation. The purpose of the study is to examine how the combination of detailed prosodic features (including pitch, silence, duration, and loudness) forms various sound patterns in reflecting important aspects of talk-in-interaction and the sequential organization of Mandarin conversation through recyclings. In the preliminary findings, 6 sound patterns were identified and each pattern corresponds to a specific interactional function while interlocutors recycle during conversation exchanges (Chen, 2011). The result from the research highlights the *intera tion spe i i* , *se en e spe i i* , and *n tion spe i i* examples of Mandarin recyclings in correlation with the use of particular prosodic patterns (Chen, 2011).

2.3 Repetition Repair in French Conversation

As for the studies on repair/disfluency in French, Henry (2002) reported a quantitative study of repetitions based on a corpus of one million-word spontaneous spoken French. Since the purpose of the study was to contribute to the improvement of speech recognition, the article focused mostly on the grammatical categories involved in the French repetitions and the syntactic locations of the repetitions (Henry, 2002). Part of the result did suggest that, other than direct repetition (i.e. when R1 is followed directly by R2), the *asso iate repetition* is another frequent type of repetitions in spoken French. Of the type of associated repetition, it was found that the repeated combination of [R1+word+R2] occurred more frequently (Henry, 2002).

Another study focusing on the prosodic parameters of disfluencies in French conversation was by Bartkova (2005). Based on the method of statistical analysis, Bartkova (2005) examined the prosodic features of French disfluencies derived from speech data consisted of telephone messages. The result from the study suggested that, of the prosodic parameters of word repetitions, 65% of the word repetitions with filled pauses could have them located between words of repetitions (Bartkova, 2005). It was further observed that, when filled pauses were not separated by silent pauses from the words, they tended to follow the final consonants or vowels of the preceding words, forming a very long schwa like vowel (Bartkova, 2005).

3 Data and Methodology

The current section introduces the data and methodology incorporated in the present study. Section 3.1 is devoted to the data, and section 3.2 introduces the methodology of *intera tiona proso* for analyzing sound realization in face-to-face interaction. Section 3.3 presents a detailed description of the annotation procedure for the prosodic profiles of and around the sites of initiation in recycling repair of both languages.

3.1 Data

Examples of French recycling repair were extracted from a Corpus of Interactional Data (CID), which consists of 8 hours of audio-video recorded spontaneous spoken French and contains about 110,000 words (cf. Bertrand et al., 2008; Blache et al., 2009). One of the features of the CID corpus is that the data has been processed automatically and annotated (both automatically and manually) on **multimodal** levels: not only the corpus metadata, but also the phonetic, prosodic/phonological, morpho-syntactic levels, as well as the level for gestures (Bertrand et al., 2008; Blache et al., 2009). Furthermore, it should be noted that the CID corpus has been annotated additionally with cases of French disfluency of different types. For the purpose of the current study, 150 instances of disfluent repetitions were selected out of the annotated instances of disfluent repetitions produced by 2 of the female French speakers who participated in the recording process for the compilation of CID.

On the other side, examples of Mandarin recycling repair were taken from two sources. The first source is a corpus of Mandarin recycling repair described in Chen (2011). The corpus consists of 260 instances of recycling repair culled from about 3.5 hours of video- and audio-taped face-to-face Mandarin interaction.[1]

[1] The 3.5-hour conversational data includes 7 segments of two or multi-party Mandarin interaction over 10 female Mandarin speakers. For the ethnographic information of the interaction participants and the selection procedures for the

The second source is an on-going project of constructing a Mandarin corpus of conversational interaction following the French CID corpus (cf. Chen et al., 2012). Together 150 instances of Mandarin recycling repair produced by 6 native Taiwanese Mandarin interlocutors were selected for further acoustic analysis of the sound profiles of sites of initiation in the repair.

3.2 Methodology: on Interactional Prosody

As mentioned in Section 1, some of the past studies on repair within the field of CA have paid attention to the discussion of the relationship between prosody and interaction in conversation (cf. Schegloff, 1979; 1987). However, it is not until recently that interactional linguists have started paying attention to the systematic organization of phonetic and prosodic details in natural conversation. The approach *intera tiona proso* (cf. Couper-Kuhlen and Selting, 1996; also *on ersationa p ono o* by Kelly and Local, 1989) suggests incorporating the following theoretical points toward the study of the sound system of conversational interaction:

- The material considered derives entirely from naturally occurring face-to-face conversational interaction
- The analysis attempts to prejudge as little as possible the salience of phonetic features
- The analysis seeks explicitly to motivate and warrant the functional categories employed by reference to the observable behaviour of the conversational participants (Kelly and Local, 1989: 263)

Thus one of the features of the interactional prosody approach is that it advocates an 'impressionistic' analysis by closely listening to the production of real speech and notating phonetic details which a trained ear could perceive, including properties such as pitch, loudness, tempo, and others (Kelly and Local, 1989).

To analyze the sound production around and for the sites of initiation in recycling repair, the current study adopts the aforementioned methodology that combines both the acoustic measurements and the impressionistic analysis. Actually, such combinational approach has been used in a previous study on word repetitions in German speech by Benkenstein and Simpson (2003). In the present study, the acoustic measurements were carried out by using the computer software Praat (© Boersma and Weenink, 2007). Additional judgments would be made based on the analyst's impressionistic interpretation of most of the auditory cues, following the impressionistic approach from interactional prosody. In the next section, various acoustic measurements made for R1 and R2 of each DR token will be described.

3.3 Annotations for Sound Profiles

In order to further compare the sound production around and at the sites of initiation in disfluent repetitions derived from both French and Mandarin interaction, the following annotations were noted for each instance of DR.

Pitch. The pitch height of the onset of R1 and R2 of each recycling repair was first measured then double-checked against the analyst's impressionistic judgments. Here the pitch height refers to fundamental frequency (F0). When recording the result of pitch height, however, we only noted the *re ati e* pitch height between R1/R2 of each DR (such as if R1 or R2 is perceived as in a higher pitch height). Furthermore, it should be mentioned that sometimes when the F0 difference between R1 and R2 was too small to be considered as hearable difference, the measurement of *se itone* would be incorporated to help determine if R1 and R2 might be perceived as realized at the same pitch height.

Duration. Duration refers to the length of R1/R2 of the repair, reported in milliseconds. The measurement of duration was taken starting from the onset to the ending of the syllable of the word or phrase in R1 and R2. Similar to the measurement for pitch height, the result of duration is reported in terms of relative duration between R1 and R2, i.e. if R1 or R2 is the longer segment of the DR.

Silence. The profile of silence recorded, in seconds, any audible pause located: a) before R1; b) in between R1 and R2; or c) after R2 of the repair. In the current research a cut-off point at 0.2-second has been applied, following Jasperson's study on focused English repair (1998). Any silent pause under 0.2 seconds was considered as part of the articulatory process (cf. Jasperson, 1998) and thus treated as having no significant impact on the processing of the repair. Silent pauses longer than 0.2 seconds, on the other hand, would be taken as serving possible function interactionally and were otherwise noted.

compilation of the recycling repair corpus, please refer to Chen (2011).

One place to point out is that, as the past discussion on French word repetitions also paid attention to filled pauses, here we took into consideration instances of DR with filled pauses located in between R1 and R2 as well.

Other prosodic cues- sound stretch and cut-off. The prosodic cue of sound stretch (or lengthening) records any perceptible prolongation on any syllable of R1 and R2 of the repair. To determine if there was perceivable sound stretches, the impressionistic judgments were made and the result was marked on the transcription of the interaction. When any lengthening has been observed, it would be marked, using the convention of the colon symbol ":".

The sound cue of cut-off is defined as an articulatory closure that interrupts the air stream, and it typically involves glottal or other stop closures (cf. Jasperson, 2002). To decide if there was a cut-off, the analyzer followed the impressionistic description of ways in which the cut-off is articulated, as proposed by Jasperson (1998; 2002). At least two types of cut-offs were distinguished: "glottalized" cut-offs, which have salient interruption glottalization, and "soft" cut-offs that have either unnoticeable or no interrupted glottalization (cf. Jasperson, 1998; 2002). The glottalized cut-offs were indicated by a percent sign "%" while the soft ones by a dash "-". Finally, as the current study concerns the sites of initiation in recycling repair, in the following results reported with regard to the sound cues of cut-off and lengthening we focus on mainly the DR instance in which R1 is followed immediately by the cut-off and/or lengthening.

4 Results

The current section describes the comparative results of acoustic measurements made on the R1/R2 of the DR in both languages. The results will be reported according to the annotation categories of acoustic measurements introduced in Section 3.3 above.

4.1 Pitch

As mentioned in 3.3, the measurement of pitch height is reported as the relative pitch realization perceived between R1/R2. Therefore the result of relative pitch height could be noted as realized in one of the following situations:

- R1 is the higher segment of the DR (Higher R1)
- R2 is the higher segment of the DR (Higher R2)
- R1 and R2 are perceived as realized in the same pitch height (Same)
- No comparable result could be yield as for which segment of R1/R2 is higher (No result)

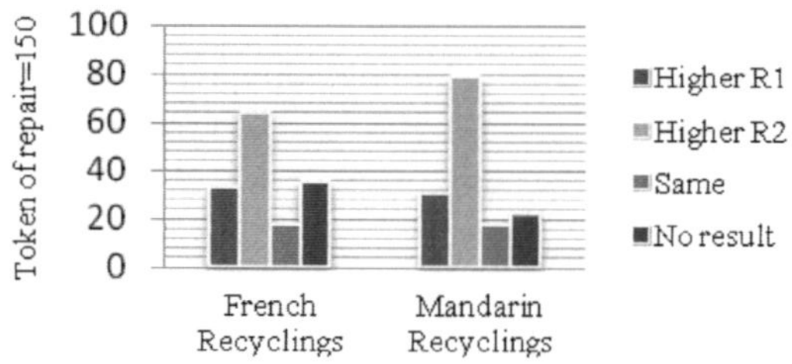

Figure 1. The Result of Relative Pitch Height Perceived between R1/R2.

From Figure 1 it is demonstrated that for most of the DR instances in both languages R2 is perceived as relatively higher when executing the repair (For French recyclings: 64/150, 42.6%; Mandarin: 79/150, 52.7%). On the other hand, about 20% of the recycling instances in both languages are realized with higher R1 (For French DRs: 33/150, 22%; Mandarin: 31/150, 20.6%). The rest of the instances could be in the situation that R1/R2 are realized at the same pitch height (For French DRs: 18/150, 12%; Mandarin: 18/150, 12%), or when the relative pitch height between R1/R2 could not be determined perceptually (For French recyclings: 35/150, 23.3%; Mandarin: 22/150, 14.7%).

4.2 Duration

The result of the relative duration between R1/R2 of the DR is presented in Table 2.

	Longer R1	Longer R2	Total
French Recyclings	125 (83.3%)	25 (16.7%)	150 (100%)
Mandarin Recyclings	126 (84%)	24 (16%)	150 (100%)

Table 2. Comparative Result of Relative Duration between R1/R2.

As can be seen, for the recycling instances in both languages over 80% are realized with longer

R1. The result thus shows a strong preference over longer R1 while executing the repair. This is actually consistent with the findings from previous studies on the relative duration between raparandum and repair of disfluency/repair in spontaneous speech of various languages (cf. Bartkova, 2005; Shriberg, 1995; Tseng, 2006).

4.3 Silence

As depicted in Section 3.3, for the measurement of silence we noted three possible locations for interlocutors to pause for accomplishing the recycling, namely before R1, in between R1 and R2, and after R2. The following Table 3-a and Table 3-b summarize the results of number of instances with pauses occurring immediately prior to R1 and after R2 of the DR respectively.

	With Pause	Without Pause	Total
French Recyclings	8 (5.3%)	142 (94.7%)	150 (100%)
Mandarin Recyclings	36 (24%)	114 (76%)	150 (100%)

Table 3-a. Occurrences of Pause Right Preceding R1.

	With Pause	Without Pause	Total
French Recyclings	9 (6.0%)	141 (94.0%)	150 (100%)
Mandarin Recyclings	11 (7.3%)	139 (92.7%)	150 (100%)

Table 3-b. Occurrences of Pause Following R2 Immediately.

From Table 3-a, the French DRs seem to differ slightly from the Mandarin instances in terms of the silent pause occurred prior to R1: French recycling repairs are less likely to be preceded by pauses longer than 0.2 seconds, while for Mandarin recyclings about a quarter of examples have their R1 preceded by longer pauses. When turning to the pauses following immediately after R2, as can be seen in Table 3-b, we find that for the majority of the recycling instances in both languages there wouldn't be any perceivable silence located right after R2.

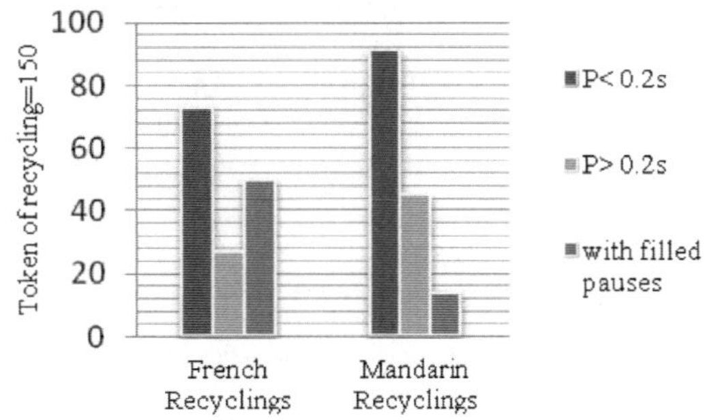

Figure 4. The Result of Pauses (P) and Filled Pauses Occurred in between R1/R2.

Figure 4 summarizes instances of recyclings with or without pauses in between R1 and R2. Based on the results, there are about 60.7% (91/150) of Mandarin recyclings that have their R1 followed directly by R2 (i.e. without additional pauses in between R1/R2 or only micro pause under 0.2 seconds), while less than half of French DR instances (48.7%, 73/150) have their R2 following R1 immediately without delay. Comparing to French recyclings, therefore, Mandarin speakers seem to have the tendency of executing the repair right after the initiation of the recycling without further delay. For recyclings with over 0.2-second pause in between R1/R2, 30% of Mandarin recyclings (45/150) have a longer, perceivable pause in between R1/R2, while about only 18% (27/150) of French DRs are realized this way. Finally, for instances with filled pauses in between R1/R2 of the DR, the two languages differ in that 33.3% (50/150) of French recycling instances were tagged with (one or more) filled pauses in between R1/R2, while this rarely happened in Mandarin recyclings (9.3%, 14/150). It is worth noting that the filled pauses located between R1/R2 of the French recyclings were found to be realized as brief as 100ms to as long as 1700ms.

4.4 Other Sound Cues: Sound Stretch and Cut-off

The annotations for the sound cues of sound stretch and cut-off at the end of R1 provide further information on how the recyclings are initiated in both languages. As presented in Table 5, speakers of the two languages seem to favor different methods of initiation: French speakers tend to initiate the recycling by the mean of prolongation at the end of R1 (59/150, 39.3%), while Mandarin speakers rely more on the cut-off at the end of R1 of the repair (67/150, 44.7%).

	Recycling initiated by lengthening	Recycling initiated by cut-off
French Recyclings	59/150 (39.3%)	18/150 (12%)
Mandarin Recyclings	41/150 (27.3%)	67/150 (44.7%)

Table 5. Summary of Tokens of Recyclings Initiated by Either Lengthening or Cut-off.

One place to add is that, from the summary presented in Table 5, by annotating instances of recycling initiated by lengthening or cut-off can only account for about half of the instances of French recyclings and about 70% of the Mandarin recyclings. Further examination shows that for French recyclings, there are about another 20% (31/150) of the instances that are realized with filled pauses in between R1/R2 of the recyclings. For the rest of the instances of DR in both languages, there can be neither cut-off nor lengthening perceived at the sites of initiation.

5 Discussion

5.1 From the Results of Acoustic Measurements

Based on the results presented in Sections 4.1 and 4.2, there seems to be a tendency for speakers of both languages to utilize the prosodic pattern of longer R1 followed by higher R2 while executing the recycling repairs. Such result is actually consistent with the general findings on the prosodic profiles for repair in French speech by Bartkova (2005) and Mandarin repair by Tseng (2006). It should be noted, however, that there are still recyclings in both languages that could be realized prosodically with R1 and R2 at the same pitch height, or when there's no perceivable result as for if R1 or R2 is realized in a relatively higher pitch. As shown in Chen (2011), Mandarin speakers can hold the same pitch height across R1/R2 of the recycling pair to reflect the specific function of *ontin ation* with the turn-so-far. Thus further exploration could be made with regard to how interlocutors in conversational interaction employ different prosodic cues while repairing in order to reflect any particular pragmatic function or in relation to interaction among the speakers and the sequential organization of the conversation. Still, there is about 23% and 14% of the French and Mandarin DR respectively that has been described as yielding no comparable result with regard to which segment of R1/R2 is higher in pitch, some possible explanations could be that, for one, the pitch realization while executing the repair could influenced by other factors such as speech rate. Another possibility could be that the pitch contour realized during recycling the word or phrase for repair is at the same time influenced by the global intonation contour from higher level discourse units.

In terms of the location of pauses, one consistent finding is that there were rarely cases in which speakers of both languages attach additional pauses after accomplishing the repair. The result implies that interlocutors simply carry on with the conversation after the recycling is accomplished without further delay. On the other hand, when turning to the pause located prior to R1, we find that for French recyclings there were rarely cases in which their R1s were preceded by perceivable pauses. Comparing to the DR instances by Mandarin interlocutors, it seems that Mandarin speakers may have slightly higher tendency of initiating the recyclings after perceivable pauses. Along the same line, it will be of further interest to explore if there exists any discrepancy between speakers of the two languages to initiate the repairs in terms of their locations within prosodic/intonation unit: i.e. if the Mandarin speakers have a higher tendency to initiate repair toward the beginning of the prosodic boundary, comparing to French interlocutors who may otherwise initiate the repair toward the middle or even later on within the intonation unit.

As for the pause located in between R1/R2 of the DR, since this is also the position for filled pauses that could be used as one of the methods of initiating repairs, we will discuss the result further in the next section.

5.2 Methods of Initiating Recycling Repair

Based on the results from Figure 4, the main differences between French and Mandarin DR in terms of the pauses located in between R1/R2 lies in that, French speakers incorporate more frequently the filled pauses while Mandarin interlocutors rarely do so in that specific location. Moreover, Mandarin interlocutors show a preference for immediately repairing right after the initiation of the DR, as demonstrated by the more frequently occurred instances with pause under 0.2 seconds in between R1/R2. Here we will discuss in detail how the result sheds light on the different methods incorporated for initiating recycling repair in the two languages.

Initiating recycling repair in French interaction. According to Table 5, French interlocutors demonstrate a preference of sound stretch or prolongation at the end of R1. One of the examples taken from the French CID corpus is presented in (3):

(3) S : mais où est– ce que tu as **des:: des** feux d'artifice
but where is- what 2Sg get **some:: some** firework
"but where did you get **some:: some** fireworks…."

As can be seen, here the speaker makes use of the lengthening at the end of R1 in order to initiate the DR. After initiating the repair, the speaker follows up by directly repeating the same word **des** to accomplish the repair. When examining further the instances of French DR, we actually find cases in which the repair is initiated by a lengthened R1 and followed by a filled pause that is often lengthened as well:

(4) S: j'ai mis mes ski sur le dos puis j'ai commencé à descendre **à pied euh::::::↓ ↓ à pied** toute la station
1sg put Poss ski Prep Det back then 1sg Aux start to descend **Prep foot euh:::::: Prep foot** all Det resort
"I put my ski on the back then I started descend **by foot euh:::::: by foot** throughout the resot."

(5) S: **et:=< euh: (.) et** en même temps euh ils se sont excusés
and: euh: (.) and Prep same time euh 3pl apologize
"**and: euh: (.) and** at the same time euh they apologized…"

One place to point out based on the above instances of French DR is that, not only do French speakers favor initiating the recyclings by lengthening at the end of R1 followed by a lengthened filled pause (such as in (4)), also they tend to attach the filled pause immediately after the lengthened R1 (as shown in (5) by the transcription notation '=<' in between *et* and *e*).[2] Actually, as mentioned in Section 2.3, Bartkova (2005) suggested that filled pauses in French speech tend to follow the final consonants or vowels of the preceding words in form of a long schwa like vowel. From the perspective of interaction and turn-taking, while French interlocutors recycle the turn for repair, they may take advantage of the prolongations at the site of initiation, plus another (optional) lengthened filled pause, to further withhold the turn in order to gain time to accomplish the repair.

Initiating recycling repair in Mandarin interaction. Turning to the DR in Mandarin interaction, based on the result from Table 5, speakers tend to incorporate a cut-off at the end of R1 to initiate the repair. Moreover, based on the result summarized in Figure 4, Mandarin interlocutors incorporate less frequently longer pauses, even rarely filled pauses in between R1/R2. Thus the more commonly used method of initiating and accomplishing recycling repair by Mandarin speakers can be described as a quick initiation by the cut-off at the end of R1, followed immediately by the direct repetition in R2 without further delay. One of such Mandarin recycling instances derived from the Mandarin CID corpus is shown in the following (6) (similarly see also the repair instance in example (2) presented previously):

(6) S:喔:那- 可是**那個- [R1] 那個[R2]**Y是%(.) 是韓國人
S: o: nà- kěshi **nàge- nàge** Y shì%(.) shì hánguórén.
Ex Det but **Det- Det** Y be% (.) be Korean
"Oh that- but **that- that** Y is% (.) is Korean."

When the speaker recycles the determiner *na e* "that" there is a cut-off at the end of R1, which otherwise facilitates a quick start at the site of initiation in repairing. To accomplish the repair process, the interlocutor immediately follows up with a direct repetition of the same lexical item without additional pause. This method of initiating the repair, therefore, is rather different from the way in which French interlocutors recycle to repair by the lengthening at the end of R1 then followed optionally by a filled pause.

Last, but not the least, as suggested from the result presented in Figure 4, Mandarin speakers rarely incorporate filled pauses in between R1 and R2 of the recyclings. The following (7) and (8) present 2 of the 14 Mandarin DR instances that were executed with filled pauses (PF) after the sites of initiation:

(7) A:然後**就是[R1]:::嗯::** (.8) **就是[R2]**要讓他們覺得有來:: (.7) 付費有收到: 實惠的那種感覺

[2] This transcription notation '=<' indicates that the immediately following talk is 'jump-started' from the syllable prior to the symbol.

A: ránhou **jìushi::: en:::** (.8) **jìushi** yào ràng tāmen juéde yǒu lái:: (.7) fùfèi yǒu shōudào: shíhuì de nàzhǒng gǎnjué

Then **just::: PF** (.8) **just** Aux let 3pl feel have come:: (.7) pay have received treat DE DET kind feeling

"Then (it's) **just::: en:::** (.8) **just** to let them feel that (since) they've paid, they should get something equal in return."

(8) X:然後所以**那個老闆-[R1]**(.)**就是** (.4) **那個老闆[R2]**跟: (.) J 說

X: ránhou suóyǐ **nàge lǎobǎn-** (.) **jìushi** (.4) **nàge lǎobǎn** gēn: (.) J ↓shūo:

Then so **Det boss** (.) **PF** (.4) **Det boss** Prep (.) J say

"And then, so, **the professor** (.) **just** (.4) **the professor** told J…"

In (7), the recycling is initiated by a lengthening at the end of R1, followed by the lengthened filled pause *en* in lengthening. Here when the speaker recycles the lexical item *s i* "just", she has incorporated a method of initiation similar to the French DR instance presented in (4). While in (8), on the other hand, the recycling of the NP *n e lǎobǎn* "the boss (lit.)/ the professor" is initiated by the cut-off at the end of R1, followed by a brief pause then the filled pause *s i*. Given that only limited number of Mandarin DR instances were identified to co-occurr with filled pauses in between R1 and R2, more data will be required to examine further how speakers in Mandarin interaction may employ filled pauses in the process of repairing and in initiating the repair.

6 Summary and Future Research

The current paper presents the study that applies the data derived from comparative corpora of interactional data in French and Mandarin for the analysis of sound profiles in and around the sites of initiation in recycling repair/disfluent repetitions. 150 examples of DR in both languages were culled from the comparative corpora of conversational interaction in both languages. By the approach of interactional prosody plus impressionistic judgments, the relative acoustic measurements of and around R1/R2 of the recycling repair were made and then compared. The goal of the comparative study is to identify the sound patterns adopted at the sites of initiation in accomplishing the DR in both languages. The findings suggest that Mandarin and French speakers may resort to different methods for initiating the recyclings: while French interlocutors may employ sound stretch at the end of R1 plus lengthened filled pause(s) at the site of initiation in repair, Mandarin speakers incorporate more frequently cut-offs at the end of R1, followed immediately by R2 for accomplishing the repair.

For future research, in addition to some possible points for further research already mentioned in the discussion sections, the result from current study may be implemented for further cross-linguistic analyses on how the sound realization for initiating the repair might be correlated with the turn-taking between the speakers and the sequential organization of the conversations: i.e. if the longer initiation process in French DR may be used by the speakers to withhold the turn and thus prevent other interlocutors from intervening the continuation of the turn-so-far by the current speaker; or if the tendency of locating Mandarin repair near pauses (cf. when the DR follows pauses) may otherwise reflect a different turn-taking system between or among interlocutors at or near to the transition-relevant places.

Acknowledgements

This research was supported in part by the Erasmus Mundus Action 2 program MULTI of the European Union, grant agreement number 2009-5259-5. The French data from the CID corpus is part of the ('Outils de traitement d'information multimodale') project supported by the ANR French agency (Grant Number: ANR-08-BLAN-0239). The author would like to thank the OTIM/ToMA team at LPL, Aix-Marseille Université & CNRS for sharing the annotated French data.

References

Bartkova, Katarina. 2005. Prosodic Cues of Spontaneous Speech in French. In *ro ee in o is en in pontaneo s pee (i*), 21-25. Aix-en-Provence, France.

Benkenstein, Ramona and Adrian Simpson. 2003. Phonetic Correlates of Self-repair Involving Word Repetition in German Spontaneous Speech. In *toria an esear Wor s op on is en in pontaneo s pee (i*), 81-84. Göteborg, Sweden.

Bertrand, Roxane, Philippe, Blache, Robert, Espesser, Gaëlle, Ferré, Christine, Meunier, Beatrice Priego-Valverde, and Stéphane Rauzy, 2008. Le CID - Corpus of Interactional Data - Annotation et Exploitation Multimodale de Parole

Conversationnelle. *raite ent to ati e es an es*, 49:105-134.

Blache, Philippe, Roxane Bertrand, and Gaëlle Ferré. 2009. Creating and Exploiting Multimodal Annotated Corpora: The ToMA Project. In M. Kipp et al. (Eds.) *ti o a orpora ro o e s o at ra ntera tion to ste s an pp i ations*. Springer Berlin Heidelberg. 38-53.

Boersma, Paul and David Weenink. 2007. *raat oin oneti s o p ter*. Online: http://www.praat.org, accessed on 20 Nov, 2007.

Chen, Helen Kai-yun. 2011. *o n atterns in an arin e in epair*. Ph.D. dissertation, University of Colorado at Boulder.

Chen, Helen Kai-yun, Laurent, Prévot, Roxane, Bertrand, Beatrice, Priego-Valverde, and Blache, Philippe. Toward a Mandarin-French Corpus of Interactional Data. 2012. In *e t Wor s op on t e e anti s an ra ati s o ia o es*. Paris, France.

Couper-Kuhlen, Elizabeth and Margret Selting. 1996. Towards an Interactional Perspective on Prosody and a Prosodic Perspective on Interaction. In Elizabeth Couper-Kuhlen and Margret Selting (Eds.) *roso in on ersation ntera tiona t ies*. Cambridge: Cambridge University Press. 11-56.

Fox, Barbara, Makoto Hayashi, and Robert Jasperson. 1996. Resources and Repair: A Cross-linguistic Study of the Syntactic Organization of Repair. In Elinor Ochs, Emanuel Schegloff, and Sandra Thompson (Eds.), *ntera tion an ra ar*. Cambridge: Cambridge University Press. 185–237.

Fox, Barbara, Fay Wouk, Makoto Hayashi, Steven Fincke, Liang Tao, Marja-leena Sorjonen, Minna Laakso, and Wilfrido Hernandez. 2009. A Cross-linguistic Investigation of the Site of Initiation in Same-turn Self-repair. In John Sidnell (Ed.), *on ersation na sis o parati e erspe ti es*. Cambridge: Cambridge University Press. 61-103.

Henry, Sandrine. 2002. Étude des répétitions en français parlé spontané pour les technologies de la parole. In *tes e a e en ontre es t iants er e rs en n or ati e po r e raite ent to ati e es an es* , 467-476.

Henry, Sandrine and Berthille Pallaud. 2003. Word Fragments and Repeats in Spontaneous Spoken French". In *toria an esear Wor s op on is en in pontaneo s pee (i),* 77-80. Göteborg, Sweden.

Jasperson, Robert. 1998. *epair a ter t o p orations in t e ra ar o o se epair o t e rn onstr tiona nit so ar*. Ph.D. dissertation, University of Colorado at Boulder.

Jasperson, Robert. 2002. Some linguistic aspects of closure cut-off. In Cecilia Ford, Barbara Fox, and Sandy Thompson (Eds.) *e an a e o t rn an se en e*. Oxford: Oxford University Press. 257–286.

Kelly, John and John, Local. 1989. *oin ono o ser in e o in nterpretin* . Manchester: Manchester University Press.

Levelt, Willem. 1983. Monitoring and Self-repair in Speech. *o nition* 14: 41–104.

Levelt, Willem and Anne Cutler. 1983. Prosodic Marking in Speech Repair. *o rna o e anti s* 2: 205-217.

Schegloff, Emanuel. 1979. The Relevance of Repair to Syntax-for-conversation. In Talmy Givón (Ed.), *is o rse an nta* . London: Academic Press. 261–286.

Schegloff, Emanuel. 1987. Recycled Turn Beginnings: A Precise Repair Mechanism in Conversation's Turn-taking Organisation. In Graham Button and John Lee (Eds.) *a an o ia r anisation*. Clevedon Avon: Multilingual Matters. 70–85.

Schegloff, Emanuel, Jefferson Gail and Sacks Harvey. 1977. The Preference for Self-correction in the Organization of Repair in Conversation. *an a e* 53: 361–382.

Shriberg, Elizabeth. 1994. *re i inaries to a eor o pee is en ies*. Ph.D. dissertation. University of California at Berkeley.

Shriberg, Elizabeth. 1995. Acoustic Properties of Disfluent Repetitions. In *ro ee in s o t e nternationa on ress o oneti ien es*, (95') 4: 384–387.

Tseng, Shu-Chuan. 2003. Repairs and Repetitions in Spontaneous Mandarin. In *toria an esear Wor s op on is en in pontaneo s pee (i),* 73-76. Göteborg, Sweden.

Tseng, Shu-Chuan. 2006. Repairs in Mandarin Conversation. *o rna o inese in isti s*, 34: 80-120.

Of-constructions in the Predicate of *demonstrate* and *show* in Academic Discourse

Liyin Chen
National Chengchi University
No.64, Sec.2, ZhiNan Rd.,
Wenshan District, Taipei City 11605,
Taiwan
98551505@nccu.edu.tw

Siaw-Fong Chung
National Chengchi University
No.64, Sec.2, ZhiNan Rd.,
Wenshan District, Taipei City 11605,
Taiwan
sfchung@nccu.edu.tw

Abstract

This study investigates *of*-constructions in the predicates of two verbs, *demonstrate* and *show*, in academic discourse. A construction perspective is taken to examine how the two predicate constructions ('*demonstrate* N1 *of* N2' and '*show* N1 *of* N2') would differ when the information-weighting of N1 and N2 are considered. The noun phrases were compared following Sinclair's (1991) conception of semantic headedness. He notes the peculiarity of *of* through the expression of double-headed constructions (i.e., considering both N1 and N2 as the semantic heads). This study adopts this framework and applies it to analyze the *of*-constructions of the two synonymous verbs. The results show that headedness of the *of*-constructions can be used to identify the subtle differences between the two synonyms. *Demonstrate* displays greater information weight predominated by double-headed constructions and tends to be associated with abstract conception. *Show* follows closely after *demonstrate,* but further analysis reveals that *show* tends to provide more 'relational' evidence described in terms of partitive uses through nouns like *variety, degree, incidence, level, rate* and *range*.

1 Introduction

In Sinclair's (1991) book chapter "The meeting of lexis and grammar", he provides his insightful analysis on the word *of* to demonstrate the fusion of lexis and grammar. The word *of*, being one of the commonest English words, is conventionally conceived as a preposition with a postmodifying function. However, Sinclair underlines the encompassing roles of *of.* In particular, nominalization structures (e.g., *the effectiveness of the telescope*; *the importance of symoblisation*) have drawn much research attention (e.g., Halliday & Martin, 1993; Kreyer, 2003; Quirk et al., 1985). For example, Quirk et al. (1985) investigate the substitutability of genitive constructions (e.g., *China's economy*) with *of*-nominalization (e.g., *the economy of China*) and the results suggest that several restrictions comply. In a similar vein, Kreyer (2003) investigates corpus data which also allow for a possible alternation between genitive and *of*-construction (e.g., *the chairman of the committee* and *the committee's chairman*) and shows that processability and degree of human involvement are two crucial factors influencing speakers' selection of the constructions. Specifically, *of*-construction is more likely to be selected when the second noun phrase is pre-modified (e.g., *the son of* ***the Royal Bucks*** *secretary*) and when the semantic relationship between the two noun phrases is more objective, attributive and partitive. In other words, in comparison with genitive constructions, *of*-constructions are hardly used when it comes to describing possessive, and kinship relations. The word *of*, along with other prepositions, also plays a role in nominalization structure. Prepositional phrases are conventionally regarded as postmodifiers (e.g., *the overall ehthalpy charge for the conversion of graphite to cardon dioxide*) to provide additional semantic content in scientific texts (Halliday & Martin, 1993). Halliday and Martin examine scientific texts and show a high degree of nominalization in such texts. They also found that objectification (e.g., *diamond is energetically unstable* can be objectified into *the energetic instability of diamond*), or object-like status as a result of nominalization, allows the nominal group to be less negotiable. They also point out that an important function of nominalization is to structure scientific knowledge in a static, synoptic representation of reality. According to these two functions, nominalization plays a crucial role in constructing scientific discourse to represent objectivity.

While previous studies have established the functions of of-constructions like demonstrating objectivity or expressing attributive and partitive relations between the two noun phrases (i.e., N1 and N2), few studies actually investigate if these functions would vary under different linguistic environment. To fill this research gap, we follow the co-occurrence approach (Gries & Otani, 2010) to examining the distributive characteristics of two verbs, namely, demonstrate and show, in academic discourse. According to Gries and Otani (2010), the co-occurrence approach takes the position that "the distributional characteristics of the use of an item reveals many of its semantic and functional properties and purposes (p. 122)". This approach follows researchers such as Firth (1957) and Bolinger (1968) to emphasize on the dependence of linguistic context for any lexical items. Gries and Otani (2010) also indicate the application of the underlying principles of this approach to a number of synonymy studies. In this study, we focus on demonstrate and show, two reporting verbs in academic discourse. A large number of studies on reporting verbs has been carried out, but they mainly focus on citational functions (e.g., Hyland, 1999), evaluation (e.g., Thompson & Ye, 1991), and disciplinary variation (e.g., Hyland, 2000; Charles, 2006). Both *demonstrate* and *show* can be considered to be in the same sub-class of reporting verbs that report research activities which have been accepted by the reporting writer (Thomas & Hawes, 1994). To the best of our knowledge, the co-occurrence approach has been rarely applied to the research of reporting verbs in academic writing.

In sum, we would like to identify if the semantic relationships of N1 and N2 in *of*-constructions (i.e., N1 *of* N2) would vary when associated with different neighboring words and if such semantic relationships can help us distinguish near-synonyms like *demonstrate* and *show*. In other words, we want to compare the types *of*-constructions predicated in *demonstrate* N1 *of* N2 and *show* N1 *of* N2. We ask the following two research questions:

(1) How do the N1 *of* N2 predicates of *demonstrate* and *show* differ in terms of their distribution of N1-N2 semantic relationships?
(2) What major functions can be found from the *of*-predicates that are associated with each verb?

The rest of the paper is organized as follows. Section two presents a brief review of semantic analyses of *of*-phrases. Section three presents the current study and criteria used and Section four introduces our methodology. Sections five and six present our results. Finally, we discuss and conclude our study in sections seven and eight.

2 Semantic Analyses of *of*-phrases

Different approaches have been taken to the semantic analysis of *of*-phrases. The following subsections briefly describe each.

2.1 A conventional account

The conventional approach treats *of*-N2 as a postmodifier. Quirk et al. (1985), for example, take such a position by comparing *of*-construction with its equivalent genitive construction as illustrated in (1a) and (1b) (examples taken from Quirk et al., 1985: 1276).

(1a) *the city's population*

(1b) *the population of the city*

Phrase (1a) can be paraphrased as (1b) to convey the same message.

(2a) *the family's car*

(2b) *?the car of the family*

(3a) *a woman of courage*

(3b) **courage's woman*

Example (2a) is a genitive construction but its equivalent *of*-construction (2b) is low in acceptability, and a reversed-direction transformation from an *of*-construction (3a) to a genitive (3b) is essentially unacceptable. Although previous work on genitive-*of*-construction alternation has drawn much research interest and shed light on the complexity of underlying mechanisms, the alternation research only characterizes partial representation of the *of*-construction (e.g., Gries & Stefanowistch, 2004; Sinclair, 1991). Sinclair (1991) points out that *of* is not limited to a post-modifying function as prevalently assumed in previous research. The following discussion will focus on Sinclair's work on *of*-constructions.

2.2 Sinclair's (1991) double-headed approach

A rather novel approach to the semantic analysis of *of*-construction is Sinclair's (1991) work. He posits that the preposition *of* behaves in a very different manner from most prepositions and demonstrates the peculiarity of *of*-construction by emphasizing the likelihood of semantic double-headedness exhibited in some *of*-constructions. Sinclair identifies three semantic heads in the N1 *of* N2 construction: (1) N1 as the head, (2) N2 as the head, and (3) both N1 and N2 as the head or double heads. While the first head class follows the conventional perspective regarding *of* as a post-modifying preposition, much of Sinclair's discussion focuses on the latter two. N2 as the head covers three major sub-categories, namely 'measure/quantifier', 'focus' nouns and 'support' nouns. 'Measure/quantifier' as N1 (bolded and underlined) can be either conventional measure (e.g., ***both*** *of them; **a couple** of weeks*) or less conventional measure with unclear boundaries (e.g., ***a series*** *of S-shaped curves; **the bulk** of their lives; **groups** of five*). 'Focus' nouns are what Sinclair refers to as "an extension of quantifier or partitive" (p. 87). There are three sub-categories, namely, focus on a part (e.g., ***the middle*** *of a sheet; **the edge** of the teeth; **the end** of the day*), focus on a more specialized part (e.g., ***the evening*** *of 5th August; **the first week** of the war; **the point** of denotation*) and focus on a component, aspect or attribute (e.g., ***the whole hull*** *of your boat; **an arrangement** of familiar figures*). The last category of N2 as the head are nouns that provide support to N2. There are also three sub-categories: (1) reduced in meaning (e.g., ***the notion*** *of machine intelligence; **various kinds** of economic sanctions*); (2) an intention to be vague (e.g., ***a sort*** *of parody; **the kind** of thing that Balzac would have called*); (3) additional grammatical support (e.g., ***a single act*** *of cheating; **the power** of speech*). This N2 head category is what Sinclair refers to as metaphorical expressions (e.g., ***the juices*** *of their imagination; **the grasp** of the undertow*).

However, further complication arises when N1 is modified. The semantic head assignment would no longer be an N2 but shift to a double head (e.g., *the **technical** resources of reconnaissance; a **comprehensive** selection of containers*). In addition to the modified N1 cases described above, there are three major categories for double-headed *of*-constructions. The first includes titles of people, places (e.g., *the Duchess of Beford; the new president of Zaire*). The second involves nominalizations or "where there is something approximating to a propositional relationship between the two nouns" (Sincliar, 1991, p. 91). One of the propositional relationships between the two nouns refers to 'verb-subject' or 'verb-object' (e.g., *the payment of Social Security* can be rephrased as *x pays Social Security*; *the enthusiastic collaboration of auctioneers* can be rephrased as *auctioneers collaborate enthusiastically*). The second propositional relationship is where N1 is a derivation of an adjective (e.g., *the **shrewdness** of the inventor*). The last category is loose association or references to common location, sponsorship, and representation (e.g., *the tea shops of Japan; the Mission to the UN of the PRC; the closed fist salute of ZANU-PF*). While Sinclair's framework provides a comprehensive analysis, Owen (2007) elaborates on Sinclair's classification of headedness with the notion of gradience.

2.3 Owen's (2007) gradience approach

Owen (2007) posits a gradience approach to *of*-construction. Table 2 presents his analysis which views semantic headedness of *of*-construction in a continuum. The author constructs an omissibility test (denoted as OT) based on the

Head?	Expression	Comment	OT
N2	*A lot of money*	Quantifier	Fail
N1?? + N2	*A load of money*	Measure	Fail
N1? + N2	*A bag of money*	Less conventional measure	Fail
N1?+ N2	*A history of money*	Focus on component, aspect or attribute	Fail
N1 + N2	*A hatred of money*	Propositional: x wastes money (fixed expression?)	Fail
N1? + N2?	*A bait of money*	a. Money laid as a bait b. Bait consisting of money	a. Fail b. Pass
N1 + N2?	*A reward of money*	*Of*-phrase seems to add secondary info., qualifying head	Pass
N1 + N2???	*A photograph of money*	Ditto,, even more so.	Pass

Table 2: Owen's gradience analysis (2007: 213)

criterion which determines the degree of damage to the meaning of the whole expression if *of* and N2 are omitted. Owen revisits Sinclair's (1991) work and notices that Sinclair's work encapsulates the notion of information-weighting. Although Owen does not elaborate on the issue, the idea will be discussed in this paper when it comes to comparing the linguistic contexts of two items.

Although Owen's analysis is effective, there are two potential problems when corpus data are to be applied. First, complexity arises when N1 and/or N2 are pre-modified.

(4) *the **family** history of obsessions*

Although the gradience analysis does not consider pre-modified cases such as (4), according to Sinclair discussed earlier, this example can be considered as a double-headed construction, since N1 (*history*) is pre-modified by *family*. In addition to pre-modification, post-modification (e.g., *the existence and persistence of inequalities **in health***) has not been dealt with in the scheme. Kreyer (2003), in his consideration of 698 instances of transformable genitives and *of*-constructions, found that approximately a fifth of the data are post-modified and the most commonly found construction is prepositional phrase (e.g., *the spread of acid precipitation **in both Europe and eastern North America***).

In addition to elucidating some unestablished grounds, further exploration of *of*-construction in the research of Natural Language Processing (NLP) is considered. Although the field of NLP has a rather different aim from linguistics, one of the ultimate goals of NLP is to provide automatic processing of language in large portion. In other words, the perspective taken in NLP studies needs to be comprehensive to facilitate various possibilities of linguistic forms. In the next section, we consider an NLP study on *of*-constructions.

2.4 Mohanty et al.'s (2004) head selection approach

The field of NLP has also paid much attention to the analysis of *of*-constructions, as the *of*-construction poses a prepositional phrase (PP) attachment problem. For example, Mohanty et al. (2004) have designed an algorithm with 92% accuracy for semantic head selection of either N1 or N2. The authors also point out that any *of*-phrase has a syntactic head and a semantic head, and these two heads may not be identical. They indicate that there are three types of *of*-constructions, namely, 'associative' (e.g., *a donation of $50,000*), 'partitive' (e.g., *a bundle of rags*) and 'kind' (e.g., *a bird of that kind*) constructions. The associative construction is equivalent to what Sinclair (1991) refers to as double-headedness, treating the second noun phrase as an argument rather than as an adjunct. The 'partitive' construction denotes categories including 'whole' and 'fractional numbers', 'aggregate numbers', 'dozen words' (e.g., *dozen, ream, quire, gross*), 'quantitative determiners' (e.g., *either, neither, each, some, all, both, half, many*), 'container words' (e.g., *can, bag, bottle, spoon, tin*), 'collection words', 'measure units' and 'indefinite amount' (e.g., *drop, pinch, dose*). In other words, the 'partitive' construction encompasses Sinclair's 'quantity/measure' and 'focus' noun groups. The last class, 'kind-construction', consists of words like *kind, type, sort, variety,* and *species*. As noted by Mohanty et al. (2004), this category is special due to its flexibility that allows alternation of the order of both NPs (e.g., *a bird of that kind* and *that kind of bird*).

In general, Mohanty et al.'s (2004) linguistic model provides us with a means of categorizing *of*-constructions that shares common grounds with Sinclair's (1991) framework. While previous work recognizes the equal importance of N2 with N1 in *of*-constructions, the extent of N2 and double semantic heads exist in real data has not yet been empirically attested.

3 Current Study

The current study is a preliminary work to investigate the distribution patterns of the three types of semantic heads. We apply the semantic head analysis to the object position of two synonymous verbs, namely, *demonstrate* and *show*, in academic discourse. We speculate that the distribution of the semantic heads would help differentiate the two verbs, serving as an additional means of analyzing words in the same synonymous set. The following demonstrates our criteria to determine a semantic head as exemplified with data from British National Corpus (BNC).

3.1 Criteria of Headedness in 'V N1 *of* N2' Construction

On the basis of previous work, the criteria of headedness in *of*-construction is established in

Figure 3. The criteria are mainly based on Sinclair's (1991) framework with minor modification. While there are mainly three categories of semantic heads, namely, N1-, N2-, and double- head categories, each category could be coming from different sources. The first step is to ask if N1 belongs to the categories of 'measure', 'support' or 'focus' nouns as discussed in more details in Section 2. If the answer is affirmative, we assign the utterance as a double head on the condition that N1 is modified (denoted as *db-mN1*). Example (5) illustrates a typical *db-mN1*.

(5) *Thin sections show a great variety of internal structures important in accurate identification.* (AMM565)

If N1 is not modified, we then assign the utterance an N2 head as shown in (6).

(6) *Given the opportunity not to be continually wrapped in a nappy a 1-year-old child will show a lot of interest in urination and indicate what has happened.* (CGT1568)

Moreover, this group of N2 heads can be further identified according to their N1 type (e.g., 'focus', 'measure' or 'support'). Example (5) is an instance of the 'measure' group where *a lot* (N1) denotes quantity.

In contrast, if N1 does not belong to the categories of 'measure', 'support' or 'focus' noun groups, we assign the utterance to the N1-head category on the condition that only N1 is modified (denoted as *m-N1*).

(7) *Such an approach is not at all for the sake of establishing some banal historical continuity, or of demonstrating a universal homogeneity of narrative*... (ARD159)

Example (7) shows a typical nominalization of the *of*-structure with N1 modified, rendering N1 heavier as far as information-weighting is concerned.

In a similar fashion, if N1 is not modified but N2 is modified, an N2 head is designated as exemplified by (8) (denoted as *m-N2*).

(8) *In R. v. Sang (H.L. , 1979) it was said that evidence should not be excluded simply to show disapproval of improper police conduct.* (EVK1311)

In this example, N2 (*police conduct*) is pre-modified by the word *improper*. If both N1 and N2 are not modified and N1 does not belong to one of the 'measure', 'support' or 'focus' groups, a double-head is found as shown in (9) (denoted as *double*).

(9 I*n both cases, extrinsic evidence could be introduced to show a want of jurisdiction.* (GU61013)

Following the categorization criteria, corpus data were analyzed and details are presented in the next sections.

4 Methodology

The data for this study were collected from the free online British National Corpus (BNCweb) with selection restricted to the written academic prose which is comprised of 15,778,028 words in 497 files. A search string was applied to query for the target 'V NP1 of NP2' constructions, as illustrated in (10) for the verb *demonstrate*.

(10) {demonstrate}_V* (no)? (any)? (_{ART})? (_{A})* (_{N})* of.

The corpus results were downloaded and

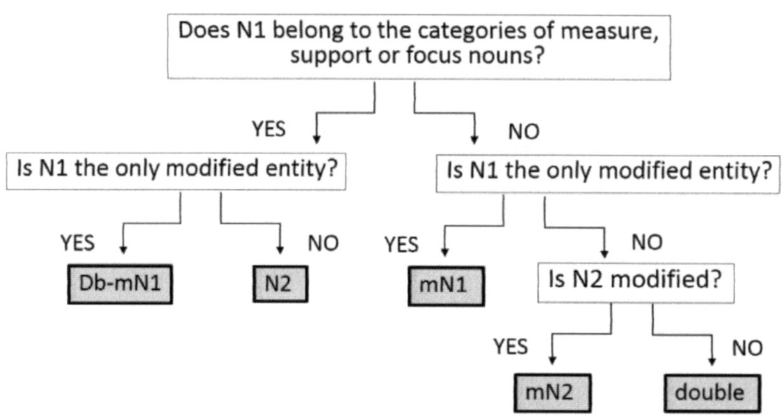

Figure 3. Flow chart to illustrate how semantic head categories are determined.

transferred to an Excel file as summarized in Table 3.

Verbs	*demonstrate*	*show*
No. of hits	313	1613
No. of texts	170	315
Frequency (/million)	19.84	102.23
Analyzed instances	313	427

Table 3: Summary of BNCweb search results

Each instance was categorized according to the semantic head of the 'N1 *of* N2' predicate following the criteria set in Table 3. Instances in an 'irrelevant' (abbreviated as irr.) category include a number of fixed expressions (e.g., *point of view*) and irrelevant structures (e.g., '*demonstrated approval of them*' EF3660) which were excluded from further analysis (see Appendix I for raw scores). Each category was counted and converted into percentage. In addition, an association plot was drawn with an R script for making a comparison between the two verbs.

5 Overall Distribution of Semantic heads in 'N1 *of* N2' Predicate Constructions

The frequency distribution of semantics heads for both *demonstrate* and *show* is presented in Table 4. Among the three types of semantic heads, the frequencies of N1-heads for both *demonstrate* and *show* (16.0% and 16.6%, respectively) are much lower than the other two categories (56.5% and 50.1% for double-heads; 25.2% and 30.9% for N2-heads). The predominant double-headed instances can be attributed to the nature of academic prose which tends to structure scientific knowledge with objectivity as previous work on nominalization have shown (*cf.* Halliday & Martin, 1993). It is more difficult to provide an explanation for a low occurrence rate of N1-heads since such construction is the conventional view on *of* (e.g., Quirk et al., 1985). It is quite interesting to find that both verbs share a common distribution pattern of the heads. As pointed out by Hyland (2002), both *demonstrate* and *show* function to imply writer's acceptance of previous claims, leaving readers with a stronger sense of writer evaluation. The proportion of N1-heads is equal in each verb, with a rate of approximately 16 percent. However, as for both the proportions of N2- and double-heads, the frequencies vary between the two classes. While double-heads occupy approximately 50 percent in *demonstrate* and *show*, N2-heads only reach 30 percent of the total. More detailed analysis for the two verbs will be presented in the next section.

Semantic Heads	*Demonstrate*	*Show*
N1	0.0%	4.4%
mN1	16.0%	12.2%
N1 Subtotal	**16.0%**	**16.6%**
double	52.1%	23.4%
db-mN1	4.5%	26.7%
Double Subtotal	**56.5%**	**50.1%**
mN2	4.2%	1.2%
N2-mea (N1='measure')	2.2%	7.3%
N2-sup (N1='support')	14.4%	19.4%
N2-foc (N1='focus')	4.5%	3.0%
N2 subtotal	**25.2%**	**30.9%**
irrelevant (irr.)	2.2%	2.3%
Total	**100.0%**	**100.0%**

Table 4: Distribution of semantic heads

6 A Comparison of semantic heads between *Demonstrate* and *Show of*-predicates

Although the overall distribution patterns of semantic heads show that *demonstrate* and *show* share some similarities, they are some striking differences. Figure 3 presents an association plot of semantic heads for both verbs. As indicated by the vertical scale on the right hand side, the darker the shade, the more significantly different a category will be found compared to its expected frequency. The graph shows that statistical significance can be found in some variables according to Pearson residuals where the p-value is less than 0.001. The following discussion is divided into three sub-sections, each designating to one category of semantic heads.

6.1 Double heads

The types of double-headed instances for *demonstrate* and *show* actually vary quite extensively. There are two major types of double-headed nouns: (1) those derived from nominalization which tend to be heavy in information weighting (denoted as *double*), and (2) those with a modified N1 that result in a category shift from an N2 head to a double head (denoted as *db-mN1*). Examples (11) and (12) represent the double heads.

(11) *The idea was to demonstrate* <u>*the solidarity*</u> *of* <u>*the NATO alliance*</u> *with a view to ensuring that negotiations with the Eastern bloc would be from a position of strength.* (ASB1450)

(12) *Adolescents may show* <u>*a combination*</u> *of* <u>*middle school age and more adult type behaviour*</u> *with depressive reactions and anxiety states (Graham et al.,…* (CN6785)

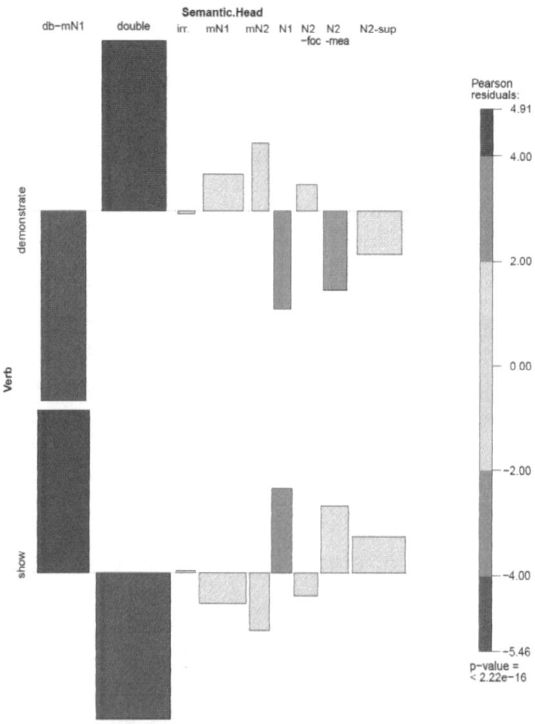

Figure 3. An association plot of semantic heads for both *demonstrate* and *show*. (*db-mN1* denotes a double head with modified N1; *double* denotes a double head; *irr.* denotes irrelevant cases; *mN1* and *mN2* denote modified N1 and N2 heads; *N2-foc* denotes an N2 head with an N1 in the 'focus' group, *N2-mea* the 'measure' group, and *N2-sup* the 'support' group.)

While N1 constitutes a large number of factual nouns like *solidarity, effect, impact,* and *disapproval*, N2 is often occupied by research entities such as v*itamin A supplementation, aphasia, a protein*, and *local political control*. N1 in the N1 *of* N2 construction could thus be used as a site of evaluation to present writer's stance.

The second group of double heads are those with a modified N1 (*db-mN1*) which can be exemplified by (13) and (14).

(13) *But they demonstrate* <u>*a fairly clear hierarchy*</u> *of* <u>*claims*</u> *to receive financial benefit from a relative which runs: spouse and/or children; parents; brothers and sisters and their children; grandparents; uncles and aunts.* (CRF108)

(14) *Secondly, however, these clusters also show* <u>*a certain degree*</u> *of* <u>*relatedness or overlap*</u>*.* (CFX439)

The frequency of db-*mN1* for *demonstrate* is as low as 4.5 percent, while that for *show* is 26.7 percent. In other words *show* tends to be used with all kinds of 'measure', 'focus' and 'support' nouns more often than *demonstrate*.

Overall, both types of double head *of*-nominals show that *demonstrate* tends to be used with information–heavy, nominalization constructions, while *show* tends to be used with nouns that are lighter in information content. In addition, *demonstrate* tends to be used more commonly with an evaluative function than *show*.

6.2 N1 heads

It came as a surprise that N1 heads constitute the smallest proportion among the three head categories. There are two types of N1 heads. The rarer type is a 'genuine' N1 head as illustrated in (15) and (16).

(15) *Although the teacher may well have introduced this later, and indeed CDL trials did show* <u>*evidence*</u> *of* <u>*this,*</u> *we decided to include some carefully graded illustrations in the documentation that…*(EUW870)

(16) *John and Mary (the two experimenters) show* <u>*a child*</u> *of* <u>*three years of age*</u> *a red box and a blue box and a pound coin.* (A0T639)

These two examples show that *of*-N2 serves a post-modifying function even though such instances are very rare in *show* and are not found in *demonstrate* at all. There are mainly two kinds of N1 heads from the corpus. The first is illustrated in (15) where N2 is a pronoun, and the second is when N2 is a quantity as shown in (16).

Another type of N1 heads is comprised of information-heavy constituents for both N1 and N2, and it is N1-headed because N1 is elaborated further with modifications. Examples (17) and (18) demonstrate this point.

(17) *...domestic dogs are descendants of wolves, to which they show many similarities of appearance and behaviour.* (FED1377)

(18) *Getting more information on comparative performance also enabled them to ask the right questions, although it also demonstrated the continuing inadequacies of data.* (HXT1193)

Difference between *demonstrate* and *show* again can be found here in terms of distribution of N1 heads. While there are more information-heavy, modified N1 instances for *demonstrate*, *show* again is much less information-driven.

6.3 N2 heads

There are four types of N2 heads in this study, namely, modified N2 heads and those with information-light N1s including 'focus', 'measure', and 'support' nouns, which are exemplified by (19) to (22), respectively.

(19) *The molecular cloning data presented in this paper not only confirm the existence of clusters of related ZNF genes on chromosome 10, but also demonstrate duplication of an entire cluster...* (K5P648)

(20) *Irving has demonstrated the tendency of investigators to employ interrogation techniques likely to accentuate rather than ameliorate these and other distorting factors.* (FBK335)

(21) *The inner core is now characterized by a preponderance of public tenants (nearly half of households), whereas the rings show a majority of owner-occupiers in line with national patterns.* (F9G766)

(22) *It follows that the snails show a pattern of prey selection.* (FU074)

Among the four groups, only the N2 heads with N1 'measure' nouns reach statistical significance for *demonstrate*. *Show* appears to co-occur more often with both 'measure' and 'support' N1 nouns than *demonstrate*, but not with 'focus' nouns.

6.4 Section Summary

In summary, semantic head categories can be viewed as providing different degrees of information weighting as addressed by Owen (2007). While double-headed *of*-constructions provide the highest information-weighting, both modified N2 heads and N1 heads also provide heavy information load. The constructions with the least information weighting are N1 heads and N1 in the 'measure' group. Moreover, the results also show significant differences between *demonstrate* and *show*. Whereas *demonstrate* is more likely to be used with information-heavy words, *show* displays the opposite trend.

7 Discussion

In this study, we have examined three types of semantic heads in two synonymous verbs. From the distribution of the three heads, we found a quite similar pattern for both verbs, with the double heads taking up half of the total instances, N2 heads about one-quarter and N1 heads about one-fifth. However, by taking a closer examination of the sub-classes of each category, differences between the two verbs can be identified. The most significant differences were the double heads and N2 heads demonstrated in the association plot. Following Sinclair's (1991) framework, the results show that it is more common for *show* to have 'measure', 'focus' and 'support' nouns in the N1 position. What these noun classes have in common is that all of them provide specificity relevant to N2. While 'measure' nouns, such as *amount* and *some*, provide information on quantity, and 'focus' nouns, such as *tendency* and *value*, specify a particular part, component, aspect or attribute of N2, 'support' nouns, such as *importance* and *extent*, are more abstract. The occurrence rate of 'focus' nouns is relatively low in the data which could be due to the functions of the construction for the two verbs. It is possible that the object position of the *of*-nominals limits its content to express a proposition or reach a conclusion (*cf.* Johns, 2001). In other words, we would expect an evaluation embedded in the *of*-nominals by means of modified N1 or factual nouns found in the 'support' group.

However, some grey areas for categorization were encountered for 'support' and 'focus' groups and nominalization. As pointed out by Owen's discussion that the semantic heads of *of*-constructions form a continuum, it is sometimes difficult to define a clear boundary between each category. Furthermore, the 'support' noun category appears to overlap with nominalization in Sinclair's classification. A more stringent criterion is therefore necessary for future work.

8 Conclusions

Contrary to the conventional view on *of*-nominals, we found a rather low percentage of N1 semantic heads (only 19 out of 723 relevant instances or approximately 3 percent) in the object position of *demonstrate* and *show* in academic discourse. The results of this study, therefore, support Sinclair's insight on the semantic role of N2 in *of*-construction. In addition, we found that the framework of semantic headedness can be used to capture the subtle variation between synonyms. In this study, significant differences were found between '*demonstrate* N1 *of* N2' and '*show* N1 *of* N2' constructions. While both *demonstrate* and *show* incorporate more than 50% of double-headed *of*-nominals, the *of*-nominals of *show* tend to occur with modified N1 heads. In other words, *demonstrate* are more likely to be used with information-heavy nominals and abstract notions. Rather than providing pieces of evidence in the object position, *demonstrate* is more often used to present propositions or observations. On the other hand, *show* is more commonly used to present specific evidence because its co-occurring nouns in the N1 position often denote specificity and/or attributes of a phenomenon, an event or a process of N2. Because present work only provides preliminary results limited to two verbs, further work is necessary to attest this position with additional evidence such as including *of*-nominals in the subject or other positions, examining a wider range of verbs, or considering genral variation.

Acknowledgement

This work was supported in part by the National Science Council under the Grants NSC101-2410-H-004-176-MY2.

References

Dwight L. Bolinger. 1968. Entailment and the meaning of structures. Glossa, 2, 119–127.

Maggie Charles. 2006. Phraseological patterns in reporting clauses used in citation: A corpus-based study of theses in two disciplines. English for Specific Purposes, 25(3), 310-331.

John R. Firth. 1957. Papers in linguistics. Oxford: Oxford University Press.

Stephan Th. Gries and Naoki Otani. 2010. Behavioral profiles: A corpus-based perspective on synonymy and antonymy. ICAME Journal, 34, 121-150.

Stephan Th. Gries and Anatol Stefanowitsch. 2004. Extending collostructional analysis: A corpus-based perspective on 'alternations'. International Journal of Corpus Linguistics, 9(1), 97-129.

Michael A. K. Halliday and James R. Martin. 1993. Writing Science. Pittsburgh: University of Pittsburgh Press.

Ken Hyland. 1999. Academic attribution: citation and the construction of disciplinary knowledge. Applied Linguistics, 23(3), 341-367.

Ken Hyland. 2000. Disciplinary discourses: Social interactions in academic writing. Edingburgh: Pearson Education.

Ken Hyland. 2002. Activity and evaluation: reporting practices in academic writing. In John Flowerdew (Ed.), Academic discourse, pp. 115-130. London: Longman.

Tim Johns. 2001. From evidence to conclusion: the case of 'indicate that'. In Martin Hewings (Ed.) Academic Writing in Context. Implications and Applications. University of Birmingham Press. 55-62.

Rolf Kreyer. 2003. Genitive and of-construction in modern written English. Processability and human involvement. International Journal of Corpus Linguistics, 8(2): 169-207.

Rajat K. Mohanty, Srinivas Samala, Ashish F. Almeida and Pushpak Bhattacharyya. 2004. The Complexity of OF in English. Proceedings of International Conference on Natural Language Processing (ICON-2004), Hyderabad, India.

Charles Owen. 2007. Notes on the ofness of *of*: Sinclair and grammar. International Journal of Corpus Linguistics, 12(2): 201-221.

Randolf Quirk, Sidney Greenbaum, Geoffrey Leech and Jan Svartvik. 1985. A Comprehensive Grammar of the English Language. London: Longman.

John M. Sinclair. 1991. Corpus, Concordance, Collocation. Oxford: Oxford University Press.

Sarah Thomas and Thomas P. Hawes. 1994. Reporting verbs in medical journal articles. English for Specific Purposes, 13(2), 129-148.

Geoff Thompson and Yiyun Ye. 1991. Evaluation in the reporting verbs used in academic papers. Applied Linguistics, 12(4), 365-382.

Appendix I: Raw scores of coded data

Heads	*Demonstrate*	*Show*
N1	0	19
mN1	50	52
N1 Subtotal	**50**	**71**
double	163	100
db-mN1	14	114
Double Subtotal	**177**	**214**
mN2	13	5
N2-mea (N1='measure')	7	31
N2-sup (N1='support')	45	83
N2-foc (N1='focus')	14	13
N2 subtotal	**79**	**132**
irrelevant (irr.)	7	10
Total	**313**	**427**

Spatial Particles in English: A Quantitative Corpus-based Approach to the Conceptualization of Symmetry in Bodily Orientation

Alvin Cheng-Hsien Chen
Department of English
National Changhua University of Education
Changhua, 500, Taiwan
alvinworks@gmail.com

Abstract

This study investigates the conceptualization of our bodily orientation in a quantitative corpus-based approach of collostructional analysis. Based on the symbolic nature of constructions, we examine the correlation patterns of the covarying collexeme NPs and 13 major spatial particles in English Preposition Construction through exploratory statistical methods. The distributional patterns of the spatial particles have far-reaching implications for the embodiment of conceptual metaphors. It is concluded that the (a)symmetry of metaphorical patterns along each spatial dimension may be attributed to the recurring (a)symmetrical daily interaction and bodily experiences with the surrounding physical environment. While cultural specificity is of great concern for future study, a hypothesis for the implicational scale of conceptual symmetry in bodily orientation is proposed.

1 Introduction

Languages differ in their granularity in dividing up various aspects of the spatial domain. Linguists seem to have agreed that languages tend to be more resistant to adding a new lexical item to the existing set of closed-class words (Tyler & Evans, 2003). Therefore, English Preposition Constructions often serve as a good candidate for the study of the conceptualization of spatial orientation.

Among all the controversial topics related to English prepositions, we would like to focus on the notion of geometrical symmetry. Spatial orientation is a projection with respect to the axes of the visual field from a personal to an impersonal perspective (Langacker, 1987). Even though spatial particles such as *p o n*, *in o t*, *e ore a ter*, contrast with one another in a geometrically symmetric way in the absolute Cartesian world, they are not necessarily defined by such oppositional features. Their meanings may be subject to the influence of the cultural-specific communities, thus lending themselves "semi-autonomous from and semi-dependent upon the conceptual space labeled by other spatial particles in the language" (Tyler & Evans, 2003, p. 108). In other words, the contrast partners of the spatial particles along the same dimensions may not be straightforwardly oppositional. Therefore, the present study would like to investigate whether bipolar spatial particles (e.g., *p o n*) on the same spatial dimension (e.g., vertical axis) exhibits a symmetrical extension to similar sets of target domains in the real language use.

2 Words, constructions, and conceptualization

In cognitive linguistics, it is hypothesized that our reasoning and knowledge are built on bodily-grounded conceptual metaphors (Grady, 1997; Johnson, 1987; Lakoff, 1993; Lakoff & Johnson, 1980), arising from a recurring instantiated correlation between sensorimotor perception and a subjective experience or judgment. This hypothesis of embodiment is further developed in Grady's theory of Primary Metaphor (Grady, 1997), which underlines a binding of our perception of the world (*so r e* domain) and our response to the perception of the world (*tar et* concept).

Take UP IS MORE for instance, a widely-discussed example in the previous literature. It is in our sensorimotor experience that the vertical elevation varies directly with quantity in many situations (e.g., filling water into a glass, or piling books on the desk). While the vertical elevation is a direct perceptual experience of our visual organs, the rise of the quantity is our cognitive response to the perception of vertical elevation. Such conceptual binding between the sensorimotor experience and the cognitive or emotional response forms the experiential basis of conceptual metaphors. Evidence for conventional conceptual metaphors has come from quite a range of studies, such as polysemy (Tyler & Evans, 2001), inference patterns between source and target domains (Fauconnier, 1998; Lakoff, 1993), novel metaphorical language (Lakoff, 1993), patterns of semantic change (Traugott, 1995), and psycholinguistic experiments (Gibbs, 1990).

Under this cognitive framework, therefore, grammatical patterns have often been studied in terms of colligations, i.e., linear co-occurrence preferences and restrictions held between words and collocates (Hunston & Francis, 1999; Sinclair, 1991), between language and genre (Biber, Johansson, Leech, Conrad, & Finegan, 1999), between words and constructional schemas (Bybee & Scheibman, 1999), or between constructions (Croft, 2001; Goldberg, 1995). More specifically, as constructional schemas often encode a relational meaning, observations on pairs of words in a construction may play a crucial role in the semantic profile of the construction, hence, a step forward toward a better understanding of our conceptualization.

The study of the correlation between a construction and its co-occurring words has been collectively referred to as *o ostr tiona* analysis by Stefanowitsch and Gries (2003). This research methodology makes theoretical commitments to a holistic and symbolic view of linguistic units and at the same time bases its quantitative methods on sophisticated statistical analyses. Words that are attracted to a particular construction are referred to as *o e e es* of the construction, whose association strength is measured by *o ostren t* — defined as the log-transformed *p*-value (to the base of 10) from the Fisher-Yates Exact test on all the raw frequency counts of each word in the specific slot of the construction. Similarly, pairs of collexemes that are statistically attracted to each other within a construction are referred as *o ar in o e e es* (Gries & Stefanowitsch, 2004). It is believed that given a partially schematic construction with at least 2 variable slots (e.g. V + *into* + V-ing), observations on the co-occurring patterns of the covarying collexemes (e.g., V and V-ing pairs in the *into*-construction) in these slots may yield useful empirical evidence for the conceptual relation encoded by the construction.

By taking English Preposition Construction (*patia arti e + ... ea o n*) as a case study, we would like to see how the covarying collexemes — preposition and the head noun — can shed light on the conceptualization of the spatial orientation in English-speaking communities. More importantly, we are interested in to what extent such covarying patterns may reveal the geometrical symmetry of the spatial particles (e.g., the English prepositions) on major cardinal spatial dimensions. Our working assumption is that the more bipolar spatial particles on the same spatial dimension are correlated with similar groups of covarying collexeme head nouns, the more likely they are metaphorically extended on a symmetrical basis.

3 Methods

The present study adopted a quantitative corpus-based approach of collostructional analysis (Gries & Stefanowitsch, 2004; Stefanowitsch & Gries, 2003). The data was first collected from British National Corpus World Edition, one of the most representative balanced English corpora. Specifically, we focused on 13 spatial particles that have been widely discussed in the previous literature: *a ter*, *e ore*, *in ront o* , *e in* , *o er*, *a o e*, *p*, *o n*, *n er*, *e o* , *in*, *o t*, and *o t o* .

These spatial particles differently referenced three cardinal spatial axes, serving to partition conceptual space on different spatial dimensions. The first dimension is the **vertical** axis, including *o er a o e p o n n er* and *e o* . The second dimension is the **horizontal** axis, including *a ter e ore in ront o* and *e in* . The third dimension includes *in o t* and *o t o* , which collectively give rise to the notion of **boundedness**. In the following, we will refer to this dimension either as the boundedness dimension or the *in o t* dimension. All the English Preposition Construction instances bearing the target spatial particles were automatically extracted via regular expressions implemented in R scripts written by the author.

Subsequently, we investigated the association between the spatial particles and the head nouns under the framework of collostructional analysis. Each spatial particle and its co-occurring head noun formed a covarying collexeme pair. In order to investigate the extent to which the physical symmetry of the spatial orientations in the real world applies to metaphorical conceptualization, we looked for potential sub-patterns or clustering of the spatial particles on the basis of their covarying collexeme head nouns. As the head nouns represent the semantic core of the NP in the English Preposition Construction, we would use the term NP instead for expository convenience.

Two exploratory statistical analyses were adopted in order to find out the sub-patterning of these 13 spatial particles, namely, hierarchical clustering and principal component analysis.

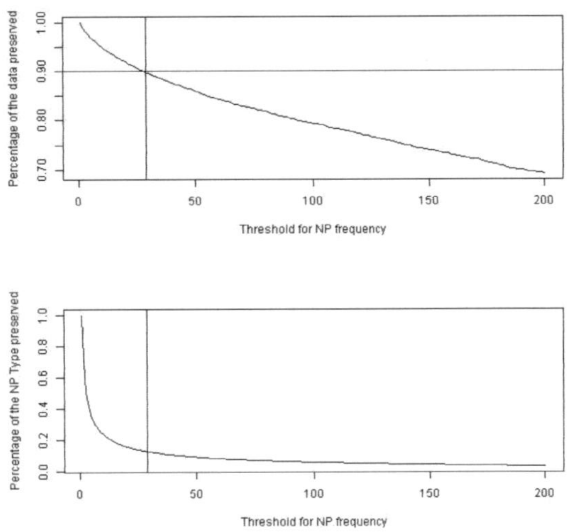

Figure 1. The percentage of the data preservation (upper panel) and the NP type frequency (lower panel) after data filtering in relation to the frequency threshold of the covarying collexeme NP. The cutting line is the threshold frequency (N=29).

Procedure of the hierarchical clustering was as follows. First each spatial particle was semantically profiled by their covarying NPs in the English Preposition Construction. As clustering was sensitive to the problem of data sparseness (Kaufman & Rousseeuw, 2005), we made a compromise between the representativeness of the sample and the efficiency of the algorithm. Figure 1 showed the relationship between covarying NP frequency threshold and data preservation percentage. We decided to include as much as 90% of the original dataset by removing covarying collexeme NPs occurring less than 29 times in the English Preposition Construction.

After data filtering, each spatial particle was transformed into vectors based on their association with each covarying collexeme NP. Such association measures indicated how much more often than chance the NP co-occurred with the spatial particle. Following Gries and Stefanowitsch (2004), we adopted collostrength as our first association measure between spatial particles and NPs. On the other hand, Curran (2004) observed that the *t*-test statistic, first proposed by Manning and Schütze (1999, pp. 162-169), performed the best as a measure of association for weighting context words in the task of profiling semantic similarity. Therefore, we also computed the *t*-test statistic as our measure of association in comparison with the collostrength.

Next we computed the pairwise similarity matrix among the 13 spatial particles. Previous research has shown that correlation-based similarity measures, as compared with distance-based similarity matrix, are more prone to detect and to use curvature of vectors in multidimensional space, thus serving as a better index for word similarity in information retrieval (Jurafsky & Martin, 2008, pp. 663-667). Among these, the cosine was the most frequently-used measure in the comparison of semantic similarity (Curran, 2004; Manning & Schütze, 1999, p. 299). Therefore, a pairwise cosine similarity matrix was generated and submitted to hierarchical clustering, using Ward's amalgamation rule. The similarity measures serve as an indicator of the degree to which each spatial particle is correlated with similar sets of NPs. A high similarity measure between two spatial terms on the same spatial dimension may suggest a symmetrical metaphorical extension, thus emerging as major clusters in early stages of the dendrogram.

Finally, we submitted this similarity matrix to Principal Component Analysis (PCA) in order to find out the cardinal spatial dimension used in the English-speaking community. With the help of dimensional reduction of the principal components, it is hoped that a study on the loadings of these 13 spatial particles on major principal components may shed light on the cultural-specific variation in the conceptualization of spatial orientation.

4 Results

4.1 Descriptive statistics

About one million instances of the English Preposition Constructions were extracted from the BNC. After data filtering, 917487 tokens (i.e., 90%) were included in the later statistical analyses, amounting to 3636 types of covarying collexeme NPs in our final dataset.

***** Formatting Issue - Best Available Paper/Graphic *****

4.2 Clustering of spatial particles in EPC

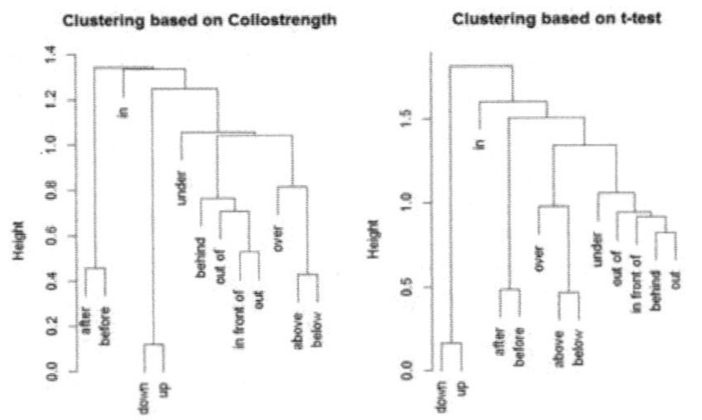

Figure 2. Dendrograms of the hierarchical clusterings based on the association measures of collostrength (left panel) and *t*-test statistics (right panel) respectively.

This 13 x 3636 contingency table yielded two similar dendrograms, as shown in Figure 2, according to the association measures of collostrength and *t*-test statistic respectively. A closer look at the resulting dendrograms has suggested a high consistency of their pairing of spatial particles.

First of all, both dendrograms have shown that *a ter/ e ore*, *p/ o n*, and *a o e/ e o* are collapsed into one small cluster at the early stages of the amalgamation (i.e., clusters at the terminal of the tree). This merging suggests that each spatial particle in the pair correlates with similar sets of covarying collexeme NPs in the English Preposition Constructions. That is, two cardinal spatial dimensions, i.e., the vertical (*p/ o n*, and *a o e/ e o*) and horizontal axes (*a ter/ e ore*) demonstrates a clear tendency of symmetry in terms of their frequent co-occurring NPs in the English Preposition Construction.

Aside from these terminal clusters on the bottom of the amalgamation, *n er/ e in /in ront o o t o o t* form a heterogeneous group, consisting of spatial particles across different spatial dimensions.

Moreover, both dendrograms suggest that *o er* patterns more similarly to the pair of *a o e e o* , emerging as its most proximal neighbor in the dendrogram. On the other hand, in both dendrograms, *in* is cast as the most distant spatial particle, amalgamated into the cluster in the final stage. This may suggest its unique semantic profile in comparison with all the other spatial particles.

4.3 Dimensional reduction of the spatial particles

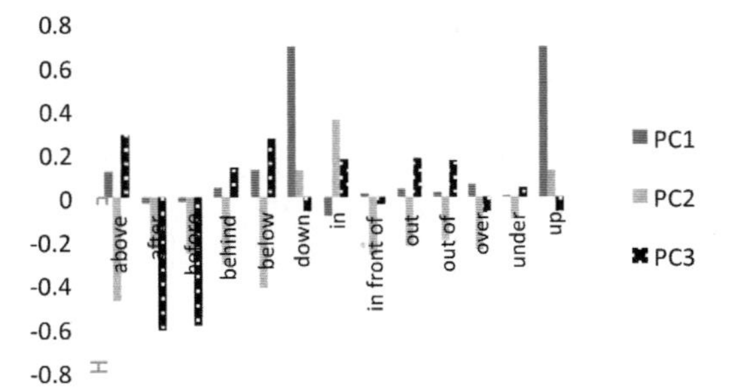

Figure 3. Loadings of each spatial particle on the first three principal components. The x-axis is the 13 spatial particles and the y-axis is the loading of each spatial particle. Each bar represents one principle component.

As both *t*-test statistic and collostrength yielded similar patterns in hierarchical clustering, our discussion of the PCA will limit to the one based on the association measure of collostrength.

Figure 3 shows the loadings of each spatial particle along the first three principal components (PC). The variation of the first PC (i.e., the solid dark grey bar in Figure 3) is clearly dominated by the spatial particles *p* and *o n*, hence, denoting an axis of verticality. The spatial particle *in* dominates the variation of the second PC (i.e., the solid light grey bar), forming a spatial contrast set between *in* vs. non-*in*, namely a boundedness dimension. Interestingly, in the third PC (i.e., the dotted black bar), high loadings of *a ter* and *e ore* suggest that this principal component majorly accounts for variation along the horizontal dimension. We, therefore, term this PC as the horizontal axis.

In comparison with the results from the hierarchical clustering, we may conclude that the spatial dimension of the vertical axis manifests a more prominent degree of symmetry in the sense that *p/ o n* and *a o e/ e o* emerge as terminal-level clusters in the early stages of the hierarchical clustering, and that *p/ o n* is found to dominate the variation of the first principal component in PCA. Secondly, the spatial dimension of the horizontal axis shows a moderate degree of symmetry in the sense that *e ore/a ter* emerges as a terminal-level cluster in the early stages of the amalgamation and also dominates the variation of the third principal component in PCA. The spatial dimension of boundedness manifests the least degree of symmetry in the sense that *in* patterns rather differently from the other spatial particles, as shown in the high loading of the second principal component and no terminal-level clusters are found on this dimension.

5 Discussions

	Terminal Clusters	**Non-terminal Clusters**	**PC Relatedness**
Vertical axis	*p o n* *a o e e o*	*o er* *n er*	PC1 (*p o n*)
Horizontal axis	*a ter e ore*	*in ront o* *e in*	PC3 (*a ter e ore*)
Boundedness		*in* *o t* *o t o*	PC2 (*in*)

Table 1. Summary of the degree of symmetry on the three cardinal spatial dimensions.

Table 1 summarizes the results of our statistical exploration on English spatial particles. While all the spatial dimensions have asymmetrical spatial particles (i.e., particles in non-terminal clusters), it has been observed that two symmetrical particle pairs on the vertical dimension have emerged in English, namely *p o n*, and *a o e e o* and one symmetrical particle pair on the horizontal dimension, i.e., *a ter e ore*. These three pairs of bipolar spatial particles manifest themselves as early terminal clusters in the dendrograms. However, no symmetry has been observed in the spatial dimension of boundedness. Our PCA also conforms to the clustering results in that two of the terminal clusters— *p o n* and *a ter e ore*—dominate the variation of PC1 and PC3 respectively while *in* stands out uniquely in PC2. We suggest that this different pattering may be attributed to our experiential interaction with each spatial dimension. The symmetry/asymmetry use of the English spatial particles may shed light on our conceptualization of the spatial dimension.

Spatial orientation is a projection of a conceptual *ront a* , *p o n* or *in o t* partitioning of a non-self entity. While this spatial partitioning may have its basis in geometry, their conceptual partitioning is often believed to be perceived on an asymmetric basis. Cognitive linguists have proposed that the asymmetry may come from the way the entity typically interacts with the environment, such as sitting, standing, or its shape (pointed ends), the way it is used by humans (building entrances), its perceived resemblance to human beings or animals. Of particular importance to the present study is the notion of embodiment.

Following the tenets in cognitive linguistics, we suggest that the attributes which give rise to the different degrees of symmetry in the conceptualization of spatial dimensions may involve how humans both perceive and interact along the spatial dimension. Accordingly, the concept of spatial conceptualization underscores the importance of embodied experience in the semantics of natural language (Svorou, 1994; Talmy, 2000; Vandeloise, 1994)

Clark (1973) has noted that our bodies are asymmetric in the sense that our legs are at one end and our head at the other. Furthermore, he argued that such physiological asymmetry had non-trivial consequences for our interaction with the environment. Secondly, our environment itself explains clearly the fact that vertical axis is asymmetric because gravity determines a natural declination.

As a living organism in the physical three-dimensional space, we are biologically programed to move along the *ront a* dimension. Even in a self-contained space, small range of space for moving around is still possible. In our experience, the flexibility of moving forward and backward is symmetrical in the sense that such dimension makes most sense biologically. Therefore, we suggest that the symmetrical embodied interaction with the two poles along the *ront a* dimension may have left its footprints in our linguistic recurring practices.

The way we interact with the environment along the vertical dimension is asymmetrical – gravity predetermines the default downward movement of all masses in the universe. However, human advances in technology have made possible an upward movement in our reality (e.g., the invention of aircraft). Therefore, a certain level of symmetry would be expected along this vertical axis. This may explain why two pairs of spatial particles have been observed to manifest symmetrical correlation with similar sets of entities.

In contrast, our interaction with the environment along the dimension of the boundedness appears rather asymmetrical. In order to understand the notion of *in*, we first have to conceptualize our body as a container with a clear boundary. Such disproportionate distribution of the inner and outer space may transform into various degrees of perceived freedom/control. Physical operations within our body are much easier to moderate and control, while the activities and developments in the outer world routinely fall outside of our sovereignty. Therefore, we suggest that this spatial dimension may be the least one to manifest a symmetrical extension on its two ends.

From the perspective of existential phenomenology (Merleau-Ponty, 1962), the meaning of the spatial particles should better be understood in terms of how they are experienced, not by the way they are described in the more objective language of psychological or physical science. Cognitive linguists have taken up this torch of embodiment and further developed the idea that linguistic meanings are grounded in our bodily experiences (Johnson, 1987; Lakoff & Johnson, 1980). One corollary is that such semantic grounding may exhibit a certain level of cultural specificity. Indeed Chen (2010) observed that in Mandarin-speaking community, only *ront a* dimension displays clear symmetrical patterning while the vertical and boundedness dimension show fewer signs of symmetrical metaphorical extension. More in-depth cross-linguistic research is needed for a better answer to the typological differences in the conceptualization of symmetry in bodily orientation.

We, however, suspect that the symmetry/asymmetry patterns of the spatial particles in a specific language may fall on an *i p i ationa* scale or an implicational universal in a typologist sense (Croft, 1990; Greenberg, 1963; Keenan & Comrie, 1977). It is hypothesized that the symmetry of the spatial dimensions may form a hierarchy— *ront a* < *p o n* < *in o t* — on which the *ront a* is the most likely to exhibit symmetrical extension to similar groups of covarying collexemes while the *in o t*, on the other hand, is the least likely. The implicational nature of this hierarchy may predict that if a language shows symmetry on the *p o n* dimension, it will also show symmetry on the *ront a* . The study on Mandarin Chinese in Chen (2010) has found that Mandarin shows symmetry only on the most probable spatial dimension, i.e., *ront a* , on the one end of the implicational scale. On the other hand, the present study has observed that English shows symmetry on both the *p o n* and the *ront a* dimensions, which bears out the prediction of the implicational scale (i.e., symmetry in *p o n* implies symmetry in *ront a*). Several cultural specificities may play a role in such typological variation on the symmetry of bodily orientation, such as the morphological productivity of the spatial particles, or the cultural preference of collectivism or individualism. The assessment of these cultural factors may deserve more additional research, which, however, is out of the scope of the present study.

6 Conclusions

The present study investigates the conceptualization of our bodily orientation in a quantitative corpus-based approach of collostructional analysis. Results have shown that the spatial dimension of the vertical axis manifests a clearer symmetry in the sense that *p/ o n* and *a o e/ e o* emerge as terminal-level clusters in the early stage of the amalgamation, and that *p/ o n* dominates the variation of the first principal component in the dimensional reduction of PCA. Secondly, the spatial dimension of the horizontal axis shows moderate degree of symmetry in the sense that *e ore/a ter* emerges as a terminal-level cluster in the early stage of the amalgamation and also dominates the variation of the third principal component. The spatial dimension of boundedness manifests the least symmetry in the sense that *in* patterns rather differently from the other spatial particles and no terminal-level clusters are found in this dimension.

The distributional patterns of the covarying collexemes in English Preposition Construction have far-reaching implications for the embodiment of spatial conceptualization. It is concluded that the symmetry of metaphorical patterns along each spatial dimension may be attributed to our recurring symmetrical daily interaction and bodily experiences with the surrounding physical environment. While cultural specificity is of great concern for future study, a hypothesis for the implicational scale of conceptual symmetry is proposed.

***** Formatting Issue - Best Available Paper/Graphic *****

References

Biber, D., Johansson, S., Leech, G., Conrad, S., & Finegan, E. (1999). *on an ra ar o po en an Written n is* . London: Longman.

Bybee, J., & Scheibman, J. (1999). The effect of usage on degree of constituency: the reduction of *on t* in American English. *in isti s* , 575-596.

Chen, A. C.-H. (2010). A conceptual understanding of bodily orientation in Mandarin: A quantitative corpus perspective. *orp s in isti s an in isti eor* (1), 1-28.

Clark, H. H. (1973). Space, time, semantics, and the child. In T. E. Moore (Ed.), *o niti e e e op ent an t e isition o an a e.* New York: Academic Press.

Croft, W. (1990). *po o an ni ersa s.* Cambridge: Cambridge University Press.

Croft, W. (2001). *a i a onstr tion ra ar nta ti t eor in t po o i a perspe ti e.* Oxford: Oxford University Press.

Curran, J. R. (2004). *ro istri tiona to se anti si i arit* (dissertation), University of Edinburgh, Edinburgh, UK.

Fauconnier, G. (1998). Mental spaces, language modalities, and conceptual integration. In M. Tomasello (Ed.), *e ne ps o o o an a e o niti e an n tiona approa es to an a e str t re* (pp. 251-279). Hillsdale, NJ: Lawrence Erlbaum.

Gibbs, R. W. (1990). Psycholinguistic studies on the conceptual basis of idiomaticity. *o niti e in isti s* (4), 417-451.

Goldberg, A. E. (1995). *onstr tions onstr tion ra ar approa to ar ent str t re.* Chicago: Chicago University Press.

Grady, J. (1997). *o n ations o eanin ri ar etap ors an pri ar s enes* (Ph.D. dissertation), University of California Berkeley, Berkeley, CA.

Greenberg, J. H. (1963). Some universals of grammar with particular reference to the order of meaningful elements. In J. H. Greenberg (Ed.), *ni ersa s o an a e* (pp. 73-113). Cambridge: MIT Press.

Gries, S. T., & Stefanowitsch, A. (2004). Co-varying collexemes in the *into*-causative. In M. Achard & S. Kemmer (Eds.), *an a e t re an in* (pp. 225-236). Stanford, CA: CSLI Publications.

Hunston, S., & Francis, G. (1999). *attern ra ar orp s ri en approa to t e e i a ra ar o n is* . Amsterdam and Philadelphia, PA.: John Benjamins.

Johnson, M. (1987). *e o in t e in* . Chicago: University of Chicago Press.

Jurafsky, D., & Martin, J. H. (2008). *pee an an a e pro essin n intro tion to nat ra an a e pro essin o p tationa in isti s an spee re o nition* (2nd edn ed.). Upper Saddle River, NJ: Prentice Hall.

Kaufman, L., & Rousseeuw, P. J. (2005). *in in ro ps in ata n intro tion to ster ana sis* (2nd edn ed.). Hoboken, NJ: Wiley.

Keenan, E. L., & Comrie, B. (1977). Noun phrase accessibility and universal grammar. *in isti n ir* (1), 63-99.

Lakoff, G. (1993). The contemporary theory of metaphor. In A. Ortony (Ed.), *etap or an o t* (2nd edn ed., pp. 202-251). Cambridge: Cambridge University Press.

Lakoff, G., & Johnson, M. (1980). *etap ors e i e* . Chicago: University of Chicago Press.

Langacker, R. W. (1987). *o n ations o o niti e ra ar eoreti a prere isites* (Vol. 1). Stanford, CA: Stanford University Press.

Manning, C. D., & Schütze, H. (1999). *o n ations o statisti a nat ra an a e pro essin .* Cambridge, MA: MIT Press.

Merleau-Ponty, M. (1962). *eno eno o o er eption.* London: Routledge.

Sinclair, J. (1991). *orp s on or an e o o ation.* Oxford: Oxford University Press.

Stefanowitsch, A., & Gries, S. T. (2003). Collostructions: Investigating the interaction between words and constructions. *nternationa o rna o orp s in isti s* (2), 209-243.

Svorou, S. (1994). *e ra ar o pa e.* Amsterdam: John Benjamins.

Talmy, L. (2000). *o ar a o niti e e anti s o e on ept tr t rin ste s.* Cambridge: MIT Press.

Traugott, E. C. (1995). Subjectification in grammaticalization. In D. Stein & S. Wright (Eds.), *e ti it an s e ti isation in isti perspe ti es* (pp. 31-54). Cambridge: Cambridge University Press.

Tyler, A., & Evans, V. (2001). Reconsidering prepositional polysemy networks: The case of over. *an a e* (4), 724-765.

Tyler, A., & Evans, V. (2003). *e se anti s o n is prepositions patia s enes e o ie eanin an o nition.* Cambridge: Cambridge University Press.

Vandeloise, C. (1994). Methodology and analyses of the preposition *in. o niti e in isti s* (2), 157-184.

Typological Stage of Counterfactuals in Chinese

Qian Yong
Ph.D . Candidate Department of Chinese, Translation and Linguistics
City University of Hong Kong
Sissy6025@gmail.com

Abstract

Wu(1994) listed ten words as CFs' markers in Chinese, they are 早 (early) ， 了 (perfect/perfective marker), 要不是/要不然 (had it not been the case), 没(didn't), 就好了 (would have been great if only)，还以为(had thought), 原来应该(should have been), ...的话 (in the case), 真的 (really). However, according to our definitions, none of them are dedicated CFs markers but only CFE [1] markers except 要不是. Several observations can be summarized from these markers: (1)although they can be applied to deliver a counterfactual reading, they can never ensure a counterfactual reading; (2) the counterfactuality delivered by them can be easily cancelled by inserting another sentence following behind; (3)counterfactuality can be expressed in absense of these CFE markers.

1 Introduction about Counterfactual Research in Chinese

The issue of different treatments of counterfactuality in Chinese and other world languages was first proposed by Bloom(1981) who made an assumption that the lack of counterfactual expressions in Chinese is a significant cognitive consequence. To support his hypothesis, he made several experiments including asking contrary-to-fact questions in HongKong and Taiwan. Comrie(1986) holds the similar opinion by arguing that Chinese is among the languages which make no distinction in terms of hypotheticality, for instance, in Chinese, where '*Zhangsan he-le jiu, wojiu mata*' can vary in interpretation from 'If Zhangsan has drunk wine, I will scold him', to 'If Zhangsan drank wine, I would scold him', and then to 'If Zhangsan had drunk wine, I would have scolded him.'

Wizerzbicka(1997) is skeptical about the accuracy of the lacking of counterfactual markings in Chinese, by illustrating:

(1) a. *Jiaru nashihou (in the past) x mei fasheng dehua, ye jiu meiyou y le.*
If X hadnot happened at that time, there would not be Y.
(Non-factual optional)

b. *Jiaru jianglai(in future) x bu fasheng de hua Jiu buhui you y.*
If X does not happen, there won't be Y.
(Non-factual impossible)

The difference between the above two sentences involves the time adverbials (nashihou implies past reference and jianglai refers to the future). In addition, the modal form *buhui* implies a real possibility.Tien(1994) gives a similar discussion about the clearly distinguished CF conditional in Taiwanese Min by considering the following examples:

(2) a. *yi lae shizwun(past) wa na wu ji, wa ae twa yi*
I will/would marry she/her.
(Non-factual optional)

b. *yihou / jionglai wa na wu ji,*
later / future I if have money
I will marry her.
(Non-factual impossible)

I agree that neither Chinese nor Taiwanese constituent an exception to the broad generalization that languages have "at least two-way distinction in terms of degrees of hypotheticality", but the complexity of counterfactual marking in Chinese has been underrated. For one thing, neither past tense nor the modal verb is sufficient to differentiate CFs from non-CFs in Chinese. The ambiguity of (2a) shows the insufficiency of the past tense as CF marking. And *buhui*(will not) is not limited to factual interpretation in Chinese as Wizerzbicka(1997) mentioned,

(3)*zao zhidao ni shi zheyang de ren,*
early know 2SG be this CLASS PTCL person,
wo jiu buhui jiagei ni.
1SG then NEG-MDL Marry for 2SG
If I had known that you were of this sort, I would not have married you.

For another thing, neither the past tense nor the modal verbs are necessary to distinguish the CFs in Chinese. CFs in Chinese can be expressed without any marking, like "*Ruguo taiyang cong xibian chulai, wojiu jiagei ni.*" (If the sun rose from the west, I will marry you.)

Leaving aside for the time being the complex counterfactual markings in Chinese, the above evidence of Chinese CF conditionals can overthrow Bloom's assumption about the lacking of CFs in

[1] CFE markers (Counterfactuality Enhancing Markers) characterize the grammatical elements whose appearence increases but not ensure the chances of expressing counterfactuality.

Chinese fully well. Other criticisms by Au(1983), Liu(1985), Wu(1994), Yeh&Gentner(2005) also report similar performances between Chinese and English speakers in CF reasoning task. But how do we account for the different responses of speakers of Chinese and English to the hypothetical questions asked by Bloom? Wu(1989) argues that these different responses could be caused by different cultural values and communicative rules that constrain the use of counterfactuality in different social contexts. Wu(1989) further provides many salient linguistic devices- lexical item, stress and intonation- in Chinese for marking counterfactuality. Then it shifts our attention from whether Chinese has counterfactual expressions to whether Chinese has dedicated CF markers. It has been admitted by Chao(1968), Chen(1988), Wu(1989), Xing(1993), Jiang(2000), Su(2008), Yeh&Gentner(2005) and Feng&Li (2006) that Chinese CFs are based on an interaction between CF markers and other variables such as semantics and contexts. Ye and Gentner(2005) divided the CFs into "transparent and non-transparent". The former can be marked through intentional violations of semantic knowledge, such as sentence "*If I you can buy a house, then I am the president of the USA*". There are obvious limitations with markings at semantic or discourse level, and they are not in the interest of our research. For the non-transparent counterfactuals, it is a cross-language phenomenon to apply the fake temporal marker. Jiang(2000) claims that the fake temporal markers also work in Chinese,

(4) a. *dangchu(in the past) yaoshi zao ting ni yi ju hua, ye bu zhi jinri.*
If I had followed your advice at that time, I would not have been so bad today.

b. *zuotian yaoshi zao zhidao hui nong cheng zheyang, wo jiu hui duo daidian qian qu.*
If I had known it was this case yesterday, I would have brought more money.

Here, zao(early) is taken by Jiang(2000) as a fake past tense in that it can point to any day in the past which can be either dangchu(that time) or zuotian(yesterday). However, I am in the view that the implicit meaning of *zao* is lexically designated and it can never alter its function of indicating PAST, such as "*(*)mingtian (tomorrow) yaoshi(if-be) zao(early) zhidao(know)...* ". Compare (4) with the following CFs with fake tense marker,

(5) *Si Pierre partait demain, il arriverait là-bas*
If Pierre left.PST.IMPF tomorrow he would arrive
le lendemain
there the next.day
If Pierre left tomorrow, he would arrive there the next day. (French)

(6) a. *zuotian yaoshi xia yi chang yu,*
Yesterday if-be fall one CLASS rain,
zhuangjia jiu buhui gan si le.
crops then NEG-MDL dry die PTCL
If it had rained yesterday, the crops would not have died from drought.

b. *zuotian yaoshi xia guo yi chang yu,*
Yesterday if-be fall PTCL one CLASS rain,
Zhuangjia jiu buhui gan si le.
crops then NEG.MDL dry die PTCL
If it rained yesterday, the crops would not die from drought.

It has been argued by Chen(1988) and Jiang(2000) that (6b) conveys the factual interpretation of the events, and the coercion on the aspect marking in (6a) is a reflex of fake aspect in Chinese CFs. I am also of a different opinion in that (6b) does convey a non-factual interpretation, and even if aspect coercion is needed for marking CFs, it will never function as a fake aspect like:

(7) *Age fardaa mi-raft hafte-ye ba'd mi-resid*
if tomorrow DUR-go.PST week-EZ next DUR-arrive.PST
If he left tomorrow, he would arrive next week.
(Persian)

Here, the durative aspect is used to indicate the perfective. The alteration of the original function of tense and aspect does not occur in Chinese CFs, and we cannot conclude that Chinese has the fake temporal marker.

However, the highly frequent occurrence of *zao* , *le*(perfect/perfective marker), *yaobushi*(if-NEG-be), *yaoburan*(if-NEG-this case), *jiuhaole*(then good-PTL), *yiwei*(had thought), ...*dehua*(in that case) and *zhende*(really) in the Chinese CFs cannot be denied, for all of which Wu(1994) included as CF markers. Jiang (2000) rejected all of them on the logical ground that each form could potentially be used in non-counterfactual contexts. Feng&Li(2006) argues CF marker may not necessarily be consistent even in English. He further concluded that the temporal reference, the aspect marker and the lexicalized phrases account for 90% of the CFs in Chinese. However, we cannot easily take all these strategies as markers for CFs in Chinese. Wang(2012) takes these carefully by referring them as CF ingredients. But do all the CF ingredients work at the same level? Like what I talked about in this paper, CF markers and CFE markers need to be differentiated and CFs in Chinese are generally expressed through CFE markers. In other words, CFs in Chinese are not determined but reinforced by the appearance of the features which can be applied to enhance the hypotheticality i.e. CFE markers. The situation in Chinese can be explained by the theory of CFI-(Counterfactual Implicature) Principle (Ziegeller,2000):

> The CFI-Principle:
> 'The strength of an implicature is directly proportional to the specificity conditions (information density) in which it is located.

Therefore, in the absence of the dedicated CF markers, the CFE markers like real past tense, objective negation (mei), first person pronoun, proximal pronouns, real perfect/perfective (le) in Chinese which are often associated with environments with high information-desity function as the potential catalyst for the extraction of the counterfactual reading. The more of the features that are present, the greater probability it implies to express counterfactuality. Therefore, the continuum nature of Comrie's description may correspond to variations in the number of features present in the sentences. And the cluster of features together may contribute to an overall optimum situation for the interpretation of counterfactual notions, like:

(8) *ruguo* ***wo(I) zuotian(yesterday) mei(did not)*** *nadao zhe(this) zhang piao, wo jiu* ***buneng(can not)*** *qu kan yanchu* ***le(perfect/perfective)***.
If I had not got this ticket yesterday, I would not have been able to see the performance.

2 Counterfactuality Enhancing Markers

The difference between CF markers and CFE markers is reflected in their exclusiveness in marking CF sentences. If A can mark B exclusively, it means A is only used to mark B but nothing else. CF markers can mark counterfactuality exclusively, like counterfactual marking in Hua (Trans-New Guinea > Eastern Highlands),

(9) *kori hu hine*
fear do.1 CTF.A
I would have run away/I almost ran away
(Haiman, 1980)

Whereas CFE markers can mark counterfactuality in a certain environment but not exclusively, the reflection of which will be found in its insufficiency of marking CFs. In Russian, the word for *if* is *esli*, which can generate open interpretation as well as the counterfactual reading, e.g.,

(10) a. *Esli* ***by*** *oni naš li étu vodu,*
if SUBJ 3PL find.PFV.PST that water.ACC
oni byli by spaseny,
3PL be-PST SUBJ save.PASS
no jia somnevajus', Č to oni ee naš li.
but 1SG doubt COMP 3PL find.PFV.PST
If they found(had found) that water, they would be (would have been) saved, but I doubt that they found(have found)it. (Non-factual optional)

b. *Esli* ***by*** *ja* ***ne*** *na naš la jabloki,*
if SUBJ 1SG NEG any find.PFV.PST apples
ja by kupila gruš i.
1SG SUB buy.PFV.PST pears
If I hadn't got(didn't get) any apples, I would have bought(would buy) pears.
(Non-factual obligatory)

By comparing these two sentences, it could be observed that the appearence of negation marker (*ne*) in Russian increases the chances of expressing counterfactuality. However, we could not easily attribute it as a CF marker because it can still occur in non-CF environment. Although there are distinct features between CFE marker and CF marker, we cannot expect a clear-cut boundary. The essential difference between each other is the different degrees of hypotheticality contained in the markers. From a historical view, we will find a process of grammaticalization from CFE markers to CF markers. Not all the CFE markers meet the requirements of changing, but for those qualified ones, some may stay at the continuum between CFE markers and CF markers, while others have already become dedicated CF makers. For convenience, some typical CFE markers will be chosen for discussion in the following passage.

2.1 Negation

Negation has a close relationship on the CF interpretation of a conditional. Wierzbicka(1997) realized the effect of negation on enhancing the hypotheticality. She even attributed the double negative CF conditionals as the hard core of the "counter-factual" category. It was further explained by her that it is easier for the common sense to accept that "facts" are positive rather than negative, that things that happen are more "real" than things that do not happen, and that our knowledge of things that have happened is more certain and reliable than the knowledge of things that haven't happened. It is well documented in many different languages that the distinction between the world of affirmative and negative sentence lies in that the negative sentences are normally connected with "irrealis", like in Nyulnyulan languages of Western Austrlia,

(11)*arri i-li-jid-an bur-ung i-ngkudal*
NEG 3SG.NOM-IRR-go-PFV camp-all 3SG.NOM-got.lost.
He didn't go to his camp; he got lost.
(McGregor ,1996)

In Chinese, negators are not regarded as grammatical contributors of counterfactuality by Jiang(2000) in that if an antecedent is introduced by negators, it always points to an event which already occurred. Negation of an already occurred event naturally generates CF interpretation. However, Wang(2012) argues that since no definite answer can be provided to prove that the use of negators will lead to a proposition containing a fact, or vice versa, it is reasonable to classify them as a CF grammatical ingredient. Likewise, negation can happen in either antecedent or consequent to enhance the hypotheticality,

(12) a. *Ruguo ni gangcai(past) lai le zher,*
jiu neng kanjian zher de bihua le.
If you came (had come) here just now, you would see (have seen) the wall painting.

b. *ruguo ni gangcai(past) mei(NEG) jiaozhu ta ,*
ta xianzai jiu yijing zai xianchang le.
If you had not stopped him just now, he would have been at the site.

(12)a with double affirmative can be interpreted either as a CF or as a non-CF, while the general reading of (12)b is only a CF. However, both of them don't entail the counterfactuality , which can be cancelled by introducing an additional clause preceding them, like "*我不知道你刚才有没有来这/叫住他，但是…… (I don't know whether you were here / stopped him just now, but...)* ". However, the counterfactuality of a CF conditional with double negation can not easily be cancelled, like,

(13)*ruguo zhongguo meiyou(NEG) guoqu sanshinian de gaigekaifang, jiu buhui(NEG) you jinri de huihuang.*

Without the policy of reform and opening up in the past thirty years, China would not have had such wonderful performance.

The speaker surely knew that China had already practiced the policy when uttering this sentence. An introducing of an additional clause used to cancel the counterfactuality will seem odd here.

2.2 Objectivity

Wierzbicka(1997) argues that it is the domain of "what happens" rather than that of what you and I may want to do , which is the realm of "factuality" par excellence. Consequently, the hard core of "counterfactuality", too, must be restricted to what happened (or didn't happen) rather than uncertain intensions. She further listed examples in Russian and Polish, where the first or second person is more difficult to get a counterfactual reading as third person or non-human subjects.

(14) a. *Esli by X ne sluČilos', Y by ne sluČilos'.(Russian)*

b. *Gdyby X sie stalto, Y by sit nie stalo.(Polish)*

If X had not happened, Y would have happened.

(Wierzbicka, 1997)

According to her, CF conditionals with a negative protasis as (14) does not necessarily have a counterfactual reading, but this case is only restricted to the first or second person. And if the third person or the non-human subjects appear, the sentence is forced to get a counterfactual reading. It can be explained in that first and second person action sentences are expected to behave differently in the respect of objectivity from "third person event sentences", since the first or second person is always bound with subjective intensions.

Similar evidence can be found in Chinese negators-mei(没) and bu(不), with the former carrying stronger counterfactuality than the latter. The differences of the two have been discussed a lot by Li and Thompson(1981), Ting-chi Tang(1994) and Yuzhi Shi and Na Li(2000). Here, we only concern the differences reflected in objectivity between mei(没) and bu(不) which will lead to the different degrees of hypotheticality for CFs. mei(没) is an objective negation of an event , while bu(不) is a negation of the subjective desire.Examples from CCL (Center for Chinese Linguistics PKU) reveal a great priority of mei(没) used in CFs over bu(不).

(15) a.*Ruguo ni bu(NEG) yuanyi jiegei wo 5 kuai qian, na wo jiu zhineng buxingzhe huiqule.*

If you are not willing to lend me 5yuan, then I have to walk home.

b.*Ruguo ta meiyou(NEG) shoushang, yiding shi NBA zuihao de zhongfeng.*

If he had not got hurt, he must have been the best center in NBA.

(15)a merely presents a possible imagination of speaker with subjective emotions. While (15)b shows an objective negation of an occurred situation, which therefore creates a possible world for the hearer through the utterance.

Considering the above examples, we can draw a brief conclusion: hypotheticality does have some relations with objectivity. Third person and un-animated subjects in Russian and Polish blessed with objective meaning work like a CFE marker. And mei(没) shows greater tendency over bu(不) to be a CFE marker in Chinese. However, as a CFE marker, mei(没) does not necessarily guarantee the counterfactual reading of the sentence, as a CFE marker cannot mark the sentence exclusively. A counterfactual interpretation should depend on the antecedent of a conditional known to be false, whereas the objective negation of an event may go beyond our shared knowledge, like:

(16)*Ruguo 2 yinian qian(past) konglong meiyou(NEG) miejue, na xianzai diqiushang hai hui you konglong.*

If dinosaurs didn't go extinct 2 hundred million years ago, then we still can find them on the earth now.

It is noteworthy that different languages may display different mechanisms in enhancing the hypotheticality. First or second person cannot be a CFE marker in Russian and Polish because of lacking objectivity, but it performs differently in other languages (which will be expound in the following passage). The role of Objectivity in enhancing the probability of counterfactual reading is also mentioned by Ziegeler(2000) who argues that the hypothesis of irrealis will be probable but not counterfactual, whereas the hypothesis of an objective known-fact will produce a counterfactual utterance.

2.3 Intimacy

As mentioned above, the interpretation of a conditional sentence is related to the personal pronouns used as subject. And the third person pronoun is more likely to appear in the CFs than the first/second person pronoun in Russian and Polish because of objectivity. But it is not always the case in other languages where the first/second person pronoun (especially the first person pronoun) bears a great priority to be a subject in CFs over others. Ziegeler(2000) argues that it is because the first or second persons are deicitically closer to speaker's immediate domain of reference, and in the case of the first person subjects, the subject and the speaker are the same. This intimacy, therefore, is in the best possible position to make a factually-based prediction about the past. She further provides two examples to prove her ideas,

(17) a.*If I had been there at the time, I would have seen the thief.*

b.*If he had been there at the time, he would have seen the thief.*

In (17)b, the cancellation of counterfactual reading can be realized by adding "*so let's go and ask him if he was there*". But in a normal circumstance, the counterfactuality of (17)a cannot be cancelled by introducing "but I didn't know where I was at the time", since I am always has the most intimate knowledge of myself under normal circumstances. Similar evidence can also be found in Chinese,

(18) a. *Ruguo ta(he) zuotian(past) qule xuexiao, jiu hui kanjian xuexiao menkou de diaoxiang.*
If he did go to school yesterday, he would see the statue at the school gate.'

b. *Ruguo ni(you) zuotian qule xuexiao, jiu hui kanjian xuexiao menkou de diaoxiang.*
then will see school gate PTCL statue
If you (had gone) did go to school yesterday, you would (have seen) see the statue at the school gate.

c. *Ruguo wo(I) zuotian qule xuexiao,*
jiu hui kanjian xuexiao menkou de diaoxiang.
If I had gone to school yesterday, I would have seen the statue at the school gate.

The third person pronoun in (18)a generates an open interpretation, since the speaker is not familiar with "*his*" situation and simply makes an open hypothesis. The second person pronoun, closer to the speaker's domain, will generate an ambiguous interpretation, either open or counterfactual, depending on whether the event in antecedent has already been presupposed to be false. Whereas, the first person pronoun in (18)c will undoubtedly produce a CF reading. Unless suffering from a memory loss and this is another case, the speaker surely knows his own situation. Any hypothesis based on a known reality will deliver a counterfactual understanding.

The influence of intimacy on enhancing the hypotheticality can also be found in the demonstrative pronouns where the proximal (this, these) is more inclined to express a CF reading than the distal (that, those). Consider the following examples in Chinese,

(19) a. *Yaoshi wo nabudao na(that) zhang piao,*
wo jiu bu neng qu kan yanchu le.
If I could(can) not get that ticket, I would(will) not go to see the performance.

b. *Yaoshi wo nabudao zhe(this) zhang piao,*
wo jiu bu neng qu kan yanchu le.
If I could not get this ticket, I would not go to see the performance.

It is because that the proximal demonstrative pronoun pulls closer the distance between the event and the speaker, and the event in the antecedent is more likely to be presupposed to be false. In contrast, the event indicated by the distal demonstrative pronoun is relatively far in the speaker's domain of reference, and less likely to be presupposed because of the remoteness. Therefore, (19)a with *na(that)* shows an ambiguous interpretation, either counterfactual or factual , while(19)b with *zhe(this)* creates a higher level of counterfactuality and can only be understood counterfactually.

The effect of intimacy can be further proved by the differences between the definite nouns and the indefinite nouns. Compare the following example with (19)a,b,

c. *Yaoshi wo nabudao piao(indefinite),*
wo jiu bu neng qu kan yanchu le.
If I cannot get ticket, I will not go to see the performance.

2.4TAM Features

The information encoded in the verbal categories-tense, aspect and mood/modality (TAM)- may be helpful in enhancing the possibility of expressing Counterfactuals. We put them together both because they interact with each other in various ways in the morpho-syntax, semantics and pragmatics and because for some languages there may not be clearly differentiated categories of these three. For instance, tense and aspect cannot be clearly distinguished in many languages, like in Spanish and Modern Greek, the imperfective aspect will be conflated with the past tense in a form traditionally called imperfect. It is also the same case in analytic languages like Chinese where aspect, lexical information and modal verbs work together to form the temporal location. Aspectual viewpoints are conveyed in Chinese by le(了), guo(过), zai(在), zhe(着) or adverbs like changchang(常常), (yijing)已经 or zero marked bare sentence. Lexicons like past/future-oriented verbs-huiyi(回忆) and jihua(计划), modal verbs-hui(会), yao(要) and jiang(将), connective adverbs-yihou(以后), jiu(就) and zao(早) all join together to help realize the temporal reference in Chinese. However, we cannot deny the theoretically ideal distinction of TAM, and there does exit many languages with separate grammatical markers for TAM.

2.4.1 Tense

It is widely believed and well documented that past tense is inextricably related to crosslinguistic notions of high hypotheticality. Presumably, it is because one should have great certainty about the past event than the future event, so that a past situation that is nonfactual will probably be hypothetical enough to be counterfactual, whereas a future situation that is nonfactual is quite likely to be just left open (Comrie,1986). Some linguists relate the past tense with high hypotheticality by proposing that "past" simply denotes remoteness, either temporal or modal (Steele,1975; Iatridou,2000; Ritter and Wiltschko,2010). It is the metaphorical device from spatial and temporal distance/proximity to abstract conceptual or coginitive distance/proximity that relates temporal distance with modal distance (Fleischman, 1989). However, we cannot easily attribute past tense as a CF marker as real past tense cannot signal unreality exclusively like fake past, e.g. in Spanish,

(20) a. *Si(es verdad que) habian llegado antes de que eso pasara,*
If arrive-3rd-PL-PST.PF-IND before of that happen-3rd-SG-PST-IMPF-SUBJ
no nos contaron nada.
not us tell-3rd-PL-PST-IND nothing
If (it's true that) they had arrived before it happened, they didn't say anything to us about it.(Factual)

b. *Si Maria hubiera llegado ayer,*
if Maria arrive-3rd-SG-PST+PF-SUBJ yesterday
se habría llevado un buen susto.

Herself carry-3rd-SG-COND+PF a good night
If Mary had arrived yesterday, she would have got a shock.

c. *Si Maria hubiera estado viviendo aquí ahora,*
if Maria live-3rd-SG-PST+PF+PROG-SUBJ here now
habría conseguido ese trabajo.
Obtain-3rd-SG-COND+PF that job
If Mary had been living here now, she would have got that job.

(Tynan&Lavin, 1997)

d. *Si los auditors hubieran venido mañana,*
if the auditors come-3rd-PL-PAST+PF-SUBJ tomorrow
habrían enconirado los libros en regla.
Find-3rd-PL-COND+PF the books in rule
If the auditors had come tomorrow, they would have found the bokks in perfect order

(Bennett, 1988)

The degree of hypotheticality contained in real past in (20)a does not reach the standard of expressing counterfactual. Considering its contribution on enhancing the hypotheticaliy, it may be more reasonable to classify them as CFE markers. However, it is not the case for the fake past which can be applied indiscriminately in sentences with various temporal references like (20)b,c,d.

Past tense labeled with real semantic values like (20)a may not necessarily occur in counterfactual environment, like in Chinese:

(21)*Yaoshi ta zuotian(past) meiyou(NEG) guandeng, na xianzai jiaoshili de deng yiding hai liangzhe.*
If he did not turn off the light yesterday, the light must be on till now in classroom. (Factual)

But considering the high frequency of real past tense in CFs, we cannot ignore the contribution of real past tenses to CFs. It may be better to term the real past tense as a CFE marker, as it really works to enhance the probability of expressing CFs.

2.4.2 Aspect: Perfect and Perfective

Like past tense, perfect/perfective can be used to locate a knowable domain. From this perspective, both perfect and perfective aspect can play the same role in enhancing the probability of expressing CFs as past tense. For example, in Welsh, according to Jones (2010), the perfect aspect has a temporal function by locating a situation in anterior time from the standpoint of reference time or, in terms of a related explanation, it provides a retrospective view of a situation from the standpoint of a reference time. And the perfect aspect with tenses other than past is problematic in Welsh,

(22) a. * *geith hi fod wedi aros.*
May.PRES.3SG she be PF stay
She can/may=permission have stayed.

b. * *all o fod weidi pasio 'r lori.*
Can.PRES.3SG he be PF pass the lorry
He can have passed the lorry.

(Jones, 2010)

The appearance of genuine perfect may enhance the degree of hypotheticality, but cannot ensure a counterfactual reading, like in Old Icelandic languages:

(23)*Þá grunaði Vani at Æsir mundi* ***hafa*** *falsat Þái mannaskiptinu*
Then the Vanir suspected that the Æsir must have played them false in exchange of men.

(Molencki, 1999)

Perfective aspect is also claimed to have equal temporal function of past tense in Nootka, where past tense can be substituted by perfective aspect in expressing the CFs, like:

(24)*wa '=' al= we' in Kʷatjat aqi-s=qu:=s naq-(y)u al*
say=TEMP=QT Kwatyat what-do=COND=1SG see-perceive.PFV
Kwatyat said, "How could I have seen him?

(Davidson, 2002)

Likewise, the information carried by real perfective aspect may enhance the hypotheticality in a sense, but it can never encode counterfactulity before it evolves into a dedicated marker with no aspectual constraints. For example, in Chinese , perfective/perfect marker *le(了)* has been taken as an important grammatical constituent by Chen(1988), (1994), Jiang(2000), Yeh&Gentner(2005) , Feng(2006) and Wang(2012), however it cannot ensure a counterfactual interpretation when delivering a perfective/perfect meaning, like:

(25)*Ruguo ni xinli yijing you bieren le(PFV), wo jiu tuichu.*
If you have already loved someone else, I will exit.

It would be better to term the real perfect/perfective aspect in Chinese as a CFE marker rather than a CF marker.

2.5 Other evidence

A cluster of CFE markers, as listed above, all contribute to an overall optimum situation for expressing hypothetical events, and the more CFE markers that are present in the sentence, the higher degree of hypotheticality implied, with counterfactuality being obtainable as an inference or implicature deriving from the highest level of hypotheticality (Comrie, 1986). Therefore, Comrie's theory of "continuum of hypotheticality" may be controlled by the choices of CFE markers in utterance. Some of the main CFE markers have been studied so far in detail with other minor features which can also be added to the cluster being left undiscussed.

Some adverbials have also been argued to contribute the hypotheticality, like *zhende(真的)*, *zao（早）* in Chinese. According to Feng&Li (2006), 10% of sentences marked by zhende(真的) in the sample will produce a counterfactual response and 83% for *zao（早）*.

zhende(真的) means *really* in English, which can enhance the hypotheticality level by introducing an unexpected event which works to increase the distance between the possible world and the reality. However, it is not restricted to the counterfactual interpretation, like:

(26)*Ruguo ta zhende(really) toule qian, iudei jin jianyu.*

Understanding I: If he had stolen the money, he would have been sent to the prison.

Understanding II: If he really has stolen the money, he will be sent to the prison.

Zao(早) means *early* in English, which can be applied to detach the possible world from the reality world by indicating a remote past. However, if co-occurred with a future tense, the "detach" function of Zao(早) will disappear, like:

(27) a.*Ruguo zao(early) zhidao jintian bu shangban, wo jiu buyong zheme zaoqi le.*
if early know today NEG work 1SG then NEG.need so early getup PTCL
If I had known I don't need to work today earlier, I would not have got up so early.

b.*Ruguo ni mingtian neng zao xiaban, jiu bang wo dai dian cai.*
If 2SG tomorrow can early get-off work then help 1SG bring some grocery
If you could get off work early tomorrow, then help me bring some groceries.

3 Typology of Languages with Counterfactual Expressions

In the languages of the world, one can come across two different major marking strategies in expressing CFs.One of them is to apply grammatical ingredients with their genuine meaning to make a hypothesis towards aknown fact. These grammatical elements are used to enhance the hypothetical effect of the sentence, therefore areattributed as CFE markers in our paper. CFE markers are commonly applied in many languages even in the so-called non-counterfactual reasoning languages like Chinese. The counterfactual sense delivered by the HE markers emerges as implicature, which can be easily cancelled. In the other type, the counterfactuality is coded by the marker (CF marker), and this is further located in time. It should, however, be noted that through language evolution, the counterfactual meaning implicated by CFE markers may be conventionalized and gradually encoded in the markers. And this leads to cross-functional uses of these grammatical elements as dedicated CF markers in marking CFs. Through the history of languages, the strive for prevailing the conventionalized implicature of grammatical ingredients always competes with their restrictions of original functions. And this abrupt shift in the function may not be achieved in languages where grammatical information is not encoded by special morphemes. For example in Chinese, past tense is expressed by the join forces of lexical items, perfective/perfect marker le(了), and other adverbials, therefore the pragmatic implicature of counterfactual meaning from those various combinations of elements may be more difficult to be strengthened and conventionalized than from a special dedicated morpheme encoding the past inflection like –ed in English. The development of a CFE marker to a CF marker, in line with the expansion of its domain of use, will be perfectly displayed by some languages with verbal inflections like Indo-European languages. However, this represents only a part of the life cycle of counterfactual marking for the relaxation of counterfactuality may be brought by the prevailing use of CF markers, which will lead to a renewal evolution from CFE marker to CF marker. The life cycle of counterfactual marking can be depicted as follows:

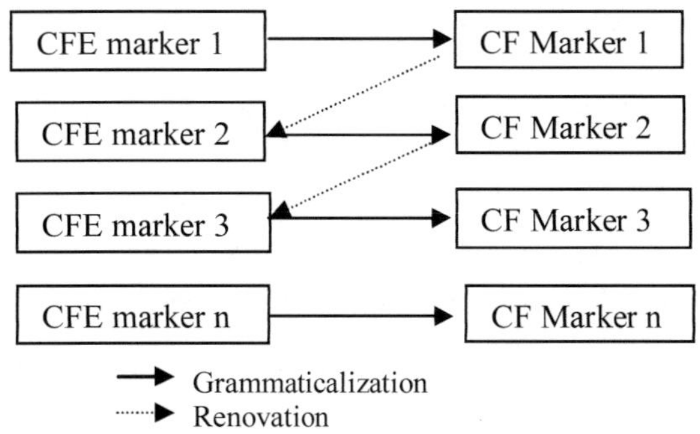

Figure 1 The Life Cycle of the Counterfactual Marking

During the language evolution, some languages may have gone through many layers of CF markers. Like English, at least three layers of CF marker-past tense, perfect, modal(would) have been formed. And the following passage will classify the world languages according to the number of CF layers.

3.1 CF_0 languages

(28)Australian>Western Nyulnyulan >Bardi

a.*Janinmarr ngalalabanjirrin miinybal*
bird sp.-SEMBL 1-UNR-have-CONT/PAST=3MIN.FOC.IO wing
'I wish I had wings like a janin bird's [because then I would fly to see my wife, but I don't]'

b. *gaadiliny nga-l-arli-n laalboo-yoon*
monkey.fish 1.MIN.NOM-UNR-eat-PRS earth.over-ABL
I would like to eat the monkey fish from an earth oven.

c. *Boowanim oolarrarlagoorr.*
ant-ERG 3-UNR-AUG-bite/eat-FUT=2AUG.DO
The ants might bite you.

(Bowern, 2004)

(29) Australian>Western Nyulnyulan>Nyulnyul

a. *Nga-li-jal-an-karr-ji kalb*
1:MIN:NOM-UNR-see-PST-SUBJ-2:MIN:ACC up
nga-li-m-an-ji mudikard-uk.
1:MIN:NOM-UNR-put-PST-2:MIN:ACC car-LOC
If I had seen you, I'd have picked you up in the car.

b. *Mi-li-jid-ikarr kinyingk-ung bur i-li-rr-ar-juy.*
2:MIN:NOM-UNR-go-SUBJ this-all
camp 3:NOM-UNR-AUG-spear-2:MIN:NOM
If you go into that country, they might spear you.

(McGregor& Wagner, 2006)

The Nyulnyulan languages show a bipartite past/non-past division or tripartite past/present/future division contrast in expressing irrealis. Counterfactuality, which is undoubtedly expressed by past irrealis in these languages, is not shared by sentences with all temporal references. Sentences with present and future references have no way to mark CFs in absence of the fake past and thus could only be interpretated hypothetically but not counterfactually, like (28)b,c and (29)b. Our argument is that although a genuine past tense can co-work with mood category to express counterfactuality, it can never ensure a counterfactual reading. And a language with only genuine temporal marking stays only at the very initial stage of counterfactual expression, normally restricted in the past reference. From above languages with genuine past tenses but no dedicated CF markers, at least some commonness can be concluded: Counterfactuality is expressed (1) through pragmatic implicature rather than morphosyntactic entailment; (2) restrictedly on sentences with past time reference; (3) most frequently with the co-work of modals.

3.2 $CF_{1/2}$ languages

CF ½ Languages refer to the languages where there are some dedicated CF modals to mark the counterfactuality regardless of the time line, but still with some restrictions. Different from CF_0 languages, counterfactual meaning is not gained through pragmatic inference from past time, neither will it be cancelled by anadditional clause.

(30) Sino-Tibeten > Chinese >Madarin

__Yaobushi__ ni mingtian wanshang yao qu meiguo,
If-not-be you tomorrow night will go America
women mingwan jiu keyi yiqi chifan le.
we tomorrow then can together have-dinner PTCL
If you weren't going to America, we would have dinner together tomorrow night.

Different from purely hypothetical conjunction ruguo, yaobushi in Chinese cannot appear in non-counterfactual environments. And the unambigious counterfactual nature of these sentences regardless of temporal reference is uniquely determined by the Yaobushi, without any contribution from aspect or tensemorphology. But the counterfactual expression is only restricted to the negative sentences.

(31)*Austronesian > Meso-Philippine > Tagalog*

__Kundi__ napakalayo ng Maynila, papag-aaralin ko sana siya roon.
If-not-that very-far Case Manila cause-study I SANA him there.
If Manila weren't so far away, I'd send him to study there.

(Nevins, 2002)

Conjunction kung…sana in Tagalog can express counterfactuality with no exception, but it has to be combined with the negation particle hindi, surfacing as kundi…sana (Schacter & Otanes, 1983). Likewise, Tagalog has a dedicated CF marker but it is also restricted to the negative sentences.

3.3 CF_1 languages

If a language has only one layer of CF marker, it must be the mood category including the irrealis marker, imaginative marker or unreal marker and so on. Different from the above languages, the mood category can mark the counterfactual without any restrictions.

(32) Indo-European > Slavic >Slovenian

a. *Da imam, bi ti posodil.*
that have-1.sg.pres would to-you lend-sg.mac
If I had it , I would lend it to you.

b. *Da je bilo deZevalo, ne bi bili Sli ven.*
that is be-part-3sg rain-part.3.sg not would be-part-pl go-part-pl out
If it had rained, we wouldn't have gone out.

da in Slovenian is applied to mark CFs even in the non-past environment, like(32)a.

(33) Afro-Asiatic >Semitic> Modern Hebrew

a. *__Ilu__ hu hayah tokeach et ha trufah, hu hayah mevri.*
CF he had taken dir-obj the medicine he would-be healthy
If he had taken the medicine, he would have been healthy.

b. *__Ilu__ hu lakach et ha trufah, hu hayah mevri.*
CF he take.PST dir-obj. the medicine he would-be healthy
If he took the medicine, he would be healthy.

In Modern Hebrew, Ilu can mark CFs even in the non-past contexts like (33)b while Im can only indicate the past CFs. According to our definition dicussed above, the former should be classified as a CF modal with the latter being a CFE modal.

3.4 CF_2 languages

I. Fake Past+ Fake Imperfective

(34) Niger-Congo > Benue-Congo > Bantoid >Zulu

a. *[ukuba __be__- ngi- phuma manje] __be__- ngi- zo- fika kusasa*
If PAST.IMPF-1SG-leave now PAST.IMPF- 1SG-FUT-arrive tomorrow
If I left now, I would arrive tomorrow.

b. *[ukuba __be__- ngi- thimul- ile] __be__-ngi- zo-dinga ithishi*
if PAST.IMPF-1SG-sneeze-PFV PAST.IMPF-1SG-FUT-need 5tissue
If I had sneezed, I would have needed a tissue.

(Halpert & Karawani, 2012)

II. Fake Past+ Fake Perfective

(35) Afro-Asiatic >Semitic >Arabic (Palestinian)

a.*[iza __ṭileʕ__ halaʔ,] __kaan__ b-iwsal ʕal waʔt la l-muħaadara*
if leave.PAST.PFV now, be,PAST.PFV B-arrive.IMPF on the-time for the-lecture
If he left now, he would arrive on time for the lecture.

b.*[iza __kanno__ b-yitlaʕ bakkeer kul yom,] __kaan__ b-iwsal ʕa l-waʔt la l-muħadaraat*
if be.PAST.PFV B-leave.IMPF early every day, be.PAST.PFV B-arrive.IMPF on the-time to the-lectures
If he were in the habit of leaving early, he would arrive to the lectures on time.

(Iatridou, 2009)

III.CF modals+ Fake Past

(36) a. *Esli by Džon umer, my poxoroni-l-I by ego na*
if SUBJ John die.PFV.PST we bury.PFV-PST-PL SUBJ he.ACC on gor-e.mountain-LOC
If John died, we would bury him on the mountain.

b. *Esli by Džon umira-l, s nim by-l by doctor.*
if SUBJ John die.IMPF-PST with he.INSTR be-PST SUBJ doctor
If John were dying, the doctor would be with him.

(Halpert & Karawani, 2012)

3.5 CF_3 languages

As its name implies, CF3 Languages refer to the languages with 3 layers of CF markers. According to diachronic data, CF conditionals in English have experienced 3 layers of development, i.e., fake past/fake perfect/would.

(37) Indo-European >Germanic >English

a. *He noere na oelmihtig, gif him oenig gefadung earfoðe woere.*
he not-were(SUBJ) no almighty if him any order difficult were(SUBJ)
He would not be almighty if any order were difficult for him to maintain
(ÆDT 80 Early 11 th c.)

Fake Past combined with subjunctive mood was applied in old and middle English to mark CFs. Then perfect gradually entered into the CF conditionals in 13th century, like:

b. *War mi hare schorn, I war noght þan stranger þan a-noþer man. Were my hair shorn I were not then stronger than another man*
If my hair were shorn, I wouldn't be stronger than anybody else.
(Cursor Mundi 7211, 1340)

It was not until mid-fourteenth century that the bleached modal (wolde-would) occurred in the CFconditionals,

c. *For had he knowen hit biforn A childe of a*
for had he known it before a childe of a

mayden born Wolde he neuer haue ȝyuen to
maiden born would he never have given to

rede þat iesu crist shulde haue ben dede
advice that Jesus Christ should have been dead
For if he had known before about a child born of a virgin, he would never have suggested that JesusChrist should die.
(Trinity MS Cursor Mundi, 10787, c1400)

Therefore, in the modern English, CF conditionals are marked through 3 layers of CF markers, like:

d. *If he had not come here, this would not have happened.*
PF.PAST MOD

Similar evidence can be found in other Indo-European languages, like

(38) Indo-European >Romance >French

Si Pierre ***partait*** *demain, il* ***arriverait*** *là-bas le lendemain*
If Pierre left.PAST.IMPF tomorrow he MOD arrive there the next.day
If Pierre left tomorrow, he would arrive there the next day.
(Halpert & Karawani, 2012)

4 Implications

Wu(1994) listed ten words as CFs' markers in Chinese, they are 早(early)， 了(perfect/perfective marker), 要不是/要不然(had it not been the case), 没(didn't), 就好了(would have been great if only)，还以为(had thought), 原来应该(should have been), ...的话(in the case), 真的(really). However, according to our definitions, none of them are dedicated CFs markers but only CFE markers except 要不是. Several observations can be found from these markers: (1)although they can be applied to deliver a counterfactual reading, they can never ensure a counterfactual reading; (2) the counterfactuality delivered by them can be easily cancelled by inserting another sentence behind; (3)counterfactuality can be expressed in absense of the CFE markers.

According to Dahl(1997), the life cycle of the CF markers is a repeated evolution from CFE markers to CF markers. At the first stage in that the markers are restrained to past time reference (a),imply couterfactuality in the strict sense (dependence on a condition known to be false)(b), are optional(c). Then, the constraints such as the temporal condition on its use would be gradually relaxed, like in English "If he had been alive next year, he would have been 200 years old." The counterfactuality constraint will be relaxed once the construction has become possible with non-past reference. Davies(1979) offers the following sentences as an apparent example of a non-counterfactual use of the "if pluperfect+would" constructions: If John had been at the scene of the crime at the time when the murder was committed, Mary would have seen him leaving. So we must get hold of her to find out if she didn't see him. If the counterfactuality cannot be sufficiently expressed, a new cycle from CFE markers to CF markers starts again from the beginning. Therefore, in some languages, CFs are expressed through many layers of CF markers.

The life cycle of CFs' markers nicely shows some potential language universals in that counterfactual thinking is shared by the world languages. However, the development of the CFs' markers is subject to the characteristics of the languages. Chinese, lacking of inflectional morphemes, shows many restrictions in forming a CF marker, therefore is less developed than other inflectional languages in counterfactual expressions.

References

Au,T. K (1983) Chinese and English counterfactuals: The Sapir-Whorf hypothesis revisited. Cognition15, 155-187.

Bloom,A.H. 1981. The Linguistic Shaping of Thought: A Study in the Impact of Language on Thinking in China and the West. Hillsdale, NJ: L. Erlbaum.

Bowern, Claire L., 2004. Bardi verb morphology in historical perspective. Ph.D. Thesis, Harvard University.

Chao,Y.R. 1968. A Grammar of Spoken Chinese. Berkeley & Los Angeles: University of California Press.

Chafe,Wallace. 1995. The Realis-Irrealis Distinction in Caddo, the Northern Iroquoian Languages, and English. In Bybee and Fleischman (eds.): 349-365.

Chen,Guohua[陈国华].1988.英汉假设条件句比较.《外语教学与研究》，73,10-19.

Comrie,B.1986. Conditionals: A Typology. In Traugott, E.(eds.) On Conditionals, 77-79. Cambridge: Cambridge University Press.

Dahl,Ősten. 1997. The Relation between Past Time Reference and Counterfactuality: a New Look. In A. Athanasiadou & R. Diven(eds.), On Conditionals Again. Amsterdam, Philadelphia: John
Benjamins Publishing Company: 97-114.

Feng,G. & Yi, L. 2006. What if Chinese had Linguistic Markers for Counterfactual Conditionals? Language and Thought Revisited. Conference paper of the 28th Annual Conference of the Cognitive Science Society.

Fleischman,Suzanne. 1989. Temporal distance: A basic linguistic metaphor. Studies in language 13:1–50.

Haiman,John. 1980. Natural Syntax. Cambridge: Cambridge University Press.

Halpert,Claire and Bjorkman, Bronwyn. 2012. In search of (im)perfection: the Illusion of Counterfactual Aspect. In Proceedings of NELS42. GLSA, Amherst, MA.

Iatridou,Sabine. 2000. The Grammatical Ingredients of Counterfactuality. Linguistic Inquiry31:231–270.

Iatridou, Sabine. 2009. Some thoughts about the imperfective in counterfactuals. Handout.

Jiang,Yan(蒋严). 2000. 汉语条件句的违实解释.《语法研究和探索》10，北京：商务印书馆， 257-279.

Jones, Bob.2010. Tense and Aspect in Informal Welsh. Berlin: Hubert & Co. GmbH & Co. KG. Göttingen.

Li,C. & Thompson S.A. 1981. Chinese Chinese: A Functional Reference Grammar. Berkeley: University of California Press.

Liu,L.G. 1985. Reasoning counterfactually in Chinese: Are there any obstacles? Cognition, 21, 239-270.

McGregor,William B. 1996. Nyulnyul. München & Newcastle: Lincom Europa.

McGregor, William B., Wagner, Tamsin, 2006. The semantics and pragmatics of irrealis mood in Nyulnyulan languages. Oceanic Linguistics 45, 339–379.

Nevins, Andrew I. 2002. Counterfactuality without past tense. In Proceedings of NELS 32 ,441–450. GLSA, University of Massachusetts/Amherst.

Ritter,Elizabeth, and Martina Wiltschko. 2010. The Composition of INFL: An exploration of Tense, Tenseless Languages and Tenseless Constructions. LingBuzz/001078, July 2010.

Schachter, Paul, and Otanes, Fe. 1983. Tagalog Reference Grammar. California: University of California Press.

Shi,Yuzhi & Li, Na. 2000. 十五世纪前后的句法变化与现代汉语否定标记系统的形成——否定标记“没（有）”产生的句法背景及语法化过程.语言研究，2：39-63.

Steele,Susan. 1975. Past and Irrealis: Just What Does it All Mean?. National Journal of merican Linguistics 41:200–217.

Su,Y. Y. 2008. Deriving Counterfactuality in Chinese Chinese yaobushi Conditionals. TOM(Toronto-Ottawa-Montreal) Semantic Workshop, University of Toronto, Toronto.

Tang,Ting-chi. 1994. 北平话否定词的语意内涵与出现分布. Studies on Chinese Morphology and Syntax: 5 Taiwan Xuesheng Shuju: 101-119.

Tien,Adrien. 1994. Semantic Primitives in Taiwanese Chinese. [BA Honours thesis, Australian National University.

Wang,Yuying. 2012. The Ingredients of Counterfactuality in Chinese Chinese. PhD. Dissertation of Poly University of Hong Kong.

Wierzbicka,Anna. 1997. Conditionals and Counterfactuals: Conceptual Primitives and Linguistic Universals. In A. Athanasiadou & R. Diven(eds.), On Conditionals Again. Amsterdam, Philadelphia: John Benjamins Publishing Company: 15-60.

Wu,Hsin-feng(吴信风).1994. “If Triangles Were Circles,…”- ‘A Study of Counterfactuals in Chinese and in English’ Taipei: The Crane Publishing Co., Ltd.

Wu,Zhaoyi. 1989. Exploring Counterfactuals in English and Chinese. PhD. Dissertation of University of Massachusatte.

Xing, Fuyi(刑福义).2001.汉语复句研究，北京：商务印书馆.

Yeh,D. & Gentner, D. (2005). Reasoning counterfactually in Chinese: Picking up the pieces. Proceedings of the Twenty-seventh Annual Meeting of the Cognitive Science Society, pp. 2410-2415.

Ziegeler,Debra P. 2000. The Role of Quantity implicatures in the Grammaticalisation of would. Language Science 22:27-61.

Event Sequence Model for Semantic Analysis of Time and Location in Dialogue System

Yasuhiro Noguchi
Faculty of Informatics
Shizuoka University
noguchi@inf.shizuoka.ac.jp

Satoru Kogure
Graduate School of Informatics
Shizuoka University

Makoto Kondo
Graduate School of Informatics
Shizuoka University

Ichiro Kobayashi
Graduate School of Humanities and Sciences,
Ochanomizu University

Hideki Asoh
Intelligent Systems Research Institute,
AIST

Akira Takagi
NLP Research Laboratory

Tatsuhiro Konishi
Graduate School of Informatics
Shizuoka University

Yukihiro Itoh
Shizuoka University

Abstract

It is important for a natural language dialogue system to interpret relations among event concepts appearing in a dialogue. The more complex a dialog becomes, the more essential it becomes for a natural language dialogue system to perform this kind of interpretation. Traditionally, many studies have focused on this problem. Some dialogue systems supported such semantic analysis by using rules and/or models designed for particular scenes involving specific type of dialogue and/or specific problem solving. However, these frameworks require system developers to reconstruct those rules/models even if a slight change is added to the targeted scene. In many cases, their rules/models heavily depend on specific type of dialogue/problem solving, and they do not have high reusability and modularity. Since those rules/models have scene-depending design, they cannot be used to incrementally construct a bigger rule or model. In this research, we focus on a set of event concepts which are usually expected to occur sequentially. In a dialogue, a spoken event concept enables the listeners to guess a sequence of events. The sequence may sometimes be logically inferred, and it may be understood based on general common sense. We believe that a concept model of sequential events can be designed for each bigger event concept that consists of a series of smaller events. Using the sequentiality of the events in the model, a dialogue system can analyze time and location of each event in a dialogue. In this paper, we design a structure of the event sequence model and propose a framework for analyzing time and location of event concepts appearing in a dialogue. We implemented this framework in a dialogue system, and designed some event sequence models. We confirmed that this system could analyze time and location of sequential events without scene-depending rules.

1 Introduction

Natural language understanding by a NLP system requires more than generating semantic representations corresponding to the user's input sentence and adding them into the dialogue context information in the system. The system is also required to interpret the semantic representations generated from the user's input sentences by comparing them with the dialogue context, the situation surrounding the user and the system, and common sense knowledge. Through these analyses, the user's input is correctly/restrictively understood beyond what is explicitly uttered.

In our previous research, we focused on the difficulty for a natural language dialogue system arising from synonymous expressions. The same semantic contents can be conveyed by different expressions with different set of words and different syntactic structures. A natural language dialogue system must obtain the same semantic contents from those synonymous expressions irrespective of their differences. The proposed method of semantic analysis allows us to obtain the same semantic contents from a variety of synonymous expressions (Takagi et al. 2006). We also developed a dialogue system based on this semantic analysis and evaluated the system (Noguchi et al. 2008). According to this framework, meanings of phrases, clauses and sentences are represented by sets of attribute-value pairs. A meaning denoted by a head (noun, verb, etc.) and its modifier is represented by a pair of the corresponding attribute and its value. We also prepared concept hierarchies for super-sub relation and whole-part relation. The concept hierarchies enable semantic comparison between different attributes, entities, or events. Accordingly, the semantic analysis in this framework consists solely of interpretation of attribute-value pairs and comparison of attribute-value pairs, and the dialogue system based on this framework obtains the same semantic contents from various synonymous expressions irrespective of their differences in their words and structures.

Semantic information explicitly conveyed in a dialogue is effectively analyzed by the above method; however, interpretation based on super-sub and whole-part relation is not enough. In this paper, we focus on a set of event concepts which are generally expected to occur sequentially. In a dialogue, a spoken event concept enables the listeners to guess a sequence of events. The sequence may sometimes be logically inferred, and it may be understood based on general common sense. Our purpose is to design a concept model of an event composed of sequential sub-events. We also propose a framework for semantic analysis of time and location based on the sequentiality in the model.

As for related research, Script (Schank and Abelson 1975) is well known for its capability to interpret relations among events involved in a dialogue. In this framework, scene-specific rules are prepared and those rules enable a dialogue system to interpret relations among event concepts in the user's input sentences, the dialogue context, the situation surrounding the user and the system, and common sense knowledge. A plan-based dialogue system (e.g. Chu-Carroll and Carberry 1998) employs a framework in which the dialogue system calculates dialogue strategy to solve the user's problem in a dialogue where a goal of the problem-solving is shared by the user and the system. Oku et al. (2004) propose a dialogue control scheme based on database and topic frames which include task-dependent knowledge. All the three frameworks require prepared task-dependent knowledge with designated structures in order to interpret semantic relations among event concepts appearing in the user's input, the dialogue context, the situation surrounding the user and the system, and common sense knowledge. Accordingly, these frameworks require system developers to reconstruct these scripts, plans or frames even if a light change is added to the dialogue situation. It is practically impossible to prepare enough knowledge to deal with every possible dialogue. Fujiki et al. (2003) propose automatic plan generation from a text corpus. Its capability of plan generation is limited, and the problem of low reusability still remains for script-based natural language understanding systems.

Some approaches have been proposed for task-independent semantic analysis (Iida et al. 2003) (Yoshimura et al. 2009) (Hayashibe et al. 2011). Unlike script-based approaches, these approaches do not deal with dialogue structure. A dialogue without a specific goal can be supported by these approaches, but they do not have enough semantic analysis for supporting task-oriented dialogues.

Tamano and Matsumoto (1996) and Noro et al. (2007) focus on time identification and time inference of sequential events based on natural language expressions in the context. These studies did not focus on preparing knowledge description of a set of event concepts which are generally expected to occur sequentially.

In linguistic fields, the discourse representation theory (Partee 1984) (Kamp and Reyle 1993) deals with dialogue structure. These theory organized the roles of tense and aspect forms for discourse representation structures including time representations. However these discourse representation structures are sometimes analyzed by hand. These approaches do not focus their computational realization for supporting task-oriented dialogues.

The purpose of this research is to design a general concept model of an event composed of sequential sub-events in such a way that the model does not depend on specific scenes or goals. In this paper, we design the general event sequence model and two specific event sequence models ("trip" event and "stay" event) based on the general model. We also propose a framework for analyzing time and location of sequential events in a dialogue. We implemented this framework in a dialogue system, and confirmed that this system could analyze time and location without scene-specific rules.

2 Event Sequence Model

2.1 Basic Concept of Event Sequence Model

An event concept in natural language input invokes a set of event concepts which are generally expected to occur sequentially. In the sequence consisting of a set of event concepts, we often understand time/location of one event by referring to time/location of the preceding or following event. Such mutual reference between two sequential events goes beyond mutual reference through super-sub/whole-part relation. For example, consider "I went to Hamamatsu city. I stayed in the Hamamatsu Hotel.". The "go" and the "stay" are different event concepts and these event concepts do not have super-sub/whole-part relation in a general concept hierarchy. In understanding these event concepts, however, we need mutual references to semantic information between the "goal" attribute of the "go" event concept and the "location" attribute of the "stay" event concept. The mutual reference is explained based on the following knowledge.

- A "go" event concept and a "stay" event concept have whole-part relationship with a "trip" event concept when the "go" event and the "stay" event are partial events of the "trip" event.
- When the "stay" event occurs after the "go" event, the "goal" attribute of the "go" event concept restricts the "location" attribute of the "stay" event concept and vice versa.

It is necessary for a natural language dialogue system to support the semantic analysis of this sort. In section 2, we discuss how sequential events should be structured and propose a general event sequence model and twin specific event sequence models based on the general model. Section 3 deals with how to perform semantic analysis based on specific event sequence models. Section 4 provides demonstration of our dialog system based on the framework to be proposed. The final section summarizes what has been achieved and what remains to be achieved.

2.2 Design Requirement of Event Sequence Model

To discuss the design requirements of the event sequence model, we focus on "trip" event concept and its related event concepts. The reason to focus on these event concepts is that "trip"-related tasks are popular in many studies about a dialogue system. In a dialogue with "trip"-related tasks, the user frequently refers to the time and location of event concepts. The purpose of this research is definitely not to design a specific model for the "trip" event concept. Therefore we should carefully design the structure of the event sequence model so that the model can be applied to a wide variety of event concepts. We should examine if the event sequence model to be proposed can be applied to many other event concepts than what is discussed in this paper. However, that is beyond the scope of this paper and we leave it for the future work.

We collected dialogue histories of hotel search/reservation dialogue systems, travel reports published on web sites, and so on. From the collected contents, we chose 62 contents which involve frequent reference to the time and location of event concepts. These contents include 399 sentences. We analyzed event concepts in the sentences and confirmed that proper interpretation of the contents requires us to assume the existence of a series of events not explicitly conveyed in the contents. We found some properties of sequential events and restrictions on the event sequence model imposed by those properties. In this section, we summarize the design requirements and conditions for the event sequence model.

In the collected contents, even events of the same type involve a wide variety of sequential events. For example, it depends on the dialogue situation whether a "trip" event contains a "stay" event as its partial event. Similarly some "trip" events include "taking a hot spring bath" or "visiting a tourist place", and others do not. If a "trip" event contains a "work" event, the "trip" event should be interpreted as a "business-trip" event and not as a "sightseeing-trip" event.

As we have just mentioned, a wide variety of "trip" event instances are made up of different combination of partial events. In addition, the chronological order of some of the partial events totally depends on the dialogue situation. It means that "(a) we cannot predefine a set and the order of partial events constituting the event sequence model in a static manner as in 'E0, E1, E2, ..., En'". A "whole" event (e.g. "trip" event) restricts the variations of its partial events. It means "(b) a set of possible partial event concepts can be defined for a specific event sequence model". Although we cannot predefine the order of all the partial events, we can still read the order of those partial events from a given content. It means "(c) an instance of a specific event sequence model should be dynamically created based on the event concepts appearing in a dialogue."

In some of the collected contents, the existence of some events are presupposed even if the events are not explicitly expressed in the contents. For example, when "taking a hot spring bath" exists as a part of a "trip" event, a "go" event must exist as a part of the "trip" event, and the value of the "goal" attribute in the implicit "go" event concept must coincide with the "location" attribute of the "hot spring bath" concept. It means "(d) when a whole event concept is conveyed or when a whole event concept is invoked from some related event concepts, a dialogue system should behave as if other event concepts essential for the explicit event concepts were conveyed in the dialogue context; hence, the structure of the event sequence model is required to define essential event concepts for the whole event concept."

A whole event concept is sometimes composed of multiple occurrences of the same type of event concept. Suppose for example that there are "a trip from A to B.", "a trip from B to C." and "a trip from C to D." in a dialogue. We can refer to each "trip" event concept as a "trip", and we can also refer to the entire event concept binding up the smaller "trip" event concepts as a "trip" as in "How much is the total cost of the trip?" It means that "(e) an event sequence model for a whole event concept includes the whole event concept itself as a part of the whole event concept."

Proper interpretation of the collected contents sometimes requires inference of the time/location of an event even if they are not explicitly expressed in the contents. The inference can be drawn from the sequentiality of the event and the preceding/following event. It means that "(f) mutual reference to semantic information between two sequential event concepts based on the spatio-temporal sequence should be defined."

Many of the collected contents contains more than one event concept each of which invokes a different series of partial events. Therefore, "(g) the framework for the event sequence model should determine how to achieve mutual reference to semantic information between different event sequences."

The discussions above are summarized in the following design requirements and conditions for the event sequence model.

(a) We cannot predefine a set and the order of partial events constituting the event sequence model in a static manner as in "E0, E1, E2, ..., En".
(b) A set of possible partial event concepts can be defined for a specific event sequence model.
(c) An instance of a specific event sequence model should be dynamically created based on the event concepts appearing in a dialogue.
(d) When a whole event concept is conveyed or when a whole event concept is invoked from some related event concepts, a dialogue system should behave as if other event concepts essential for the explicit event concepts were conveyed in the dialogue context; hence, the structure of the event sequence model is required to define essential event concepts for the whole event concept.
(e) An event sequence model for a whole event concept includes the whole event concept itself as a part of the whole event concept.
(f) Mutual reference to semantic information between two sequential event concepts based on the spatio-temporal sequence should be defined.
(g) The framework for the event sequence model should determine how to achieve mutual reference to semantic information between different event sequences.

2.3 Structure of Event Sequence Model

Figure 1 shows the general structure of event sequence models based on requirements (a-g) discussed in previous section.

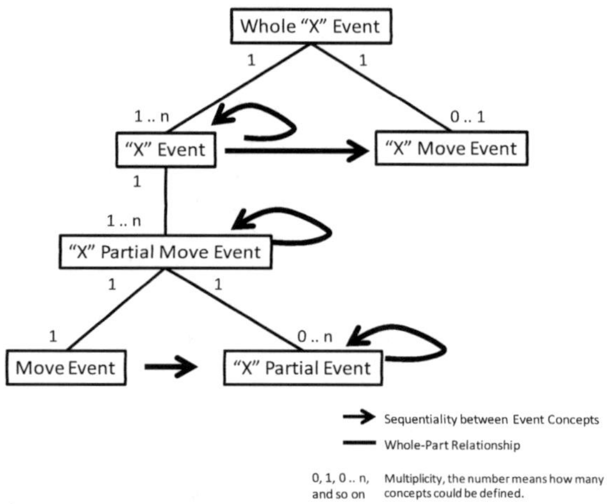

Figure 1. General Structure of Event Sequence Model

As for the requirement (e), we designed a 4 -layered whole-part relationship tree structure as the general structure of the event sequence model. In this model, the multiplicity definitions at both ends of a whole-part relation line mean how many concepts are possibly defined at the ends. Each event sequence model according to an event is defined based on this general structure by each word concept as Figure 2. "X" in Figure 1 is transferred to the name of each event concept.

In this framework for the requirement (a) and (c), an instance of an event sequence model is dynamically created based on the event concepts appearing in a dialogue. The "X Partial Event" in Figure 1 means that a set of event concepts is possible to be a part of the "X Event", discussed in requirement (b). For example, a set of "Trip Partial Event" concepts includes "eat", "sightseeing", "drive", and so on.

The arrow line in Figure 1 means the sequentiality between two events for the requirement (f). For example, the arrow line from "Move Event" to "X Partial Event" means that an "X Partial Event" will be occurred after the "Move event". In Figure 2, "Trip Event" has the sequentiality with "Return Event", and next "Trip Event".

The general structure of the event sequence model expressly includes the "Move Event" because each event concept, in general, has the "location" attribute. In this structure, every "X Partial Event" with changing its location accompanies "Move Event" before it. A "X Partial Move Event" bounds a pair of a "Move Event" and arbitrary number of "X Partial Event" concepts. This pair can define a partial event sequence that arbitrary number of events involved in a set of "X Partial Event" occur after the "Move Event".

Figure 3 is an example of the instance of the event sequence model for "trip" event in Figure 3. This instance is created by "trip advisory" dialogue. As a dialogue continues, an event concept used in the dialogue is judges whether it is capable to join the existing instance of the event sequence model or not. If the event concept can join to the existing instance, the event concept is joined as a "X Partial Event" in the existing instance. If the event concept cannot join to the existing instance, the instance should be extended. For example, as a new "trip" event, the "Trip Event 2", the "Trip Partial Event 2_1", the "Move Event 2_1" are created in Figure 4. After that, the "Attend Event" is joined as the "Trip Partial Event" after the "Move Event 2_1".

The other sequentiality of two event concepts depends on the type of the event concepts. When the event sequence model for an whole event is defined, the sequentiality between the essential partial events for the whole event are expressly defined. In Figure 4, "check-in" and "check-out" events are essential partial events for the "stay" event, and the sequentiality between them are defined.

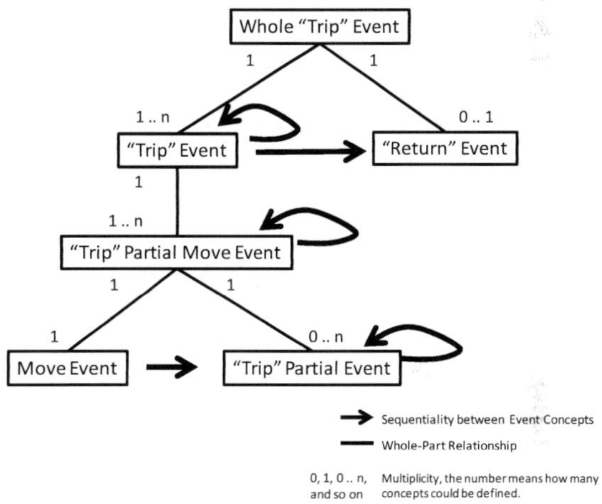

Figure 2. Example of Event Sequence Model of "trip" Event

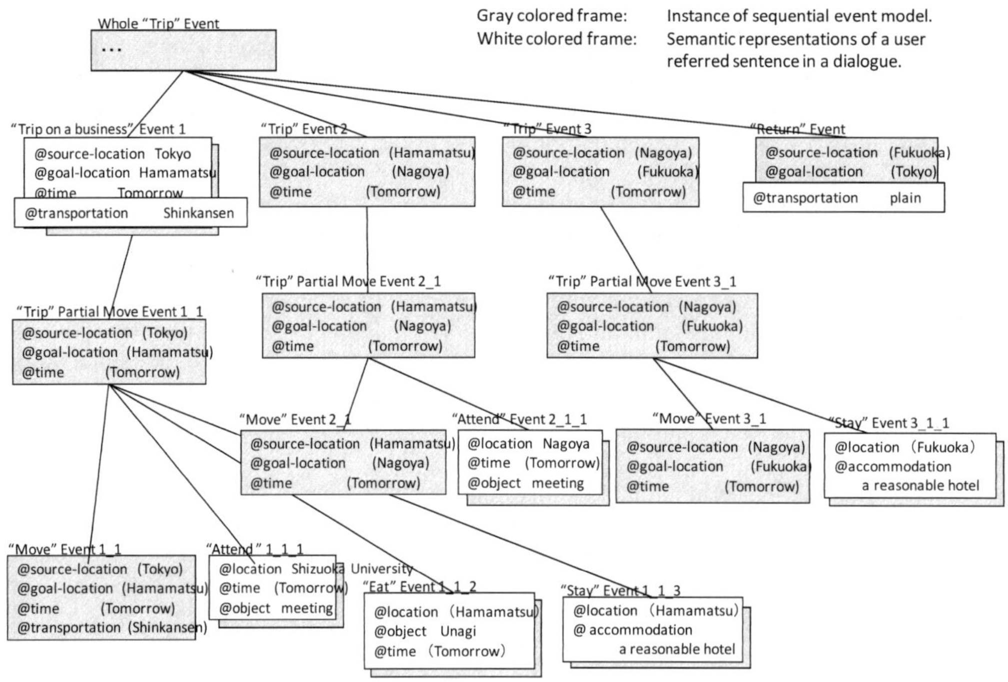

Figure 3. Instance of Event Sequence Model (e.g. "trip advisory" dialogue)

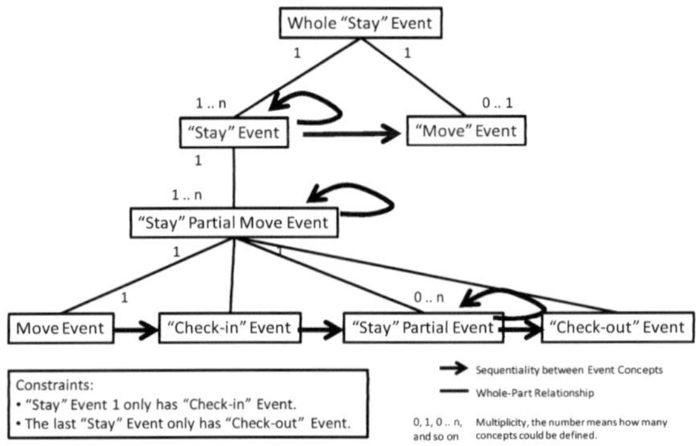

Figure 4. Example of Event Sequence Model of "stay" Event

As for the requirement (d), some event concepts are presupposed in a dialogue, even if the event concepts are not explicitly expressed in the dialogue. From the analysis of the collected context, some event concepts are usually known as essential partial event concepts for their whole event. In Figure 4, "check-in" and "check-out" events are essential partial events for the "stay" event. The dialogue system with this framework should presuppose these essential events and structural essential events of the event sequence model like "Move Event", "Stay Partial Move Event", "Stay Event", and "Whole Stay Event".

3 Semantic Analysis with Event Sequence Model

3.1 Semantic Analysis in Event Sequence Model

In this section, we explain a method in a instance of an event sequence model based on the requirement (f) discussed in previous section.

In an event sequence model, we defined two types of relationship between event concepts: whole-part relationship and sequentiality between two events. Following mutual references of semantic information are applied to two events which have whole-part relationship. These references must be restricted their semantic information to ensure consistency of time and location in the whole instance of the event sequence model.

- The value of the "location" attribute or the "goal-location" attribute in a partial event is restricted to the part of the value of correspondent attribute in the whole event.
- The value of the "time" attribute is restricted to the part of the value of correspondent attribute in the whole event.

These results of semantic analysis are used for the restrictions to judge whether an event concept could join the existing instance of an event sequence model or not, discussed in previous section. The value of "location" attribute of "Attend Event 2_1_1" in Figure 3 is restricted based on the value of "location" or "goal-location" attribute of "Trip Partial Event 2_1". The "Trip Partial Move Event 2_1" is simultaneously restricted based on the "Trip Event 2". In Figure 3, when the user explicitly expressed his/her business trip to "Hamamatsu" city, the value of the "location" attribute of the "Attend Event 2_1_1" is restricted on the part of "Hamamatsu" city. It enable the dialogue system to identify the location of the meeting, and to presuppose the "attend" event.

Based on the sequentiality between two events in an event sequence model, following references are applied to ensure consistency of time and location in the whole instance of the event sequence model.

- The value of the "location" attribute or the attribute "source-location" in an event at the origin of an arrow line is semantically restricted by the value of the "location" attribute or the "goal-location" attribute in an event at the end of the arrow line, regardless of difference of the type of event concepts.
- The value of the "time" attribute in an event at the end of an arrow line is semantically restricted around the same time or future time of the value of the "time" attribute in an event at the origin of the arrow line.

The sequentiality among the "Trip Event 1", "Trip Event 2", "Trip Event 3" and "Return Event" in Figure 3 restricted their "time" attribute and "location" attribute. The value of the "goal-location" attribute in the "Trip Event 1" restricted the value of the "location" attribute in the "Trip Event 2". In the "Trip Event 2", "Trip Event 3", "Trip Event 3", and "Return Event", same kinds of restrictions are applied.

3.2 Semantic Analysis between Event Sequence Models

In this section, we explain a semantic analysis method among multiple event sequence models in a dialogue based on the requirement (g) discussed in previous section. The result for analyzing collected contents indicated the requirements of following operations as Figure 5 when more than 1 instances of event sequence models in a dialogue.

- When some events are shared in among multiple event sequence models, the semantic information of these events are mutual referred from these event sequence models.
- An event is occurred at the point on the event sequence of the other event sequence model. The sequentiality including the event is dynamically generated, when the event has enough semantic information to determine the sequence where the event occurs.

When the user expressed an event which is capable to join both event sequence models in a dialogue, in each event sequence model, the relations with the event and the existing event sequence model are interpreted as section 3.1. The event which joined both event sequence models (as dark gray colored frame in Figure 5) shared the mutual references of semantic information. If the consistency of these event sequence models including the shared event could not be ensured, the capability that the event concept joined into both event sequence models should be rejected. If the consistency of them could be ensured, the events of "Check-in", "Bath", "Sleep", "Eat" and "Buy" have similar sequentiality that these events occurred after "Move Event" and before "Check-out Event". The sequence of them will be determined by more detailed semantic information explicitly expressed by the user. It is also important for a dialogue system to tentatively suppose the sequence to decide next system's behavior based on the result of semantic analysis.

There are logically following relationships among the event sequence models defined by the requirement (b).

(A) The instances of event sequence models are subset/superset relationship.

(B) The instances of event sequence models have intersection.

(C) The instances of event sequence models do not have intersection (all instances of an event sequence model are occurred before/after all instances of the other event sequence model).

In case (A) and (B), an event is capable to be simultaneously both sequences of some event sequence models. A natural language processing system should determine the order of the event on the sequentiality of event sequence models. Current implementation demonstrated in section 0, the implemented system determines the order of the event concept based on the consistency of time and location of the sequentiality in the event sequence models.

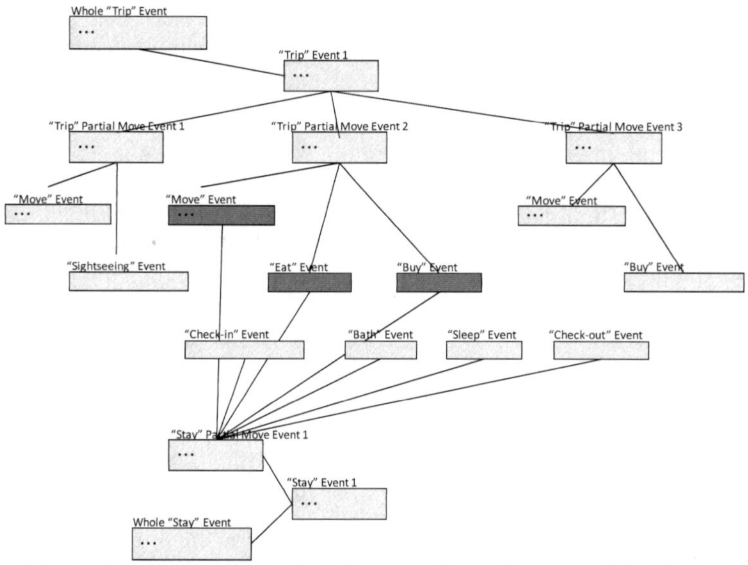

Figure 5. Model for Semantic Analysis between Event Sequence Models in a Dialogue

4 Demonstration

We implemented a framework for a semantic analysis method using event sequence models in a dialogue system. We defined some event sequence models according to event concepts appearing in "trip advisory" dialogues. Figure 6 shows an example of dialogue with this dialogue system, and Figure 7 shows the extracted part of instances of event sequence models generated in this dialogue.

In the dialogue in Figure 6, "trip" event concept and "stay" event concept invoke the instances of these event sequence models like Figure 5. The underlined system's replies are generated using these models.

When the user would like to eat unagi (cooked eel) in "Unahamaken (a restaurant)", the instance of "Move Event 1_2" and others are created to keep the consistency of the location which is changed from "Shizuoka University" to "Unahamaken". So, the dialogue system can identify that the user must be going to move from "Shizuoka University" to "Unahamaken" and can intend to give the travel time from Shizuoka University to "Unahamaken" to the user.

U	asu, hamamatsu-ni syucho shimasu. (I will travel to hamamatsu city tommorrow for business.)
S	kashikomari-mashita. goyoken-ha? (OK. Do you have a requests?)
U	"Shizudai"-de uchiawase-wo shimasu. ato, unagi-wo tabe-tai. (I'll have a meeting in Shizuoka University. I want to eat unagi at lunch.)
S	"Unahamaken"-ga osusume-desu. Shizudai-kara basu-de 5 fun-de yukemasu. unajyu jo-dato 2,800 yen desu. (I suggest you "Unahamaken". You can go there from Shizuoka University for 5 minutes by bus. Unajyu jo is 2,800 yen.)
U	wakarimashita. yasui hotel-ni tomaritai no dake-do. (I see. Could you tell me a reasonable hotel?)
S	hamamatsueki-mae-no ippaku 4,800 yen no "Hotel Hamana"-ha ikagadesu-ka? ("Hotel Hamana" near Hamamatsu station is 4,800 yen by a day.)
U	arigatou. soko-ni tomarimasu. sore-to "Station Hotel"-de 7:00-ni Sato-san-to yusyoku-wo torimasu. (Thanks. I'll stay there. I'll got dinner with Mr. Sato in Station Hotel.)
S	"Hotel Hamana"-kara "Station Hotel"-heha toho-de 5 fun desu. "Hotel Hamana"-no checkin-ha 6:30-de yoi-desune. (You can go Station Hotel from Hotel Hamana on walk for 5 minutes. The time of check-in in Hotel Hamana is 6:30 p.m., isn't it?)
U	arigatou. yokujitsu-ha, nagoya-de kaigi-ni sanka shite-kara, fukuoka-ni mou ippaku shimasu. (OK. Next day, I have a meeting in Nagoya city, and stay in Fukuoka city.)
S	wakari-mashita. fukuokaeki-mae ippaku 5,600 yen no "Fukufukutei"-ga osusume desu. (I see. I suggest "Fukufukutei" on the front of Fukuoka station whose price is 5,600 yen by a day.)
U	arigatou. (Thanks.)

Figure 6. Dialogue Example with Implemented Dialogue System

When the system suggested "Hotel Hamana" to the user, the instance of "stay" event sequence model are created. When the user told the system that the user have an appointment to take dinner with Mr. Sato in the Station Hotel, the "Trip Partial Event 1_3" and its branches are created. The part of the forth layer (bottom layer) instances of "stay" model are located between "Eat Event 1_2_1" and "Move Event 1_3". As another interpretations, the part of the forth layer instances of "stay" model could be located after "Eat Event 1_1_1". In this case, the former interpretations were tentatively adopted by the system. These instances are set mutual references based on sequentiality among the "Eat Event 1_2_1", the "Move Event 1_1", the "Check-in Event 1_1_1", the "Move Event 1_3" and the "Eat Event 1_3_1". The "Move Event 1_3" enables the system to intend to give the travel time from the "Hotel Hamana" to the Station Hotel to the user. The "Check-in Event 1_1_1" enables the system to intend to confirm the user's check-in time to the "Hotel Hamana".

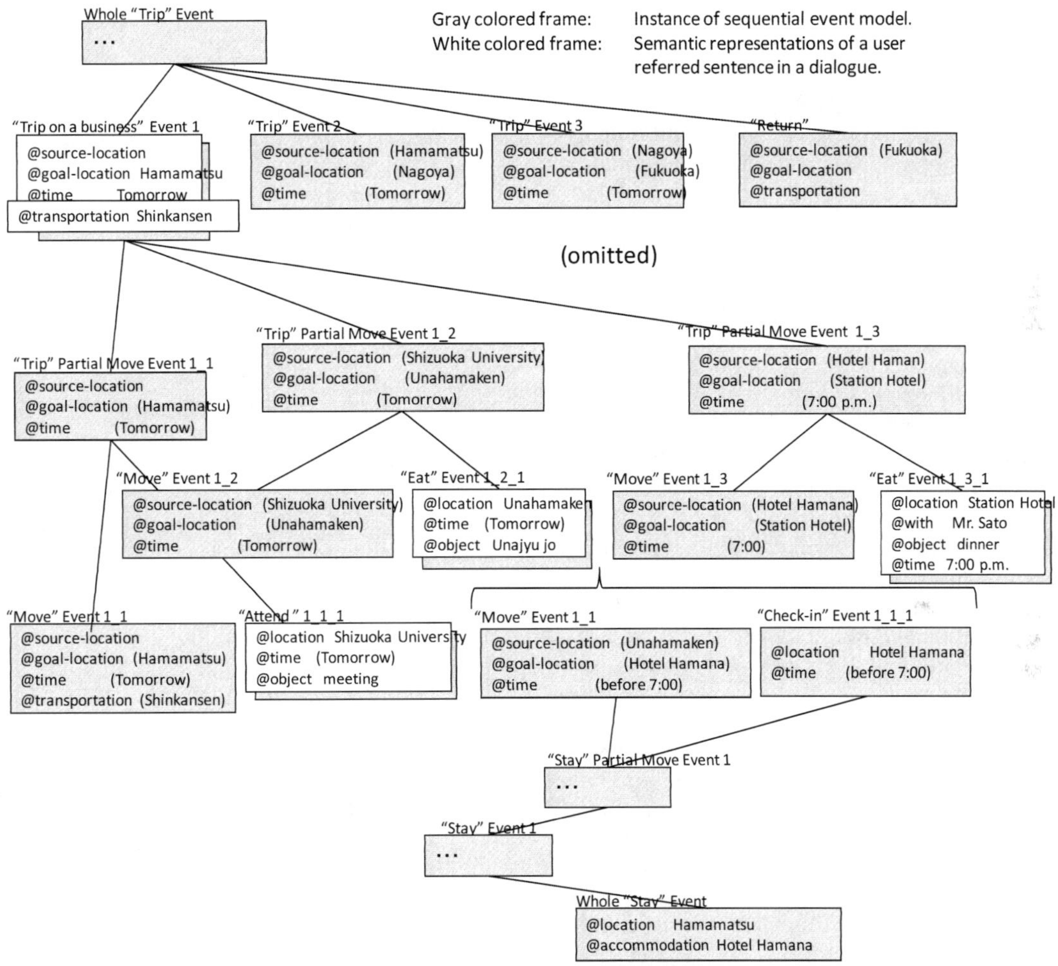

Figure 7. Extracted Instances of Event Sequence Models on the Dialogue Example

5 Conclusion

This paper described the design of the general event sequence model and two specific event sequence models ("trip" event and "stay" event) based on the general model. We also propose a framework for analyzing time and location of sequential events in a dialogue. We implemented this framework in a dialogue system, and confirmed that this system could analyze time and location without scene-specific rules.

We analyzed "trip" event contents to design the general event sequence model. These contents were collected from hotel search/reservation dialogues, travel reports on web sites and so on. We think that the high applicability of the suggested event sequence model was not enough to be confirmed. Especially for many event sequence models exist in a dialogue. In this paper, we demonstrated with "trip" and some other event concepts however the demonstrated event sequence models are subset/superset relationship. The instance of event sequence models with intersection and without intersection are not demonstrated. As future works, the applicability of the suggested models with these conditions should be evaluated. Naturally, it is necessary to evaluate even more event concepts in many varieties of dialogues.

References

A. Takagi, H. Asoh, Y. Itoh, M. Kondo and I. Kobayashi. 2006. Semantic Representation for Understanding Meaning Based on Correspondence between Meanings, Journal of Advanced Computational Intelligence and Intelligent Informatics, 10(6): 876-912.

Y. Noguchi, Y. Ikegaya, S. Kogure, M. Kondo, H. Asoh, I. Kobayashi, T. Konishi, A. Takagi and Y. Itoh. 2008. Construction and Evaluation of a Dialog System Based on Mapping Sentence Meanings to the Dialog Context, Journal of Japan Society for Fuzzy Theory and Intelligent Informatics, 20(5): 732-756. (in Japanese)

R. C. Schank and R. P. Abelson. 1975. Scripts, plans, and knowledge, Proceedings of the 4th international joint conference on Artificial intelligence, 1:151-157.

J. Chu-Carroll and S. Carberry. 1998. Collaborative Response Generation in Planning Dialogues, Computational Linguistics, 24(3): 355-400.

T. Oku, T. Nishimoto, M. Araki and Y. Niimi. 2004. A task-independent control method for spoken dialogs, Systems and Computers in Japan, 35(14):87-95. (in Japanese)

E. Yoshimura, S. Tsuchiya and H. Watabe. 2009. A Method of Association Response Based on Commonsense in Chatting System, Forum on Information Technology, 8(2):303-306. (in Japanese)

R. Iida, K. Inui, H. Takamura and Y. Matsumoto. 2003. Incorporating contextual cues in trainable models for coreference resolution, Proceedings of the 10th EACL Workshop on the Computational Treatment of Anaphora, 23-30. (in Japanese)

Y. Hayashibe, M. Komachi and Y. Matusmoto. 2011. Improving Japanese Inter-sentential Predicate Argument Structure Analysis with Contextual Information and Similarity between Case Structures, IPSJ SIG-SLP, 2011-SLP-86(10):1-8. (in Japanese)

T. Fujiki, H. Nanba and M. Okumura. 2003. Automatic acquisition of script knowledge from a text collection, Proceedings of the tenth conference on European chapter of the Association for Computational Linguistics, 2:91-94.

K. Tamano and Y. Matsumoto. 1996. A study of constraint based description of temporal structure, IPSJ SIG-NL, 115(2):9-14.

T. Noro, K. Inui, H. Takamura and M. Okumura. 2007. Time Period Identification of Events in Text, IPSJ, 48(10):3405-3414. (in Japanese)B. Partee. 1984. Nominal and temporal anaphora, Linguistic and Philosophy, 7, 243-286.

H. Kamp and U. Reyle. 1993. Form Discourse to Logic. Kluwer.

#Irony or #Sarcasm— A Quantitative and Qualitative Study Based on Twitter

Po-Ya Angela Wang
Graduate Institute of Linguistics, National Taiwan University, Taiwan
3F,Le-Xue Building, No.1, Sec.4,Roosevelt Road, Taipei Taiwan
r01142009@ntu.edu.tw

Abstract

Current study is with the aim to identify similarities and distinctions between irony and sarcasm by adopting quantitative sentiment analysis as well as qualitative content analysis. The result of quantitative sentiment analysis shows that sarcastic tweets are used with more positive tweets than ironic tweets. The result of content analysis corresponds to the result of quantitative sentiment analysis in identifying the aggressiveness of sarcasm. On the other hand, from content analysis it shows that irony owns two senses. The first sense of irony is equal to aggressive sarcasm with speaker awareness. Thus, tweets of first sense of irony may attack a specific target, and the speaker may tag his/her tweet irony because the tweet itself is ironic. These tweets though tagged as irony are in fact sarcastic tweets. Different from this, the tweets of second sense of irony is tagged to classify an event to be ironic. However, from the distribution in sentiment analysis and examples in content analysis, irony seems to be more broadly used in its second sense.

1 Introduction

Philosophers and rhetoricians have been interested in irony and sarcasm for over 2500 years (Katz, 2000). In recent years, irony and sarcasm have been popular issues discussed qualitatively and quantitatively. Being a special way of language creativity, irony and sarcasm provide the opportunity to explore the interaction between cognition and language. Many frameworks have been proposed to illustrate the mechanisms underlying, such as Echoic Mention (Sperber and Wilson, 1981, 1986), Echoic Reminder (Kreuz and Glucksberg, 1989), Allusional Pretense (Kumon-Nakamura et al., 1995), Pretense (Clark and Gerrig, 1984), Standard Pragmatic Model (Grice,1975; Searle, 1978), Traditional Oppositional Model reviewed by Clift (1999), and Framing and Footing (Clift, 1999). Empirical psycholinguistic studies are also conducted to understand what should be recognized as irony or sarcasm from hearer angle. Computational linguistics have devoted in related studies in order to develop refined machine program in detecting human˘s real intention that is coated by used words.

Though many insightful works have been done, current study is still with the intention to further explore this issue. The quantitative sentiment analysis and qualitative content analysis are adopted in probing the similarities and distinctions between irony and sarcasm. Current study provides another angle to understand irony and sarcasm by adopting both qualitative and quantitative methodology in exploring this issue from speakers˘ performance in a different genre, internet language.

2 Literature Review

Irony is a term used to describe unscrupulous trickery in its Greek term *eironeia*. Sarcasm, on the other hand, means to speak bitterly, and to tear flesh like dogs in its Greek word origin *sarazein*. (Katz, 2000). The two seem to be slightly different in their meanings from word origin; however, with the progress of language using, how these two terms reflect different cognition and language creativity as well as how language is achieved to this creativity is worth of further discussion. In this section, scetion2.1 and section 2.2 would separately introduce previous qualitatively and quantitatively studies. Section

2.3 would illustrate the research question in current study.

2.1 Previous Qualitative Studies on Irony or Sarcasm

There are many frameworks in accounting the mechanism of ironic effects. The review from Clift (1999) on the Traditional Oppositional Model (TOM) has critically pointed out the advantage of TOM locates at its illustration in the divergence between a speaker˘s words, and what he/she might mean by his/her words. However, this two-stage mechanism is criticized for ignoring the fact that two aspects of meaning must be perceived simultaneously to make an utterance as irony. Correspondingly, the Echoic / Interpretation model (Sperber and Wilson, 1981, 1986) is also criticized because the model claims that listeners process only what the ironic meaning, not the literal meaning the speaker said. Another echoic account is the `Echoic Reminder_ (Kreuz and Glucksberg, 1989; Colston, 1997). In this account rather than directly mentioning another person˘s comments, a speaker can mention generally accepted beliefs about a situation, like a social norm, to remind the addressee of those beliefs when they have not showed up in the ongoing situation. On the other hand, Kumon-Nakamura et al. (1995) has proposed that irony is achieved by directly mentioning part of the expected situation that actually has occurred, when the remaining part of the expected situation has been violated. Colston (2000) has evaluated previous accounts and partially agreed that the two conditions for verbal irony comprehension are the violation on expectation, and the pragmatically insincere, the `counterfactual_, `insincere_ or `contrary_ relationship between what is uttered and what is ironically intended. This pragmatically insincere also echoes to the divergence of speaker intention and utterance form proposed by TOM. Though Colston has proposed counter examples in pointing the limitations of these two mechanisms˘ accountability, the examples proposed are still worth more discussion because they do not take the real conversation context, and the speakers˘ real intentions into consideration.

The results from reviewed previous qualitative content analysis are based on the analytic induction from observations. Though the proposed frameworks, Echoic Mention (Sperber and Wilson, 1981, 1986), Echoic Reminder (Kreuz and Glucksberg, 1989), Allusional Pretense (Kumon-Nakamura et al., 1995), Pretense (Clark and Gerrig, 1984), Standard Pragmatic Model (Grice,1975; Searle, 1978), Traditional Oppositional Model reviewed by Clift (1999), and Framing and Footing (Clift, 1999), all reflect the mechanisms that achieve ironic effects, they are limited in several ways. First, what they mainly concentrate on is irony. There is less illustration on the subtle distinct between irony and sarcasm. Second, each of the account is limited in the type(s) of irony that they can account. Third, the focus is mainly on how the interaction in communication reaches the effect of irony, but how the hearers perceive or process irony and sarcasm, or how the speakers deliver ironic or sarcastic messages need to further explore. Fourth, though Colston (2000) has not directly identified this fact, but from the comparison chart Colston has made, it shows that each framework can just illustrate certain type of irony, so instead of focusing on discussion frameworks, it would be more inspiring to explore the mechanisms operated in these two types of linguistic devices first.

Though rarely studies have been done in understanding the distinctive features between irony and sarcasm, the insightful observation from the footnotes of Clift (1999) indicates that speaker intention plays an important role; however, from the discussion in her footnotes, the two concepts seems to be overlapped because though sarcasm is defined as the hostile false words the speaker is aware of when uttering out, irony could be the false words the speaker may be aware of, or may be not aware of. Clift has claimed that sarcasm is one type of irony that is aggressive. The overlapped area, speaker awareness, implied from Clift˘s footnote seems to explain why previous studies reviewed by Clift(1999) tend to take the hostility of sarcasm as the attribute of irony. To briefly sum up, from Clift˘s point it seems that `irony_ has two senses: in one sense it is an umbrella term that covers sarcasm. In another sense it is the linguistics creative device featured with unawareness and no aggressiveness in speaker intention. Whether the speaker is aware of or not and whether the utterance involves aggressive emotion or not should be further examined from speaker angle.

2.2 Previous Quantitative Studies on Irony or Sarcasm

Quantitative Studies in its controllable designs provide another point of view to understand the issue of irony and sarcasm. The rich quantitative experimental investigations provide chances to control complicated linguistic variables in order to precisely perceive more straightforward relationship between the factors underlying the operation of irony and sarcasm. The quantitative studies can be discussed from two directions, psycholinguistic studies and computational linguistics.

In psycholinguistic studies, the designed materials or neurological equipment are used to measure the hypothesis formed on irony or on sarcasm (Gibbs, 1986; Bryant and Tree, 2002; McDonald, 2002; Bowes and Katz 2011). For example, what Clift (1999) has proposed as simultaneous processing on both literal and non-literal meanings in ironic statement has gained support from experimental studies (Schwoebel, Dews, Winner and Srinivas 2000). Besides, hostility as the feature to distinguish sarcasm from irony is testified in study conducted from Lee and Katz (1998). However, the pretense theory of verbal irony has not been supported much in some experimental designs (Gibbs and O˜Brien,1991).

In computational linguistics (Burfootand and Baldwin, 2009; González-Ibáñez et al., 2011; Reyes et al., 2013), huge data processing on Internet language provides the opportunity to retrieve the features in irony and sarcasm directly as well as to practically apply the results in machine learning. The motivation to study irony and sarcasm is often originated from the interest in opinion mining in product reviews in order to understand the evaluation from users. Though multimodal approach has been adopted, the popular methodology that has been widely used is sentiment analysis´ to detect the positive and negative emotion words used to understand what the messages conveyed is positive or negative. The investigation on irony and sarcasm has been richly discussed because as Bowes and Katz (2011) stated, `When an individual is sarcastic or ironic, he or she is expressing a sentiment (often superficially positive) but intending the opposite._ This divergence in ironic and sarcastic utterance would cause difficulty in machine opinion detection.

However, the psycholinguistic studies focus more on retrieving hearers˘ comprehension to ironic and sarcastic statement because the participants are the recipients of the presented designed materials. Second, the materials manipulated do not include all types of irony and sarcasm. For example, the materials Lee and Katz (1998) designed are descriptions on events with direct echoic remark to previous statement, though the form of irony and sarcasm is clear; however, the application of the results may only limited to this form of irony and sarcasm. Kreuz (2000) has pointed out that psycholinguistic researchers focus more on `top-down_ strategy in studying irony by manipulating key phrases in materials, instead of studying verbal irony `in the wild._ Thus, complementary studies are needed to form the whole picture and to include other variety of the phenomenon. On the other hand, in computational linguistics irony and sarcasm are lack of quantitative distinction, but are viewed as the same in data processing (Elena 2012), which may with the danger that the true intention of the speakers on their opinions may be wrongly captured because psychological studies (Lee and Katz 1998) and qualitative study (Clift 1999) have discovered that sarcasm is the real aggressive one, but irony is not necessarily meant to attack.

2.3 Research Question

Given the fact that reviewed qualitative studies focus more on the interaction in communication, the reviewed psycholinguistic studies pay more attention on hearers˘ understanding to designed materials, and the reviewed computational linguistic studies do not distinguish irony and sarcasm, current studies would like to probe this issue from speaker angle in wild data from both qualitative and quantitative directions. The purpose of current study and the reason to take Twitter as the research target are illustrated in following discussion.

The Purpose is To Explore Features of Irony and Sarcasm: Current study is going to explore the features of irony and sarcasm from four questions, which are based on the claims and results from Clift (1999) and Lee and Katz (1998). The approaches adopted to answer these questions are content analysis and sentiment analysis on retrieved data. The four questions to be solved in current study are: (1) Is sarcasm more aggressive than irony? (2) Is there a specific target attacked in sarcasm, but not in irony? (3) Is the tweeter aware of his/her sarcastic or ironic tweets? (4) Are there any overlapped features between sarcasm and irony? The first question is going to be evaluated by sentiment analysis, and the later three questions are going to be evaluated by content analysis.

The first question is that Clift as well as Lee and Katz have pointed out that sarcasm owns aggressiveness, but irony does not. Based on the basic idea pointed by Bowes and Katz (2011), `When an individual is sarcastic or ironic, he or she is expressing a sentiment (often superficially positive) but intending the opposite,_ the formal sentiment characteristic of sarcasm and irony is going to be explored in current study. To put the hypothesis in more detailed, given the fact that sarcasm is being identified as more aggressive than irony, the sentiment score in it should be more positive.

The second question is based on Lee and Katz (1998). Their study is conducted by asking participants to judge the degree of goodness of the examples to be ironic or sarcastic. The results have shown that sarcasm is with a specific target to attack, but irony is not. Given the fact that the result comes from audience˘s judgment, it is with interest to understand this issue from the speakers˘ angle, the tweeter.

The third question is based on Clift (1999) who claims that in irony the speaker may or may not be aware of false words he/she uttered, but the speaker is always aware of his/her own sarcastic utterance. The awareness of speaker can be identified by analyzing the contents of the tweets tagged with irony or sarcasm. If a speaker is aware of his/her false words, then the tag should be used in order to identify his/her own utterance stated in the tagged tweets is ironic or sarcastic because to tag a thing is to be aware of its quality; however, if the tweeter is unaware of his/her false words, then what is being tagged should not be his/her own utterance, but at this moment the tweeter is at the audience˘s angle to evaluate a thing as being ironic or sarcastic. This is what Clift (1999) has pointed as `To be ironic, a speaker need not be aware that his words are :false˘ ¯ it is sufficient that his interlocutors or his audience be aware of thisŭ .,_ thus the content of the tagged tweets should be the description on an event because the tag is just the revelation of the judgment from the tweeter. Namely, the speaker˘s intention revealed in the tag is his/her attitude to the event he/she perceives when he/she is the audience.

The fourth question is that Clift (1999) thinks sarcasm is one type of irony. The speaker may be or may be not aware of ironic utterance, but the/she must be aware of his/her sarcastic utterance. Thus, there should be overlapped feature between sarcasm and irony based on the speaker awareness. However, `aggressiveness_ has been pointed out from Clift as well as Lee and Katz to be the feature distinguishes sarcasm from irony. Hence, it should be reasonable to hypothesize that irony should have two senses. In one sense, the speaker is aware of what he/she says is opposite to what is intended to mean. The second sense is to be distinct from sarcasm in being not aggressive and without awareness.

The Reason to Take Twitter as the study target: Current study is going to explore the characteristics of sarcasm and irony from speaker angle by adopting quantitatively computational sentiment analysis and qualitatively content analysis. The data used in current study is collected from social network Twitter because it provides the function of #hashtag, which allows the users to classify their tweets at their will by using the sign `#_ plus the label name they like. Hence, with collecting the tweets labeled as #sarcasm or #irony we can anchor the speakers˘ intention. The tagging is a kind of crowdsourcing (Elena, 2012). The crowdsourcing is similar to the psycholinguistic studies that ask participants to judge how good the example is to be ironic/sarcastic as in the study conducted by Lee and Katz (1998), but it is different from previous studies in that the judges are not the hearers, but the speakers themselves. Language speakers may not be able to precisely define what irony and what sarcasm is; however, the labels should be reliable to reflect the nature of irony and sarcasm from speaker angle because the labels used are the most natural language performance from language users. Besides, the collected data are not transcription from oral data that needs auditory paralinguistic cues, but the original written messages employing visual cues, so the strategies adopted in expressing the speaker˘s true intention as well as in achieving ironic or sarcastic effects can be more clearly perceived and understood in current study.

3 Quantitatively Sentiment Analysis

This section would be divided into two parts: the adopted methodology as well as the discussion on the retrieved result.

3.1 Method

The sentiment analysis in current study adopts Breen's approach (Miner et al. 2011) with the opinion lexicon that contains 2,006 positive words and 4,783 negative words proposed from Hu and Liu (2004). Examples of positive words are `a+,_ `revitalize,_ or `whoooa_ etc. Examples of negative words are `zombie,_ `blab,_ or `fuck_ etc. The amount of positive words deducts the amount of negative words in a single tweet would be the sentiment score of the tweet. Based on the sentiment score current study classifies the tweets into positive (sentiment score > 0), negative (sentiment score < 0), or neutral tweet (sentiment score = 0). When counting the score, the labels #irony and # sarcasm would be removed to avoid influencing the scoring results. 500 #irony tweets and 500 #sarcasm tweets have been randomly sampled for current study.

From previous theoretical discussion, it implies that sarcastic statements are more aggressive than ironic ones. Though Clift (1999) takes sarcasm as one type of irony, empirical psycholinguistic study from Lee and Katz (1998) shows that hearers perceive aggressiveness as the feature that distinguishes sarcasm from irony. Thus, it is with interest to understand how speakers use emotion words in these two types of language creativity. The mechanism operated in sarcasm and irony involves pragmatic insincerity, the divergence between what the speakers intend to mean and how the expression the speaker presents, so the tweet that with more aggressive intention should be sugar coated with more positive emotion words. It is with interest that in speaker performance whether the type of the tweet (sarcastic or ironic tweet) would affect the sentiment score of the tweet. The mean in group irony is -0.176, and the mean in group sarcasm is 0.514.

The alternative hypothesis specifies that the type of the tweet (ironic tweet or sarcastic tweet) affects the sentiment score of the tweet. The sample mean difference of -0.338 is due to random sampling from populations where ≒þ. ≒.The null hypothesis states that the type of the tweet (ironic tweet or sarcastic tweet) is not related to the sentiment score of the tweet. The sample mean difference of -0.338 is due to random sampling from populations where ≒=. ≒.The conclusion would be made by using $= 0.05_{2\ tail}$.

3.2 Results and Discussion

The two samples are independently retrieved, so the independent t-test should be adopted. The result of t test indicates that the null hypothesis is rejected [t = -10.68, p < 0.01].However, even though the sampling size is large, the departure from the normality is too significant as shown in Fig.1. The densities of irony and sarcasm both are not symmetrical distribution. Thus, the nonparametric test, the Wilcoxon test is used when there is serious violation on normality assumption. The result of Wilcoxon test indicates that the null hypothesis is rejected [W= 78916, p < 0.01], so we can conclude that the type of the tweet (ironic tweet or sarcastic tweet) affects the sentiment score of the tweet.

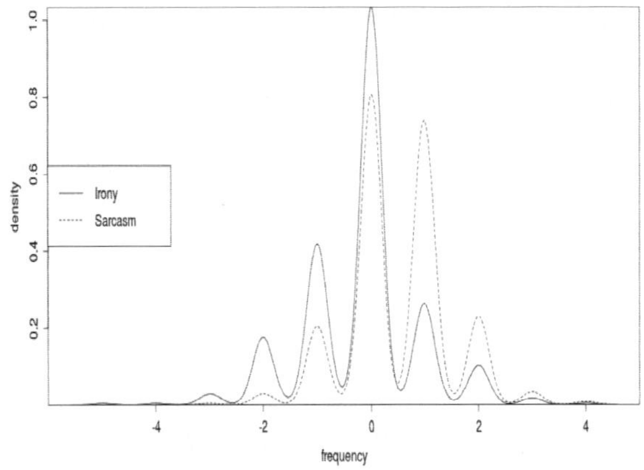

Fig. 1. Estimated Probability Density of Ironic and Sarcastic tweets

On the other hand, from Fig.1 it shows that the distribution patterns of the two linguistic devices are different. In Fig.2 it further illustrates that sarcastic tweets use more positive tweets, but ironic tweets use more neutral tweets. There is a distinct in these two types of tweets.

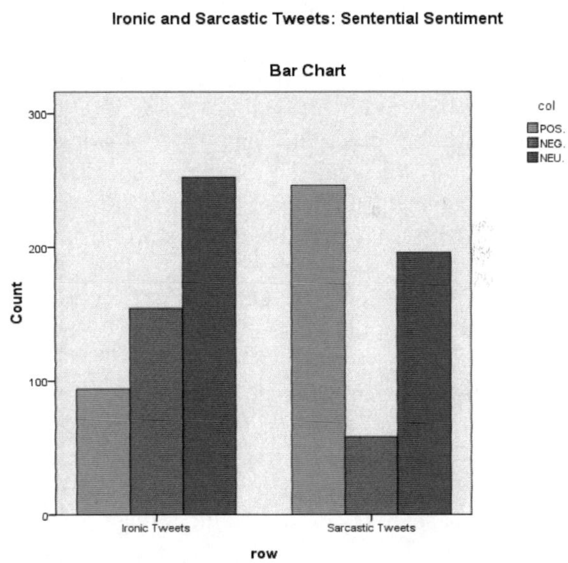

Fig. 2. Frequency of Positive, Negative, and Neutral Tweets in Ironic and Sarcastic Tweets

Hence, the result from current study manifests two important points. First, irony and sarcasm are different in their emotion express from speaker˘s angle. The speakers tend to use more positive tweets to convey sarcasm, but more natural tweets to convey irony. Second, based on the underlying mechanism of sarcasm and irony, there is a divergence between what the speaker said and what he/she intended to mean, thus the positive words used in tweets seems to represent the aggressive intention. It has shown that sarcasm is more aggressive than irony from speakers˘ natural language performance. This result corresponds to the study on hearers˘ comprehension conducted by Lee and Katz (1998).

4 Qualitatively Content Analysis

The discussion in current study would be divided into three sections to separately answer following questions: (1) Is there a specific target attacked in sarcasm, but not in irony? (2) Is the tweeter aware of his/her sarcastic or ironic tweets? (3) Are there any overlapped features between sarcasm and irony?

4.1 Is there a specific target attacked in sarcasm, but not in irony?

From the listed examples (1-f) to (1-j), it shows that the target of utterance are not limited to others, but also the speaker himself/herself in sarcastic tweets. On the other hand, in ironic tweets though the attack on specific target is rarely few, it does exist. For example, the `Our prof_ in (1-a) is a specific target to be talked about in the tweet tagged as irony. This fact seems to be different from the result of Lee and Katz (1998). With or without a specific target could not be powerful enough to distinguish irony from sarcasm. To be more specifically, sarcastic tweets do have a specific target, but ironic tweets may also have a specific target to attack.

(1-a) RT @matthewyabs: Our prof in CRITHIN has the initials MAD.... #irony

(1-b) The only man who can save Max Cliffords public relations is.......Max Clifford #irony

(1-c) "@JustTheJay: A slut calling other's 'flirt ' . #irony"

(1-d) @SillyLiberals @SouthernCharm @pari123awaaz u do realise US made these extremist, through its foreign policy and amp; created your "enemies" #Irony

(1-e) Worrying about weight gain while happily eating 5 slices of pizza and a doughnut. #irony food is my love.

(1-f) This play is amazingly good. #sarcasm

(1-g) i really have fantasssstic friends.. #sarcasm

(1-h) Boyfriend of the year award. #sarcasm

(1-i) you always find a way to ruin my night! #thankyou #sarcasm

(1-j) I ordered 6 new pairs of shoes...this saving money thing is going pretty good for me #Sarcasm

(1-k)Oh! there's water coming out of the smoke alarm. :) cool! #sarcasm #irony

4.2 Is the tweeter aware of his/her sarcastic or ironic tweets?

From tweets (1-f) to (1-j), it can be observed that the tagged utterances are the words from the speakers rather than the description on an event. As example (1-f), though the tweet says `the play is amazingly good,_ the tag `#sarcasm_ indicates what the speaker really intend to mean is the opposite. The sarcastic effect is built based on what is said by the tweeter, and the speaker is aware of what he/she has said. On the other hand, the contents of ironic tweets are more about a general event, such as (1-a) to (1-e). For example, in (1-d) the ironic effect locates in the nature of the contrast between `foreign policy_ and `create enemies._ Hence, it shows that ironic effect is less built by the tweeters˘ own words in tweets, but the event the tweeters point out.

However, there is case that the tweeter is aware of his/her words to be ironic. Example (1-e) omits the subject, so the whole utterance is more like a narration of an event. However, the `food is my love._ with the put of the period inside seems to be aimed to complete the whole utterance. The `my_ does indicate the subjectivity of the utterance. Thus, the tweet is not to objectively describe an event. The speaker is aware of what his/her has tweeted is ironic. This shows that ironic tweets can contain the tweets that are with speaker˘s awareness. Namely, the speaker could be aware of his/her own words as an irony. This result evidences the hypothesis of Clift (1999) that irony can be aware or not be aware by the speaker.

4.3 Are there any overlapped features Between sarcasm and irony?

In example (1-k), the speaker tags a tweet simultaneously as irony and sarcasm. This coexistence of these two linguistic devices as the tag marker to a single tweet shows that sarcasm and irony could be overlapped. Though `Oh! there's water coming out of the smoke alarm._ seems to be a general description to this event, the emoticon `:)_ and the comment `cool!_ are subjective. The whole content, the descriptive words and the subjective comments should be viewed as a whole utterance that is to express subjectively that the speaker does not really think the coming out of water from the smoke alarm is cool. This subjective expression contributes to being tagged as both sarcasm and irony. It should not to view separately that the descriptive words is the reason to be tagged as irony, and the subjective comment is the reason to be tagged as sarcasm. This is because if there is a correspondence between the order of content and the order of tag, and the order of the tags reflects the progress of the speaker˘s cognition, then what corresponds to sarcasm should be the subjective comments, `:) cool!_ and what corresponds to the irony should be the descriptive words, `Oh! there's water coming out of the smoke alarm._ However, there is not such case. In this case, the speaker seems to be hard to decide whether it is an irony or sarcasm, so he/she tagged them both, which indicates that these two terms are not distinguished in their functions in this example.

Evaluating this case with the cases illustrated in 4.2, it shows that the content of sarcastic tweets are built on what the speaker said, but ironic tweets can be general description, or the speaker˘s own words. Hence, it is more appropriate to propose that irony has two senses. The first sense is that it is equal to the sarcasm in being aggressive and with self-awareness. This is different from the hypothesis made by Clift (1999) that sarcasm is a type of irony. There is a single tweet tagged simultaneously with irony and sarcasm in, it does not show that irony is the hypernym of sarcasm, but implies the interchangeability between the two. The second sense is the exclusive one that specifies the utterance about ironic events, so it is nonaggressive and without speaker awareness.

5 General Conclusion

The quantitative sentiment analysis and qualitative content are used complementarily in current study to probe distinctions and similarities between irony and sarcasm

The quantitative sentiment score has illustrated that sarcastic tweets are more positive, but ironic tweets are more neutral. This echoes to the claim that sarcasm is more aggressive because being more aggressive in emotion should be sugar coated with more positive emotion words. This result also corresponds to the finding in content analysis of sarcastic tweets and ironic tweets. Most of the content of the tweets tagged # sarcasm are subjective utterance from the speaker, but to tweets tagged with #irony, the content is more about the description of an event. Thus, the tag #irony is more used by the users˘ to classify an event as irony. At this moment the tweeter is at the audience˘s angle to evaluate a thing as being ironic. Besides, this less subjective content corresponds to its result of sentiment analysis in being more neutral. Hence, the quantitative sentiment analysis and qualitative content analysis both identify that being aggressive can be effectively distinguish sarcasm from irony.

However, there are also examples that the speaker is aware of his/her tweets as ironic, or the speakers mark his/her own subjective words as #sarcasm #irony simultaneously. This illustrates that irony owns two senses. The first sense of irony is equal to the more aggressive and `awareness_ sarcasm. However, this is different from the hypothesis made by Clift (1999) that sarcasm is a type of irony. There is a single tweet tagged simultaneously with irony and sarcasm in, it does not show that irony is the hypernym of sarcasm, but implies the undistinguishable between the two. This also accounts why some ironic tweets may include a specific attacking target, which is different from the result of Lee and Katz (1998). However, it is noticeable that the result of content analysis and quantitative statistics both indicate that irony may be more widely to be used in neutrally classifying an event rather than being interchangeable with sarcasm.

Current study has identified the distinctions and similarities between irony and sarcasm. The features that differentiate irony and sarcasm: the degree of aggressiveness and the content of the utterance. The degree of aggressiveness is evidenced by the using of more positive emotion words in sarcastic tweets. The content of the utterance is about description on ironic event or sarcastic self-utterance. However, there still leaves room for future study on irony and sarcasm. For example, Internet language is hard to operate auditory paralinguistic cues, but to utilize visual cues as in capitalization, emoticons, punctuation, and hashtags to show the real intention of the speaker in order to achieve the effect of sarcasm and irony. Thus, to make comparison between the paralinguistic cues used in oral and internet language is a direction to further understand this issue. Meanwhile, the details about how these two linguistic devices operate their effects should be further investigated with more various examples. The results of the studies can be further applied on opinion mining and instructions on language learning in information structuring.

References

Albert N. Katz. 2000. Introduction to the Special Issue: The Uses and Processing of Irony and Sarcasm. Metaphor and Symbol, 15:1-2, 1-3

Antonio Reyes, Paolo Rosso, and Tony Veale.2013. Multidimensional Approach for Detecting Irony in Twitter. Lang Resources and Evaluation, 47:239¯268

Bowes Andrea and Albert Katz .2011. When Sarcasm Stings. Discourse Processes, 48:4, 215-236

C.Burfoot and T. Baldwin. 2009. Automatic Satire Detection: Are You Having a Laugh? In: ACL-IJCNLP '09: Proceedings of the ACL-IJCNLP 2009 conference short papers, 161¯164.

Christopher J. Lee and Albert N. Katz.1998. The Differential Role of Ridicule in Sarcasm and Irony. Metaphor and Symbol, 13(1): 1-15

D. Sperber and D.Wilson. 1981. Irony and the Use-mention Distinction. In P. Cole (ed), Radical Pragmatics. New York: Academic Press, 295¯318.

D. Sperber and D.Wilson. 1986. Relevance: Communication and Cognition. Cambridge, MA: Harvard University Press.

Elena Filatova. 2012. Irony and Sarcasm: Corpus Generation and Analysis Using Crowdsourcing. Presented in 8th International conference on Language Resources and Evaluation (LREC)

Gary Miner, John Elder IV , Thomas Hill, Robert Nisbet, Dursun Delen, and Andrew Fast. 2012. Practical Text Mining and Statistical Analysis for Non-structured Text Data Applications. Online reference:

http://www.sciencedirect.com/science/book/9780123869791

Gregory Bryant and Jean E. Fox Tree. 2002. Recognizing Verbal Irony in Spontaneous Speech, Metaphor and Symbol, 17(2): 99-119.

H. H. Clark and R. J. Gerrig. 1984. On the pretense theory of irony. Journal of Experimental Psychology: General, 113: 121¯126.

H. L.Colston. 1997. Salting a wound or sugaring a pill: The pragmatic functions of ironic criticism. Discourse Processes, 23: 25¯45.

H. L. Colston. 2000. On necessary Conditions for Verbal Irony Comprehension. Pragmatics and Cognition, 8(2), 277-324.

H. P.Grice. 1975. Logic and conversation. In P. Cole and J. L. Morgan (eds). Syntax and Semantics, Volume 3: Speech Acts. New York: Academic Press, 41¯58.

J. Schwoebel, S. Dews, E. Winner, and K. Srinivas. 2000. Obligatory processing of the literal meaning of ironic utterances: Further evidence. Metaphor and Symbol, 15: 47¯61.

Jr. R. Gibbs. 1986. On the psycholinguistics of sarcasm. Journal of Experimental Psychology: General, 115: 3-15

Jr. R. Gibbs and J. O'Brien. 1991. Psychological aspects of irony understanding. Journal of Pragmatics, 16:523¯530.

J. R. Searle. 1978. Utterance Meaning. Erkenntnis 13: 207¯224.

Minqing Hu and Bing Liu. Mining and Summarizing Customer Reviews. Proceedings of the ACM SIGKDD International Conference on Knowledge Discoveryand Data Mining (KDD-2004), Aug 22-25, 2004, Seattle, Washington, USA.

Rebecca Clift. 1999. Irony in Conversation. Language in Society, 28:523¯553

R. J. Kreuz, and S. Glucksberg. 1989. How to be Sarcastic: The Echoic Reminder theory of Verbal Irony. Journal of Experimental Psychology: General, 118:374¯386.

R. J. Kreuz. 2000. The Production and Processing of Verbal Irony. Metaphor and Symbol, 15:1-2, 99-107

Roberto González-Ibáñez, Smaranda Muresan,and Nina Wacholder. 2011.Identifying Sarcasm in Twitter: A Closer Look. Proceedings of the 49th Annual Meeting of the Association for Computational Linguistics: short papers, 581¯586

S. Kumon-Nakamura, S. Glucksberg, and M. Brown. 1995. How About Another Piece of Pie? The Allusional Pretense Theory of Discourse Irony. Journal of Experimental Psychology: General, 124: 3¯21.

S. McDonald. 2000. Neuropsychological studies of sarcasm. Metaphor and Symbol, 15:85¯98.

Collective Sentiment Classification Based on User Leniency and Product Popularity

Wenliang Gao[*], **Naoki Yoshinaga**[†], **Nobuhiro Kaji**[†] **and Masaru Kitsuregawa**[†‡]

[*]Graduate School of Information Science and Technology, The University of Tokyo
[†]Institute of Industrial Science, The University of Tokyo
[‡]National Institute of Informatics
{wl-gao, ynaga, kaji, kitsure}@tkl.iis.u-tokyo.ac.jp

Abstract

We propose a method of collective sentiment classification that assumes dependencies among labels of an input set of reviews. The key observation behind our method is that the distribution of polarity labels over reviews written by each user or written on each product is often skewed in the real world; intolerant users tend to report complaints while popular products are likely to receive praise. We encode these characteristics of users and products (referred to as *user leniency* and *product popularity*) by introducing global features in supervised learning. To resolve dependencies among labels of a given set of reviews, we explore two approximated decoding algorithms, "easiest-first decoding" and "two-stage decoding". Experimental results on two real-world datasets with product and user/product information confirmed that our method contributed greatly to the classification accuracy.

1 Introduction

In document-level sentiment classification, early studies have exploited language-based clues (e.g., n-grams) extracted from the textual content (Turney, 2002; Pang et al., 2002), followed by recent studies which adapt the classifier to the reviews written by a specific user or written on a specific product (Tan et al., 2011; Seroussi et al., 2010; Speriosu et al., 2011; Li et al., 2011). Although the user- and product-aware methods exhibited better performance over the methods based on purely textual clues, most of them use only the user information (Tan et al., 2011; Seroussi et al., 2010; Speriosu et al., 2011), or they assume that the user and the product of a test review is known in advance (Li et al., 2011). These assumptions heavily limit their applicability in a real-world scenario where new users and new products are ceaselessly emerging.

This paper proposes a method of collective sentiment classification that is aware of the user and the product of the target review, which benefits from the skewed distributions of polarity labels: intolerant users tend to report complaints while popular products are likely to receive praise. We introduce global features to encode these characteristics of a user and a product (referred to as user leniency and product popularity), and then compute the values of global features along with testing. Our method is therefore applicable to reviews written by users and on products that are not observed in the training data.

Because global features depend on labels of test reviews while the labels reversely depend on the global features, we need to globally optimize a label configuration for a given set of reviews. In this study, we resort to approximate algorithms, easiest-first (Tsuruoka and Tsujii, 2005) and two-stage strategies (Krishnan and Manning, 2006), in decoding labels, and empirically compare their speed and accuracy.

We evaluated our method on two real-world datasets with product (Maas et al., 2011) and user/product information (Blitzer et al., 2007). Experimental results demonstrated that the collective sentiment classification significantly improved the classification accuracy against the state-of-the-art methods, regardless of the choice of decoding strategy.

The remainder of this paper is organized as follows. Section 2 discusses related work that exploits user and product information in a sentiment classification task. Then, Section 3 proposes a method that collectively classifies polarity of given set of reviews. Section 4 reports experimental results. Finally, Section 5 concludes this study and addresses future work.

2 Related Work

Early studies on sentiment analysis considers only textual content for classifying the sentiment of a given review (Pang and Lee, 2008). Pang *et al.* (2002) developed a supervised sentiment classifier which only takes n-gram features. Nakagawa *et al.* (2010) and Socher *et al.* (2011) considered structural interaction among words to capture complex intra-sentential phenomena such as polarity shifting (Li et al., 2010).

On the other hand, recent studies started exploring the effectiveness of user and/or product information. Tan *et al.,* (2011) and Speriosu *et al.,* (2011) exploited user network behind a social media (Twitter in their case) and assumed that friends give similar ratings towards similar products. Seroussi *et al.* (2010) proposed a framework that computes users' similarity on the basis of text and their rating histories. Then, they classify a given review by referring to ratings given for the same product by other users who are similar to the user in question. However, such user networks are not always available in the real world.

Li *et al.* (2011) incorporate user- or product-dependent n-gram features into a classifier. They argue that users use a personalized language to express their sentiment, while the sentiment toward a product is described by product-specific language. This approach, however, requires the training data to contain reviews written by test users and written for test products. This is infeasible since labeling reviews requires too much manual work.

3 Method

This section describes our method of collective sentiment classification that uses user leniency and product popularity.

3.1 Overview

Our task is, given a set of N reviews $\mathcal{R}$, to predict labels $\mathcal{Y}$, where $y_r \in \{+1, -1\}$[1] for each given review $r \in \mathcal{R}$. The label of each review is predicted based on the following scoring function:

$$s_r = score(\boldsymbol{x}_r) = \boldsymbol{w}^T \boldsymbol{x}_r, \qquad (1)$$

[1]The labels, +1 and -1, represent positive and negative polarity, respectively.

where $\boldsymbol{x}_r$ is feature vector representation of the review r and $\boldsymbol{w}$ is the weight vector. With this scoring function, the label is predicted as follows:

$$y_r = \text{sgn}(s_r) = \begin{cases} +1 & if\ s_r > 0, \\ -1 & otherwise. \end{cases}$$

Our interest is to exploit user leniency and product popularity for improving sentiment classification. We realize this by encoding such biases as two global features, as detailed in Section 3.2. Since global features make it impossible to independently predict the labels of reviews, we explored two approximate decoding strategies in Section 3.3.

Note that we assume the review is associated with the user who wrote that review, the product on which that review is written, or both. This assumption is not unrealistic nowadays. User information is available in many standard dataset (Blitzer et al., 2007; Pang and Lee, 2004). Moreover, as for product information, even if such information is not available, it is possible to extract it (Qiu et al., 2011). We should emphasize here that our method does not require user profiles, product descriptions, or any sort of extrinsic knowledge on the users and the products.

3.2 Features

Our features can be divided into local and global ones such that $\boldsymbol{x}_r = \{\boldsymbol{x}_r^l, \boldsymbol{x}_r^g\}$. While local features ($\boldsymbol{x}_r^l$) are conventional word n-grams ($n = 1$ and $n = 2$), global features ($\boldsymbol{x}_r^g$) represent the user leniency and product popularity.

Our global features are computed as:

$$\boldsymbol{x}_r^g = \{f\_u^+(r), f\_u^-(r), f\_p^+(r), f\_p^-(r)\},$$
$$where$$
$$f\_u^+(r) = \frac{|\{r_j \mid y_j = +1, r_j \in \mathcal{N}_u(r)\}|}{|\mathcal{N}_u(r)|},$$
$$f\_u^-(r) = \frac{|\{r_j \mid y_j = -1, r_j \in \mathcal{N}_u(r)\}|}{|\mathcal{N}_u(r)|},$$
$$f\_p^+(r) = \frac{|\{r_j \mid y_j = +1, r_j \in \mathcal{N}_p(r)\}|}{|\mathcal{N}_p(r)|},$$
$$f\_p^-(r) = \frac{|\{r_j \mid y_j = -1, r_j \in \mathcal{N}_p(r)\}|}{|\mathcal{N}_p(r)|}.$$

$\mathcal{N}_u(r)$, the user-related neighbors, is the set of reviews, excluding r, written by the user who wrote the review r, and $\mathcal{N}_p(r)$, the product-related neighbors, is the set of reviews, excluding r, on the same product as the review r, respectively.

Algorithm 1 Easiest-first strategy

1: **for** $r \in \mathcal{R}$ **do**
2: initialize the global features to 0
3: compute $score(\boldsymbol{x}_r)$
4: **while** $\mathcal{R} \neq \emptyset$ **do**
5: $r_{max} = \arg\max_{r_i \in \mathcal{R}} |score(\boldsymbol{x}_{r_i})|$
6: $y_{r_{max}} = \text{sgn}(score(\boldsymbol{x}_{r_{max}}))$
7: **for** $r_j \in (\mathcal{N}_u(r_{max}) \cup \mathcal{N}_p(r_{max})) \cap \mathcal{R}$ **do**
8: update global features
9: re-compute $score(\boldsymbol{x}_{r_j})$
10: $\mathcal{R} = \mathcal{R} \backslash \{r_{max}\}$
11: **return** $\mathcal{Y}$

The first two features capture user leniency, i.e., how likely the user is to write positive and negative reviews, respectively. The other features capture product popularity, i.e., how likely positive and negative reviews on the product at hand are to be written.

3.3 Two Approximate Decoding Strategies

The global features make it difficult to perform decoding, i.e., labeling reviews, since each review can no longer be labeled independently. Exact decoding algorithms based on dynamic programming are not feasible in our case, because the search space grows exponentially as the number of test reviews increases. So instead, we explore and empirically compare two approximate algorithms: easy-first (Tsuruoka and Tsujii, 2005) and two-stage strategy (Krishnan and Manning, 2006).

Algorithm 1 depicts the easiest-first decoding algorithm. This strategy iteratively determines the label of each review one by one. In each iteration step, a review that is the easiest to label , i.e., the review with the highest score, is picked up (line 5 in Algorithm 1), and then its label is determined (line 6 in Algorithm 1). This process is repeated until all the reviews are labeled. The global features are computed by using the labels of reviews that are already assigned with labels. That is, at the beginning of decoding, no global features are fired; more global features are fired as the labeling process proceeds. The score of the review is computed in a different way depending on how global features are fired, as analogous to (Tsuruoka and Tsujii, 2005). Specifically, we prepare four classifiers, and those classifiers are used when (1) no global features are fired, (2) only user leniency features are fired, (3) only product popularity features are fired, and (4) both global features are fired, respectively.

Algorithm 2 Two-stage strategy

1: **for** $r \in \mathcal{R}$ **do**
2: $y_r = \text{sgn}(score(\boldsymbol{x}_r))$
3: **for** $r \in \mathcal{R}$ **do**
4: compute global features
5: $y_r = \text{sgn}(score(\boldsymbol{x}_r))$
6: **return** $\mathcal{Y}$

Next, we introduce a two-stage strategy (Krishnan and Manning, 2006), which has better scalability than easy-first strategy. It is depicted in Algorithm 2. This strategy performs decoding twice. In the first stage (line 1 to line 2 in Algorithm 2), we ignore all the global features, and use only local features to classify all the reviews. In the second stage (line 3 to line 5 in Algorithm 2), labels predicted in the first stage are used to compute global features and the labels are re-assigned by using both global features and local features. In our case, two-stage at first only uses word n-gram features to estimate the labels of reviews. Thereafter, those labels are used to compute global features in the second stage.

3.4 Time Complexity

This subsection analyzes the time complexity of the two decoding strategy with respect to the number of reviews, N.

In easiest-first strategy, two processes consume most of the computing time. One is choosing the easiest review label (line 5 in Algorithm 1). The $arg\,max$ operation takes $O(\log \mathcal{N})$ time in each iteration by using a heap structure. Thus, the total time complexity in this step is $O(\mathcal{N} \log \mathcal{N})$ for N iteration. Another bottleneck is score recomputation (line 9 in Algorithm 1). To update the score for each review $r_j \in \mathcal{N}_u(r_{max}) \cap \mathcal{N}_p(r_{max})$, we need at most $|\mathcal{N}_u(r_{max}) \cap \mathcal{N}_p(r_{max})|$ times *delete* and *insert* operations to the heap. Since we could limit the number of reviews for each user or each product, $|\mathcal{N}_u(r_{max}) \cap \mathcal{N}_p(r_{max})|$ is treated as a constant C.[2] The overall time complexity sums up to $O(\mathcal{N}(\log \mathcal{N} + C \log \mathcal{N})) = O(\mathcal{N} \log \mathcal{N})$.

In two-stage strategy, the complexity is $O(N)$ for both stages. Then the total complexity is also $O(N)$, which is the same as the existing method

[2]However, based on our experiment as shown in Figure 2, the number $|\mathcal{N}_u(r_{max}) \cap \mathcal{N}_p(r_{max})|$ is weakly related to N.

Dataset	Blitzer	Maas
No. of reviews	188,350	50,000
No. of users	123,584	n/a
No. of products	101,021	7,036
No. of reviews/user	1.5	n/a
No. of reviews/products	1.9	7.1

Table 1: Dataset statistics.

that uses only local textual features.

3.5 Training

It is straightforward to train the parameters of the scoring functions. We train a binary classifier as the score estimation function in Eq. 1, considering word n-gram features, user leniency features, and product popularity features. The values of global features are computed by using the gold labels. We assume that a value of the user leniency feature or product popularity feature for a review whose user has no other reviews or whose product has no other reviews is set to 0.

4 Experiments

In this section, we evaluate our method of collective sentiment classification on two real-world review datasets with user/product or product information (Blitzer et al., 2007; Maas et al., 2011).

We preprocessed each review in the datasets by OpenNLP[3] toolkit to detect sentence boundaries and to tokenize n-grams. Following Pang *et al.* (2002), we induce word unigrams and bigrams as local features, taking negation into account. We ignored n-grams that appeared less than six times in the training data.

We adopted a confidence-weighted linear classifier (Dredze et al., 2008) with n-gram features as our baseline. To make the comparison fair, we used the same classifier, which despite of local features also considers global features, as the local classifier in our method. We used the default hyper-parameters to this classifier. Note that the confidence-weighted algorithm performed as good as SVM (Dredze et al., 2008) so it constructs a strong baseline.

4.1 Datasets

Blitzer *et al.* (2007) and Maas *et al.* (2011) collected two datasets which contain user/product or product information respectively. Table 1 summarizes the statistics of the two datasets. We should mention that the original Blitzer dataset contains more than 780k reviews collected from Amazon.com on several domains (e.g. books, movies and games). We automatically delete replicated reviews written by the same author on the same product (resulting in 740k raw reviews). Then the reviews are balanced for positive and negative labels (over 90k reviews for each) to maintain consistency with the Maas dataset.

The Maas dataset has 25,000 positive and 25,000 negative reviews on movies. We have used a URL (linked to the move title) provided with each review as the identifier of the product movie. Because user information cannot be fully recovered, we only model the product popularity on this dataset.

In the two datasets, the reviews were ordered by

Method	Blitzer	Maas
Seroussi *et al.*, (2010)	89.37	n/a
Maas *et al.*, (2011)	n/a	88.89[4]
baseline	90.13	91.41
proposed (easiest-first)		
+user	91.04$^{\gg}$	n/a
+product	90.16$^{>}$	**92.73**
+user +product	**91.11**$^{\gg}$	n/a
proposed (two-stage)[5]		
+user	90.95$^{\gg}$	n/a
+product	90.15	92.68
+user +product	91.02$^{\gg}$	n/a

Table 2: Accuracy (%) on review datasets. *+user*/*+product* means modeling the user leniency / product popularity features. Accuracy marked with "$\gg$" or "$>$" was significantly better than baseline ($p < 0.01$ or $0.01 \leq p < 0.05$ assessed by McNemar's test).

[3] `http://opennlp.apache.org/`

[4] This results uses different 2-fold splitting from ours. Under their splitting, our accuracies (+user+product) are 91.02%, 92.54% and 92.28% for baseline, easiest-first and two-stage with product popularity features respectively. Both strategies easily beat Maas *et al.*, (2011)'s accuracy, 88.89%. The main difference between our baseline and their baseline is the features. They use only unigram features (baseline accuracy is 87.80%), while we use unigram and bigram (which considers negation) as features.

[5] The two-stage implementation in Gao *et al.* (2013) used a different setting. In that paper, the classifiers for the first stage and second stage are the same one considering local and global features. While in this paper, the classifier used in the first stage only considers local features and the classifier for the second stage considers both.

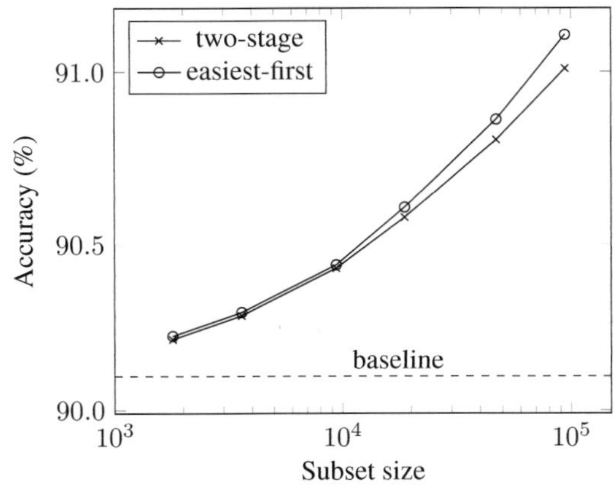

Figure 1: Average accuracy when we changed the size of subset on test reviews.

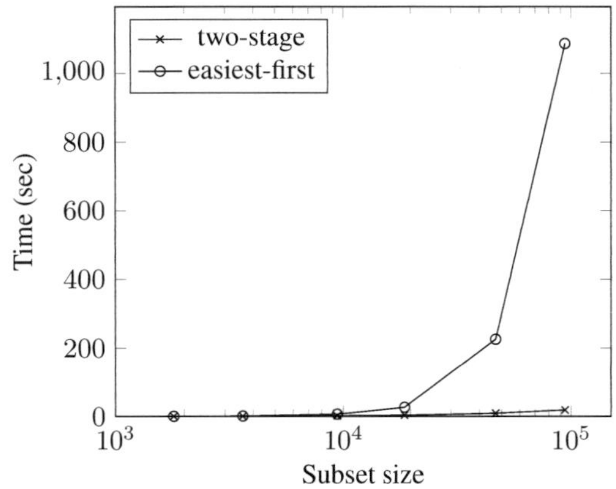

Figure 2: Average computation time when we changed the size of subset on test reviews.

user and product. In order to prevent the seemingly unfair accuracy gain under this particular splitting, we performed a 2-fold cross-validation after randomly splitting reviews, rather than using the split provided by the authors.

4.2 Results

We then compared the accuracy of our method with the two baseline methods on the two datasets: a confidence-weighted linear classifier with n-gram features and a user-aware sentiment classifier proposed by Seroussi *et al.* (2010).

In Seroussi's method, we need to fix the threshold to the number of reviews written by the same user to prepare and train a personalized classifier. After several test, the threshold is set to be 5 to gain a better performance[6]. Similarity of users is computed by word n-gram jaccard distance (called "AIT" in their paper). When the user of the test review is unseen in the training set, the default classifier trained on all the training reviews (identical to the other baseline classifier based on n-grams) is used to determine the label.

Table 2 shows the experimental results. Our method significantly improved accuracies across the two datasets against the baseline classifier. A larger improvement is acquired on the Maas dataset probably because the average number of reviews for each product is higher than that on the Blitzer dataset so we could estimate more reliable global features.

On the Blitzer dataset, the user leniency was more helpful than the product popularity. This is probably because the Blitzer dataset had been collected for users, which means to collect all the reviews written by each user. While on the Maas dataset, product information plays a important role because the reviews are collected for each product.

Among the two decoding methods, the easiest-first decoding achieved better for this test. This conforms our expectation that the easiest-first decoding is more cautious than the other. However, easiest-first decoding has it's own weakness. In what follows, we investigate the speed and accuracy trade-off of the two decoding methods.

Impact of test review size on speed and accuracy: Next, we investigate the impact of the number of test reviews on speed and accuracy in our collective sentiment classification. We use Blitzer dataset for evaluation because of its larger review size. The two types of global features are both considered.

We performed 2-fold cross-validation with the same splitting for the Blitzer dataset, while changing the size of test reviews processed at once to investigate the impact of test review size on classification accuracy. In this experiment, we split the test reviews into equal-sized smaller subsets and applied our classifier independently to each of the subsets. We average the result for all the subsets to get a stable accuracy. Figure 1 shows the experimental results. When we process a larger number of reviews at once, the accuracies of the two methods increase because of more reliable global features.

We then performed the speed test using the same setting as the previous test, but measured the average time consumed by one single subset. As

[6]Seroussi *et al.*, chose users who have more than 50 positive and 50 negative reviews. Few users or product in

	(sp)	(up)	total
No. of reviews	46,397	3,603	50,000
Ave. No. of reviews/product	4.82	1.62	4.22
baseline	91.87	85.51	91.41
proposed (easiest-first)	93.11 (+1.24)	87.73 (+2.22)	92.73 (+1.32)
proposed (two-stage)	93.09 (+1.22)	87.48 (+1.97)	92.68 (+1.21)

Table 3: Accuracy (%) on known/unknown product splits on Maas dataset. *sp* and *up* stand for *seen product* and *unseen product*. Float inside parenthesizes is the difference compared to the baseline classifier.

	(su, sp)	(uu, sp)	(su, up)	(uu, up)	total
No. of reviews	35,689	60,775	36,895	55,027	188,350
Ave. No. of reviews/user	2.04	1.04	2.14	1.04	1.40
Ave. No. of reviews/product	1.20	1.39	1.14	1.20	1.43
baseline	89.71	90.45	90.37	89.95	90.13
proposed (easiest-first)	91.42 (+1.71)	90.93 (+0.59)	92.19 (+1.82)	90.76 (+0.81)	91.11 (+0.98)
proposed (two-stage)	91.23 (+1.52)	90.88 (+0.54)	92.09 (+1.72)	90.30 (+0.35)	91.02 (+0.89)

Table 4: Accuracy (%) on known/unknown user/product splits on Blitzer dataset. *su*, *uu*, *sp* and *up* stand for *seen user*, *unseen user*, *seen product* and *unseen product* respectively. Float inside parenthesises is the difference compared to the baseline classifier.

shown in Figure 2, the speed of the easiest-first decoding significantly slows down as the number of processed reviews grows, whereas the speed of the two-stage decoding increases compute time linearly. Meanwhile, the accuracy of the two strategies are competitive as shown in Figure 1.

These results confirm the analysis in Section 3.4 that the easiest-first decoding takes most of the time in re-computing and sorting the scores. More specifically, if the user has plenty of reviews or the product has been rated by plenty of reviews, the score frequently changes in each iteration in response to the change of global features' values. Based on these observations, when the amount of test data is large, the two-stage decoding is tremendously faster with only a little loss of accuracy. When the dataset is small, to fully utilize the user leniency and product popularity properties, easiest-first decoding should be adopted.

Impact of user/product-awareness: We investigate the performance on the test reviews when we observed the user/product or not in the training data. We use the leniency and popularity global features on the Blitzer dataset, while we consider only product popularity features on the Maas dataset.

The baseline classifier is expected to better estimate the labels of reviews written by known user or written on known product because similar *n*-grams would be contained in the training. On the other hand, in our model's setting, more reviews per user (or per product) should lead to more reliable leniency (or popularity) features thus better accuracy.

On the Maas dataset as shown in Table 3, the improvement on unknown product set is larger than that on known product set. We have to note here that the improvement on the unknown product set is greater while the review number for each product is smaller, which seems to violate our assumption. The reason is that baseline on the unknown product set performed poorly, which left our method larger space for improvement, even without enough global features.

On the Blitzer dataset as shown in Table 4, improvement is higher on known user sets. We find that average review number for each user is extremely low (1.04 reviews). Then lacking reliable global features may be the main reason for the poor performance on unknown user sets. We next investigate how many reviews are needed to compute reliable global features.

Accuracy Distribution: We here investigate how the reliability of the global features would influence the accuracy improvement. We exploit the accuracies with respect to how many reviews

		No. of product-related neighbors ($\|\mathcal{N}_p(r)\|$)			
		0	**1**	**2**	**3-**
No. of user-related neighbors ($\|\mathcal{N}_u(r)\|$)	**0**	55,043 90.11 (+0.03)	34,735 90.13 (+0.26)	16,601 90.80 (+0.53)	9,630 92.48 (+0.58)
	1	10,768 91.18 (+1.37)	6,530 91.24 (+2.11)	2,974 91.32 (+1.17)	1,536 92.12 (+1.04)
	2	4,595 91.28 (+1.55)	2,711 91.26(+2.66)	1,292 90.56 (+1.71)	663 92.14 (+2.36)
	3-7	8,120 92.48 (+2.33)	4,974 91.19 (+2.27)	2,174 92.18 (**+3.31**)	998 90.18 (+1.50)
	8-	13,243 **93.73** (+2.2)	7,484 92.28 (+1.74)	3,017 91.28 (+1.52)	1,289 90.22 (+1.62)

Table 5: Accuracy (%, downer inside cell) of proposed method (two-stage) and review size (upper inside cell) on Blitzer dataset separated according to the number of reviews written by the user and the number of reviews on the product.The float inside parenthesizes is the difference from the baseline method.

No. of product-related neighbors ($\|\mathcal{N}_p(r)\|$)				
0	1	2-5	6-10	11-
3,597 86.41 (+0.42)	4,646 90.94 (+1.96)	14,394 92.59 (+1.75)	10,444 93.98 (+1.31)	16,919 93.78 (+0.83)

Table 6: Accuracy (%, downer inside cell) of proposed method (two-stage) and the review size (upper inside cell) on Blitzer dataset separated according to the number of reviews on the product. The float inside parenthesizes is the difference from the baseline method.

each user or product has. More reviews means that more reliable global features will be extracted by our model.

Since user leniency is the dominant influential global feature on the Blitzer dataset, Table 5 shows the leniency features is related to the improvement. Product popularity has limited influence on this dataset because it is collected according to users. On the Maas dataset, popularity features play an important role as shown in Table 6.

We noticed that when the review number of a user or a product reaches some point ($|\mathcal{N}_u(r)| = 3-7$ in the Blitzer dataset and $|\mathcal{N}_p(r)| = 2-5$ in the Maas dataset), having more reviews does not improve the accuracy any further. However, higher $|\mathcal{N}_u(r)|$ or $|\mathcal{N}_p(r)|$ number induces lower speed of easiest-first decoding as we analyzed in Section 3.4. Then, we could collect a bounded number of reviews for each user or product to cost less time and acquire better accuracy.

Examples: Some examples are given here to explain how our model would work. As shown in Table 7, it is sometimes hard to correctly classify labels when only the text is given.

In the first two examples, weak negative textual features are found in the test instance. However, since the two users are lenient and the first product is relatively popular (these characteristics are captured by our proposed method), these two reviews should still be given positive labels.

Frequently, sentiment expressed inside a review is not obvious if the classifier does not know the latent meaning of the words (sometimes, even real person feels hard to extract sentiment from these words). As we can see in the third example in Table 7, the baseline classifier could recognize no obvious sentiment evidence from the textual features, while our method classified it as negative by detecting that its on a notorious product and the user is critical.

These examples illustrate that our model can successfully use the user and product-based dependencies to improve sentiment classification accuracy. Nowadays, in the big data background, this method could be more useful with huge amount of unlabeled data.

5 Conclusion

We have presented collective sentiment classification which captures and utilizes user leniency and product popularity. Different from the previous studies that are aware of the user and product of

leniency	popularity	content	labels golden	baseline	proposed
f_u^+: **0.92** f_u^-: 0.08	f_p^+: **0.67** f_p^-: 0.33	... The book would deserve 5 stars is the author had compared several popular jurisdictions **instead of** focusing solely on Nevada	+1	-1	+1
f_u^+: **0.81** f_u^-: 0.19	f_p^+: 0.50 f_p^-: 0.50	... I am using Windows XP with office Pro 2003 and today was **disappointed to** find that the Help menu is not as user friendly or helpfulas earlier editions	+1	-1	+1
f_u^+: 0.18 f_u^-: **0.82**	f_p^+: 0.00 f_p^-: **1.00**	ooo! see Halle act. act, halle, act. emote. emote. see halle act drunk. see halle act crying. see halle act nympho. ... but what does it matter, since we get to see halle act ...	-1	+1	-1

Table 7: Examples show the influence of leniency and popularity global features. The **bold** content is the negative evidence learned by classifier.

the review, our model does not assume the training data to contain the reviews written by the same user of test reviews or written on the same product of test reviews. To decode a labels configuration for a given set of reviews, we adopted and compared two strategies, namely "easiest-first decoding" and "two-stage decoding".

We conducted experiments on two real-world review datasets to compare our method with the existing methods. The proposed method performed more accurately than the baseline methods that uses word n-gram as features. It also outperforms another state-of-the-art method which trains personalized sentiment classifiers significantly. The more reviews per-user/product possesses, the larger improvement our model would gain. Two-stage strategy gains less accuracy than easiest-first, however, consumes only linear time in terms of the test review size (expected to be the same order of speed as the baseline classifiers). We plan to publish the code and datasets[7].

A future extension of this work is to use this on other task, such as classifying the subjectivity of a given document. We also plan to use dual decomposition as an advanced decoding strategy on our model.

[7] http://www.tkl.iis.u-tokyo.ac.jp/~wl-gao/

References

John Blitzer, Mark Dredze, and Fernando Pereira. 2007. Biographies, bollywood, boom-boxes and blenders: Domain adaptation for sentiment classification. In *Proceedings of ACL*, pages 440–447, Prague, Czech Republic.

Mark Dredze, Koby Crammer, and Fernando Pereira. 2008. Confidence-weighted linear classification. In *Proceedings of ICML*, pages 264–271, Helsinki, Finland.

Wenliang Gao, Naoki Yoshinaga, Nobuhiro Kaji, and Masaru Kitsuregawa. 2013. Modeling user leniency and product popularity for sentiment classification. In *Proceedings of IJCNLP*, Nagoya, Japan. to appear.

Vijay Krishnan and Christopher D. Manning. 2006. An effective two-stage model for exploiting non-local dependencies in named entity recognition. In *Proceedings of COLING-ACL*, pages 1121–1128, Sydney, NSW, Australia.

Shoushan Li, Sophia Y. M. Lee, Ying Chen, Chu-Ren Huang, and Guodong Zhou. 2010. Sentiment classification and polarity shifting. In *Proceedings of COLING*, pages 635–643, Beijing, China.

Fangtao Li, Nathan Liu, Hongwei Jin, Kai Zhao, Qiang Yang, and Xiaoyan Zhu. 2011. Incorporating reviewer and product information for review rating prediction. In *Proceedings of IJCAI*, pages 1820–1825, Barcelona, Spain.

Andrew L. Maas, Raymond E. Daly, Peter T. Pham, Dan Huang, Andrew Y. Ng, and Christopher Potts. 2011. Learning word vectors for sentiment analysis. In *Proceedings of ACL-HLT*, pages 142–150, Portland, Oregon, USA.

Tetsuji Nakagawa, Kentaro Inui, and Sadao Kurohashi. 2010. Dependency tree-based sentiment classification using crfs with hidden variables. In *Proceedings of NAACL-HLT*, pages 786–794, Los Angeles, CA, USA.

Bo Pang and Lillian Lee. 2004. A sentimental education: sentiment analysis using subjectivity summarization based on minimum cuts. In *Proceedings of ACL*, pages 271–278, Barcelona, Spain.

Bo Pang and Lillian Lee. 2008. Opinion mining and sentiment analysis. *Foundation and Trends in Information Retrieval*, 2(1-2):1–135.

Bo Pang, Lillian Lee, and Shivakumar Vaithyanathan. 2002. Thumbs up? sentiment classification using machine learning techniques. In *Proceedings of EMNLP*, pages 79–86, Pennsylvania, PA, USA.

Guang Qiu, Bing Liu, Jiajun Bu, and Chun Chen. 2011. Opinion word expansion and target extraction through double propagation. *Computational Linguistics*, 37(1):9–27.

Yanir Seroussi, Ingrid Zukerman, and Fabian Bohnert. 2010. Collaborative inference of sentiments from texts. In *Proceedings of UMAP*, pages 195–206, Big Island, HI, USA.

Richard Socher, Jeffrey Pennington, Eric H. Huang, Andrew Y. Ng, and Christopher D. Manning. 2011. Semi-supervised recursive autoencoders for predicting sentiment distributions. In *Proceedings of EMNLP*, pages 151–161, Edinburgh, Scotland, UK., July.

Michael Speriosu, Nikita Sudan, Sid Upadhyay, and Jason Baldridge. 2011. Twitter polarity classification with label propagation over lexical links and the follower graph. In *Proceedings of EMNLP, workshop on Unsupervised Learning in NLP*, pages 53–63, Edinburgh, UK.

Chenhao Tan, Lillian Lee, Jie Tang, Long Jiang, Ming Zhou, and Ping Li. 2011. User-level sentiment analysis incorporating social networks. In *Proceedings of KDD*, pages 1397–1405, San Diego, California, USA.

Yoshimasa Tsuruoka and Jun'ichi Tsujii. 2005. Bidirectional inference with the easiest-first strategy for tagging sequence data. In *In Proceedings of HLT-EMNLP*, pages 467–474, Vancouver, B.C., Canada.

Peter D. Turney. 2002. Thumbs up or thumbs down?: semantic orientation applied to unsupervised classification of reviews. In *Proceedings of ACL*, pages 417–424, Pennsylvania, PA, USA.

KOSAC: A Full-fledged Korean Sentiment Analysis Corpus

Hayeon Jang, Munhyong Kim, and Hyopil Shin

Department of Linguistics, Seoul National University
Gwanak-no Gwanak-gu, Seoul 151-741
{hyan05, likerainsun, hpshin}@snu.ac.kr

Abstract

This paper aims to introduce the Korean Sentiment Analysis Corpus named KOSAC. KOSAC is a corpus consisting of 332 news articles taken from the Sejong Syntactic Parsed Corpus. These sentences have been manually-tagged for sentimental features. The corpus includes 7,713 sentence subjectivity tags and 17,615 opinionated expression tags based on the annotation scheme called KSML which reflects the characteristics of the Korean language. The results of sentence subjectivity and polarity classification experiements using the corpus show the wide possibilities of application the KSML scheme and the tagged information of the KOSAC comprehensively to other corpus. What is innovative about our work is that it pulls together both the concept of private states and nested-sources into one linguistic annotation scheme. We believe that this corpus could be used by researchers as a gold standard for various NLP tasks related to sentiment analysis.

1 Introduction

There has been much research on the automatic identification and extraction of opinions and sentiments in text. Researchers from many subareas of Artificial Intelligence and Natural Language Processing (NLP) have been working on the automatic identification of opinions and related tasks. To date, most such work has focused on opinion, sentiment or subjectivity classification at the document or sentence level. A common sentiment analysis task is to classify documents or sentences by whether they are subjective or objective, and, if the target text is subjective, to classify it as positive or negative (Pang et al., 2002; Wiebe et al., 2005).

Along with these lines of research, a need for corpora annotated with rich information about opinions and emotions has emerged. In particular, statistical and machine learning approaches have become the method of choice for constructing a wide variety of practical NLP applications. These methods, however, typically require training and test corpora that have been manually annotated with respect to each language-processing task to be acquired. As such a resource, the Multi-perspective Question Answering (MPQA) Opinion Corpus plays an important role in sentiment analysis.

The goal of this paper is to introduce the Korean Sentiment Analysis Corpus, KOSAC[1]. We received two years of support (May, 2011-April, 2013) in this corpus construction project from the Korean Research Foundation (KRF). In the first year of the project, we focused on a fine-grained annotation scheme called KSML (Shin et al., 2012) that identifies key components and properties of sentiments based on solid theoretical background. The annotation scheme has been employed in the manual annotation of a 7,713-sentence corpus of 332 news articles from the Sejong syntactic parsed corpus. This manually-tagged corpus includes 17,615 opinionated expression tags.

The remainder of this paper is organized as follows. Section 2 gives an overview of KSML focused on differences with the annotation scheme of the MPQA. Section 3 describes observations about KOSAC. Section 4 presents the results of subjectivity and polarity classification experiments using the corpus. Section 5 presents conclusions and discusses future work.

[1] http://word.snu.ac.kr/kosac

2 Markup Language: KSML

The MPQA Opinion Corpus began with the conceptual structure for private states in Wiebe (2002) and developed manual annotation instructions (Wiebe et al., 2005; Wilson, 2008). Documents contained in the MPQA version 2.0 corpus are mostly news articles. It contains 461 documents spanning 80,706 sentences, 216,080 tokens, and 10,315 subjective expressions annotated with links. These subjective expressions are annotated with "attitude types" indicating what type of subjectivity they invoked. 5,127 of these subjective expressions convey sentiment. Since this corpus provides rich annotated expressions based on a fine-grained annotation scheme, it is widely used as a source for training data in machine learning approaches and serves as the gold standard in many sentiment analysis tasks. Since, we took advantage of the MPQA as a fundamental resource for sentiment corpus construction in Korean.

In the first year of the project constructing the Korean Sentiment Analysis Corpus, we focused on the theoretical background for the annotation scheme named the Korean Subjectivity Markup Language (KSML). Shin et al. (2012) provides a solid theoretical background for the corpus and described the results of inter-annotator agreement test with a view to improving the annotation scheme. Our work essentially follows the idea of the annotation scheme of the MPQA, but we have modified the existing framework and attributes in order to address the characteristics of Korean. In this section, we give an overview of KSML focused on differences with the annotation scheme of the MPQA.

2.1 Annotation Framework

First of all, the annotation frame of the MPQA is classified as six types by functions and meanings of the expressions regardless of the tagging unit: *t pe a ent e pressi e s e ti it ire t s e ti e o e ti e spee e ent attit e*, and *tar et*. Each unit could connect by various links such as target-links or attitude-links.

The KSML, however, divides tagging units as the whole sentences and smaller expressions included in the sentences. The *s e ti it* and *o e ti it* present the subjectivity of the whole sentence by reflecting whether an annotator feel the sentence is objectively true or not in terms of the speech event.

```
anchor: morpheme id(s)
id: tag id
nested-source: w-(morpheme id(s)
        |implicit|out)-...-
        (morpheme id(s)|implicit|out)
target: morpheme id(s)
type: direct-explicit,direct-speech,
      direct-action,indirect,
      writing-device
subjectivity-type: emotion-{pos,neg,
      complex,neutral},judgment-{pos,
      neg,complex,neutral},argument-
      {pos,neg,complex,neutral},
      agreement-{pos,neg,neutral},
      intention-{pos,neg},
      speculation-{pos,neg}, others
polarity: positive,negative,complex,
          neutral
intensity: low,medium,high
```

Table 1: The list of SEED tag attributes

In a SEED tag, each individual unit which is smaller than a sentence expresses a private state. The KSML describes information related to subjectivity such as source, target, and subjectivity-type by using attributes of a SEED tag without any links. Table 1 shows the attributes.

2.2 Change of Attributes

`Type` attributes specify either speech events (acts) that express private states or non-speech events. These fit into five subtypes: `direct-explicit`, `direct-speech`, `direct-action`, `indirect`, and `writing-device`. The *e pressi e s e ti it* of the MPQA corpus matches the `indirect` type in the KSML. The *attit e* of the MPQA is expressed by `subjectivity-type` in the KSML. The *ire t s e ti e* of the MPQA corpus classifies `direct-explicit`, `action`, or `speech` types in the KSML depending on the exact nature of the subjectivity. These tags group direct expressions together by the way of express opinions or emotions. Such classification could show different shades of expressed sentiments. The MPQA does not have a specific tag for direct subjective speech events. The *o e ti e spee e ent* of the MPQA is `direct-speech` type expressions of a sentence having an `objectivity` tag in the KSML frame.

The `writing-device` is a newly added attribute to KSML in order to show writers' own subjectivity through non-predicate expressions.

Modal expressions, speaker-oriented adverbials, conjunctive endings, and special functional particles get `writing-device` tags as kinds of devices reflecting sentiments in texts. As a basic annotation unit, we chose a morpheme rather than a word because Korean is an agglutinative language having many meaning-bearing particles and sentence endings which can carry private states. We need to be able to pinpoint precise segments as a basic unit, especially when finding `writing-device` expressions. Since some endings and particles show the subjectivity of a sentence having no direct opinionated expressions, `writing-device` expressions usually have high intensity of subjectivity. Various expressive techniques like *ontrast in erre repetition*, and *sar asti* of the MPQA could be classified as `writing-device` in the KSML.

The framework of the MPQA is similar to that of Appraisal Theory by Martin (2002) and White (2002). The Appraisal framework is composed of concepts including *e t ent ppre iation n a e ent*, and *p i i ation*. *e t ent*, and *ppre iation* represent different types of positive and negative attitudes. Nonetheless, the MPQA corpus does not distinguish different types of private states like *e t* and *ent*, which can provide useful information in sentiment analysis. On the other hand, the MPQA corpus distinguished different ways that private states may be expressed, such as *ire t* or *in ire t* . The KSML, however, not only cover many types of attitudes as in Appraisal theory but also several expressive types as in the MPQA corpus. For example, we added a `Judgment` attribute to the `subjectivity-type` in KSML.

Each attributes of `subjectivity-type` except `others` has directional cues like `positive`, `negative`, `complex`, and `neutral`. Unlike the MPQA, the KSML adds `neutral` and `complex` directional cues. In addition, the `speculation` attribute also has directional cues. Directional cues express semantic orientations of `subjectivity-type` tags. Such detailed classification provides the benefits in the process of sentiment analysis.

2.3 Sentence Tagging Examples

So far we describe the KSML as an annotation scheme for the Korean Sentiment Analysis Corpus with a focus on the differences with the MPQA annotation scheme.

n at r a e et representati es o t o ar or s o as e io ent ast ee o er o s o e o ernor in eastern a tia pro in e
The MPQA annotation scheme
GATE_objective-speech-event nested-source=w implicit=true GATE_direct-subjective: *as e io ent* nested-souce=w, *ar or s* polarity=negative expression-intensity=high intensity=high GATE_agent: *t o ar or s* id= *ar or s* nested-source=w, *ar or s*
The KSML annotation scheme
Objectivity tag SEED: *as e o er* nested-souce=w, *ar or s* type=dir-explicit subjectivity-type=agreement-negative polarity=negative intensity=high target= *o s o e o ernor in eastern a tia pro in e* SEED: *io ent* nested-souce=w type=indirect subjectivity-type=judgment-negative polarity=negative intensity=high target= *as e o er*

Table 2: Tagging examples of the MPQA and KSML

As an end of this section, the sentence tagging examples in Table 2 show the different tagging aspects according to the annotation schemes. The sample sentence and the example tags of the MPQA are brought from the existing MPQA corpus, and the tagging example of the KSML is made by an annotator who participated in the project constructing the Korean Sentiment Analysis Corpus. Compared to the MPQA scheme, the frame of the KSML is simpler and easier to understand in terms of subjectivity included in the sentence because the KSML grabs opinionated expressions in detail.

3 Sentiment Corpus: KOSAC

3.1 Corpus Selection

Unlike English, Korean is a morphologically rich language, so, rather than words, morphemes should be the units of annotations. However, it is too time consuming to build a flawless morphologically parsed corpus due to the inaccuracy of part of speech (POS) taggers. For this reason, the Sejong syntactic parsed corpus, which is semi-automatically built, was used as the basis for the sentiment annotation corpus. Syntactic information of sentences is also available, enabling further logical inference on agents or targets of sentimental expressions.

A subset containing a total of 332 articles made up of 7,713 sentences was selected from the Sejong corpus newspaper articles. These articles were taken from the society and life subsections of Hankyoreh and Chosun, the editorial section of Hankook.

3.2 Annotation Process

The size of corpus largely depends on the speed of annotation work. Without an appropriate annotation tool, it is almost impossible to build a large annotated corpus.

Though the MPQA opinion corpus was built with GATE annotation tool, we developed a morpheme based annotation tool for Korean text (Cattle et al., 2013) for three reasons. First, none of current annotation tools, such as GATE or brat, supported switching between word and morpheme views. Second, there are non-continuous sentiment expressions that cannot be annotated by current tools. Third, targets and nested-sources of sentiment expressions need to be annotated in advance of sentiment expressions within those tools, which is not intuitive and in turn makes process of annotation slow. Moreover, to ensure the quality of annotations, three well-trained linguistics students annotated separately, and then double cross-checked the annotations until all annotators agree on the same annotations.

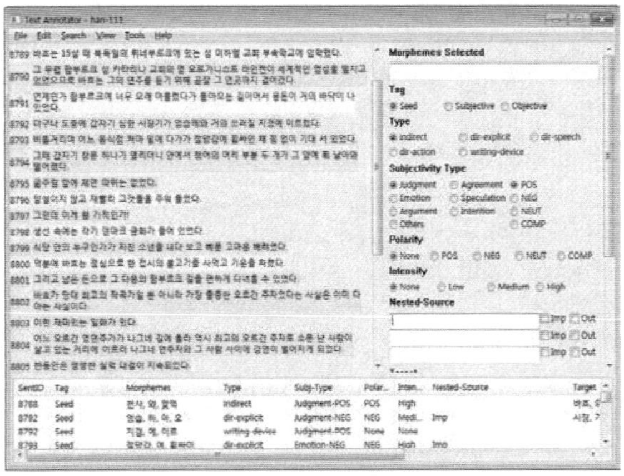

Figure 1: Morpheme Based Annotation Tool

3.3 Annotated Expressions

The accuracy of an annotated corpus is difficult to measure. For KOSAC, twenty frequently occurring sentiment expressions were chosen from six subjectivity types to see how consistently people annotated those expressions. For measurement, the ratio of annotated times to the number of occurring times for each of those expressions is shown in Table 3.

Emotion	ratio	Agreement	ratio	Argument	ratio
두렵- twulyep- 'fear'	1.00	합의하- hapuyha- 'agree'	0.86	주장하- cwucangha- 'insisit'	0.98
분노 pwunno 'anger'	0.93	인정하- incengha- 'admit'	0.90	지적하- cicekha- 'point out'	0.90
사랑하- salangha- 'love'	0.94	반대하- pantayha- 'disagree'	1.00	제시하- ceysiha- 'suggest'	0.82
행복하- hayngpokha- 'happy'	0.94	거부하- kepwuha- 'deny'	0.90		

Intention	ratio	Judgement	ratio	Speculation	ratio
-고 싶- -ko siph- 'want'	0.88	인기 inki 'popular'	0.87	-는 것 같- -nun kes kath- 'might'	0.50
-기 위하- -ki wiha- 'purpose'	0.63	재미 caymi 'fun'	0.59	-을 것 -ul kes 'would'	0.20
-도록 -tolok 'purpose'	0.52	중요하- Cwungyoha- 'important'	0.90	예상 되- yeysang toy- 'expected'	1.00
예정 yeyceng 'plan'	0.61	풍부하- Phwungpwuha- 'plentiful'	0.91		

Table 3: Frequency Cross Table of Expressive and Subjectivity Type

	Agree.	Argu.	Emotion	Intention	Judgment	Speculation	Others
Dir-Action	1	9	71	8	38	0	1
Dir-Explicit	156	277	341	276	2740	157	40
Dir-Speech	8	1149	22	28	86	13	7
Indirect	255	321	720	409	6086	63	22
Writing-Device	5	98	9	306	764	172	2957

Table 4: Frequency Cross Table of Expressive and Subjectivity Type

Among the 7,713 sentences, 2,658 are annotated as subjective and 5,055 sentences as objective. There are 17,615 SEED tags, indicating on average 2.3 expressions tagged as SEED per sentence.

Of the 17,615 SEED annotations, the frequencies of `type` and `subjectivity-type` are given in Table 4. As seen above, the `judgment` subjectivity type is the most predominant type since `judgment` subjectivity type expressions include not just short sentiment words or phrases, but also clauses that show speakers' judgments. Among subtypes of `type`, `indirect` expressions include all sentiment expressions except all main predicates and `writing-device` expressions; accordingly `indirect` type is also the most frequent type of all. A large portion of `writing-device` expressions are categorized `others` subjectivity type because they do not usually belong to any other subjectivity types. To help understand which expressions belong to such types above and how they are annotated, Table 5 shows some examples of some types.

`Direct-explicit` & `Agreement`		
뜻을 모으-	ttusul mou-	'agree'
결의하-	kyeluyha-	'resolve'
반발이 강하-	panpali kangha-	'strongly oppose'
`Direct-action` & `Emotion`		
눈물이 흐르-	nwunmwuli hulu-	'tear drops'
얼싸안-	elssaan-	'hug'
킥킥거리-	khikkhikkeli-	'giggle'
`Writing-device` & `Judgment`		
하지못하면	haci moshamyen	'if do not do (it)'
제아무리	ceyamwuli	'even if'
오히려	ohilye	'rather'

Table 5: Examples of Annotated Expressions

From the examples above, it can be seen that annotated expressions are not restricted to specific syntactic segments, but rather capture segments which reveal one's subjectivity. Also, it is noticeable that intensifiers are not separated from sentiment expressions.

From the fine-grained annotated corpus, characteristics of a subjective or an objective sentence could be described by frequencies of type and subjectivity types.

Type	Objective	Subjective
direct-action	0.015772	0.017097
direct-explicit	0.374925	0.794073
direct-speech	0.225594	0.067629
indirect	0.678179	1.679711
writing-device	0.354761	0.946809
Subjectivity Type	Objective	Subjective
Agreement	0.041925	0.079787
Argument	0.270313	0.18845
Emotion	0.116191	0.216565
Intention	0.118387	0.162234
Judgment	0.830904	2.087006
Speculation	0.030146	0.094225
Others	0.241366	0.677052
Number of SEEDs	1.649231	3.505319

Table 6: Average Frequencies of Types for Objective and Subjective Sentences.

For an objective or a subjective sentence, how many types and subjectivity types it has on average is shown in Table 6. A subjective sentence tends to have more `direct-explicit`, `indirect`, `writing-device` types than an objective sentence. The frequency of the `direct-speech` type is higher for objective sentences due to the reporting predicates. For subjectivity type, a subjective sentence has particularly higher frequency of `judgment`, `speculation`, `emotion`, and `others` than an objective sentence. Also the number of SEED tags for a subjective sentence is the double of that for an objective.

4 Experiments

4.1 Subjectivity Classification

Firstly, a subjectivity classification test was done by using frequency features from sentence tag attributes. To guarantee the experiment result, a 10-fold cross validation was used; 1/10 is used as a test set and 9/10 as a training set. As a classification model, SVMlight (Joachims, 2002) was chosen using a linear kernel and default options.

Since there could be too many frequency features from attributes, a pair of features was tested to classify sentence subjectivity, and then features were added one by one until the accuracy of SVM began to drop to find the most effective feature set. In detail, we identified the effectiveness of the attributes of SEED tags in terms of classifying polarity of a sentence by adding each attribute feature to the most efficient pairs as per the previous experiment. If an added attribute showed a better result, the combination would be the base pair for the next experiment.

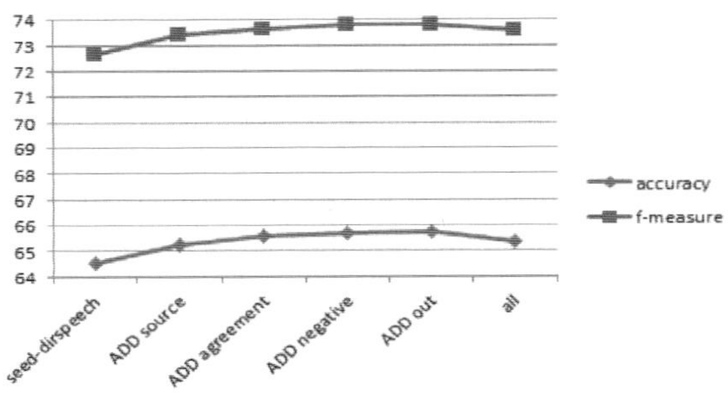

Figure 2: The result of polarity classification tests

Figure 2 shows experimental results of subjectivity classification. The best pair of features was the number of SEED tags and the `direct-speech` frequency, so another feature was added to the pair until the accuracy dropped. In the end, it was found that the best result was a feature set of the number of SEEDs, `direct-speech`, `nested-source`, `agreement`, `out (nested-source)`, and `negative` value of `polarity`. The best performance of the SVM classifier was accuracy 65.72%, precision 59.76%, recall 96.41%, F-measure 73.78%.

However, the best classification result by SVM is not satisfactory, even though this test was done within a gold standard data. The reason was that sentence subjectivity surprisingly does not depend on the frequency of attributes. Rather, it is decided how a sentence ends. It is intuitively noticeable that a subjective sentence has features that make it subjective, and an objective sentence does not. We found almost all subjective sentences end with expressions that have a `direct-explicit` tag or include a `writing-device` seed. Among subjective sentences, 84.9% included a `direct-explicit` or `writing-device` seed. Table 7 shows how much sentence subjectivity depends on `direct-explicit` and `writing-device` expressions. Furthermore, the position of `writing-device` expression is important for the subjectivity of a sentence; a subjective sentence tends to have it within a main clause or close to main predicate.

Type	Subjective Sent.(1)	Objective Sent	(1) / Total Subj Sent
D-E	2102	935	2102/2658 (79.08%)
W-D	1543	1197	1543/2658 (58.05%)

Table 7: Ratio of `direct-explicit` and `writing-device` for Sentence Subjectivity

4.2 Polarity Classification

Secondly, sentence polarity classification experiments were conducted. The experimental method was the same as the sentence subjectivity classification experiments. The following Figure 3 shows the best results and the experimental result of using all attributes.

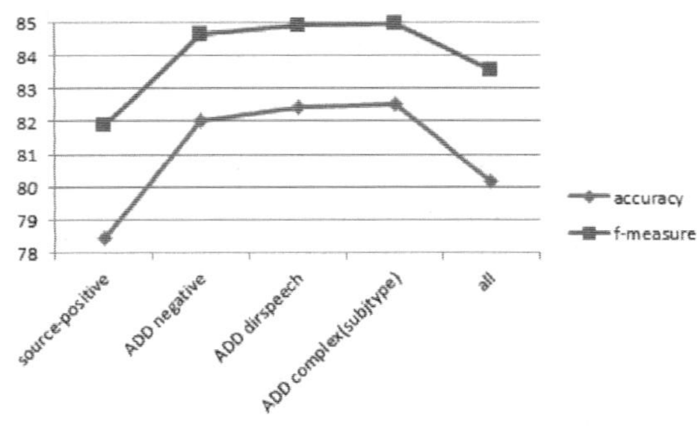

Figure 3: The result of polarity classification tests

Attributes leading the best results (Accuracy 82.52%, Precision 77.64%, Recall 93.93%, F-measure 84.96%) in the sentence polarity classification experiments were the number of `nested-source`, `positive` (`polarity`), `negative` (`polarity`), `direct-speech` (`type`), and `complex` (directional cue of `subjectivity-type`).

Among the contributory features in the experiment, the directional cue `complex`, which combines only with `emotion`, `judgment`, and `argument` subtype of `subjectivity-type`, is worthy of notice. These subtypes express private states in a relatively direct way and so the intensity of expressions is usually higher than other subtypes. In such aspects, polarity of expressions classified as these subtypes would be easier.

We suppose that the characteristics of news articles are the reason why `nested-source` and `direct-speech` (`type`) are the main features in the experimental results. In general, writers of news articles try to maintain objective distance. When citing other people's comments or statements, however, they have to convey the exact words of the speaker. Therefore, cited sentences could include more direct opinionated expressions showing obvious polarity. A number of `nested-source` and `direct-speech` (`type`) are important factors to distinguish whether an expression is a writer's own thinking or a citation of another's utterance.

In another manner, we can classify polarity of a sentence simply by checking for the inclusion of specific attributes. Checking attributes can be different according to the corpus. In the experiment using KOSAC corpus, we only used three attributes of SEED tags: `type` (only `direct` subtypes), `polarity`, and `intensity`. Table 8 describes the algorithm to classify polarity of a sentence by checking these attributes.

Through this checking algorithm, we obtained an 82.15% accuracy on sentence polarity classification. This result is slightly lower than the best experimental result using the SVMlight. However, considering that many sentences could slip through the net of checking at any phase of the algorithm since the algorithm is too simple, such accuracy can be rated high. In addition, this method does not need any other classifier, and we can get good results by using attributes which are understood intuitively as important factors in classification of polarity.

For all sentences in the KOSAC corpus,

1. if a sentences have SEED tags of `direct` subtypes,
   for only corresponding SEED tags,
   A. if a number of `positive` polarity tags and a number of `negative` polarity tags are different, classify the sentence as the bigger polarity.
   B. else,
      i. if `intensity` values of the polarity tags are different, classify the sentence as the polarity having the highest intensity value.
      ii. else, classify the sentence as the polarity having `dir-explicit` type value.
2. else,
   for every SEED tags,
   do the same process of phase 1.

Table 8: Checking algorithm for polarity classification

Therefore, we confirm that the theoretical background forming the KSML annotation scheme is highly effective at describing subjectivity and polarity of opinionated expressions.

5 Conclusion and Future Work

This paper described a fine-grained annotation scheme KSML and the manually-annotated Korean Sentiment Analysis Corpus, KOSAC. This scheme pulls together into one linguistic annotation scheme both the concept of private states and nested source based on the MPQA. However, the frame and some attributes were modified in order to reflect the characteristics of Korean language. The scheme was applied comprehensively to a large 7,713-sentence corpus. Several examples illustrating the scheme and basic observations of the corpus were described in section 3. The results of sentence subjectivity and polarity classification experiments using the corpus were also presented in section 4. Such experimental results show wide possibilities of application of the KSML annotation scheme and the KOSAC corpus.

The main goal behind the KSML and KOSAC is to support the development and evaluation of NLP systems that exploit opinions and sentiments in applications. Our hope is that including rich information of opinionated expressions in our corpus annotations will contribute to a new understanding of how sentiments are expressed linguistically in Korean language. We hope this work will be useful to others working in corpus-based explorations of subjective language and that it will encourage NLP researchers to experiment with subjective language in their applications.

Acknowledgments

This work was supported by the National Research Foundation of Korea Grant funded by the Korean Government (NRF-2011-327-A00322).

References

Cattle, Andrew, Munhyong Kim, and Hyopil Shin. 2013. Morpheme-based Annotation Tool for Korean Text. In Proceedings of the American Association for Corpus Linguistics.

Joachims, Thorsten. 2002. Learning to Classify Text Using Support Vector Machines. Ph.D Dissertation, Cornell University.

Martin, J.R. 2002. Appraisal: An overview. http://www.grammatics.com/appraisal/AppraisalGuide/UnFramed/Appraisal-Overview.htm

Pang, Bo, Lillian Lee, and Shivakumar Vaithyanathan. 2002. Thumbs up? Sentiment Classification Using Machine Learning Techniques. In Proceedings of the Conference on Empirical Methods in Natural Language Processing, pages 79-86.

Shin, Hyopil, Munhyong Kim, Yu-Mi Jo, Hayeon Jang, and Andrew Cattle. 2012. Annotation Scheme for Constructing Sentiment Corpus in Korean. In proceedings of the 26th Pacific Asia Conference on Language, Information and Compuation, pages 181-190.

White, P.R. 2002. Appraisal-the language of evaluation and stance. In Jef Verschueren, Jan-Ola Ostman, Jan Blommaert, and Chris Bulcaen, editors, Handbook of Pragmatics, pages 1-27.

Wiebe, Janyce. 2002. Instructions for Annotating Opinions in Newspaper Articles. Departiment of Computer Science Technical Report TR-02-101, University of Pittsburgh.

Wiebe, Janyce, Theresa Wilson, and Claire Cardie. 2005. Annotating Expressions of Opinions and Emotions in Language. Language Resources and Evaluation, 39(2/3):164-210.

Wilson, Theresa Ann. 2008. Fine-grained Subjectivity and Sentiment Analysis: Recognizing the Intensity, Polarity, and Attitudes of Private States. Ph.D Dissertation, Brandeis University.

*** Formatting Issue - Best Available Paper/Graphic ***

Cross-lingual Link Discovery between Chinese and English Wiki Knowledge Bases

Qingliang Miao, Huayu Lu, Shu Zhang, Yao Meng
Fujitsu R&D Center Co., Ltd.
No.56 Dong Si Huan Zhong Rd, Chaoyang District, Beijing P.R. China
{qingliang.miao, zhangshu, mengyao}@cn.fujitsu.com
lvhuayu@gmail.com

Abstract

Wikipedia is an online multilingual encyclopedia that contains a very large number of articles covering most written languages. However, one critical issue for Wikipedia is that the pages in different languages are rarely linked except for the cross-lingual link between pages about the same subject. This could pose serious difficulties to humans and machines who try to seek information from different lingual sources. In order to address above issue, we propose a hybrid approach that exploits anchor strength, topic relevance and entity knowledge graph to automatically discovery cross-lingual links. In addition, we develop CELD, a system for automatically linking key terms in Chinese documents with English Concepts. As demonstrated in the experiment evaluation, the proposed model outperforms several baselines on the NTCIR data set, which has been designed especially for the cross-lingual link discovery evaluation.

1 Introduction

Wikipedia is the largest multilingual encyclopedia online with over 19 million articles in 218 written languages. However, the anchored links in Wikipedia articles are mainly created within the same language. Consequently, knowledge sharing and discovery could be impeded by the absence of links between different languages. Figure 1 shows the statistics of monolingual and cross-lingual alignment in Chinese and English Wikipedia. As it can be seen that there are 2.6 millions internal links within English Wikipedia and 0.32 millions internal links within Chinese Wikipedia, but only 0.18 millions links between Chinese Wikipedia pages to English ones. For example, in Chinese Wikipedia page "武术(Martial arts)", anchors are only linked to related Chinese articles about different kinds of martial arts such as "拳击(Boxing)", "柔道(Judo)" and "击剑(Fencing)". But, there is no anchors linked to other related English articles such as "Boxing", "Judo and "Fencing". This makes information flow and knowledge propagation could be easily blocked between articles of different languages.

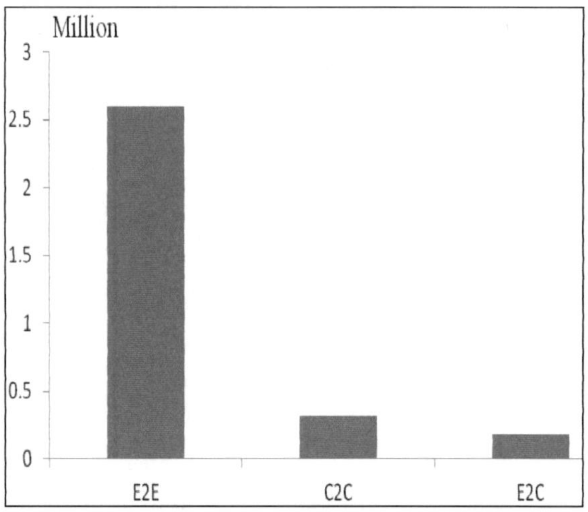

Figure 1. Statistics of English to English links (E2E), Chinese to Chinese links (C2C) and Chinese to English links (C2E).

Consequently, automatically creating cross-lingual links between Chinese and English Wikipedia would be very useful in information flow and knowledge sharing. At present, there are several monolingual link discovery tools for English Wikipedia, which assist topic curators in discovering prospective anchors and targets for a given Wikipedia pages. However, no such cross-lingual tools yet exist, that support the cross-lingual linking of documents from multiple languages (Tang et al., 2012). As a result, the work is mainly taken by manual, which is obviously tedious, time consuming, and error prone.

One way to solve above issue is cross-lingual link discovery technology, which automatically creates potential links between documents in different languages. Cross-lingual link discovery not only accelerates the knowledge sharing in different languages on the Web, but also benefits many practical applications such as information retrieval and machine translation (Wang et al., 2012). In existing literature, a few approaches have been proposed for linking English Wikipedia to other languages (Kim and Gurevych, 2011; Fahrni et al., 2011). Generally speaking, there are three steps for Cross-lingual link discovery: (1) Apply information extraction techniques to extract key terms from source language documents. (2) Utilize machine translation systems to translate key terms and source documents into target language. (3) Apply entity resolution methods to identify the corresponding concepts in target language. However, in key term extraction step, most works rely on statistical characteristics of anchor text (Tang et al., 2012), but ignore the topic relevance. In this case, common concepts are selected as key terms, but these terms are not related to the topic of the Wikipedia page. For example, in Chinese Wikipedia page "武术 (Martial arts)", some countries' name such as "中国 (China)", "日本 (Japan)" and "韩国 (Korea)" are also selected as key terms when using anchor statistics. For term translation, existing methods usually depends on machine translation, and suffers from translation errors, particularly those involving named entities, such as person names (Cassidy et al., 2012). Moreover, machine translation systems are prone to introduce translation ambiguities. In entity resolution step, some works use simple title matching to find concept in target languages, which could not distinguish ambiguous entities effectively (Kim and Gurevych, 2011).

In this paper, we try to investigate the problem of cross-lingual link discovery from Chinese Wikipedia pages to English ones. The problem is non-trivial and poses a set of challenges.

Linguistic complexity

Chinese Wikipedia is more complex, because contributors of Chinese Wikipedia are from different Chinese spoken geographic areas and language variations. For example, Yue dialect[1] is a primary branch of Chinese spoken in southern China and Wu[2] is a Sino-Tibetan language spoken in most of southeast. Moreover, these contributors cite modern and ancient sources combining simplified and traditional Chinese text, as well as regional variants (Tang et al., 2012). Consequently, it is necessary to normalize words into simple Chinese before cross-lingual linking.

Key Term Extraction

There are different kinds of key term ranking methods that could be used in key term extraction, such as tf-idf, information gain, anchor probability and anchor strength (Kim and Gurevych, 2011). How to define a model to incorporate both the global statistical characteristics and topically related context together?

Translation

Key term translation could rely on bilingual dictionary and machine translation. This kind of methods could obtain high precision, while suffer from low recall. When using larger dictionaries or corpus for translation, it is prone to introduce translation ambiguities. How to increase recall without introducing additional ambiguities?

In order to solve the above challenges, we investigate several important factors of cross-lingual link discovery problem and propose a hybrid approach to solve the above issues. Our contributions include:

(1) We develop a normalization lexicon for Chinese variant character. This lexicon could be used for traditional and simplified Chinese transformation and other variations normalization. We also discovery entity knowledge from Wikipedia, Chinese encyclopedia, and then we build a knowledge graph that includes mentions, concepts, translations and corresponding confidence scores.

(2) We present an integrated model for key terms extraction, which leverages anchor

[1] http://zh-yue.wikipedia.org
[2] http://wuu.wikipedia.org

statistical probability information and topical relevance. Efficient candidate selection method and distinguishing algorithm enable this model meet the real-time requirements.

(3) We implement a system and evaluate it using NTCIR cross-lingual links discovery dataset. Comparing with several baselines, our system achieves high precision and recall.

The remainder of the paper is organized as follows. In the following section we review the existing literature. Then, we formally introduce the problem of cross-lingual link discovery and some related concepts in section 3. We introduce the proposed approach in section 4. We conduct comparative experiments and present the experiment results in section 5. At last, we conclude the paper with a summary of our work and give our future working directions.

2 Related Works

Generally speaking, link discovery is a kind of semantic annotation (Kiryakov et al., 2004), which is characterized as the dynamic creation of interrelationships between concepts in knowledge base and mentions in unstructured or semi-structured documents (Bontcheva and Rout, 2012).

In particular, most existing monolingual semantic annotation (MLSA) approaches annotate documents with links to Wikipedia or DBPedia. Mihalcea and Csomai (2007) first attempt to use Wikipedia to annotate monolingual text is their Wikify system. Wikify system includes two main steps, key term detection and disambiguation. The system identifies key terms according to link probabilities obtained from Wikipedia pages. In order to link key term to the appropriate concept, Wikify extracts features from the key term and its context, and compares these features to training examples obtained from the Wikipedia. Milne and Witten (2008) implement a similar system called Wikipedia Miner, which adopts supervised disambiguation approach using Wikipedia hyperlinks as training data. There are also some semantic annotation contests. For example, TAC's entity linking task[3] focuses on the linkage of named entities such as persons, organizations and geo-political entities to English Wikipedia concepts. Given a query that consists of a name string and a background document ID, the system is required to provide the ID of the knowledge base entry to which the name refers; or NIL if there is no such knowledge base entry. Due to the intrinsic ambiguity of named entities, most works in entity linking task focus on named entity disambiguation. For example, Han and Sun (2012) propose a generative entity-topic model that effectively joins context compatibility and topic coherence. Their model can accurately disambiguate most mentions in a document using both the local information and the global consistency.

Following this research stream, researchers have been paying more and more attention on cross-lingual semantic annotation (CLSA). Knowledge Base Population (KBP2011) evaluations propose a cross-lingual entity link task, which aims to find link between Chinese queries and English concepts. NTCIR9 cross-lingual link discovery task is another kind of cross-lingual semantic annotation. These two tasks are different in query selection criteria, leading to different technical difficulties and concerns. In KBP2011, key terms are manually selected to cover many ambiguous entities and name variants. Consequently, disambiguation is crucial in KBP2011. While in NTCIR9, participants have to extract key terms from given documents first. Since these extracted key terms are less ambiguous than KBP's entities, disambiguation has less effect on final performance (Kim and Gurevych, 2011). In contrast, translation plays an important role in NTCIR9 task. Another direction is cross-lingual knowledge linking across web knowledge bases. Wang et al. (2012) study the problem of creating cross-lingual links between English Wikipedia and Chinese encyclopedia Baidu Baike [4] and propose a linkage factor graph model.

Although CLSA is a new task, efforts in MLSA could be adopted. In particular, there are two conventional way to extend MLSA systems to the cross-lingual setting: the first one is applying MLSA method to link source language entity mentions to source language knowledge base concepts, and then link the source language knowledge base concepts to the corresponding target language knowledge base concepts. This strategy relies heavily on the existence of a reliable mapping between source language knowledge base and target language knowledge base. The second one is utilizing machine translation techniques to translate the source

[3] http://www.nist.gov/tac/2012/KBP/workshop/index.html

[4] http://baike.baidu.com/

language document or mentions into the target language, and then apply a MLSA method in the target language side. This process relies on machine translation output, and it will suffer from translation errors inevitably, particularly those involving named entities (Cassidy et al., 2012). In this paper, we leverage anchor probability information and topic relevance to extract key terms from Chinese documents. And then, we build a knowledge graph, and use this graph to translate key terms to English. Finally, cross-lingual links are identified by concept resolution model.

3 Problem Definition

In this section, we define the problem of cross-lingual link discovery and some related concepts.

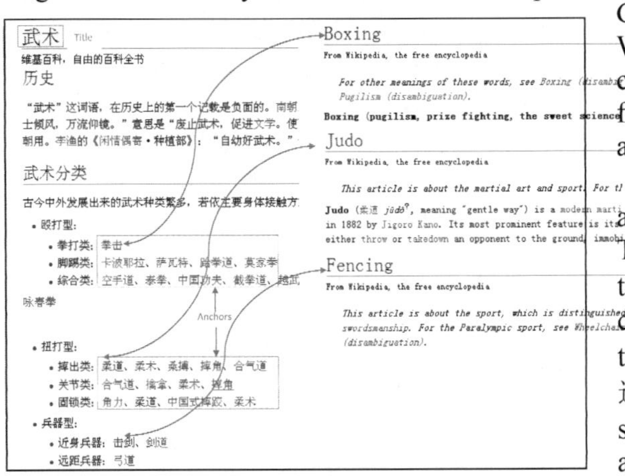

Figure 2. An Example of cross-lingual link discovery, Chinese to English links (C2E).

Definition 1: Wikipedia Knowledge Base

Wikipedia knowledge base is a collection of collaboratively written articles, each of which defines a specific concept. It can be formally represented as $K=\{a_i\}, i \in [1,n]$, where a_i is an article in K and n is the size of K. Each article a_i describes a specific concept. Each article includes four key elements, title name, textual content, anchors and categories and can be represented as $\{N(a_i), T(a_i), A(a_i), C(a_i)\}$, where $N(a_i)$ and $T(a_i)$ are the title name and textual content of the article a_i respectively; $A(a_i)$ denotes the set of anchors of the a_i, and $C(a_i)$ is the category tags of a_i.

Definition 2: Topic document

The topic documents are actual Wikipedia articles selected for link discovery. Anchors in topic documents are removed in the test data. For example, in Chinese to English link discovery task. Topic documents are Chinese articles without existing anchors. Topic document could be represented as $\{N(a_i), T(a_i), C(a_i)\}$, where $N(a_i)$ is the title name of the document, $T(a_i)$ is the textual content of the document a_i; and $C(a_i)$ is the category tags of the document a_i.

Definition 3: Anchor

An anchor is a piece of text that is relevant to the topic and worthy of being linked to other articles for further reading. Anchor text usually gives the user relevant descriptive or contextual information about the content of the link's destination.

Definition 4: Cross-lingual Link

Given one topic t in source language and a Wikipedia knowledge base K in target language, cross-lingual link discovery is the process of finding potential anchors in t and link to appropriate articles in K.

As shown in Figure 2, the topic "武术(Martial arts)" is from Chinese Wikipedia documents. There is no anchors (cross-lingual link) from topic "武术" to English Wikipedia articles. In the cross-lingual link discovery problem, our goal is to extract anchors such as "拳击(Boxing)", "柔道(Judo)" and "击剑(Fencing)", and then find semantic equivalent articles for all the extracted anchors in English Wikipedia knowledge base.

4 The Approach

In this section, we will first introduce the overview of the system. And then, we present key term extraction and translation and concept resolution.

4.1 System Overview

Figure 3 illustrates the overview of the cross-lingual link discovery system. The inputs of the system are Chinese topic documents and English Wikipedia knowledge base, and the outputs are anchors of Chinese topic documents and their linking concepts in English Wikipedia knowledge base.

The system consists of four parts: (1) key term extraction module (KEM); (2) knowledge mining module (KMM); (3) key term translation module (KTM) and (4) concept resolution module (CRM).

KEM first extracts key term candidates from the main text of Chinese topic documents. And then, KEM refines key term candidates according to anchor statistical probability and topic similarity. Finally, key terms are normalized by normalization lexicon.

KMM extracts mentions, concepts and translations from Wikipedia dumps and Chinese encyclopedia. Then translation of concept is obtained by cross-lingual links and heuristic patterns. Finally, KMM builds knowledge graph including mentions, concepts and translations with corresponding confidence.

KTM has two inputs, one is key terms from KEM and the other one is knowledge graph from KMM. KTM first map key term (mention) to corresponding concept, and then find the translation of concept. In case we cannot find the mentions in the knowledge graph, we use machine translation systems to translate the key terms.

CRM first searches concept candidates from knowledge graph. This process could also be viewed as query expansion. After that, CRM ranks the concept candidates according to weighted sum of similarities including lexical similarity, local context similarity and category similarity. And then, CRM selects the one with highest similarity score as the final linking target and generates cross-lingual links.

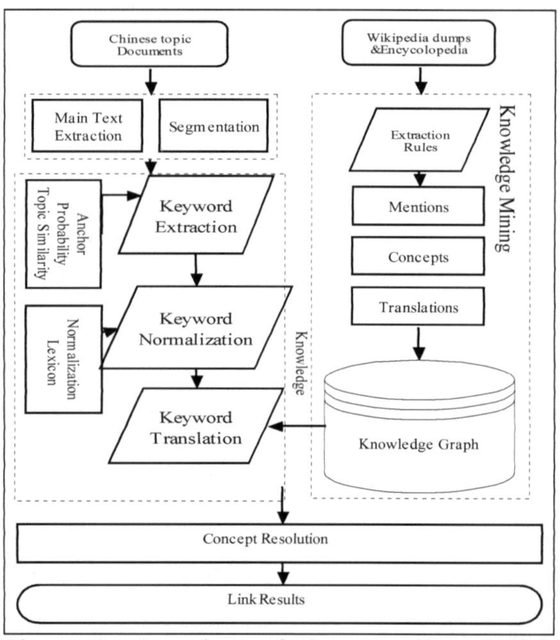

Figure 3. Overview of the cross-lingual link discovery system.

4.2 Key Term Extraction

In this section, we introduce the method for key term extraction. Key term extraction includes three steps: (1) key term candidate extraction from Chinese topic document; (2) key term candidate ranking according to importance and topic relevance; (3) key term normalization.

Kim and Gurevych (2011) introduce several key term candidate selection methods, such as noun phrases, named entities and anchor text. They also present some key term candidate ranking method such as tf-idf, anchor probability. In order to obtain topic-related and important terms, we leverage anchor strength and topic relatedness to rank key term candidates in this paper. In particular, we extract all n-grams of size 1 to 5, because n-grams subsume most key term candidates, which could obtain a high recall. Then, we compute anchor strength and topic relevance. Anchor strength measures the probability of the given text being used as an anchor text to its most frequent target in the Wikipedia corpus. Anchor strength could be computed as follows:

$$anchorStrength = \frac{count(c, d_{anchor})}{count(c,d)} \quad (1)$$

where $count(c.d_{anchor})$ denotes the count of anchor candidate c being used as an anchor in a document d, and $count(c.d)$ is the count of c appearing in a document d. In this paper, we filter out the key term candidates whose anchor strength is low than 0.001.

Topic relevance is computed as follows:

$$relatedness(a,b) = \frac{\log(\max(|A|,|B|)) - \log(|A \cap B|)}{\log(|W|) - \log(\min(|A|,|B|))} \quad (2)$$

where a and b are two articles, A and B are the sets of all articles that link to a and b respectively, and W is set of all articles in Wikipedia. In this paper, we compute the semantic relatedness between each key term candidate and the topic. In particular, we first map the key term candidate to its corresponding concept, and then compute the semantic relatedness with the topic. If the key term candidate does not have any associated concept, we discard it. For example, given the topic document t and key term candidate a, we first find the concept c of a, and then compute the semantic relatedness between t and c. Finally, we filter out some key term candidates whose semantic relatedness is low than a threshold.

After that, we normalize the key terms according to the normalization lexicon. The normalization lexicon is derived from Wiktionary[5], which is a multilingual, web-based project to create a free content dictionary,

[5] http://zh.wiktionary.org/zh/

available in 158 languages. The lexicon contains 4747 traditional and simple Chinese character pairs. Most key terms could be normalized by simply looking up the normalization lexicon except for some cases. For example, in phrase "乾燥 (Drying)", character "乾" should be convert to "干", while in phrase "乾隆 (Qianlong_Emperor)" character "乾" should not be convert to "干". For these special cases, we have to build another dictionary, which includes the special phrases.

4.3 Key Term Translation

In this section, we first introduce how to mine entity knowledge from Wikipedia dumps and Chinese encyclopedia. And then, we introduce the structure of the knowledge graph. Finally, we illustrate how to use this knowledge graph to translate key terms. In particular, the knowledge can be built in two steps:

(1) Extracting mentions and concepts;
(2) Extract concepts and corresponding translations.

KMM extracts mentions and corresponding concepts by using redirection links, anchor links and pre-defined extraction patterns. Redirections in Wikipedia and encyclopedia are good indicators for mentions and concepts. Anchor links could also be used to trace to which concepts the mention links. In this paper, we use anchor links in Chinese Wikipedia and encyclopedia such as Baidu Baike and Hudong Baike[6]. We also exploit synonyms and linguistic patterns such as such as "A also called B", "A known as B", "A is referred to as B". After mention and concept extraction, we compute the confidence score that measures how confident the mention referring to concepts. For redirection links and linguist patterns, the confident score is assigned 1.0, since they are manually annotated. For anchor links, we assign the linking frequency as confident scores for corresponding mention and concept pairs.

KMM extracts concepts and their translations according to cross-lingual links and linguistic patterns. Cross-lingual links connect articles on the same concept in different languages, therefore concept and their translation pairs could be extracted. Besides cross-lingual links, we also discovery translations from Chinese encyclopedia through linguistic patterns, such as "A's English name is B", "A's abbreviation is C". The confident scores are set to 1.0.

After that, we built mention, concept and translation graph MCTG. MCTG includes mention, concept and translation layers. The associations between different layers are represented as interlayer links, and each association is assigned a confident score.

In key term translation, we adopt a cascade translation strategy. For a key term (mention), we first obtain the corresponding concepts and their confident scores. Then, we search the graph to find the translations for each concept. If the knowledge graph does not contain the mention, concept or translation, we use a machine translation system to translate the mention. Figure 4 illustrates a translation example. Given a mention such as "和阗玉" or "昆仑玉", we first find corresponding concept "和田玉", and then map the concept "和田玉" to its translation "Hetian jade" and "nephrite".

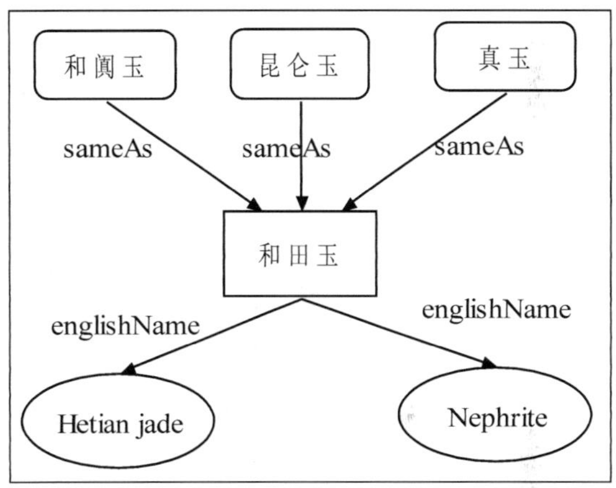

Figure 4. A key term translation example

4.4 Concept Resolution

After key term translation, we use the knowledge graph to select concept candidates for each mention and obtain a concept candidate set *S*. To identify the exact concept the key term refers, our system uses the weighted sum of similarities including lexical similarity, local context similarity and category similarity to determine which concept is the right one. In particular, we adopt Levenshtein distance[7] based algorithm to compute lexical similarity between mentions and concepts' titles. We also adopt vector-space model using bag-of-words to compute the textual similarity. Besides local similarity, we also

[6] http://www.baike.com/

[7] http://en.wikipedia.org/wiki/Levenshtein_distance

consider category similarity, for each concept candidate c_c in S, we find the English concept c_e whose title exactly matches the concept candidate. When multiple English concepts match the concept candidate, we find the most specific common class that subsumes c_c and c_e in the class taxonomy of Wikipedia. And then, we compute the path length between c_c and c_e. Finally, we select the one with largest similarity as the final linking target and generate cross-lingual links. In this work, the weight of each similarity is estimated from a manually collected training data set.

5 Experiments

In this section, we report a primary experiment aimed at evaluating the proposed method and system. We first describe the datasets used in our study and then we give experiment setup and results to demonstrate the effectiveness of our method for cross-lingual link discovery task.

5.1 Experimental Setup

In this experiment, we use the same dataset in (Tang et al., 2012), which is provided by NTCIR. The dumps of the Chinese and English Wikipedia are downloaded in June 2010. There are 3,484,250 English articles and 316,251 Chinese articles respectively. The test data contains a set of 36 Chinese topics[8]. The ground-truth is derived from Wikipedia dumps.

For evaluation, we adopt two metrics, Precision@N and Mean Average Precision (MAP) to quantify the performance of different methods. In this experiment, we adopt six methods as baselines. For detailed information about the baseline methods, please refer to (Tang et al., 2012).

5.2 Experimental Results

Table 1 shows the experiment results of different methods. From Table 1, we can see that the proposed approach outperforms all the baselines. Through analyzing the experiments, we find anchor probability is very efficient in key term selection, since it could filter out most unimportant key term candidates. Topical relevance and key term normalization could also improve the performance. Knowledge graph based method translation could get high precision results, and machine translation system could provide complementary information for knowledge graph based translation.

Method	**MAP**	**P@5**	**P@10**	**P@20**
CELD	**0.217**	0.767	**0.733**	**0.653**
LinkProb	0.168	**0.800**	0.694	0.546
PNM	0.123	0.667	0.567	0.499
LinkProbEn2	0.095	0.456	0.428	0.338
LinkProbEn	0.085	0.489	0.394	0.315
LinkProb_S	0.059	0.411	0.322	0.268
LinkProbEn_S	0.033	0.233	0.186	0.144

Table 1. Experiment results

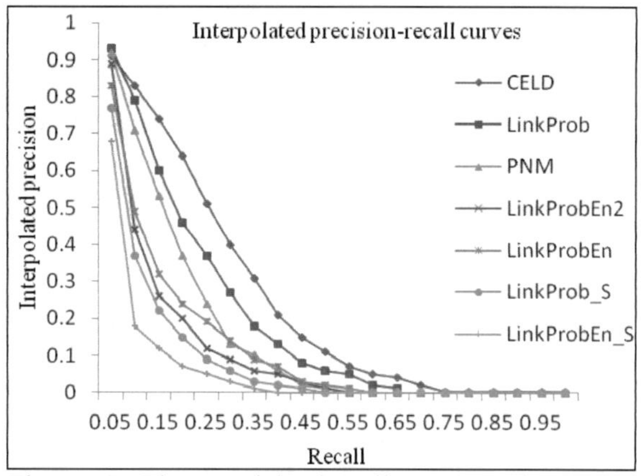

Figure 5. The precision/recall curves of CELD system

Figure 5 shows the interpolated precision-recall curves of CELD and other baseline methods. From Figure 5, we can see the proposed system outperforms all the baseline methods.

6 Conclusion

In this paper we present a hybrid approach for Chinese to English link discovery. This approach can automatically identify anchors in Chinese document and link to target concepts in English Wikipedia. To solve the Chinese character variant issues, we develop a normalization lexicon. We also build a knowledge graph for key term translation. Experimental results on real world datasets show promising results and demonstrate the proposed approach is efficient. As a future research, we plan to use more sophisticated nature language processing techniques to key term extraction and translation. We also plan to integrating linking and contextual information for concept resolution.

[8] http://crosslink.googlecode.com/files/zh-topics-36.zip

*** Formatting Issue - Best Available Paper/Graphic ***

References

Bontcheva, K., and Rout, D. 2012. Making Sense of Social Media Streams through Semantics: a Survey. Semantic Web journal.

Cassidy, T., Ji, H., Deng, H. B., Zheng, J., and Han, J. W. 2012. Analysis and Refinement of Cross-Lingual Entity Linking. In Proceedings of the third International Conference on Information Access Evaluation: Multilinguality, Multimodality, and Visual Analytics,2012. CLEF'12. Springer-Verlag Berlin, Heidelberg, 1-12.

Fahrni, A., Nastase, V., and Strube, M., 2011. HITS' Graph-based System at the NTCIR-9 Cross-lingual Link Discovery Task. In Proceedings of ntcir-9 workshop meeting, 2011. NTCIR'9.

Han, X. P., and Sun, L. 2012. An Entity-Topic Model for Entity Linking. In Proceedings of the 2012 Joint Conference on Empirical Methods in Natural Language Processing and Computational Natural Language Learning, 105-115.

Kim, J., and Gurevych, I. 2011. UKP at CrossLink: Anchor Text Translation for Cross-lingual Link Discovery. In Proceedings of ntcir-9 workshop meeting, 2011. NTCIR'9.

Kiryakov, A., Popov, B., Ognyanoff, D., Manov, D., Kirilov, A., and Goranov, M. 2004. Semantic Annotation, Indexing and Retrieval. Journal of Web Semantics, ISWC 2003 Special Issue, 1(2): 49-79, 2004.

Mihalcea, R., and Csomai, A. 2007. Wikify! Linking Documents to Encyclopedic Knowledge. In Proceedings of the 17th ACM Conference on Information and Knowledge Management, 2007, CIKM'07. ACM New York, NY, 233-242.

Milne, D., and Witten, I. H. 2008. Learning to link with Wikipedia. In Proceedings of the 17th ACM Conference on Information and Knowledge Management, 2008. CIKM'08. ACM New York, NY, 509-518.

Tang, L. X., Geva, S., Trotman, A., Xu, Y., and Itakura, K. Y. 2011. Overview of the NTCIR-9 Cross-link Task: Cross-lingual Link Discovery. In Proceedings of ntcir-9 workshop meeting, 2011. NTCIR'9.

Tang, L. X., Trotman, A., Geva, S., and Xu, Y. 2012. Cross-Lingual Knowledge Discovery: Chinese-to-English Article Linking in Wikipedia. Lecture Notes in Computer Science Volume 7675, 2012, 286-295.

Wang, Z. C., Li, J. Z., Wang, Z. G., and Tang, J.2012. Cross-lingual Knowledge Linking across Wiki Knowledge Bases. In Proceedings of the 21st International Conference on World Wide Web, 2012. WWW'12. ACM New York, NY, 459-468.

Locative Postpositions and Conceptual Structure in Japanese

Akira Ohtani
Faculty of Informatics, Osaka Gakuin University
2-36-1 Kishibe-minami, Suita-shi, Osaka, 564-8511, Japan
ohtani@ogu.ac.jp

Abstract

This paper proposes two syntax-semantics correspondence rules which consistently account for the distribution of Japanese locative postpositions *ni* and *de*. We demonstrate how to adapt the machinery of the occurrence of the postpositions based on the assumption of Conceptual Semantics (Jackendoff, 1983; 1990; 1991) to fit the organization of Japanese grammar. The correspondence rules correlate with semantic distinction of verb classes: the semantic field distinction between Spatial and Temporal with respect to the BE-function encoded in the lexical conceptual structure of several verbs. As a result, this paper elucidates the mechanism of locative alternation of the verb *aru* 'be', which has not been fully explicated.

1 Introduction

Japanese postpositions *ni* and *de* indicate locations, which are exemplified below.

(1) a. Kauntaa-no-ue-{*ni/*de*} gurasu-ga aru.
bar-GEN-on glass-NOM is
'There is a glass on the bar.'

b. Kauntaa-no-ue-{**ni/de*} gurasu-ga subetta.
bar-GEN-on glass-NOM slid
'A glass slid on the bar.'

As shown in (1a) *de* cannot be used with the stative verb *aru* 'be' to indicate a location where an object exists, and as shown in (1b) *ni* cannot occur with non-stative verb *suberu* 'slide' which expresses motion of an object. It can be argued that *ni* indicates "location of a state", while *de* indicates "location of an event or action".

However, the locational verb *aru* 'be' shows the following alternation between *ni* and *de*.

(2) a. Kono hoteru-{*ni/*de*} hooru-ga aru.
This hotel-in hall-NOM is
'There is a hall in this hotel.'

b. Kono hoteru-{**ni/de*} konsaato-ga aru.
This hotel-in concert-NOM is
'There is a concert in this hotel.'

Since the postposition *de* can be used with the stative verb *aru* 'be' as shown in (2b), we cannot simply refer to the stative/non-stative distinction of the predicate involved in order to predict the distribution of *ni* and *de*.

Although many descriptive and theoretical studies have discussed the syntactic and semantic properties of these postpositions (e.g. Kageyama, 1974; Kamio, 1980; Martin, 1987; Moriyama, 1988; Nakau, 1994a; 1994b; 1995; 1998; Teramura, 1982, among others), none of them have fully accounted for the distribution of the postposition *ni* and *de* and the semantic difference between them.

In this paper we consider the semantic difference between the two locative postpositions and give an account of the semantic structures for sentences involving locative *ni*- or *de*-phrases within the framework of Jackendoff's (1983; 1990; 1991) Conceptual Semantics.

2 Distribution of *Ni* and *De*

2.1 Two Types of Location

There are cases where *ni* can occur with a non-stative verb as in (3a), and *de* can appear with a stative verb as in (3b).

(3) a. Kauntaa-no-naka-*ni* baaten-ga tatta.
bar-GEN-inside barman-NOM stood
'A barman stood inside the bar.'

b. Raunji-*de*-wa biiru-no nedan-ga takai.
lounge-at-TOP beer-GEN price-NOM high
'The price of beer is high at the lounge.'

In (3a), the entity *baaten* 'barman' occupies the place denoted by the *ni*-phrase. In (3b), 'the price of beer being high' obtains at the location denoted by the *de*-phrase.

2.2 Locational Verb *Aru*

On the semantic level, there are two points to be addressed with regard to the examples in (2). The first point to be noted is that the choice between *ni* in (4a) and *de* in (4b) below seems to be related to the ontological category of the nominative NP.

(4) a. Kono hoteru-{*ni/*de*}
This hotel-in
[$_{\text{NP}}$ hooru/steeji/raunji]-ga aru.
hall/stage/lounge-NOM is
'There is a {hall/stage/lounge} in this hotel.'

b. Kono hoteru-{**ni/de*}
This hotel-in
[$_{\text{NP}}$ konsaato/kekkonshiki/kaigi]-ga aru.
concert/wedding/meeting-NOM is
'There will be a {concert/wedding/meeting} in this hotel.'

That is, the nominative NP denoting a location of an "individual" co-occurs with a PP headed by *ni*, while the nominative NP denoting a location of a "situation" co-occurs with a PP headed by *de*, as Nakau (1998) claims.

The second point is the semantic relatedness of the two instances of the same verb *aru* 'be' in (4a) and (4b). There is a clear intuition about the relatedness between the two, so that one may reasonably assume that they are two different realizations of the same verb *aru*: both of them mean that some "entities" are located at some "locations", though they differ in what are counted as "entity" and "location". The *aru* in (4a) means that some Things are located at some spatial "locations", while the *aru* in (4b) means that some Events are located at some temporal "locations" that are not expressed.[1]

The semantic relatedness between the two uses of *aru* as mentioned above should be reflected in the lexical conceptual structure (henceforth, LCS) of the verb.

3 Two Types of Location

3.1 Two Types of Location in English

Jackendoff (1983; 1990) distinguishes two types of "location" by assuming that the conceptual category [PLACE] can appear either as an argument or a modifier in conceptual structure.

(5) a. The mouse is under the table.

$$[_{\text{State}}\ \text{BE}\ ([_{\text{Thing}}\ \text{MOUSE}],\ [_{\text{Place}}\ \text{UNDER}\ ([_{\text{Thing}}\ \text{TABLE}])])]$$

(Jackendoff, 1990: 72)

b. The mouse stayed under the table.

$$[_{\text{Event}}\ \text{STAY}\ ([_{\text{Thing}}\ \text{MOUSE}],\ [_{\text{Place}}\ \text{UNDER}\ ([_{\text{Thing}}\ \text{TABLE}])])]$$

(cf. Jackendoff, 1983: 163, 172)

(6) The mouse ran around under the table.

$$\begin{bmatrix} \text{GO}\ ([_{\text{Thing}}\ \text{MOUSE}],\ [_{\text{Path}}\ \text{AROUND}]) \\ _{\text{Event}}\ [_{\text{Place}}\ \text{UNDER}\ ([_{\text{Thing}}\ \text{TABLE}])] \end{bmatrix}$$

(Jackendoff, 1990: 72)

In (5), [PLACE] appears as the second argument of the locational function BE as (5a) or STAY as (5b), which shows that the [PLACE] is the location where the Thing involved exists. The Place-arguments in (5) are licensed by one of *the innate formation rules for the conceptual structure* shown in (7a).

In (6), on the other hand, the [PLACE] is not an argument of the Event-function GO, but appears as a restrictive modifier, designating the location where the whole Event occurs. The conceptual structure in (6) is licensed by *the restrictive modification schema* shown in (8):

(8) *Restrictive Modification Schema*

$$[\text{Entity}_1] \rightarrow \begin{bmatrix} \text{X} \\ [\text{Entity}_2] \end{bmatrix}$$

(Jackendoff, 1990: 56)

[1]When the temporal location is expressed, it is realized as a PP headed by *ni*, the same phonetic form as that of the head of the spatial locative *ni*-phrase, as shown in (i).

(i) 7 ji-*ni* kono hoteru-de konsaato-ga aru.
7:00-at this hotel-in concert-NOM is
'There is a concert in this hotel at 7:00.'

We will discuss the realization of the temporal location in Section 4.3.

(7) a. $[\text{PLACE}] \rightarrow [_{\text{Place}}\ \text{PLACE-FUNCTION}\ ([_{\text{Thing}}\ \ ])]$

b. $$[\text{PATH}] \rightarrow \left[_{\text{Path}} \begin{Bmatrix} \text{TO} \\ \text{FROM} \\ \text{TOWARD} \\ \text{AWAY-FROM} \\ \text{VIA} \end{Bmatrix} \left(\begin{Bmatrix} [_{\text{Thing}}\ \ ] \\ [_{\text{Place}}\ \ ] \end{Bmatrix} \right) \right]$$

c. $$[\text{EVENT}] \rightarrow \begin{Bmatrix} [_{\text{Event}}\ \text{GO}\ ([_{\text{Thing}}\ \ ], [_{\text{Place}}\ \ ])] \\ [_{\text{Event}}\ \text{STAY}\ ([_{\text{Thing}}\ \ ], [_{\text{Place}}\ \ ])] \end{Bmatrix}$$

d. $$[\text{STATE}] \rightarrow \begin{Bmatrix} [_{\text{State}}\ \text{BE}\ ([_{\text{Thing}}\ \ ]\ [_{\text{Place}}\ \ ])] \\ [_{\text{State}}\ \text{ORIENT}\ ([_{\text{Thing}}\ \ ]\ [_{\text{Place}}\ \ ])] \\ [_{\text{State}}\ \text{EXT}\ ([_{\text{Thing}}\ \ ]\ [_{\text{Place}}\ \ ])] \end{Bmatrix}$$

e. $$[\text{EVENT}] \rightarrow \left[_{\text{Event}}\ \text{CAUSE} \left(\begin{Bmatrix} [_{\text{Thing}}\ \ ] \\ [_{\text{Event}}\ \ ] \end{Bmatrix}, [_{\text{Event}}\ \ ] \right) \right]$$

(Jackendoff, 1990: 43)

(9) a. $[_{\text{Situation}}\ \text{SITUATION-FUNCTION}\ ([_{\text{Thing}}\ x\ ], [_{\text{Place}}\ y\ ])\ \ ]$: Conceptual Structure

$\updownarrow$

$[_{\text{S}} \ldots [_{\text{PP}}\ [_{\text{NP}}\ y\ ]\ ni\ ] \ldots]$: Syntactic Structure

b. $\left[_{\text{Situation}}\ \text{SITUATION-FUNCTION}\ (\ \underset{[_{\text{Place}}\ z\ ]}{\ldots}\ )\ \right]$: Conceptual Structure

$\updownarrow$

$[_{\text{S}} \ldots [_{\text{PP}}\ [_{\text{NP}}\ z\ ]\ de\ ] \ldots]$: Syntactic Structure

In (8), $[\text{Entity}_2]$ modifies X, which represents the rest of the constituent $[\text{Entity}_1]$. According to this schema, the constituent $[_{\text{Place}}$ UNDER $([_{\text{Thing}}$ TABLE$])]$ in (6) is considered to modify the whole function-argument structure: GO($[_{\text{Thing}}$ MOUSE$]$, $[_{\text{Path}}$ AROUND$]$) in the $[_{\text{Event}}\ ]$.

3.2 Linking of Spatial Concepts in Japanese

We claim that the difference between *ni* and *de* shown in the previous sections can be encoded as the structural distinction between arguments and modifiers in conceptual structure. *Ni* indicates the location of a "Thing" whereas *de* indicates the location of a "Situation" which subsumes states, events, actions, and so on in Jackendoff's (1983) terms. In Japanese the Place-argument in (5) is realized as a *ni*-phrase while the Place-modifier in (6) as a *de*-phrase, though in English they can be expressed by the same PP.

Regarding the linking of conceptual categories [PLACE] with Japanese postpositional phrases, we propose the correspondence rules in (9).

The category [SITUATION] in (9) is a supercategory which subsumes Events and States (Jackendoff, 1991). In (9a), a conceptual constituent [PLACE] that appears in conceptual structure as the second argument of a two-place Situation-function (i.e. Event- or State-function) corresponds to a PP headed by *ni* in syntactic structure. On the other hand, in (9b) a [PLACE] that appears as a restrictive modifier in a [SITUATION] in conceptual structure corresponds to a PP headed by *de* in syntactic structure.

The rule (9a) provides an account for the difference in grammaticality between *ni* and *de* in (1a) repeated as (10).

(10) Kauntaa-no-ue-{*ni/*de*} gurasu-ga aru.
bar-GEN-on glass-NOM is
'There is a glass on the bar.'

The conceptual structure for the verb *aru* 'be' in (10) is represented as (11) by the BE-function, which is the same as the conceptual structure for its English counterpart *be* in (5a).

(11) Kauntaa-no-ue-*ni* gurasu-ga aru.
bar-GEN-on glass-NOM is

$[_{State}\,BE\,([_{Thing}GLASS], [_{Place}ON\,([_{Thing}BAR])])]$: CS
↕
$[_{S}\ \dots\ [_{PP}\ [_{NP}$ kauntaa-no-ue $]$ *ni* $]\ \dots\ ]$: SS

In the framework of Conceptual Semantics, the correspondence rules (9a) and (9b) belong to the class of syntax-semantics correspondence rules in Japanese grammar.

4 Locational Verb *Aru* and Semantic Fields

4.1 Spatial and Temporal Fields

Following the basic assumption of Conceptual Semantics, we account for the difference and the relatedness between the two uses of the locational verb *aru* 'be' in (2a) and (2b), repeated as (12a) and (12b), respectively.

(12) a. Kono hoteru-{*ni/*de*} hooru-ga aru.
This hotel-in hall-NOM is
'There is a hall in this hotel.'

b. Kono hoteru-{**ni/de*} konsaato-ga aru.
This hotel-in concert-NOM is
'There is a concert in this hotel.'

We claim that both instances of the verb *aru* 'is' are realizations of the semantic function BE, and are distinguished from each other by the kind of *semantic field* (Jackendoff, 1983), more precisely Spatial field or Temporal field, in which the Event or the State is defined.

Thematic Relations Hypothesis (henceforth, TRH) in (13), which was originally suggested by Gruber (1976) and developed by Jackendoff (1983) to explore the parallelism across different semantic fields.

One of the evidence for TRH is the fact that many verbs appear in two or more semantic fields, forming intuitively related paradigms. Here we deal only with Spatial and Temporal fields that are relevant to the present discussion.

(14) Spatial field
a. The statue is in the park. (BE)
b. We moved the statue from the park to the zoo. (GO)
c. Despite the weather, we kept the statue on its pedestal. (STAY)
(Jackendoff, 1983: 190)

(15) Temporal field
a. The meeting is at 6:00. (BE)
b. We moved the meeting from Tuesday to Thursday. (GO)
c. Despite the weather, we kept the meeting at 6:00. (STAY) (Jackendoff, 1983: 190)

The conceptual structures for (14) and (15) are represented as (16) and (17), respectively.

These two semantic fields have parallel conceptual structures. They are realizations of the basic conceptual functions BE (for stative location), GO (for transition), and STAY (for eventive, durational location). They differ only in what is counted as an entity being located in a Place. In terms of the TRH, Temporal field is defined as follows:

(18) Temporal field:
a. [EVENTS] and [STATES] appear as theme.
b. [TIMES] appear as reference object.
c. Time of occurrence plays the role of location. (Jackendoff, 1983: 189)

The semantic relatedness of the two variants of the same verb serves to restrict the ranges of possible ontological and conceptual categories (i.e. Thing, Event, Place, and so on) that can appear as Theme and as reference object of Event- or State-functions in each semantic field.

4.2 Two Variants of the Verb *Aru*

The semantic relatedness of the two variants of the verb *aru* in (12a) and (12b) is postulated as (19).

(19) Lexical Entry for the Verb *Aru*

$$\begin{bmatrix} \textit{aru} \\ \text{V} \\ \text{<PP}_j\text{>\_} \\ \begin{bmatrix} \left\{ \begin{array}{l} \text{BE}_{\text{Spat}}\ ([\text{THING}]_i, \\ \quad [_{\text{Place}}\text{PLACE-FUNCTION}_{\text{Spat}}([\text{THING}])]_j) \end{array} \right\} \\ \left\{ \begin{array}{l} \text{BE}_{\text{Temp}}\ ([\text{EVENT}]_i, \\ \quad [_{\text{Place}}\text{PLACE-FUNCTION}_{\text{Temp}}([\text{TIME}])]_j) \end{array} \right\} \end{bmatrix} \end{bmatrix}$$

The LCS in (19) consists of two alternating variants of the same BE-function: BE_{Spat} and BE_{Temp}. They are distinguished from each other by the kind of semantic field features shown as subscripts attached to the functions, i.e. spatial or temporal. These two functions, each enclosed in curly brackets { }, are interpreted as mutually exclusive (cf. Jackendoff, 1990: 76–77).

(13) *Thematic Relations Hypothesis (TRH)*

In any semantic field of [EVENTS] and [STATES], the principal event-, state-, path-, and place-functions are a subset of those used for the analysis of spatial location and motion. Fields differ in only three possible ways:

a. what sorts of entities may appear as theme;
b. what sorts of entities may appear as reference object;
c. what kind of relation assumes the role played by location in the field of spatial expressions.

(Jackendoff, 1983: 188)

(16) a. $[_{\text{State}}\ \text{BE}_{\text{Spat}}\ ([_{\text{Thing}}\ \text{STATUE}], [_{\text{Place}}\ \text{IN}\ ([_{\text{Thing}}\ \text{PARK}])])]$

b. $$[_{\text{Event}}\ \text{CAUSE}\ ([_{\text{Thing}}\ \text{WE}], [_{\text{Event}}\ \text{GO}_{\text{Spat}}\ ([_{\text{Thing}}\ \text{STATUE}], \left[\begin{array}{c}\text{FROM}\ ([_{\text{Place}}\ \text{PARK}])\\ _{\text{Path}}\ \text{TO}\ ([_{\text{Place}}\ \text{ZOO}])\end{array}\right])])]$$

c. $[_{\text{Event}}\ \text{CAUSE}\ ([_{\text{Thing}}\ \text{WE}], [_{\text{Event}}\ \text{STAY}_{\text{Spat}}\ ([_{\text{Thing}}\ \text{STATUE}], [_{\text{Place}}\ \text{ON}\ ([_{\text{Thing}}\ \text{PEDESTAL}])]\ )])]$

(17) a. $[_{\text{State}}\ \text{BE}_{\text{Temp}}\ ([_{\text{Event}}\ \text{MEETING}], [_{\text{Place}}\ \text{AT}_{\text{Temp}}\ ([_{\text{Time}}\ 6{:}00])])]$

b. $$[_{\text{Event}}\ \text{CAUSE}\ ([_{\text{Thing}}\ \text{WE}], [_{\text{Event}}\ \text{GO}_{\text{Temp}}\ ([_{\text{Event}}\ \text{MEETING}], \left[\begin{array}{c}\text{FROM}_{\text{Temp}}\ ([_{\text{Time}}\ \text{TUESDAY}])\\ _{\text{Path}}\ \text{TO}_{\text{Temp}}\ ([_{\text{Time}}\ \text{THURSDAY}])\end{array}\right])])]$$

c. $[_{\text{Event}}\ \text{CAUSE}\ ([_{\text{Thing}}\ \text{WE}], [_{\text{Event}}\ \text{STAY}_{\text{Temp}}\ ([_{\text{Event}}\ \text{MEETING}], [_{\text{Place}}\ \text{AT}_{\text{Temp}}\ ([_{\text{Time}}\ 6{:}00])])])]$

(Jackendoff, 1983: 190–191)

These conceptual-categorial restrictions, being fully integrated into the LCS for the verb, serve as the selectional restrictions with which the verb constrains its arguments. We can present the conceptual structures of sentences (12a) and (12b) as in (20a) and (20b), respectively.

(20) a. Kono hoteru-*ni* $[_{\text{NP}}$ hooru]-ga aru.
This hotel-in hall-NOM is

$$[_{\text{State}}\ \text{BE}_{\text{Spat}}\ ([_{\text{Thing}}\ \text{HALL}], [_{\text{Place}}\ \text{IN}_{\text{Spat}}\ ([_{\text{Thing}}\ \text{HOTEL}])])]$$
$$\updownarrow$$
$$[_{\text{S}}\ \ldots\ [_{\text{PP}}\ [_{\text{NP}}\ \text{kono hoteru}\ ]\ \textit{ni}\ ]\ \ldots\ ]$$

b. Kono hoteru-*de* $[_{\text{NP}}$ konsaato]-ga aru.
This hotel-in concert-NOM is

$$\left[\begin{array}{l}\text{BE}_{\text{Temp}}\ ([_{\text{Event}}\ \text{CONCERT}],\\ \quad [_{\text{Place}}\ \text{AT}_{\text{Temp}}\ ([_{\text{Time}}\ \ ])])\\ _{\text{State}}\ [_{\text{Place}}\ \text{IN}_{\text{Spat}}\ ([_{\text{Thing}}\ \text{HOTEL}])]\end{array}\right]$$
$$\updownarrow$$
$$[_{\text{S}}\ \ldots\ [_{\text{PP}}\ [_{\text{NP}}\ \text{kono hoteru}\ ]\ \textit{de}\ ]\ \ldots\ ]$$

In (20a) the verb *aru* is a realization of the spatial function BE_{Spat} that takes a Thing as its Theme-argument and a spatial location as its Place-argument. The latter argument is realized as the locative PP headed by *ni*, whose realization is consistent with (9a). In (20b) the verb *aru*, on the other hand, corresponds to the temporal function BE_{Temp} which requires an Event as its Theme-argument and a Time as the reference object.

4.3 Locative *Ni/De* Alternation

As the definition of the Temporal field in (18) states, BE_{Temp} cannot take any Place-argument designating a spatial location of the Theme. This is the crucial difference between BE_{Spat} and BE_{Temp}, which triggers *ni/de* alternation in syntax.

If the semantic field changes from spatial to temporal, the kind of the ontological category required as the reference object of the BE-function also changes from Thing to Time. The Place-constituent designating a spatial location can no longer work as the second argument of the BE_{Temp}, and therefore it is demoted to the restrictive-modifier position in conceptual structure, which is syntactically realized as a PP headed by *de*, as the rule (9b) predicts.

In sentence (21) below, the BE_{Temp} takes as its second argument a temporal Place-constituent $[_{\text{Place}}\ \text{AT}_{\text{Temp}}\ ([_{\text{Time}}\ 7{:}00])]$, which corresponding to *7 ji-ni* 'at 7:00', a syntactic PP headed by *ni*.

(21) 7 ji-*ni* kono hoteru-de konsaato-ga aru.
7:00-at this hotel-in concert-NOM is
'There is a concert in this hotel at 7:00.'

$$\begin{bmatrix} BE_{Temp}\ ([_{Event}\ CONCERT], \\ \quad [_{Place}\ AT_{Temp}\ ([_{Time}\ 7{:}00])]) \\ _{State}\ [_{Place}\ IN_{Spat}\ ([_{Thing}\ HOTEL])] \end{bmatrix}$$

In the Temporal field, as defined in (18), the BE_{Temp} requires as its reference object a [TIME].

5 Verb Classes and the Occurrence of PP

This section deals with the LCS of some verb classes which are exemplified in (1b), (3a) and (3b), and are repeated here as (22), (23) and (24).

(22) Kauntaa-no-ue-*de* gurasu-ga
bar-GEN-on glass-NOM
subetta/korogatta/yuraida.
slid/fell/wobbled
'A glass {slid/fell/wobbled} on the bar.'

(23) Kauntaa-no-naka-{*de/ni*} baaten-ga
bar-GEN-inside barman-NOM
tatta/suwatta/nekoronda.
stood/sat/lay
'A barman {stood/sat/lay} inside the bar.'

(24) Raunji-*de*-wa biiru-no nedan-ga takai.
lounge-at-TOP beer-GEN price-NOM high
'The price of beer is high at the lounge.'

5.1 Object-internal Motion Verbs

The verb in (22) is semantically characterized as a verb of object-internal motion (Jackendoff, 1990: 89). The conceptual structure for verbs in this class is represented by the one-place Event-function MOVE that takes only a Theme-argument, as shown in (25).

(25) $[_{Event}\ MOVE\ ([_{Thing}\quad])]$

Since MOVE does not take a Place-argument, any Place-constituent co-occurring with the verb must occupy the modifier position in conceptual structure as in (26).

(26) Kauntaa-no-ue-*de* gurasu-ga subetta.
bar-GEN-on glass-NOM slid

$$\begin{bmatrix} MOVE\ ([_{Thing}\ GLASS]) \\ _{Event}\ [_{Place}\ ON\ ([_{Thing}\ BAR])] \end{bmatrix}$$
$$\updownarrow$$
$$[_S \ldots [_{PP}\ [_{NP}\ \text{kauntaa-no-ue}\ ]\ de\ ] \ldots]$$

Consequently, a Place-constituent co-occurring with MOVE is always syntactically realized as a PP headed by *de* by the correspondence rule (9b).

5.2 Verbs of Configuration

The essential part of the LCS for the verb in (23) is represented as (27).

(27) $[_{Event}\ INCH\ ([_{State}\ CONF\ ([_{Thing}\quad])])]$

INCH is the Event-function denoting an inchoative Event and it maps its State-argument into an Event that terminates in that State (Jackendoff, 1990: 92). CONF is the one-place State-function that expresses the internal spatial configuration of its Theme (Jackendoff, 1990: 91). The co-occurrence of a *de*-phrase with the verbs in (23) is also licensed by the rule (9b).

However, some verbs in this class can also take a locative *ni*-phrase as well as a *de*-phrase.[2] Since the LCS (27) does not contain a BE_{Spat}, a problem arises as to how the co-occurrence of a *ni*-phrase with the verbs in (23) is licensed.

On the intuitive understanding of sentence (23), Ueno (2007) points out that *baaten* 'barman' changed not only his configuration but also his his spatial location.[3] According Ueno (2007), when verbs in this class take a locative *ni*-phrase, its inherent meaning is subordinated in terms of conceptual-structure configuration (backgrounded), whereas the meaning of "change of location" yielded by conflation is superordinated (foregrounded) as (28).

(28) LCS for the Verbs of Configuration

$$\begin{bmatrix} INCH\left(\begin{bmatrix} BE_{Spat}\ ([_{Thing}\quad]^{\alpha}{}_{j},\ [_{Place}\quad]) \\ _{State}\ [WITH\ [_{State}\ CONF([\alpha])]] \end{bmatrix}\right) \\ _{Event} \end{bmatrix}$$

If the correspondence rule (9a) is applied to (28), the Place-argument of the BE_{Spat} is realized as the locative PP headed by *ni* as follows.

[2]The other verbs in this class cannot take a locative *ni*-phrase, as shown in (ii).

(ii) Kauntaa-no-naka-{**ni/de*} baaten-ga
bar-GEN-inside barman-NOM
syaganda/ojigishita/senobishita.
crouched/bowed/stretched himself
'A barman {crouched/bowed/stretched himself} inside the bar.'

[3]The sentence with *de*-phrase as in (ii) implies that barman changes his configuration but does not imply that he changes his spatial location.

(29) Kauntaa-no-naka-*ni* baaten-ga tatta.
bar-GEN-inside barman-NOM stood

$$\left[_{\text{Event}} \text{INCH}\left(\left[_{\text{State}} \begin{array}{l} \text{BE}_{\text{Spat}}\left(\begin{array}{l}[_{\text{Thing}}\text{BARMAN}]^{\alpha}{}_{j},\\ \quad [_{\text{Place}}\ \text{IN}([_{\text{Thing}}\ \text{BAR}])]\end{array}\right)\\ \text{[WITH } [_{\text{State}}\text{CONF}([\alpha])]] \uparrow \end{array}\right]\right)\right]$$

$$\downarrow$$

$$[_{S} \ldots [_{PP}\ [_{NP}\ \text{kauntaa-no-ue}]\ \textit{ni}] \ldots]$$

Thus, the desired syntactic realization of PP and semantic interpretation of the sentence are obtained by the correspondence rule (9a).

5.3 Identificational Field

To deal with sentence (24), another semantic field *identificational*, which concerns the categorization and ascription of properties, is needed. In terms of the TRH, Identificational field is defined as follows:

(30) Identificational field:

a. [THINGS] appear as theme.

b. [THING TYPES] and [PROPERTIES] appear as reference object.

c. Being an instance of category or having a property plays the role of location.
(Jackendoff, 1983: 194)

The conceptual structure for the adjective *takai* 'high' in (24) is represented as the following (31) by the finction BE_{Ident}.

(31) Raunji-*de*-wa biiru-no nedan-ga takai.
lounge-at-TOP beer-GEN price-NOM high

$$\left[_{\text{State}} \begin{array}{l} \text{BE}_{\text{Ident}}\ ([_{\text{Thing}}\ \text{BEER}],\\ \quad [_{\text{Place}}\ \text{AT}_{\text{Ident}}\ ([_{\text{Property}}\ \text{HIGH}])])\\ [_{\text{Place}}\ \text{AT}_{\text{Spat}}\ ([_{\text{Thing}}\ \text{LOUNGE}])] \end{array}\right]$$

$$\updownarrow$$

$$[_{S}\ \ldots\ [_{PP}\ [_{NP}\ \text{raunji}\ ]\ \textit{de}\ ] \ldots\ ]$$

Since BE_{Ident} requires a Thing as its Theme-argument and a Property as the reference object, any Place-constituent co-occurring with the verb must occupy the modifier position in conceptual structure by the rule (9b).

6 Concluding Remarks

In this paper, we have proposed two kinds of syntax-semantics correspondence rules within the framework of Conceptual Semantics. We have observed the distribution of locative postpositional *ni*-marked and *de*-marked phrases and the semantic difference between them in Section 1 and 2.

In Section 3, we have demonstrated how to adapt the machinery of the occurrence of the spatial postpositional phrases based on the assumption of Conceptual Semantics to fit the organization of Japanese grammar. The conceptual-categorial restrictions, being fully integrated into the LCS for the verb, serve as selectional restrictions that the verb imposes on its Place-argument, which is realized as *ni*-phrase in Japanese.

We have also explicated the mechanism of the locative *ni/de* alternation seen with the verb *aru* 'be' in Section 4, and co-occurrence of the spatial and temporal locative postpositional phrases in Section 5 on the basis of the correspondence rules and the semantic field distinction with respect to the BE-function encoded in the LCS of several verbs.

In this paper, we have only provided the account of syntax and semantics conditions for the distribution of locative phrases marked with the postpositions *ni* and *de*. One of the reviewers pointed out that *wo*-marked locative phrase, the presence of Goal-reading with *ni*-phrases and the absence of such a reading with *de*-phrases should be explained within our framework. We will leave the analysis of the issue for future work.

Acknowledgments

We are indebted to three anonymous PACLIC reviewers, Pilar Valverde and Robert Logie for their invaluable comments on an earlier version of this paper. All remaining inadequacies are our own. This research is partially supported by the Grant-in-Aid for Scientific Research (C), 24500189 of the Japan Society for the Promotion of Science (JSPS).

References

Jeffrey S. Gruber. 1976. *Lexical Structures in Syntax and Semantics*. North-Holland Publishing Company, Amsterdam.

Ray Jackendoff. 1983. *Semantics and Cognition*. MIT Press, Cambridge, MA.

Ray Jackendoff. 1990. *Semantic Structures*. MIT Press, Cambridge, MA.

Ray Jackendoff. 1991. Parts and Boundaries. *Cognition*, 41:9–45.

Taro Kageyama. 1974. Basyo-rironteki Kenchi kara [From a Localistic Point of View]. *Gengo no Kagaku [Sciences of language]*, 5:39–77. Tokyo Institute for Advanced Studies of Language, Tokyo.

Akio Kamio. 1980. 'Ni' to 'De' — Nihongo niokeru Kuukanteki Ichi no Hyoogen [*Ni* and *De*: Spatial Locative Expressions in Japanese]. *Gengo [Language]*, 9/9: 55–63.

Samuel E. Martin. 1987. *A Reference Grammar of Japanese*. Charles E. Tuttle Company, Inc., Rutland, Vermont & Tokyo, Japan.

Takuro Moriyama. 1988. *Nihongo Dooshi-jutsugo-bun no Kenkyuu [Studies on Japanese Sentences with Verbal Predicates]*. Meiji Shoin, Tokyo.

Minoru Nakau. 1994a. Basyo no *Ni* to *De*: Nihongo Kaku-joshi no Ninchi Chizu [Locative *Ni* and *De*: the Cognitive Map of Japanese Case Particles]. *Eigo Seinen [The Rising Generation]*, 140/2:28–30.

Minoru Nakau. 1994b. *Ninchi Imiron no Genri [Principles of Cognitive Semantics]*. Taishukan, Tokyo.

Minoru Nakau. 1995. Nichi-Eigo no Kuukan Ninshiki no Kata (1)–(3) [Patterns of Spatial Cognition in Japanese and English (1)–(3)]. *Eigo Seinen [The Rising Generation]*, 140/10:20–22; 140/11:22–24; 140/12:22–24.

Minoru Nakau. 1998. Kuukan to Sonzai no Koozu [The Architecture of Space and Existence]. *In: Minoru Nakau and Yoshiki Nishimura, Koobun to jisyoo-koozoo [Constructions and Event Structures]*, 1–106

Hideo Teramura. 1982. *Nihongo no Shintakusu to Imi, I [Japanese Syntax and Meaning, vol. I]*. Kurosio Publishers, Tokyo.

Seiji Ueno. 2007. *Nihongo niokeru Kuukan Hyoogen to Ido Hyoogen no Gainen Imironteki Kenkyu [Studies on Spatial Expressions and Motion Expressions in Japanese in Conceptual Semantics]*. Hituzi Syobo, Tokyo.

Transliteration Systems Across Indian Languages Using Parallel Corpora

Rishabh Srivastava and **Riyaz Ahmad Bhat**
Language Technologies Research Center
IIIT-Hyderabad, India
{rishabh.srivastava, riyaz.bhat}@research.iiit.ac.in

Abstract

Hindi is the lingua-franca of India. Although all non-native speakers can communicate well in Hindi, there are only a few who can read and write in it. In this work, we aim to bridge this gap by building transliteration systems that could transliterate Hindi into at-least 7 other Indian languages. The transliteration systems are developed as a reading aid for non-Hindi readers. The systems are trained on the transliteration pairs extracted automatically from a parallel corpora. All the transliteration systems perform satisfactorily for a non-Hindi reader to understand a Hindi text.

1 Introduction

India is home to languages from four language families namely Indo-Aryan, Dravidian, Austroasiatic and Tibeto-Burman. There are 22 official languages and more than 1000 dialects, which are written in more than 14 different scripts[1] in this country. Hindi, an Indo-Aryan language, written in Devanagari, is the lingua-franca of India (Masica, 1993, p. 6). Most Indians are orally proficient in Hindi while they lack a good proficiency in reading and writing it. In this work, we come up with transliteration systems, so that non-native speakers of Hindi don't face a problem in reading Hindi script. We considered 7 Indian languages, including 4 Indo-Aryan (Punjabi, Gujarati, Urdu and Bengali) and 3 Dravidian (Telugu, Tamil and Malayalam) languages, for this task. The quantity of Hindi literature (especially online) is more than twice as in any other Indian language. There are approximately 107 newspapers[2], 15 online newspapers[3] and 94067 Wikipedia articles[4] (reported in March 2013), which are published in Hindi. The transliteration systems will be helpful for non-Hindi readers to understand these as well as various other existing Hindi resources.

As the transliteration task has to be done for 7 languages, a rule-based system would become very expensive. The cost associated with crafting exhaustive rule-sets for transliteration has already been demostrated in works on Hindi-Punjabi (Goyal and Lehal, 2009), Hindi-Gujarati (Patel and Pareek, 2009) and Hindi-Urdu (Malik et al., 2009; Lehal and Saini, 2010). In this work, we have modelled the task of transliteration as a noisy channel model with minimum error rate training (Och, 2003). However, such a statistical modelling needs an ample amount of data for training and testing. The data is extracted from an Indian language sentence aligned parallel corpora available for 10 Indian languages. These sentences are automatically word aligned across the languages. Since these languages are written in different scripts, we have used an Indian modification of the soundex algorithm (Russell and Odell, 1918) (henceforth Indic-Soundex) for a normalized language representation. Extraction of the transliteration pairs (two words having the similar pronunciation) is then followed by Longest Common Subsequence (henceforth LCS) algorithm, a string similarity algorithm. The extracted pairs are evaluated manually by annotators and the accuracies are calculated. We found promising results as far as the accuracies of these extracted pairs are concerned. These transliteration pairs are then used to train the transliteration systems. Various evaluation tests are performed on these transliteration systems which confirm the high accuracy of these transliteration systems. Though the best system was nearly 70% accurate on word-level, the character-level accuracies (greater than 70% for all systems) along with the encouraging results from the human evaluations, clearly show

[1] http://en.wikipedia.org/wiki/Languages of India

[2] http://en.wikipedia.org/wiki/List_of_newspapers_in_India

[3] http://www.indiapress.org/

[4] http://stats.wikimedia.org/EN_India/Sitemap.htm

that these transliterations are good enough for a typical Indian reader to easily interpret the text.

1.1 Related Work

Knight (1998) provides a deep insight on how transliteration can be thought of as translation. Zhang et al.(2010) have proposed 2 approaches, for machine transliteration among English, Chinese, Japanese and Korean language pairs when extraction/creation of parallel data is expensive. Tiedemann (1998) has worked on text-based multi-language transliteration exploiting short aligned units and structural & orthographic similarities in a corpus. Indirect generation of Chinese text from English transliterated counter-part (Kuo and Yang, 2004) discusses the changes that happen in a borrowed word. Matthews (2007) has created statistical model for transliteration of proper names in English-Chinese and English-Arabic.

As Indian languages are written in different scripts, they must be converted to some common representation before comparison can be made between them. Grapheme to Phoneme conversion (Pagel et al., 1998) is one of the ways to do this. Gupta et al. (2010) have used WX notation as the common representation to transliterate among various Indian languages including Hindi, Bengali, Punjabi, Telugu, Malayalam and Kannada. Soundex algorithm (Russell and Odell, 1918) converts words into a common representation for comparison. Levenshtein distance (Levenshtein, 1966) between two strings has long been established as a distance function. It calculates the minimum number of insertions, deletions and substitutions needed to convert a string into another. Longest Common Subsequence (LCS) algorithm is similar to Levenshtein distance with the difference being that it does not consider substitution as a distance metric.

Zahid et al. (2010) have applied Soundex algorithm for extraction of English-Urdu transliteration pairs. An attempt towards a rule based phonetic matching algorithm for Hindi and Marathi using Soundex algorithm (Chaware and Rao, 2011) has given quite promising results. Soundex has already been used in many Indian language systems including Named entity recognition (Nayan et al., 2008) and cross-language information retrieval (Jagarlamudi and Kumaran, 2008). Although they applied soundex after transliteration from Indian language to English. Named-entity transliteration pairs mining from Tamil and English corpora has been performed earlier using a linear classifier (Saravanan and Kumaran, 2008). Sajjad et al. (2012) have mined transliteration pairs independent of the language pair using both supervised and unsupervised models. Transliteration pairs have also been mined from online Hindi song lyrics noting the word-by-word transliteration of Hindi songs which maintain the word order (Gupta et al., 2012).

In what follows, we present our methodology to extract transliteration pairs in section 2. The next section, Section 3, talks about the details of the creation and evaluation of transliteration systems. We conclude the paper in section 4.

2 Extraction of transliteration pairs

We first align the words for all the languages with Hindi in the parallel corpora. Phoneme matching techniques are applied to these pairs and the pairs satisfying the set threshold are selected. Given these pairs, transliteration systems are trained for all the 7 language pairs with Hindi as the source language.

2.1 Corpora

We have used the ILCI corpora (Jha, 2010) which contains 30000 parallel sentences per language for 11 languages (we have not considered English. Neither are Marathi and Konkani as the latter 2 are written in Devanagari script, which is same for Hindi). The corpora contains sentences from the domain of tourism and health with Hindi as their source language. Table 1 shows the various scripts in which these languages are written. All the sentences are encoded in utf-8 format.

2.2 Word Alignment

The first task is to align words from the parallel corpora between Hindi and the other languages. We have used IBM model 1 to 5 and HMM model to align the words using Giza++ (Och and Ney, 2000). Hindi shows a remarkable similarity with the other 4 Indo-Aryan languages considered for this work (Masica, 1993). With the other 3 Dravidian languages Hindi shares typological properties like word order, head directionality, parameters, etc (Krishnamurti, 2003). Being so similar in structure, these language pairs exhibit high alignment accuracies. The extracted translation

Table 1: Written scripts of various Indian languages

Language	Script
Bengali(Ben)	Bengali alphabet
Gujarati(Guj)	Gujarati alphabet
Hindi(Hin)	Devanagari
Konkani(Kon)	Devanagari
Malayalam(Mal)	Malayalam alphabet
Marathi(Mar)	Devanagari
Punjabi(Pun)	Gurmukhi
Tamil(Tam)	Tamil alphabet
Telugu(Tel)	Telugu alphabet
Urdu(Urd)	Arabic
English(Eng)	Latin (English alphabet)

pairs are then matched for phonetic similarity using LCS algorithm, as discussed in the following section.

2.3 Phonetic Matching

In the extracted translation pairs, we have to find whether these words are transliteration pairs or just translation pairs. The major issue in finding these pairs is that the languages are in different scripts and no distance matching algorithm can be applied directly. Using Roman as a common representation (Gupta et al., 2010), however, is not a solution either. A Roman representation will miss out issues like short vowel drop. For example, $ktAb$ (Urdu, book) and $kitAb$ (Hindi, book) (Figure 1), essentially same, are marked as non-transliteration pairs due to short vowel drop in Urdu (Kulkarni et al., 2012). We opt for a phoneme matching algorithm to bring all the languages into a single representation and then apply a distance matching algorithm to extract the transliteration pairs. Fortunately, such a scheme for Indian languages exists, which will be addressed in the 2.3.1.

2.3.1 Indic-Soundex

Soundex algorithm (Russell and Odell, 1918) developed for English is often used for phoneme matching. Soundex is an optimal algorithm when we just have to compare if two words in English sound same. Swathanthra Indian Language Computing Project (Silpa[5]) (Silpa, 2010) has proposed

Word	किताब	کتاب
characters	क ि त ा ब	ک ت ا ب
Gloss	k i t A b	k t a b

Figure 1: Figure shows $kitAb$ (book), written in Hindi and Urdu respectively, with their gloss (Hindi is written in Devanagari script from left to right while Urdu is written in Persio-Arabic script from right to left. The gloss is given from left to right in both). As is clear that if a both are transliterated into a common representation, they wont result into a transliteration pair

an Indic-Soundex system to map words phonetically in many Indian languages. Currently, mappings for Hindi, Bengali, Punjabi, Gujarati, Oriya, Tamil, Telugu, Kannada and Malayalam are handled in the Silpa system. Since Urdu is one of the languages we are working on, we introduced the mapping of its character set in the system. The task is convoluted, since with the other Indian languages, mapping direct Unicode is possible, but Urdu script being a derivative from Arabic modification of Persian script, has a completely different Unicode mapping[6] (BIS, 1991). Also there were some minor issues with Silpa system which we corrected. Figure 2 shows the various character mappings of languages to a common representation. Some of the differences from Silpa system include:

- mapping for long vowels.
  - U, o, au, are mapped to v.
  - E and ae are mapped to y.
  - A is mapped to a.
- $bindu$ and $chandrabindu$ in Hindi are mapped to n.
- ah and $halant$ are mapped to null (as they have no sound).
- Short vowels like a, e, u are mapped to null.
- h is mapped to null as it does not contribute much to the sound. It is just a emphasis marker.
- To make Silpa mappings readable every sound is mapped to its correspoding character in Roman.

[5]The Silpa Soundex description, algorithm and code can be found from http://thottingal.in/blog/2009/07/26/indicsoundex/. The Silpa character mapping can be found at http://thottingal.in/soundex/soundex.html

[6]Source: http://en.wikipedia.org/wiki/Indian_Script_Code_for_Information_Interchange

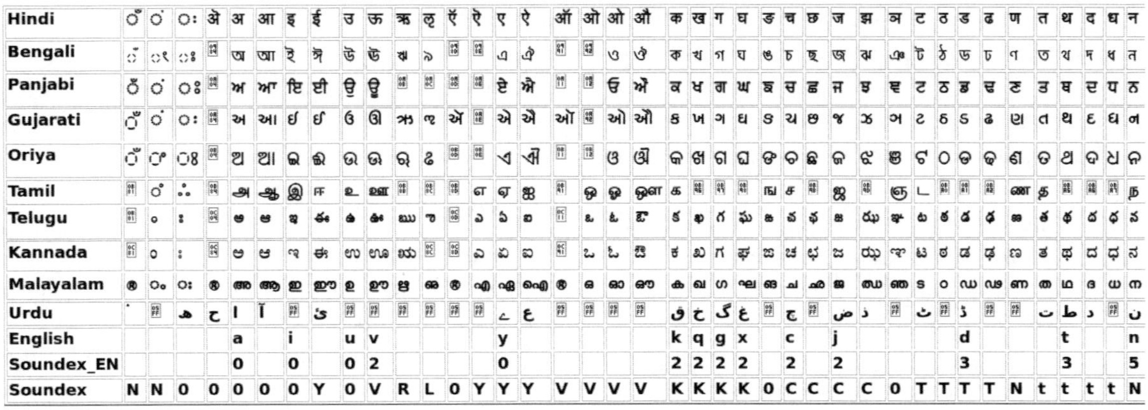

Figure 2: A part of Indic-Soundex, mappings of various Indian characters to a common representation, English Soundex is also shown as a mapping. This is modified from one given by (Silpa, 2010)

In the following, we discuss the computation and extraction of phonetically similar word pairs using LCS algorithm.

2.3.2 Word-pair Similarity

Aligned word pairs, with soundex representation, are further checked for character level similarity. Strings with LCS distance 0 or 1 are considered as transliteration pairs. We also consider strings with distance 1 because there is a possibility that some sound sequence is a bit different from the other in two different languages. This window of 1 is permitted to allow extraction of pairs with slight variations. If pairs are not found to be exact match but at a difference of 1 from each other, they are checked if their translation probability (obtained after alignment of the corpora) is more than 50% (empirically chosen). If this condition is satisfied, the words are taken as transliteration pairs (Figure 3). This increases the recall of transliteration pair extraction reducing precision by a slight percentage. Table 2 presents the statistics of extracted transliteration pairs using LCS.

Word	विक्रम	বিক্রম
characters	व ि क ् र म	ব ি ক ্ র ম
Gloss	Vikram	Bikram
Soundex	वKRM0000	বKRM0000

Figure 3: Figure shows $Vikram$, a person name, written in Hindi and Bengali respectively, with their gloss and soundex code. The two forms are considered transliteration pairs if they have a high translation probability and don't differ by more than 1 character.

A detailed algorithm using translation probabilities obtained during alignment phase is provided in Algorithm 1.

Algorithm 1 match(w1, w2, translation-probability (w1,w2))

1. Find the language of both the words by using the 1st character of each and checking in the character list.
2. Calculate Soundex equivalent of w1 and w2 using Soundex algorithm.
3. Check if both the soundex codes are equal.
4. If yes, return both as transliteration pairs.
5. else, check the LCS between the soundex codes of w1 and w2.
6. If the distance is found to be 1,
7. check if the translation probability for w1 to w2 is more than 0.5.
8. if Yes, return both are transliteration pairs.
9. else both are not transliteration pairs.

2.4 Evaluation of Transliteration Pairs

To evaluate the phonetic similarity of the extracted aligned word pairs by LCS algorithm, a small subset (10%) from each language pair is given for Human evaluation. Annotators[7] are asked to judge whether the extracted word pairs are in fact transliterations of each other or not, based on the way the word pairs are pronounced in the respective languages. The results for the transliteration pairs for a given language pair extracted by

[7]Annotators were bi-literate graduates or undergraduate students, in the age of 20-24 with either Hindi or the transliterated language as their mother tongue

LCS algorithm are reported in Table 2. Hindi-Urdu and Hindi-Telugu (even though Hindi and Telugu do not belong to the same family of languages) demonstrate a remarkably high accuracy. Hindi-Bengali, Hindi-Punjabi, Hindi-Malayalam and Hindi-Gujarati have mild accuracies while Hindi-Tamil is the least accurate pair. Not only Tamil and Hindi do not belong to the same family, the lexical diffusion between these two languages is very less. For automatic evaluation of alignment quality we calculated the alignment entropy of all the transliteration pairs (Pervouchine et al., 2009). These have also been listed in Table 2. Tamil, Telugu and Urdu have a relatively high entropy indicating a low quality alignment.

Table 2: This table shows various language pairs with the number of word-pairs, accuracies of manually annotated pairs and the alignment entropy of all the languages. Here accu. represents average accuracy of the language-pairs

pair	#pairs	accu.	entropy
Hin-Ben	103706	0.84	0.44
Hin-Guj	107677	0.89	0.28
Hin-Mal	20143	0.86	0.55
Hin-Pun	23098	0.84	0.39
Hin-Tam	10741	0.68	0.73
Hin-Tel	45890	0.95	0.76
Hin-Urd	284932	0.91	0.79

3 Transliteration with Hindi as the Source Language

After the transliteration pairs are extracted and evaluated, we train transliteration systems for 7 languages with Hindi as the source language. In the following section, we explain the training of these transliteration systems in detail.

3.1 Creation of data-sets

All the extracted transliteration word pairs of a particular language pair are split into their corresponding characters to create a parallel data set, for building the transliteration system. The data-set of a given language pair is further split into training and development sets. 90% data is randomly selected for training and the remaining 10% is kept for development. Evaluation set is created separately because of two reasons; firstly we don't want to reduce the size of the training data by splitting the data set into training, testing and development, secondly evaluating the results on a gold data set would give us a clear picture of the performance of our system. Section 3.3 explans various evaluation methodologies for our transliteration systems.

3.2 Training of transliteration systems

We model transliteration as a translation problem, treating a word as a sentence and a character as a word using the aforementioned data-sets (Matthews, 2007, ch. 2,3) (Chinnakotla and Damani, 2009). We train machine transliteration systems with Hindi as a source language and others as target (all in different models), using Moses (Koehn et al., 2007). Giza++ (Och and Ney, 2000) is used for character-level alignments (Matthews, 2007, ch. 2,3). Phrase-based alignment model (Figure 4) (Koehn et al., 2003) is used with a trigram language model of the target side to train the transliteration models. Phrase translations probabilities are calculated employing the noisy channel model and Mert is used for minimum error-rate training to tune the model using the development data-set. Top 1 result is considered as the default output (Och, 2003; Bertoldi et al., 2009).

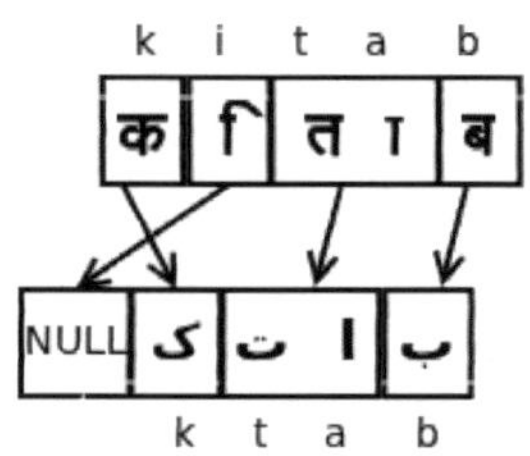

Figure 4: Figure depicts an example of phrase-based alignment on *kitAb* (book), written in Hindi (top) and Urdu (bottom).

3.3 Evaluation

In this section we will do an in-depth evaluation of all the transliteration systems that we reported in this work.

3.3.1 Creation of Evaluation Sets

We used two data-sets for the evaluation. The creation of these data-sets is discussed below:

- **Gold test-set**: Nearly 25 sentences in Hindi, containing an approximate of 500 words (unique 260 words) were randomly extracted from a text and given to human annotators for preparing gold data. The annotators[7] were given full sentences rather than individual words, so that they could decide the correct transliteration according to the context. We were not able to create gold test-set for Tamil.

- **WordNet based test-set**: For automatic evaluation, the evaluation set is created from the synsets of Indian languages present in Hindi WordNet (Sinha et al., 2006). A Hindi word and its corresponding synsets in other languages (except Gujarati) are extracted and represented in a common format using Indic-Soundex and then among the synsets only exact match(s), if any, with the corresponding Hindi word, are picked. In this way, we ensure that the evaluation set is perfect. The set mainly contains cognate words (words of similar origin) and named entities.

3.3.2 Evaluation Metrics

We evaluated the transliteration systems on the above-discussed test-sets following the metrics discussed below:

- We used the evaluation metrics like ACC, Mean Fscore, MRR and MAP_{ref}, which refer to Word-accuracy in Top1, Fuzziness in Top1, Mean-reciprocal rank and precision in the n-best candidates repectively (Zhang et al., 2012).

- Keeping in view the actual goal of the task, we also evaluated the systems based on the readability of their top output (1-best) based on the transliteration of consonants. Consonants have a higher role in lexical access than vowels (New et al., 2008), if the consonants of a word are transliterated correctly, the word is most likely to be accessed and thus maintaining readability of the text. So, we evaluated the systems based on the transliteration of consonants.

3.3.3 Results

We present consolidated results in Table 3 and Table 4. Apart from standard metrics i.e., metrics 1, metrics 2 captures character-level and word-level accuracies considering the complete word and only the consonants of that word with the number of testing pairs for all the transliteration systems. The character-level accuracies are calculated according to the percentage of insertions and deletions required to convert a transliterated word to a gold word. Accuracy of all the transliteration systems is greater than 70%, i.e. even a worst transliteration system would return a string with 7 correct characters, out of 10, on an average. The accuracies at the character-level of only the consonants ranges from 75-95% which clearly proves our systems to be of good quality. It is clear from the results that these systems can be used as a reading aid by a non-Hindi reader.

As the table shows, all the transliteration systems have shown similar results on both the test-sets. These results clearly show that all the systems except Malayalam, Tamil and Telugu perform rather well. This can be attributed to the fact that these languages belong to the Dravidian family while Hindi is an Indo-Aryan language. Although, as per Metrics 1, the results are not promising for these languages, the consonant-based evaluation, i.e. Metrics 2, shows that the performance is not that bad.

Perfect match of the transliterated and gold word is considered for word-level accuracy. Bengali, Gujarati, Punjabi and Urdu yield the very high transliteration accuracy. The best system (Hindi-Pujabi) gives an accuracy of nearly 70% on word-level whereas Hindi-Urdu gives the highest accuracy on character-level. Urdu transliteration accuracy being so high is strengthened from the fact that linguistically the division between Hindi and Urdu is not well-founded (Masica, 1993, p. 27-30) (Rai, 2001). We can infer from the results of the word-level accuracies of the whole word that these transliteration systems cannot be directly used by a system for further processing.

3.3.4 Human Evaluation

In order to re-confirm the validity of the output in practical scenarios, we also performed human-based evaluation. For human evaluations 10 short Hindi sentences, with an average length of 10 words, were randomly selected. All these sentences were transliterated by all the 7 transliteration systems and the results of each were given to several evaluators [8] to rate the sentences on the scale of 0 to 4.

- *Score 0*: Non-Sense. If the sentence makes no sense to one at all.

[8] Annotators were bi-literate, some of who did not know how to read Hindi, graduates or undergraduate students, in the age of 20-24 with the transliterated language as their mother tongue

Table 3: Evaluation Metrics on Gold data.

	Metrics 1				Metrics 2			
Lang	ACC[9]	Mean F-score	MRR	Map_{ref}	Char (all)	Char (consonant)	Word (consonant)	#Pairs
Ben	0.50	0.89	0.57	0.73	0.89	0.94	0.72	260
Guj	0.59	0.89	0.67	0.84	0.91	0.97	0.86	260
Mal	0.11	0.69	0.26	0.55	0.73	0.94	0.40	260
Pun	0.60	0.90	0.69	0.83	0.89	0.93	0.81	260
Tel	0.27	0.75	0.32	0.49	0.78	0.93	0.71	260
Urd	0.58	0.89	0.67	0.81	0.88	0.89	0.70	260

Table 4: Evaluation Metrics on Indo-WordNet data.

	Metrics 1				Metrics 2			
Lang	ACC	Mean F-score	MRR	Map_{ref}	Char (all)	Char (consonant)	Word (consonant)	#Pairs
Ben	0.60	0.91	0.70	0.87	0.93	0.95	0.87	1263
Mal	0.15	0.78	0.31	0.61	0.83	0.88	0.71	198
Pun	0.69	0.92	0.76	0.88	0.70	0.73	0.47	1475
Tam	0.31	0.82	0.38	0.57	0.82	0.86	0.58	58
Tel	0.34	0.87	0.49	0.76	0.87	0.93	0.82	528
Urd	0.67	0.92	0.73	0.84	0.92	0.94	0.83	720

- *Score 1*: Some parts make sense but is not comprehensible over all.
- *Score 2*: Comprehensible but has quite few errors.
- *Score 3*: Comprehensible, containing an error or two.
- *Score 4*: Perfect. Contains minute errors, if any.

Table 5 contains the average scores given by evaluators for the outputs of various transliteration systems. The results clearly depict the ease that a reader faced while evaluating the sentences. According to these scores, Gujarati, Bengali and Telugu transliteration system gives nearly perfect outputs, followed by the transliteration systems of Urdu and Malayalam which can be directly used as a reading aid. Tamil and Punjabi transliterations were comprehensible but contained a considerable number of errors.

[9]ACC stands for Word level accuracy; Char(all) stands for Character level accuracy; Char(consonant) stands for Character level accuracy considering only the consonants; Word(consonant) stands for Word level accuracy considering only the consonants

Table 5: Average score (out of 4) by evaluators for various transliteration systems

language	avg. score
Bengali	3.6
Gujarati	3.8
Malayalam	3.3
Punjabi	1.9
Tamil	2.5
Telugu	3.6
Urdu	3.2

4 Conclusion

We have proposed a method for transliteration of Hindi into various other Indian languages as a reading aid for non-Hindi readers. We have chosen a complete statistical approach for the same and extracted training data automatically from parallel corpora. An adaptation of Soundex algorithm for a normalized language representation has been integrated with LCS algorithm to extract training transliteration pairs from the aligned language-pairs. All the transliteration systems return transliterations, good enough to understand the text, which is strengthened from the evaluators' score as well as from the character-level accuracies. However, word-level accuracies of these transliteration systems prompt them not to be used as a tool for text processing applications. Further, we are training transliteration models between all these 8 Indian languages.

References

Nicola Bertoldi, Barry Haddow, and Jean-Baptiste Fouet. 2009. Improved minimum error rate training in moses. *The Prague Bulletin of Mathematical Linguistics*, 91(1):7–16.

Bureau of Indian Standards BIS. 1991. *Indian Script Code for Information Interchange, ISCII*. IS 13194.

Sandeep Chaware and Srikantha Rao. 2011. Rule-Based Phonetic Matching Approach for Hindi and Marathi. *Computer Science & Engineering*, 1(3).

Manoj Kumar Chinnakotla and Om P Damani. 2009. Experiences with english-hindi, english-tamil and english-kannada transliteration tasks at news 2009. In *Proceedings of the 2009 Named Entities Workshop Shared Task on Transliteration*, pages 44–47. Association for Computational Linguistics.

Vishal Goyal and Gurpreet Singh Lehal. 2009. Hindi-punjabi machine transliteration system (for machine translation system). *George Ronchi Foundation Journal, Italy*, 64(1):2009.

Rohit Gupta, Pulkit Goyal, Allahabad IIIT, and Sapan Diwakar. 2010. Transliteration among indian languages using wx notation. *g Semantic Approaches in Natural Language Processing*, page 147.

Kanika Gupta, Monojit Choudhury, and Kalika Bali. 2012. Mining hindi-english transliteration pairs from online hindi lyrics. In *Proceedings of the 8th International Conference on Language Resources and Evaluation (LREC 2012)*, pages 23–25.

Jagadeesh Jagarlamudi and A Kumaran. 2008. Cross-Lingual Information Retrieval System for Indian Languages. In *Advances in Multilingual and Multimodal Information Retrieval*, pages 80–87. Springer.

Girish Nath Jha. 2010. The tdil program and the indian language corpora initiative (ilci). In *Proceedings of the Seventh Conference on International Language Resources and Evaluation (LREC 2010). European Language Resources Association (ELRA)*.

Kevin Knight and Jonathan Graehl. 1998. Machine transliteration. *Computational Linguistics*, 24(4):599–612.

Philipp Koehn, Franz Josef Och, and Daniel Marcu. 2003. Statistical phrase-based translation. In *Proceedings of the 2003 Conference of the North American Chapter of the Association for Computational Linguistics on Human Language Technology-Volume 1*, pages 48–54. Association for Computational Linguistics.

Philipp Koehn, Hieu Hoang, Alexandra Birch, Chris Callison-Burch, Marcello Federico, Nicola Bertoldi, Brooke Cowan, Wade Shen, Christine Moran, Richard Zens, et al. 2007. Moses: Open source toolkit for statistical machine translation. In *Proceedings of the 45th Annual Meeting of the ACL on Interactive Poster and Demonstration Sessions*, pages 177–180. Association for Computational Linguistics.

Bhadriraju Krishnamurti. 2003. *The Dravidian Languages*. Cambridge University Press.

Amba Kulkarni, Rahmat Yousufzai, and Pervez Ahmed Azmi. 2012. Urdu-hindi-urdu machine translation: Some problems. *Health*, 666:99–1.

Jin-Shea Kuo and Ying-Kuei Yang. 2004. Generating paired transliterated-cognates using multiple pronunciation characteristics from Web Corpora. In *PACLIC*, volume 18, pages 275–282.

Gurpreet S Lehal and Tejinder S Saini. 2010. A hindi to urdu transliteration system. In *Proceedings of ICON-2010: 8th International Conference on Natural Language Processing, Kharagpur*.

Vladimir I Levenshtein. 1966. Binary codes capable of correcting deletions, insertions and reversals. In *Soviet physics doklady*, volume 10, page 707.

Abbas Malik, Laurent Besacier, Christian Boitet, and Pushpak Bhattacharyya. 2009. A hybrid model for urdu hindi transliteration. In *Proceedings of the 2009 Named Entities Workshop: Shared Task on Transliteration*, pages 177–185. Association for Computational Linguistics.

Colin P Masica. 1993. *The Indo-Aryan Languages*. Cambridge University Press.

David Matthews. 2007. Machine transliteration of proper names. *Master's Thesis, University of Edinburgh, Edinburgh, United Kingdom*.

Animesh Nayan, B Ravi Kiran Rao, Pawandeep Singh, Sudip Sanyal, and Ratna Sanyal. 2008. Named entity recognition for Indian languages. *NER for South and South East Asian Languages*, page 97.

Boris New, Verónica Araújo, and Thierry Nazzi. 2008. Differential processing of consonants and vowels in lexical access through reading. *Psychological Science*, 19(12):1223–1227.

F. J. Och and H. Ney. 2000. Improved Statistical Alignment Models. pages 440–447, Hongkong, China, October.

Franz Josef Och. 2003. Minimum error rate training in statistical machine translation. In *Proceedings of the 41st Annual Meeting on Association for Computational Linguistics-Volume 1*, pages 160–167. Association for Computational Linguistics.

Vincent Pagel, Kevin Lenzo, and Alan Black. 1998. Letter to sound rules for accented lexicon compression. *arXiv preprint cmp-lg/9808010*.

Kalyani Patel and Jyoti Pareek. 2009. Gh-map-rule based token mapping for translation between sibling language pair: Gujarati–hindi. In *Proceedings of International Conference on Natural Language Processing*.

Vladimir Pervouchine, Haizhou Li, and Bo Lin. 2009. Transliteration alignment. In *Proceedings of the Joint Conference of the 47th Annual Meeting of the ACL and the 4th International Joint Conference on Natural Language Processing of the AFNLP: Volume 1-Volume 1*, pages 136–144. Association for Computational Linguistics.

Alok Rai. 2001. *Hindi nationalism*, volume 13. Orient Blackswan.

R Russell and M Odell. 1918. Soundex. *US Patent*, 1.

Hassan Sajjad, Alexander Fraser, and Helmut Schmid. 2012. A statistical model for unsupervised and semi-supervised transliteration mining. In *Proceedings of the 50th Annual Meeting of the Association for Computational Linguistics: Long Papers-Volume 1*, pages 469–477. Association for Computational Linguistics.

K Saravanan and A Kumaran. 2008. Some experiments in mining named entity transliteration pairs from comparable corpora. *CLIA 2008*, page 26.

Silpa. 2010. Swathanthra Indian Language Computing Project. [Online].

Manish Sinha, Mahesh Reddy, and Pushpak Bhattacharyya. 2006. An approach towards construction and application of multilingual indo-wordnet. In *3rd Global Wordnet Conference (GWC 06), Jeju Island, Korea*.

Jörg Tiedemann. 1998. Extraction of translation equivalents from parallel corpora. In *Proceedings of the 11th Nordic conference on computational linguistics*, pages 120–128. Center för Sprogteknologi and Department of Genral and Applied Lingusitcs (IAAS), University of Copenhagen, Njalsgade 80, DK-2300 Copenhagen S, Denmark.

Muhammad Adeel Zahid, Naveed Iqbal Rao, and Adil Masood Siddiqui. 2010. English to Urdu transliteration: An application of Soundex algorithm. In *Information and Emerging Technologies (ICIET), 2010 International Conference on*, pages 1–5. IEEE.

Min Zhang, Xiangyu Duan, Vladimir Pervouchine, and Haizhou Li. 2010. Machine transliteration: Leveraging on third languages. In *Proceedings of the 23rd International Conference on Computational Linguistics: Posters*, pages 1444–1452. Association for Computational Linguistics.

Min Zhang, Haizhou Li, Ming Liu, and A Kumaran. 2012. Whitepaper of news 2012 shared task on machine transliteration. In *Proceedings of the 4th Named Entity Workshop*, pages 1–9. Association for Computational Linguistics.

Exploiting Parallel Corpus for Handling Out-of-vocabulary Words

Juan Luo
IPS
Waseda University
Fukuoka, Japan
juan.luo@suou.waseda.jp

John Tinsley
CNGL
Dublin City University
Dublin, Ireland
jtinsley@computing.dcu.ie

Yves Lepage
IPS
Waseda University
Fukuoka, Japan
yves.lepage@waseda.jp

Abstract

This paper presents a hybrid model for handling out-of-vocabulary words in Japanese-to-English statistical machine translation output by exploiting parallel corpus. As the Japanese writing system makes use of four different script sets (*kanji*, *hiragana*, *katakana*, and *romaji*), we treat these scripts differently. A machine transliteration model is built to transliterate out-of-vocabulary Japanese *katakana* words into English words. A Japanese dependency structure analyzer is employed to tackle out-of-vocabulary *kanji* and *hiragana* words. The evaluation results demonstrate that it is an effective approach for addressing out-of-vocabulary word problems and decreasing the OOVs rate in the Japanese-to-English machine translation tasks.

1 Introduction

Phrase-based statistical machine translation systems rely on parallel corpora for learning translation rules and phrases, which are stored in "phrase tables". Words that cannot be found in phrase tables thus result in out-of-vocabulary words (OOVs) for a machine translation system. The large number of loanwords and orthographic variants in Japanese makes the OOVs problem more severe than in other languages. As stated in (Oh et al., 2006), most of out-of-vocabulary words in translations from Japanese are made up of proper nouns and technical terms, which are phonetically transliterated from other languages. In addition, the highly irregular Japanese orthography as is analyzed in (Halpern, 2002) poses a challenge for machine translation tasks.

Japanese is written in four different sets of scripts: *kanji*, *hiragana*, *katakana*, and *romaji* (Halpern, 2002). *Kanji* is a logographic system consisting of characters borrowed from the Chinese characters. *Hiragana* is a syllabary system used mainly for functional elements. *Katakana* is also a syllabary system. Along with *hiragana*, they are generally referred as *kana*. *Katakana* is used to write new words or loan words, i.e., words that are borrowed and transliterated from foreign languages. *Romaji* is just the Latin alphabet.

In this paper, we present a method of tackling out-of-vocabulary words to improve the performance of machine translation. This method consists of two components. The first component relies on a machine transliteration model for *katakana* words that is based on the phrase-based machine translation framework. Furthermore, by making use of limited resources, i.e., the same parallel corpus used to build the machine translation system, a method of automatically acquiring bilingual word pairs for transliteration training data from this parallel corpus is used. With these enriched bilingual pairs, the transliteration model is further improved. In the second component, a Japanese dependency structure analyzer is used to build a *kanji-hiragana* system for handling orthographic variants.

The structure of the paper is as follows. Section 2 reviews related works. In Section 3, we present a back-transliteration model which is based on the SMT framework for handling *katakana* OOV words. Section 4 describes a method of tackling *kanji* and *hiragana* OOV words. Section 5 and 6 deal with the experiments and error analysis. Conclusion and future directions are drawn in Section 7.

2 Related Work

A number of works have been proposed to tackle the *katakana* out-of-vocabulary words by making use of machine transliteration. According to (Oh et al., 2006), machine transliteraion can be classified into four models: grapheme-based transliteration model, phoneme-based transliteration model, hybrid transliteration model, and correspondence-based transliteration model.

A grapheme-based transliteration model tries to map directly from source graphemes to target graphemes (Li et al., 2004; Sherif and Kondrak, 2007; Garain et al., 2012; Lehal and Saini, 2012b). In the phoneme-based model, phonetic information or pronunciation is used, and thus additional processing step of converting source grapheme to source phoneme is required. It tries to transform the source graphemes to target graphemes via phonemes as a pivot (Knight and Graehl, 1998; Gao et al., 2004; Ravi and Knight, 2009). A hybrid transliteration approach tries to use both the grapheme-based transliteration model and the phoneme-based model (Bilac and Tanaka, 2004; Lehal and Saini, 2012a). As described in (Oh et al., 2006), the correspondence-based transliteration model (Oh and Choi, 2002) is also considered as a hybrid approach. However, it differs from the others in that it takes into consideration of the correspondence between a source grapheme and a source phoneme, while a general hybrid approach simply uses a combination of grapheme-based model and phoneme-based model through linear interpolation.

Machine transliteration, especially those methods that adopt statistical models, rely on training data to learn transliteration rules. Several studies on the automatic acquisition of transliteration pairs for different language pairs (e.g., English - Chinese, English - Japanese, English - Korean) have been proposed in recent years.

Tsuji (2002) proposed a rule-based method of extracting *katakana* and English word pairs from bilingual corpora. A generative model is used to model transliteration rules, which are determined manually. As pointed out by Bilac and Tanaka (2005), there are two limitations of the method. One is the manually determined transliteration rules, which may pose the question of reduplication. The other is the efficiency problem of the generation of transliteration candidates. Brill et al. (2001) exploited non-aligned monolingual web search engine query logs to acquire *katakana* - English transliteration pairs. They firstly converted the *katakana* form to Latin script. A trainable noisy channel error model was then employed to map and harvest (*katakana*, English) pairs. The method, however, failed to deal with compounds, i.e., a single *katakana* word may match more than one English words. Lee and Chang (2003) proposed using a statistical machine transliteration model to identify English - Chinese word pairs from parallel texts by exploiting phonetic similarities. Oh and Isahara (2006) presented a transliteration lexicon acquisition model to extract transliteration pairs from mining the web by relying on phonetic similarity and joint-validation.

While many techniques have been proposed to handle Japanese *katakana* words and translate these words into English, few works have focused on *kanji* and *hiragana*. As is shown in (Halpern, 2002), the Japanese orthography is highly irregular, which contributes to a substantial number of out-of-vocabulary words in the machine translation output. A number of orthographic variation patterns have been analyzed by Halpern (2002): (1) okurigana variants, which are usually attached to a *kanji* stem; (2) cross-script orthographic variants, in which the same word can be written in a mixture of several scripts; (3) kanji variants, which can be written in different forms; (4) *kun* homophones, which means word pronounced the same but written differently.

In this paper, we use a grapheme-based transliteration model to transform Japanese *katakana* out-of-vocabulary words to English, i.e., a model that maps directly from *katakana* characters to English characters without phonetic conversion. Furthermore, this model is used to acquire *katakana* and English transliteration word pairs from parallel corpus for enlarging the training data, which, in turn, improves the performance of the grapheme-based model. For handling *kanji* and *hiragana* out-of-vocabulary words, we propose to use a Japanese dependency structure analyzer and the source (i.e., Japanese) part of a parallel corpus to build a model for normalizing orthographic variants and translate them into English words.

3 Katakana OOV Model

Machine transliteration is the process of automatically converting terms in the source language into those terms that are phonetically equivalent in the target language. For example, the English word "chromatography" is transliterated in Japanese *katakana* word as "クロマトグラフィー". The task of transliterating the Japanese words (e.g., クロマトグラフィー) back into English words (e.g., chromatography) is refered in (Knight and Graehl, 1998) as *back-transliteration*.

We view the back-transliteration of unknown Japanese *katakana* words into English words as the task of performing character-level phrase-based statistical machine translation. It is based on the SMT framework as described in (Koehn et al., 2003). The task is defined as translating a Japanese *katakana* word $J_1^n = \{J_1, ..., J_n\}$ to a English word $E_1^i = \{E_1, ..., E_i\}$, where each element of J_1^n and E_1^i is Japanese grapheme and English character. For a given Japanese *katakana* J, one tries to find out the most probable English word E. The process is formulated as

$$\arg\max_E P(E|J) = \arg\max_E P(J|E)P(E) \quad (1)$$

where $P(J|E)$ is translation model and $P(E)$ is the language model. Here the translation unit is considered to be graphemes or characters instead of words, and alignment is between graphemes and characters as is shown in Figure 1.

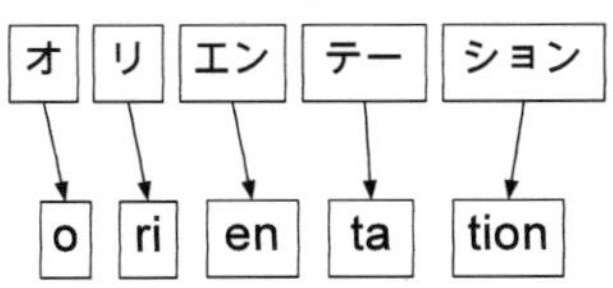

Figure 1: Character alignment

As the statistical model requires bilingual training data, a method of acquiring Japanese *katakana* - English word pairs from parallel corpus will be presented in the following section. The structure of the proposed method is summarized in Figure 2.

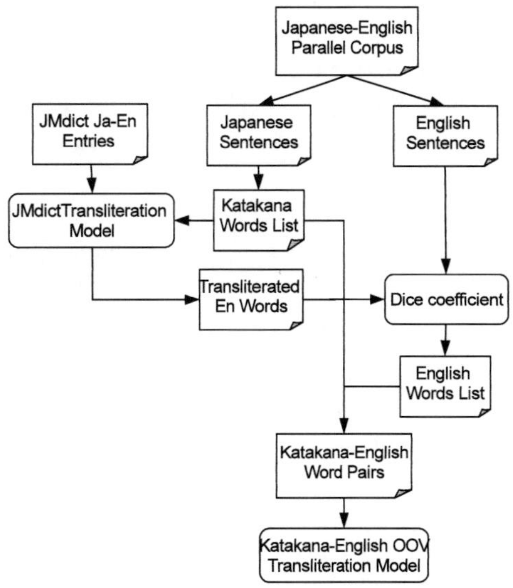

Figure 2: Illustration of katakana OOV model

3.1 Acquisition of Word Pairs

In this section, we will describe our method of obtaining *katakana* - English word pairs by making use of parallel corpus.

The procedure consists of two stages. In the first stage, bilingual entries from a freely-available dictionary, JMdict (Japanese - Multilingual dictionary) (Breen, 2004), are first employed to construct a *seed* training data. By making use of this *seed* training set, a back-transliteration model that is based on the phrase-based SMT framework is then built. In the second stage, a list of *katakana* words is firstly extracted from the Japanese (source) part of the parallel corpus. These *katakana* words are then taken as the input of the back-transliteration model, which generate "transliterated" English words. After computing the Dice coefficient between the "transliterated" word and candidate words from the English (target) part of the parallel corpus, a list of pairs of *katakana* - English words is finally generated.

To measure the similarities between the transliterated word w_x and target candidate word w_y, the Dice coefficient (Dice, 1945) is used. It is defined as

$$Dice(w_x, w_y) = \frac{2n(w_x, w_y)}{n(w_x) + n(w_y)} \quad (2)$$

where $n(w_x)$ and $n(w_y)$ are the number of bigram occurrences in word w_x and w_y respectively, and $n(w_x, w_y)$ represents the number of bigram occurrences found in both words.

3.1.1 One-to-many Correspondence

There is the case where a single *katakana* word may match a sequence of English words. Examples are shown in Table 1. In order to take into consideration of one-to-many match and extract those word pairs from parallel corpus, we preprocessed the English part of the corpus. Given a *katakana* word, for its counterpart, the English sentence, we segment it into n-grams, where $n \leq 3$. The Dice coefficient is then calculated between the "transliterated" word of this *katakana* and English n-grams (i.e., unigrams, bigrams, and trigrams) to measure the similarities. This method allows to harvest not only one-to-one but also one-to-many (*katakana*, English) word pairs from parallel corpus.

Katakana	English
トナーパターン	toner pattern
フラッシュメモリ	flash memory
アイスクリーム	ice cream
グラフィックユーザインタフェース	graphic user interface
デジタルシグナルプロセッサ	digital signal processor
プロダクトライフサイクル	product life cycle

Table 1: One-to-many correspondence

4 Kanji-hiragana OOV Model

Japanese is written in four scripts (*kanji*, *hiragana*, *katakana*, and *romaji*). Use of these sets of scripts in a mixture causes the highly irregular orthography. As analyzed in (Halpern, 2002), there are a number of orthographic variation patterns: okurigana variants, cross-script orthographic variants, kana variants, kun homophones, and so on. Table 2 shows an example of okurigana variants and kun homophones. These Japanese orthographic variants pose a special challenge for machine translation tasks.

Patterns	English	Reading	Variants
Okurigana variants	'moving'	/hikkoshi/	引越し 引っ越し 引越
	'effort'	/torikumi/	取り組み 取組み 取組
Kun homophones	'bridge' 'chopsticks'	/hashi/	橋 箸
	'account' 'course'	/kouza/	口座 講座

Table 2: Orthographic variants

In this section, we will present our approach for tackling and normalizing out-of-vocabulary *kanji* and *hiragana* words. The architecture of the approach is summarized in Figure 3. The method comprises two processes: (a) building a model; (b) normalizing and translating *kanji-hiragana* OOVs. In the first process, firstly, we use the Japanese part of the parallel corpus (the same Japanese-English parallel corpus used for training in the standard phrase-based SMT) as the input to the Japanese dependency structure analyzer CaboCha (Kudo and Matsumoto, 2002). A phonetic-to-standard Japanese parallel corpus (Figure 4) is then obtained to train a monolingual Japanese model which is also built upon a phrase-based statistical machine translation framework. In the second process, the dependency structure analyzer CaboCha

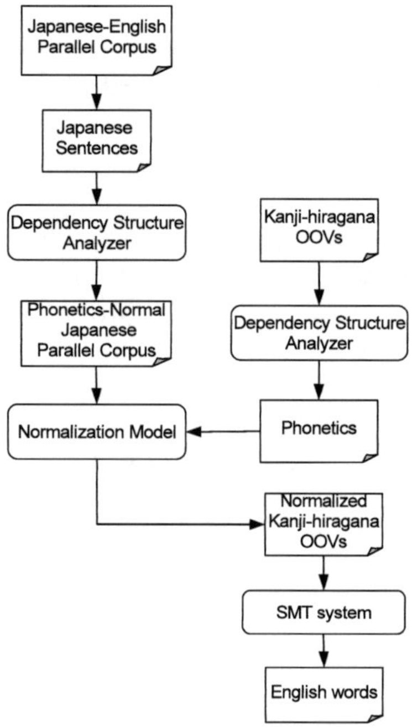

Figure 3: Illustration of kanji-hiragana OOV model

フカ オウトウ セイギョ ヲ	負荷 応答 制御 を
アイドル カイテン スウ セイギョ ヲ	アイドル 回転 数 制御 を
ティック ワリコミ ショリ ガ	ティック 割り込み 処理 が
ホウデン デンリュウ ヲ	放電 電流 を
カイシ サ レル 。	開始 さ れる 。
モール ド ブ デ アル 。	モール ド 部 で ある 。
シュツリョク ベースアドレス ヲ	出力 ベースアドレス を
ドウヨウ ナイブ シンゴウ モ	同様 内部 信号 も
ゲンテイ サ レル	限定 さ れる
キリカエル	切り換える
クミアワセ ニヨル	組み合わせ による

Figure 4: Sample of phonetic-to-standard Japanese parallel corpus

is applied to generate corresponding phonetics from a list of *kanji-hiragana* out-of-vocabulary words. These OOVs in the phonetic forms are then input to the monolingual model to produce a list of normalized *kanji-hiragana* words. Finally, the normalized OOV words will be translated into English.

5 Experiments

In this section, we will present the results of three experiments. In the first setting, we evaluate the performance of back-transliteration model. The data sets used in the back-transliteration system comprise one-to-one or one-to-many *Katakana*-English word pairs, which are segmented at the character level. In the second setting, the performance of the model for normalizing *kanji-hiragana* is assessed. In the third setting, the performance of handling both *Katakana* and *kanji-hiragana* out-of-vocabulary words in a machine translation output will be evaluated.

5.1 Katakana Transliteration Test

To train a back-transliteration model which is built upon a phrase-based statistical machine translation framework, we used the state-of-the-art machine translation toolkit: Moses decoder (Koehn et al., 2007), alignment tool GIZA++ (Och and Ney, 2003), MERT (Minimum Error Rate Training) (Och, 2003) to tune the parameters, and the SRI Language Modeling toolkit (Stolcke, 2002) to build character-level target language model.

The data set for training (499,871 entries) we used in the experiment contains the JMdict entries and word pairs extracted from parallel corpus. The JMdict consists of 166,794 Japanese - English entries. 19,132 *katakana* - English entries are extracted from the dictionary. We also extracted 480,739 *katakana* - English word pairs from NTCIR Japanese - English parallel corpus. The development set is made of 500 word pairs, and 500 entries are used for test set.

The experimental results are shown in Table 3. For evaluation metric, we used BLEU at the character level (Papineni et al., 2002; Denoual and Lepage, 2005; Li et al., 2011). Word accuracy and character accuracy (Karimi et al., 2011) are also used to assess the performance of the system. Word accuracy (WA) is calculated as:

$$WA = \frac{\text{number of correct transliterations}}{\text{total number of test words}} \quad (3)$$

Character accuracy (CA) is based on the Levenshtein edit distance (Levenshtein, 1966) and it is defined as:

$$CA = \frac{len(T) - ED(T, L(T_i))}{len(T)} \quad (4)$$

where $len(T)$ is the length of reference word T. $L(T_i)$ is the suggested transliteration at rank i, and ED is the Levenshtein edit distance (insertion, deletion, and substitution) between two words. The character accuracy takes an average of all the test entries.

System	BLEU	WA	CA
Katakana transli.	80.56	50.60%	86.33%

Table 3: Evaluation results of transliteration test

An analysis of number of character errors in entry strings is shown in Table 4. 253 out of 500 entries (50.60%) match exactly the same as the reference words. Strings contain one and two character errors are 86 (17.20%) and 56 (11.20%), respectively. In total, strings with less than two character errors represent 79.00% of overall test entries. There are 50 (10.00%) and 55 (11.00%) entries contain three or more character errors.

Examples of *katakana* - English transliteration output are given in Table 5. For some *katakana* words, they are transliterated correctly as references. For other *katakana* words, it shows that the output of transliteration contain spelling errors. For example, the grapheme "アン" can be transliterated into "an", "en", or "un". For the *katakana* word "アンハッピー" (unhappy), it is erroneously transliterated into "anhappy" .

Character errors	Entries	Percentage
0 character error	253	50.60%
1 character error	86	17.20%
2 character error	56	11.20%
3 character error	50	10.00%
Others	55	11.00%

Table 4: Analysis of number of character errors

	Katakana	Reference	Output
0	インベンション	invention	invention
0	インプット	input	input
0	アンカー	anchor	anchor
1	アンカーマン	anchorman	ancherman
1	アンハッピー	unhappy	anhappy
1	アントレ	entree	entre
2	インテルクチュアル	intellectual	intelctual
2	インビジブル	invisible	inbsible
2	インテリア	interior	interia
n	インターフェアランス	interference	interfealance
n	アンフェア	unfair	anfare
n	アンタッチャブル	untouchable	antatchable

Table 5: Examples of character errors

5.2 Kanji-hiragana Normalization Test

In the second setting, we will assess the performance of *kanji-hiragana* normalization model as it is described in Section 4. As the monolingual Japanese normalization model is also built upon the statistical machine translation framework, we used the same toolkit as those in Section 5.1. For the training set, we applied the Japanese dependency structure analyzer CaboCha on the Japanese part of the parallel corpus (300,000 lines) and obtained a phonetic-to-standard Japanese parallel corpus (see Figure 4). The development set and test set consist of 1,000 lines and 5,000 words, respectively. Since this experiment is not a task of measuring the accuracy of the output of the model (i.e., it is a test of how the monolingual model can normalize the Japanese *kanji-hiragana* words), we did not use any evaluation metrics, such as BLEU, WA, and CA.

Table 6 shows an analysis of number of character differences between *kanji-hiragana* words and their normalized forms. The number of entries matches exactly the same as the original Japanese words is 3908, which represents 78.16% of all test entries. There are 21.84% of the entries which are normalized to different forms. Examples of number of character differences is shown in Table 7. The normalized output forms can generally be categorized into three types: *kun homophones*, *okurigana variants*, and others. *Kun homophones* would cause orthographic ambiguity. Words in the category *okurigana variants* are normalized into different forms but they have the same meaning. It shows that the monolingual normalization model is useful for solving out-of-vocabulary *okurigana variants* and helps reducing the out-of-vocabulary words rate. There are other words that are not normalized for which the phonetic representations is output directly.

Character diff.	Entries	Percentage
0 character diff.	3,908	78.16%
1 character diff.	424	8.48%
2 character diff.	509	10.18%
3 character diff.	44	0.88%
Others	115	2.30%

Table 6: Analysis of number of character differences

	Japanese	Phonetics	Norm. output
0	駐車 (parking)	チュウシャ	駐車 (parking)
0	飲み物 (beverage)	ノミモノ	飲み物 (beverage)
0	電極 (electrode)	デンキョク	電極 (electrode)
	kun homophones		
1	視点 (perspective)	シテン	支点 (fulcrum)
1	通貨 (currency)	ツウカ	通過 (pass)
1	講座 (course)	コウザ	口座 (account)
2	注視 (gaze)	チュウシ	中止 (stop)
2	意思 (intention)	イシ	医師 (doctor)
2	近郊 (suburbs)	キンコウ	均衡 (balance)
n	当たり (per)	アタリ	辺 (side)
	okurigana variants		
1	読みとり (read)	ヨミトリ	読み取り
1	繰返し (repeat)	クリカエシ	繰り返し
1	呼出し (call)	ヨビダシ	呼び出し
2	纏め (collect)	マトメ	まとめ
2	釣合 (balance)	ツリアイ	釣り合い
2	振替 (transfer)	フリカエ	振り替え
n	うま味 (umami)	ウマミ	旨み
	others		
n	切替 (switch)	キリカエ	切り換え
n	雪崩 (avalanche)	ナダレ	ナダレ
n	藤木 (personal name)	フジキ	フジキ

Table 7: Examples of character differences can be seen by comparing the Japanese column with the Normalized output column

5.3 Out-of-vocabulary Words Test

In the third setting, we evaluate the performance of handling out-of-vocabulary words for machine translation by making use of *katakana* OOV model and *kanji-hiragana* OOV model. The system architecture is summarized in Figure 5. From the output of a machine translation system, out-of-vocabulary words are firstly extracted. OOV *katakana* words are then transliterated into English by using the back-transliteration model and OOV *kanji-hiragana* words are normalized and translated into English words by using the normalization model. A standard phrase-based statistical machine translation system is built by making use of the same toolkit as described in Section 5.1. KyTea (Neubig et al., 2011) is used to perform segmentation on *katakana* OOV words.

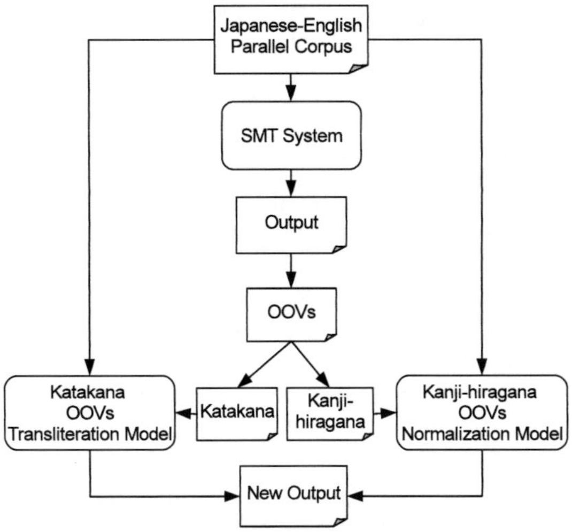

Figure 5: Illustration of system architecture

For data sets in the baseline SMT system, we used a sample of NTCIR Japanese - English parallel corpus. The training set is made of 300,000 lines. The development set contains 1,000 lines, and 10,000 lines are used for test set.

As for the evaluation, while the quality of a machine translation system is usually measured in BLEU scores, it may not be fair to examine the results in BLEU scores for measuring the improvement and contribution of out-of-vocabulary *katakana* transliteration and *kanji-hiragana* normalization to a machine translation system. Here we provide the BLEU scores as a reference. Table 8 shows the evaluation results of OOV words test. By comparing with the baseline system, it shows that there is a slight gain in BLEU for transliterating out-of-vocabulary *katakana* words and normalizing and translating *kanji-hiragana* words. We also extracted sentences that contain out-of-vocabulary words (813 lines) from the test set. In comparison with the baseline, sentences with translated out-of-vocabulary words give better result.

System	BLEU
Japanese - English MT baseline	24.72
MT with translated OOV word	24.77
Sentence with OOV (MT baseline)	16.04
Sentence with OOV (translated OOV word)	16.57

Table 8: Evaluation results of OOV words test

An analysis of out-of-vocabulary words in the machine translation output is presented in Table 9. In the output of a test set of 10,000 sentences, there are 1,105 out-of-vocabulary Japanese words. Among these OOV words, 447 out of 1,105 are *katakana* words, which is 40.45%. The number of OOV *kanji-hiragana* words are 658 (59.55%).

	Data
Test sentences	10,000
Out-of-vocabulary words	1,105
OOV *katakana*	447
OOV *kanji-hiragana*	658

Table 9: Analysis of out-of-vocabulary words

6 Error Analysis

The main points observed from a scrutinous analysis of the results of *katakana* OOV model and *kanji-hiragana* OOV model and countermeausures against them are as follows:

Katakana OOV model: some compound *katakana* words are not segmented appropriately, which result in erroneous English transliteration. Further improvement on back-transliteration model would be expected when the accuracy of segmentation of *katakana* words is improved.

- the word: インストルメンタルパネル
  segment: インストル | メンタル | パネル
  transliterate: instru mental panel
- the word: レイティングデイスクリプタ
  segment: レイティング | デイス | クリプタ
  transliterate: rating dis criptor
- the word: カムセンサ
  segment: カムセンサ
  transliterate: camsensor

Kanji-hiragana OOV model: handling *kanji-hiragana* words is very difficult due to the orthographic variants and the complexity of the

Japanese writing system. The model is useful for handling *okurigana variants*. For example, the word “閉込め” is normalized into “閉じ込め” and translated correctly into “confinement”. However, 68% (447) of the normalized *kanji-hiragana* words cannot be translated into English. Some words are normalized and transformed into different written forms as they are pronouned the same (*kun homophones*), which leads to ambiguity. Further classification and treatment of *kanji-hiragana* words is needed as it is observed from the machine translation output that 145 out of 658 out-of-vocabulary words (22.04%) are personal names, place names, and organization names, i.e., named entities. Building a mapping table between the phonetics of words and their romanization representations might be effective for tackling names, which may further improve the performance of *kanji-hiragana* model.

- *kun homophones*: 変事
  phonetics: ヘンジ
  normalize: 返事
  translate: reply
- name: 宗二
  phonetics: ソウジ
  normalize: 相似
  translate: analogous
- name: 富士通
  phonetics: フジツウ
  normalize: 富士通
  translate: 富士通

7 Conclusion and Future Work

We have described a method of handling both *katakana* and *kanji-hiragana* out-of-vocabulary words by exploiting parallel corpus. A grapheme-based back-transliteration model is built upon the phrase-based statistical machine translation framework for transliterating *katakana* into English words. This model is also used to enriching training set by extracting Japanese *katakana* and English word pairs from parallel corpus. A normalization model is built to tackle and translate *kanji-hiragana* words. While there are limitations of the model, it can be an aid to normalize and translate *okurigana variants*.

It is summarized in (Karimi et al., 2011) that grapheme-based models tend to provide better performance than phoneme-based models. This is because that the transliteration process consists of fewer steps and that there is less reliance on external pronunciation dictionaries. They also pointed out that transliteration models can usually be used in combination to improve the performance. In the future, we would like to try to use the transliteration models in a complimentary manner. The experimental results reveal that segmentation of Japanese *katakana* words should be improved, which will be our future work. We also plan to investigate the effects of handling of names in reduction of out-of-vocabulary words.

References

Slaven Bilac and Hozumi Tanaka. 2004. A hybrid back-transliteration system for Japanese. In *Proceedings of the 20th international conference on Computational Linguistics (COLING 2004)*, pages 597–603, Stroudsburg, PA, USA. Association for Computational Linguistics.

Slaven Bilac and Hozumi Tanaka. 2005. Extracting transliteration pairs from comparable corpora. In *Proceedings of the Annual Meeting of the Natural Language Processing Society*, Japan.

James Breen. 2004. Jmdict: a Japanese - Multilingual dictionary. In *Proceedings of the Coling 2004 Workshop on Multilingual Linguistic Resources*, pages 71–78, Geneva.

Eric Brill, Gary Kacmarcik, and Chris Brockett. 2001. Automatically harvesting katakana-English term pairs from search engine query logs. In *Proceedings of the Sixth Natural Language Processing Pacific Rim Symposium (NLPRS 2001)*, pages 393–399, Tokyo, Japan.

Etienne Denoual and Yves Lepage. 2005. BLEU in characters: towards automatic MT evaluation in languages without word delimiters. In *Proceedings of the Second International Joint Conference on Natural Language Processing (IJCNLP 2005)*, pages 79–84, Jeju Island, Republic of Kore, October.

Lee R. Dice. 1945. Measures of the amount of ecologic association between species. *Journal of Ecology*, 26(3):297–302.

Wei Gao, Kam-Fai Wong, and Wai Lam. 2004. Phoneme-based transliteration of foreign names for oov problem. In *Proceedings of the First international joint conference on Natural Language Processing (IJCNLP 2004)*, pages 110–119, Berlin, Heidelberg. Springer-Verlag.

Utpal Garain, Arjun Das, David Doermann, and Douglas Oard. 2012. Leveraging statistical transliteration for dictionary-based English-Bengali CLIR of OCR'd text. In *Proceedings of the 24th Internatiional Conference on Computational Linguistics (COLING 2012)*, pages 339–348, Mumbai, India,

December. The COLING 2012 Organizing Committee.

Jack Halpern. 2002. Lexicon-based orthographic disambiguation in cjk intelligent information retrieval. In *Proceedings of the 3rd Workshop on Asian Language Resources and International Standardization - Volume 12*, pages 1–7, Stroudsburg, PA, USA. Association for Computational Linguistics.

Sarvnaz Karimi, Falk Scholer, and Andrew Turpin. 2011. Machine transliteration survey. *ACM Computing Surveys*, 43(3):17:1–17:46, April.

Kevin Knight and Jonathan Graehl. 1998. Machine transliteration. *Computational Linguistics*, 24(4):599–612, December.

Philipp Koehn, Franz J. Och, and Daniel Marcu. 2003. Statistical phrase-based translation. In *Proceedings of the 2003 Human Language Technology Conference of the North American Chapter of the Association for Computational Linguistics (HLT-NAACL 2003)*, pages 48–54, Edmonton.

Philipp Koehn, Hieu Hoang, Alexandra Birch, Chris Callison-Burch, Marcello Federico, Nicola Bertoldi, Brooke Cowan, Wade Shen, Christine Moran, Richard Zens, Chris Dyer, Ondrej Bojar, Alexandra Constantin, and Evan Herbst. 2007. Moses: Open source toolkit for statistical machine translation. In *Proceedings of the 45th Annual Meeting of the Association for Computational Linguistics (ACL 2007)*, pages 177–180, Prague, Czech Republic.

Taku Kudo and Yuji Matsumoto. 2002. Japanese dependency analysis using cascaded chunking. In *CoNLL 2002: Proceedings of the 6th Conference on Natural Language Learning 2002 (COLING 2002 Post-Conference Workshops)*, pages 63–69, Taipei, Taiwan.

Chun-Jen Lee and Jason S. Chang. 2003. Acquisition of English-Chinese transliterated word pairs from parallel-aligned texts using a statistical machine transliteration model. In *Proceedings of the HLT-NAACL 2003 Workshop on Building and using parallel texts: data driven machine translation and beyond - Volume 3*, HLT-NAACL-PARALLEL '03, pages 96–103, Stroudsburg, PA, USA. Association for Computational Linguistics.

Gurpreet Singh Lehal and Tejinder Singh Saini. 2012a. Conversion between scripts of Punjabi: Beyond simple transliteration. In *Proceedings of the 24th International Conference on Computational Linguistics (COLING 2012)*, pages 633–642, Mumbai, India, December. The COLING 2012 Organizing Committee.

Gurpreet Singh Lehal and Tejinder Singh Saini. 2012b. Development of a complete Urdu-Hindi transliteration system. In *Proceedings of the 24th International Conference on Computational Linguistics (COLING 2012)*, pages 643–652, Mumbai, India, December. The COLING 2012 Organizing Committee.

Vladimir I. Levenshtein. 1966. Binary codes capable of correcting deletions, insertions and reversals. *Soviet Physics-doklady*, 10(8):707–710.

Haizhou Li, Min Zhang, and Jian Su. 2004. A joint source-channel model for machine transliteration. In *Proceedings of the 42nd Annual Meeting on Association for Computational Linguistics (ACL 2004)*, pages 159–166, Stroudsburg, PA, USA. Association for Computational Linguistics.

Maoxi Li, Chengqing Zong, and Hwee Tou Ng. 2011. Automatic evaluation of Chinese translation output: word-level or character-level? In *Proceedings of the 49th Annual Meeting of the Association for Computational Linguistics: Human Language Technologies (ACL-HLT 2011)*, pages 159–164, Portland, Oregon, USA.

Graham Neubig, Yosuke Nakata, and Shinsuke Mori. 2011. Pointwise prediction for robust, adaptable japanese morphological analysis. In *Proceedings of the 49th Annual Meeting of the Association for Computational Linguistics: Human Language Technologies (ACL-HLT 2011)*, pages 529–533, Portland, Oregon, USA.

Franz Josef Och and Hermann Ney. 2003. A systematic comparison of various statistical alignment models. *Computational Linguistics*, 29(1):19–51.

Franz Josef Och. 2003. Minimum error rate training in statistical machine translation. In *Proceedings of the 41st Annual Meeting on Association for Computational Linguistics - Volume 1 (ACL 2003)*, pages 160–167, Stroudsburg, PA, USA. Association for Computational Linguistics.

Jong-Hoon Oh and Key-Sun Choi. 2002. An English-Korean transliteration model using pronunciation and contextual rules. In *Proceedings of the 19th International Conference on Computational linguistics (COLING 2002)*, pages 1–7, Stroudsburg, PA, USA. Association for Computational Linguistics.

Jong-Hoon Oh and Hitoshi Isahara. 2006. Mining the web for transliteration lexicons: Joint-validation approach. In *Proceedings of the 2006 IEEE/WIC/ACM International Conference on Web Intelligence*, WI '06, pages 254–261, Washington, DC, USA. IEEE Computer Society.

Jong-Hoon Oh, Key-Sun Choi, and Hitoshi Isahara. 2006. A comparison of different machine transliteration models. *Journal of Artificial Intelligence Research*, 27(1):119–151, October.

Kishore Papineni, Salim Roukos, Todd Ward, and Wei-Jing Zhu. 2002. BLEU: a method for automatic evaluation of machine translation. In *Proceedings of the 40th Annual Meeting of the Association for Computational Linguistics (ACL 2002)*, pages 311–318, Philadelphia.

Sujith Ravi and Kevin Knight. 2009. Learning phoneme mappings for transliteration without parallel data. In *Proceedings of Human Language Technologies: The 2009 Annual Conference of the North*

American Chapter of the Association for Computational Linguistics (NAACL 2009), pages 37–45, Stroudsburg, PA, USA. Association for Computational Linguistics.

Tarek Sherif and Grzegorz Kondrak. 2007. Substring-based transliteration. In *Proceedings of the 45th Annual Meeting of the Association of Computational Linguistics (ACL 2007)*, pages 944–951, Prague, Czech Republic, June. Association for Computational Linguistics.

A. Stolcke. 2002. SRILM-an extensible language modeling toolkit. In *Proceedings of the Seventh International Conference on Spoken Language Processing (ICSLP 2002)*, volume 2, pages 901–904, Denver, Colorado.

Keita Tsuji. 2002. Automatic extraction of translational Japanese-katakana and English word pairs from bilingual corpora. *International Journal of Computer Processing of Oriental Languages*, 15(3):261–279.

Classifying Questions in Question Answering System Using Finite State Machines with a Simple Learning Approach

Mohammad Moinul Hoque
University of Evora, Evora, Portugal
moincse@yahoo.com

Teresa Goncalves
University of Evora, Evora, Portugal
tcg@uevora.pt

Paulo Quaresma
L2F/INESC-ID & University of Évora, Portugal
pq@uevora.pt

Abstract

Question Classification plays a significant part in Question Answering system. In order to obtain a classifier, we present in this paper[1] a pragmatic approach that utilizes simple sentence structures observed and learned from the question sentence patterns, trains a set of Finite State Machines (FSM) based on keywords appearing in the sentences and uses the trained FSMs to classify various questions to their relevant classes. Although, questions can be placed using various syntactic structures and keywords, we have carefully observed that this variation is within a small finite limit and can be traced down using a limited number of FSMs and a simple semantic understanding instead of using complex semantic analysis. WordNet semantic meaning of various keywords to extend the FSMs capability to accept a wide variety of wording used in the questions. Various kinds of questions written in English language and belonging to diverse classes from the Conference and Labs of the Evaluation Forum's Question Answering track are used for the training purpose and a separate set of questions from the same track is used for analyzing the FSMs competence to map the questions to one of the recognizable classes. With the use of learning strategies and application of simple voting functions along with training the weights for the keywords appearing in the questions, we have managed to achieve a classification accuracy as high as 94%. The system was trained by placing questions in various orders to see if the system built up from those orders have any subtle impact on the accuracy rate. The usability of this approach lies in its simplicity and yet it performs well to cope up with various sentence patterns.

1 Introduction

Classifying a question to its appropriate class in an important subtask and plays a substantial role in the Question Answering (QA) systems. It can provide some useful clues for identifying potential answers in large collections of texts. The goal of this current work is to develop a classifier using Finite State Machines (FSM) to classify a set of questions into their relevant classes. Various techniques have already been tried by the community either to classify a question to its relevant class or to a finer subclass of a specific class. Results of the error analysis acquired from an open domain QA system demonstrates that more or less 36.4% of the errors were generated due to the wrong classification of questions (Moldovan et al., 2003). So, this issue can be highlighted as a subject of interest and has arisen the aim of developing more accurate question classifiers (Zhang and W. Sun Lee, 2003). Usually the answers generated from the classified questions have to be exact in nature and the size of the answer has to be within a restricted size (Peters et al., 2002; Voorhees, 2001) which greatly emphasizes the need of an accurate question classifier. Techniques involving Support Vector Machines (Dell Zhang and Wee Sun Lee, 2003; K. Hacioglu and W. Ward, 2003) showed a good accuracy rate of over 96% in classifying questions to their finer classes instead of diverse super classes. Li and Roth (2002) investigated a variety of feature combinations using their Sparse Network of Winnows algorithm (A. Carlson et al., 1999). The Decision Tree algorithm (Mitchell, 2002) was also used for question classification with fair amount of accuracy rate. It is a method for approximating discrete valued target function where the learned function is presented in a tree which classifies instances. Naïve Bayes (Mitchell, 2002) method was also used in the question classification task with limited accuracy rate of around 79.2%. In another work (Fan Bu et al., 2010), where a function-based question classifi-

[1] This work was supported by national funds through FCT – Fundação para a Ciência e a Tecnologia, under project PEst-OE/EEI/LA0021/2013

cation technique is proposed, the authors of that paper claimed to have achieved as high as 86% precision levels for some classes of questions. Some attempts have been made to develop a language independent question classifier (Thamar Solorio et al., 2004) with not a mentionable success rate.

This work[1] focuses on the questions posed only in English language and uses questions from the Question Answering (QA) track of the Conference and Labs of the Evaluation Forum (CLEF) (QA4MRE, 2013). It classifies the questions into 5 major classes namely Factoid (FA), Definition (DE), Reason/Purpose (RP), Procedure (PR) and Opinion (OP) Class. CLEF QA track have some diverse types of questions and we are required to fit each of the questions into any of the above mentioned classes. Factoid class of questions are mainly fact oriented questions, asking for the name of a person, a location, some numerical quantity, the day on which something happened such as 'What percentage of people in Bangladesh relies on medical insurance for health care?', 'What is the price of an air-conditioning system?' etc. Definition questions such as 'What/Who is XYZ?' asks for the meaning of something or important information about someone or an organization. 'What is avian influenza?', 'Define SME', 'What is the meaning of Bluetooth signal?' are some examples of the definition class questions. Reason/Purpose questions ask for the reasons/goals for something happening. 'Why was Ziaur Karim sentenced to death?' and 'What were the objectives of the National meeting?' are the example questions of this class. Procedural questions ask for a set of actions which is an accepted way of doing something. Such as: 'How do you calculate the monthly gross salary in your office?' Opinion questions ask for the opinions, feelings, ideas about people, topics or events. An example question of this type may be like 'What did the Academic Council think about the syllabus of informatics department?' A question is either mapped to only one class or may be classified as 'other'.

The next section of the paper describes the procedure used to create the states and transitions in the FSMs involving a simple learning mechanism and the section 3 presents the data set for the experimental verification of the procedures and outcome of the experiments followed by a section covering a discussion about the future works.

2 Classification using Finite State Machines (FSM) with learning strategy

From a large number of questions derived from the gold standard set of QA track of CLEF 2008 - 2011 and observing them manually, we came to a conclusion that it is possible to classify a set a questions using a set of FSMs and the FSMs can be automatically built and adjusted according to the questions in the training set and later on can be used to classify the questions appearing in the test set. Initially we start off with some elementary states for each of the FSMs beginning with different headwords. The headwords are usually What, Why, How, When, Where etc. Questions that do not begin with a known headword can be restructured to a suitable form. For example, 'In which country was the Vasco da Gama born?' can be changed to 'What country was the Vasco da Gama born?'. Similarly, 'What does SME stand for?' can be reformatted to 'What is SME?' and so on. The initial preprocessing module performs this question restructuring step. A set of non stops words of English language are extracted from the question instances which we call a Keyword set. The preprocessing module also converts the keywords into its present tense and singular form to make sure that the keywords 'thought' and 'think' are treated similarly. It also reduces the number of keywords in the set. Each FSM is represented with a directed graph and may have more than one state for each question class. Those states are called final states. Rests of the intermediate states are called 'undefined' (UN).

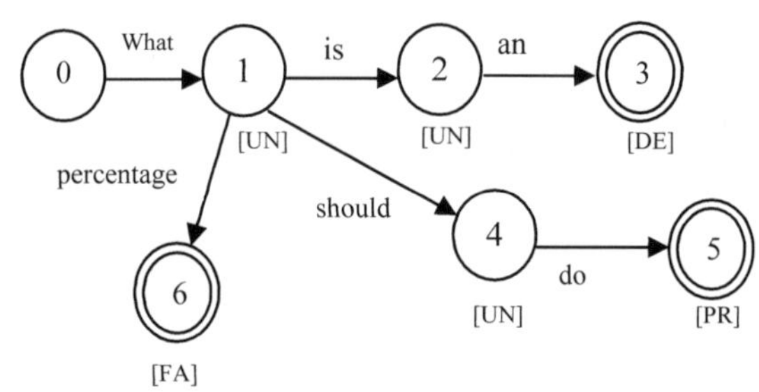

Figure 1. An FSM accepting questions Q1 and Q2.

An FSM can have many intermediate and undefined states as well as transitions between them. The inputs to a FSM are keyword tokens extracted from the question. An example FSM beginning with the headword 'What' and accepting the questions Q1: 'What is an SME?' and Q2: 'What percentage of people relies on TV for news?' is depicted in the figure 1.

2.1 Learning new states and transitions in the FSM using keywords

FSMs continue to build up the states and transitions as it encounters more new question instances. Each of the questions in the training set is tokenized removing a few English stop words and the keywords are then isolated from each of the questions to form a keyword structure (KS). Every keyword in the KS has a weight in context with the other keywords appearing in the question. In order to calculate the relevant weights of the n number of keywords, a Keyword Frequency Matrix (KFM) of n *x* n dimension is created first and the frequency of every keyword appearing before and after of every other ones is stored in the matrix. This KFM is prebuilt from all the question instances of the training set. Table 1 shows a dummy KFM with some sample frequency values.

before \ after	*What*	*The*	*Is*	*Meaning*	*Think*
What	5	80	90	16	8
The	1	5	120	16	8
Is	2	71	6	12	6
Meaning	0	0	1	0	0
Think	0	3	2	0	0

Table 1. A sample 5x5 Keyword frequency matrix (KFM)

When we are using a sentence to build or train up the FSMs, a subset of the KFM is created using only those keywords which are appearing in the question sentence and the weights of each keyword Z in the question sentence is calculated in context with other keywords appearing in that sentence using the formula followed. The formula sums up all the frequency values where the keyword Z appears after each of the other keywords in the sentence and subtracts from it the sum of the frequency values where Z appears before each of the other keywords in that question sentence. There are many keywords in various question sentences which appear more frequently than some other rarely used keywords. In order to make sure that such keywords do not receive highest weights all the time compared to the other significant but less frequently used keywords, we divide the weight value with the sum of the frequency value of Z where Z appears after each of the other keywords in the question sentence. This process normalizes the weight value of a keyword within the range 0.0 to 1. In case of a negative weight, the weight is set to 0.0.

Probable Weight (Z) =

$$\frac{\left[\sum_{j\in row} KFM(j)(index\ of\ Z\ in\ column) - \sum_{j\in col} KFM(index\ of\ Z\ in\ row)(j)\right]}{\sum_{j\in row} KFM(j)(index\ of\ Z\ in\ column)}$$

Finally, the keyword structure (KS) is built from the question sentence and it comprises of the keywords along with their weights. An FSM is selected based on the headword appearing in the question sentence and it is built using the *Algorithm1*.

The *Algorithm1* detects the keyword boundary from the Keyword Structure (KS) which is the position of the keyword having the highest weight value. If there are multiple keywords having the same highest weights, the position of the first keyword with the highest weight value is marked as the keyword boundary position. The FSM does not take any keyword as input beyond this boundary position to build up on its own. When creating a transition to a state for an input keyword, synonyms of the keyword if there are any are also derived with the help of WordNet (George A. Miller, 1995; Christiane Fellbaum, 1998) and are added as inputs to that transition to extend the machines capability significantly.

<u>*Major steps of Algorithm1:*</u>

For *every keyword* K_i in the KS of a question sentence
  Mark the keyword boundary which is the first position of the highest weighted keyword
End for
For *every keyword* K_i within the keyword boundary position in the KS
  Try to go through the FSM states using K_i as input to the FSM starting from the state S_0
    If a valid state S_j can be reached using a transition path with K_i as input
      Continue to repeat the above step with the next K_i from the state S_j
    Else
      If for the input K_i, no transition path can be found from state S_f
        If K_i and K_{i-1} were same
          Create a loop transition in that state S_f
        Else
          Create a new state and add a transition from the current state S_f to that new state
          Set the input of the transition as K_i and also the synsets(K_i) using WORDNET
        End if
      End if

If K_i appears at the keyword boundary
Set the class of the state S_f according to the already labeled class of the question.
Else
Set the class of the state S_f to 'UNDEFINED'
End if
End for

2.2 Voting function for a state

Different ordering of the similar kind of question sentences belonging to different classes can mislead the development of an FSM with wrong classification states. For example, the question, 'What is the aim of the raid spectrum policy?' may be classified as a factoid question in one training set where as there may be 5 more questions of similar pattern that are classified as Reason/Purpose question in another training set. In this case, we propose a simple voting algorithm approach. In the voting process, every question in the training set which terminates at a final state with a keyword appearing at the keyword boundary will vote for the class of the state class in the questions labeled class. The class of that state of the FSM will finally be determined according to the class that gets the maximum vote. Voting function ensures that an FSM does not label one of its final states to a wrong class because of the different ordering of the questions appearing in the training set.

Major steps of the Voting Algorithm:

For every FSM_i in the FSM set
For Every Question Q_i in the question set
For Every Keyword K_i in the Q_i appearing at the keyword boundary and terminating at a final state S_f in the FSM_i
Cast a vote for that state S_f in favor of the class that Q_i itself belongs to
End for
End for
Update each of the states of the FSM_i to that class which gets the maximum vote
End for

3 Experimental verification

For the experimental purpose, we took questions from CLEF question answering track for the year 2008-2011. A total number of 850 questions of various classes were selected for the evaluation purpose. Around 400 questions from various years were selected for the training purpose and a test set was created with the rest of the questions. The system was trained with a training set and a test set was used to test the capability of the system. Effectiveness of the classification was calculated in terms of precision and recall and the accuracy was calculated from the confusion matrix (Kohavi R., and F. Provost, 1998).

In order to make sure that the system does not get biased with specific question patterns, we have trained and tested the system in various ways to see if any subtle changes occur in the case of precision and recall. We also trained the system with 50% questions from one year mixed up with the 50% question from another year to cope up with the variations used in question wording and syntactic structure. We also changed the question order to see if the FSMs built from different order cause any considerable error or not. Keyword frequency matrix was trained using a dataset and it continued to update itself with the introduction of new questions from the training set. The data set and the result is presented in table 2. Throughout the training process, voting function was kept activated.

Year	No. of Questions for training	No. of Questions for testing	Accuracy
2008	50	50	96.5190%
2009	250	250	94.1777%
2010	80	90	95.1278%
2011	40	40	90.6014%
Mixed Set of questions	400	450	93.2111%

Table 2. Data set for the question classification using FSMs

Precision and Recall for each class is calculated and is shown in Table 3 followed. From the data in Table 3, we can see that most of the questions were correctly classified by the FSMs, because it could find correct patterns for the questions belonging to specific classes. Wrong classifications were made in some cases where almost similar pattern existed in questions belonging to two different classes. Fortunately, our voting function took the feedback from the questions and responded accordingly to reduce the classification error by a margin. Because of the inaccurate calculation of weights for some keywords in context with the other also played a role to the errors, though most of the time, the weight calculation function provided near correct assumption. In order to check the building procedure of the FSM during the training stage using the training data, we were concerned about the question ordering. We have created an $n \times n$ question index matrix with each of the questions in the training set having an index number in that question matrix. We have randomly selected a question index and started to train the system from there on. The next question selected for the training was the question that was most similar to the previously selected one.

Question Class	2008	2009	2010	2011	Mixed
DE (Precision)	1.0	1.0	1.0	0.811	0.981
DE (Recall)	1.0	0.938	0.966	0.721	0.921
FA (Precision)	1.0	0.899	0.903	0.904	0.967
FA (Recall)	1.0	0.955	1.0	0.964	0.911
OP(Precision)	0.0	0.0	1.0	1.0	1.0
OP (Recall)	0.0	0.0	1.0	1.0	1.0
PR(Precision)	0.0	0.977	1.0	0.89	0.965
PR(Recall)	0.0	0.957	0.939	0.85	0.991
RP(Precision)	0.0	0.959	1.0	1.0	0.978
RP(Recall)	0.0	0.967	1.0	1.0	0.988

Table 3. Measure of precision and recall for every class of questions based on the data in the test set

The similarity was calculated in terms of most similar words or their synonyms appearing in two of those questions.

Question Class	Trained with most similar ones. Overall Accuracy 92.1%	Trained with most dissimilar ones Overall Accuracy 94.1%
DE (Precision)	0.942	0.962
DE (Recall)	0.943	0.943
FA (Precision)	0.913	0.921
FA(Recall)	0.891	0.890
OP(Precision)	1.0	1.0
OP(Recall)	1.0	1.0
PR(Precision)	0.911	0.925
PR(Recall)	0.986	0.962
PR(Precision)	0.912	0.911
RP(Recall)	0.912	0.921

Table 4. Precision and recall measure for every class of questions with a change in question order.

We did 4 runs and in every run, we have selected the first question to train randomly and made sure that the same question does not get selected twice. We did the same kind of training by picking the most dissimilar questions to train the system and did 4 runs for that case as well.

The average of the runs is listed in table 4. We can observe from the average run that, no significant change in accuracy, precision and recall are noticed with the change occurring in the question order although the FSMs built from different ordering of the questions had different states or transitions.

4 Discussion and future works

In this current work we have tried to take a practical yet simpler approach towards the question classification problem. The approach came into existence when we realized that most of the time, we don't need to go through all the words and their semantic meanings in detail to map the questions to different classes. We thought it may be useful to give the machine this kind syntactic knowledge and a little semantic understanding to some extent to make it capable of classifying questions to its various classes. Instead of deriving handcrafted rules by watching each of the questions manually, we tried to establish a formalism through the Finite State Machines where the syntactic structure of the sentences could be learnt gradually with the example instances.

The state of the art techniques used so far have already used various mechanisms for addressing question classification problem. Support Vector Machine (SVM) and Conditional Random field used for classifying questions in 6 major classes have achieved an accuracy rate of 93.4% (Zhiheng Huang et al., 2008) whereas, the use of SVM for coarse grain questions have achieved an accuracy rate as high as 97%. Maximum Entropy Model could achieve an accuracy rate around 93.6% and the combined approach of Decision tree and SVM demonstrated a 90% accuracy rate.

The result that we achieved in this work shows that, the approach can be handy and may cope with various types of syntactic structure used for creating question sentences.

Because of not using deep semantic meaning analysis, our system failed to classify some of the questions to their corresponding classes. Lack of a proper recognizable structure was responsible for the failure in those cases. The system also made a few wrong classifications when some very similar structures belonging to two different classes of questions came into existence and this can be observed from the result that we achieved from the recall parameter measurement of the each of the classes. The voting function we used rescued us to some extent to handle such situations.

The result that we achieved encourages us to carry on with this approach further to improve it and use it in the other problem domain such as identifying question focus or may be in classifying questions to their finer classes.

References

A. Carlson, C. Cumby, J. Rosen, and D. Roth. 1999. *The snow learning architecture*, Technical Report UIUCDCS-R99-2101, University of Illinois at Urbana-Champaign.

Christiane Fellbaum. 1998. *WordNet: An Electronic Lexical Database. Cambridge*, MA: MIT Press.

Dell Zhang and Wee Sun Lee. 2003. *Question Classification using Support Vector Machines*, In Proceedings of the 26th annual international ACM SIGIR conference on Research and development in information retrieval.

Fan Bu, Xingwei Zhu, Yu Hao and Xiaoyan Zhu. 2010. *Function-based question classification*, In Proceedings of the Conference on Empirical Methods in Natural Language Processing, MIT, Massachusetts, USA, pages 1119–1128.

George A. Miller. 1995. *WordNet: A Lexical Database for English,* Communications of the ACM Vol. 38, No. 11: 39-41.

K. Hacioglu and W. Ward. 2003. *Question classification with support vector machines and error correcting codes*, In Proceedings of NAACL/HLT-2003, Edmonton, Alberta, Canada, pages 28–30.

Kohavi R., and F. Provost. 1998. *On Applied Research in Machine Learning,* In Editorial for the Special Issue on Applications of Machine Learning and the Knowledge Discovery Process, Columbia University, volume 30, New York.

Mitchell Tom M. 2002. 2nd edition, *Machine Learning*, McGraw-Hill, New York.

Moldovan, M. Pasca, S. Harabagiu, and M. Surdeanu. 2003. *Performance issues and error analysis in an open domain question answering system*, ACM Trans. Inf. Syst., 21(2):133–154.

Peters, M. Braschler, J. Gonzalo, and M. Kluck. 2002. *Advances in Cross-Language Information Retrieval*, Third Workshop of the Cross-Language Evaluation Forum (CLEF), Rome, Italy.

QA4MRE. 2013. *Question Answering for machine reading evaluation track of CLEF*, http://celct.fbk.eu/ResPubliQA/index.php?page=Pages/pastCampaigns.php, accessed on May 29, 2013.

Thamar Solorio, Manuel Perez, Manuel Montes-y-G´omez, Luis Villasenor-Pineda and Aurelio L´opez. 2004. *A Language Independent Method for Question Classification*, Proceedings of the 20th international conference on Computational Linguistics, Article No. 1374.

Voorhees. 2001. *Overview of the TREC 2001 question answering track*, In Proceedings of the 10th Text Retrieval Conference (TREC01), NIST, Gaithersburg, pages 157–165.

X. Li and D. Roth. 2002. *Learning question classifiers*. In Proceedings of the 19th International Conference on Computational Linguistics (COLING'02).

Zhang and W. Sun Lee. 2003. *Question classification using support vector machines*, In Proceedings of the 26th Annual International ACM SIGIR Conference on Research and Development in Information Retrieval, pages 26–32, Toronto, Canada. ACM Press.

Zhiheng Huang, Marcus Thint and Zengchang Qin. 2008. Question *Classification using Head Words and their Hypernyms*, In Proceedings of Empirical Methods in Natural Language Processing, pages 927–936, Honolulu.

Use of Combined Topic Models in Unsupervised Domain Adaptation for Word Sense Disambiguation

Shinya Kunii
Ibaraki University
4-12-1 Nakanarusawa, Hitachi,
Ibaraki 316–8511, Japan
13nm707sl@hcs.ibaraki.ac.jp

Hiroyuki Shinnou
Ibaraki University
4-12-1 Nakanarusawa, Hitachi,
Ibaraki 316–8511, Japan
shinnou@mx.ibaraki.ac.jp

Abstract

Topic models can be used in an unsupervised domain adaptation for Word Sense Disambiguation (WSD). In the domain adaptation task, three types of topic models are available: (1) a topic model constructed from the source domain corpus: (2) a topic model constructed from the target domain corpus, and (3) a topic model constructed from both domains. Basically, three topic features made from each topic model are added to the normal feature used for WSD. By using the extended features, SVM learns and solves WSD. However, the topic features constructed from source domain have weights describing the similarity between the source corpus and the entire corpus because the topic features made from the source domain can reduce the accuracy of WSD. In six transitions of domain adaptation using three domains, we conducted experiments by varying the combination of topic features, and show the effectiveness of the proposed method.

1 Introduction

In this paper, we propose an unsupervised method of domain adaptation for Word Sense Disambiguation (WSD) using topic models.

An inductive learning method is used in many tasks of natural language processing. In inductive learning, training data is created from corpus A, and a classifier learns from the training data. A original task is solved by using the classifier. During this analysis, the data for the task is in corpus B that differs from the domain of corpus A. In cases, the classifier learned from corpus A (i.e., the source domain) cannot analyze the data of corpus B (i.e., the target domain). This problem is called the domain adaptation problem, which is also regarded as a component of transfer learning in the field of machine learning. The domain adaptation problem has been extensively researched in recent years.

The methods of domain adaptation can be divided into two groups from the viewpoint of whether labeled data is to be used in the target domain. When using labeled data, it is called supervised learning, while unsupervised learning does not use labeled data. There is substantial research on supervised learning techniques. Conversely, not much attention has been paid to unsupervised learning because of low precision; however, we adopt the unsupervised learning approach because it is does not require labeling.

Shinnou and Sasaki examined the unsupervised domain adaptation for WSD (Shinnou and Sasaki, 2013). In their study, the topic model is built from the target domain corpus, and topic features constructed from the topic model are added to training data in both source and target domains. As a result, the accuracy of the classifier made by training data in the source domain is improved; however, in their study, the topic model is made by only the target domain. As indicated by Shinnou, it is unclear how topic models can be used for WSD. Further, in the domain adaptation task for WSD, the following three types of topic models are available: (1) a topic model constructed from the source domain corpus; (2) a topic model constructed from the target domain corpus, and (3) a topic model constructed from both domains. It is also unclear whether there is an effective combination of these topic models. The aim of this paper is to illuminate the latter problem.

The use of topic models in this paper adopts a similar approach to Shinnou (Shinnou and Sasaki, 2013). Basically, three topic features made from each topic model are added to the normal features used for WSD, and a classifier learns using the extended features; however, the topic features constructed from the source domain have weights describing the similarity between the source corpus and the entire corpus because the topic features made from the source domain do not necessarily improve the accuracy of WSD, and sometimes actually reduce the accuracy. When it can be determined that the topic features made from the source domain are effective for WSD, the value of weight r is approximately 1. In contrast, when it can be determined that the topic features made from the source domain are not effective for WSD, the value of the weight r is approximately 0.

The weight r is set by following equation:

$$r = \frac{KL(T, S+T)}{KL(T, S+T) + KL(S, S+T)}$$

where S is the source domain corpus, T is the target domain corpus, and S+T is the combined domain corpus; further, KL(A,B) is the Kullback Leibler (KL) divergence of A on criterion B.

In our experiments, we chose three domains, PB (books), OC (Yahoo! Chie Bukuro), and PN (news) in the BCCWJ corpus, and selected 17 ambiguous words that had a comparatively high frequency of appearance in each domain.

Domain adaptation has the following six transitions: (1) from PB to OC, (2), from OC to PB, (3), from PB to PN, (4), from PN to PB, (5), from OC to PN, and (6) from PN to OC. In every domain adaptation, we conducted experiments by varying the combination of the topic features. Through our experiments, we show the effectiveness of our proposed method.

2 Use of Topic Model for WSD

In recent years, supervised learning approach has a great success for WSD, but this approach has a data sparseness problem. Generally, a thesaurus is used for the data sparseness problem. There are two types of the thesaurus that is constructed by hand and automatically from a corpus. The former has a high quality, but has the domain dependence problem.The latter is not so high quality, and has an advantage that can be constructed from each domain. In this paper, the latter is used in oder to deal with the domain adaption problem.

Topic model is a stochastic model that introduced K-dimensional latent topics z_i into generation of documents d.

$$p(d) = \sum_{i=1}^{K} p(z_i)p(d|z_i)$$

$p(w|z_i)$ for each word can be obtained by using Latent Dirichlet Allocation (LDA) (Blei et al., 2003)that is one of the topic models. Soft clustering can be done by using LDA and regarding the topic z_i as a cluster.

Suitable $p(w|z_i)$ in each domain is obtained by using each domain corpus and LDA. There are several studies (Li et al.,)(Boyd-Graber et al., 2007)(Boyd-Graber and Blei,) that use information of $p(w|z_i)$ for WSD, and a hard tagging approach (Cai et al., 2007) is used in this paper . The hard tagging approach is a method that give the word w the topic of the highest relevance $z_{\hat{i}}$.

$$\hat{i} = \arg\max_i p(w|z_i)$$

First, when the number of topic is fixed K, a K-dimensional vectort$t$ is prepared. Second, the topic of the highest relevance for each word $w_j (j = 1 \sim n)$ in an input example is evaluate, and the value of $\hat{i}$-dimension on the vector t is set 1. Then, this operation proceed from w_1 to w_n. The vector made by this process is called topic features. The topic features made are added to the normal feature used for WSD, and extended features are used in learning and discrimination.

The normal features in this paper are the word in front of and behind the target word, part-of-speech in front of and behind the target word, and three content words in front of and behind the target word.

3 Three Types of Topic Features

In domain adaptation, the following three types of topic models are available: (1) a topic model constructed from the source domain corpus; (2) a topic model constructed from the target domain corpus, and (3) a topic model constructed from the both domains corpus. Three types of topic features can be made from three topic models.

The topic features made from the source domain are denoted by tp(S). The topic features made from the target domain are denoted by tp(T). The topic features made from the both domain are denoted by tp(S+T). The normal features used for WSD are denoted by B.

The following cases using the topic features for WSD are considered:

1. B + tp(T)
2. B + tp(S+T)
3. B + tp(T) + tp(S+T)
4. B + tp(T) + tp(S)
5. B + tp(T) + tp(S+T) + tp(S)
6. B + tp(T) + tp(S+T) + r * tp(S)

(1) and (2) are simply uses of the topic features for reflecting the knowledge of the target domain. (3) , which has the weight of the knowledge of the target domain, is also a promising method. A problem occurs that how tp(S) is used.

Currently, the key to a solution is how the knowledge of the source domain is used in domain adaptation. When the knowledge of the source domain is used, it does not necessarily improve the accuracy of WSD, and sometimes actually reduce the accuracy. Because of this, there is no guarantee that (4) is better than (1), (2) and (3).

(5) that uses tp(S) is a promising method. This idea is similar to Daumé (Daumé III, Hal, 2007). In study of Daumé, vector x_s of training data in the source domain is mapped to augmented input space $(x_s, x_s, 0)$, and vector x_t of test data in the target domain is mapped to augmented input space $(0, x_t, x_t)$. Classification problems are solved by using the augmented vector. This is known as the very simply and the high effectiveness method. This method is thought that an effect shows up in domain adaptation because the weight is learned by overlapping the characteristics common to the source and the target domain. It can be considered that (5) is added the knowledge tp(S+T) common to the knowledge of the source domain tp(S) and the knowledge of the target domain tp(T).

The proposed method in this paper is (6), and is the amended (5). As mentioned above, the weight has in (6) because the knowledge of the source domain tp(S) can have a bad influence on accuracy of WSD.

4 The Weight in the Source Domain

In this paper, the topic features are used as follows:

B + tp(T) + tp(S+T) + r * tp(S)

A problem occurs a apposite setting of the weight r.

It is considered that the weight r is the degree of the general knowledge which the source domain has.

Generally, in domain adaptation, the key to the solution is how the knowledge of the source domain is used. This problem is closely related to the similarity of the source domain and the target domain.

4.1 Similarity Between Domains

In domain adaptation, it is necessary that the source domain is somewhat similar to the target domain. When the source domain is not similar to the target domain completely, it is clear that the source domain data is not useful in the target domain. It is difficult to define formally the degree of the similarity, and it is recognized one of the most important issues in domain adaptation since the dawn of domain adaptation.

Kamishima did not dare to give a concept of this similarity a universal definition, and did presuppose how the knowledge of the source domain is used in the target domain, and did point out that it is important how this assumption is modeled mathematically (Kamishima, 2010). From this point of view, the similarity between the source and the target domains is measured, and it is normal to use the degree of this similarity for learning.

Asch measured the similarity among each the domain in part-of-speech tagging task, and showed that how the accuracy is reduced in domain adaptation by using the similarity (Van Asch and Daelemans, 2010). Harimoto examined factors of performance decrement by varying the target domain in parsing (Harimoto et al., 2010). Plank measured the similarity among each the domain in parsing, and chose the most suitable source domain in oder to analyze the target domain (Plank and van Noord, 2011). Ponomareva (Ponomareva and Thelwall, 2012) and Remus (Remus, 2012) used the similarity among the domains for parameter of learning in sentiment classification. Those studies measured the similarity for every task. It is thought that the similarity among the domains depend on the target words in WSD. Komiya changed the learning methods for each target word by using the property[1] including the distance between domains (Komiya and Okumura, 2012) (Komiya and Okumura, 2011).

[1] All those property can be called the similarity among the domains

4.2 Setting of the weight r

Measuring between the source and the target domains is mean that separating the common knowledge of the both domains and the specific knowledge because the similarity is intrinsically measured by comparing the common and the specific knowledge.

The weight r is considered to be the degree of the general knowledge that the source domain has. Because of this, it is important that how the general knowledge is set for calculating the weight r. The general knowledge is expressed by the combined domain corpus, that is contracted the the source and the target domain corpus. By combining two corpus, weights of the common part in two corpus is increased, and it is thought that the combined domain corpus approximates to the common part. By using KL divergence, $KL(S, S{+}T)$ is the distance between Corpus S and the general knowledge, and $KL(T, S+T)$ is the distance between Corpus T and the general knowledge. The following relationship is assumed:

$$r - 1 : r = KL(S, S+T) : KL(T, S+T)$$

By this assumption, r is calculated by the following equation:

$$r = \frac{KL(T, S+T)}{KL(T, S+T) + KL(S, S+T)}$$

Here, how to measure $KL(S, S{+}T)$ is describe in the following. Frequency of the nouns w in the corpus $S+T$ and in the corpus S is checked. The definition of $KL(S, S+T)$ is the following equation:

$$KL(S, S+T) = \sum_{w} p_s(w) \log \frac{p_s(w)}{p_{s+t}(w)}$$

where $p_{s+t}(w)$ is an occurrence probability in the corpus $S+T$, and is the following equation:

$$p_{s+t}(w) = \frac{f_{s+t}(w)}{N_{s+t}}$$

where $N_{s+t} = \sum_w f_{s+t}(w)$. $p_s(w)$ is an occurrence probability of the words w in the corpus S, and is defined by the following equation:

$$p_s(w) = \frac{f_s(w) + 1}{N_s + V}$$

where $N_s = \sum_w f_s(w)$, and V is the number of types of nouns in the corpus $S+T$.

5 Experiments

In our experiments, we chose three domains, PB (books), OC (Yahoo! Chie Bukuro), and PN (news) in the BCCWJ corpus (Maekawa, 2007), and selected 17 ambiguous words that had a comparatively high frequency of appearance in each domain. Table 1[2] shows words and the number of word sense on dictionary in our experiments. PB and OC corpus are gotten from BCCWJ corpus, and PN is gotten from Mainichi newspaper in 1995.

Table 1: Target words

word	PB freq. of word	PB # of senses	OC freq. of word	OC # of senses	PN freq. of word	PN # of senses
言う (iu)	1114	2	666	2	363	2
入れる (ireru)	56	3	73	2	32	2
書く (kaku)	62	2	99	2	27	2
聞く (kiku)	123	2	124	2	52	2
来る (kuru)	104	2	189	2	19	1
子供 (kodomo)	93	2	77	2	29	2
時間 (jikan)	74	2	53	2	59	2
自分 (jibun)	308	2	128	2	71	2
出る (deru)	152	3	131	3	89	3
取る (toru)	81	7	61	7	43	7
場合 (bai)	137	2	126	2	73	2
入る (hairu)	118	4	68	4	65	3
前 (mae)	160	2	105	3	106	4
見る (miru)	273	6	262	5	87	3
持つ (motu)	153	3	62	4	59	3
やる (yaru)	156	4	117	3	27	2
ゆく (yuku)	133	2	219	2	27	2
Average	193.9	2.94	150.6	2.88	72.2	2.59

We conduct six transitions since there are three domains. We conducted experiments by varying the combination of the topic features (as mentioned section 3) for above target words on each method, and obtained the averaged accuracy rate for the words.

Topic model learned by using LDA [3], and the number of topics was fixed 100. Table 2 shows the result of our experiments.

The accuracy rate of method that does not use topic model is lower than the other, and showed the effectiveness of topic model for WSD. The proposed method (7) is the highest accuracy rate, and showed the effectiveness.

[2]word sense is underlain the Iwanami Kokugo Jiten in the Japanese dictionary and middle level sense is targeted in our experiments. 「入る (hairu)」 is defined three word sense in the dictionary, but is defined four word sense in PB and PB because a novel sense of the word appears in BCCWJ corpus.

[3]http://chasen.org/˜daiti-m/dist/lda/

Table 2: Experimental result (averaged accuracy rate %)

	OC→PB	OC→PN	PB→OC	PB→PN	PN→OC	PN→PB	Average
(1) B	74.18	70.18	70.38	76.94	69.25	74.88	72.64
(2) B + tp(T)	74.58	68.40	70.89	77.78	70.13	75.80	72.93
(3) B + tp(S+T)	73.48	70.46	72.70	78.50	70.25	76.24	73.61
(4) B + tp(T) + tp(S+T)	73.61	69.88	72.45	78.90	70.36	76.86	73.68
(5) B + tp(T) + tp(S)	73.61	68.79	72.09	78.91	70.17	76.48	73.34
(6) B + tp(T) + tp(S+T) + tp(S)	73.92	68.70	72.18	79.41	70.53	76.71	73.58
(7) B + tp(T) + tp(S+T) + r *tp(S) (proposed method)	73.63	69.89	72.14	79.08	70.58	77.17	73.75
Weight r	0.0174	0.01139	0.9825	0.35655	0.98861	0.6434	

6 Discussions

6.1 Use of the Topic Model

In this paper, the topic features are made from topic models, and added to the normal features. Several uses of the topic model for WSD have been suggested.

Use of the topic model for WSD can be divided into direct and indirect uses.

The indirect use is to fortify the resource used for WSD. Cai used Bayesian Network for WSD, and improved the original Bayesian Network by innovating the topic features made from topic model to Bayesian Network (Cai et al., 2007). Boyd-Graber introduced the word sense of WordNet as the additional latent variable into LDA, and used topic model to search synset from WordNet (Boyd-Graber et al., 2007). Li proposed a method of constructing a probability model for WSD depending on three circumstances, which Prior probability distribution of word sense was obtained from the corpus or not and the resource of paraphrase in corpus was lacked (Li et al.,).

The direct use is directly using the topic features made from topic model for WSD. The proposed method belongs to this type. Boyd-Graber estimated marginal probability distribution of the word using LDA, and estimated word sense from the probability distribution (Boyd-Graber and Blei,). However, due to unsupervised learning, the normal features were not used for WSD, and it was not study that improved a classifier made from supervised learning by using topic model. Cai's paper described above, a method that the topic features are added to the normal features was implemented as a comparison method with the proposed method (Cai et al., 2007). Cai conducted two experiments, which hard tag was a method that give the word w the topic of the highest relevance, and soft tag was a method that use all topic of relevance. He pointed out that the soft tag is better.

From the viewpoint of easiness of implement, the direct use is better; however, in this case, the corpus domain which builds topic model, the size of the corpus and the number of topic have a great influence for the accuracy, and it is necessary to estimate the value of those. Especially, the corpus used in our experiments was 26.8MB in PB, was 0.4MB in OC and was 52.4MB in PN. The size of OC was smaller than the other. Therefore, the similarity between the OC and other was so small. When the source domain was OC, the weight r was also small.

6.2 Comparison with Existing Thesaurus

In this paper, topic models were used as thesaurus. We compared the proposed method and a method that uses existing thesaurus. We used Bunrui-goi-hyou[4] as Existing thesaurus. Table 3 shows the

[4]Japanese standard thesaurus

result.

Table 3: Comparison with existing thesaurus

	the propose method	B + thesaurus
OC→PB	73.63	72.85
OC→PN	69.89	70.64
PB→OC	72.14	70.68
PB→PN	79.08	78.13
PN→OC	70.58	69.72
PN→PB	77.17	75.87
Average	73.75	72.98

The accuracy rate of the method that use topic models is higher than using existing thesaurus.

This result suggest that it is better to use the topic models constructed from the corpus of domain that is targeted in the task than to use existing thesaurus when solving WSD. Moreover, considering this result, use of a combination of topic models and existing thesaurus can have a effectiveness. This point is for further study.

6.3 Domain Dependence of Thesaurus

When considering a domain adaptation problem, there is an idea that the common knowledge constructed from all domains can use for each domain in common. In fact, there are such tasks. For example, Mori improved the accuracy using the labeled data of each domain, and pointed outs that it is better to use the labeled data of all domains than using the labeled data of each domain(Mori,).

For the task in this paper, if the topic model is made from the combined corpus of all domains is made, it is thought that the topic model can be used in each domain. This idea is the method (3) , B + tp(S+T), which achieved good evaluation value in the experiments results. Moreover, it is clear that the knowledge of the target domain has a effectiveness in the target domain, and it can be envisioned that the method (4), B + tp(T) + tp(S+T) , has a effectiveness rather than the method (3). The experiments results shows also that.

A problem is the way of using tp(S). Basically, tp(S) need not to be used; however, when the source domain corpus S is similar to the combined corpus S+T, the topic feature tp(S) has benefit in domain adaptation. In particular, when $KL(S, S+T)$ is only bigger than $KL(T, S+T)$, the topic features tp(S) have benefit in domain adaptation.

6.4 Domain Dependence of Thesaurus of Each Target Word

The weight r of tp(S) on the proposed method in this paper was set for each domain. There is an idea that the optimum method of domain adaptation for each target word is different. We examined that whether optimal use of the topic models is different in each target word.

Table 4 shows the method of the highest accuracy rate in domain adaptation for each word. In addition, the number of table 4 corresponds to the number of methods in table2 Seen Table4, several words have the effective methods regardless of the combination of the domains. For example, method (4) is better in the words 「ゆく (yuku) 」 and 「自分 (jibun) 」,and the method (5) is better in the word 「書く (kaku) 」. 「やる (yaru)」 and 「来る (kuru)」 do not depend substantially on the methods, and the other words do not depend on the certain method. Table4 also shows that the effective methods depends on the domains. In other words, it is thought that the effective use of the topic models in domain adaptation for WSD is determined from the target words and the domains.

7 Conclusions

In this paper, we proposed an unsupervised method of domain adaptation for word sense disambiguation using topic models. Concretely, each topic model is constructed from the source domain corpus, the target domain corpus and the both domain corpus.The topic features are made by each topic model. Therefore. three topic features are available. Three topic features made from each topic model are added to the normal features, and the extended feature are used in learning for WSD. However, regarding the topic features made from the source domain, this topic features have the weight because this topic features reduce the accuracy of WSD. This weight is obtained from the similarity between the two domains, and the similarity is measured by Kullback-Leibler divergence. In our experiments, we chose three domains, and selected 17 ambiguous words that had a comparatively high frequency of appearance in each domain. In every domain adaptation, we conducted experiments by varying the combination of topic features, and estimated the average accuracy rate of WSD. Eventually,the effectiveness of the proposed method is showed. In future, we will examine the more effective use of the topic models

Table 4: the best method of each word

word	OC→PB	OC→PN	PB→OC	PB→PN	PN→OC	PN→PB
言う (iu)	1	2	3	1	6 7	3 5
入れる (ireru)	2	5	4	6	3	7
書く (kaku)	5	3	1 ∼ 7	1 2 3 4 5 7	2	3 5 6 7
聞く (kiku)	6	4 7	3	2	2 4	3
来る (kuru)	3 4	1 2 4 5 6 7	1 ∼ 7	1 ∼ 7	1 ∼ 7	1 ∼ 7
子供 (kodomo)	5	1 2 3 5 6	4	4 7	4	3
時間 (jikan)	2 6	6	1 ∼ 7	6	2 4 5 6 7	3
自分 (jibun)	4	1	4	1 ∼ 7	1 ∼ 7	1 ∼ 7
出る (deru)	2	3 4 7	6	2 3 4	5	4
取る (toru)	1 2 4 5 6	4 7	3	6	5	2
場合 (bai)	1 3 4 6	1	2	1	3 6 7	3
入る (hairu)	4	1	5	6	3 5 6 7	7
前 (mae)	4	1 3	1	5 6	6 7	6
見る (miru)	1	1	1 3	1	3	2
持つ (motu)	1	2 6	3	3	2 3 4	1 ∼ 7
やる (yaru)	1 2 3 5	1 ∼ 7	1 ∼ 7	1 ∼ 7	1 ∼ 7	1 ∼ 7
ゆく (yuku)	4	1 ∼ 7	4 6 7	1 3 4 5 6 7	1 ∼ 7	2 4

in the WSD task.

References

D. M. Blei, A. Y. Ng, and M. I. Jordan. 2003. Latent dirichlet allocation. *Machine Learning Reseach*, 3:993–1022.

Jordan Boyd-Graber and David Blei. Putop: Turning Predominant Senses into a Topic Model for Word Sense Disambiguation. In *SemEval-2007*.

Jordan Boyd-Graber, David Blei, and Xiaojin Zhu. 2007. A Topic Model for Word Sense Disambiguation. In *EMNLP-CoNLL-2007*, pages 1024–1033.

Jun Fu Cai, Wee Sun Lee, and Yee Whye Teh. 2007. Improving Word Sense Disambiguation using Topic Features. In *EMNLP-CoNLL-2007*, pages 1015–1023.

Daumé III, Hal. 2007. Frustratingly Easy Domain Adaptation. In *ACL-2007*, pages 256–263.

Keiko Harimoto, Yusuke Miyao, and Junichi Tsujii. 2010. Kobunkaiseki no bunyatekiou ni okeru seido teika youin no bunseki oyobi bunyakan kyori no sokutei syuhou (in japanese). In *The 16th Annual Meeting on Journal of Natural Language Processing*, pages 27–30.

Toshihiro Kamishima. 2010. Transfer learning (in japanese). *The Japanese Society for Artificial Intelligence*, 25(4):572–580.

Kanako Komiya and Manabu Okumura. 2011. Automatic Determination of a Domain Adaptation Method for Word Sense Disambiguation using Decision Tree Learning. In *IJCNLP-2011*, pages 1107–1115.

Kanako Komiya and Manabu Okumura. 2012. Automatic Domain Adaptation for Word Sense Disambiguation Based on Comparison of Multiple Classifiers. In *PACLIC-2012*, pages 75–85.

Linlin Li, Benjamin Roth, and Caroline Sporleder. Topic Models for Word Sense Disambiguation and Token-based Idiom Detection. In *ACL-2010*, pages 1138–1147.

Kikuo Maekawa. 2007. Design of a Balanced Corpus of Contemporary Written Japanese. In *Symposium on Large-Scale Knowledge Resources (LKR2007)*, pages 55–58.

Shinsuke Mori. Domain adaptation in natural language processing (in japanese). *The Japanese Society for Artificial Intelligence*, 27(4):365–372.

Barbara Plank and Gertjan van Noord. 2011. Effective measures of domain similarity for parsing. In *ACL-2011*, pages 1566–1576.

Natalia Ponomareva and Mike Thelwall. 2012. Which resource is best for cross-domain sentiment analysis? In *CICLing-2012*.

Robert Remus. 2012. Domain adaptation using domain similarity- and domain complexity-based instance selection for cross-domain sentiment analysis. In *Proceedings of the 2012 IEEE 12th International Conference on Data Mining Workshops (ICDMW 2012) Workshop on Sentiment Elicitation from Natural Text for Information Retrieval and Extraction (SENTIRE)*, pages 717–723.

Hiroyuki Shinnou and Minoru Sasaki. 2013. Domain Adaptation for Word Sense Disambiguation using k-Nearest Neighbors Method and Topic Model (In Japanese). pages NL–211.

Vincent Van Asch and Walter Daelemans. 2010. Using domain similarity for performance estimation. In *Proceedings of the 2010 Workshop on Domain Adaptation for Natural Language Processing*, pages 31–36.

Vietnamese Text Accent Restoration With Statistical Machine Translation

Luan-Nghia Pham
Department of Information Technology
Haiphong University
Haiphong,Vietnam
nghialuan@gmail.com

Viet-Hong Tran
University of Economic
And Technical Industries
Hanoi,Vietnam
thviet@uneti.edu.vn

Vinh-Van Nguyen
University of Engineering and Technology
Vietnam National University
Hanoi,Vietnam
vinhnv@vnu.edu.vn

Abstract

Vietnamese accentless texts exist on parallel with official vietnamese documents and play an important role in instant message, mobile SMS and online searching. Understanding correctly these texts is not simple because of the lexical ambiguity caused by the diversity in adding diacritics to a given accentless sequence. There have been some methods for solving the vietnamese accentless texts problem known as accent prediction and they have obtained promising results. Those methods are usually based on distance matching, n-gram, dictionary of words and phrases and heuristic techniques. In this paper, we propose a new method solving the accent prediction. Our method combine the strength of previous methods (combining n-gram method and phrase dictionary in general). This method considers the accent predicting as statistical machine translation (SMT) problem with source language as accentless texts and target language as accent texts, respectively. We also improve quality of accent predicting by applying some techniques such as adding dictionary, changing order of language model and tuning. The achieved result and the ability to enhance proposed system are obviously promising.

1 Introduction

Accent predicting problem refers to the situation where accents are removed (e.g. by some email preprocessing systems), cannot be entered (e.g. by standard English keyboards), or not explicitly represented in the text (e.g. in Arabic). We resolve the languages using Roman characters in writing together with additional accent and diacritical marks. These languages include European languages such as Spanish and French and Asian languages such as Chinese Pinyin and Vietnamese.

Vietnamese accentless texts coexist with official Vietnamese texts and it is relatively common texts on the internet. Official Vietnamese language is a complex language with many accent (including acute, grave, hook, tilder, and dot-below) and Latinh alphabets. These are two inseparable components in Vietnamese. However, many Vietnamese choose to use accentless Vietnamese because it is easier and quickly to type. For example, a official Vietnamese sentence: *chúng tôi sẽ bay tới Hà Nội vào chủ nhật* ('We will fly to Hanoi on Sunday') will be written as an Vietnamese accentless sentence as *chung toi se bay toi Ha Noi vao chu nhat*. Decoding such a sentence could be quite hard for both human and machine because of lexical ambiguity. For instance, the accentless term "*toi*" can easily lead to confusion between the original Vietnamese "*tôi*" ('we') and the plausible alternative "*tới*" ('to').

Nowadays, the application of information technology to exchanging information is more and more popular. We daily receive many of emails, SMS but the majority of them are without accents which may cause troubles for interpreting the meaning. Therefore, automatic accent restoration of accentless Vietnamese texts have many of applications such as automatically inserting accent to emails, instant message, SMS are written without diacritics Vietnamese, or assistant for website administration in which accent Vietnamese is required. Therefore, it is essential to develop supporting tools which can automatically insert accent to Vietnamese texts.

Accent predicting problem is the particular problem of lexical disambiguation. The recent approach to lexical disambiguation is corpus-based such as n-gram, dictionary of phrases, ...

In this paper, we propose the method for automatic accent restoration using Phrase-based SMT. Vietnamese accentless sentence and Vietnamese accent sentence (office Vietnamese sentence) will be source and target sentence in Phrase based SMT, respectively. We also improve quality of accent predicting by applying some techniques such as adding dictionary, changing size of n-gram of language model. The experiment results with Vietnamese corpus showed that our approach achieves promising results.

The rest of this paper is organised as follows. Related works are mentioned in Section 2. The methods for accent restoration using SMT are proposed in Section 3. In Section 4, we describe the experiments and results for evaluating the proposed methods. Finally, Section 5 concludes the paper.

2 Related works

In the recent years, several different methods were proposed to automatically restore accent for Vietnamese texts.

The VietPad (Quan, 2002) used a dictionary file and this one is stored all of words in Vietnamese. The idea of VietPad is based on the use of dictionary file and each non-diacritic word is mapped 1-1 into diacritic word. However, the dictionary file also is stored many words which are rarely used so these words is incorrectly restored accent. Therefore, VietPad can only restore Vietnamese accent texts with accuracy about 60-85% and this accuracy is depended on content of text.

The AMPad (Tam, 2008) is an efficiency Vietnamese accent restoration tool and texts can be restored online. The idea of AMPad is based on the statistical frequency of diacritics words which correspond with non-diacritics word. The program used selection algorithm and the most appropriate word is chosen. AMPad can restore Vietnamese accent texts with accuracy about 80% or higher for political commentary and popular science domain. However, It also restore Vietnamese accent with accuracy about 50% for specialized documents or literature and poetry documents which have complex sentence structure and multiple meaning.

The VietEditor (Lan, 2005) is based on the idea of VietPad but it is improved. This program used a dictionary file and this file is stored all of phrase which are often used in Vietnamese texts. This file is called phrase dictionary. After each non-diacritic word is mapped 1-1 into diacritic word, the program check the phrase dictionary to find the most appropriate word. VietEditor restore Vietnamese accent texts more flexibly and accurately than VietPad.

The viAccent (Truyen et al., 2008) allows you to restore Vietnamese accent texts online and with several different speed. Generally, the slower speed is the better result is. The idea of program used n-gram language model and it is reported at the conference PRICAI 2008 (The Pacific Rim International Conference on Artificial Intelligence).

The VnMark (Toan, 2008) used n-gram language model to create a dictionary file. It is VNMarkDic.txt file. This file shows occurrence probability of phrase in Vietnamese texts and it will build the case restoration for word or phrase. This combination will create sentences which are restored Vietnamese accents. When the weight of each sentence is identified, the best way will be selected accent restoration for Vietnamese text. However, Accuracy depends on the sentences of the dictionary file. Because the number of sentence is few so the result is still limited.

3 Our method

As mentioned in the section 2, the studies about accent restoration for Vietnamese text are based on experience. These studies used the dictionary file (such as VietPad) or n-gram language model with phrase (such as VnMark, AmPad, viAccent ...) but They are not yet generalized because this combination has some limitation as following:

- The number of phrases are few (each phrase is only 2 words, 3 words) and there are no priority when each phrase is chosen.
- The combination of language model and phrase dictionary is simple and It is mainly based on experience.

To overcome the above limitation, we present a general approach to restore accent for Vietnamese text. This method is viewed as machine translation from non-diacritical Vietnamese language (source language) into diacritical Vietnamese language (target language). This method has solved two above limitation by the use of phrase-table with the priority levels (the length of the phrase is arbitrary and the corresponding translation probability value) and It is combined language model with phrase-table by log-linear model (adding and turning of parameters for combination).

3.1 Overview of Phrase-table Statistical Machine Translation

In this section, we will present the basics of Phrase-based SMT toolkit(Koehn et al., 2003). The goal of the model is translating a text from source language to target language. As described by (1), we have sentences in source language (English) $e_1^I = e_1, \ldots e_j, \ldots, e_I$ which are translated into target language (Vietnamese) $v_1^J = v_1, \ldots, v_j, \ldots v_J$. Each sentence can be found in the target text then the we will choose sentence so that:

$$V_1^J = argmax_{v_1^I} \Pr(v_1^J / e_1^J) \qquad (1)$$

The figure below illustrates the process of phrase-based translation:

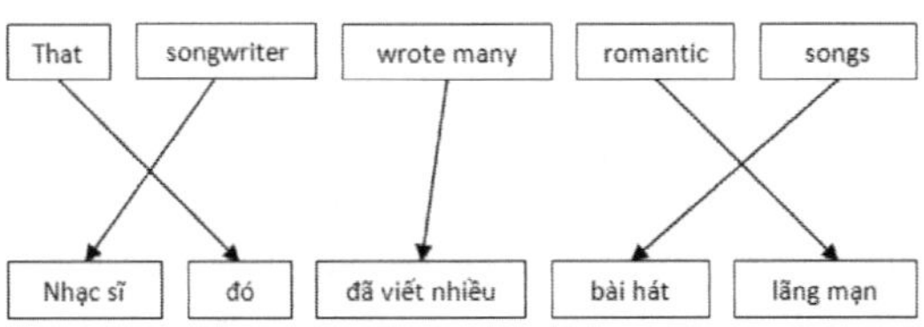

Figure 1: Phrase-based translation model

In phrase translation model, sequence of consecutive words (phrases) are translated into the target language. The length of source phrase can be different from target phrase. We divide source sentence into several phrases and each phrase is translated into a target language, then it reorder the phrases so that the target sentence to satisfy the formula (1) and then they are grafted together. Finally, we get a translation in the target language.

Figure 2 shows the phrase-based statistical translation model. There are many translation knowledge which can be used as language models, translation models, etc. The combination of component models (language model, translation model, word sense disambiguation, reordering model...) is based on log-linear model (Koehn et al., 2003).

3.2 Accent prediction based on Phrase Statistical Machine Translation.

Vietnamese texts with accent are collected from newspapers, books, the internet, etc., and they are reprocessed to remove the excess characters. Then

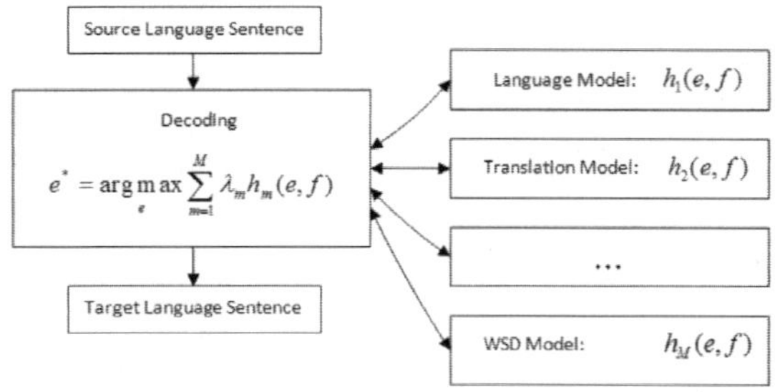

Figure 2: Diagram Phrase-based SMT translation based on log-linear model

vnTokenizer tool (Hong et al., 2008) is used to segment words in Vietnamese language. After that, the text file with accent and a corresponding accentless text fileis are created. Two text files are the same number of line and each line of accent text file corresponds with an accentless line in another text file. Figure 3 shows some sentences in corpus.

Accentless Vietnamese	Accent Vietnamese
cai ban_nay hinh ban_nguyet .	cái bàn_này hình bán_nguyệt .
toc_do truyen_thong se tang_cao .	tốc_độ truyền_thông sẽ tăng_cao .
toi_nay toi đi_choi .	tối_nay tôi đi_chơi .
nhung van_de lien_quan toi nguoi dong_tinh luyen_ai duoc ban_bac soi_noi trong buoi_hop nhom toi hom_qua	những vấn_đề liên_quan tới người đồng_tính luyến_ái được bàn_bạc sôi_nổi trong buổi_họp nhóm tối hôm_qua .

Figure 3: Some sentences in corpus

The accents removal is processed by building mapping table between the accents words and corresponding accentless Vietnamese words . For example:

a = {a, á, à, ạ, ả, ă, ắ, ặ, ẳ, â, ầ, ấ, ậ, ẩ}

Mapping table of characters include uppercase and lowercase letters in Vietnamese. After preprocessing we have a corpus file and we processed training data. Finish, we received phrase table and language model for machine learning. This phrase table is stored phrases with the different length. Language model with n-grams is covered nearly all Vietnamese sentences and this training process is automatically executed.

The general architecture of our method is described on Figure 4:

Phrase-based Statistical Translation model has three important components. They include translation model, language model and decoder. Translation results are calculated with parameters in the

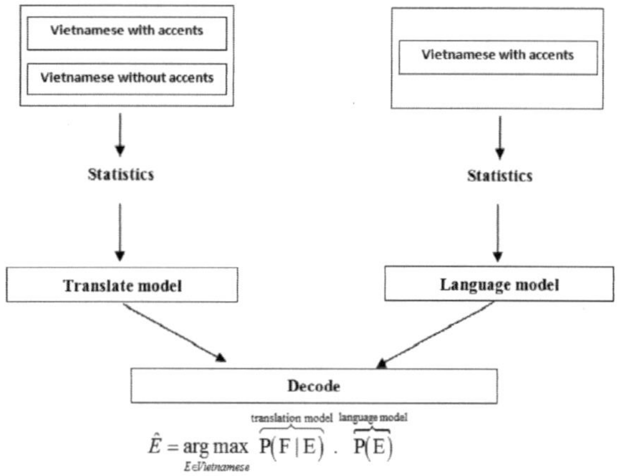

Figure 4: Accents restoration base on Phrase-based SMT

phrase table and language model. Example, accentless sentence restoration in Vietnamese:
neil Young da bieu dien nhieu the loai nhac rock va blue.
After the phrases is segmented. This sentence is:
neil_Young da bieu_dien nhieu the loai nhac rock va blue.
Results after the translation:
neil_Young đã biểu_diễn nhiều thể loại nhạc rock và blue .

First, the source sentence will be divided into phrases neil_Young, neil_Young da, neil_Young da bieu_dien, da bieu_dien, bieu_dien, bieu_dien nhieu,. . . .

After that, the system find the probability of each phrase in the phrase table and language model then the weight of sentence is computed . Example:
We found weight of above phrases in the phrase table and language model:
da bieu_dien ||| đã biểu_diễn ||| 1 1 1 0.857179 2.718 ||| 1 1
the loai ||| thể loại ||| 1 1 1 0.0362146 2.718 ||| 2 2

-3.436823 đá -0.3055001
-2.309609 đã -0.5276677
-4.109961 biểu_diễn -0.2860174
-4.168163 đã biểu_diễn
-2.227281 biểu_diễn nhiều
-1.628649 thể loại

Finally, the system is implemented by the decoder process. For each translation choice will have a hypothesis. Suppose first selection word is the neil_Young, this word is translated into neil_Young (unchanged) because it do not find corresponding word. For simplicity, we translate from left to right of sentence. Next, da word is translated, for example, it can be đá or đã. The probability of each hypothesis is calculated and updated for the each new hypothesis. Next, bieu_dien is translated, this phrase is found in the phrase table, language model and a phrase is chosen that is biểu_diễn phrase. Combining hypotheses can happen, da bieu_dien phrase is restored to đã biểu_diễn. Continue until all the words of sentence are translated.

4 Experiment Results

4.1 Corpus Statistics and Experiments

For evaluation, we used an accentless Vietnamese corpus with 206000 pairs, including 200000 pairs for training, 1000 pairs for tunning and 5000 pairs for development test set.

The corpus for experiments was collected from newspapers, books,. . . on the internet with topics such as social, sports, science (Nguyen et al., 2008). The Table 1 shows the summary statistical of our data sets. Several experiments are processed on the basis of Phrase-based Statistical Machine Translation model with MOSES open-source decoder (Koehn et al., 2007). For training data and turning parameters, we used standard settings in the Moses toolkit (GIZA++ alignment, grow-diagfinal-and, lexical reordering models, MERT turning). To build the language model, we used SRILM toolkit (Stolcke, 2002) with 3 and 4-gram. In this experiments, we evaluated the quality of the translation results by BLEU score (Papineni et al., 2002) and accuracy sentences.

We performed experiments on MT_VR system and MT_VR+Dict system:

- MT_VR is a baseline Vietnamese restoration system. This system uses phrase-based statistical machine translation with standard settings in the Moses toolkit.
- MT_VR+Dict is a baseline Vietnamese restoration combine with dictionary information.

4.2 Results

- We experimented on several different corpus and we evaluated translation quality.

Corpus Statistical		Vietnamese with accents	Vietnamese without accents
Training	Sentences	200000	
	Average Length	22.3	22.3
	Word	4474378	4474378
Development	Sentences	1000	
	Average Length	24,3	24,3
	Word	24343	24343
Test	Sentences	5000	
	Average Length	22,1	22,1
	Word	110729	110729

Table 1: The Summary statistical of data sets

- Translate model with the corpus include 50.000, 100.000, 150.000 and 200.000 sentence pairs. After successful training, we tested with 5.000 pairs of sentence.

To improve the quality of the system we need to build a corpus with better quality as well as greater coverage and we need to process accurately data. We have improved on some of the approach

4.2.1 Improved models using dictionary

The training from the raw corpus may have some limitations due to the size of the corpus. If the corpus is too small, the possibility of useful phrases are not learned when building phrase table. However, if corpus is too larger could in excess. In addition, we used the automatic segment of phrase tool so that it can be some errors in the analysis. We added Vietnamese dictionary of compound and syllable word into the phrase translation table and we assigned weight 1 into the each word, we solved this problem. Results as following:

System	BLEU score			
	Corpus 50.000	Corpus 100.000	Corpus 150.000	Corpus 200.000
MT_VR *(Baseline Vietnamese restoration)*	0.9744	0.9800	0.9830	0.9848
MT_VR+Dict *(Baseline Vietnamese restoration combine Dictionary)*	0.9748	0.9803	0.9832	0.9850

Table 2: The accuracy of experiment systems

Training	MT_VR		MT_VR+Dict	
	Complete correct sentences	Accuracy(%)	Complete correct sentences	Accuracy(%)
50.000	4120	82.40%	4533	90.66%
100.000	4291	85.82%	4558	91.16%
150.000	4300	86.00%	4585	91.70%
200.000	4352	87.04%	4628	92.00%

Table 3: The accuracy of experiment systems

4.2.2 Improved model using n-gram level changes

Changing n-gram level, the increased level of language model improved translation results. However, with level 4 or higher then the results has not been almost changed. Because in the Vietnamese language, the phrases including 3 or 4 words are more related than each other. The result with the weight assigned to 1 and level of language model 4: BLEU score=0.9850; accuracy when using MT_VR combine dictionary information: 92%.

Corpus	BLUE score		
	MT_VR	MT_VR+Dict3ngram	MT_VR+Dict4ngram
50.000	0.9744	0.9748	0.9743
100.000	0.9800	0.9803	0.9830
150.000	0.9830	0.9832	0.9826
200.000	0.9848	0.9850	0.9844

Table 4: Results with different n-grams levels

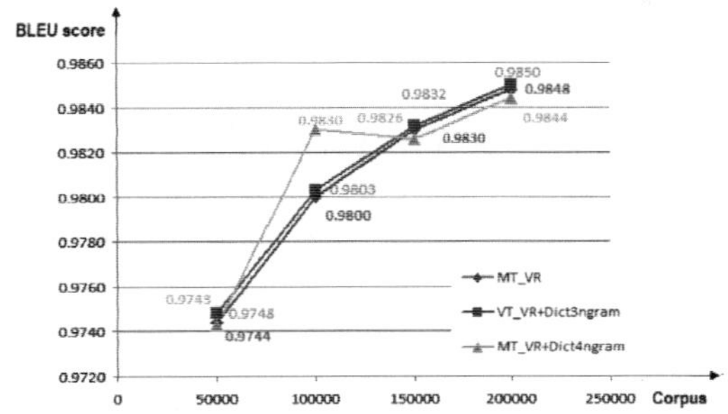

Figure 5: Compare BLUE score with experiment systems

Table 3 shows experimental results with different training corpus. Experimental results show that using MT_VR combine dictionary infomation with 3-gram have the best result. Table 4 and Figure 5 show that training with 200.000 pairs of sentence will have the best accuracy accents prediction.

Accentless Vietnamese	MT VR+Dict	viAccent	Reference Sentences
trong khu vuc choi game chinh , ban se su dung chuot de click vao bat ky nhan vat nao ban muon chon (co the chon mot luc mot hoac nhieu nhan vat den toi da la 9) .	trong khu vực chơi game chính , bạn sẽ sử dụng chuột để click vào bất kỳ nhân vật nào bạn muốn chọn (có thể chọn một lúc một hoặc nhiều nhân vật đến tối đa là 9) .	trong khu vực chơi game chính, bạn sẽ sử dụng chuột để click vào bất kỳ nhân vật nào bạn muốn chọn(có thể chọn một lúc một hoặc nhiều nhân vật đến tôi đã là 9).	trong khu vực chơi game chính , bạn sẽ sử dụng chuột để click vào bất kỳ nhân vật nào bạn muốn chọn (có thể chọn một lúc một hoặc nhiều nhân vật đến tối đa là 9) .
Tiep theo , ban se co ba cach khac nhau de dieu khien cac nhan vat nay .	tiếp theo , bạn sẽ có ba cách khác nhau để điều khiển các nhân vật này .	tiếp theo, bạn sẽ có ba cách khác nhau để điều khiến các nhân vật này.	tiếp theo , bạn sẽ có ba cách khác nhau để điều khiển các nhân vật này .
cach thu nhat : su dung cac nut de ra lenh cho nhan vat hanh dong bang cach nhap chuot trai vao chung .	cách thứ nhất : sử dụng các nút để ra lệnh cho nhân vật hành động bằng cách nhắp chuột trái vào chúng .	cách thứ nhất: sử dụng các nút đề ra lệnh cho nhân vật hành động bằng cách nhấp chuột trái vào chung.	cách thứ nhất : sử dụng các nút để ra lệnh cho nhân vật hành động bằng cách nhắp chuột trái vào chúng .
cach thu hai : ngoai ra , de tiet kiem thoi gian , co the nhan thang phim tat cua cac nut .	cách thứ hai : ngoài ra , để tiết kiệm thời gian , có thể nhấn thẳng phím tắt của các nút .	cách thứ hai: ngoài ra, để tiết kiệm thời gian, có thể nhận thẳng phim tật của các nút.	cách thứ hai : ngoài ra , để tiết kiệm thời gian , có thể nhấn thẳng phím tắt của các nút .
muon biet cac phim tat , ban hay de chuot tren nut tuong ung , lap tuc duoi day man hinh se xuat hien mot dong chu thong bao cho y nghia cua nut va phim tat .	muốn biết các phím tắt , bạn hãy để chuột trên nút tương ứng , lập tức dưới đáy màn hình sẽ xuất hiện một dòng chữ thông báo cho ý nghĩa của nút và phím tắt .	muốn biết các phim tật, bạn hãy để chuột trên nút tương ứng, lập tức dưới đây màn hình sẽ xuất hiện một dòng chữ thông báo cho ý nghĩa của nút và phim tất.	muốn biết các phím tắt , bạn hãy để chuột trên nút tương ứng , lập tức dưới đáy màn hình sẽ xuất hiện một dòng chữ thông báo cho ý nghĩa của nút và phím tắt .
cach thu ba : ngoai cach nhap chuot vao cac nut , chung ta co the su dung phim phai cua chuot nhu mot cach dieu khien tat .	cách thứ ba : ngoài cách nhấp chuột vào các nút , chúng ta có thể sử dụng phím phải của chuột như một cách điều khiển tắt .	cách thứ ba: ngoài cách nhấp chuột vào các nút, chúng ta có thể sử dụng phim phải của chuột như một cách điều khiển tật.	cách thứ ba : ngoài cách nhấp chuột vào các nút , chúng ta có thể sử dụng phím phải của chuột như một cách điều khiển tắt .
cai ban nay hinh ban nguyet.	cái bàn này hình bán nguyệt	cái bản này hình ban nguyệt	cái bàn này hình bán nguyệt
toi nay toi di choi.	tối nay tôi đi chơi	tới nay tôi đi chơi	tối nay tôi đi chơi
toc do truyen thong se tang cao	tốc độ truyền thông sẽ tăng cao	tốc độ truyền thống sẽ tăng cao	tốc độ truyền thông sẽ tăng cao

Table 5: Accent prediction of some sentences

4.2.3 Comparison with other methods

We also compared our method with viAccent system(Truyen et al., 2008) because viAccent is the newest and efficient method for Vietnamese accent prediction. We conducted the experiment with the same test corpus (5000 sentences) for viAccent. Bleu scores of both MT_VR+Dict and viAccent system were showed on Table 6.

System	BLEU score
MT_VR+Dic	0.9850
viAccent	0.8875

Table 6: Compared our method with viAccent system

5 Conclusion

The experimental results showed that our approach achieves significant improvements over viAccent system. Performance of accent prediction with our method achieves better accuracy than that and some examples in test corpus was showed on Table 5.

In this paper, we introduced the issues of accents prediction for accentless Vietnamese texts and proposed a novel method to resolve this problem. The our idea is based on Phrase-based Statistical Machine Translation to develop a Vietnamese text accent restoration system.

We combined the advantage of previous approach such as n-gram languages model and phrase dictionary. In general, experimental results showed that our approach achieves promised performance. The quality of accents prediction can be improved if we have a better corpus or assigned appropriate weight to dictionary.

6 Acknowledgments

This work is funded by the Vietnam National Foundation for Science and Technology Development (NAFOSTED) under grant number 102.01-2011.08

References

Phuong-Le Hong, Huyen-Nguyen Thi Minh, Azim Roussanaly, and Vinh-Ho Tuong. 2008. *A Hybrid Approach to Word Segmentation of Vietnamese Texts*. In Proceedings of the 2nd International Conference on Language and Automata Theory and Applications, Springer, LNCS 5196.

Philipp Koehn, Franz Josef Och, and Daniel Marcu. 2003. Statistical phrase-based translation. In Proceedings of HLT-NAACL 2003, pages 127–133. Edmonton, Canada.

Philipp Koehn, Hieu Hoang, Alexandra Birch, Chris Callison-Burch, Marcello Federico, Nicola Bertoldi, Brooke Cowan, Wade Shen, Christine Moran, Richard Zens, Chris Dyer, Ondrej Bojar, Alexandra Constantin, and Evan Herbst. 2007. Moses: Open source toolkit for statistical machine translation. Proceedings of ACL, Demonstration Session.

Phan Quoc Lan. 2005. *Approach to add accents for Vietnamese text without accent.* Informatics Bachelor's thesis, VietNam National University of Ho Chi Minh City.

Thai Phuong Nguyen, Akira Shimazu, Tu Bao Ho, Minh Le Nguyen, and Vinh Van Nguyen. 2008. *A tree-to-string phrase-based model for statistical machine translation.* In Proceedings of the Twelfth Conference on Computational Natural Language Learning (CoNLL 2008), pages 143–150, Manchester, England, August. Coling 2008 Organizing Committee.

Papineni, Kishore, Salim Roukos, Todd Ward, and Wei-Jing Zhu. 2002. *BLEU: A Method for Automatic Evaluation of Machine Translation.* ACL.

Nguyen Quan. 2002. *VietPad.* http://vietpad .sourceforge.net.

A. Stolcke. 2002. *"Srilm - an extensible language modeling toolkit," in Proceedings of International Conference on Spoken Lan-guage Processing.*

Tran Triet Tam. 2008. *AMPad.* http://www.echip .com.vn/echiproot/weblh/qcbg/duynghi/automark.

Nguyen Van Toan. 2008. *VnMark.*

Tran The Truyen, Dinh Q. Phung, and Svetha Venkatesh. 2008. *Constrained Sequence Classification for Lexical Disambiguation.* In Proceedings of PRICAI 2008, pages 430–441.

A Compact FP-tree for Fast Frequent Pattern Retrieval

Tri Thanh Nguyen
Vietnam National University, Hanoi (VNUH)
University of Engineering and Technology (UET)
ntthanh@vnu.edu.vn

Abstract

Frequent patterns are useful in many data mining problems including query suggestion. Frequent patterns can be mined through frequent pattern tree (FP-tree) data structure which is used to store the compact (or compressed) representation of a transaction database (Han, et al, 2000). In this paper, we propose an algorithm to *o press* frequent pattern set into a smaller one, and store the set in a modified version of FP-tree (called compact FP-tree) as an inverted indexing of patterns for later quick retrieval (for query suggestion). With the compact FP-tree, we can also restore the original frequent pattern set. Our experiment results show that our compact FP-tree has a very good compression ratio, especially on sparse dataset which is the nature of query log.

1 Introduction

Frequent pattern mining is an important task because its results can be used in a wide range of mining tasks, such as association rule, correlation, causality, sequential pattern, etc. as reviewed by Han (2000). In some mining tasks (e.g. association rule, correlation, or causality), frequent patterns are used as intermediate data for computing final results, so there is no need to access these patterns again. However, in some other tasks, such as *er s estion* (or *er re o en ation*) (Li, 2008), when a user enter a keyword, the search engine will recommend the potential phrases (or patterns) the user may want to use, in order to: (a) save time for users, (b) make the convenience of use, and even (c) guide the user in case he/she is not sure about what to search for. In such tasks, we need to frequently search for frequent patterns containing a certain keyword (or phrase), hence, we want to have a method that supports quick retrieval of patterns. In information retrieval, one of the contemporary methods for fast retrieval of documents containing a certain word (or phrase) is *in erte in e in* (Manning, et al, 2008), which manages a mapping from a keyword to a set of documents containing it. Thus, given a keyword, we will quickly have the list of related documents.

We found that FP-tree can be used as an inverted indexing which can provide us a list of patterns containing a certain item. Thus, we propose to modify FP-tree to store the frequent patterns for later fast retrieval. The difference between our FP-tree and the original one is:

- The original FP-tree stores the compact version of a transaction database, and an algorithm (called *ro t*) is used to find out the frequent patterns;
- Our FP-tree stores the frequent patterns for quick access, so each path in the tree is already a pattern.

Since the number of frequent patterns generated from a transaction database can be very large, we propose an algorithm to compress them into a much smaller (compact) set and store in FP-tree data structure. We also propose to modify related algorithms to make FP-tree compatible with frequent patterns instead of transaction data. We call the tree of compact pattern set *o pa t tree*. With the compact FP-tree, it is easily to restore the original frequent pattern set. The results of the experiments on benchmark transaction database show that our compact FP-tree has very good compression ratio.

Our paper is organized as follows: Section 2 introduces about FP-tree, and summarizes some typical literature; Section 3 introduces our compact FP-tree and the algorithms for compressing frequent patterns as well as restoring the original pattern set; Experiment and evaluation is discussed in Section 4 while conclusion and future work are provided in Section 5.

2 Background and related work

In this section, to make the paper self-containing, we will introduce frequent pattern mining problem, some detail of FP-tree, and some typical studies.

2.1 Frequent pattern mining problem

Let = {a_1, a_2, ..., a } be the **set of items** (which can be the list of goods in a supermarket), and a **transaction database** =⟨ $_1$, $_2$, ..., $_n$ ⟩, where each $_i$ ($1 \le i \le n$) is a **transaction** which contains a subset of items in . An example of a transaction $_i$ is the list of goods in a shopping basket. Define the **support count** (or the absolute support, i.e. the absolute occurrence frequency/count) of a pattern (is a subset of) is the number of transactions in that contains . Note that, in other studies, relative support is used (i.e. the percentage of a pattern in DB). It is easily to convert from absolute to relative support, and vice versa using the formula:

re ati e s pport=a so te s pport /| |

In this paper, the term *s pport o nt* is used to: (a) refer to absolute occurrence frequency, (b) distinguish from relative support, and (c) make it easier to follow the examples. Pattern is called a *re ent pattern* (or *re ent ite set* – the term used in some other literature) if ' support count is greater than or equal a predefined minimum support count (*ins p o nt*) ξ. The task of finding the *o p ete set o re ent patterns* in a DB with a *ins p o nt* ξ is called frequent pattern mining problem. This task is claimed to be time-consuming, hence, there are many algorithms having proposed to solve the task.

One of the algorithms, that has high attention of study is frequent pattern tree (or FP-tree for short) proposed by (Han, 2000). One of the advantages of FP-tree over previous algorithms is the reduction of the number of database scans. In FP-tree construction phrase, it needs only two scans over the database. The definition of FP-tree data structure and its related algorithms are given in next subsection.

2.2 FP-tree introduction

Han, et al, proposed the FP-tree data structure that can store the *o p ete set o re ent patterns* using only *t o s ans* over the . The biggest contribution to speed up the frequent pattern mining task is reduction of the number of scans over the DB down to only 2, since the speed of reading data in the secondary storage is slow. FP-tree is a tree structure as defined below:

1. It consists of one root labeled as "null", a set of **item prefix subtrees** as the children of the root, and a **frequent-item header table**.
2. Each node in the **item prefix subtree** consists of 4 fields: *ite na e*, (support) *o nt*, *parent in* , and *no e in* , where item-name registers which item this node represents, count registers the number of transactions represented by the portion of the path reaching this node, and node-link links to the next node in the FP-tree carrying the same item-name, or null if there is none, the parent-link links to the parent node[1].
3. Each entry in the **frequent-item header table** consists of three fields: (1) *ite na e*, (2) the (support) *o nt* , and *ea o no e in* which points to the first node in the FP-tree carrying the *ite na e*.

An example of a FP-tree is given in Figure 1, now we will study how to construct the FP-tree in this figure. With the *ins p o nt* ξ based on the listed in Table 1. This table shows a simple database of transactions of a supermarket, where the first column is the transaction identification, each row in the second column is the list of items that were bought by a customer. The FP-tree construction is described briefly as follows:

TID	Items Bought	(Ordered) Frequent Items
100	*a i p*	*a p*
200	*a o*	*a*
300	*o*	
400	*s p*	*p*
500	*a e p n*	*a p*
600	*s*	

Table 1. Transactions in DB and their frequent items

FP-tree construction starts with the first scan over the to find the list of frequent items (i.e. frequent itemsets with the cardinality of 1 having the support no less than ξ). The result of the scan over the DB in Table 1 is the list of ⟨(: 5), (: 5), (*a*: 3), (: 3), (: 3), (*p*: 3)⟩,

[1] Though this field is not clearly mentioned in Han's paper, it is important in forming the tree, so we list it here for the sake of completeness.

[2] This field is not clearly mentioned in Han's paper neither, we list it here for later use.

where the number after the colon ":" is the support count of items, and the is sorted in support count descending order denoted as . is used to build the *re ent ite ea er ta e* (or header table for short), where each entry in the table consists of the *ite na e* and a pointer (called *ea o no e in s*) to the first (appeared) node having the same item-name in the FP-tree as depicted in Figure 1. The second scan will get the list of frequent items of each transaction, sort it according to , and insert it into the FP-tree. To make it easier to observe, this list of each transaction is showed in the third column of Table 1. The tree construction algorithm is listed in Algorithm 1.

Algorithm 1: FP-tree_construction

Input: A transaction database DB and a *minsupcount* ξ.

Output: The frequent pattern tree *F*

(1) 1. Scan the *DB* to get the list *L* of frequent items, and sort it in support descending order.
(2) Create a FP-tree *F* by:
(3) Create the header table, and set all the *head-of-node-links* to null.
(4) Create *the* root node *T* of the tree having the item-name of null.
(5) Set the *parent-link* and *node-link* of *T* to null.
(6) 2. Scan the *DB* again
(7) **For each** transaction *Tran* in *DB* **do**
(8) Get the list of frequent items.
(9) Sort it according to the order *L*.
(10) Let this list be [*p*|*P*], where *p* is the first item and *P* is the remaining items.
(11) Call *insert_tree*([*p*|*P*], *T*).

where the insert_tree(.) procedure is defined in Algorithm 2.

Algorithm 2: insert_tree

Input: the ordered list [*p*|*P*] of frequent items, and a node *T* of a FP-tree.

Output: the updated FP-tree.

(1) **if** *T* has a child node *N* such that the item name of *N* and *p* is the same **then**
(2) Increase the count of *N* by 1
(3) **else**
(4) Create a new node *N*.
(5) Set the *item_name* of *N* to *p.item_name*.
(6) Set the count of *N* to 1.
(7) Link the *parent-link* of *N* to *T*.
(8) Set the *node-link* of *N* to null.
(9) **if** the *head-of-node-links* of the item *h* in the header table having the same name as *p* is null **then**
(10) Set *head-of-node-links* of *h* to *p*;
(11) **else**
(12) Traverse through the *head-of-node-links* of *h* to the end of the list, and link the *node-link* of the end-node to *p*.
(13) **if** *P* is not empty **then**
(14) Let $P=[p_1|P_1]$
(15) Call *insert_tree*($[p_1|P_1]$, *N*).

The key idea why the algorithm needs to sort the items in a transaction in the order is: the more frequent an item is, the more common it is in transactions, hence the transactions will share the items as a prefix. And such transactions will be "compressed" in the prefix, and make the tree compact.

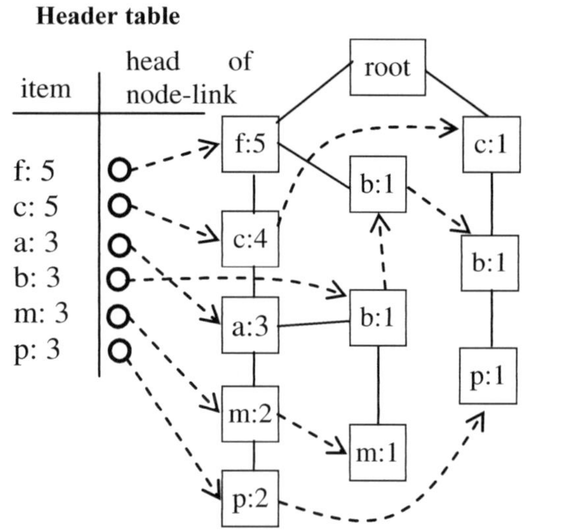

Figure 1. FPTree corresponding to the DB in Table 1

Han (2000) proved that FP-tree has both compactness (i.e. it has a compact representation) and completeness (i.e. it stores the complete information of the database in relevant to frequent pattern mining).

After having built the FP-tree, frequent patterns can be extracted from the item at the bottom of the header table (i.e. the item having the smallest count) (Han, 2000). For example, from the FP-tree in Fig. 1, we start with item *p* in the header table, and have one frequent pattern (*p*: 3) and two paths: ⟨(: 5), (: 5), (*a*: 3), (: 3), (: 2), (*p*: 2)⟩ and ⟨(: 1), (: 1), (*p*: 1)⟩. The items (called *p*'s prefix) that appear *to et er* with *p* in the two paths are ⟨(: 2), (: 2), (*a*: 2), (: 2), (: 2) ⟩ and ⟨(: 1), (: 1)⟩, correspondingly. The prefix set of *p* {⟨(: 2), (: 2), (*a*: 2), (: 2), (: 2)⟩, ⟨(: 1), (: 1)⟩} is called *p*'s conditional pattern base (i.e. the sub-pattern base under the condition of *p*'s existence). This set is used as a set of transactions to construct another FP-tree called p's conditional FP-tree with respect to minimum support count: ξ. The only frequent item in p's conditional pattern base is (: 3), hence we can produce one frequent pattern (p :3). Table 2 lists the conditional pattern bases, conditional FP-trees, and frequent patterns of other items of the FP-tree in Fig. 1.

Ite m	Conditional pattern base	Cond' FP-tree	Frequent pattern
p	{(2 2 a 2 2), (:1, b:1)}	{(:3)}|p	{(p:3), (p :3)}
	{(: 2, :2, a:2), (:1, :1, a:1, b:1)}	{(:3, :3, a:3)}|	{(:3), (a :3, (a :3), (a :3), (a:3), (:3), (:3), (:3)}
	{(:1, :1, a:1, :1), (:1, :1), (:1)}	{}	{(:3)}
a	{(:3, :3)}	{(:3, :3)}|a	{(a:3), (a :3), (a :3), (a :3)}
c	{(:4)}	{(:4)}|	{(:5), (:4)}
f	{}	{}	{ :5}

Table 2. Frequent pattern generation

When a single path in one item's conditional FP-tree having the length greater than 1 as in case of and a (see Table 2), a set of combinations of items (i.e. the non-empty subsets) in the path is generated as frequent patterns with the same support as the considered item's. For example, the item a has the conditional FP-tree consisting of only one path (:3), and the combinations of the items in this path are {(:3), (:3), (:3)}. These combinations are used as a prefix of a to produce frequent patterns: (a :3), (a :3), (a :3). The algorithm to extract frequent patterns from a FP-tree is given in Algorithm 3.

Algorithm 3: FP_growth

Input: FP-tree constructed based on Algorithm 1, using *DB* and a *minsupcount* ξ, and a pattern prefix α

Output: The complete set of frequent patterns.

Procedure FP-growth (*Tree*, α)

(1) **if** Tree contains a single path *P* **then**

(2) **for each** combination (denoted as β) of the nodes in the path P **do**

(3) Generate pattern $\beta \cup \alpha$ with support =minimum support of nodes in β;

(4) **else for each** a_i in the header of Tree **do**

(5) Generate pattern $\beta = a_i \cup \alpha$ with support = a_i.support;

(6) Construct β's conditional pattern base and then β's conditional FP-tree $Tree_\beta$ with respect to *minsupcount* ξ;

(7) **If** $Tree_\beta \neq \emptyset$ **then** call FP-growth ($Tree_\beta$, β)

To extract patterns from a FP-tree , we call FP-growth(, null).

FP-tree data structure has attracted many studies in both application and modification (improvement) aspects. Li, et al (2008) parallelized FP-tree and pattern generation to detect relation among tags and and webpages for query recommendation. Kumar and Rukmani, (2010) used both FP-tree and Apriori for web usage mining problem. Xu, et al (2011) mined associated factors about emotional disease based on FP-tree growing algorithm. Patro, et al, (2012) proposed to use Huffman coding to compress FP-tree. Yen, et al (2012) proposed Search Space Reduced (SSR) algorithm to speed up the pattern extraction from FP-tree. Bernecker, et al (2010) added probability to FP-tree to mine uncertain databases. Concretely, the authors proposed the first probabilistic FP-Growth (ProFP-Growth) and associated probabilistic FP-Tree (ProFP-Tree), which we use to mine all probabilistic frequent patterns in uncertain transaction databases without candidate generation. Shrivastava, et al (2010) mined multiple level association rules based on FP-tree and co-occurrence frequent item tree (CFI). Lin, et al (2010) added constraints on FP-tree for multi-constraint pattern discovery.

2.3 Inverted indexing

In document representation, a document can be represented as a vector of which each element is a feature (e.g. a binary value indicating whether a word appears in the document or not). Vector representation of document is suitable for computation, such as classification. However, it is not good for searching (i.e. given a keyword, find all the documents containing it). Inverted indexing is a data structure that stores a mapping from content (e.g. keywords) to documents. All the distinct keywords in the universal document set are used to form a dictionary. Each keyword in the dictionary is attached a list of document identifiers (doc_id) called *postin ist*. For example, given a set of 3 documents:

{ T[0]= "What is inverted indexing?"
T[1]= "Inverted indexing is a data structure"
T[2]= "Inverted indexing is used in search engine"}

The distinct keywords in the document set is {"a", "data", "engine", "in", "indexing", "inverted", "is", "search", "structure", "used", "what"}, and the inverted indexing of the document set is[3]:

"a"	=> {1}
"data"	=> {1}
"engine"	=> {2}
"in"	=> {2}
"indexing"	=> {0, 1, 2}
"inverted"	=> {0, 1, 2}
"is"	=> {0, 1, 2}
"search"	=> {2}
"structure"	=> {1}
"used"	=> {2}
"what"	=> {0}

With this data structure, given a keyword we will quickly have the list of documents containing it. When we want to find documents that contain some keywords all together, we simply find out the document list of each keyword and calculate the intersection. Inverted indexing is usually employed in search engines (Manning, et al, 2008).

3 Compact FP-tree

When the frequent pattern set generated from a transaction database is large, while we need to access the frequent patterns regularly, is it possible to: (a) compress the set into a smaller one, and (b) facilitate the access to frequent patterns? In this section, we will address the two questions through: (a) frequent pattern compression method, and (b) compact FP-tree.

3.1 Frequent pattern set compression

Given a set of frequent patterns =$\{ p_1{:}s_1, p_2{:}s_2, ..., p_n{:}s_n\}$, where p_i is a frequent pattern and s_i is its support. The frequent pattern set compression is defined as:

Find another frequent pattern set ' such that | | < | |, and it is possible to restore the from . Formally, we need to find to procedure compress(.) and uncompress(.) such that: if =compress( ), then | | < | | and uncompress(')=

Our compression idea is based on the fact that if there are two frequent patterns p_i s_i and p s (where s_i is the support of the pattern) such that s_i=s_j and $p_i \subset p$ then we can remove the pattern p_i

For example, from the set of frequent patterns generated from the item in Table 2 {(:3), (*a*:3), (*a* :3), (*a* :3), (*a* :3), (*a*:3), (:3), (:3), (:3)}, since the pattern is a subset of pattern with the same support of 3, we can remove from the set. Similarly, is a subset of , we remove Repeating this process exhaustively, the above set is reduced to the set {(*a* :3)}.

A heuristic method to reduce the search space to find out the frequent patterns of which one can be a subset of another is to sort the patterns according to the support, and then the frequent patterns. After sorting, patterns having the same support and prefix will be grouped into a segment. The search performed per segment will be faster, since it has a smaller search space.

To uncompress the pattern set, we reverse the compress process. For a pattern p_i s_i whose cardinality is greater than 1, we generate a set of all the combinations (i.e. the non-empty subsets) of its items: { p_{i1} p_{i2}, ..., p_{in}}, each combination p_i is assigned the support s_i to form a frequent pattern. Added the pattern p_i s_i to the generated set we produce the output set { p_{i1}: s_i p_{i2}: s_i, ..., p_{in}: s_i, p_i:s_i }.

The above output set sometimes is not original set due to the fact that some combination in the original set can have a bigger support count. For example, the uncompressed set of the pattern (*a* :3) is {(*a* :3), (*a* :3), (*a* :3), (*a*:3), (:3), (:3), (:3), (:3), (*a*:3), (:3), (:3)}. However, in the compressed set we have the frequent pattern (:5), so the pattern (:3) is redundant and need to remove. We call this phenomenon *re n ant pattern* for later reference.

Based on the above discussion, we first introduce the compress(.), uncompress(.) procedures, and prove the correctness later.

[3] We ignore additional techniques while building the dictionary as well as the inverted indexing for simplicity. Interested readers can refer to (Manning, et al, 2008)

*** Formatting Issue - Best Available Paper/Graphic ***

The compress(.) procedure is defined as Algorithm 4.

Algorithm 4: compress(.)

Input: a set of frequent patterns *FP*
Output: a compact set of frequent patterns
(1) **while** exist two patterns $fp_i{:}s_i$ and $fp_j{:}s_j$ in *FP* such that $s_i{=}s_j$ and fp_i is a subset of fp_j **do**
(2) $= \backslash\{ p_i : s_i\}$
(3) **return** *FP*

And the uncompress(.) procedure is defined as Algorithm 5.

Algorithm 5: uncompress(.)

Input: a set of compact frequent patterns *FP*
Output: the original set of frequent patterns
(1) *FP'*={}
(2) **while** exist a pattern $fp_i{:}s_i$ in *FP* such that s_i >1 **do**
(3) Let F_i be the set of all frequent patterns that are combinations of items in fp_i with the support s_i
(4) $= \backslash\{ p_i : s_i\}$
(5) $'= \ '\cup \ _i \cup\{ p_i : s_i\}$
(6) $'= \ '\cup$
(7) **while** exist two pattern $fp_i{:}s_i$ and $fp_j{:}s_j$ in *FP'* such that $s_i < s_j$ and $fp_i = fp_j$ **do** $'= \ '\backslash\{ p_i : s_i\}$
(8) **return** *FP'*

Lemma 3.1: Given a set of frequent patterns generated from a transaction database, after having compressed by the above compress(.) procedure, the uncompress(.) procedure will produce the original frequent pattern set.

Proof: According to *priori* property (Agrawal, et al 1993): if a pattern *p* is frequent, then all of its subsets are frequent, thus, if there is a pattern $fp_j{:}s_j$ is compressed by compress(.), then all the combinations of the items in fp_j { p_{i1}: s_i p_{i2}: s_i, ..., p_{in}: s_i,} are frequent. The only phenomenon is the *re n ant pattern* discussed earlier. However, this phenomenon can be solved by simply removing the pattern with lower support count (in line 7 of Algorithm 5). □

Applying the compress(.) procedure to the frequent pattern set generated from the FP-tree in Fig. 1, we have the compressed set {(:5), (:5), (:4), (*a* :3)}. We can see that the compressed set is much smaller than the original one. Our compression algorithm produces the *ose an a i a ite set* as (Grahne and Zhu, 2003). Grahne and Zhu proposed an algorithm based on FP-tree called FPClose to mine closed and maximal item set. The compressed set will be stored in the compact FP-tree, which *a ain* helps to reduce the storage as discussed in Section 3.2.

3.2 Compact FP-tree

From the definition of FP-tree data structure, it has a header table containing all the frequent items. Each item has a pointer that links all its occurrences in the patterns of the tree. This header table is similar to inverted indexing mechanism discussed in Section 2.3. The only difference is: each item in header table maintains a list of patterns (not a list of *pattern i* s as in inverted indexing). Therefore, FP-tree data structure has the same characteristics of inverted indexing, i.e. it facilitates the fast retrieval of patterns containing a certain item, and we propose to use FP-tree to store the compressed frequent pattern set. Since, we can not use the original FP-tree as well as its related algorithms, we define another version of FP-tree called *o pa t tree* (with the differences from the original of FP-tree definition are in bold):

1. It consists of one root labeled as "null", a set of item prefix subtrees as the children of the root, and a frequent-item header table.
2. Each node in the item prefix subtree consists of 4 fields: *ite na e*, ***support***[4], *parent in* , and *no e in* , where *ite na e* registers which item this node represents, ***support* is used to calculate the support of the pattern containing this item**, and node-link links to the next node in the compact FP-tree carrying the same item-name, or null if there is none, the parent-link links to the parent node.
3. Each entry in the frequent-item header table consists of three fields: (1) *ite na e*, (2) the ***support***, and *ea o no e in* which points to the first node in the compact FP-tree carrying the *ite na e*.

Lemma 3.2: The order of frequent items in FP-tree storing the compressed frequent pattern set is the same as that of the original FP-tree (i.e. the FP-tree corresponding to the uncompressed pattern set).

Proof: the items in header table of the FP-tree constructed from a transaction database are themselves frequent, hence, their order remains the same if we copy them to another FP-tree. □

[4] This can be relative or absolute support, in this paper we use absolute support for consistency

The algorithm to construct a compact FP-tree is defined as:

Algorithm 6: FP-tree_construction

Input: A compressed pattern set *S*.
Output: The compact FP-tree *F*
(1) Generate the list *L* of frequent items from *S*, and sort L in descending order of support.
(2) Create a FP-tree *F* by:
(3) Create the header table based on *L*, and set all the *head-of-node-links* to null.
(4) Create *the* root node *T* of the tree having the item-name of null.
(5) Set the *parent-link* and *node-link* of *T* to null.
(6) Remove all frequent items from *S*.
(7) **for each** pattern *fp*:s in *S* **do**
(8) Sort the items in *fp* according to the order *L*.
(9) Let this list be [*p* | *P*], where *p* is the first item and *P* is the remaining items.
(10) Call *insert_pattern*([*p* | *P*], *T*,*s*).

where insert_pattern(.) is defined as:

Algorithm 7: insert_pattern

Input: the ordered list [*p* | *P*] of frequent items, a node *T* of a compact FP-tree, and the support *s*.
Output: the updated compact FP-tree.
(1) **if** *T* has a child node *N* such that the item name of *N* and *p* is the same **then**
(2) **if** p.support>N. support **then** N. support =p. support
(3) **else**
(4) Create a new node *N*.
(5) Set the *item_name* of *N* to *p.item_name*.
(6) *N*. support =*p*. support
(7) Link the *parent-link* of *N* to *T*.
(8) Set the *node-link* of *N* to null.
(9) **if** the *head-of-node-links* of the item *h* in the header table having the same name as *p* is null **then**
(10) Set *head-of-node-links* of *h* to *p*;
(11) **else**
(12) Traverse through the *head-of-node-links* of *h* to the end of the list, and link the *node-link* of the end-node to *p*.
(13) **if** *P* is not empty **then**
(14) Let *P*=[p_1 | P_1]
(15) Call *insert_pattern*([p_1 | P_1], *N*, *s*)

The compressed pattern set of the FP-tree in Fig. 1 as discussed in Section 3.1 has the compact FP-tree as Fig. 2.

3.3 Searching in compact FP-tree

Given an item, we follow the node-link pointer from the header table to get all the patterns containing it. If we want to search for patterns containing more than one item (e.g. this case is frequently occurs in web search, where users can search for a phrase instead of a keyword), then we search for patterns containing the lowest support item, then filter out the patterns containing all the given items. For example, if we want to search for patterns containing {*a*, , }, we just search for patterns containing , then filter out the patterns containing both *a* and .

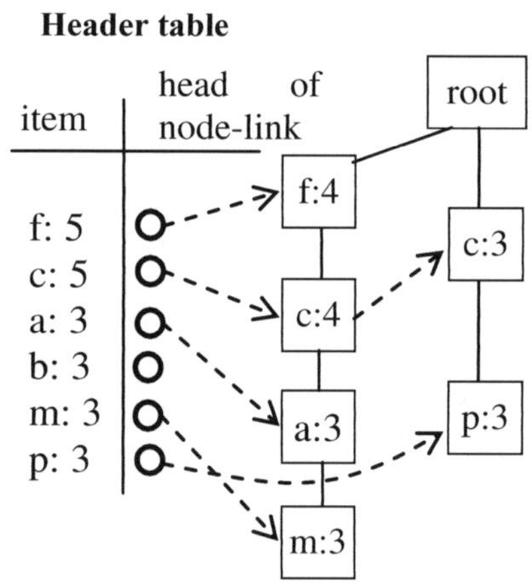

Figure 2: A compact FP-tree

However, there is a limitation of current compact FP-tree, i.e. if we search for patterns containing an item that is not a leaf node, then we can not extract the whole pattern (from the root to the leaf). For example, in the compact FP-tree in Fig. 2, if we search the tree based on item *a*, then we can only extract a pattern (*a* :3), is absent in the pattern. Fortunately, we can overcome this limitation by adding pointers from a parent node to its children nodes, so we can traverse in both directions from a leaf to the root and vice versa.

In some situations, we want to get the patterns with higher support first, i.e. in query suggestion, we want to suggest users with more frequent keywords first. To support this situation, we simply reorder the node-link of nodes so that the highest support pattern is pointed by the head-of-node-link (i.e. the pointer of the header table).

3.4 Original frequent pattern set recovery

In case we want to restore the original frequent pattern set (the uncompressed one) we can easily do through the compact FP-tree. For each path in the compact FP-tree, we generate the combinations of its items with the lowest support of the item in the combination. After generation, we also face *re n ant pattern* problem, which can be solved by a removal step. The recovery algorithm is described in Algorithm 8.

Algorithm Pattern_extraction

Input: a compact FP-tree *Tree*
Output: The complete set *S* of frequent patterns.
(1) *S*={all items in the header table}
(2) **for each** *path* in *Tree* **do**
(3) Generate the set *P* of all combinations with the length>1, each of which has the support of the lowest support item.
(4) $S = S \cup P$
(5) **while** exist two pattern $fp_i{:}s_i$ and $fp_j{:}s_j$ in *S* such that $s_i < s_j$ and $fp_i = fp_j$ **do** $= \ \backslash\{ \ p_i : s_i\}$

---

4 Experiments

We used the open source FP-growth package[5] developed by (Borgelt, 2005). The patterns having the same support are generated in next to each other as a group as listed in Table 2, where the number in the parenthesis is the (relative) support (in percent) of the pattern.

Frequent Pattern
m (60.0)
m a (60.0)
m a c (60.0)
m a c f (60.0)
m a f (60.0)
m c (60.0)
m c f (60.0)
m f (60.0)

Table 2. Frequent patterns generated from FP-growth

By exploiting this characteristic, we simply find the longest pattern in the group which will be the compressed pattern of the group. Hence, we wrote another algorithm as Algorithm 8 which has the complexity of ( ).

Algorithm 8: Pattern_compression

Input: a list *P* of frequent patterns
Output: The set *S* of compressed frequent patterns having the length>1, and a list *L* of frequent items for building header table
(1) *L*={} ;
(2) *S*={}
(3) iterate through the list *P*
(5) **if** the current pattern *p* has the length=1 **then**
(6) *L*=*L* + *p*
(7) **else** this is the starting of a group with the same support, so find the longest pattern *p* in this group
(9) $S = S \cup p$

We used two types of transaction databases that are published as benchmark datasets[6]: sparse (i.e. T10I4D100 and T20I6D100) and dense (i.e. mushroom and C20D10). For evaluation, we compare the size (in term of the total of nodes) of the compact FP-tree and its original FP-tree called *o pression ratio* (in %) as follows:

$$ratio = \frac{\sum no\ es\_in\_\ o\ \ pa\ t\_\quad -tree}{\sum no\ es\_in\_ori\ \ ina\ \_\quad -tree} * 100\%$$

The smaller the ratio is, the better compression is.

With sparse databases, we had to use very small relative minimum support thresholds ranging from 0.1% to 1%. The compression ratio of sparse databases is given in Fig. 3 where we can see that the compact FP-tree is drastically reduced. With the relative support of 0.1%, the size of compact FP-tree is reduced to 8% and 2% on T20I6D100 and T10I4D100, correspondingly. With the relative support of 1%, the compression ratio is extremely good: 0.05% on both transaction databases.

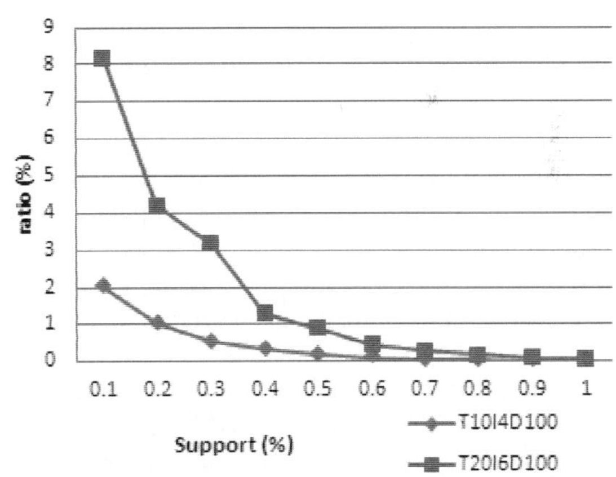

Figure 3: The compression ratio on sparse databases

With dense databases, we used big relative minimum support thresholds ranging from 10% to 40%. The results of the experiments are given in Fig. 4. Compact FP-tree does not have much

[5] http://www.borgelt.net/fpgrowth.html

[6] http://keia.i3s.unice.fr/?Jeux_de_Données___Benchmark_Datasets

power with dense databases, since the compression ratio is not good.

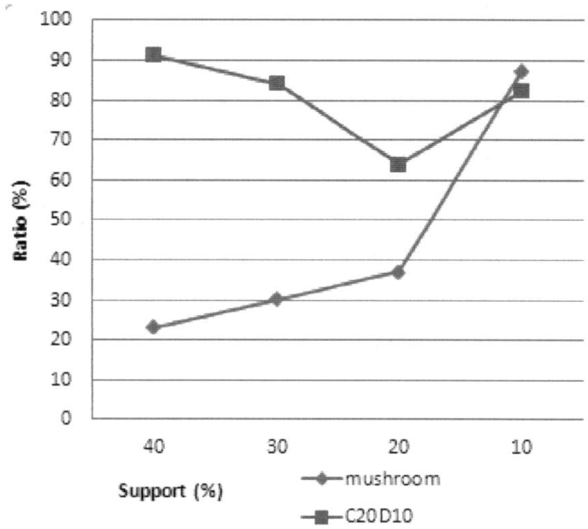

Figure 4: The compression ratio on dense databases

From experimental results, we can see that, on sparse databases, the compact FP-tree has very good compression ratio, whereas, it does not expose its power in dense databases. There are many domains, where the data is sparse, such as text document collections of which the number of dimension is so big that the data is very sparse. Another example of domain is query logs, where the queries are diverse, especially on multi-language search engines (e.g. Google). Thus, the application of compact FP-tree is very promising.

5 Conclusion and future direction

In this paper, we proposed to compress the frequent pattern set mined from a transaction database to a compact set. The compact set is useful in application where the longest pattern is usually used, such as query suggestion (i.e. we prefer to suggest the longest frequent pattern containing a certain word/phrase to users). The practical compression algorithm is very effective with the low complexity of ( ). In order to speed up the retrieval of frequent patterns, we proposed to modify the FP-tree into compact FP-tree which stores the compressed pattern set as an inverted indexing data structure.

Our experimental results on benchmark databases show that the proposed method is very useful in sparse databases.

In the future direction, we will study the method to construct the compact FP-tree directly form its FP-tree.

References

A. P. Xu, et al, 2011. *inin sso iate a tors a o t otiona isease ases on ree ro in orit* , International Journal of Engineering and Manufacturing, vol. 4, pp. 25-31.

B. S. Kumar and K. V. Rukmani, 2010. *p e entation o We sa e inin sin an ro t orit s* Int. J. of Advanced Networking and Applications, Vol 01, Issue: 06, pp 400-404.

C. Borgelt, 2005. *n p e entation o t e ro t orit* . Workshop Open Source Data Mining Software (OSDM'05, Chicago, IL), pp. 1-5, ACM Press.

C. D. Manning, et al, 2008. *ntro tion to n or ation etrie a* , Cambridge University Press.

G. Grahne and J. Zhu, 2003. *i ient sin re i trees in inin re ent te sets*, Proceedings of the ICDM 2003 Workshop on Frequent Itemset Mining Implementations, vol. 17, no. 10, pp. 1347-1362.

H. Li, et al, 2008. *ara e ro t or er e o en ation*, Proceedings of the 2008 ACM conference on Recommender systems, pp 107-114.

J. Han, et al, 2000. *inin re ent atterns it o t an i ate eneration*, Proc. Conf. on the Management of Data (SIGMOD'00, Dallas, TX.

M. Singh, et al, 2010. *ree pro e i ien n rease a a i it pp in ara e ro e te* , Binary Journal of Data Mining & Networking, Vol 1, No 1. pp 14-16.

R. Agrawal, et al, 1993. *inin asso iation r es et een sets o ite s in ar e ata ases*, Proceedings of the 1993 ACM SIGMOD international conference on Management of data pp. 207-216.

S. J. Yen, et al, 2009. *e t ies o inin re ent atterns ase on re ent attern ree*, Lecture Notes in Computer Science Volume 5476, pp. 232-241.

S. J. Yen, et al, 2012. *ear pa e e e orit or inin re ent atterns*, Journal Of Information Science And Engineering, Vol 28, pp 177-191.

S. N. Patro, et al, 2012. *onstr tion o ree sin an o in* , International Journal of Computer Science Issues, Vol 9, Issue 3, pp 446-469.

T. Bernecker, et al, 2010. *ro a i isti re ent attern ro t or te set inin in n ertain* Databases, Cornell University Technical Report.

***** Formatting Issue - Best Available Paper/Graphic *****

V. K. Shrivastava, et al, 2010. *tree an ase pproa or inin o tip e e e sso iation* Rules *in ar e ata ases*, International Journal of Computer Science and Information Security, Vol. 7 No. 2, pp. 273-279.

W. Y. Lin, et al, 2010. *ree n tree ase a orit or ti onstraint patterns is o er* , Int. J. of Business Intelligence and Data Mining, Vol. 5, No 3, pp. 231 – 246.

ML-Tuned Constraint Grammars

Eckhard Bick
Institute of Language and Communication
University of Southern Denmark, Odense
eckhard.bick@mail.dk

Abstract

In this paper we present a new method for machine learning-based optimization of linguist-written Constraint Grammars. The effect of rule ordering/sorting, grammar-sectioning and systematic rule changes is discussed and quantitatively evaluated. The F-score improvement was 0.41 percentage points for a mature (Danish) tagging grammar, and 1.36 percentage points for a half-size grammar, translating into a 7-15% error reduction relative to the performance of the untuned grammars.

1 Introduction

Constraint Grammar (CG) is a rule-based paradigm for Natural Language Parsing (NLP), first introduced by Karlsson et al. (1995). Part-of-speech tagging and syntactic parses are achieved by adding, removing, selecting or substituting form and function tags on tokens in running text. Rules express linguistic contextual constraints and are written by hand and applied sequentially and iteratively, ordered in batches of increasing heuristicity and incrementally reducing ambiguity from morphologically analyzed input by removing (or changing) readings from so-called readings cohorts (consisting of all possible readings for a given token), - optimally until only one (correct) reading remains for each token. The method draws robustness from the fact that it is reductionist rather than generative - even unforeseen or erroneous input can be parsed by letting the last reading survive even if there are rules that would have removed it in a different context. Typical CG rules consist of an operator (e.g. REMOVE, SELECT), a target and one or more contextual constraints that may be linked to each other:

(a) REMOVE VFIN (-1C ART OR DET) ;

(b) SELECT VFIN (-1 PERS/NOM) (NOT *1 VFIN)

Rule (a), for instance, removes a target finite verb reading (VFIN) if there is an unambiguous (C) article or determiner 1 position to the left (-), while rule (b) selects a finite verb reading, if there is a personal pronoun in the nominative immediately to the left, and no (NOT) other finite verb is found anywhere to the right (*1).

Mature Constraint Grammars can achieve very high accuracy, but contain thousands of rules and are expensive to build from scratch, traditionally requiring extensive lexica and years of expert labor. Since grammars are not data-driven in the statistical sense of the word, domain adaptation, for instance for speech (Bick 2011) or historical texts (Bick 2005), is traditionally achieved by extending an existing general grammar for the language in question, and by using specialized lexica or two-level text normalization. However, due to its innate complexity, the general underlying grammar *as a o e* has properties that do not easily lend themselves to manual modification. Changes and extensions will usually be made at the level of individual rules, not rule interactions or rule regrouping. Thus, with thousands of interacting rules, it is difficult for a human grammarian to exactly predict the effect of rule placement, i.e. if a rule is run earlier or later in the sequence. In particular, rules with so-called C-conditions (asking for unambiguous context), may profit from another, earlier rule acting on the context tokens involved in the C-condition. Feed-back from corpus runs will pinpoint rules that make errors, and even allow to trace the effect on other rules applied later on the same sentence, but such debugging is cumbersome and will not provide information on missed-out positive, rather than negative, rule interaction. The question is therefore, whether a hand-corrected gold corpus and machine-learning techniques could be used to improve performance by data-driven rule ordering or rule adaptation, applied to existing, manual grammars. The method would not only allow to optimize general-purpose grammars, but also to adapt a grammar in the face of domain variation without actually changing or adding any rules manually. Of course the technique will only work if a compatible gold-annotation corpus exists for the target domain, but even creating manually-revised training data from scratch for the task at hand, may be warranted if it then allows using an existing unmaintained or "black box" grammar. Other areas where ML rule tuning of existing grammars may be of use, is cross-language porting of grammars between closely related languages, and so-called bare-bones Constraint Grammars (Bick 2012), where grammars have to cope with heuristically analyzed input and correspondingly skewed ambiguity patterns. In such grammars, linguistic intuition may not adequately reflect input-specific disambiguation needs, and profit from data-driven tuning.

2 Prior research

To date, little work on CG rule tuning has been published. A notable exception is the μ-TBL system proposed in (Lager 1999), a transformation-based learner working with 4 different rule operators, and supporting not only traditional Brill-taggers but also Constraint Grammars. The system could be seeded with simple CG rule templates with conditions on numbered context positions, but for complexity reasons it did not support more advanced CG rules with unbounded, sentence-wide contexts, barrier conditions or linked contexts, all of which are common in hand-written Constraint Grammars. Therefore, while capable of building automatic grammars from rule templates and modeling them on a gold corpus, the system was not applicable to existing, linguist-designed CGs.

That automatic rule tuning can capture systematic differences between data sets, was shown by Rögnvaldsson (2002), who compared English and Icelandic μ-TBL grammars seeded with the same templates, finding that the system prioritized right context and longer-distance context templates more for English than Icelandic. For hand-written grammars, rather than template expression, a similar tuning effect can be expected by prioritizing/deprioritizing certain rule or context types by moving them to higher or lower rule sections, respectively, or by inactivating certain rules entirely.

Lindberg & Eineborg (1998) conducted a performance evaluation with a CG-learning Progol system on Swedish data from the Stockholm-Umeå corpus. With 7000 induced REMOVE rules, their system achieved a recall of 98%. An F-Score was not given, but since residual ambiguity was 1.13 readings per word (i.e. a precision of 98/113=86.7%), it can be estimated at 92%. Also, the lexicon was built from the corpus, so performance can be expected to be lower on lexically independent data.

Though all three of the above reports show that machine learning can be applied to CG-style grammars, none of them addresses the tuning of human-written, complete grammars rather than lists of rule templates[1]. In this paper, we will argue that the latter is possible, too, and that it can lead to better results than both automatic and human grammars seen in isolation.

3 Grammar Tuning Experiments

As target grammar for our experiments we chose the morphological disambiguation module of the Danish DanGram[2] system and the CG3 Constraint Grammar compiler[3]. For most languages, manually revised CG corpora are small and used only for internal development purposes, but because Constraint Grammar was used in the construction of the 400.000 word Danish Arboretum treebank (Bick 2003), part of the data (70.800 tokens) was still accessible in CG-input format and could be aligned to the finished treebank, making it possible to automatically mark the correct reading lines in the input cohorts. Of course the current DanGram system has evolved and is quite different from the one used 10 years ago to help with treebank construction, a circumstance

[1] One author, Padró (1996), using CG-reminiscent constraints made up of close PoS contexts, envisioned a combination of automatically learned and linguistically learned rules for his relaxation labelling algorithm, but did not report any actual work on human-built grammars.

[2] An description of the system, and an online interface can be found at: http://beta.visl.sdu.dk/visl/da/parsing/automatic/parse.php

[3] The CG3 compiler is developed by GrammarSoft ApS and supported by the University of Southern Denmark. It is open source and can be downloaded at http://beta.visl.sdu.dk/cg3.html

affecting both tokenization (name fusing and other multiple-word expressions), primary tags and secondary tags. Primary tags are tags intended to be disambiguated and evaluated, and differences in e.g. which kind of nouns are regarded as proper nouns, may therefore affect evaluation. But even secondary tags may have an adverse effect on performance. Secondary tags are lexicon-provided tags, e.g. valency and semantic tags not themselves intended for disambiguation, but used by the grammar to contextually assign primary tags. Most importantly, the gold corpus derived from the treebank does not contain semantic tags, while current DanGram rules rely on them for disambiguation. However, this is not relevant to the experiments we will be discussing in this paper - any accuracy figures are not intended to grade the performance of DanGram as such, but only to demonstrate possible performance improvements triggered by our grammar tuning. For this purpose, a certain amount of errors in the base system is desirable rather than problematic. In fact, for one of the experiments we intentionally degraded the base grammar by removing every second rule from it.

3.1 Training process and evaluation set-up

The available revised CG corpus was split randomly into 10 equal sections, reserving in turn each section as test data, and using the remaining 9 jointly as training data, a method known as 10-fold cross-validation.

For training, grammar changes (first of all, rule movements) were applied based on a performance rating of a run with the unchanged grammar (0-iteration) on the training data [4]. After a test run, the resulting, changed grammar-1 was then itself applied to the training data, and a further round of changes introduced based on the updated performance. At first, we repeated these steps until results from the test runs stabilized in a narrow F-score band. Though with certain parameter combinations this might take dozens of rounds, and though secondary, relative performance peaks were observed, we never actually found absolute maximum values beyond the 3rd iteration for either recall or precision. Therefore, most later runs were limited to 3 iterations in order to save processing time.

[4] This unchanged run also served as the baseline for our experiments (cp. dR, dP and dF in the tables).

3.2 Exploiting section structure

Constraint Grammar allows for section-grouping of rules, where the rules in each section will be iterated, gradually removing ambiguity from the input, until none of the rules in the section can find any further fully satisfied context matches. After that, the next batch of rules is run, and the first set repeated, and so on. For 6 sections, this means running them as 1, 1-2, 1-3, 1-4, 1-5, 1-6. CG grammarians use sectionizing to prioritize safe rules, and defer heuristic rules, so one obvious machine learning technique is to move rules to neighbouring sections according to how well they perform, our basic set-up being a so-called PDK-run (**P**romoting, **D**emoting, **K**illing):

- if a rule does not make errors or if its error percentage is lower than a pre-set threshold, promote the rule 1 section up[5]
- if a rule makes more wrong changes than correct changes, kill it altogether
- in all other cases, demote the rule 1 section down

The table below lists results (**R**ecall, **P**recision and **F**-score) for this basic method for all subsections of the corpus, with a rule error threshold of 0.25 (i.e. at most 1 error for every 4 times the rule was used). Apart from considerable cross-data variation in terms of recall improvement (dR), precision improvement (dP) and F-score improvement (dF), it can be seen that recall profits more from this setup than precision, with the best run for the former adding 0.8 percentage points and the worst run for the latter losing 0.09 percentage points.

	R	dR	P	dP	F	dF
part 1	98.11	0.22	94.6	-0.07	96.30	0.07
part 2	97.90	0.42	94.21	0.04	96.78	0.23
part 3	98.26	0.51	94.56	-0.06	96.37	0.25
part 4	97.80	0.36	93.08	-0.09	95.38	0.13
part 5	97.78	0.59	92.94	0.09	95.30	0.33
part 6	97.72	0.48	93.74	0.16	95.69	0.31
part 7	97.89	0.40	94.78	0.04	96.31	0.21

[5] First section rules can also be promoted, the effect being that they go to the head of the first section, bypassing the other rules in the section.

part 8	97.07	0.67	94.30	0.19	96.15	0.42
part 9	97.99	0.63	94.63	0.20	96.28	0.41
part 10	97.69	0.80	93.52	0.28	95.56	0.53
average	97.92	0.51	94.03	0.08	95.94	0.29

Table 1: Break-down of 10-fold cross-validation for a simple PDK run

Changing the error threshold up or down (table 2, 10-part average), decreased performance[6]:

average	R	dR	P	dP	F	dF
th=0.10	97.88	0.471	94.00	0.045	95.90	0.250
th=**0.25**	97.92	**0.509**	94.03	0.082	95.93	**0.288**
th=0.40	97.88	0.475	94.00	0.047	95.90	0.253

Table 2: Effect of changed rule error threshold (th) for a simple PDK run

We expected that iterative runs would correct initial detrimental role movements, while leaving beneficial ones in place, but for almost all parameter settings, further iterations did more harm than good. We tried to dampen this effect by reducing the rule error threshold with each iteration (dividing it by the number of iterations), but the measure did not reverse the general falling tendency of the iterated performance curve. In fact, the curve had a steeper decline, possibly because the falling threshold prevented the grammar from reversing bad rule movements.

run	0	1	2	3	4	5
th=0.25	96.12	**96.36**	96.21	96.18	96.13	**96.20**
th=*1/it	96.12	**96.36**	96.06	95.33	95.47	95.55

Table 3: F-scores for test chunk 3, per iteration

Suspecting, that hand-annotation errors in the gold corpus might cause iteration decreases by overtraining, we changed all rule-error counts by -1, among other effects permitting promoting of single-error rules, but this was overall detrimental[7].

In order to isolate the relative contributions of promoting, demoting and rule killing, these were also run in isolation:

	R	dR	P	dP	F	dF
promote	97.41	0.005	94.18	0.232	95.77	0.123
demote	97.41	0.015	94.21	**0.259**	95.77	0.127
kill	97.85	**0.440**	93.97	0.021	95.87	**0.227**

Table 4: Individual contribution of P, D and K

The results show that killing bad rules is by far the most effective of the three steps[8]. Interestingly, the three methods have different effects on recall and precision. Thus, killing bad rules prioritizes recall, simply by preventing the rules from removing correct readings. The effect of promoting and demoting almost exclusively affected precision, with demoting having a somewhat bigger effect. It should also be noted that though killing bad rules is quite effective, this does not hold for the "less bad than good" demoting category (see definition in 3.1), since killing demotable rules, too (PKK, i.e. promote-kill-kill, table 5), while marginally increasing recall, had an adverse effect on overall performance, as compared with a full PDK run. On the other hand, killing cannot be replaced by demoting, either: In a test run where bad>good rules were not killed, but instead simply demoted (PDD1) or - preferably - moved to the last section (PDD6), the expected slight increase in precision gain was more than offset by a larger decrease in recall gain. Finally, the third factor, promoting, can be shown to be essential, too, since removing it altogether (DK) is detrimental to performance.

	R	dR	P	dP	F	dF
PDK	97.92	0.509	94.03	0.082	95.93	**0.288**
PKK	**98.02**	0.611	93.86	-0.193	95.84	0.193
PDD1	97.52	0.115	94.31	**0.355**	95.89	0.239
PDD6	97.52	0.107	94.32	**0.373**	95.89	0.245
DK	97.91	0.504	94.00	0.051	95.92	0.269

Table 5: Killing instead of demoting (PKK), and demoting (PDD) instead of killing

[6] Further continuous 0.05 step variation was performed, but followed the general tendency and were left out in table 2.

[7] There was only one of the 10 sets, where error count reducing had a slight positive effect.

[8] Killed rules might be an area where human intervention might be of interest, in part because rules that do more bad than good, probably do not belong even in an untuned grammar, and in part, because a human would be able to improve the rule by adding NOT contexts etc, rather than killing it altogether.

3.3 Sorting rules

Another way of re-ordering rules is sorting all rules rather than moving individual rules. As a sorting parameter we calculated the worth W of a given rules as

$$W(\text{rule}) = G(\text{rule})^{a} / (G(\text{rule}) + B(\text{rule}))$$

where G (=good) is the number of instances where the rule removed a wrong reading, and B (=bad) the number of instances where the rule removed a correct reading[9]. The exponent a defaults to 1, but can be set higher if one wants to put extra weight on the rule being used at all.

The most radical solution would be to sort all rules in one go, then introduce section boundaries in (six) equal intervals to prevent heuristic rules from being used in too early a pass (exploiting the 1, 1-2, 1-3 ... rule batching property of CG compilers). However, this sorting & resectioning algorithm produced poor results when used on its own - only when the original human sectionizing information was factored in by dividing rule worth by section number, was some improvement achieved (0.1 percentage points). A third option investigated was ordering rules one section at a time, which didn't help much, but was assumed to be easier to combine with rule movements in one and the same run.

	R	dR	P	dP	F	dF
resec-tioning	97.41	0.005	93.95	0.007	95.65	0.007
resect.+ /section weighti.	97.51	**0.103**	94.05	**0.106**	95.74	**0.104**
sort by section	97.44	0.033	93.98	0.031	95.67	0.031

Table 6: sorting-only performance

Putting extra weight on rule use, i.e. increasing the a exponent variable, did not increase performance, cp. the results below (with sorting performed section-wise after rule movement):

average	R	dR	P	dP	F	dF
10/10						
a=**1**	97.72	**0.312**	94.00	**0.058**	95.81	**0.173**
a=1.2	97.58	0.171	93.96	0.019	95.73	0.094

Table 7: Effect of used-rule weighting

3.4 Rule relaxation and rule strictening

The third optimization tool, after rule movement and sorting, was rule relaxation, the rationale being that some (human) rules might be over-cautious not only in the sense that they are placed in too heuristic a rule section, but also in having too cautious context conditions. A typical CG rule uses contexts like the following:

1. (-1C ART)
2. (-1 ART)
3. (*1C VFIN BARRIER CLB)
4. (*1 VFIN BARRIER CLB)
5. (*1 VFIN CBARRIER CLB)

Rule 1 looks for an article immediately to the right, while rule 3 looks for a finite verb (VFIN) anywhere to the right (*1) but with clause boundaries (CLB) as a search-blocking barrier. In both rules the 'C' means cautious, and the compiler will instantiate the context in question only if it is unambiguous. Hence, a verb like 'to house' or 'to run' that can also be a noun, can act as context once another rule has removed the noun reading. Without the C (examples 2 and 4), rules with these contexts do not have to wait for such disambiguation, and will thus apply earlier, the expected overall effect being first of all improved precision, and possibly recall, especially if the change indirectly facilitates other rules, too. BARRIER conditions work in the opposite way, they are *ess* cautious, if only fully disambiguated words can instantiate them[10].

To explore the effect of rule relaxation, well-performing rules with C-contexts were duplicated[11] at the end of the grammar after stripping them of any such C-markers.

[9] What is counted here, are actual instances. Counting rule actions in isolation, i.e. what the rule would have done had it been the first to be applied, was also evaluated, but had a negative effect on almost all test subsets for both P, R and F.

[10] The same holds, in principle, for NOT contexts, but since these are mostly introduced as exceptions, their very nature is to make a rule more cautious, and most CGs will not contain examples where NOT and C are combined.

[11] The original rules were still promoted - in their original forms, on top of relaxation. Blocking the originals of relaxed-duplicated rules from promoting decreased performance.

for rules with:	R	dR	P	dP	F	dF
PDK	97.92	0.509	94.03	0.082	95.93	0.288
PDK r<1	97.86	**0.456**	94.13	0.180	95.95	0.311
PDK r<5	97.85	0.441	94.18	0.230	95.97	0.330
PDKR	97.85	0.442	94.25	**0.302**	95.65	**0.370**

Table 8: C-relaxation (added rules) instead of (pDKr), or on top of promotion (PDKr)

As can be seen, performance was clearly higher than for role movement alone, (PDKr). Setting the "well-performing"-threshold at either < 1 or < 5 errors for the rule in question, made almost no difference for recall, but showed a slight precision bias in favour of the latter. On the whole, the success of C-relaxation resides in its precision gain, which more than outweighed a moderate loss in recall.

We also experimented with relaxing such rules in situ, rather than duplicating them at the end of the grammar, but without positve effects. Similarly, no positive effect was measured when relaxing BARRIER contexts into CBARRIERs, or with combinations of C- and BARRIER-relaxation. Finally, adding in-section sorting to the C-relaxation was tried, but did not have a systematic positive effect either.

Of course, the opposite of rule relaxation, something we here will call "rule strictening" might also be able to contribute to performance, improving recall by making bad rules more cautious, waiting for unambiguous context. In this vein, we tried to add C conditions to all rules slated for demoting[12]. However, for most runs there was no overall F-score improvent over the corresponding non-stricting runs, independently of whether C-strictening was performed in situ or in combination with demoting. The only exception was PDKR(s), where stricting worked as a counter-balance to the threshold-less relaxation. As expected, recall and precision were very unequally affected by this method, and as a recall-increasing method, C-strictening *i* improve performance.

	R	dR	P	dP	F	dF
PDKR	97.85	0.442	94.25	**0.302**	95.65	0.370
PDKRs	97.88	**0.475**	94.25	0.297	96.03	**0.383**

[12] Stricting instead of killing was also tried, but without success.

PDK	97.92	0.509	94.03	**0.082**	95.93	**0.288**
PDKs	97.98	**0,571**	93.95	-0.053	95.89	0.246
PDKs in situ	97.95	0.538	93.86	-0.086	95.86	0.213
PDKr5	97.85	0.441	94.18	**0.230**	95.97	**0.330**
PDKr5s	97.89	**0.486**	94.12	0.168	95.97	0.321

Table 9: PDK rule-moving with C-relaxation (r) and strictening (s)

Combining the best stricting option with ordinary PDK and C-relaxation produced a better F-score than either method on its own, and presented a reasonable compromise on recall and precision .

3.5 PDK & rule-sorting combinations

We tested a number of further combinations of rule movement, sorting and rule relaxation/stricting, finding that sorting cannot be successfully combined with either simple rule movement (PDK, table 10) or relaxation/stricting-enhanced rule movements (PDKrs, table 11), performance being lower than for rule movement alone. If sorting is used, it should be used with the existing sectioning (sort-s) rather than resectioning (sort-S).

for rules with:	R	dR	P	dP	F	dF
PDK	97.92	**0.509**	94.03	**0.082**	95.93	**0.288**
sortPDK	97.73	**0.323**	93.96	0.014	95.80	0.162
PDKsort	97.72	0.312	94.00	**0.058**	95.81	**0.173**
sort-S + PDK	97.56	0.154	93.94	0.000	95.71	0.074
PDK + sort-S	97.41	0.006	93.96	0.012	95.65	0.009

Table 10: Effect of combining PDK and sorting, without and sort-resectioning (sort-S)

Sorting before PDK movements preserves recall better and adapts itself better to new sectioning, but the overall result is best for sorting after PDK (boldface in table 10). The only measure that could be improved by sorting, was precision in the case of sorting after a PDKr combination (bold in table 11). This effect is strongest (0.209) when resectioning is part of the sorting process (sort-S).

	R	dR	P	dP	F	dF
PDKrs	97.89	**0.486**	94.12	0.168	95.97	**0.321**
PDKrs + sort	97.85	0.444	94.07	0.117	95.92	0.274
sort + PDKrs	97.79	0.382	94.03	0.087	95.87	0.227
PDKrs + sort-S	97.47	0.064	94.15	**0.209**	95.78	0.137
sort-S + PDKrs	97.67	0.260	94.10	0.155	95.85	0.205

Table 11: Effect of combining PDKr/s and sorting

One interesting combinatorial factor is sectionizing, i.e. the creation of different or additional sections breaks in the grammar. We have already seen that sort-sectionizing (sort-S) cannot compete with the original human sectionizing, at least not with the rule sorting algorithm used in this experiment. However, sort-s is sensitive to sectionizing, too, if it is performed in connection with rule movements. To test this scenario, we introduced new start- and end-sections for rules moved to the top or bottom of the grammar, affecting especially error-free rules (top) and C-relaxed rules (bottom). The added sectioning did improve performance, but only marginally, and with no added positive effect from sorting. A more marked effect was seen when combining total C-relaxation with top/bottom-sectioning. With stricting this combination achieved the largest F-score gain of all runs (0.407 percentage points), without stricting the largest precision gain (0.318).

	R	dR	P	dP	F	dF
PDK	97.92	0.509	94.03	0.082	95.93	0.288
PDKr5s	97.89	0.486	94.12	0.168	95.97	0.321
PDKr5	97.85	0.441	94.18	0.230	95.97	0.330
PDKrSta	97.90	0.489	94.16	0.202	95.99	0.340
PDKrsS	97.93	**0.518**	94.11	0.162	95.98	0.337
PDKrS	97.89	0.480	94.18	0.227	96.00	0.349
PDKRS	97.89	0.486	94.27	**0.318**	96.05	0.399
PDKRsS	97.92	**0.518**	94.25	0.304	96.05	**0.407**
PDKRsS +sort	97.88	0.475	94.21	0.262	96.01	0.364

Table 12: PDKrs and PDKRs with new separate sections for moved start & end rules (PDKrsS)

3.6 Robustness

It is possible to overtrain a machine learning model by allowing it to adapt too much to its training data. When tuning a grammar to an annotated text corpus the risk is that rare, but possible human annotation errors will help to kill or demote a rule with very few use instances, or prevent a more frequent rule from being promoted as error-free. We were able to document this effect by comparing "corpus-true" runs with runs where all rule-error counts had been decreased by 1. The latter made the grammar tuning more robust, and led to performance improvements independently of other parameter settings, and was factored in for all results discussed in the previous sections.

Another problem is that when a large grammar is run on a relatively small one-domain training corpus, less than half[13] the rules will actually be used in any given run - which does not mean, of course that the rule will not be needed in the test corpus run. We therefore added a minimum value of 0.1 to the "good use" counter of such rules to prevent them from being weighted down as unused [14] . A corresponding minimum counter could have been added to the rule's error count, too, but given that on average rules trigger much more correct actions than errors, and assuming that the human grammarian made the rule for a reason, a small good-rule bias seems acceptable.

Finally, we had to make a decision on whether to score a rule's performance only on the instances where the rule was actually used, or whether to count instances, too, where the rule *o* *a e* been used, if other rules had not already completely disambiguated the word in question. It is an important robustness feature of CG compilers that - with default settings - they do not allow a rule to remove the last reading of a given word, making parses robust in the face of unorthodox language use or outright grammatical errors. This robustness effect seemed to carry over into our tuned grammars - so when we tried to include 'would-discard-last-reading' counts into the rule weighting, performance decreased. The likely explanation

[13] For the 10 training corpus combinations used hear, the initial percentage of used rules was 46-47%, and considerably lower for the changed grammars in later iterations.

[14] Depending on the weighting algorithm, non-zero values are necessary anyway, on order to prevent "division-by-zero" program breakdowns.

is that rules are designed with a certain section placement in mind, so demoting rules from their current section because they would have made errors at the top of the grammar, does not make sense[15].

3.7 Grammar Efficiency

In a CG setup, grammar efficiency depends on three main parameters: First, and most obviously, it depends on the size of the grammar, and - even more - on the size of the rules actually used on a given corpus[16]. Secondly, the order of rules is also important. Thus, running efficient rules first, will increase speed, i.e. SELECT rules before REMOTE rules, short rules before long rules, high-gain/high-frequency rules before rare rules. Thirdly, a large number of sections can lead to a geometric growth in rule repetitions, and lead to a conssiderable slow down, since even if a repeated rule remains unused, it needs to run at least some negative target or context checks before it knows that it doesn't apply. In this light it is of interest, if grammar tuning has a side effect on any of these efficiency parameters. Since we have shown that neither re-sectioning nor used-rule weighting has a positive effect on perfomance, and since the relative proportion of SELECT[17] rules (SEL% in table 13) remained fairly constant, tuning is neutral with regard to the second and third parameters.

	rules	used	killed	promote (use)	demote (use)	SEL %
0	4840	2278	-	-	-	38.5
1	4734	2157	105	4581-45%	153-51%	38.2
2	4724	2163	9	3676-49%	90-73%	37.8
3	4701	2051	22	2273-46%	97-57%	37.3
4	4687	2135	13	2984-50%	100-60%	37.5
5	4678	1987	8	2008-49%	87-61%	36.3

Table 13: PDK rule use statistics, for 10-3 training corpus (Fmax=96.36 at iteration 1)

There was, however, a falling tendency in the number of used rules with increasing iterations, in part due to rule-pruning by killing, but probably also to the promotion of safe rules that could then "take work" from later rules. For the first 2 iterations, where optimal performance usually occured, this amounts to 6-7% fewer rules.

The better-performing PDKRsS method led to a much smaller reduction in active rules (2-3%, table 14), because of the added relaxed rules that contributed to improved precision by cleaning up ambiguity after ordinary rules. Also, for the same reason, the absolute number of rules increased considerably, and because even unused rules have to be checked at least for their target condition, there actually was a 9% increase in CPU usage.

	rules	used	killed	promote (use %)	demote (use %)	SEL %
0	4840	2278	-	-	-	38.5
1	7625	2232	105	4581-45%	153-35%	38.0
2	7715	2204	21	3676-46%	84-43%	38.0
3	7821	2209	21	7481-29%	44-43%	38.0
4	7831	2217	9	7608-29%	52-44%	37.7
5	7837	2194	12	7722-28%	47-30%	38.0

Table 14: PDKRsS rule use statistics, for 10-3 training corpus (Fmax=96.43, iteration 3)

3.8 Smaller-scale grammars

In this paper, we have so far discussed the effect of tuning on full-size, mature Constraint Grammars, determining which parameters are most likely to have a positive effect. In quantitative terms, however, the improvement potential of a smaller-scale, immature grammar is much bigger. We therefore created an artificially reduced grammar by removing every second rule from the original grammar, on which we ran the PDK+relaxation/stricting setup that had performed best on the full grammar, with optional pre- and postsorting.

	R	dR	P	dP	F	dF
original	97.41	-	93.95	-	95.65	-

[15] More specifically, it would make sense only in one scenario - section-less sorting of all rules, which proved to be an unsuccessful strategy for other reasons.

[16] Of course, independently of rule number, the disambiguation load of a corpus remains the same, and hence the number of times some rule removes a reading. However, fewer rules used means that superfluous rules could be removed from grammar, rather than trying to match their targets and contexts in vain.

[17] A SELECT rule is more efficient, because it can resolve a 3-way ambiguity in one go, while it will take 2 REMOVE rules to achieve the same.

grammar						
untuned 1/2 gr.	97.48	.	85.55	-	91.12	-
PDKr1s	97.59	0.113	86.23	0.474	91.44	0.318
PDKr1sS	97.48	0.222	85.88	0.327	91.41	0.282
PDKr5s	97.56	0.083	86.26	0.708	91.56	0.436
PDKr5sS	97.73	**0.247**	86.19	0.638	91.59	0.469
PDKRs	97.52	0.045	87.84	2.289	92.43	1.303
DKr1s	97.57	0.095	86.00	0.449	91.12	0.295
DKr5s	97.52	0.040	86.45	0.906	91.65	0.529
DKR	97.54	0.066	87.90	2.345	92.47	1.343
DKRs	97.52	0.037	87.96	**2.417**	92.42	**1.369**
DKRsS	97.92	**0.441**	85.36	-0.185	91.21	0.086
DKRs + sort	97.54	0.062	87.87	2.330	92.45	1.329

Table 15: Effects on half-sized grammar

Like for the original grammar, PDK performed best without sorting. However, a number of performance differences can be noted. First, performance maxima were achieved later, often on the third iteration rather than the first, as was common for the original grammar. Second, as might be expected, F-scores improved 4 x more in absolute, and 2 x more in relative terms, than for the full grammar. More surprisingly, the gain is entirely due to precision gains, with a small fall in recall for most runs[18]. This can probably be explained by the fact that a Constraint Grammar is in its essence reductionist - it reduces ambiguity. Inactivating part of the rules, will simply leave more ambiguity (i.e. lower precision), but not necessarily have a corresponding influence on recall, since recall depends more on the quality of the individual rule. Given this dominating importance of precision, we tried to create a precision bias by inactivating the recall-favoring choices of stricting (PDKr) and rule-killing (PDr), but for the incomplete grammar reducing recall did not automatically mean increased precision, and these combinations did not work. Surprisingly, and contrary to what was expected from the full-grammar runs, the most beneficial measure was to inactivate promoting (DKrs), and to create maximally many relaxed rules (DKRs), by removing the relaxation threshold, allowing all rules with C-conditions to relax as long as their original versions did more good than bad. Adding new top/bottom-sections produced the highest recall gains (0.441 for DKRsS), but these did not translate into corresponding F-score gains.

The iteration profile for the succesful DKR run does not show the falling oscillation curve for F-scores seen for PDK runs (table 16). Rather, there is a shallow-top maximum stretching over serveral iterations, and than a slow fall-off with late oscillation. In terms of efficiency, the iteration pattern is also quite flat, with a fairly constant SELECT-rule percentage, and a slowly falling number of used rules, with relaxed-duplicated rules compensating for the disappearance of killed rules and demoted rules.

	rules	used	killed	demote (use)	SEL%	F-score
0	2420	1383	-	-	37.7	91.55
1	3011	1670	66	100-93%	35.9	92.70
2	3821	1661	40	120-77%	36.2	92.73
3	3012	1639	23	94-83%	36.3	92.74
4	3936	1630	8	83-82%	36.6	92.75
5	3936	1624	5	73-74%	36.5	92.71

Table 16: DKR rule use statistics, for 10-3 training corpus on reduced grammar

4 Conclusion

In this paper, we have proposed and investigated various machine learning options to increase the performance of linguist-written Constraint Grammars, using 10-fold cross-validation on a gold-standard corpus to evaluate which methods and parameters had a positive effect. We showed that by error-rate-triggered rule-reordering alone (promoting, demoting and killing rules), an F-score improvement of 0.29 could be achieved. With an F-score around 96% this corresponds roughly to a 7.5 % lower error rate in relative terms. However, we found that a careful balance had to be struck for individual rule movements, with a demoting threshold of 0.25% errors being the most effective, and that general performance-driven rule sorting was less effective than threshold-based individual movements. Likewise, the original human grammar sectioning and rule order is important and could not be improved by adding new sectioning, or even by in-section rule sorting.

[18] The only recall-preserving combination was DKr, i.e. without promoting and without stricting.

Apart from rule movements, rule changes were explored as a means of grammar optimization, by either increasing (for well-performing rules) or decreasing (for badly performing rules) the amount of permitted ambiguity in rule contexts. Thus, removing C (unambiguity) conditions was beneficial for precision, while adding C-conditions ("stricting") improved recall. Finally, section-delimiting of moved top- and bottom rules also helped. Altogether, the best combination of these methods achieved an average F-score improvement of 0.41 percentage points (10 percent fewer errors in relative terms). For a randomly reduced, half-size grammar, F-score gains are about three times as high - 1.36 percentage points or 15% in relative terms, an important difference being that for the mature grammar recall improvement contributed more than recall, while gains in the reduced grammar were overwhelmingly based on precision.

Obviously, the grammar tuning achieved with the methods presented here does not represent an upper ceiling for performance increases. First, with more processing power, rule movements could be evaluated against the training corpus individually and in all possible permutations, rather than in-batch, eliminating the risk of negative rule-interaction from other simultaneously moved rules[19]. Second, multi-iteration runs showed an oscillating performance curve finally settling into a narrow band *e o* the first maximum (usually achieved already in iteration 1 or 2, and never after 3). This raises the question of local/relative maxima, and should be further examined by making changes in smaller steps. Finally, while large scale rule reordering is difficult to perform for a human, the opposite is true of rule killing and rule changes such as adding or removing C-conditions. Rather than kill a rule outright or change *a* C-conditions in a given rule, a linguist would change or add individual context conditions to make the rule perform better, observing the effect on relevant sentences rather than indirectly through global test corpus performance measures. Future research should therefore explore possible trade-off gains resulting from the interaction between machine-learned and human-revised grammar changes.

[19] With over 4,000 rules and a 3-iteration training run taking 30 minutes for most parameter combinations, this was not possible in our current set-up.

References

Eckhard Bick, Heliana Mello, A. Panunzi and Tommaso Raso. 2012. The Annotation of the C-ORAL-Brasil through the Implementation of the Palavras Parser. In: Calzolari, Nicoletta et al. (eds.), Proceedings LREC2012 (Istanbul, May 23-25). pp. 3382-3386. ISBN 978-2-9517408-7-7

Eckhard Bick. 2011. A Barebones Constraint Grammar, In: Helena Hong Gao & Minghui Dong (eds), Proceedings of the 25th Pacific Asia Conference on Language, Information and Computation (Singapore, 16-18 December, 2011). pp. 226-235, ISBN 978-4-905166-02-3

Eckhard Bick & Marcelo Módolo. 2005. Letters and Editorials: A grammatically annotated corpus of 19th century Brazilian Portuguese. In: Claus Pusch & Johannes Kabatek & Wolfgang Raible (eds.) Romance Corpus Linguistics II: Corpora and Historical Linguistics (Proceedings of the 2nd Freiburg Workshop on Romance Corpus Linguistics, Sept. 2003). pp. 271-280. Tübingen: Gunther Narr Verlag.

Eckhard Bick. 2003. Arboretum, a Hybrid Treebank for Danish, in: Joakim Nivre & Erhard Hinrich (eds.), Proceedings of TLT 2003 (2nd Workshop on Treebanks and Linguistic Theory, Växjö, November 14-15, 2003), pp.9-20. Växjö University Press

Fred Karlsson, Atro Voutilainen, Juha Heikkilä and Arto Anttila. 1995. Constraint Grammar: A Language-Independent System for Parsing Unrestricted Text. Natural Language Processing, No 4. Mouton de Gruyter, Berlin and New York

Torbjörn Lager. 1999. The μ-TBL System: Logic Programming Tools for Transformation-Based Learning. In: Proceedings of CoNLL'99, Bergen.

Nikolaj Lindberg, Martin Eineborg. 1998. Learning Constraint Grammar-style Disambiguation Rules using Inductive Logic Programming. COLING-ACL 1998: 775-779

Lluís Padró. 1996.. POS Tagging Using Relaxation Labelling. In: Proceedings of the 16th International Conference on Computational Linguistics, COLING (Copenhagen, Denmark). pp. 877--882.

Eirikur Rögnvaldsson. 2002. The Icelandic μ-TBL Experiment: μ-TBL Rules for Icelandic Compared to English Rules. Retrieved 2013-05-12 from [http://hi.academia.edu/EirikurRognvaldsson/Papers]

Comparative Analyses of Textual Contents and Styles of Five Major Japanese Newspapers

Takafumi Suzuki
Faculty of Sociology, Toyo University / 5-28-20, Hakusan, Bunkyo-ku, Tokyo, Japan
takafumi_s@toyo.jp

Erina Kanou
Faculty of Sociology, Toyo University / 5-28-20, Hakusan, Bunkyo-ku, Tokyo, Japan
k_69en@yahoo.co.jp

Yui Arakawa
Graduate School of Library Information and Media Studies, University of Tsukuba / 1-2 Kasuga, Tsukuba, Ibaraki, Japan
s1221577@u.tsukuba.ac.jp

Abstract

Newspapers remain an important media from which people obtain a wide variety of information. In Japan, there are five major newspapers, having their own opinions and ideologies. Although these are readily recognized, they are infrequently investigated from the viewpoint of their textual characteristics. This study analyzes these differences among the five newspaper editorials. We apply morphological analysis and count the frequency of morphemes within the text data. We then apply principal component analysis and random forests classification experiments to examine their similarities and differences. Throughout these statistical analyses, we use function words and content words as features, which enables us to determine which of the two characteristics -styles or content- more powerfully affects the classification types. This study contributes to text classification studies by deliberately comparing the classification performances provided by different feature sets, function words and content words. In addition, this study will provide an empirical basis for understanding the similarities and differences among the five newspapers.

1. Introduction

Newspapers are an important media from which people obtain a wide variety of information, ranging from contemporary political and economic issues to ordinary incidents. Particularly in Japan, where newspapers delivery remains popular, many people read them in their own spaces and have continued to use them as popular information resources, even after the advent and spread of the Web. According to Nihon Shinbun Kyokai (2012), 87.3 percent people in Japan read newspapers, which is second only to television (98.7 percent) among the five surveyed media including newspaper, television, radio, magazines, and Internet.

There are five major newspapers in Japan: Asahi, Mainichi, Nikkei, Sankei, and Yomiuri, which have publication offices in Tokyo, Osaka, and other areas, and are distributed to almost all regions of Japan. Though all of these newspapers regard correctness, neutrality and unbiased reporting as important, they have their own opinions and ideologies. According to the Hosyu (conservative)-Kakushin (liberal) image survey by Shinbun Tsushin Chosakai (2009), the five major newspapers scored as follows: Yomiuri 5.6, Sankei 5.3, Nikkei 5.2, Mainichi 5.0, and Asahi 4.4, where larger numbers indicate a newspaper perceived as more conservative and smaller numbers indicate a newspaper perceived as more liberal. Excluding Nikkei, which is a specialized newspaper that focuses on economic issues, the survey results show that people see Yomiuri and Sankei as more conservative and Mainichi and Asahi as more liberal. These differences might affect the textual characteristics of newspapers; however, they have not been investigated in a comprehensive and systematic manner.

With the development of natural language processing techniques and the creation of many online text corpora, quantitative text analysis has been expanding in scope. Such methods have begun to be recognized as important tools for solving many theoretical and practical social science research questions.

Particular to newspapers, some studies have applied these quantitative text analysis methods. For example, Newman and Block (2006) determined topics using a probabilistic mixture decomposition method with the Pennsylvania Gazette, a major colonial U.S. newspaper that was in publication from 1728 to 1800. Higuchi (2011) investigated whether there is significant association between the content of newspaper articles and social consciousness trends by using three Japanese newspapers, Asahi, Yomiuri, and Mainichi. However, these previous newspaper text analyses focused only on the content. Examination of textual characteristics, such as styles of texts, which can reveal attitudes, personalities, psychologies, emotions, text genres, and authors (Argamon et al., 2007; Suzuki, 2009), have rarely been focused despite being intriguing aspects for analysis.

Therefore, this study analyzes the differences among editorials in the five major Japanese newspapers. Among the many types of articles, editorials are one of the most intriguing and colorful, wherein respective viewpoints are expressed (Goto, 1999), and thus are good materials for investigation. We first apply principal component analysis (PCA) to observe the overall distribution of these texts in scatter plots and investigate the factors affecting the textual characteristics. Next, we apply random forests classification experiments using newspapers, editorial dates, and ideology types as classes in order to examine the classification performance and important features of these experiments. Throughout these analyses, we use function words as well as content words as features, which is useful for investigating the similarities and differences of these classes. In addition, these features enable us to clarify which of the two characteristics-styles or content-more powerfully affects these classification types, which is also an interesting text analysis topic. This study contributes to text classification studies by deliberately comparing the classification performance provided by different feature sets, function words and content words. In addition, this study provides empirical findings useful for understanding the characteristics of the five newspapers.

2. Data and methods

2.1. Data

This study focused on the five major Japanese newspapers: Asahi, Mainichi, Nikkei, Sankei, and Yomiuri. We constructed the editorial texts using the following databases.

Yomiuri: Yomidasu Rekishikan (1874-now)

Asahi: Kikuzo II Visual for Libraries (1945-1984, pocket edition 1985-now)

Mainichi: Mainichi News Pack (1987-now)

Nikkei: Nikkei Terekon 21 (1975-now)

Sankei: The Sankei Archives (1992.9-now)

We selected two editorial dates for each newspaper, Jan. 1 and Aug. 15 from 2000 to 2010. As Jan. 1 is New Year's Day, each newspaper runs an editorial reflecting their primary opinions and interests. The Aug. 15 is the anniversary of the end of the Pacific War in Japan, and each newspaper runs an editorial reflecting their view on the war. New Year's Day editorials reflect the general vision of each newspaper and the end-of-war editorials reflect specific visions of the newspapers. In this study, we used 31 editorials from Nikkei and 22 editorials from each of the other newspapers.[1] We removed symbols, lines, and parentheses, i.e., analysis noises, and applied morphological analysis using MeCab.[2] We divided the morphemes into content words and function words using the tags assigned by MeCab.[3] The relative frequencies of morphemes were counted; three types of text-feature matrices (bag-of-words models) were constructed using all morphemes, content words, and function words as features.

2.2. Methods

2.2.1. Principal component analysis

We applied PCA using the variances-covariance matrices constructed from three types of text-feature matrices in order to observe the distribution of the newspaper texts and to examine the factors affecting their textual characteristics.

2.2.2. Random forests

Next, we applied random forests (Breiman, 2001) for classification experiments. Random forests is an improved means of bagging (Breiman, 1996), which is an ensemble-learning method. The basic objective of ensemble learning is to improve the classification performance of previous statistical methods, i.e. decision trees in this case, by repeatedly performing the experiments and calculating the mean or majority votes of the results. However,

---

[1] Nikkei has two editorials in Aug. 15, and we regard them as separate ones.

[2] mecab.sourceforge.net

[3] We regard noun-dependent, noun-pronominals, adnominals, conjunctions, particles, auxiliary verbs, signs as function words, and others as content words.

the results will always be the same when using exactly the same data. Therefore, ensemble learning methods such as bagging usually use bootstrap samplings from the original data to repeat the experiments. The main improvement in random forests over bagging is the extraction of a random subset from each bootstrapping sample that enlarges the variances in the bootstrapping samples (Breiman, 2001; Jin, 2007). Firstly, we randomly sampled i cases from the original text-feature matrix $M_{i,j}$ with replacements to create a bootstrap sample and extracted square root random subsets of j variables from the bootstrap sample to create a sample for constructing an unpruned decision tree. We used the Gini index, formalized as follows, to split the nodes.

$$Q_\tau(T) = \sum_{k=1}^{K} p_{\tau k}(1 - p_{\tau k}) ,$$

where $p_{\tau k}$ denotes the proportion of data points in region R_τ assigned to class k (k = 1, ... , K), which vanishes for $p_{\tau k}$ = 0 and $p_{\tau k}$= 1 and has a maximum at $p_{\tau k}$ = 0.5 (Bishop, 2006). These sampling, extraction, and tree-constructing processes were repeated 1, 000 times, and a new classifier was constructed by a majority vote of the set of trees. When the training set for the current tree was drawn by sampling with replacements, one-third of the cases were omitted from the sample. This is referred to as the out-of-bag (OOB) data, and is used to obtain a running unbiased estimate of the classification errors as trees are added to the forest. It is also used to obtain estimates of variable importance (Breiman and Cutler, 2004). An important characteristic of random forests is that it returns variable importance (VI_{acu}) for classification experiments. To calculate variable importance, we first determined the OOB cases and counted the number of votes cast for the correct class. Next, we randomly permutated the values of the variable m in the OOB cases and placed these cases further down the tree. We subtracted the number of votes for the correct class in the variable-m-permuted OOB data from the number of votes for the correct class in the original untouched OOB data. We calculated the average of this number for all trees in the forest and determined the raw importance score for each variable. Finally, we divided the raw score by the standard error of the variable in the calculation over all trees, which is denoted as VI_{acu} for each variable (Breiman, 2001; Breiman and Cutler, 2004). The VI_{acu} value represents the degree to which a class loses its specific character when one type of morpheme changes to another type. We used precisions, recall rates, and F1 values for evaluation (Tokunaga, 1999). As random forests use random digits for their experiments, we used the mean values from 100 experiments for these evaluation scores (Jin & Murakami, 2007; Suzuki, 2012).

We used four types of classifications, i.e., five newspaper classes, two editorial date classes, ten editorial classes (two editorial dates from the five newspapers), and three ideology types (Sankei-Yomiuri, Asahi-Mainichi, and Nikkei). We also used three types of features: all morphemes, content words, and function words. We conducted the following 12 types of experiments.

Exp. 1: five newspaper classes, all morpheme features
Exp. 2: ten classes (two editorial dates from five newspaper classes), all morpheme features
Exp. 3: two editorials date classes, all morpheme features
Exp. 4: five newspaper classes, content word features
Exp. 5: ten classes (two editorial dates from five newspaper classes), content word features
Exp. 6: two editorial date classes, content word features
Exp. 7: five newspaper classes, function word features
Exp. 8: ten classes (two editorial dates from five newspaper classes), function word features
Exp. 9: two editorial date classes, function word features
Exp. 10: three ideology type classes, all morpheme features
Exp. 11: three ideology type classes, content word features
Exp. 12: three ideology type classes, function word features

3. Results and discussion

3.1. Basic results

Table 1 shows the mean number of tokens and types of morphemes of two editorials from the five newspapers. It shows that Yomiuri has the longest editorials, which indicates that Yomiuri strives to express their opinions using New Year's editorials more ardently than others. In addition, it shows that all but Mainichi and

Nikkei have longer Jan. 1 editorials than Aug. 15 editorials. This indicates that New Year's editorials cover more general and diverse content than the end-of-war anniversary editorials.

3.2. Principal component analysis

Figure 1-3 shows PCA scatter plots (x axis: PC1 and y axis: PC2) using all morphemes, content words, and function words, respectively, as features. Each editorial text was plotted using labels representing the five newspapers (a: Asahi, m: Mainichi, n: Nikkei, s: Sankei, Y: Yomiuri) with the editorial date (1: Jan. 1 and 8: Aug. 15). Figure 1 and Figure 3 are similar, which indicates that function words affect the PCA results more strongly than content words when we use all morphemes (simple bag-of-words) are used as features.

The results show that Yomiuri's Jan. 1 editorials were plotted in a larger area as compared to the other editorials. When we calculated the coefficients of variances using the number of tokens in 11 texts (2000-2010) from each class, Yomiuri's Jan. 1 editorials had the largest value (.180). The large variance in editorial length explains this PCA result.

Yomiuri, Nikkei, and Sankei's Jan. 1 and Aug. 15 editorials were grouped respectively. The grouping of editorials from Asahi and Mainichi, for the same dates, was not clearly differentiated, suggesting that Asahi's and Mainichi's contents and styles were similar.

Though previous survey results (Shinbun Tsushin Chosakai, 2009) indicated the similarity between Asahi and Mainichi, and Yomiuri and Sankei, the PCA results do not show this point clearly. Instead the results indicate the differences between Yomiuri's Jan. 1 and Nikkei's Aug. 15 editorials.

	Number of tokens		Number of types	
	Jan. 1	Aug. 15	Jan. 1	Aug. 15
Asahi	14, 722	13, 722	5, 364	5, 015
Mainichi	13, 589	14, 313	4, 975	4, 964
Nikkei	11, 879	12, 625	4, 365	5, 296
Sankei	14, 015	11, 265	5, 249	4, 526
Yomiuri	20, 595	13, 120	6, 510	4, 424
mean	14, 960	13, 009	5, 292.6	4, 845

Table 1: Basic results

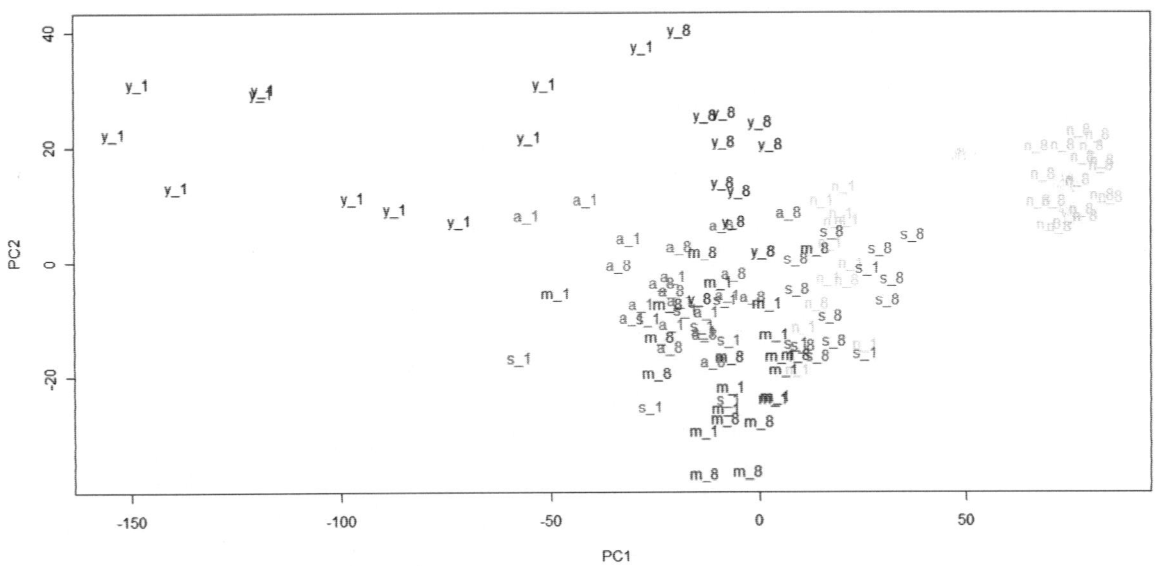

Figure 1: PCA scatter plot (all morphemes)

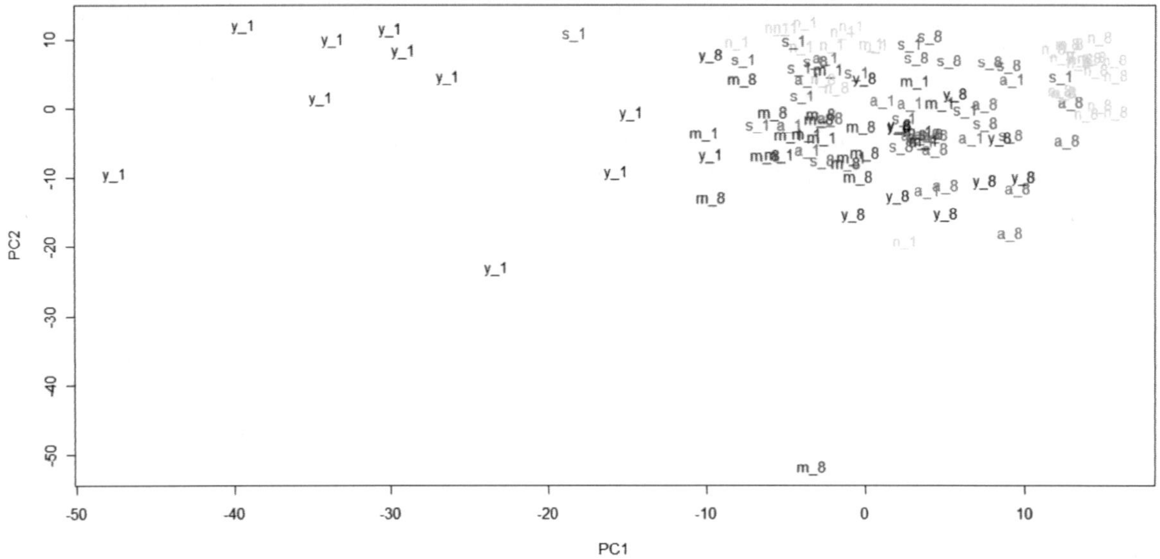

Figure 2: PCA scatter plot (content words)

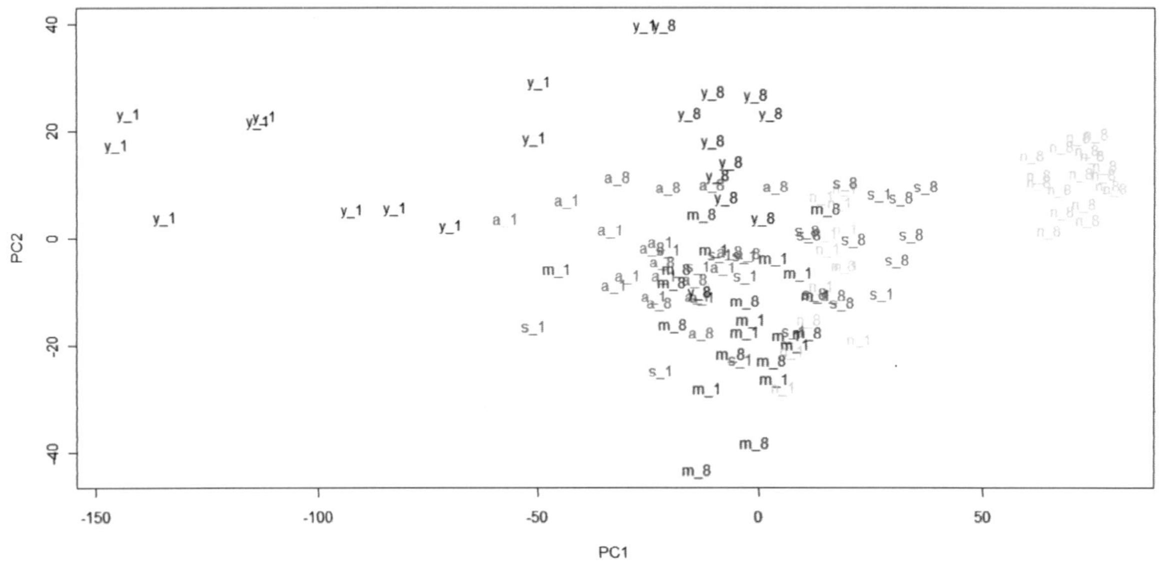

Figure 3: PCA scatter plot (function words)

3.3. Classification experiments by random forests

3. 3. 1. Experimental results

Table 2 presents the precision, recall rates, and F1 values given by the random forests classification experiments.[4] The results show that Exp. 3 (class: date, features: all morphemes) provided the best performance, probably, because the objective of Exp. 3 was to classify the minimum number of classes using the maximum number of features.

[4] Some values are missing because they can not be calculated.

In the newspaper classification experiments (Exps. 1, 4, and 7), the results show that Exp. 7 (function words) provided better performance than Exp. 4 (content words), which indicates that the main differences among the newspapers are stylistic. This finding is consistent with that given by PCA.

In contrast, in the editorial date classification experiments (Exps. 3, 6, and 9), the results show that Exp. 6 (content words) provided better performance than Exp. 9 (function words), which indicates that content is the main difference between New Year's editorials and the end-of-war anniversary editorials.

The results of the newspaper classification experiments (Exp.1, 4, and 7) show that Nikkei and Yomiuri have special content and styles characteristics because both newspapers obtain rather high classification performances in experiments using three types of features.

The results of the editorial date experiments (Exps. 2, 5, and 8) show that Aug. 15 editorials have higher classification performance than Jan. 1 editorials for all morphemes and content word classifications. However, when using function words as the feature, the former has lower classification performance than the latter, which indicates that Aug. 15 editorials have specific end-of-war content characteristic.

The results of ideology-type classification experiments (Exps. 10, 11, and 12) show that Asahi-Mainichi types have higher classification performance than Yomiuri-Sankei types, which suggest that , with regard to content and styles, Asahi and Mainichi are more similar to each other than they are to Yomiuri and Sankei. The result is also consistent with PCA results.

	precision	**recall rates**	***F1***
Exp. 1	88.865	87.377	87.747
Exp. 2	68.015	67.406	66.360
Exp. 3	92.278	92.025	92.118
Exp. 4	74.369	66.029	65.877
Exp. 5	—	46.702	—
Exp. 6	89.763	88.508	88.805
Exp. 7	87.809	87.368	87.424
Exp. 8	67.520	66.963	—
Exp. 9	78.918	79.028	78.919
Exp. 10	91.199	89.377	89.842
Exp. 11	83.295	81.765	81.975
Exp. 12	92.977	91.352	91.901

Table 2: Precision, recall rates, *F1* values

3.3.2. Important classification variables

Table 3 represents the top 20 important variables contributing to classification (Exps. 1-12), with their part of speeches and variable importance values. Among the experiments using all morphemes as features (Exps. 1, 2, and 3), many function words appear in the table for Exps. 1 and 2 (including newspaper classification), while many content words appear in the table for Exp. 3, (editorial date classification). In particular, '戦争' (war) and '終戦' (end of war) appear as the top two variables, representing the special topics that appear in Aug. 15 editorials. These results are consistent with the classification performance given by random forests.

Among the experiments using content words (Exps. 4, 5, and 6), many war-related morphemes appear in Exps. 5 and 6, (including editorial date classification), but not in Exp. 4 (newspaper classification). In Exp. 4, content words that have general meanings or functional roles appear in the lists, which indicates that style affects classification to a greater extent than content even when content words are used as the feature.

Among the ideology-types classification experiments (Exps. 10, 11, and 12), many function words appear in Exp. 10. In Exp. 11, content words that have general meanings or functional roles appear in the list. Therefore, it is evident that the identification of ideological differences is primarily a function of style.

4. Conclusion

This study analyzed the differences among newspaper editorials, focusing on five newspapers, two editorial dates, and ideology types. We applied PCA and constructed scatter plots to observe the overall distribution of these texts and investigated the factors affecting textual characteristics. We also conducted random forests classification experiments using the newspapers, editorial dates, and ideology types as classes to examine the classification performance and identify important features. In these analyses, we used function words and content words as features. These features facilitated the investigation of similarities and differences among the classes and helped determine which of the two characteristics, styles or content, more powerfully affected the classification types.

The PCA results showed that function words affect the textual characteristics more strongly than content words, Yomiuri's Jan. 1 editorials and Nikkei's Aug. 15 editorials had distinctive characteristics; Asahi's and Mainichi's Jan. 1 and Aug. 15 editorials had similar characteristics. The random forests results showed that function words strongly affect newspaper classification and content words strongly affect editorial date classification. Nikkei and Yomiuri had distinctive style and content characteristics. Asahi-Mainichi types were more similar to each other than Yomiuri-Sankei types.

We clarified the similarities and differences among newspapers, editorial dates and ideology types by textual characteristics. In particular, our results showed that function words had rather important roles for these classifications. This study contributes to text classification studies by deliberately comparing the classification performances determined by different feature sets, function words, and content words. In addition, this study provides empirical evidence that will increase understanding of the characteristics of the five major Japanese newspapers.

In the future, we will investigate the similarities and differences between these five newspapers using a wider variety of editorials and we will compare our results to newspapers in other countries.

Acknowledgements

This study was supported by Grant-in-Aid for Scientific Research 23700288 for Young Scientists (B), from the Ministry of Education, Culture, Sports, Science and Technology, Japan. We would like to express our gratitude for these supports. This research includes revised and expanded content based on gradation thesis presented by Erina Kanou to the Faculty of Sociology, Toyo University. An earlier version of this study was presented at the 19th Annual Meeting of the Association for Natural Language Processing (NLP2013) at Nagoya University. We would like to thank the participants for their useful comments.

References

Shlomo, Argamon, Casey Whitelaw, Paul Chase, Sobhan Raj Hota, Navendu Garg and shlomo Levitan 2007. Stylistic text classification using functional lexical features, *Journal of the American Society for Information Science and Technology*, 58(6):802-822.

Leo Breiman. 1996. Bagging predictors, *Machine Learning*, 24:123-140.

Leo Breiman. 2001. Random forests, *Machine Learning*, 45:5-32.

Leo Breiman and Adele Cutler. 2004. Random Forests, www.stat.berkeley.edu/ ~breiman/ RandomForests (7 March 2013 last access).

Masayuki Goto. 1999. Mass Media Ron, Yuhikaku, Tokyo.

Koichi Higuchi. 2011. Contemporary national newspapers and social consciousness: Efficiency and limitations of newspaper content analysis, *Kodo Keiryogaku (The Japanese Journal of Behaviormetrics)*, 38 (1):1-12.

Mingzhe Jin and Masakatsu Murakami. 2007. Authorship identification using random forests, *Proceedings of the Institute of Statistical Mathematics*, 55(2):255-268.

Mingzhe Jin. 2007. *R ni yoru Deta Saiensu*, Morikita Shuppan, Tokyo.

David J. Newman and Sharon Block. 2006. Probabilistic topic decomposition of an eighteenth-century American newspaper, *Journal of the American Society for Information Science and Technology*, 57(6):753-767.

Nihon Shinbun Kyokai. 2012. '2011nen Zenkoku Media Sessyoku / Hyoka Cyosa' Hokokusyo, Nihon Shinbun Kyokai, www.pressnet.or.jp/ adarc/ data/rep/files/2011media.pdf (21 Feb. 2013 last access).

Shinbun Tsushin Cyosakai. 2009. 2008 Nen Media ni Kansuru Zenkoku Seron Cyosa, Shinbun Tsushin Cyosakai, www.chosakai.gr.jp/ notification/ pdf/ report.pdf (21 Feb. 2013 last access).

Takafumi Suzuki. 2009. Extracting speaker-specific functional expressions from political speeches using random forests in order to investigate speakers' political styles, *Journal of the American Society for Information Science and Technology*, 60(8):1596-1606.

Takafumi, Suzuki, Shuntaro Kawamura, Fuyuki Yoshikane, Kyo Kageura, and Akiko Aizawa. 2012. Co-occurrence-based indicators for authorship analysis, *Literary & Linguistic Computing*, 27(2):197-214.

Tokunaga, Takenobu. 1999. *Joho Kensaku to Gengo Syori*, University of Tokyo Press, Tokyo

	Exp.1			Exp.2			Exp.3		
ranks	**variables**	**pos**	***VI(acu)***	**variables**	**pos**	***VI(acu)***	**variables**	**pos**	***VI(acu)***
1	、	s	0.007347	、	s	0.008540	終戦	n	0.009378
2	。	s	0.007220	て	p	0.008524	戦争	n	0.004674
3	の	p	0.006187	。	s	0.005433	で	p	0.004177
4	て	p	0.006137	の	p	0.005224	地球	n	0.004117
5	は	p	0.006038	と	p	0.004725	日	n	0.004096
6	で	p	0.005795	も	p	0.004528	は	p	0.004028
7	を	p	0.004759	う	av	0.003771	戦没	n	0.004005
8	も	p	0.004098	1	n	0.003551	経済	n	0.003615
9	に	p	0.003836	だ	av	0.003433	。	s	0.003399
10	と	p	0.003699	として	p	0.003427	ある	av	0.003329
11	経済	n	0.003564	を	p	0.00319	世界	n	0.003168
12	が	p	0.003390	は	p	0.003181	が	p	0.003069
13	ない	av	0.003262	た	p	0.003152	な	av	0.002888
14	た	av	0.002878	で	p	0.003145	8月	n	0.002810
15	だ	av	0.002861	いる	v	0.003133	化	n	0.002605
16	終戦	n	0.002749	“	s	0.003120	の	p	0.002493
17	う	av	0.002469	”	s	0.003070	記念	n	0.002491
18	「	s	0.002346	いわゆる	adn	0.002907	財政	n	0.002308
19	」	s	0.002284	が	p	0.002902	追悼	n	0.002306
20	な	av	0.002072	他方	n	0.002748	を	p	0.002205

	Exp.4			Exp.5			Exp.6		
ranks	**variables**	**pos**	***VI(acu)***	**variables**	**pos**	***VI(acu)***	**variables**	**pos**	***VI(acu)***
1	1	n	0.005865	経済	n	0.004497	終戦	n	0.009168
2	いる	v	0.004690	し	v	0.003920	地球	n	0.005378
3	し	v	0.004178	1	n	0.002834	戦争	n	0.004735
4	0	n	0.004095	いる	v	0.002770	経済	n	0.004725
5	られ	v	0.003961	日本	n	0.002714	世界	n	0.004338
6	他方	n	0.003723	必要	n	0.002568	戦没	n	0.003815
7	平成	n	0.003223	終戦	n	0.002556	化	n	0.003486
8	れ	v	0.002953	的	n	0.002298	財政	n	0.003066
9	さ	v	0.002820	世界	n	0.002291	ある	av	0.002929
10	9	n	0.002459	する	v	0.002206	8月	n	0.002735
11	する	v	0.002450	平成	n	0.001967	必要	n	0.002705
12	日本人	n	0.002253	追悼	n	0.001876	先進	n	0.002574
13	なら	v	0.002251	れ	v	0.001829	改革	n	0.002548
14	九	n	0.002181	0	n	0.001805	記念	n	0.002443
15	2	n	0.002077	戦争	n	0.001775	危機	n	0.002408
16	軍事	n	0.001720	られ	v	0.001708	企業	n	0.002292
17	現実	n	0.001692	級	n	0.001640	する	v	0.002096
18	国民	n	0.001548	さ	v	0.001633	日	n	0.001989
19	必要	n	0.001547	地球	n	0.001633	追悼	n	0.001978
20	6	n	0.001512	他方	n	0.001587	成長	n	0.001965

	Exp.7			Exp.8			Exp.9		
ranks	**variables**	**pos**	***VI(acu)***	**variables**	**pos**	***VI(acu)***	**variables**	**pos**	***VI(acu)***
1	、	s	0.027852	、	s	0.022828	日	n	0.023632
2	て	p	0.025036	。	s	0.019897	は	p	0.012206
3	。	s	0.014986	て	p	0.016021	で	p	0.011571
4	の	p	0.012213	の	p	0.015435	。	s	0.010696
5	も	p	0.011241	は	p	0.015083	が	p	0.009095
6	と	p	0.011084	で	p	0.012908	な	av	0.008524
7	”	s	0.009826	を	p	0.010720	あの	adn	0.008178
8	“	s	0.009797	も	p	0.008508	を	p	0.006522
9	だ	av	0.009260	に	p	0.008464	の	p	0.006168
10	いわゆる	adn	0.009048	と	p	0.008185	から	p	0.005435
11	として	p	0.008002	が	p	0.008161	だ	av	0.004824
12	そんな	adn	0.007842	だ	av	0.007798	、	s	0.004327
13	う	av	0.007481	た	p	0.007187	に	p	0.004008
14	が	p	0.007178	日	n	0.006392	ば	p	0.003672
15	は	p	0.006455	な	av	0.005604	なく	av	0.003326
16	た	p	0.006170	A	s	0.005494	ある	av	0.003173
17	を	p	0.005930	いわゆる	adn	0.004757	この	adn	0.002610
18	で	p	0.005830	ない	av	0.004568	ない	av	0.002530
19	「	s	0.005461	「	s	0.004521	A	s	0.002420
20	」	s	0.005459	“	s	0.004468	た	p	0.002257

	Exp.10			Exp.11			Exp.12		
ranks	**variables**	**pos**	***VI(acu)***	**variables**	**pos**	***VI(acu)***	**variables**	**pos**	***VI(acu)***
1	て	p	0.008789	1	n	0.007746	て	p	0.025149
2	。	s	0.006295	0	n	0.005372	。	s	0.017149
3	の	p	0.006063	し	v	0.004070	だ	av	0.014567
4	と	p	0.005060	九	n	0.003963	の	p	0.013545
5	1	n	0.005036	られ	v	0.003553	、	s	0.011640
6	だ	av	0.004911	十	n	0.003462	として	p	0.011371
7	、	s	0.004875	いる	v	0.003348	と	p	0.011303
8	として	p	0.004566	れ	v	0.003225	も	p	0.010391
9	も	p	0.004481	さ	v	0.003062	“	s	0.008768
10	う	av	0.004167	2	n	0.003005	”	s	0.008683
11	を	p	0.003919	五	n	0.002776	が	p	0.008508
12	は	p	0.003807	9	n	0.002385	う	av	0.007858
13	が	p	0.003738	国際	n	0.002329	を	p	0.007856
14	で	p	0.003572	たち	n	0.002291	いわゆる	adn	0.007799
15	九	n	0.003441	なら	v	0.002270	私	n	0.007716
16	0	n	0.003137	6	n	0.002038	は	p	0.007055
17	ない	av	0.003039	日本	n	0.002030	で	p	0.006175
18	”	s	0.003034	三	n	0.001901	こと	n	0.005993
19	いわゆる	adn	0.003024	現実	n	0.001824	ある	av	0.005894
20	こと	n	0.002916	国民	n	0.001760	た	p	0.005048

Table 3: Important variables

The Island Effect in Postverbal Constructions in Japanese

Kohji Kamada
Chiba University
1-33, Yayoicho, Inage Ward, Chiba-shi, Chiba, 263-8522 Japan
k-kamada@L.chiba-u.ac.jp

Abstract

It has been generally assumed that a violation of island constraints indicates that the relevant syntactic phenomena involves movement. That is, if what look like displacements violate island constraints but remain acceptable, this means that they should not be derived by movement. A careful examination of postverbal constructions in Japanese reveals that no movement is involved in the derivation of the construction despite the fact that in some cases island effects are observed. The effects, which have up to now been dealt with purely in syntax, can receive a better account in terms of language processing. This suggests that the human parser should undertake explanations of part of the output of the competence system.

1 Introduction

Japanese is descriptively a verb-final language. In some cases, however, non-verbal elements come at the end of sentences, as shown in (1).[1, 2]

(1) a. *Taro-ga ano mise de tabe-ta yo,*
Taro-NOM that shop at eat-PAST FP
***susi-o*.**
sushi-ACC
'Taro ate sushi at that shop.'
b. *Taro-ga susi-o tabe-ta yo,*
Taro-NOM sushi-ACC eat-PAST FP,
***ano mise de*.**
that shop at

In (1a), the object *susi-o* 'sushi-ACC' appears in postverbal position, and in (1b), the adverbial phrase *ano mise de* 'at that shop' does so. I refer to these phenomena as the postverbal construction in Japanese (JPVC), and refer to elements in sentence-final position as postverbal elements (PVE).[3]

Some researchers (e.g., Endo, 1989; Kaiser, 1999; Whitman, 2000; Tanaka, 2001; and Abe, 2004) claim that the PVE is derived by movement because of the obedience of the PVE to island constraints such as the so-called Complex NP Constraint (CNPC), as shown in (2). In (2), *e* is used to mark the position associated with the moved element, namely the PVE, and the identical subscript indicates that the PVE corresponds to *e*.

(2) *?[$_{NP}$ [$_{CP}$ [e_i *Sonkeisiteiru*] *sensei*]-*ga*
respect teacher-NOM
fueteimasu yo, ***gakuseitati-ga***$_i$.
increase FP students-NOM
'The number of the teachers who *they*$_i$ respect is increasing, **students**$_i$.'

In (2), the PVE is extracted out of the NP that contains the relative clause, thereby violating the CNPC. The example in (3), however, is acceptable although it violates the CNPC.

(3) [$_{NP}$ [$_{CP}$ e_i *Sonkeisiteiru*] *gakuseitati*]-*ga*
respect students -NOM
fueteimasu yo, ***Tanaka sensei-o***$_i$.
increase FP Tanaka teacher-ACC
'The number of the students who respect *him*$_i$ is increasing, **Mr. Tanaka**$_i$.'

It has been generally assumed that a violation of island constraints indicates that the relevant syntactic phenomena involves movement. That is, if what look like displacements violate island constraints but are still acceptable, this means that they should not be derived by movement.

[1] The relevant elements are in boldface.

[2] The abbreviations used in glossing the data are as follows: ACC = accusative, DAT =dative, FP = sentence-final particle, NEG = negative, NOM = nominative, TOP = topic.

[3] I do not deal with the case in which clauses appear in postverbal position, as shown below.

(i) Watashi-wa sitteiru yo, **Taro-ga susi-o tabe-ta**
I -TOP know FP Taro-Nom sushi-ACC eat-PAST
koto-o.
that-ACC
'I know that Taro ate sushi.'

The example in (3) is hence problematic for movement approaches. I therefore propose the statement given in (4) concerning the derivation of the JPVC:

(4) The PVE is adjoined to a CP via External Merge.

The purpose of this paper is to argue, through analysis of the island effect in the JPVC, that the human parser should undertake explanations of part of the output of the competence system.[4] The outline of this paper is as follows. In section 2, I propose/adopt a licensing condition and interpretive rules for adjoined phrases, as well as two parsing strategies. In sections 3 and 4, I demonstrate that the presence or absence of the island effect observed in the JPVC can be accounted for in terms of the interaction of the licensing condition with the parsing strategies. Finally, in section 5, I deal with the case in which adjuncts appear in postverbal position.

2 Hypotheses[5]

I propose the licensing condition for adjoined elements in (5).

(5) The licensing condition for adjoined phrases (where X= any syntactic category):
A phrase α adjoined to XP is licensed only if α is associated with β such that
(i) α c-commands β,[6] and
(ii) α is non-distinct from β in terms of Case features.

In light of the condition in (5), I propose interpretive rules concerning adjoined phrases as shown informally in (6):

(6) Interpretive rules about adjoined phrases
Suppose that α is adjoined to XP (where X= any syntactic category), then
(i) α is construed as an argument sharing properties with β,[7] only if
a. α is an NP or a CP, and
b. α is non-distinct from β in terms of referentiality,[8] and
c. β is in A(rgument)-position (i.e., subject and object).
(ii) α is construed as a potential modifier of β only if α is not construed as an argument.

With respect to parsing strategies, I first follow Pritchett (1992) in adopting the *Generalized Theta Attachment* formulated in (7):

(7) Generalized Theta Attachment:
Every principle of the Syntax attempts to be maximally satisfied at every point during processing. (Pritchett, 1992: 138)

Although the name of (7) contains *theta attachment*, Pritchett notes that this heuristic should be understood in the sense that the parser attempts to maximally satisfy all syntactic principles. Furthermore, I propose a condition applicable to reinterpretations in (8):

(8) Unconscious Reinterpretation Condition (UREC)
It is impossible for the human parser to associate a syntactic object X with α, if there is β such that α is similar to β and β is closer to X than α is.

"Similar" and "closer" are defined in (9) and (10), respectively:

(9) α is similar to β iff
a. α, β, and X are non-distinct in terms of categorial features (i.e., syntactic categories) and Case features (e.g., nominative, accusative), or
b. both α and β are potential modifiees of X.[9]

(10) Suppose that X c-commands α and β. Then, β is closer to X than α is iff
a. β contains α, or
b. β c-commands α unless every phase (i.e., *v*P, CP) containing α contains β,[10] or

[4] See also Ackema and Neeleman (2002).

[5] In Kamada (2009), I demonstrate that the licensing condition in (5) is applicable to English Rightward Movement constructions (ERMC) as well and account for island effects in ERMCs in terms of language processing.

[6] *C-command* is defined as (i) based on *contain* as defined in (ii) (see Chomsky, 2001: 116):
(i) X c-commands Y if X is a sister of K that contains Y, where K may or may not be Y, (ii) K contains Y if K immediately contains Y or immediately contains L that contains Y.

[7] α and β share properties including theta-roles and semantic features unless semantic conflicts occur.

[8] α is non-distinct from β as long as they do not refer to different persons, things, or events. Hence, α can be construed as an argument even if it is non-referential (see footnote 15).

[9] The problem of giving a precise formulation of *potential modifiees* will be left to future research.

[10] The conditional clause in (10b) makes it difficult to unify the three relations in terms of a path between a PVE and the

c. otherwise (i.e., if β neither contains nor c-commands α), a path between β and X is shorter than the one between α and X.

To put it in another way, the UREC states that attempts can be made to associate X with α without conscious efforts (i.e., in a low-cost manner) until an appropriate interpretation is given to X unless there are competing elements such as β.

To show how the assumptions proposed above apply, I analyze the JPVC in (11).[11, 12]

(11) *Taro-ga* e_i *tabe-ta yo,* ***susi$_i$-o***
Taro-NOM eat-PAST FP, **sushi-ACC**
'Taro ate *it*$_i$, **sushi$_i$**.'

When encountering *Taro-ga* 'Taro-NOM,' the parser classifies it as a nominative Case marked NP to which no theta-role is assigned.[13] According to (7), to maximally satisfy syntactic principles (e.g., the theta-criterion), *Taro-ga* is kept in storage (i.e., left unattached to anything) until a theta-role assigner (i.e., a predicate) is encountered; otherwise, the theta criterion would not be locally satisfied.[14]

When encountering the verb *tabe-ta* 'ate,' the parser identifies it as a verb that has two theta-roles. To maximally satisfy syntactic principles, the parser postulates a gap as a null argument (i.e., object) while at the same time integrating *Taro-ga* as an argument so that *Taro-ga* can receive a theta-role from the verb.[15, 16] The postulated null object is also assigned a theta-role such as an overt counterpart. Then, *yo* 'COMP' is encountered, and C and TP are merged.[17] The parser thus contains a structure like (12).

(12)

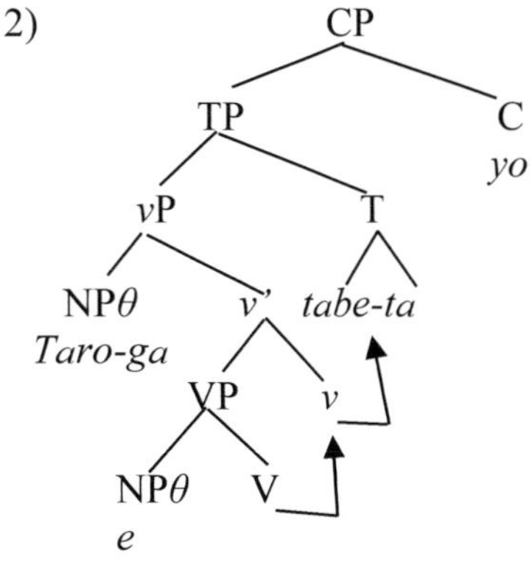

When *susi-o* 'sushi-ACC' is encountered, it is identified as an NP that has no theta-role assigned. However, it is impossible to make a structural reanalysis such that the PVE can receive a theta-role. Otherwise, word order would be rearranged. Thus, the NP is adjoined to a root CP, and the licensing condition in (5) subsequently attempts to apply in order to assure that the PVE can be licensed. The final parse tree is given in (13).

---

relevant element. I will later give evidence for the necessity of this condition (see (24)).

[11] It is assumed that in Japanese, nominative Case checking should be done in the specifier of *v*P without movement to the specifier of TP (see Fukui, 1995; Kuroda, 1992). That is, a subject does not move to the specifier position of TP unless T has an EPP feature (cf. Miyagawa, 2001).

[12] Here, I assume that T (=Tense) must be amalgamated with V at the Interfaces.

[13] For convenience, I take only the theta-theory into consideration.

[14] In accordance with a head-driven parsing strategy, T in Japanese should not appear in the parse tree until a predicate is encountered.

[15] The theta-theoretic principle: External Merge in theta-position is required of (and restricted to) arguments.
Adapted from Chomsky (2000: 103)

[16] It is not appropriate to assume that null arguments are *pro*. One of the reasons is that non-referential NPs such as idiom chunks can appear in postverbal position:

(i) *Taro-wa e nage-ta yo,* ***saji-o***
Taro-TOP throw-PAST FP **spoon-ACC**
'Taro gave up.' [Lit. 'Taro threw a spoon.']

The idiom chunk *saji* cannot be the antecedent of an overt pronoun *sore* 'it,' as shown below:

(ii) **Taro-wa saji-o nage-ta kedo Hanako wa*
Taro-TOP spoon-ACC throw-PAST but Hanako-TOP
sore-o nage-nakat-ta.
it-ACC throw-NEG-PAST
'Taro gave up but Hanako did not give up.'

Example (i) would hence be unacceptable in the idiomatic reading if the null argument *e* were *pro*. The idiomatic interpretation, however, is available in (i). Accordingly, *pro* in (i) is inappropriate (pace Tanaka, 2001; Soshi & Hagiwara, 2004). Here, I assume that *e* is an underspecified null argument in the sense that it has no inherently specified features such as [+pronominal].

It may be worth mentioning, in passing, that as one of the reviewers claims, the displacement of idiom chunks of the sort in (i) is usually evidence for movement because idioms are often assumed to be treated as non-compositional. However, I follow Nunberg, Sag and Wasow (1994) in arguing that idioms should be treated as compositional, i.e., an idiomatic meaning is composed from idiomatic interpretations of the parts of an idiom. For a detailed discussion, see Kamada (2009, chapter 4).

[17] The parse tree in (12) is the same as that of a normal sentence which ends with the final particle, as shown in (i).

(i) [$_{CP}$ [$_{TP}$ [$_{vP}$ *Taro-ga* [$_{VP}$ *e tabe-ta*]]] *yo*]
Taro-NOM eat-PAST FP

(13)

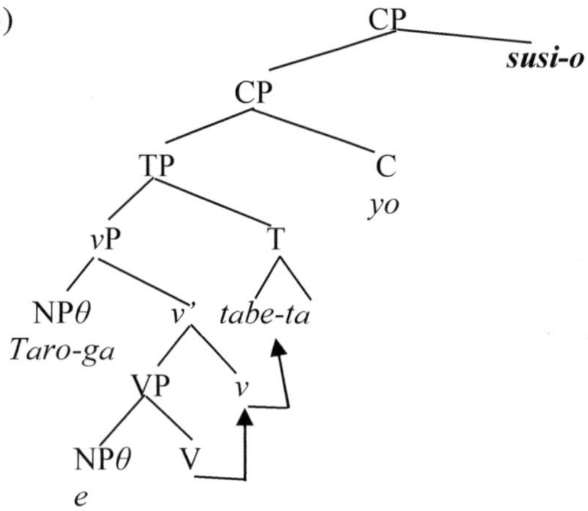

In (13), *susi-o* c-commands *e* and it is non-distinct from *e* in terms of Case features. The PVE can hence be associated with *e*, and thus it is licensed, because in (13), there is no element corresponding to β in (8). Furthermore, according to the interpretive rules in (6), the PVE may be construed as if it is an argument of the verb *tabe-ta* 'ate' because it is non-distinct from *e* in terms of referentiality.[18]

3. The Island Effect[19]

In light of the UREC in (8), it is now possible to consider the island effect observed in the JPVC. For convenience, I will describe island effects according to the structural relation between α, the potential associate and β, a potential intervener, in (8) which is divided into three types in (10). That is, Type I: β contains α; Type II: β c-commands α; and Type III: β neither contains nor c-commands α.

3.1 Type I: β containing α

I will begin with the type shown in (10a). Let us consider the example in (14) where a phrase containing a null argument is non-distinct, in the sense of (9a), from the PVE which is expected to be associated with the null argument.[20]

(14) *?[$_{NP}$ [$_{CP}$ [e_i *sonkeisiteiru*] *sensei*]-*ga*
respect teacher-NOM
fueteimasu yo, ***gakuseitati-ga***$_i$. (=(2))
increase FP **students-NOM**
'The number of the teachers who *they*$_i$ respect is increasing, **students**$_i$.'

In (14), the matrix subject is the complex NP [$_{NP}$ [$_{CP}$ [*e sonkeisiteiru*] *sensei*]-*ga*, which has nominative Case as well as contains a null argument. The nominative Case marked postverbal NP *gakuseitati-ga* 'students-NOM' c-commands the null argument and they are non-distinct with respect to Case features (see (5)). According to the UREC in (8), however, the complex NP has priority over the null argument for association with the PVE, because the complex NP contains the null argument and they are non-distinct in terms of categorial features and Case features. That is, the parser cannot associate the PVE with the null argument. Example (14a) is thus unacceptable.

3.2 Type II: β c-commanding α

I will now turn to the case of (10b) in which the association of a PVE with a null subject inside a complex NP is blocked by an element c-commanding the null subject.[21]

(15) &[$_{NP}$[$_{CP}$ e_i *Tanaka sensei-o sonkeisiteiru*
Tanaka teacher-ACC respect
toiu] *uwasa*]-*o sitteiru yo,* ***Taro$_i$-ga.***
COMP rumor-ACC (I) know FP **Taro-NOM**
'(I) know the rumor that *he*$_i$ respects Mr. Tanaka, **Taro**$_i$.'

In (15), when the verb *sonkeisiteiru* 'respect' is encountered, a null subject is postulated, and

[18] There is no way in my proposed analysis to exclude examples such as (i):

(i) *e_i Kokoni ki-ta yo, **Taro$_i$-o.**
here came FP **Taro-ACC**
'Taro came here.'
Cf. e_i Kokoni ki-ta yo, **Taro$_i$-ga.**
here came FP **Taro-NOM**

In (i), the verb *kita* 'came' is an intransitive verb and an accusative Case marked NP *Taro-o* ''Taro-ACC'' appears in postverbal position. The licensing condition would allow *Taro-o* to be associated with a null argument *e* in subject position because they are non-distinct in terms of Case features, and *Taro-o* would thus be licensed. Then, following the interpretive rules, *Taro* would share properties with the null argument, and hence the example would have the reading that *Taro came*. This, however, is contrary to fact. This problem seems to come from the assumption that the Case features of null arguments should be uninterpretable. If Case features in Japanese were interpretable whether or not they are morphologically realized, this problem would be dissolved. This possibility should be explored in future research.

[19] For more details and many more examples, see Kamada (2009).

[20] *? indicates relatively unacceptable examples.

[21] & indicates that a PVE is associated with a wrong element, resulting in a different interpretation from what is intended.

subsequently the null subject and *Tanaka sensei-o* 'Mr. Tanaka-ACC' have theta-roles assigned, respectively. On reaching *toiu* 'COMP', the parser reanalyzes the main clause as an embedded clause, and hence keeps it in storage until a theta-role assigner appears. When *uwasa*-o 'rumor-ACC' is encountered, it is merged to the embedded clause, creating a complex NP. The complex NP does not have a theta-role, and therefore it is kept in storage. As soon as the parser encounters the matrix verb *sitteiru* 'know,' it postulates a null argument as a matrix subject. Then, the null matrix subject and the stored complex NP are integrated and theta-roles are assigned. Afterwards, the final particle *yo* is merged with the matrix TP, and the postverbal NP is adjoined to the root CP. The final parse tree is informally represented in (16).

(16)

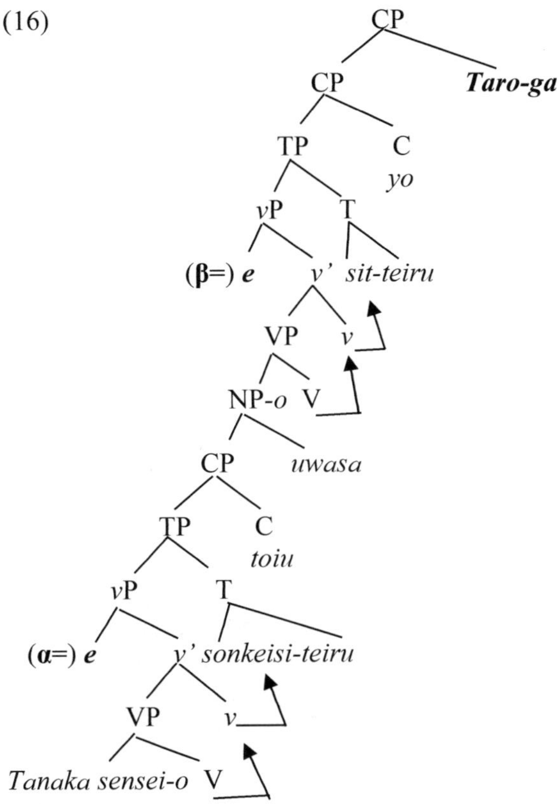

In (16), the null subject *e* (=β) in the main clause c-commands the null subject *e* (=α) in the embedded clause. They are non-distinct in terms of Case features. Thus, the matrix subject has priority over the embedded counterpart for association with the PVE. Therefore, (15) would have the reading that *Taro knows the rumor that someone respects Mr. Tanaka*, which is different from what is expected.

3.3 Type III: β neither containing nor c-commanding α

Let us then consider the type shown in (10c) (i.e., the case where β neither contains nor c-commands α). Observe (17), where the PVE has an accusative Case, the matrix subject is a complex NP containing a null object, and the matrix object appears in the initial position of a sentence by undergoing the operation of scrambling.

(17) & *Minna-o* [NP[CP *Taro-ga* e_i *sonkeisiteiru*
Everyone-ACC Tar -NOM respect
toiu] *uwasa*]-*ga* *odorokaseta yo,*
Comp rumor -NOM surprised FP
Tanaka ***sensei$_i$-o***.
Tanaka **teacher-ACC**
'The rumor that Taro respects *him$_i$* surprised everyone, **Mr. Tanaka$_i$**.'

In (17), when the embedded verb *sonkeisiteiru* 'respect' is encountered, the parser incorrectly analyzes *minna-o* 'everyone-ACC' and *Taro-ga* 'Taro-NOM' as arguments of the embedded clause verb. The parse tree at this point thus contains no null arguments. *Minna-o* should also be construed as a scrambled element.

On reaching *toiu* 'COMP,' the parser amends the main clause analysis such that the clause can be assigned a theta-role, and thereby the clause is kept in storage until a theta-role assigner appears.

When encountered, the theta-role assigner *uwasa-ga* 'rumor-NOM' is merged to the stored clause, and assigns the clause a theta-role. Thus, the complex NP is created. However, the complex NP has no theta-role at this stage, and hence it is stored.

When reaching a matrix verb, the parser postulates a null object as an argument of the matrix verb, and subsequently integrates both the null object and the complex NP to the matrix verb, so that both of them can be assigned theta-roles.

As soon as the postverbal NP is attached to a root CP, the licensing condition attempts to apply in order to guarantee that the postverbal NP is licensed. The parse tree at this point is illustrated in (18). There, the PVE *Tanaka sensei-o* 'Mr. Tanaka-ACC' fails to be associated with the embedded object t_I (=α), which is incorrectly analyzed as the trace of the scrambled object *minna-o* 'everyone-ACC.' Furthermore, the null object *e* (=β) of the matrix verb is closer to the PVE than any other element non-distinct from it.

The matrix object hence takes precedence over such elements for association with the PVE. The alternative analysis would reattach *minna-o* to the matrix TP as a scrambled element. This reanalysis, however, is costly. The PVE in the above example is hence difficult to associate with the null object within the complex NP.

(18)

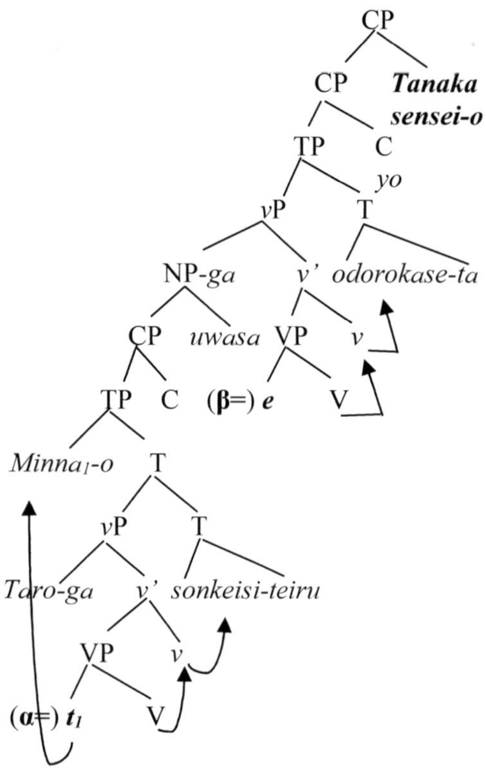

I will turn to another example in which an incorrect syntactic-analysis leads to the wrong association. Consider the sentence in (19).[22]

(19) *? *Hanako-ga* [NP[CP *Taro-ga* *e*$_i$
Hanako-NOM Taro-NOM
sonkeisiteiru toiu] *uwasa*]-*o*
respect COMP rumor- ACC
sitteiru yo, ***Tanaka sensei***$_i$***-o.***
know FP **Tanaka teacher-ACC**
'Hanako knows the rumor that Taro respects *him*$_i$, **Mr. Tanaka**$_i$.'

[22] The example in (i) is unacceptable, probably because the complex NP containing a null argument has the same type of Case as the PVE:

(i) *? *Hanako-wa* [NP[CP *Taro-ga* *e*$_i$ *sonkeisiteiru toiu*]
Hanako-TOP Taro-NOM respect COMP
uwasa]-*o sitteiru yo,* ***Tanaka sensei***$_i$***-o***
rumor-ACC know FP **Tanaka teacher-ACC**
'Hanako knows the rumor that Taro respects *him*$_i$, **Mr. Tanaka**$_i$.'

In (19), *Hanako-ga* 'Hanako-NOM' is incorrectly analyzed as an element in the embedded clause. In other words, *Hanako-ga* is construed as an argument of *sonkeisiteiru* 'respect.' Thus, there are no appropriate elements with which the PVE can be associated. That is, the PVE is difficult to associate with the null object in the embedded clause.

4. The Absence of the Island Effect

In this section, I will discuss acceptable examples where PVEs can be associated with null arguments that are contained embedded clauses such as complement clauses and relative clauses. These examples are grouped into three types as listed below:

Type A: Phrases containing null arguments are different from PVEs with respect to categorial features.
Type B: Phrases containing null arguments are different from PVEs with respect to Case features.
Type C: Phrases containing null arguments are different from PVEs with respect to both categorial features and Case features.

These three types will be presented in turn.

4.1 Type A: Different Categorial Features

I will first consider Type A: phrases containing null arguments that are different from PVEs with respect to categorial features.

(20) [CP *e*$_i$ *Tanaka sensei-o* *sonkeisiteiru*
Tanaka teacher-ACC respect
koto]-*ga* *hontoo dat-ta yo,* ***Taro***$_i$***-ga.***
COMP -NOM true was FP **Taro**$_i$**-NOM**
'That *he*$_i$ respect Mr. Tanaka was true, **Taro**$_i$.'

In (20), a nominative Case marked NP *Taro-ga* 'Taro-NOM' appears in postverbal position. It is different in terms of categorial features from the clause [CP *Tanaka sensei-o sonkeisiteiru koto*]-*ga* '[that *e* respect Mr. Tanaka]-NOM,' which contains a null argument. That is, the clause is not similar to the null argument in the sense of (9). Thus, the clause does not prevent the PVE from being associated with the null argument, and hence (20) is acceptable.

4.2 Type B: Different Case Features

Next, I will consider Type B: phrases containing null arguments that are different from PVEs with respect to Case features.

Let us look at the examples in (21).

(21) [NP [CP e_i *Sonkeisiteiru*] *gakuseitati*]-*ga*
respect students -NOM
fueteimasu yo, ***Tanaka sensei-o***$_i$. (=(3))
increase FP Tanaka teacher-ACC
'The number of the students who respect *him*$_i$ is increasing, **Mr. Tanaka**$_i$.'

In (21), an accusative Case marked NP *Tanaka sensei-o* 'Mr. Tanaka-ACC' appears in postverbal position. It is different in terms of Case features from the complex NP [NP [CP *Sonkeisiteiru*] *gakuseitati*]-*ga* '[the students who respect *e*]-NOM' which contains a null argument. In other words, the complex NP is not similar to the null argument in the sense of (9). Thus, the complex NP does not block the PVE from being associated with the null argument, and hence (21) is acceptable.[23]

4.3 Type C: Different Categorial and Case Features

Now let us turn to Type C. Observe the example in (22).

(22) [CP *Taro-ga* e_i *sonkeisiteiru koto*]-*ga*
Taro-NOM respect Comp -NOM
hontoo dat-ta yo, ***Tanaka sensei***$_i$***-o***
true was FP **Tanaka teacher-ACC**
'That Taro respects *him*$_i$ was true, **Mr. Tanaka**$_i$.'

In (22), an accusative Case marked NP *Tanaka sensei-o* 'Mr. Tanaka-ACC' appears in postverbal position. The PVE is different from the clause [*Taro-ga sonkeisiteiru koto*]-*ga* '[Taro respects *e*]-NOM' which contains a null argument with respect to not only categorial features but also Case features. Hence, the clause is not similar to the null argument in the sense of (9), resulting in failure to block the association of the PVE with the null argument. Thus, (22) is acceptable.

5. Postverbal Adjuncts

In this section, I will deal with the case where adjuncts appear in postverbal position. Let us consider the example in (23) that displays island effects.

(23) &[*Shushou-ga kinoo at-ta*
Prime minister-Nom yesterday met with
josei]-*o mitanda yo,* ***Shinbashino-no***
woman-Acc saw FP **Shinbashi -Gen**
ryoutei-de.
Japanese-style restaurant at
'(I) saw the woman whom [the prime minister met with **at a Japanese-style restaurant in Shinbashi** yesterday].'
(Soshi and Hagiwara (2004: 423))

In (23), after encountering the postverbal PP, the parser realizes that there are no following elements, and it then starts to associate the PVE with a modifiee. The matrix verb *mita* 'saw' can be modified by the locative PP, and it also contains the complex NP that includes the other verb *atta* 'met with;' hence, the matrix verb is chosen as a modifiee over the embedded one. In other words, the postverbal locative PP is difficult to associate with the verb *at-ta* 'met with' within the relative clause.

Finally, I discuss the case where evidence is given for the necessity of the conditional clause in (10b). Let us consider the example in (24) where, although a subject asymmetrically c-commands an object, the former has no priority over the latter for association (see footnote 10):

(24) *Kyooju-ga kuruma-o kat-ta yo,*
Professor-NOM car -ACC bought FP,
yuumei-na
well-known
'A professor bought a car, **well-known**.'

Example (24) has two readings: the postverbal adjective *yuumei-na* 'well-known' may modify *kyooju-ga* 'professor-NOM' or *kuruma-o* 'car-ACC'. This ambiguity can be derived from the UREC in (8). That is, the subject does not block

---

[23] The example in (i) is less acceptable than that in (21) although the postverbal phrase is different from the complex NP that contains a null argument in terms of Case features:

(i) *? John-ga [NP[CPMary-ga e_i age-ta] hon]-o nusunda
John-NOM Mary-NOM gave book-ACC stole
yo, **Bill**$_i$**-ni**.
FP **Bill-DAT**
'John stole a book that Mary gave to him$_i$, **to Bill**$_i$.'

The reason that (i) is unacceptable may be that an NP marked with a dative particle *ni* is likely to be analyzed as a locative PP, and that *Bill-ni* 'Bill-DAT' is interpreted as a potential modifier of the matrix predicate.

the association between the object and the PVE because the subject is contained in every phase (i.e., *v*P) that contains the object (note that *kyooju-ga* occupies the specifier position of *v*P). Hence, *yuumei-na* may be associated with both arguments without conscious efforts. This account is further supported by the following unambiguous example in (25).

(25) *Kuruma$_i$-o kyooju-ga t_i kat-ta yo,*
car- ACC Professor-Nom bought FP,
yuumei-na
well-known
'A car$_i$, a professor bought t_i, **well-known**.'

In (25), the object *kuruma-o* 'car-ACC' is moved to the specifier position of TP by scrambling. The scrambled NP c-commands *kyooju-ga* 'professor-NOM,' and is not contained in every phase that contains *kyooju-ga*. Hence, *kuruma-o* has priority over *kyooju-ga* for association with the PVE *yuumei-na*, resulting in the absence of ambiguity.

6. Conclusion

In this paper, I first proposed that the PVE is adjoined to a CP via External Merge given the assumption that the derivation of the JPVC involves no movement. Then, I demonstrated that the presence or absence of the island effect observed in the JPVC can be accounted for in terms of the interaction of the licensing condition with the parsing strategies I have proposed/adopted here. This analysis suggested that the human parser should undertake explanations of part of the output of the competence system.

Acknowledgments

An earlier version of this paper was read at the 27th meeting of the Sophia University Linguistic Society held at Sophia University, Tokyo on July 21, 2012. I would like to thank the participants in the meeting as well as the three PACLIC 27 reviewers for their comments.

References

Abe, Jun. 2004. On Directionality of Movement: A Case of Japanese Right Dislocation. *Proceedings of the 58th Conference, The Tohoku English Lieteracy Society*: 54-61.

Ackema, Peter and Ad Neeleman. 2002. Effects of Short-Term Storage in Processing Rightward Movement. In Sieb Nooteboom, Fred Weerman and Frank Wijnen (eds.), *Storage and Computation in the Language Faculty* (*Studies in Theoretical Psycholinguistics*). Dordrecht: Kluwer. pp. 219-256.

Chomsky, Noam. 2000. Minimalist Inquiries: The Framework. In Martin, Roger, David Michaels and Juan Uriagereka (eds.), *Step by Step: Essays on Minimalist Syntax in Honor of Howard Lasnik*. Cambridge, Mass.: MIT Press. pp. 89-155.

Chomsky, Noam. 2001. Derivation by Phase. In Michael Kenstowicz, (ed.), *Ken Hale: A life in language*. Cambridge, Mass: MIT Press. pp. 1-52.

Endo, Simon, Mutsuko. 1989. *An analysis of the postposing construction in Japanese,* PhD Thesis, the University of Michigan.

Fukui, Naoki. 1995. *Theory of Projection in Syntax*. California: CSLI.

Kaiser, Lizanne. 1999. Representing the Structure-Discourse Iconicity of the Japanese Post-Verbal Construction. In Darnell, Michael, Edith Moravcsik, Frederic Newmeyer, Michael Noonan, and Kathleen Wheatley (eds.), *Functionalism and Formalism in Linguistics, Volume II: Case Studies.* Amsterdam: John Benjamins Publishing Company. pp. 107-129.

Kamada, Kohji. 2009. *Rightward Movement Phenomena in Human Language*, PhD Thesis, the University of Edinburgh.

Kuroda, Shigeyuki. 1992. *Japanese Syntax and Semantics, Collected Papers*. Dordrecht: Kluwer Academic Publishers.

Miyagawa, Shigeru. 2001. The EPP, Scrambling, and Wh-in-Situ. In Michael Kenstowicz (ed.), *Ken Hale: A life in language*. Cambridge, Mass: MIT Press. pp. 293-338.

Nunberg, Geoffrey, Ivan A. Sag and Thomas Wasow. 1994. Idioms. *Language*, 70(3): 491-538.

Pritchett, Bradley. 1992. *Grammatical Competence and Parsing Performance*, Chicago: University of Chicago Press.

Soshi, Takahiro and Hiroko Hagiwara. 2004. Asymmetry in Linguistic Dependency: Linguistic and Psychophysiological Studies of Japanese Right Dislocation. *English Lingusitics*, 21(2): 409-453.

Tanaka, Hidekazu. 2001. Right-Dislocation as scrambling. *Journal of Linguistics*, 37: 551-579.

Whitman, John. 2000. Right Dislocation in English and Japanese. In Ken-ichi Takami, Akio Kamio and John Whitman (eds.), *Syntactic and Functional Explorations in Honor of Susumu Kuno.* Tokyo: Kurosio Publishers. pp. 445-470.

Evaluation of Corpus-Assisted Spanish Learning

Hui-Chuan Lu
FLLD, NCKU / No. 1 University Road
701 Tainan, Taiwan
huichuanlu1@gmail.com

Yu-Hsin Chu
FLLD, NCKU / No. 1 University Road
701 Tainan, Taiwan
katy0806@gmail.com

Abstract

In the development of corpus linguistics, the creation of corpora has had a critical role in corpus-based studies. The majority of created corpora have been associated with English and native languages, while other languages and types of corpora have received relatively less attention. Because an increasing number of corpora have been constructed, and each corpus is constructed for a definite purpose, this study identifies the functions of corpora and combines the values of various types of corpora for auto-learning based on the existing corpora. Specifically, the following three corpora are adopted: (a) the *Corpus of Spanish*; (b) the *Corpus of Taiwanese Learners of Spanish*; and (c) the *Parallel Corpus of Spanish, English, and Chinese*. These corpora represent a type of native, learner, and parallel language, respectively. We apply these corpora as auxiliary resources to identify the advantages of applying various types of corpora in language learning from a learner's perspective. In the environment of auto-learning, 28 participants completed frequency questions related to semantic and lexical aspects. After analyzing the questionnaire data, we obtained the following findings: (a) the native corpus requires a more advanced level of Spanish proficiency to manage ampler and deeper context; (b) the learners' corpus facilitates the distinction between error and correction during the learning process; (c) the parallel corpus assists learners in connecting form and meaning; (d) learning is more efficient if the learner can capitalizes on specific functions provided by various corpora in the application order of parallel, learner and native corpora.

1 Introduction

The trend of using corpus has expanded into all sub-areas of linguistics, including applied fields such as foreign language teaching and learning. According to Lee (2010), almost 360 corpora have been constructed for various purposes in 57 languages. Sixty-three percent of these corpora have been analyzed in previous research on language analysis and English teaching. In the past decade, the majority of corpus users have been researchers and teachers. Therefore, we are interested in extending the usage of corpus to foreign language learners, and studying how the perspective of corpus application can benefit these learners. Moreover, instead of English, we have selected Spanish as the target language of this research because the popularity of second foreign language acquisition is increasing in Taiwan, and multilingualism has become a novel research topic in applied linguistics.

Among the related literature, the application of existing corpora in teaching or learning has focused primarily on native corpus. Moreover, although there have been several studies on parallel corpus, very few have examined learners' corpus. The reason that less attention has been drawn to the evaluation of effectiveness might be attributable to the lack of access to parallel and learners' corpora. Moreover, to our knowledge, no study has compared the various types of corpora. The discussed reasons have motivated us to conduct this research. This study examines the advantages and disadvantages of the three types of corpora from the learners' perspective, and applies them complementarily to maximize the learning outcomes.

By applying extant sources, language learners can learn how to apply created corpora for the self-learning of foreign languages. As the final goal, we hope that learners can capitalize on the complementary merits of various types of corpora to achieve the best results, and maximize the efficiency of their learning through the application of information technology.

2 Literature review

With the era of information technology, the corpus approach has developed rapidly over the past four decades. The first milestone of corpus research can be traced back to Kucera and Francis (1967). They constructed the Brown Corpus, which comprised one million words of modern American English. Thereafter, the interest in the study of corpus linguistics has increased over time. Kennedy (1998) stated that the corpus approach has been employed for linguistic analyses by collecting and organizing data. According to the sub-database of Proquest, *Linguistics and Language Behavior Abstracts* (*LLBA*) had exhibited an increasing publication rate from 1970 to 2010. For example, we entered "corpus" as keyword to obtain the distribution of publications during the 1970s (588 publications), 1980s (1,365 publications), 1990s (4,452 publications), and 2000s (10,886 publications). Lee (2010) indicated that the various corpus types include diachronic, contemporary, native, learner, specialized, web, monolingual, multilingual, parallel, spoken and annotated, and multimedia corpora, among others.

Focusing on the target language of Spanish, *Reference Corpus of Current Spanish* and *Corpus of Spanish* are two well-known Spanish corpora of Hispanic native speakers. Howe and Ranson (2010) and Lavid, Arús, and Zamorano-Mansilla (2010) applied native corpus by extracting and analyzing the data from both of these corpora for different linguistic purposes. Howe and Ranson (2010) analyzed temporal modifiers in Spanish, whereas Zamorano–Mansilla (2010) contrasted Spanish grammar usage with English. Although previous studies have utilized existing corpora for research; investigations on the application of corpus to facilitate language learning are scarce. Therefore, we selected *Corpus of Spanish* because it has rich data and offers powerful search functions, as one of the linguistic resource to evaluate the effectiveness of using this corpus for assisting learning.

Different from native corpus as *Corpus of Spanish*, the learners' corpus, which is the collection of production of foreign language learners has its distinguished characteristics. Granger, Kraif, Ponton, Antoniadis, and Zampa (2007) indicated the help of error-tagged learners' corpora in both teaching and learning languages. Gilquin, Granger, and Paquot (2007) emphasized the importance of learners' corpora in English for academic writing purposes. A variety of data can be drawn from learners' corpus to discover leaner-specific patterns such as lexical, grammatical, wording and reliance, etc. Teachers and researchers can identify the tendency of the language usage of learners through corpus. Mukherjee (2008) showed that learners should take advantage of the resources of the learners' corpora. Dalziel and Helm (2008) indicated that the learners' corpora can guide learners through self-inquiry. These studies confirmed the positive value of utilizing the learners' corpora. However, few empirical studies have provided concrete evidence to prove its effectiveness in assisting learning. *L2 Spanish Written Corpus* and *Spanish Learner Language Oral Corpora* are representative of two learners' corpora of Spanish. Both collected data from learners whose native language is English. However, the *L2 Spanish Written Corpus* is not available to the public, whereas *Spanish Learner Language Oral Corpora* only contains spoken data. Therefore, we applied our constructed learners' corpus to research taking the learners' background and resource availability into consideration.

Moreover, using parallel corpus as a reference database is beneficial for contrastive analysis, translation study and language learning (Baker, 1993; Malmkjaer, 2005). Zhang, Wu, Gao and Vines (2006) suggested that parallel corpora can be used for various purposes, such as cross-language information retrieval, and data-driven natural language processing systems. Because Spanish is the target language and Chinese as the first language of our learners, we required a parallel corpus containing Spanish and Chinese. Although Spanish–English or English–Chinese parallel corpora could be found, we could not locate a Spanish–Chinese parallel corpus for us to employ before we dedicated to its construction.

Consequently, in this paper, besides (a) the *Corpus of Spanish*, we introduce (b) the *Corpus of Taiwanese Learners of Spanish*, and (c) the *Parallel Corpus of Spanish, English and Chinese*. Furthermore, we compare the effectiveness of their utilization as assistant resource for language learning. By investigating various types of corpora, this study answers the following research questions: (a) by comparing three types of corpora, what are the advantages and disadvantages of each corpus from the users' point of view? (b) by combining three types of corpora, how do they complement each other to obtain the optimum learning result?

3 Methodology

3.1 Participants

Twenty-eight Taiwanese learners of Spanish who studied in the Department of Foreign Languages and Literature participated in the survey. Their mother tongue is Chinese, and English and Spanish were learned as their first and second foreign languages, respectively. They learned Spanish in a classroom for 300 to 400 hours, and *Dos Mundos* was used as the textbook for learning Spanish in a classroom environment. The Wisconsin Placement Test was administered to identify the Spanish proficiency level of all participants. Table 1 shows the characteristics of the participants.

	Type			
Year	Third year		Forth year	
	20 (71%)		8 (29%)	
Sex	Female		Male	
	23 (82%)		5 (18%)	
Profic	1	2	3	4
.level	0 (0%)	19 (68%)	8 (29%)	1 (3%)

Table 1. Characteristics of Participants.

3.2 Instruments

The following three corpora were adopted as assisting resources; (a) the *Corpus of Spanish*, (b) the *Corpus of Taiwanese Learners of Spanish* and (c) the *Parallel Corpus of Spanish, English, and Chinese*; that represent a type of native, learners and parallel language, respectively. The first one was created by Mark Davies of BYU, and the other two were constructed by the National Cheng Kung University (NCKU) team in Taiwan.

The *Corpus of Spanish* ("Corpus del Español" in Spanish, CdE) comprises 100 million words. The powerful search functions of the corpus such as lemma and collocation surpass other available native corpora of Spanish. We set data of the year 1900 as our source for users' searches to obtain more contemporary data.

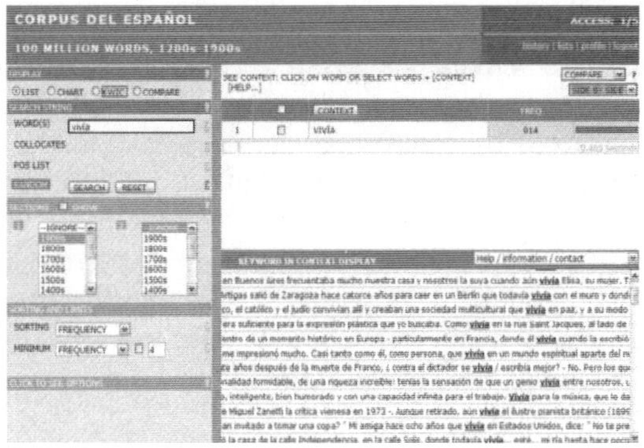

Figure 1. The Interface of CdE.

The second corpus is the *Written Corpus of Taiwanese Learners of Spanish* ("Corpus Escrito de Aprendices Taiwaneses de Español", CEATE). It was created by the NCKU corpus team in 2005, and contains 2,425 texts, and approximately 446,694 words. It was POS-tagged and corrections were added for every error made in the learners' version. For the questionnaire, "revised compositions" were chosen as a condition set for users' searches.

Figure 2. The Interface of CEATE.

The third corpus is the *Parallel Corpus of Spanish, English, and Chinese* ("Corpus Paralelo de Español, Inglés y Chino", CPEIC). It was constructed by the NCKU corpus team in 2012. A tri-lingual parallel corpus contains written data from the Bible and various fairy tales, with 755,461 words in Spanish, 794,571 words in Engish, and 923,509 words in Chinese. Data of Spanish, English, and Chinese were individually POS-tagged and word-aligned among these three languages. Searches can be conducted by setting single or multiple keywords of various languages, and their part of speech. From the search result, it can be observed that the syntactic and lexical contrasts of parallel meanings among them.

Figure 3. The Interface of CPEIC.

3.3 Exercise and evaluation

To ensure that participants were familiar with the search functions of various corpora, they practiced with an exercise prior to the formal evaluation. In the exercise, participants were required to do at home a similar practice (Appendix A) in which eight pairs of words were listed to be differentiated and selected according to their frequency of usage. These questions can be classified into the following two groups: (a) past tense, preterit or imperfect: *vivió/vivía* \`lived´, *comió/comía* \`ate´, *preguntó/preguntaba* \`asked´, *murió/moría* \`died´; and (b) copular verbs SER or ESTAR ´to be´ with the adjectives: *ser/estar possible* ´to be possible´, *ser/estar feliz* \`to be happy´, *ser/estar limpio* \`to be clean´, *ser/estar enamorado* \`to fall in love´. Finally, the participants needed to evaluate different corpora in a questionnaire with open questions after experiencing the practice process for each question.

One week later, in the classroom, participants were limited to 45 minutes to finish evaluating these corpora through searching seven pairs of words that appeared in the formal evaluation. As those questions listed in the exercise, these questions were grouped into two categories: (a) past tense: *hubo/había* \`there was´ + *N*, *fui/iba a* + *destino* \`went to + destination´, *dijo/decía* \`said´, *llegó/llegaba* \`arrived´; and (b) copular verbs SER or ESTAR ´to be´ with adjectives: *ser/estar conveniente* \`to be convenient´, *ser/estar seguro* \`to be sure´, *ser/estar contento* \`to be glad´. Upon completion, the survey participants were asked to evaluate three corpora by contrasting their advantages and disadvantages.

The pairs of words used in this exercise and the formal evaluation were selected based on the frequency of search result from *Corpus of Spanish*. Two specific categories, past tense and copular verb, were included in the exercise and evaluation because both are difficult for learners to distinguish the two similar elements of each pair according to our teaching experience. Moreover, a contrast exists among the three languages; that is, there are two copular verbs (SER/ESTAR) in Spanish, one (BE) in English, and none in Chinese. The same occurs for past tense. Two (preterit and imperfect) in Spanish, one in English, and zero in Chinese. And these three languages are target language (L3), first foreign language (L2) and mother language (L1) of our participants respectively.

Compared with English learners, the number of Spanish learners is relatively less in Taiwan. Moreover, a complete exercise and training program for using the corpus tools should be addressed to participants before the formal evaluation. Furthermore, although only seven or eight questions were listed in the exercise and the formal evaluation, each question took a participant at least five minutes to complete the search activity, fill the result, and write down the user experience.. Hence, considering these limitations, we only had two Spanish classes with a total number of 28 students from the same university for this preliminary study of evaluation work covering only two Spanish grammatical categories.

4 Results and discussion

4.1 Exercise and evaluation

Tables 2 and 3 show the search results and user satisfaction, respectively.

Q	CdE	CEATE	CPEIC
	indefinido/imperfecto		
1	*había* (100%)	*había* (96%)	*había* (53%)
2	*iba* (77%)	*fui* (100%)	*iba* (67%)
3	*dijo* (100%)	*dijo* (100%)	*dijo* (86%)
4	*llegó* (100%)	*llegó* (100%)	*llegó* (79%)
	SER/ESTAR		
5	*Ser* (100%)	*Ser* (100%)	*Ser* (100%)
6	*estar* (96%)	*ser* (100%)	*estar* (100%)
7	*estar* (100%)	*estar* (100%)	*estar* (100%)

Table 2. Search Results of Frequency.

The search result for the frequency shown in Table 2 indicates the inclination of high frequency usage in two related elements of one pair. From this table, we observe the similarities (Questions 1, 3, 4, 5, and 7) and differences (Questions 2 and 6) for usage inclination among the three corpora through the participants' search results. Learners' corpus seems to have different result from the other two types of corpora, the native and parallel corpora. The participants had the chance to understand that different results could be searched with distinct corpora used. Generally speaking three types of corpora would help, in different degrees, the distinction between two elements of each pair. All three corpora could provide information of sentence and paragraph levels for learners to obtain more details and lexical meanings to distinguish two elements of the same pair.

Q	CdE	CEATE	CPEIC
1	80%	92%	78%
2	75%	89%	76%
3	86%	93%	69%
4	87%	88%	83%
5	96%	100%	93%
6	90%	60%	91%
7	91%	100%	100%

Table 3. User Satisfaction.

Then, based on the search experience, the majority of participants (> 60%) consented that these three corpora, CdE, CEATE, and CPEIC, were useful in helping learners to gain linguistic knowledge, as shown in Table 3.

4.2 General evaluation

General evaluation regarding to three different types of corpora is shown in Table 4.

	Advantages	Disadvantages
CdE	* rich examples * POS and lemma tagging * frequency order	* difficult vocabulary and sentence structure
CEATE	* errors vs. correction * easy comprehension * context	* lack of diversification * insufficient examples
CPEIC	* three languages	* lack of diversification * insufficient examples * not applicable to daily usage (Bible)

Table 4. Advantages and Disadvantages of 3 Corpora.

To answer research Question 1, we discuss the advantages and disadvantages of each corpus. Through various powerful search functions, CdE provided numerous systematic examples for learners. However, overly complex functions and an excessive number of examples sometimes causes more difficulties and obstacles for learners.

CEATE facilitated the distinction of contrasting usages between two aspects of the past tense (preterit and imperfect) or two copular verbs (SER/ESTAR) through the errors made by students, and the correction revised by Spanish native speakers. However, limited examples could not cover the infinite possibilities of learning situations because of the arduous work of corpus creation.

CPEIC was especially helpful in distinguishing contrastive types of adjectives such as "listo" ("intelligent and ready" in English) because different meanings were clearly revealed in English and Chinese in word level with no need of going further to the sentence or paragraph level. The main problem of this corpus was related to the technical problem of correctly matching the parallel meanings among the three languages.

With respect to research Question 2, learning could be more efficient if the complementary advantages of specific functions were provided by the various corpora. The parallel corpus assisted in forming connections between form and meaning. The learners' corpus facilitated the distinction of error and correction in the learning process, and the native corpus required a more advanced level of Spanish to manage an ampler context. Therefore, the recommended order of using these three types of corpora is (1) parallel corpus, (2) learners' corpus, and (3) native corpus. Without the first two types of corpora, only more advanced learners can be benefited because the native corpus required a higher level of language knowledge.

5 Limitation and Future Works

The first limitation was related to the participants. We only had 28 Spanish language learners who participated in evaluating the three corpora. The results are not representative enough; in future studies, we plan to conduct an evaluation task with more participants to make the conclusion more valid and reliable. Moreover, our participants were from the Department of Foreign Languages, and they were enrolled at the same university. We need to expand the evaluation work to learners of multiple universities and from different levels of language proficiency, including learners in Spanish departments and other universities in Taiwan.

Second, in the environment of a computer room, when more than 20 participants worked simultaneously using the three corpora, the corpora might collapse and so intervened the search process. This situation did not occur when the exercises were conducted individually at home, or when less than 10 users were working simultaneously. A technical team is currently taking the responsibility to determine and solve the problem.

Finally, the questions listed in the exercise and formal evaluation were limited to only two types: past tense and copular verbs. Future studies should include more linguistic varieties such as various syntactic and semantic aspects for users to evaluate the general effectiveness of the three corpora.

6 Conclusion

Existing constructed corpora have contributed to corpus-based studies. Their applied value should not be restricted to only researchers or teachers. Foreign language learners should also be considered as beneficial users if they are pre-trained and familiar with instructions and functions of distinct corpora.

Various types of corpora can benefit users in learning foreign languages if they are applied in a complementary way to capitalize on the best results of various functions and purposes of existing corpora. Parallel corpus can supply the translation of parallel meanings through similarities or differences of structures and lexical expressions. Learners' corpus can offer a base to contrast the errors made by learners and corrections revised by natives to impress the learners, and the numerous examples of native corpus provide a helpful source to enrich learners' linguistic knowledge and performance.

In future studies, a greater number of participants with various language proficiencies and from different campuses should be included in such studies to make the findings more generalizable.

References

Baker, M. 1993. Corpora in translation studies: An overview and some suggestions for future research. Target, 7(2): 223-243.

Dalziel, F. and Helm, F. 2008. Exploring modality in a learner corpus of online writing. Linguistic Insights - Studies in Language and Communication, 74: 287-302.

Gilquin, G., Granger, S., and Paquot, M. 2007. Learner corpora: The missing link in EAP pedagogy. Journal of English for Academic Purposes, 6(4): 319-335.

Granger, S., Kraif, O., Ponton, C., Antoniadis, G., and Zampa, V. 2007. Integrating learner corpora and natural language processing: A crucial step towards reconciling technological sophistication and pedagogical effectiveness. ReCALL, 19(3): 252-268.

Howe, Chad and Ranson, L. D. 2010. The evolution of clausal temporal modifiers in Spanish and French. Romance Philology, 64(2): 197-207.

Kennedy, G. 1998. Introduction to Corpus Linguistics. London: Longman.

Kucera, H., and Francis, W. N. 1967. Computational analysis of present-day American English. Providence, RI: Brown University Press.

Lavid, J., Arús, J., and Zamorano-Mansilla, J. R. 2010. Systemic functional grammar of Spanish: A contrastive study with English. London: Continuum International Publishing Group.

Lee, D. 2010. Bookmarks for Corpus-based Linguists. Retrieved from http://www.uow.edu.au/~dlee/CBLLinks.htm

Malmkjaer, K. 2005. Linguistics and the language of translation. UK: Edinburgh University Press.

Mukherjee, J. 2008. English corpus linguistics and foreign language research: Line of development and perspectives. ZFF, Zeitschrift fur Fremdsprachenforschung, 19(1): 31-60.

Zhang, Y., Wu, K., Gao, J., Vines, P. 2006. Automatic acquisition of Chinese–English parallel corpus from the web. In Advances in Information Retrieval (pp. 420-431). London: Springer. doi: 10.1007/11735106_37.

CEATE, http://corpora.flld.ncku.edu.tw

CEDEL2, http://www.uam.es/proyectosinv/woslac/cedel2.htm

Corpus del Español, http://www.corpusdelespanol.org/

CPEIC, http://140.116.245.228/FW/tri_lingual_index.html

CREA, http://corpus.rae.es/creanet.html

Linguistics and Language Behavior Abstracts (LLBA) http://search.proquest.com/

SPLLOC, http://www.splloc.soton.ac.uk/

Appendices

Appendix A: Pre-training

Aplicación de 3 córpora (Frec. de uso)-preprueba

Número: Nombre:

Pregunta 1: *vivió/vivía*...

Explicación: ¿Por qué se selecciona? ¿Qué diferencia hay en el sentido o uso? Evaluación de ayuda: Sí o No ¿Cómo? ¿En qué aspecto?		
A. CdE: vivió & vivía	*vivió/vivía*	□ No □ Sí
B. CEATE: vivió & vivía	*vivió/vivía*	□ No □ Sí
C. CPEIC: vivió & vivía	*vivió/vivía*	□ No □ Sí

Pregunta 2: *comió/comía*...

Pregunta 3: *preguntó/preguntaba*...

Pregunta 4: *murió/moría*...

Pregunta 5: *ser/estar posible*...

Explicación: ¿Por qué se selecciona? ¿Qué diferencia hay en el sentido o uso? Evaluación de ayuda: Sí o No ¿Cómo? ¿En qué aspecto?		
A. CdE: [ser] posible & [estar] posible	*ser/estar*	□ No □ Sí
B. CEATE: posible	*ser/estar*	□ No □ Sí
C. CPEIC: posible	*ser/estar*	□ No □ Sí

Pregunta 6: *ser/estar feliz*...

Pregunta 7: *ser/estar limpio*...

Pregunta 8: *ser/estar enamorado*...

Appendix B: Questionnaire

Aplicación de 3 córpora (Frec. de uso)

Pregunta 1: *hubo/había + N*

Selección: Circule el que se usa con más frecuencia y tache el que no se usa. Evaluación de ayuda: ¿ayuda o no? (X vs. Y)		
A. CdE: hubo [NN*] 和 había [NN*]	*hubo/había*	□ No □ Sí
B. CEATE: hubo 和 había	*hubo/había*	□ No □ Sí
C. CPEIC: hubo 和 había	*hubo/había*	□ No □ Sí

Pregunta 2: *fui/iba a + destino*

Pregunta 3: *dijo/decía*...

Pregunta 4: *llegó/llegaba*...

A. CdE: [ser] conveniente & [estar] conveniente	*ser/estar*	□ No □ Sí
B. CEATE : conveniente	*ser/estar*	□ No □ Sí
C. CPEIC : conveniente	*ser/estar*	□ No □ Sí

Pregunta 5: *ser/estar conveniente*...

Pregunta 6: *ser/estar seguro*...

Pregunta 7: *ser/estar contento*...

Evaluación en general:

Córpora	Ventajas	Desventajas
A. CdE		
B. CEATE		
C. CPEIC		

Augmented Parsing of Unknown Word by Graph-based Semi-supervised Learning

Qiuping Huang Derek F. Wong Lidia S. Chao Xiaodong Zeng Liangye He
NLP^{2}CT Laboratory / Department of Computer and Information Science University of Macau
Macau S.A.R., China
michellehuang718@gmail.com,{derekfw,lidiasc}@umac.mo,
nlp2ct.samuel@gmail.com,wutianshui0515@gmail.com

Abstract

This paper presents a novel method using graph-based semi-supervised learning (SSL) to improve the syntax parsing of unknown words. Different from conventional approaches that uses hand-crafted rules, rich morphological features, or a character-based model to handle unknown words, this method is based on a graph-based label propagation technique. It gives greater improvement on grammars trained on a smaller amount of labeled data and a large amount of unlabeled one. A transductiv[1] graph-based SSL method is employed to propagate POS and derive the emission distributions from labeled data to unlabeled one. The derived distributions are incorporated into the parsing process. The proposed method effectively augments the original supervised parsing model by contributing 2.28% and 1.72% absolute improvement on the accuracy of POS tagging and syntax parsing for Penn Chinese Treebank respectively.

1 Introduction

Parsing is an important and fundamental task in natural language processing. In the past years, many researches focusing on building high quality parsers for English (Charniak, 2000; Collins, 2003; Charniak and Johnson, 2005; Petrov et al., 2006) and these parsers obtain the state-of-the-art performance up to 92% accuracy. Recently, Chinese parsing has received more and more attention, and several researchers attempt to develop accurate parsers for Chinese (Klein and Manning, 2003; Charniak and Johnson, 2005; Petrov and Klein, 2007). Inspired from their works, Huang et al., (2012) design a head propagation table to improve the parsing performance with a factored model. Nevertheless, as pointed out in (Harper and Huang, 2009), the improved performance around 84% F-measure that still falls far short of performance on English. This leaves a large space for the further improvement of Chinese parsing.

As far as we known, there is a large portion of fixed errors stemming from unknown words in Chinese parsing. Therefore, a robust parser must have a mechanism of processing unknown words, where it discovers the POS tag and features information about unknown words during parsing. A number of researches design hand-crafted rules or make use of rich morphological features to handle them. It is well known that Chinese words tend to have greater POS tag ambiguities than English and the morphological properties of Chinese words are complicated to be predicted of POS type for unknown words. For this reason, Harper and Huang (2007) present a character-based model to handle Chinese unknown words. Similar to their work, He et al., (2012) propose a more effective method. They mainly use an exponential function to represent the distance between the head character and other characters in an unknown word and use the geometric average to estimate the emission probability of it. However, in this paper, we focus on using a graph-based label

[1]Transductive learning is used to contrast inductive learning. A learner is transductive if it only works on the labeled and unlabeled training data, and cannot handle unseen data.

propagation method to deal with unknown words. Graph-based label propagation methods have made a remarkable improvement in several natural language processing tasks, e.g. knowledge acquisition (Talukar et al., 2008), Chinese word segmentation and POS tagging (Zeng et al., 2013) and etc. As far as we known, this study is the first attempt at applying graph-based label propagation to resolve the problem of unknown word, which is mainly used to propagate POS tag and derive the emission probabilities to the large amount of unlabeled data by utilizing the limited resource (e.g. POS information from the labeled data, i.e. Penn Chinese Treebank and lexical emission probability learned by the PCFG-LA model). Then the derived unlabeled information generated by graph-based knowledge will be incorporated into the parser. In fact, this method explores a new way to exploit the use of unlabeled data to strengthen the supervised model in parsing.

This paper is structured as follows. Section 2 reviews the background, including the lexical model in the Berkeley PCFG-LA model and the graph-based label propagation methods. Section 3 presents the details of our proposed model based on graph-based semi-supervised learning approach and compares with other unknown word recognition models. Experiments setup and result analysis are reported in section 4. The last section draws the conclusion and future work.

2 Background

2.1 Lexical Model in Berkeley Parser

The Berkeley parser (Petrov et al., 2006; Petrov and Klein, 2007) is an efficient and effective parser that introduces latent annotations to learn high accurate context-free grammars (CFG) directly from a Treebank. Nevertheless, the lexical model of grammar is not well designed to effectively handle the out-of-vocabulary (OOV) words (aka unknown words) universally and the OOV model of Berkeley parser has proved to be more suitable for English in (Huang and Harper, 2009; Attia et al., 2010). The built-in treatment to unseen words of Berkeley parser can be concluded as: utilizing the estimation of rare words[2] to reflect the appearance likelihood of OOV words.

In order to get the more refine and accurate grammar, Petrov et al., (2006) developed a simple split-merge-smooth training procedure. In order to counteract over-fitting problem, they introduced a linear smoothing method to smooth the lexical emission probabilities:

$$\overline{P} = \frac{1}{|t|}\sum_x P_\theta(w|t_x) \quad (1)$$

$$P_\theta(w|t_x) \leftarrow \varepsilon\overline{P} + (1-\varepsilon)P_\theta(w|t_x) \quad (2)$$

where $|t|$ denotes the number of latent tags from t and t_x means a set of latent subcategories $\{t_x|x = 1, \dots, |t|\}$. In Equation (1), θ is the model parameters which can be optimized by EM-algorithm. In Equation (2), ε is a smoothing parameter.

Since the lexical model can only generate words observed in the training data, a separate module is needed to handle the OOV words that appear in the test sentences. There are two ways to estimate an OOV word w based on a specific latent tag t_x. One is assigning the probability of generating rare words in the training data by t_x: $P_\theta(rare|t_x)$; another is, suggested by the Berkeley parser as *Sophisticated Lexicon*, to calculate the emission probability through analysing the morphological features of the OOV words. In the Berkeley parser, English words are classified into a set of signatures based on the presence of characters, especially on a list of inherent suffixes (e.g., *-ed, -ing*), then the estimation of w/t_xpair is:

$$P_\theta(w|t_x) \propto P_\theta(s|t_x) \quad (3)$$

where s is the OOV signature for w and $P_\theta(s|t_x)$ is computed by $e_{t_x,s}/e_{t_x}$.

Nevertheless, the features applied to Chinese word are simpler than English. Only the last character of word will be taken into account in estimating emission probabilities of rare word. Before applying such model, OOV words will be checked if they belong to temporal noun (NT)[3], cardinal number (CD)[4], ordinal number (OD)[5] or proper noun (NR)[6] preferentially.

2.2 Graph-based Label Propagation

Graph-based label propagation, a critical subclass of semi-supervised learning (SSL), has

[2]In the newest version of Berkeley parser, words with frequent less than 10 will be regarded as rare words acquiescently.

[3]By checking if the word contains characters like "年" (year), "月" (month), or "日""号"(day).

[4]By checking if the word contains character of number.

[5]By checking if the word contains character, such as "第".

[6]By checking if the word contains character, such as " • "

Algorithm 1: Words Label Propagation Algorithm

Input:

- $_{l} = \{w_i\}_{i=1}^{l}$: labeled texts
- $_{u} = \{w_i\}_{i=l+1}^{l+u}$: unlabeled texts
- $E_l = \{P_\theta(w_i, t_i)\}_{i=1...l}$: emission probabilities trained by Berkeley parser

Run:

1. $\{G\}$ = construct_POSTagGraph (T_l,T_u)
2. $\{Q\}$ = propagate_POSTagProbability ($\{G\}$,E_l)
3. $\{D_l, D_u\}$ = propagate_POSTag ($\{Q\}$, E_l,T_u)
4. For $i = 1, 2, \dots, N$
5. $\{g_i\}$ = construct_latentGraph (D_l, D_u)
6. $\{q_i\}$ = propagate_latentTagProbability ($\{g_i\}$)
7. E_u = combine ($\{q_i\}_{i=1}^{N}$)

Output:

$E_u = \{P_\theta(w_i, t_i)\}_{i=1...u}$: emission probabilities of unknown words

End

been widely used and shown to outperform other SSL methods (Chapelle et al., 2006). Most of these algorithms are transductive in nature, so they cannot be used to predict an unseen test example in the future (Belkin et al., 2006). Typically, graph-based label propagation algorithms are run in two main steps: graph construction and label propagation. The graph construction provides a natural way to represent data in a variety of target domains. One constructs a graph whose vertices consist of labeled and unlabeled data. Pairs of vertices are connected by weighted edges which encode the degree to which they are expected to have the same label (Zhu et al., 2003). The great importance of graph construction methods leads to a number of graph construction algorithms in the past years. Popular graph construction methods include *k*-nearest neighbors (*k*-NN), *e*-neighborhood, and local reconstruction. In this paper , the *k*-NN method is used to construct the graph. Besides, label propagation operates on the constructed graph. Its primary objective is to propagate labels from a few labeled vertices to the entire graph by optimizing a loss function based on the constraints or properties derived from the graph, e.g. smoothness (Zhu et al., 2003; Subramanya and Bilmes, 2008; Talukdar and Crammer, 2009) or sparsity (Das and Smith, 2012). State-of-the-art label propagation algorithms include LP-ZGL (Zhu et al., 2003), Adsorption (Baluja et al., 2008), MAD (Talukdarand and Crammer, 2009) and Sparse Inducing Penalties (Das and Smith, 2012). The Sparse Inducing Penalties algorithm is used in this study.

3 The Proposed Approach

The emphasis of this paper is on presenting a method to recognize Chinese unknown words by using two different kinds of data sources, e.g. labeled texts and unlabeled texts, to construct a specific similarity graph. In essence, this problem can be treated as incorporating gainful information, e.g. prior knowledge or label constraints, of unlabeled data into the supervised model. In our approach, we employ a transductive graph-based label propagation method to achieve such gainful information, e.g. label distributions are inferred from a similarity graph constructed over labeled and unlabeled data. Then, the derived label distributions are regarded as "soft evidence" to augment the parsing of Chinese unknown words based on a new learning objective function. The algorithm contains the following two stages (see Algorithm 1). Firstly, given labeled data and unlabeled data, i.e. $_{l} = \{w_i\}_{i=1}^{l}$ with l labeled words and $_{u} = \{w_i\}_{i=l+1}^{l+u}$ with u unlabeled words, a specific similarity graph $\{G\}$ representing T_l and T_u is constructed (POS tag graph). In this stage, we construct one graph over all of labeled data and unlabeled data and propagate one POS tag for each unlabeled word (see section 3.1). Secondly, probabilities of latent tag $P_\theta(w|t_x)$ are estimated subsequently. In this application, we will generate N graphs. Where N stands for the number of POS types, each graph is aimed at propagating latent tag for the unlabeled words in their most probable POS tag, which can be determined from the graph in first stage (see section 3.2).

Feature	Example
Trigram + Context	我非常开心
Trigram	非常开
Left Context	我非
Right Context	开心
Center Word	常
Left Word + Right Word	非开
Left Word + Right Context	非开心
Left Context + Right Word	我非开

Table 1: Features employed to measure the similarity between two vertices, in a given text example "我非常开心" (I am very happy), where the trigram is "非常开".

3.1 Assigning POS Tags to Unlabeled Words

In this stage (corresponding to procedure 1-3 in Algorithm 1), the common practice is to construct a similarity graph for the labeled data and unlabeled data, and aim at assigning a POS tag to unlabeled data in a vertex constructing and label propagation tradition. The effect of the label propagation depends heavily on the the quality of the graph. Thus graph construction plays a central role in graph-based label propagation (Zhu et al., 2003).

In this stage, we represent vertices by all of the word trigrams with occurrences in labeled and unlabeled sentences to construct the first graph. The graph construction is non-trivial. As Das and Petrov (2011) mentioned that taking individual words as the vertices would result in various ambiguities and the similarity measurement is still challenging. Therefore, in this paper, we follow the same intuitions of graph construction from (Subramanya et al., 2010) by using trigram and the objective focuses on the center word in each vertex. Formally, we are given a set of labeled texts $T_l = \{w_i\}_{i=1}^{l}$, and a set of unlabeled texts $T_u = \{w_i\}_{i=l+1}^{l+u}$. The goal is to form an undirected weighted graph $G = (V, E)$, in which V as the set of vertices, which covers all trigrams extracted from T_l and T_u. Here $V = V_l \cup V_u$, where V_l refers to trigrams that occurs at least once in labeled data and V_u refers to trigrams that occurs only in the unlabeled data. The edge $E \in V \times V$. In our case, we make use of the k-nearest neighbors (k-NN) (k=5) method to construct the graph and the edge weights are measured by a symmetric similarity function as follows:

$$w_{i,j} = \begin{cases} sim(x_i, x_j), & if\ j \in K(i) or\ i \in K(j) \\ 0, & otherwise \end{cases} \tag{4}$$

where x denotes one vertex in the graph, $K(i)$ is the k nearest neighbors of x_i ($|K(i) = k, \forall i|$) and $sim(x_i, x_j)$ is a symmetric similarity measure between two vertices. The similarity function is computed based on the co-occurrence statistics over the features shown in Table 1.

To induce label distributions of unlabeled word from labeled vertices to entire graph, the label propagation algorithm, Sparsity-Inducing Penalties (Sparsity) proposed by (Das and Smith, 2012) is employed in this study. The following convex objective function is optimized in our case:

$$\arg\min_q \sum_{j=1}^{l} \|q_j - r_j\|^2 + \mu \sum_{i=1, k\in N(i)}^{m} w_{ik} \|q_i - q_k\|^2 + \lambda \sum_{i=1}^{m} {q_i}^2$$

$$s.t.\ q \geq 0,\ \forall i \in V,\ \|q_i\|_1 = 1. \tag{5}$$

where r_j denotes empirical label distributions of labeled vertices and q_i denotes unnormalized estimate measures in every vertex. The w_{ik} refers the similarity between trigram i and trigram k, and $N(i)$ is a set of neighbors of trigram i. μ and λ are two hyperparameters. The squared-loss[7] criterion is used to formulate the objective function. The first term in Equation (5) is the seed match loss which penalizes q_j if they go too far away from the empirical labeled distribution r_j. The second term is the edge smoothness loss that requires q_i to be smoothed with respect to the graph, such that two vertices connected by an edge with high weight should be assigned similar labels. The final term is a regularizer to incorporate the prior knowledge, e.g. uniform distributions used in (Das and Petrov, 2011; Subramanya et al., 2010).

The estimated label distribution q_i in Equation (5) is relaxed to be unnormalized, which simplifies the optimization. Thus, the objective function in Equation (5) can be optimized by

[7]E.g. $\|p\|^2 = \sum_y p^2(y)$, it can be seen as a multi-class extension of the quadratic cost criterion (Bengio et al., 2007) or as a variant of one of the objectives in (Zhu et al., 2003).

LBFGS-B (Zhu et al., 1997), a generic quasi-Newton gradient-based optimizer.

Mathematically, the problem of label propagation is to get the optimal emission label distribution q_i of every labeled vertex. Integrating the similarity between every two vertices, we can project the most probable POS (selection from the q_i) tag to the unlabeled words.

Through the construction of similarity graph and propagation of labels in this stage, each unlabeled word will get a POS tag.

3.2 Generating Latent Tag and Emission Probability to Unlabeled Words

In this stage (corresponding to procedure 4-7 in Algorithm 1), we mainly construct another type of graph $\{g\}$ to generate latent tag and emission probability to unlabeled words. As mentioned, each unlabeled word gets only one POS tag in stage one. Consequently, we build a graph for each type POS tag respectively in order to obtain an optimal emission probability distribution for each unlabeled word at this stage. When constructing the similarity graph, each vertex represents a word instead of a trigram. Because we only need to consider this word's latent tags and emission probability distribution based on its POS tag generated in the stage one. The graph construction and label propagation procedures are similar to that of the previous stage. It is worth noting that $||q_i||_1 \neq 1$ in the Equation (5) that differs from the previous stage. The emission distribution q_i is generated from all possible vertices with the same POS tag in a similarity graph instead of all of possible POS types of a vertex. Finally, the label distributions can be propagated to the unlabeled words, and the label distribution content is same as the Berkeley lexicon (contain the respective rule scores and words) trained by Berkeley parser.

3.3 Incorporation

After the former steps, we can get a lexicon of unlabeled words with label distribution. The lexicon is treated as an OOV lexicon which covers most of OOV words that appear in testing data but not in the training data in our system. Then this OOV lexicon should be incorporated into the Berkeley parser. Our strategy of insertion is that: when an OOV word is detected, it should be firstly examined if the OOV lexicon contains such word, then corresponding estimation will be used; otherwise, the built-in OOV word model (mentioned in the section 2.1) will be used. During the parameter tuning phase, we try to use linear incorporation to inspect the impact of our OOV model to the whole parsing model:

$$\alpha\theta_o + (1-\alpha)\theta_b \quad (6)$$
$$s.t.\ 0 \leq \alpha \leq 1$$

where θ_o, θ_b denote the estimation generated by our proposed OOV model and the Berkeley model respectively.

3.4 Comparison with Other OOV Recognition Models

The proposed approach in this paper differs from previous OOV recognition models. Collins (2003) assigned the UNKNOWN token to unknown words, and any $tag/word$ pairs not seen in training data would give a zero of estimation. While in (Klein and Manning, 2003), the unknown words were split into one of several word-class categories, based on capitalization, suffix, digit, and other character features. For each of these categories, they took the maximum-likelihood estimation of $P(tag|wordclass)$ and add a parameter k to smooth and accommodate unknown words. In (Petrov et al., 2006), they mainly utilized the estimation of rare words to reflect the appearance likelihood of OOV words and the details of the method have been mentioned in section 2.1. In fact, Chinese words are quite different from English, and the word formation processing for Chinese can be quite complex. Huang et al., (2007) reflected the fact that the characters in any position (prefix, infix, or suffix) can be predictive of the POS type for Chinese words. Inspired by their work, Huang and Harper (2009) improved Chinese unknown word parsing performance by using the geometric average of emission probabilities of all of the characters in the word. Differing from their concerns, we make use of a new perspective to employ unlabeled data to augment the supervised model and to handle the OOV word by graph-based semi-supervised learning. Our emphasis is to learn the semi-supervised model by smoothing the label distributions that are derived from a specific graph constructed with labeled and unlabeled data. Though graph-based knowledge, the OOV label distribution can be generated. It is worth nothing that the selection of unlabeled data should cover OOV words as much as possible. Because this approach is mainly used to assign a POS tag and emission probabilities to each

	Train	Unlabeled	Dev	Test
#Sentence	7,176	19,075	893	912
#Word	201,460	1,110,947	26,170	26,134
#OOV	-	-	2,168	2,223

Table 2: The statistics summary of data.

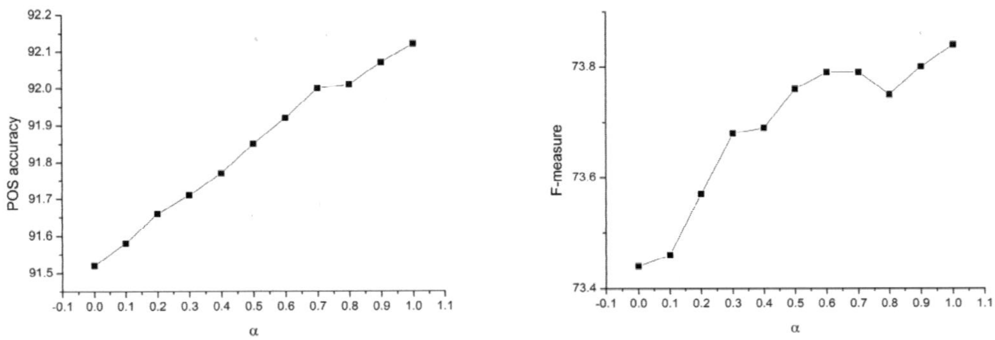

Figure 1: POS and parsing accuracy on development set, corresponding to different α.

unlabeled data according to the similarity between any two vertices in a graph constructing among labeled data and unlabeled data. If all of OOV words are found in the unlabeled data, then each OOV word would be recognized by our model. When we construct a graph where a portion of vertices correspond to labeled instances, and the rest is unlabeled. Pairs of vertices are connected by a weighted edge denoting the similarity between the pair. In this process, optimization of a loss function based on smoothness properties of the graph is performed to propagate labels from the labeled vertices to the unlabeled ones. Overall, our method differs in three important aspects: firstly, the existing resource (e.g. annotated Treebank and the latent variable grammars induced by Berkeley parsing model) is well utilized. Secondly, the training procedure is simpler than the (Huang and Harper, 2011). Thirdly, the derived label information from the graph is smoothed into the model by optimizing a modified objective function.

4 Experiment

4.1 Settings

In our experiment, Xinhua news and Sinorama magazine portions of the most recently released Penn Chinese Treebank 7.0 (CTB 7.0) (Xue et al., 2002) are used as labeled text T_l. Besides, the Peking University Corpus in Second International Chinese Word Segmentation Bakeoff[8] is utilized as unlabeled data T_u. The unlabeled data has been word-segmented with Stanford segmenter (Chang et al., 2008) because it adopts the same segmentation scheme used in the Treebank. The CTB 7.0 corpus was collected during different time periods from different sources with a diversity of articles. In order to obtain a representative experimental data, we refer to the splitting standard of (Huang et al., 2007; Huang and Harper, 2009), dividing the whole corpus into blocks of 10 files sorted by ascending order. For each block, the first file is used for development, the second file is used for testing, and the remaining 8 files are used for training. The corresponding statistic information on the data is shown in Table 2. The development set is used to determine the optimal α value to reflect our OOV model. EVALB (Sekine and Collins, 1997) is used for the evaluation.

4.2 Experiment Results

We firstly run the experiment on development set, the Berkeley baseline model has an overall POS tags accuracy of 91.51% on the development set, which is fairly low compared to the accuracies of importing the graph-based OOV model. In our model, the parameter α is smoothed to accommodate OOV model used in Equation 6. Figure 1 depicts the impact of combining the baseline model (lexical model in Berkeley) and

[8]http://www.sighan.org/bakeoff2005/

	Length	R	P	F	POS
Baseline	All	73.34	75.20	74.25	91.51
	<=40	75.48	76.02	75.75	91.87
$\alpha = 1$	All	75.12	76.83	75.97	93.79
	<=40	77.34	77.71	77.52	94.19

Table 3: POS and parsing accuracy on testing set.

Models	Parsing
Answer:	(IP (NP (NR 河南) (NR 西峡)) (VP (VV 发现) (NP (NN 恐龙) (NN 骨骼) (NN 化石))))
Baseline:	((IP (NP (NP (NR 河南))(NP (NN 西峡))) (VP (VV 发现) (IP (NP (NN 恐龙)(NN 骨骼)) (VP (VV 化石)))))
Our model:	(IP (NP (NR 河南) (NR 西峡)) (VP (VV 发现) (NP (NN 恐龙) (NN 骨骼) (NN 化石))))

Table 4: The parsing results for sentence: 河南西峡发现恐龙骨骼化石 (The dinosaur bone fossils were found in XiXia, Henan province).

#Words in testing set	#Tag in baseline model	Our model	Golden
王翔-12	6-*NR*,4-*NN*,1-*VV*, 1-*AD*	12-*NR*	12-*NR*
书展-12	9-*NN*, 1-*NR*,1-*CD*,1-*JJ*	12-*NN*	12-*NN*
地对-7	5-*NN*, 1-*NR*,1-*JJ*	7-*JJ*	7-*JJ*
捐助-3	1-*VV*, 1-*NN*, 1-*VA*	3-*VV*	3-*VV*
次日-2	2-*AD*	2-*NT*	2-*NT*
轻便-1	1-*AD*	1-*VA*	1-*VA*
多所-1	1-*VV*	1-*AD*	1-*AD*

Table 5: The OOV words correctly tagged by our model.

graph-based OOV model using different α values. When $\alpha = 0$, the model uses only the lexical model estimation. While $\alpha = 1$, it uses only the graph-based OOV model prediction of words. It is interesting to note that the combination model results in significant improvement over the baseline lexical model in terms of F-score and OOV accuracy. When $\alpha = 1$, the estimation performs the best result. This strongly reveals that the knowledge derived from the similarity graph does effectively strengthen the model.

Table 3 demonstrates the parsing result in the testing set. The best improvements in POS tagging and parsing are 2.28% and 1.72% respectively, which are statistically significant.

4.3 Discussion

By incorporating unlabeled data to boost the supervised model, our model outperforms the baseline. The main reason is that unlabeled data lack information, we use transductive graph-based label distributions derived from labeled data. The derived label information is considered as prior knowledge relative to unlabeled data, thereby enriching the training data. Most importantly, the similarity graph can also be allowed to propagate the label distributions for unknown words. The improved performance of the described model can be illustrated by the excerpt in Table 4, extracted from the test data. The table shows the golden parsing in the first line, and the parsing results given by the Berkeley baseline model and our OOV model in the following lines. Parsing errors are marked in red bold. The results achieved by our model for this example are totally correct, whereas the baseline model get the erroneous parsing mainly occurred in generating extra phrasal tags (e.g. NP, IP, VP) and mis-tagging a POS tag (e.g. VV). In which the word "化石" (fossil) is an OOV word in the test data. Our model can properly determine the POS tag for this word with the help of the label distribution by constructing the similarity graph. As mentioned before the OOV lexicon which concludes almost OOV words, and we found the word "化石" (fossil) has assigned with the *NN* tag. So the corresponding estimation with this tag will be used firstly by our model during the parsing. According to the result shown in the Table 3, the POS tag has about 2.3%

improvement. To a great extent, it mainly contributes to the incorporating of the OOV lexicon into the Berkeley parser. The Table 5 shows the sample OOV words are correctly tagged by utilizing the OOV lexicon in parsing. The first column stands for the number of times the word appears in the test data (e.g. 王翔 (WangXiang) - 12 means the word "王翔 (WangXiang)" appears 12 times in the test set). The other three columns stand for the times of this word's with certain POS tag type when paring in the baseline model, our model and golden file respectively. From the table, we can see our OOV model has a high POS accuracy by incorporating the OOV lexicon into the parser. Simultaneously, it proves that the label distribution derived from the similarity graph can augment the parsing of unknown words.

5 Conclusion

In this paper, we show for the first time that the graph-based semi-supervised learning is able to improve the performance of a PCFG-LA parser on OOV words. The approach mainly uses a k-nearest-neighbor algorithm to construct a similarity graph based on labeled and unlabeled data and then incorporates the graph knowledge into the Berkeley parser. Experimental comparisons on the Chinese Treebank corpus indicate that the proposed approach yields much better results than the baseline case without using unlabeled data.

In future work, we will concentrate on applying the graph-based OOV model into other parsing model (e.g. coarse-to-fine) and apply the model to other languages.

Acknowledgments

The authors are grateful to the Science and Technology Development Fund of Macau and the Research Committee of the University of Macau for the funding support for our research, under the reference No. 017/2009/A and MYRG076(Y1-L2)-FST13-WF. The authors also wish to thank the anonymous reviewers for many helpful comments.

References

Mohammed Attia, Jennifer Foster, Deirdre Hogan, Joseph Le Roux, Lamia Tounsi, and Josef Van Genabith. 2010. Handling unknown words in statistical latent-variable parsing models for Arabic, English and French. In *Proceedings of the NAACL HLT 2010 First Workshop on Statistical Parsing of Morphologically-Rich Languages*, pp. 67–75.

Shumeet Baluja, Rohan Seth, D. Sivakumar, Yushi Jing, Jay Yagnik, Shankar Kumar, Deepak Ravichandran, and Mohamed Aly. 2008. Video suggestion and discovery for youtube: taking random walks through the view graph. In *Proceedings of the 17th international conference on World Wide Web*, pp. 895–904.

Mikhail Belkin, Partha Niyogi, and Vikas Sindhwani. 2006. Manifold regularization: A geometric framework for learning from labeled and unlabeled examples. *The Journal of Machine Learning Research*, 7, 2399–2434.

Pi-Chuan Chang, Michel Galley, and Christopher D. Manning. 2008. Optimizing Chinese word segmentation for machine translation performance. In *Proceedings of the Third Workshop on Statistical Machine Translation*, pp. 224–232.

Olivier Chapelle, Bernhard Schölkopf, Alexander Zien. 2006. *Semi-supervised learning*. MIT press Cambridge.

Eugene Charniak. 2000. A maximum-entropy-inspired parser. In *Proceedings of the 1st North American chapter of the Association for Computational Linguistics conference*, pp. 132–139.

Eugene Charniak and Mark Johnson. 2005. Coarse-to-fine n-best parsing and MaxEnt discriminative reranking. In *Proceedings of the 43rd Annual Meeting on Association for Computational Linguistics*, pp. 173–180.

Michael Collins. 2003. Head-driven statistical models for natural language parsing. *Computational linguistics*, 29(4), 589–637.

Dipanjan Das and Slav Petrov. 2011. Unsupervised part-of-speech tagging with bilingual graph-based projections. In *Proceedings of the 49th Annual Meeting of the Association for Computational Linguistics: Human Language Technologies*, pp. 600–609.

Dipanjan Das and Noah A. Smith. 2012. Graph-based lexicon expansion with sparsity-inducing penalties. In *Proceedings of the 2012 Conference of the North American Chapter of the Association for Computational Linguistics: Human Language Technologies*, pp. 677–687.

Mary Harper and Zhongqiang Huang. 2011. Chinese statistic parsing. In Joseph Olive, Caitlin Christianson, and John McCary, editors, *Handbook of Natural Language Processing and Machine Translation*. Springer Verlag.

Liangye He, Derek F. Wong, and Lidia S. Chao. 2012. Adapting multilingual parsing models to Sinica treebank. In *Proceedings of the Second CIPS-SIGHAN Joint Conference on Chinese Language Processing*, pp. 211-215.

Qiuping Huang, Liangye He, Derek F. Wong, and Lidia S. Chao. 2012. A simplified Chinese parser with factored model. In *Proceedings of the Second CIPS-SIGHAN Joint Conference on Chinese Language Processing*, pp. 188-193.

Zhongqiang Huang and Mary Harper. 2009. Self-Training PCFG grammars with latent annotations across languages. In *Proceedings of the 2009 Conference on Empirical Methods in Natural Language Processing: Volume 2-Volume 2*, pp. 832–841.

Zhongqiang Huang and Mary Harper. 2011. Feature-rich log-linear lexical model for latent variable PCFG grammars. In *Proceedings of 5th International Joint Conference on Natural Language Processing*, pp. 219–227.

Zhongqiang Huang, Mary Harper, and Wen Wang. 2007. Mandarin part-of-speech tagging and discriminative reranking. In *Proceedings of the 2007 Joint Conference on Empirical Methods in Natural Language Processing and Computational Natural Language Learning (EMNLP-CoNLL)*, pp. 1093–1102.

Dan Klein and Christopher D. Manning. 2003. Accurate unlexicalized parsing. In *Proceedings of the 41st Annual Meeting on Association for Computational Linguistics-Volume 1*, pp. 423–430.

Roger Levy and Christopher Manning. 2003. Is it harder to parse Chinese, or the Chinese Treebank? In *Proceedings of the 41st Annual Meeting on Association for Computational Linguistics-Volume 1*, pp. 439–446.

Slav Petrov, Leon Barrett, Romain Thibaux, and Dan Klein. 2006. Learning accurate, compact, and interpretable tree annotation. In *Proceedings of the 21st International Conference on Computational Linguistics and the 44th annual meeting of the Association for Computational Linguistics*, pp. 433–440.

Slav Petrov and Dan Klein. 2007. Improved inference for unlexicalized parsing. *Human language technologies 2007: the conference of the North American chapter of the Association for Computational Linguistics*, pp. 404–411.

Satoshi Sekine and Michael Collins. 1997. *Evalb*. Available at nlp.cs.nyu.edu/evalb.

Amarnag Subramanya and Jeff Bilmes. 2008. Soft-supervised learning for text classification. In *Proceedings of the Conference on Empirical Methods in Natural Language Processing*, pp. 1090–1099.

Amarnag Subramanya, Slav Petrov, and Fernando Pereira. 2010. Efficient graph-based semi-supervised learning of structured tagging models. In *Proceedings of the 2010 Conference on Empirical Methods in Natural Language Processing*, pp. 167–176.

Partha Pratim Talukdar and Koby Crammer. 2009. New regularized algorithms for transductive learning. *Machine Learning and Knowledge Discovery in Databases*, pp. 442–457.

Nianwen Xue, Fu-Dong Chiou, and Martha Palmer. 2002. Building a large-scale annotated Chinese corpus. In *Proceedings of the 19th international conference on Computational linguistics-Volume 1*, pp. 1–8.

Xiaodong Zeng, Derek F. Wong, Lidia S. Chao, and Isabel Trancoso. 2013. Graph-based semi-supervised model for Joint Chinese word segmentation and part-of-speech tagging. In *Proceeding of the 51st Annual Meeting of the Association for Computational Linguistics*, pp. 770–779. Sofia, Bulgaria.

Ciyou Zhu, Richard H. Byrd, Peihuang Lu, and Jorge Nocedal. 1997. L-BFGS-B: Fortran subroutines for large scale bound constrained optimization. *ACM Transactions on Mathematical Software*, 23:550–560.

Xiaojin Zhu, John Lafferty, and Zoubin Ghahramani. 2003. Combining active learning and semi-supervised learning using Gaussian fields and harmonic functions. *ICML 2003 workshop on the continuum from labeled to unlabeled data in machine learning and data mining*, pp. 58–65.

Tonal Patterns in the 15th Century: a Corpus-based Approach

Chihkai Lin
East Asian Languages and Literatures, University of Hawai'i at Mānoa
Moore Hall 382, 1890 East-West Road, Honolulu, HI 96822, USA
linchihkai@gmail.com

Abstract

This paper investigates the tonal patterns in the 15th century from a corpus-based approach, focusing on two historical sources, 日本館譯語 *Rìběn kuǎn yìyǔ* 'A Wordlist of Chinese-Japanese Phrases' and 朝鮮館譯語 *Cháoxiān kuǎn yìyǔ* 'A Wordlist of Chinese-Korean Phrases'. The results suggest that Japanese and Korean are signiifcantly different in the phonetic transcription of low tone in monosyllabic words and in the first syllable of a disyllabic word. The results also suggest that Mandarin Chinese in the 15th century tends to be a falling tone in the second syllable of a disyllabic word.

1 Introduction

The issue concerned with the phonetic value of Early Ming Phonology in the 15th century can be investigated from two sources: a) traditional Chinese rhyme books and b) wordlists for foreign languages transcribed logographically by using Chinese characters. The traditional Chinese rhyme books include 洪武正韻 *Hóngwǔ zhèngyùn* (1375) 'The Standard Rhyme of Hóngwǔ' and 韻略易通 *Yùnluè yìtōng* (1445) 'The Easy Access to Rhymes'; the wordlists for foreign languages include 日本館譯語 *Rìběn kuǎn yìyǔ* 'A Wordlist of Chinese-Japanese Phrases' and 朝鮮館譯語 *Cháoxiān kuǎn yìyǔ* 'A Wordlist of Chinese-Korean Phrases',[1] for example. When it comes to the two types of sources, the main concern has been segments rather than prosody, given that in traditional Chinese phonology, it is difficult to present prosody by using Chinese characters. Besides, Chinese rhyme books are often compiled in such a way that presents initials, rhymes and tones separately. Such presentation is significantly different from the wordlists for foreign languages, which show no distinction of initials, rhymes and tones, and are transcribed by using Chinese characters for the foreign phrases. The wordlists for foreign languages could preserve different information from the traditional rhyme books not only in the reconstruction of segments, but also in the correspondence of prosody, since prosodic similarity should also be taken into consideration when the compliers were transcribing foreign languages by Chinese characters.

Speaking of the prosodic system, it is certain that Early Mandarin Chinese in the 14th - 15th century[2] has at least five tones, as suggested by the rhyme books, 洪武正韻 *Hóngwǔ zhèngyùn* (1375) 'The Standard Rhyme of Hóngwǔ' and 韻略易通 *Yùnluè yìtōng* (1445) 'The Easy Access to Rhymes'. On the other hand, Japanese and Korean also have their own prosodic systems. Japanese is a language with pitch-accent, marked by high pitch-accent and low pitch-accent. The prosodic system of Korean, however, has dramatically changed from Middle Korean to Modern Korean. Middle Korean is a language with three tones: level tone, falling tone and rising tone (Lee and Ramsay, 2011: 123).[3]

Nevertheless, previous studies based on the wordlists for foreign languages seldom touch upon prosody in 日本館譯語 *Rìběn kuǎn yìyǔ* 'A Wordlist of Chinese-Japanese Phrases' (e.g., Ding, 2008 and Lin, 2009) and in 朝鮮館譯語 *Cháoxiān kuǎn yìyǔ* 'A Wordlist of Chinese-

[1] The real publication data is not clear for the two wordlists, but it is certain that they are published in early years of Ming dynasty.

[2] In traditional Chinese phonology, Mandarin Chinese starts from 中原音韻 *Zhōngyuán yīnyùn* 'The Standard Rhyme in Central Plain' (1324 AD), in Yuan Dynasty (1271AD – 1368 AD).

[3] The notation of the three tones in Middle Korean is based on Chinese tradition, 平 *píng* 'level', 上 *shǎng* 'rising', 去 *qù* 'falling' and 入 *rù* 'entering'. However the real tonal values of the three tones are somehow different from Chinese tones. According to Chong (1976: 22) and Lee (1990: 147), a level tone has low level value (L), a falling tone has high level value (H) and a rising tone is a combination of low and high tone (LH).

Korean Phrases' (e.g., Kang 1995), all of which put more stress on segments. Besides, it is not clear whether or not in the two historical sources Chinese tones can represent Japanese pitch-accent and Korean tones. Therefore the goal of this study is to investigate prosody in Early Ming dynasty based on the historical records for foreign languages, and I would like to address two questions:

a) Do tones in Early Ming phonology represent Japanese pitch-accent and Korean tones?

b) Is there any difference between the transcription in Japanese and Korean?

In order to answer the two research questions, I adopt a corpus-based approach and deal with monosyllabic and disyllabic phrases in the two historical resources for foreign languages in the 15th century, 日本館譯語 *Rìběn kuăn yìyŭ* 'A Wordlist of Chinese-Japanese Phrases' and 朝鮮館譯語 *Cháoxiān kuăn yìyŭ* 'A Wordlist of Chinese-Korean Phrases'. The results shown in this study will have implication not only for the phonology of the source language, namely, Early Ming phonology, but also for the phonology of the target languages, that is, Japanese and Korean in the 15th century.

The paper is organized as follows. Section 2 introduces the data examined in this study. Section 3 presents the results, followed by a general discussion in section 4. Section 5 provides the conclusion and some suggestions for future studies.

2 Methodology

The main sources for this study are 日本館譯語 *Rìběn kuăn yìyŭ* 'A Wordlist of Chinese-Japanese Phrases' and 朝鮮館譯語 *Cháoxiān kuăn yìyŭ* 'A Wordlist of Chinese-Korean Phrases'. The two sources are compiled in such a way that a Chinese word/phrase is provided first and then followed by a phonetic transcription of Japanese or Korean, using Chinese characters. For example, Chinese 風 'wind' is logographically transcribed by 刊節 for Japanese かぜ *kaze* 'wind' and by 把論 for Korean 바람 *param*[4] 'wind'.

The two major sources include different types of entries. The majority is a single word and then phrases. There are some sentences in the two sources. In total, 日本館譯語 *Rìběn kuăn yìyŭ* 'A Wordlist of Chinese-Japanese Phrases' has 566 entries; 朝鮮館譯語 *Cháoxiān kuăn yìyŭ* 'A Wordlist of Chinese-Korean Phrases' contains 596 entries.

In this study, I will use Ding's (2008) notation for 日本館譯語 *Rìběn kuăn yìyŭ* 'A Wordlist of Chinese-Japanese Phrases' and Kang's (1995) notation for 朝鮮館譯語 *Cháoxiān kuăn yìyŭ* 'A Wordlist of Chinese-Korean Phrases'.

In this study, I will primarily cope with two types of syllable structures, monosyllabic and disyllabic words, by which I refer to the entries that correspond to one/two Japanese kana or one/two Korean Hangeul. Table 1 present the entries found in the two historical resources.

	One	Two
Japanese Kana	34	142
Korean Hangeul	71	115

Table 1. The tokens of the entries analyzed in this study

Attention should be given here. Japanese kana can perfectly correspond to Chinese characters one by one. In other words, one Japanese kana can be presented by one Chinese character. As for Korean, one Korean Hangeul sometimes corresponds to one Chinese character and sometimes to two Chinese characters. Such correspondences usually result from Korean coda *-l*, which is not attested in Chinese phonology. Korean coda *-l* is then transcribed by Chinese character, 二, in particular. For instance, Korean 하늘 *ha.neul* 'sky, heaven', which is a disyllabic word, is transcribed by three Chinese characters, 哈嫩二. The first Chinese character, 哈, is associated with the first syllable, *ha*, and the second Chinese character, 嫩, is aligned with the second syllable, *neu*, without including the coda *-l*. The third Chinese character, 二, specifically represents coda *-l* in the second syllable.

The two-to-one correspondences are also found in other codas, such as -s, which is also not attested in Chinese phonology. In this case, it has to be again transcribed by an extra Chinese character, as seen in 花 'flower', which is transcribed by two Chinese characters, 果思, for Korean 꽃 *kkos* 'flower'.

In this study, the two-to-one correspondences are included in the token calculation, but the tonal values of the Chinese characters that are

[4] The spelling conventions for Korean follow Sohn (2001: 139-141).

used to present the Korean codas which are not attested in Chinese will be disregarded. That is to say, while 哈嫩二 'sky, heaven' for Korean 하늘 is considered one token, only the tonal values of the first and second Chinese characters, 哈嫩, are taken into account.

How the tonal values of the selected entries are determined depends on two criteria: a) the classification in Middle Chinese, that is, 廣韻 *Kuǎng yùn* (1008 AD), and b) the tonal value of modern Mandarin Chinese. Of course, from Middle Chinese to modern Mandarin Chinese, there is a drastic change in tonal value. In Middle Chinese there are four tones, 平 *píng* 'level', 上 *shǎng* 'rising', 去 *qù* 'falling' and 入 *rù* 'entering'.[5] Later, the four tones split depending on the voicing of initials, 陰 *yīn* 'voiceless' and 陽 *yáng* 'voiced'. Theoretically there should be eight tones.[6] Later in the 14th century, according to 中原音韻 *Zhōngyuán yīnyùn* (1324) 'Phonology of the Central Plain', the eight tones underwent merger and then reduced to five tones,[7] which are close to the number of tones in modern Mandarin Chinese.

The fact that Early Mandarin Chinese in the 14th - 15th century is close to modern Mandarin Chinese in the numbers and types of tones does not necessarily indicate that the tonal values are identical with each other in the two different periods of Chinese. Therefore, when transcribing the tonal values of the selected entries, I will pay more attention to categories instead of the real tonal value, even though the tonal values of modern Mandarin Chinese tones are also helpful in determining the categories.

The tonal patterns of the selected entries will be presented in section 3.

[5] Entering tone differs from the other three tones, because entering tone essentially refers to a syllable ending in voiceless stops, -p, -t, and -k.

[6] The eight tones are 陰平 *yīn píng* 'level tone with voiceless initial', 陽平 *yáng píng* 'level tone with voiced initial', 陰上 *yīn shǎng* 'rising tone with voiceless initial', 陽上 *yáng shǎng* 'rising tone with voiced initial', 陰去 *yīn qù* 'falling tone with voiceless initial', 陽去 *yáng qù* 'falling tone with voiced initial', 陰入 *yīn rù* 'entering tone with voiceless initial' and 陽入 *yáng rù* 'entering tone with voiced initial'.

[7] In traditional Chinese phonology, the merger of eight tones to four tones from Middle Chinese to Modern Mandarin Chinese could be summarized as three processes: a) level tones have phonation distinction, b) a rising tone with voiced initial becomes a falling tone and c) entering tones have dropped the coda and merged with the other three tones.

3 Results

Results are presented in two parts. Section 3.1 presents the tonal patterns of one kana and Hangeul, and section 3.2 shows the tonal patterns of two kana and Hangeul.

3.1 Tonal Patterns of One Kana and Hangeul

Table 2[8] and Table 3 show the tonal patterns of one kana in Japanese and one Hangeul in Korean, respectively.

Tones	Tokens
1	8 (23.5%)
2	10 (29.4%)
3	6 (17.6%)
4	10 (29.4%)
Total	34 (100%)

Table 2. The distribution of one kana

Tones	Tokens
1	12 (16.9%)
2	15 (21.1%)
3	23 (32.4%)
4	21 (29.6%)
Total	71 (100%)

Table 3. The distribution of one Hangeul

The attestations in Table 2 and Table 3 vary from each other. In Japanese, there are 34 entries in total, while in Table 3 there are 71 entries in total. In Tone 1, there are 8 attestations in Japanese (23.5%) and 12 attestations in Korean (16.9%). For Tone 2, there are 10 attestations in Japanese (29.4%) and 15 attestations in Korean (21.1%). An obvious difference between Japanese and Korean consists in Tone 3.

[8] In Table 2 and the following tables, I number the four tones, 陰平 *yīn píng* 'level tone with voiceless onset' as 1, 陽平 *yáng píng* 'level tone with voiced onset' as 2, 陰上 *yīn shǎng* 'rising tone with voiceless onset' as 3, and 去 *qù* 'falling tone' as 4. This system is commonly used in Taiwan for the four tones.

It is necessary to explain why there are five tones in previous section, but I only mark four tones in this section. There is no need to separate entering tones from other tones, since the codas in entering tones are not counted in transcription for Japanese and Korean. For instance, Chinese 霜 'frost' for Korean 서리 *se.li* 'frost' is transcribed by 色立. These two Chinese characters belong to entering tones in Middle Chinese. It is clear that the codas in the entering tones are either ignored purposefully or disappeared in the 15th century.

Japanese mono kana is least transcribed by Chinese Tone 3, whereas the most frequently used tone for transcribing Korean mono Hangeul is Tone 3. The distribution in the two languages is almost identical in Tone 4, the falling tone, both of which are more than one-quarter, approximately 29%.

3.2 Tonal Patterns of Two Kana and Hangeul

Tonal patterns of two kana and Hangeul are provided below. First of all, Table 4 and Table 5 demonstrate the distributions of tonal patterns of the first and the second kana in Japanese, respectively.

Tones	Tokens
1	38 (26.8%)
2	38 (26.8%)
3	23 (16.2%)
4	43 (30.2%)
Total	142 (100%)

Table 4. The distribution of the first kana in a two-kana phrase

Tones	Tokens
1	34 (23.9%)
2	28 (19.7%)
3	20 (14.1%)
4	60 (42.3%)
Total	142 (100%)

Table 5. The distribution of the second kana in a two-kana phrase

In Table 4 and Table 5, the distributions of tonal patterns of the first and the second kana in Japanese show similar tendency to the distribution in Table 2. In either the first kana or the second kana, Tone 3, that is, 陰上 *yīn shǎng* 'rising tone with voiceless onset', is the least favored tone for transcribing Japanese. In Table 5, more than forty percent of attestations appear in Tone 4, suggesting that the tonal pattern of the second kana in a two-kana phrase should be different from the tonal pattern of mono kana or the first kana in a two-kana phrase.

The distributions of tonal patterns of the first and the second Hangeul in Korean are shown in Table 6 and Table 7.

Tones	Tokens
1	18 (15.6%)
2	24 (20.9%)
3	46 (40.0%)
4	27 (23.5%)
Total	115 (100%)

Table 6. The distribution of the first Hangeul in a two-Hangeul phrase

Tones	Tokens
1	8 (7.0%)
2	11 (9.6%)
3	28 (24.3%)
4	68 (59.1%)
Total	115 (100%)

Table 7. The distribution of the second Hangeul in a two-Hangeul phrase

In Korean, the distribution of the first Hangeul in a two-Hangeul phrase, as shown in Table 6, is similar to the distribution of a single Hangeul in Table 3 where Tone 3 is the most favored tone and Tone 1 is the least favored one.

The distribution of the second Hangeul in a two-Hangeul is skewed, however, as Table 7 suggests. About sixty percent of the second Hangeul is transcribed by Tone 4. This skewed distribution of the tonal pattern of the second Hangeul in a two-Hangeul phrase significantly differs from the distribution of tonal pattern in a single Hangeul and the first Hangeul in a two-Hangeul phrase, since both of them prefer Tone 3 to other tones.

It could be tentatively concluded here. When Japanese kana and Korean Hangeul are transcribed in the historical sources in the 15th century, there is a major difference in Tone 3, 陰上 *yīn shǎng* 'rising tone with voiceless onset' which is the least favored tone for Japanese, but is the most favored tone for Korean, for a single kana/Hangeul and the first kana/Hangeul in a two-kana/Hangeul phrase. As for the second kana/Hangeul in a two-kana/Hangeul phrase, it is Tone 4, 去 *qù* 'falling tone', that is the most preferred tone. The differences are discussed in the next section.

4 Discussion

This study addresses two research questions: a) Do tones in Early Ming phonology represent

Japanese pitch-accent and Korean tones? b) Is there any difference between the transcription in Japanese and Korean?

Results in section 3 have suggested that there are two significant differences in Chinese and Japanese/Korean. First of all, the results are of great help in understanding the prosodic system of Japanese and Korean in the 15th century as well as the behavior of Chinese tones. Although the real phonetic value of each tone is unknown, Tone 3, 陰上 *yīn shǎng* 'rising tone with voiceless onset', in Early Mandarin Chinese behaves differently from the other tones, as reflected in the transcription of Japanese kana and Korean Hangeul. As suggested by Table 2 and Table 4, Tone 3 in Early Mandarin Chinese is not preferred for Japanese kana, whereas it is suggested by Table 3 and Table 6 that Tone 3 is favored to transcribe Korean Hangeul. The differences draw the attention.

Japanese pitch-accent has only two types of register, low (L) and high (H). Contour types, such as rising (R = L+H) and falling (F = H+L), are also attested in Old Japanese (Okumura 1995). However, in the 11th-12th century, contour types started to disappear (Okumura 1995: 188).[9] Only falling contour type is persevered in modern Kyoto Japanese. It could be surmised from the prosodic change that Japanese disfavored a contour like rising, and in the 15th century, a rising type might have disappeared, resulting in the fact that Tone 3, which is a rising contour starting with a low pitch, is not preferred for Japanese.

In contrast, Tone 3 in Chinese is preferable to other tones for Korean.[10] This corresponds to the fact that Korean in the 15th century tends to have more tones that start with a low level pitch. Korean tones are comprised by a low level tone (L) and a high level tone (H), and a rising tone stems from the combination of low + high (L + H).

How Tone 3 in Chinese is used differently to transcribe Japanese kana and Korean Hangeul reflects the prosodic difference of Japanese and Korean in the 15th century. A contour like LH in Japanese might have disappeared so that Tone 3 in Chinese became the least favored choice for Japanese. On the other hand, Tone 3 in Chinese is preferred in Korean, due to the fact that Korean has a rising tone like LH.

This distinction of Tone 3 in Japanese and Korean, however, is not found in the second kana of Japanese and Hangeul of Korean, since the second kana/Hangeul is often transcribed by Chinese Tone 4. This might be due to a tendency that in Chinese, especially in a phrase with two syllables, the second syllable is preferred to be a falling tone.

Table 8 and Table 9 show the tokens of the possible combination of tones in a phrase with two Japanese kana and Korean Hangeul.

1st / 2nd	1	2	3	4	Total
1	9	7	8	10	34
	6.3%	4.9%	5.6%	7.1%	23.9%
2	8	9	1	10	28
	5.6%	6.3%	0.7%	7.1%	19.7%
3	3	7	7	3	20
	2.1%	4.9%	4.9%	2.1%	14.1%
4	18	15	7	20	60
	12.7%	**10.6%**	4.9%	**14.1%**	42.3%
Total	38	38	23	43	142
	26.7%	26.7%	16.2%	30.4%	100%

Table 8. The tokens of all possible combination of tones in a phrase with two Japanese kana

1st / 2nd	1	2	3	4	Total
1	1	1	3	3	8
	0.9%	0.9%	2.6%	2.6%	7.0%
2	2	5	3	1	11
	1.7%	4.3%	2.6%	0.9%	9.5%
3	3	3	14	8	28
	2.6%	2.6%	**12.2%**	7.0%	24.3%
4	12	15	26	15	68
	10.4%	**13.0%**	**22.6%**	**13.0%**	59.1%
Total	18	24	46	27	115
	15.7%	20.8%	40%	23.5%	100%

Table 9. The tokens of all possible combination of tones in a phrase with two Korean Hangeul

As discussed in Table 5 and Table 7, the distribution is skewed. The second kana in a two-kana phrase and the second Hangeul in a two Hangeul phrase are often transcribed by Chinese Tone 4, which is a falling tone. The reason why

[9] Modern Kyoto Japanese preserves the falling contour, as in LF, suggesting that rising contour disappears faster than falling contour.

[10] Most modern Korean dialects have lost tones, except for Kyengsang Korean, which preserves three tones: high tone, mid tone and low tone (Sohn 2001: 200). Unlike the tones in Middle Korean, the phonetic value of the tones in Kyengsang Korean is more like modern Japanese pitch-accent, which tends to be register.

the second kana/Hangeul is often transcribed by Tone 4 attributes to the preferred tonal combination in Chinese. Ding (2008) provided a diachronic survey of Chinese tonal development and a synchronic investigation of possible combinations of different tones. In a phrase with two Chinese characters, the first Chinese character is often a high level tone and the second character is often a falling tone.[11] In addition to Ding's (2008) study, Wang (2011: 133-134) reported that in modern Mandarin Chinese, the most prominent combination is a falling tone + a falling tone (15.2%) and the percentage of the combination that the second word is a falling tone is about 35%.

Taking the diachronic and synchronic studies together, the tendency that the second kana in Japanese and Hangeul in Korean are transcribed by Tone 4, which is a falling tone, is affected by Chinese tonal pattern, instead of any Japanese or Korean prosodic features. A question arises, however. Could it be possible that the tendency that the second kana/Hangeul is often transcribed by Tone 4 results from the patterns of Japanese pitch-accent or Korean tones? The answer is no, because how a two-kana/Hangeul phrase is transcribed should be consistent. That is to say, how a single Japanese kana or Korean Hangeul is transcribed follows the target language's prosodic system in a two-kana/Hangeul phrase. The results presented in section 3, nevertheless, suggest that a single kana/Hangeul and the first kana/Hangeul in a two-kana/Hangeul phrase behave similarly, while the second kana/Hangeul significantly differs. In addition, as discussed above, Japanese has stronger disfavor of rising contour (LH) over falling contour (HL), so Chinese falling tone should be the least optimal candidate for Japanese. The different strategy of transcription for a single kana/Hangeul and a two-kana/Hangeul phrase indicates that the compilers of 日本館譯語 *Rìběn kuǎn yìyǔ* 'A Wordlist of Chinese-Japanese Phrases' and 朝鮮館譯語 *Cháoxiān kuǎn yìyǔ* 'A Wordlist of Chinese-Korean Phrases' tried their best to be faithful to Japanese and Korean when they were transcribing a single kana/Hangeul and the first kana/Hangeul, whereas the compilers were unable to distinguish the pitch-accent or tones in the second kana/Hangeul. Instead, the compilers replaced the second kana/Hangeul in a two-kana/Hangeul phrase with the tonal pattern for Chinese two-character phrases, which consists of a falling tone in the second character.

In Table 9, the combination of Tone 3 and Tone 3 (12.2%) in Korean draws our attention. This combination discloses another phenomenon. When two third tones can appear consecutively, the second one should be relatively higher than the first Tone 3 so that the phrase with two third tones is similar to the combination of Tone 3 and Tone 4. This change suggests that in the 15th century, there might be tone sandhi in Chinese.[12]

The processes could be briefly presented in Table 10.

Monosyllabic	Single	
Disyllabic	First	Second
	↑ Japanese/Korean	↑ Chinese

Table 10. The prosodic patterns of Japanese kana and Korean Hangeul by Chinese tones

Although according to the corpus, it could be tentatively summarized that there are two types of transcribing Japanese kana and Korean Hangeul by Chinese characters, in the corpus, a minimal pair is attested, as shown in (1) for Japanese.

(1)

Examples	花 *hana*	鼻 *hana*
Meaning	'flower'	'nose'
Chinese character	法納	法納
Chinese tones	3+4	3+4
Tokyo Japanese	LH	LH
Kyoto Japanese	HL	HH

In (1), the two examples, 花 *hana* 'flower' and 鼻 *hana* 'nose' have different representations in pitch-accent, regardless of regional differences. The two examples, however, are transcribed by identical Chinese characters. This phenomenon is also found in (2) for Korean.

[11] The first character is often a level tone with voiceless onset.

[12] The tone sandhi process should be also attested in Japanese sources, since this phonological process is a Chinese phenomenon. In Table 8, it should be reasonable to assume that this tone sandhi takes place as well. However, since Japanese does not favor Tone 3, the chance becomes low that Tone 3 + Tone 3, which is phonetically more like Tone 3 + Tone 4, is chosen.

(2)

Examples	一 *hanʌ*	天 *hanʌl*
Meaning	'one'	'heaven, sky'
Chinese character	哈那	哈嫩(二)
Chinese tones	1+4	1+4
Middle Korean	LL	LH

Although examples in (2) are not perfect minimal pair, they serve well enough to demonstrate the differences. In Middle Korean, 一 *hanʌ* 'one' and 天 *hanʌl* 'heaven, sky' are different in their tones of the second Hangeul. 一 *hanʌ* 'one' has a low tone, whereas 天 *hanʌl* 'heaven, sky' has a high tone. However, the two examples are identically transcribed by the combination of Tone 1 and Tone 4.

Examples in (1) and (2) infer that Chinese in the 15th century might have different level tone, Tone 1 as high level tone and Tone 3 as low level tone.[13] The two pairs also suggest that the Chinese compilers of the two books in the 15th century showed less distinction in the second kana/Hangeul than in the first kana/Hangeul and the mono kana/Hangeul.

5 Conclusion

This study starts from a simple question that how Chinese compliers of the wordlists of Chinese-Japanese and Chinese-Korean in the 15th century transcribes Japanese pitch accent and Korean tones by using Chinese characters. The analysis and results lead us to believe that the Chinese compilers had noticed the prosodic differences between Chinese, Japanese and Korean.

The findings in this study have implications for the understanding of Japanese and Korean prosodic systems in the 15th century. Japanese disfavors a low pitch-accent for mono kana and the first kana in a two-kana phrase, whereas Korean prefers a low tone for mono Hangeul and the first Hangeul in a two-Hangeul phrase. With respect to the second kana/Hangeul, it tends to begin with a high pitch, as suggested by the frequent use of a falling tone for the second kana/ Hangeul.

Further studies are still needed and can be done by including more historical sources from the neighborhood. This current study has probed into only two languages, Japanese and Korean, yet it would be helpful to include 琉球館譯語 *Liúqiú kuǎn yìyǔ* 'A Wordlist of Chinese-Okinawan Phrases', which is also compiled in the 15th century. Besides, to gain a more general picture of Chinese phonology, prosodic system in particular, it is definitely more reliable to compare 日本館譯語 *Rìběn kuǎn yìyǔ* 'A Wordlist of Chinese-Japanese Phrases', 朝鮮館譯語 *Cháoxiān kuǎn yìyǔ* 'A Wordlist of Chinese-Korean Phrases' and 琉球館譯語 *Liúqiú kuǎn yìyǔ* 'A Wordlist of Chinese-Okinawan Phrases'.

[13] In Modern Mandarin Chinese, Tone 1 is a high level tone, marked as 55 and Tone 3 is a contour tone that is 214. It is not clear when Tone 3 becomes a contour like 214, which is not a common phenomenon among Chinese dialects. In the 15th century, Tone 3 might not be a contour type like 214. A more reliable scenario is that Tone 1 is a high level tone, Tone 3 is a rising tone, Tone 3 is a low level tone and Tone 4 is a falling tone.

References

葉寶奎 [Bao-kui Ye]. 2001. 明清官話音系 [Phonology of Ming and Qing Mandarin Chinese]. Xiamen University Press, Xiamen.

林慶勳 [Ching-hsiun Lin]. 2009.寄語集的華語詞彙探討──以《日本館譯語》與《琉球館譯語》比較為對象 [Chinese Vocabulary during the Period of Ming-Study Based on the "Ji-yu" in Chinese-Japanese and Chinese-Ryukyu Dictionaries]. 國立台灣師範大學國文學報 [Bulletin of Chinese, National Taiwan Norma University] 46: 95-128 .

Chong, Yon-chan. 1976. *Kwuke Sengcho e kwanhan yenku [Study on the Tone in Korean]*. Ilchwokak, Seoul.

丁峰 [Feng Ding]. 2008. 日漢琉漢對音與明清關話對音研究 [A Comparative Study of Japanese-Chinese, Ryukyuan-Chinese correspondences and Ming-Qing Mandarin Chinese]. Zhonghua Books, Beijing.

Kang, Shin-hang. 1995. *Cheungpwo Chwoswonkwan eke Yenku [A Study of Chwoswonkwan eke]*. Sungkyunkwan University Press, Seoul.

Lee, Ki-moon. 1990. *Kwuke Eumwunsa Yonku [A Study of the History of Korean Phonology]*. Tap Press, Seoul.

Lee, Ki-moon and Robert Ramsey. 2011. *A History of*

the Korean Language. Cambridge University Press, Cambridge.

王茂林 [Mao-ling Wang]. 2011. 漢語自然話語韻律模式研究 [A Study of Chinese Prosody in Spontaneous Speech]. Jinan University Press, Guangzhou, China.

Okumura, Mitsuo. 1995. *Nihongo Akusentoshi Kenkyu [A Study of the History of Japanese Accent]*. Kazamashobo, Tokyo.

丁邦新 [Pang-hsin Ding]. 2008. 國語中雙音節並列語兩成分間的聲調關係 [The relation of the two components in Mandarin Chinese disyllabic phrases], in 中國語言學論文集 *[A Collection of Chinese Linguistics]*. Zhonghua Books, Beijing.

Sohn, Ho-min. 2001. *The Korean Language*. Cambridge University Press, Cambridge.

Basic Principles for Segmenting Thai EDUs

Nalinee Intasaw
Department of Linguistics,
Faculty of Arts, Chulalongkorn University,
Bangkok 10330, THAILAND
nalinee.int@gmail.com

Wirote Aroonmanakun
Department of Linguistics,
Faculty of Arts, Chulalongkorn University,
Bangkok 10330, THAILAND
awirote@chula.ac.th

Abstract

This paper proposes a guideline to determine Thai elementary discourse units (EDUs) based on rhetorical structure theory. Carson and Marcu's (2001) guideline for segmenting English EDUs is modified to propose a suitable guideline for segmenting EDUs in Thai. The proposed principles are used in tagging EDUs for constructing a corpus of discourse tree structures. It can also be used as the basis for implementing automatic Thai EDU segmentation. The problems of determining Thai EDUs both manually and automatically are also explored and discussed in this paper.

1 Introduction

Elementary discourse unit or EDU is a building block that can combine together to form a larger unit or structure in discourse. It is significant to applications that process discourse such as text summarization, machine translation, text generation, and discourse parsing. In some applications e.g. text summarization and machine translation, an EDU is suitable to be used as an input than a sentence or a paragraph since it is smaller and contains a single piece of information, In addition, in languages in which sentence boundaries are not clearly marked like Thai, determining an EDU would be more practical and more useful since an EDU serves as a building block for constructing the discourse structure. However, little study has been devoted to Thai elementary discourse unit. Previous research on Thai discourse structure (Charoensuk, 2005; Sinthupoun, 2009; Katui et al., 2012) did not clearly discussed how to determine an EDU in Thai. Determining an EDU is not an easy task. As a result, Carson and Marcu (2001) had developed a guideline for determining an EDU in English, which is used for tagging discourse tree structure. In this paper, our objective is to propose a guideline to determine Thai EDUs. The proposal is grounded on the framework of rhetorical structure theory by Mann and Thomson (1988). The background knowledge related to our paper will be discussed in section 2. Data used in this work is described in section 3. In section 4, principles for segmenting Thai EDU are proposed. Problems arisen with Thai EDU segmentation are explored in section 5. The last section will be the conclusion.

2 Background knowledge

To analyze the structure of text, the text has to be segmented into pieces of information and linked together to reflect the coherence of text. Rhetorical structure theory (RST), one of the most widely used in both linguistics and computational linguistics, was proposed by Mann and Thomson (1988) to explain discourse structure of written texts. Briefly, RST explains the discourse relation of two spans of texts. It explains how parts of text are organized and formed into a larger structure of text which can be represented as a tree structure. For any two spans of text, one of them will have a specific relation to the other. The one that is more essential is the nucleus while the other one functioning as a supporting text is a satellite unit. The discourse tree is described on the basis of successive rhetorical relation between these discourse units. The terminal node of the tree structure represents the minimal unit of the discourse called elementary discourse unit or EDU. Relation that holds between two EDUs can be mononuclear or multinuclear. Mononuclear relation holds between two units which are a nucleus and a satellite. Multinuclear relation holds between two units which are both nucleus. An example of RST analysis of an English text is shown in Figure 1. In this example, the structure is composed of six discourse unit. Units 2-6 are hold together with the relation LIST. All of these units then have a relation PURPOSE with the first discourse unit.

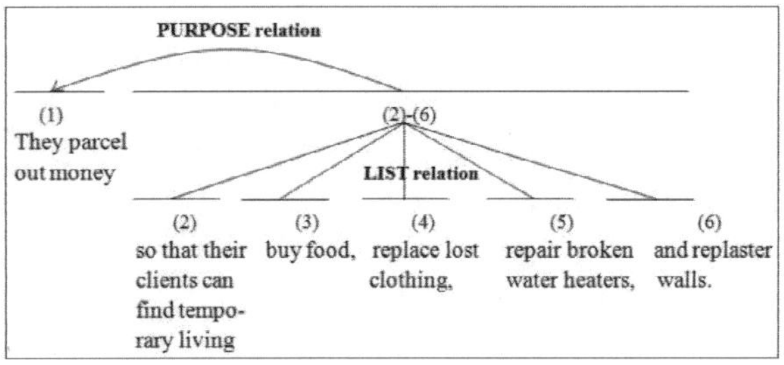

Figure 1. RST tree structure of English text "They parcel out money so that their clients can find temporary living, buy food, replace lost clothing, repair broken water heaters, and replaster walls." (Carson and Marcu, 2001)

However, RST does not specify what minimal discourse unit should look like. It only provides general explanation of the relation among those units in discourse. Later, Carson and Marcu (2001) who were trying to interpret and make use of the theory, proposed a guideline to determine an EDU in English in his discourse tagging reference manual for building an annotated RST corpus (Carson et al., 2001; Carson and Marcu, 2001). Their EDUs were based on the balance between granularity of tagging and ability to identify units consistently. It is well-recognized that their EDU determination is widely accepted, and thus, has been adapted in other research concerning the use of EDU. Carson and Marcu's EDU is not always a clause or sentence. Phrases can be EDU too but with restricted conditions. Coordinated verb phrases are not treated as separate EDUs if they are transitive verbs sharing the same direct object or intransitive verbs sharing a modifier.

There are a few studies on Thai discourse structure in computational aspect. Those studies determined an EDU differently. That is, Sinthupoun (2009) and Katui et al. (2012) took only clauses as EDUs while Charoensuk (2005) took clauses and phrases with strong discourse markers as EDUs. Charoensuk and Katui et al.'s works are based on RST. However, they did not provide a clear explanation of what should be considered an EDU in Thai. In this paper, our focus is proposing a guideline for determining Thai EDUs boundaries and exploring problems in segmenting Thai EDUs.

3 Data collection

The data used in this paper are collected from the Thai National Corpus (TNC). We choose only written academic texts because written and spoken languages differ on the structure of discourse. Our written data are randomly selected from 3 domains which are liberal arts, social sciences, and sciences, about 2,000 EDUs in total. Carson and Marcu's principles for English EDU determination are adapted and adjusted to suit the Thai data. At the end, the basic principles for Thai EDU segmentation are listed as the guideline for segmentation. The guideline will be discussed in the next section following by problems of Thai EDU segmentation.

4 Basic principles for Thai EDU segmentation

In this section, we present a guideline for segmenting Thai EDUs on the basis of the data as described in the previous section. Our goal is to determine the minimal units in every possible structure in discourse. The proposed principles to segment Thai EDU must be clear enough to be used consistently. After segmenting, those EDUs should be able to combine together to reflect the rhetorical relation holding between them.

In this study, the conventions used in our examples are as follows. The EDUs are marked in square brackets. Boldface and italic are used to highlight items being mentioned. Subscripts indicate the number of unit. We follow Carlson and Marcu's (2001) basic idea that clauses and noun phrases with strong markers are treated as EDUs. The proposed principles to determine what is or is not a Thai EDU are listed below.

4.1 Finite clauses

Finite verb is a verb form that can function as a root of a clause. In some languages, finite verb can be inflected for gender, person, number, tense, aspect, mood, and/or voice. However, Thai is an isolating language, its verbs do not inflect to show whether they are finite or non-finite. The criterion to test whether the verb in question is finite or non-finite is to insert an auxiliary such as ต้อง-'must', ควร-'should', จะ-'irrealis marker', เคย-'perfective marker' or กำลัง-'progressive marker'. Only finite verbs can co-occur with those words (Hoonchamlong, 1991; Yaowapat and Prasithrathsint, 2008). A clause can be classified into a finite clause and a non-finite clause according to finiteness of verb. Like Carson and Marcu's basic principle, we treat a finite clause as EDU but with some exception which will be discussed later. If it starts with a discourse marker, that marker is treated as a part of EDU. In contrast, non-finite clause is not treated as EDU.

A finite clause can be independent or dependent clause. Independent or main clause is a clause that can stand alone while dependent or subordinate clause cannot stand alone and always depends on the main clause. Independent and dependent clauses can link together with a subordinate conjunction and hold mononuclear relation whereas two independent clauses can be combined with a coordinate conjunction and hold multinuclear relation between them.

On the basis of function, a dependent clause can be divided into **subject/object clause**, **finite relative clause,** and **adverbial clause.** According to Carson and Marcu's EDU determination, relative clause and adverbial clause are marked as EDUs while subject or object clause is not EDU. Furthermore, **coordinate clauses** are also treated as EDUs while **coordinate verb phrases** are not. We will discuss more about these types of dependent clause below.

4.1.1 Subject and object clause

A clause functioning as subject or object of predicate is not treated as separate EDU because it is not a modifying part of any text portion and cannot be omitted or separated into a stand-alone unit. Moreover, subject or object clause does not hold any relation to the matrix clause. Example of subject clause is shown below in boldface.

[**ผู้จบปริญญาเอกด้านวิทยาศาสตร์**ต้องมีคุณสมบัติอย่างไรบ้าง]$_1$

[What qualification should **one who receives a doctorate of science** have?]$_1$

4.1.2 Finite relative clause

A finite relative clause is a type of dependent clause and also a noun modifying clause. It will be treated as an EDU. In Thai, relative clause can be formed by either gap strategy or pronoun retention strategy. A relative clause formed by gap strategy does not contain any overt coreference to the head noun while a relative clause formed by pronoun retention contains a pronoun realizing the head noun in the relative clause. The clause may or may not be introduced by a relativizer. Thai relativizers include ที่-'that', ซึ่ง-'that', and อัน-'that'. (Yaowapat and Prasithrathsint, 2008). Example is shown below with relative clause in boldface.

[เนื่องจากขาดการศึกษาและวางนโยบาย]$_1$[**ที่ชัดเจน**]$_2$[**อันจะทำให้ประชาชนสามารถตัดสินใจได้**]$_3$

[since Ø lack of studying and planning policy]$_1$[**that is clear**]$_2$[**which will make people be able to decide**]$_3$

4.1.3 Adverbial clauses

Adverbial clause is a clause that combines with the other clause to give additional information through some rhetorical relation of time, manner, condition, reason, etc. Generally, this type of dependent clause is marked by a subordinate conjunction. Each type of subordinate conjunction is an important clue for identifying rhetorical relation because its grammatical meaning can tell what kind of rhetorical relation two clauses are holding. For instance, purposive conjunctions เพื่อ-'for' and เพื่อว่า-'for that' show purpose relation while contrastive conjunctions แต่-'but' and ส่วน-'whereas' show contrast relation between two clauses. (Chanawangsa, 1986; Matthiessen, 2002) The following example shows how adverbial clause in boldface is segmented into EDU.

[ให้ความสำคัญแก่การวางโครงเรื่อง]$_1$[ที่สลับซับซ้อน]$_2$[**เพื่อหลอกล่อให้คนอ่านเดาเรื่องไม่ออก**]$_3$

[Ø emphasize on plot planning]$_1$[which is complicated]$_2$[**in order to make the readers unable to predict the story**]$_3$

4.1.4 Coordinate clauses

Coordinate clauses are composed of two independent clauses with or without a coordinate conjunction. Note that coordinate clauses are different from coordinate verb phrases in the way that verbs in coordinate clauses do not share the same object or modifier while verbs in coordinate verb phrases always share the same object and modifier. We treat coordinate clauses as EDUs since they hold elaboration relation. On the other hand, we do not separate coordinate verb phrases because they do not have any rhetorical relation to one another. The following examples show how coordinate clauses and coordinate verb phrases are segmented respectively.

[ความยากจนเป็นปัจจัยนำไปสู่การเกิดพยาธิสภาพแก่ปัจเจกบุคคล]$_1$ [และมีผลกระทบต่อส่วนรวม]$_2$

[Poverty is a cause of individual pathology]$_1$[and affects the community at large]$_2$

[แต่หลายส่วนลอกและเพิ่มเติมมาจากกฎหมายตราสามดวง]$_1$

[But many parts were copied and inserted from the Three Emblems Law]$_1$

4.2 Non-finite relative clauses

We do not treat non-finite relative clause as a separate EDU because of its non-finite status of verb. Non-finite relative clause or reduced relative clause is a type of noun modifier without a relativizer. The verb in this type of relative clause is non-finite, therefore, cannot co-occur with auxiliaries or tense-aspect markers. For instance, "ดี "in "คนดี"-'nice people' is a non-finite relative clause used for modifying the head noun "คน" (Yaowapat and Prasithrathsint, 2006). Example of non-finite clause is show below. Text in boldface is considered a non-finite clause.

[โดยได้แสดงวิธีการวิเคราะห์สาร**สำคัญ**จากตำนานเรื่องอีดีพุส]$_1$

[By demonstrating an analysis of **important** contents from the Oedipus myth]$_1$

4.3 Clausal complements

A complement is a constituent of a clause and an obligatory element that completes the meaning of its head (Dowty, 2003). It can be in the form of phrase or clause. In case of clausal complement, its verb can be either finite or non-finite. Finite causal complements are found in complements of attributive verbs. Attributive verbs include verbs of reporting speech and verbs of cognition. Examples of attributive verb in Thai are ยอมรับ-'accept', คิด-'think', เชื่อ-'believe', แสดง-'show', สันนิษฐาน-'assume', เสนอ-'propose', รู้-'know', อธิบาย-'explain', แนะนำ-'suggest', ตัดสินใจ-'decide', สมมติ-'suppose', ถาม-'ask', สงสัย-'doubt', etc. The clausal complements may be introduced by a complementizer ว่า or ที่. We treat clausal complement of attributive verb as a separate EDU since it shows attributive relation to its verb head. The following example shows EDUs with attributive verb in italic and its clausal complement in boldface.

[ชี้ให้เห็น*ชัดเจน*]$_1$[**ว่ามีการละเมิดสิทธิขั้นพื้นฐานของประชาชน**]$_2$

[Ø point out *clearly*]$_1$[**that there is violation of citizens' fundamental rights**]$_2$

In contrast, non-finite clausal complement is not treated as EDU. According to Jenks (2006), the complements in Thai are usually introduced by infinitival complementizer. The complementizer ที่จะ-'that+irrealis marker' and ที่ว่า-'that+say' is used to introduce the clausal complement of noun while ที่จะ and จะ is found in the clausal complement of verbs, except for that of attributive verbs mentioned above. The following examples show an EDU containing clausal complement of noun and of verb in boldface and their heads in italic.

[บทความนี้มี*วัตถุประสงค์***ที่จะศึกษาเปรียบเทียบลักษณะเด่นและลักษณะร่วมระหว่างเรือนพื้นถิ่นของกลุ่มไทลาว**]$_1$

[This article has *an objective* **to compare outstanding characteristics and common characteristics among local houses of Lao Tai people**]$_1$

[หาก*พร้อม***ที่จะปลูกสร้างเรือนใหม่**]$_1$[จึงแยกเรือน]$_2$

[if Ø *(be) ready* **to build a new house**]$_1$[then Ø separate the house ('move to the new house']$_2$

4.4 Serial verb construction

Serial verb construction (SVC) is one of the common characteristics of the Thai language. Thai SVC can be classified into basic and non-basic types. The basic SVC consists of two contiguous verb phrases with no overt linker while non-basic type consists of two or more verbs interrupted by markers or objects of verb (Thepkanjana, 1986; Takahashi, 2009). According to Foley and Olson (1985), each verb in SVC has the same status as predicate and they are all finite. Moreover, there are some studies about negation in Thai SVC. It is found that negation word ไม่-'not' can occur in front of the first verb and also in the middle of serial verbs (Takahashi, 1996). Though this evidence proves the finiteness status of Thai verbs in serial, SVC expresses only one unite single event and represents one piece of information. This comes to our decision that SVC should be treated as a single clause and segmented into a single EDU. The following example is Thai SVC with direct object in the middle of two verbs. The whole construction is treated as one EDU with serial verbs in boldface.

[ขณะเดียวกันก็**รอคอย**โชคชะตา**มาพลิกผัน**ชีวิตให้แปรเปลี่ยนไป]$_1$

[Meanwhile, Ø **waiting** for the destiny to **come** and **change** the life]$_1$

However, if there is an attributive verb within SVC, that SVC should be broken into separate EDUs. This only occurs with grammaticalized SVC which contains a grammaticalized verb ว่า-'say/complementizer' The following example shows SVC that is broken into two EDUs because it contains an attributive verb คิด-'think'. The grammaticalized verb ว่า-'say/comp.' plays a role of a complementizer rather than a verb since it cannot co-occur with negation word.

[เพราะเขา**คิด**]$_1$[**ว่า**เขา**ขาด**โอกาสทางธุรกิจ]$_2$

(Literally) because + he + **thinks** + **say/that** + he + **lacks** + opportunity + business

(Translation) Because he thinks that he lacks business opportunity.

*เพราะเขาคิดไม่ว่าเขาขาดโอกาสทางธุรกิจ

(Literally) because + he + think + not + say/that + he + lacks + opportunity + business

4.5 Cleft

Cleft is one of focusing devices used to emphasize a particular element. Although it appears as a complex clause consisting of one independent and one dependent clause, there is no rhetorical relation between them. Like Carson and Marcu's criteria for English, Thai cleft is not treated as a separate EDU. Thai cleft construction can be noticed by the copula เป็น-'be' or คือ-'be', which is the main verb of the whole cleft construction followed by a cleft clause, which is usually a relative clause (Taladngoen, 2012). Thai cleft is treated as a part of one EDU as in the following example.

[เขาเป็นคนที่ทอดทิ้งภรรยาให้เดียวดาย]$_1$

[He is the one who abandons the wife]$_1$

[คนไหนคือคนที่นิดแอบชอบ]$_1$

[Which one is the man whom Nid like]$_1$

4.6 Phrases with strong markers

Phrases can be EDUs if they are preceded by strong discourse markers. The strong discourse markers are markers that not only function as connectors but also have strong meaning to show relation to other units in discourse. These markers are important clues to identify EDU boundaries and discourse relation between discourse units. In Thai, we found two kinds of strong markers. One shows example relation and the other shows purpose relation. Examples of Thai strong discourse markers are เช่น...ฯลฯ-'for example…etc', ได้แก่...เป็นต้น-'for example…etc', ยกตัวอย่างเช่น-'for example', อย่างเช่น-'for example', เพื่อ-'for', etc. The markers are not strong makers and do not make the following phrases an EDU if they do not show neither example nor purpose relation. The boldface in the following examples show strong discourse markers followed by noun phrases.

[ตำนานปรัมปราเป็นการอธิบายถึงกำเนิดของจักรวาล โครงสร้าง และระบบของจักรวาล มนุษย์ สัตว์ ปรากฏการณ์ทางธรรมชาติ]^1[**เช่น** ลม ฝน กลางวัน กลางคืน ฟ้าร้อง ฟ้าผ่า]^2

[Legend is the explanation about the creation, structure, and system of the universe, human beings, animals, natural phenomenon]$_1$[**such as** wind, rain, day, night, thunder, and lightning]$_2$

[กู้หนี้ยืมสินมา]^1[**เพื่อ**การต่อสู้คดี]^2

[Ø borrow money]$_1$[**for** fighting the case]$_2$

In addition, noun phrases in the form of parentheticals, name of the title and author, and other nominal units linking with the body of the text are possible to be EDUs. The following example shows how noun phrase in parenthesis is marked as an EDU.

[อพยพมาจากเวียงจันทร์]$_1$ [**(ลาวเวียง)**]$_2$

[Ø migrated from Vientiane]$_1$[**(Lao Vieng)**]$_2$

4.7 Same unit construction

Sometimes, a clause is split up by an insertion of another clause. Carson and Marcu (2001) proposed a multinuclear pseudo-relation called "same-unit" which is the relation holding between two parts of the clause that is being interrupted. Though being separated part, the same-unit construction is treated as one single EDU. Same unit constructions can be found in construction with relative clauses, appositives, and parentheticals. The following example shows an embedded unit in normal font and a split EDU in boldface. The units subscripted as 1 and 3 are same unit constructions and are treated as one EDU.

[**ต่อมาในสมัยหลังสมัยใหม่**]$_1$ [(Post-modern)]$_2$ [**ได้เกิดวรรณกรรมแนวทดลอง**]$_3$

[**Later in post-modern period**]$_1$ [Post-modern]$_2$ [**there comes an experimental literature**]$_3$

4.8 Punctuation

Punctuation is treated as a part of EDU. In Thai, some punctuation can be used to identify EDU boundary. From the data, we observed that punctuation that is always at the end of EDU is question mark (?). Punctuation that is in pairs and usually found at the beginning and the end of EDU is parenthesis ((…)) and quotation marks ("…"). Other punctuation such as dash (-), separator in numbered lists, comma (,), period (.), colon (:), semi colon (;), Thai punctuation used to abbreviate certain words (ฯ), Thai punctuation used to indicate more of a like kind (ฯลฯ), and Thai punctuation used to indicate repetition (ๆ) usually appear inside EDU and do not play a role in EDU boundary identification.

5 Implementation

To ensure that the proposed principles above are suitable for automatic segmentation, we did a pilot on automatic EDU segmentation. A set of training data (90%) and testing data (10%) are prepared using this guideline. The system relies on Thai word segmentation and POS tagging as preprocessing. We used support vector machine training algorithm to build a model that assigns EDU boundaries of strings of texts. In a preliminary experiment in which 240 EDUs are used in the testing, the precision is 95% and the recall is 70%. This indicates that the proposed principles are practical for automatic EDU segmentation.

6 Problem with Thai EDUs segmentation

Based on the use of the proposed principles on the test data, we found some characteristics of the Thai language that pose difficulties in identifying EDU boundaries. The problems we encountered are as follows.

First, Thai verbs have only one form and are not inflected for any grammatical information. Therefore, they are difficult to be determined whether they are finite or non-finite. But since finiteness of verb is the main criterion for EDU determination, this topic becomes an issue for both manual and automatic EDU segmentation. For manual EDU segmentation, it can be solved because there are criteria to test whether the verb is finite or non-finite. Since a finite verb is the locus of grammatical information such as tense, aspect, and mood, we can test finiteness of verb by observing whether the verb in question co-occur with time adverbs and aspect/mood markers such as จะ-'irrealis marker', เคย-'perfective marker', กำลัง-'progressive marker', and แล้ว-'perfective marker'. In the case that there is no overt marker, we can try inserting some of those markers to verify its finiteness. In a similar way, we can test whether the verb is non-finite by inserting infinitival markers จะ‘irrealis marker’, ที่จะ-‘that+irrealis marker’ and ที่ว่า-‘that+say’ since a non-finite clause is usually introduced by these markers

However, testing finiteness of verb by inserting tense, aspect, mood markers, and infinitival markers requires Thai native speaker to judge whether the sentence is valid or not. This method is not suitable for automatic segmentation. How to determine finiteness automatically is a challenging task.

The second problem is about Thai compound noun. In Thai, a new word can be created by forming a compound noun. One pattern of noun compound is a noun + a transitive verb (+ a noun). For example, หม้อกรองอากาศ-‘air filter’ is composed of a noun หม้อ-‘pot’, a transitive verb กรอง-‘filter’, and a noun อากาศ-‘air’. This compound noun may be incorrectly detected as a sentence by a machine because its pattern is the same as a sentence (Kriengket et al., 2007). Thus, to avoid this kind of mistake in EDU segmentation, compound noun boundary must be disambiguated first.

The third problem is about syntactic ambiguity of a relative clause as in this example ลูกหลานของ*คน***ยากจน**-‘descendants of *people* **that are poor**’. The verb ยากจน-‘poor’ in boldface can be analyzed as a relative clause without a relativizer or a non-finite relative clause with คน-‘people’ in italic as its head noun. The difficulty in EDU segmentation is that this type of relative clause does not have any clue to show that it is a non-finite clause and should not be marked as EDU. Moreover, the word ยากจน-‘poor’ can be seen as a modifying verb and the string คนยากจน-‘people + poor’ can be analyzed as a compound noun-‘poor people’. In the latter case, it will be the problem of compound noun identification discussed earlier.

The fourth problem is concerned with Thai SVC. This is not quite a problem when segmenting EDUs manually. But when it comes to segmenting EDUs by a machine, Thai SVC identification can be a difficult task. Since Thai SVC is a complex predicate structure consisting of two or more finite verbs in which each verb can have its object, it can be very confusing whether each verb phrase should be segmented into separate EDU or not. For example from the previous section, the verb รอคอย-‘wait’ takes โชคชะตา-‘destiny’ as its direct object, serialized verbs มาพลิกผัน-‘come + change’ takes ชีวิต-‘life’ as its direct object, and serialized verbs ให้แปรเปลี่ยนไป-

'give + alter + go' has no object. The correct EDU segmentation is that the whole SVC should be marked as one single EDU. This is why automatic segmenting SVC is a challenging task.

[ขณะเดียวกันก็**รอคอย**โชคชะตา**มาพลิกผัน**ชีวิต**ให้แปรเปลี่ยนไป**]

(Literally) meanwhile + discourse marker + **wait** + destiny + **come** + **change** + life + give + alter + go

(Translation) Meanwhile, Ø wait for the destiny to come and change the life.

The fifth problem is about clauses with no overt discourse marker. Discourse marker is not only an important clue to help identify the EDU boundary but it also signals the type of rhetorical relation holding between clauses. Normally, a subordinate clause and coordinate clause are linked to the other clause by a discourse marker. However, it is possible for two clauses to have rhetorical relation to each other without a discourse marker between them. As in the example below, two clauses are holding consequence relation between them without a consequence marker. Without the presence of overt marker, a machine may find it difficult to identify EDU boundary.

[นโยบายพลังงานเป็นเรื่องใหญ่]$_1$ [สามารถกระทบชีวิตคนทุกคนทั้งโดยตรงและโดยอ้อม]$_2$

(Literally) [policy + energy + be + big deal] [Ø + can + affect + every life + both + directly + and + indirectly]

(Translation) Energy policy is a big deal (because it) can affect everyone both directly and indirectly.

The ambiguity of spaces can also cause a big problem for EDU segmentation. In Thai, text is written without a space between words. Instead, a space is used in Thai text to segment parts of discourse. However, the use of space in Thai text can be ambiguous because not every space functions as a sentence or clause separator. This is because Thai does not have strict and precise convention of using a space. Thus, we cannot rely on every space to determine EDU boundaries. To illustrate, the following sentences are all correct and the meanings are the same, even though the spaces are placed in different positions. Still, their EDU boundaries are all the same.

[คนเล่านิทานไม่ได้เล่า]^1[ว่านางเอื้อยในนิทานเรื่อง "ปลาบู่ทอง" มีหน้าตารูปร่างหรือมีนิสัยใจคออย่างไร]^2

[คนเล่านิทานไม่ได้เล่า]^1[ว่านางเอื้อยในนิทานเรื่อง "ปลาบู่ทอง" มีหน้าตา รูปร่าง หรือมีนิสัยใจคออย่างไร]^2

[คนเล่านิทานไม่ได้เล่า]^1[ว่า นางเอื้อยในนิทานเรื่อง "ปลาบู่ทอง" มีหน้าตา รูปร่าง หรือมีนิสัยใจคออย่างไร]^2

(Translation) The story teller did not tell how Nang Uay in "Pla Boo Thong" looks like or what personality she has.

In addition, Thai words can have multiple meanings. For instance, a discourse marker ส่วน- 'whereas' can also be a noun meaning 'part'. Yet, a discourse marker of one form may have several functions. For example, the word แล้ว can be a sequential marker meaning 'then' and also a perfective marker meaning 'already'. Therefore, POS tagging has to be applied correctly before doing automatic EDU segmentation.

7 Conclusion

The principles of Thai EDU determination proposed in this paper can be used as a guideline to segment Thai EDUs in written text. The creation of EDU segmented corpus is the first step in building a resource for the study of Thai discourse structure and automatically EDU segmentation. We believe that EDU is a suitable unit to be an input for Thai text processing because Thai writing system does not use any explicit marker for sentence boundary. Thai discourse is a continuation of text chunks holding together with or without a connection or a discourse marker. However, we found that determining EDUs in Thai text is not clear and easy especially for a machine. Further studies on automatic EDU segmentation using machine learning algorithms should be explored. But in order to do this, a corpus which is EDU segmented using the principles proposed in this study has to be built first. Therefore, the guideline proposed in this paper is the essential first step for this line of study.

Acknowledgments

This research is a part of the first author's thesis. It is partially supported by the Chulalongkorn University Centenary Academic Development Project and by the Ratchadaphiseksomphot Endowment Fund of Chulalongkorn University (RES560530179-HS).

References

Carlson, L. and Marcu, D. 2001. Discourse Tagging Manual. ISI Tech Report ISI-TR-545. July 2001.

Carlson, L., Marcu, D., and Okurowski, M.E. 2001. Building a DiscourseTagged Corpus in the

Framework of Rhetorical Structure Theory. In Proceedings of the 2nd SIGdial Workshop on Discourse and Dialog, Aalborg, Denmark.

Chanawangsa, W. 1986. Cohesion in Thai. Ph.D. dissertation, Georgetown University.

Charoensuk, J. 2005. Thai Elementary Discourse Unit Segmentation by Discourse Segmentation Cues and Syntactic Information. Master's thesis, Kasetsart University, Bangkok.

Dowty, D. 2003. The Dual Analysis of Adjuncts/Complements in Categorial Grammar. In Ewald Lang, et. al. (eds.) Modifying Adjuncts. NewYork: MoutondeGruyter.

Foley, W.A. and Mike, O.1985. Clausehood and verb serialization. In Nichols, Johanna and Anthony C. Woodbury (eds.) Grammar Inside and Outside the Clause: Some Approaches to Theory from the Field, 17-60. Cambridge, Cambridge University Press.

Hoonchamlong, Y. 1991. Some issues in Thai anaphora: A government and binding approach. Ph.D.dissertation, University of Wisconson-Madison.

Jenks, P. 2006. Control in Thai. In Variation in control structures, ed. M. Polinksy and E. Potsdam.

Ketui, N., Theeramunkong, T., and Onsuwan, C. 2012. A rule-based method for Thai Elementary Discourse Unit Segmentation (TED-Seg). Proceedings of the 7th International Conference on Knowledge Information and Creativity Support Systems (KICSS) 2012, Melbourne, Australia.

Kriengket, K., Kosawat, K., and Anchaleenukul, S. 2007. A Computational Linguistics Study of Compound Nouns in Thai, In Proceedings of the Seventh International Symposium on Natural Language Processing (SNLP 2007), pp. 31–36.

Mann, W. and Thompson, S.1988. Rhetorical structure theory: Toward a functional theory of text organization. Text, 8(3).

Mann, W., Matthiessen, C., and Thompson, S.1992. Rhetorical structure theory and text analysis. In Mann and Thompson (eds.) Discourse Description: Diverse Linguistc Analyses of a Fund-raising Text. Amsterdam: John Benjamins.

Matthiessen, Christian M.I.M. 2002. Combining clauses into clause complexes: a multifaceted view. In Joan Bybee & Michael Noonan (eds.), Complex sentences in grammar and discourse: essays in honor of Sandra A. Thompson. Amsterdam:Benjamins. 237-322.

Taladngoen. U. 2012. The Semantics-Syntax Analysis of 'pen' in Thai. M.A.thesis, Srinakharinwirot University.

Takahashi, K. 1996. Negation in Thai Basic Serial Verb Constructions. M.A. thesis, Chulalongkorn University.

Takahashi, K. 2009. Basic Serial Verb Constructions in Thai. Journal of the Southeast Asian Linguistics Society 1.

Thepkanjana, K.1986. Serial Verb Constructions in Thai. Ph.D. dissertation, University of Michigan.

Sinthupoun, S. 2009. Thai Rhetorical Structure Analysis. (Ph.D dissertation). National Institute of Development Administration, Bangkok.

Stowell, T. 2005. Appositive and Parenthetical Relative Clauses. In Hans Broekhuis, Norbert Corver, Jan Koster, Riny Huybregts and Ursula Kleinhenz (eds.) Organizing Grammar: Linguistic Studies in Honor of Henk van Riemsdijk, Berlin/New York, Mouton de Gruyter.

Yaowapat, N. and Prasithrathsint, A. 2006. Reduced relative clauses in Thai and Vietnamese. In Sidwell, Paul, and Uri Tadmor (eds.) SEALS XVI: Papers from the Sixteenth Annual Meeting of the Southeast Asian Linguistics Society. Canberra: Pacific Linguistics.

Yaowapat, N. and Prasithrathsint, A. 2008. A typology of relative clauses in mainland Southeast Asian languages, in The Mon-Khmer Studies Journal, vol. 38, pp. 1-23.

Automatic Clause Boundary Annotation in the Hindi Treebank

Rahul Sharma, Soma Paul, Riyaz Ahmad Bhat and Sambhav Jain
Language Technology Research Centre, IIIT-Hyderabad, India
{rahul.sharma, riyaz.bhat, sambhav.jain}@research.iiit.ac.in, soma@iiit.ac.in

Abstract

In this paper, we propose a method for automatic clause boundary annotation in the Hindi Dependency Treebank. We show that the clausal information implicitly encoded in a dependency structure can be made explicit with no or less human intervention. We exercised the proposed approach on 16,000 sentences of Hindi Dependency Treebank. Our approach gives an accuracy of 94.44% for clause boundary identification evaluated over 238 clauses. The resultant corpus has varied usages and can be utilized for developing a statistical clause boundary identifier.

1 Introduction

Clause boundary is important for various NLP systems like machine translation, parallel corpora alignment, parsing etc. (Leffa, 1998; Gadde et al., 2010; Ejerhed, 1988). This information is furnished by an automatic tool often called *clause boundary identifier*. Both data driven (Puscasu, 2004) and rule based (Leffa, 1998) approaches have been explored in past for building such a system, however recent inclination has been towards the data-driven approaches due to their robustness. In order to built a clause boundary identifier, using data driven approach, one needs to have a good clause boundary annotated corpus for training. At present, such a resource is not available in Hindi. However, the syntactic treebank with dependency relations annotated has been developed. We wish to expand this manually annotated treebank with the clause boundary annotation in this work.

Several insightful approaches, in past, have enriched existing resources by first utilizing the explicit information available to derive new implicit information (Klein and Manning, 2003; Kosaraju et al., 2012) and then explicitly annotating it back into the original resource. Conversion of a treebank from one grammatical formalism to the other serves as a good example of how an implicit information can be mapped and extracted (Xia and Palmer, 2001). Instead of starting from scratch, an already existing treebank is transformed into a new grammatical formalism. Bhatt et al. (2009) is one such effort for Hindi. They have automatically transformed dependency structures to phrase structure utilizing Hindi Dependency Treebank and Hindi PropBank (Palmer et al., 2009). Following such insights, we attempt to automatically generate the clause marked data from existing resources for Hindi. We propose that the clause information is implicitly encoded in the Hindi Dependency Treebank and thus, can be extracted and explicitly specified as an additional layer of annotation in the treebank. This paper presents a systematic approach towards incorporating clausal information in the Hindi Dependency Treebank utilizing the information (mopho-syntactic, dependency etc.) already available in the treebank.

This paper is structured as follows: In Section 2, we discuss the related works that have been done earlier on clause identification and classification. In Section 3, we talk about clause and its types. In Section 4, we discuss about Hindi-Urdu treebank. Section 5 describes our methodology and in Section 6 we discuss the results achieved and outline the issues faced. In Section 7, we conclude with some future directions.

2 Related Work

In this section, we report some of the works related to clause boundary marking. In general, for the task of clause boundary identification two kinds of resources are used: (a) typed dependency structures; (b) lexical cues such as subordinate and coordinate conjuncts. However, the works reported on Indian languages have mainly used typed dependency structures. Ghosh et al. (2010) has developed a rule based system for identifying clause boundary for Bangla. They have defined clause as a composite construction of a verb along with its dependent chunks. The rules are designed on the basis of dependency relation in an annotated corpus. They use CRF based statistical system for labeling different clauses. Dhivya et al. (2012) reports the task of identifying clauses in Tamil. They first preprocess the input sentence using Maltparser which gives dependency tree as its output. They have proposed 11 different dependency tags. Using those dependency tags marked by Maltparser, they try to find clause boundary in a sentence. Another work on Tamil (Ram and Devi, 2008) have proposed a hybrid approach for detecting clause boundaries in a sentence. They have used CRF based system which uses different linguistic cues for the task. After identification of the clause boundaries they run error analyzer module to find the false boundaries, which are then corrected by the rule based system built using linguistic cues.

Leffa (1998) has proposed a rule based system for English. This system uses lexical cues such as subordination conjuncts, coordination conjuncts etc. for indentification of clause boundaries and the type of a clause. Puscasu (2004) proposed a multilingual method of combining language independent machine learning techniques with language specific rules to detect clause boundaries in unrestricted texts. The rules identify the finite verbs and clause boundaries not included in learning process. Gadde et al. (2010) used some heuristic rules for clause boundary marking in Hindi. Their aim was to see the impact of clausal information on parser performance.

3 Clause and its Classification

A clause is a group of words consisting of a verb (or a verb group) and its arguments (explicit and implicit). Depending on the type of the verb, a clause is classified either as finite or non-finite based on the finiteness of the head verb. For example:

(1) raam khana khaakar ghar gayaa.
Ram food eat+do home go+past.
'Ram went home after eating.'

In this example (1), *khana khaakar* is a non-finite clause since 'khaakar' is a non-finite verb. Similarly, *raam ghar gayaa* is a finite clause as 'gayaa' is a finite verb. A sentence can have more than one clauses in it. These clauses are classified in to two types as:

1. Main clause, which is an independent clause, is also called Superordinate clause,

2. Subordinate clause, which is dependent on the main clause.

Clauses can also be classified based on their function in a sentence such as complement clause, adverbial clause, relative clause etc. (discussed shortly). Based on the relative position of clauses with respect to each other, clauses can either be nested or non-nested. Nested here means one clause is embedded in another clause, while non-nested means they lie adjacent to each other. For example,

(2) raam jo khela , ghar gayaa
Ram who play+past , home go+past
'Ram who played , went home.'

In example (2) the two clauses are: 1) *raam ghar gayaa* (a non-embedded clause) 2) *jo khela* (an embedded clause), which is embedded in *raam ghar gayaa.*

Below, we discuss some of the clause types mentioned earlier.

(a) **Complement Clause**

These clauses are introduced by complementizer 'ki' (that) and generally follow the verb of main clause (Koul, 2009).

(3) yaha sach hai ki mohan bimaara hai
It true is that Mohan sick is
'It is true that Mohan is sick'

In example (3), *ki mohan bimaar hai* is a Complement clause and 'ki' is a complementizer.

It must be noted that 'complement clause' may also act an argument of the main clause verb. So, in example (3), the main clause is *yaha sach hai ki mohan bimaara hai*, which contains the complement clause *ki mohan bimaara hai*, in it. This is considered to be a special case where a clause comes as an argument of a verb and becomes a part of the main clause. We have handled this type of construction separately (discussed in section 5).

(b) **Relative Clause**

Finite relative clauses occur as a modifier of verb's argument and contain a relative pronoun (Koul, 2009). Such clauses can be either nested or non-nested. For example:

(4) vaha ladkaa jo khel rahaa thaa ghar
that boy who play+past+conti. home
gayaa
go+past
'That boy who was playing went home'

In example (4), the nested relative clause is *jo khel rahaa thaa* (who was playing) with 'jo' as a relative marker. 'jo' modifies 'vaha', the argument of the verb 'gayaa'.

Consider another example:

(5) vaha ladkaa ghar gayaa jo
that boy home go+past who
khel rahaa thaa
play+past+conti.
'That boy who was playing went home'

In example (5) relative clause *jo khel rahaa thaa* is an example of an extraposed relative clause.

(c) **Coordinate Clause**

It is one of the independent clauses in a sentence belonging to a series of two or more independent clauses co-ordinated by a coordinating conjunction (Koul, 2009). For example:

(6) main ghar jaaungaa aur raam
I home go+fut. and Ram delhi
dillii jaayegaa
go+fut
'I will go home and Raam will go to Delhi'

mai ghar jaaungaa and *raam dillii jaayegaa* are two independent clauses with the same status in example (6). In our work, we consider both clause as coordinate clauses, and the coordinating conjunct is not taken to be part of any of the two clauses. There is thus no hierarchy in these clauses.

4 Hindi Dependency Treebank

In this section, we give an overview of Hindi Treebank (HTB ver-0.51) a part of which was released for Hindi Dependency Parsing shared task, MTPIL, COLING 2012 (Sharma et al., 2012). It is a multi-layered dependency treebank with morphological, part-of-speech and dependency annotations based on the Computational Pāṇinian Grammatical (CPG) framework. In the dependency annotation, relations are mainly verb-centric. The relation that holds between a verb and its arguments is called a *kaṛaka* relation. Besides *kaṛaka* relations, dependency relations also exist between nouns (genitives), between nouns and their modifiers (adjectival modification, relativization), between verbs and their modifiers (adverbial modification including subordination). CPG provides an essentially syntactico-semantic dependency annotation, incorporating *kaṛaka* (e.g., agent, theme, etc.), non-*kaṛaka* (e.g. possession, purpose) and other (part of) relations. A complete tagset of dependency relations based on CPG can be found in (Bharati et al., 2009), the ones starting with 'k' are largely Pāṇinian *kaṛaka* relations, and are assigned to the arguments of a verb. Example (7) shows the three levels of information discussed above encoded in the SSF format.

(7) raam ne khaanaa khaayaa aur paani
Ram+erg food ea+past and water
piyaa.
drink+past
'Raam who ate food and drank water, went home'

Offset	**Token**	**Tag**	**Feature structure**
1	((	NP	<fs name=NP drel=k1:VGF>
1.1	raama	NNP	<fs af='raama,n,m,sg,3,d,0,0'>
1.2	ne	PSP	<fs af='ne,psp,,,,,'>
	))		
1 2	((	NP	<fs name=NP2 drel=k2:VGF>
2.1	khaanaa	NN	<fs af='khaanaa,n,m,sg,3,d,0,0' name="khaanaa">
	))		
3	((	VGF	<¡fs name=VGF drel=ccof:CCP>
3.1	khaayaa	VM	<fs af='KA,v,m,sg,any,,yA,yA' name="khaayaa">
	))		
4	((	CCP	<¡fs name=CCP>
4.1	aur	CC	<fs af='Ora,avy,,,,,' name="aur">
	))		
5	((	NP	<¡fs name=NP3 drel=k2:VGF2>
5.1	paani	NN	<fs af='pAnI,n,m,sg,3,d,0,0' name="paani">
	))		
6	((	VGF	<¡fs name=VGF2 drel=ccof:CCP>
6.1	piyaa	VM	<fs af='pIyA,unk,,,,,' name="piyaa">
	))		

Figure 1: SSF representation for example 7

In figure 1, the preterminal node is a part of speech (POS) of a lexical item. These parts of speech are grouped together to form chunks (eg. NP, VGF, CCP, VGNF etc.) as a part of sentence analysis. The dependency relations are marked at chunk level, marked with drel in above SSF format. $k1$ is the agent of the action and $k2$ is the object of the verb. There are two $k2's$ for two different verbs, $khaanaa$ 'food' is $k2$ for $khaayaa$ 'eat' verb and $paani$ 'water' is $k2$ for $piyaa$ 'drink' verb.

5 Method

As we discussed earlier, we use dependency attachments and dependency relations annotated in the treebank to automatically mark the clause boundaries. The assumption is that the left most and the right most projections (dependents) of a verb are the extremes of a clause it heads.

Our approach is composed of two steps which execute sequentially to identify boundaries of a clause. Step 1 identifies the clause boundary in general, while Step 2 is a post-processing step which do adjustments specifically to handle 'ki' (that) complement clauses.

STEP 1: In this step, we first extract all verbs in a sentence using POS tag and chunk information and then traverse the dependency tree to extract their dependents recursively one by one. For each verb in the list, we stop traversing if either we exhaust the nodes dominated by the verb or find another verb in its dominance. However, when a complement clause introduced by complementizer 'ki' is annotated as an argument of a verb we will continue traversing till we exhaust all the nodes dominated by the complementizer 'ki'. This will ensure that the complement clause be treated as part of the main clause, more like an embedded clause. Once verb and its dependents are obtained, we sort them by their offsets. The lowest offset is considered as the start of a clause and the highest offset marks its end. This way we determine boundaries of each clause in a sentence.

Example (8) illustrates STEP 1:

(8) raam ghar gayaa aur khaanaa khaayaa.
Ram home go+past and food eat+past
'Ram went home and ate food.'

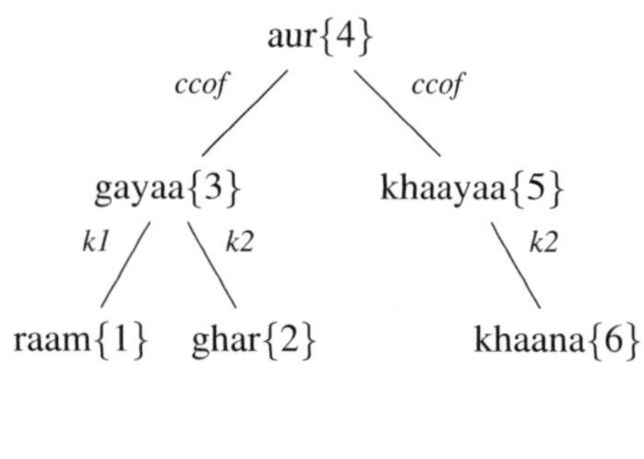

Figure 2: Dependency Tree

Figure 2 shows the dependency tree of example (8). Relations (k1, k2 etc.) are marked on edges and Offsets of different chunks are shown in brackets with the words. Following STEP 1, a verb list containing two verbs–'gayaa' and 'khaayaa' is formed. Then, after traversing the dependency tree of example (8) for verb 'gayaa', a list, containing verb 'gayaa' and its arguments–'raam' and 'ghar' is built. This list is, then, sorted by the offsets of words contained in it. After sorting, the words corresponding to the lower and higher offsets are treated as the boundaries of the clause headed by the verb 'gayaa'. Similarly for 'khaayaa' verb, words at offset 5 and offset 6 mark the boundaries. Thus, the clause boundaries for example (8) will be marked as:

(raam ghar gayaa) aur (khaanaa khaayaa.)

STEP 2: This step, as a postprocessing step, handles the exceptional case of 'ki' (that) complex complement clauses. As mentioned earlier, 'ki' complement clause may occur as an argument of a verb and could be thus a part of its clause. Although, in STEP 1 we will accurately include the complement clause as a part of the main clause, we don't mark the scope of complement clause itself, if it is complex i.e., made of more than one clause. This step marks the scope of complex complement clauses based on the output of STEP 1. Example (9) explains this further.

(9) raam ne kahaa ki tum ghar jaao or
ram+erg say+past that you home go and
aaraam karloo
rest do
'Ram said that you go home and take rest.'

After STEP 1, the clause boundaries for the sentence (9) would be like:

(raam ne kahaa ki (tum ghar jaao) or (aaraam karloo))

In STEP 2, we iterate over the output of STEP 1 and mark the boundaries of the complement clause starting from the word imediately following the 'ki' complementizer and the ending with the end of main clause of which complement clause is a part. The modified boundaries will be:

(raam ne kahaa ki ((tum ghar jaao) or (aaraam karloo)))

6 Results and Discussion

A testing set of 100 sentences containing 288 clauses randomly selected from a section of the Hindi Dependency Treebank is used to evaluate the performance of our approach. The accuracies are calculated on the basis of the following aspects of a clause:

- Start of clause
- End of clause
- Whole clause
- Finite clause
- Non-finite clause
- Embedded clause
- Non-embedded clause

Table 1 shows the accuracies of our approach for different aspects of clause marking.

Different aspects	Accuracy%
Start of clause	97.91
End of Clause	94.44
Whole clause	94.44
Finite clause	93.88
Non-Finite clause	98.30
Embedded clause	94.32
Non-Embedded clause	94.55

Table 1: Results of different aspect of clause

While evaluating our approach, we come across some constructions which were not handled by it. They are:

1. **Topicalisation**: Extraction of a constituent from in its canonical position to clause initial position may sometimes affect the representation of actual clause boundaries. Extraction from subordinate clause to sentence initial position provides such an example:

   (10) raam$_i$ maine kahaa ki t_i ghar gayaa.
   Ram I+Erg say+past that home go+past
   'I said that raam went home.'

   In example (10) 'raam' moved from its default position t_i to the sentence initial position. The overlap in the constituents of main and subordinate clauses in (10) makes the representation of clause boundaries in such sentences difficult.

2. **Inconsistencies in the treebank**: Since we rely on manually annotated dependency structures to identify the clause boundaries, any inconsistency in the structure would affect the accurate marking of such information. We spotted some errors which were due to the inconsistencies in the annotation in the treebank like part of speech and attachment errors.

7 Conclusion and future work

In this paper, we showed how implicit clausal information captured in a dependency tree can be extracted and added back to the original resource. We worked with the Hindi Dependency Treebank and automatically added the clausal information using the dependencies between constituents in the treebank. We discussed some of the issues in identifying clause boundaries using our approach. In the future, we plan to use the clause boundary annotated corpus furnished in this work for the task of clause boundary identification in raw text using machine learning.

Acknowledgments

The work reported in this paper is supported by the NSF grant (Award Number: CNS 0751202; CFDA Number: 47.070). [1]

References

Akshar Bharati, Dipti Misra Sharma, Samar Husain, Lakshmi Bai, Rafiya Begum, and Rajeev Sangal. 2009. Anncorra: Treebanks for indian languages guidelines for annotating hindi treebank (version–2.0).

Rajesh Bhatt, Bhuvana Narasimhan, Martha Palmer, Owen Rambow, Dipti Misra Sharma, and Fei Xia. 2009. A multi-representational and multi-layered treebank for hindi/urdu. In *Proceedings of the Third Linguistic Annotation Workshop*, pages 186–189. Association for Computational Linguistics.

R Dhivya, V Dhanalakshmi, M Anand Kumar, and KP Soman. 2012. Clause boundary identification for tamil language using dependency parsing. In *Signal Processing and Information Technology*, pages 195–197. Springer.

Eva I Ejerhed. 1988. Finding clauses in unrestricted text by finitary and stochastic methods. In *Proceedings of the second conference on Applied natural language processing*, pages 219–227. Association for Computational Linguistics.

Phani Gadde, Karan Jindal, Samar Husain, Dipti Misra Sharma, and Rajeev Sangal. 2010. Improving data driven dependency parsing using clausal information. In *Human Language Technologies: The 2010 Annual Conference of the North American Chapter of the Association for Computational Linguistics*, pages 657–660. Association for Computational Linguistics.

[1]Any opinions, findings, and conclusions or recommendations expressed in this material are those of the author(s) and do not necessarily reflect the views of the National Science Foundation.

Aniruddha Ghosh, Amitava Das, and Sivaji Bandyopadhyay. 2010. Clause identification and classification in bengali. In *23rd International Conference on Computational Linguistics*, page 17.

Dan Klein and Christopher D Manning. 2003. Accurate unlexicalized parsing. In *Proceedings of the 41st Annual Meeting on Association for Computational Linguistics-Volume 1*, pages 423–430. Association for Computational Linguistics.

Prudhvi Kosaraju, Samar Husain, Bharat Ram Ambati, Dipti Misra Sharma, and Rajeev Sangal. 2012. Intra-chunk dependency annotation: expanding hindi inter-chunk annotated treebank. In *Proceedings of the Sixth Linguistic Annotation Workshop*, pages 49–56. Association for Computational Linguistics.

Omkar Nath Koul. 2009. *Modern Hindi Grammar*. Indian Institute of Language Studies.

Vilson J Leffa. 1998. Clause processing in complex sentences. In *Proceedings of the First International Conference on Language Resources and Evaluation*, volume 1, pages 937–943.

Martha Palmer, Rajesh Bhatt, Bhuvana Narasimhan, Owen Rambow, Dipti Misra Sharma, and Fei Xia. 2009. Hindi syntax: Annotating dependency, lexical predicate-argument structure, and phrase structure. In *The 7th International Conference on Natural Language Processing*, pages 14–17.

Georgiana Puscasu. 2004. A multilingual method for clause splitting. In *Proceedings of the 7th Annual Colloquium for the UK Special Interest Group for Computational Linguistics*.

R Vijay Sundar Ram and Sobha Lalitha Devi. 2008. Clause boundary identification using conditional random fields. In *Computational Linguistics and Intelligent Text Processing*, pages 140–150. Springer.

Dipti Misra Sharma, Prashanth Mannem, Joseph van-Genabith, Sobha Lalitha Devi, Radhika Mamidi, and Ranjani Parthasarathi, editors. 2012. *Proceedings of the Workshop on Machine Translation and Parsing in Indian Languages*. The COLING 2012 Organizing Committee, Mumbai, India, December.

Fei Xia and Martha Palmer. 2001. Converting dependency structures to phrase structures. In *Proceedings of the first international conference on Human language technology research*, pages 1–5. Association for Computational Linguistics.

Myths in Korean Morphology and Their Computational Implications

Hee-Rahk Chae
Department of Linguistics and Cognitive Science
Hankuk University of Foreign Studies
Yongin, Gyeonggi, 449-791, Korea
hrchae@hufs.ac.kr

Abstract

This paper examines some popular misanalyses in Korean morphology. For example, contrary to popular myth, the verbal *ha-* and the element *-(nu)n-* cannot be analyzed as a derivational affix and as a present tense marker, respectively. We will see that *ha-* is an independent word and that *-(nu)n-* is part of a portmanteau morph. In providing reasonable analyses of them, we will consider some computational implications of the misanalyses. It is really mysterious that such wrong analyses can become so popular in a scientific field of linguistics.

1 Introduction

This paper aims at examining some popular misanalyses in Korean morphology. Focusing on the verbal *ha-* and what is called the present tense marker *-(nu)n-*, we will see that, contrary to popular myth, they cannot be analyzed as a derivational affix and as a present tense marker, respectively. In providing reasonable analyses of them, we will consider some implications of the misanalyses, especially from a computational point of view.

Most Korean linguists assume that the *ha-* in *kongpwu-ha-* ('to study'), for example, is a derivational affix and, hence, *kongpwu-ha-* as a whole is a verb.[1] However, as we can see shortly, *ha-* itself is an independent word and [*kongpwu ha-*] is a phrase. More Korean linguists assume that the element *-(nu)n-* is a present tense marker. However, the Korean tense system becomes far simpler, if we assume that the present tense marker is null (-ø-) rather than *-(nu)n-*.

2 The Morpho-syntactic Status of Some Dependent Elements

As an agglutinative language, Korean has rather complex structures of word-like expressions. Hence, it is not always easy to determine the

---

[1] Noticeable exceptions are Song (1967: 64-71), Suh (1991: 486, 1994: 578, 1996: 346), Chae (1996) and some others. They have shown, for example, that *ha-* in *kongpwu-ha-* cannot be a derivational affix and that [*kongpwu ha-*] and [*kongpwu-lul ha-*] are realizations of the same syntactic structure.

The Japanese counterpart of the Korean *ha-* is *suru*. The unit of verbal noun plus *suru* is also regarded as a word by most Japanese linguists. However, this is very dubious.

a) bengkyou-bakari/wa/... suru
   study -only/Contr do
b) ??bengkyou yoku/nagaku/... suru
   well/long time
c) [bengkyou-to undou]-bakari/wa/... suru
   -and exercise

Although it is not very natural for such independent words as *yoku* and *nagaku* to come between the two elements, as we can see in (b), delimiters like *-bakari* and *-wa* are allowed as in (a). In addition, the verbal noun before *suru* can be conjoined, as we can see in (c). These facts show that *bengkyou-suru* is not a word but a phrase (and, hence, such expressions should not be registered as head words in dictionaries).

morpho-syntactic status of a dependent element, whether it is a derivational affix, an inflectional affix or something else.

When a root/stem and another element which seems to be dependent on it stand next to each other, the dependent element can usually be analyzed either as a derivational affix or as an inflectional affix. In Korean, however, many such elements cannot be analyzed as either of them. For example, postpositions are neither derivational affixes nor inflectional affixes (Chae and No 1998: 73).[2]

(1) [[nae-ka nol-te-n] kos-eyse
I-Nom play-Retro-Rel place-at
chac-ass-ta]
find-Past-Decl
'(I) found (it) in the place where I used to play.'

The postposition *-eyse* is not a derivational affix. If it is, we have to assume that the relative clause [*nae-ka nol-ten*] in (1) modifies an adverb (i.e. *kos-eyse*) rather than a noun (i.e. *kos*). It is very clear that relative clauses cannot modify adverbs. Postpositions, including *-eyse*, cannot be analyzed as inflectional affixes, either. Firstly, they make nominal expressions have adverbial functions. Although it is true that some nouns have adverbial functions (especially, those which represent time or space), it would be very unnatural to argue that the "inflected forms" of pronouns and proper nouns can have all the adverbial functions which are expressed by the postpositions. Secondly, the whole range of different postpositions is not likely to form an inflectional paradigm. There are more than ten atomic postpositions and more than dozens of (even hundreds of) complex postpositions in Korean.

Elements like postpositions can best be analyzed as clitics,[3] i.e. those units which are separate words syntactically but are not independent phonologically. Korean has a variety of clitics. However, their existence has not been duly appreciated in the tradition of Korean linguistics (cf. Chae and No 1998: sec. III, Chae 2007: sec. II). According to Chae (2007), all the members of postpositions and delimiters are clitics, and nouns, adjectives (or descriptive verbs), adnominals and adverbs have clitic members as well as regular members. Based on these observations, he provides a new classification system of parts of speech in Korean. This system comprises not only regular words but also clitics because both of them are words syntactically.

Taking clitics into consideration, we can distinguish three different types of dependent elements: derivational affixes (DA), inflectional affixes (IA) and clitics.

(2) $[[X_{root}\text{-DA}]_{stem}\text{-IA}]$ - Clitics ... (Words)

The former two constitute parts of words, while the latter, i.e. clitics, are words themselves even though they are dependent on neighboring elements phonologically. Among the two word-internal elements, derivational affixes are more closely related to their roots than inflectional affixes to their stems.

It is rather unfortunate that clitics have not been seriously taken into account in analyzing Korean sentences, which means that the very building blocks of sentences, i.e. (regular and clitic) words, have not been recognized properly. Of course, the main reason for this unfortunate tradition is due to the fact that clitics are not independent phonologically. That is, the very nature of the language itself is partly responsible for such a tradition.

It is not easily understandable, however, that many regular words are also considered as dependent elements in Korean. Firstly, such expressions as the following are assumed to be compounds (Lee 2005: 44).

(3) a. nach-sel-ta, pich-na-ta
face-[]-Decl light-[]-Decl
'to be unfamiliar' 'to shine'
b. nach-i (manhi) sel-ta, pich-i na-nta
-Nom -Nom

It may be true that the predicates in such verbal expressions as those in (a) have some degree of idiomatic meanings. However, (the degree of) idiomaticity has nothing to do with the morpho-syntactic status of expressions (cf. Roh 2013: 37). Please note that, as we can see in (b), the nominative marker *-i* can be attached to the noun

[2] The abbreviations used for grammatical terms in this paper are as follows. Nom: Nominative, Acc: Accusative, Retro: Retrospective, Rel: Relativizer, Past: Past Tense, Pres: Present Tense, Decl: Declarative, Progr: Progressive.

[3] Clitics are "grammatical units with some properties of inflectional morphology and some of independent words" (Zwicky and Pullum 1983, Zwicky 1985). They have the former properties as far as phonological phenomena are concerned and the latter properties when syntactic phenomena are concerned.

before the predicate. In addition, such adverbs as *manhi* 'many/much' can be inserted between the noun and the predicate. These facts clearly indicate that the expressions in (a) are all phrases rather than compound words. Secondly, such verbal elements as *ha-*, *toy-* and *sikhi-* are assumed to be derivational affixes not only in most Korean grammar books and dictionaries but also in most research papers (cf. footnote 1).

(4) a. phakoy-ha-ta
    destruction-do-Decl 'to destroy'
  b. phakoy-toy-ta
    -become 'to be destroyed'
  c. phakoy-sikhi-ta
    -let … do 'to (let …) destroy'

(5) a. phakoy-lul ha-ta
    -Acc
  b. phakoy-ka toy-ta
    -Nom
  c. phakoy-lul sikhi-ta
    -Acc

As they are analyzed as derivational affixes, all the expressions in (4) are regarded as verbs rather than verb phrases. However, they cannot be verbs as we can see from the data in (5), which show that accusative or nominative markers, which can only come at the end of object/subject phrases, can be inserted in between.

Among the numerous examples of misanalyses (cf. Chae 2010), the type in (4) is the least expected one, because a regular word is analyzed as a derivational affix. Regular words are completely independent from the preceding root/word and, hence, they do not belong to the dependent elements listed in (2). They are more independent units than clitics. Derivational affixes are the least independent from its root. There is another unexpected type of misanalysis. In this type part of a word which cannot be a separate morpheme is analyzed as one. Although there are not many examples of this type, it is also unusual in the sense that morphemes are not difficult to factor out, especially in an agglutinative language. In the remaining sections of this paper, we will focus on only one example from each of these two types of misanalyses: the "light verb" *ha-* and the assumed present tense marker *-(nu)n-*. We will not only elucidate their morpho-syntactic statuses but also consider computational implications of the misanalysis.

3 The Verbal *ha-*

In this section, we will firstly examine the morpho-syntactic status of the verbal *ha-*. Then, we will consider what kinds of implications the popular misanalysis has for automatic analyses.

3.1 The Morpho-syntactic Status

The agglutinative nature of Korean makes it difficult to distinguish between word-internal elements like (derivational and inflectional) affixes and word-external elements like clitics. What makes the belief that the verbal *ha-* is a derivational affix be mysterious is that it is not even a clitic but a wholly independent word. Let us examine the following examples:

(6) cyon-i kongpwu-ha-ko
  John-Nom study do-Progr
  iss-ta
  be-(Pres)-Decl
  'John is studying.'

(7) cyon-i kongpwu(-lul) cal/manhi/…
    -Acc well/much/…
  ha-ko iss-ta
  'John is studying well/much/…'

Judging from the data in (7), which show that external elements can be inserted between *kongpwu* and *ha-*, it becomes clear that *ha-* is a word and [*kongpwu ha-*] is a phrase. That is, *kongpwu* and *ha-* are two independent words (Song 1967, Suh 1991, Chae 1996, Chae and Chong 2011, among others). Firstly, the accusative marker *-(l)ul* can be inserted between them. Secondly, such adverbs as *cal* and *manhi* can also be inserted between them freely. We do not need any more evidence to establish the morpho-syntactic status of *ha-* as an independent word.

Those who take the wordhood of *kongpwu-ha-* for granted argue that such expressions as [*kongpwu cal ha-*] are derived from the phrase [*kongpwu-lul ha-*], deleting the accusative marker *-lul* and adding the adverb *cal*. Under this kind of argumentation, it is assumed that [*kongpwu cal ha-*] has nothing to do with the "word" *kongpwu-ha-*. However, there are serious problems with such an approach. First of all, it is not understandable at all that *kongpwu-ha-* does not have any (formal) relationship with [*kongpwu-lul ha-*] or [*kongpwu cal ha-*]. These latter expressions have no special meanings different from that of the former expression, except that they contain *-lul* and *cal*, respectively. Secondly, the argument is not falsifiable, which leads to a non-scientific research. It is not falsifiable because all units of [NP V] can be argued to be words rather than phrases:

(8) a. pap-ul (cal) mek-ta
rice-Acc well eat-Decl
b. pap (cal) mek-ta
'to eat boiled rice (well)'

(9) a. hakkyo-ey (cacu) ka-ta
school-to often go-Decl
b. hakkyo (cacu) ka-ta
'to go to school (often)'

If *kongpwu-ha-* is argued to be a word despite such expressions as [*kongpwu-lul ha-*] and [*kongpwu cal ha-*],[4] it can also be argued that [*pap mek-*] in (8b) and [*hakkyo ka-*] in (9b) are words rather than phrases. Under this kind of argumentation, we can say that [*pap cal mek-*] and [*hakkyo cacu ka-*] are derived from [*pap-ul mek-*] in (8a) and [*hakkyo-ey ka-*] in (9a), respectively, rather than from the "words" [*pap mek-*] and [*hakkyo ka-*]. However, even those who assume that *kongpwu-ha-* is a word will not accept that [*pap mek-*] and [*hakkyo ka-*] are words.

3.2 Computational Implications

If we cannot factor out a regular word *ha-* from expressions like *kongpwu-ha-*, we cannot provide a systematic analysis of the expressions containing it. In that case, *kongpwu-ha-* and [*kongpwu cal ha-*], for example, can only be analyzed with reference to two unrelated mechanisms. The former should be listed in the dictionary because it is assumed to be a word. The latter, on the other hand, should be treated in the syntactic component on the basis of the three lexical items *kongpwu, cal,* and *ha-* and relevant syntactic rules and/or principles.

The situation becomes more serious in automatic analyses than in manual analyses. First of all, it is impossible to capture any formal relationships between *kongpwu-ha-* and [*kongpwu cal ha-*], because they are outputs of two different components and they do not even share any lexical items. However, it is clear that the only difference between them is due to the (non-)existence of the adverb *cal*, which is impossible to capture under the popular approach. Secondly, it is very difficult, though may not be impossible, to capture the semantic relationship between the two expressions. Thirdly, all the lexical entries involved have to be registered twice, leading to a significant amount of redundancy (Chae 2010). Although *kongpwu-ha-* is registered in the dictionary, *kongpwu* and *ha-* have to be registered as well. Notice that these words appear in the phrase [*kongpwu cal ha-*], in which the adverb *cal* is in between the two words. Lastly, the system will produce two different analyses of *kongpwu-ha-*: as a lexical item and as a syntactic construct. As we have *kongpwu* and *ha-* as separate lexical items, there is no reasonable way of preventing the combination of them to produce [*kongpwu ha-*], which is the same as the lexical item *kongpwu-ha-*.

We have seen problems with only one example. From a computational point of view, the sheer number of *ha*-expressions in Korean makes the popular misanalysis more difficult to maintain. It may be the case that expressions containing *ha-* would be more than half of the whole verbal expressions in representative Korean corpora.

4 The Verbal Element *-(nu)n-*

In this section, we will examine the behavior of the verbal element *-(nu)n-*. Although it is usually assumed to be a present tense marker, the assumption is based on superficial observations. A more careful observation will lead to the conclusion that the present tense marker, more accurately, the non-past tense marker is null (-ø-) rather than *-(nu)n-*. Of course, there are some previous works which argue for this position like Kang (1988), Suh (1994) and others. However, the argument has not been taken seriously in Korean linguistics, just like that for the wordhood of *ha-* in *kongpwu-ha-* (cf. footnote 1).

4.1 The Morpho-syntactic Status

The popular belief that *-(nu)n-* is a present tense marker is based on such data as the following:[5]

[4] One might argue that the verbal *ha-* cannot be regarded as an independent word because it does not have its own meaning. However, semantic facts do not necessarily go together with morpho-syntactic facts. That is, the meaning of a unit cannot tell whether it is a word or not.

[5] The verbal marker *-(nu)n* has two variants: *-nun* after a verb ending in a consonant and *-n* after a verb ending in a vowel.

(10) a. cyon-i cip-ey ka-n-ta
John-Nom house-to go-Pres-Decl

b. cyon-i cip-ey ka-ass-ta
-Past
'John goes/went home.'

(11) a. cyon-i pap-ul mek-nun-ta
John-Nom rice-Acc eat-Pres-Decl
b. cyon-i pap-ul mek-ess-ta
-Past
'John eats/ate boiled rice.'

When we compare the two sentences in (10) and in (11), it seems to be very obvious that *-(nu)n-* is in a paradigmatic relation with the past tense marker *-ass/ess*.

However, if we observe the behavior of the element *-(nu)n-* more carefully, we will see that there are many problems with the popular belief. First of all, *-(nu)n-* is not actually in a paradigmatic relation with the past tense marker.

(12) a. ka(*-n)-keyss-ta
Go -Modality-Decl
ka(-ass)-keyss-ta
b. mek(*-nun)-keyss-ta
eat
mek(-ess)-keyss-ta

The past tense marker can occur before the irrealis modality marker *-keyss*, but the assumed present tense marker cannot.

Secondly, the distribution of *-(nu)n-* is very limited:

(13) a. ka(*-n)-(nu)nya, mek(*-nun)-(nu)nya
-Interrogative
b. ka(*-n)-kela, mek(*-nun)-ela
-Directive
c. ka(*-n)-ca, mek(*-nun)-ca
-Propositive

(14) a. ka(*-n/ok-ass)-a/e,
mek(*-nun/ok-ess)-e
b. ka(*-n/ok-ass)-ney,
mek(*-nun/ok-ess)-ney
c. ka(*-n/ok-ass)-o,
mek(*-nun/ok-ess)-uo/o
d. ka(*-n/ok-ass)-a/e-yo,
mek(*-nun/ok-ess)-e-yo
e. ka(*-n/ok-ass)-pnita/supnita,
mek(*-nun/ok-ess)-supnita

Korean verbal endings have different forms according to sentence type and speech level. There are at least four different sentence types: declaratives, interrogatives, directives and propositives. There are six different speech levels, from the least formal to the most formal. Among the twenty four possible combinations of the two grammatical categories, only one combination requires the element *-n-* or *-nun-*: that of the declarative sentence[6] and the (least formal) plain level sentence, as we can see in (10a) and (11a). The element does not appear in the other combinations. As we can see in (13), it cannot combine with the interrogative, directive or propositive ending, even when the speech level concerned is the plain level. In addition, as we can see in (14), it cannot combine with any of the other speech level endings.

We can easily solve these problems if we assume that the non-past tense marker is *-ø-*. Under this assumption, the variants of *-(nu)n-*, i.e. *-n-* and *-nun-*, are just parts of the (present) declarative endings of verbs in the plain speech level. That is, we can assume that *-nta* and *-nunta* are "portmanteau" morphs,[7] i.e. those morphs which can be analyzed into more than one morpheme (Crystal 1980, Spencer 1991).[8] The

---

6 What seems to be "exclamative endings," among others, also contain *-nun-*.

a) cip-ey ka-nunkwuna/nunkwun.
house-to go-Ending
'(He/She) does go home!'
b) cal mek-nunkwuna/nunkwun.
well eat-Ending
'How well (he/she) eats!'
c) san-i khu/cak-kwuna/kwun.
mountain-Nom be big/small-Ending
'How big/small the mountain is!'

Compared with the endings after adjectives (or descriptive verbs) in (c), those after verbs have the extra element *-nun-* in (a-b). However, there is enough evidence to show that Korean does not have a separate sentence type of exclamative. What seems to be exclamative sentences have the formal properties of declarative sentences. Hence, the sentences above belong to declaratives in Korean (Lee 2005: 170-171).

7 We are in line with Yongkyoon No's assumption in "... the selection from allomorphs *-nunta/nta/ta* ..." (Chae and No 1998: 91). He regards *-nunta, -nta* and *-ta* as allomorphs of one and same morpheme.

8 Portmanteau morphs are defined/described in the literature as follows: "A term used in morphological analysis referring to cases where a single morph can be analysed into more than one morpheme, ..." (Crystal 1980: 276); "... the term portmanteau, which in this context means type of fusion of two morphemes into one. ... we have four morphemes all realized by a single portmanteau morph ... In a portmanteau morph, then,

two portmanteau morphs indicate the present tense of the plain level declarative sentence. The former is used when the stem of the verb concerned ends in a vowel, and the latter when it ends in a consonant. The point here is that they are indivisible morphs which contain not only the information about the sentence type and the sentence level but also the information about the tense of the verb concerned.

Under the *-ø*-tense marker approach, *-(nu)n-* is inseparable from the predicative ending *-ta* and, hence, cannot take the position of tense markers. In addition, the non-past and the past tense markers take the same position:

(15) a. ka-ø-nta, mek-ø-nunta (cf. (10-11))
b. ka-ø-keyss-ta, mek-ø-keyss-ta (cf. (12))
c. ka-ø-(nu)nya, mek-ø-(nu)nya (cf. (13a))
d. ka-ø/ass-e, mek-ø/ess-e (cf. (14a))

As we can see from this reanalysis of the data in (10-14), we can account for the ungrammatical data in (12-14) very naturally. In (12), the inseparable *-(nu)n-* and *-ta* are separated from each other. In (13) and (14), *-(nu)n-* stands alone without its inseparable "partner" *-ta*.

Before leaving this section, we need to introduce a constraint, with reference to the following data:

(16) a. *ka-ass-nunta, *mek-ess-nunta
b. *ka-ø-keyss-nunta, *mek-ø-keyss-nunta

In (a), although the past tense marker takes the same position as that of the non-past tense marker (cf. (15a)), the expressions concerned are ungrammatical. They are ungrammatical just because the portmanteau morph *-nunta* occurs with the past tense marker. In (b), although the morph *-nunta* occurs with the non-past marker, the expressions are ungrammatical as well. We need to postulate that the morph has to be immediately preceded by the non-past tense marker. Notice that this constraint accounts for both types of data in (16).

several categories are realized by one surface formative, an instance of a one-many correspondence between form and function" (Spencer 1991: 50-51).

4.2 Computational Implications

As we have seen with reference to the data in (13) and (14), among dozens of possible combinations of speech level and sentence type, only one combination of the plain level and the declarative sentence requires *-n-* or *-nun-*. All the other combinations cannot have the element. Then, it would be very difficult to account for the distribution of *-(nu)n-* computationally, if we assume that it is a present tense marker. Please notice that, as is shown in (14), the past tense marker *-ass/ess* can occur in the position where the element *-(nu)n-* is not allowed to occur.

When we deal with computational systems, we have to consider the understanding process and the productions process separately, just as the two areas of speech recognition and speech synthesis show. From an understanding point of view, the traditional approach fails to interpret many present tense forms. For example, *ka-a* and *mek-e* are correct present tense forms, although they do not have *-(nu)n-* (cf. (14)). From a production point of view, the approach produces a lot of ill-formed expressions: including all the ill-formed ones in (12-14). It would not be easy to filter out these expressions.

5 Conclusion

In this paper, we have surveyed some popular misanalyses in Korean morphology, focusing on two unexpected ones: the verbal *ha-* as a derivational affix and the verbal element *-(nu)n-* as a present tense marker. We have shown that careful observations reveal that *ha-* is an independent verb and that *-nun-* and *-n-* are parts of portmanteau morphs rather than independent morphemes themselves. It is really mysterious that such wrong analyses can become so popular in a scientific field of linguistics.

Acknowledgments

We are thankful to the anonymous reviewers, whose valuable comments have been very helpful in improving the quality of this paper. This work was supported by a 2013 research grant from Hankuk University of Foreign Studies.

References

Chae, Hee-Rahk. 1996. Properties of *ha-* and Light Predicate Constructions [written in Korean]. *Language Research*, 32(3), 409-476.

Chae, Hee-Rahk. 2007. Clitics and a Classification of Parts of Speech in Korean [written in Korean]. *Korean Journal of Linguistics*, 32(4), 803-826.

Chae, Hee-Rahk. 2010. Basic Units of Lexicons and Ontologies: Words, Senses and Concepts. *Proceedings of the 24th Pacific Asia Conference on Language, Information and Computation*, 35-44, Tohoku University.

Chae, Hee-Rahk and Wuk-Jae Chong. 2011. A Procedure for the Identification of Word Units in Korean. *Harvard Studies in Korean Linguistics* XIV, 67-76, Harvard-Yenching Institute.

Chae, Hee-Rahk and Yongkyoon No. 1998. A Survey of Morphological Issues in Korean: Focusing on Syntactically Relevant Phenomena. *Korean Linguistics* 9, International Circle of Korean Linguistics.

Crystal, David. 1980. *A First Dictionary of Linguistics and Phonetics*. Blackwell.

Kang, Beom-mo. 1988. *Functional Inheritance, Anaphora, and Semantic Interpretation*. Ph.D. dissertation, Brown University.

Lee, Iksop. 2005. *A Korean Grammar* [written in Korean]. Seoul National University Press.

Roh, Chang-Hwa. 2013. *A Study of Verb Sequences in Korean: Focusing on [V-e V] Expressions* [written in Korean]. Ph.D. dissertation, Hankuk University of Foreign Studies.

Sepencer, Andrew. 1991. *Morphological Theory*. Blackwell.

Song, Seok-Choong. 1967. *Some Transformational Rules in Korean*. Ph.D. dissertation, Indiana University.

Suh, Cheong-Soo. 1991. On the Korean Verbs Ha and TOY [written in Korean]. *Language Research* 27(3), 481-505.

Suh, Cheong-Soo. 1994. *Korean Grammar* [written in Korean]. The Deep-Rooted Tree Publishing.

Suh, Chong-Soo. 1996. *Contemporary Korean Grammar* [written in Korean]. Hanyang University Press.

Zwicky, Arnold. M. 1985. Clitics and Particles. *Language*, 61(2), 283-305.

Zwicky, Arnold M. and Geoffrey K. Pullum. 1983. Cliticization vs. Inflection: English *n't*. *Language* 59(3), 502-513.

*** Formatting Issue - Best Available Paper/Graphic ***

Creative Language Learning Projects with Emerging Digital Media

Chin-chi Chao
National Chengchi University
NO.64, Sec.2, ZhiNan Rd., Wenshan District,
Taipei City 11605,Taiwan (R.O.C)
cchao@nccu.edu.tw

Abstract

This paper introduces seven genres of the digital media projects that can help the 21st century EFL learner develop intercultural communication capability (ICC) in English with creativity afforded by emerging digital media. It is based on a project by the author and a group of pre-service teachers during the Fall semester of 2012-2013. Guided by a list of suggested topics and the concept of learner-centeredness, the team discovered many useful project ideas. Although communicative language teaching, task-based language teaching, and multiple intelligences are all behind the applications, we found that when learner-centeredness is the guiding principle and ICC is the goal, possibilities are abundant. It is true that we are only limited by our imagination when it comes to teaching a language with digital media. The purpose of this workshop is not to exhaust all the possibilities, but to help the audience become aware of the availability of the many language learning projects which afford opportunities for the key principle and the goal. As new tools emerge, the particular digital media introduced might become obsolete, but the key concepts presented here will make sure that new tools will be used in a creative and meaningful way to support language learning.

1 Introduction

Software applications for second and foreign language learning purposes have come a long way. Warschauser (1996), among others, has categorized the evolution of computer assisted language learning into different stages: behavioristic, communicative, and integrative. Whatever the changes and no matter what new tools are emerging, suggestions made by language educators have been relatively stable for the past two decades. In fact, the key pedagogical philosophy that has been advocated for the best classroom integration is always along the line of constructivism and learner-centeredness. It is found that teachers who operate based on these concepts often could provide students with the 21st-century learning experiences, combining media technology and master expertise to motivate students to inquire, to find answers, and to learn. One important characteristic for this kind of learning experience is creativity afforded by a project-based approach which allows sufficient room for learners to use the digital media to express themselves in the target language and experience the target culture, no matter how limited the learner's proficiency is.

Although many forms of software application have emerged in recent years and used widely in everyday life and work, research continuously finds that they are not used much in everyday language classroom. One of the reasons is that teachers do not have the time to explore and create ways to integrate the tools into classroom instruction. In addition, many language teachers tend to think of applications too narrowly: only those with language learning content are considered worthwhile, missing out a large number of other possibilities. There is a need for language teachers to understand the variety of genres of language learning project available in order to bring active and fulfilling learning experiences to the learner and make the most of the digital media.

The seven genres discussed in this paper were identified and carefully examined by the author with the help from a group of pre-service language teachers during the school year 2012-2013. Guided by a list of suggested topics and the concept of learner-centeredness, the team explored and then discovered many useful project ideas that encourage creativity in learning English. Although communicative language teaching, task-based language teaching, and multiple intelligences are all behind the applications, we found that when learner-centeredness and creativity are the guiding instructional principle and intercultural communication competence (ICC, Fantini, n/a, cited in Godwin-Jones, 2013) is the learning goal, possibilities are abundant. It is true that we are only limited by our imagination when it comes to teaching a language with the digital media.

2 The Rationale

Although there are many different types of applications on the internet that can be used for language learning, it is possible to think of them as affording two major types of language learning experiences: One is those that abide to a drill-and-practice or paper-and-pencil quiz or exercise mode of language practice. This more familiar method can come in many different forms including, for example, multiple choice, matching, and many other quiz types that created by the *ot otatoes* suite or a simple shooting game that involves one learner interacting with a digital media. It is obvious that these applications emphasize mastery of basic language skills. With intercultural communication competence, however, such discrete level or fact-oriented exercises without the learner's personal engagement in the target culture may not be the best option. For the purpose of developing cultural understanding, learners need the experience "to approach, appreciate, and bond with people from other cultures" (Shrum & Glisan, 2005, p. 136), and the project-based approach is considered more appropriate. It treats the language learner as a language user, not learner, allowing them to make use of everyday digital tools and to take many different paths to use their language in order to develop intercultural communication competence.

There are multiple theoretical originations for project-based learning. John Dewey (1859-1952), American psychologist, philosopher, educator, social critic and political activist is the key scholar project-based learning was attributed to. In TESOL, project-based language learning can also be supported by the communicative language teaching (CLT) approach and the philosophy of learner-centeredness with much emphasis on giving sufficient room for the production of language and learner autonomy. CLT as an umbrella term for many of the recent language teaching methods such as task-based language learning is often used to characterize a language classroom that has a large amount of interaction among students, rather than merely between a teacher and a class of students. The teacher is not the only person that is active while the learner passively listening to organized materials that have already been selected and processed for them, as in a lecture hall. On the contrary, the learner is engaged in meaningful communication and learning to fulfill daily functions in the target language, as which are the main goal of CLT. Authentic language is emphasized, and accuracy and fluency are both important. Communication skills are developed mostly through group or pair work, roleplays, games, and simulations that have some kind of information gaps which students must work out collaboratively using the target language in its four integrated skills. It brings the focus of learning and instruction to production, making it clear that language learning must develop both active productive and receptive skills (Larsen-Freeman and Anderson, 2011).

However, if students only work through information gaps, this is still a teacher-controlled form of practice with limited language learning outcomes. Using project-based learning it is possible to develop expert knowledge and cultural understanding in the new language, which becomes the stronger version of CLT: i.e., content-based language learning (Larsen-Freeman and Anderson, 2011, p. 131): learners are not learning to use English, but using English to learn something new. It also does not have 'predetermined linguistic content' as the weak version of CLT. The goal is mastering both the content cultural, and language in an authentic context. Thus, content-based language learning also lends a strong support to project-based learning, an approach that has often been considered the best use of technology in education.

3 Features of Project-based Language Learning

Project-based language learning is actually a challenging and time consuming process, but it could lead to rewarding results that are not possible with more traditional methods. In Boss and Krauss's approach to projects, five features are emphasized (2007, p. 12):

- Projects form the centerpiece of the curriculum – they are not an add-on or extra at the end of a "real" unit.
- Students engage in real-world activities and practice the strategies of authentic disciplines.
- Students work collaboratively to solve problems that matter to them.
- Technology is integrated as a tool for

discovery, collaboration, and communication, taking learners places they could not otherwise go and helping teachers achieve essential learning goals in new ways.
- Increasingly, teachers collaborate to design and implement projects that cross geographic boundaries or even jump time zones.

Dudeney and Hockly (2007), on the other hand, has provided the following as the features:

- Both short-term and long-term
- Group activities
- Communication & Sharing of knowledge
- Cooperative & Interaction
- No specialist technical knowledge is needed
- Real-world
- Greater motivation
- Encourage critical thinking skills
- Ss do not just regurgitate information, but have to transform that information in order to achieve a given task

There are many different forms of projects, including creative writing projects, computer-mediated communication projects, or inquiry projects. It can be for language learning purposes only, interdisciplinary, or requiring integrated language skills. Successful projects have to be structured, and it needs time to plan and design. Dudeney and Hockly specified four basic steps for implementing a successful project:

1. Choose the project topic: Will your learners be researching famous people, an event or an issue?
2. Make the task clear: What information will they need to find – biographical, factual, views and opinions?
3. Find the resources: Which websites will your learners need to visit? Do these websites contain the information they need and are they at the right level?
4. Decide on the outcome: What is the final purpose of the project? For example, will your learners be making a poster, a presentation or holding a debate?

This list is similar to the steps for a WebQuest project, a web-based inquiry project that aims to make the best use of online resources for all subject areas. Bernie Dodge (1997) defines Webquest as "an inquiry-oriented activity in which some or all of the information that learners interact with comes from resources on the internet, optionally supplemented with videoconferencing." It is structured as a series of webpage which present the project information as the introduction, question & task, the process, resources, and conclusion (March, n/d). These steps can be considered the basic components of project-based instructional design. One important aspect is to decide a project genre. There have been many different projects genres developed by language educators all over the world, but the seven below all use emerging digital media in some way and have been advocated as creative yet useful for foreign language learning.

.

4 Seven Genres of Creative Project-based FL Learning with Digital Media

Although information sources for project-based learning such as the WebQuest Central provide many project design patterns, not all of them are useful for FL (Foreign language learning) or EFL (English as a foreign language) learners. EFL is similar to FL but is very different from all the other school subjects. Most significantly, learners are supposed to *se* a language that they are not familiar with. Thus, Sox and Rubinstein-Avila (2009) assert that WebQuest projects (WQs) for English language learners have to have three extra features in addition to those for conventional WQs: linguistic, multimedia, and organizational. That is, the language used for explaining the project has to be simple and concise, information must be presented with multiple modality, and pages and information must be consistently organized in order to assist comprehension. Other researchers (Koenraad and Westhoff, 2003; Koenraad, 2005) also specified the importance of attending to SLA and CLT theoretical considerations such as having sufficient language input and output opportunities. Drawing on the unique needs for foreign language learners, seven project genres are presented below.

4.1 Genre 1: Language Quest

Seeing the uniqueness of foreign language learning process, language educators in Netherland first developed Language Quest as a special form of WebQuest (Koenraad and Westhoff, 2003; Koenraad, 2005). In addition to following the principles of a WebQuest as developed by Dodge, Language Quest also have the following features based on CLT:

- The task should encourage the use of the target language as instruction language and language in use for the duration of the task and for the end products of the Language Quest.
- The material presented in the Language Quest should be authentic. The tasks within the Language Quest should be functional and realistic.
- The task should be learner-oriented and should therefore be attractive and related to the learner's reality.
- Students can work on the task in a flexible way. The task offers different routes, media, procedures and ways of collaborating.
- The task should encourage students to exchange information and expertise, preferably in the target language.

Koenraad and Westhoff (2003, 2005) used a webquest that plans a visit to the Disneyland as an example of the Language Quest project. Levi Altstaedter and Jones (2009) used the same travelling theme with a group of Spanish learners who designed a brochure, created a concept map, and wrote a reflective essay in Spanish for a trip to Argentina. In a study with language teachers (Chao, 2006), it was found that designing itineraries for overseas trips is indeed the particular WebQuest pattern most often chosen by EFL teachers. The final product of such projects allows the learner to introduce the target country with multiple modality of literacy, making use of texts, pictures, photos, videos, or sound tracks that they found on the Internet representing various places that they mean to visit. Other LanguageQuest products are reports, videos, plays, or exhibitions, which involve the learner in reading authentic information (authentic input), planning based on their understanding of the target language culture, linking language learning with a real-world context, and finally engaging in creating the product through the pushed output process (Swain, 1995; Swain and Lapkin, 1995). All the materials the learner use is authentic, functional, and indeed realistic. The active construction process can be attractive and motivating to the learner and thus are considered a useful project genre for foreign language learners.

4.2 Genre 2: Virtual Quest

Although LanguageQuest is promising for language learning, there is one key problem: FL or EFL learners tend not to communicate in the target language (TL) among themselves in the process. To create reasons to use the TL during the project, teachers need to make use of computer-mediated community, or CMC, a form of digital projects that has in recent years generated a large number of studies among language educators and researchers (e.g., Jin, 2013; Liaw, 2006; Stockwell and Stockwell, 2003; Warschauer, 1995). With CMC, language learners have the opportunity to work with another group of learners who may or may be native speakers but are from a different geographical location. In order to create a product for the project collaboratively, the learners have no choice but to communicate with one another in the target language, and the interaction between the local and the distanced partner is made through the internet communication tools, such as email, Facebook, conferencing tools, or Skype.

One unique CMC study which made use of the 3D virtual environment, *e on i e*, to engage foreign language learners in a *an a e est* is Vickers (2010), who called his project *irt a est*. Usually when creating a product is the focus, both teachers and learners tend to overlook the learning opportunities in the process. VirtualQuest allows learners to first experience and then stop to reflect on the experience and learn from it. Different from *We ests* or *an a e ests* which aim to create a product, *irt a ests* are exploratory in nature and aim to create language learning content from unplanned dialogues, conversations, and cultural experiences that occur in *e on i e* as the learner interact with others. Learners define their tasks in the virtual environment, which then lead to a product output as well as learning materials for the whole class. This practice is supported by a language teaching approach called the Dogme language learning (Meddings and Thornbury, 2009), which aims to draw learning materials from the learner's experience interacting with others instead of depending on a textbook. The example provided by Victers is an English learner who investigated a variety of ways to use SL in order meet people, get an understanding of the environment, explore places, and learn English. Although the learner had difficulty using voice chats and participating in group talks with a large number of native speakers in SL, in his final presentation he reported his experiences and evaluated SL as "a good way to learn English." This learner's experience reminds this author of many other ways to use MOOs (Multi-user, Object-Oriented) or text-based virtual realities for language learning in the early days of CALL. For example, learners can use SL to perform a soap opera (Turner, 1998), to enact a historical event, or to engage in collaborative writing projects. This emergent and dialogic pedagogy can also creation cultural immersion opportunities for FL as well as EFL learners. It also features autonomy, relevance and motivation and thus is recognized as very appropriate for learning ICC with web2.0 tools.

4.3 Genre 3: Presentation Projects

Depending on the level of learners, it is also possible to engage learners in a presentation genre of projects, such as having the learner use digital media to introduce their country, their family, their favorite person, and their room. For WebQuest scholars and practitioners such as Bonnie Dudge and Tom March, this task may not be considered a Webquest because there seems not much critical thinking and web resources involved. However, with such projects EFL learners could engage in pushed or comprehensible output (Swain, 1995; Swain and Lapkin, 1995), which is a process that allows learners to experiment with the new language by actually using it while getting necessary feedback from interlocutors. In this indispensible process for language development, the learner may look as if only copying and pasting what they see on the Internet, but the selection of information, figuring out the written information, reorganizing and restructuring the material, and presenting the material in written or oral production using appropriate language forms to an audience are important and difficult literacy to develop.

In this author's oral training classes, EFL learners have been asked to engage in such projects. The topics used include " *is is a orite* " in which the learner presents a topic that they like, such as their favorite vocal artists, dance genres, and sports, while " *o a not no t is t* " allow students to present a new piece information to the class and involve the class in hands-on learning activities. With the focus on fluency, the principle for selecting a topic is that every learner must have something to say about the topic. Selection of tools is of the students' choice. They could use all the audio-visual media that they think useful, but it is specified that video clips and songs cannot be played more than one fifth of the whole presentation time (i.e., 4 minutes out of the total 20) since most of the time should be used for the presenter to speak in person in the target language. Tools that students use for these presentations are many, including the camera and video functions in their own smartphones, *o er oint* and *rezi*. Oftentimes students would also create a short movie with Movie Maker or download one from *o t e*. These presentations, although do not require collaboration, are challenging and rewarding to the presenter because of the hard work involved before, during and after the presentation. Students usually are nervous and stiff at the first presentation during the school year, and gradually become more comfortable and feel proud of their own ability to present an extensive topic with reputable performance. For learners of weaker language skills, the topics can be less challenging and the presentation can be made less lengthy, and the effects can be expected to be equally positive.

4.4 Genre 4: Visual Projects

Visual projects for the purpose of develop intercultural communicative competence do not simply put learners at the position of a consumer of ready-made graphics or visuals. Instead, it is important to engage learners in playful, creative use of language using various visual tools and artifacts, such as images, photos, videos, maps, ads. With these visuals, learners can also be encouraged to express their feelings by telling a story, writing a poem, creating a fairy tale, making a drawing, or creating a comic (Godwin-Jones, 2013)

Many digital applications have recently become available which allow users to create graphics and visuals with great convenience. These tools are useful both when the learner creates their own graphics (i.e., learners engage in production) or when they are given graphics to mediate understanding (i.e., learners in comprehension). With self-created visuals such as pictures and photos, it is possible for the learner to accomplish two goals in the language learning process: arousing interest and mediating text-based language development with an alternative mode of expression – one that feels natural and comfortable for most youngsters and visual learners. On the other hand, compared with words and abstract symbols, graphics and images can also help the learner construct a concrete understanding even when they are struggling with an unfamiliar foreign language discourse.

Two recent tools can best represent such a graphic-creating genre: *oon oo* and *i roso t oto tor* . The former is an online website for creating cartoons. Instead of drawing from scratch with an electronic pen brush as the simple drawing tool available in every computer, the user of *oon oo* is now given a wide variety of ready-made graphic components, such as different natural scenes, backgrounds, buildings, furniture, everyday objects, animals, as well as bodies, noses and eyes of different shapes and colors. To get started, the user first selects one, two, three, or four frames as well as a horizontal or vertical page layout; it is also possible to create cartoon e-books, which are formed by connecting a series of one-frame cartoon pages. Most importantly, a feature of *oon oo* is its community undertone, a common feature for all Web 2.0 tools. In the case of *oon oo*, the community feature means that all the created works can be shared or made available to all visitors, registered members, or designated individuals, giving an authentic reason to engage in creation. Members can also give others' works their appraisal, comment, and support so that real communication functions can be achieved. In addition, with this community feature, users and members can interact and learn from one another, generating a lot of creativity among users.

Another widely used tool in this genre is *otostor* , a familiar software application for producing photo slideshows. As *otostor* is a piece of stand-alone software, it does not have the community feature. However, as it is readily available in every computer, there is no worry about network failure. It is also a lot faster to put together a finished product than *oon oo*. The user first needs to select and input photos, and then with a few keystrokes and selecting actions, all photos will be displayed according to the user-assigned order creating a connected slideshow with proper transition effects. Appropriate background music could also make the slideshow look even more professional.

In terms of language classroom application, projects can be so designed that learner groups are asked to use *oon oo* in creating cartoon stories, which can later be used in speaking or writing assignments. Instead of the usual practice of writing or speaking in responding to teacher-created or professionally created cartoons, learners can be expected to feel more motivated to respond to peer-created cartoons. With *otostor* , project ideas include "My Favorite Home Cooking" or "My Dream Life." With teenager learners, it is important to make sure that every student has something to say about the topic and that no negative feelings could be generated because of the theme.

4.5 Genre 5: Journalism Projects

Having students work as a journalist could make use of all four language skills. Examples include creating a narrated tour, oral history, or digital storytelling, as Godwin-Jones (2013) suggested. Learners could also interview native speakers or other people to collect data for a written or oral report on a topic of interest to themselves. Gardener (1995), for example, reported how the learner's production of video documentary could lead to authentic language use. *i eport* is a website in which students can submit their news stories and get published. The types of digital media that could be used to support journalism projects are plenty, including all those available in a smartphone such as a camera, video, sound recording, note-taking functions and applications. For EFL or FL learners, the challenge of finding people for such a project can be met by conducting interviews with native speaker interviewees online or with local people and then translate the discussion into English. Another way of creating journalist content is using 'Scoop it', which allows the user to put together a page of specific information searched on the internet. All of these will be motivating projects for EFL learners.

4.6 Genre 6: Cultural Immersion Projects

Cultural immersion is difficult to achieve with EFL environments if not for networked digital devices. When learners explore and interact in the *e on i e*, for example, the whole experience could give the strong feeling of being immersed in a different country or culture. *e on i e* suggests some interesting and popular places to visit ranked according to topics (available at http://secondlife.com/destinations/learning). Websites that introduce overseas trips such as *ee o* are useful for a vicarious cultural immersion experience. With *ta o* , learners could also get to know all the tourist attractions in 140 cities of the world.

In addition, interactive videos can also bring cultural immersion when experts, guests, and other classrooms are invited through interactive video conferencing tools to interact with the learner in real time. Recently, mobile devices have also played a role in providing cultural immersion opportunities, as Godwin-Johns stated that students on a field trip or during study abroad could use the mobile device to interact with peers at home, engaging all the students in the overseas experience. These applications, however, have not been taken advantage of by many EFL classes, perhaps due to the high demand for technical stability for people to interact synchronously and through video signals.

4.7 Genre 7: Real-world Problem-solving Projects

Foreign language learners often do not think of themselves as having the ability to participate in world-world problem solving projects due to the perceived lack of sufficient language proficiency, but the Internet has created many such opportunities for everybody, including, of course, foreign language learners. There have been many K-12 EFL teachers from Taiwan and many parts of the world participating in world-wide problem-solving projects such as those sponsored by international organizations such as iEarn- International Education and Resource Network (http://www.iearn.org/). Students solve a real-world problem by working with other students from all over the world. As of September 2013- January 2014, project teams are solicited for producing a newspaper, regional history, creative writing, reporting on a hero, and discussing global issues in education and environment. Many of these will be real-world issues that students need to engage in inquiry and develop solutions. It is also possible to engage in local public service and then present or write about this experience. Liu (2012), for example, reported a project in which EFL university students wrote about their experience in real-world public service experiences.

5 Conclusion

This paper introduces seven genres of project-based foreign language learning. There are of course many other possibilities with other emerging tools. For example, Baralt, Pennestri, & Selvandin (2011) used *or es* in teaching writing, a tool that generates "word clouds" from text. Coniam (2008) reported the use of *at ots*, or online robots, as language learners' conversation partners. Music production with *in n* or *o e ition* are also possible to lead to EFL learning project ideas, although there have not been many researchers reporting the use music as a creative project with language learners.

With the newer tools constantly coming to the market, more creative project ideas can be expected. Language teachers could get inspirations from project information for other subject matters such as the Twenty Ideas for Engaging Projects by Edutopia or a PBS video documentary titled, Digital Media – New Learners of the 21st Century. The purpose of this paper is not to exhaust all the possibilities, but to help the reader become aware of (1) the importance of a guiding principle in selecting CALL tools, (2) the availability of the type of projects that afford the possibilities of using digital media for developing intercultural communication competence as well as language learning. As newer tools emerge, the particular digital media introduced here may become obsolete but the key concept of creative project-based learning will make sure that new tools will be used in a creative, productive, and meaningful way to support not just the more traditional concept of language development but also intercultural communication competence.

References

Baralt, M., Pennestri, S., & Selvandin, M. (2011). Using *or ess* to teach foreign language writing. *an a e earnin e no o*

Beckett, G. H. & Miller, P. C. (Eds.) (2006). *ro e t ase e on an orei n an a e ation ast resent an t re.* Greenwich, CN: Information Age Publishing. (available in the library as an e-book).

Boss, S., & Krauss, J. (2007). *ein entin pro e t ase earnin* . Eugene, OR: International Society for Technology in Education.

Chao, C. (2006). How WebQuests send technology to the background: Scaffolding EFL teacher professional development in CALL. In P.

Hubbard and M. Levy (Eds.), *ea er ation in* . John Benjamins.

Coniam, D. (2008). An evaluation of *at ots* as software aids to learning English as a second language . *e ro a e ie* , 13. Available online at http://www.eurocall-language.org.

Dodge, B. (1997). *o e t o ts a o t We ests*. San Diego, CA: San Diego State University. [Online.] Available at http://webquest.sdsu.edu/about_webquests.html (Dead link as of August 29, 2013).

Dudeney, G., & Hockly, N. (2007). *o to tea n is it te no o* . Pearson.

Edutopia (2011), *ent eas or n a in ro e ts*. Available at http://www.edutopia.org/blog/20-ideas-for-engaging-projects-suzie-boss .

Fried-Booth. D. L. (2002). *ro e t or* (2nd ed.). New York: Oxford University Press.

Gardner, D. (1995). Student produced video documentary provides a real reason for using the target language. *an a e earnin o rna* , 12, 54-56.

Godwin-Jones, R. (2013). Integrating intercultural competence into language learning through technology. *an a e earnin e no o* , 17(2), 1–11. Retrieved from http://llt.msu.edu/issues/june2013/emerging.pdf .

Jin, L. (2013). Language development and scaffolding in a Sino-American telecollaborative project. *an a e earnin e no o* , 17(2), 193–219. Retrieved from http://llt.msu.edu/issues/june2013/jin.pdf .

Kemaloğlu, E. (2010). *ro e t ase orei n an a e earnin* . Lambert Academic Publishing.

Koenraad, T. (2005). *e or s op an a e est nternationa isin t e pro e t a en est* . Occasional paper presented at the CONTEXT event. Graz, Austria: European Centre for Modern Languages.

Koenraad, T. & Westhoff, G. J. (2003). *an o te a an a e est en o see one esi n riteria or a en ests*. Paper presented at the 2003 Conference of the European Association for Computer Assisted Language Learning. University of Limerick, Ireland, 3-6 September 2003.

Krauss, J. & Boss, S. (2013). *in in ro ro e t ase earnin i in eeper n ir* .

Larsen-Freeman, D. & Anderson, M. (2011). *Te ni es an rin ip es in an a e ea in* . Oxford: Oxford University Press.

Levi Altstaedter, L., & Jones, B. (2009) Motivating students' foreign language and culture acquisition through Web-based inquiry. *orei n an a e nna s* 42(4), 640-657.

Liao, M. (2006). E-learning and the development of intercultural competence. *an a e earnin e no o* ,10(3), pp. 49-64.

Liu, Y. C. (2012). Incorporation of Service Learning with EFL academic writing: Experience transfer for invention. *ai an o rna o* . 9, 1.

Meddings, L. & Thornbury, S. (2009). *ea in np e o e in n is an a e tea in* . Delta Publishing.

March, T. (n/d). *We ests e p ate*. Retrieved August 29, 2013 from http://tommarch.com/strategies/webquests/webquests-template/ .

PBS (2011). *i ita e ia ne earners o t e st ent r* . [video documentary] Available at http://video.pbs.org/video/1797357384/ .

Shrum, J. & Glisan, E. (2005). *ea er s an oo onte t a ize an a e instr tion* (3rd Ed.). Boston: Thompson Heinle.

Sox, A. & Rubinstein-Avila, E. (2009). WebQuests for English-language learners: Essential elements for design. *o rna o o es ent t itera* , 53(1), 38-48.

Soykurt, M. (2011). *ro e t ase earnin in ea in n is* . LAP Lambert Academy Publish.

Stockwell, E., & Stockwell, G. (2003). Using email for enhanced cultural awareness. *stra ian an a e atters*, 11(1), 3-4.

Swain, M. (1995). Three functions of output in second language learning. In G. Cook & B. Seidlhofer (Eds.), *rin ip e an pra ti e in app ie in isti s t ies in ono r o Wi o son*. Oxford: Oxford University Press.

Swain, M., & Lapkin, S. (1995). Problems in output and the cognitive processes they generate. A step towards second language learning. *pp ie in isti s*, 16, 371-391.

Turner, J. (1998). A walk on ice. *n a* , 12(3), pp. 20-24.

Vickers, H. (2010). VirtualQuests: Dialogic Language Learning with 3D Virtual Worlds. *o p ter eso r es or an a e earnin* , 3, 75-81. (Available online at http://www.ucam.edu/corell/issues/Vickers.pdf.)

Warschauer, M. (1995). *irt a onne tions n ine a ti ities an pro e ts or net or in an a e earners*. University of Hawaii Press.

*** Formatting Issue - Best Available Paper/Graphic ***

iPad Reading: An Innovative Approach to New Literacies

Hsin-chou Huang

National Taiwan Ocean University/2, Pei-ning Road, Keelung202, Taiwan

joehuang@ntou.edu.tw

Abstract

This study aimed to investigate the use of iPads as a learning tool for college-level EFL students and to explore these language learners' perceptions of iPad reading. Drawn from an intermediate EFL reading class, three students with limited experiences of iPad reading participated in this study. Data from weekly journals and interviews showed that the iPads' palm size, light weight, and accessibility to the Internet through wireless connections not only promoted mobile learning outside the classroom but also achieved learning goals inside the classroom. The various iPad applications enabled students to learn English through games and easy access to helpful resources and thereby increased their motivation to learn. Students also improved their communication skills by using iPads to create videos. iPads have provided useful opportunities for new literacy instruction.

1 Introduction

New technologies provide new ways to read, and how readers interact with electronic texts—through such new devices as iPads, Tablet PCs, Amazon Kindle, and Sony's Reader Digital Book--is worthy of further exploration (Larson, 2010). The emergence of these mobile devices intensifies the need to integrate digital technologies and equip learners with new literacy skills that are different from traditional printed reading and writing skills (Coiro, Knobel, Lankshere, and Leu, 2008). Among these new devices, iPads--equipped with LCDs, Internet surfing functions, e-books, and application (app) downloading capabilities--are the most popular medium of screen-based reading (Connell, Bayliss, and Famer, 2012) and can facilitate new literacy practices (Coiro, et al., 2008). Godwin-Jones (2010) pointed out that iPads have contributed to the rise of e-books because they are portable, have off-line reading functions, and provide a huge storage capacity within a small device. Apple applications, such as games and incorporating audio functions into e-books, have also created learning opportunities (Godwin-Jones, 2011). The personal profiles archived in iPads, including the history of browsing pages and look-up behaviors in online dictionaries, can create a personal learning history. Moreover, the iPad's built-in camera enables users to capture pictures or videos to use in creating responses to readings (Hutchison, Beschorner, and Schmide-Crawford, 2012). The convenience of such mobile devices as iPads has the potential to encourage learner autonomy and combine formal and informal learning (Godwin-Jones, 2011).

Studies of iPad reading mostly focus on how iPads support L1 readers in primary literacy programs (Ellis, 2011); relatively few examine how iPads can assist L2 learners' language learning in tertiary education (Sekiguchi, 2011). One exception is Sekiguchi (2011), who experimented with the use of iPads as a learning resource outside the classroom with 20 EFL undergraduate students in Japan. The results showed that students improved their self-regulated learning by using iPads to tweet about their learning experiences.

The general trend has been to use iPads to replace textbooks or to provide supplementary reading material outside classrooms. Few studies have examined the use of iPads as a major learning instrument or as part of the curriculum to facilitate learning (Hutchison, et al., 2012). Hutchison et al. (2012) reported on the exploratory use of iPads among fourth graders for literacy instruction. Students read a story and used graphic organizer apps to create a visual diagram to describe it, which led to the creative presentation of ideas. Students also drew illustrations using the Doodle Buddy app to show their understanding, which provided opportunities to reread materials and thereby promoted better reading comprehension. These activities, which successfully met multi-literacy goals and helped learners convey meaning digitally, inspired this researcher to design iPad reading activities to promote literacy instruction. Because the integration of iPads into language education is relatively new and still underexplored, this iPad project aimed to investigate the use of iPads as a learning tool in a college EFL reading class and to explore these language learners' perceptions of iPad reading. The researcher posed two questions:

1. How can iPads be integrated into EFL reading instruction?
2. What characterized students' iPad learning experiences?

2. Methodology

Three Taiwanese EFL learners with intermediate English proficiency and limited experiences with iPad reading participated in this study. Prior to this project, they had learned English for at least 6 years; they volunteered to participate in this after-class iPad reading activity within the regular freshman English curriculum. During this semester-long project, the researcher first investigated students' impressions of iPads through a background questionnaire that elicited their preliminary views on the usefulness and usability of iPads. After the students were familiar with this new medium, the researcher investigated students' actual use of iPads as a learning tool by inviting them to surf and read online materials, to experiment with language learning app resources, and finally to create a video that integrated the information they had collected during the semester. In each two-hour iPad session, students completed a reflective journal on how they used iPads to locate information, integrate resources, and make videos. Students also wrote about the problems they encountered and what they most enjoyed about iPad reading. At the end of the semester, the students attended a semi-structured interview that elicited comments about iPads' specific features, the advantages and disadvantages of using iPads to read, how iPad reading could enhance the acquisition of language skills, and overall suggestions for this project. This case study adopted a qualitative approach in which qualitative data from reflection journals and interviews were transcribed, coded, and sorted into categorized segments (Guba and Lincoln, 1981). The qualitative data gathered from this in-depth investigation of three participants' iPad usage suggested effective ways to integrate mobile technology into language instruction.

3. Results and Discussion

A description of the sequence of iPad literacy activities by each participant is followed by an analysis of the themes that emerged from the three participants' feedback and reflections on their iPad reading experiences. Pseudonyms are used for the student's names.

3.1 Andy: An enthusiastic iPad reader

The first stage of this iPad project was e-book reading. Andy selected several favorite books to read from iBooks. He read stories from *esop s a es* including *e at an t e Wease s e ss an t e rass opper e are an t e ortoise an e o ntin o sts* To understand the story quickly, Andy also downloaded several English-Chinese and English-English dictionaries and used them to find the meanings of idioms and new vocabulary. He highlighted and color-coded these items and the sentences worthy of re-reading or for taking notes. During the process of reading, he searched online and watched videos of *e is er an ipin* and *er es an t e Wa oner* on Youtube, which provided the context of these stories. He also searched Google for illustrations of *e are an t e ortoise* as a way to preview its storyline.

In his reflection journal, Andy wrote that he enjoyed reading and being able to check unfamiliar words easily with the help of dictionary apps or online dictionaries and noted that paper-based reading does not provide such ready accessibility to these resources. In his interview, he also praised the convenience of being able to access more information and background knowledge about these stories through the iPad's wireless connection.

During the second stage of this project, Andy used the iPad to explore apps for English word learning games. He accessed *Wor a s* which asks learners to assemble letters into the correct spelling of words. When learners get the correct answer, they score and are allowed to move to the next game. In the interview, Andy said he enjoyed this game because getting a high score in a short time challenged his familiarity with the words and with English spelling rules.

The final stage was to make a video using the iPad to integrate the information gathered online and then to record their own voices and present their understanding of a given topic in a video format. It took Andy 11 days, averaging an hour each day, to use an iPad to complete this video project. His video focused on three tourist spots: London, the host city of the 2012 Olympics; Taiwan, his home country; and China, which he was going to visit the following summer. He began by downloading an app that displayed the scenery of famous tour spots. Then he found an ebook, *ootprints o ra e o rne in in an an s* by Maturin Murray Ballou, which presented a lot of travel information about famous scenic spots. When Andy clicked on the picture of a scenic spot, he was led to more detailed information. In his interview, Andy described how accessing these multi-links helped him learn to quickly scan for major information, grasp the main ideas, and increase the efficiency of his learning process. By using the Google search engine to access online information about London, he found useful information about Heathrow airport, the history of England, and England's food culture. The many hyperlinks allowed Andy to develop a well-rounded understanding of London. To get information about tour spots in China and Taiwan, Andy discovered the webpages of the *one anet* (www.lonelyplanet.com), and Wikitravel also offered useful travel information. He digested a huge amount of information by reading the table of contents on the left side to gain an overview of the text and to decide whether he would read entire texts or jump to the parts that interested him. The next step was to organize the information he found. He used the Idea Sketch app to outline his ideas and then wrote a draft for his narration of the video. The final stage involved using Blurb, a video-making app, to integrate the pictures, videos, and his voiceover.

In the interview, Andy stated that this video project enabled him to read extensively to gather information, to organize details, and to make decisions on what pictures and images to include in his video to best illustrate his ideas. This involved creativity and critically evaluating the information he read. He felt that the project involved a lot of effort, but he had a sense of achievement when he completed it. He appreciated the portability of the iPad. The only inconvenience was that the dorm he lived in did not have a stable wireless connection. He also suggested that the workload might have been lighter if he had been able to work with a partner. Overall, he felt that this iPad project provided extensive reading benefits through videos, texts, and hyperlinks and promoted his independent learning, which was a new experience for him compared with his experience in traditional language classes.

3.2 Sharon: A meticulous iPad user

Sharon carried out e-book reading for seven sessions, each of which lasted for 50 minutes. She read such fairy tales as *e o en ir ans in* and *orin a an orin e* She summarized these e-book stories in English. For *e o en ir* she wrote, "There were 3 brothers looking for a golden bird, but only the youngest one found it." For *ans in* she wrote, "Hans left his lord, who gave him a stump of silver. During his journey, Hans kept exchanging what he had to get something else. However, all the things that he got did not work as he wished." For *orin a an orin e* Sharon wrote, "Two lovers wandered into a forest. The girl was captured and turned into a bird locked in a cage, and the boy was forced to do some boring chores. One day he dreamed about a purple flower with a costly pearl inside which could rescue his girlfriend from the cage. Then he found it indeed when he woke up. He walked into the castle with the pearl, and his girlfriend was released, and so were the other birds which all turned back to humans."

In her e-book reading reflection, she mentioned that initially she was not quite sure how to use all the functions on the iPad, but she picked them up quickly after 2 days of practice and started to make a word list for memorizing vocabulary. To check unfamiliar words, she used online English-English and English-Chinese dictionaries and Google translator. The ease and convenience of checking unfamiliar words online enabled Sharon to finish reading her first four-page fairytale on the second day of the project, which gave her a sense of accomplishment and increased her confidence about reading English materials.

Sharon's e-book reading summaries got longer, and her writing skills matured as she read more stories on the iPad. In her comments on iPad's grammar and dictionary tools, she felt that the availability of checking the meaning of unfamiliar words immediately enabled her to increase her English reading speed and facilitated her reading comprehension. As she gradually adapted to iPad reading and its functions, she was willing to spend more time on iPad reading, and she improved her reading speed. She was full of hope that she could improve her English reading, and her motivation to read English materials increased day by day during the e-book reading project period. She wrote, "I feel happy when reading e-books on the iPad because I can read 9 pages in 100 minutes… I never knew there are so many details in the story of *e o en ir* That's terrific! I have a sense of achievement." On the final day of the project, Sharon actually critiqued the story she had read. She wrote, "At the end, the plot of *orin a an orin e* was not described in detail. How his girlfriend was released was still not mentioned in detail. In contrast, how they entered the forest and met the nightingale has more detailed description. I still think it is an interesting story." It appears that Sharon had entered the world of English reading and that this reading experience had fostered critical thinking in making judgments about how the story was told.

As for using learning resources during the second stage of the project, Sharon tried an app called Free Grammar. This app provides brief explanations of such grammar issues as verb tenses, causative verbs, and conjunctions, and conditionals. She chose a tutorial on prepositions listed in the left column in the app's screenshot, and then took a grammar test. It was an interactive game-like tutorial.

For her video production, Sharon spent 4 hours each day for 5 days to complete her video on the iPad. She chose to introduce the *n er a es* movie because she had read the novel before and felt it was a sensational topic. She began by using the Yahoo search engine to explore information related to this movie, a process that she considered the most difficult part of the project. She looked at the overview of the plot and the characters on Wikipedia and then watched the movie's trailer on Youtube to understand more about the story. On the second day, she started to collect pictures for each character because she planned to describe them in her digital storytelling. She placed the characters' pictures and brief character descriptions on PowerPoint (PPT).

On the following day, she began writing her storytelling script. She said she spent lots of time brainstorming how to organize it. To include more information about the movie, she read many online articles, such as a movie review from IMDB, (http://www.imdb.com/title/tt1392170/), articles from Wikipedia (http://en.wikipedia.org/wiki/The_Hunger_Games), and the movie's official website (http://www.thehungergames.co.uk/). Her final product was a 451-word script that she typed and saved either on a PC or the iPad. On the fourth day, she used the Blurb app to combine all of the data she had collected, including the story's plot from Wikipedia, the online trailer, and the recording of her own narration.

In her reflection sheet, she mentioned some difficulties she encountered during the video-making process. The first problem was insufficient access to Wi-Fi in her dorm. She needed to complete her project in the library. In addition, she needed a quiet place to record her narration, which was inconvenient because she was concerned about possible interruptions in the recording. The third problem was the capacity of the video-making app, Blurb. This software was easy to use, but because it was free, users could not upload more than 8 pictures at a time. Sharon separated the entire video into 4 segments, uploaded them separately, and then combined them at the end. It took the subject quite a long time to complete this procedure.

Overall, Sharon recognized the advantages of using iPads for completing this reading and video project because iPads are very light and can be carried anywhere. She appreciated the apps for playing games, which increased her motivation to use the iPad. Despite the limitations of the Blurb software, Sharon felt the video project enabled her to read more fluently during the process of searching information online to enrich her video content, improved her writing and reading skills as she sought more background information for her script, and enhanced her aesthetic sense as she combined her images and narration to report on this movie in a coherent and organized way.

3.3 Jo: An ambivalent iPad user

Jo spent six iPad sessions reading a classic novel, *ri e an re i e* from iBook. She read 65 minutes on average during each of the six sections. Because it is a classic novel with more than 1000 pages and lots of difficult vocabulary and grammar, she did not finish reading it by the final day of the project. During her reading process, she annotated the book with the words she did not understand. She reflected in your journal that the words she looked up mostly occurred in literature--such as scrupulous, vexing, and caprice—and not as often in everyday language. She consulted Youtube to find videos to assist her comprehension. In her reflection journal, she indicated her frustration with trying to read a novel that was far beyond her current proficiency level and with the need to constantly look up new words in the iPad's English-English dictionary to help her comprehension. Her Youtube searches did support her reading and helped her gain an overview of the story.

As for learning game apps, Jo loves music, so she tried to find several songs from *in a a n is ite* from iTunes to improve her listening ability. This site turns the captions on and off to help train listening comprehension. In her reflection journal, Jo indicated that she felt she improved her listening ability by constantly turning off the captions and trying to guess the lyrics.

Her final video was about travel. As a keen traveler, Jo decided to introduce special scenic spots. To enrich her content, she read traveling articles on the *e s* website, chose those that interested her, and summarized the important parts of the articles she read. She introduced the catacombs in Paris, The Land of Nod's Toy Shop in New York, and Micronesia's ghost ship. She used pictures from Google and used Blurb to effectively integrate them with her narration. In her reflection, she indicated that her English language reading improved when using iPads to create her work because she read articles written in English once a week. She did feel, however, that the on-screen glare hurt her eyes. Generally, she quite enjoyed the "touching" function of iPad when creating her video, but this convenient function also created a major problem when the excellent quality of the touch screen accidentally deleted her first video and she had to redo her project. It seems that technology provides both convenience and some unpredictable pitfalls.

3.4 Emerging themes from iPad learning activities

Three themes emerged from these iPad e-book reading, language game apps, and video-making activities.

i a s it ne earnin too s rin res an npre e ente earnin e perien es an oti ate st ents to earn

These students regarded learning with iPads as new and fresh experiences that piqued their curiosity and desire to learn. With the flicks of their fingers, they entered a world of knowledge without boundaries. They could easily find definitions for unknown words and access ebooks from the iBook library. The learning software apps gave them tutorials that never tired of the teaching process. The easy image capturing of iPads enabled them to store their favorite images either by searching online or by taking their own pictures for later retrieval. They could also record their voices, assemble the images, and streamline the images and their narration into an interactive video. These new learning opportunities cannot be found in a traditional language classroom.

i a s pro i e e tensi e rea in opport nities it o t t e i itations o ti e an spa e

As suggested by previous studies (Connell et al., 2012; Ellis, 2011), iPads with wireless connections can promote learning at any time and at any place. Reading e-books with iPads can also give students extensive reading opportunities, as evidenced by Sekiguchi (2011) and Larson (2010). From a wide selection of iBooks, students can read more easily using such multiple tools as dictionaries and highlighting functions. Students can also find additional information online. Because iPads are free of space and time boundaries, students are able to cultivate their reading habits and read whatever books interest them and whenever they want to read them. Reading becomes pleasurable rather than stressful.

ro in i eos it i a s e pe st ents onstr t t eir o n no e e

This iPad video project provided useful opportunities for these students to construct their own knowledge. The video was a synthesized product that intertwined students' enthusiasm for the topics, their understanding of the online articles they read, their writing skills as they composed their scripts, and their critical judgments of the information they needed to combine their materials and create a coherent project. Activities like these go beyond traditional teacher-centered classrooms.

Students learn to express their ideas with digital artifacts. The iPad supports learning aligned with instructional goals when teachers select appropriate activities and assessment strategies (Hutchison, et al. 2012).

4. Conclusion

This exploratory study provided empirical evidence of how iPads can be integrated into language instruction, with practical suggestions for designing instructional activities that meet curricular goals. Three case studies cannot represent the entire EFL population, but the hands-on learning experiences with these iPads, together with students' feedback, may provide clues for how EFL teachers can design similar activities that engage learners. iPads' flexibility of access and abundant applications for mobile learning constitute a catalyst for learning. With more advances in iPad applications, it will be exciting to witness more learners adapting to the use of iPads and interacting with texts in more creative ways.

Acknowledgments

This study was supported by the National Science Council, Taiwan, ROC, Project No. NSC 100-2410-H-019-012 and 101-2410-H-019-015.

References

Coiro, J., Knobel, M., Lankshear, C., and Leu, D. 2008. Central issues in new literacies and new literacies research. In J. Coiro, M. Knobel, C. Lankshear, and D. Leu (Eds.), Handbook of Research on New Literacies (pp.1–21). New York: Erlbaum.

Connell, C. Bayliss, L., and Farmer, W. 2012. Effect of eBook readers and tablet Computers on reading comprehension. International Journal of Instructional Media, 39 (2):131-140.

Ellis, S. 2011. Teaching the future: How iPads are being used to engage learners with special needs. Screen Education, 63: 61-64.

Godwin-Jones, R. 2010. Emerging technologies literacies and technologies revisited. Language Learning and Technology, 14 (3): 2-9.

Godwin-Jones, R. 2011. Emerging technologies mobile apps for language learning. Language Learning & Technology, 15 (2): 2-11.

Hutchison, A., Beschorner, B., and Schmidt-Frawford, D. 2012. Exploring the use of the iPad for literacy learning. The Reading Teacher, 66 (1): 15-23.

Larson, L. 2012. Digital readers: The next chapter in e-book reading and response. The Reading Teacher, 64 (1): 15-22.

Sekiguchi, S. 2011 Investigating effects of the iPad on Japanese EFL students' self-regulated study. Retrieved from http://www.pixel-online.org/ICT4LL2011/common/download/Paper_pdf/IBL33-246-FP-Sekiguchi-ICT4LL.pdf

A Generic Cognitively Motivated Web-Environment to Help People to Become Quickly Fluent in a New Language

Michael Zock
CNRS & LIF
Aix-Marseille Université
Marseille, France
michael.zock
@lif.univ-mrs.fr

Guy Lapalme
RALI-DIRO
Université de Montréal
Montréal, Québec, Canada
lapalme
@iro.umontreal.ca

Lih-Juang Fang
LaLIC
Université Paris Sorbonne
Paris, France
fanglihjuang
@yahoo.com

Abstract

To speak fluently is a complex skill. In order to help the learner to acquire it we propose an electronic version of an age old method: *pattern drills* (PD). While being highly regarded in the fifties, pattern drills have become unpopular since then. Despite certain shortcomings we do believe in the virtues of this approach, at least with regard to the memorization of basic structures and the acquisition of fluency, the skill to produce language at a 'normal' rate. Of course, the method has to be improved, and we will show here how this can be achieved. Unlike tapes or books, computers are open media, allowing for dynamic changes, taking users' performances and preferences into account. Our drill-tutor, a small web-application still in its prototype phase, allows for this. It is a free, electronic version of pattern drills, i.e. an exercise generator, open and adaptable to the users' ever changing needs.

1 Problem

To produce language spontaneously and at a normal rate is a challenging problem requiring the solution of several complex tasks: (a) content determination, (b) lexical choice, (c) morphological adjustments[1] and (d) articulation (Reiter & Dale, 2000; Fromkin, 1993; Levelt, 1993, 1989).

There are various reasons why language production is such a difficult process. For example, a speaker has to make quickly a great number of choices of various kind (conceptual, pragmatic, linguistic), leading to results which are highly unpredictable. Hence it is hard, if not impossible to make a causal analysis on the basis of correlations between an input and an output (a change of the former causing a change at the latter), as the relationship between the two may be unsystematic (no one-to-one mapping) and the result of the choices may show up not only at the final output, the only one accessible to our senses, but also at the intermediate stages (Zock, 1994, 1988). Figure-1 illustrates this for the input : `[help (Paul, Marie)]` which after multiple specifications at the intermediate steps yields: *Paul l'aide* (Paul helps her).

There are also time- and space-management problems. Speaking is basically a sequential process, component *b* relying on the results of component *a*. Hence, any hesitation in one component, say, lexical choice, may yield a delay of the next lower component (syntax or morphology). Also, the results of a higher component may need to be revised in the light of results coming from a lower component (retroaction). Correlated to the *time problem* (delay) there is also a *space problem*. Any symbol waiting for translation (say, the mapping of a concept into a word) needs to be stored,

[1] Not all of these components present the same level of difficulty. For example, morphology is hardly a problem for languages like Chinese or Japanese, while the production of the final output (spoken or written words) may be very demanding. It certainly is a challenge for Europeans learning Chinese, while the very same persons may have little problems with Italian, Spanish, or Japanese. Also, none of the European languages can compete with the logic of the Chinese lexicon, which make it particularly suitable for look-up (Zock et Schwab, 2010) and the learning of words, be it only for those describing objects.

taxing short-term memory, a very scarce resource.

If speaking in one's mother tongue is already a daunting task, to do so in a foreign language can be overwhelming (Bock, 1995). Language production is a skill (Levelt, 1975; de Keyser, 2007a) whose *elements* (words, rules, etc.) and *order* (staging; what is to be processed when) have to be learned, and this is hard work, requiring a lot of practice in various situations.

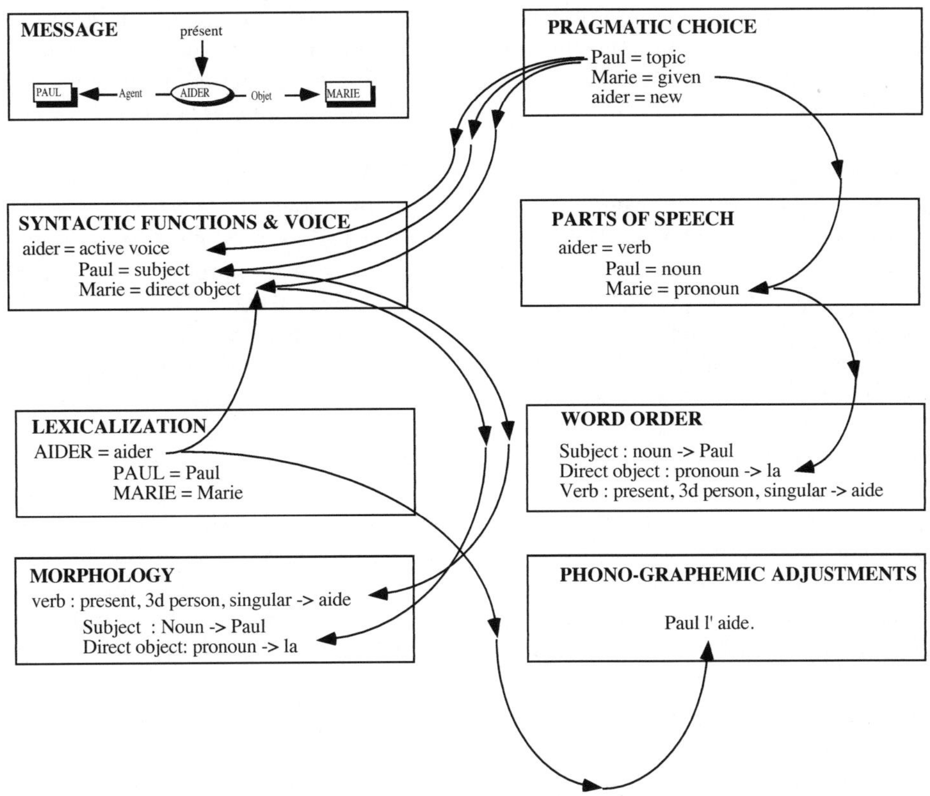

Figure 1 : Language production as a glass box, revealing the multiple dependencies and interactions at various levels.

2 Our model or approach : patterns, rules or both?

As you will see, we will take a hybrid approach. If spontaneous language production is such a complex process the question arises whether it can be made feasible, and if so, how. This is precisely the point we will try to address in this paper, be it only briefly. We would like to stress though, that we deal here only with the survival level (go shopping, ask for information, ...)

To illustrate our approach let us recast it into one of the major frameworks used for language production, the Reiter & Dale model (Reiter & Dale, 2000). Hence we will take on board some of their terminology like macro/micro-level, conceptual input, lexicalization, morphology, etc.

However, before proceeding and present our approach, we would like to emphasize another point. Going through the steps depicted in Figure-1 and applying all the rules implied by natural language generators is highly unrealistic for people trying to learn a foreign language. There are various good reasons to doubt:

- *memory*: people do not have in their mind all the knowledge described by linguists, neither can they hold all the required information in their working memory (Baddeley, 1970);
- *attention*: people can focus only on a small set of items at a time;
- *time*: speech, i.e. the conception of a message and its translation into language is extremely fast. Speakers do not have the time to perform all the computations, i.e. search and apply the needed rules.

Linguists describe languages in terms of rules, but people hardly ever learn such descriptions, leave alone apply all of them, at least not at the initial stages of acquiring a new language. What people do learn though are *patterns* complying with these rules. Of course, people do use rules, but in conjunction with patterns.

Patterns can be seen as frozen instances of a given step in the derivational process. They can also be abstracted at any level of the process. They can be of any sort, hybrid, mixing semantic and syntactic information. Patterns are global structures, which can be built dynamically by applying a set of rules, moreover, they can also be stored as ready made sentence plans or templates in which case they behave somehow like words: they can be retrieved at once, sparing us the trouble to have to go through the cumbersome process of structure creation. Obviously, access, i.e. pattern retrieval, is much faster than the computation of its corresponding structure. There are simply too many steps involved. This is probably the reason why so many people use them for language (learners, interpreters, journalists, etc.) or other tasks (music, programming, chess playing, etc.) without even being aware of it (Nagao, 1984).

Of course, there is a price to be paid : patterns need to be accessed (see below) and they may need to be accommodated. In other words, patterns have qualities, but also certain shortcomings: they are rigid and tax memory. Imagine someone abstracting a pattern for every morphological variation. Take for example the following two sentences: 'I've attended PACLIC 2012 in Bali' *vs.* 'I'll attend PACLIC 2013 in Taipei'. They basically instantiate the same pattern [(I've attended/ I'll attend <conference name> <place> <time>)]). In other words, it does not make sense in this case to abstract two patterns, since the two are so much alike. It would be much more reasonable to have one general pattern for the global structure and a set parameters, i.e. rules for local adjustments, like agreement, tense, etc.

Just like patterns, rules do have certain shortcomings. While they may account for the expressive power and all the regularities of a given language, they may prevent us from getting the job done in time, in particular if there are too many of them. This being so, we suggest to use a hybrid approach, resorting to each strategy when they are at their best, patterns for *global structures*, the syntactic layout, i.e. sentence frame, and rules for *local adjustments*. This combination gives us the best of both worlds, minimizing the use of computational resources (attention, memory), while maximizing the power (speed) and flexibility of output (possibly needed accommodations).

When people learn a new language, they build some kind of database composed of words, patterns and phrases. This memory (pattern-library) can consist of translation pairs, or, pairs of conceptual patterns and corresponding linguistic forms (sentences). One can also think of conceptual patterns as a pivot, mediating between translations of languages.

There is one problem though with this kind of approach. As the number of patterns grows, grows the problem of accessing them. This is where indexing plays a role. Patterns can be indexed from various points of view: *semantically* (thematically, i.e. by domain), via their components (words), *syntactically*, etc. While we index our patterns pragmatically, i.e. in terms of communicative goals (function that the pattern is to fulfill), we allow their access also via other means: navigation in a goal hierarchy.

To see how our model relates to the generation model mentioned earlier, we try to recast it in those terms. The tool we are building can be used as a translation aid, as an exercise generator (our concern in this paper), or as a tool to extend the current database (this is work for the future).

In the first case it would function in the following way: given some user input (sentence), the system tries to find the corresponding translation, which is trivial if the translation is stored in the DB.[2]

In the second case, the assumption is that the user knows the goal s/he'd like to achieve. Hence, the dialogue goes as follows (see table-1, next page). Given some goal (step-1), the system presents a list of patterns from which the user must choose (step-2), and instantiate then the pattern's variables with lexical items (step-3) and morphological values (step-4, or the steps A-D in figure 2 here below). Note, that some of these choices could be considered as optional, as they are performed by the system. This is typically the case in traditional pattern drills, where the user has no choice soever concerning the input, the words to use, ...

Note also, that the *conceptual input* (see table-

[2] If the goal is the extension of the database by finding similar sentences in a corpus, i.e. sentences built on the same pattern, the problem will be harder. The program must infer or abstract the input's underlying pattern and find a corresponding sentence in the target language. This sentence can be either the translation of the input or a somehow similar sentence extracted automatically from the corpus. This is clearly work for the future. The main part of this paper deals with the *exercise generator*.

1) is distributed over three layers: at a global level (macro-level) the speaker chooses the pattern via a *goal* by providing incrementally *lexical values* (for the pattern's variables) and *morphological parameters* (number, tense) to refine gradually the initially underspecified message. This kind of distribution has several advantages. Information is requested only when relevant and needed. There is better control in terms of access, storage and processing load. Obviously, this approach is better than storing a pattern for every morphological variant. Last, but not least, this method is faster for conveying a message than navigating through a huge *lexical* or *conceptual ontology*, as suggested elsewhere (Zock,1991; Power et al., 1998; or Zock et al. 2009).

task	input	output
MACRO-LEVEL	1) choice of *goal*	set of sentence frames 1 <OBJECT$_1$> is more <ATTRIBUT> than <OBJECT$_2$> 2 <OBJECT$_2$> is less <ATTRIBUT> than <OBJECT$_1$>
	2) choice of *sentence frame*	<OBJECT-$_1$> is more <ATTRIBUT> than <OBJECT$_2$>
MICRO-LEVEL	3) choice of *lexical value*	lexically specified structure *Cigar* is more *expensive* than *perfume*.
	4) morphological parameter	morphologically specified structure <OBJECT$_1$>: plural Fully specified conceptual, syntactic and morphological structure

Table 1: Conceptual input as a four-step process for the following output : "Cigars are more expensive than perfume"

3 Goal and scope

In order to reach the above mentioned goal, help people to acquire quickly the skill of speaking, we propose a very simple solution: the development of an open (i.e. customizable), generic, web-based environment. Put differently, we propose an electronic version of a well-known method called "pattern drill" (Chastaing, 1969). This method has been criticized for various reasons (see section 6). Despite this fact we do believe in its virtues provided that the method is adapted and properly used.

Obviously, in order to be able to perform ***automatically***, that is, without having to think about the various tasks mentioned, we must **exercise** them, as otherwise we will forget or be unable to integrate them into a well staged whole, a prerequisite for **fluency** (deKeyser, 2007).

Learning should be made simple and possible in a reasonably short time. Our goal is to help the learner reach the level of fluency needed to express his/her basic needs: ask for information, answer a question, solve a concrete problem, etc. by using language. In other words, our scope is the **survival level**.

4 Method

To achieve our goal, we suggest to build a *template-based sentence generator*. Patterns or templates are abstractions over concrete linguistic instances, i.e. sentences (I prefer beer to wine => < SPEAKER> prefer < DRINK$_1$> to < DRINK$_2$>). Patterns are linked to *communicative goals*, for example, 'comparison', the speaker's starting point (see table 2, next page). Our approach is based on the following assumptions :

Resource limitations: given the limitations of our brain (space and time), speakers cannot afford to perform very complex operations, especially not during learning;

Decomposition: speaking being a complex process, we have to decompose it, allowing the speaker to focus selectively on a limited number of issues: *meaning*, *form*, or *sound*. Since people can focus only on few items at the same time, it makes sense to put them into a situation, where they can rely upon a set of ready-made building blocks (the 'constants' of the pattern), computing only part(s) of the whole structure (the values of the patterns' variables).

Open-endedness: different people have *different needs*. This being so, we propose to build an *open system*, allowing the user to tailor the tool to fit his or her needs.

Contextualization: words are not learned in isolation, they are learned in the context of a sentence pattern, which may form even larger structures (scripts, discourse patterns).

Grounding: words and sentence structures are linguistic resources used to achieve specific communicative goals. By indexing our patterns in terms of goals and by presenting words in the context of sentence patterns, we achieve this kind of communicative grounding (pragmatic competency). The student learns when to use what specific resource.

	goal	*associated pattern*	*example of instantiated pattern*
1°	Identity (name)	My name is <NAME>, <FIRST NAME> <LAST NAME>.	My name is *Bond, James Bond.*
2°	Presentation (full name)	This is <FIRST NAME> <LAST NAME> also called the <SUR-NAME>.	This is *Bjorn Borg*, also called the *iceberg.*
3°	Origin (country)	I am from <COUNTRY> and you?	I am from *Portugal*, and you?
4°	Q-A : preference	Q : What do you like better <DRINK$_1$><DRINK$_2$>. A : I prefer <DRINK$_1$> to <DRINK$_2$>.	Q : What do you like better, *tea* or *coffee*? A : I prefer *tea* to *coffee.*
5°	Q-A : comparison	Q : Which city is bigger, <PLACE$_1$> or <PLACE$_2$> ? A : <PLACE$_1$> is bigger than <PLACE$_2$>.	Q : Which city is bigger, *Tainan* or *Taipei* ? A : *Taipei* is bigger than *Tainan.*

Table 2 : Patterns indexed in terms of goals

The **need of practice**: words have to be memorized, so do syntactic structures. Speaking is fast and various component tasks have to be carried out quasi-simultaneously. Hence we need to automate some of them (conversion meaning => form => sound). All these operations require practice (de Keyser, 2007), as without it we may not only forget, but also be unable to integrate the components into a well staged whole and to deliver the result in time.

Holism: rather than assembling words into sentences we instantiate patterns. Instead of proceeding word by word, the learner operates on larger chunks, sentence patterns. In doing so, we buy what is needed next to knowledge, *space* (intentional resources) and *time*.

5 Discussion

While there are many good teaching methods, there is at least one point where nearly all of them (books, tapes) fall short: due to the media constraints they are closed. In consequence, everything has to be anticipated, which implies that all students have to take the same route, in spite of the diversity of their ever changing needs. This is a pitfall we try to avoid in our sentence and exercise generator, an open, customizable, web-based tool designed for novices studying foreign languages. The generator's **inputs** are *communicative goals* and *conceptual information*, the **output** is text (i.e. written form) or synthesized speech.

To summarize, we propose the building of an exercise generator to help people to develop basic communication skills in a foreign language (in our case the Chinese). The goal is to assist the *memorization* of words and the acquisition of fundamental sentence patterns to become sufficiently *fluent* in the new language to participate in a simple conversation.

6 Building and using the resource

There are two aspects to be considered: *building* the resource and *using* it.

To **build the resource** (construction phase), we index a list of fundamental sentence *patterns* with *goals* from which the learner will choose during the exercice phase (Table 2). Since different people have different needs we keep the system open so that the user can customize it according to his needs. In other words, the user can change certain parameters:

- the link between *patterns* and *goals*;
- the *names* of the *goals* (if s/he doesn't like our metalanguage);
- the *words* with which s/he'd like to instantiate a given pattern;
- the *number of times* s/he'd like to work on

a given pattern;

- the *time delay* between a stimulus (question) and a response (answer);
- etc.

To **use** the **resource:** having chosen the *goal*, the system will display the according pattern(s). If there is more than one, then the learner will choose among them the one s/he wants to learn, communicating the system the specific words s/he would like the pattern to be instantiated with (see Figures 2-3).

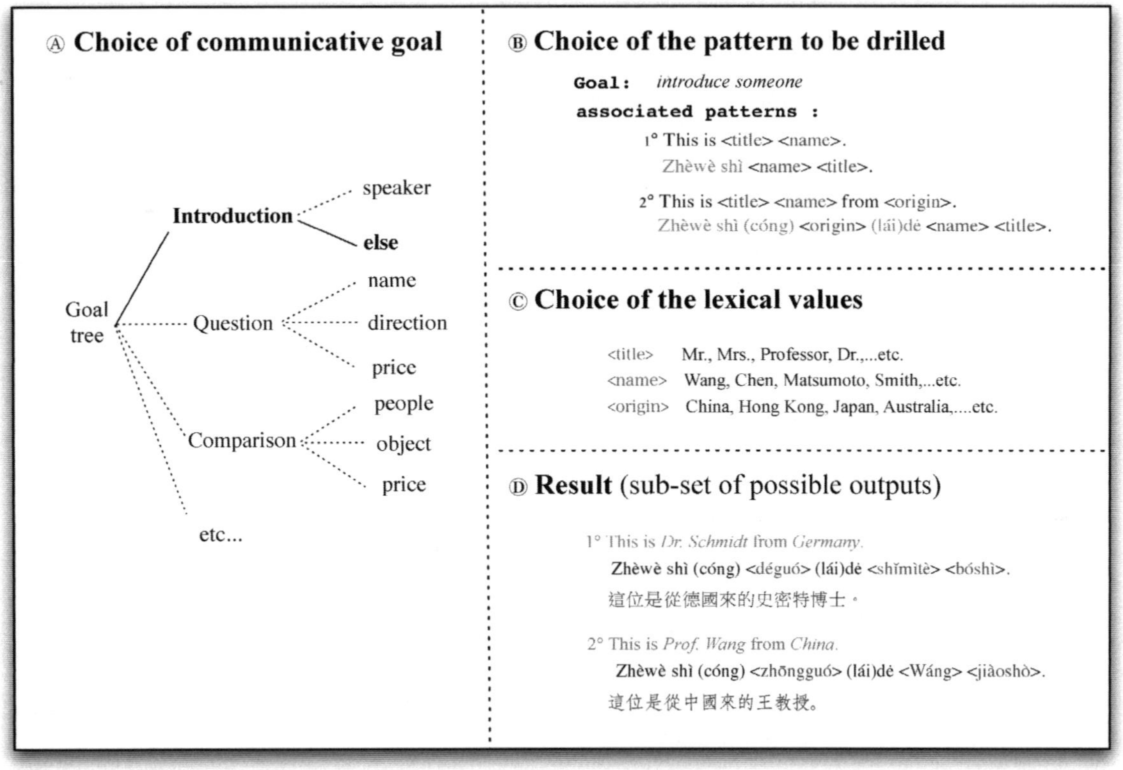

Fig. 2 : Communication Flow

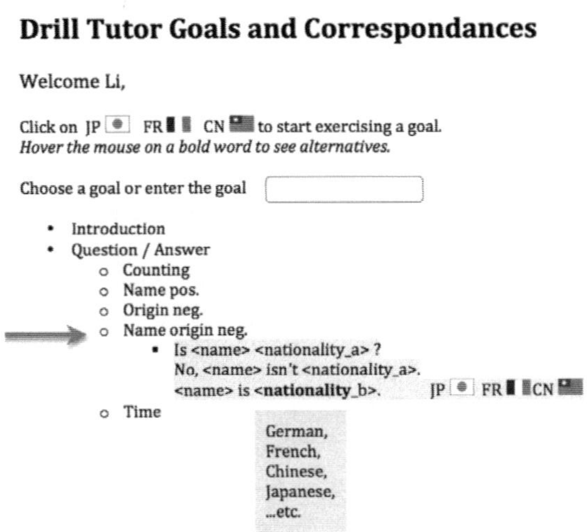

Fig. 3 : Lexical choice

The system has now all it needs to produce sentences of a specific kind/class (pattern) taking the user's preferences (chosen words) into account. Yet, before doing so it will invite the learner to try by herself[3]. Once this is done, he can compare his results with the system's outputs. By seeing which pattern achieves which discourse goal and by being able to produce the required form he can now compare his/her outputs with those of the system. Hence s/he learns not only to express himself in a foreign language, but also, and more importantly, how to achieve quickly a specific communicative goal.

7 A short note concerning the criticism against pattern drills

After having been very popular for many years, pattern drills and repetition which they rely upon have been discredited by linguists, —see Chomsky's violent criticism (Chomsky, 1959) of

[3] Note that in this particular case the output is subvocal, as unlike in the case of the language laboratory we cannot record it and written output would be too time-consuming.

Skinner's book *Verbal Behavior*,— by psychologists (Levelt, 1970, Herriot, 1971; Leont'ev, 1974; Krashen, 1981) and pedagogues (Rivers, 1964, 1972; Spolsky, 1966; Chastain, 1969; Savignon, 1983; Stevens, 1989, Wong and vanPatten, 2003).

While we partially agree with these criticisms with respect to the *creative aspects* of language production, we do not share them at all when *habit formation* or the *acquisition of automatisms* are the learning goal Actually, it seems that we are not the only ones to hold this view, see for example: deKeyser (2007a, 2007b, 2001), Fitts, (1964), Garrod & Pickering (2007), Gatbonton & Segalowitz (2005, 1988), Guillaume (1973), Hulstijn (2001), Segalowitz (2007, 2003, 2000), Segalowitz and Hulstijn (2005), to name just those.

At least partial automatization of the process is necessary to become fluent in speaking. Automatisms are the speakers' means to buy time, allowing them to focus on another, possibly more demanding component, for example, the next conceptual fragment, i.e. message, to be uttered. Put differently, in order to achieve the skill of fluent speaking, that is, fast conversion of ideas into sounds (Zock, 1997), we do believe that well-staged repetitions of stimulus-response patterns in a clear communicative setting, together with feedback are a valuable learning method. Of course, they are not the whole story. Interestingly enough, patterns have been rehabilitated by well-known linguists like Goldberg (1998) and by Ray Jackendoff (1993) one of Chomsky's most brilliant students.

8 Conclusion

We have started the paper by stressing the fact that speaking is difficult. We have tried then to show that the acquisition of this skill could be made feasible by blending an old theory and new technology. While the current prototype is fairly small (15 goals, a dozen of patterns and 300 words, in four languages), this should not be taken as a decisive argument against the potential usefulness of our approach. Our focus was not on scope but on generality. We wanted to see how difficult it would be to use the very same approach for typologically different languages. We were pleasantly surprised to see that even adding Chinese after having tried the system for French and Japanese, was quite simple.

In sum, the number of patterns and the size of the vocabulary is not really our major concern at this stage, the focus being on the implementation of an editor designed for building, modifying and using a database. The database can easily be extended. Note also that our system is not only an exercise generator, but also a language generator, simple as it may be. In sum, our drill tutor has several features that set it apart from traditional pattern drills, user-controlled input being just one of them.

To conclude, we do believe in the virtuosity of our approach : the system is open and customizable (concerning input, linguistic knowledge, processing preferences, interface, etc.). It is generic and it can be built and extended quite easily, by allowing to add various plug-ins : synthesized speech, automatic creation of patterns or automatic building of a pattern library. Obviously, the ultimate judge of the qualities of the system is the user, but since we are still in the development phase, this has to be left for the future.

Obviously, pattern drills are not a panacea. They can even be harmful it not used properly (parroting, mindless repetition), but used in the right way, that is, at the right moment, with the right goals and at the right proportion, they can do wonders. Just like a tennis player might want to go back to the court and train his basic strokes, a language learner may feel the need to drill resisting patterns. Whoever has tried to become skillful in a language fundamentally different from his own can't but agree with deKeyser's (2001) words when he writes: "Without automatization no amount of knowledge will ever translate into the levels of skill required for real life use".

References

Baddeley, A. (1990). Human memory: theory and practice. Hillsdale: Erlbaum.

Bock, J.K. (1995). Sentence production: From mind to mouth. In J. L. Miller & P.D. Eimas (Ed.), Handbook of perception and cognition. Vol. 11: Speech, language and communication. Orlando, FL: Academic Press.

Chastain, K. (1969). The audio-lingual habit learning theory vs. the code-cognitif learning theory. IRAL, 7(2), 97–107.

Chomsky, N. (1959). A review of B. F. Skinner's Verbal Behavior. Language, 31(1), 26–58.

deKeyser, R. (2001). Automaticity and automatization. In P. Robinson (Ed.), Cognition and second language instruction (pp. 125-151). New York: Cambridge University Press.

deKeyser, R. (2007a). Skill acquisition theory. In J. Williams & B. VanPatten (Eds.), Theories in Second

Language Acquisition: An introduction (pp. 97-113). Mahwah, NJ: Erlbaum.

deKeyser, R. (Ed.). (2007b). Practicing in a second language: Perspectives from applied linguistics and cognitive psychology. Cambridge University Press

Fitts, P. (1964). Perceptual motor skill learning. In A. Melton (Ed.), Categories of human learning (pp. 243–285). New York: Academic press.

Fromkin, V. (1993). Speech Production. In Psycholinguistics. J. Berko Gleason & N. Bernstein Ratner, Eds. Fort Worth, TX: Harcourt, Brace, Jovanovich.

Garrod, S. & Pickering, M.J. (2007). Automaticity in language production in monologue and dialogue. In A.S. Meyer, L.R. Wheeldon, & A. Krott (Eds.), Automaticity and control in language processing (pp. 1-21). Hove: Psychology Press.

Gatbonton, E., & Segalowitz, N. (1988). Creative automatization: Principles for promoting fluency within a communicative framework. TESOL Quarterly, 22, 473-492.

Gatbonton, E., & Segalowitz, N. (2005). Rethinking communicative language teaching: a focus on access to fluency. Canadian Modern Language Review, 61, 325-353.

Guillaume, P. (1973). La formation des habitudes. PUF, Paris.

Herriot, P. (1971). Language and Teaching: A Psychological View. London: Methuen and Co.

Hulstijn, J.H. (2001). Intentional and incidental second-language vocabulary learning: A reappraisal of elaboration, rehearsal and automaticity. In P. Robinson (Ed.), Cognition and second language instruction (pp. 258-286). Cambridge, UK: Cambridge University Press.

Jackendoff, R. (1993). Patterns in the Mind: Language and Human Nature. London: Harvester-Wheatsheaf.

Krashen, S. (1981). Second Language Acquisition and Second Language Learning. http://www.sdkrashen.com/SL_Acquisition_and_Learning/index.html

Leont'ev, A. (1974). Psycholinguistik und Sprachunterricht. Stuttgart, Germany: Kohlhammer.

Levelt, W. (1989). Speaking. MIT Press, Cambridge, Mass.

Levelt, W. (1993) The architecture of normal spoken language use. In Blanken G., J. Dittmann, H. Grimm, J. Marshall & C. Wallesch (eds.) Linguistic Disorders and pathologies. W. de Gruyter, Berlin, New York

Levelt, W.J.M., (1975). Systems, skills and language learning. In A. van Essen & J.P. Menting (Eds.), The Context of Foreign Language Learning (pp. 83-99). Assen: Van Gorcum.

Nagao, M. (1984). A framework of a mechanical translation between Japanese and English by analogy principle. In A. Elithorn & R. Banerji (Eds.), Artificial and Human Intelligence (pp. 173–180). Amsterdam: Elsevier.

Power, R., Scott, D. & Evans, R. (1998). What you see is what you meant: direct knowledge editings with natural language feedback. In H. Prade (Ed.), 13th European conference on artificial intelligence (ECAI'98) (pp. 677–681). Chichester: Wiley.

Reiter, E., & Dale, R. (2000). Building natural language generation systems. Cambridge: Cambridge University Press.

Rivers, W. (1964). The Psychologist and the Foreign Language Teacher. University of Chicago Press,.

Rivers, W. (1972). Speaking in Many Tongues: Essays in Foreign Language Teaching. Rowley: Newbury House.

Savignon, S. (1983). Communicative Competence: Theory and Classroom Practice. Reading, MA: Addison-Wesley.

Segalowitz, N. (2000). Automaticity and attentional skill in fluent performance. In H. Riggenbach (Ed.), Perspectives on fluency (pp. 200-219). Ann Arbor, MI: University of Michigan Press.

Segalowitz, N. (2003). Automaticity and second language learning. In C. Doughty & M. Long (Eds.), The handbook of second language acquisition (pp. 382-408). Oxford, UK: Blackwell.

Segalowitz, N. (2007). Access fluidity, attention control, and the acquisition of fluency in a second language. TESOL Quarterly, 41, 181-186.

Segalowitz, N., & Hulstijn, J. (2005). Automaticity in second language learning. In J. Kroll & A. De Groot (Eds.), Handbook of bilingualism: Psycholinguistic approaches (pp. 371-388). New York: Oxford University Press.

Spolsky, B. (1966). A psycholinguistic critique of programmed foreign language instruction. IRAL, 4(2).

Stevens, V. (1989). A direction for CALL: From behavioristic to humanistic courseware. In M. Pennington (Ed.), Teaching Languages with Computers (pp. 31–43). La Jolla, CA: Athelstan.

Weir, R. (1962). Language in the Crib. Mouton, La Haye.

Wong, W., & B. VanPatten. (2003). The Evidence is IN: Drills are Out. Foreign Language Annals, 36(3), 403-23.

Zock, M. (1997) Sentence Generation by Pattern Matching: the Problem of Syntactic Choice. In R. Mitkov & N. Nicolov (Eds.), Recent Advances in Natural Language Processing. (pp. 317-352).

Zock, M. (1994) Language in action, or, learning a language by watching it work. 7th Twente Workshop on Language Technology: Computer-Assisted Language Learning, Twente, pp. 101-111

Zock, M. (1991). Swim or sink: the problem of communicating thought. In M. Swartz & M. Yazdani (Eds.), Intelligent tutoring systems for foreign language learning (pp. 235–247). New York: Springer.

Zock, M. (1988) Natural languages are flexible tools, that's what makes them so hard to explain, to learn and to use. In Zock, M. & Sabah, G. (eds.), Advances in Natural Language Generation: an Interdisciplinary Perspective, Ablex, Norwood, N.J., Vol. 1, pp. 181-196.

Zock, M. & D. Schwab (2011). *Storage does not guarantee access. The problem of organizing and accessing words in a speaker's lexicon*. In Journal of Cognitive Science 12, 3, pp. 233-259, Institute for Cognitive Science, Seoul

Zock, M., Sabatier, P. and L. Jakubiec. (2008). Message Composition Based on Concepts and Goals. International Journal of Speech Technology, 11(3-4):181–193.

Evaluation on Second Language Collocational Congruency with Computational Semantic Similarity

Ching-Ying Lee **Chih-cheng Lin**
Department of English, National Taiwan Normal University
Department of Applied Foreign Languages, Kang Ning Junior College
collocation354@gmail.com

Abstract

Collocation learning is one of the important building blocks for the development of language competence. Remarkably, it is influenced by L1 and L2 congruency. The present study thus focused on the distinguishability of the computational similarity values between L2 collocates and L1 counterparts to establish the use of semantic similarity measure as a research instrument. The results showed that the inconsistency between human (subjective) and computational (objective) congruency classification of verb-noun collocations.

1 Introduction

Collocation learning is an important research area because it involves structural, semantic and cognitive variations in lexical components which underpin the foundation of language competence. The notion of collocational congruency distinguishes whether an L2 collocation is congruent or incongruent with L1 counterpart. Evaluation of collocational congruency is currently performed by human judgment. This subjective evaluation mostly depends on individual lexical knowledge and word meaning interpretation. Human judgment on meaning accordance lacks a clear criterion as to clear-cut L2 collocation in congruency. How much similar in word meaning can be considered as congruent collocation? How much different should be regarded as incongruent? This vagueness is not resolvable by human judgment and can only expect inconsistent evaluation.

The current study identified a research gap in the literature of L2 collocation where theoretical concepts of collocation congruency remain vague and lack explicit criteria for subjectively dichotomous congruency classification (Koya, 2005; Webb & Kagimoto, 2009; Yamashita & Jiang, 2010; Wolter & Gyllstad, 2011). This research proposed an objective and systematic method for congruency evaluation by exploiting computational measures of lexical semantic similarity. Based on literature review, it was found that *WordNet* (Miller, 1995) incorporated eight computational algorithms of semantic similarity measures and provided convenient online use. Of the eight algorithms, two (*Adapted Lesk* and *Gloss Vectors*) were selected in terms of their computational features and measuring stability. Three sets of word pairs with different semantic relations were composed and tested for lexical similarity values by the two measures.

The current study further applied the two similarity measures to the experimental set of collocation so as to objectively evaluate the properties of congruency. Semantic similarity between a collocate and an L2 transferred word with L1 word sense was quantified by the two computational similarity measures. Statistical and analytical comparisons were made, which led to further understanding of the potential advantage of exploiting semantic similarity for congruency evaluation.

2 Instruments and Data Collection

The research instruments included two semantic similarity measures and a set of collocation test. By the operational definition, a collocation is formed by a collocate and a base. Given a pair of equivalent L2 and L1 collocations, the subject of study is usually the semantic relation between the pair of cross-linguistic collocates. However, currently all semantic similarity measures were designed to operate on word pairs of the same language. To evaluate the semantic relation between the pair of cross-linguistic collocates by semantic similarity measures, an L2 transferred word of the L1 collocate was used as a surrogate that embedded the word sense of the L1 collocate.

As a design feature, semantic similarity measures also allowed semantic similarity evaluation between word pairs in both contexts of all word senses or designated word senses. When operated in all word senses, semantic similarity measures computed all possible combinations of word senses and gave the highest value that reflected the most similar senses of the two words. Alternatively, when a particular sense of each word was selected, semantic similarity measures provided similarity values of the two designated word senses.

As a convenient and useful semantic search instrument, *WordNet Search-3.1* was employed to consult for word senses in glossary. The online system of *WordNet Search-3.1* (Miller, 1995) was different from other online dictionaries because it showed not only lexical meanings and part of speech, but also its synset relation and word relation. For the purpose of this study, *WordNet Search-3.1* provided word sense observation and selection for both L2 collocates and L2 transferred words as surrogates of L1 collocates.

The use of the two semantic similarity measures, *Adapted Lesk* and *Gloss Vectors*, as a research instrument was operationalized with the online service of *WordNet::Similarity*. In fact, *WordNet::Similarity* conveniently integrated the online service of *WordNet Search-3.1* (Miller, 1995) with hyperlinks and provided semantic similarity calculation by a straightforward process of data input and results output. The process of calculating and retrieving lexical similarity values was as follows.

A. In the context of all word senses:

1. Key-in the L2 collocate in the Word1 slot with the format word#part_of_speech, for example, *observe#v*.
2. Key-in the L2 transferred word from the L1 counterpart in the Word2 slot with the format word#part_of_speech, for example, *celebrate#v*.
3. Select one of the embedded measures, for example, *Gloss Vectors*, with a pull-down menu to calculate the semantic similarity of input words in Word1 and Word2.
4. Press the "Compute" button.
5. Receive the results, e.g, "the relatedness of *observe#v#6* and *celebrate#v#1* using vector is 1". This showed that, among all word sense combination, word sense #6 of *observe* had the highest similarity to word sense #1 of *celebrate*, rated as 1 by the *(Gloss) vector* measure.

B. In the context of single word sense: (with the results from the all word sense context)

1. Click on the "View glosses (definitions)" link.
2. Inspect all word senses of the two words and determine a particular word sense for each word.
3. Key-in the L2 collocate in the Word1 slot with the format word#part_of_speech#sense, for example, *observe#v#7* (follow with the eyes or the mind).
4. Key-in the L2 transferred word from the L1 counterpart in the Word2 slot with the format word#part_of_speech#sense, for example, *celebrate#v#1* (behave as expected during of holidays or rites).
5. Select one of the embedded measures, for example, *Gloss Vectors*, with a pull-down menu to calculate the semantic similarity of input words in Word1 and Word2.
6. Press the "Compute" button.
7. Receive the results, e.g, "the relatedness of *observe#v#7* and *celebrate#v#1* using vector is 0.1822". This showed that, for this specific word sense combination, the semantic similarity between *observe* and *celebrate* was rated as 0.1822 by the *(Gloss) vector* measure.

The second instrument was a set of collocation candidates were extracted from the collocation lists of previous studies on common miscollocations. The final set of collocation test included two categories of collocation items, congruent verb-noun collocations and incongruent verb-noun collocations. Each category consisted of ten collocation items, as shown in Table 3, with given bases and expected collocates.

3 Verification on the Lexical Similarity Measures

The first quantitative study verified the effectiveness of the two similarity measures, *Adapted Lesk* and *Gloss Vector* based on WordNet, in evaluating semantic similarity. The semantic evaluation test was performed on three sets of ten word pairs. The first set consisted of word pairs that were near synonyms or semantically similar. The second set included word pairs that were semantically related, e.g., they were likely to appear in the same context, but not synonyms. Word pairs in the third set were neither synonyms nor context-related. Table 1 shows the three sets of word pairs designed to manifest differences in semantic distance.

Similar	Related	Unrelated
close, shut	woman, man	door, fish
start, begin	dog, cat	lock, cloth
big, large	tree, leaf	box, eye
end, finish	sun, rain	book, cake
small, tiny	food, eat	bag, road
salary, wage	day, night	brain, cook
injure, harm	body, mind	computer, shoes
grow, raise	animal, human	float, card
exam, test	earth, solar	law, sea
opinion, view	music, melody	color, friend

Table 1. Word Pairs Test Set for Semantic Similarity Measures

The purpose of the semantic evaluation test was to observe how the two similarity measures performed in providing a quantifiable and distinguishable judgment on semantic similarity. Table 2 summarizes statistical descriptions of semantic similarity values calculated by the two similarity measures within the all-word-sense context for each set of word pairs. For each combination of word pair set and similarity measure, the statistical description included mean similarity values and standard deviation in parenthesis.

Type / Measure	Similar	Related	Un-related	Numerical Range
Adapted Lesk	429.6 (358.94)	81.2 (97.41)	19.2 (11.42)	$0 \rightarrow N$
Gloss Vectors	0.91 (0.183)	0.46 (0.179)	0.21 (0.072)	$0 \rightarrow 1$

Table 2. Statistical Descriptions of Semantic Similarity Values on Semantic Evaluation Test

Note that *Adapted Lesk* was designed to measure semantic similarity with a numerical range from zero to a very large number, with larger number indicating higher similarity. On the other hand, the numerical range of *Gloss Vectors* was normalized to reside in the range of zero and one, with one being the highest similarity. The results showed that both measures of *Adapted Lesk* and *Gloss Vectors* were able to provide reliable and effective indication to semantic similarity and to distinguish semantic relation with the notion of semantic distance. The resulting evidences of the first quantitative study provided support for adopting computational measures of semantic similarity, such as *Adapted Lesk* (abbreviated as *Lesk* in the following sections) and *Gloss Vectors* (abbreviated as *Vector* in the following sections), as objective and systematic method for congruency evaluation.

4 Collocational Congruency Classification by Semantic Similarity Values

As indicated in the previous discussion, current notion of congruency primarily depends on individual researcher's subjective judgment to give a binary classification of congruent and incongruent collocations. This leads to ambiguity as to whether collocations can be consistently classified. Further studies on congruency factor in L2 collocation learning seem to be somewhat problematic in deriving theory with an indeterministic basis. The result of the first study suggested that the values of lexical semantic similarity measures could be considered as effective indicators of the collocation congruency. They are objective and systematic as the numerical values are calculated by computational algorithms and a proper threshold for congruency classification can be ascertained and applied to all evaluation targets, which also lead to consistent classification results.

The second study was designed to demonstrate the application of semantic similarity measures to classification of L2 collocation congruency and to derive empirical results for further deduction. As an operational definition, an L2 collocation is formed by a collocate and a base. In most cases, the base is fully transparent between L2 and L1 and is straightforward to cross-linguistic translation. The collocate, on the other hand, is subjective to cross-linguistic semantic variation and is the sole determinant of congruency. Given an equivalent pair of L2 and L1 collocations, such as "*seek information*" and "尋找資訊 (xyun zhiao zi xyung)", congruency of the L2 collocation is determined by whether the L2 collocate "*seek*" and the L1 collocate "尋找 (xyun zhiao)" are conceptually equivalent or similar at the semantic level. However, current computational similarity measures are designed for two words of the same language. To evaluate semantic similarity between L2 collocate and L1 collocate, a surrogate of L1 collocate in L2 must be used. This L2 surrogate in semantic similarity evaluation with L2 collocate can be represented by one of the synonymous transferred words from L1 counterpart. For example, the transferred word "*find*" of the L1 collocate "尋找(xyun zhiao)" can be used as a surrogate to compute the semantic similarity with the L2 collocate "*seek*".

On the surface, the requirement of an L2 surrogate for an L1 collocate seemed to be a potential shortcoming. There may be several synonymous transferred words eligible as candidates for the L2 surrogate of an L1 collocate. Semantic similarity may vary with the selection of a transferred word as the surrogate, thus, leading to variable congruency evaluation between an L2 collocate and an L1 collocate. A deeper analysis revealed that the use of an L2 surrogate for an L1 collocate was actually advantageous in providing *learner-centered* congruency evaluation. First, the selection of a transferred word for an L1 collocate reflects the L2 lexical knowledge of a learner. Collocational congruency, thus, depends on L2 learners' proficiency level and becomes relevant to learners' individual status. Second, the process of selecting a transferred word involves the activation of conceptual links in learners' cross-linguistic lexical networks, and thus, closely simulates the actual context of learners' L2 collocation use. Third, the decision of a transferred word also incorporates potential L1 influence on individual learners, and thus, embeds the critical factor into congruency evaluation in real context of L2 learning. All these favorable attributes of adopting semantic similarity measures for congruency evaluation provide strong support for better analysis of realistic congruency effects on L2 collocation performance.

The research design of adopting two semantic similarity measures, e.g., *Adapted Lesk* and *Gloss Vectors*, was based on the consideration of providing more evidences of semantic similarity evaluation on a cross-linguistic collocate pair. Evaluation from both measures can be cross-examined for consistency so as to establish larger confidence on the subsequent congruency classification. Experimental results from the first quantitative study partially verified the evaluative consistency of these two measures. The adoption of two semantic similarity measures in the quantitative studies also allowed the construction of a conceptual space of semantic similarity where distribution of semantic similarity values and area of congruency classification can be figuratively observed.

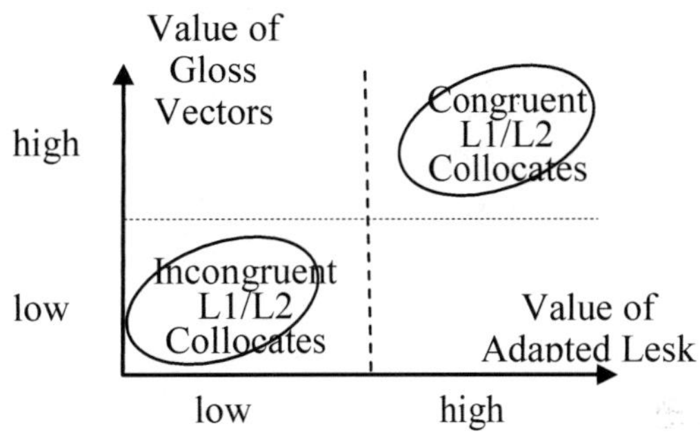

Figure 1. Ideal Semantic Similarity Distribution and Congruency Classification

Figure 1 shows the conceptual space of semantic similarity formed by orthogonal dimensions of the two semantic similarity measures, *Adapted Lesk* and *Gloss Vectors*. It was assumed that incongruent L1/L2 collocates would be given low similarity values from both measures, while congruent collocate pair would receive high values. This would result in an ideal bi-polar distribution of two clearly separated clusters and distinct classification of congruency.

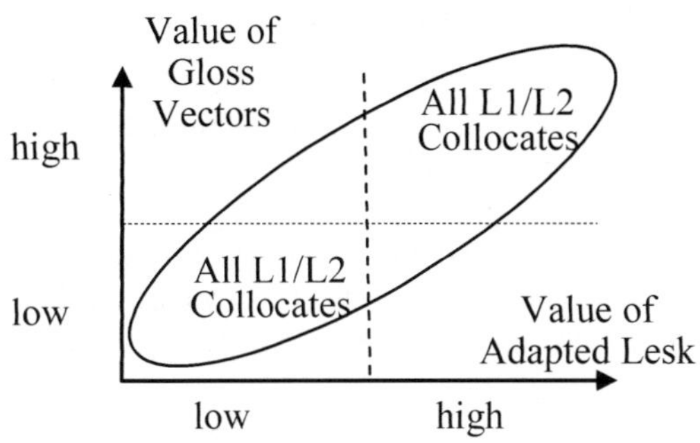

Figure 2. Expectation of Semantic Similarity Distribution

However, this extreme convergence of similarity values may not be realistic. It was expected that some similarity values would fall in the middle range. Thus, actual semantic similarity distribution of cross-linguistic collocate pairs may form a continuous band tilted from lower left corner to upper right end, as shown in Figure 2. In addition, it was conjectured that actual plotting of similarity values of cross-linguistic collocate pairs along with their subjective congruency classification based on human judgment may show an overlapping area.

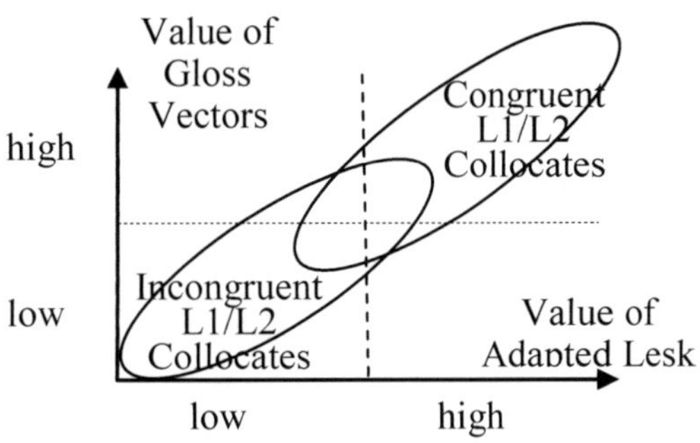

Figure 3. Disagreement between Objective Similarity Evaluation and Subjective Human Classification

This area, as shown in Figure 3, exhibited a boundary crossing disagreement between objective similarity evaluation and subjective human classification where some collocate pairs were humanly judged as congruent but were computationally evaluated as relatively low similarity and some were subjectively incongruent but were objectively of moderate similarity. This mutual middle ground suggested that current practices of subjective human judgment on congruency might actually be partially inconsistent, inaccurate, and unreliable.

5 Applying Sematic Similarity Values and Examining Congruency

The second study applied the semantic similarity measures to the collocation sets so as to provide empirical evidences for the conjectured semantic similarity distribution. Subjective congruency classification of collocations was then cross examined with their computational semantic similarity. Statistical analysis was then performed on the congruency categories for significance of difference in the numerical values of computational semantic similarity. The purpose was to evaluate the consistency of subjective congruency classification from the perspective of objective semantic similarity and to reveal potential classification conflicts.

As noted previously, the congruency classification on the collocation sets was based on an initial and subjective judgment by the researcher. The transferred word from each L1 collocate in the test set was also provided by the participants' most common choice as an exemplar learner's selection. The computation of semantic similarity measures between two words also involves the selection of word sense in two modes. In the single-word-sense mode, each polysemous word was assigned a particular word sense for semantic similarity evaluation. In the all-word-sense mode, no word sense was assigned and all word meanings of the word pairs are considered so as to match the closest word meanings. In other words, the semantic similarity evaluation, when operated in the all-word-sense mode, gives the highest value to represent the most similar word senses of the two polysemous words. In the L2 learning context, semantic similarity evaluation in the single-word-sense mode can be used to simulate lexical knowledge of low-level to mid-level learners, while the all-word-sense mode may assume the characteristics of more advanced learners. When selecting a particular word sense in the single-word-sense mode, L2 learners' primary perception of word meaning would usually be a good consideration.

As introduced previously, the measures of semantic similarity, *Gloss Vectors* and *Adapted Lesk*, provided a deterministic and algorithmic evaluation of semantic similarity between any pair of English words. However, the two measures did not produce a similar range of values. To provide a more convenient and complementary similarity observation of the two measures, the values of the *Adapted Lesk* measure were converted by logarithm, as *Log (Lesk+1)*. The addition of one to the *Lesk* values before logarithmic conversion was to avoid mathematic peculiarity because *Lesk* value started from zero.

For binary classification of similarity level, the thresholds were judiciously ascertained at 0.6 for the *Gloss Vectors* measure and 99 for the *Adapted Lesk* measure (i.e., 2 for *Log (Lesk+1)*). In other words, semantic similarity of a pair of L1/L2 collocates was classified as high if the evaluated value of *Gloss Vectors* measure was higher than 0.6 and/or if the evaluated value of *Log (Lesk+1)* was higher than 2. In a few cases when the evaluative grades were not consistent

Subjective Congruency	L2 Collocate (base)	L1 Transferred Word	Semantic Similarity			
			Single Word Sense		All Word Sense	
			Vector	Lesk	Vector	Lesk
congruent	*acquire* (knowledge)	*get*	1.0	3.364	1.0	3.364
	seek (information)	*search*	1.0	3.018	1.0	3.018
	make (efforts)	*do*	1.0	2.905	1.0	2.905
	see play	*watch*	1.0	2.696	1.0	2.696
	increase (abilities)	*increase*	1.0	3.112	1.0	3.112
	maintain (relationship)	*keep*	1.0	2.560	1.0	2.560
	preserve (culture)	*conserve*	1.0	2.839	1.0	2.839
	make (troubles)	*make*	1.0	2.967	1.0	2.967
	take (actions)	*do*	0.695	2.121	0.695	2.121
	overcome (challenges)	*conquer*	0.750	1.491	0.750	1.491
Incongruent	*surf* (Internet)	*browse*	0.066	1.0	1.0	2.517
	solve (crimes)	*break*	0.731	2.412	0.731	2.412
	make (apology)	*say*	0.421	1.845	0.421	1.845
	study (English)	*read*	0.201	1.462	1.0	2.501
	carry (lanterns)	*hold*	0.141	2.017	1.0	2.605
	ease (worries)	*relieve*	0.249	0.903	1.0	2.220
	make (conclusion)	*get*	1.0	2.967	1.0	2.967
	conduct (heat)	*transmit*	0.083	1.204	1.0	2.452
	make (impression)	*leave*	0.465	1.342	0.583	2.312
	restore (vitality)	*recover*	0.197	1.591	0.197	1.591

Table 3. Semantic Similarity Values of Verb-Noun L2/L1 Collocates in Subjective Congruency Classification

between the two measures, the grade (high similarity or low) given by the *Gloss Vectors* measure was adopted.

Table 3 reports the similarity values of both the subjectively congruent and subjectively incongruent verb-noun L2/L1 collocate pairs in the collocation test set based on the two semantic measures, *Gloss Vectors* and *Adpated Lesk*, in both contexts of single word sense and all word senses.

In Table 3, it was noted that all subjectively congruent L1/L2 verb collocates were indeed of high semantic similarity. In addition, eight out of the ten verb collocate pairs received the highest similarity value in the *Gloss Vectors* measure. The similarity evaluations were also not affected by difference in learners' lexical knowledge as the similarity values were the same in the two modes of single-word-sense and all-word-sense. The experiments showed that subjective and objective evaluations for congruency were consistent on semantically similar pairs of verb collocate. However, most transferred words from participants' common choice were incorrect use. This indicated congruent verb-noun collocations may not be assumed to be easy and straightforward for L2 learners.

For subjectively incongruence, some variations were observed. In the single-word-sense mode, e.g., learners' lexical knowledge on the collocates was assumed to be limited to primary word meaning, most subjectively incongruent verb collocate pairs were indeed of low semantic similarity. The collocate pairs of "*solve* and *break*", "*make* and *get*", were the only two exceptions and surprisingly showed high similarity. In the all-word-sense mode,

Word Sense	Subjective Congruency	N	Gloss Vectors				Log (Lesk+1)			
			Mean	Std. Dev.	Min.	Max.	Mean	Std. Dev.	Min.	Max.
Single	Congruent	10	0.945	0.118	0.695	1.0	2.707	0.544	1.491	3.364
	Incongruent	10	0.355	0.305	0.066	1.0	1.674	0.649	0.903	2.967
All	Congruent	10	0.945	0.118	0.695	1.0	2.707	0.544	1.491	3.364
	Incongruent	10	0.793	0.094	0.197	1.0	2.342	0.389	1.591	2.967

Table 4. Descriptive Summary of Computational Semantic Similarity in Verb Noun Collocations

when assumption of learners' lexical knowledge on the collocates was extended to comprehensive word meanings, however, most subjectively incongruent verb collocate pairs showed high semantic similarity. Only three collocate pairs, e.g., "*make* and *say*", "*leave* and *make*", "*restore* and *recover*", remained of low semantic similarity. This empirical results showed that congruency might depend on learners' lexical knowledge on the candidate collocates.

The semantic similarity analysis on verb-noun collocations revealed a problematic pattern of inconsistent classification between human (subjective) and computational (objective) evaluations. This inconsistency of congruency evaluation was further aggravated by the different conditions of learners' word sense level. For verb-noun collocations, the worst inconsistency occurred in the subjectively incongruent category with the assumption of learners' all word senses, where seven out of ten collocations that were humanly judged as of low similarity, were instead, computationally considered as of high similarity.

For further verification, a statistical analysis was also performed on the semantic similarity differences between congruency categories. Table 4 reported the descriptive summary of the computational semantic similarity in verb-noun collocations. Mean values of the *Vector* measures of subjectively congruent collocations, in both contexts of learners' single word sense, and all word sense, was very close to 1.0, indicating that semantics of the L2 collocates and the transferred words from the L1 counterpart were almost identical. indicating that semantics of the L2 collocates and the transferred words from the L1 counterpart were almost identical. For subjectively incongruent verb noun collocations, mean values of the *Vector* measures in the context of learners' single word sense indicated low similarity. However, in the context of learners' all word senses, mean values of the *Vector* measures of subjectively incongruent verb-noun collocations more than doubled and indicated high similarity. A similar pattern of varying similarity evaluation between subjectively congruent and incongruent verb-noun collocations under different contexts of learners' proficiency levels was also observed on the *Lesk* measures.

Table 5 reports the statistical comparison between subjective congruency categories by two computational measures of semantic similarity under learners' different proficiency contexts. It has shown that semantic similarity differences between subjective congruency categories were statistically significant by both measures in the context of learners' single word sense, e.g., $F(1, 18) = 32.448$, $p = 0.000 < 0.05$, and $F(1, 18) = 14.877$, $p = 0.001 < 0.05$. However, in the context of learners' all word senses, there was no statistically significant difference in the semantic similarity by both measures between congruency categories, e.g., $F(1, 18) = 2.228$, $p = 0.153 > 0.05$, and $F(1, 18) = 2.984$, $p = 0.101 > 0.05$.

The inconsistency between human (subjective) and computational (objective) congruency classification was manifested in verb noun collocations. Both the item-level and the category-level examination showed that computational and human congruency evaluations might not share the same view. In addition, human congruency evaluation might not account for learners' varying proficiency levels. This analysis revealed that congruency could become ambiguous and disconcerted in the contexts of human evaluation and learners' various proficiency levels. Further studies on better congruency classification and its effects on L2 learners' collocation performance were required.

Word Sense	Subjective Congruency		Sum of Squares	df	Mean Square	F	Sig.
Single	Vector	Between Groups	1.735	1	1.735	32.448	.000
		Within Groups	.962	18	.053		
		Total	2.698	19			
	Lesk	Between Groups	5.334	1	5.334	14.877	.001
		Within Groups	6.454	18	.359		
		Total	11.787	19			
All	Vector	Between Groups	.114	1	.114	2.228	.153
		Within Groups	.924	18	.051		
		Total	1.038	19			
	Lesk	Between Groups	.666	1	.666	2.984	.101
		Within Groups	4.019	18	.223		
		Total	4.685	19			

Table 5. One-Way ANOVA on Computational Semantic Similarity between Subjective Congruency Categories in Verb Noun Collocations

6 Conclusion

The quantitative study empirically verified the applicability of computational semantic measures in classification of L2 collocation congruency. It has shown that objective evaluation of congruency required an input of transferred words from L1 collocate and then operated purely on the L2. This might avoid the fallacy of subjective and cross-linguistic evaluation of congruency. In addition, this *learner-centered* congruency evaluation more closely simulated the context of L2 learners' lexical decision process.

References

B. Wolter and H. Gyllstad. 2011. Collocational links in the L2 mental lexicon and the influence of L1 intralexical knowledge. Applied Linguistics, 32(4), 430-449.

C. Lin. 1997. Semantic network for vocabulary teaching. *Journal of Taiwan Normal University: Humanities & Social Science*, 42, 43-54.

G. A. Miller. 1995. WordNet: A Lexical Database for English. Communications of the ACM (11).

H. J. Chen. 2011. Developing and Evaluating a Web-based Collocation Retrieval Tool for EFL Students and Teachers. Computer Assisted Language Learning, 24(1), 63-79.

J. Yamashita and N. Jiang. 2010. L1 influence on the acquisition of L2 collocations: Japanese ESL users and EFL learners acquiring English collocations. TESOL Quarterly, 44(4), 647-668.

L. J. Brinton and D. M. Brinton. 2010. The lingustic structure of modern language. Philadelphia: John Benjamins.

S. Webb and E. Kagimoto. 2009. The effects of vocabulary learning on collocation and meaning. TESOL Quarterly, 43(1), 55-77.

T. Koya. 2005. The acquisition of basic collocations by Japanese learners of English. Unpublished dissertation. Waseda University.

A Corpus-Based Tool for Exploring Domain-Specific Collocations in English

Ping-Yu Huang[1], Chien-Ming Chen[2], Nai-Lung Tsao[3] and David Wible[3]

[1]General Education Center, Ming Chi University of Technology
alanhuang25@hotmail.com

[2] Institute of Information Science, Academia Sinica
virtualorz@gmail.com

[3] Graduate Institute of Learning and Instruction, National Central University
{beaktsao, wible}@stringnet.org

Abstract

Coxhead's (2000) Academic Word List (AWL) has been frequently used in EAP classrooms and re-examined in light of various domain-specific corpora. Although well-received, the AWL has been criticized for ignoring the fact that words tend to show irregular distributions and be used in different ways across disciplines (Hyland and Tse, 2007). One such difference concerns collocations. Academic words (e.g. *analyze*) often co-occur with different words across domains and contain different meanings. What EAP students need is a "discipline-based lexical repertoire" (p.235). Inspired by Hyland and Tse, we develop an online corpus-based tool, *TechCollo*, which is meant for EAP students to explore collocations in one domain or compare collocations across disciplines. It runs on textual data from six specialized corpora and utilizes frequency, traditional mutual information, and normalized MI (Wible et al., 2004) as measures to decide whether co-occurring word pairs constitute collocations. In this article we describe the current released version of TechCollo and how to use it in EAP studies. Additionally, we discuss a pilot study in which we used TechCollo to investigate whether the AWL words take different collocates in different domain-specific corpora. This pilot basically confirmed Hyland and Tse and demonstrates that many AWL words show uneven distributions and collocational differences across domains.

1 Introduction

There has long been a shared belief among English for academic or specific purposes (EAP and ESP) instructors that it is necessary to provide students with a list of academic vocabulary[1] irrespective of their specialized domain(s). There are two main reasons why academic vocabulary receives so much attention in EAP instruction. First, academic vocabulary accounts for a substantial proportion of words in academic texts (Nation, 2001). Sutarsyah et al. (1994), for example, found that about 8.4% of the tokens in the Learned and Scientific sections of the Lancaster-Oslo/Bergen (Johansson, 1978) and Wellington corpora (Bauer, 1993). Second, academic words very often are non-salient in written texts and less likely to be emphasized by content teachers in class (Flowerdew, 1993). Consequently, EAP researchers have been convinced that students need a complete list of academic vocabulary, and several lists were thus compiled. Among the attempts to collect academic lexical items, Coxhead's (2000) Academic Word List (AWL) has been considered the most successful work to date. In the AWL, Coxhead offered 570 word families which were relatively frequent in a 3.5-million-token corpus of academic texts. The corpus was composed of writings from four disciplines: arts, commerce, law, and science. By considering certain selection principles such as frequency and range, Coxhead gathered a group of word families which were *specialized* in academic discourse and *generalized* across different fields of specialization. On average, the AWL accounted for 10% of Coxhead's academic corpus and showed distributions of 9.1-12% of the four disciplines. Since its publishment, the AWL has been frequently used in EAP classes,

[1] Academic words are also variously termed *sub-technical vocabulary* (Yang, 1986), *semi-technical vocabulary* (Farrell, 1990), or *specialized non-technical lexis* (Cohen et al., 1979) in the literature. They generally refer to words which are common in academic discourse but not so common in other types of texts.

covered by numerous teaching materials, and re-examined by various domain-specific corpora (e.g. Vongpumivitch et al., 2009; Ward, 2009). The AWL, as Coxhead (2011) herself claims, indeed exerts much greater effects that the author ever imagined.

Although well-received, the AWL is not without criticisms. For instance, Chen and Ge (2007), while confirming the significant proportion of the AWL in medical texts (10.07%), found that only half of the AWL words were frequent in the field of medicine. In Hancioğlu et al. (2008), the authors criticized that the distinction that Coxhead (2000) made into academic and general service words was questionable. In actuality, there were several general service words contained in the AWL (e.g. *drama* and *injure*). Arguably the strongest criticism came from Hyland and Tse (2007), who questioned whether there was a single core academic word list. Hyland and Tse called Coxhead's corpus compilation "opportunistic" (p. 239) and built a new database better controlled for its selection of texts to examine Coxhead's findings. Utilizing a more rigorous standard, Hyland and Tse found that only 192 families in the AWL were frequent in their corpus. Furthermore, numerous most frequent AWL families did not show such high-frequency distributions in Hyland and Tse's dataset. In addition to these methodological problems, as Hyland and Tse emphasized, the AWL as well as those previous academic word lists ignored an important fact that words tend to behave semantically and phraseologically differently across disciplines. Many academic words, such as *analyze*, tend to co-occur with different words and contain different meanings across research areas. What EAP learners actually need and have to study, accordingly, should be "a more restricted, discipline-based lexical repertoire" (p. 235).

Inspired by Hyland and Tse's (2007) insights and analyses, we devise and create a learning tool which is able to generate domain-specific lexico-grammatical knowledge for EAP students. The knowledge that we focus on here concerns collocations. Specifically, we develop an online corpus-based tool, *TechCollo*, which can be used by EAP students to search for and explore frequent word combinations in their specialized area(s). The tool, by processing written texts in several medium-sized domain-specific corpora, enables students to study collocational patterns in their own domain, compare collocations in different disciplines, and check whether certain combinations or word usages are restricted to a specific field. To decide whether a pair of co-occurring words constitutes a candidate collocation, TechCollo uses measures such as frequency, traditional mutual information (MI) (Church and Hanks, 1990), and normalized MI (Wible et al., 2004). We will discuss these measures in more detail in Section 3.

This paper is structured as follows. In Section 2 we briefly discuss some related work. Section 3 describes the online learning tool and the corpora from which TechCollo extracts collocations. In Section 4, we present results of a pilot study to exemplify how to exploit TechCollo to discover differences in collocations across two domains. Finally, we propose our future plans for improving TechCollo in Section 5.

2 Related Work

In electronic lexicography or automatic term recognition (ATR), a number of studies have investigated how to retrieve multiword terminology from texts (e.g. Collier et al., 2002; Rindflesch et al., 1999). Basically, those studies identified candidate patterns of words (e.g. noun-noun or adjective-noun combinations) from texts and used various frequency-based or association-based measures to determine the *termhood* of those candidates. Other ATR studies took more sophisticated approaches. Wermter and Hahn (2005), for example, distinguished domain-specific from non-domain-specific multiword terms on the basis of *paradigmatic modifiability* degrees. The assumption behind this approach was that the component words of a multiword term had stronger association strength and thus any component of it was less likely to be substituted by other words. However, although the identification of multiword terms has been an active field of research, few studies have explored ways of making the terminology accessible to EAP students. To our knowledge, Barrière's (2009) TerminoWeb has been the only work addressing this issue in the literature. Below we describe Barrière's platform.

TerminoWeb, as its name suggests, was created with an aim to help learners of different professional areas explore and learn domain-specific knowledge from the Web. To get access to the knowledge, a user had to follow several steps. The starting point was to upload a technical paper to the platform. This paper was used as a source text in which the user selected unknown terms and the TerminoWeb also automatically identified certain terms. Then, a set of queries were performed on the Web to collect texts relevant to the source text (i.e. belonging to the same domain) or including the same user-selected and computer-identified terms. Those collected texts were then a large domain-specific corpus. Within the corpus, the user could do concordance searches to understand word usages of an unknown term in larger contexts. The user could also make collocation searches for this term. The calculation of collocations performed by Barrière (2009) was based on Smadja's (1993) algorithm, which, as Smadja claimed, reached a precision rate of 80% for extracting collocations.

Unlike the technical corpora compiled via the TerminoWeb with texts from the whole Web and were likely to include lots of messy data, the corpora underlying TechCollo basically were composed of texts edited in advance which were assumed to be *cleaner* and more reliable. TechCollo, furthermore, offers an interface which allows users to compare collocations in two different specialized domains or in a specialized and a general-purpose corpus. These convenient search functions will more effectively enable EAP learners to discover and explore specialized collocational knowledge online.

3 TechCollo: A Corpus-Based Domain-Specific Collocation Learning Tool

TechCollo, which stands for *technical collocations*, is an online tool with which EAP students can explore specialized collocations. To illustrate the functions of TechCollo, we respectively describe: (1) the compilation of ESP corpora underlying it, (2) the determination of a word pair as a candidate for a true collocation, and (3) the interface designed for EAP students.

3.1 Corpora

Currently, TechCollo extracts collocations from six domain-specific corpora. All of the six databases are medium-sized, containing 1.8-5.5 million running tokens. Among them, three were composed of texts coming from the largest online encyclopedia, Wikipedia. Specifically, the Wikipedia texts that we processed were provided by the Wacky team of linguists and information technology specialists (Baroni et al., 2009),[2] who compiled large Wikipedia corpora for various European languages such as English, Italian, and French. Based on an English corpus created by the Wacky team, we established corpora for three domains: medicine, engineering, and law, which were named Medical Wiki, Engineering Wiki, and Legal Wiki Corpora, respectively. The other three ESP textual archives contained writings from high-quality academic journals. That is, for the same medical, engineering, and legal domains, we consulted sixty academic journals and respectively downloaded 280, 408, and 106 articles from those journals online. We utilized the tools offered by Stanford CoreNLP (Klein and Manning, 2003) to POS-tag and parse the three academic corpora. The three corpora then were termed: Medical Academic, Engineering Academic, and Legal Academic Corpora.

In addition to the domain-specific corpora, TechCollo also provides collocation searches in two general-purpose corpora: Wikipedia and British National Corpus (2001). We offer collocation exploration for the two corpora for users to compare and identify collocations in subject areas and general use. Table 1 shows the corpus sizes of the six technical and two general-purpose corpora behind TechCollo.

Corpus	Token Count
Medical Wiki Corpus (MWC)	2,812,082
Engineering Wiki Corpus (EWC)	3,706,525
Legal Wiki Corpus (LWC)	5,556,661
Medical Academic Corpus (MAC)	1,821,254
Engineering Academic Corpus (EAC)	1,989,115
Legal Academic Corpus (LAC)	2,232,982
Wikipedia	833,666,975
British National Corpus (BNC)	94,956,136

Table 1: Sizes for Domain-Specific and General-Purpose Corpora

3.2 Collocation Extraction

In computational linguistics, various measures have been utilized in order to automatically extract collocations from texts. Those measures can be roughly divided into three categories (Wermter and Hahn, 2004): (1) frequency-based measures, (2) information-theoretical measures (e.g. mutual information), and (3) statistical

[2] The corpus that we downloaded from the Wacky website (http://wacky.sslmit.unibo.it/) was WaCkypedia_EN, which was POS-tagged, lemmatized, and syntactically parsed with TreeTagger and MaltParser. We thank Baroni et al. (2009) for offering the WaCkypedia_EN corpus.

measures (e.g. t test and log-likelihood test). To evaluate whether a measure is effective or to compare the effectiveness of several measures, one often needs to collect a set of true collocations and non-collocations and examine how a measure ranks those word combinations (see, for example, Pecina, 2008). An important lesson learned from the examinations of those measures is that there is no single measure which is perfect in all situations. To identify target collocations, one is suggested to exploit several association measures with a correct understanding of their notions and behaviors.

TechCollo employs three main measures to decide whether a two-word combination constitutes a candidate collocation in a five-word window in our textual databases: frequency, traditional mutual information (*tradMI*) (Church and Hanks, 1990), and normalized MI (*normMI*, Wible et al., 2004). A learner using TechCollo can set or change the values of these measures to show candidate collocations in the six technical corpora (a detailed description of the user interface for TechCollo is given in section 3.3). First, the measure of frequency refers to raw co-occurrence count of a word pair. However, to filter out the pairs which are extremely frequent as a result of one or both of their component words but are not true collocations,[3] TechCollo offers the common association measure: *tradMI*, which is formulated as follows:

$$tradMI(x,y) = \log_2 \frac{P(x,y)}{P(x)\,P(y)}$$

This information-theoretical measure works by comparing the joint probability of two expressions *x* and *y* (i.e. the probability of two expressions appearing together) with the independent probabilities of *x* and *y*. In other words, MI expresses to what extent the observed frequency of a combination differs from expected. Although *tradMI* effectively removes word pairs containing high-frequency words, it inevitably suffers from a problem that it also filters out certain pairs which contain high-frequency words but are interesting and actual collocations. In English, for example, word combinations such as *take medicine, make (a) decision, and run (a) risk* are real collocations which include very frequent component words. To solve the problem with the *tradMI*, Wible et al. introduces the alternative association measure *normMI*, which attempts to minimize the effects caused by sheer high frequency words. To achieve this, Wible et al. normalizes the *tradMI* by dividing the lexeme frequency by its number of senses (based on WordNet). The formula for the *normMI* is shown below. Basically, the notion of *normMI* is based on the *one sense per collocation* assumption proposed by Yarowsky (1995). A highly frequent word (e.g. *take, make,* and *run*) is generally polysemous. However, as Wible et al. indicates, as the word appears in a collocation, it is very common that only one of its senses is used (e.g. the word *run* in the collocation *run a risk*). Wible et al. compares the *tradMI* with *normMI* using several pairs containing high-frequency words (e.g. *make effort* and *make decision*) and found that these combinations are ranked higher among the identified candidate collocations. It is important to note that, although the *normMI* produces higher recall than the *tradMI*, precision does not decrease accordingly. On our TechCollo interface, we provide the *normMI* to enable EAP learners to find and learn some word combinations which include high frequent words but are still true and specialized collocations in their domain(s).

$$normMI(x,y) = \log_2 \frac{P(x,y)}{\left(\frac{P(x)}{sn(x)}\right) * \left(\frac{P(y)}{sn(y)}\right)}$$

3.3 User Interface

The main page of TechCollo is shown in Figure 1. Basically, this online collocation exploration tool allows users to choose from the six medium-sized domain-specific corpora: MWC, EWC, LWC, MAC, EAC, and LAC, and the two large-scale general-purpose corpora: BNC and Wikipedia. A user accessing the website can key in a keyword that he/she intends to study and the system will automatically search for words which tend to co-occur with the keyword in the selected databases. The current released version of TechCollo (i.e. TechCollo 1.0) provides searches of verb-noun collocations. The

[3] A typical example of the frequent non-collocational pairs is the string *of the*, which appears more than 2.7 million times in Corpus of Contemporary American English (Davies, 2008).

measures of frequency and *tradMI*, as specified earlier, can be changed and decided by users so that the system will respond with either a shorter list of word pairs with higher frequency counts and MI or a longer list containing more candidate collocations.

Here we take the noun *procedure* and its verb collocates in MWC and EWC as examples. We feed this word into the TechCollo system with the frequency and *tradMI* set at 1 and 4, respectively. That is, only the verbs which appear together with *procedure* at least two times and having mutual information larger than 4 will be identified as candidate collocates. The search results are demonstrated in Figure 2.

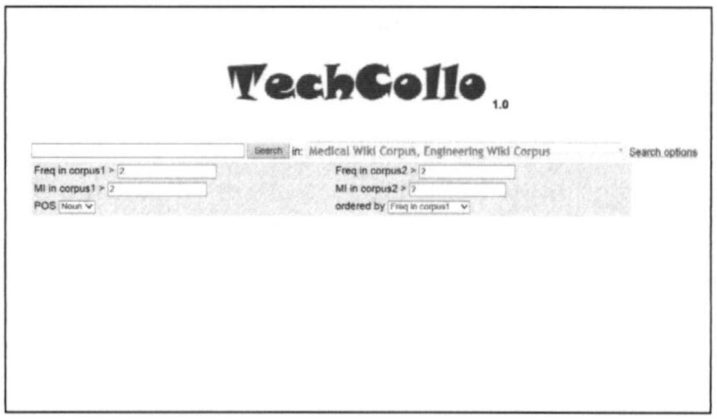

Figure 1: Main Page of TechCollo

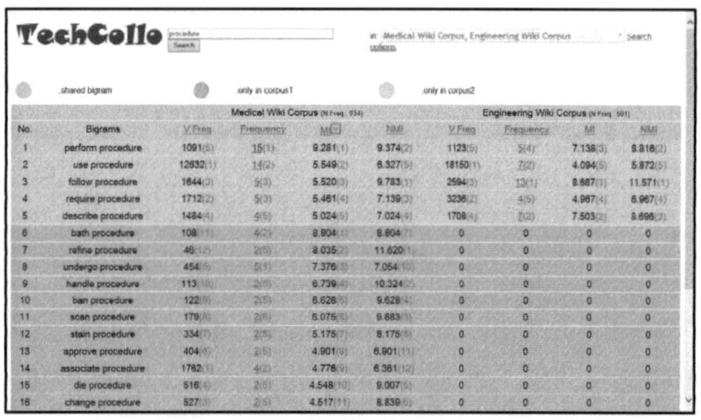

Figure 2: Search Results for *procedure*

According to the results offered by TechCollo, there are, respectively, 934 and 591 tokens of *procedure* in Medical Wiki and Engineering Wiki. Furthermore, the two corpora (or the two fields of profession) share several common collocations, including: *perform procedure, follow procedure, describe procedure*, etc. Taking a closer look at the *unshared* verb collocates in the two corpora (i.e. only in MWC or EWC), however, we find that *procedure* tends to co-occur with *undergo* and *die* only in MWC. These specialized collocations suggest that *procedure* is a technical term in medicine which refers to an operation. We expect and encourage EAP students to use TechCollo to explore and further discover such specialized collocations by: (1) searching collocations in a specific domain, (2) comparing collocations in two domain-specific corpora (e.g. MWC vs. EWC), and (3) comparing collocations in a specialized and a general-purpose corpora (e.g. MWC vs. BNC).

On TechCollo, for the extracted candidate collocations, a user can change their ordering(s) by clicking on the icons *frequency* or *MI* (which refers to *tradMI*). The other measure offered by TechCollo is *NMI*, which is the *normMI* that we described earlier and provide on our website in the hope that it allows EAP learners to find certain collocations containing high frequency component words. To examine the effectiveness of the *normMI*, we test it with certain legal collocations in the LAC, with the results shown in Table 2.

Collocation	*tradMI* ranking for the verb	*normMI* ranking for the verb
break *law*	63	1
push *trial*	14	7
carry *obligation*	5	1

Table 2: Comparison of *tradMI* and *normMI* with Legal Collocations

In the three cases, specifically, we use the three nouns: *law, trial,* and *obligation* as keywords to search in the LAC and examine how the *tradMI* and *normMI* decide the rankings of the three high-frequency verb collocates: *break, push,* and *carry*. As Table 2 shows, *normMI* changes the rankings of these collocations with the three verbs being ranked in higher positions. The three verbs might not be noticed by learners using the *tradMI* and the *normMI* successfully raises them into more advantaged positions for learners. A more thorough examination, nevertheless, is required to investigate whether the *normMI* is indeed an effective measure of identifying collocations in domain-specific texts.

4. Comparing Collocational Patterns across Disciplines: A Pilot Study

To specify and illustrate how to use TechCollo in EAP studies, we ran a pilot study in which we examined the verb-noun collocations in two different domains: medicine and engineering. More specifically, we focused on the nouns included in the Sublist 1 of the Academic Word List[4] (Coxhead, 2000) and explored and analyzed their verb collocates in the MWC and EWC. Our purpose, then, was to investigate whether it is true that words tend to show differences in collocations in different professional areas, as Hyland and Tse (2007) point out.

First, from the sixty word families contained in the Sublist 1, we identified 109 nouns. Those nouns were fed into TechCollo in order to extract their frequent co-occurring verbs in MWC and EWC. The very first observation that we made in the data generated by TechCollo was that many nouns showed uneven distributions in the two domain-specific corpora. Some examples of those nouns are given in Table 3. These distributional variations suggest that an academic word which is highly frequent and important in one discipline may be less important for students in another domain (e.g. the words *contractor, finance,* and *specification* for medical school students). EAP students who are required to study the AWL for their academic studies are very likely to be exposed to more lexical items than they actually need (Hyland and Tse, 2007).

Word	Frequency (per million tokens) in MWC	Frequency (per million tokens) in EWC
concept	115	332
contractor	1	53
contract	32	109
creation	35	90
datum	192	732
derivative	135	45
economy	18	100
evidence	329	93
finance	2	21
indication	104	29
methodology	13	60
policy	26	140
principle	96	214
processing	89	190
requirement	66	349
sector	10	135
specification	9	196
specificity	38	6
variable	25	128

Table 3: Nouns with Irregular Distributions in MWC and EWC

In addition to the comparisons of numbers of occurrence, what interests us more concerns their relations with verbs in medicine and engineering. We present some of the verb-noun collocation data in Table 4.

Noun	Shared Collocates	Verbs in MWC Only	Verbs in EWC Only
analysis	perform		conduct
area		rub, scratch	
assessment			allow, perform
benefit	receive	confer	provide, offer
concept	use	employ	utilize
consistency		boil	
context	depend		
contract			negotiate, cancel
creation	result	induce	lead
environment	create		build
evidence	show	yield, reinforce	trace
factor		activate, inhibit	
formula		feed, determine	derive
function		affect, impair	replicate
issue	address	approach	deal
majority	make	constitute	
method	devise, employ		
policy			influence, implement
principle	operate		apply
procedure		undergo, die	
requirement	meet, fulfill		satisfy, comply
research	conduct	undergo	undertake
response	trigger, evoke	induce, stimulate	
role	play, fulfill		
structure	describe	elucidate, depict	
theory	develop, propose		formulate
variation	show	exhibit	display

Table 4: Verb Collocates in MWC and EWC

As Table 4 displays, there are several nouns which *share* verb collocates in the MWC and EWC, including: *context, method,* and *role*. In other words, these verb-noun combinations are of equal importance for EAP students, at least for

[4] As Coxhead (2000) explains, the word families of the AWL are categorized into ten sublists according to their frequency. Each of the sublists contains sixty families with the last one containing thirty.

medicine and engineering majors. This table, however, reveals that there are many more so-called *generalized* academic words which tend to take different collocates and even refer to different meanings across disciplines. The word *area*, for example, co-occurs with *rub* and *scratch* in MWC and not in EWC and refers to the specialized meaning of a part on the surface of human body. Several other nouns, such as *consistency, formula, function, procedure,* and *response* also contain such medicine-specific senses as they co-occur with *boil, feed, impair, die,* and *induce*, respectively. Another notable cross-disciplinary difference based on these collocations is, while expressing a similar idea, people in medicine and engineering appear to prefer different verbs. Examples for this include: *confer/offer benefit, employ/utilize concept, induce/lead creation, approach/deal issue, undergo/undertake research, exhibit/display variation*, etc. These field-specific idiomatic and habitual usages do not suggest that they are the only expressions that people in medicine or engineering use. Rather, they provide evidence showing that people in different areas tend to select different word combinations which form "a variety of subject-specific literacies" (Hyland and Tse, 2007: p.247). What EAP students need to study, then, should be these common specialized collocations and usages which make their writings and speech *professional* in their own domain(s).

5. Conclusion

The pilot study reported in this article basically suggests that academic words, though being collected for EAP students irrespective of their subject areas, tend to have different numbers of occurrence and co-occur with different words in different domains. If students depend on word lists such as the AWL to learn academic words, they are very likely to memorize more lexical items than they actually need for studies in their own domain. Plus they will not be familiar with the common collocations that their colleagues frequently use in speech or writing. What the students need, or more specifically, what EAP researchers are suggested to develop, should be discipline-based vocabulary and collocation lists. Accordingly, we develop the online corpus-based collocation exploration tool, TechCollo, with the aim of providing the specialized lexico-grammatical knowledge that EAP students need to master at college. The tool, with its ability to allow students to learn specialized collocations in a discipline, compare collocations across disciplines, and explore collocations in domain-specific and general-purpose corpora, is of great help for EAP students to check word usages as they write technical papers. Furthermore, as we can expect, TechCollo will be very useful for researchers doing interdisciplinary studies and having to check word combinations across disciplines.

We have made several plans for improving TechCollo. First, for pedagogical purposes, we plan to provide discipline-specific word lists on the TechCollo website. Those lists, compiled based on our domain-specific corpora, will be indexed with frequency information for various domains (e.g. in MWC, academic corpora, or BNC). EAP students can conveniently click on each listed word and study its collocational patterns in different areas. Second, for technical purposes, we will continue to improve our techniques of extracting domain-specific collocations. We plan to use the techniques and methods developed by, for example, Wermter and Hahn (2005) and Pecina (2008) and examine whether the revised techniques increase the precision of collocation extractions. Specifically, we intend to investigate whether taking into account paradigmatic modifiability degrees and combining several association measures outperform the *tradMI* and *normMI* measures used by the current version of TechCollo. These new techniques will further be tested on various domain-specific corpora which may enable us to make some interesting discoveries in terminology extraction.

Acknowledgements

The research reported in this paper was supported in part by a grant from Taiwan 's National Science Council, Grant #NSC 100-2511-S-008-005-MY3.

References

Marco Baroni, Silvia Bernardini, Adriano Ferraresi, and Eros Zanchetta. 2009. The WaCky Wide Web: A Collection of Very Large Linguistically Processed Web-crawled Corpora. Language Resources and Evaluation 43(3): 209-226.

Caroline Barrière. 2009. Finding Domain Specific Collocations and Concordances on the Web. Proceedings of the Workshop on Natural Language Processing Methods and Corpora in Translation, Lexicography, and Language Learning.

Laurie Bauer. 1993. Manual of Information to Accompany the Wellington Corpus of Written New Zealand English. Victoria University of Wellington.

British National Corpus, Version 2 (BNC World). 2001. Distributed by Oxford University Computing Services on behalf of the BNC Consortium. URL: http://www.natcorp.ox.ac.uk/

Qi Chen and Guang-Chun Ge. 2007. A Corpus-Based Lexical Study on Frequency and Distribution of Coxhead's AWL Word Families in Medical Research Articles (RAs). English for Specific Purposes 26(4): 502-514.

Kenneth Ward Church and Patrick Hanks. 1990. Word Association Norms, Mutual Information, and Lexicography. Computational Linguistics 16(1): 22-29.

Andrew Cohen, Hilary Glasman, Phyllis R. Rosenbaum-Cohen, Jonathan Ferrara, and Jonathan Fine. 1979 Reading English for Specialized Purposes: Discourse Analysis and the Use of Student Informants. TESOL Quarterly, 34: 551-564.

Nigel Collier, Chikashi Nobata, and Junichi Tsujii. 2002. Automatic Acquisition and Classification of Terminology Using a Tagged Corpus in the Molecular Biology Domain. Terminology 7(2): 239-257.

Averil Coxhead. 2000. A New Academic Word List. TESOL Quarterly, 34(2): 213-238.

Mark Davies. 2008. The Corpus of Contemporary American English (COCA): 400+ Million Words, 1990-present. http://www.americancorpus.org

Paul Farrell. 1990. Vocabulary in ESP: A Lexical Analysis of the English of Electronics and a Study of Semi-Technical Vocabulary. CLCS Occasional Paper No. 25.

John Flowerdew. 1993. Concordancing as a Tool in Course Design. System 21(2): 231-244.

Nilgün Hancioğlu, Steven Neufeld, and John Eldridge. 2008. Through the Looking Glass and into the Land of Lexico-Grammar. English for Specific Purposes 27(4): 459-479.

Dan Klein and Christopher D. Manning. 2003. Accurate Unlexicalized Parsing. Proceedings of the 41st Annual Meeting on Association for Computational Linguistics-Volume 1.

Ken Hyland and Polly Tse. 2007. Is there an "academic vocabulary"?." TESOL Quarterly 41(2): 235-253.

I. S. P. Nation. 2001. Learning Vocabulary in Another Language. Cambridge University Press, Cambridge, UK.

Stig Johansson. 1978. Manual of Information to Accompany the Lancaster-Oslo/Bergen Corpus of British English, for Use with Digital Computers. University of Oslo. Oslo, Norway.

Pavel Pecina. 2008. A Machine Learning Approach to Multiword Expression Extraction. Proceedings of the LREC MWE 2008 Workshop.

Thomas C. Rindflesch, Lawrence Hunter, and Alan R. Aronson. 1999, Mining Molecular Binding Terminology from Biomedical Text. Proceedings of the AMIA Symposium. American Medical Informatics Association.

Frank Smadja. 1993. Retrieving Collocations from Text: Xtract. Computational Linguistics 19(1): 143-177.

Cucu Sutarsyah, Paul Nation, and Graeme Kennedy. 1994. How Useful Is EAP Vocabulary for ESP? A Corpus Based Case Study. RELC Journal 25(2): 34-50.

Viphavee Vongpumivitch, Ju-yu Huang, and Yu-Chia Chang. 2009. Frequency Analysis of the Words in the Academic Word List (AWL) and Non-AWL Content Words in Applied Linguistics Research Papers. English for Specific Purposes 28(1): 33-41.

Jeremy Ward. 2009. A Basic Engineering English Word List for Less Proficient Foundation Engineering Undergraduates. English for Specific Purposes 28(3): 170-182.

Joachim Wermter and Udo Hahn. 2004. Collocation Extraction Based on Modifiability Statistics. Proceedings of the 20th International Conference on Computational Linguistics. Association for Computational Linguistics.

Joachim Wermter and Udo Hahn. 2005. Paradigmatic Modifiability Statistics for the Extraction of Complex Multi-word Terms. Proceedings of the Conference on Human Language Technology and Empirical Methods in Natural Language Processing. Association for Computational Linguistics.

David Wible, Chin-Hwa Kuo, and Nai-Lung Tsao. 2004. Improving the Extraction of Collocations with High Frequency Words. Proceedings of International Conference on LREC.

Huizhong Yang. 1986. A New Technique for Identifying Scientific/Technical Terms and Describing Science Texts. Literary and Linguistic Computing 1: 93-103.

David Yarowsky. 1995. Unsupervised Word Sense Disambiguation Rivaling Supervised Methods. Proceedings of the 33rd Annual Meeting on Association for Computational Linguistics. Association for Computational Linguistics.

Automatic Identification of English Collocation Errors based on Dependency Relations

Zhao-Ming Gao
National Taiwan University
zmgao@ntu.edu.tw

Abstract

We present an English miscollocation identification system based on dependency relations drawn from the Stanford parser. We test our system against a subset of error-tagged Chinese Learner English Corpus (CLEC)and obtain an overall precision of 0.75. We describe some applications and limitations of our system and suggest directions for future research.

1. Introduction

Collocations play a very important role in second language learning (cf. Lewis, 1993). They reflect users'depth of vocabulary knowledge as well as their language proficiency levels (cf.Schimitt, 2000, 2010; Nation, 2001; Nation and Webb, 2011).Researchhas shown that collocations are one of the most significant feature which distinguishes native from non-native writings. Furthermore, non-native writers tend to makecollocation errors unconsciously, many of which arise from first language interference. All these suggest the necessity of developing a miscollocation identification system to help learners detect their collocation errors as well as raise their language awareness. .Such a system might also havegreat impact for second language acquisition (SLA) research, as collections and analyses of collocation errors are vital to our understanding of the difficulties and problems learners encounter (cf. Nesselhauf, 2005). Just like other errors in learner corpora, error-tagged miscollocations are not widely and readily accessible to researchers. Traditionally, miscollocations can only be identified viavery time-consuming process of manual error tagging. Thanks to recent advance in natural language processing (NLP), automatic identification of miscollocations has been made possible. This paper presents an English miscollocation identification system by drawing on NLP tools and resources such as the Stanford parser, Google 1T ngrams, and WordNet. We will show that such a system not only has pedagogical valuebut also can facilitate the study of English miscollocations by non-native speakers.

2. Literature Review

There are two approaches to the study of collocations, namely, the frequency-based approach (Sinclair, 1987) and the phraseological approach (Cowie, 1981; Benson, 1989). Drawing on natural language processing tools, researchers have proposed automated procedures to retrieve collocations from corpora by using statistical methods such as mutual information and t-score (Church and Hanks, 1990) as well as log likelihood ratio (Dunning , 1993).In addition to statistical measures, dependency relations derived from parsers play an important role in identifying collocations (cf. Church and Hanks, 1990; Smadja, 1993;Kilgarriff, 2004).

(Jian, Chang, and Chang, 2003) present TANGO, a program which given a keyword and its part-of-speech can extract English example of four English collocation patterns (i.e. v-n, n-p, v-n-p, a-n) together with their Chinese translations from parallel corpora.

(Shei and Pain, 2000) present a conceptual frameworkto detect and correct collocation errors by Chinese learners of English. They draw on a learner corpus, a reference corpus, a dictionary of synonyms derived from WordNet, and a paraphrase database compiled using learner data. Addressing the same problem of miscollocations caused by first language interference, (Chang et al., 2008) focus on the identification and correction of V-N miscollocations by Chinese learners of English. They extract V-N collocations from British National Corpus (BNC) and leaner corpora and use a bilingual English-Chinese dictionary to identify the meanings intended by the learners. They then use the collocations extracted from BNC to pinpoint the miscollocations in the learner corpora and suggest correct collocations which learners intended to use. (Futagi et al. 2008)notice that some collocation errors are in fact due to spelling errors. They use spelling checkers to identify and correct misspelled words. They then identify miscollocation candidates by part-of-speech tags and rank-ratio statistics calculated over 1 billion word corpus by native speakers.

3. Using Dependency Relations to Identify Collocations

We follow the phraseological approach taken by(Cowie, 1981; Benson, 1989) and consider collocations a type of word combinations. As pointed out by Smadja (1993), many collocations involve pedicative relations such as subject-verb, verb-object, adjective-noun. These word combinations are easier to identify by using dependency parsers than statistical measures such as mutual information and t-score, which are useful to finding significant collocations and idioms. Our proposed miscollocation identification system is based on authentic English corpora of 14.5 million words. The system follows the lines of (Church, 1990; Smadja, 1993, Lin, 1998; Kilgarriff, 2004) in using parsers to retrieve collocations. Our approach consists of three major steps. The first step is to identify and correct spelling errors. The second step is.to identify and store the predicative relations (also known as dependency relations) occurring in the reference corpus in a dependency relation database The third step is to identify the dependency relations in a learner sentence and check them against the database of dependency relations derived from reference corpus. The technology underlying the system is similar to (Lin, 1998; Kilgarriff, 2004).

To identify dependency relations in an English sentence, the Stanford parser is used (c.f.de Marneffe, 2006). Stanford parser can identify numerous dependency relations, including modifier-noun, subject-verb, verb-noun, etc. (1) is the output of the Stanford parser, which outputs the part-of-speech tags of each word in the sentence, its syntactic structures, and dependency relations. For example, the relationnn (prices-2, Stock-1) in (1)indicates that the first word 'Stock' modifies the second word 'prices' and form a N-N dependency relation. Similarly, the second word 'prices' and the third word 'plunged' form a subject-verb relation.

(1) Stock prices plunged on many global markets Monday.

Stock/NNP prices/NNS plunged/VBD on/IN many/JJ global/JJ markets/NNS Monday/NNP

```
(ROOT
  (S
    (NP (NNP Stock) (NNS prices))
    (VP (VBD plunged)
      (PP (IN on)
        (NP (JJ many) (JJ global) (NNS
markets)))
      (NP (NNP Monday)))))
```

```
nn(prices-2, Stock-1)
nsubj(plunged-3, prices-2)
prep(plunged-3, on-4)
amod(markets-7, many-5)
amod(markets-7, global-6)
pobj(on-4, markets-7)
dobj(plunged-3, Monday-8)
```

The performance of the Stanford parser varies with the complexity of the input sentence. If the sentence is short and the structure is not ambiguous or complicated, it can achieve relatively high accuracy.

There are six major types of dependency relations stored in our database, namely, subject-verb, verb-object, verb-adverb, noun-noun, adjective-noun, and adverb-adjective.

We use two corpora. The first is a reference corpus totaling 14.5 million words extracted from authentic English texts (i.e. the reference corpus). The second is an error-tagged learner corpus used to evaluate the accuracy of our system. The learner corpus is the subcorpus st2 in the Chinese Learner English Corpus (CLEC) and totals 251558 tokens. Each sentence in the reference corpus has been parsed by the Stanford parser to extract the dependency relations. Important dependency relations such as subject-verb, verb-object, adjective-noun, verb-adverb, and noun-noun are identified and stored in the dependency relation database for the reference corpus. The tables of.dependency relation database include the information of ahead word (the primary key in the database), its part-of-speech, the dependency relation between the headword and its collocation, the collocate of the headword, as well as the part-of-speech of the collocate. The part-of-speech information of the keyword includes noun, verb, adjective, adverb, and preposition. Nouns in the subject and object positions are distinguished to facilitate the retrieval of subject-verb and verb-object relation. Preposition is included for collocational patterns involving a verb and a preposition (e.g. 'rely on') or a noun and a preposition (e.g. 'under attack').

4. Identifying Miscollocations

A program is written which converts the dependency relation database into a collocation database. When a query is made, the program will search the collocation database, find all the collocations of the word in accordance with the conditions input by the user. Figure 1 is the interface of the collocation retrieval system. If the user inputs the keyword "responsibility", "noun in the object position' as its part-of-speech, and "verb" as the part-of-speech of the collocate, the system will return a list of potential verb collocates of the noun 'responsibility' such as: 'take', 'shoulder', 'fulfill', 'bear', 'assume', 'accept', 'have', 'evade', 'shirk'. 'avoid'.

It should be noted that the frequency information and the dependency relations we use in our program are based on lemmas (i.e. the basic form of a word). For instance, *ta e*, *too* , *ta en*, *ta in* , *ta es* all have the same lemma 'take'. We use WordNet 3.1 for converting a word into its lemma.

Following (Futagi, 2008), we identify and correct spelling errors in learner sentences in order to identify more miscollocations. We incorporate the open source spelling checker A spell and the information of language model based on the Google 1T ngram data. The correct spelling is chosen if the candidate word is the closest to the wrongly spelled word in terms of minimal edit distance and ngram probabilities.

Figure 1. The Inteface of our collocation retrieval system

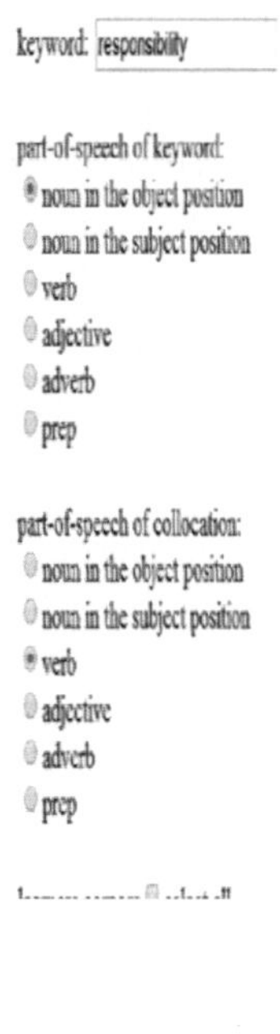

Each of the dependency relations extracted from learners' sentences not involving a personal pronoun or a proper name is checked against our English collocation retrieval program. Personal pronouns and proper names are identified by using the part-of-speech tag information output by the Stanford parser. Dependency relations with these tags are directly ignored by our collocation checker.

If a dependency relation in a learner sentence cannot be found in our English collocation database, it is considered a candidate of miscollocation.

5. Evaluations

We test our proposed system usingst2, a 251558 token subcorpus of the Chinese Learner English Corpus (CLEC)(cf. Gui and Yang, 2003), whose error tags facilitate automatic evaluation of our system. There are six types of collocation errors in the CLEC including CC1 (noun-noun), CC2 (noun-verb), CC3 (verb-noun), CC4 (adjective-noun), CC5 (verb-adverb), and CC6 (adverb-adjective). The precision rates of the six types of collocation errors are 0.77, 0.87, 0.72, 0.75, 0.83, and 0.63, respectively. Our system performs the best with CC2 (noun-verb), which has0.87 accuracy. The lowest precision is 0.63 found in CC6 (Adverb Adjective). The overall precision rate is about 0.75.

Table 1. Precision of our proposed method

	CC1 NN	CC2 NV	CC3 VN	CC4 AN	CC5 V adv	CC6 Adv A
precision	0.77	0.87	0.72	0.75	0.83	0.63

The recall rateis much lower than the precision rate, suggesting that there are many miscollocations that cannot be identified by our program.

Our dependency-based collocation extraction program has a number of limitations. As with the other collocation extraction programs, our program is not entirely reliable. Our approach fails (1) when the parser does not derive the correct dependency relations (2) or when the collocation does not belong to any dependency relation in the Stanford Parser (3)or when certain correct collocations do not occur in the reference corpus. Incorrect analyses of dependency relations typically result from sentences which have ellipsis or complicated structures. Some errors in the dependency relations are caused by the incorrect identification of the head noun in a noun phrase. One major problem with our system is the relatively small size of our reference corpus, which hasonly 14.5 million words. Another problem of using dependency relations to identify miscollocations arises from the multiple meanings and constructions a word might be associated with. Consider the word combinations of 'make stomach' and 'take university'. At first sight, they seem odd. However, inspection of the examples in (2) suggest that these word combinations are appropriate in the following contexts.

(2) (a). So I devour those buns and noodle and this fast movement of mouth makes my stomach uncomfortable a whole morning.
(b). TakeNational Don HuaUniversityfor instance.

In other words, using dependency relations to identify miscollocations might be inadequate when the keyword in question has different meanings and can appear in different constructions. This is a serious limitation to the dependency-based approach to miscollocation identification. Solution to this problem might require identification of different constructions a word can occur in. This, however, cannot be easily achieved at present. Another limitation to our approach is that a phrase may be inappropriate even if all its parts seem acceptable, because the correctness of all the smaller parts of the phrase cannot entail the correctness of the larger units. The same applies to ngrams and dependency relations. Just like ngrams, dependency relations are approximations to larger units such as a phrase or a sentence. They alone cannot give us all the information about their grammatical status or contextual appropriateness of which they are a part.

6. Applications

One of the applications of our program is automatic identification of collocational differences in learner and authentic corpora. With this function, we are able to automatically collect miscollocationsfrom learner corpora. For example, by inputting the verb 'take' and the part-of-speech of a noun in the object position, we extract 'take exercise', 'take adventure', 'take reform', 'take lecture', 'take grade', and 'take travel'asmiscollocations.'Some examples containing thesemiscollocations in the learner corpora are listed in (3).

3. (a). Theytakemore**exercises**than ever.
(b). They like new things and like taking **adventure**.
(c). We take the **reform** and open policy.
(d).I have to take the economic **lectures** and learn to use computer in order to gain more knowledge and keep up with the society.
(e). In junior high school, the English teacher only taught you how to take good **grade** in the test.

Some other examples of miscollocations identified by our system are provided in (4).

(4) (a). That will open our sights of the world.
(b). Since we have faced the cricis of fresh water, we should do what we can to release the **problem**.
(c). Meanwhile, on the way to Belcy I planned to **take**a travel in the famous cities.
(d). What defines a really alive **person** is his personal functions but not physiological ones.
(e). Nonprofit organizations do many **efforts** to the world.
(f). We not only learn the knowledge of financial management but also make **action** for it.
(h). It has long been a controversy that a teacher should take physical **punishment** or education by love to teach their students.

With our system, it is relatively easy to find general patterns about learners' miscollocations. First, learners have difficulties in collocations involving support verbs, such as 'take', 'make', and 'do'. They are often confused about which support verb they should use in a certain context (cf. (3a)-(3e), (4e)-(4h)).Second, learners are heavily influenced by their first language and cannot distinguish the subtle nuances between near synonyms (e.g. 'widen' or 'broaden' vs. 'open', 'vision' vs. 'sight' in (4a), 'trip' vs. 'travel' in (4c), and 'living' vs. 'alive' in (4d)). Third, learners are not only confused by semantically similar words but also phonetically or orthographically similar words (e.g. 'relieve' vs. 'release' in (4b)).
The examples in (3) and (4) show that our systems can efficiently and effectively identify common miscollocation patterns and facilitate research in L2 miscollocations in a way similar to (Nesselhauf, 2005). Clearly, our system ismuch more efficient than traditional method of manual error tagging in identifying miscollocations as well as differences between native and non-native usage.

7. Conclusions and Future Research

The proposed English miscollocation checker might help learners reduce collocation errors and develop learner autonomy. It has the potential of alleviating teachers' burden in correcting students' English miscollocations.The proposed system can automatically collect and characterize the collocational differences used in learner and authentic corpora. Thisfeature might have positive impact for the teaching, learning, and research of collocations and miscollocations.

There are a number of limitations to our approach. For example, the corpus size of our reference corpus is not large enough. The accuracy of the dependency relations derived from the Stanford parser should also be improved. There are also constructions which cannot be adequately analyzed by dependency relations. These constructions allow greater flexibility than dependency relations.

While our proposed system for identifying collocation errors are not completely reliable, they might help learners improve their writing if the tool is used properly. Future research includes (1). qualitative and quantitative evidence of the learning effects of the proposed system in second language writing (2).development of an intelligent system that can not only detect but also correct collocation errors (3). investigation of the relationships between miscollocation types, error gravity, and learners' proficiency levels.

References

Benson, M. 1989. The Structure of the Collocational Dictionary."International Journal of Lexicography, Vol. 2, No. 1, pp. 1-14.

Cowie, A. P. 1981. The Treatment of Collocations and Idioms in Learner's Dictionaries. Applied Linguistics, Vol. 2, No, 3, pp. 223-235.

Chang, Y.-C., Chang Jason, Chen Hao-Jan, & Liou, H.C. 2008. An automatic collocation writing assistant for Taiwanese EFL learners: A case of corpus-based NLP technology. Computer Assisted Language Learning 21(3), 283-299.

Church, Ken. and Hanks, Patrick. 1990 Word Association Norms, Mutual Information, and Lexicography." Computational Linguistics, Vol. 16, No. 1, pp. 22-29.

Cowie, Anthony. 1981. The Treatment of Collocations and Idioms in Learner's Dictionaries.Applied Linguistics, Vol. 2, No, 3, pp. 223-235.

Chang, Yu.-Chia., Chang, Jason, Chen Hao-Jan, & Liou, Hsien-Chin. (2008). An automatic collocation writing assistant for Taiwanese EFL learners: A case of corpus-based NLP technology. *o p ter ssiste an a e earning* 21(3), 283-299.

deMarneffe, Marie-Catherine, MacCartney, Bill and Manning, Christopher. 2006. Generating typed dependency parses from phrase structure parses. In .

Futagi, Yoko, et al. 2008. A computational approach to detecting collocation errors in the writing of non-native speakers of English. Computer-Assisted Language Learning, Vol. 21, No. 4, pp.353 – 367.

Gui, Shicun and Yang, Huizhong. 2002. Chinese Learner English Corpus. Foreign Language Education Press, Shanghai.

Jian, J.-Y., Chang, Y.-C., Chang, J.-S. 2004. Tango: Bilingual Collocational Concordancer. Poster presented at the Annual Conference of the Association for Computational Linguistics.

Kilgarriff, Adam et al. 2004. The Sketch Engine.In Proceedings of EURALEX, Lorient, France.

Lewis, Michalel. 1993. The Lexical Approach: the State of ELT and a Way Forward.: Thompson/Heinle, Boston.

Lin, Dekang. 1998. Extracting Collocations from Text Corpora. First Workshop on Computational Terminology, Montreal, Canada, August, 1998.

Nation, Paul. 2001. Learning Vocabulary in Another Language. Cambridge: University Press, Cambridge.

Nation, Paul, and Webb, Stuart. 2011. Researching and Analyzing Vocabulary.Heinle, Boston

Nesselhauf, N. 2005.Collocations in a Learner Corpus. John Benjaimins. Amsterdam.

Schmitt, Norbert. 2000. Vocabulary in Language Learning.

Schimitt,Nobert. 2010. Researching Vocabulary: a Vocabulary Research Manual. Palgrave Macmillian, London.

Smadja, Frank. 1993Retrieving Collocations from Text: Xtract. ComputationalLinguistics, Vol. 19, No. 1, pp. 143 - 177.

Shei, Chi.-Chiang.and Pain, Helen. 2000. An ESL Writer's Collocation Aid Computer-Assisted Language Learning, Vol. 13, No. 2, pp. 167-182.

Sinclair, John. 1987. Collocations: a Progress Report. In Steele and Thrreadgold (eds.) , 1987, Language Topics: Essays in Honour of Michael Halliday. John Benjamins, Amsterdam and Philadelphia.

Software Used in this Study

Aspellhttp://aspell.net/

Chinese Learner English Corpus. CD accompanying (Gui and Yang, 2003)

Google 1T ngramshttp://www.ldc.upenn.edu/Catalog/CatalogEntry.jsp?catalogId=LDC2006T13

The Stanford Parser.http://webdocs.cs.ualberta.ca/~lindek/Stanford.htm

WordNet 3.1http://wordnet.princeton.edu/

A Japanese Learning Support System Matching Individual Abilities

Takahiro Ohno
Graduate School of Integrated Basic Sciences
Nihon University
Tokyo, JAPAN

Zyunitiro Edani
Graduate School of Integrated Basic Sciences
Nihon University
Tokyo, JAPAN

Ayato Inoue
Department of Information Science
College of Humanities and Sciences
Nihon University,
Tokyo, JAPAN

Dongli Han
Department of Information Science
College of Humanities and Sciences
Nihon University,
Tokyo, JAPAN
han@chs.nihon-u.ac.jp

Abstract

With the growing popularity of Japanese learning, a large number of learning support tools or systems have been developed to help Japanese learners in various situations. We have particularly noticed the increasing necessity of systems developed as web applications, most of which are free and easily accessed, and hence regarded to be the most significant resources for Japanese learners. However, noun of the existing studies has considered the difference in language ability among Japanese learners. Learning contents and instructional method in these systems usually remain unchanged at all times without taking account of individual variations while in some cases they are supposed to vary with the real language ability of each Japanese learner. In this paper, we have developed a web application to provide appropriate suggestions and different learning materials for each Japanese learner based on their individual Japanese abilities. Specifically, we divide the language ability into several elements, propose different methods to quantify each element, and generate feedbacks or training questions for the Japanese learners. Experimental results have partially shown the effectiveness of our methods.

1 Introduction

More and more people are learning Japanese as the second or foreign language. According to a report issued by the Japan Foundation, Japanese learners have increased 9.1% all over the world since 2009 [1]. With the growing popularity of Japanese learning, a large number of learning support tools or systems have been developed to help Japanese learners in various situations (Liu et al, 1999; Fujita, 2001; Suwa, 2006; Zhang, 2006; Gao, 2005; Kakegawa, 2000; Nakano and Tomiura, 2011). We have particularly noticed the increasing necessity of systems developed as web applications, most of which are free and easily accessed, and hence regarded to be the most significant resources for Japanese learners. Here are some examples. Asunaro[2] presents the dependency relations between phrases in a given Japanese sentence, Obi[3] classifies the difficulty of a given text into 13 levels, Reading Tutor[4] analyzes a given text and shows the difficulty level of each morpheme in it, and Chantokun[5] discovers the misuse of a case particle in a user's input and shows the potential alternatives as well.

However, noun of the existing studies has considered the difference in language ability among Japanese learners. Learning contents and instructional method in these systems usually remain unchanged at all times without taking account of individual variations while in some cases they are supposed to vary with the real

[1] http://www.jpf.go.jp/j/japanese/survey/result/survey12.html
[2] http://hinoki.ryu.titech.ac.jp/asunaro/main.php?lang=jp
[3] http://kotoba.nuee.nagoya-u.ac.jp/sc/obi2/
[4] http://language.tiu.ac.jp/
[5] http://cl.naist.jp/chantokun/index.html

language ability of each Japanese learner. Capturing the personal feature of a learner's language ability and providing her with the most appropriate learning contents in the most proper way will definitely make the learning procedure more efficient.

Our final goal in this work is to develop a web application to provide appropriate suggestions and different learning materials for each Japanese learner based on their individual Japanese abilities. Specifically, we divide the language ability into several elements, propose different methods to quantify each element, and generate feedbacks or training questions for the Japanese learners. Here in this paper, we describe the basic idea in Section 2, and describe a few modules we have developed as the first step of the whole system in Section 3, 4, and 5. Finally, we end this paper with a conclusion in Section 6.

2 The Basic Idea

The general framework is composed of two main parts: the interactive interface and the background processing platform. When the learner inputs some words, the system will carry out two kinds of analysis in turn: morphological analysis and syntactic parsing. Here, we use the free Japanese analyzing tools, Cabocha[6] and Knp[7], to carry out the analytical tasks.

Then the system tries to figure out the linguistic ability of the current user. The linguistic ability structure is divided into several elements: Kanji character, vocabulary, case particle, sentence pattern, inflection, and honorific expression. So far, we have developed two modules for case particles and sentence patterns respectively.

Finally, based on the analytical results, the system generates different feedbacks or practice questions for each Japanese learner trying to provide her with the most appropriate learning contents in the most proper way, which might make the learning procedure more efficient.

3 Usage of Case Particles

We have mentioned Chantokun, a previous web application, in Section 1, where wrong usages of case particles could be discovered and corrected. Case particles are the most important components in Japanese sentences. It is impossible to generate a grammatically correct sentence without using any case particles. We in this work consider case particles as one of the most critical factors to analyze the linguistic ability of Japanese learners, and propose a method to conduct a profound analysis on their usages of case particles.

Here, similar to Chantokun, we also use 3-gram data from Google N-gram Corpus[8] to discover and modify the wrong usages of case particles. The 3-gram corpus is extracted mainly from web pages containing a large number of 3-continuous-word fragments in the form of "W1 CP W2". Here, CP indicates a case particle, W1 and W2 represent the two words surrounding it. However, the difference between our work and Chantokun lies in that we incorporate dependency relation analysis into the error checking task as shown in Figure 1.

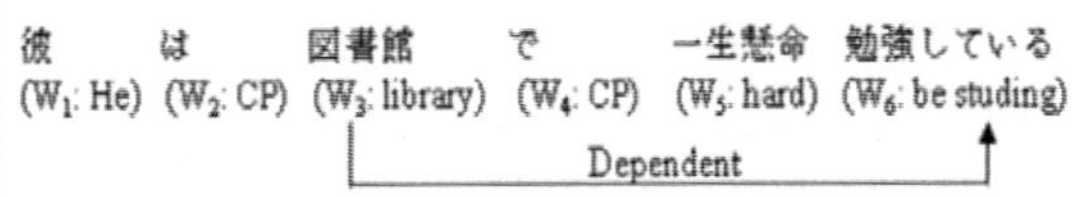

Fig. 1. The dependency relation analysis

Besides the error check and correction, we have developed another function involving the case particles. Through the correct use cases of case particles from the user's input texts, we try to estimate the user's level of dealing with case particles. Here we define two kinds of measurements: GUR (General Understanding Rates), and GER (General Error Rates) as shown below.

$$= \frac{\sum_{i}}{_{\max} \times}$$

$$= \frac{\sum_{i}}{_{\max} \times}$$

Here, $_i$ and $_i$ stand for the occurrence frequency of the correctly used 3-gram and the modified 3-gram in the 3-gram corpus. is the number of correctly used case particles in the user's input texts, and represents the number of case particles that have been modified. $_a$ is the highest occurrence frequency in the 3-gram corpus. We try to reflect the user's understanding ability towards the frequently used case particles, and the tendency to make mistakes with these formulas.

In the experiments for wrong-usage detection of case particles with 100 sentences extracted

[6] http://code.google.com/p/cabocha/
[7] http://nlp.ist.i.kyoto-u.ac.jp/index.php?KNP

[8] http://www.gsk.or.jp/catalog/GSK2007-C/GSK2007C_README.utf8.txt

from Lang8[9], we get the results as shown in Table 1 with different experimental arguments. Here, "Abs" indicates the absolute threshold value. For example, "Abs(0)" means the case where a wrongly used case particle is detected without considering the difference between the wrong usage and the most frequent usage in the corpus. On the other hand, "Rel" indicates the cases where a specific magnitude relationship between the wrong usage and the most frequent usage has to be taken into consideration. Generally, "Rel(10)" is the most effective one among all the argument sets.

	Precision	Recall	MissRate	F-value
Abs(0)	0.69	0.42	0.19	0.51
Abs(100)	0.66	0.60	0.31	0.63
Abs(500)	0.65	0.74	0.39	0.69
Rel(10)	0.76	0.75	0.23	0.75
Rel(50)	0.75	0.60	0.20	0.67
Rel(100)	0.73	0.53	0.19	0.61

Table. 1. Experimental results for case particles

4 Usage of Sentence Patterns

A sentence pattern indicates some specific usage of certain words to express some particular context or meaning (Han and Song, 2011). Here is a very simple example: "～あげく" meaning "in the end". The signal "～" acts as a placeholder with certain strict conditions. In this sentence pattern, only two kinds of expressions could be used to replace "～" in front of "あげく" : past tenses of verbs or a particular formal noun in Japanese, "の" . Whether a Japanese learner is able to use a sentence pattern correctly is considered as another significant indicator of her real Japanese linguistic ability.

To the best of our knowledge, Reading Tutor is the only web system which has made contributions on learning sentence patterns. Reading Tutor analyzes the input sentence, recognizes the sentence patterns used in it, and elaborates the usage of each sentence pattern found. However, Reading Tutor is not able to recognize the wrong sentence-pattern usages. In other words, even if an expression other than the past tense of a verb or the particular formal noun "の" appears in front of "あげく" , Reading Tutor is not able to indicate the mistake.

[9]http://lang-8.com/

During the practical sentence-pattern learning process, compared with the simple and outward sentence-pattern searching function, it is usually more important to tell the user whether the sentence she has just composed using a particular sentence pattern is correct, and where the problem is lying if the answer is no. Our study differs from Reading Tutor on this aspect.

1. ～○
2. ～○～
3. ～～○
4. ○～△
5. ～○～△
6. ～○～△～□
7. ～○～△～□～◎

Fig. 2. Main structures of sentence patterns

Generally, there are seven kinds of structures lying in all sentence patterns as shown Figure 2. Here, the signal "～" is a placeholder as described above, and each signal except "～" indicates a partial expression of the whole sentence pattern. During the analytical procedure, we use Cabocha to obtain the conjugated form for each "～" . Meanwhile, we create a huge table containing all the combining rules in advance based on a sentence-pattern dictionary (Ask Shuppan, 2008), and develop a module to discover the wrong usages of sentence patterns and provide feedbacks on correct usage based on the combination-rule table.

Specifically, we follow the steps below to accomplish this task taking "～あげく" as the specific case here.

Step1. Search the input sentence for "あげく"

Step2. Obtain the part-of-speech (POS) and conjugation information of "～" , the expressions in front of "あげく" using Cabocha.

Step3. Compare the POS of "～" and that in the combination-rule table.

Step4. Exit the process and present the user with the message "POS Error" if they do not match.

Step5. Compare the conjugation information of "～" and that in the combination-rule table.

Step6. Exit the process and present the user with the message "Conjugation Error" if they do not match.

The above process will be iterated for all the signals including "○", "△", "□", and "◎" for all the other patterns in Figure 2.

We have conducted a simple experiment to examine the effectiveness of our sentence-pattern processing module. Here, we extract 200 correct sample sentences each containing at least one sentence pattern from another Japanese sentence-pattern dictionary (Ask Shuppan, 2007). Table 2 shows the experimental results.

Recognized Sentence Patterns	328(100%)
Correctly recognized sentence patterns	279 (85%)
Wrongly Recognized Sentence Patterns	49(15%)

Table. 2. Experimental results for sentence pattern

Cases of failure have been observed with the following reasons.

1. Delicate difference lies between the sentence pattern dictionary and the Morphological analyzer.
2. Oral Expressions are used instead of the formal ones in "○", "△", "□", and "◎".
3. The sentence pattern dictionary is non-exhaustive.
4. Normal usages are incorrectly equated to certain sentence patterns

The first three issues come from the inadequacy of the sentence-pattern dictionary, and are possible to be addressed completely or partially through incorporating other dictionaries and complementing the current one simultaneously.

The last issue indicates the case where a normal expression containing one of four special signals ("○", "△", "□", and "◎") is misattributed to a sentence pattern. Here is an example.

Input:
私は大学を卒業<u>するまで</u>そこで過ごしました。
(I lived there until I graduated from the college)
Feedback:
「～て」を接続しなければいけません
(The「する」connection must be replaced by the「～て」connection)

According to the Feedback, the input sentence should be modified as "私は大学を卒業<u>してまで</u>そこで過ごしました" meaning *ra ate ro t e o e e to i e t ere*. The modified sentence has a completely different nuance from the input sentence which is also correct. Our future task includes figuring out strategies to address this kind of problems.

5 Practice-question Generation

Another significant difference between our system and other previous studies lies in the function of providing practice questions and feedbacks based on the user's linguistic ability and self-assessment. Specifically, practice questions are provided to help the learners improve their abilities to use a certain case-particle or sentence pattern. On the other hand, feedbacks are given to the learners to indicate their scores and what they should pay particular attention to during the practicing process.

5.1 Determination of Question Form

Some existing studies have mentioned the relation between the learning effect and the learning method or feedbacks during the process of foreign language learning. Yokoyama analyzed the effectiveness of negative feedbacks (NFs) and represented some perceptions on the difference between explicit and implicit NFs (Yokoyama, 1996). In another study, Nishitani and Matsuda explored the possibility to manage the language-anxiety level of the learners (Nishitani and Matsuda, 2008). Profound survey on the above studies leads us to the following ideas.

1. Feedbacks are generally effective for foreign language learning
2. Expositions tailored for a particular learner is necessary.
3. Different Question forms should be provided to learners of different levels
4. Language-anxiety element might be taken into consideration to select the most appropriate learning method.

Based on the above considerations, we have developed three modules for our practice-question generation function: Character Judgement, Question-form Determination, and Feedback Generation. Character Judgement conducts a questionnaire with each learner having an assessment page filled out in the system. Questions contained in the assessment page come from Motoda's study (Motoda, 2000), and are used to assess the user's language-anxiety and feelings of self-esteem. Figure 3 shows the screen shot of the questionnaire in our web system.

Fig. 3. Screen shot of the questionnaire

Average assessments from the questionnaire are used to estimate the user's character and self-perception, which will be used in the Question-form Determination module.

In our system, four forms are used to provide practice questions: multiple-choice question, fill-in-the-blank question, true-false question, and error-correction question. Following the idea suggested by Yokoyama, we assign difficulty levels from 1 to 4 to each of the four forms. For example, multiple-choice questions are comparatively simple, and error-correction questions are usually difficult compared with others.

In the Question-form Determination module, judgement on question form is carried out based mainly on the user's total accuracy so far. For example, if the learner has achieved a total accuracy of 90%, she will be given the chance to step on to the higher difficult level. Similarly, the user will be forced to reduce her difficulty level to an easier question form. This is the basic policy to adjust the question form for each learner. However, there are situations where we must consider users' characters as well. For instance, if the user's language-anxiety is comparatively high, we will set a stricter condition for her to raise the difficulty level. The most appropriate form will be selected for a particular user in accordance with her character and self-perception.

The third module, Feedback Generation, applies the opinions of Nishitani and Matsuda on the effects of feedbacks, and outputs a feedback sentence according to the user's character.

5.2 Extraction of Question Source

As described in Section 3, we use the Google 3-gram Corpus to discover and modify the wrong usages of case particles. Here we extract 3-grams from the same corpus as the source of practice questions. When the system decides to generate a practice question regarding a particular case particle according to the result of a first-time ability test, the context of the particular case particle is also employed.

For example, if the user messes up with the 3-gram "W_1+CP+W_2", the user will receive a set of 3-grams as the practice questions with similar contexts. Specifically, 3-grams in the following form are randomly extracted from the Google Corpus and used to generate practice questions for "W_1+CP+W_2".

$$W_{1SP}/W_{N1SS} + CP + W_{2SP}/W_{N2SS}$$

Here, W_{NSP} indicates the words holding the same POS as W_N, and W_{N1SS} indicates the words holding the same semantic feature as W_N. We use Juman [10] to extract semantic features for nouns, and Japanese Wordnet [11] to extract semantic features for verbs.

On the other hand, we generate practice questions for sentence patterns from a news corpus [12]. Specifically, we take the following steps to accomplish this task.

Step1. Extract the body text from the corpus.
Step2. Segment the body text into sentences.
Step3. Clip the sentences containing at least one sentence pattern.
Step4. Examine the correctness of the sentence-pattern usage with the program described in Section 4.
Step5. Change the inflected form of the verb around the special signals in a sentence pattern to another.
Step6. Present the whole sentence containing a blank or a wrong verbal inflected form to the user as a practice question.

[10]http://nlp.ist.i.kyoto-u.ac.jp/index.php?cmd=read&page=JUMAN&alias%5B%5D=%E6%97%A5%E6%9C%AC%E8%AA%9E%E5%BD%A2%E6%85%8B%E7%B4%A0%E8%A7%A3%E6%9E%90%E3%82%B7%E3%82%B9%E3%83%86%E3%83%A0JUMAN

[11]http://nlpwww.nict.go.jp/wn-ja/

[12]http://www.nichigai.co.jp/sales/mainichi/mainichi-data.html

Some practice-question examples generated in this way for multiple-choice practice question and true-false question are shown in Figure 4 and 5.

Comparing with the web text, news articles are more formal which indicates the ease to find appropriate sample sentences, whereas facing the risk that extracted sentences tend to be long and thus comparatively difficult for entrance-level users.

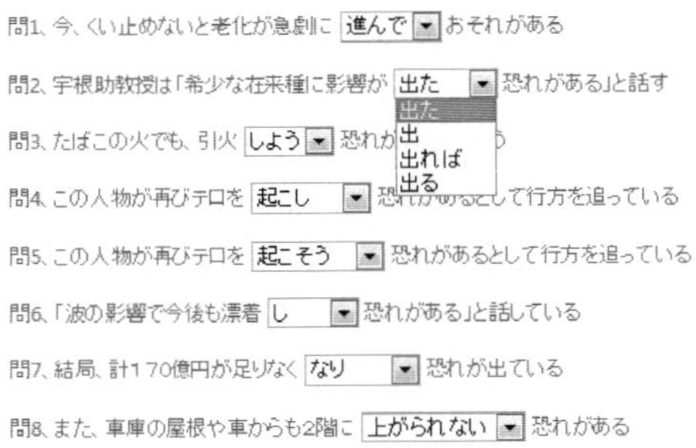

Fig. 4. Screen shot of the multiple-choice practice questions

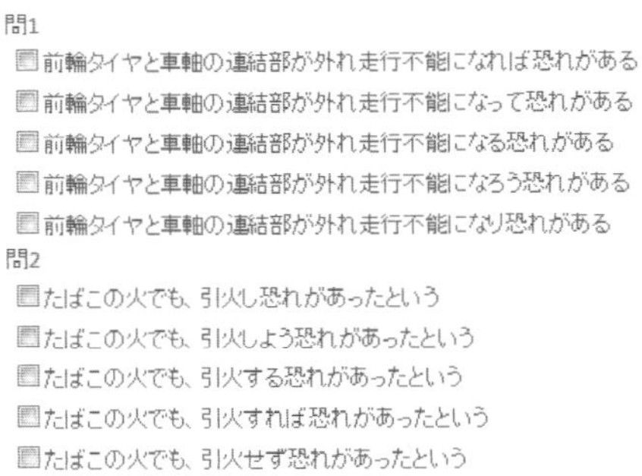

Fig. 5. Screen shot of the true-false questions

6 Conclusion

This paper describes some work we have been doing towards the development of a Japanese learning system. The principal difference between this work and the previous studies lies in the linguistic ability structure we have defined, and the idea that each learner is able to obtain his or her own linguistic-ability evaluation and customized learning contents. We have implemented three modules to help users with their usage of case particles and sentence grammars so far. Some evaluations have shown the effectiveness of our strategies. Figure 6 is the screen shot of our web system

However, as elaborated in Section 4 and 5, we still have ways to improve the method and obtain better results. Also, some ongoing modules including those for Kanji character, vocabulary and honorific expression are to be finished as soon as possible. What matters most of all, is a questionnaire targeted toward the JSL learners to examine the learning effectiveness for them with the help of our web application.

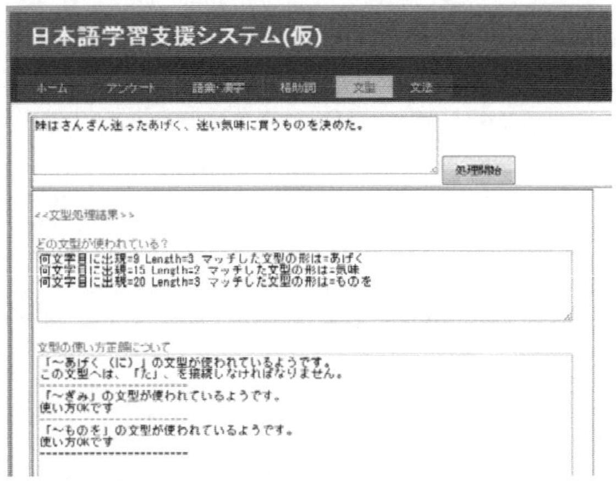

Fig. 6. Screen shot of our web interface

Acknowledgments

This research is supported in part by JSPS Grant-in-Aid for Young Scientists (B) Grant Number 24700914.

References

Ask Shuppan. 2008. "Ikita Reibun De Manabu Nihongo Hyougen Bunkei Jiten". Japan. (in Japanese)

Ask Shuppan. 2007. "Donna Toki Dou Tsukawu Nihongo Hyougen Bunkei Jiten". Japan. (in Japanese)

Fujita, S., Lin, C., and Narita, S. 2001. "An Instruction System of Hand-writing Chinese Character for Non-Japanese". Journal of Japan Society for Educational Technology. Vol. 25, No. 2, pp. 129-138. (in Japanese)

Gao, J., Takahashi, I., Kuroiwa, J., Odaka, T., and Ogura, H. 2005. "The Feature Extracted for Evaluating Japanese-Learners' Composition in China". IEICE Trans. Vol.J88-D-I, No.4, pp.882-890. (in Japanese).

Han, D., and Song, X. 2011. "Japanese Sentence Pattern Learning with the Use of Illustrative Examples Extracted from the Web", IEEJ Transactions on Electrical and Electronic Engineering, Vol.6, No.5, pp.490-496.

Kakegawa, D., Kanda, H., Fujioka, E., Itami, M., and Itoh, K. 2000. "Diagnostic Processing of Japanese for Computer-Assisted Second Language Learning", IEICE Trans. Vol.J83-D-I, No.6, pp.693-701. (in Japanese).

Liu, Y., Ogata, H., Ochi, Y., and Yano, Y. 1999. "Anckle: Agent-Based Communicative Kanji Learning Environment Focusing on the Difference between Japanese and Chinese Kanji Meaning", IEICE Trans. Vol.J82-D-II, No.10, pp.1645-1654. (in Japanese).

Motoda, S. 2000. "Measurement of Second Language Anxiety in the Target Language Environment: the Japanese Language Anxiety Scale – Test construction, Reliability, and Validity", Japanese Journal of Educational Psychology. Vol.48. pp.422-432. (in Japanese)

Nakano, T. and Tomiura, Y. 2011. "Relationship between Errors and Corrections in Verb Selection: Basic Research for Composition Support", Journal of Natural Language Processing. Vol.18, No.1, pp.3-29. (in Japanese)

Nishitani, M., and Matsuda, T. 2008. "Providing feedback to manage foreign language learners' anxiety level", Center for Student Exchange journal (Hitotsubashi University), 11, pp.35-46. (in Japanese)

Suwa, I., Takahashi, I., Kuroiwa, J., Odaka, T., and Ogura, H. 2006. "A Support System of Understanding Katakana Loan Words for Learners of Japanese". IEICE Trans. Vol.J89-D, No.4, pp.797-806. (in Japanese).

Yokoyama. 1996. "Daini Gengo Gakushu Ni Okeru Negative Feedback No Yakuwari: Gaikan", http://teapot.lib.ocha.ac.jp/ocha/bitstream/10083/50204/1/01_001-011.pdf (in Japanese)

Zhang, X., Takahashi, I., Kuroiwa, J., Odaka, T., and Ogura, H. 2006. "A System of Supporting Japanese Input and Japanese Learning for Foreign Students". IEICE Trans. Vol.J89-D, No.12, pp.2734-2743. (in Japanese).

PADS Restoration and Its Importance in Reading Comprehension and Meaning Representation

Shian-jung Chen
National Taiwan University of Science and Technology
shianjungchen@yahoo.com

Abstract

Unlike competent human readers capable of inferring, tracing, and filling out gaps or hurdles left behind by authors' use of transformations in their writing such as permutation, addition, deletion, and substitution (PADS), these operations are challenging to computer readers and new foreign language learners. This paper reports a parser's use of a suite of NLP technologies - clause boundary detection, resolution of different anaphors, inter-event relation finding, and case frame building - to fill out PADS gaps and output a much more explicit kernel-like meaning representation that includes case relation tuples of "Who Did What to Whom" and the inter-event relations based on conjoining, embedding, branching, insertion and apposition. According to Halliday and Hasan (1976), those gaps serve as cohesive devices to achieve better texture of the text organization. The transformations are ruled-based and they are important part of native speakers' competence. Though the rule-based parser is still short of perfection, the necessary design is in place and it has quite a few encouraging results. This report will also show the usefulness of PADS restoration technology in CALL and information extraction.

Key words: English parser, PADS gaps, PADS restoration, case frame building, clause boundary detection, zero anaphor resolution, anaphor resolution, event relation finding, pronoun co-reference resolution, PP attachment, garden-path, information extraction, computer reading, meaning representation, CALL

1 Introduction

According to Lyons (1977), two different conceptions of kernel-sentences have been formalized in transformational grammar: one by Harris and the other by Chomsky. Zellig Harris defined a kernel as one that is not derived from any other sentence by means of a transformation rule; while Chomsky (1957) regarded a kernel as one generated in the grammar without the operation of "optional" transformations. Without looking into how kernels are conceptualized differently, kernels refer to "simple, complete, active, affirmative declaratives (or statements)", from which surface structures are derived. When Chomsky postulated theory of transformational grammar, he has PADS (permutation, addition, deletion and substitution) in mind as the stumbling rules that alienate Deep Structure from Surface Structure. For example, active sentences are transformed into passive either because the Agent is unknown or so that the Agent is moved to the end of a clause to serve as a link to the following clause. This need to link in texture organization might cause a careless reader to misread since the Agent and the Patient are swapped. Misreading is even more likely if the passive is in a participial, in which the verb-to-be is deleted. Ambiguity or misreading caused by PADS is sometimes referred to by reading researchers as the garden-path phenomenon.

Whether they are called PADS gaps or garden-path, the derivations are causes of misinterpretation for computer reading and for underachieved readers. Nevertheless, for Halliday and Hasan (1976), they are great devices for cohesion, which refers to "the relations of meaning that exist within the text". Halliday and Hasan classify cohesive devices into five categories: reference, ellipsis, substitution, lexical cohesion, and conjunction. The mechanism "reference" relates one element of the text to another for its interpretation because they express the same referent. "Ellipsis" is used to omit an item to avoid repetition. "Substitution" refers to the use of pronouns or pro-forms to avoid using the same phrase for the same referent mentioned earlier. "Lexical cohesion" refers to two elements that share a lexical field or collocation. "Conjunction" refers to particular expressions used to create parallel connections.

It's interesting to note that two linguistic schools established two decades away from each other should use similar mechanisms to refer to two very different concepts, one for generating surface sentences and the other in achieving text meaning. Chomskyan Generative Grammar and Hallidayan cohesion concept are mentioned here to draw attention to two things: 1) they point out that transformation rules and cohesive devices both involve missing, displaced or surrogate words or phrases that are extremely difficult for sequential or distance-based computation or for L2 learners; 2) the answer to their restoration should be in the study of language knowledge.

In the following sections, the author will first point out that the occurrences of PADS gaps are almost entirely predictable. In other words, we know where they are from and how they are used. With this, how the English parser achieves different goals of PADS restoration, namely, clause boundary detection, PP attachment, zero anaphor resolution, anaphor resolution, pronoun co-reference resolution, event relation finding, will be reported. I will then show that the problems addressed are also causes of garden-path phenomena. The next section illustrates an explicit kernel-like meaning representation that is used to integrate PADS restoration and highlight explicit referents as well as intra-event and inter-event relations. Then, some preliminary results and evaluation methods will be reported. At the end, the paper will show how the parsing outputs in XML form can be used to help with CALL (computer-aided language learning), information extraction and knowledge discovery.

2 Kernels and derived sentences

Kernels are simple, complete, active, affirmative statements. From them compound, complex, incomplete, passive, negative statements, or questions and commands are derived. Although not all derivations have all PADS gaps and not each PADS gap occurs solely to a single derivation, the co-occurrence of a derivation with a PADS transformation is basically predictable.

Kernel	Derivation	PADS	Issues
simple	compound complex	deletion substitution deletion permutation deletion	zero-anaphor relative-anaphor trace
complete	incomplete	deletion	zero-anaphor
active	passive	addition permutation deletion	discontinuity trace anaphor
affirmative	negative	addition permutation	discontinuity trace
statement	question command	addition permutation deletion	discontinuity trace zero-anaphor
reference	pronoun	substitution	anaphor co-reference

Table 1

Table 1 shows the correspondence between PADS operations and constituent types in English. It also shows that the phrase structure type in English dictates the occurrence of PADS or language mechanisms. A relative clause either has a relative pronoun or it can be omitted. The existence of a relative pronoun is the result of substitution. And it's likely that the Object inside the relative is moved (permuted) to the left of the clause. On the other hand, the omission of the relative clause implies an extra operation of deletion, so zero anaphor resolution, rather than relative-anaphor resolution is needed to restore PADS gaps. For passive reduced relative or past participial, deletion and zero-anaphor resolution will be involved because both the Subject and verb-to-be are missing. Permutation also occurs in this situation. Subject- or object-control infinitival also involves zero anaphor and it is the control type that decides which referent to be restored in zero anaphor resolution. Compounds or other kinds of conjoining often involve zero-anaphor, meaning that Subject or Verb or Object might be omitted if repetition is sensed.

3 English parser and NLP resolutions

The deep parser built by the author (Wasson et al. 2010, Chen & Lu 2012) is a spin-off of the parser family based on the generalized transition network grammar (GTN) parsers of Loritz's (1992) which in turn were built on the framework of an augmented transition network (ATN). Some new designs are implemented to enable the parser to do integrated meaning representation and PADS restoration. To attain these two goals, the parser needs near perfect constituency (deciding the beginning and end of a constituent and its structure type) and the finding of intra-event relations of "Who Did What to Whom" as well as inter-event relations of conjoining, embedding, branching, insertion and apposition.

3.1 Clause boundary detection

Unlike most clause boundary detection tasks reported, the parser here uses case frame as the ultimate judge of clause boundaries because not every clause has a salient boundary marker and most clause markers are ambiguous themselves. This implementation is driven by the idea that if a clause has got enough case roles required by a predicate, a new clause will be expected.

Clause boundary detection is important in this study because the finding of both intra-event and inter-event relations depends on it. So far the parser returns an accuracy rate of over 90%. Its evaluation is simple and clear. (see Table 4).

3.2 Different anaphor resolutions

There are three kinds of anaphor resolution implemented in this parser -- relative anaphor for relative clauses, co-reference resolution for personal pronouns, and zero-anaphor resolution for conjoining construction, pronoun-less relatives, reduced relatives, etc. As mentioned in section 2, most anaphor resolutions are not so hard to implement because their restoration clues are predictable. The difficult parts of anaphor resolution lie in pronoun co-reference resolution and the zero-anaphor resolution that is related to scope of coordination.

The concept behind pronoun resolution is easy if adequate mention-lists are built and the priority of different mention-lists is set. The difficulty lies in the fact that it takes time to subcategorize all nouns as person or non-person and to add features of male or female. Scope of coordination is easier for omitted Subject or Verb, but very difficult for omitted Object in parallel construction. It is further complicated by morphological conversion, meaning so many English nouns also function as verbs.

The most important thing for anaphor resolution is the use of the "carry-over" of some register of Subject or Object right at the moment when the old clause ends and a new clause is introduced. At that moment, the co-referent of an anaphor is used to restore the empty element or take the place of *which* or *he*.

3.3 PP attachment

The success or failure of PP attachment is critical to clause boundary detection and constituency in general. Its difficulty mainly lies in the context of a preposition following the grammatical NP object of a verb. The parser makes use of event classification of the object NP as well as the information of two-word verbs to determine whether a PP is attached to an NP or a Verb. So far the only thing that is still troubling the parser's PP attachment is in the case where the PP of interest is itself a parallel construction.

3.4 Case frame building

For the intra-event relation or case relation, according to case grammar (Fillmore 1968), the parser's representation of "Who Did What to Whom" is laid out under the label of Agent, Predicate, MainVerb, Patient and Goal. Among them, Agent refers to Doer or the only participant of the event. By default, it should be the grammatical Subject of the clause unless a passive voice is detected, which in turn moves the Subject to the Patient position. Most PP participants (an NP marked with a case marking preposition) are placed under the label Goal, except when a two-word verb is identified. Goal position is also saved for marginal participants if no other case role is found. This is aimed at accommodating as many participants as possible. It should be noted that embedded noun clauses or non-finite clauses are also included in the case frame representation.

3.5 Inter-event relation finding

Aside from using different kinds of anaphor resolution to upgrade the parser to do more than sentence parsing, the parser is further developed to find inter-event relations. In English, there are actually three relations between events or referents: that of equivalence, embedment and dependency. However, following Chen (2010), "insertion" joins "branching" for the dependency relation and "apposition" is added to share with "conjoining" the equivalence relation. At the junction of clause boundary, a principle of sentence construction is selected among conjoining, embedding, branching, insertion and apposition to describe how the current event is related to another one. It should be noted that only five principles are needed to capture all inter-event relations in English (Chen 2010).

3.6 Garden-path phenomena

From the parser design and implementation of all kinds of resolution, the author notices that relational function words are the most ambiguous in English. Comma(,) tops the list of ambiguous words. As a boundary marker, it can lead to a new clause, a new phrase, a series of parallel constituents, an insertion or an apposition. Any decision made at the junction of a comma might guarantee a successful parse or ruin the whole thing. Comma junction is a key cross-road of garden-path.

Part-of-speech (POS) ambiguity is ubiquitous among English words. A noun is often a verb or an adjective. The parser is often puzzled by such words when it cannot decide whether to start parsing an NP or a VP, or whether to end an NP for a possible VP or go on taking one more noun for the current NP. The most notorious POS ambiguity is that of verbs with -ed or -ing ending. Words ending with -ing are potential noun, verb or adjective. The ambiguity affects constituency as well as relation type assignment. Words ending with -ed add an extra layer of ambiguity between active and passive. In terms of constituency ambiguity, words of multiple POS's involve garden-path because they put the parser at a cross-road all the time.

A special kind of POS ambiguity involves function words such as *that, as, for, to*, etc. The word *that* might begin an NP, a relative clause or a noun clause. The preposition *to* signifies the beginning of a PP or an infinitival, whereas *as* might start a PP, a subordinate clause or a relative clause. These words lead to garden-path of all kinds.

3.7 Context Grammar Parser

The parser is based on a context grammar for several reasons: 1) The parser lets the context disambiguate POS and word senses by giving each word only one entry in the lexicon so as to free the parsing from selecting a sense out of several lexical meanings; 2) Each entry of word is provided with multiple POS's if the word has more than one possible syntactic category so that the parser can test on possible POS and pick one among the candidates according to the context; 3) Different senses of the same part of speech will be disambiguated based on different lexical features or subcategories. For example, most verbs are potentially transitive and intransitive, but only transitive verbs can be passive. A passive context will decide that the verb is transitive. Similarly, a verb taking a person Patient, an event Patient or a clause Patient will eventually let the collocation context decides its own lexical sense. In other words, there is no need to burden the lexicon with several predetermined senses and further burden the parser with unnecessary decision making that is unattainable without accommodating the lexicon with the entire world knowledge.

The parser is taught to use the left context that has been decided by the words already parsed and the right context made available by all the unparsed words. The parser can check on every word in the sentence in terms of POS, subcategories and any other lexical feature. For the words in the left context, the information derived from the grammar and the finished parse will tell the parser where the current word is situated, in what type of clause or phrase it is, inside a Subject or still expecting an Object, inside a series of NPs or parallel clauses, and so on. All these are made possible by having the parser registers structured hierarchically.

4 Meaning representation

Historically, many AI or NLP (natural language processing) systems preferred logical forms to other forms of meaning representation for an obvious reason in accessibility. However, this advantage can also be achieved even with natural-language-like representation if it turns into a structured data type from the unstructured text. For this very reason, the parser in this study outputs Excel-like tables to represent the meaning of each sentence with its automatic annotation, i.e. adding new derived information back to the document.

As for the content, the meaning representation used here is based on the author's three aspects of meaning (Chen 1996): referential, relational and specificational. The author believes every text or sentence is all about referents and relations among them. However, words, phrases or clauses only go so far as designating possible entities and possible worlds. This is why specificational meaning is added to referents and relations. In this parser's output representation, three tables are generated from parsing: an NP table that annotates all NPs discovered; a case frame table that annotates each new-found clause with "Who Did What to Whom" event representation plus an inter-event relation; a term definition table that annotates sentences in which certain terms are defined.

Four advantages result from this meaning representation. First, it outputs searchable data which can be merged easily. Second, the three tables are present in a single XML file, i.e. the database contains everything that is needed for information extraction. Third, it is natural-language-like. There is no need to depend on some artificial symbolic forms to make it accessible or readable only by machines. Human readers or reviewers need no additional training to use the database or evaluate the system performance. Four, necessary PADS restorations have been done in the annotation so that no gaps will hinder human comprehension or machine reading. For underachieved readers, the filling of the gaps makes the sentences easy to understand. For computer systems or search engines, the explicit information added by PADS restoration makes it a powerful tool for unearthing buried information and hidden links.

Table 2 shows the case frames of the sentence *He first examined his childhood memories and came to realize the intense hostility he had felt for his father.* Three rows of "Who Did What to Who" are shown in the table. They indicate a success in doing clause boundary detection. In terms of PADS restoration, two pronouns are found in the sentence. The nominative *he* is given back its co-referent *Freud*, which is absent in this sentence. However, the parser manages to restore the co-reference by getting the right one from previous sentences.

Agent	Predicate	Main Verb	Patient	Goal	EventRelation
He: Freud {pro-ana}	examined	examined	his childhood memories		m-clause=
He: Freud {zero -ana}	came to realize	realize	the intense hostility		conjoin= m-clause=
He: Freud {pro-ana}	had felt	felt	the intense hostility {zero-ana} {rel-ana} {trace}	for his father	branch=rel

Table 2: case frame

The annotation {pro=ana} is to show that co-referent *Freud* is restored for pronoun *he* while {zero-ana} is to show that Subject of the second clause is missing because the first two clauses conjoin to each other by *and*, meaning that the Subject of the second clause is omitted to avoid repetition and it is restored by zero-anaphor resolution. The conjoining of these two clauses is indicated by inter-event relation "conjoin" while "m-clause" is to signify "main clause". A relative clause is added to the second clause as the right-branched modifier of *the intense hostility*. Since the relative pronoun is omitted, {zero-ana} is used to show the effect of zero-anaphor resolution. While the omitted relative pronoun is supposed to replace the antecedent, relative anaphor resolution is involved. Furthermore, since the antecedent is originally the Object of the kernel relative, a trace is left behind. It is then moved back to the Object position, thanks to successful case frame building. As to sentence construction principle, it's a branching relation between the head NP and the relative clause. Table 2 shows that the parser is able to capture both referential meaning in each Case Role and relational meaning inside the case frame (intra-event relation) and between two events (inter-event relation). The aspect of specificational meaning is evident in this table from having *came to realize* as the filler of the Predicate slot. There is no event of *coming* here. The parser treats *came to* as a specifier of the verb *realize*. *Came to realize* presents a particular world out of the possible worlds denoted by *realizing*.

5 Effects of PADS restoration

Up to now, most language parsers only do sentence parsing. A system can go around the limitation of sentence parsing by using mention-lists to do co-reference resolution for pronouns. As emphasized by Halliday and Hasan (1976), text meaning should be treated as going beyond sentence boundaries. They treat cohesive devices as the texture to better organize the text. The use of PADS restoration by this parser identifies cohesive devices or PADS transformations from parsing and restores what are made implicit. Such a technology benefits both computer systems in information extraction or any search engine, and human readers in overcoming the comprehension gaps left behind by PADS. Here are some examples of its application.

5.1 Extended definition

Typically researchers rely on definition words to find defined terms in sentences. However, to avoid repeating a term so often in writing, the original term is replaced by a pronoun or omitted as known. When *it* is defined, the definition will be missed. This is why PADS restoration finds itself a good use, that is, to find extended definitions for a given term. This is also made possible by the structured meaning representation that is sorted and searchable. Notice that the examples underlined in Table 3 might be past unnoticed because of the missing of the term *the id* or because it is not in a position indicating that a term is defined.

Term	Cohesion	S
the id		The id is ***the biological component***, the ego is the psychological component, and the superego is the social component.
the id		THE ID -- The id is ***the original system of personality***; at birth a person is all id.
the id		The id is ***the primary source of psychic energy and the seat of the instincts***.
the id	it: the id	It ***lacks organization and is blind, demanding, and insistent***.
the id	it: the id	***A cauldron of seething excitement***, the id ***cannot tolerate tension***, and *it* ***functions to discharge tension immediately***.
the id	(the id) ruled by	***Ruled by the pleasure principle, which is aimed at reducing tension, avoiding pain, and gaining pleasure***, the id is ***illogical, amoral, and driven to satisfy instinctual needs***.
the id	(the id) remaining	The id ***never matures, remaining the spoiled brat of personality***.
the id	it: the id	It ***does not think but only wishes or acts***.
the id		The id is ***largely unconscious, or out of awareness***.
the id		***The ego***, as the seat of intelligence and rationality, ***checks and controls the blind impulses*** of the id.
the id		Whereas the id ***knows only subjective reality***, the ego distinguishes between mental images and things in the external world.
the id	it: anxiety	***It develops out of a conflict among the id***, ego, and superego over control of the available psychic energy.

Table 3: Extended definition

5.2 Debugging tool

Three sentences are used in this section to show why the parser's meaning representation is a great tool for evaluation and debugging. In Table 4, the underlined words and phrases are erroneous. In the first clause of the sentence *Freud's family background is a factor to consider in understanding the development of his theory*, the infinitival should not be placed under label Goal because it is the modifier of the NP *a factor*, which should be a non-finite clause "branching" from the NP. In other words, it should be part of Patient and there should be no Goal in this clause. This is a mistake of attachment and constituency. The error comes from the parser's negligence to attach an infinitival to verb-to-be. Adding a test for the verb-to-be not to take a Goal and forcing the NP following verb-to-be to take the modifier, the parser should be able to make it right.

Agent	Predicate	Main Verb	Patient	Goal	EventRelation
Freud's family background	is	is	a factor	***to consider in understanding the development of his theory***	m-clause=
Freud's family background	to consider	consider	———	in understanding the development of his theory.	branch=to
dummy-subject	understanding	understanding	the development of his theory		embed=ing
Freud's family	***had limited***	***limited***	***finances***		branch=sub
Freud's family	was forced to live	live		in a crowded apartment	conjoin= branch=sub
his parents	made	made	every effort	to foster his obvious intellectual capacities	m-clause=

his parents	to foster	foster	his obvious intellectual capacities		branch=to
	settled	settled	***He: Freud***	on medicine	branch=ed

Table 4: Evaluation and debugging

The second mistake comes from whether verb-to-be is subject-control or object-control. For subject-control verbs, the parser is taught to restore the Subject of the infinitival by using the Subject of the matrix clause, whereas an object-control verb will cause the parser to borrow matrix Object to be the Subject. Unfortunately such a consideration forces the parser to make a wrong decision and take *Freud's family background* as the Subject. In fact, verb-to-be is neither a subject-control verb nor an object-control verb. The burden is still on verb-to-be. By then, the consideration of the NP modifier will force *the factor* to be the Patient because *the factor* is a non-person. This one is very difficult for most parsers.

In terms of clause boundary detection, Table 4 shows a 100% recall of 8/8 but only an 87.5% precision of 7/8 from parsing the three sentences.

For sentence *Even though Freud's family had limited finances and was forced to live in a crowded apartment, his parents made every effort to foster his obvious intellectual capacities*, the only mistake actually comes from POS ambiguity for the word ending with -ed. Since verb-to-have is usually followed by past participle to form a perfective aspect and the plural noun *finances* does not require a determiner, the right constituency of "*had* + *limited finances*" is mistaken as "*had limited* + *finances*." This error caused by ambiguous -ed is hard to do right. The only solution might come from using the very low possibility for the word *finances* to function as a countable noun. Nevertheless, the possibility is still not zero.

Similar -ed ambiguity occurs to the third sentence *He finally settled on medicine*. There are more transitive verbs than intransitive in English. Although not all transitive verbs can be passive, a majority of them have passive form. The ambiguity between active and passive has the potential to ruin case role assignment. Passive reduced relatives cannot rely on verb-to-be to pronounce passiveness because it is omitted. As a result, the parser usually depends on a preposition right behind the -ed verb to make the right call, as in this case. However, it is not entirely dependable with the complication caused by two-word verbs. Two-word verbs refer to transitive phrasal verbs, which are passive only when there is another preposition following the second element of the phrasal verbs. In this case, *settled on* should be active because it is a two-word verb.

6 Building of knowledge base out of automatic computer reading

Although the rule-based parser used in this study is slow comparing with most statistical shallow parsers. It is less ambiguous and more powerful in terms of the range of NLP tasks it is able to perform. Nevertheless, it is still faster than human readers. In addition, human reading is characteristic of leaving no record after reading. When a reader finishes reading a book, everything he or she has learned is inside the brain as invisible imprint and only the reader can access it mentally. Computer reading is different. The parser is taught to keep all the reading "results", filed and well-structured for open access. From all the Excel-like tables, we can create knowledge base to serve as annotated surrogate documents for an article, a book, or even a corpus. The knowledge base will then become very powerful corpus to support CALL, information extraction or even knowledge discovery. Such knowledge bases are different from most available corpus tools in that they have precise pieces of information as to telling exactly "Who Did What to Whom" in each clause or event and how events are related and linked, not relying mainly on distance or regular-expression rules to do concordance, collocation, chunking or bag-of-terms search.

6.1 Writing tool for CALL

With all the inter-event relations annotated, the knowledge base can be used to teach how to use different kinds of structure to do, for instance, embedding in an English writing class aimed at teaching sentence making rules.

embed=ing	Freud devoted most of his life to ***formulating and extending his theory of psychoanalysis***.
embed=to	It is a mistake ***to assume that all feelings clients have toward their therapists are manifestations of transference***.
embed=n-	It is a mistake to assume ***that all feelings***

cl	***clients have toward their therapists are manifestations of transference.***
embed=np	The ego has ***contact with the external world of reality.***
embed=to	One of the central functions of analysis is ***to help clients acquire the freedom to love, work, and play.***

Table 5: How to do embedding

6.2 Knowledge discovery

Table 6 provides enough knowledge about what therapists do in counseling. With the database such knowledge is always ready for extraction.

therapist	developing	the therapeutic relationship
therapists	share	their personal reactions
therapists	dealt with	these personal issues / in their own intensive therapy
therapists	become aware of	the countertransference
therapists	study	their internal reactions
therapists	use	their internal reactions / to understand their clients
therapists	understand	their clients
therapists	monitor	their feelings / during therapy sessions
therapists	develop	some level of objectivity
therapists	not react	defensively and subjectively
therapists	ask	clients / to free associate to some aspect of the manifest content of a dream
therapists	interpret	the most obvious resistances
therapists	lessen	the possibility of clients' rejecting the interpretation
therapists	increase	the chance that they will begin to look at their resistive behavior.
therapists	respect	the resistances of clients
therapists	assist	clients / in working with their defenses
therapists	become aware of	their own sources of countertransference
therapists	broaden	their understanding of clients' struggles
therapists	understanding	clients' struggles
Therapists	exploring	clients' associations with them: symbols
Therapists	help	their clients / review environmental situations
Therapists	work	from a developmental perspective
Therapists	adopt	the blank-screen aloofness typical of the "pure" context of classical psychoanalysis
Therapists	hidden	themselves / as persons in the guise of "being professional"
Therapists	see	continuity / in life
Therapists	see	certain directions their clients have taken

Table 6: What do therapists do?

7 Conclusion

This paper reports the use of PADS restoration technology, which consists of clause boundary detection, resolution of anaphors, PP attachment, case frame building and so on, to help an English parser to fill out comprehension gaps left behind by PADS transformations. This technology is helpful to beginning English learners who have difficulty in reading because of PADS gaps. The surrogate structured database created by the parser's annotation proves to be useful to help CALL, information extraction, and knowledge discovery because PADS gaps are made explicit.

References

Chen, S.-J. 1996. *Analysis of Chinese for Chinese-English Machine Translation*. Ph.D. dissertation. Georgetown University, Washington, DC.

Chen, S.-J. 2010. Linguistic relativity revisited, *2010年跨文化研究國際研討會論文集*. 輔仁大學.

Chen, S.-J. & Lu, S.-K. 2012. Clause boundary detection and relational marking for MT reordering. *2012 International Conference on Applied Linguistics & Language Teaching (ALLT).*

Chomsky, N. 1957. *Syntactic Structures*. The Hague: Mouton & Co.

Fillmore, C. 1968. "The Case for Case" In Bach and Harms (Ed.): *Universals in Linguistic Theory*. New York: Holt, Rinehart, and Winston. 1-88.

Halliday M. A. K., & R. Hasan. 1976. *Cohesion in English.* London: Longman.

Loritz, D. 1992. Generalized transition network parsing for language study: the GPARS systems for English, Russian, Japanese and Chinese. *CALICO Journal, Volume 10 Number 1*

Lyons, J. 1977. *Semantics*, 2 vols. Cambridge: Cambridge University Press.

Wasson, M., D. Loritz, S.-J. Chen, et al. 2005. *System and Method for Extracting Information from Text Using Text Annotation and Fact Extraction*, US Patent *US7912705*, 19 Jan 2010.

Association for Computational Linguistics
209 N. Eighth Street
Stroudsburg, Pennsylvania 18360

CURRAN ASSOCIATES INC
proceedings.com